HISTORY OF ITALIAN RENAISSANCE ART

PAINTING • SCULPTURE • ARCHITECTURE

HISTORY OF ITALIAN

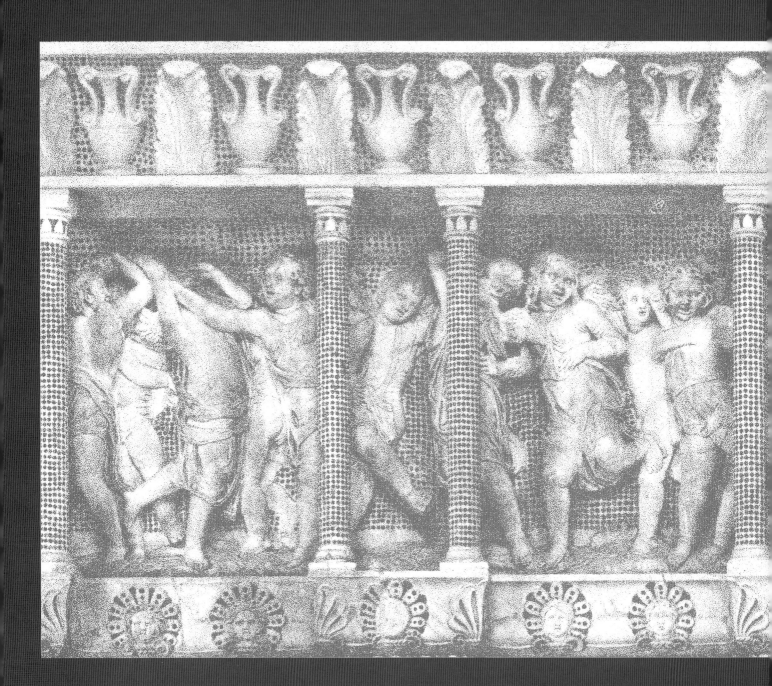

RENAISSANCE ART

PAINTING · SCULPTURE · ARCHITECTURE

FREDERICK HARTT

REVISED BY DAVID G. WILKINS
UNIVERSITY OF PITTSBURGH

FOURTH EDITION

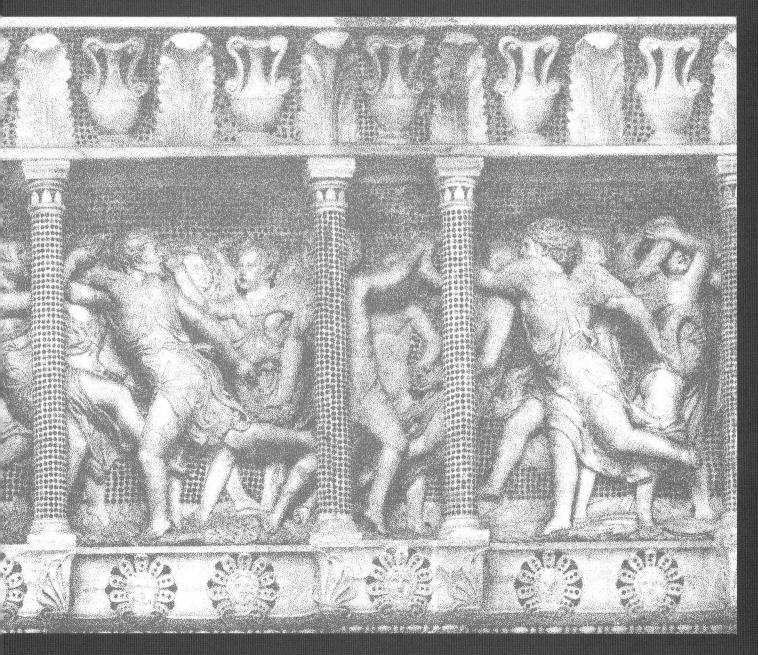

PRENTICE HALL, INC., AND
HARRY N. ABRAMS, INC., PUBLISHERS

Project manager: Eve Sinaiko
Editor: Joanne Greenspun
Art direction: Dirk Luykx
Design: Communigraph, Lydia Gershey
    and Yonah Schurink
Picture research: Uta Hoffmann

Library of Congress Cataloguing-in-Publication Data
Hartt, Frederick.
    History of Italian Renaissance art : painting, sculpture,
architecture/Frederick Hartt.—4th ed./revised by David G. Wilkins.
        p.   cm.
    Includes bibliographical references and index.
    ISBN 0–13–393380–6
    1. Art, Italian 2. Art, Renaissance—Italy. I. Wilkins, David
G. II. Title.
N6915.H37 1993b
709'.45'09024—dc20   93–1145

Fourth Edition 1994

Published in 1994 by Harry N. Abrams, Incorporated, New York
A Times Mirror Company

Prentice Hall, Inc.
A Simon & Schuster Company
Englewood Cliffs, New Jersey 07632

Printed and bound in Japan

Title page: Donatello, detail of the *Cantoria*, 1433–39, marble and
mosaic, from the Cathedral of Florence. See fig. 243

Page 9: Andrea del Verrocchio, *Doubting of Thomas,* 1465–83, bronze,
Orsanmichele, Florence. See fig. 333

Page 25: Lorenzo Maitani, detail of *Creation of the Birds and Fishes*,
from *Scenes from Genesis*, c. 1310–before 1316, marble façade relief,
Cathedral of Orvieto. See figs. 110, 111

Page 151: Lorenzo Ghiberti, detail of *Jacob and Esau*, 1425–52, panel
from the *Gates of Paradise* (East Doors), Baptistery of Florence, 1425–52.
Gilded bronze. See fig. 239, colorplate 46

Page 429: Benvenuto Cellini, *Perseus Freeing Andromeda*, bronze relief plaque
from the pedestal of *Perseus and Medusa*, 1545–54, Florence. See fig. 694

Contents

PART ONE: THE LATE MIDDLE AGES

PART TWO: THE QUATTROCENTO

PART THREE: THE CINQUECENTO

Preface to the Fourth Edition

This revision of Frederick Hartt's magisterial *History of Italian Renaissance Art* was scheduled at the time Professor Hartt died, unexpectedly, on October 31, 1991. It had already been decided that there would not be major changes to the text, and the revision maintains the canon of works selected by Hartt to characterize the development of Italian Renaissance art as well as the sequence in which he ordered them. New photographs have been substituted when works have been restored, and color-plate portfolios of Renaissance art in context and of Michelangelo's restored Sistine Ceiling have been added. The text has been somewhat tightened to conform to the book's new design, and new ideas and scholarship have been included where possible. It was agreed from the beginning that the inimitable voice of Frederick Hartt, discussing the works and landscape that he loved so much, should continue to speak clearly in this revision. I hope you will agree that this has been accomplished.

A few changes have been introduced to make the book more useful for today's students and general readers and to conform to new interests that are developing in art history. Because location was such an important consideration in the design of Renaissance works of art, paintings and sculptures that are still in their original settings—with the exception of obvious examples of frescoes, mosaics, and façade sculptures—are indicated by a 🏛 in the captions. For works today in private collections or museums, the original locations, if known, have been added to the captions.

In addition, an effort has been made to include in each caption a reference to the patron, when the name of the particular individual, family, or commissioning body is known. Although some patrons are today no more than a name, even the name serves as a reminder of the formative and essential role that the patron so often played in the creation of a Renaissance work of art.

Earlier editions included occasional references to specific scholars, but as the increasing complexity and richness of Renaissance scholarship threatened to bury this revision under an avalanche of names, it was decided to eliminate this information. The revised glossary now keys terms to the illustrations, and an updated bibliography guides interested readers to the sources that support, critique, and expand upon the information presented in this book.

I owe special thanks to many colleagues in the Renaissance field who have advised me during this process, especially Bernard Schultz of West Virginia University and Roger Crum of the University of Dayton. Additional ideas for improvements were made by Ann Sutherland Harris and by many members of the Italian Art Society. For insight into the student's point of view and for research and editorial assistance I am indebted to Rebecca Wilkins, Chris Colborn, and Katherine Wilkins. The updated bibliography profited from the attention of Ray Anne Lockhard, Librarian at the Henry Clay Frick Fine Arts Library at the University of Pittsburgh. At Harry N. Abrams, Inc., I received good advice, encouragement, and direction from Julia Moore and Eve Sinaiko. Uta Hoffmann located the splendid new photographs, and I owe a special debt to Joanne Greenspun, whose subtle editorial skills have been crucial throughout this endeavor. The artists for the handsome new design were Lydia Gershey and Yonah Schurink. The fine jacket design is by Dirk Luykx.

It was my intention from the beginning that Frederick Hartt's personal and inspiring approach to the Renaissance remain intact. As I read his text again and again, I continued to be impressed by the breadth and depth of his knowledge, by the manner in which he encourages us to examine each work in detail, and how he tries to persuade us to experience each work as fully as he did. My hope is that this revision will demonstrate my respect for his authority and vision.

David G. Wilkins
University of Pittsburgh
August 1993

Reprinted here are excerpts from Frederick Hartt's Forewords and Prefaces to earlier editions. It is our belief that Professor Hartt's own words, both illuminating and instructive, will be of interest to the reader. They also provide a framework for and an important record of the changes that were made to this book over the course of three editions. For the full texts, the reader is referred to the original editions.

Foreword to the First Edition, 1969

A book in English dealing with the art of the Italian Renaissance—painting, sculpture, and architecture—needs no apology for its existence . . . all three were closely related in Renaissance Italy. Often the same master practiced two of the major arts with equal success; sometimes he achieved commanding stature in all of them. And, especially in the early Renaissance, architects, sculptors, and painters interchanged their ideas with the greatest freedom, often going so far as to borrow for exploitation in their own arts effects which seem more appropriate to other techniques and other media. . . .

The organization of the book has precipitated a series of difficult choices. A comprehensive treatment of all the gifted masters at work from the Alps to Sicily, during the period of roughly three centuries which can be embraced by the term Renaissance, the whole compressed between one pair of covers, might have produced a useful handbook but not a readable account. Worse, it would not have been possible to illustrate all the works of art mentioned in the text with photographs of legible scale and quality. I chose, instead, the twin principles of extended discussion and adequate illustration. In fact, no work of art treated in the book is left unillustrated.

In making my choices I have tried to leave some for other teachers. While my own undergraduate course in Italian Renaissance art covers many more works than can possibly be discussed or illustrated in a single book, I have never attempted to treat in my lectures all the masters who appear in the following pages. Individual teachers may wish to take up artists I omit, or vice versa, and the general reader—whose rights should be respected—ought also to be able, if he wishes, to get a wider view of the subject than can be fitted into any college course.

Reasons could be advanced for every inclusion, every omission; but equally persuasive arguments will doubtless be produced by critics who do not agree with my judgments. Neither they nor I can claim complete objectivity. First, for instance, I admit to a personal slant in favor of Tuscany, and especially Florence, which I would be willing to relinquish if it could be proved to me that the Renaissance originated anywhere else. Second, it has seemed to me more important to write at length about revolutionary figures and major movements than to include certain minor masters, no matter how delightful their works may be. I have tried to be fair, despite my Tuscan bias. . . .

My guiding principle of selection has meant that certain pictures have had to be reproduced here no matter how often the reader may have seen them elsewhere; otherwise I would have had to refer him to a library of other volumes. But even here, from time to time I have changed the traditional emphasis, and put in fresh works that I thought deserved to be better known, and left out some familiar warhorses. Sometimes it has been impossible to give a fair account of the work of an artist with so few examples. *Pazienza*, as the Italians would say; the works of art themselves are in the galleries and churches to be enjoyed and thought about, and the rich literature about them is on the shelves to be read. My goal will be attained if I have stimulated the reader's appetite to do both.

Throughout the book I have attempted, where possible, to present the individual work of art in its context of contemporary history, to show how it fulfilled specific needs on the part of artist and patron, and how its meaning was intended to be interpreted. Sometimes the texts I quote may seem abstruse and remote from our own experience; that is not their fault. An iconologist (one who interprets the meaning of works of art through texts) often meets with the objection, "But aren't you reading all this into the work of art?" If the iconologist has found the right texts, he has discovered only what was intended to be seen in the work of art, and what the forgetfulness of centuries has caused to be read *out* of it. Aesthetically, of course, a work of art is no less interesting if we do not know what it represented. But a knowledge of its meaning can admit us into realms of experience, in both the personality of the artist and the period to which he was speaking, that would otherwise have been inaccessible. Such knowledge can also open our eyes to previously unobserved qualities of form and color in the work of art. And it can tell us much about why the artist did certain things the way he did—and even, at times, give us a flash of insight into the forces which cause styles to change or disappear and new ones to take their places.

In quite a number of instances I have presented tentative ideas, labeled as such, which will eventually, I hope, be more completely expounded elsewhere, supported by all the necessary evidence. Would it have been better to leave them out? Rightly or wrongly, I have always felt that I owed the student in my courses the benefits of my thoughts even when not fully tested by proof, and I saw no reason why I should not follow the same principle in this book. . . .

Foreword to the Second Edition, 1979

. . . My generous publishers have permitted my considerable expansion in both text and illustrations in this Second Edition. As a result, I have been able to rectify to a considerable extent my Tuscan bias and to include a number of important Northern Italian painters, sculptors, and architects for the first time. I have also been able to extend the treatment of both the Trecento and the Cinquecento by the inclusion of more artists and of additional works by some masters already present. Alas, if all the artists I would like now to have included were to make their way into these pages, the Second Edition would require two volumes! . . .

There is little necessity to justify an attempt to bring a book such as this one abreast of recent literature. Bernard Berenson once quipped that his *Italian Painters of the Renaissance* was a literary classic and he had no right to touch it. No such claim can be made for this volume. . . My professional colleagues will be the first to recognize that this goal cannot be fully achieved. The outpouring of books and articles dealing with all aspects of Italian Renaissance art in the past ten years has been immense, and new discoveries have changed radically our ideas about many works of art treated in these pages. Inevitably, today's commonplace is tomorrow's antique. . . .

If I have learned one lesson in a long professional career, it is the danger of faith in one's own infallibility. Anyone can be proved wrong. Investigators who devote a disproportionate amount of their energy to pursuing the mistakes of others pay the penalty of slighting the larger issues of aesthetics, meaning, social relationships, and historical development that are the central mission of art history, and they also run the risk of slipping or being pushed, sometimes spectacularly, into the pit of error over which we must all thread our way along such slender bridges. . . .

Preface to the Third Edition, 1986

. . . Works of art, like all human productions and like ourselves, are bound in time. . . . Their history, therefore, is a part of their very nature, if by history we mean their place in the development of art, and their relation to the circumstances under which they were produced. The history of works of art *after* creation is another story. It should not be essential to their appearance, but it too often is, in the case of damage or other alteration, and that also must be at least mentioned.

In determining historical importance, paternalism again sets in. The writer of a general text has to make difficult choices, and must often leave out works of high quality in favor of others somewhat less attractive in order to provide a reasonable account of historical situations and their development. The reader, then, is asked to trust the writer's judgment based on experience, and to recognize that sometimes these choices were painful.

In the forewords to earlier editions I have admitted to a personal slant in favor of Tuscany and especially Florence, which I would be willing to relinquish if it would be proved to me that the Renaissance originated anywhere else. I must also confess to greater excitement in contemplating the beginning of an important cycle than its end, and thus, according to some colleagues with later interests, have slighted the Cinquecento. In the second edition I included for the first time a number of important North Italian painters, sculptors, and architects, and in this one I have brought into the fold several more painters and sculptors, all from the Cinquecento and mostly from the North. In order to include these masters without increasing the size of the book unreasonably I have been obliged to eliminate two or three earlier and lesser artists as well as some important works, such as Giotto's frescoes in the Peruzzi Chapel, which are in such poor condition that they cannot be appreciated in small reproductions. . . .

A PORTFOLIO OF THE ITALIAN RENAISSANCE

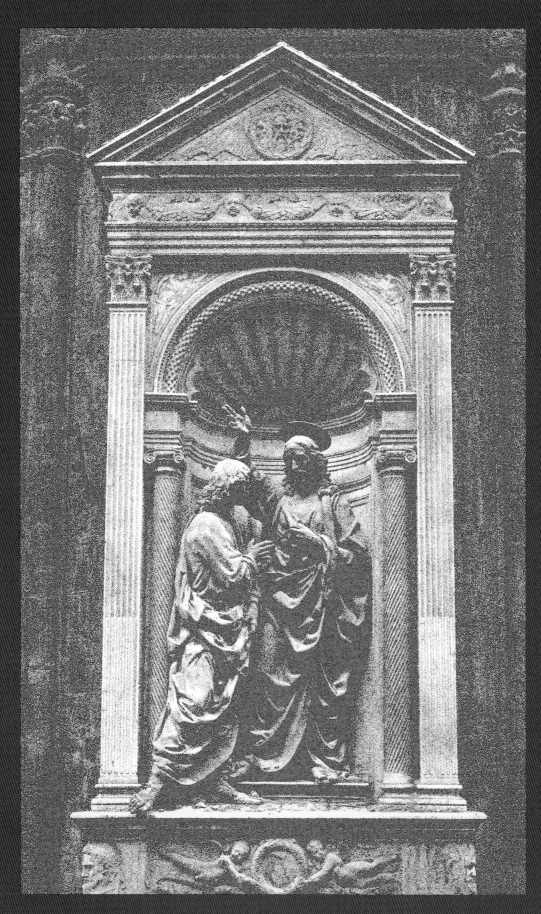

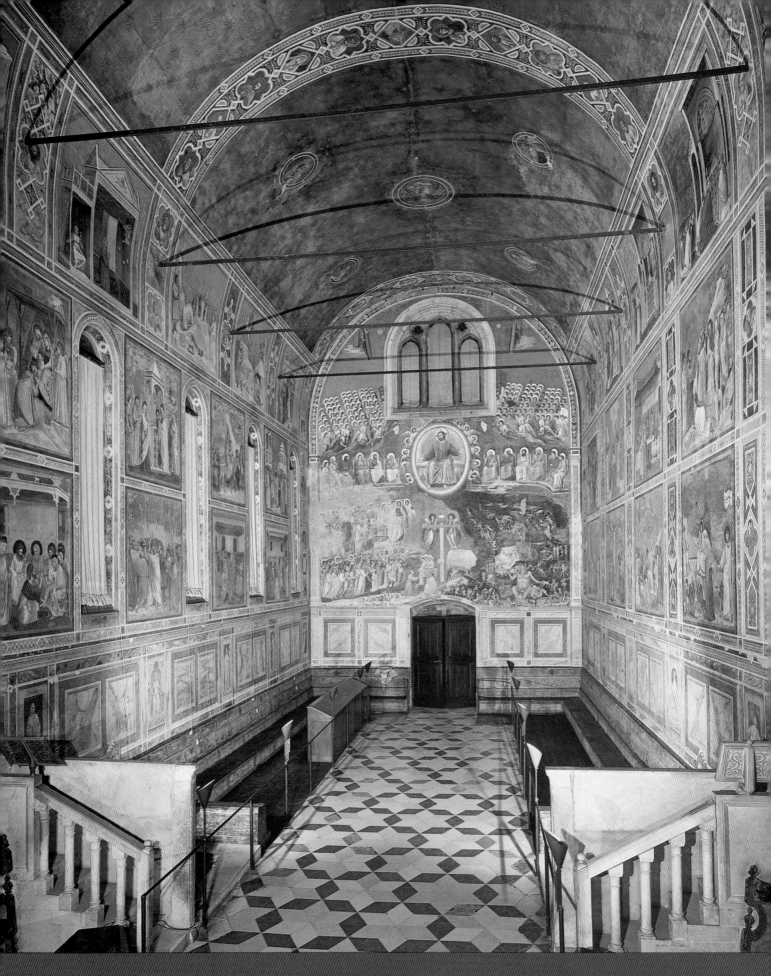

Colorplate 1. GIOTTO. Arena Chapel, Padua, looking toward the fresco of the *Last Judgment* over the entrance door. Consecrated 1305. Commissioned by Enrico Scrovegni

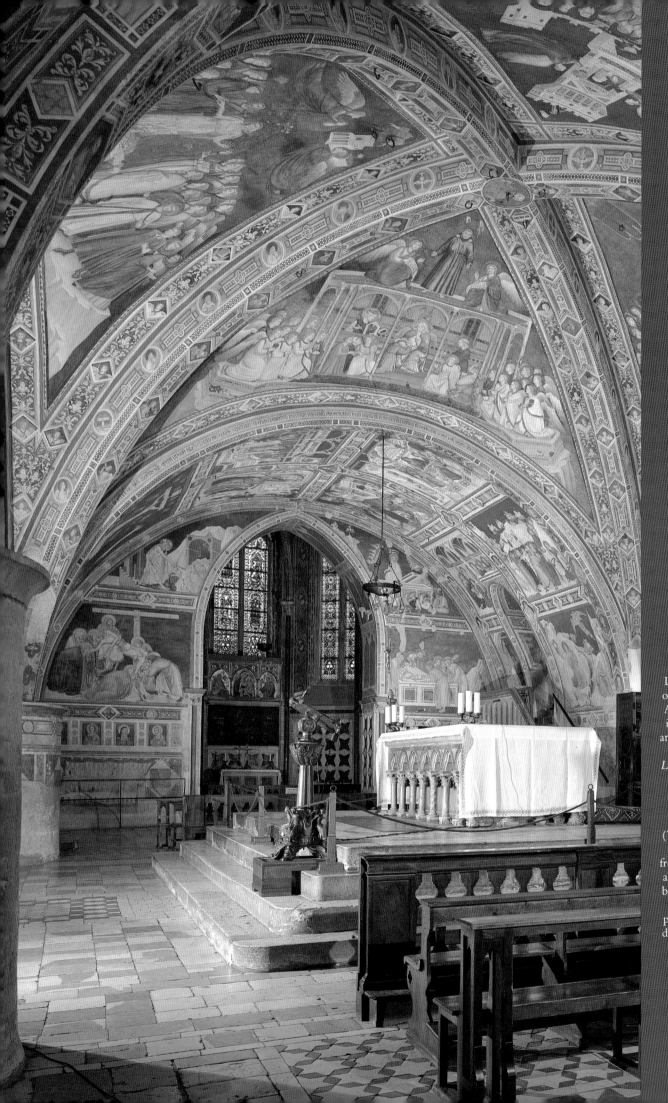

Colorplate 2. PIETRO LORENZETTI and assistants. Lower Church of S. Francesco, Assisi. Frescoes in the transept arm: *Descent from the Cross*, the *Lamentation*, and other scenes from Christ's Passion. 1320s–1330s. (The allegorical Franciscan frescoes over the altar, which are by an unknown Trecento painter, are not discussed in this book.)

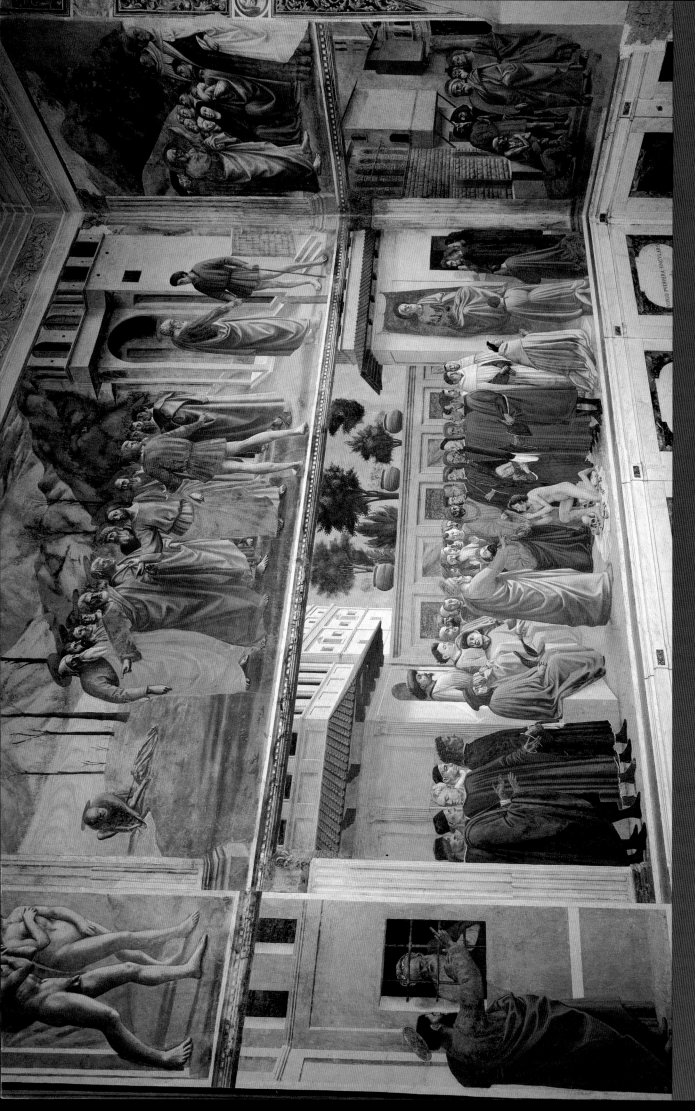

Colorplate 3. MASACCIO, MASOLINO, and FILIPPINO LIPPI. Brancacci Chapel. Sta. Maria del Carmine, Florence. Frescoes in upper register: *Expulsion* (Masaccio), *Tribute Money* (Masaccio), and *St. Peter Preaching* (Masolino); in lower register: *St. Paul Visiting St. Peter in Prison* (Filippino Lippi), *Raising of the Son of Theophilus* (Masaccio, completed by Filippino Lippi), and *St. Peter Healing with His Shadow* (Masaccio). Probably 1425–28(?) and early 1480s. Perhaps commissioned by Felice Brancacci

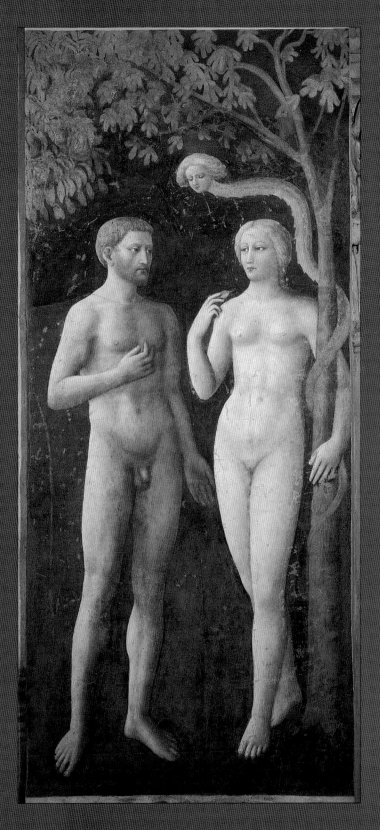

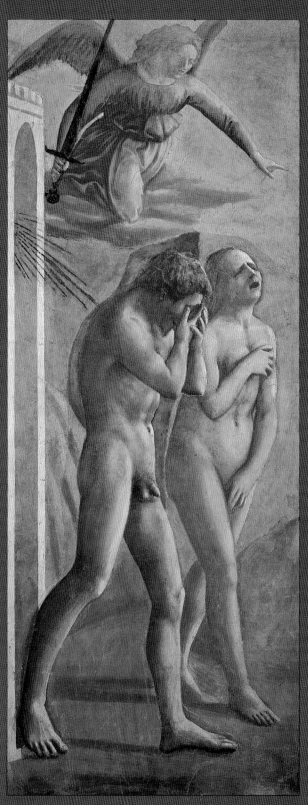

Colorplate 4. MASOLINO. *Temptation*. Probably 1425. Fresco, 7' x 2' 11". Brancacci Chapel

Colorplate 5. MASACCIO. *Expulsion*. Probably 1425. Fresco, 7' x 2' 11". Brancacci Chapel. See also figs. 196, 197

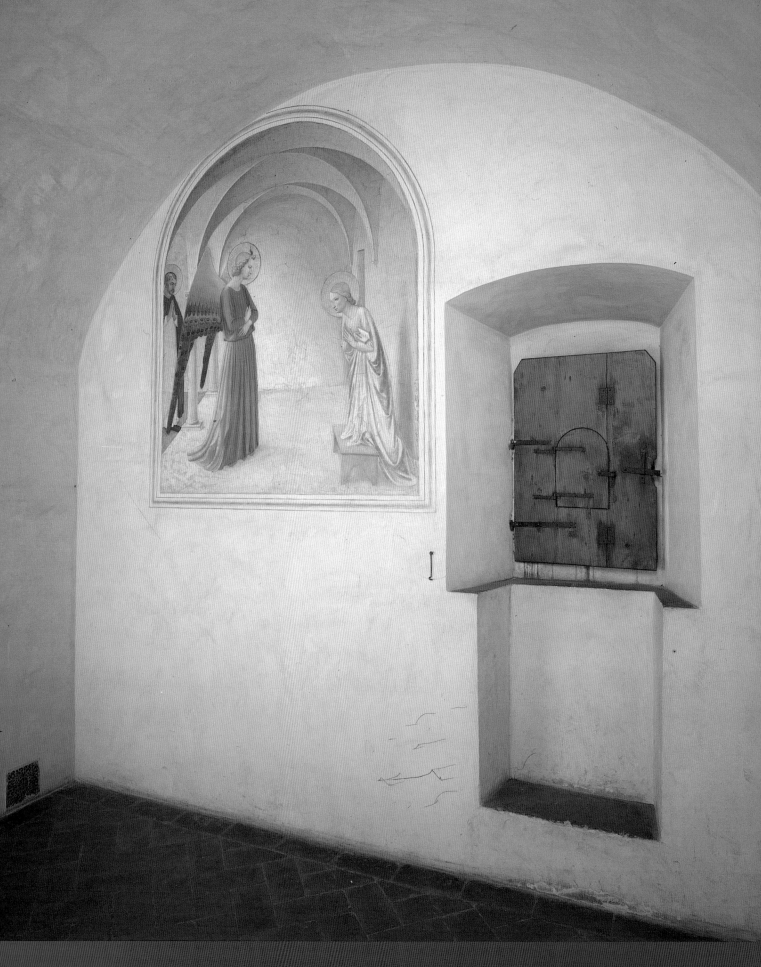

Colorplate 6. FRA ANGELICO. *Annunciation* in Monk's cell, Monastery of S. Marco, Florence. 1438–45. Fresco,
6' 1½" x 5' 2". Probably commissioned by Cosimo de' Medici

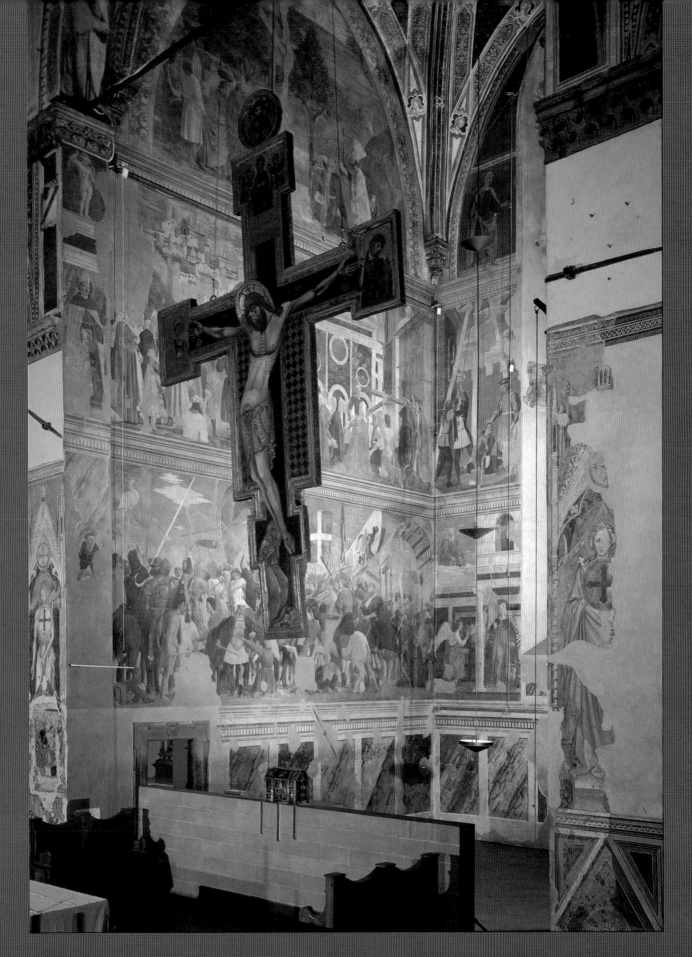

Colorplate 7. PIERO DELLA FRANCESCA. Chapel, S. Francesco, Arezzo. Frescoes of the Legend of the True Cross.
Lunette: *Heraclius Restoring the Cross to Jerusalem*; middle register: *Invention of the True Cross* and *Recognition of the True Cross and Judas Taken from the Well*; lower register: *Battle of Constantine and Maxentius* and *Annunciation*. c. 1454–58. Width of wall 24' 6". Commissioned by members of the Bacci family

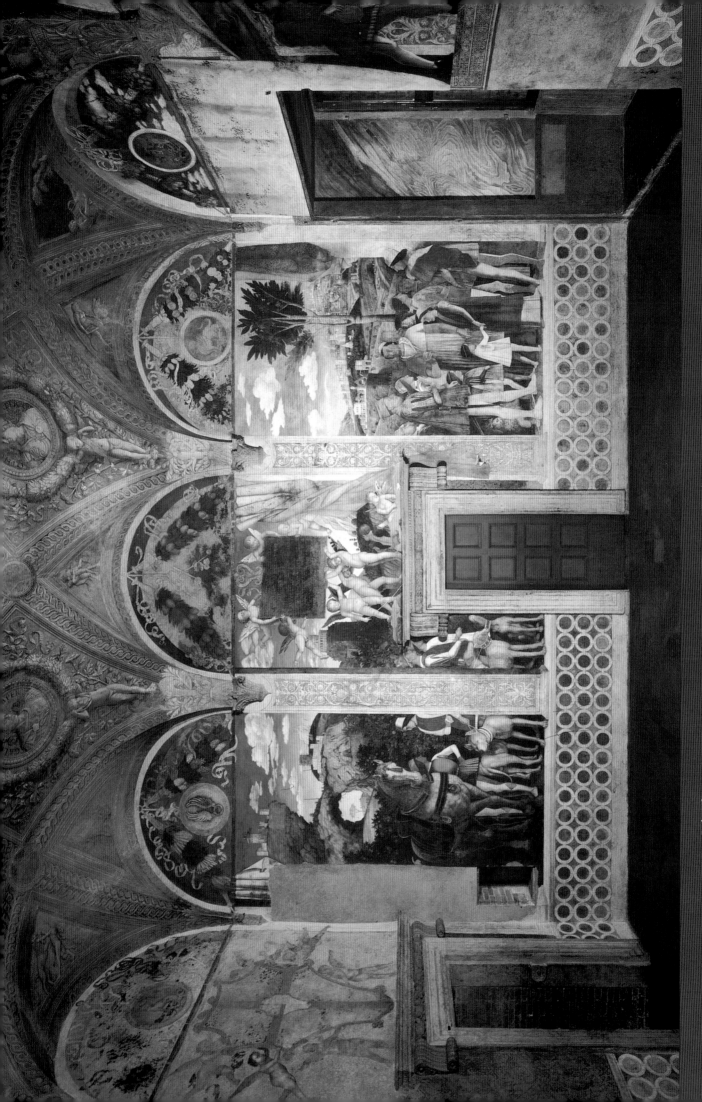

Colorplate 8. ANDREA MANTEGNA. Camera Picta, Palazzo Ducale, Mantua. *Arrival of Cardinal Francesco Gonzaga.*
Completed 1465–74. Walnut oil on plaster. Commissioned by Ludovico Gonzaga

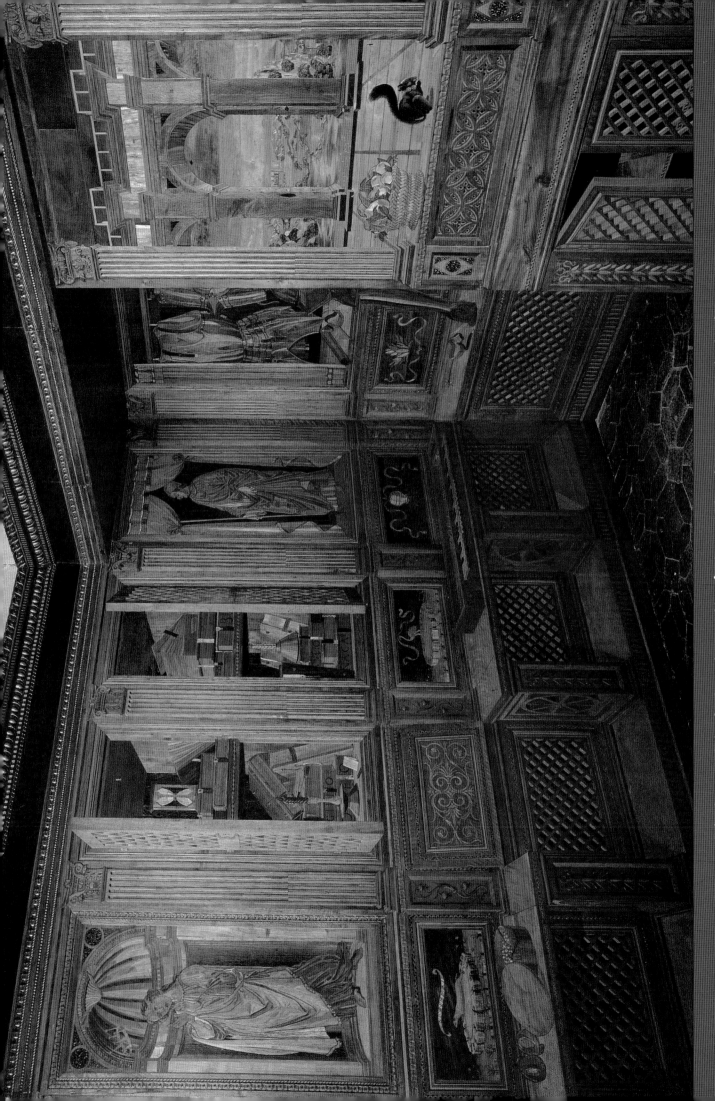

Colorplate 9: Studiolo of Federico da Montefeltro. Palazzo Ducale, Urbino. 1470s. Intarsia, height of intarsia 7' 3"

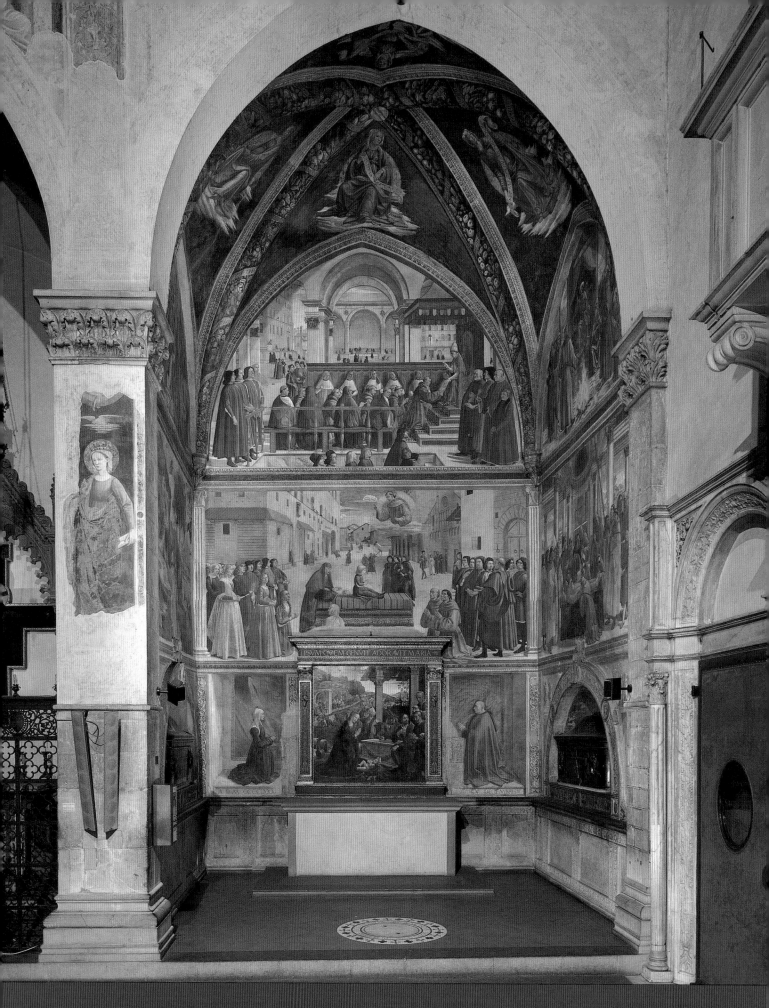

Colorplate 10. DOMENICO DEL GHIRLANDAIO. Sassetti Chapel, Sta. Trinita, Florence. Frescoes of scenes from the legend of St. Francis; *Nativity and Adoration of the Shepherds* (see colorplate 64, p. 353). 1483–86. Commissioned by Francesco Sassetti. The basalt tombs at the sides are attributed to GIULIANO DA SANGALLO

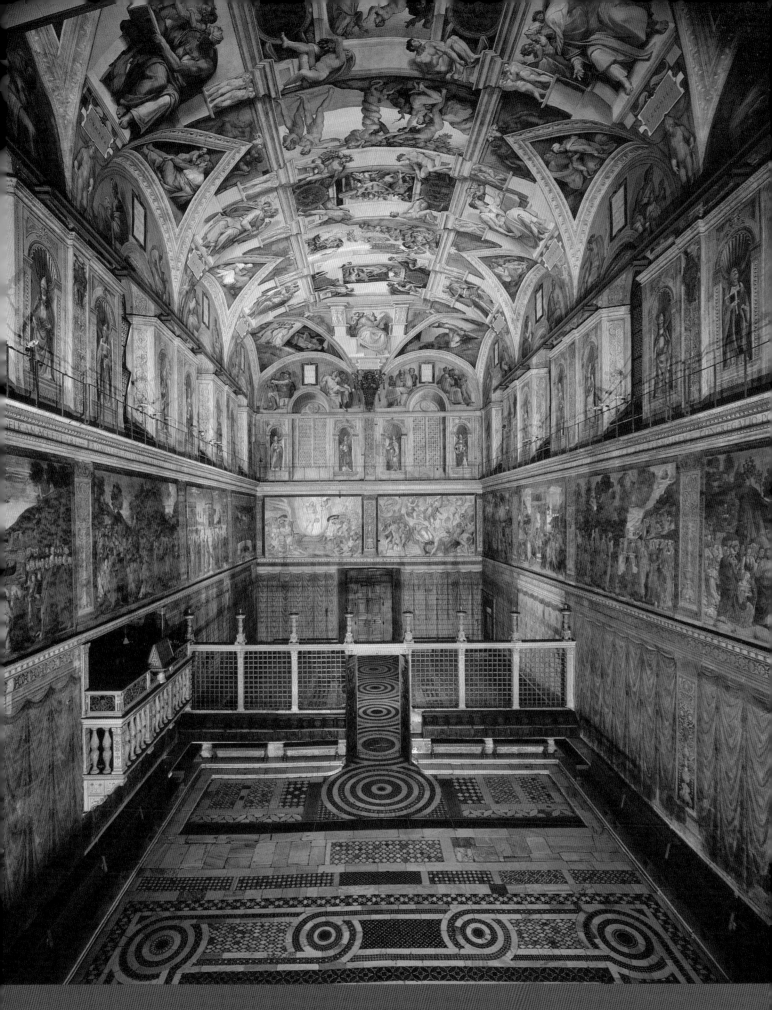

Colorplate 11. MICHELANGELO and others. Sistine Chapel, Vatican, Rome. General view showing
frescoes on the ceiling and side walls (see also colorplate 90, pp. 490–91). The ceiling measures 45 x 128'

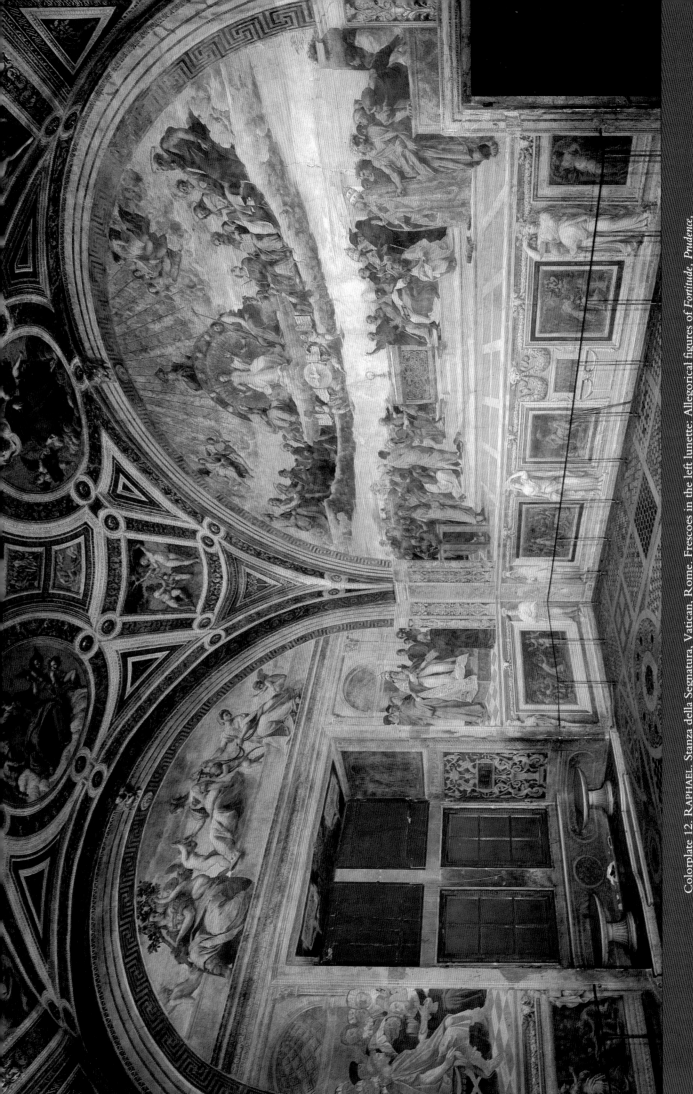

Colorplate 12. RAPHAEL. Stanza della Segnatura, Vatican, Rome. Frescoes in the left lunette: Allegorical figures of *Fortitude, Prudence, and Temperance*; above: *Allegory of Justice*; left of window: *Tribonian Handing the Law Code to Justinian*; right of window: *Gregory IX Approving the Decretals*, with portraits of Julius II as Gregory IX, and of Cardinals Giovanni de' Medici and Alessandro Farnese; right wall: *Disputà (Disputation over the Sacrament)* or *Theology*; above: *Allegory of Theology*. 1510–11. Size of *Disputà*, 19 x 27'. Commissioned by Pope Julius II

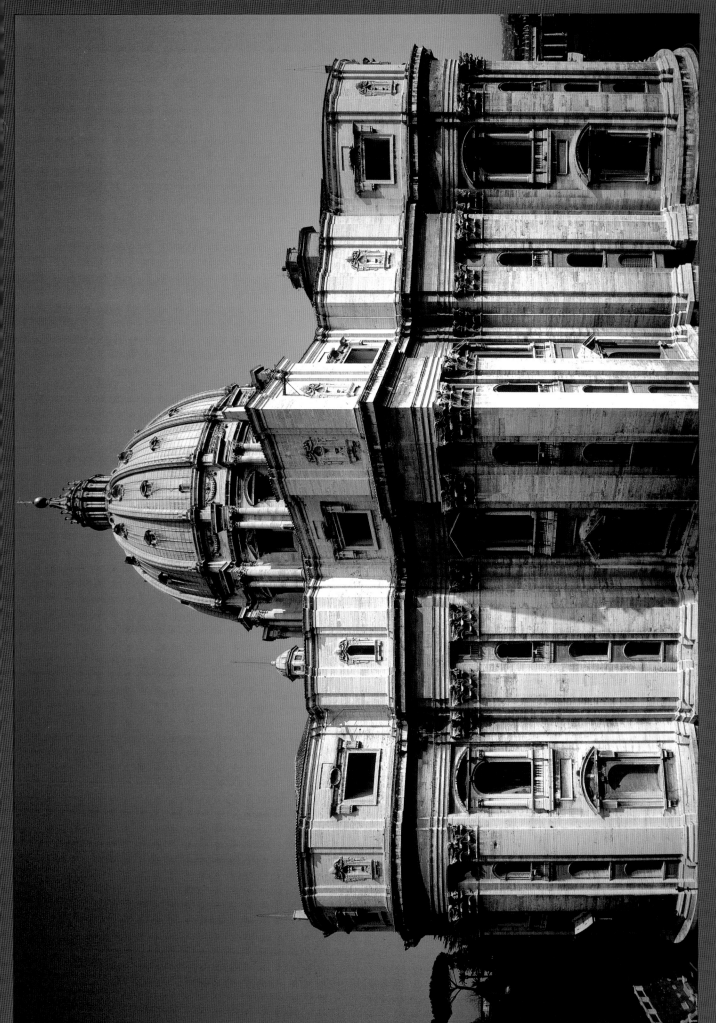

Colorplate 13. MICHELANGELO. St. Peter's, Vatican, Rome. View of apse. 1546–64

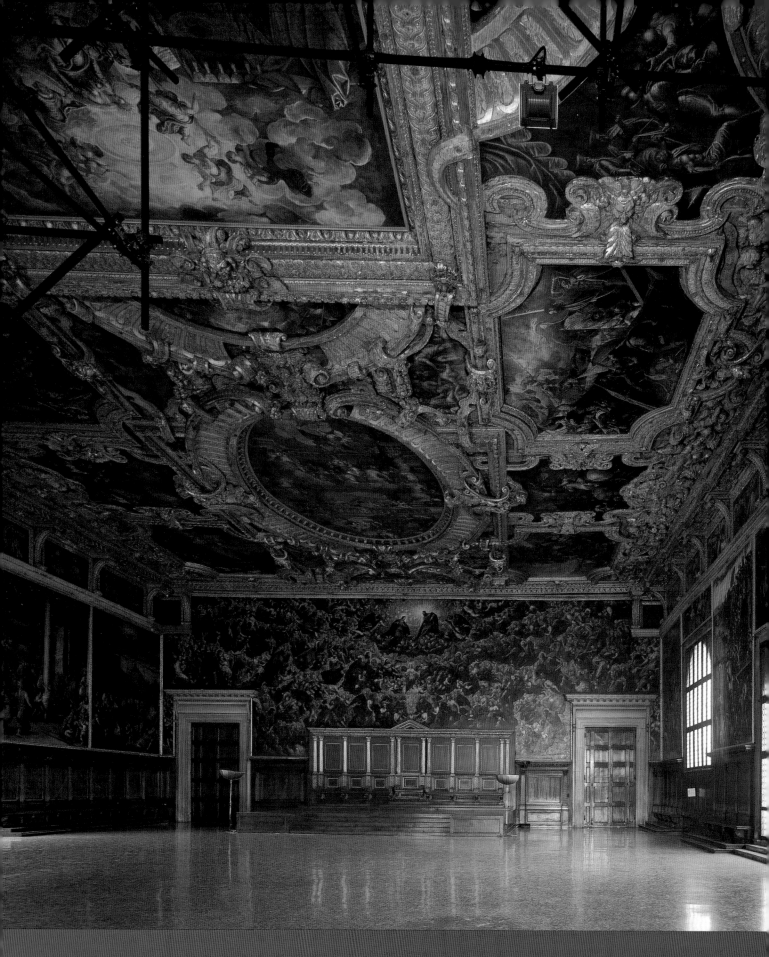

Colorplate 14. Hall of the Great Council, Doges' Palace, Venice. The oval ceiling painting visible here is the 🏛 *Triumph of Venice*, by VERONESE and pupils (see fig. 659); end wall painting, 🏛 *Paradise*, by TINTORETTO and pupils. 1585–90. Commissioned by the city government of Venice

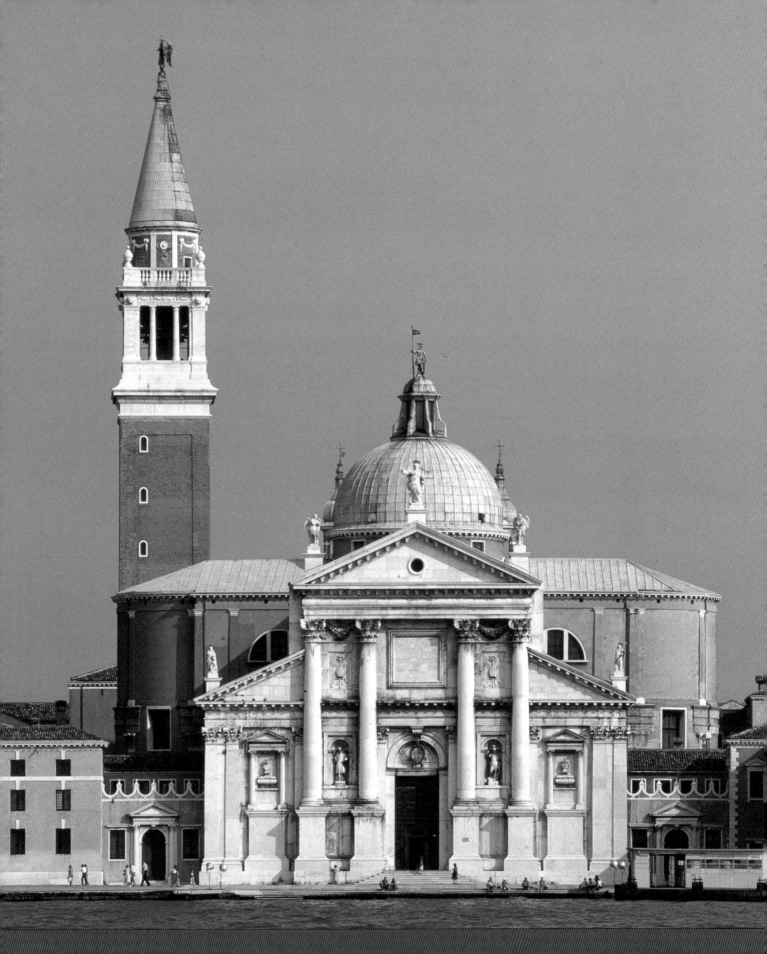

Colorplate 15. PALLADIO. Façade of S. Giorgio Maggiore, Venice. Completed by VINCENZO SCAMOZZI, 1610

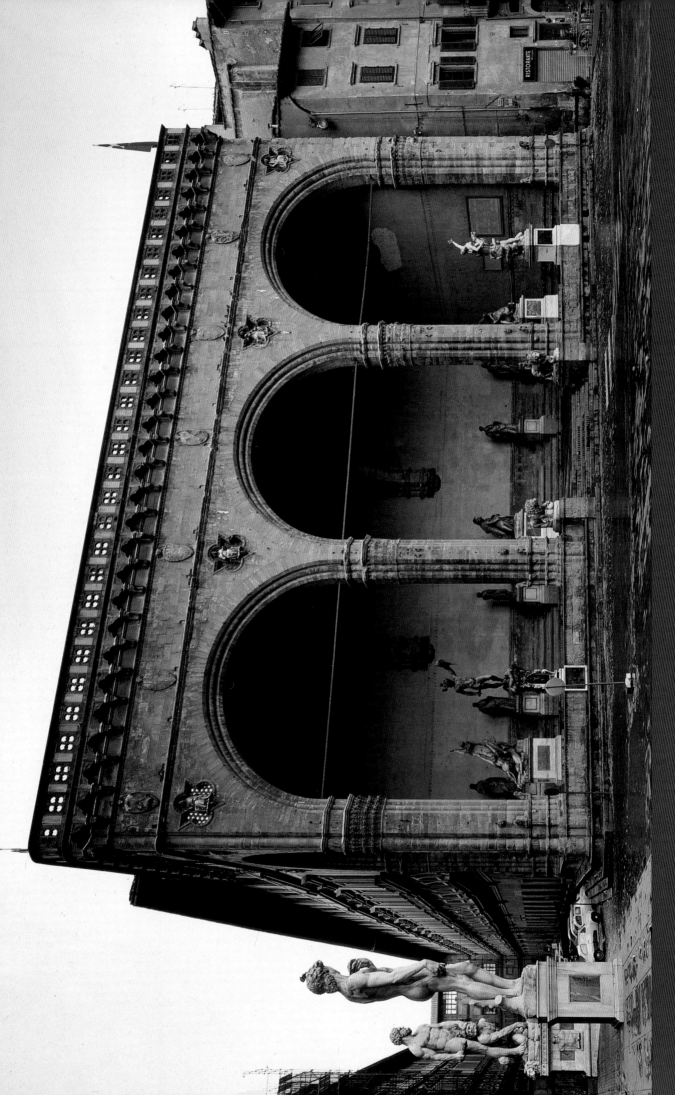

Colorplate 16. Piazza della Signoria, with a view of the Uffizi (see fig. 705) and the Loggia della Signoria (dei Lanzi). Built 1376–c. 1381 under the supervision of BENCI DI CIONE and SIMONE TALENTI. Underneath left arch of the loggia: ▥ *Perseus and Medusa*, by BENVENUTO CELLINI (see fig. 694); under right arch: ▥ *Rape of the Sabine Woman*, by GIOVANNI BOLOGNA (see figs. 698, 699); to the left is a copy of Michelangelo's *David* (see fig. 477), placed on the statue's original site

THE LATE MIDDLE AGES

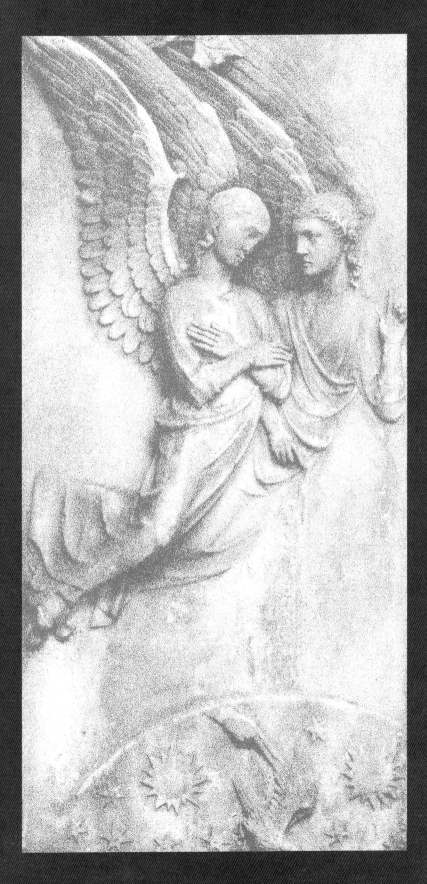

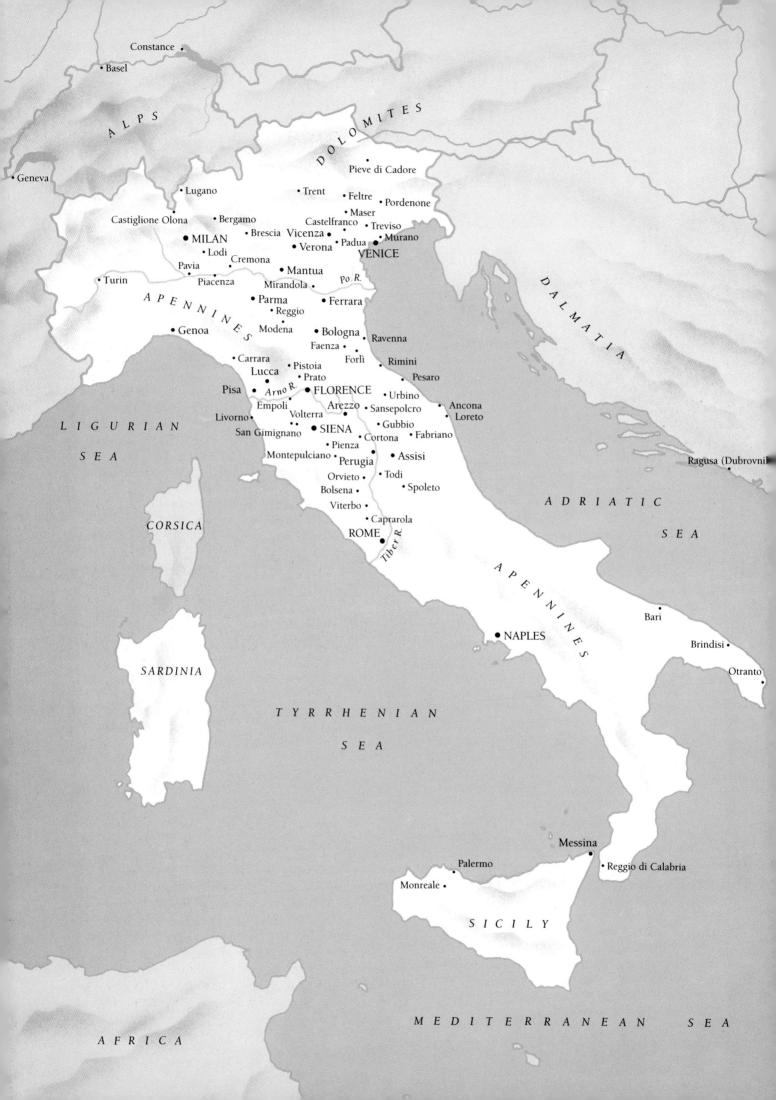

1
Italy and Italian Art

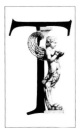he matrix of Italian art is Italy itself (fig. 1), a land whose physical beauty has attracted visitors from time immemorial. The variety of the Italian landscape, even over short distances, transforms a country roughly the size of California into a subcontinent, harboring a seeming infinity of pictorial surprises. Alpine masses shining with snow in midsummer, fantastic Dolomitic crags, turquoise lakes reflecting sunlight onto precipices, wide plains of profound fertility, poplar-bordered rivers, sandy beaches, Apennine chains enclosing green valleys, vast pasture lands, glittering bays enclosed by mountains, volcanic islands, dark forests, eroded deserts, gentle hills—all these combine to make up the inexhaustible Italy that rewards and defeats a lifetime of explorations.

But not all the beauty of Italy was provided by nature. Perhaps more than any other country in the Western world, Italy may be said to have been humanized. The country and its people have made their peace in an extraordinary way. Many towns and even some large cities do not lie in the valleys as we think they should, but are perched on hilltops, sometimes at dizzying heights. The reason for such positions is not hard to discover, for most Italian towns were founded when defense was essential. But the views from their ramparts offered the inhabitants not only a military but also an intellectual command of surrounding nature. Even the hills that are not crowned with cities, villages, castles, or villas—and most of those that are—have been turned into stepped gardens, terraces that hold, growing constantly and together, those essentials of Italian civilization—wheat, the olive, and the vine. Only here and there does one come across wild tracts whose rocks or sand have defied attempts at cultivation.

Everywhere cities can be seen from cities, towns from towns. Agriculture and forests are submitted to the ordering intelligence of human activity. On the Lombard plains the plots of woodland are marshaled in battalions; like perfect sentinels the disciplined cypresses guard the Tuscan hills. Three-hundred-year-old olive trees shimmer in gray and silver, winter and summer alike. The gardens are not flowerbeds but hedged and terraced evidences of human planning, patience, and skill. The Italian climate is less gentle than its reputation. Although

opposite: 1. Map of Italy

the winters seldom match the severity of those in the United States or Northern Europe, neither can they offer brilliant days of blue skies and flashing snowfields. Even in southern Italy and Sicily, winter is dark, wet, and interminable. Summer is hot, autumn rainy, and spring capricious. Yet in three millennia or so of constant and often stormy marriage with the land, the Italians have created a kind of harmony between human life and the natural world that is not met with elsewhere.

In the second half of the twentieth century, the relentless forces of industrialization are draining the hill farms of their population. Stone farmhouses stand abandoned among untended olive trees and weedy, crumbling terraces. With endless blocks of apartment houses and factories, modern suburbs have marred the beauty of many a valley and plain. The cancer of the modern motor highway, metastasizing throughout the peninsula and inevitably accompanied by factories and warehouses, has devoured many a magical vista. Automobile smog has fouled the once-clear skies over Florence, Rome, and Naples. The façades of Roman churches and palaces are often blackened by exhaust fumes. But one can still experience the Italian concord with nature. Country roads are still traveled, and hill farms still worked by pairs of colossal long-horned oxen. The smoke still rises from the ancient towns on their hilltops. And views across lines of cypresses and up rocky ledges reveal what might be the background of a fresco by Benozzo Gozzoli. The vast Umbrian spaces are much as Perugino saw them, and the rustling woods in the Venetian plain seem ready to disclose a nymph and satyr from the paintings of Giovanni Bellini.

THE CITIES

It is the hard-won harmony with nature that makes not only the landscape of the Italian peninsula but also the art of its people different from any other in the world. But this art in its entirety predates the rise of the national state of Italy in the nineteenth century. The Italian language uses the same word (*paese*) both for village and for country in the sense of nation, and to the medieval Italian and to millions of Italian peasants and villagers today, the boundaries of "country" do not extend beyond what can be seen from a hilltop village. A map of Italy in the Late Middle Ages or Early Renaissance would look like a mosaic, the pieces representing sepa-

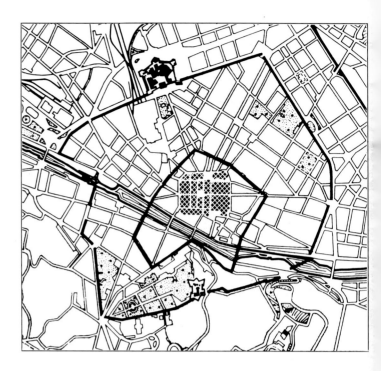

2. Plan of Florence. Crosshatched area,
original Roman city; inner black line, 13th-century walls;
outer black line, 14th-century walls and fortifications

rate political entities that were sometimes hardly larger than the village. These communes, which have often been compared to the city-states of ancient Greece, were all that was left of the Roman Empire, or of the kingdoms and dukedoms founded in the disorders following the barbarian invasions and the ensuing breakup of ancient Roman society. During the Late Middle Ages, from the eleventh through the fourteenth century, these city-states were quite independent of one another. Each had its own peculiar polity, at least outside of the fairly monolithic south, the so-called Kingdom of the Two Sicilies, or Kingdom of Naples. Each ruled its surrounding area of farmland and villages from the central city. Each spoke a different, sometimes a sharply individual, dialect, and not until the Renaissance did the modern Italian language begin to emerge, based on the Tuscan dialect. Although undermined by radio and television, many of these dialects are spoken (though not written) today.

At the outset of the Late Middle Ages, most of the city-states were republics, but in Lombardy many were ruled by their bishops. In general, they were merchant cities, and the republican governments were dominated by manufacturers, traders, and bankers. These republics were in a state of endemic if sporadic war with each other, even with visible neighbors (Florence with Fiesole, Assisi with Perugia). Fiercer even than the intercommunal wars, however, were the civil eruptions of family against family, party against party. Under such conditions, it was easy for powerful individuals to undermine the independence of a city-state. Nobles in their castles, mercenary generals ostensibly hired to protect the republic, and powerful merchants struggled to gain control of the prosperous towns, and their rate of success in the fourteenth and fifteenth centuries measures that of the destruction of communal liberties. The most successful of all these superpolities was the papacy, which maintained varying degrees of control over a wide belt of central Italian states.

Some of the republics were destined for greatness. Venice, at the top of the Adriatic, had by the thirteenth century established an enormous colonial empire, largely in order to maintain its commercial ties with the East. By the end of the thirteenth century, Florence, in Tuscany, was trading with Northern Europe and Asia and had so many branches of its banking firms in Europe that Pope Innocent III declared that there must be five elements, rather than four, because wherever Earth, Water, Fire, and Air were found in combination, one also saw Florentines. There were other important republics as well: Siena, Lucca, Pisa, Genoa—all separate, proud, independent states—and many that were smaller. Each state, whether a republic or ruled by a despot (duchy, marquisate, county, or merely signoria-lordship), tended to absorb its smaller neighbors by conquest or purchase, and by the end of the fifteenth century the

peninsula was divided into a decreasing number of polities, each dominating a considerable subject territory. Yet they were unable to unite against the menace of the increasingly centralized monarchies of the rest of Europe which, in the sixteenth century, were to submerge Italy almost entirely.

The most striking phenomenon of any one of these Italian city-states is a dense huddle of houses of almost uniform height—regulated by law—crowding up the slopes and toward the summits of the hills chosen for defense, often still surrounded by city walls with gates and towers. The jumbled planes of the tiled roofs are punctuated here and there by the loftier walls and towers of churches and civic buildings. The town houses of the great noble and commercial families also generally culminated in towers, built to secure the fortunes—and sometimes the lives—of their owners. Only in a few isolated towns are some of these house-towers preserved to their full height; in the Late Renaissance, when the small republics had coalesced into a few larger princedoms, the owners were forced by decree to truncate these symbols of family power and means of defense.

In or near the center of every town is the piazza, an open space that is the focus of civic life and as such is essential to understanding the civic nature of Italian art. Italian art is based in part on communication between people in the square and its adjoining streets, the sites where the life of the community takes place. Wherever the great squares have not become parking lots, this is still true.

In even the earliest Italian paintings, it is striking how immediately the circumstances of life, the people, and the architecture are transported into the works of art. Under the guise of religious or historical narrative, the painting or the work of sculpture presents an image of the continuing reality of everyday life—the contact, conversation, and conflict between people that constitute the drama of the piazza.

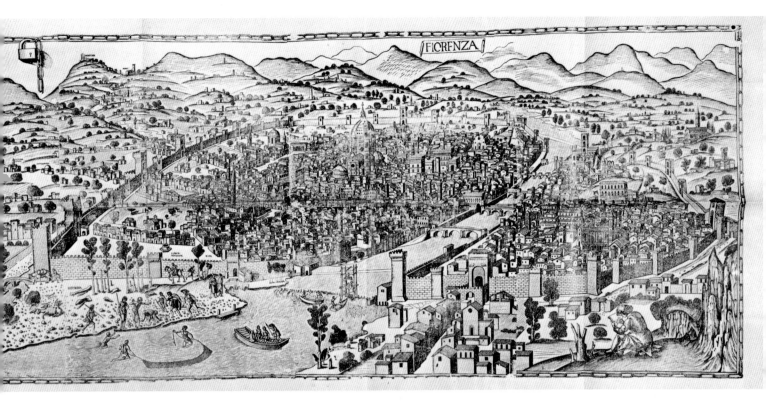

3. Florence as seen by an artist of the Quattrocento. Florentine wood engraving of c. 1480

In its ground plan, Florence reveals the nature of the expansion of the Italian city-state (fig. 2). A view (fig. 3) shows the city in the fifteenth century, when it was the largest in Europe. A century earlier, when London and Paris were towns of twenty thousand or so and Bruges and Ghent, the trading cities of the North, did not surpass forty thousand, Florence had more than one hundred thousand inhabitants. The colossal dome, whose construction we will presently follow, forms a focus for the city, which is surrounded by the circle of walls and then by the Tuscan hills. In the plan, roughly oriented from east to west in the manner of an ancient Roman town of the plains, one can see how the metropolis grew. The area of the original Roman city plan is indicated by crosshatched lines. This area was originally crisscrossed with straight streets that intersected at right angles. By the thirteenth century there were more inhabitants in the suburbs clustering around the gates than inside the Roman walls, and a second circle of fortifications, much less regular, was built. The third, fourteenth-century circle of walls encompassed an area so large that the city had not filled it by the nineteenth century. Its towered gates were decorated with paintings and sculpture.

Even today, when Florence has grown to half a million, a few large gardens remain inside the boulevards that, except on the south bank, have largely replaced the walls. The narrow streets must have been overcrowded even during the Middle Ages and the Renaissance. They are flanked by stone buildings that present a forbidding appearance in their present, largely stripped state (or with, at most, tan stucco), but that were originally coated with gray, white, or even brightly colored stucco, if we can believe the representations in old

paintings. The more splendid houses were sometimes decorated with simulated architectural elements, ornament, and figures incised in the plaster, of which a few examples remain.

Siena (fig. 4) is some forty-five miles to the south over winding roads—in the Middle Ages probably a day's journey by post-horses. An intermittent commercial and political rival of Florence, Siena was eventually to succumb to her hated enemy in the middle of the sixteenth century. To a degree difficult for a foreigner to conceive, Siena is still the archetype of the resentful vanquished. It is a hill town, straggling in the shape of a Y along the crest of three hills, in the midst of a magnificent landscape. Instead of the foursquare intersections and powerful cubic masses of Florence, Siena presents us with climbs and descents, winding streets, and unexpected vistas. In comparison with the logic of Florentine architecture and planning, it appears illogical and spontaneous.

The third city that will concern us chiefly, Venice (fig. 5), needs scarcely to be described, save to emphasize that its position, supported on wooden piles on hundreds of marshy islets in a sheltered lagoon along the Adriatic shore, rendered unnecessary either the city walls or the massive house construction of the mainland towns. The result was an architecture whose freedom and openness come as a release after the fortresslike character seen in so many other Italian cities.

THE ARTIST AND THE GUILDS

The typical central and north Italian city-state of the Late Middle Ages was dominated by the guilds in virtually every phase of its commercial and political life.

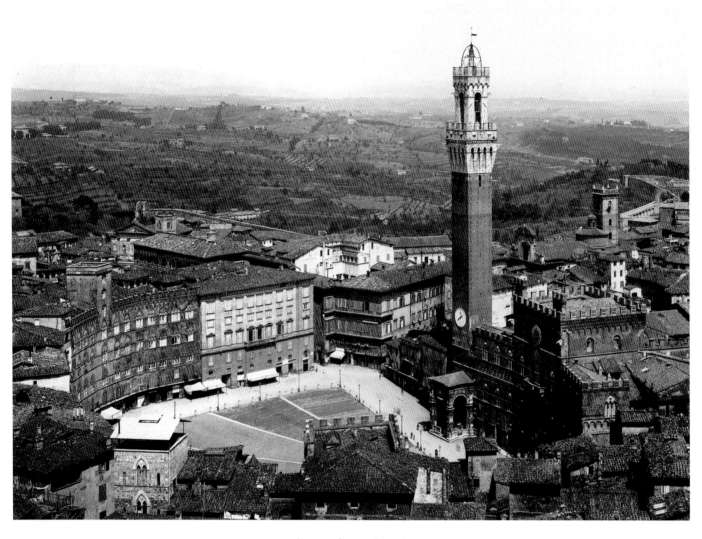

4. Aerial view of Siena from the west

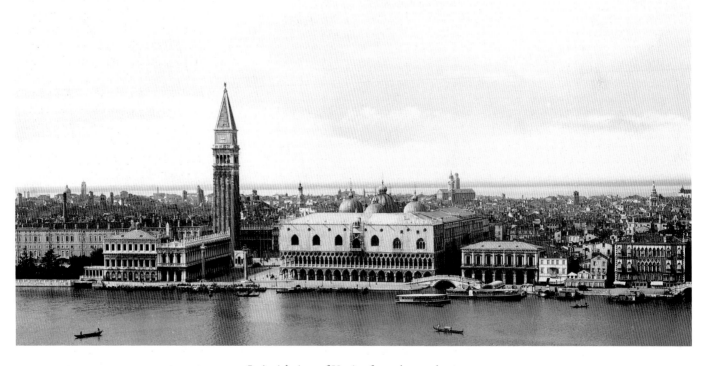

5. Aerial view of Venice from the southeast

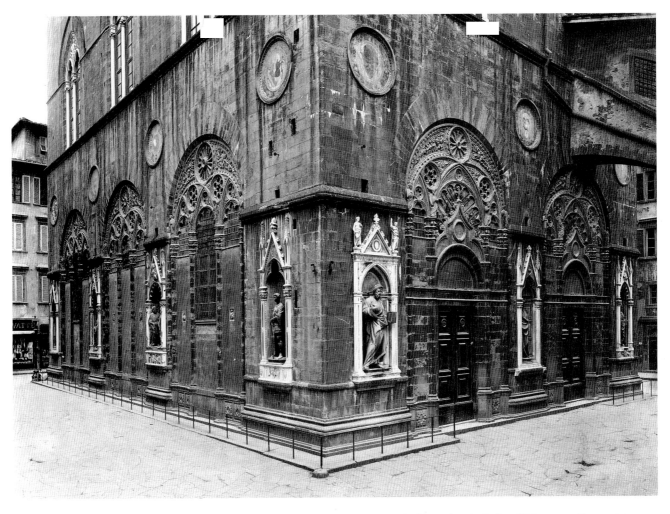

6. Orsanmichele, Florence, southeast corner with guild patron saints and tabernacles, including 🏛 NANNI DI BANCO's *Four Crowned Martyrs* (third niche from left, see fig. 168), DONATELLO's *St. George* (fourth from left, fig. 164), and 🏛 GHIBERTI's *St. Matthew* (fifth from left, fig. 160). Rebuilt 1337; arches closed, later 14th century; niches and sculptures, 14th–16th centuries

Florence was a republic founded on commerce and ruled by an organization of guilds—independent associations of bankers and artisan-manufacturers. The guilds were self-perpetuating and self-regulating, but they had to accept the domination of the Guelph party, the single political entity permitted in a democracy that, however restrictive by modern standards, was in advance of anything conceived in Western Europe since the days of Pericles. In Florence the position of the guilds was symbolized by the niches reserved for them in a building that was the center of the food supply of the Republic in an era threatened constantly by famine—the combined grain exchange and shrine known as Orsanmichele (fig. 6). The arches of this enormous three-story structure in the center of the city were, in those days, still open to the streets, and between the arches were niches in which each principal guild had the civic responsibility to place a statue of its patron saint.

The seven major guilds (*Arti*, as they were called) included the Arte di Calimala, the refiners of imported woolen cloth; the Arte della Lana, the wool merchants who manufactured their own cloth; the Arte dei Giudici e Notai, or judges and notaries; the Arte del Cambio, or bankers' and money changers' guild; the Arte della Seta,

or silk weavers; the Arte dei Medici e Speziali, or doctors and pharmacists; and the Arte dei Vaiai e Pellicciai, or furriers. The painters, oddly enough, belonged to the guild of the doctors and pharmacists, to which they were admitted in 1314, perhaps—as is generally believed—because they ground their colors as the pharmacists ground materials for medicines. In the 1340s the painters were classified as dependents of the physicians, perhaps because painters and doctors enjoyed the protection of the same patron saint, St. Luke, who was reputedly both an artist and a physician. And in 1378 the painters became an independent branch of the Medici e Speziali.

There was a constantly shifting number of intermediate and minor guilds. Among the former, and never admitted to the rank of the major guilds, was the Arte di Pietra e Legname, the guild of workers in stone and wood. This comprised all sculptors who worked in these two materials, but a sculptor trained to work in metals, such as bronze (and there was a completely different attitude on the part of the citizens toward this material and those who knew how to manipulate it), was a member of a major guild, the Arte della Seta.

At the bottom of the social structure, outside the

guilds, were the wool carders, on whose labors much of the fortune of the city depended. Their situation in some ways was comparable to that of the slaves of ancient Athens, for although the Ciompi, as they were called, were permitted to leave their employment, their activities were strictly circumscribed by law. These workers, who constantly hovered on the brink of starvation, revolted in 1378 and founded a guild of their own, but their guild and participation in the government were both short-lived. The oligarchy resumed control, put down the Ciompi by mass slaughter and individual execution, and resumed control over the economy and political fortunes of the Republic.

Through membership in one or more guilds, the artist's social position was established not in the Liberal Arts—grammar, logic, rhetoric, arithmetic, geometry, astronomy, and music—which were considered the only arts suitable for a gentleman either in antiquity or in medieval feudal societies, but in the Mechanical Arts. In the Italian city-states, however, classification among the Mechanical Arts represented a positive advantage to painters, sculptors, and architects. In 1334 the painter Giotto (see pp. 76, 92–93) is believed to have designed a set of reliefs for the *campanile* (bell tower) of the Cathedral of Florence that were intended to be seen and read by the working citizen in the street; they were carved by Andrea Pisano. The series begins with the *Creation of Adam* (see fig. 84) and the *Creation of Eve*, skips the episodes of the temptation and expulsion, and goes on to show the first labors of Adam and Eve. Next, going round the tower, the early activities of humanity are shown, with the Mechanical Arts among them, including painting, sculpture, and architecture (see figs. 7, 16, 17).

Late in the fourteenth century, the Florentine writer Filippo Villani devoted a chapter to the painters of his era, comparing them to those who practice the Liberal Arts. In 1404 the Paduan humanist Pier Paolo Vergerio claimed (erroneously) that painting was one of the four Liberal Arts taught to Greek boys. At the end of the fifteenth century, Leonardo da Vinci took up the struggle in earnest (see p. 432). The stakes were economic as well as social. The fifteenth-century artist, with some outstanding exceptions, was not well paid and often complained of poverty, but in the sixteenth century Michelangelo (who claimed noble ancestry), Titian (who was actually ennobled), Raphael, and many other artists attained international fame, respect, and wealth. Artists who could attach themselves to the court of a prince occupied positions of prosperity and had the power to enforce their style on others. By the late sixteenth century, academies under princely patronage (see p. 631) began to replace the long-moribund guilds.

Artists were an essential part of a closely knit society, and they usually worked on commission. It would hardly have occurred to an artist of the thirteenth or fourteenth century to paint a picture or carve a statue for any other reason than to satisfy a patron, and an artist who was a good manager would have a backlog of commissions awaiting execution. Artists did not work in the studios common to later traditions. The word itself, which means "study" in Italian, only came into use in the seventeenth century, when the artists joined and were dominated by academies. In the Late Middle Ages and throughout much of the Renaissance, the artist worked in a *bottega* (shop); this word is also used to signify the organized body of paid assistants and apprentices who worked under the direction of the master. Apprentices entering the system could be as young as seven or eight, and their instruction was paid for by their families. Until the late sixteenth century, women were excluded, in part because they were forbidden to join the appropriate guilds.

Sometimes the *bottega* was entered, like a shop, from the street. Artists might even exhibit finished work to the public in their shops. Masaccio, Ghiberti, Castagno, and Antonio del Pollaiuolo, as well as other important artists, would accept commissions for jewelry, for painted wooden trays customarily given new mothers, for painted shields for tournaments or ceremonials, for processional banners, or for designs for embroidered vestments or other garments. Artists were also employed designing triumphal arches, floats, and costumes for the festivals that celebrated civic, religious, and private events. In his old age, in a period dominated by the new academic conception of the artist as well as by the new autocracies, Michelangelo protested that he "was never a painter or a sculptor like those who keep shops."

For our purposes, the principal object made by a painter in a *bottega* was the movable picture, above all, the altarpiece. This work stands as a religious image upon the altar: it may use symbols to represent the doctrine underlying the Mass, or depict the saint to whom a particular church or altar was dedicated, together with scenes from his or her life. Up to the thirteenth century or so, the exact date varying from place to place, the priest stood behind the altar, facing the congregation, and it is to this early form of the liturgy that many churches have returned in our own day. With the celebrant in such a position, there was room on the altar for nothing but the required crucifix, missal, candles, and vessels of the Mass. Decoration—and this could include images and narrative scenes—was limited to the front of the altar and perhaps the sides and back. Sometimes the decoration was sculpted, in stone or even precious metals. Often it was painted on wooden panels known as altar frontals.

In the thirteenth century, the ritual was moved around to the front of the altar, so that the priest had his back to the congregation except when he turned to it for responses or readings. This change was a direct result of the growth of the city throughout Western Europe but especially in Italy, which placed wealthy burgher families in the position of donors to the new and often large church buildings. The belief in the efficacy of the Mass as an instrument for salvation gave rise to chapels

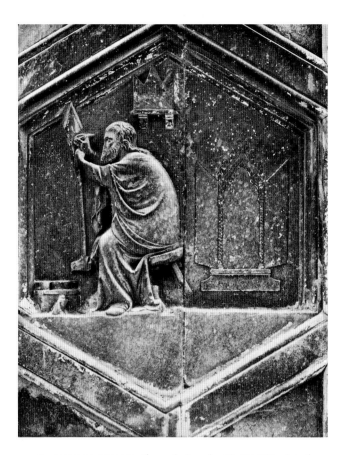

7. ANDREA PISANO (from designs by GIOTTO?). *Art of Painting*. c. 1334–37. Marble, 32³/4 x 27¹/4". Removed from original location on the Campanile, Florence (see fig. 77). Museo dell'Opera del Duomo, Florence

could be painted in fresco with subjects related to that of the altarpiece, and by the same artist. Many of the paintings and sculptures treated in this book come from such family chapels, and some are still in place.

Large churches were generally divided by a massive wood or stone screen into the choir, where the clergy, monks, or nuns celebrated the Divine Office (prayers and psalms sung seven times daily), and the nave for the laity, which sometimes included the crossing of nave and transept and was often provided with its own altar. This choir screen was treated as an important architectural element and included small family chapels. It was often surmounted by religious images, usually crucifixes, sometimes of great size and often tilted forward so that they could be seen more easily. (Colorplate 18, p. 58, shows an example.) After the almost universal destruction of the choir screens in the sixteenth century, the crucifixes wound up elsewhere in the church, or eventually on museum walls.

Both altarpieces and the smaller devotional pictures made to be set up in private homes as aids to devotions were almost always composed of wooden panels. Sometimes two panels were joined together, in which case the work is called a diptych. More common, however, were the triptychs (three panels) and polyptychs (many panels), whose design within architectural frames often suggests the façades of Gothic or Renaissance churches. An altarpiece on a high altar might also have painted images and scenes on the back. The custom of painting the predella, or base of the altarpiece, with small narrative scenes, visible only at close range by the clergy and faithful, began early in the fourteenth century. And at about the same time the Gothic pinnacles, set between or above the arches and their architectural gables, also began to provide fields for painting. The iconography of the altarpiece was determined by the clergy, or by the wealthy family who had ordered it, and even its shape could be subject to the patron's tastes. The panels of the altarpiece, complete with frames, were sometimes manufactured outside the painter's studio by a professional carpenter and woodcarver who, on occasion, might also be a well-known architect; sometimes this occurred even before the painter had signed a contract to gild its background, frame, and ornaments and to paint pictures on its surfaces. Sometimes the painter was also an architect and would thus probably have provided the design no matter who carved and assembled the panels. Painters might even be confronted with ready-made panels in little harmony with their own style. One of the Giotto-Pisano reliefs (fig. 7) shows the interior of a painter's *bottega* with an artist earnestly at work.

THE PRACTICE OF PAINTING

The intricate procedures of the painter's craft, as practiced in Florence and northern Italy, are described in detail by Cennino Cennini in *Il libro dell'arte* (*The Book*

in which Mass could be said daily, sometimes many times a day, for the souls of departed members of these families. Such chapels ranged from altars along the inner walls of the side aisles to structures like small churches in themselves, but most were rooms of standard size and architectural character that lined the side aisles and transepts of churches. Sometimes chapter houses, for the meetings of a community of monks or nuns, and sacristies, where the vessels, books, and vestments of the liturgy were kept, were endowed as family chapels and provided with altars. Family chapels might outnumber by twenty or thirty to one the high altar at which Mass was said for the entire congregation, and in very few chapels was there enough space for the priest to stand behind the altar.

The new position of the priest left the altar-table open for large-scale religious images, and these developed with rapidity in the thirteenth and fourteenth centuries. The crucifix, required for every altar, was the most logical theme. A crucifix stands on an altar in the fourteenth-century fresco shown in colorplate 27 (p. 114). The thirteenth century also saw tremendous growth in the veneration of the Virgin Mary, and patrons began to commission the images of the Madonna and Child, protectors of the Christian family, that play so large a part in Italian art and are still to be found in Catholic homes. If the chapel was large, the side walls, the space above the altarpiece, and the vaulted ceiling

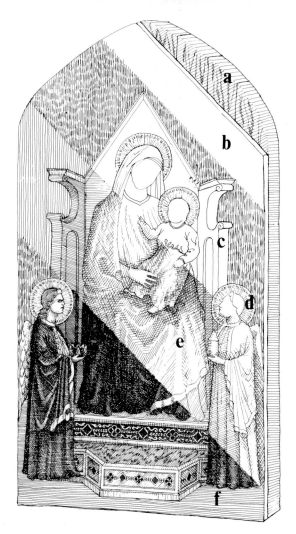

8. Tempera panel dissected to show principal layers:
a. wooden panel; *b.* gesso, sometimes reinforced with linen;
c. underdrawing; *d.* gold leaf; *e.* underpainting;
f. final layers of tempera

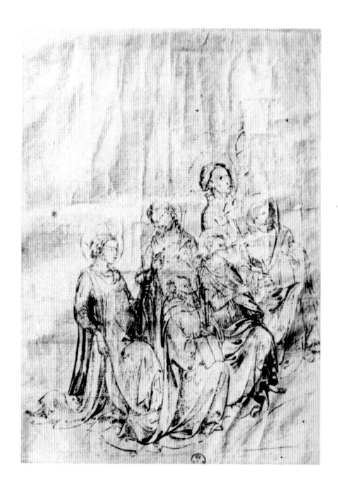

9. Workshop of Lorenzo Monaco. *Six Saints,*
study for the San Benedetto *Coronation of the Virgin.* c. 1415.
Silverpoint and pen on paper, 9⁵/₈ x 6⁷/₈". Uffizi Gallery,
Florence

of Art), written about 1400. Although he boasts that he studied with Agnolo Gaddi, the son and pupil of Taddeo Gaddi, who had been an assistant of Giotto, no evidence or paintings back up this claim. The book was written in Padua, in northern Italy, where Cennino had lived long enough to write in the local dialect rather than in Tuscan. All we know for certain is that the art of painting as described by Cennino is how things were done in his own Paduan *bottega.* Nonetheless, we have no other technical treatise from this period, and what Cennino says, although not necessarily relevant to earlier periods—and sometimes certainly in error—must be read seriously.

The first step in the making of a tempera painting was the construction of the panels. Once joined and framed by the carpenter, the panels, of finely morticed and sanded poplar, linden, or willow wood, were taken to the painter's shop (see fig. 8). They were then spread with gesso, a mixture of finely ground plaster and animal glue. Sometimes the gesso was covered with a surface of linen soaked in gesso and still more gesso was applied to the linen. When dry, the final gesso surface could be given a finish as smooth as ivory. Then came the procedure of drawing, whose exact role in the fourteenth and early fifteenth centuries is still debated among scholars.

Relatively few Italian drawings dating before the 1430s are preserved, and quite a number of these are apparently leaves from artists' pattern books that represent copies of works of art, models for standard compositions, and drawings of animals, birds, figures, and heads. Many, however, show signs of being sketches for actual compositions, and some can be securely identified as such, although only one, by a member of Lorenzo Monaco's workshop (fig. 9), is for an altarpiece, one portion of which is sketched out in silverpoint and light strokes of the quill pen. If these few survive from a period when drawings themselves were neither prized nor collected, there must originally have been many more.

Drawing is regarded as the foundation of art by Cennino, who devotes twenty-eight brief chapters to the subject, advising the painter to draw daily on paper, parchment, or panel with pen, charcoal, chalk, or brush. He urges the artist to draw from nature, from the paintings of the masters, or from the imagination. A generation later the architect and theorist Leonbattista Alberti (see pp. 229–31), writing in Florence, speaks of "concepts" and "models" (doubtless sketches and detailed drawings) as customary preparations for painting and for *storie* (figural compositions). In the mid-sixteenth century, Giorgio Vasari, the painter, architect, and first histo-

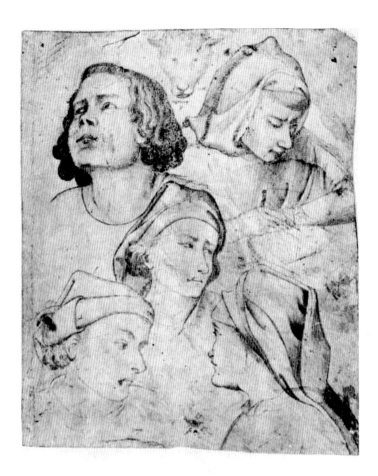

10. AGNOLO GADDI (attributed to). *Life Studies of Five Heads.*
c. 1380. Pen and wash on parchment, 7³/4 x 6¹/4".
Castello Sforzesco, Milan

rian of Italian art, describes sketches as "a first sort of drawings that are made to find the poses and the first composition," dashed down in haste by the artist, from which drawings "in good form" will later be made.

The importance of preparatory drawings may well have varied considerably from *bottega* to *bottega*, but the evidence suggests that the fourteenth-century painter drew such standard subjects as Madonnas, saints, or crucifixes directly on the panel before beginning to paint. The painter must also have sketched out, or even studied in detail, complex figure compositions in small scale, on paper or parchment, to be kept next to the painting as a guide in the early stages. Dust, paint drippings, and the wear and tear of the *bottega* (Cennino warns painters to cover ornaments and gilding with a sheet while painting) would have rendered such sketches hardly worth preserving. This paragraph represents the author's hypothesis, but it seems preferable to the claim that suddenly, in 1430, painters discovered the utility of the preliminary drawing, which architects and sculptors (often the selfsame individuals) had been employing for more than a hundred years (see figs. 76, 156) and which painters were often required by contract to submit to patrons for approval. Nor is there any other reasonable explanation for the surviving composition sketches, certain or probable. Other studies, involving the play of light on figures and groups (fig. 10), also survive, and

some of these may have been drawn for panels.

By the mid-fifteenth century, the *spolvero* (Italian for "dust off"), a new technique previously used for ornamental borders, came into broader usage. The *spolvero* was a full-scale drawing of complex details, such as the heads of the main figures. The outlines of the *spolvero* were transferred by "pouncing," or dusting. The outlines of a drawing would be pricked with a sharp point and, after the drawing was placed on the surface to be painted, it would be tapped with a sponge or bag loaded with charcoal dust so that rows of dots would transfer the design to the surface. Sometimes these dots can still be made out. The preliminary compositional sketch and other drawings were thus relegated to a safer stage of the work, resulting in their more frequent preservation, while the *spolvero* in turn was exposed to the dangers of the *bottega* (no *spolvero* remains intact). In the early sixteenth century even the pouncing was skipped. The *spolvero* was replaced by the cartoon (from the Italian word *cartone*, a heavy paper), a full-scale drawing made on sheets of heavy paper glued together, whose outlines were transferred by means of a metal point, or stylus, pressing through the cartoon. Several cartoons and fragments of cartoons remain, but they are few compared to the thousands that must have been executed.

Cennino is explicit on how to compose a single figure on a panel. The underdrawing began with a piece of charcoal tied to a reed or stick in order to gain a little distance from the panel and thus enjoy greater ease in composing. Shading was done by means of light strokes, and erasures were made with a feather. When the design of the figure was determined, the feather could erase all but dim traces of the original strokes, and the drawing was then reinforced with a pointed brush dipped in a wash of ink and water; the brush was made of hairs from the tail of a gray squirrel. After the panel was swept free of charcoal, the painter shaded in the drapery folds and some of the shadow on the face with a blunt brush loaded with the same wash, "and thus," Cennino says, "there will remain to you a drawing that will make everyone fall in love with your work."

In panel paintings of the thirteenth, fourteenth, and early fifteenth centuries, the backgrounds behind the figures and the haloes around the heads of saints were almost invariably gold leaf, applied in sheets over a red sizing or glue called *bole*. Lines incised around the contours of the figures and halos guided the gilder. In many paintings the edges of the sheets can still be made out, and as the gold leaf tends to wear off with rubbing, damaged backgrounds often display areas of the underlying red. Gold was used because of its precious and beautiful character and because its luminosity suggested the light of Heaven. In the thirteenth century, gold haloes, and sometimes parts of the background, were incised to make a pattern in relief, but by about 1330 these areas were being decorated using low-relief punches shaped like flowers, stars, and other patterns to emboss these designs into the gold and gesso surface.

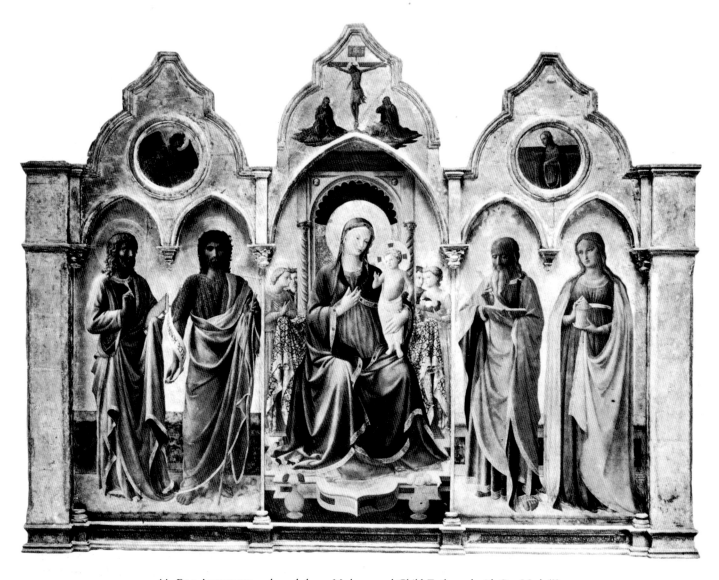

11. FRA ANGELICO and workshop. *Madonna and Child Enthroned with Sts. Mark (?),*
John the Baptist, John the Evangelist, and Mary Magdalen. c. 1436. Panel, transferred from original panel,
54 x 81¼". Museo Diocesano, Cortona. Commissioned for S. Domenico, Cortona

When the gilding of the background was complete, the painter could proceed with underpainting, usually in *terra verde* (green earth) for the flesh, but even the drapery was often outlined in this color. When the underpainting was completed, the artist would build up the actual painting in layer after thin layer of tempera—ground colors mixed with egg yolk as a vehicle. Yolk of egg dries rapidly and becomes extremely hard, and as a result, the painter could not easily change a form or correct mistakes. The strokes, applied with a sharply pointed brush of gray squirrel hairs, had to be accurate, neat, and final, and although Cennino does not say so, the brushstrokes are generally parallel and seldom overlap, following in concentric curves each form of flesh or drapery.

Cennino instructs the painter to make three dishes of each drapery color, the first full strength, the second mixed half-and-half with white, and the third an equal mixture of the first two, thus accounting for darks, lights, and intermediate tones. The highlights, brushed on last in white or near-white, or sometimes even in yellow or gold, are inevitably the first to disappear in the rough cleaning to which almost all old pictures were subjected in the past. Cennino also instructs the painter how to achieve an effect of iridescent drapery by using a different color for highlights from that employed for darker areas. The methods he describes reveal the slow, painstaking approach required by the art of painting in tempera, and the Giotto-Pisano relief (see fig. 7) shows a painter working on a small panel as closely as if it were a miniature.

Blue was a special problem. The two available pigments were both imported and expensive: azurite came from Germany, and ultramarine, which was as costly as gold and sometimes more so, was produced by grinding lapis lazuli imported from Afghanistan. Both were customarily mixed with a little white. In the case of the Virgin's mantle, which was typically painted blue to represent her as Queen of Heaven, the white was usually omitted. In most early altarpieces this mantle has turned dark grayish green through the action of the egg, and the viewer has to imagine the effect of the original blue. By the end of the Trecento, apparently, painters began to notice what was happening, and in most later paintings the Virgin's mantle is as blue as one could desire.

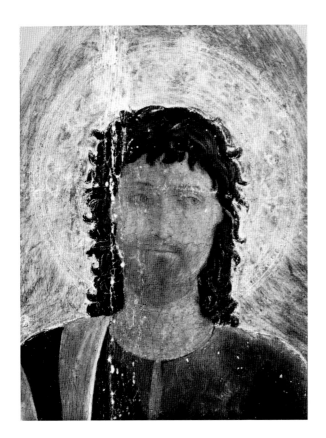

12. FRA ANGELICO. Head of St. John the Baptist, detail of fig. 11. Underpainting, seen from reverse side during restoration

A major restoration performed on an altarpiece after damage in World War II affords an opportunity to reconstruct the procedure of the artist. A *Madonna and Child Enthroned with Saints* by Fra Angelico (fig. 11) that was heavily damaged by mold had to be transferred to a new panel; this is a difficult but not unusual procedure. After the mold and dirt were removed, the surface was covered with sheets of cheesecloth dipped in a plastic adhesive that hardened sufficiently to maintain the integrity of the painted surface. The panels were then detached from the frame, turned over, and the diseased wood and gesso picked off or scraped away, leaving only the veil of pigment adhering to the hardened cheesecloth and adhesive. In the final stages of this process, the underpainting was revealed from the back side, as Fra Angelico himself never could have seen it (fig. 12). The *terra verde* used for underpainting the flesh was intact, as were the broad areas of solid color under the drapery passages. Because all the diseased gesso was removed from the haloes, the punched patterns stand up in reverse in the photograph, which even shows Fra Angelico's delicate brush underdrawing adhering to the underside of the film of tempera. After the paint was adhered to a new surface, the plastic adhesive was dissolved and the layers of cheesecloth removed.

The fresh bright colors and flashing gold of the altarpieces were slightly toned down by the application of varnish; varnish has even been found on thirteen-century panels beneath a layer of fourteenth-century re-

paint. While a painting was in use in a church or elsewhere, the colors would slowly be obscured by candle smoke, and it sometimes takes a considerable mental effort to restore a darkened picture in a museum or church to its original brilliance. We have a few instances of old pictures that have suffered hardly at all: one notable example is a *Madonna and Child with Saints* by Nardo di Cione (colorplate 17, p. 57). A domestic devotional image, this picture apparently remained closed for centuries, preserving the surface from dirt, fading, or other discoloration, as well as from rubbing or retouching. This is one of the best preserved of Italian fourteenth-century pictures, and it should be studied by visitors to the National Gallery in Washington, D.C., as a standard against which to measure the condition and original qualities of other tempera paintings.

Altarpieces forced painters to work with meticulous care over months and years, but they had a chance to express themselves more freely in the medium of fresco. According to Cennino Cennini, who seems to have described many of the standard procedures of Giotto and his followers, fresco (the Italian word means "fresh") was the most delightful technique of all, probably because the painter could work fast, pouring out ideas with the immediacy, vivacity, and intensity for which the Italians are well known. A fresco may appear detailed and exact when viewed from the floor, but when examined closely, it reveals at once that it was executed at considerable speed. Most Italian fresco painters could manage an approximately life-sized figure in two days—one for the head and shoulders, the other for all the rest. Counting an additional day for the background architecture or landscape, one can devise a rule of thumb that arrives at the amount of time involved in painting a fresco by multiplying the number of foreground figures by three days. More exact methods are possible, as we shall presently see, but this simple system corresponds roughly to the usual state of affairs, at least among experienced fresco painters. Some painters, such as Masaccio, who finished the *Expulsion* in only four days, worked even faster (see colorplate 5, p. 13; figs. 196, 197).

In creating a fresco (fig. 13), the thirteenth- or fourteenth-century painter seems to have painted directly on the wall without preparatory drawings on paper beyond the kind needed for a painting on panel. But if the subject was unusual, requiring new compositional inventions or perhaps prior approval of the patron, more detailed drawings may well have been made. The early painter drew on the wall rapidly, standing on a scaffolding before a wall whose masonry had been covered with a rough coat of plaster called *arriccio*. On this surface the painter could make, often with the aid of rules or chalk lines tied to nails, the principal divisions of the area to be painted. Then, with or without the aid of preliminary sketches, the painter drew the composition rapidly, first with a brush dipped into pale, watery earth color that would leave only faint marks.

Over these first ocher indications, the painter could

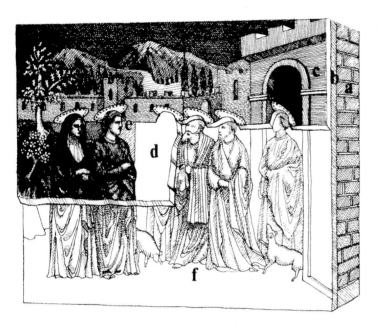

13. Partially finished fresco at beginning of a day's work. Joints between previous days' work indicated in heavy lines. *a.* masonry wall; *b. arriccio*; *c.* painted *intonaco* of upper tier; *d. giornata* of new *intonaco* ready for color; *e.* previous day's *giornata*; *f.* underdrawing in *sinopia* on *arriccio* layer

draw the rough outlines of the figures lightly with a stick of charcoal, further establishing the poses and principal masses of drapery. The third stage was a drawing in red earth called *sinopia*, after the name of the Greek city Sinope, in Asia Minor, from which the finest red-earth color was thought to come. Mixed with water, the red earth made an excellent material in which to establish musculature, features, and ornament, sometimes with the broad strokes of a coarse-bristle brush, sometimes with shorter, finer strokes. In the process of detaching threatened frescoes from the walls, many of these *sinopie* have been brought to light (fig. 14). In their freshness and freedom, *sinopie* are sometimes more attractive to modern eyes than the more finished frescoes that covered them. If a *sinopia* varies considerably from its fresco, this may be because the painter decided to change the position of a limb or a piece of drapery, or because the patron complained that a saint was wrongly dressed or placed. We possess a letter in which Benozzo Gozzoli informed Piero de' Medici that he had just painted a cloud over an angel to which the patron had objected—presumably in the *sinopia*.

As the work continued, the artist or an assistant covered a section of *sinopia* each morning (or the previous evening) with an area of fresh, smooth plaster called *intonaco*, covering the *sinopia* and leaving the painter with nothing but memory (or some good working drawings) as a guide to paint that area. Each new patch of *intonaco* is called a *giornata* (pl. *giornate*). On any given day, a fresco in progress would consist of a certain proportion of finished work, a certain proportion of *sinopia*, and one blank, challenging *giornata* of fresh *intonaco* that had to

be painted before the end of that day. The joints between each *giornata* are often visible and palpable because the painter cleaned off with a knife whatever *intonaco* remained unpainted when the light failed so as to have a clean edge to start on the next day. To keep the edge from crumbling, it was beveled. When the new *giornata* was laid on, it inevitably left a soft and rounded edge adjoining the bevel. One can therefore often determine not only the limits of each *giornata*, but also the order in which they were done. Individual painters varied in how much work they could do in a day and in how they placed their joints. Sometimes the joints follow the contours of a head or figure, but more frequently the joints fall between two figures or heads.

In the course of painting, the colors in their water vehicle would sink into the fresh *intonaco*. At this point a chemical reaction takes place: the carbon dioxide of the air combines with the calcium hydrate in the plaster, producing calcium carbonate as the plaster hardens. When dry, fresco colors no longer look the same as when they were first laid down on the wet plaster, and the quality and luminosity of color depend on the exact stage of the drying process of the plaster when the painter applied that color. The painter also had to consider the humidity of the interior, and it goes without saying that frescoes could not be painted in cold weather in unheated interiors. Not all colors were water soluble, and some had to be painted *a secco*, that is, on the dry plaster from which they were, sooner or later, in danger of peeling off.

Painters worked from the top down to keep from dropping paint on completed sections, and the floorboards of the scaffolding had to be lowered as they moved on to paint successively lower levels. The result is a tendency to compose in horizontal strips. The background landscape and architecture, sometimes including the haloes, were almost invariably painted before the heads of the foreground figures. Sometimes the painter started in the center and worked out, sometimes from the sides toward the center. At best it was piecemeal work, and this became a drawback during the fifteenth century, when visual unity, including light and atmosphere, was considered essential to good painting. The limits of the scaffolding prevented the painter from stepping back to get a view of the whole, and occasionally an impulsive painter went over the edge and was injured, as was Michelangelo when he was painting the *Last Judgment* (see colorplate 131, p. 652). According to Vasari, Barna da Siena (see p. 138) was killed in such a fall. Many of the older masters, particularly when faced with a hurried commission that had to be carried out with the aid of many assistants, did a great deal of *secco* painting over fresco underpainting. In the fifteenth century, painters carried out experiments, some of them ruinous, in attempts to discover a compromise between the demands of the new style and the limitations of the old method. As in any form of painting during the Middle Ages and the Renaissance, technical skill and ex-

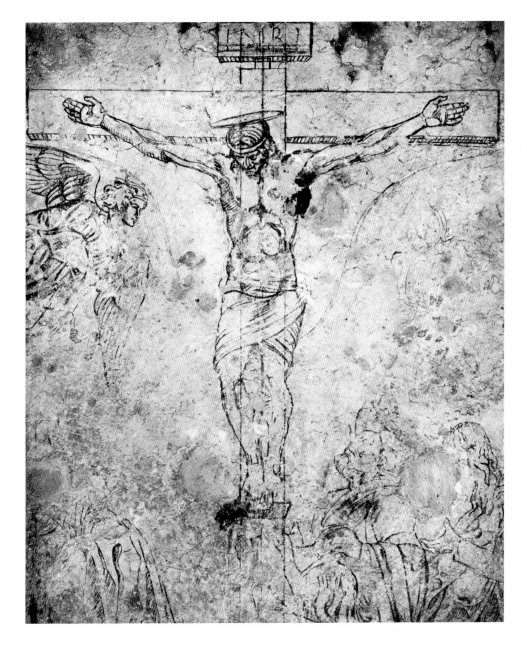

14. ANDREA DEL
CASTAGNO. *Crucifixion.*
1445–47. *Sinopia* drawing
(portion) for fresco.
Cenacolo of Sant'Apollonia,
Florence (see colorplate 50,
p. 260)

perience were required at every stage. Only at the point of the sketches and *sinopia* and during the painting of faces and details was inspiration of much importance.

With the combined evidence of Cennino's testimony and the *sinopie* themselves, which have been rediscovered in some abundance, scholars have come to accept the notions that before the mid-fifteenth century *sinopie* were universally employed and that painters customarily worked directly on the *intonaco* without preparatory drawings of any kind. In recent years, however, conservation work has shown that a number of fourteenth-century fresco cycles, including both of those by Giotto in Santa Croce in Florence (see figs. 73–75), had no preparatory drawings on the wall under the *intonaco*. The frescoes by Nardo di Cione in Santa Maria Novella (see figs. 115, 116) have rough indications on the *intonaco* that are insufficient to guide the artist. It was physically impossible to carry out *sinopie* for huge frescoes, such as those in figures 107, 108, 121, 123 and colorplates 1,

32, 34 (pp. 10, 118, 120), while running up and down the scaffolding because only a small portion of the wall could be seen through the scaffolding, whose beams and boards concealed any view of the whole from the floor. For such colossal paintings, detailed preparatory plans were indispensable. That Cennino does not mention them may indicate that at his modest artistic level in Padua, preparatory drawings were customarily skipped. In the opinion of the present writer, the interest in light shown by Giotto and his immediate followers would also have required preparatory studies of the behavior of light on faces, drapery, and perhaps even backgrounds. A number of such drawings survive, including the sheet attributed to Giotto's pupil Maso di Banco (fig. 15). Any preparatory drawings actually used in painting a fresco would have been exposed to damage on the scaffolding, and it is no surprise that preserved examples cannot be connected with known frescoes.

The death knell of the *sinopia* was sounded by the

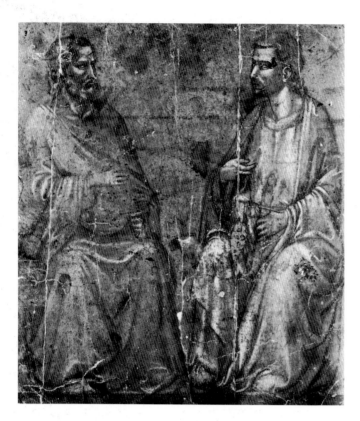

15. MASO DI BANCO (attributed to). *Sts. Paul and Julian.*
c. 1340. Silverpoint, wash and white on green-tinted paper,
8¼ x 7⁵/₁₆". The Louvre, Paris

spolvero, although there was a period, in the middle of the Quattrocento, when both were used in the same fresco. The *spolvero*—and later the cartoon, if necessary cut into sections—was brought onto the scaffolding and the outlines transferred by pouncing, or with a stylus in the case of the cartoon, as each section of *intonaco* went on the wall. The painter was then free to lay on colors without having to remember a hidden section of *sinopia* under the *intonaco*, and with the *spolvero* or cartoon at hand for guidance. Even with these techniques, however, it is fascinating to note how often painters varied from the contours they had pounced or incised when they actually came to paint.

THE PRACTICE OF SCULPTURE

Giotto and Andrea Pisano show us a sculptor (fig. 16) at work on a statue that is not standing vertically in its final position, but in the most convenient position for carving—reclining at a diagonal. Even as late as the sixteenth century, Michelangelo worked on some of his statues in this manner, which permitted the sculptor to approach every section easily without climbing and which also gave every hammer blow the benefit of gravity.

Sculptors too began by drawing. The outlines of the figure or figures were sketched in charcoal on the surfaces of the block, from which the sculptor then began to create the work by carving away, first with a pointed,

then with a toothed, chisel. The parallel marks left by the latter were removed with files and the surface was then polished with pumice and straw. Before undertaking a statue in marble or any other material, a sculptor usually made a small model in clay, then sometimes a full-scale statue in clay. A device composed of adjustable iron rods jointed together and ending in points could be used to transfer the shape and proportions from the model to the block and, ultimately, to the finished work. The word "sculptor," incidentally, did not come into common use until the late fifteenth century; older documents use the term *tagliapietra* (stonecutter).

A bronze sculpture was approximately ten times as expensive as one in marble. Sculptors were generally but not always their own bronze founders, carrying out in person every stage of the difficult and dangerous operation. The initial step in casting is the artist's production of a full-scale clay model, around which a plaster mold would be constructed so that it could be removed in sections. These sections were removed and coated inside with a thick layer of melted wax. Separately, a core of clay and shavings was built on a framework of iron to provide support during the casting process; the core is necessary so that the bronze statue could be hollow, for otherwise both weight and cost would be prohibitive. The wax sections, removed from the plaster mold, were fixed to the core with wires to make a statue of wax around the core. This wax statue was then brushed with a paste made of fine ash mixed with water, and around it was made an exterior mold of clay and shavings that was supported by an iron framework pinned and jointed to that of the core. When this construction was heated, the wax ran out, leaving a space between core and outer mold for the melted bronze, which was conducted through pipes from a furnace.

After the bronze had cooled, both core and mold could be chipped away, leaving a hollow statue whose thickness depended on the bronze founder's accuracy in measuring the core. In the Gothic and Early Renaissance periods, the rough surfaces of the bronze were filed away by a process known as chasing, and details such as strands of hair and the decorative edging of garments would be added through incising, similar to an engraver's incising on a copper plate or an armorer's incising designs on steel. Much fine detail could be added to the statue or relief by these laborious means. Later, in the sixteenth century, only the mold marks, bubbles, and other imperfections were removed, and the surface remained otherwise much as it had left the sculptor's hands in the original, modeled clay.

In the fourteenth and fifteenth centuries, the entire statue or relief, or selected details, was gilded. This was an elaborate process; details could be gilded by a means similar to that used for panels, but larger areas were usually fire-gilt. This technique required the application of an alloy of gold and mercury; when heated, the mercury ran out, leaving the sculpture covered with a thin but durable coating of gold.

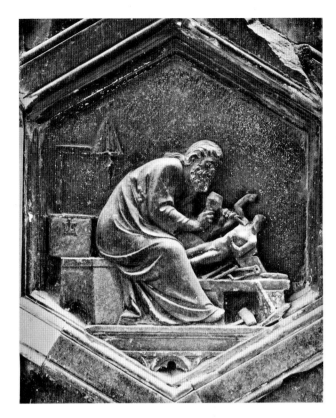

16. ANDREA PISANO (from designs by GIOTTO?).
Art of Sculpture. c. 1334–37. Marble, 32³/4 x 27¹/4". Removed
from original location on the Campanile, Florence
(see fig. 77). Museo dell'Opera del Duomo, Florence

THE PRACTICE OF ARCHITECTURE

For Italians during the Renaissance, architecture was the
leading art. New buildings went up everywhere, and old
ones were remodeled. New city centers were constructed, and ideal cities—destined to remain dreams—reached
the level of theoretical definition. In these structures and
groups of structures reference was made to classical antiquity through the use of classical proportions and revived Roman orders, arches, and decoration. Squares
that recall Roman forums were built, and direct imitations of Roman triumphal arches were created for the
festivities of Renaissance sovereigns. Italian architects
were inspired by the buildings of ancient Rome, many
of which were visible in more nearly complete state
during the Renaissance than they are today (see fig.
310). The new classicizing buildings, based on drawings
of Roman structures, could vary from exactly measured,
archaeologically correct views to designs that added
highly personal embellishments to the original structure.

Yet, in the long view, it is remarkable how little
Italian architects before the High Renaissance understood the fundamentals of Roman Imperial building, especially the system of vaulting used by the Romans to
roof permanently, and yet still light adequately, vast interior spaces. In spite of the development of an influential
new vaulting system in Lombardy in the late eleventh

and early twelfth centuries that was destined to remain
without issue in Italy itself, Italian architecture of the
Late Middle Ages and the Early Renaissance remained
an architecture of walls. In fact, the word used by
Renaissance architects, patrons, and theorists for "to
build" was *murare* (literally, "to wall"), and in Italy a
builder is still a *muratore.*

In comparison with the richly articulated architecture
of masses and spaces developed during the Roman
Empire, followed at Ravenna, and—technically at least—
surpassed in the Gothic cathedrals of France and other
countries in Northern Europe, Italian buildings of the
fourteenth and fifteenth centuries are simple and relatively barren. They are vast spaces enclosed by flat walls
that are pierced, at not necessarily regular intervals, by
doors and windows and, nine times out of ten, roofed
by the same simple timber constructions used in Early
Christian basilicas, and with at most a flat, wooden ceiling suspended from the timbers.

Even when constructing a vault, the Italian architect
was averse to the rich system of supports—the so-called
exoskeleton—of a French Gothic church with its flying
buttresses and pinnacles. The massive masonry vaults of
the cathedrals of Florence and Siena would collapse if it
were not for the iron tie-rods that from the beginning
have helped to hold the structure together (see fig. 126,
where the tie-rods are visible in the nave and side aisles).
French visitors to Italy often consider such a visible device a confession of incompetency, but this contempt is
equaled by the Italians' revulsion from the complexity of
the French system, which spoils, in their eyes, the simple beauty of the walls.

It seems that the builders of very large Italian churches
often were far from sure, when they laid out the foundations of their structures, exactly how high the walls
and columns were to go or how the interior spaces were
to be vaulted. To an extent that astonishes the twentieth-century observer indoctrinated with the ideals of
functionalism, the calculation of spaces and forms was
based on mathematical principles of sequence and proportion, rather than on the practical requirements of
day-to-day living. Elaborate drawings of architectural
plans, elevations, perspectives, and details (see figs. 449,
502, 503, 550) survive in vast numbers and form one of
the most striking categories of Renaissance artistic creation, especially when, as too often happened, the actual
building was never built. Also, architectural backgrounds, frequently unbuildable, provide a setting for
the dramas of Italian Renaissance pictorial compositions
(colorplate 67, p. 356; figs. 386, 488). Sadly enough,
most of the dreams of Italian Renaissance architects for
the rebuilding of Italian cities were prevented by circumstances—wars, personal quarrels, lack of funds—
from becoming anything but dreams (see figs. 386, 436),
but they have inspired actual projects of urban design
ever since.

Although the work was carried out under the general
direction of an architect, the key personality might well

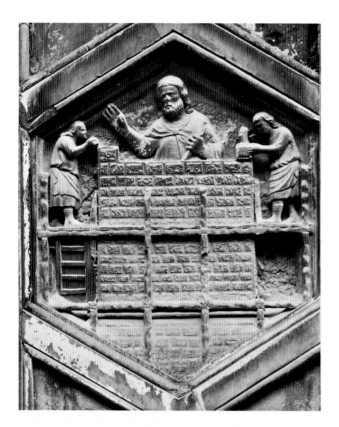

17. ANDREA PISANO (from designs by GIOTTO?).
Art of Architecture. After 1343–before 1348. Marble,
32³/4 x 27¹/4". Removed from original location
on the Campanile, Florence (see fig. 77). Museo
dell'Opera del Duomo, Florence

be a mason or builder—a member of the Arte di Pietra e Legname. Rarely did such a technician, however, rise to the status of designing architect. There was, in fact, no word for architect in the fourteenth century, only *capomaestro* (literally, "head-master"). Almost all the most inventive architects discussed in this book began and continued as painters, sculptors, or, in the case of Michelangelo, both; many came to architecture relatively late and, impressive as their architectural achievements were, they continued to paint or sculpt. Often they were appointed *capomaestro* without either training or experience in building. The modern institution of an architectural office was unknown in the Renaissance, and the principal method of communication between architect and builder was a detailed wooden model, a number of which survive (see fig. 551). Military architecture, a category of building that was extremely important to the Italians of the Renaissance, was given over to untrained builders, who made themselves into expert engineers.

Unfortunately, there is no room in this volume to discuss Renaissance fortifications, whose beauty, brilliance, and practicality have attracted increasing notice.

Another relief from the Florence Campanile (fig. 17) shows the construction of a building with the rough-cut blocks characteristic of Florentine houses and Florentine military architecture of the Late Middle Ages and Early Renaissance, the so-called rusticated masonry. The architect, holding a scroll that might be a plan or other calculations, is visibly directing the procedure; masons, shown in a smaller scale, are standing on the scaffolding and laying the stones around its beams. As the wall rose, these beams would be raised to a new level, leaving holes in the structure. These square holes are still visible in many medieval structures. The all-important wall, freestanding with a minimum of external buttressing or none at all, was the basis of Italian architectural thinking until it was replaced by the elaborate radial organizations of spaces in the High Renaissance.

The concept of the flat wall plane dominates the architecture of Italy to an extent inconceivable elsewhere. It is fascinating, for example, to note how often the façade of an Italian church or palace seems to have little to do with the building behind it. Although the façade of a church may try to prepare the observer for the spaces and architectural motives of the interior, the tissue of delicate elements that makes up the façade may do little more than turn the corner before stopping. There a flat, untreated wall continues, abundantly visible from the sides of the building and as acceptable to Italian eyes as it is startling to foreigners. The façade is not considered an essential part of the building but is, rather, a ceremonial decoration for the piazza before it, like the huge shrines still erected in south Italian streets to celebrate the festival of a saint. The façade sometimes does not even have the same number of stories as the building behind it, and it may tower far above and be supported from behind by iron rods fastened to the roof beams; sometimes it is even embarrassingly lower than the bulk of the actual building. Often the façade has never been built at all.

In a sense, the wall is the beginning and the end of Italian architecture, and it forms as well a broad field for fresco painting and a background for altarpieces and sculpture. The wall is the plane from which perspective thinking starts, when new, harmonious spaces are created in a world projected within and beyond its surface and into which the observer is visually invited to step. The wall is the screen on which Italian civic life and the Italian landscape are preserved through the fertility of the Italian imagination.

2

Duecento Art
in Tuscany and Rome

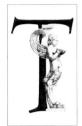he first manifestations of an independent
new style in painting and sculpture seem
to have taken place in Tuscany, a region in
central Italy embraced between the Apennines and the Tyrrhenian Sea; it corresponds in general to the area inhabited in
ancient times by the Etruscans, from whom
the medieval Tuscans were in part de-
scended. Shortly after the year 1000, this region became
the scene of new political developments; one by one the
cities of Pisa, Lucca, Pistoia, Prato, and Florence constituted themselves free communes or republics, liberated
from domination by the counts of Tuscany after the
death of Countess Matilda in 1115, and owing a somewhat shadowy allegiance to either the emperor or, in
the case of Florence, the pope. Somewhat later in the
century, Siena established itself as an independent republic free from the domination of the bishop and neighboring feudal lords. These Tuscan city-states were the
theater of the constant struggle for power between the
merchant class and the old nobility, a struggle in which a
premium was placed on the value and initiative of the
individual; they provided a rich market and a powerful
incentive for the new art.

Duecento (two hundred) is used in Italian to designate
the thirteenth century (the 1200s), as *Trecento* is used for
the fourteenth century, *Quattrocento* for the fifteenth,
and *Cinquecento* for the sixteenth. The quality and quantity of panel painting (the frescoes have largely disappeared) in the Duecento have come to be appreciated
only in the middle of the twentieth century; earlier this
period was generally accepted as one of stagnation,
under the influence of Byzantine art—the painting of
the Eastern or Greek Empire, centering on Constantinople. According to Vasari, Greek (Byzantine) painters
were even called to Florence, where Cimabue, whom
Vasari considered the first of the truly Florentine painters, saw them at work and surpassed their "rude" manner. Vasari knew little, of course, about the intellectual
and refined quality of later Byzantine painting, but there
is a germ of truth in his legend. Greek mosaicists were
indeed called to the court of King Roger II of Sicily in
the twelfth century (fig. 18) and founded a new school
of Italo-Byzantine art. Byzantine influence in thirteenth-
century Europe is explained by the sack of Constantinople in 1204 by the Crusaders, who devastated the

churches and the Great Palace. Their artistic booty—
painted icons, manuscripts, ivory carvings, enamels, fabrics with woven pictures—was scattered throughout
Europe, and objects from the sack are still visible in Italy
today.

Byzantine artistic ideas were imprinted on European
imagination through the richness of Byzantine style and
materials. Greek painters themselves, with few opportunities in ruined Constantinople, left to work in Serbia
for the kings there, and they were probably also attracted

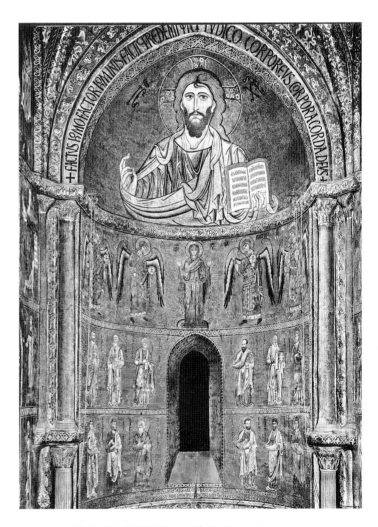

18. ITALO-BYZANTINE. *Christ Pantocrator,*
the *Virgin Mary, Angels, Saints,* and *Prophets.* 1148.
Apse mosaic. Cathedral, Cefalù, Sicily

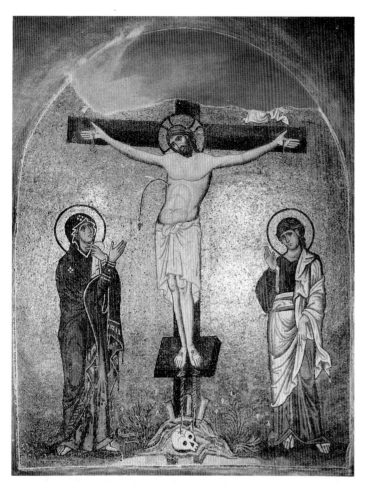

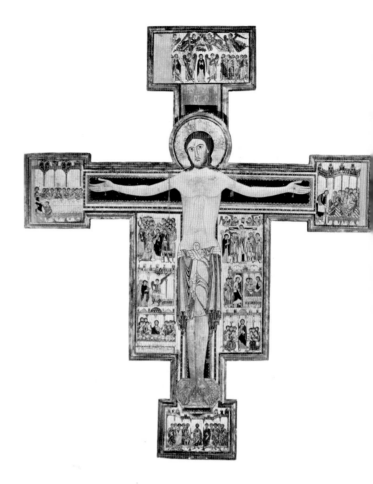

19. BYZANTINE. *Crucifixion*. 11th century. Mosaic. Monastery Church, Daphni, Greece

20. SCHOOL OF PISA. *Cross No. 15*. Late 12th century. Panel, 9' 3" x 7' 9¾". Pinacoteca, Pisa

by the wealth of Venice and the Tuscan cities. They brought with them Byzantine style in the formalized and linear "Comnenian" phase, which is named after the dynasty of Byzantine emperors that came to an end in 1204. But for all their initial reliance on Greek models, on the Greek methods of dividing the anatomy into clearly demarcated and delicately shaded portions, and on the Greek way of rendering light on drapery by means of parallel striations of color or gold, even the earliest productions of Italo-Byzantine paintings show a vigor and tension that distinguish them from their Eastern models (fig. 19).

PAINTING IN PISA

So little is left of twelfth-century Tuscan painting that it is impossible to determine the main currents of its development and the complex problem of its origins, but the earliest examples seem closer to the art of Romanesque Europe than to that of the Byzantine East. Probably as a result of the conquest of Constantinople, however, Byzantine influence in the Duecento rapidly becomes unmistakable. Pisa had been a rich, powerful seaport since Roman times, when it was the capital of the Province of Tuscany. In 1133, under Pope Innocent

II, Pisa was briefly the seat of the papacy, and St. Bernard called it a new Rome. The republic was in constant commercial competition and naval warfare with the rival ports of Genoa, to the northwest, and Amalfi, south of Naples.

One of the earliest surviving Italian panel pictures is probably the anonymous, undated *Cross No. 15* in Pisa (fig. 20). This large work, probably for a choir screen, shows an alive Christ on the cross; scenes from the Passion and subsequent events are placed to either side of his body and at the ends of the bars of the cross. The type of cross with a living Christ—the *Christus triumphans* (Christ triumphant)—appears in a number of other examples. The purpose of these images was not to show the agony of the Crucifixion as a specific incident, but to present a symbolic image of the sacrifice of Christ as part of doctrine and to dramatize for the worshiper the significance of the Mass. In the backgrounds the architectural shapes, with their arches and columns, and the repeated vertical elements of the lateral scenes, recall the Romanesque architecture of the Cathedral, Baptistery, and Bell Tower (Leaning Tower) of Pisa.

It was the necessity of viewing the painting from a distance that doubtless led the artist to consider carefully the architectural structure of the composition and also

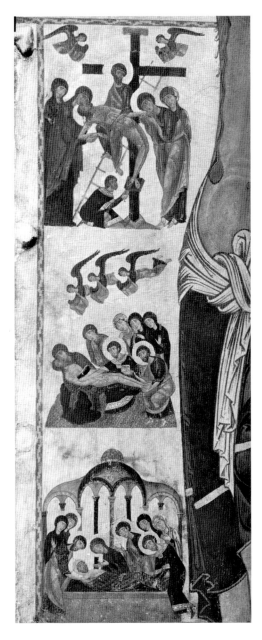

21. SCHOOL OF PISA. Deposition, Lamentation, and Entombment, details of *Cross No. 20* (see colorplate 18, p. 58). c. 1230. Parchment on panel. Pinacoteca, Pisa

scenes from the Passion are treated as if they were incidents from a codified ritual. All in all, the style recalls the manuscript painting of the Romanesque period in Italy more than anything Byzantine.

Against this static and largely symbolic painting, another and even more beautiful example, *Cross No. 20* in Pisa (colorplate 18, p. 58; fig. 21), sets forth an unexpected range of emotional values. Christ is shown dead, hanging lightly upon the cross as if opening his arms to embrace all humanity. With its direct appeal to the personal feelings of the spectator, this type, known as the *Christus patiens* (suffering Christ), rapidly replaced the *Christus triumphans*. Again we know neither the date of the painting nor the identity of the artist, but it is evident that the painter was strongly influenced by Byzantine art. The pose of the body, with the hips curving to the figure's right, is common in Byzantine representations, such as the mosaic at Daphni (see fig. 19) and examples in Serbia. The drawing of the anatomy and drapery betrays a knowledge of Greek style, but even more important than the Byzantine elements, which never reach the point of strict imitation, is the intensity of feeling that is derived from a personal style of lyric beauty and tragic power. By analogy with dated works, it is possible to suggest a date of about 1230. The change in content and style between the two Pisan crosses is probably explained by the spread of the doctrine of St. Francis of Assisi (d. 1226), who preached and practiced a direct devotion to Christ and who, in 1224, is said to have received the stigmata, wounds that paralleled those of Christ.

The new emotional content is evident throughout: in the expression of sadness, rather than physical torment, on the countenance of Christ, and in the dramatic effectiveness of the scenes from the Passion, in which architectural backgrounds are subordinated to human content. Everywhere the flow of line, in the hair and the delicately delineated features, in the long and slender fingers, and in the composition of the scenes silhouetted against gold, reaches a pitch seldom achieved again in Italian art until Botticelli, in the Quattrocento. In the Lamentation (fig. 21), long delicate lines move downward with increasing rapidity through the angels' wings to Mary and her Son, whose dead body rests on her lap as in no scriptural account. This group was surely derived from Byzantine sources. The tenth-century theologian Simeon Metaphrastes was apparently the first to describe Mary holding the dead Christ on her lap as she had held him as a child, and as early as the twelfth century the scene was represented in Byzantine art. The passionately intense fresco of about 1164 at Nerezi shows this scene (fig. 22); another example may have migrated to Pisa. *Cross No. 20* is one of the earliest of those tragic evocations of the relation between Mary and the dead Christ that will form so important a subject for Italian artists of the Renaissance. By the late years of the Trecento, this theme will be known as the Pietà (Italian for both "piety" and "pity").

the colors, which are evenly spaced and repeated to achieve an all-over harmony among a few simple colors—blue, rose, white, tan, gold. Considering the potential drama of the subjects, the style is restrained. Clear contours outline major elements, and the linear drapery style is related to that of contemporary Tuscan Romanesque sculpture. The artist has modeled the figure—whose arms seem stretched voluntarily against the cross—with delicacy, as though it were carved in low relief. The wide-open eyes, in their curious squared lids, stare impassively outward. Against the elaborate architectural structures, within which we are supposed to imagine the stiff little figures to stand and move, the

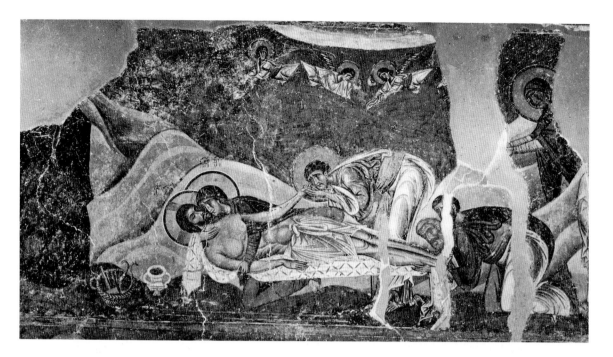

PAINTING IN LUCCA

Similar stages may be discerned in the painting of Lucca, a rival republic about fifteen miles from Pisa; separated from the sea by the mass of Monte San Giuliano, Lucca was for centuries able to carry on a splendid existence through its banking activities. A group of crosses of the *Christus triumphans* type culminates in an example (fig. 23) by one of the earliest Italian artists known to us by name. Berlinghiero Berlinghieri, born in Milan, founded a family of painters active in Lucca in the Duecento. In his signed *Cross*, Christ looks out at the observer with wide-open eyes. The small figures of Mary and John under the arms of the cross replace the narrative scenes customary in earlier examples. The crossarms, as in many earlier examples, culminate in the symbols of the four evangelists. The impact of Byzantine style is evident in the striated drapery and the division of Christ's body into separately modeled segments.

An altarpiece of *St. Francis with Scenes from His Life* (fig. 24) in San Francesco at Pescia, a town about halfway between Lucca and Pistoia, is signed by Berlinghiero's son, Bonaventura, and dated 1235, only nine years after the death of St. Francis. Although it is the earliest known image of the saint, there is no evidence that Tuscans in the Duecento attached any importance to portrait likeness. We can, however, deduce from the intensity of the face, with its emaciated cheeks and piercing gaze, a great deal about the meaning of St. Francis's message to his contemporaries. Bonaventura has shown us the ascetic Francis of private meditations and ecstatic prayers. The harsh power of the forms and the solemnity of content come as a surprise if we know only the gentler representations of St. Francis and his life from the Trecento and Quattrocento.

The placement of the lateral scenes from the life of the saint to either side of a large central figure is inspired by painted crosses. The triangular top, however, is like

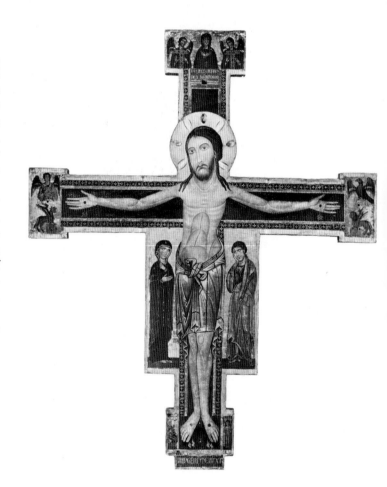

the gable of a church or a shrine, and this is the shape that will be followed in altarpieces representing the enthroned Madonna and Child until the mid-Trecento, when it will be replaced by rich Gothic shapes imported from French art. Two of the narrative scenes have landscape backgrounds and, although the Byzantine models for painting hills are schematized and reduced to repeated, superimposed formulae, there is something about

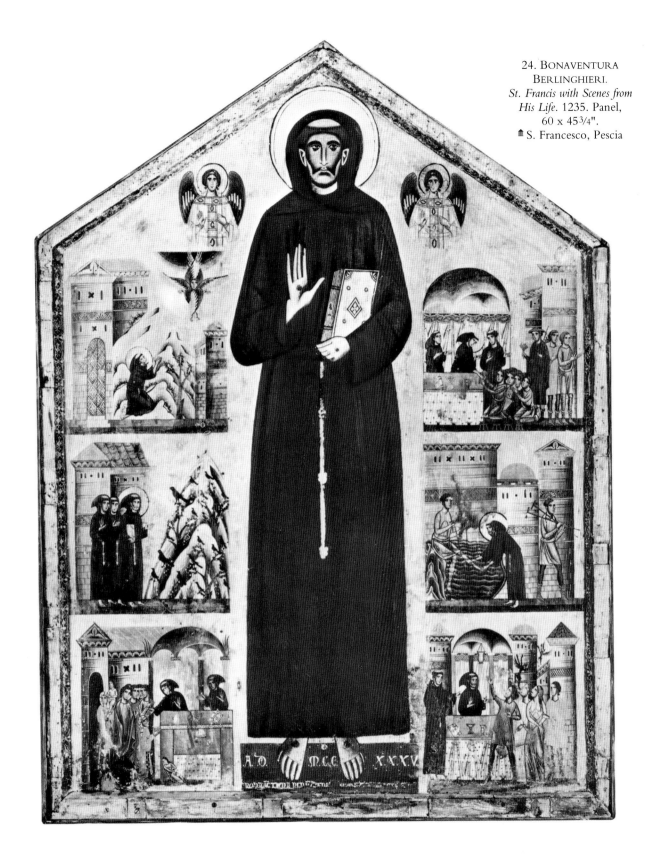

24. BONAVENTURA
BERLINGHIERI.
*St. Francis with Scenes from
His Life*. 1235. Panel,
60 x 45¾".
🏛 S. Francesco, Pescia

the color and shapes that suggests a new feeling for nature that is accompanying the new interest in human emotional reactions. The *Preaching to the Birds* and the *Stigmatization* are engaging, both artistically and poetically. The architectural settings, on the other hand, were adopted almost without change from Byzantine models and show no relation to the Lucchese architecture of Bonaventura's day.

PAINTING IN FLORENCE

Until the Duecento, Pisa and Lucca were more populous and powerful than Florence, and Florentine painting seems to have had a slightly later start. But even the earliest examples show a greater directness, power, and plasticity than is found in the works of the two rival schools. An impressive early work is a *Cross* of the *Christ-*

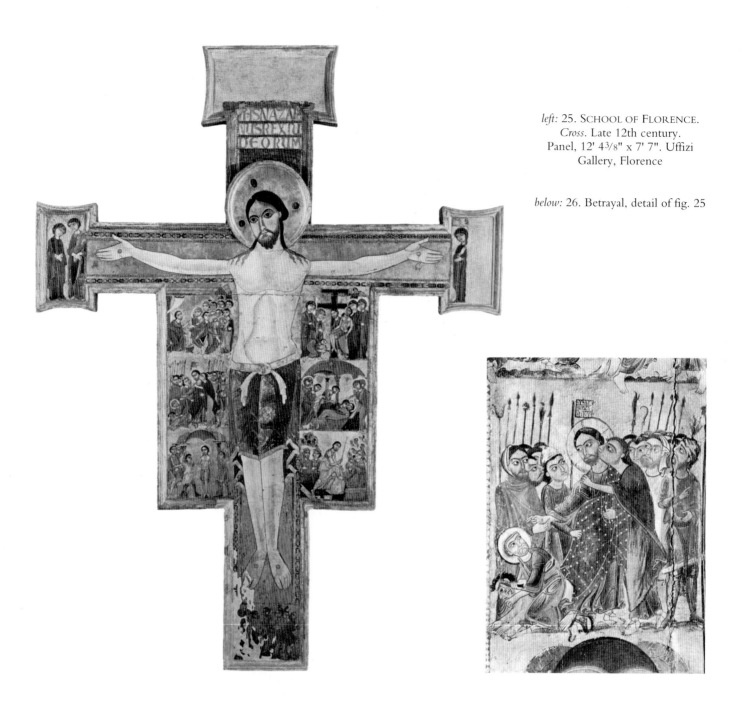

us triumphans type (fig. 25) whose affinities are with works located in or around Florence. The Christ seems almost to be soaring, and there is no indication of the original wood of the cross, which is dissolved into a background field of flat gold. The firmly modeled and strongly constructed forms culminate in a somber head, whose eyes gaze calmly outward. The powerful shapes contrast with the delicacy of detail in the dotted loincloth and in the subdued colors. The narrative scenes make no effort to compete with the modeling of the central figure. Almost flat in their silhouetted shapes, they are, nonetheless, sharply alive, owing to the vivid contrasts in linear direction and to the flashing glances of the eyes (fig. 26). As in Romanesque painting elsewhere in Europe, the heads in the small dramatic scenes are enlarged so that the facial expressions will not be lost. Byzantine canons of proportion, inherited from the

Hellenic and Roman world, did not permit such violations. This artist, like the master of *Cross No. 20,* was a strong artistic personality and the first of the innovative Florentine artists we are to encounter.

Coppo di Marcovaldo (active 1260s–70s), a Florentine painter, is generally accepted as the artist of the harrowing *Crucifix* (fig. 27) in San Gimignano, which was then in Sienese territory. Coppo is even more deeply influenced by the Byzantine style than was the painter of *Cross No. 20,* but he turns the linearity, compartmentalized forms, and striated drapery construction to a different end. Coppo shows us a Christ whose sculptural body and face are convulsed and distorted with suffering, and whose loincloth, powerfully rendered to show depth at the waist, is broken into almost cubistic angles that are projected with a violence unusual in Italian art. The closed eyes are treated as two fierce, dark, hooked

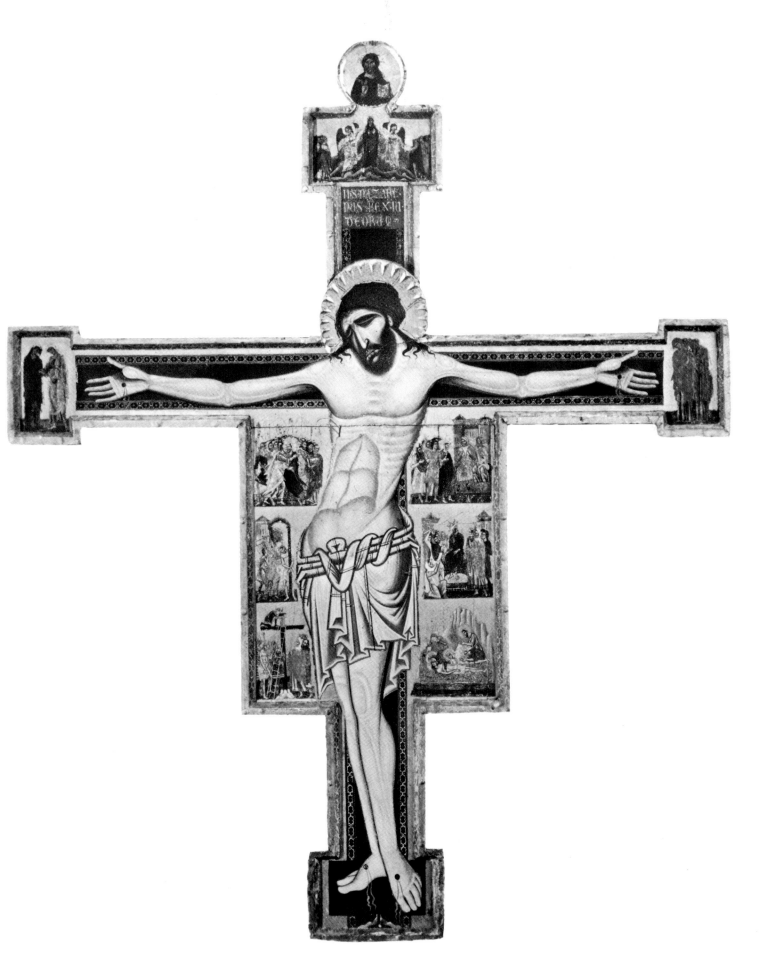

27. COPPO DI MARCOVALDO. *Crucifix*. Second half of 13th century.
Panel, 9' 7³/₈" x 8' 1¹/₄". Pinacoteca, San Gimignano

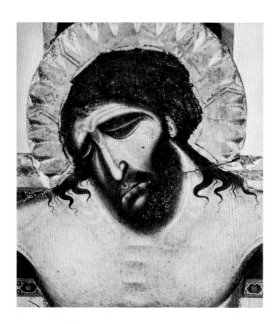

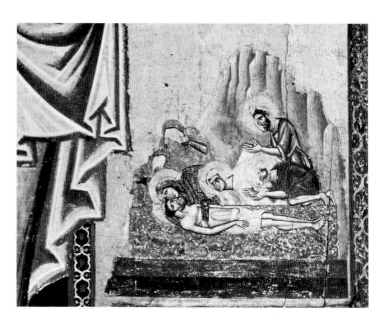

28. Head of Christ, detail of fig. 27

29. Lamentation, detail of fig. 27

slashes (fig. 28), the pale mouth seems to quiver against the sweat-soaked locks of the beard, and the hair seems to writhe like snakes against the tormented body. Even the halo, carved into a raised disk that is broken by wedgelike indentations, plays a part in a total effect of great expressive power. Because the head of the Christ was painted over a layer of gold leaf, some of the hair has crusted off, spoiling the long curves of the contours.

Coppo fought as a Florentine soldier in the Battle of Montaperti in 1260 and was taken prisoner by the Sienese after the Florentine defeat; it is sometimes suggested that the emotional content of his *Crucifix* reflects his wartime experiences. As compared with the Lamentation in *Cross No. 20* (see fig. 21), Coppo's scene almost has the immediacy of a television shot of street violence (fig. 29). The dead Christ lies rigid on the ground, his head held by his mother; the surrounding figures seem to explode with emotion and so does the landscape, with its dramatic verticals.

Among the other surviving works by Coppo is a *Madonna and Child* (fig. 30). The subject does not allow the expressionistic outbursts seen in the *Crucifix*, but Coppo's intensity of feeling is transferred to the form and design. The Virgin is shown as in many Byzantine representations, seated on a lyre-backed throne, crowned as Queen of Heaven and holding her Son, his hand raised in blessing, upon her knee. Two small angels are shown behind the throne. The Virgin's sad expression reveals an emotional content not explained either by the relationship of mother and child or by the ritual purpose of the image; like many other Italian Madonna and

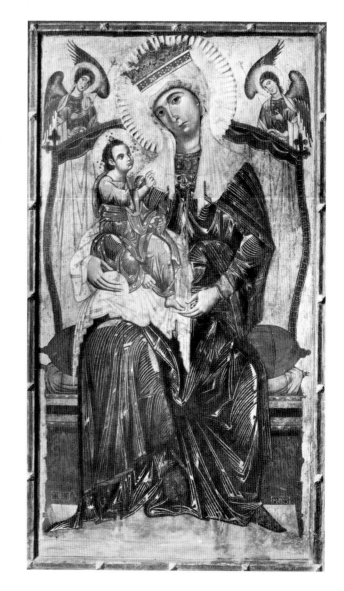

30. COPPO DI MARCOVALDO. *Madonna and Child.* c. 1265.
Panel, 7' 9 3/4" x 4' 5 1/8". S. Martino dei Servi, Orvieto

Child compositions, this is a reference to the Passion and death of Christ. Coppo's Madonna is mournful because she is endowed with the ability to prophesy the tragic events to come.

As in the *Crucifix*, Coppo has divided the face into compartments by sharp, linear accents in the nose, lips, and eyes, and these divisions are strengthened by the modeling of the masses in light and dark. But here every shape is treated as an abstract form, severe and clearcut—like elements of architecture. Here, too, Coppo has used wedge-shaped depressions in the halo, but they are smaller and more numerous than those in the *Crucifix*, creating a glitter of gold around the face. The energetic Christ Child, remarkably unchildlike in appearance and holding a scroll in his left hand, is represented as the Savior and teacher.

Coppo's dramatic style is evident in the drapery, which is cut up in folds that are outlined and patched by gold striations. These sharp, intense, and irregular sunburst shapes have little to do with the behavior of cloth, and the crackling striations, seen alone, could almost be mistaken for a work of twentieth-century abstract painting, so strong an independent life do these forms lead. Few of Coppo's works can be securely dated, but the one picture that is inscribed and some documentary references indicate a relatively brief artistic activity, centering around the late 1250s, 1260s, and early 1270s.

The extensive cycle of mosaics in the octagonal pyramid of the Baptistery of Florence is the most important pictorial undertaking of the Duecento that remains in the Tuscan metropolis. On the west face is the *Last Judgment* (colorplate 19, p. 59), which is attributed to Coppo di Marcovaldo. The commission for a work of such prominence provided an opportunity for Coppo to display the vigor of his imagination and the power of his forms on an unprecedented scale. The colossal central figure, more than twenty-five feet in height, is designed with simplicity and clarity, and the anatomical masses are broken into segments that are richly modeled in color. Christ is enthroned in a glory whose border is adorned with foliate ornament that is perfectly visible from the floor. Below the seat of his throne are the seven blue arcs of the seven heavens. Gazing outward, Christ beckons with his right arm toward the blessed, while with his left he casts the damned into eternal fire. The athletic figures leaping from their tombs are convincing as Coppo's design, as is the terrifying Hell scene, in which a few punishments and demons, clearly decipherable from the floor of the Baptistery, do duty for the whole. Around Satan, writhing serpents and monstrous toads devour the damned, which are rendered with the broad, clear, zigzag shapes characteristic of Coppo's style. Coppo's mosaic of Christ is the most awe-inspiring representation of divinity in Italian art until Michelangelo. Although his name, forgotten by tradition, was not even mentioned in later sources, Coppo's vision remained to inspire, directly or indirectly, generations of Florentine artists.

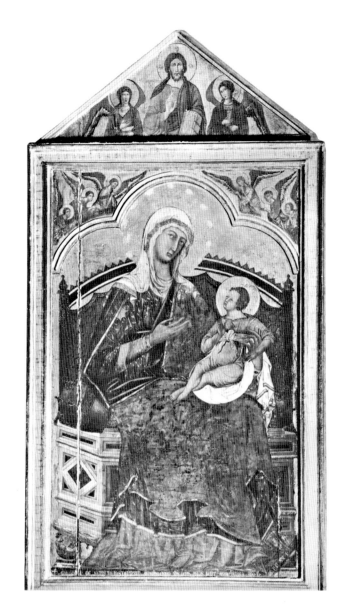

31. GUIDO DA SIENA (Madonna's face and Child repainted, probably by DUCCIO, early 14th century). *Enthroned Madonna*. Second half of 13th century. Panel, 9' 4 1/2" x 6' 4". Palazzo Pubblico, Siena. Commissioned for the high altar of S. Domenico, Siena

PAINTING IN SIENA

During his stay in Siena, Coppo had considerable influence, especially on Guido da Siena (active c. 1260), the leading painter of the previously archaic Sienese School. For San Domenico, Guido painted a huge *Enthroned Madonna* (fig. 31). The face of the Madonna and the figure of the Christ Child were repainted in the early Trecento, but the original portions of the picture show the adaptation of Italo-Byzantine motifs to Sienese taste, which has been described as more refined and delicate than that of Florence. In other works, Guido appears to have been strongly influenced by the style of Bonaventura Berlinghieri. The *Madonna* has been the subject of a prolonged controversy dating back to the eighteenth century, because the painting bears an inscription declaring that Guido da Siena painted it in the "happy days" of 1221. This gave Sienese antiquarians ammunition in their battle to assert the cultural priority of Siena over Florence. Although the inscription has been proved old and unaltered, most modern scholars are unable to date this accomplished painting at the same time as the crude efforts of the Sienese School in the early Duecento, about fifty years earlier than dated paintings that are almost identical with it in style. The inscription is lettered in a manner common in the early Trecento and was added, for commemorative purposes, when the faces were repainted and Guido's exact dates had long been forgotten.

CIMABUE

The painter Cenni di Pepi (active c. 1272–1302) is better known by the nickname Cimabue, a name of difficult etymology that could be translated as "ox head" or "dehorner of oxen." The latter interpretation might refer to Cimabue's personality, which in an early source is described as proud and arrogant. In most introductions to the history of art, Cimabue appears as the earliest of Florentine and therefore of Italian painters. This is where Vasari, who considered everything before Cimabue's time to be clumsy, placed him. In reality, Cimabue comes not at the beginning of a development but at its end. His altarpieces show him to be the last thoroughly Italo-Byzantine painter. Others who carried Cimabue's style into the Trecento were minor masters whose activity was relegated to the villages and soon ceased altogether. Cimabue sums up an Italo-Byzantine tradition that had been going on for nearly a century in Tuscany, and elaborate and splendid though his creations are, he begins nothing essentially new.

The huge *Enthroned Madonna and Child with Angels and Prophets* (colorplate 20, p. 60), painted for Santa Trinita in Florence, has always been attributed to Cimabue by Florentine tradition and is not now doubted, although no document connects it with the master, and we are not even sure of the date. Probably it was done a few years before Duccio's *Madonna* of 1285 (see fig. 89). It is even larger than the *Madonna* by Guido, and by far the most ambitious panel painting attempted by any Italian master up until that time. Inside the dark, narrow, and lofty church and seen properly by candlelight, it must have made an overwhelming impression. The enthroned Madonna, shown without a crown, presents her Child to the viewer. The throne is held by eight angels, while in the arches below, Old Testament prophets display scrolls with prophecies of the Virgin Birth. The throne is so fantastic that any attempt to figure out purposes and relationships is fruitless. Each form can be traced back through Byzantine art to classical sources, but the result is the antithesis of classical art. One is constantly aware of shifting shapes and floating forms, of figures that have no ground to stand on yet assume the duty of support, or of figures that suddenly appear from

below as if on elevators that have stopped halfway up. Cimabue does not even seem to have made up his mind whether the curves beneath the throne are arches in elevation, niches in depth, or both.

The Christ Child, seated on the Virgin's left, holds his scroll and looks directly out toward the observer. This is a ceremonial subject depicting a court ritual in which none of Coppo di Marcovaldo's emotional power could be tolerated. The gold striations of the drapery have proliferated, and hundreds of lines weave a shifting, glittering network of shapes, as if the artist were trying to overwhelm the faithful with his image of regal majesty. The Virgin's heavenly mantle was originally a brilliant blue, the customary color, as is the rose tone of her tunic. The coloristic effect when the painting was fresh must have been impressive, especially as the blue was brought into relief by the flickering flame colors of the angels' wings.

Cimabue's nervous and delicate drawing style is very different from the raw power of Coppo's broad lines. The eye structure is characteristic, with the lower lid almost level, the upper lid shaped like a circumflex, and the sidelong glance contrasting with the downward tilt of the head. Cimabue has a keen sense of modeling within definite limits, and he delicately shades the drapery save for the gold-striated garments of Christ and the Virgin, but no form seems to occupy space and no head is really round. He wishes to show everything he knows to exist, making both ears appear even in a three-quarters view of the face, as though no solid mass of the head intervened to hide one of them. The idea that the image of an object was received by the human eye as a reflection of light had, at this time, occurred to no one. In his zeal to inform us, Cimabue gives us a kind of Mercator's projection of a global head on a flat surface. At the same time, however, Cimabue differentiates psychological types with considerable effect, as in the distinction between the youthful angels and the somewhat weary, disillusioned prophets. He delights in complicated shapes, long slender fingers, and the complex ornament derived from classical sources. Even when he gets to the gold background, he does not stop inventing. This background, including the haloes, is enriched with shifting patterns of incised lines and a series of punched dots.

Cimabue was also a monumental artist, and he probably continued the Baptistery mosaics started by Coppo and others. His abilities as a fresco painter can be suggested only dimly here by photographs of his poorly preserved cycle of frescoes in the apse and transept of the Upper Church of San Francesco at Assisi. Even when one stands before the originals, little comes through beyond the unity of the frescoes with the walls they decorate and the spaces they dominate.

St. Francis, the *Poverello* (little poor man) of Assisi, who married Lady Poverty and renounced all possessions, is enshrined in a huge double church, one above the other, erected over his tomb. Probably built with the collaboration of French and German architects, the

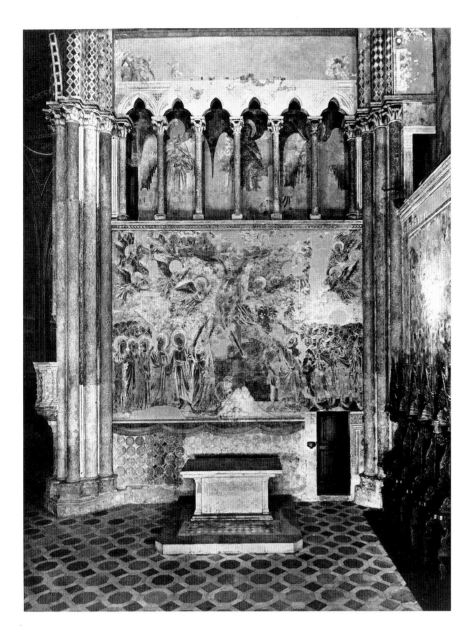

32. CIMABUE. *Crucifixion*. After 1279.
Fresco, c. 17 x 24'.
Upper Church of S. Francesco,
Assisi. Perhaps commissioned by
Pope Nicholas III

Upper Church is almost completely lined with frescoes, and its window openings are filled with stained glass, making it the most nearly complete large-scale cycle of religious imagery in Italy before the Sistine Chapel. Cimabue's *Crucifixion* (fig. 32) is difficult to decipher because the whites, painted with white lead, have oxidized and turned black with time; Cimabue's fresco is even sometimes reproduced as a photographic negative. Later Cennino would warn painters against using white lead on walls. Cimabue has conceived the Crucifixion as a universal catastrophe. Christ writhes on the cross, his head bent in pain—perhaps already in death, although this is impossible to determine in the present state of the fresco. A great wind seems to have broken loose, as if produced by the earthquake recorded in the Gospels, sweeping the folds of the loincloth off to one side. Angels hover in the air, their drapery blown by the wind, and hands reach upward from the crowd below toward the crucified Christ. From his side pour blood

and water—allusions to the sacraments of the Eucharist and Baptism—into a cup held by a flying angel. On our left appears Mary, the other holy women, and the apostles; on our right are the Romans and the chief priests and elders, including the Roman centurion in the foreground, who has recognized that Christ was the Son of God. Even from this wrecked fresco we can understand that Cimabue was an artist of great dramatic capacity, endowed with the ability to grasp and project the intensity of a moment of revelation.

PAINTING IN ROME

While Cimabue was ruling the Florentine scene, a remarkable school of painters was working in Rome, where the practice of mural decoration in fresco and mosaic had continued in an unbroken tradition since the Early Christian period. The late thirteenth century saw

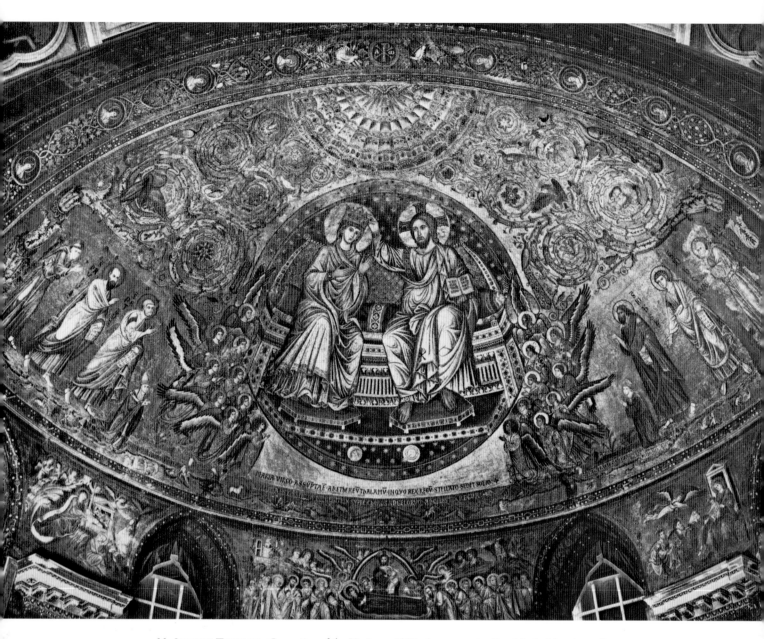

33. JACOPO TORRITI. *Coronation of the Virgin*. c. 1294. Apse mosaic. Sta. Maria Maggiore, Rome

an upsurge in pictorial activity in Rome that continued until 1305, when the seat of the papacy was removed from Rome to Avignon in southern France. A certain impetus may have been given to Roman artists by the arrival of exiled Greek masters from Constantinople, and there are documents that Pope Honorius III imported mosaicists, probably either Greek or Greek-trained, from Venice. The climax of Duecento monumental art in Rome is the apse mosaic of Santa Maria Maggiore (fig. 33), signed by Jacopo Torriti and executed during the pontificate of Nicholas IV (1285–94). Christ and the Virgin, robed in gold with blue shadows and seated on a rose-colored cushion with their feet on sky-blue footstools, appear against a deep-blue mandorla studded with gold stars and framed in sky blue with silver stars that seems to float in the golden empyrean of the background.

As in certain earlier Roman medieval apse mosaics,

the gold ground is crowded with curling acanthus scrolls populated by ducks, doves, parrots, pheasants, cranes, and peacocks. The shell-niche at the crown of the apse moves through a startling succession of colors—gold, sky blue, rose, and green. The mosaic is astonishing in the richness of the sources from which it derives: the subject of the Coronation of the Virgin is French and had appeared in Gothic cathedral sculpture for more than a century, while the linear style is related to Byzantine mosaic art and the acanthus scrolls are based on late classical originals, probably of the mid-fifth century. The mosaic even embodies fragments of a fifth-century mosaic, including a river-god and a sailing ship that are barely visible below the angels at the left. More important than these diverse origins is the ease with which they are harmonized. The drapery motifs, for example, are at once Byzantine in their linearity, Gothic in their amplitude, and classical in their harmony. A new

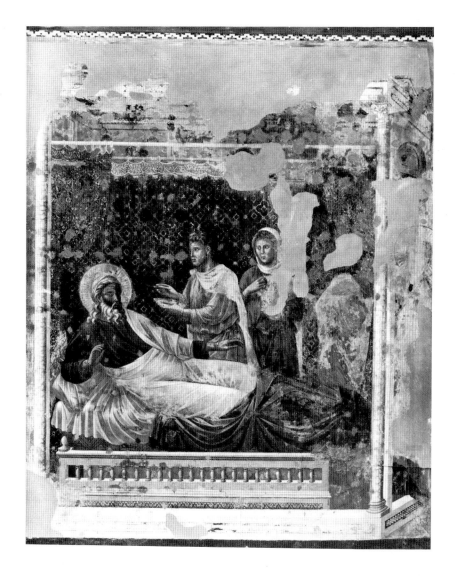

34. ISAAC MASTER. *Isaac and Esau*. 1280s or early 1290s. Fresco, 10 x 10'. Upper Church of S. Francesco, Assisi

style is emerging in Rome, in which the three currents most active in the formation of the Italian Renaissance are already approaching fusion.

Several Roman painters, including Torriti, were active in the nave of the Upper Church of San Francesco at Assisi, probably after Cimabue had finished his work in the transept and choir. One of these is called the Isaac Master on account of two scenes from the story of Isaac and Jacob (fig. 34) that are the best preserved of the works painted by this artist in the upper level of frescoes, above the series of the Life of St. Francis. The flat ceiling with a diamond pattern in dark and light to indicate coffering, the elaborate hangings of the bed, and the little colonnade at its base seen in the painting illustrated here are often found in Roman thirteenth-century art (see fig. 35), while the majestic drapery curves, at once classical, Byzantine, and Gothic, recall those of Torriti.

The scene is tense. In the adjoining fresco Jacob, abetted by Rebecca, has received the blessing of the blind Isaac by fraudulent means, presenting a gift of meat as venison. Here Esau, Isaac's favorite son, returns with the real gift, expecting the blessing; Isaac, realizing that he has been tricked, says to Esau, "Who art thou?" and

"trembled very exceedingly" (Genesis 27:32–33). His right hand is raised, his left extended in confusion. Oddly enough, Esau, who should be looking at his father in dismay, gazes straight past him, while an unidentified young woman, holding a pitcher to her bosom (cf. fig. 35), looks on unmoved, and Jacob, now almost destroyed, hustles off the scene at the extreme right. Stiff as the scene may be in poses and gestures, and imperfectly realized in the weightlessness of the figures under their drapery, the painter was able to model faces and hands to indicate the play of light with great subtlety. A date in the 1280s or early 1290s seems likely.

CAVALLINI

It is the new discovery of the meaning and function of light in the realization of form, although still carried out in a manner that takes no account of the sources of light, that transfigures Roman mural art in the work of the artist known as Pietro Cavallini (Pietro de' Cerroni, nicknamed Cavallino, "little horse"). Born sometime between 1240 and 1250, he was active until about 1330.

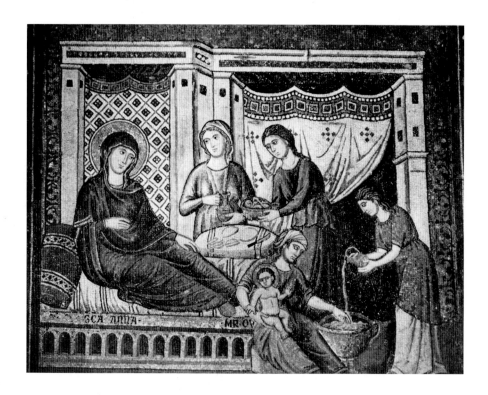

35. PIETRO CAVALLINI. *Birth of the Virgin*. 1290s. Mosaic. Sta. Maria in Trastevere, Rome. Commissioned by Bertoldo Stefaneschi

A notation by his son tells us that he lived to a hundred and never covered his head, even in the worst days of winter. The Florentine sculptor Ghiberti, who knew frescoes and mosaics by Cavallini that are still preserved and others that have perished, including cycles in Old St. Peter's, San Paolo fuori le Mura, San Francesco, and San Crisogono, called him a "most noble master" and praised his work for its "great relief."

The most important achievements by Cavallini still visible in Rome are the mosaics in the apse of Santa Maria in Trastevere ("across the Tiber") and the fragmentary frescoes in Santa Cecilia in Trastevere, both of which Ghiberti mentions, but neither of which can be securely dated beyond the probability they were done in the 1290s. Ghiberti discerned in Cavallini's frescoes in Old St. Peter's "a little of the ancient manner, that is, Greek." The circumstances of Cavallini's lost work in the Early Christian basilica of San Paolo fuori le Mura elucidate Ghiberti's assessment. As Early Christian frescoes suffered from the passage of time, they were repainted again and again throughout the Middle Ages, and this was what Cavallini was commissioned to do, maintaining the late classical qualities of the original compositions, but substituting his own ideas where little or nothing of the original was left.

The classic quality of style he learned in the process is evident in the *Birth of the Virgin* (fig. 35) from the series of the Life of the Virgin in Santa Maria in Trastevere. The color creates a soft radiance that fills the apse with shifting, subtle variations of hue and value. The background is a templelike structure, like a stage set that is related in its shapes to ancient Roman domestic architecture and shrines, but its inlaid ornament derives from Roman medieval sources. The women setting a table by

the mother's couch and the two midwives about to bathe the newborn Mary (a theme borrowed from representations of the Nativity of Christ; see p. 66) carry their bread, wine, and water with the solemnity of a ritual. The figures are imbued with classic grace and simplicity, and though the gold striations persist in the mantle about St. Anne's legs, the other drapery masses recall Greek and Roman sculpture in the breadth of their forms and the ease with which the folds fall, in sharp contrast to the tension and complexity of the drapery of Torriti or the Isaac Master. Most important of all, the rounded heads, tubular arms, and cylindrical bodies seem to owe their existence in space largely to the play of light.

This is a fundamental revolution in artistic vision, and it is clear that it came about through intimate acquaintance with Early Christian models. An even sharper transformation is visible in Cavallini's fragmentary fresco of the *Last Judgment* in Santa Cecilia in Trastevere (colorplate 21, p. 61), which is all that is left of a cycle that once covered the entrance and nave walls of the church. In the enthroned Christ and apostles, whose rich coloristic harmonies are dominated by soft orange and green, and in the angels with feathers in graduated colors, there is a remarkable step beyond even the mosaics of Santa Maria, resulting in a wholly new sense of real rather than schematic volumes, of surfaces, and of textures in light. Cavallini's illumination still does not come from one identifiable source, but it plays richly on the drapery of the seated apostles, and above all on the faces. Forms seem to have roundness in depth through the action of light. The linear compartmentalization of the necks has been replaced by a columnar roundness that allows the anatomical structure of the neck to be felt in

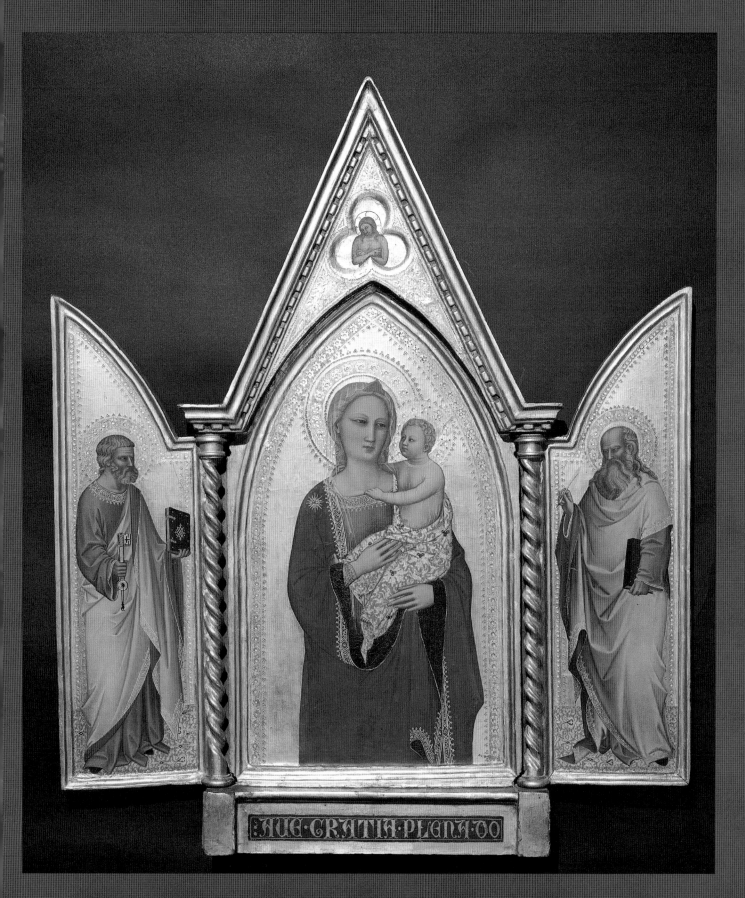

Colorplate 17. NARDO DI CIONE. *Madonna and Child with Sts. Peter and John the Evangelist.* Probably c. 1360.
Panel, height 30". National Gallery of Art, Washington, D.C. (Kress Collection)

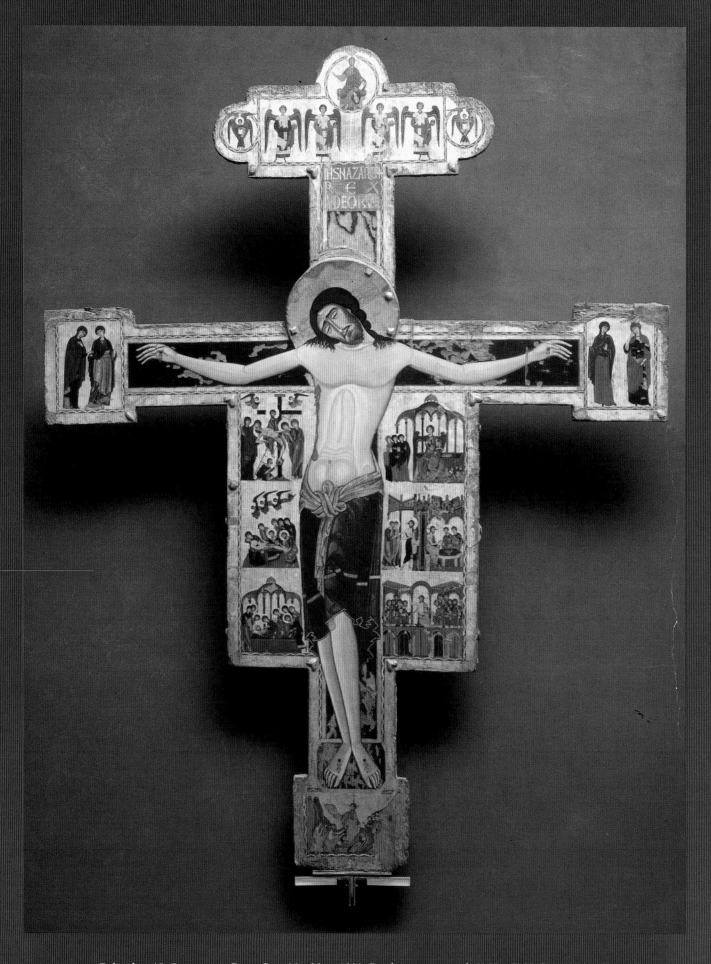

Colorplate 18. SCHOOL OF PISA. *Cross No. 20.* c. 1230. Parchment on panel, 9' 9" x 7' 8". Pinacoteca, Pisa

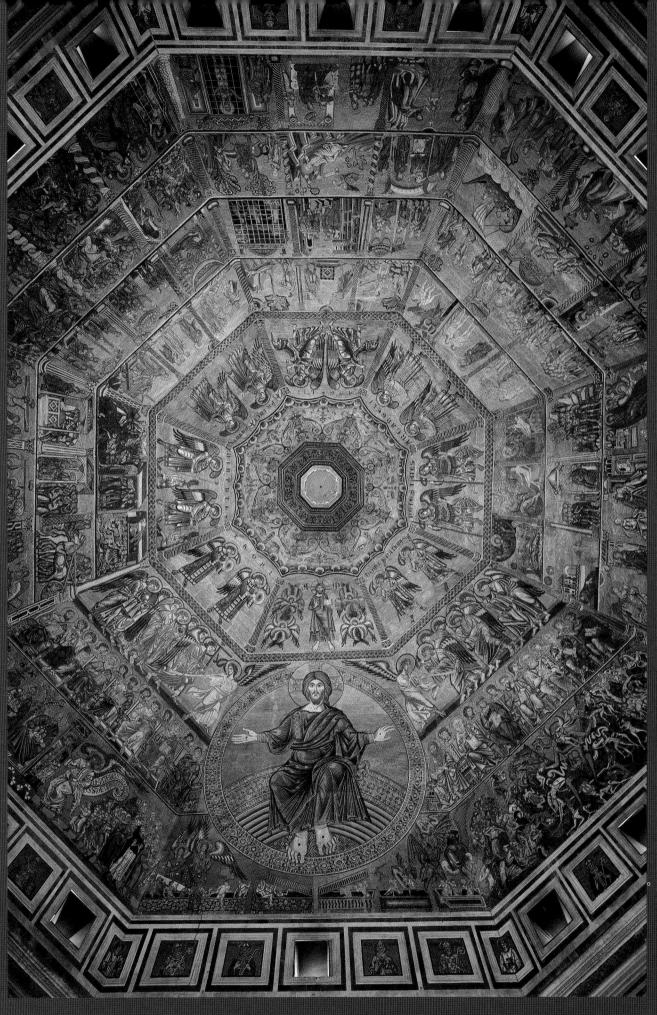

Colorplate 19. Mosaics of the *Last Judgment, Ranks of Angels,* and *Scenes from the Lives of Christ and St. John the Baptist*;
the central figure of Christ in the *Last Judgment* has been attributed to COPPO DI MARCOVALDO. Second half of 13th century.
Baptistery, Florence

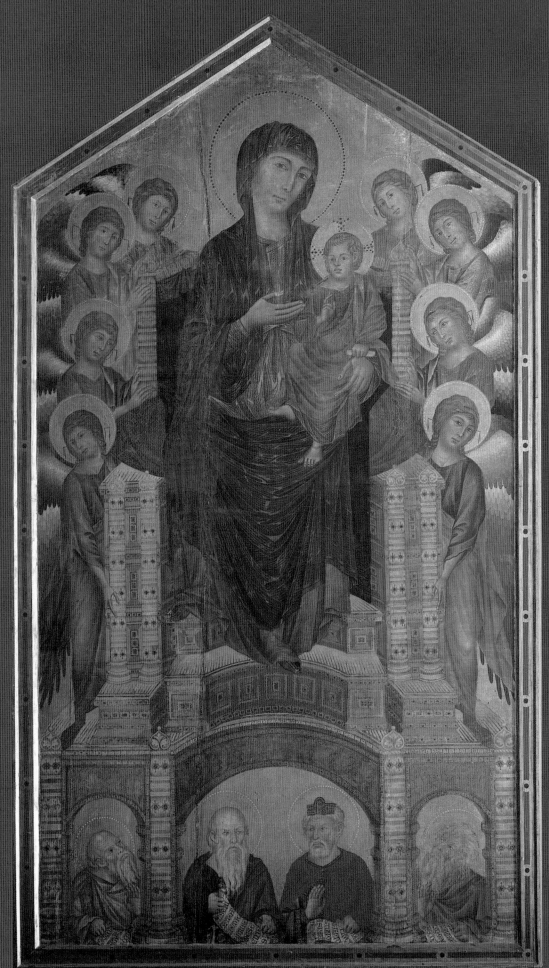

Colorplate 20.
CIMABUE. *Enthroned Madonna and Child with Angels and Prophets.* c. 1280. Panel, 11' 7" x 7' 4". Uffizi Gallery, Florence. Commissioned for the high altar of Sta. Trinita, Florence

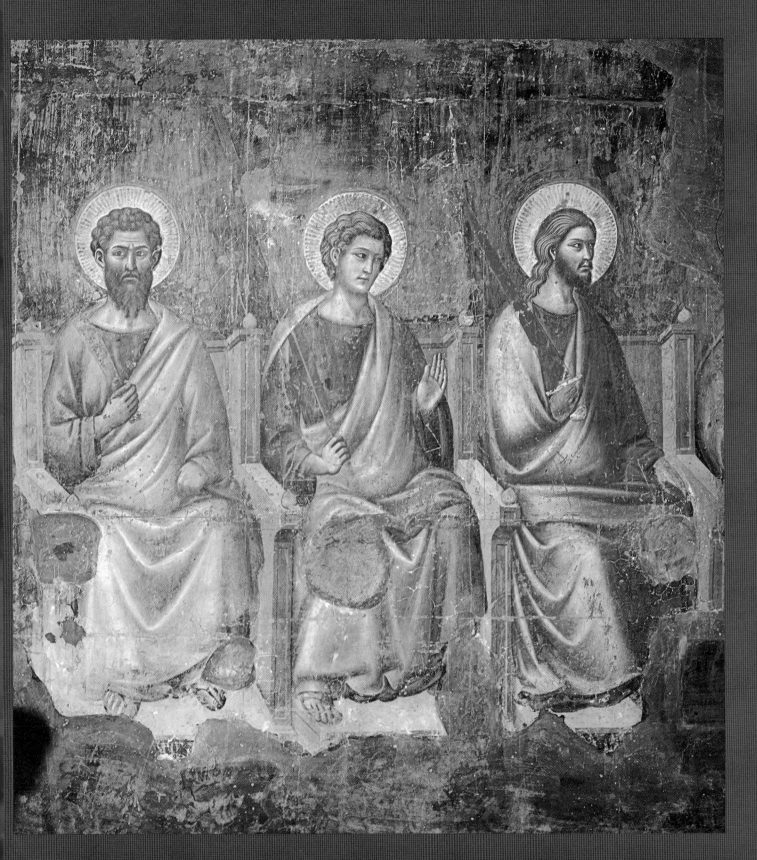

Colorplate 21. PIETRO CAVALLINI. *Last Judgment* (portion). c. 1290. Fresco. Sta. Cecilia in Trastevere, Rome

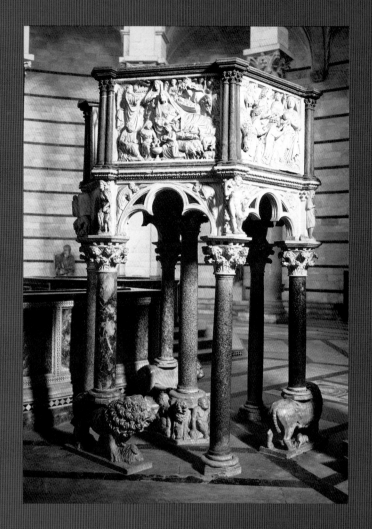

Colorplate 22. NICOLA PISANO. Marble pulpit. 1260. 🏛 Baptistery, Pisa. Commissioned by Archbishop Federigo Visconti

Colorplate 23. GIOVANNI PISANO. Lower half of façade, including statuary. 1284–99. Cathedral, Siena. Most of the sculptures are copies; originals now in the Museo dell'Opera del Duomo, Siena (see fig. 43)

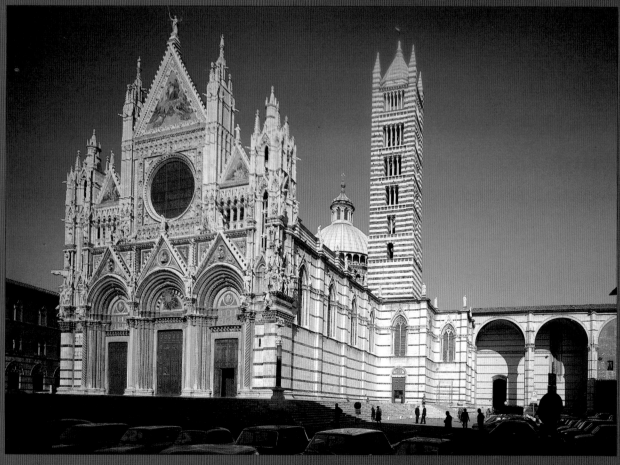

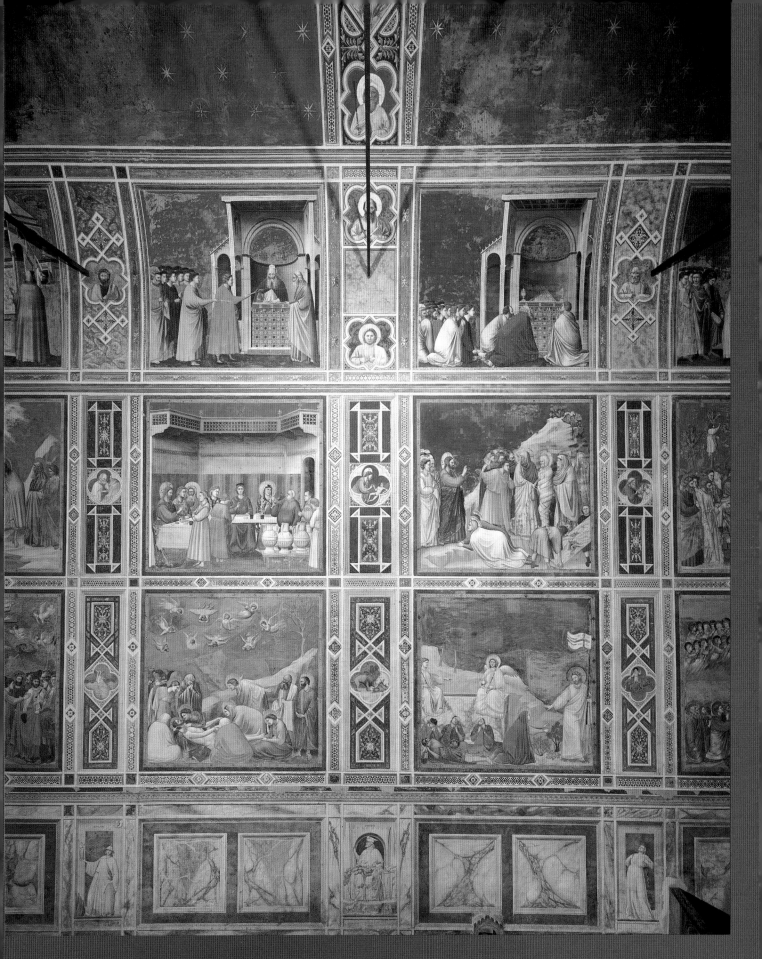

Colorplate 24. GIOTTO. Arena Chapel, Padua. Portion of the wall. Frescoes in the top register: *Suitors Presenting the Rods* and the *Prayer Before the Rods;* in the middle register: *Marriage at Cana* and *Raising of Lazarus;* in the lower register: *Lamentation* and *Noli Me Tangere;* at the bottom: figures of the vices of Infidelity, Injustice, and Wrath. After 1305. Commissioned by Enrico Scrovegni

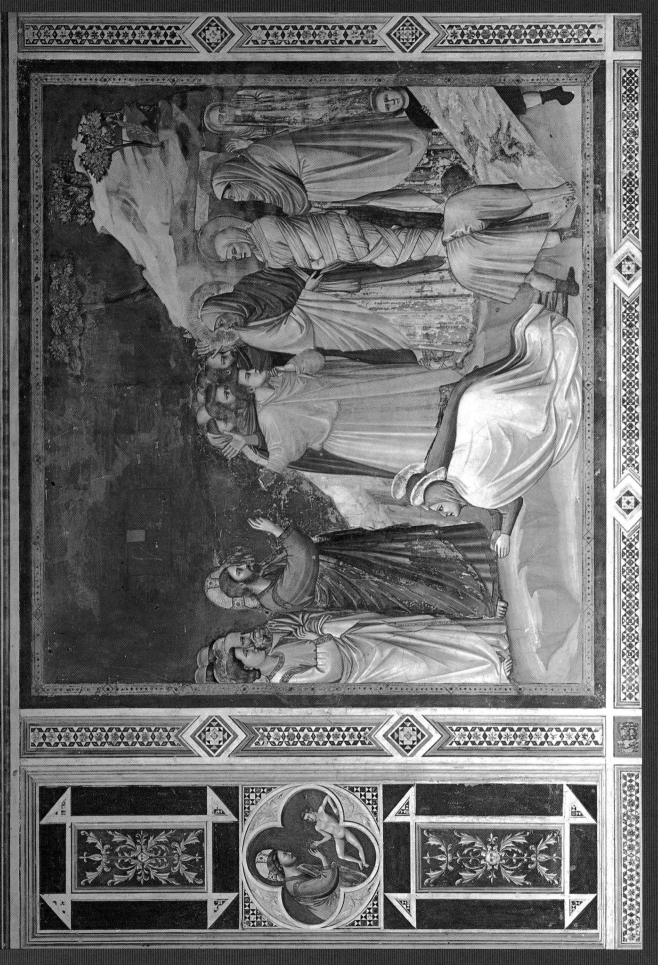

Colorplate 25. GIOTTO. *Raising of Lazarus*. After 1305. Fresco. Arena Chapel, Padua

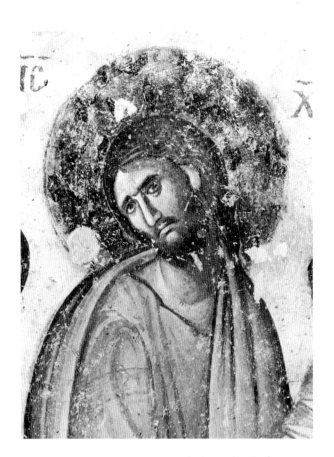

36. BYZANTINE. Head of Christ, detail of
Dormition of the Virgin. Probably 1263–68. Fresco.
Church of the Trinity, Sopočani

Italian architects. Cavallini's apostles resemble the Christ in the Sopočani *Dormition of the Virgin* in facial type, handling of beard and hair, expression, drapery masses, and above all in the manner in which form is created by light, but there are also many important differences.

The innovations of Cavallini provided a strong incentive, perhaps even inspiration, for the Florentine master Giotto, who must have seen and studied Cavallini's work in Rome. It is disappointing that, in spite of his longevity, Cavallini was not able to keep pace with the rapid changes in style he had been instrumental in setting in motion. His later works, in Rome and Naples, show only occasional flashes of the old fire.

SCULPTURE

While the Italo-Byzantine movement was reaching its height in Italian painting in the second half of the Duecento, Nicola d'Apulia, the sculptor known to us today as Nicola Pisano (active 1258–78) from his adopted city, arrived in Pisa from southern Italy. He was the first of many sculptural innovators, and his unexpected classicism of motifs and style has often been attributed to a supposed connection with the classicizing culture of the court of Emperor Frederick II, who ruled in Nicola's native Apulia. But Pisa, with its Roman history and pretensions, had a strong classical tradition of its own, and its ancient monuments had been copied by Nicola's sculptural predecessors earlier in the century. His first known work, a marble pulpit for the Baptistery of the Cathedral of Pisa (colorplate 22, p. 62), was signed with an inscription in which the artist proclaimed himself the greatest sculptor of his day, in keeping with the self-laudatory inscriptions common in medieval Tuscany. Busketus, the architect of the Cathedral of Pisa, had even compared himself to Ulysses and Daedalus.

The presence of a pulpit in a baptistery can be understood through the special importance of the baptistery in the Italian city-states, where it was the only place to celebrate Baptism, the sacrament that brought a child into the Christian community and into citizenship in the Commune. The baptistery, usually a separate building, thus had a civic as well as a religious importance. Sermons by Archbishop Federigo Visconti, who commissioned Nicola's pulpit, contain vivid symbolism of water as a vehicle for divine grace. Nicola's hexagonal pulpit, which is directly alongside the font, is a magnificent construction of white marble from the quarries at nearby Carrara, with columns and colonnettes of polished granite and variegated red marble. Every other column is short and supported on the back of a white marble lion, while the central column stands on a base enriched by seated sculptural figures. The pulpit shows the same juxtaposition of Northern European and Mediterranean elements we have noticed in contemporary Italo-Byzantine art (see pp. 43–44).

a manner not seen in art since ancient times. Although the locks of hair are still formalized, the beards are naturalistic in texture and the mantles have a soft and silky sheen, no doubt due in part to Cavallini's adoption of the Roman use of marble dust in his *intonaco*. The naturalism of the seated apostles, whose facial expressions betray deep and subtle states of feeling, owes little to antiquity and nothing to Tuscany, but much to a new stylistic current that made its appearance during the 1260s in portions of the Byzantinized world under the Palaeologan dynasty. There is a striking relationship between Cavallini's style at Santa Cecilia and that of the damaged frescoes in the Church of the Trinity at Sopočani in Serbia, built in the early thirteenth century and decorated at the order of King Uroš I, probably between 1263 and 1268, by Greek painters in the new, luminary style (fig. 36).

Cavallini may have seen Palaeologan icons in Italy, but it is perfectly possible, considering the migrations of artists in the Middle Ages and Renaissance, that he went to Sopočani to absorb the new style in its full sweep. There were rich and continuous relations between Serbia and Western Europe. Uroš had a French wife and his Venetian mother, Queen Anna Dandolo, daughter of a doge, was buried at Sopočani, which was built by

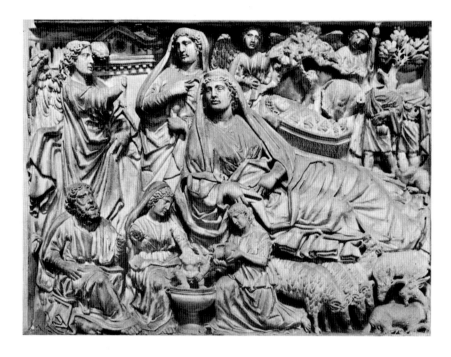

37. NICOLA PISANO. *Annunciation, Nativity,* and *Annunciation to the Shepherds,* panel on the marble pulpit, ⛪ Baptistery, Pisa (see colorplate 22, p. 62). 1260. 33½ x 44½". Commissioned by Archbishop Federigo Visconti

Nicola's study of the ancient Roman Corinthian capitals found in abundance in Pisa gives his capitals classical firmness and precision, but their acanthus leaves resemble the freer and more naturalistic ornament on French Gothic cathedrals, especially that at Reims, with which Nicola's ornament shows many affinities. While his arches are barely pointed in the Gothic manner, they are enriched with the cusping developed in French cathedral architecture. The hexagonal parapet behind which the preacher stands provides fields for five marble high-relief panels (the sixth being used for the opening from the staircase); the spandrels, filled with reliefs of Old Testament prophets, are separated by figures in high relief standing over the capitals. The pupils of the eyes were inset in some cases and painted in others, and the backgrounds of the scenes were decorated with patterned glazes on a gesso foundation, creating an effect not unlike the overall patterns that decorate the backgrounds of French Gothic manuscript paintings. The compact structure, rich in detail, culminates in the white marble eagle that serves as the lectern, doubtless because the eagle is the symbol of St. John, whose Gospel commences, "In the beginning was the Word, and the Word was with God, and the Word was God."

Nicola was apparently required by his archepiscopal patron to compress a number of separate incidents into the same frame: the initial panel includes the *Annunciation,* the *Nativity,* and the *Annunciation to the Shepherds* (fig. 37). The Annunciation, of course, is one of the most important events in the Christian cycle, when the Angel Gabriel brought to the Virgin Mary the tidings of her miraculous maternity. According to theologians, it was when Gabriel's words struck her ear that the human body of Christ was conceived in Mary's womb. One of the reasons for dating Christmas on December 25 was the custom of celebrating the feast of the Annunciation nine months previously, on March 25, the first day of

the Roman year. In fact, throughout Tuscany the new year began on March 25 until the Gregorian calendar was adopted in the late sixteenth century; Florence reckoned the new year from the feast of the Annunciation until 1750.

In the *Nativity,* Mary reclines upon a mattress before a suggestion of the cave used in Byzantine representations of this event, a reference to the cave still shown to visitors in Bethlehem. The two midwives who test the temperature of the bath are derived from a tradition preserved in an apocryphal gospel, but here on a baptismal font this scene is doubtless also connected with the idea of Baptism. At the lower left, Joseph sits as a silent spectator. The shepherds, although damaged, can be seen at the upper right-hand corner. These peripheral scenes act as a kind of frame for the enormous figure of the reclining Virgin, much as narrative scenes flank a Duecento cross or a standing saint. The style suggests that Nicola drew his figures on the marble slab and then cut in to free heads, arms, and trees from the background or from each other. No attempt was made to suggest distant space, and all the heads lie on the surface plane no matter how much the figures may overlap. Yet this also means that the crowded relief is responsive to the inner forces of the enclosing architecture, a feature impossible to observe in separate photographs but effective when facing the actual pulpit.

Not only the dense packing of the figures but, much more important, the rendering of their heads can be traced to classical models, especially to figures on Roman sarcophagi, of which a number had remained in Pisa since antiquity or been brought there more recently to be reutilized as Christian tombs. These provided Nicola with authoritative models. His Virgin has often been characterized as a Roman Juno, and the straight nose, full lips, broad cheeks, and hair waving back from a low forehead come directly from classical art. But for

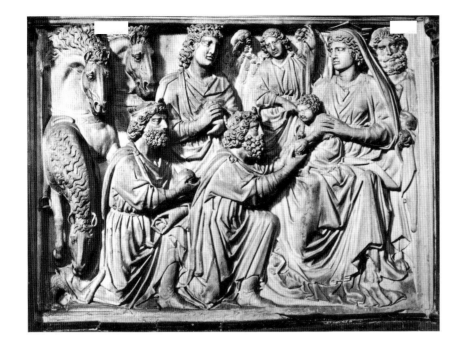

38. NICOLA PISANO. *Adoration of the Magi*, panel on the marble pulpit, 🏛 Baptistery, Pisa (see colorplate 22, p. 62). 33¹/₂ x 44¹/₂"

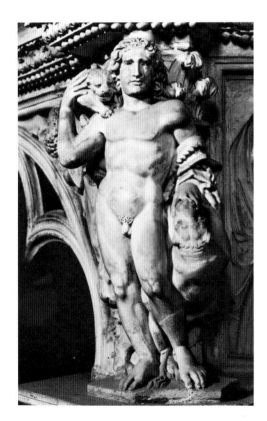

39. NICOLA PISANO. *Daniel*, on the marble pulpit, 🏛 Baptistery, Pisa (see colorplate 22, p. 62). Height 22"

all these detailed and specific references to antiquity, and the figures' classical weight and dignity, the whole is strangely unclassical. The drapery breaks into sharp angles, creating an all-over network reminiscent of the Italo-Byzantine forms in contemporary Duecento painting. The general compositional principles in the Baptistery pulpit reliefs are not far from those of Coppo di Marcovaldo and Cimabue. Classical and Gothic details alike seem intrusions at this stage.

In the *Adoration of the Magi* (fig. 38), the seated Virgin is imitated, almost line for line, from the seated Phaedra on a Roman sarcophagus representing the legend of Hippolytus that is still in Pisa and which in Nicola's day was on the façade of the Cathedral. The borrowing was first noticed, apparently, by Vasari. The three kings who come to adore Christ look like Roman bearded figures, but again the drapery shows the staccato breaks of Italo-Byzantine style rather than the fluidity of even the mass-produced Roman sculpture available to Nicola. Most striking of all is the nude male figure, below the left-hand corner of the *Adoration*, who is now identified as *Daniel* (fig. 39). He was imitated from a figure on a Roman Hercules sarcophagus. In spite of the Christian horror of nudity, naked figures do turn up in medieval art, especially in scenes of the Last Judgment, where all are naked before God. In the Trecento, in fact, nude figures are more common than one might at first think. Andrea Pisano's sculptor (see fig. 16) is carving a male nude, and Cennino Cennini describes the proportions and construction of the male nude in detail. But this *Daniel* is the first heroic nude in Italian art.

Nicola's interest in the classical may be the result of a number of factors. Pisans traditionally thought of their city as a new Rome, and classical sarcophaghi were used for burials in churches throughout the city. In addition, Nicola's use of the classical gives his scenes a majesty and dignity not seen in earlier Italian reliefs, and his motivation in looking to the antique may have been based on a desire to find sculptural models that offered a mood and character that he thought appropriate for Christian subject matter.

Five years after he completed the Pisa pulpit, Nicola was called to Siena, where he executed an even more ambitious pulpit for the Cathedral (fig. 40). In this octagonal and much more richly decorated work, Gothic and classical elements blend effortlessly in a style of un-

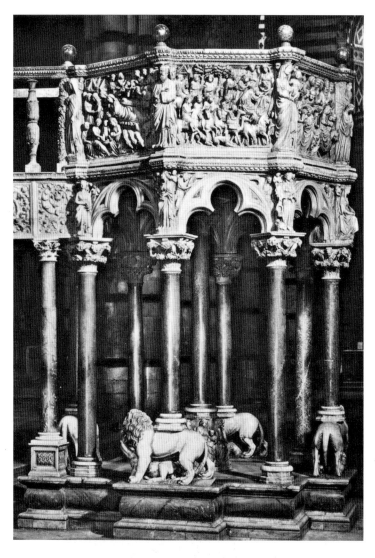

precedented serenity and dramatic resonance. Nicola worked on this immense undertaking from 1265 to 1268 with the assistance of a group of pupils that included his son Giovanni and three other sculptors who would later become well known, including Arnolfo di Cambio. These assistants were necessary to complete so elaborate a project in so short a time, but the general style of the work and probably even the execution of most of the principal sculptural portions show the style of Nicola himself. Here the abrupt compositions and technique of the Pisa Baptistery pulpit have given way to a broader, smoother, and more unified treatment of shapes and surfaces. Standing statues separate curved reliefs with the result that the flow of sculpted forms appears continuous. Nine columns of granite and porphyry support the pulpit; the four shorter ones rest on the backs of lions or lionesses who stand over animals they have struck down. Around the base of the central column sit the Liberal Arts, their number here augmented to eight. The pulpit was at one time dismantled, and all the statues are not now in their proper positions; furthermore not all the figures have been clearly identified.

Nicola, like so many artists from the Middle Ages to the Baroque, must have had pattern books for stock scenes, and some of the events are here represented in compositions that are similar to those in the Pisa Baptistery pulpit. The most spectacular of the scenes is the *Last Judgment* (fig. 41), which comprises two relief panels flanking the central sculptural group of the enthroned Christ with angels. The richness of the panoramic composition depends on the combination of various degrees of sculptural projection and on a new, vivid conception of the muscular surface of the human figure, especially in the relief that shows the damned about to be dragged to Hell—figures whose freedom of pose and

40. NICOLA PISANO. Marble pulpit. 1265–68.
🏛 Cathedral, Siena. Commissioned by Fra Melano, the Operaio of Siena Cathedral

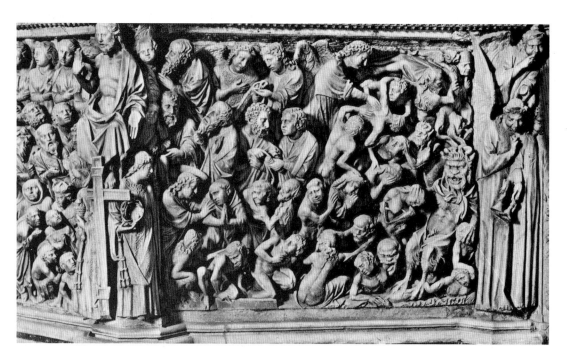

41. NICOLA PISANO. *Last Judgment* (portion), panels on the marble pulpit, 🏛 Cathedral, Siena. Each panel, 33 1/2 x 38 1/4"

THE LATE MIDDLE AGES

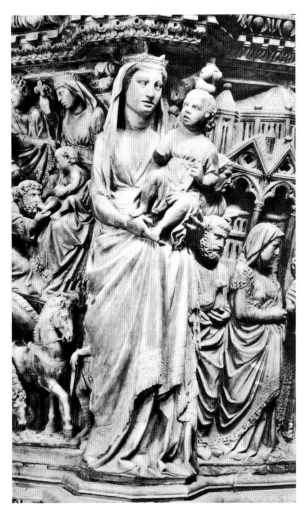

42. NICOLA PISANO. *Madonna and Child*, on the marble pulpit,
🏛 Cathedral, Siena. Height 33¹/₂"

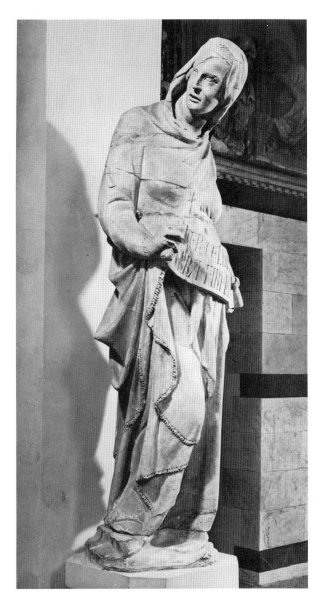

43. GIOVANNI PISANO. *Mary, Sister of Moses.* 1284–99.
Marble, height 74³/₈". Removed from original location on
the façade of the Duomo, Siena (see colorplate 23, p. 62).
Museo dell'Opera del Duomo, Siena

action gave inspiration to later artists, particularly the
Sienese painter Duccio. All traces of Italo-Byzantine
compartmentalization of form have been swept away by
the vigor of Nicola's surface. Now drapery flows as easily
as in the classical originals he admired, and a new softness
of flesh and a grace of expression are evident, particularly
in the *Madonna* (fig. 42), who has a new physicality. Her
breasts are visible through the drapery, as in the French
Gothic statues of Reims Cathedral. The question of
French influence is still open, but Nicola's art, a strongly
individual creation, is full of premonitions of the Renaissance and forms a parallel to the innovations of Cavallini in painting.

Nicola's son Giovanni inherited the shop after his father's death, at some time between 1278 and 1287. Giovanni Pisano (c. 1250–c. 1314) designed the lower half
of the magnificent façade of Siena Cathedral (colorplate
23, p. 62) and carried out some of its finest sculpture
before returning to Pisa. In contrast to Nicola, Giovanni
is determinedly Gothic, but it is a Gothic far removed
from the courtly style as we know it in France; it is closer to the expressionistic Gothic of German sculpture.
The powerful statues of prophets and saints on the Siena

façade twist and turn as if to declare their independence
from the confining rules of architecture, even though it
was Giovanni himself who laid out the arches, gables,
and pinnacles that surround them. The statues, of colossal size, recall the loftiest figures from the pinnacles of
Reims Cathedral, carved only a few years earlier, but
Giovanni's figures express a more powerful sense of
movement that is most evident in his figure of *Mary,
Sister of Moses* (fig. 43).

The abrupt tensions of her pose—especially the neck
projecting sharply from the torso and then twisted to
one side—are to be explained in part by a sensitivity to
the spectator's position that was apparent even in the art
of Nicola, whose reliefs were clearly designed to be seen
from below, their shapes responding to those of the
arches. Giovanni was well aware that unsatisfactory ef-

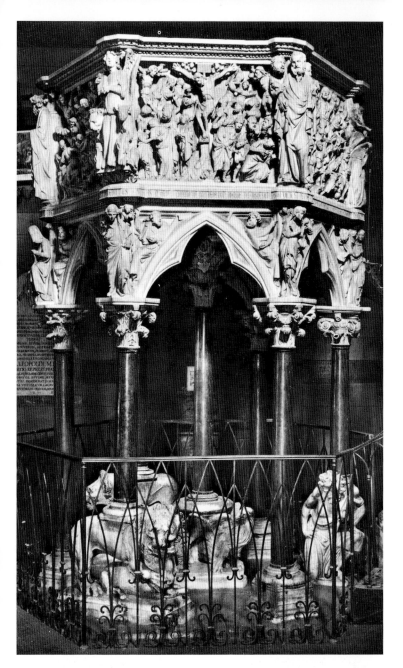

fects would result if a sculptor did not take the visual angle into account when planning statues intended for a lofty position. He therefore brought the neck outward so that when the figure was seen from the piazza below, the face would not be hidden by the breasts and knees. Mary's dramatic pose may also be related to her original position on the side of the façade; she leans aggressively forward as if to communicate with her fellow prophets and sibyls. Giovanni also—and this is common in Italian sculpture designed for such spots—reduced the figure and its features to their essentials, because at a distance fine detail would be lost and only the most powerful masses and movements could register on the eye. Today the badly eroded originals, taken down for safekeeping, have been replaced by copies on the façade. In their present setting in the Museo dell'Opera del Duomo, near or in some cases even below eye level from the entrance, the rationale for their extraordinary appearance has evaporated.

The self-laudatory inscription placed by his father on the Pisa Baptistery pulpit is exceeded by the inscription Giovanni carved on the pulpit he created between 1298 and 1301 for the Romanesque Church of Sant'Andrea in Pistoia (fig. 44). While Nicola had claimed to be the greatest living sculptor, Giovanni states that he has surpassed Nicola, which in some respects is true—although he never approached the subtlety of his father's late style. Although hexagonal, the Pistoia pulpit gives a totally different impression from the Pisa Baptistery pulpit. The cusped arches are sharply pointed and the leaves of the capitals more strongly projecting, while the classical elements so important in Nicola's art have been submerged by a rising tide of emotionalism. The projections are sharper, the undercuttings of heads, arms, and other projecting elements deeper. The free, zigzag movement of

above: 44. GIOVANNI PISANO.
Marble pulpit. 1298–1301.
🏛 Sant'Andrea, Pistoia.
Commissioned by Canon Arnoldus

right: 45. NICOLA PISANO.
Massacre of the Innocents, panel on
the marble pulpit, 🏛 Cathedral,
Siena (see fig. 40). 33¹/₂ x 38¹/₄"

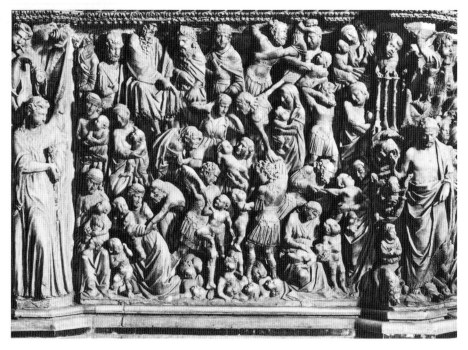

THE LATE MIDDLE AGES

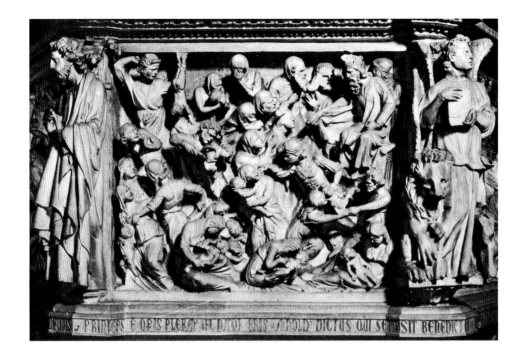

left: 46. GIOVANNI PISANO.
Massacre of the Innocents,
panel on the marble pulpit,
⛫ Sant'Andrea,
Pistoia. 33 x 40¹/8"

below: 47. GIOVANNI PISANO.
Sibyl, on the marble pulpit,
⛫ Sant'Andrea, Pistoia.
Height 24³/8"

the drapery has little in common with Nicola's carefully balanced folds. Even when the arrangement of figures and scenes appears to be derived from Nicola's pattern book, the effect is one of deep hollows enclosed by fluid shapes in continuous motion.

A scene especially suited to Giovanni's new style is the *Massacre of the Innocents,* those children under the age of two who were slain at the command of King Herod to destroy the infant he feared would usurp his power. Represented in a restrained way by Nicola, this scene becomes an orgy of sadism in Giovanni's relief (figs. 45, 46). On the upper right, Herod is giving the order; the stage is filled with wailing mothers, screaming children, and soldiers holding up children and stabbing them with swords; below, mothers cradle their dead children and weep over them. Even the lesser figures—the prophets in the spandrels and sibyls between the capitals and the parapet—share in the general agitation. The sibyls, Greek and Roman prophetesses who were believed to have foretold the coming of Christ, will be seen again and again throughout Italian art, culminating in their representation by Michelangelo on the Sistine Ceiling. One dramatic figure (fig. 47), inspired by an angel who appears over her shoulder, can be compared to Michelangelo's *Libyan Sibyl* (see fig. 513). Her excitement is communicated by the turn of her head, the zigzag movement of the figure, and the flow and flicker of the drapery. Giovanni's most unexpected figure is the one who supports a column on the nape of his neck (fig. 48), forcing severe contortions on the figure and a disturbing empathetic effect on the observer.

It is perhaps characteristic of the mélange of styles that coexisted in Duecento Tuscany that the Pistoia pulpit should be roughly contemporary with the last manifestations of the Italo-Byzantine style in painting. But we have seen that Cimabue was, at Assisi, capable of

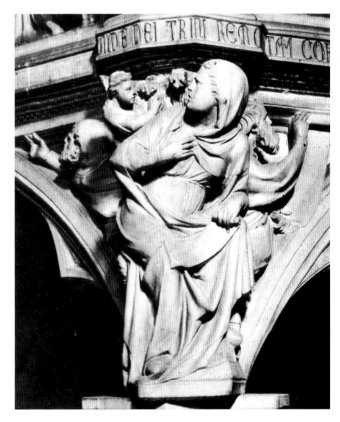

projecting emotional dramas on a large scale in fresco compositions. At this particular moment in Italian art, Gothic sculpture and Italo-Byzantine painting are allies. The last manifestations of Giovanni Pisano's art, however, really belong to the next chapter. The grand simplicity of his *Madonna and Child* on the altar of the Arena Chapel in Padua (fig. 49), her clear-cut profile so different from the Romanizing profiles by Nicola, the broad sweep of the drapery masses enhancing the vol-

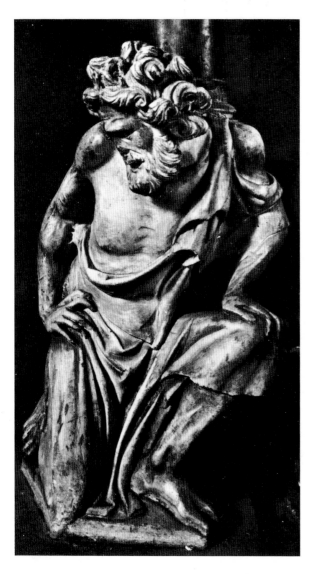

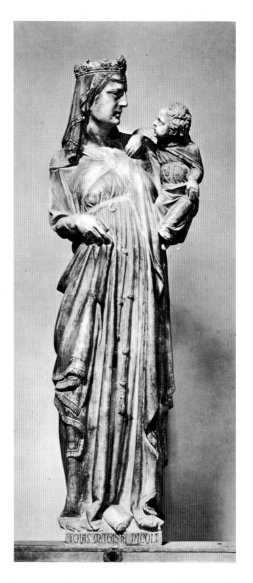

48. GIOVANNI PISANO. *Supporting Figure*, on the marble pulpit, ⌂ Sant'Andrea, Pistoia. Height 34³/4".

49. GIOVANNI PISANO. *Madonna and Child*. c. 1305–6. Marble, height 50³/4". ⌂ Arena Chapel, Padua. Commissioned by Enrico Scrovegni

ume of the figure beneath them, the geniality and human directness of the expressions—all suggest a close familiarity with the art of Giotto, the master whose frescoes fill the walls and ceiling of the same chapel. For the moment, at least, the harsh expressionism of the Pistoia pulpit is in abeyance, but this vein flows just below the surface of Italian art and life, and under circumstances of stress will reappear again and again.

ARCHITECTURE

At this point we face a dilemma. It is logical enough to consider the great painters and sculptors of the Duecento and the Trecento as precursors of the Renaissance and, in their own right, as leaders of an artistic revival that is not directly comparable with the Gothic style that prevailed elsewhere in Europe. Despite their ties with

the Middle Ages, their work, as will be seen in later chapters, is inseparable from that of the Renaissance masters of the Quattrocento and Cinquecento. The same cannot be said of Duecento architecture—an Italian version of the Gothic without the organic complexity of French Gothic, to be sure, but Gothic nonetheless. Yet the figurative artists of the period worked within this architectural context, and many of its preconceptions governed their frescoes, statues, and reliefs. In fact, they sometimes took part in the construction of Duecento buildings.

The great thirteenth-century religious movements, Dominican as well as Franciscan, required ecclesiastical buildings on an entirely new scale to accommodate their unprecedented congregations. The Florentine churches of Santa Maria Novella and Santa Croce owe their existence to the preaching orders that still occupy them. Santa Maria Novella (figs. 50, 51), founded by the

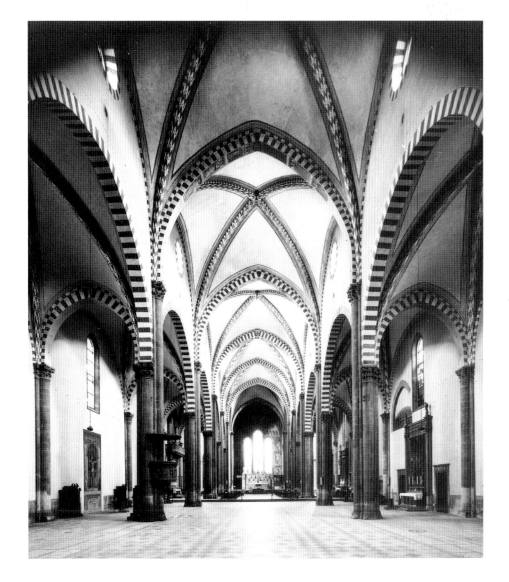

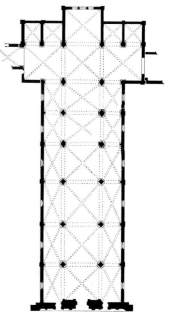

Dominicans before 1246 but constructed from 1279 into the early Trecento, is perhaps the supreme example of the simplicity of plan, organization, and detail that characterizes Italian Gothic architecture as a whole. The plan is derived from those developed for churches of the Cistercian Order, which was founded earlier in France; in its monasteries throughout France, England, and Italy, a flat east end was substituted for the rounded or polygonal apse generally used in cathedral churches. But the relatively high side aisles, leaving little room for a clerestory and none for a triforium, are typically Italian. So is the contrast of the stone of the supports and arches with the *intonaco* that covers the walls and vaulting surfaces. These plastered surfaces create a continuous membrane that encloses and harmonizes with the ascending and descending forms of the pointed arches, which are striped in stone like the façade. Arches and vault ribs are flat, wall ribs are almost nonexistent, and compound piers are as simple as those of Romanesque buildings in France.

There is, moreover, no formal separation between the nave arcade and the wall above, which is pierced by simple oculi instead of the usual pointed Gothic windows. As a result nothing interrupts the unifying membrane of the wall, which creates a feeling of calm repose. This is in striking contrast to the energetic pictorial art and the rich sculpture of the period. However different the architectural forms of Santa Maria Novella may be from the later, classically derived elements of the Renaissance, the harmony of its lines and spaces renders it a fitting precursor of such Quattrocento churches as San Lorenzo and Santo Spirito (see figs. 140, 141). At a moment when French architects had dissolved the wall entirely, converting whole churches into elaborate stone cages to enclose surfaces of colored glass, the unknown—possibly monastic—builders of Santa Maria

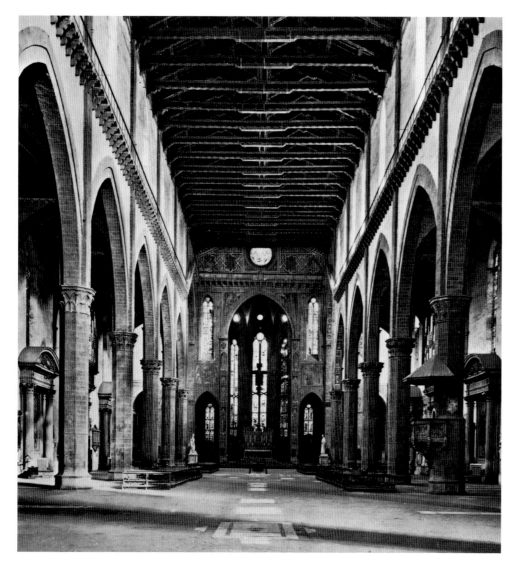

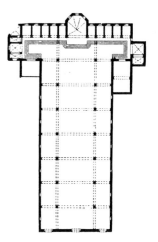

left: 52. ARNOLFO DI CAMBIO (attributed to). Nave and choir, Sta. Croce, Florence. Begun 1294

below: 53. Plan of Sta. Croce

Novella proclaimed the quintessentially Italian supremacy of the wall.

So did the architect of Santa Croce (figs. 52, 53), the Franciscan church on the opposite side of the city, but in a very different way. In all probability this master was Arnolfo di Cambio, who was also important as a sculptor, as a pupil and co-worker of Nicola Pisano, and as the first architect of the new Cathedral of Florence (see fig. 126). The construction of Santa Croce, founded in 1294, continued well into the Trecento. The plan combines a long, timber-roofed nave of seven bays with a lower, vaulted polygonal apse that is separated from the nave by a triumphal arch somewhat like those of the Early Christian basilicas in Rome but with pointed arches and windows. A choir screen containing chapels once separated the crossing from the nave. Octagonal columns replace the compound piers used in Santa Maria Novella, which are needless here since there is no vaulting. A catwalk carried on corbels separates the small clerestory from the nave arcade, and carries the eye down the nave and up over the crossing to the triumphal arch.

Santa Croce's loftiness and the openness of its arches make it seem almost endless. From the very start, the wall surfaces were intended for painting, as were the windows for stained glass. In fact, the nave was still being built when Giotto and his followers were at work painting frescoes on the walls of some of the transept chapels. The early Trecento painted decoration of the ceiling beams is still largely intact. The splendor of Santa Croce, of which this brightly painted roofing is an essential part, gives us some insight into how the nave of the Duomo of Florence (*duomo* is the Italian term for "cathedral") might have looked had Arnolfo's plan been followed.

In the Italian city-states the building that housed the government competed in physical bulk and artistic magnificence with the principal churches, and Florence was no exception. Also attributed to Arnolfo is the Palazzo dei Priori, or Palace of the Priors, as the principal governing body of Florence was called (fig. 54); it is now popularly and inappropriately known as the Palazzo Vecchio, a name it was given in the sixteenth century when the Medici family, who had lived in the republi-

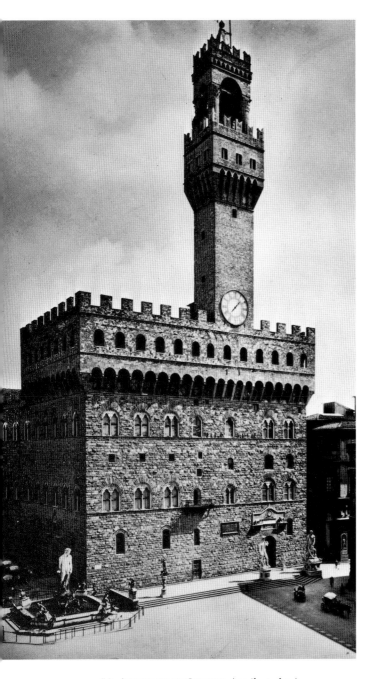

54. ARNOLFO DI CAMBIO (attributed to).
Palazzo dei Priori (now known as Palazzo Vecchio),
Florence. 1299–1310

can city hall for a period, moved across the river to their "new" palace, the Palazzo Pitti.

The Palazzo dei Priori dominates a whole section of the city and in popular imagination its tower is grouped with the dome of the Cathedral as a symbol of the city. It is not only the largest but also one of the last built of the Italian medieval communal palaces. It was erected in an astonishingly short space of time, only eleven years from the laying of its foundations in 1299 to the completion of the bell tower in 1310. From the start the building was intended to help define the piazza produced by the destruction, in 1258, of the houses of the traitorous Uberti family, who had fled Florence and later fought with the Sienese at the Battle of Montaperti. The Priori had declared that no buildings would ever stand on their property, which was confiscated by the Commune. The new communal palace was built of *pietra forte*, a tan-colored local stone. It appears as a gigantic block, divided by stringcourses into a ground floor and two main stories, each of colossal proportions, and crowned by powerfully projecting machicolations carried on corbels and culminating in a crenellated parapet. The great tower is placed off-center, perhaps to make use of the foundations of earlier house towers. It is thrust aggressively forward, out over the corbelled arcade, and terminates in more corbelled machicolations, another crenellated parapet, and a baldacchino-like bell chamber supported on four huge columns.

The brutal power of the building mass is accentuated by the roughness of the huge blocks, which are rusticated, as in Roman military architecture. And the building seems even more impregnable by virtue of the relative delicacy of the mullioned windows with their trefoil arches, in imitation of French Gothic models. Its simplicity and force, its triumphant assertion of the noble human capacity to govern, were intended to symbolize the victory of civic harmony over the internal strife that tore the Republic apart in the late Duecento. The building may also serve as an introduction to the artistic ideals of one of the greatest periods in Florentine art, the Trecento, and to the style of Giotto, its leading master.

3
Florentine Art of the Early Trecento

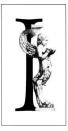n the early Trecento, a new style of painting emerged that was to revolutionize the art of Florence, of Tuscany, and in fact of Italy and eventually of the entire western world. This new style was initiated by the first Italian master to achieve universal importance, who became one of the most influential artists who ever lived.

GIOTTO

The fame and significance of Giotto di Bondone (c. 1277–1337), born in the village of Colle di Vespignano north of Florence, were recognized by his contemporaries. The *Chronicle* of Giovanni Villani, written a few years after Giotto's death, rates him among the great personalities of the day. Boccaccio claims that Giotto "brought back to light" the art of painting "that for many centuries had been buried under the errors of some who painted more to delight the eyes of the ignorant than to please the intellect of the wise" (*Decameron*, VI, 5). In a famous passage in the *Divine Comedy* (XI, 94–96), Dante relates his encounter in Purgatory with the miniaturist Oderisi da Gubbio, who bewails his own fall from popularity, comparing it with that of Cimabue as an example of the transience of worldly fame and fortune. As Dante makes clear, it was Giotto who stole the fame from Cimabue:

> In painting Cimabue thought he held the field
> And now it's Giotto they acclaim—
> The former only keeps a shadowed fame.

Similar, according to Dante, was the success of the poet Guido Cavalcanti, inventor of the *dolce stil nuovo* (beautiful new style), whose revolutionary use of the Tuscan language chased his competitors from the field.

Dante's statements are literally true. Within a few years after the appearance of Giotto, the style of Cimabue was banished to the villages, where it lingered only a decade or so. Most painters in Florence began to imitate Giotto's new style, which spread to other centers in Tuscany, including Siena, and then up and down the Adriatic coast, capturing one provincial school after another. Within a generation it met resistance only in Venice, which was strongly tied to the Greek East, and in Piedmont and Lombardy, where the Northern Goth-

ic was deeply influential. The basic conceptions of Giotto's art remained dominant into the Quattrocento, despite the personal variants of individual painters; Renaissance artists and writers were emphatic in their insistence that Giotto was their true artistic ancestor. At few other moments in the history of painting has a single idea achieved so rapid, widespread, and virtually complete a change.

What was this new style? Cennino Cennini, who claimed to have been the pupil of Agnolo Gaddi (himself the son and pupil of Taddeo Gaddi, one of Giotto's closest followers), expressed the matter succinctly when he declared that Giotto had translated painting from Greek (by which he meant Byzantine) into Latin. Later Vasari declared that Giotto had revived painting after it had languished in Italy since ancient times on account of the many wars that had overwhelmed the peninsula. Giotto, he said, abandoned the "rude manner" of the Greeks, and since he continued to "derive from Nature, he deserves to be called the pupil of Nature and no other." No one, not even in Cennini's time, was in a position to realize what Italian painting had gained from Byzantine examples and, perhaps, from actual Greek (Byzantine) masters. To all commentators naturalness was equated with Latinity, which meant, of course, Roman culture in the larger sense—Italy and, as we shall see, France. The virtue of Giotto's style for his contemporaries and successors lay in its fidelity to the human, natural, Italian world they knew, as against the artificial manner imported from the Byzantine East. Although Cennini does not say that Giotto drew from posed models, Villani suggests this when he refers to Giotto as "he who drew every figure and action from nature," depending on the precise significance one attaches to his word *trasse*, which can mean "drew" in two different senses. So pungent and convincing are Giotto's figures that we are almost compelled to presuppose such drawings.

The surviving work of the Italian masters of the period we are studying is a mere fraction of what they actually painted. But as we read Vasari's accounts of Giotto's work—even knowing that some of the paintings he mentions may have been by other artists—we realize how little remains of what Giotto produced in the course of a long and honored lifetime. He is reported to have worked throughout Tuscany, northern Italy, and the Kingdom of Naples, including its capital, then ruled by a French dynasty. The great master was said even to have gone to France to work in Avignon, the new seat of the papacy after 1305, and elsewhere. French contacts are abundantly visible in Giotto's style, and commercial relations between Florence and all parts of Europe were so routine during the Trecento that we would be daring indeed to deny the possibility, even the ease, of a trip to France for so prosperous and universally desired a master. Whether or not Giotto studied with Cimabue in Florence, as Vasari says he did, the older master can have played little part in the formation of the young artist's style as we now know it. The dominant influences were the sculpture of the Pisano family, the painting of Cavallini, French sculpture either in France itself or through small, imported works—and the rediscovery of nature.

During most of the Duecento, Florence and its territory had been the scene of bitter warfare between opposing factions: the Guelphs, who favored the pope, and the Ghibellines, who were attached to the Holy Roman Emperor. In reality, this was a class conflict, because the Ghibellines were the feudal nobility, and they and their supporters looked to the emperor to maintain them in their fiefs. The Guelphs, on the other hand, comprised the bulk of the city dwellers—artisans and merchants for the most part—who succeeded in establishing their guilds by the Ordinances of Justice in 1293; to all intents and purposes these ordinances disenfranchised the nobles unless, as many were eventually constrained to do, they were willing to adopt a trade and join a guild. An attempt by the nobles to regain power was put down in 1302, and hundreds of Ghibellines, including Dante, were exiled from the city. It is against this triumph of the energetic, prosperous, commercial and artisan class, who equated their values with the highest ideals of the state, that one must understand the art of Giotto, with its emphasis on clarity, measure, balance, order, and on the carefully observed drama that develops between human beings who live and work at close quarters.

THE ARENA CHAPEL. In this same period Padua, a university city not far from Venice, had regained its republican independence and created a considerable state in the flat Venetian plain. In 1300 a wealthy Paduan merchant, Enrico Scrovegni, acquired the ruins of the ancient Roman arena, where a chapel dedicated to the Virgin Annunciate was located, as a site for a palace. Scrovegni began building a new chapel, probably in the hope of atoning for the sin of usury committed by his deceased father, Reginaldo, in 1303; in 1305 it was consecrated. A series of manuscript copies of the chapel's frescoes can be dated in 1306. From the very start, apparently, Scrovegni had the idea of asking Giotto, who according to one account was *satis iuvenis* (fairly young) and who was then at work on a fresco series in the Franciscan Basilica of Sant'Antonio in Padua, to paint the interior of the chapel. Whether Giotto planned the fresco cycle of the nave (those of the chancel are later) by himself or with the aid and advice of Scrovegni and

theological advisers is unknown. Although he undoubtedly had assistants working with him, Giotto certainly painted the principal figures and much of the rest with his own hand.

The frescoes of the Arena Chapel are his greatest preserved achievement and one of the most wonderful fresco cycles anywhere (fig. 55; colorplates 1, 24, 25, pp. 10, 63, 64). They are astonishing in their completeness and state of preservation, despite the recent menace from industrial fumes. The frescoes are somewhat smaller than they seem to be in reproductions; the figures are about half life-sized. On the north side the chapel was attached to the palace and thus there are windows on the south wall only. These were kept small in order to provide as much wall space as possible for the sequence of narrative frescoes. The frescoes are designed in three superimposed rows of scenes. To enclose the scenes Giotto designed delicately ornamented frames that form a continuous structure of simulated architecture. On the north wall, these frames enclose smaller scenes in French Gothic quatrefoil frames that act as commentaries on the larger ones (fig. 67; colorplate 24, p. 63). The vault is painted the same bright unifying blue as the background color in all the frescoes—naturally enough, since vaults and domes were traditionally held to be symbolic of Heaven, and Italian documents show that the vault of an interior was often referred to as *il cielo* (the sky). This one is covered with gold stars, and bust portraits of Christ and the four evangelists, and the Virgin and four prophets, appear in circular frames that seem to pierce the sky to reveal the glories of Heaven beyond.

The chapel is dedicated to the Virgin of Charity. The wall surfaces are so divided that the Lives of the Virgin and Christ are told on three levels in thirty-eight scenes. The incidents chosen emphasize the Life of the Virgin as told in the *Golden Legend* by the thirteenth-century Genoese bishop Jacobus de Voragine, and generally omit from Christ's life scenes in which the Virgin plays no role. Narration begins on the upper level, to the right of the chancel arch, with the events of the lives of Joachim and Anna, the Virgin's parents, on the right-hand wall and the Life of the Virgin on the left, ending with God the Father enthroned in the center over the arch, sending the Archangel Gabriel on his mission, and the Annunciation on either side of the sanctuary. On the second level, the Infancy of Christ on the right-hand wall culminates in his adult mission, on the left. On the lowest tier, the Passion of Christ on the right is followed on the left by his Crucifixion and Resurrection. The lowest level, like wainscoting or a dado, is painted in imitation of panels of veined marble that enframe images in grisaille of the Seven Virtues on the right and the Seven Vices on the left. The drama of human salvation comes to its climax in the *Last Judgment*, which covers the entrance wall (see colorplate 1, p. 10). In a sense, the narration can be compared to that of the cinema, so exact is Giotto's sense of timing and so clear is his presentation of each dramatic incident. Unfortunately, in a

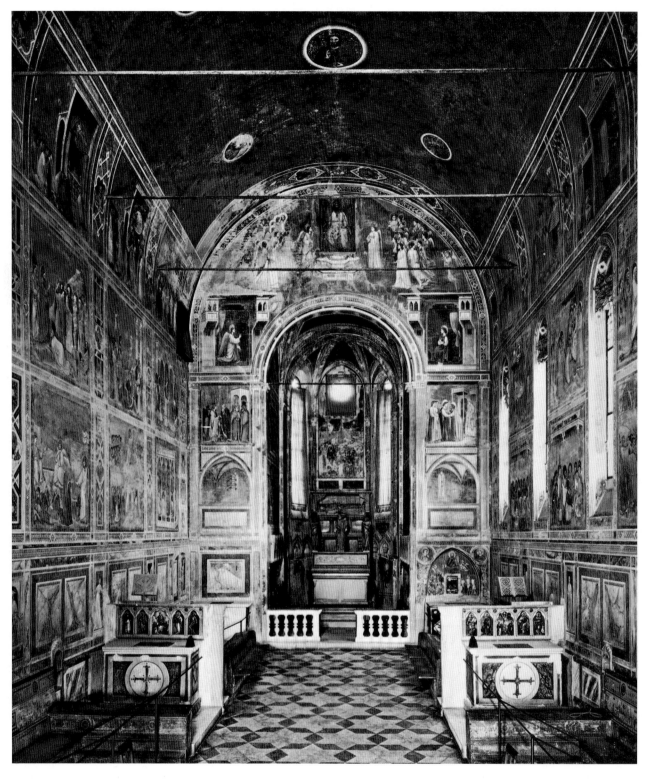

55. Giotto. Arena Chapel, Padua. Interior, facing altar. Consecrated 1305. Commissioned by Enrico Scrovegni

book of this scope all of the scenes cannot be illustrated or discussed.

Most observers entering the chapel probably do not immediately recognize the element of time, but they are at once aware that they have stepped into a world of order and balance. The Byzantine fabric of compartmentalized figures and gold-striated drapery has vanished. All is clear light, definite statement, strong form, firm ground, carefully modulated ornament, simply de-

fined masses, and beautiful glowing color, the colors of spring flowers. One is reminded of John Ruskin's phrase, "the April freshness of Giotto."

In many scenes, the dignity and balance of Giotto as a narrator make one think of Sophocles, who "saw life steadily and saw it whole." Italian documents and sources contain no word for our "scene": scenes are invariably called *storie* (stories), and that is what they are throughout Italian art. Each *storia* is an incident from a continu-

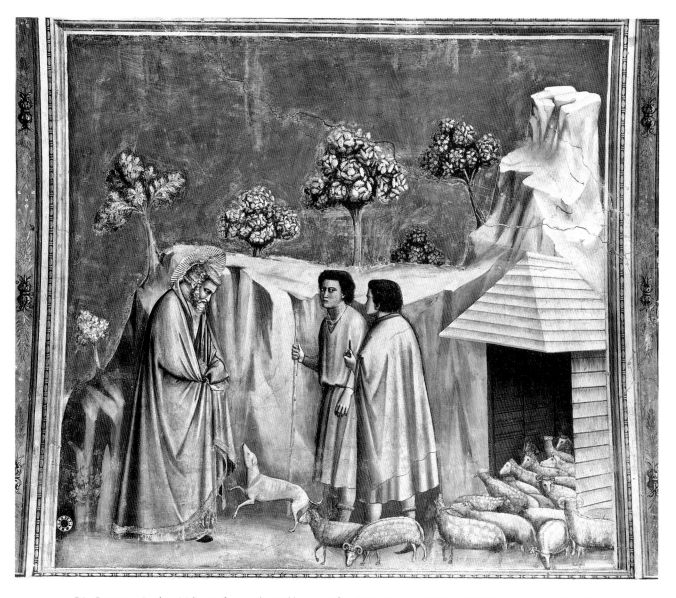

56. GIOTTO. *Joachim Takes Refuge in the Wilderness*. After 1305. Fresco, 78³/₄ x 72⁷/₈". Arena Chapel, Padua

ous drama and is based on the human relationships of the figures. We can follow the plot, generally accompanied in the Shakespearean sense by one or two subplots as well, in great or delicate, but seldom excessive, detail as we move through the series. In an incident from the Life of the Virgin, for example (fig. 56), the aged Joachim, who will later become her father, has been expelled from the Temple on account of his childlessness and has taken refuge with shepherds in the wilderness. This is the principal plot, and the composition is founded on the relationships among the figures. Joachim looks downward, overcome by humiliation. The youthful shepherds accept him only with reluctance; one looks toward the other, attempting to gauge his response and judge whether it is safe to take in this outcast. The landscape frames and accentuates this tense moment. Then comes the subplot; the sheep, symbols of the Christian flock (priests and ministers are still called pastors, "shepherds"), pour out of their sheepfold, and the dog, an age-old symbol of fidelity in Christian art, leaps upward in joyful recognition of Joachim's sacred role.

The landscape, the most advanced known at that time, is powerfully projected but deliberately restricted in scope. Cennini instructs his readers that, to paint a landscape, it is necessary only to set up some rocks in the studio to stand for mountains and a few branches for a forest. Yet Giotto's iceberglike, rocky backgrounds form an effective stage setting for his dramas, and in successive scenes that supposedly take place in the same spot he does not hesitate to rearrange the rocks a bit to bring out the inner meaning of the particular moment of action. The rocks enclose a distinct space that is limited, in all the scenes, by the continuous blue background that as yet does not contain clouds or suggestions of other atmospheric phenomena, except where they are needed to indicate the angels' celestial origin.

Within this shallow box of space, the figures stand forth in three dimensions like so many columns, the drapery masses simplified to bring out the cylindrical masses of the figures, which show profile, one-quarter, and even back views instead of the customary three-quarter aspect of figures in Duecento painting. In deli-

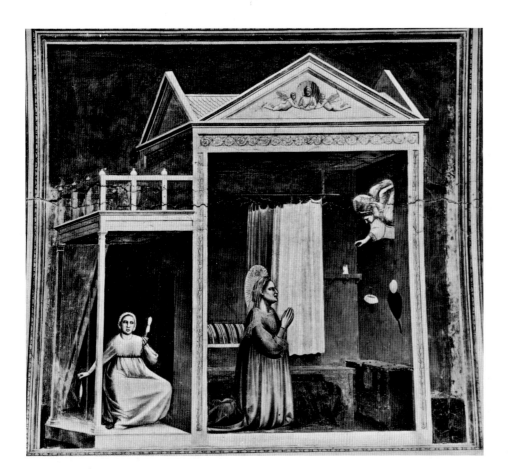

57. GIOTTO. *Vision of Anna.*
Fresco, 78³/4 x 72⁷/8".
Arena Chapel, Padua

cate gradations, the light models faces, drapery, rocks, and trees with a precision and delicacy that establishes their existence in space. But—and this is of prime importance—no source is yet shown for the light. A uniform illumination bathes all scenes alike, regardless of the time of day, and this, of course, helps maintain the unity of the compositions within the space of the chapel. Giotto's light, having no source, casts no shadows and makes no reflections. With few exceptions, cast shadows do not appear in painting until the Quattrocento, yet we can hardly imagine that Trecento painters were unaware of shadows. In a famous passage in the *Inferno* one of the damned asked who Dante is, since he—unlike the dead—casts a shadow; this is only one example from a rich medieval tradition of literature on light and its behavior. But for some reason as yet unexplained, painters did not consider natural light effects suitable for representation. Although Giotto's realism is limited, like his space, by a set of conventions, he often suggests a broader or more distant space; some trees are shown cut off by the rocks, so that we read them as growing on the other side of the hill, and figures sometimes disappear behind the frame at the sides of his scenes. And there is no limitation whatever to the depth and subtlety of his observation of the reactions of human beings.

The next scene is the *Vision of Anna* (fig. 57), back in Jerusalem, where she is visited by an angel who flies in through a window to announce that she will conceive and bear a child. Out on the back porch a servant who is spinning pays no attention. The setting is charming,

but it is not meant to indicate an actual building. Its jambs and entablature are enriched with ancient Roman carved acanthus scrolls instead of Cavallini's mosaic inserts, and it is roofed with marble plaques in a scale pattern rather than with Italian roof tiles. Its classical pediment contains a medallion with a bust portrait uplifted by angels that is imitated from a Roman sarcophagus; the figure is probably meant to represent God the Father. Probably this exterior is symbolic, a shrine within which the Immaculate Conception of Mary can take place. Like the rocks in the landscape backgrounds, a few simple architectural elements symbolize a complex reality. The front wall is removed as in a stage setting to show the interior of the house, and Giotto has treated us to a view of a Trecento Florentine room with a bed and its curtains, a little chest for clothing, shelves, and various objects hanging on the wall. The cube of space is turned at a slight angle so that we can see two sides at once, and the head of the angel, seen from above, is foreshortened as a powerful volume in space.

Vasari is eloquent on the subject of Giotto's foreshortenings, and he is probably right in claiming that Giotto was the first to be able to do them. Cennini tells us that the distant objects should always be represented darker than those in the foreground; this must have been another convention derived from Giotto, and it will be noted that the elegant frame of the architecture is more brightly lighted than the recesses of the interior, just as the foremost leaves on Giotto's trees are lighter than those farther away (see fig. 56).

The final scene of this group is the *Meeting at the*

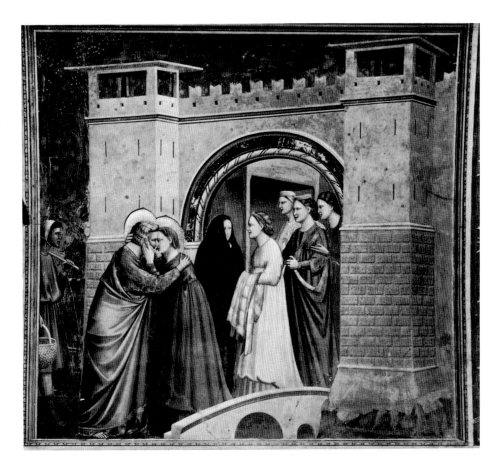

58. GIOTTO. *Meeting at the Golden Gate*. Fresco, 78³/4 x 72⁷/8". Arena Chapel, Padua

Golden Gate (fig. 58). Meanwhile Joachim has also received a revelation from an angel and returns to Jerusalem to tell Anna, just as she rushes out to break her identical news to him. Their encounter occurs on a bridge outside the Golden Gate of Jerusalem. The small scale of the architecture as compared with the figures is explained by another Trecento convention. Architecture, especially Italian architecture, is relatively large and people are small; to apply the same scale to architecture and figures would result either in reducing the figures to a point where the story could be read only from close up, or in omitting all but the lower portions of the buildings. Giotto and his followers—in fact all artists, well into the Quattrocento—were content with a double scale that presented the story in all its force within reduced architectural settings.

In this case the architecture, in particular the shape of the arch, reflects the emotions of the figures. In this reunion of husband and wife, Anna puts one hand around Joachim's head, drawing his face toward hers for a long embrace. As always, Giotto's draftsmanship is broad and simple, leaving out details that might interrupt his message of sincere human feeling or the powerful clarity of his form. One subplot, of course, can be sensed in the happy neighbors; another appears in the shepherd who accompanies Joachim to carry his belongings.

Turning to the events directly connected with the Life of Christ, we find the *Annunciation* (figs. 59, 60), divided into two sections, in the spandrels flanking the sanctuary arch. This position was designated for the Annunciation by a Byzantine tradition that was based on

Ezekiel's vision of the sanctuary of the Temple, whose gate was shut: "And no man shall enter in by it; because the Lord, the God of Israel, hath entered in by it, therefore it shall be shut. It is for the prince; the prince, he shall sit in it to eat bread before the Lord; he shall enter by way of the porch of that gate, and shall go out by the way of the same" (Ezekiel 44:2–3). To Christian theologians the closed gate (*porta clausa*) of the sanctuary, which only the Lord both entered and left, stood for the virginity of Mary; the prince was Christ, and the bread the Eucharist. The use of a cusped Gothic arch for the balconies to either side is important, for throughout the chapel Giotto uses the round arch to refer to the Old Law and the pointed, Gothic arch as a symbol for the New Testament; here, at the moment of the conception of Christ, we see the first Gothic arches in the cycle.

Giotto has represented the Annunciation, the moment of the Incarnation of Christ in human form, in a new and intimate way that is in keeping with his profound understanding not only of religion but also of the human heart. He has laid stress on the moment in which Mary accepts her responsibility: "Be it done to me according to thy will." In a token of resignation she crosses her hands upon her chest and kneels, as does the angel, as if enacting the widespread practice of genuflection on one or both knees that was introduced in the eleventh century as an act of adoration of the Eucharist. A flood of light, painted in clustering rays with a soft orange-yellow pigment, descends on the figure of the Virgin. This suggests actual light, not golden rays or masses of gold leaf (even though the haloes are still ren-

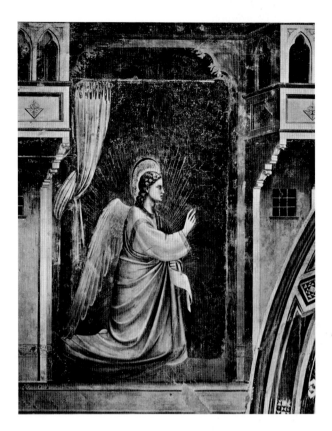
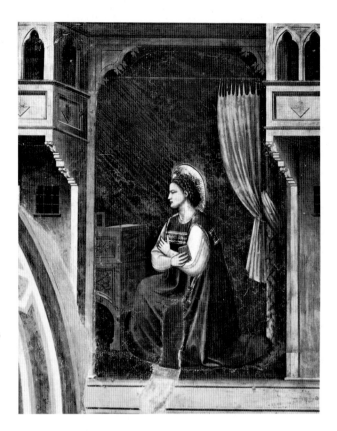

59, 60. Giotto. *Annunciation*. Fresco; each scene: 76³/4 x 59". Arena Chapel, Padua

dered as gold disks). Yet there are no sources of natural light anywhere in Giotto's art, and this must be the light of Heaven. Light is identified mystically with the Second Person of the Trinity: "In him was life; and the life was the light of men. . . . That is the true Light which lights every man who comes into the world." These words, repeated as a private devotion at the close of the Mass, eventually entered the liturgy.

The two stages on which Giotto has placed the participants of the Annunciation are probably derived from constructions used in the dramatizations of the Annunciation that took place during the Trecento in Padua, starting at the Cathedral and culminating in performances in the Arena Chapel. But Giotto has filled his spaces with the radiance of Divine Light that comes from the throne of God the Father in the arch above. In his *Annunciation* we have emerged from a world where every scene is bathed in the same dispassionate light into a world of mysticism and revelation that is unexpected for an artist so classical and self-possessed as Giotto. The effects seen here are prophetic of the mystical paintings of the Late Renaissance and the Baroque, when light again will play a catalytic role. It is important for the deeper understanding of Giotto's style and personality to recognize that even he found a point at which he was willing to disrupt the rational order of his universe, to submerge clear shapes in a tide of shadow and light for a scene of revelation.

Before Giotto, Italian artists had always placed the Nativity in the cave required by Byzantine tradition

(now less familiar to us than the stable of the European tradition). Although the cave still exists in Bethlehem—authentic or otherwise—the Gospel account specifies no precise setting. Giotto, perhaps after his visit to France, adopted the shed usually depicted in Gothic art (fig. 61). He also eliminated the apocryphal account of the baby's bath. The midwives are still there, however; one is handing the Christ Child, already washed and wrapped, to Mary. The ox and ass, who almost invariably appear in Western Nativities, look on. They are a fulfillment of the prophecy of Isaiah: "The ox knoweth his owner, and the ass his master's crib" (1:3). Joseph is sleeping in the foreground. The Annunciation to the Shepherds is taking place around and above; rejoicing angels are scattered in a variety of positions against the blue, and one leans downward to give the tidings to two shepherds. One shepherd has turned his back to us—a simple device, yet it is impossible to overestimate what this implies for Giotto's attitude toward space; he now can turn and move his figures in any direction. Giotto's backs, moreover, can be extremely expressive: the shepherd's astonishment seems evident in the set of his shoulders, the back of his head, the calves of his legs, and even the hang of his garment.

In the *Flight into Egypt* (fig. 62), the family moves calmly and intrepidly off to the distant land. They are led by an angel who, visible only to the waist, seems to emerge from a trailing cloud. Mary, seen in complete profile, holds the infant Christ to her bosom. Giotto's awareness of the meaning of time is indicated by the fact

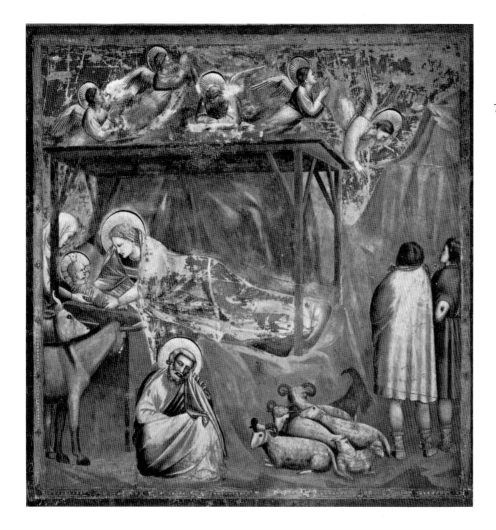

61. GIOTTO. *Nativity*. Fresco,
78³/4 x 72⁷/8". Arena Chapel, Padua

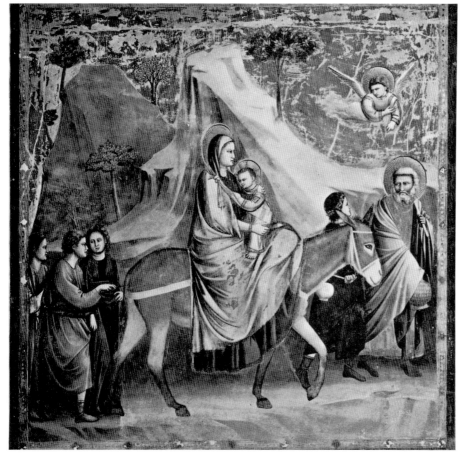

62. GIOTTO. *Flight into Egypt*.
Fresco, 78³/4 x 72⁷/8".
Arena Chapel, Padua

Florentine Art of the Early Trecento

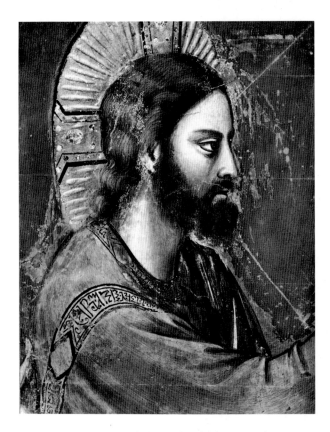

63. GIOTTO. Head of Christ, detail of *Raising of Lazarus*
(see colorplate 25, p. 64). Arena Chapel, Padua

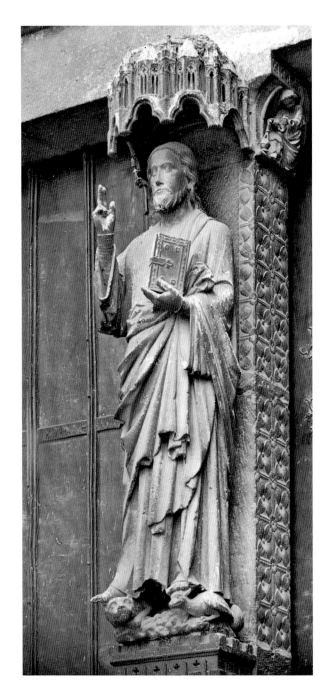

64. FRENCH GOTHIC. *Christ Treading on the Lion and the
Basilisk* ("*Beau Dieu*"). c. 1220. Cathedral of Notre Dame,
Amiens, France

that the previously almost bald Child has now grown dark hair. The pyramidal group is echoed in the structure of the background rocks. Giotto again suggests movement in space by cutting off the last figures, to show that they have come from outside the frame. Giotto's animals are delightful, and this patient donkey is one of his most convincing, a complete animal personality.

The adult Christ in the *Raising of Lazarus* (colorplate 25, p. 64; fig. 63) is the shortbearded Christ of French Gothic tradition, as at Amiens Cathedral (fig. 64). He is more naturalistic than the Byzantine type favored by Coppo and Cimabue. Lazarus's sisters, Mary and Martha, prostrate themselves before Christ in supplication, while he calls their brother from the dead with a simple gesture of his right hand. Giotto includes the traditional figures who cover their noses ("by this time he stinketh"; John 11:39), yet such details never seem distracting. Despite the considerable number of elements, the scene is clearly and simply composed, divided into blocks of figures by broad diagonals, verticals, and rhythmic curves.

In the workman at the right, Giotto has again exploited the back of the figure as an expressive device. The vivid color includes iridescent passages (the bending workman is dressed in pale pea green with rust-colored shadows), the formula for which is recorded in Cennini's handbook. An especially striking bit of coloristic freedom is the veined marble of the tomb slab. Christ's blue garment was rendered in one of the pigments that, Cen-

nini tells us, could not be painted in true fresco and therefore had to be added *a secco*. As a result of peeling, the brushstrokes of the underlying drawing have been revealed. In a striking, but by no means unusual, balancing of New Testament events with those of the Old that were believed to have foreshadowed them, the adjacent quatrefoil in the border represents the *Creation of Adam*, the design of which is close to that carved later by Andrea Pisano, possibly from Giotto's designs, for the Campanile of Florence Cathedral (see fig. 84). Here God raises Adam from the dust, as Christ—obviously the same face—raises Lazarus.

We now turn to the story of the Passion; in the *Betra-*

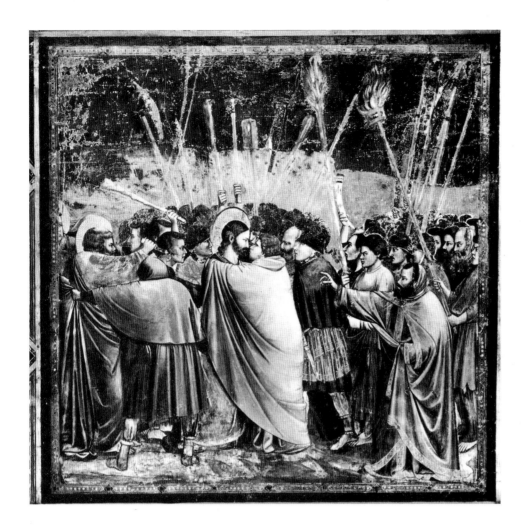

yal (fig. 65), Giotto follows the general compositional arrangement of the scene in the Uffizi *Cross* (see fig. 26). The nucleus of the drama is the group of Christ and Judas. Even though his body almost disappears in the sweep of Judas's cloak, Christ stands as firmly as in the *Raising of Lazarus* and with the same calm gaze. Giotto exploits the contrast between the regular profile of Christ and the bestial features of Judas, his lips pursed for the treacherous kiss, as a confrontation of good and evil. The contrast is especially striking since, in the preceding scene of the *Last Supper*, Judas had the same handsome, youthful face as many of the other apostles. But the Gospel account tells us that the devil entered into Judas when he took the sop in wine (John 13:27; see p. 270). Giotto has increased the impact of the drama by inserting the faces of two Roman soldiers between the confronted Judas and Christ.

The main group is flanked by two sharply different subplots. Required by iconographic tradition to depict the episode of Peter cutting off the ear of Malchus, the high priest's servant, Giotto has almost concealed it behind another of his expressive backs, that of a hooded attendant at the left who is trying to restrain one of the fleeing, terrified apostles. Especially telling is Giotto's exploration of the character and feelings of the high priest at the right, which are revealed entirely through his pose. He points toward the treacherous embrace in the center yet vacillates as he does so, as if unable to face the full wickedness of Judas's betrayal. His crooked finger begins to contract, and the masses of his garments break up into little shivering folds that deliberately contrast with the sharp, forward lunge of Judas's cloak. It will be noticed that Christ's halo, modeled in plaster, is shown in perspective. Some of the effect of the composition has become dissipated by the loss of the swords, halberds, and torches that, painted *a secco*, have largely peeled off.

In the *Crucifixion* (fig. 66), Giotto has shown the *Christus mortuus*, not the triumphant, alive Christ of the liturgical crosses of the late twelfth and early thirteenth centuries nor the agonized victim in Italo-Byzantine representations. Here he is dead, quietly and absolutely. He hangs there; one is made to feel the actual weight of the body suspended from the arms. No one screams and there are few gestures, but Mary collapses, losing the columnar entity, the firmness, the grandeur with which Giotto endowed humanity.

Mary Magdalen kneels before the cross, her long golden hair unbound, gazing at the feet she once washed with her tears and dried with her hair. At the right, the Roman soldiers are disputing over Christ's seamless robe, mentioned in the gospels (John 19:23–24); one, dressed in a gilded cuirass, argues with a companion, who is about to cut the robe with a knife. Above, the grieving angels recall their rejoicing counterparts in the *Nativity*. Some hold chalices to catch Christ's

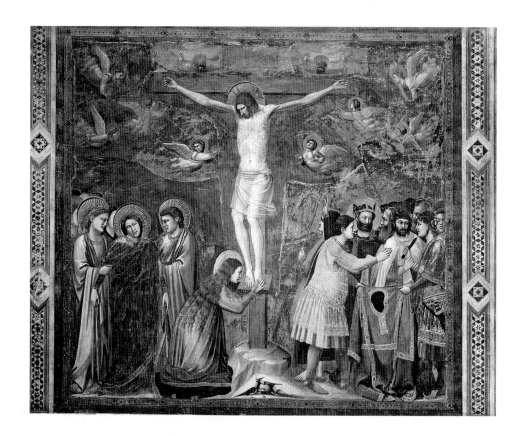

66. GIOTTO. *Crucifixion*. Fresco, 78³/4 x 72⁷/8". Arena Chapel, Padua

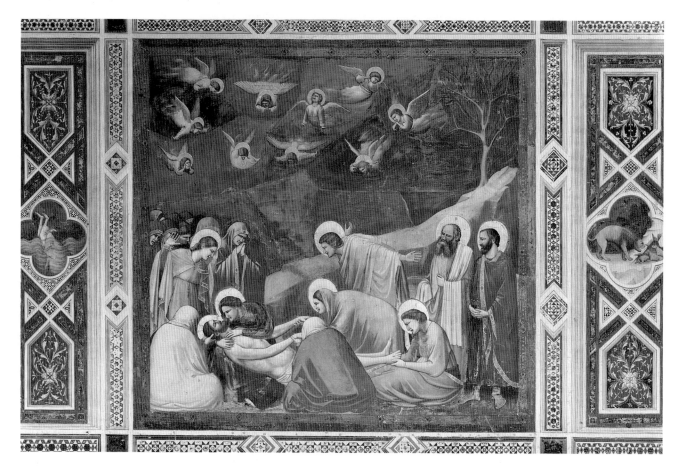

67. GIOTTO. *Lamentation* (see also colorplate 24, p. 63). Fresco, 78³/4 x 72⁷/8". Arena Chapel, Padua

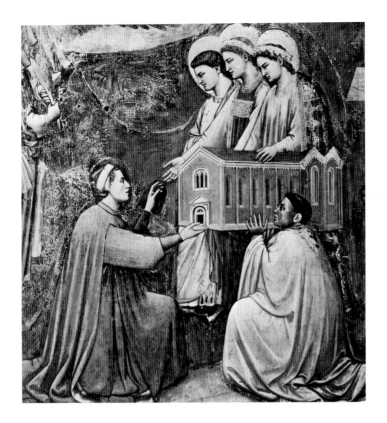

68. GIOTTO. Enrico Scrovegni Offering the
Model of the Arena Chapel to the Virgin Mary,
detail of *Last Judgment* (see colorplate 1, p. 10).
Arena Chapel, Padua

blood, others rend their garments or wring their hands. Directly above the cross two angels fly straight toward the observer so that their heads are foreshortened from above. Even this scene of deepest tragedy is presented with the same quiet firmness of composition—two blocks of figures, at once divided and united by the cross—and the same fresh beauty of color we find throughout the cycle.

The famous *Lamentation* (fig. 67; colorplate 24, p. 63), like the *Betrayal*, follows a traditional Byzantine type, as at Nerezi (see fig. 22), common in Duecento Italy (see figs. 21, 29). The dead Christ is stretched across the lap of Mary, his head upheld by a mourning figure seen only from the back, while another holds up one of his hands; Mary Magdalen gazes down at his feet. John stands with arms outstretched, and the long line of the barren rock behind him emphasizes the interchange between Mary and Christ, she searching his face as if to elicit an answer from beyond the barrier that separates life and death. The angels here move discordantly, twisting and turning first toward us, then away. But the drapery lines of all the main figures point sharply down, toward earth. Here and there some startling bits of Giotto's coloristic freedom are visible, especially the apostle wringing his hands, whose gray-blue cloak has plum-colored shadows.

The *Last Judgment* (colorplate 1, p. 10) fills the entire entrance wall, save for the window around which Giotto deployed battalions of the heavenly host. On either side of the window archangels roll away the sun, the moon, and the heavens like a scroll (Isaiah 34:4; Revelation 6:14), revealing the golden gates of Paradise. The *Divine Comedy*, begun by Dante at about this same time, was to provide later painters with an inexhaustible sup-

ply of details about the torments of Hell, but Giotto has selected a limited number of punishments.

In the center of the wall, Christ, wearing the seamless robe, is enthroned as judge of all creation. His rainbow throne and the rainbow glory around him are made up of tiny, colored feathers that are graduated in tone like those in the wings of Duecento angels; they recall references in the Psalms to God's wings and feathers (for example, Psalms 17:8, 91:4). The seat is upheld by the beasts of the four evangelists. The glory is attended by angels on either side, and cohorts of angels float above. Whereas Coppo's terrifying Judge (see colorplate 19, p. 59) stares impassively, Giotto's compassionate Christ averts his face from the damned and seems to betray grief over their fate. The apostles are enthroned to the sides. Below, the dead rise from their graves and are welcomed into Heaven or consigned to Hell; among the blessed can be seen the soldier who saved the seamless robe. Rivers of red and orange fire proceed from the throne of Christ to engulf the damned.

Directly over the door of the chapel, the cross of Christ is upheld by angels, and directly below the cross kneels Enrico Scrovegni and an Augustinian monk (fig. 68), who uphold a model of the Arena Chapel as Scrovegni's expiatory offering. These two portraits and others within the ranks of the blessed are among the earliest convincing examples of portraiture, as distinguished from the stock effigies common in medieval art, which may or may not have resembled their subjects. One has the feeling that Enrico Scrovegni must have looked like Giotto's portrait of him. The precise identity of the figures who accept the model has been a matter of controversy, but the central one is certainly the Virgin Mary, to whom the chapel was dedicated.

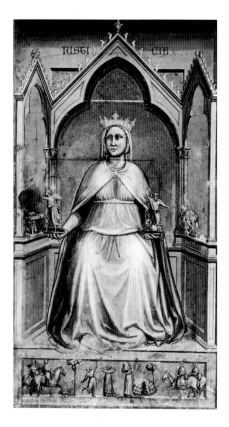
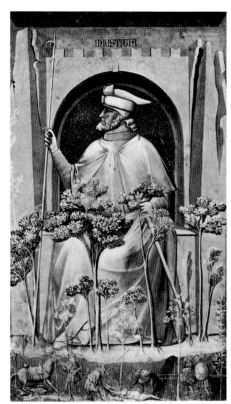
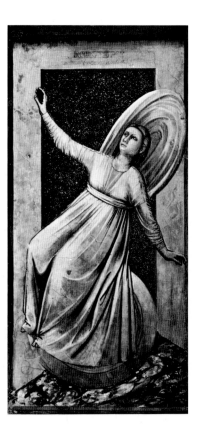

69, 70, 71. GIOTTO. *Justice, Injustice* (see colorplate 24, p. 63), and *Inconstancy*.
Fresco; each figure 47 1/4 x 215/8". Arena Chapel, Padua

The Virtues and Vices on the lower sections of the walls recall a tradition common in French Gothic portal sculpture. *Justice* (fig. 69) is a regal female figure before whom commerce, agriculture, and travel, the essential human activities of Italian corporate life, proceed undisturbed. Her male counterpart, *Injustice* (fig. 70), is a robber baron (reminding us that Padua and Florence were both merchant republics organized against the nobility) who, from his castle gates surrounded by rocks and forests, presides over rape and murder. Giotto represents the vice of Inconstancy (fig. 71) on a precarious wheel, losing the very balance that for Giotto is the essential of existence.

THE OGNISSANTI MADONNA. Although not dated precisely, the *Enthroned Madonna with Saints* (fig. 72), painted for the Church of Ognissanti (All Saints), is believed to have been done between 1305 and 1310, not long after the completion of the Arena Chapel. The gabled shape is similar to that of Cimabue's Santa Trinita *Enthroned Madonna and Child* (see colorplate 20, p. 60) and other Duecento altarpieces. Giotto has placed the Virgin on a Gothic throne, like that of *Justice* in the Arena Chapel—another instance of his interest in French inventions. This throne, with its pointed vault, delicate gable ornamented with crockets, and open arched wings, provides a cubic space for the Madonna that is utterly different from the elaborate Byzantine thrones of the Duecento. Access to the throne is provided by a mar-

ble step. Narrow panels are filled with delicate, controlled ornament painted to resemble inlaid geometrical shapes that alternate with foliate motifs, and both contrast with the free forms of the marble veining, which is surprisingly fluid and brilliant in color.

The Virgin gazes outward with the calm dignity we expect from Giotto, but her lips are parted to give the effect of the natural passage of breath. Christ lifts his right hand in the two-finger gesture of teaching, holds the scroll lightly in his left, and opens his mouth as if speaking. As in the frescoes, Giotto has abandoned the anatomical compartmentalization of the Italo-Byzantine style. The clear-cut existence of the massive bodies in depth is enhanced by the delicate forms of the throne. The robust Christ Child is lightly but firmly held by his mother, whose fingertips press against his waist. Her right hand is truly sculptural in its apparent roundness, and the cylindrical shape of her neck is brought out by the clean, round neckline of the tunic. His head is a definite block in space, completely hiding the right ear from our sight.

On each side of the throne saints are grouped with angels, but all of these figures are smaller in scale than Mary, Queen of Heaven. The two foremost standing angels, dressed in a beautiful, clear green, offer Mary a crown and a box. They are in profile, as are the kneeling angels before the throne who present crystal vases of lilies and roses, both symbols of the Virgin. The clarity of their profiles, strikingly similar to that of Giovanni

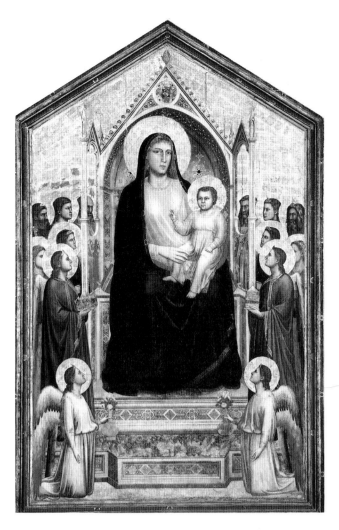

72. GIOTTO. *Enthroned Madonna with Saints*
(*Ognissanti Madonna*). c. 1305–10. Panel, 10' 8" x 6' 8¼".
Uffizi Gallery, Florence. Commissioned for the high altar
of the Church of Ognissanti in Florence

Pisano's *Madonna* in the Arena Chapel (see fig. 49), and the glowing white of their tunics, with shadows of soft lavender-gray, make these among the most beautiful of Giotto's figures. When compared with such complex visionary altarpieces of the later Duecento as Cimabue's *Enthroned Madonna*, Giotto's *Ognissanti Madonna* seems the quintessence of stability, harmony, and warm humanity.

THE BARDI AND PERUZZI CHAPELS. After the fresco cycle in Padua and the *Ognissanti Madonna*, Giotto's style underwent a change. Of the four fresco cycles he and his workshop painted in the Franciscan Church of Santa Croce in Florence, the chapels of the Bardi and the Peruzzi families, who controlled the two greatest banking houses in Italy, survive. The dates of the frescoes, painted when the other end of the church was still unfinished, are as controversial as the order in which the two chapels were painted. Both would appear to date from the 1320s, a period of turmoil and difficulty during which the popular government was threatened from within and the territory of the Republic diminished by attacks from the Ghibelline forces of Pisa and Lucca. Under such circumstances, perhaps the heroic harmo-

nies of the Arena Chapel could not be recaptured.

Both chapels were whitewashed in the eighteenth century and cleaned and overpainted in the nineteenth, but a careful twentieth-century restoration has removed all or most of the repaint, revealing a different situation in each chapel. The Bardi Chapel, frescoed with scenes from the Life of St. Francis, reappeared in good condition, save for gaps left by earlier mutilations. But the Peruzzi Chapel is a ghost of its former self and no scenes from this chapel are illustrated or discussed here; apparently it was painted largely *a secco*. In all his fresco cycles Giotto must have had assistance in laying out the surface and in the actual painting, especially of the background figures and less important details. Conservation work in both chapels has shown that there were no underdrawings on the wall, so preparatory drawings on paper or parchment were probably used to transfer the ideas from the mind of the painter to the pictorial surface. At least one other fresco cycle and a considerable number of panel paintings, some of them very fine, betray the same collaboration between the popular master and the army of helpers necessary for the execution of all the commissions he accepted in his later years.

St. Francis Undergoing the Test by Fire Before the Sultan (fig. 73) in the Bardi Chapel shows some renunciation of the controlled dramatic intensity that made the Arena Chapel frescoes so powerful. At first sight very little appears to be going on in the Bardi frescoes, which are often divided symmetrically as if they were altarpieces, but a closer look discloses that Giotto's dramatic and human style has merely become subdued in his later years. In the center the sultan is seated on his throne while on the right St. Francis calmly prepares to undergo the test by fire. He will, of course, emerge unharmed, to the discomfiture of the Muslims who are creeping away on the left, their fright indicated by their expressions and the patterns of their drapery folds. The two servants beside them, who are among the earliest known representations of black persons in Western art, are sensitively rendered not only in their rich coloring, set off by the luminous white and soft gray of their garments, but also in the naturalistic analysis of their facial structure.

The *Funeral of St. Francis* (fig. 74) was badly mutilated when the frescoes were whitewashed and a tomb, long since removed, was added. What remains, if fragmentary, is at least entirely by Giotto's hand. The saint lies upon a simple bier; the other friars crowd around him, weeping, kissing his hands and feet, or gazing into his eyes. Priests and monks at the saint's head intone the Office of the Dead, the service for funerals. A richly dressed knight of Assisi, his back to the spectator, kneels beside Francis and, like a new St. Thomas, thrusts his hand into the wound in the saint's side. Above, angels bear the released soul heavenward, his drab Franciscan habit now transformed into a celestial lavender. The composition is static, symmetrical, and carefully balanced, but a closer view shows that the drama still goes

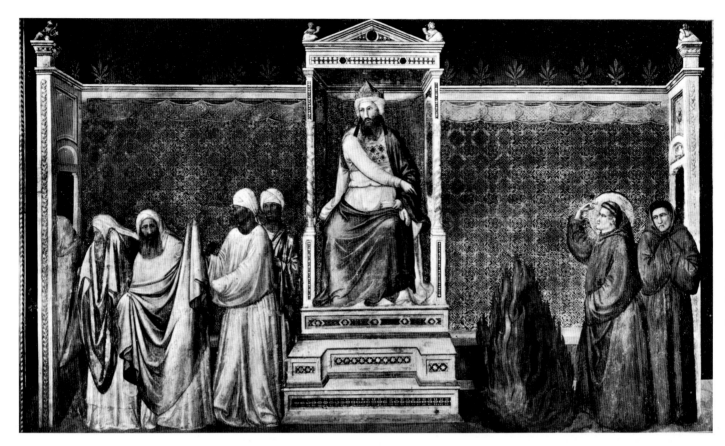

73. GIOTTO. *St. Francis Undergoing the Test by Fire Before the Sultan*. Probably 1320s.
Fresco, 9' 2" x 14' 9". Bardi Chapel, Sta. Croce, Florence. Commissioned by a member of the Bardi family

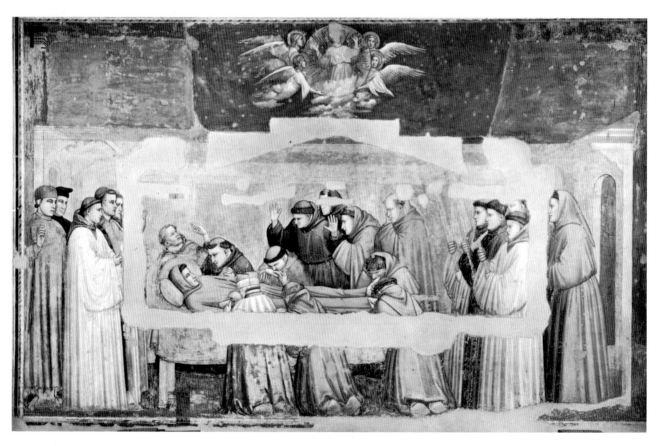

74. GIOTTO. *Funeral of St. Francis* (see also colorplate 26, p. 113). Probably 1320s.
Fresco, 9' 2" x 14' 9". Bardi Chapel, Sta. Croce, Florence

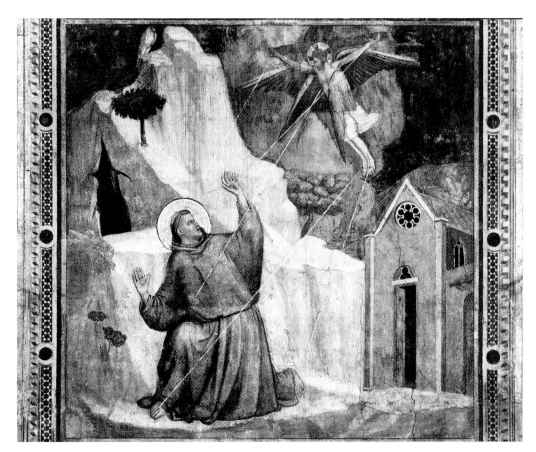

75. GIOTTO.
*Stigmatization of St.
Francis*. Probably 1320s.
Fresco, 12' 9" x 12' 2".
Bardi Chapel, Sta. Croce,
Florence

on (colorplate 26, p. 113). The face of the saint and those of the mourners—even the characteristic Giotto backs—betray an inner feeling too deep for overt expression. In this fresco the late style of Giotto reaches a new stage of calm, purity, and breadth. Sometimes we seem able to watch him at work; the head of the brother looking upward in wonder at the soul carried to Heaven was painted at great speed, and the artist did not erase his preliminary lines or paint over the quick touches of the brush in which the cowl is indicated. The result is a head of astonishing freshness and freedom.

Above the entrance to the chapel is Giotto's *Stigmatization of St. Francis* (fig. 75; this scene is visible in the view of Santa Croce in fig. 52, to the right of the chancel opening). This subject had been represented many times since its earliest known depiction by Bonaventura Berlinghieri (see fig. 24, upper left-hand corner), and two altarpieces on the subject from Giotto's studio, but not by his own hand, also survive, as well as a fresco at San Francesco in Assisi. According to the *Legenda Maior*, the official life of St. Francis written by St. Bonaventura (see p. 94), while Francis was meditating on the lofty peak of La Verna in western Tuscany he asked a follower to bring him the Gospels from the chapel altar and open them at random. Three times the leaves parted at the Passion. At that moment Francis knew he had been chosen to undergo the sufferings of Christ. He then became aware of a six-winged flaming seraph coming toward him through the heavens, and in the midst of the wings appeared a crucified figure. Christ's Crucifixion pierced St. Francis's soul "with a sword of compassionate grief," and when the vision disappeared, the marks of the nails began to appear in his hands and feet, turning rapidly into the nails themselves, the heads on one side, the bent-down points on the other, and his right side was marked with a scar that often bled. A later version of the life of St. Francis, the anonymous *Fioretti* (*Little Flowers*), speaks of a light that illuminated the surrounding mountains.

Berlinghieri does not show this light in any way, but other Duecento painters represent it as stripes of gold descending toward the kneeling saint. In the two works from Giotto's shop and in this fresco, gold rays descend from the five wounds of Christ to the corresponding spots in St. Francis's hands, feet, and side, forming, as it were, a network of golden wires. Like some earlier painters, Giotto omits Francis's follower, whose presence could only have detracted from the sublime theme of this fresco—the man adopted by God, to both his suffering and his glory. In all earlier representations, St. Francis kneels before the vision on one knee or both; here he seems to be forced to one knee on what Dante called the "raw rock" of La Verna by the sheer force of the apparition. He turns away and then, raising his right knee, turns toward the vision in combined surprise, pain, and loving acceptance. Not until Michelangelo will we find a colossal figure of such complexity or of so rich an interrelation of changing spiritual states and violent physical movement.

The light described by the *Fioretti* radiates from the figure of Christ, whose loincloth streams behind him against what was once a soft, blue cloud that is now badly eroded. This same light, whose source, as in the *Annunciation* in Padua, is spiritual, is the sole source of light in the picture. A tree to the right bends as if with the storm of the apparition. On the left appears the saint's cave, and on a ledge just below the summit of the peak perches the falcon who awakened Francis each morning.

THE DESIGN FOR THE CAMPANILE OF FLORENCE CATHEDRAL. The principal surviving achievement of Giotto's last years is his design for the Campanile of the Cathedral of Florence (fig. 76). In January 1334, the Commune appointed Giotto *capomaestro* of the Cathedral in an extraordinary document that extols his fame as a painter but mentions no architectural training or experience; by this time the only parts of the Cathedral that had been built were the partially completed façade and the south wall, which had reached the level of the side-aisle roof. In April 1334, the Campanile, the only portion of the Cathedral with which the aging master was involved, was mentioned again, and by January 1337 Giotto was dead. In the brief intervening period, however, work proceeded at a rapid pace. A massive foundation was laid, and the first story constructed in exact correspondence with that of a large, tinted drawing on parchment. The drawing itself involves much mechanical repetition of identical elements and was probably carried out by assistants using Giotto's sketches and calculations, and under his direction. We would be foolish to suggest that his hand can be detected in any part of it, but it is his creation nonetheless, in the same sense as is the decorative framework of the Arena Chapel.

The design commences in the tradition of a common Tuscan campanile type, whose windows multiply as its stories rise. The final story is an octagonal bell chamber flanked by cylindrical pinnacles on the corners that are set on octagonal buttresses that start from the ground. Giotto's solution corresponds to that of the slightly earlier tower of the Cathedral of Freiburg im Breisgau, Germany, but the appearance of the two buildings is entirely different; Giotto's spire and pinnacles are solid, while those at Freiburg, as in other German cathedrals, are open tracery. Actually, both the pitch of Giotto's spire and the character of its crockets correspond to those of the solid spires begun, but never carried out, on the towers of Reims Cathedral, a work that greatly influenced Italian artists. Moreover, the tracery of Giotto's windows, with their beautiful pointed arches and crocketed gables, is also close to that at Reims.

The lower story of the Campanile as actually built (fig. 77) makes sense only in relation to Giotto's design, in which hexagons of white marble are suspended against pink marble panels (it is unclear whether or not at this stage of the design reliefs were intended). These hexagons would have been repeated in the second story in three squares, one inside the other, centering on a quatrefoil window. Two such frames apiece appear on the third and fourth stories, one on the fifth, and none

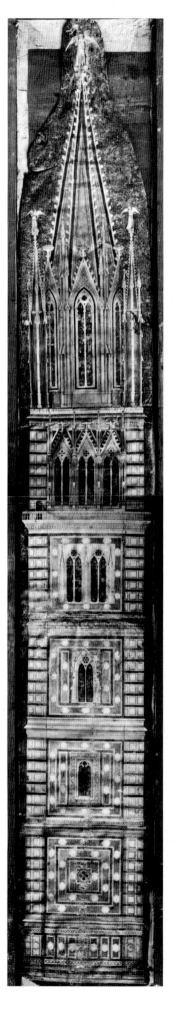

left: 76. GIOTTO (attributed to). Design for the Campanile of the Cathedral, Florence. c. 1334. Tinted drawing on parchment, height of image 6' 10". Museo dell'Opera del Duomo, Siena. Commissioned by the Arte della Lana

opposite: 77. Campanile of the Cathedral, Florence. Lowest story by GIOTTO, 1334–37; next three stories by ANDREA PISANO, c. 1337–43; remainder by FRANCESCO TALENTI, 1350s. Commissioned by the Arte della Lana

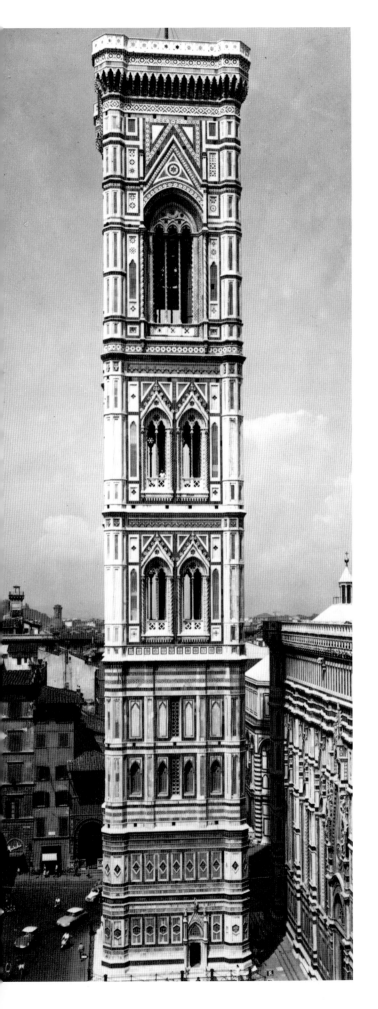

thereafter. Since the hexagons are off-axis with each other from panel to panel, the effect looking up would have been an exquisite oscillation of white hexagons against pink to the height of about two hundred feet. There would have been seventy-five hexagons on each face of the Campanile, or exactly three hundred for the entire structure, which tells us something about Giotto's desire for arithmetical simplicity. But there may be much more. In a medieval structure it is difficult to overlook the fact that Giotto's tower has four sides, the number of the Gospels (it could have been octagonal, like its top story, or round like the Leaning Tower of Pisa), and seven stories, the number of the Gifts of the Holy Spirit and of the Joys and of the Sorrows of the Virgin; the hexagons are grouped in sevens, fours, eights (the numbers of the Resurrection), and twelves (the number of the apostles and of the gates of the New Jerusalem); and the perfect number one hundred is multiplied in their total by the number of the Trinity.

Giotto, aware of the force of wind pressure on such a lofty bell chamber, drew iron tie-rods running from the pinnacles through the oculi of the corner windows, possibly to some stabilizing framework inside. Given this caution, it is surprising that he places enormous marble baskets of fruit on the three gables of his sixth story, crowns his slender pinnacles with marble angels with widespread wings, and poises a colossal Archangel Michael with wings and a banner on the tip of his spire, some three hundred feet above the ground, all of them exposed to the wind and to the disintegrative action of the rain, ice, and snow of Florentine winters. His design was not followed by his successors, only plundered (see fig. 77 and p. 144), and after his death it was discovered that the walls of his first story were insubstantial and their thickness had to be doubled. After all, he was a painter, and his tower was a painter's tribute to the glory of his beloved Florence.

THE UPPER CHURCH OF SAN FRANCESCO, ASSISI. The matter of Giotto's early style has been left until this point because it is one of the vexing questions in the history of painting, and there is still no general agreement. The crucial problem revolves around the twenty-eight scenes of the Life of St. Francis in the nave of the Upper Church of San Francesco at Assisi. In each bay the wall is divided into three or four scenes by painted spiral colonnettes standing on a corbel table (see colorplate 27, p. 114). The painted colonnettes appear to support a characteristic Roman architrave, which is ornamented with simulated inlaid mosaic and surmounted by a cornice on painted consoles. The soffit of the entablature is coffered in two parallel strips so that it looks quite deep. In an approach to one-point perspective, centered on the middle of each bay, all those elements appear to emerge from the wall, and their relief is enhanced by a systematic use of sharp light on the supposed projections and soft shadow on the under surfaces. By these means the artist responsible for the general layout has established an illusion of a continuous portico as deep as the real catwalk above it; through this portico we read the vivid scenes that record, with brusque naturalism and intense conviction, the Life of St. Francis, largely according to the *Legenda Maior* of St. Bonaventura.

In general, Italian scholars regard all but four of the scenes as early works of Giotto, before the Arena Chapel, though with a large amount of participation by pupils in some of the scenes. Foreign scholars tend to reject all of the scenes as by Giotto and to date them somewhat later. One's views on the matter affect, of course, one's estimate of Giotto's style and personality. Just as important, the series itself is one of the most prominent, most extensive, largest (the figures, for the most part, are approximately life-size), and most interesting Italian fresco cycles of the Middle Ages. There were few and archaic models for some scenes (see fig. 24)—none at all for most of them—and the solutions to narrative problems are often of striking originality, conceived in terms of a fresh, new naturalism.

There are no documents regarding the series. A Ferrarese chronicler called Riccobaldo wrote about 1313 (or so the passage is now reconstructed, since the original manuscript is lost) that the quality of Giotto's art is witnessed by "the works made by him in the churches of the Franciscans at Assisi, Rimini, and Padua, and in the church of the Arena." Since the Arena Chapel frescoes are preserved, and since we know that paintings by Giotto once decorated the Franciscan churches of San Francesco at Rimini and Sant'Antonio in Padua, it is argued that Riccobaldo, writing while Giotto was still alive and working, was correct about Assisi as well, and that his remarks could only refer to the St. Francis cycle. In the fifteenth century Ghiberti wrote that Giotto "painted almost all the lower part," and in the second edition of his *Lives* in 1568 Vasari assigned the St. Francis series to Giotto. A recently discovered document shows that in 1309 Giotto repaid in Assisi a debt he had contracted there, but it does not mention the frescoes.

Neither Riccobaldo, Ghiberti, nor Vasari provides any solid evidence. The proponents of Riccobaldo do not point out that he may have been referring to the paintings in the Magdalen Chapel in the Lower Church, quite possibly commissioned from Giotto and executed partly by him but largely by pupils. Nor has the question been examined of an altarpiece for the Upper Church, whose absence is one of the strangest phenomena at Assisi; such an altarpiece, presumably a polyptych, might have been by Giotto. Ghiberti's ambiguous remark might also refer to the paintings in the Magdalen Chapel or to other frescoes in the Lower Church painted by followers of Giotto. As for Vasari, the extent of his information regarding works painted nearly three hundred years earlier at Assisi may be measured by the fact that he assigned Pietro Lorenzetti's *Crucifixion* to Cavallini.

In the St. Francis cycle, each bay is organized as a

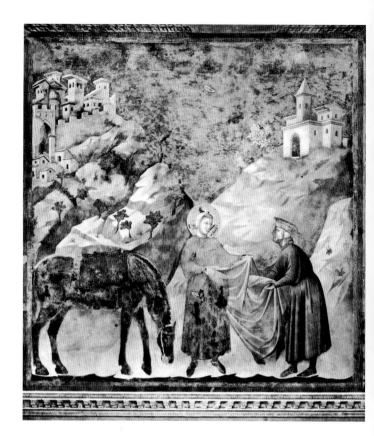

78. MASTER OF THE ST. FRANCIS CYCLE. *St. Francis Giving His Cloak to the Beggar.* Early 14th century. Fresco, 8' 10" x 7' 7". Upper Church of S. Francesco, Assisi

triptych, as in Scenes IV–VI (colorplate 27, p. 114), in which two incidents involving collapsing churches flank a central event taking place in an open piazza. The actual sequence of incidents in the *Legenda Maior* was sometimes altered to bring out an underlying spiritual structure through arrangements of parallel scenes from side to side of the nave. In Scene IV, *St. Francis Praying Before the Crucifix at San Damiano*, the eye is assailed by the jagged masses of fragmentary walls, although the rubble has been neatly cleared away. In the second, *St. Francis Renouncing His Worldly Goods*, the piazza is split vertically, leaving on one side the raging father, on the other the naked saint cloaked by an embarrassed bishop; above, at the left, can just be made out the hand of God to which Francis stretches out both his own in prayer. The *Dream of Innocent III* shows the pope reclining in a sumptuous interior framed by typically Roman architecture and ornament, while a serene Francis upholds the collapsing Basilica of San Giovanni in Laterano, identifiable with the appearance of this church at that time. Throughout the cycle, the color is crisp, clear, and decorative.

The setting of Scene II, *St. Francis Giving His Cloak to the Beggar* (fig. 78), is delightful, with its delicate color and the charm of a hillside town complete with suburbs outside the gates, but this is also a far cry from Giotto's rudimentary architectural forms. The upward flow of the hillside—its cliffs, scattered trees, town, and chapel—is unconvincing compared with the hard, simple masses of Giotto's rocks. Such complexities are alien not only to Giotto's landscape as we know it, but also to the directions that Cennino Cennini said were derived from Giotto. The landscape masses converge on St. Francis's head in a kind of X-shape that is uncomfortable and not especially dramatic.

Throughout the series, however, despite the originality of the conceptions and often brilliant bits of observation, the compositions are staccato and abrupt, in contrast to the balance characteristic of Giotto. Facial expressions are uncommunicative and often inert, while the figures themselves are often not coherent in structure. Neither the impact nor the force of Giotto's figures can be felt. Profiles, so characteristic of Giotto, are rare in the St. Francis cycle. When Giotto's eloquent backs are imitated, the artist also gets the faces into view. Giotto's one-quarter views of faces rarely appear, and then awkwardly. Most of the faces are in Byzantine three-quarters view. Eyes are shown full-face, whatever the angle of the head; in three-quarters faces, the distant eye remains flat, while Giotto's distant eyes show his distinct awareness of three-dimensionality by being cut into the profile. To many critics, including the author of this book, the differences in style and quality between the St. Francis cycle and the known works of Giotto are too great to be embraced by the style of a single artist.

All scholars are agreed that Scene I and Scenes XXVI–XXVIII were painted by the St. Cecilia Master (see pp. 101–3). Who, then, painted the other twenty-four? The consistency of the compositions throughout the entire cycle, including those by the St. Cecilia Master, has suggested to many authors that one artist made designs for all twenty-eight, to be approved by the superior general of the Franciscan Order, and that these were followed in general and in most details. Probably these designs were on parchment or paper, since no *sinopie* have come to light. Two major painters have been distinguished in addition to the St. Cecilia Master: one was active from Scene II through Scene XIX; the second, less experienced in fresco, from Scene XX through Scene XXV, in addition to a host of assistants. The two masters used white lead for highlights, with the same disastrous results as Cimabue encountered. Neither the St. Cecilia Master nor Giotto in his undoubted works ever used this pigment, which, as we have seen, Cennini will later condemn. The connections with Roman architecture and Roman painting are so strong that the first and second masters may well have been Roman, of a generation following that of Torriti and Cavallini, and left unemployed in Rome by the move of the papacy to Avignon in 1305.

FLORENTINE PAINTERS AFTER GIOTTO

The authority of Giotto's style in Florence may well have impeded the emergence of other personalities of

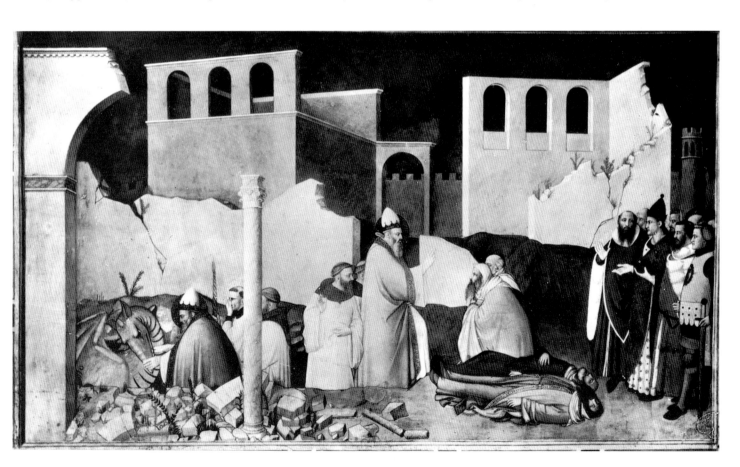

79. MASO DI BANCO. *St. Sylvester Sealing the Dragon's Mouth and Resuscitating Two Pagan Magicians.* c. 1336–39. Fresco, width 17' 6". Bardi-Bardi di Vernio Chapel, Sta. Croce, Florence

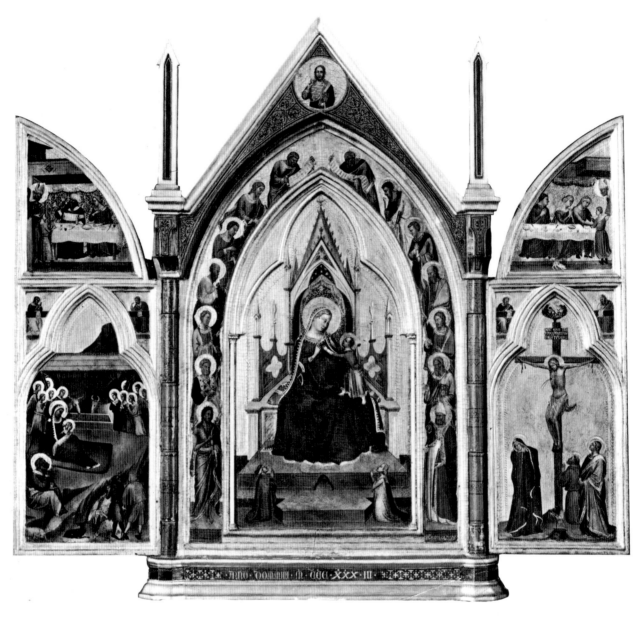

80. BERNARDO DADDI. *Triptych.* 1333. Central panel, 35 3/8 x 38 1/8". Loggia del Bigallo, Florence

the first order. Nonetheless, three of Giotto's Florentine assistants became important painters in their own right. Closest to the master, perhaps, is Maso di Banco (active 1330s and 1340s), whose work has been convincingly reconstructed. Although Maso did not, for whatever reason, approach Giotto's breadth and harmony, he did achieve a handsome narrative and decorative style, especially in the frescoes of the Bardi-Bardi di Vernio Chapel in Santa Croce. The chapel is decorated with scenes from the Lives of the emperor Constantine and of St. Sylvester, the pope who was believed to have baptized the emperor. One miracle of St. Sylvester was the sealing of the mouth of a dragon whose breath had killed two pagan magicians in the Roman Forum, and their resuscitation (fig. 79). Among Roman ruins, one sees the magicians lying on their backs, then suddenly alive and kneeling in thankfulness. This before-and-after

representation is typical of Trecento miracle paintings. The massive figures and the unified space and lighting are all learned from Giotto, but Maso has gone further in the spatial complexity of the background and the evocative quality of the Roman ruins, with their flat wall planes and empty arches, enhanced by the plants that grow in the cracks. Maso's facial types reflect Giotto's style of the Santa Croce chapels, where Maso may well have assisted him.

A study of *Sts. Paul and Julian* (fig. 15) has been attributed to Maso on the basis of the resemblance of the facial types and expressions, and the style of the hands and the drapery forms, to passages in Maso's work. The two saints are shown seated, apparently on a bench. Each holds a sword, but for opposite reasons; St. Paul, who is called the sword of the Church, grasps his weapon with both hands, but Julian, who committed parricide, holds the instrument of his crime downward with his left (see p. 273) while with his right he strikes his breast in repentance. Except for the deep and wordless communication between them, the two saints recall their direct ancestors in the *Last Judgments* by Cavallini and Giotto.

Like many such detailed studies from the Trecento and later, the drawing is done with wash over preparations in silverpoint on tinted paper, and the lights are picked out with white, thus approximating the three gradations of value Cennini describes in his directions for painting a fresco. Since no figure drawings attributable to Giotto are known, this carefully rendered work is witness to the probable role of drawing in Giotto's art, as well as to the draftsmanly procedures of the great master. Intense psychological interchange, the basic principle of Giotto's compositions, is established from the start. Then, after the general proportions and contours had been fixed by line, light, gliding across faces and drapery masses with silken grace, projects the larger volumes and smaller forms in depth.

Giotto's follower, Bernardo Daddi (active c. 1312–48), is a painter whose sensitivity was more suited to panel paintings than to frescoes, which in fact he rarely painted. The little triptych (fig. 80) is typical; his pictures are intimate, even those intended for important public positions, and show a different aspect of the Virgin and Child from the majestic images in the tradition that runs from Coppo di Marcovaldo to Giotto. Daddi's Virgin smiles gently as she admonishes the playful Christ Child. The delicate Gothic forms of the throne provide an ample space for her and diminish her apparent size, even though the two donors are even smaller. In a space seemingly outside that of the inner image, the surrounding saints and prophets rise like a rose trellis. In the *Nativity* in the left wing, Mary has taken Christ out of the manger and holds him on her lap. Even the *Crucifixion* on the right wing is not treated as a tragic event, and the eye is at once drawn to the apex of the cross, where a pelican, following medieval legend, strikes her breast to feed her young, a symbol of the self-sacrifice of Christ.

Daddi's lyric sweetness has been traced to the influence of Sienese art, but this is difficult to justify; most likely it is a happy conjunction between his own temperament, the rather relaxed taste of the 1340s, and the example of Gothic ivory carvings brought from France, which often show a similar sweetness and playfulness. But Daddi is never sentimental: his forms are as round and firm as one could wish from Giotto's protégé, his drawing is precise, his modeling clear, his color resonant. The facial types, with their short noses and round cheeks, are his own, and his drapery folds confer on his compositions a melodic beauty.

The latest known work of Bernardo is a large *Madonna and Child Enthroned with Angels* (fig. 81), painted in 1347 for the altar in the shrine of Orsanmichele (see fig. 6) and later enclosed in an elaborate marble

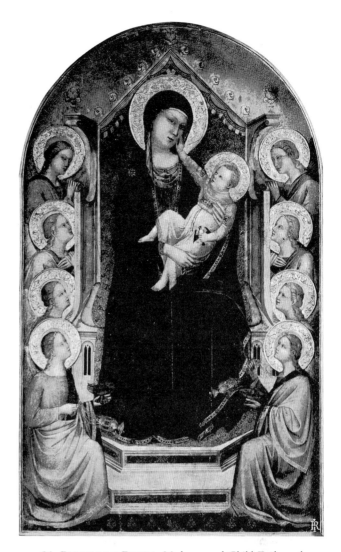

81. BERNARDO DADDI. *Madonna and Child Enthroned with Angels*. 1347. Panel, 8' 2³/8" x 5' 10⁷/8". 🏛 Orsanmichele, Florence. Commissioned by the Capitani of the Compagnia di Orsanmichele

tabernacle by Andrea Orcagna (see fig. 113). Clearly something very strange has come over the Giottesque style. True, the Virgin still sits on a grand Gothic throne, modeled in three dimensions, and is adored by angels. And in a manner typical of Daddi, the Christ Child reaches for his mother's cheek—but here he only touches it with the tips of his thumb and two fingers instead of showing Daddi's usual caress. The Virgin pays no attention to him, but looks out at us in a manner suggestive of Cimabue. Aside from the modeling of the throne, there is little indication of space. The carpet is parallel to the picture plane and, as in Cimabue, the angels rise in vertical superimposition while their drapery is modeled with the full resources of Giotto's style. A chill seems to have fallen upon Daddi's spontaneous sweetness. The most likely explanation is that he was required to repeat the composition of a miracle-working Duecento *Madonna* that had been damaged in the fire of

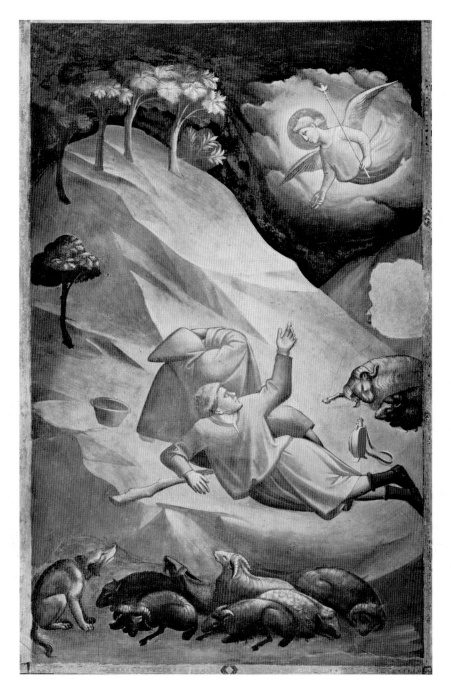

82. TADDEO GADDI. *Annunciation to the Shepherds*. c. 1328–30. Fresco. Baroncelli Chapel, Sta. Croce, Florence. Commissioned by Bivigliano, Bartolo, and Salvestro Manetti and Vanni and Piero Bandini de' Baroncelli

1304 at Orsanmichele, but this does not fully explain why he has taken so resolute a step backward into the spaceless world of the Italo-Byzantine style.

The Madonnas of Taddeo Gaddi (active c. 1328–c. 1366), another faithful follower of Giotto and father of Agnolo Gaddi, have the virtue of a rustic honesty, and his frescoes, for all their abruptness of form, can be impressive. Taddeo's principal achievement in the field of fresco painting is the Baroncelli Chapel, one of the larger chapels in Santa Croce. As much of the work was done during Giotto's last years, it may reflect his ideas. Giotto even "signed" the chapel's altarpiece, though few believe he painted much of it with his own hand. The *Annunciation to the Shepherds* (fig. 82) is notable for its dramatic effect of night light, a vivid and important

forerunner of later efforts in this direction, including Correggio's Cinquecento *Holy Night* (see fig. 590), with all its Baroque descendants. The angel casts a strong light onto the dark hillside, where the shepherds are guarding their sheep.

Taddeo's enormous *Last Supper with the Tree of Life* in the refectory of Santa Croce shows the robust vigor of this painter, as well as a fascinating display of iconographic richness (fig. 83). The fresco illustrates one of the major works of St. Bonaventura. Christ hangs not upon the conventional cross but upon the symbolic Tree of Life, which grew alongside the Tree of Knowledge in the Garden of Eden (Genesis 2:9). The medallions hanging from it, the fruits of this marvelous tree, contain bust portraits of the four evangelists and twelve

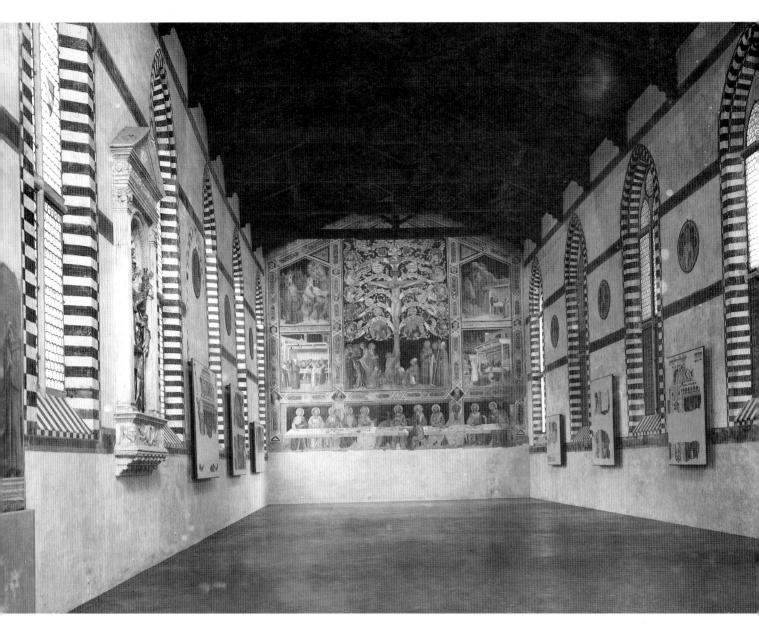

83. TADDEO GADDI. Refectory, Sta. Croce, Florence. Frescoes of the *Last Supper with the Tree of Life and Other Scenes.* c. 1360. Width 39'. Commissioned by the woman in the garments of a Franciscan tertiary kneeling at the foot of the cross, behind St. Francis

prophets. At the right are *The Priest at His Easter Meal Receiving Word of St. Benedict's Hunger in the Wilderness* and *The Magdalen Washing the Feet of Christ,* at the left the *Stigmatization of St. Francis* and *St. Louis of Toulouse Feeding the Poor and Sick of Toulouse.* The *Last Supper,* below, is the earliest survivor of the many that still decorate the refectories of Florentine monasteries and convents. The strong, simple, clear-cut figures, with their relatively coarse features and harsh expressions, form a strong contrast to the refinements of Bernardo Daddi and are almost a caricature of Giotto's powerful forms. In its rejection of the optimism of the Baroncelli Chapel, the austere style of the Santa Croce refectory is related to later developments that will form the subject of Chapter 5.

SCULPTURE

Giotto's style dominates the art of the Trecento, including sculpture. The work of Andrea Pisano has a special relationship to Giotto's shop. Andrea Pisano (c. 1290–1348) is no relation to Nicola and Giovanni Pisano, but acquired his name through the fact that he came from a town then in Pisan territory. We have already noted the reliefs representing painting, sculpture, and architecture (see figs. 7, 16, 17) with which Andrea ornamented Giotto's Campanile. Ghiberti claimed to have seen Giotto's designs for these reliefs, which he says were "most exceptionally drawn." The *Creation of Adam* (fig. 84), which begins the series, obviously comes straight from Giotto's quatrefoil representing the same subject in the

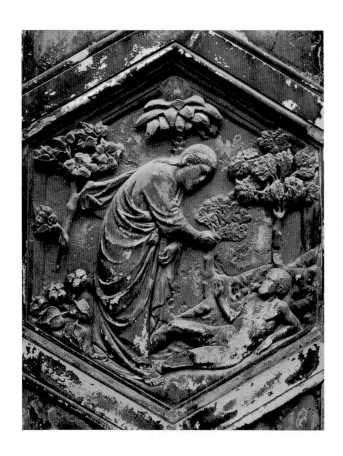

left: 84. ANDREA PISANO (from designs by GIOTTO?).
Creation of Adam. c. 1334–37. Marble, 32¾ x 27¼".
Removed from original location on the Campanile, Florence
(see fig. 77). Museo dell'Opera del Duomo, Florence

below: 85. Baptistery, Florence. c. 1060–1150.
🏛 South Doors (left), ANDREA PISANO, 1330–36; East Doors
(right; now removed), LORENZO GHIBERTI, 1425–52

opposite: 86. ANDREA PISANO (after a design by GIOTTO).
Salome Presenting the Baptist's Head to Herodias,
panel on the South Doors, 🏛Baptistery, Florence. 1330–36.
Bronze with gilding, 19¼ x 17". Commissioned
by the Arte di Calimala

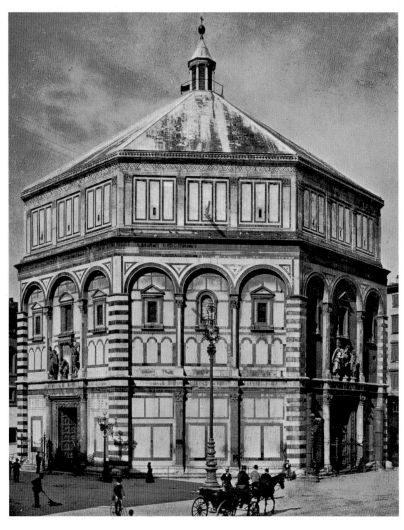

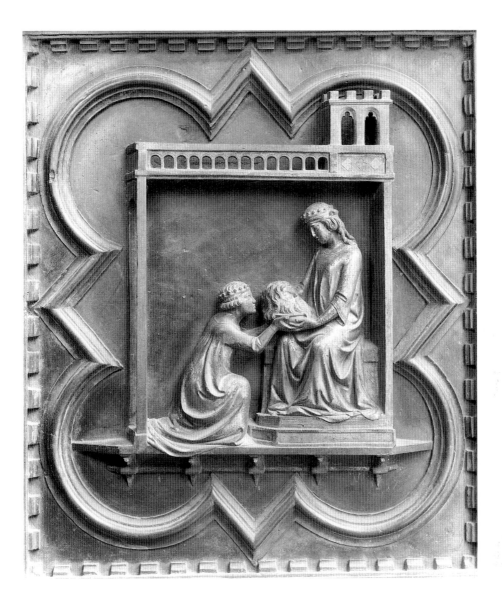

decorative framework of the Arena Chapel (see color-plate 24, p. 63). The figures and their poses are almost identical, although the increased size of the image permits the figure of God the Creator to be shown in its entirety, as well as allowing the addition of a splendid array of trees, including both the Tree of Knowledge and the Tree of Life.

Andrea had been brought to Florence as a specialist in bronze casting to make a set of bronze doors for one of the three portals of the Florentine Baptistery (fig. 85). These doors include figures of eight Virtues and twenty scenes from the Life of St. John the Baptist. Like Ghiberti's two sets of doors that followed in the Quattrocento, they consist of bronze panels in a bronze frame. The figures and many of the raised elements of ornament, architecture, and landscape are covered with gold leaf and burnished. The individual compositions of the scenes from the Life of the Baptist are, with one exception, directly derived from either the Baptistery mosaics or Giotto's fresco cycle in the Peruzzi Chapel at Santa Croce; perhaps as an outsider Andrea's contract to create

the doors constrained him to employ these Florentine sources in representing the life of Florence's patron saint. Or, since Giotto was the *capomaestro* of the Cathedral complex at this time, it is possible that he provided drawings for Andrea to follow. The limited depth, well-spaced compositions, and simple stagelike sets are directly related to Giotto's new vision of form and space, and especially to his economy of statement. The delicate and lucid scene of *Salome Presenting the Baptist's Head to Herodias* (fig. 86) is neatly balanced inside the fashionable quatrefoil form imported from Gothic France; the composition is derived from Giotto's Peruzzi fresco.

MASTER OF ST. CECILIA

Up to this moment we have followed only the grand new style in Florentine painting that was dominated by Giotto and his followers. But there were other artists who did not capitulate entirely. One of these, a distinct and delightful artistic personality, is the Master of St. Cecilia, not otherwise identified, whose principal work

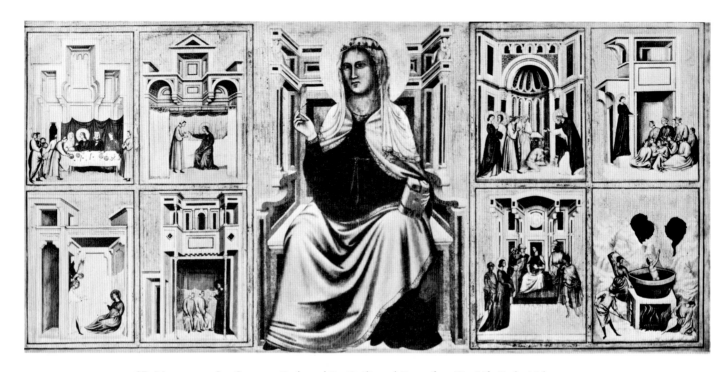

87. MASTER OF ST. CECILIA. *Enthroned St. Cecilia and Scenes from Her Life.* Early 14th century.
Panel, 33 1/2 x 71 1/4". Uffizi Gallery, Florence. Commissioned for Sta. Cecilia, Florence

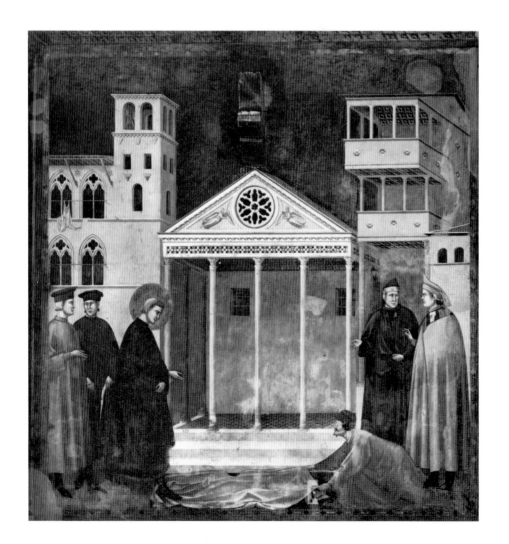

88. MASTER OF ST. CECILIA.
St. Francis and the Madman.
Early 14th century. Fresco,
8' 10" x 7' 7". Upper Church
of S. Francesco, Assisi

is the altarpiece that shows the *Enthroned St. Cecilia and Scenes from Her Life* (fig. 87). The monumentality of the saint recalls Giotto, but the facial type is entirely different, as is the lack of Giotto's precision of form. The figures of the St. Cecilia Master enact their narratives at the bottom of well-like spaces; understanding the risks of the traditional double scale for architecture and figures, the painter has created rooms that are more naturalistically proportioned to his figures. The stories cannot be so easily read as Giotto's, and there is none of the grand drama of Giotto's scenes. But the lively figures, with their long bodies, tiny heads, and explicit gestures, and the freely invented architectural shapes, so strongly projected and illuminated, form a pleasant antidote to the grand official style.

The St. Cecilia Master painted Scene I (fig. 88) and Scenes XXVI–XXVIII in the Life of St. Francis in the Upper Church of San Francesco at Assisi, the last to be done. The incident represented is the recognition of the future sanctity of Francis, who was at the time still a high-living youth, by a simple man of Assisi. He spreads a cloak before Francis to honor him. The narrative, which has been described as the first modern street scene in Italian art, takes place in the principal piazza of Assisi. Some of the buildings shown here are still standing, but the painter has transformed them. The Torre del Comune, brought to its first story of open arches in 1305 (another indication of an early Trecento date for the cycle), is shown without its present final story, but it is also embellished with an adjacent Gothic palazzo that may have been planned but never built. On the right is a structure of superimposed porticoes supported on delicate columns that never could have been built.

In the center stands the Temple of Minerva Asisium, a well-preserved ancient Roman building, which is here given five columns instead of its actual six; inserted in the pediment is a Gothic rose window flanked by soaring angels in simulated relief. The painter has also substituted a strip of medieval Roman mosaic inlay for the actual Corinthian entablature and, in keeping with his special taste, has slenderized the Augustan columns to mere colonnettes. His scene, characteristically dominated by empty space, is carpeted by the simple man's cloak, and the figures on either side, with their elongated bodies, small heads, and delicately drawn faces, correspond to those of the *Enthroned St. Cecilia*. We must mourn the loss of other frescoes by this highly individual artistic personality.

4
Sienese Art of the Early Trecento

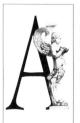As in Florence, Sienese painters moved decisively away from the Byzantine style. During the late Duecento and early Trecento, the only Sienese painter who can withstand close comparison with Giotto, the Florentine, was Duccio di Buoninsegna (active 1278–1318). The full story of the formation of his art is known, but it is clear that his highly personal style was shaped in varying respects by influences from other centers.

DUCCIO

Among the documents that survive about Duccio's life are eleven fines levied against the painter for breaking the curfew, for not swearing allegiance to an important official, for an unwillingness to fulfill military service, and other such behavior. He did not pay some of the fines for years, and when he died his children renounced his will, possibly because it consisted mostly of debts. In Siena, Duccio may well have witnessed the carving of the Cathedral pulpit by Nicola Pisano and his assistants, including his son Giovanni (see fig. 40). In Florence, Cimabue's Enthroned *Madonna and Child* in Santa Trinita (see colorplate 20, p. 60) must have excited the young painter.

The earliest major work we know by Duccio is a Florentine commission, the huge *Madonna* (fig. 89) popularly (and inappropriately) known as the *Rucellai Madonna* because it once stood in the Rucellai family chapel in Santa Maria Novella. It is probably to be identified with a large Madonna commissioned by the Society of the Virgin Mary, known as the Laudesi, in 1285.

In the Uffizi today, Cimabue's and Duccio's *Madonna*s are displayed in the same room, enabling us to contrast the differences in style between them. Duccio's Virgin is seated sideways on a throne seen slightly from the right while the surrounding angels kneel naturalistically on one knee but are superimposed against the gold background as if floating. Except for the cloth around the legs of the Christ Child, Duccio has abandoned the traditional Byzantine gold striations still used by Cimabue to indicate drapery. The gold border of the Virgin's cloak, embellished with a delicate golden fringe, assumes an important role as a carrier of energy. On the Virgin's shoulder and over her brow glow stars whose sixteen points suggest the points of the compass; Mary's name had been translated as "Star of the Sea" by St. Ambrose. The colors of the angels' robes offer a springlike freshness and refinement new to Italian panel paint-

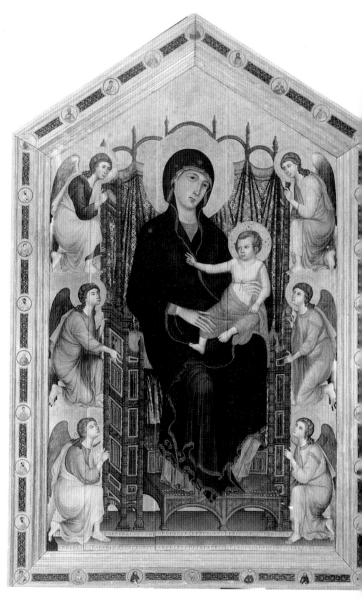

89. DUCCIO. *Rucellai Madonna*. Commissioned 1285. Panel, 14' 9 1/8" x 9' 6 1/8". Uffizi Gallery, Florence. Commissioned by the Società della Vergine

ing; their flowerlike tones include lavender, yellow, rose, and luminous gray-blues and gray-lavenders.

Refinement of surface is pushed to a new extreme. The arches of the Virgin's throne are hung with a splendid patterned silk, its folds indicated by strokes of wash over the design. The same pattern reappears in the fragmentary frescoes in the chapel used by the Laudesi at Santa Maria Novella, suggesting that Duccio's Madonna was originally part of a wider decorative program. The frescoes have been attributed to both Duccio and Cimabue.

The ovoid shapes in the Virgin's face are derived from those of Coppo di Marcovaldo (see fig. 30), but they are more organic, in keeping with Duccio's undulating line and new coloristic refinement. Curving contours outline the eyes and unite the brow with the long, slender nose. The upper lip protrudes slightly and the chin recedes to blend with the slender neck. The angels, whose faces are similarly constructed, gaze in reverence toward the Christ Child, who turns to address them with outstretched hand.

Tooling covers the gold haloes with a pattern of interlocking circles and foliate designs derived, like the patterns of the silk, from French Gothic sources, and tiny French Gothic arches decorate the spindles of the throne. The usual dot-dash motif in the frame is replaced by a series of bust portraits of saints in medallions alternating with richly ornamented bands. Duccio's new, slightly Gothicized phase of Italo-Byzantine style must have had an effect on contemporary Florentine painters, including the youthful Giotto.

For Siena, the Virgin Mary was the Mother of God, the Queen of Heaven, and the patron saint of the Sienese Republic. Siena's title, in fact, was *vetusta civitas virginis* (ancient city of the Virgin). In 1308 Duccio was commissioned to create the high altarpiece for the Cathedral, a striped marble structure at the apex of the city's highest hill (colorplate 23, p. 62). In 1311 this colossal altarpiece was carried in triumphal procession to the Cathedral "accompanied by the members of the government, the clergy, and the people, carrying lighted candles and torches, to the sound of all the bells of the city, and the music of trumpets and bagpipes." The altarpiece was not only a religious triumph for the city, but also an artistic one for the painter. In 1506 it was replaced by a fashionable new ciborium, statues, and candlesticks, and when Vasari wrote his *Lives* in 1550 he was not even able to discover its location.

Originally the *Virgin in Majesty*—or simply the *Maestà*, to give the work its Italian title—was a superaltarpiece. Its central panel (colorplate 28, p. 115) represents the enthroned Virgin adored by saints and angels; above is a row of bust-length prophets. On the predella at the base, a sequence of panels illustrated scenes from the Infancy of Christ and scenes from the Life of the Virgin on the pinnacles at the top were surmounted by bust-length angels. Since the high altar stood under the dome of the Cathedral, the back of the altarpiece, including predella panels and pinnacles, was covered with scenes depicting the Passion of Christ. It was the center of a cluster of Marian works—the pulpit by Nicola Pisano, and later narrative altarpieces by Simone Martini (colorplate 30, p. 116), Pietro Lorenzetti (fig. 105), Ambrogio Lorenzetti (colorplate 31, p. 117), and Bartolommeo Bulgarini. Most of the major panels of Duccio's altarpiece remain in Siena, but some of the predella panels have been scattered to other collections. The central pinnacles, front and back, have never been found, and their subjects are conjectural.

Sienese saints kneel in the front row of the central panel; more saints and four archangels stand in a row behind them. Four angels rest their hands and chins on Mary's intricately inlaid marble throne. In the resulting interlace of figures, heads, and haloes—all united by the flow of drapery lines, ornamental masses, and brilliant color—separate elements do not stand out as they would in Giotto's compositions. Rather, the panel takes on the appearance of a length of rich and splendid fabric. The Christ Child seems to have relinquished his teaching function and gazes directly outward at the observer; he is a more natural, human baby. In line with the artist's decreasing reliance on Byzantine motifs, gold striations appear only here and there in the richly modeled drapery that courses about clearly felt, if somewhat attenuated, bodies. The Virgin's face has suffered from a disastrous overcleaning in the distant past, but judging from better-preserved Madonnas by Duccio, she must have showed still further refinement of curvilinear motifs. The inscription includes Duccio's only known signature: "Holy Mother of God be thou the cause of peace for Siena and, because he painted thee thus, of life for Duccio."

The head of St. Catherine of Alexandria (fig. 90), at the extreme left of the panel, demonstrates how the Byzantine demarcation of surface forms, including all but a hint of the characteristic formation at the juncture of the eyebrows, is swept away in a new, unified surface. The mournful gaze of Catherine's eyes is characteristic of Duccio's figures, as is the Byzantine treatment of the eye so that the white continues across the bottom, below the pupil. His treatment of the fabrics of her garments is particularly refined. The gold-embroidered scarf seems translucent, and we sense the shape of the saint's head and see her hair through its flowing folds. Her mantle is painted over gold, and the paint has been tooled away to suggest the sparkle of a gold-thread damask cloth.

The *Nativity* flanked by prophets from the front predella (fig. 91) preserves its original, simple framing. Duccio keeps the cave of the Byzantine tradition, but inserts the shed imported from French Gothic representations, a compromise symptomatic of his artistic position, which draws upon both the Byzantine and Gothic traditions. Mary, enveloped in her bright blue mantle, reclines on a scarlet mattress; following Byzantine tradition, she pays no attention to the Christ Child in the manger. In the bath scene the Christ Child is plunged by the midwives into a chalicelike tub, as in Nicola Pisano's Pisa Baptistery pulpit (fig. 37). Some of the angels behind the cave look up toward the arc of Heaven, others bend over like the angels behind Mary's throne in the central panel. One angel waves a scroll announcing the event to the shepherds, whose sheep have already arrived upon the scene. The brilliant colors of Mary's cloak and mattress are set off by softer colors, such as the rose of Joseph's cloak. Isaiah's lavender mantle covers a tunic of an entirely different rose, and the powdery blue

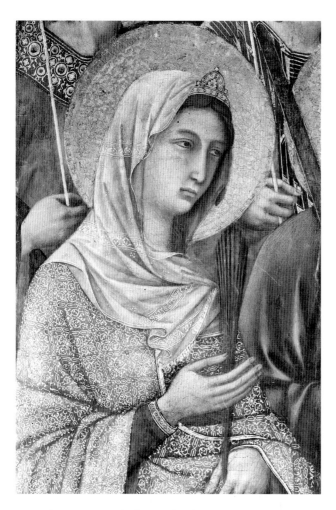

90. DUCCIO. Head of St. Catherine, detail of the front of *Maestà* (see colorplate 28, p. 115). 1308–11. Museo dell'Opera del Duomo, Siena. Commissioned by the Opera of the Opera del Duomo for the high altar of Siena Cathedral

of the angels' garments contrasts with the stronger blue of Ezekiel's cloak.

A panel from the back predella (fig. 92) shows how Satan tempted Christ by leading him up a high mountain and offering him all the kingdoms of the world. Duccio represents the kingdoms as Italian city-states with walls, gates, streets, and public and religious buildings with towers, domes, roof tiles, and battlements. The colorful architecture of those in the foreground is picked out delicately in light, while the distant cities are almost lost in shadow. The illusion of space is limited, but the sense of distance is enhanced by the tiny scale of the cities. While we may feel that we can enter the reasonable, tangible environment Giotto created for his narratives (see figs. 56, 57), we cannot penetrate the complex, elusive world of Duccio's creation. Duccio's rocks, for example, seem almost fluid when compared with Giotto's mountains: their surfaces seem to twist and ripple, and they break upward toward the standing figures. On this moving ground the figures cannot stand with the firmness and decision of Giotto's people; they maintain an uncertain footing, as if walking on waves. In the drapery of Christ, the usual liquid fluidity of Duccio's line is transformed into straight lines and sharp points that reinforce Christ's gesture and words: "Get thee behind me, Satan" (Luke 4:8). Even in this scene, however, Duccio's slender, sad Christ is utterly different from the majestic, forthright Christ of Giotto.

On the main panel on the back of the *Maestà*, the story of the Passion is told in thirty-four scenes, beginning with the *Entry into Jerusalem* (colorplate 29, p. 115). The hilltop setting, similar to that of Siena itself, reflects a Sienese Palm Sunday procession in which the bishop led a throng to one of the city gates to meet an actor

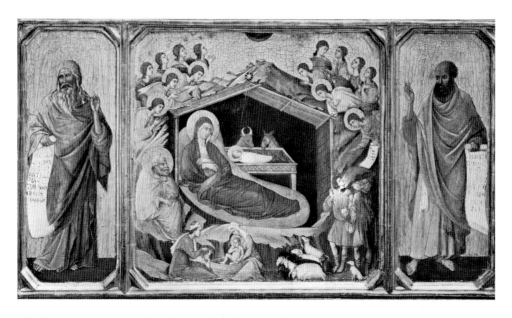

91. DUCCIO. *Nativity* and *Prophets Isaiah and Ezekiel*, from the front predella of *Maestà*. 1308–11.
Panels: *Nativity*, 17¼ x 17½"; *Prophets*, each 17¼ x 6½". National Gallery of Art, Washington, D.C.
(Mellon Collection)

garbed as Christ. Duccio has placed us in a field that is separated from the highway by a wall with an open gate, over which we watch the procession winding up along the highway to the towering city gate. We can see over the wall on the other side of the road into an orchard where people climb trees, as in Byzantine representations of the scene. As the text of the Gospel requires, some onlookers remove their mantles and spread them on the road. Christ rides on a donkey, fulfilling the prophecy of Zechariah: "Behold, thy King cometh . . . lowly, and riding upon an ass" (9:9). The crowd surges out of the gate chattering and gesticulating, the apostles follow Christ up the road. In these two human rivers about to meet we get all the feeling of a mob scene in an Italian medieval city. We can look through the gate into the main street; there is even a balcony with a head protruding through a window. The Temple, strikingly like a Tuscan baptistery, rises in the distance over trees and rooftops.

In the *Crucifixion* (fig. 93), Duccio has depicted a scene of mass violence and tragedy. All three crosses are

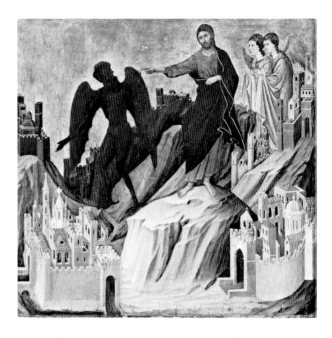

92. DUCCIO. *Temptation of Christ*, from the back predella of *Maestà*. 1308–11. Panel, 17 x 18 1/8". Copyright The Frick Collection, New York

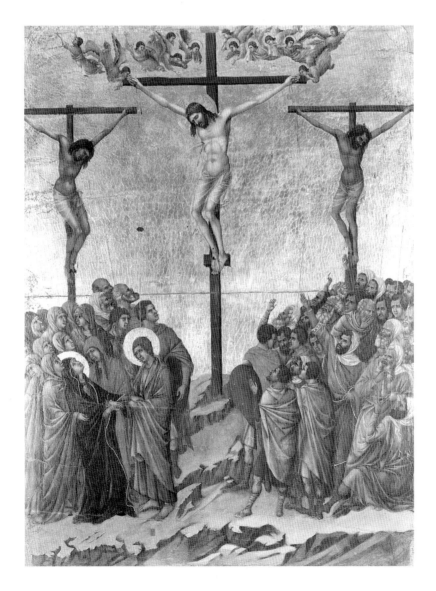

93. DUCCIO. *Crucifixion*, from the back of *Maestà*. 1308–11. Panel, 40 1/8 x 29 7/8". Museo dell'Opera del Duomo, Siena

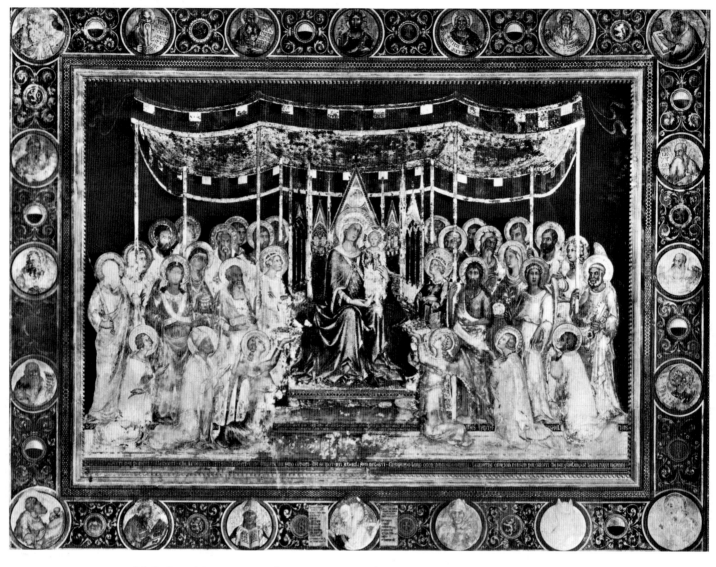

94. SIMONE MARTINI. *Maestà*. Between 1311 and 1317; repaired 1321. Fresco, 25' x 31' 9".
Council Chamber, Palazzo Pubblico, Siena. Commissioned by the Commune of Siena

shown and, following the Gospels, the legs of the thieves have been broken to ease their agony, while Christ's legs were left intact in fulfillment of a prophecy that "a bone of him shall not be broken" (John 19:36). The lofty, slender crosses soar against the gold background, into which the eye seems to be able to penetrate as into golden air. Duccio distinguishes the penitent thief, who is turned toward Christ, from the impenitent thief, who faces away and is represented in a darker color. The angels do not form definite groups about Christ, as in Giotto's *Crucifixion* (see fig. 66), but gather above him, almost like a flock of birds. Below, the crowds of the apostles, Mary, the holy women, the chief priests and elders, and the Roman soldiers are separated into two waves, like the Red Sea before the Israelites. As in the *Meditations on the Life of Christ*, a text written by a Franciscan mystic living in Tuscany at the end of the thirteenth or the beginning of the fourteenth century, Mary swoons below the cross, sinking powerless into the arms of the holy women as she looks up-

ward toward the body of her agonized Son, from whose side blood and water gush in powerful streams. Duccio's mastery of crowds and his ability to project naturalistic human feeling are effectively shown in this scene, with its flashing eyes and reaching hands.

SIMONE MARTINI

Like Giotto in Florence, Duccio had a number of pupils and close imitators in Siena. Their works suggest that he was a liberating teacher, for each of the pupils developed a style independent of the master and of each other. One of the most original was Simone Martini (active 1315–44), who most likely worked on Duccio's later commissions, including the *Maestà*, and later achieved fame and influence far beyond the borders of Siena. Shortly after Duccio's *Maestà* was completed, Simone was commissioned to paint a *Maestà* of his own (fig. 94), a large fresco that covers the end wall of the Council Chamber in the Palazzo Pubblico in Siena. From this vantage point, the Virgin could watch over the deliberations of the Council of the Sienese Republic. The kneeling saints in the foreground reveal the influence of Duccio, but the kneeling angels in profile follow the innovations of Giotto. Duccio's thrones, Byzantine with occasional Gothic details, are here replaced by a completely Gothic throne with wings whose open tracery recalls the windows of French cathedrals.

Simone has unified the loosely grouped throng of saints and angels by a spacious cloth canopy similar to the ones that shelter the Eucharist today when it is carried in procession in Italian churches or through streets and country roads. Simone's canopy is carried by saints, who turn to gaze outward toward the observer. Some portions of the work were painted *a secco* and have peeled off in the course of time, showing the underdrawing on the *intonaco*. For reasons unknown today, Simone repaired certain sections in 1321; perhaps they were already in bad condition, or they may not have been satisfactory to the patrons or the painter. The repairs have been connected to the two different head styles evident in the fresco. In the rear ranks of the Virgin's attendants some Duccio-inspired heads are still to be seen, their eyes almond-shaped and their hair covered with mantles. The heads of the Virgin and Child and of the two female saints that flank them show the more Gothic type characteristic of Simone's later works; they have broad full cheeks, pursed mouths, and wavy or curly blond hair.

Between the two campaigns on the *Maestà*, Simone was invited to Naples by the French king of that country, Robert of Anjou. While there he painted a large dynastic icon that depicts the king kneeling to receive the crown from his brother, St. Louis of Toulouse (fig. 95), who was canonized in 1317; motifs from the family's coat of arms decorate the frame, the background, and the garments. The artist has reconciled the conflict between the vertical, frontal, centralized image of the saint and the kneeling king, who is placed to one side. Simone unites the composition through the subtle relation of interweaving diagonals and diagonally directed curves; these are carried out with remarkable consistency in the figures and drapery patterns, from the base line up to the off-center placing of the angels who hold a heavenly crown above the enthroned saint. In this original, and at times almost abstract, composition Simone displays his ingenuity in handling boldly silhouetted areas and in creating surface patterns that are even richer and more delicate than those of Duccio. The morse on the saint's chest, which is made of glass decorated with paint and gold leaf, is boldly attached to the surface of the panel; the original decoration also included the application of precious gems. The richly embossed surface patterns are never permitted to compete with the basic element in Simone's maturing style—a taut, harsh, linear contour, almost as if the shapes were cut from sheet metal.

Simone's frescoes in the St. Martin Chapel in San Francesco in Assisi have recently been assigned to the

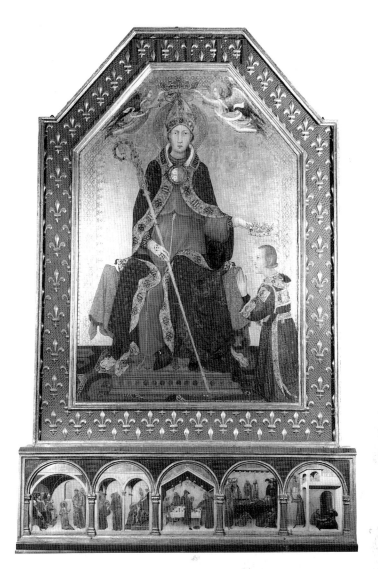

95. SIMONE MARTINI. *St. Louis of Toulouse Crowning Robert of Anjou, King of Naples,* and *Scenes from the Life of St. Louis of Toulouse.* c. 1317. Panel with gold and silver leaf, originally embellished with gold work and precious stones, 78 3/4 x 54 1/4". Museo di Capodimonte, Naples. Commissioned by Robert of Anjou

period between 1312 and 1319. Here Simone showed his narrative ability, enchanting colorism, and decorative talents in such scenes as the *Dream of St. Martin* and the *Funeral of St. Martin* (figs. 96, 97). In the former, an aloof and princely Christ appears to the saint, who sleeps under a rose and blue plaid silk coverlet heightened by gold threads. Simone's linear organization and the expressiveness of the faces reveal the best qualities of his style; less expected is the rather salty naturalism of observation in the *Funeral*. The saint lies in a Gothic chapel with lofty spiral colonnettes and Gothic tracery. With evident relish Simone emphasizes such details as the youth kissing the ring of St. Ambrose, who has miraculously appeared to conduct the rite; the monks singing enthusiastically; and the humble attendants, dressed in animal skins, who lift with difficulty gigantic wax torches at the foot of the bier.

The most famous of Simone's surviving works is the *Annunciation* (colorplate 30, p. 116) painted for Siena

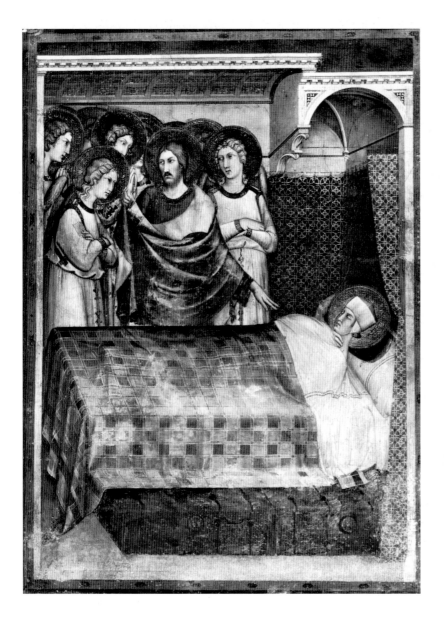

96. SIMONE MARTINI. *Dream of St. Martin.*
Between 1312 and 1319(?). Fresco,
8' 8" x 6' 7". St. Martin Chapel, Lower
Church of S. Francesco, Assisi.
Commissioned by Cardinal Gentile
Partino da Montefiore dell'Aso

Cathedral in 1333. He signed it jointly with his brother-in-law Lippo Memmi; this signature and the joint payments for the work attest to their collaboration, but it is not clear what role Lippo played in the execution of the work. This is the earliest known example in which the Annunciation was the subject of an entire altarpiece. The elaborate frame is not the original, and the different floor design and angle of view suggest that the side saints were not attached in this manner to the Annunciation panel. The blank gold background is traversed by raised gesso words that stretch from Gabriel's mouth to Mary's ear: *"Ave gratia plena dominus tecum"* ("Hail, thou that art highly favoured, the Lord is with thee"; Luke 1:28).

As in Giotto's fresco the heavenly messenger kneels, but here the suddenness of his arrival is indicated by the device of a cloak that still floats in the breeze. The Virgin shrinks backward at the news; the Gospel account says that she was disturbed at the appearance and salutation of the angel. The violence of her movement increases the explosive immediacy of the effect. The

sharp, taut curves of her body are contrasted to the masses of the angel, who is crowned with the olive leaves of the Prince of Peace and bears an olive branch in his hand. In the center of a richly veined marble floor is a golden vase of lilies that symbolize Mary's purity. The lilies, the olive leaves, the curves of the drapery, and even the features of Mary and Gabriel display the same sharp, metallic quality seen in Simone's *St. Louis of Toulouse*. The dove of the Holy Spirit bursts forth from a group of bodiless angels with crossed wings. The hard, crisp lines of Simone's faces emphasize the suspicious expression of Mary, with her puckered brows and pursed lips. Glittering sunburst shapes incised in the gold background burst out around the tooled haloes.

Simone reveals his skill as a narrator in the altarpiece representing the Blessed Agostino Novello with scenes of his miracles (fig. 98). The centralized placement of the monk, which may have been requested by the patron, follows the tradition of Bonaventura Berlinghieri's *St. Francis* (see fig. 24) and other Duecento images, but Simone has transformed the stiffness of his prototypes

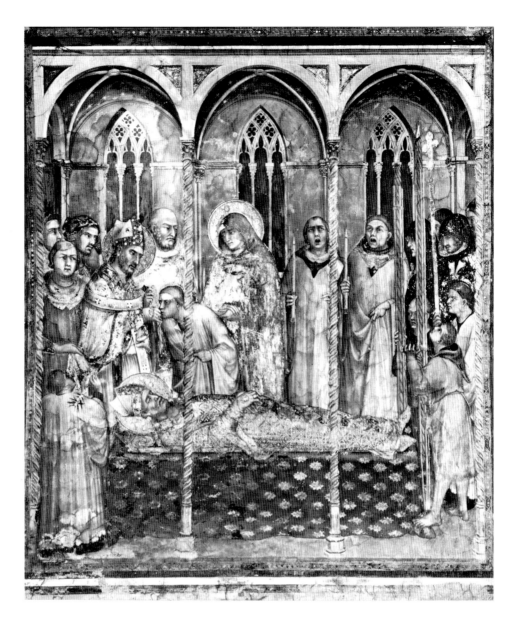

97. SIMONE MARTINI.
Funeral of St. Martin.
Between 1312 and 1319(?).
Fresco, 9' 4" x 7' 7".
St. Martin Chapel, Lower
Church of
S. Francesco, Assisi

into a gentle, swaying pose. The book the monk holds may be symbolic of the juridical learning for which Novello, briefly prior general of the Augustinian Order, was respected. He is seen among the trees of a forest, lost in meditation, while an angel whispers in his ear. The subtlety of Simone's sense of line and space is evident in the flattened curves and the suggestion of diagonal motion into depth. The stubble on the monk's jaw and chin is a rare naturalistic detail that foreshadows realistic effects that will be further exploited by Netherlandish artists in the following century. The lateral scenes represent Agostino Novello's posthumous miraculous appearances, in which he heals a boy who had been attacked by a wolf and restores to life a traveler who had fallen from his horse and a baby who had fallen from a broken hammock. In one scene the monk intervenes to grab a board dislodged from a balcony and to revive a child who had fallen (fig. 99). Wood-grained balconies, nail-studded doors, and views into staircase halls recapture the Siena of Simone's day without sacrificing his austerity of pattern and delicacy of color.

Simone's last years were spent in Avignon, a Provençal city then the seat of the papacy. Simone's followers left a number of works from this period, but only a few by Simone remain, notably a series of panels from a small folding devotional work representing the Passion; the most dramatic of these is the *Way to Calvary* (fig. 100). Paradoxically enough, in these works painted in France, Simone's Francophile elegance is replaced by an interest in immediate, naturalistic, and even violent action. Christ is led forth from a very Sienese Jerusalem, seen from below, but he is almost overwhelmed by the mob of loving, grieving apostles and friends and by mocking Romans and Hebrews, including two irreverent children. In the new interest in passionate drama, even Simone's delicate color has given way to a fierce brilliance centering on the scarlet robe of Christ. Simone's late style had no immediate issue in Italy, but it must have been a revelation to Northern European painters; certainly his art and that of his compatriots working in Avignon played a role in the development of the new naturalism with which, under Jan van Eyck and

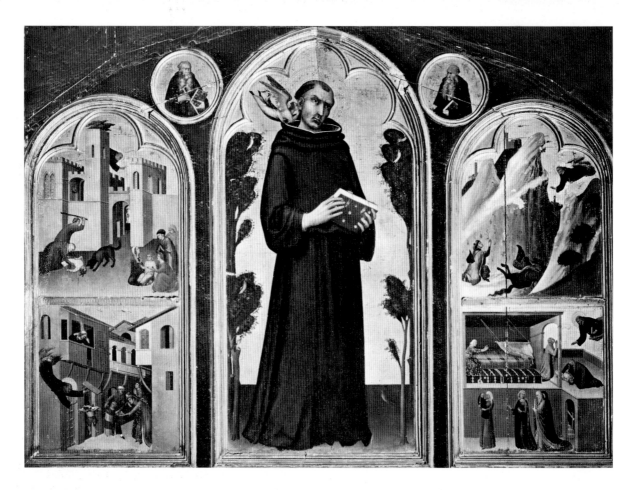

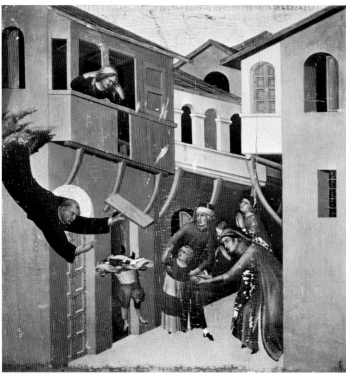

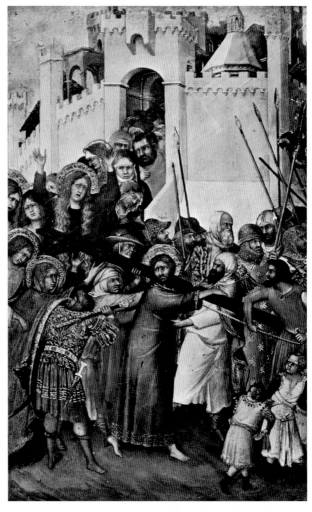

above: 98. SIMONE MARTINI. *The Blessed Agostino Novello and Four of His Miracles.* c. 1324. Panel, 6' 6" x 8' 5". 🏛 Sant'Agostino, Siena

below left: 99. The Blessed Agostino Novello Saves a Child who Fell from a Balcony, detail of fig. 98

below right: 100. SIMONE MARTINI. *Way to Calvary.* c. 1340–44. Panel, 9⁷/8 x 6¹/4". The Louvre, Paris. Originally part of a small folding devotional work commissioned by an Orsini cardinal

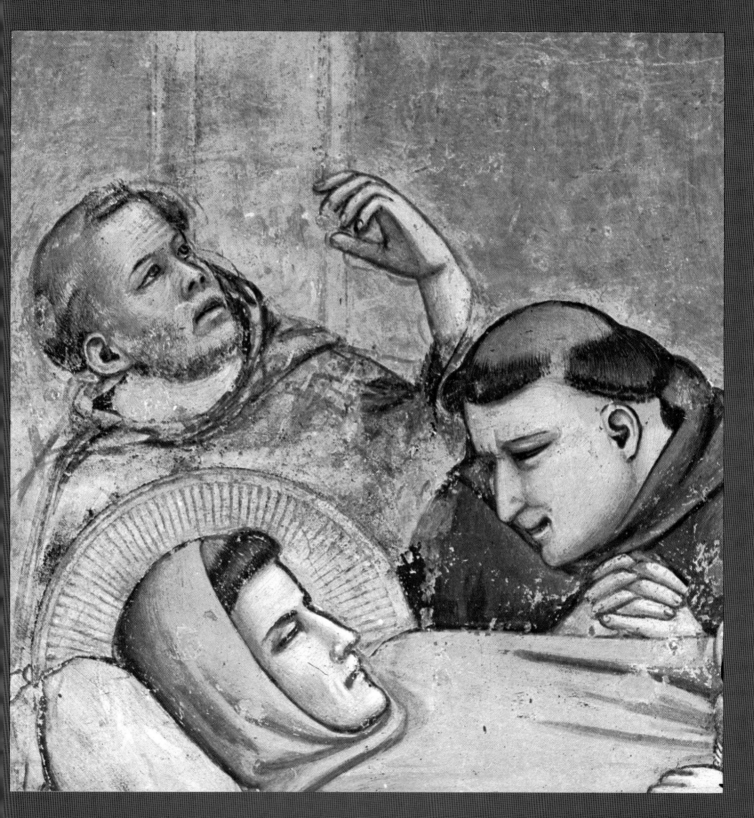

Colorplate 26. GIOTTO. *Funeral of St. Francis* (detail of fig. 74). Probably 1320s. Fresco. Bardi Chapel, Sta. Croce, Florence.
Commissioned by a member of the Bardi family

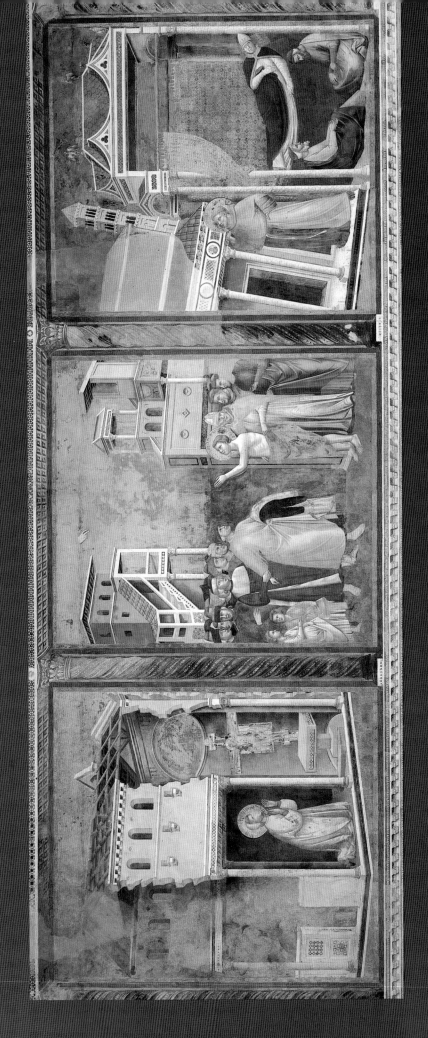

Colorplate 27. MASTER OF THE ST. FRANCIS CYCLE. *St. Francis Praying Before the Crucifix at San Damiano; St. Francis Renouncing His Worldly Goods; Dream of Innocent III.* Early 14th century. Fresco; each scene: 8' 10" x 7' 7". Upper Church of S. Francesco, Assisi

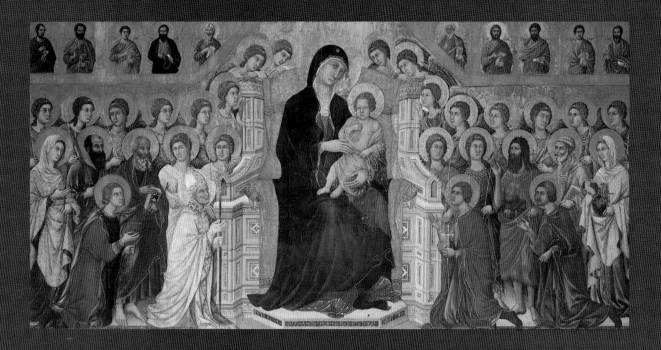

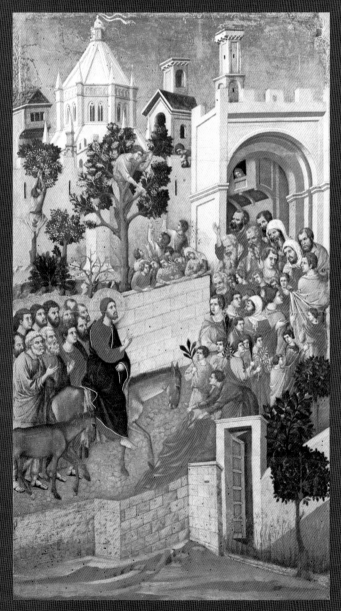

Colorplate 28. DUCCIO. *Maestà*.
1308–11. Central front panel,
7 x 13'. Museo dell'Opera del Duomo,
Siena. Commissioned by the Opera
of the Opera del Duomo
for the high altar of Siena Cathedral

Colorplate 29. DUCCIO. *Entry into
Jerusalem*, from the back of *Maestà*.
1308–11. Panel, 40¹⁄₈ x 21¹⁄₈". Museo
dell'Opera del Duomo, Siena

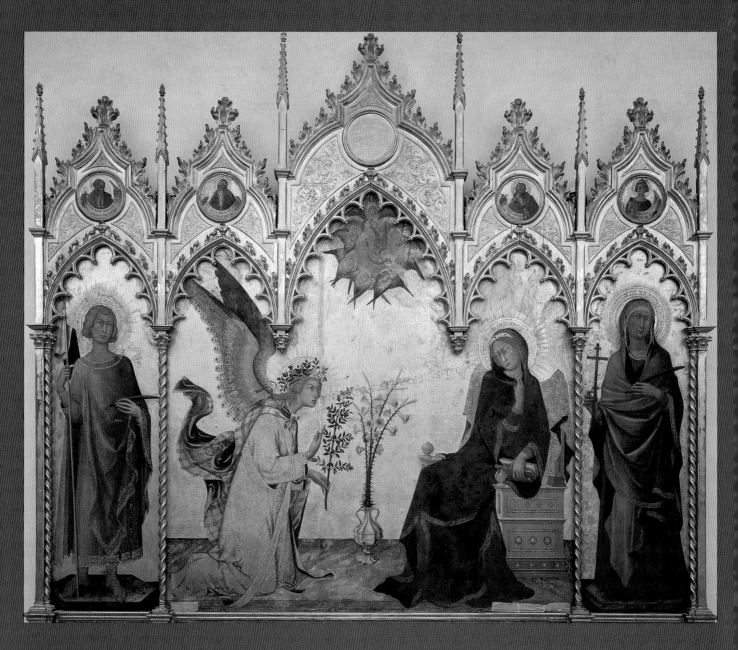

Colorplate 30. SIMONE MARTINI and LIPPO MEMMI. *Annunciation with Two Saints*. 1333. Panel, 10' x 8' 9".
Uffizi Gallery, Florence. Commissioned by the Opera del Duomo for the Cathedral of Siena

opposite: Colorplate 31. AMBROGIO LORENZETTI.
Presentation in the Temple. 1342. Panel, 8' 5¹/8" x 5' 6¹/8".
Uffizi Gallery, Florence. Commissioned by the Opera del
Duomo for the Cathedral of Siena

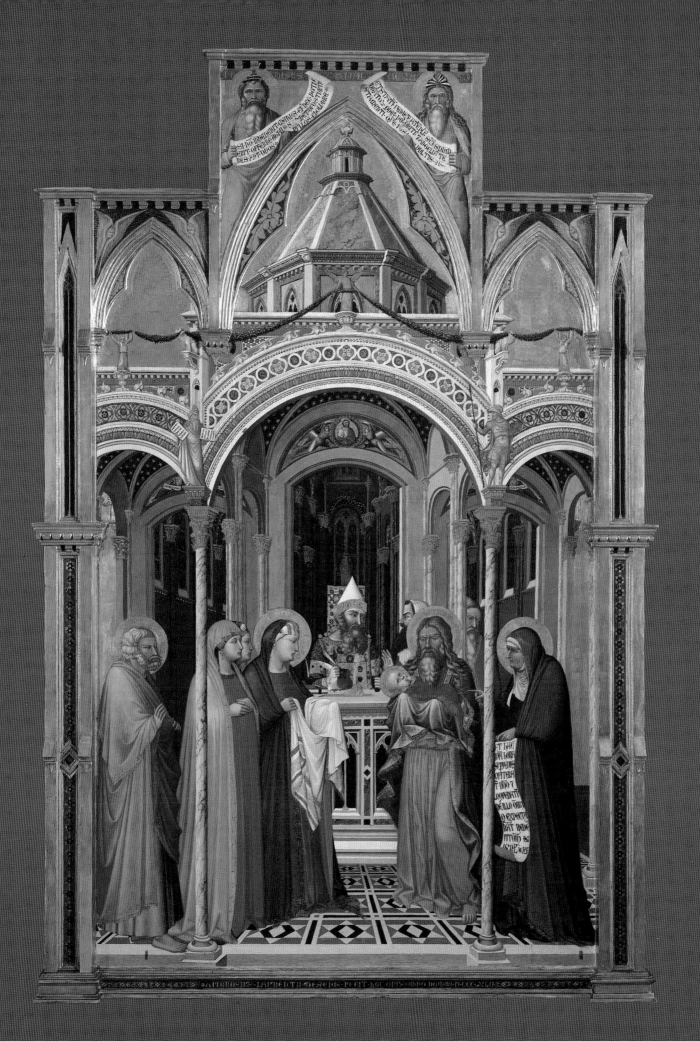

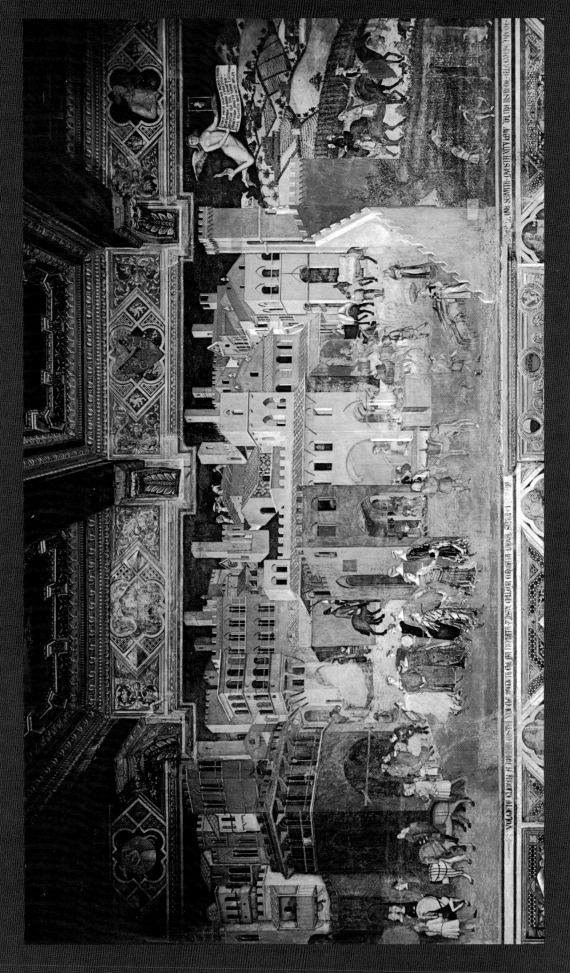

Colorplate 32. AMBROGIO LORENZETTI. *Allegory of Good Government: Effects of Good Government in the City and the Country*
(portion; see figs. 107–9). 1338–39. Fresco. Sala dei Nove, Palazzo Pubblico, Siena

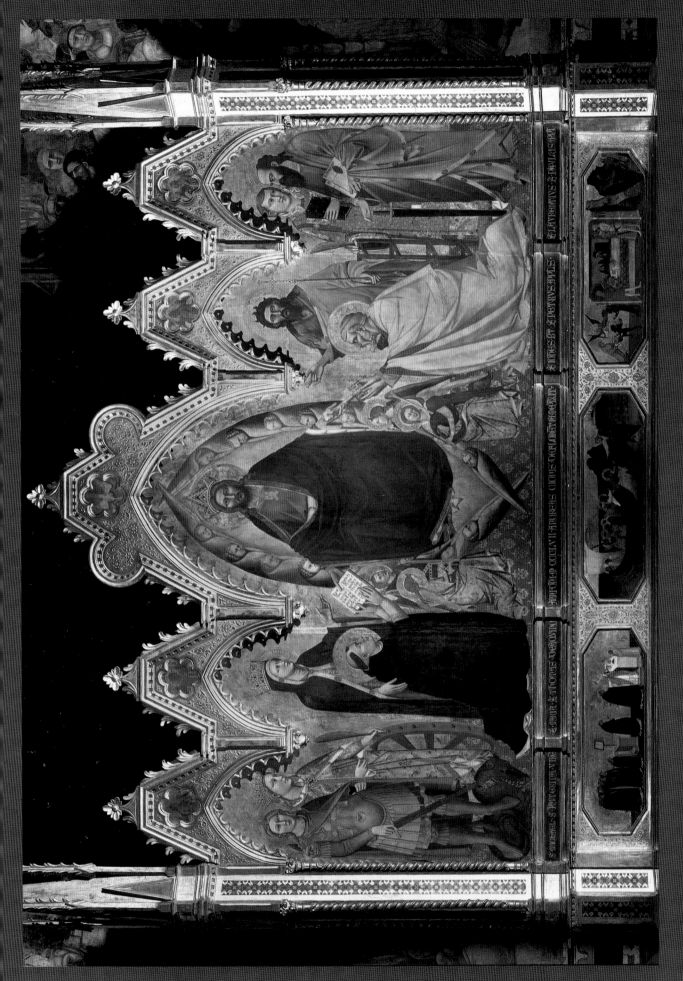

Colorplate 33. ANDREA ORCAGNA. *Enthroned Christ with Madonna and Saints.* 1354–57. Panel, c. 9′ x 9′ 8″. Strozzi Chapel, Sta. Maria Novella, Florence. Commissioned by Tommaso di Rossello Strozzi

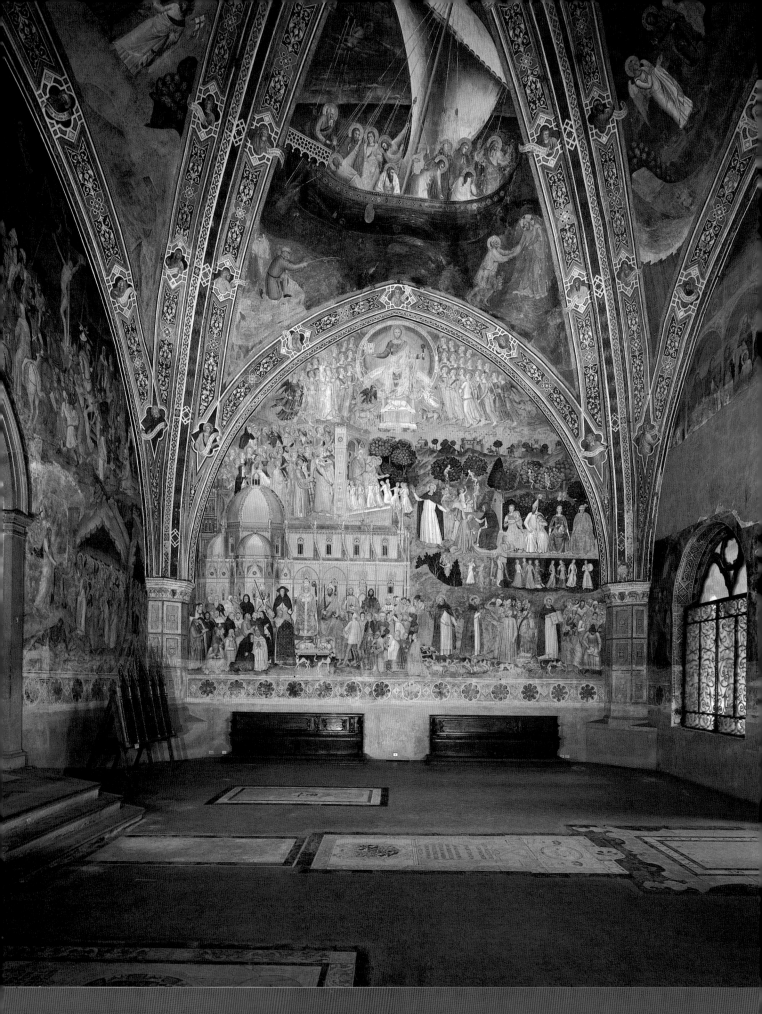

Colorplate 34. ANDREA DA FIRENZE. *Triumph of the Church* (below) and the *Navicella* (above). c. 1366–68.
Fresco, width of wall 31' 6". Chapter House (now known as the Spanish Chapel), Sta. Maria Novella, Florence.
Commissioned by Buonamico Guidalotti

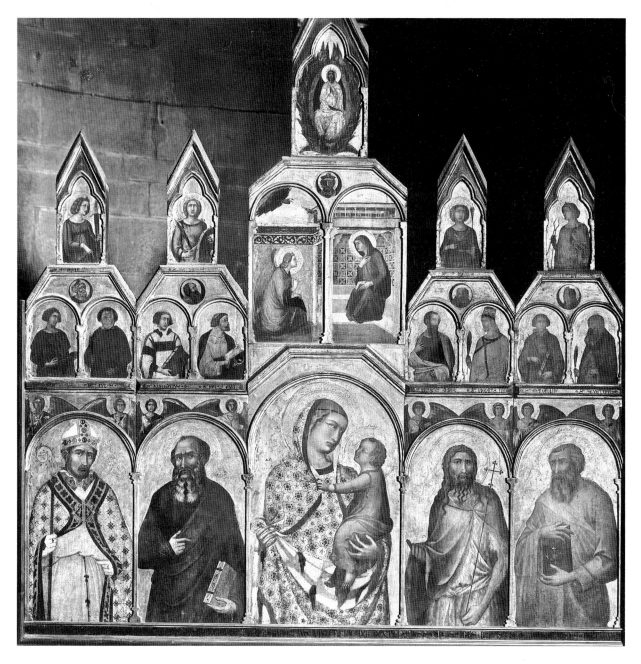

101. PIETRO LORENZETTI. *Madonna and Child with Saints, Annunciation*, and *Assumption*. 1320. Panel, 9' 9½" x 10' 1½".
🏛 Pieve di Sta. Maria, Arezzo. Commissioned by Bishop Guido

Robert Campin (the Master of Flemalle), Netherlandish painters transformed Northern painting in the opening decades of the fifteenth century.

PIETRO LORENZETTI

Simone's chief competitors in Siena, the brothers Pietro and Ambrogio Lorenzetti, exercised undisputed domination over Sienese style after Simone's departure (Pietro, c. 1290–1348?; Ambrogio, d. 1348?). Although the brothers almost always worked and signed their paintings independently, they show an affinity of style that is distinct from both the lingering Byzantinism of the Duccio School and the Francophile elegance of Simone. In Pietro's earliest known work, the polyptych (fig. 101) still on the high altar of the Romanesque Pieve di Santa Maria in Arezzo, the artist shows himself

to be a mature master in control of a new style. Pietro must have visited Florence, for the Gothicism and humanity of his art, not to mention the clear-cut features, strong hands, and ample proportions of his figures, reveal an acquaintance with the art of Giotto and his followers. In the central panel the Christ Child looks upward at his mother with a gaze whose happiness is answered by a look of searching, foreboding depth typical of the passionate intensity that characterizes Pietro's art. The saints in the lateral panels turn toward each other as if in conversation even as they look out questioningly toward the observer; in the upper register, just to the left of the *Annunciation*, St. Luke, closing his book, looks upward at the event about which he had written so beautifully—perhaps also to remind us that he, too, was a painter and, according to tradition, painted the Virgin's portrait.

Sienese Art of the Early Trecento

121

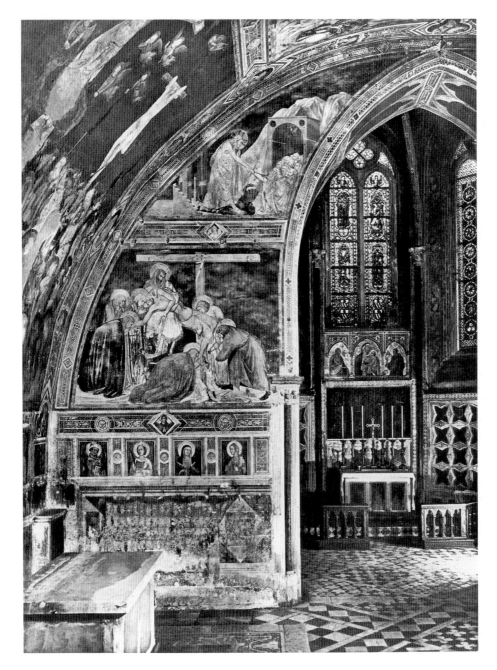

102. PIETRO LORENZETTI and assistants. Lower Church of S. Francesco, Assisi. Frescoes of the *Descent into Limbo, Descent from the Cross,* and *Madonna with Two Saints* (see colorplate 2, p. 11). 1320s–1330s. Width at base 12' 4"

Compared with the massive figures of the Giottesque tradition, however, Pietro's personages are less massive; rather than assessing their volumes, we are invited to explore the richness of the patterned fabrics. Instead of her customary blue mantle, the Virgin wears a tunic and cloak of white patterned silk, the latter lined with ermine, its dark tails punctuating the flow of surface design. In this work there is little to suggest that Duccio's *Maestà* was finished only nine years before and that Simone had still to complete his own version of that subject.

The extent of Pietro's participation in the Passion cycle in the Lower Church of San Francesco at Assisi, as well as the date of the series, remains in doubt. His authorship of the *Descent from the Cross* (fig. 102; see colorplate 2, p. 11), however, is beyond question, as are its dramatic power and bold originality of composition. The upper portion of the cross is cut off by the border of the fresco, leaving the long horizontal of the crossbar against a background that, on the right, is completely vacant. The gaunt body of Christ, the effects of rigor mortis indicated in its harsh lines and angles, is lowered by his friends: Joseph of Arimathea holds the torso; St. John embraces the legs, pressing his cheek to one thigh; and Nicodemus, holding an immense pair of tongs, attempts to withdraw the spike from one pierced foot while Mary Magdalen prostrates herself to kiss the other. Another of the Marys holds Christ's right hand, and—most shattering of all—the Virgin presses the head of her Son to her cheek in a way that unites the two heads, one right side up, the other upside down, the dead and the living eyes seemingly threaded on the same line. The broad, columnar masses of Giotto's figures, which undoubtedly influenced Pietro's repertory of forms, are simplified into vertical drapery lines that suggest little or no volume beneath them, yet they bind the fabric of the

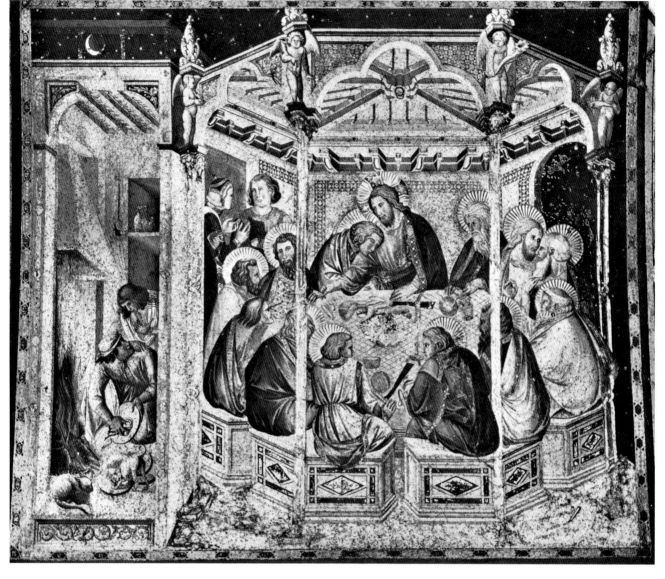

103. PIETRO LORENZETTI (design; executed by a pupil). *Last Supper*. 1320s–1330s.
Fresco, 8' x 10' 2". Lower Church of S. Francesco, Assisi

composition into a unity of almost unbearable tension.

Many of the other scenes are of lesser interest, but the *Last Supper* (fig. 103) is one of the most striking examples of the observation of light in Trecento art. Christ and the apostles are gathered in a hexagonal upper loggia that is almost filled by the table. The rich ornament of this structure unexpectedly includes nude baby angels inspired by the putti that often appear in ancient Roman works. Judas at the left reaches greedily for the sop in wine that Christ hands to him to identify his betrayer, but the reactions of the other apostles to Christ's revelation is contrasted with the lack of concern on the part of the servants conversing in the doorway, just as the spiritual food of the Last Supper is contrasted with the greedy dog licking the plates being scraped in the kitchen. Even more striking is the contrast of material and spiritual light. The kitchen is illuminated by the fire in the fireplace, and the moon and stars are shown in a naturalistic sky outside, a detail that will not reappear until the 1420s (see fig. 185). But what source lights the ceiling of the loggia from below when there is neither candle nor lamp? It can only be the light from the haloes of Christ and the apostles.

Pietro's *Enthroned Madonna* (fig. 104) was painted in 1340 for San Francesco in Pistoia, in Florentine territory. Although the simple columnar forms of the figures abound in references to the Giottesque tradition, the softness with which the surfaces are modeled makes it impossible to mistake the picture for a Florentine work, even in a generation when Bernardo Daddi had already altered the grandeur of Giotto's heritage. The Christ Child playfully pushes his mother's chin and toys with one of her fingers. The blond angels have almost Greek profiles, with straight noses and jaws, derived from the tradition of Giotto and the Pisani but softer in definition than anything from the Florentine School. The color is

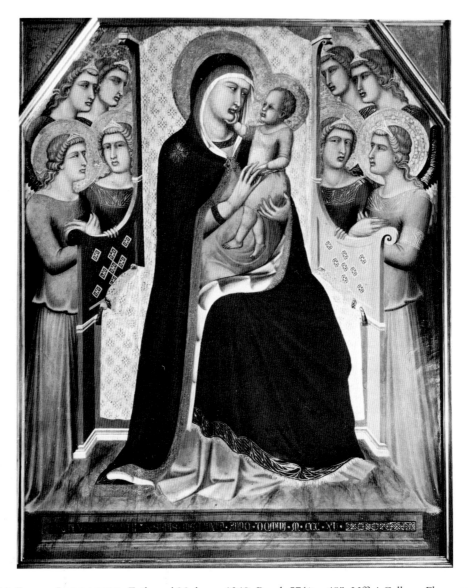

104. Pietro Lorenzetti. *Enthroned Madonna*. 1340. Panel, 57 1/8 x 48". Uffizi Gallery, Florence.
Commissioned for S. Francesco, Pistoia

well preserved, and the blue of the Virgin's ermine-lined mantle harmonizes with the powdery, paler blues of the angels' tunics. A bit of gold striation lingers in the embroidered patterns at the neck and sleeves.

Two years later Pietro painted the *Birth of the Virgin* (fig. 105) as his contribution to the cycle of Marian altarpieces for the Cathedral of Siena; this triptych, perhaps in competition with one by his brother Ambrogio (see colorplate 31, p. 117), established a new standard in the definition of space. The altarpiece is treated as if it were a stage or even an actual building, with the colonnettes, pointed arches, and pinnacles of the frame becoming the outward projection of the painted architecture (the present Italian policy of removing all restorations has left us with no outer edges, no pinnacles, and no colonnettes to support the arches). Or, conversely, we can view each arch of the frame as the foremost arch of the vault beyond it. It is an astonishing bit of illusion that gives us the feeling that we could enter the room where

St. Anne lies on her bed with its checkered spread, while the baby Virgin is being bathed and neighbors arrive bearing gifts. One woman holds a striped fan to cool St. Anne (the Virgin's birthday was traditionally set at September 8, still the hot season in Tuscany). In the antechamber on the left St. Joachim receives the good news, and behind him we look into a space that might belong to some ecclesiastical building—a towering Gothic structure of at least three stories, the upper one cut off by the vault of the antechamber. This tall structure must be a reference to the Temple in which Mary was to be presented three years later.

Pietro's triptych is the first of a series of Italian paintings that presents the illusionistic space of the picture as an inward extension of the frame. In his perspective formulation Pietro at times comes close to the one-point perspective system that rules pictorial art during the following century, but analysis will show that the floors in the side panels have separate vanishing points that do

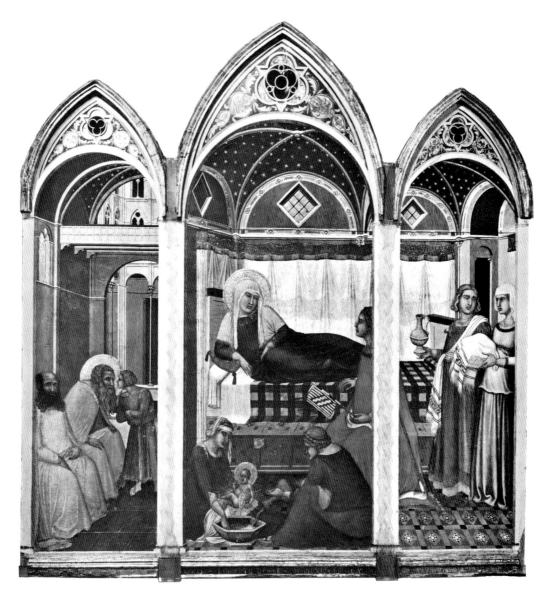

105. PIETRO LORENZETTI. *Birth of the Virgin.* 1342. Panel, 73½ x 71½". Museo dell'Opera del Duomo, Siena. Commissioned by the Opera del Duomo for the Cathedral of Siena

not correspond to the single vanishing point used for the three vaults. Nonetheless, the Sienese Trecento painters, recklessly plunging into the unexplored realm of the rational formulation of pictorial space, were moving toward the art of the Renaissance.

AMBROGIO LORENZETTI

Ambrogio Lorenzetti seems to have visited Florence on at least two occasions—in 1319, when he painted a *Madonna* for the Pieve in Vico l'Abate outside Florence, and in 1332–34, when he painted a polyptych for the Church of San Procolo, and joined, possibly because he had to in order to work in Florence, the Arte dei Medici e Speziali. Typical of the warmth and emotional richness of his altarpieces is the group of panels from a polyptych Ambrogio painted for the convent of Santa Petronilla in Siena (fig. 106). In the central panel Mary presses the Christ Child to her cheek. Mary Magdalen

lifts her left hand as if in delight at this image of maternal tenderness and holds forth her jar of precious ointment, while on her breast shines the face of the mature Christ in the center of a cruciform burst of rays; St. Dorothy, who demonstrated the directness of her route to Paradise by a miraculous growth of flowers on her path, has picked some and made a nosegay in tribute to the Madonna. In the flowers, an almost Impressionist sense of the value of each brushstroke creates points of color, bright and clear and pure, against the soft gray-lavender tunic and mantle of the saint. The color composition receives an unexpected accent in the black-and-orange ribbon wound in St. Dorothy's hair.

Ambrogio's female forms are fuller than those of Pietro, his faces and throats seem softer, and his coloring is even warmer. Rich rose tones enliven the flesh. At the same time, even the apparent spontaneity of his figural relationships produces delicate adjustments of linear pattern in, for example, the haloes and the tooled borders

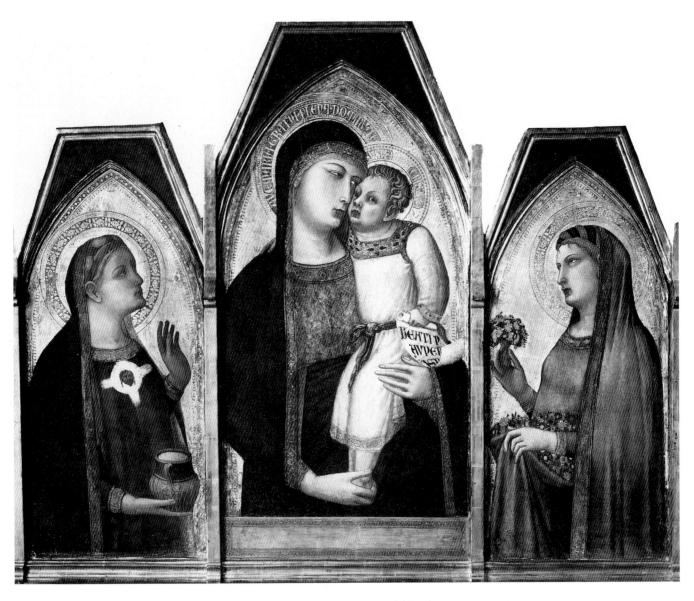

106. AMBROGIO LORENZETTI. *Madonna and Child with Saints*. Late 1330s.
Panel, 58 x 89 ½". Pinacoteca, Siena

that they intersect. The message of the altarpiece is summed up in the inscriptions—the "AVE MARIA" incised in Mary's halo and the scroll held by the round-eyed, curly-headed Child: "BEAUTI PAUPER . . . ISP . . . ," referring to the first Beatitude, "Blessed are the poor in spirit, for theirs is the kingdom of heaven."

In the competition with his brother in 1342, Ambrogio seems to have been the victor, for his *Presentation in the Temple* (colorplate 31, p. 117) for the Cathedral of Siena penetrates architectural space in a manner unprecedented since Roman antiquity. The complex Gothic frame, now shorn of its superstructure, is not an integral part of the architecture, but the frame gives the impression of a lofty gateway. Within and beyond the frame we gaze into an interior where the light is dimmed by a stained-glass window. While Ambrogio still maintains the double scale of medieval art—one scale for the figures, another for the setting—he has reduced the fig-

ures so as to make the architecture more credible. Slender columns uphold the blue, gold-starred, ribbed vaults of the nave. Behind the altar we look into the dimness of the sanctuary, with its black marble columns and gilded capitals, and for the first time in any Italian painting we sense the immensity of a cathedral interior.

The architecture is a strange amalgam of Romanesque and Gothic. In the Late Middle Ages, Romanesque architecture was considered to be of Eastern origin, so that the Temple in Jerusalem was generally represented with Romanesque round arches rather than Gothic pointed ones. Also, the polygonal building we see in the backgrounds of such Trecento paintings as Duccio's *Entry into Jerusalem* (colorplate 29, p. 115) is always the Temple, since the Crusaders had brought back descriptions of the Dome of the Rock in Jerusalem, the central-plan mosque built on the site of Solomon's Temple. In Ambrogio's picture, we also see beyond the roof of

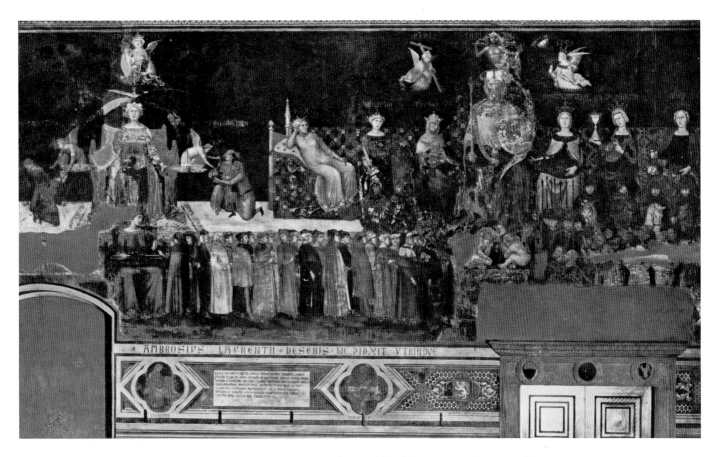

107. AMBROGIO LORENZETTI. *Allegory of Good Government: Commune of Siena*
(see also colorplate 32, p. 118). 1338–39. Fresco; size of the room, c. 46' x 25' 3". Sala dei Nove,
Palazzo Pubblico, Siena

the building to the great polygonal dome behind, which is provided with Gothic windows in spite of the Romanesque arches of the nave.

For all his quiet drama, Ambrogio has precisely illustrated the Gospel text (Luke 2:22–38). We see the gift of two turtle doves upon the altar, according to the Law. The aged Simeon, who had been told by the Holy Spirit that he would not die until he had seen the Messiah, holds the Christ Child in his arms and murmurs the words of the "Nunc Dimittis": "Lord, now lettest thou thy servant depart in peace, according to thy word: For mine eyes have seen thy salvation, Which thou hast prepared before the face of all people; A light to lighten the Gentiles, and the glory of thy people Israel" (Luke 2:29–32).

At the left stand Joseph, Mary, and two attendants; on the right the eighty-four-year-old prophetess Anna holds a scroll with the last verse of the passage from St. Luke: "And she coming in that instant gave thanks likewise unto the Lord, and spake of him to all them that looked for redemption in Jerusalem" (Luke 2:38). Ambrogio has depicted all the differences in age and feelings, from the tiny Child blissfully sucking his thumb and the gentle pride of his mother, her arms now momentarily empty, to the wrinkled age of the prophetess

Anna and the weariness of Simeon, now to be released from the burden of life. Cleaning has revealed colors of unexpected brilliance—crisp whites against clear primary tones—that compete with the splendor of Duccio and Simone.

Ambrogio's most revolutionary achievement is the fresco series that lines three walls of the Sala dei Nove, where Siena's chief magistrates held their meetings, in the Palazzo Pubblico. Ambrogio's task was unprecedented. He apparently was called upon to depict allegorically Good Government and Bad Government—subjects of intense significance to medieval Italian communes—and to represent the effects these regimes would have in the town and the country. Today the cycle is usually identified simply as "Good and Bad Government," but in 1427 St. Bernardino of Siena referred to them as "War and Peace." Ambrogio chose the most strongly illuminated walls for Good Government and its effects, leaving Bad Government to languish in the shadows on a wall that has also suffered considerable damage, some of it perhaps intentional because of its subject. Faced with such extensive surfaces, Ambrogio composed freely, following a panoramic principle that he seems to have invented.

The compositions flow in a relaxed manner, without

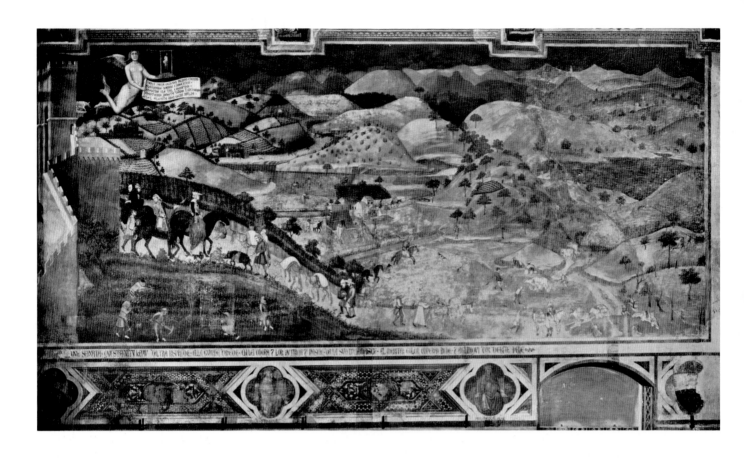

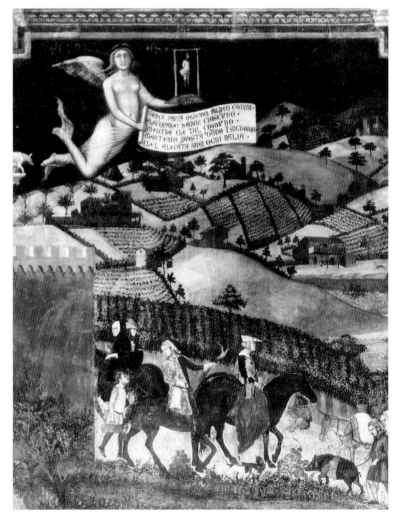

above: 108. AMBROGIO LORENZETTI.
*Allegory of Good Government: Effects of Good
Government in the Country* (see also
colorplate 32, p. 118). 1338–39. Fresco.
Sala dei Nove, Palazzo Pubblico, Siena

right: 109. Securitas and Sienese landscape,
detail of fig. 108

set geometric relationships, much like the spontaneous city plan of Siena itself. On one wall Ambrogio has enthroned the majestic figure of the Commune of Siena, who holds the orb and scepter and is dressed in the communal colors of black and white. He is guided by Faith, Hope, and Charity, who soar above his head (fig. 107). On either side of Commune are other Virtues, chosen for their civic significance, who sit or lounge on a damasked bench. To the left, Justice, above whose head floats Wisdom, dispenses rewards and punishments through winged figures that represent Commutative Justice, who gives arms to a noble and money to a merchant, and Distributive Justice, who crowns a kneeling figure with her left hand as she lops off the head of another with her right. Below the throne of Justice, Concord presides over the twenty-four magistrates of the Sienese Republic, one of whom grips the cord that extends from Justice and Concord back to the scepter of the personification of the Sienese Commune. The reclining figure of Peace is taken from a Roman sarcophagus fragment today in the Palazzo Pubblico, but if the original were not preserved, Ambrogio's drapery is so medieval that one would scarcely suspect a classical prototype.

The fresco of Good Government in town and country (colorplate 32, p. 118; fig. 108) is a delightful, continuous vista so wide that no photograph can contain it all. We are taken through the streets, alleys, and squares of Siena (much as it still stands), over the city walls, and out into the Tuscan countryside. This is an amazing panorama, and to show us as much as possible of town and country and of what goes on in every corner, Ambrogio, still a medieval painter, constantly shifts his viewpoint. His world is complete with buildings, people, trees, hills, farms, waterways, animals, and birds.

Since the subject is life in the city and the country, Ambrogio is almost able to abandon the double scale. Actually, the buildings are smaller than they would be in relation to people, but if Ambrogio had painted the people and animals in scale to the architecture, they could hardly have been made out in so vast a worldscape. He has boldly represented the entire city of Siena as it climbs up its hillside, with its towers, crenellated parapets, and windows both simple and mullioned. He shows us the beams outside the windows for hanging out clothing or providing leverage to haul things up from the street below, and streets with people conversing, entering houses, or cut off from our view as they ride behind buildings. Through the open arches of the large building in the foreground we gain access to the interior of an elegant shop displaying shoes and hosiery, a school where the master teaches attentive pupils from a raised desk, and a tavern with flasks of wine set on an outdoor bar. We can also see a house in the process of construction; the workmen, standing on the scaffolding they had probably put in place only the day before, are carrying building materials in baskets on their heads and laying new courses of masonry. A young woman plays a tambourine and sings while her elegantly dressed companions dance a kind of figure eight in the street. Nearby farmers arrive from the prosperous countryside, leading donkeys, driving herds of sheep, and carrying produce in baskets on their heads. All have come through the city gate—probably the recently completed Porta Romana in the walls of Siena. This wall zigzags freely from the lower border to the gate, which is surmounted by a representation of the wolf with Romulus and Remus, a Sienese symbol because the Sienese believed themselves to be descended from Remus.

The pastoral view shown in figure 109 is perhaps the most daring of all. Ambrogio seems to have wanted to bring in the Sienese territory as far as the sea at Talamone, Siena's ambitious new port, in order to display the prosperity of the Republic. Vines are tended, grain is harvested and threshed. As the peasants, conversing happily, bring their produce and their animals (including a saddlebacked black-and-white hog) up the steep incline into the city, men and women descend into the country to go hawking. They indulge in this sport only in the fields of stubble and *never* in the standing grain.

The apparently random activities depicted in city and country correspond to the seven Mechanical Arts, according to Hugh of St. Victor. For example, dancing in the street, actually forbidden in medieval Siena, is related to the art of Music. Medicine, another Mechanical Art, includes both shopkeeping and spice selling and is personified between them, for the teacher visible in the central arch wears a doctor's red gown. Presiding over these activities is a virtually nude figure of Securitas, who floats through the air holding a gallows and a scroll: "Without fear, let each man freely walk, and working let everyone sow, while such a commune this personage will keep under her rule because she has removed all power from the guilty." Her hideous counterpart on the opposite wall is Fear, who can only be banished by Good Government.

Our eye follows the vista off over hill after towered hill, farm after farm, but this spectacle terminates against the traditional unmodulated blue of the wall itself at the horizon. It is too early, apparently, for the artist to want to paint the sky with clouds. But as the landscape moves into the distance, it is clear that Gothic linear techniques no longer suffice for Ambrogio. He now represents details of plants and stubble with a few quick, sketchy strokes, a kind of shorthand that will have to await the Quattrocento and Masaccio for fuller exploration.

LORENZO MAITANI

At the end of the Duecento and in the early Trecento, Sienese sculpture was dominated by Nicola and Giovanni Pisano, and although some local sculptors managed to free themselves from the Pisani tradition, the appearance of Lorenzo Maitani in Siena in the first third of the Trecento comes as a surprise. This extraordinary man was responsible for the finest carving on the four huge marble panels on the façade of Orvieto Cathedral,

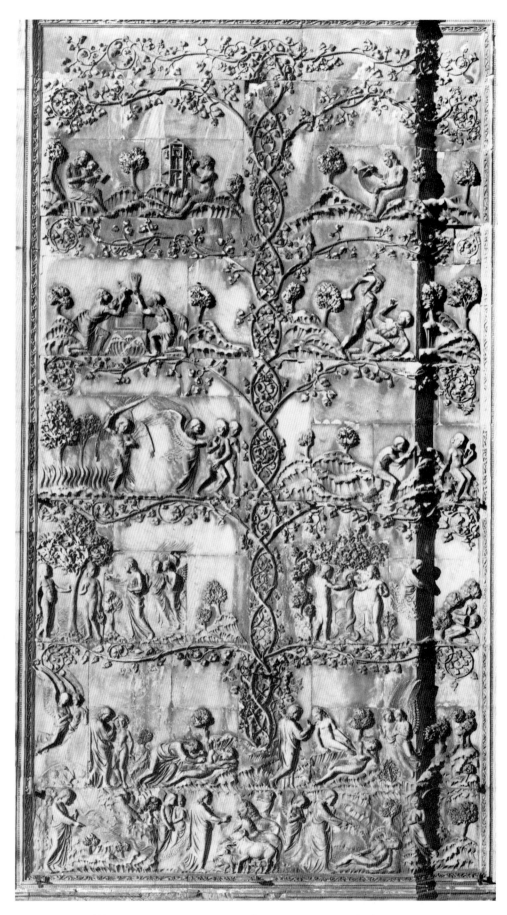

110. LORENZO MAITANI. *Scenes from Genesis*. c. 1310–before 1316.
Marble. Façade, Cathedral, Orvieto

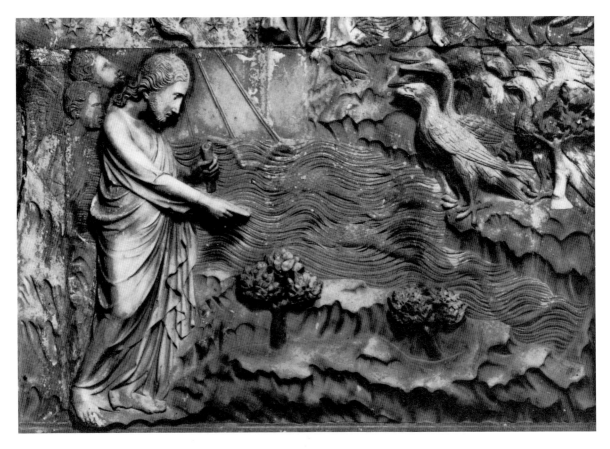

111. LORENZO MAITANI. Creation of the Birds and Fishes,
detail of fig. 110

and he probably also created the general design of all four. In 1263 the bloodstained corporal (Eucharistic cloth), the relic of the miraculous Mass of Bolsena (see p. 510), was carried to Orvieto for presentation to Pope Urban IV, then in temporary residence there. In 1264 the pope proclaimed the Feast of Corpus Christi from Orvieto. A vast cathedral was built to enshrine the relic, and in 1310 the Sienese architect and sculptor Lorenzo Maitani, about whom we know little except the dates of his marriage in 1302 and death in 1330, was named *capomaestro*. One of his responsibilities was the "wall figured with beauty, which wall must be made on the front part," clearly the four reliefs, each over thirty feet high. One of Maitani's drawings for the façade survives. The leading position he holds in the documents has caused him to be identified with the most gifted of the sculptors at work on the panels, the upper portions of which, here and there, are still unfinished.

The reliefs represent the story of Adam and Eve (figs. 110, 111), the Life of Christ, the Tree of Jesse, and the Last Judgment (fig. 112). The first and last reliefs display the vision of an artist who could create images of exquisite poetry and of the utmost horror. Unlike fresco, the work proceeded from the bottom up, as the façade rose. From the start Maitani and his collaborators dispensed with the customary enframements and composed the scenes in continuous strips, like those on the ancient Roman columns of Trajan and of Marcus Aurelius, and with figures as closely packed as in the work of the Pisani. But in the second row a change takes place: in the center of each relief sprouts an immense vine, whose branches and tendrils form growing supports and frames for the scenes. In the two central panels the vine is an acanthus, as in Roman medieval apse mosaics, and the scrolls curl tightly. But the branches of the vines in the right and left panels are more widely separated, leaving airy spaces above and around the figures. On the left the vine is ivy—the plant from which ancient victors' wreaths were formed (an odd accompaniment to the Creation story)—but on the right it is the grapevine, recalling the Eucharistic miracle of Bolsena.

The Creation scenes are imaginative (fig. 111). God

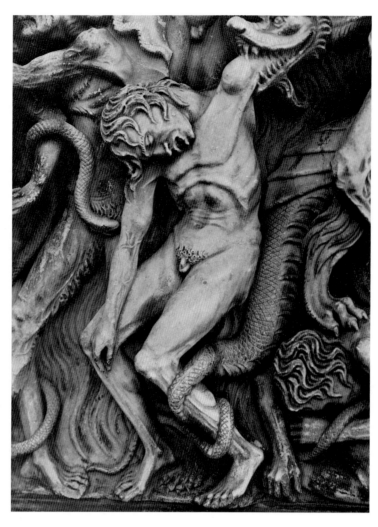

112. LORENZO MAITANI. Detail of the Damned in Hell
from the *Last Judgment*. c. 1310–30. Marble. Façade, Cathedral, Orvieto

moves with grace across the primal rocks, calling the fish to life in the swirls of marble water and the birds to attention in miniature forests. Maitani—if indeed this is he—has taken a tremendous step, in a direction not to be fully exploited until Donatello and Ghiberti, by lowering the projection of distant figures and birds to a fraction of an inch above the background elements, in contrast to the almost freestanding, heavily undercut foreground figures. The airy movements and diaphanous

mantle of God the Creator, moving among his works, hardly prepare us for the shock of Maitani's view of Hell. Here, barely above eye level (fig. 112), the tormented figure of one of the damned hangs by his arm from the jaws of a demon—a pose so compelling that, as the author noted to his astonishment many years ago, it impressed Michelangelo, who transfigured it in his dead Christ in the Florentine *Pietà* (see fig. 689).

5

Later Gothic Art in Tuscany and Northern Italy

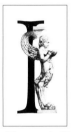n the first half of the Trecento, the masters of Florence and Siena, especially the painters, created a new art that revolutionized the vision of Western Europe and that seems to lead toward the Early Renaissance—some of whose major discoveries, indeed, Trecento artists in large measure anticipated. Without Giotto, Nicola and Giovanni Pisano, and Ambrogio Lorenzetti, the work of such leaders of the Early Renaissance as Donatello, Ghiberti, and Masaccio would be hard to imagine. Yet the history of art, like that of humanity itself, avoids straight lines and is seldom predictable. In some ways, the art of the second half of the Trecento seems like a renunciation of the achievements of the first half and to have little to do with the Renaissance that followed; thus it is often passed over with a few perfunctory phrases. Nonetheless, during this period artists produced works of striking originality and expressive depth.

For both Florence and Siena, the 1330s and 1340s were decades of calamities of increasing intensity. In Florence the flood of 1333, exceeded in height only by that of 1966, struck the city with such violence that it tore down six hundred feet of city walls and towers along the Arno and brought havoc to commerce, buildings, and, doubtless, works of art. Costly and frustrating military activities and a succession of political and economic crises were followed in the mid-1340s by the failures of the Peruzzi and Bardi banks, chiefly due to the bankruptcy of their English branches, which were involved in the military adventures of King Edward III. Soon every major banking house in Florence and Siena was drawn into ruin, with serious consequences for economic and cultural life. A brief experiment with dictatorship under the duke of Athens in 1342–43 did little to help, and agricultural disasters during 1346 and 1347 brought widespread famine.

The weakened and demoralized populations of Florence and Siena were in no position to resist when in 1348 the bubonic plague—the so-called Black Death, which had already caused heavy mortality in 1340—struck again with unbelievable intensity. There is no accurate way of measuring the human toll; estimates vary from fifty percent mortality in both cities to seventy-five or even eighty percent of the population, all swept away in one hot, terrible summer. Chronicles written by the survivors present a horrifying picture of streets piled high with rotting corpses, bodies stacked in immense ditches, complete economic stasis, runaway inflation, and general terror. The work force was decimated, and the effects on every aspect of culture were devastating.

The artists suffered as bitterly as anyone else. Bernardo Daddi, Andrea Pisano, and probably Pietro and Ambrogio Lorenzetti died in the plague. Only Taddeo Gaddi survived to carry the tradition of Giotto into the second half of the century. The demands for works of art seem also to have changed radically. In the general wave of self-castigation that follows catastrophe, religion offered an explanation in terms of divine wrath, as well as a refuge from the consequences of that wrath. The ground was prepared for a new style that turned toward the supernatural and the Italo-Byzantine past, rejecting as perilous the humanity and naturalism of the early Trecento.

MID-TRECENTO PAINTING IN FLORENCE

Both the neomedievalism of the mid-Trecento and the more positive qualities of the period are visible in an altarpiece painted by Andrea Orcagna (active c. 1343–68) for the Strozzi Chapel in the Dominican Church of Santa Maria Novella in Florence (colorplate 33, p. 119). Although at first glance the elements of Giotto's style seem still to be present, this picture soon discloses that most of what Giotto and his contemporaries had tried to build up has been abandoned. Within the discordant rhythms of the frame, the figures seem locked in a predetermined pattern that suggests stasis and denies the mobility of early Trecento figures. In the center Christ is frontally enthroned, staring ahead, but no throne is visible. He appears as an apparition in a mandorla bordered by seraphim. Without looking at either of the kneeling saints, Christ hands the keys to St. Peter, the Rock on whom the Church was founded, and presents a book to St. Thomas Aquinas, one of the most important Dominican saints and patron of the donor, Tommaso Strozzi. Behind these symbols of ecclesiastical authority stand Mary, patron of the church, and St. John the Baptist, patron of Florence. Space is not clear, and instead of a receding ground we find a gold-figured carpet that is parallel to the picture plane.

The humanity and naturalism of the early Trecento

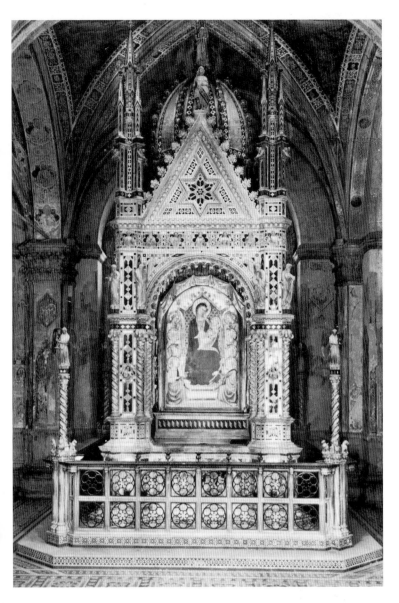

113. ANDREA ORCAGNA. Tabernacle. Probably begun 1355;
finished 1359. Marble, mosaic, gold, lapis lazuli.
🏛 Orsanmichele, Florence. (*Madonna and Child Enthroned*
by BERNARDO DADDI, 1347; see fig. 81.) Commissioned
by the Compagnia di Orsanmichele

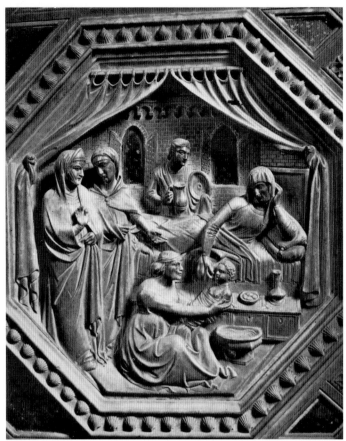

114. ANDREA ORCAGNA. *Birth of the Virgin*,
detail of fig. 113. Marble on mosaic background.
🏛 Orsanmichele, Florence

have been replaced by the authority of doctrine and the
immediacy of religious vision. The pyramid of the central group is abutted in the lateral panels by pairs of
standing figures crammed into spaces that seem too
small to hold them. The arrangement is ostensibly symmetrical: the saints holding swords guard the flanks (St.
Michael and St. Paul), those with tiered instruments of
martyrdom (St. Catherine and St. Lawrence) stand next
to them. But asymmetries appear: on the right side, the
saints turn their heads toward each other in conversation; on the left, St. Catherine looks inward, St. Michael out toward the spectator. The heads, still within
the general repertory of Giottesque forms, show nonetheless a wholly un-Giottesque tension of expression
and form and a sharp concentration on linear detail.
Christ stares outward with the impersonality of a Duecento Pantocrator (All-Ruler; see fig. 18). Frowns puck-
er the foreheads of the older saints: St. Peter, looking

fixedly at Christ with an expression of deep emotion, is
drawn with a typical thirteenth-century insistence on
every line of the intricately curled beard and waved,
crisply cut hair. A hint of Duecento compartmentalism
reappears in the armor-plate divisions of the hair and
the sharply demarcated structure of the features and
neck. St. John the Baptist, his locks of hair writhing like
flames, looks outward and partly upward with an expression of mystic exaltation. Only the female or youthful
faces are calm. Thomas Aquinas's face is so distinctive that
it seems to be a portrait of a living individual. Throughout the composition the flowing drapery rhythms of the
early Trecento are replaced by harsh and complex shapes.

Two predella scenes depict St. Thomas Aquinas in
ecstasy during the celebration of Mass and Christ walking on the water to save Peter. These are directly related
to the saints above. The third scene, the saving of the
soul of the emperor Henry II, is unexpected and unrelated to any figure above. According to the story preserved in the *Golden Legend*, Henry II's soul hung in the
balance until he made a gift of a golden chalice to the
Cathedral of Bamberg. Presumably Tommaso Strozzi
expected his gift of this altarpiece to determine matters
in his own favor at a similar moment, which occurred a
few years later.

Orcagna joined the Arte di Pietra e Legname in 1352
and in 1355 was made *capomaestro* of Orsanmichele.
Probably in that very year he began a fantastic taberna-

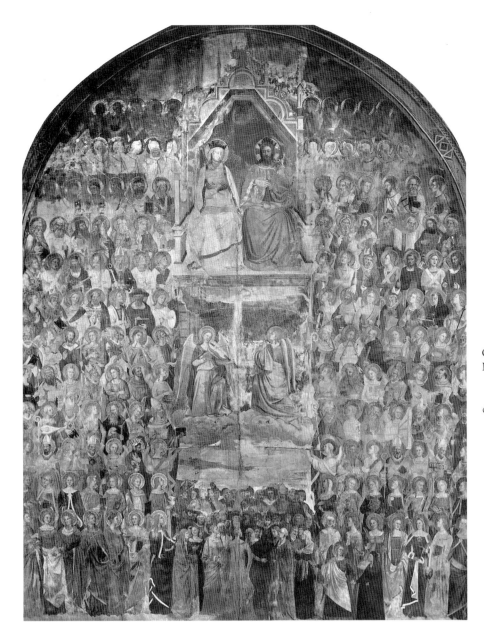

115. NARDO
DI CIONE.
Paradise. 1350s.
Fresco. Strozzi
Chapel, Sta. Maria
Novella, Florence.
Commissioned
by Tommaso
di Rossello Strozzi

cle (fig. 113) to enshrine Daddi's huge *Madonna and Child Enthroned* (see fig. 81), for which money was collected in 1348, just after the passage of the Black Death. The work is overwhelming in size and magnificence. Its pinnacles nearly touch the vault, and its white marble is encrusted with mosaic ornament in blue, gold, and patterned glass. The transformation in style in only twenty years can be illustrated by a comparison between the lucidity of Giotto's design for the Campanile of the Cathedral of Florence (see fig. 76) and the complexity of this structure. The dome may be Orcagna's documented entry in the contest for that of the Cathedral, as we suspect is the case with the dome portrayed in a fresco by Andrea da Firenze (see colorplate 34, p. 120); in 1357 Orcagna submitted models for the piers of the Cathedral, but he was passed over in favor of Francesco Talenti. The smaller scenes in relief, especially the *Birth of the Virgin* (fig. 114), should be compared with Cavallini's mosaic of the same subject (see fig. 35). Here the floor is tilted and the bed curtains parted like those of a stage to display every detail—the midwife admiring the swaddled child, the background figure with the in-

evitable pitcher in one hand and in the other a tray (similar to one customarily given to a Florentine mother after the birth of a male child), the bedroom walls of unplastered masonry, the open *imposte* (inner, solid shutters, still used in Italy and a necessity in the era before window glass) with even their nailheads showing—down to the keyholes in the linen chest, which formed the pedestal of an Italian bed of the period (see figs. 96, 208). All this represents as sharp a departure from the ordered reliefs of Andrea Pisano as do Orcagna's dissonant drapery rhythms from the harmonious ones of Giotto.

Orcagna, whose real name was Andrea di Cione, was one of three brothers (Andrea, Nardo, Jacopo) whose studios dominated much of the painting of the third quarter of the Trecento in Florence. Nardo di Cione (active c. 1343–66) produced the *Last Judgment with Paradise and Hell* that fills the walls of the Strozzi Chapel, where Orcagna's painting is the altarpiece. The Last Judgment is shown on the window wall, behind the altarpiece, and the side walls are given over to panoramic representations of Paradise and Hell. *Paradise* (fig. 115) contains many beautiful individual heads, but it is hardly

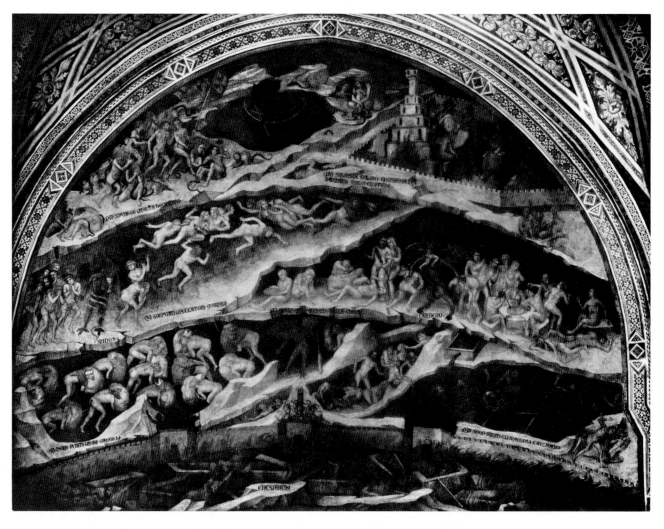

116. NARDO DI CIONE. *Hell* (portion). 1350s. Fresco. Strozzi Chapel, Sta. Maria Novella, Florence

more than a mass of costumed figures, row on row as if in church. But *Hell* (fig. 116) is the first attempt at an encyclopedic illustration of the punishments described by Dante in the *Inferno*. The explicit and detailed representation of these torments in separate circles may be another sign of the times.

Nardo's Washington triptych (see colorplate 17, p. 57) is typical of the small-scale folding paintings used to aid private devotions in the Trecento and may well have been painted in a happier period. Here the influence of Bernardo Daddi is evident in the delicacy of execution and detail and also in the square-jawed, large-eyed facial type. There is a softness and dreaminess about Nardo's people that are not found in the works of other painters, save the imitators who made of Nardo's art a graceful countercurrent to the *terribilità* of his brother.

A fascinating figure in the complex picture of the third quarter of the Trecento in Florence is Andrea Bonaiuti, known as Andrea da Firenze (active c. 1343–77). Relatively little of his work survives save for a vast fresco cycle in the chapter house at Santa Maria Novella, which is now misleadingly known as the Spanish Chapel because of its later use by the Spanish community in Florence. Andrea converted the whole interior into an allegorical diorama surpassing in scale even the *Government* frescoes by Ambrogio Lorenzetti. Now, however, the theme is ecclesiastical rather than secular government, and it was clearly the intent of the patron, a wealthy merchant, and of the Dominican monks to emphasize the role of the Dominican Order in establishing a new ecclesiastical orthodoxy. All the frescoes make reference to the sacred origins and supreme power of the Church in general, and the importance of the Dominican Order in particular. The most unusual is the scene known as the *Triumph of the Church* (colorplate 34, p. 120).

This fresco covers one entire wall of the chapel. The lower part is concerned with religious life on earth, the upper part with Heaven, and the area between the two seems to be controlled by the Dominican Order. In the lower left a detailed representation of the Duomo of Florence, then incomplete and never to be finished according to this plan, refers to the Church on earth—a reminder, perhaps, that when the money was donated

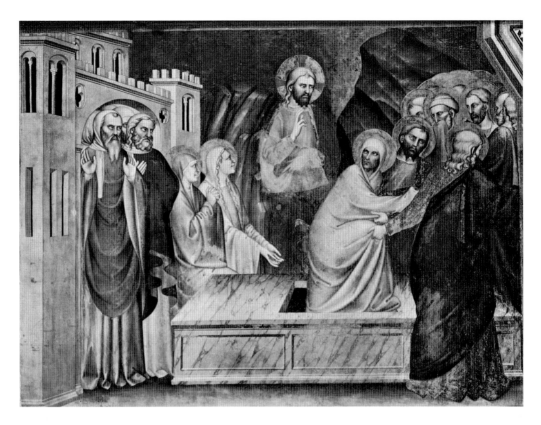

117. GIOVANNI
DA MILANO.
*Resurrection
of Lazarus.* 1365.
Fresco. Rinuccini
Chapel, Sta.
Croce, Florence.
Probably
commissioned
by Lapo di Lizio
Guidalotti

for the frescoes the archbishop of Florence was a Dominican, and that Andrea da Firenze himself was one of the consulting architects for the Duomo. The reigning pope, Urban V, is enthroned in the center of this section, with a cardinal and a bishop on his right, Emperor Charles IV and the King of Cyprus on his left. The sheep at his feet, symbolizing the Christian flock, are guarded by black-and-white dogs—the *domini canes* (Dominicans, "dogs of the Lord")—and a crowd of ecclesiastical and secular figures gathers before the thrones.

On the right-hand side is the world outside the fortress of the Church, where black-and-white dogs attack wolves and Dominican saints admonish heretics and refute pagans. Above these groups, worldly figures are dancing in the fields, making music, and embracing in the bushes. From this blind alley, humanity can be rescued only by the sacrament of Penance, administered by a Dominican, while another Dominican saint then shows humanity the way to Heaven. Before the splendid gates, opened by a somewhat reluctant St. Peter, angels crown the little souls, who then disappear; Heaven, it seems, is the exclusive province of rejoicing saints, all drawn to a much larger scale. Only the saints in Heaven can behold Christ who, with book and key as in Orcagna's Strozzi altarpiece, floats far above in his mandorla-shaped glory; below him the apocalyptic Lamb on his altar-throne is guarded by symbols of the four evangelists, and angelic attendants praise God.

While Andrea da Firenze seems disinterested in the naturalism that delighted us in the frescoes of Ambrogio Lorenzetti, he relies on the same vast visual sweep as Ambrogio. His detailed landscape moves past distant ranges to culminate in castles and a little chapel. The foliage, however, is represented entirely according to formula, without any of the delicate observations and sketchy brushwork of Ambrogio. The landscapes of the Spanish Chapel were imitated into the early Quattrocento in Florence, when they were gradually supplanted by the new visual realism of the Early Renaissance. The space represented in the landscape is curiously negated by the composition and the coloring, which produce an effect of all-over patterning. The colors, although often bright and clear, run to grayish reds, harsh oranges and greens, and unusual and not easily definable intermediate tones, rather than to the primary and secondary colors that often dominate Giottesque schemes. Andrea has a keen eye for unusual facial types, but his figures sometimes appear flat and wooden.

Giovanni da Milano (active 1346–66), an outsider from Lombardy working in Florence in the middle of the Trecento, began a splendid series of frescoes in the Rinuccini Chapel in the sacristy of Santa Croce in 1365. In the *Resurrection of Lazarus* (fig. 117), Giottesque space is denied, as are the dignity and physical beauty of early Trecento figures. Scowling bystanders, who emerge from a city gate that is tiny even by Trecento pictorial standards, look on with Giovanni's characteristic feral expressions. Christ looks powerless, devoid of the handsome features given him by the Gothic tradition, and Lazarus seems to be hustled out of the tomb. Giovanni da Milano's *Pietà* (fig. 118), which shows the dead Christ upheld by the Virgin, Magdalen, and St.

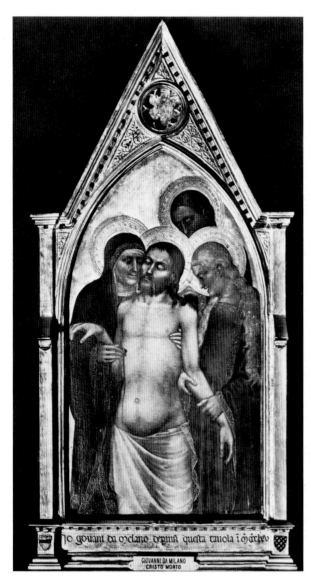

118. GIOVANNI DA MILANO. *Pietà*. 1365.
Panel, 43¼ x 18⅛". Accademia, Florence

Martini and to have died in a fall from scaffolding. To him is traditionally attributed a frescoed Life of Christ on the right side aisle wall of the Collegiate Church at San Gimignano. It is generally dated between 1350 and 1355, although there is little evidence to support this. Here the Passion scenes are rendered with a new emotional immediacy. The *Pact of Judas* (fig. 119) represents the moment when the high priests give Judas thirty pieces of silver to betray Christ, and while this composition recalls earlier compositions of this subject, the incident is converted into a rite of diabolical perversity. The architecture soars above the figures and reaches outward to embrace the spectator, while Judas and the priests are drawn together into a huddle so that their heads seem to form a human arch.

In all the Passion scenes Christ is alone, but never more so than in the *Betrayal* (fig. 120). Even Judas's treachery seems scarcely more contemptible than Peter's mayhem on Malchus in the foreground, which fills one-third of the scene—or the cowardice of the other apostles, who abandon Christ to his fate. Even St. John gathers his cloak about him and darts a look of terror over his shoulder as he scurries away. Christ is abandoned to an avalanche of steel. His quiet face resists Judas's glare although he is cut off from the outside world by helmets, spears, and shields. The artist retains Simone's crisp linearism and idiosyncrasies of facial construction, but he uses these for new expressive purposes. In greater measure than perhaps any other master of his time, Barna reflects the tragic tensions of the Tuscan environment after the Black Death.

Another work of capital importance because of the subject and the spectacular scale and position of the work is the series of frescoes that includes the *Triumph of Death* and the *Last Judgment* that decorated the cemetery known as the Camposanto ("holy field," so called because it contained earth brought from the Holy Land) at Pisa. Scholars are not in agreement on the authorship of the cycle; the traditional attribution is to the Pisan painter Francesco Traini (active c. 1321–63). The *Triumph of Death* (fig. 121) reflects the panoramic schemes of Ambrogio Lorenzetti. At the lower left (fig. 122) is shown the traditional meeting of the three living and the three dead. While hunting, three splendidly dressed noblemen and their friends and attendants come upon three open coffins, each occupied by a corpse, one still bloated, the next half-rotted, the third reduced to a skeleton. Worms and serpents play over all three; one of the noblemen holds his nose at the stench, and even the horses and hunting dogs sniff and draw back in disgust. To the right young men and women sit in a grove playing music, caressing pets and each other, and paying no heed to the approach of Death, a terrifying white-haired hag flying toward them on bat wings and brandishing the huge scythe with which she will cut them down.

In the center is a heap of Death's recent victims, all richly dressed, while above demons carry off their helpless souls. The escape from this horror, apparently, is to

John, is one of the earliest representations of this subject painted in Florence. Its expressive depth is typical of the contemporary interest in a harrowing representation of the sacrifice of Christ. His body is held up by the grieving figures to remind the observer of the suffering Christ endured for humanity. The face of the dead Christ is haunting in its intensity.

MID-TRECENTO PAINTING IN SIENA AND PISA

Although Siena produced a number of painters in the third quarter of the Trecento, none are as interesting as the masters of the first four decades of the century. Only the works of an artist traditionally known as Barna da Siena can compete with Giovanni da Milano in depth and intensity. We know little about Barna—not a single date—but he is assumed to have been a pupil of Simone

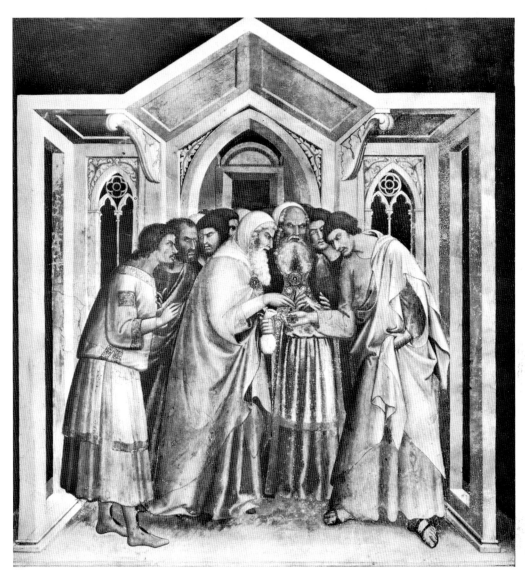

119. BARNA DA SIENA(?). *Pact of Judas*. 1350s(?). Fresco, 8' 6" x 7' 9".
Collegiate Church, San Gimignano

be sought in the life of hermits in the wilderness, where they read, work, and contemplate on rocky heights, fed by milk furnished by a doe. The accompanying *Last Judgment* (fig. 123) shows a regally crowned Christ acting as the condemning judge, with no concern for salvation. Christ, seated in a mandorla, uses his left hand to display the wound in his side; Mary, raised to new pre-eminence in a twin mandorla, puts her hand to her chest and shrinks back in fear. A tempest of emotion sweeps both the terrified damned, expelled by archangels armed with huge swords, and the blessed, even the apostles. Earth is reduced to one great tomb of square holes from which the dead arise. Recent research has shown that these frescoes were painted not after, but before, the Black Death of 1348, but it should be recalled that the plague had already struck in 1340. These, like the other mural paintings of the Pisa Camposanto, were irreparably damaged during World War II and al-

though much was saved by prompt conservation efforts after the liberation of Pisa, the frescoes are only pale reflections of what prewar visitors remember.

LATE TRECENTO ART

In the last quarter of the Trecento, no new figures of the first rank emerge in the other arts, either in Florence or Siena. Government by committee was the order of the day in both centers, as a method of forestalling either dictatorship or revolution, though the personnel of any given committee might often rotate. Applied to artistic projects, the result of this patronage was a leveling process that stressed conformity at the expense of individuality. Accomplished painters and sculptors flourished, but their works, when compared with those of the Cione brothers, Giovanni da Milano, and Barna da Siena, not to mention the masters of the earlier Tre-

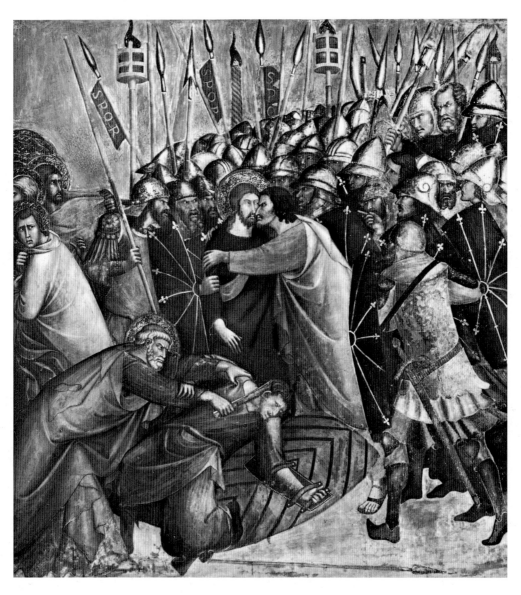

120. Barna da Siena(?). *Betrayal*. 1350s(?). Fresco, 8' 6" x 7' 9".
Collegiate Church, San Gimignano

cento, present a parade of craftsmanly skill rather than imaginative freshness or continuing sensitivity to the visual world. In this bureaucratic society, which held oligarchical control over all activities of the state, the most characteristic painter in Florence was Agnolo Gaddi (active c. 1369–96), the son of Taddeo Gaddi and the artist whose precepts appear to be recorded in Cennino Cennini's book. In some ways Agnolo's artistic role, even his pictorial style, could be compared to that of Domenico del Ghirlandaio in the late Quattrocento, or of Vasari in the late Cinquecento. Agnolo was far from being a revolutionary artist, but he had at his fingertips the resources of Trecento tradition; he could fuse his Giottesque inheritance with the compositional and expressive devices of the mid-century artists.

Agnolo's principal work, for which he must have needed a number of assistants, is a vast fresco cycle of the Legend of the True Cross for the Church of Santa Croce at Florence. On the huge walls of the choir (see figs. 52, 53), Agnolo composed and narrated on a gigantic scale. The story is told in four superimposed registers, and within each composition two or three separate episodes may take place side by side, sometimes almost overlapping. Landscape or architectural elements serve as dividers, in a manner reminiscent of the packed compositions of Nicola and Giovanni Pisano a century or so earlier. It has been claimed that the juxtapositions of large and small, near and distant, in scenes such as the *Triumph of Heraclius over Chosroes* (fig. 124) indicate Agnolo's denial or even ignorance of pictorial space, but these are conventions that enable him to narrate all parts of the complex story with equal visibility and to preserve the decorative unity of the wall.

A dispassionate observer in the choir of Santa Croce must acknowledge the decorative beauty of Agnolo's fresh, clear color and the manner in which his surfaces,

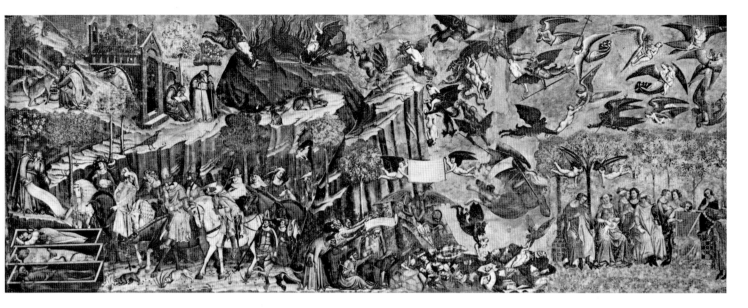

121. Francesco Traini (?). *Triumph of Death*. Mid–14th century.
Fresco, 18' 6" x 49' 2". Camposanto, Pisa

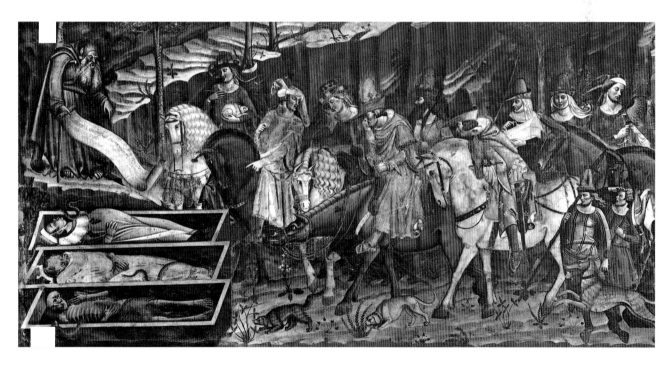

122. Detail of fig. 121

treated almost like tapestry, maintain the integrity of the building. In those scenes that did not have to contain more than one incident, Agnolo showed his mastery of spatial recession and even in the landscape dividers of the *Chosroes* scene, he utilizes many suggestions of depth. Agnolo's landscape devices, drapery forms, and compositional methods seem to have determined the representation of such elements in Florentine painting until Gentile da Fabriano and Masaccio arrived on the scene. A lively pen-and-wash drawing attributed to Agnolo is

probably the earliest Italian drawing from life preserved to us (see fig. 10), and it seems to have been made in preparation for some of the heads that crowd the frescoes in this series. One bareheaded young man is shown slightly foreshortened from below as he looks upward. The others wear the customary Florentine *cappuccio*; one bends over as he writes or perhaps draws; the other three are seen in variants of profile view, including the one-quarter aspect that appears often in Giotto's frescoes. At the top of the drawing a lamb's head is provid-

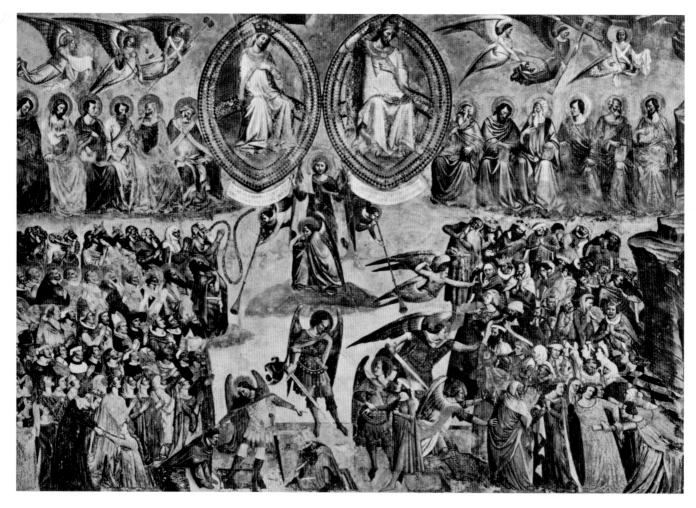

123. FRANCESCO TRAINI(?). *Last Judgment*. Mid–14th century. Fresco, 19' 8" x 28' 3". Camposanto, Pisa

ed with the word *agnolo*, which can mean "angel" or "lamb" but which in this context could also be a signature or a notation of authorship by a later owner.

The Late Gothic style of Agnolo and his followers and contemporaries remains, at least in quantity of production, the dominant pictorial style in Florence well into the Quattrocento: it was what patrons wanted, and what the painters gave them, for an industrious half century or so. Among the host of competent practitioners of the craft of painting in this final phase of the Gothic style in Florence, a single artist stands out who is known to us today as Lorenzo Monaco (Lawrence the Monk). Lorenzo was probably born in the mid-1370s and he died (or ceased working) in 1423 or 1424. His early works are influenced by Agnolo Gaddi in their color, drapery rhythms, and landscape motifs.

But the sudden burst of linear patterning in the attenuated poses and sweeping curves of drapery betrays the arrival on the scene of a new factor, the fantastic, gorgeous style known to scholars as the International Gothic because it flourished over all of Northern Europe, from London to Prague. As far as Tuscan art is concerned, the term "international" is somewhat of a

misnomer. It is often difficult to tell what center, in some cases even what country, some Northern pictures of this style actually come from. This is not the case with Tuscan paintings, for the clarity of Tuscan forms and the firmness of Tuscan statement always prevail over the most exuberant Gothic movement. The dominant influence in Lorenzo Monaco's mature style is that of the sculptor Lorenzo Ghiberti, which explains the vigorous sculptural quality of the flowing drapery folds. These resemble the drapery folds in Ghiberti's contemporary sculpture and those in some works by Ghiberti's rival, Nanni di Banco, and are also related to certain aspects of the art of the most revolutionary artist of the Quattrocento, Donatello.

But to place Lorenzo Monaco in the next chapter would ignore one factor: the first masters of the new style of the Early Renaissance were concerned with naturalism, basing their art on observation, and this to Lorenzo Monaco meant very little. It is not easy to reconstruct his environment. We know that he joined the Camaldolite Order at Santa Maria degli Angeli in Florence in 1390, rising to the rank of deacon in 1396. Yet by 1402 he was enrolled in the Arte dei Medici e Spe-

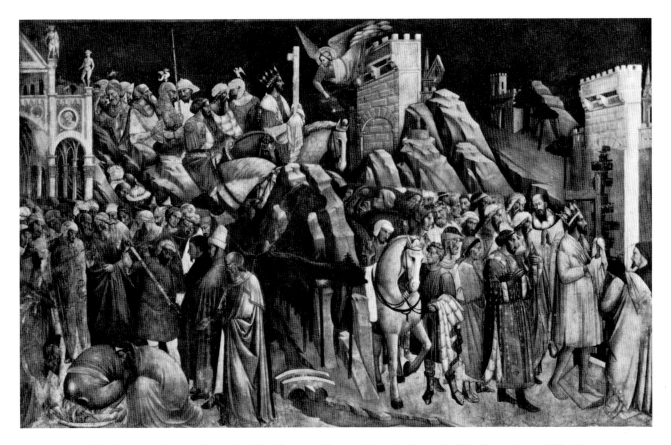

124. AGNOLO GADDI. *Triumph of Heraclius over Chosroes*, from the Legend of the True Cross. 1388–93. Fresco. Sta. Croce, Florence. Commissioned by Benedetto di Nerozzo degli Alberti

ziali under his lay name, Piero di Giovanni, and was living outside the monastery. Apparently he retained his habit and monastic status while painting a splendid array of altarpieces, frescoes, and illuminated manuscripts.

The Camaldolite Order was the most mystical of the Tuscan religious communities, and this mysticism received expression in Lorenzo's altarpiece, the *Coronation of the Virgin*, which is dated February 1414 (1413 in the Florentine calendar, since their year began on March 25) for the high altar of Santa Maria degli Angeli (colorplate 35, p. 201). In the central panel all divisions are swept aside by the onrushing tide of colors and forms. We are lifted into the empyrean, above the dome of the heavens, which we see in cross section, its component arches shaded in tones of piercing blue and studded with golden stars. At the apex of the heavenly vault stands a Gothic tabernacle culminating in a dome on a drum that is reminiscent of Orcagna's shrine at Orsanmichele (see fig. 113). On a double throne in front of the tabernacle Christ turns to place a crown on the head of his mother. In the central gable God the Father, appearing on clouds flanked by seraphim, confers his blessing on the scene, while in the lateral gables are represented Gabriel, flying against the gold background and trailing clouds, and the seated Mary.

For all their solidity as abstract shapes, the figures seem essentially bodiless; it is the crispness of the metal-

lic contours and the power of line and shading that achieve the strong, sculptural effect. The dazzling color composition is based on a splendid bouquet of blues—the dome of the heavens, the blue clouds, and blue shadows, not to speak of Christ's azure mantle—in combination with the gold background and the unexpected, dazzling whites of the mantles. Far below, at the springing points of the outermost arches, kneel St. Benedict, of whose order the Camaldolites were a branch, and St. Romuald, founder of the Camaldolite community. Mary seems to have honored the Benedictine Order by adopting its white for her mantle, instead of the traditional blue. These whites are anything but inert: a rainbow of colors from the surrounding saints and angels is reflected into their shadows, and even the lights are often picked out in glowing yellow. Rainbow-winged angels swing censers below the throne, but the angelic organist in the center was, unfortunately, cut away at a later period to accommodate a tabernacle for the Eucharist. How the composition of such altarpieces as this took shape can be followed in a vivid pen sketch (see fig. 9) probably done in preparation for a similar altarpiece now in London. The rhythmic surge from figure to figure takes shape with the first rapid strokes of the quill pen, breaking into ripples as the folds and borders of individual tunics and mantles are defined.

The exalted mood in the central panel of the *Coro-*

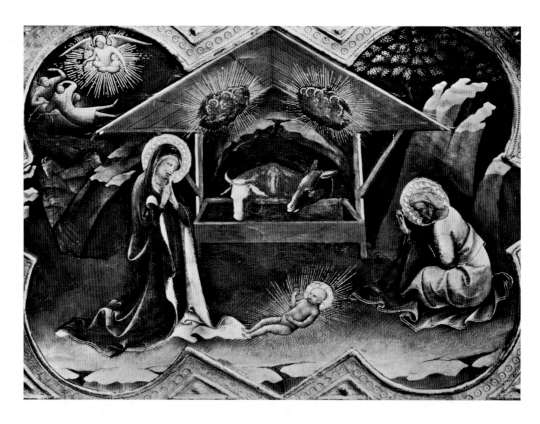

125. LORENZO MONACO. *Nativity*, on the predella of the *Coronation of the Virgin* (see colorplate 35, p. 201). 1414. Panel, 12½ x 21". Uffizi Gallery, Florence. Commissioned for the high altar of Sta. Maria degli Angeli, Florence

nation is sustained, if in a lower key, in the predellas below, especially in the *Nativity* (fig. 125). While Lorenzo has adopted for these predella panels the French Gothic quatrefoil shape used by Giotto and Andrea Pisano (see colorplate 24, p. 63; fig. 86), it is symptomatic of the new freedom of Lorenzo's style that he has transformed it into a rectangle. The *Nativity* is based partly on the writings of St. Bridget, a fourteenth-century Swedish princess who, during a visit to Bethlehem, had a vision of the Nativity while in the cave that traditionally marks the site. Bridget was canonized in Florence in 1420–22 by Pope Martin V. Not everything in her vision is taken up by Lorenzo, but the principal elements that he represents led to a new version of the Nativity in the art of the Quattrocento—the Adoration of the Child (see figs. 221, 290, 318, 394, 423). Mary kneels to worship her Child, who lies naked before her on the floor of the cave, shining with golden rays. Lorenzo has added to the cave of St. Bridget's vision the shed from Western tradition, matching its shape to the angles of the quatrefoil. In the dark night outside, a luminous angel awakens the shepherds.

This and Lorenzo Monaco's other works represent a glorious, last flowering of the Gothic style in Florence. How strongly his luminary display in the predella panel differs from the treatment of the same scene by Gentile da Fabriano nine years later (see fig. 185), and how much less real it seems than the rendering of supernatural light by Giotto in the Arena Chapel (see figs. 59, 60)! Lorenzo Monaco's visual poetry is essentially imaginative and unreal; the crucial developments of the early Quattrocento, on the other hand, were based on a new

evaluation of the reality of day-to-day experience and of the human beings who experience it.

ARCHITECTURE

The major architectural monument of the period, the Cathedral of Florence (figs. 126, 127), had been commenced in 1296 by Arnolfo di Cambio to replace the Church of Santa Reparata, but work came practically to a standstill after Arnolfo's death in 1302. The work continued sporadically under Giotto, who began the Campanile, and Andrea Pisano, who designed its second and third stories (see fig. 77). After the Black Death, however, the project for the Cathedral underwent modification. During the 1350s, Francesco Talenti completed the Campanile, changing the design yet again. A comparison with Giotto's design (see fig. 76) will show how Talenti adapted Giotto's French Gothic windows to the taste of the late Trecento. Talenti is only one of the personalities involved in the complex picture of group activity at the Cathedral. In 1355 a commission was appointed; its personnel was to change, but it included the painters Taddeo Gaddi, Orcagna, and Andrea da Firenze, as well as well-known sculptors and prominent citizens. Model after model for the church and its details was submitted to the commission and accepted or rejected; somehow the work went on, although rejected ideas kept reappearing.

One of these may well be the design recorded in Andrea da Firenze's fresco of the *Triumph of the Church* (see colorplate 34, p. 120). It is not clear how much, if any, of Arnolfo's original design was kept, and how

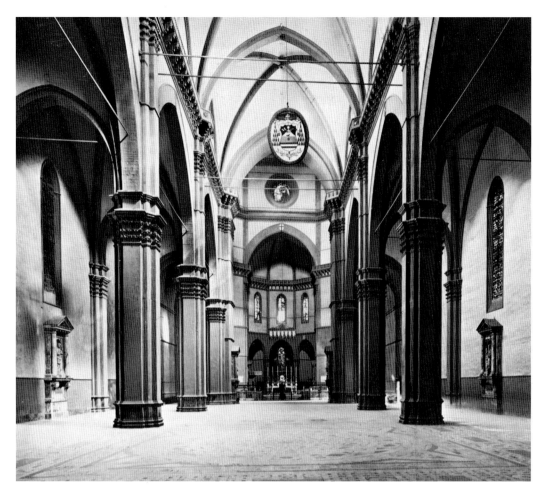

126. Nave and choir, Cathedral, Florence. Begun by Arnolfo di Cambio, 1296; present appearance due to Francesco Talenti and others

much of the present Duomo can be attributed to the documented activity there of Francesco Talenti, Fra Jacopo Talenti (no relation), Simone Talenti (Francesco's son), and the painters. A definitive project embodying the piers and cornice designed by Francesco Talenti was adopted by the commission in 1364 and embodied in a model constructed after the final decisions of 1367 on the designs of Neri di Fioravante. The commission ordered the destruction of all competing designs and models and absolute adherence to the official project. This included the commission's requirement that the bracketed cornice above the nave arcade be kept as close as possible to the arches and that the vault rise directly from the cornice, effectively eliminating a pointed clerestory, for which oculi were substituted. The plan was a striking compromise between a central plan and a Latin cross. Three polygonal apses, each with five radiating chapels, surround the octagonal dome, under which the high altar was placed. On the outside, these tribunes culminate in semidomes intended to buttress the central dome, but at the time no one had the faintest notion how the great dome itself could be constructed.

The interior of the Cathedral consists of a nave composed of four huge bays, its lofty arches opening onto

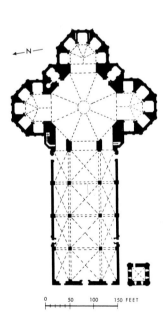

127. Plan of Cathedral and Campanile, Florence

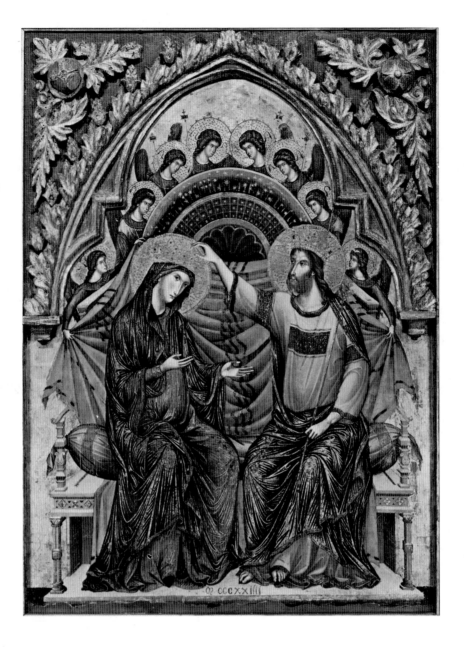

128. PAOLO
VENEZIANO.
*Coronation of the
Virgin.* 1324.
Panel, 39 x 30½".
National Gallery
of Art, Washington,
D.C. (Kress
Collection)

side aisles half the width of the nave. The nave leads to the octagon of the dome and provides the principal entrance to this majestic, centralized space. The building was planned so that vast crowds could move from one area to the next without disturbing ceremonies at the high altar or in the fifteen surrounding chapels. The plan has a masterly simplicity and utility and, at times, great beauty.

PAINTING AND SCULPTURE IN NORTHERN ITALY

In the Late Middle Ages and the Early Renaissance, the political life of northern Italy was dominated by the relations between the two major city-states of Venice and Milan and such smaller centers as Mantua, Ferrara, Padua, and Brescia, whose communal governments had, at varying moments, been taken over by princes, founders of hereditary dynasties. Milan, near the north-

ern edge of the Lombard plain, controlled trade routes to Northern Europe. Once the capital of the Western Roman Empire, it became a flourishing commercial center. Its territory, however, was landlocked until the expansionist attempts of Duke Giangaleazzo Visconti gained temporary control of Pisa in the opening years of the Quattrocento. The opposition to Milanese imperialism, aimed at domination of the Italian peninsula, came from Florence and was eventually successful. Florence found its only ally in republican Venice, whose outburst of independent artistic activity began in the middle of the Quattrocento and continued throughout the Cinquecento.

THE VENETIAN REPUBLIC. The existence of Venice is one of the miracles of history. The city was founded in the fifth and sixth centuries on marshy islets of the Adriatic by refugees from the Roman cities of the Po Valley who were fleeing the barbarian invasions. Deprived of their territory and homes, these remnants of a formerly great culture learned to think of the sea as their sole resource and protection and of continental Italy, at their backs, as essentially hostile. The Venetian Republic, an oligarchy with an elected duke (*doge*, in Venetian dialect), became the only state in Western Europe that survived from antiquity into modern times without revolution, invasion, or conquest: from the last years of the Roman Empire it endured until Napoleon abolished it in 1792. Venice was, moreover, the only Italian state to achieve an empire, but it was a peculiar sort of empire. For many centuries the Venetians disliked and distrusted land power. Their interest was in commerce and their riches were fantastic, and both had to be protected. The security of the city was not hard to maintain; its lagoons were superior to any fortifications devised by land-based states. The Venetian navy was the equal, at times the superior, of that supported by Genoa, its only serious maritime rival. But sea commerce needed bases, and the Venetians developed these throughout the Adriatic, Ionian, and Aegean seas, which became, to all intents and purposes, Venetian lakes. The Most Serene Republic of St. Mark, to give the Venetian state its full title, took over ports down the Dalmatian coast and throughout the Greek islands, and, after the capture of Constantinople by the Crusaders in 1204, Venice enjoyed extraterritorial possession of one-quarter of that imperial city.

In its initial stages, the Venetian Renaissance was nourished by contacts with Florence. But before Florentine artists arrived in Venice in the first half of the Quattrocento, Venetian art had turned toward the East. In Greece and in the churches and palaces of Constantinople, the Venetians witnessed the effect of Byzantine mosaics at their grandest, and in the Duecento the Venetians set to work clothing the interior of the Ducal Basilica of San Marco with mosaics, relying more on Byzantine examples and training, and even on actual Greek mosaicists, than on the Early Christian prototypes still visible in Venetian controlled or dominated areas. The general effect of the church, its every wall and vaulting surface covered by slabs of veined marble or mosaics with glimmering gold backgrounds, is still enthralling.

It has been asserted that the situation of Venice gave the inhabitants a predisposition toward values of color and light rather than those of form and mass. At all times in its history the appearance of the city has presented an amazing spectacle (see fig. 5). From the start, water formed the thoroughfares for the inhabitants. Larger passages became major canals, some of which still provide anchorage for shipping. The others made up a labyrinth of small canals and basins. These at first were bridged by wooden structures, but gradually wood gave place to stone, which also came into use for the embankments of the canals. Land space was at a premium, so there were few open squares and almost no true streets. Narrow alleys separated houses and provided passage for pedestrians. The houses of the great families,

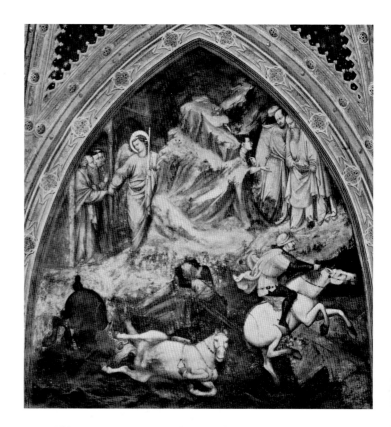

129. JACOPO AVANZO. *Liberation of the Companions of St. James.* c. 1374. Fresco. Chapel of St. Felix, Sant'Antonio, Padua

who alone were allowed to participate in the government, faced the major canals and were approached by water, thus rendering unnecessary the massive exterior walls of the Florentine palaces, which were built for defense against civil unrest. Construction was founded on wooden piles driven into the muddy islets or the underwater subsoil. The city's canals and basins, alleys and squares overflowed with a continuous and colorful pageant. Ships, flags, exotic garments, and wares of all nations mingled here, and the palaces of brick, limestone, or marble are illuminated almost as much by reflections from the water as by the direct light of the sun.

In the Duecento, a lively school of panel painting arose in Venice, but Venetian painting found its first authoritative voice in Paolo Veneziano, whose signed works range from the 1320s to the 1360s. Paolo could hardly have been unaware of the achievements of Giotto in nearby Padua, but there is no indication that if he actually saw Giotto's frescoes they meant much to him. His pictures represent the high refinement of Italo-Byzantine style, in all its familiar elements. In Paolo's earliest dated work, the *Coronation of the Virgin* (fig. 128) of 1324, the only foreign intrusions are the French or German Gothic decorative elements of the frame, but the freedom, freshness, and brilliance of Paolo's color epitomize the special quality of Venetian taste. The whole picture is organized in terms of waves of different colors and patterns. Unlike Tuscan painting, no clear-cut forms emerge; the picture is a web of color and

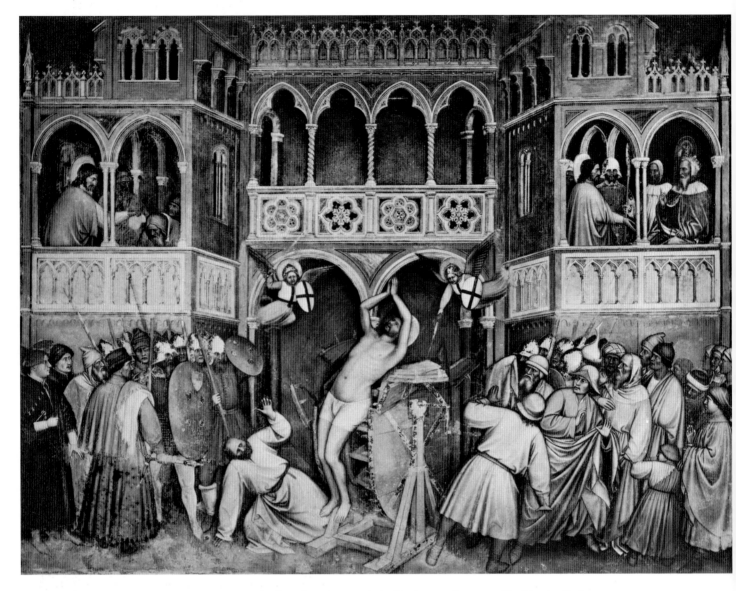

130. ALTICHIERO. *Martyrdom of St. George.* 1380–84. Fresco. Oratory of S. Giorgio, Padua.
Commissioned by Raimondino Lupi di Soragna

lines, like a luxurious fabric. It is perhaps not irrelevant to the splendid surfaces of Venetian art that, while the Florentines based their fortunes on banking and woolen cloth, the Venetians dealt principally in spices and silks.

PADUA. Independent of the immediate sphere of Venetian influence in the late Trecento, the school of Padua is certainly entitled to be ranked as the most vigorous of north Italian schools. The painters of Padua built upon Giotto's achievements in that city; indeed their art may in some aspects be considered a Giottesque revival. Not only Giotto but also his followers, and especially Maso, may be sensed in these prolific fresco painters, who added striking naturalistic observations of their own in landscape, in the painting of animals, and in portraiture. The most successful painters of the period both came to Padua from outside—Altichiero from Verona and Jacopo

Avanzo from Bologna. To Avanzo have been attributed most of the lunettes of the Life of St. James, painted about 1374 in the Chapel of St. James in Sant'Antonio in Padua, while to Altichiero has been assigned the huge *Crucifixion* in the same chapel, some of the other lunettes, and all of the frescoes in the nearby Oratory of San Giorgio.

Avanzo's *Liberation of the Companions of St. James* (fig. 129) shows some of the qualities of the Paduan style. Ambrogio Lorenzetti and Francesco Traini had, of course, developed the panoramic background (see figs. 108, 121), but no Tuscan painter presents us with this kind of nature—impassable, impenetrable, indecipherable. The human figures, many showing traits of physiognomy and drapery that remind us of Giotto and Maso, are dominated by a central mass of rocks. The foreground is even more hostile. A bridge has collapsed, and the persecutors of the saint's companions fall into a stream. The floundering horses and humans are represented with striking fidelity. It seems unlikely that a Tuscan painter in the Trecento would have put a horse, seen from below, in the most prominent spot in the painting. In the Quattrocento, however, Paolo Uccello did exactly that in his *Battle of San Romano* (see fig. 263), and considering the time he spent in Padua it is possible that Avanzo's daring fresco put the idea in his mind.

In its density and richness Altichiero's *Martyrdom of St. George* (fig. 130) is equally non-Tuscan, in spite of occasional echoes of Giotto in the faces. A palace with loggie and Late Gothic parapets fills the scene and provides smaller stages for various episodes of the saint's life. The attempt to break him on the wheel fills the center foreground. The crowds of executioners and townspeople are terrified at the intervention of the angels, who smash the wheel with their swords. As in Avanzo's frescoes, the complexity of the background, this time architectural rather than natural, envelops and dominates the figures. Altichiero's color, gorgeous in its muted tones of rose, green, and gold, is as foreign to Tuscan art as is the extreme naturalism of the portrait types that emerge from the crowd. Especially striking is the almost nude body of the saint on the wheel, which is sharply real in its emphasis on details of anatomical modeling and physical stress.

MILAN. In 1387 Milan lost its communal liberties to the Visconti family, and for the next two centuries the Visconti, succeeded by their relatives the Sforza, held absolute sovereignty over a fluctuating territory including, at times, all of Lombardy and much of central Italy as well. At Milan and Pavia these rulers held courts whose magnificence was rivaled in Italy only by those of the Vatican and the Kingdom of Naples. Bernabò Visconti, count of Milan, is represented in a tomb monument by the Lombard sculptor Bonino da Campione (active 1357–85), carved before 1363, when the count still had more than twenty years to live (fig. 131). The base of the monument is a sarcophagus, carved in a style derived from that of Nicola Pisano, who, with his pupils, had worked in north Italian centers. On the sarcophagus stands an over-life-sized statue of Bernabò on horseback, the ancestor of the famous Quattrocento equestrian monuments by Donatello and Verrocchio (see figs. 249, 337, 338), also commemorating north Italian leaders. But in contrast to these dynamic Renaissance successors, imbued with the influence of ancient Rome, the equestrian statue by Bonino, like those he made for other north Italian centers, remains absolutely immobile. The steed plants all four feet firmly on the base, and the rider stares grimly ahead. Nonetheless, it is impressive through the sheer power of its presence and the typical north Italian attention paid to the anatomy of the horse. According to Trecento sources, the statue was covered with silver and gold and the figure held a flag or pennant.

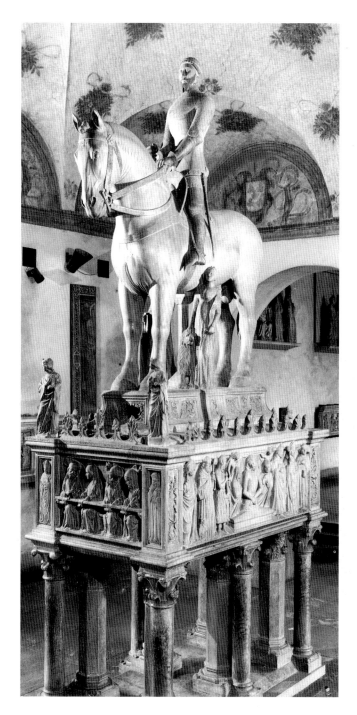

131. BONINO DA CAMPIONE. *Equestrian Monument to Bernabò Visconti*. Before 1363. Workshop of BONINO DA CAMPIONE, *Sarcophagus of Bernabò Visconti*. c. 1385. Marble, originally with gilding and silver decoration; overall height 19' 8". Museo del Castello Sforzesco, Milan. Equestrian monument commissioned by Bernabò Visconti for S. Giovanni in Conca, Milan

In 1385 Bernabò was imprisoned by his own nephew, Giangaleazzo Visconti, who assumed total power and in 1395 bought from the impoverished Holy Roman Emperor Wenceslas the title of hereditary duke of Milan. Aspiring to rule over all of Italy, Giangaleazzo became, as we shall see in the next chapter, a mortal threat to the Florentine Republic. The duke gathered about himself a talented and original group of artists from Lombardy, France, Germany, and the Netherlands to build the Visconti funeral monastery, the Certosa of Pavia, and the ambitious Cathedral of Milan, which was still far from completion when Leonardo da Vinci worked in that city a century later.

Animals constituted one of the favorite delights of north Italian courts. The pleasures of the chase and the joys of collecting rare animals and birds from as far away as Africa and the Near East enliven the art created for the new tyrants. Giovannino de' Grassi (active 1380s, d. 1398) was architect, sculptor, and painter to Giangaleazzo, and for a while *capomaestro* over the host of artists working on the Cathedral of Milan. He was also responsible for a beautiful book of animal studies now in Bergamo, and for the first half of a magnificent prayer book of the type known as a Book of Hours. The pages decorated by Giovannino in the *Visconti Hours*, as the book came to be known, are among the most alluring products of Italian manuscript art. A sample page (color-plate 36, p. 202) shows a portion of Psalm 118, but the illustrations have nothing to do with the scriptural lines.

In the middle of the huge initial "D" sits King David, clothed in red, blue, and gold, in a gorgeous Gothic interior. He reaches out his left hand while God, a bit hard to find among the ornament at the right, upholds the orb of power.

The border ornaments are two conventional tree trunks of gold, entwined with ivy with golden leaves, that grow from soft, green grass at the left and rocky slopes at the right, both sparkling with wildflowers. The grass is inhabited by Giangaleazzo's hunting dogs, who already sniff their prey, and three handsome stags and a doe, crouching, climbing, grazing, and even foreshortened from the rear. The animals and flowers are painted with an extraordinary freedom and freshness distinct from the stiffness characteristic of earlier Milanese art. Between the hunters and the hunted a sunburst encloses a portrait of Giangaleazzo. The entrancing naturalism of Giovannino and other Lombard illuminators, known to contemporary French artists as the *ouvraige de Lombardie*, appears to have inspired the art of the Limbourg brothers in Burgundy, and in Italy it exercised an incalculable influence on Gentile da Fabriano (see Chapter 8).

PART TWO

THE QUATTROCENTO

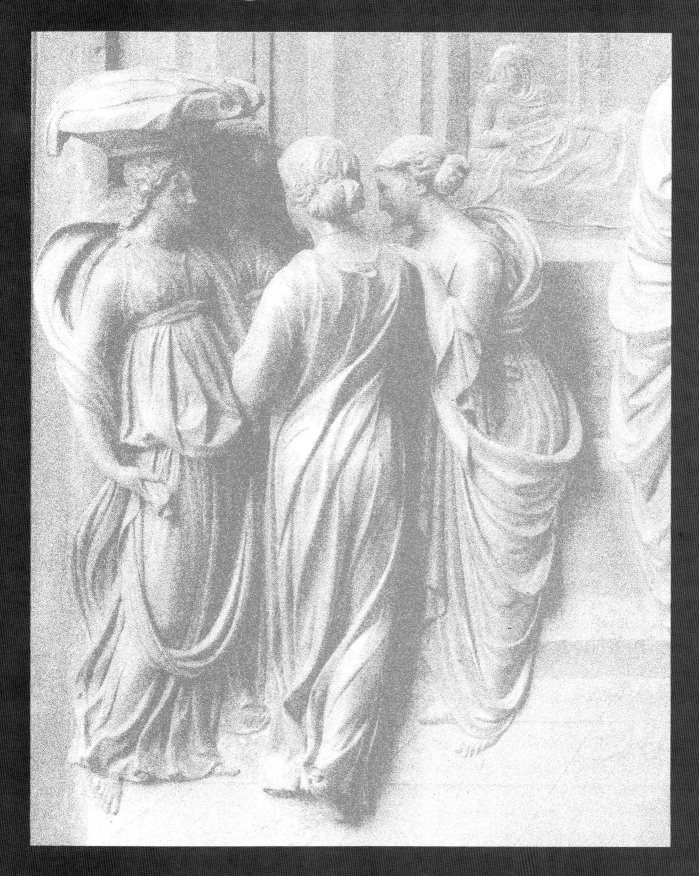

6

The Beginnings of Renaissance Architecture

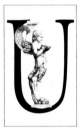p to this point we have been considering what might be referred to as premonitions of the Renaissance—the new light and humanism of the Trecento, and the Trecento artists' occasional imitation of works of classical art. Architecture remained Gothic, although a Gothic modified by Italian ideas of clarity and simplicity. In the early Quattrocento in Florence, we can trace the development of a new art dedicated to human potential and human standards and inspired by forms and ideas drawn from the civilizations of Greek and Roman antiquity in which these human standards had been raised to a high level of expression. Leonbattista Alberti, who formulated the theoretical principles of the new style in books written some twenty years after the first new stylistic statements of the Renaissance, refers to antiquity at almost every point. At the same time, he is proud of the new ideas of his own period. In his treatise *On Painting*, written in Latin in 1435 and translated into Italian as *Della pittura*, he claimed that "it was less difficult for the Ancients—because they had models to imitate and from which they could learn—to come to a knowledge of those supreme arts which today are most difficult for us. Our fame ought to be much greater, then, if we discover unheard-of and never-before-seen arts and sciences without teachers or without any model whatsoever."

As a supreme example of the new art, Alberti submits the dome of the Cathedral of Florence (fig. 132), then being completed by Filippo Brunelleschi (1377–1446), to whom the prologue was addressed. "Who could be hard or envious enough to fail to praise [Filippo] the architect on seeing here such a large structure, rising above the skies, ample to cover with its shadow all the Tuscan people, and constructed without the aid of centering or great quantity of wood? Since this work seems impossible of execution in our time, if I judge rightly, it was probably unknown and unthought of among the Ancients."

As we look at this dome, whose shape and proportions vie in grandeur with the hills surrounding Florence, it seems the product of a serene and harmonious period consecrated to the kind of intellectual activities that Alberti and his fellow humanists extol, but nothing could be further from the truth. Like so many creative periods, the Early Renaissance, which covered roughly

the fifteenth century in most major centers, was an era of bitter conflict and of challenges never more than partly met. Seldom, however, in history is the gap between human problems and their solutions more evident than during the Italian Renaissance. Florence in particular, whose role in the modern world has often been compared with that of Athens in antiquity, resembled Athens in this respect as well. Only on an ideal plane, in their great monuments and works of art, did the Florentine people achieve the harmony, dignity, and balance that were denied them by the turbulent realities of their epoch.

During the formative period of the Early Renaissance, in the first third of the Quattrocento, the continued existence of the Florentine Republic and even of Florence as an independent state was in doubt. In 1378 the guild system had come under attack in the short-lived revolt of the Ciompi—the impoverished wool carders who occupied the bottom rung of the social and economic ladder. After ruthless suppression of the Ciompi, the oligarchy reestablished its domination through the major guilds and the Guelph party. The next threats came from without, from the rapidly expanding duchy of Milan, which, under the Visconti family, seemed ready to engulf most of the Italian peninsula. By a system of alliances, threats, and intimidations, as well as by conquest, Duke Giangaleazzo Visconti gained control over all northern Italy, save only the republics of Genoa and Venice, and much of central Italy, including Siena, the ancient rival of Florence; Florence thus was surrounded on three sides. Eventually Giangaleazzo succeeded in cutting Florence off from the sea, and in the summer of 1402 he was poised in the Apennines, ready to descend on Florence and wipe out that hotbed of bourgeois liberty. At that moment the plague, always smoldering, erupted among his armies and by September Giangaleazzo was dead and his jerry-built empire fell apart. The Florentines rejoiced at their deliverance and returned to their normal commercial and intellectual activities.

And then another threatening tyrant emerged. King Ladislaus of Naples, having conquered Rome three times (on the third he put the city to fire and sword), threatened Florence from the south. Again disease came to the aid of the Florentines, and in 1414 Ladislaus died. It is important to remember that despite these two de-

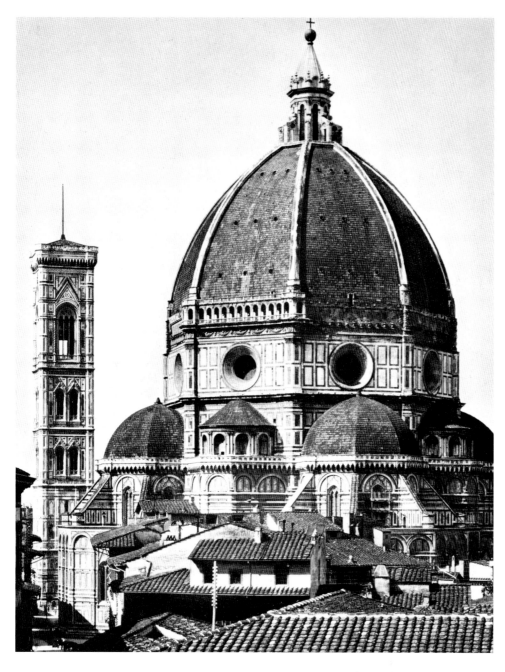

liverances, which many Florentines ascribed to divine intervention, the city had been ready to defend itself against these tyrants. With no alliances save an uncertain one with Venice, no military tradition to speak of, modest resources, and no standing army, the Florentines, armed only with their commercial power and their courage, prepared for the onslaught.

In the 1420s arose the third danger, and this time no convenient disease saved the Florentines. Filippo Maria, the son of Giangaleazzo Visconti, undertook to finish off his father's work, directing his politics from his castle at Pavia, a center of espionage and intrigue. The inexperienced Florentines suffered one defeat after another before they managed to pull together all the resources of the Republic. In 1427, to obtain the necessary sums for the war, the Florentines instituted the *catasto*, the first graduated tax in history. The *catasto* was a tax on wealth,

but it was also the ancestor of the modern income tax in the sense that it was calculated according to the productivity of property, including artists' tools and materials; it had a system of exemptions and deductions and required a personal, written declaration. Large numbers of these survive from 1427 and later assessments, and they form an invaluable source of information (although often deliberately misstated by the taxpayers themselves) about Florentine citizens of all ranks. The new system replaced the capricious exactions of earlier tax collectors with a workable, if far from watertight, mechanism for defining the financial responsibilities of every citizen to the threatened Republic.

The war dragged on; Filippo Maria did not descend on Florence, but neither did the Florentines defeat him. The situation that developed was a prolonged stalemate; nobody really won, yet danger overshadowed the people

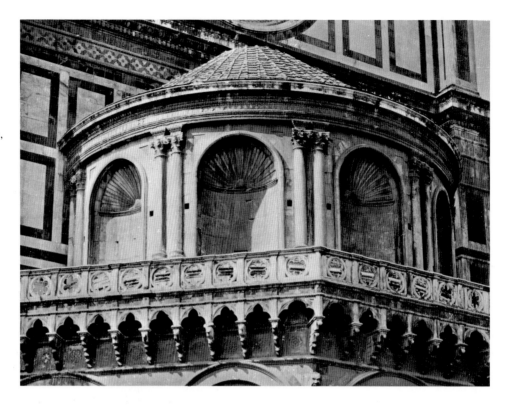

133. FILIPPO
BRUNELLESCHI.
Buttress in the
shape of an exedra,
Cathedral,
Florence. 1440s

of Florence for years. It was in this atmosphere of crisis that some of the important works of Early Renaissance art were created. Military expenditures notwithstanding, the Florentines were able and willing to pay for costly structures and large works of sculpture in marble or bronze. One reason for this seeming extravagance was the civic orientation of the new commissions. Works of art could also function as soldiers in the continuing struggle against absorption and dictatorship by galvanizing popular support for the life-and-death struggle of Florence through their profoundly felt, yet easily recognizable, symbolic content. These new public works were unusual in that they were meant for the person in the street, not for the pious in the churches.

THE DOME OF FLORENCE CATHEDRAL

Brunelleschi's dome for the Cathedral (fig. 132), completed in spite of Florentine defeats, addresses not only the citizens of Florence, but also the inhabitants of the Arno Valley from which its bulk was visible. In 1403, after Brunelleschi lost the competition for a set of bronze doors for the Florentine Baptistery to Lorenzo Ghiberti (see figs. 151, 153), he largely abandoned the art of sculpture, at which he had been proficient, and dedicated himself to architecture. Vasari tells us that Brunelleschi went to Rome to study and measure the remains of ancient architecture. He came back to Florence with ideas on how ancient elements could be utilized in the new art of the day. It is most likely that he also brought back with him measured drawings and views of the great Roman monuments.

We do not know when Brunelleschi actually designed the dome, but his father had served on the Duomo committee of 1367. Brunelleschi must have been brought up with the model of 1367, and both he and Ghiberti took part in the committee of 1404, which obliged the architect Giovanni d'Ambrogio to lower his projected semidomes to their present level. Vasari says that it was Brunelleschi who, in 1407, advised the Opera del Duomo (Board of Works of the Cathedral) to "lift the weight off the shoulders of the semidomes," in other words to insert a drum between the central dome and the surrounding semidomes. In 1410 the Opera authorized just such a drum. A wooden model, still in the Opera Museum, seems to represent this stage. In 1417 the Opera hired Brunelleschi as an adviser, and in 1420 a masonry model of the dome was finally accepted.

Brunelleschi was limited by the nature of the existing structure, for the plan of the Cathedral, commenced by Arnolfo di Cambio and expanded in the Trecento by his successors, could not be changed (see fig. 127): the octagonal base for the crowning dome was already established; the nave, choir, and transepts had been built; and the marble incrustation of the exterior, with its intricate Gothic ornamental shapes, was largely complete. The idea of oculi (round windows) instead of Gothic pointed ones had been adopted in 1367, and the building of the clerestory was apparently completed by 1390. But the exterior decoration of the clerestory as we see it today and of the finished portions of the dome present a consistent appearance whose harmony, clarity, and simplicity are strikingly different from the complexity of the Gothic shapes of the lower areas. The marble incrustation around the dome was carried out during 1452–59, after Brunelleschi's death, but most of the incrustations on the clerestory and drum probably reflect his designs.

In both the clerestory and the drum, the bays are decorated with rows of rectangular panels over which the oculi windows seem to be superimposed. Rectangles and circles are elements of architectural draftsmanship created with the compass and square: Brunelleschi's architecture has been called "paper architecture," and to some degree it does preserve in stone the procedures of laying out architectural shapes on paper. Indeed, this simple partitioning conveys the principles and the message of Brunelleschi's architecture, with its simplicity and order, clear-cut proportions, and exact relationships.

The shape of Brunelleschi's dome has an inherent tension that relates it more to a Gothic vault than to the hemispherical dome of the Pantheon, which Brunelleschi had studied and measured in Rome. The eight massive ribs seem to be held together at the top by the marble lantern, designed to admit light into the interior. In the taut curves of its profile, the force of its volume, and the dynamism of its upward leap, the shape of Brunelleschi's dome can even be compared to the Early Renaissance idea of the indomitable individual will.

The construction, started in 1420, was completed in 1436 with an octagonal oculus at the summit that was temporary until the lantern could be built. It was under this dome that, three years later, the Roman pope and Greek patriarch signed a treaty designed—uselessly, as it soon appeared—to end the centuries-old schism between the two branches of Christianity. The dome remains a symbol today. The Florentine equivalent to a London cockney's declaration of being born within the sound of Bow bells is *Io son fiorentino di Cupolone* (I am a Florentine from the great dome).

The crowning lantern and the four semicylindrical exedrae that function as buttresses (figs. 133, 134) represent another period in Brunelleschi's development and are executed in a different style. The exedrae recall circular temples Brunelleschi had seen in and near Rome, but with the columns paired and alternating with shell-headed niches. No longer is there any trace of Gothicism; the capitals harmonize perfectly with shafts, bases, and entablature. But Brunelleschi has introduced an unexpected variant. Between the capitals and the entablature he has inserted impost blocks that give a lift to the half-circle of the entablature and the cone of roof above.

The lantern (fig. 134) that brings the shapes and forces of the building to a climax abounds in fantastic variations on classical vocabulary. The eight ribs of the dome culminate in eight buttresses, each surmounted by a volute, that support the angles of the octagonal lantern. Each angle is decorated with a Corinthian pilaster, while the stilted window arches between them rest on capitals invented by Brunelleschi. Each buttress is pierced by a portal-like opening surmounted by a classicizing shell form, while the volutes curl downward and upward. Brunelleschi died before the lantern was begun, and some details not seen in the original model may be due to Michelozzo di Bartolommeo, who finished the

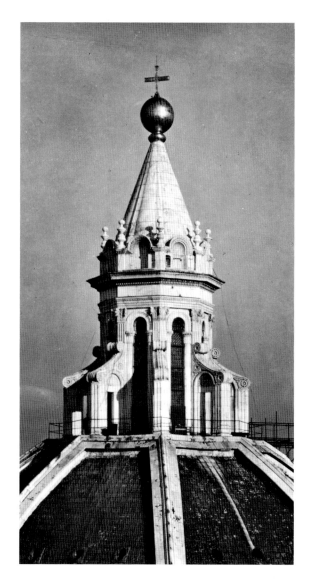

134. FILIPPO BRUNELLESCHI and MICHELOZZO DI BARTOLOMMEO. Lantern, Cathedral, Florence. After 1446

work. The lantern as built by Michelozzo culminates in a burst of delightful forms: an attic, composed of alternating niches and balusters surmounted by balls, supports a fluted cone, gold orb, and cross.

No one knows how Brunelleschi intended to complete the section separating the drum and the dome, which is now a stretch of rough masonry save for a later gallery on one face (fig. 132). A Cinquecento competition for this area was won by Baccio d'Agnolo, but after one section of his design was carried out, Michelangelo reportedly compared it to a cricket cage, and work came to a stop. The bare masonry is perhaps preferable for, despite its handsome classical forms, Baccio's gallery is so out of scale that it seems as relevant to Brunelleschi's design as a patch of scrub vegetation on the face of a cliff.

Brunelleschi's fame among his contemporaries was largely based on his ability to solve the constructional problems of so great a dome—the largest since the

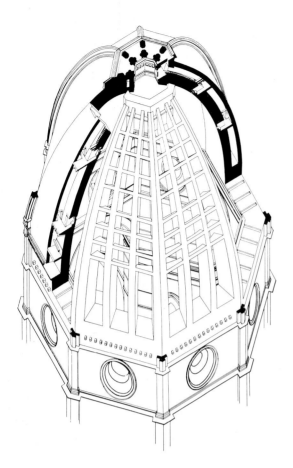

135. Diagram showing construction of Brunelleschi's
Cathedral Dome, Florence

brick; these were laid in staggered vertical rows to produce a diagonal whorl that converged on the keystone. He used this method for his other domical constructions, but here, for an octagonal dome, he employed a strong and interlocking herringbone pattern. The lower levels of the dome were laid in *pietra forte*, the traditional stone of the Florentine builders, the higher in brick.

The dome is composed of an inner and an outer shell (fig. 135), both of which are anchored to the eight ribs; between the shells are sixteen smaller ribs visible only to those who climb up between the two domes. They are connected to one another and to the main ribs by arc-shaped bands of stone; the strength of this interlocking grid was reinforced at the springing of the dome by an encircling chain of gigantic oaken beams held together by iron links.

Originally there were seventy-two oculi in three superimposed tiers in both shells of the dome. The ones in the outer shell are still visible, but those in the inner shell were closed in the sixteenth century so that the inner surface could be frescoed. Originally they must have provided dazzling crowns of light that would have transformed the effect of the now rather dark interior. It has been suggested that the Florentines may have entertained the idea of leaving the dome without a lantern, lighting the interior by the pinpoints of light from the oculi and the shaft of light that would have come from the octagonal oculus at the summit.

In all the buildings that he designed from the outset, Brunelleschi abandoned the Gothic compound pier and Gothic pointed arch, substituting a vocabulary imitated—but simplified—from classical antiquity and from the Baptistery of Florence (see fig. 85) and the Church of San Miniato, two classicizing Romanesque buildings that in his day were thought to be Roman. In all of his buildings, round arches are supported on columns derived from one of the Roman orders, usually the Corinthian. This new vocabulary soon became standard, and the architecture built in Florence became responsive to the current ideals of measure and proportion.

THE OSPEDALE DEGLI INNOCENTI

The most striking embodiment of Brunelleschi's style in the crucial years around 1420 was the Ospedale degli Innocenti, the foundling hospital for orphans and abandoned children (fig. 136). The role of this hospital in the evolution of the Florentine citizenry is attested by nearly eight columns of persons named Innocenti or its derivatives in a recent telephone directory. Although orphanages had existed previously, the Ospedale degli Innocenti was dedicated to caring for an increasing number of foundlings, including guaranteeing their education and vocational training until they reached the age of eighteen. The Innocenti was built on one side of a piazza at the end of the Via dei Servi, a new street that led from the Duomo to the Church of the Santissima Annunziata. Today matching loggias on two other sides of

Roman Pantheon and the highest ever built until that time. The officials of the Opera del Duomo were especially concerned about the colossal expense of erecting the temporary centering of timber that was the tradtional means of supporting the masonry of a dome as it went up. Centering for a dome of this scale would have required an entire forest. One of Brunelleschi's competitors even suggested building a core of earth, sown with silver and gold coins; when the dome was finished and the doors opened, it was argued that the Florentines would rapidly remove the dirt to search for the coins.

Brunelleschi's scheme made it possible to construct the dome without centering, and the masons worked from a scaffolding, reproduced in drawings and engravings, that could be suspended from recently completed sections of the dome; beams supporting narrow platforms would be lifted as the work progressed. So that the masons would not have to carry all the building materials on their shoulders to great heights, Brunelleschi invented a hoisting machine that was such a success that the Opera del Duomo had to publish an order forbidding adventurous Florentines from hooking rides on it.

Brunelleschi the engineer had designed his own method of laying brickwork in rings of horizontal masonry, but with each ring cut occasionally with a vertical

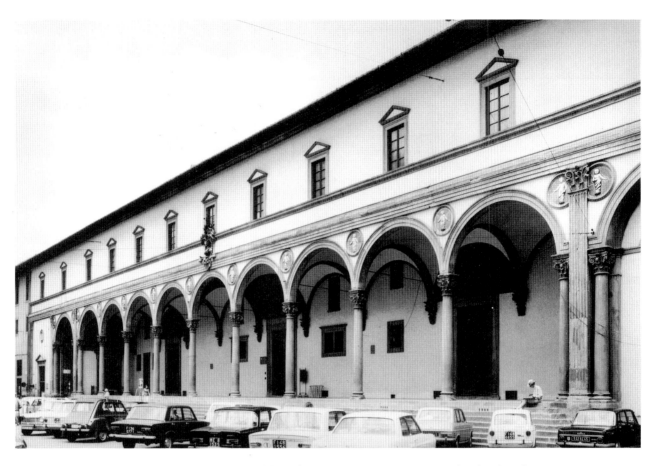

136. FILIPPO BRUNELLESCHI. Ospedale degli Innocenti. Begun 1419; completed mid-15th century.
Piazza della SS. Annunziata, Florence. Commissioned by the Arte della Seta

the piazza help to create the first of the great unified squares of modern urban design, and we suspect that this harmonious series of arcades was probably planned from the first.

Brunelleschi's science of measure and proportion dominates the apparent simplicity of his design, in which Corinthian columns support round arches and an entablature. The cornice above the frieze serves as the base for a row of pedimented windows, one above the keystone of each arch. Since he was obliged to be absent from Florence during the crucial phase of construction, Brunelleschi provided the builders with something they had never seen, a measured scale drawing, and, according to his biography, they had difficulty with the measurements and deplored the absence of the customary wooden model. Worse, Brunelleschi's name eventually disappears from the documents concerning the hospital's erection, and the new supervisor eliminated from Brunelleschi's design roundels in the frieze and pilasters between the windows of the second story. Only the arcade and the Corinthian pilasters embracing the terminal arches are as Brunelleschi planned them.

In both plan and elevation, the structure is founded on modules. The system of proportions used by Brunelleschi is based on the sixth century B.C. writings of Pythagoras. Pythagoras noted that when plucked a

stretched string produces by vibration a note, and that when the string is measured and plucked at points which correspond to exact divisions by whole numbers—$1/2$, $1/3$, $1/4$, etc.—the vibrations will produce a harmonious chord.

Brunelleschi's modular system starts with equivilancies. The distance between the centers of the columns, for example, equals the distance between the center of a column and the back wall of the loggia. This same distance equals the height of the vertical support from the floor of the loggia to the sharp point where the arches seem to coalesce, just over the impost block that Brunelleschi generally liked to place above his capitals. The choice of this junction point, rather than the springing point of the semicircular arches, is apparently Brunelleschi's way of taming the always inconvenient factor π, which is essential in determining the measurement of a circle. By this means the distance between the junction point and the base of the architrave may be established as one-half the height of a column, including capital and base (but without plinth or impost block)—or two-fifths the height of an entire support. Now we can understand the location of the cornice on which the windows rest: the distance from the top of the cornice to the base of the architrave equals the distance from the base of the architrave to the junction point of the arches. This same

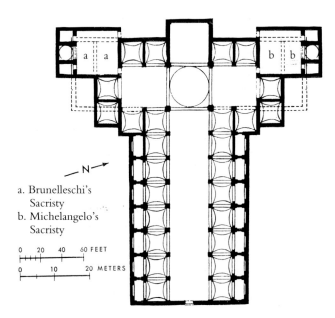

137. FILIPPO BRUNELLESCHI. Plan of S. Lorenzo, including First Sacristy (Old) and New Sacristy or Medici Chapel by MICHELANGELO. Commissioned by Giovanni di Bicci de' Medici

a. Brunelleschi's Sacristy
b. Michelangelo's Sacristy

0   20   40   60 FEET

0   10   20 METERS

clarified his Roman models, as can be seen in comparing his capitals, in which the forms are set separately against a plain ground, with the richness and technical virtuosity of Roman Corinthian capitals.

BRUNELLESCHI'S SACRISTY FOR SAN LORENZO

The sacristy that Brunelleschi designed for San Lorenzo is now often called the Old Sacristy to distinguish it from its later counterpart at the other end of the transept, the New Sacristy, designed by Michelangelo (also known as the Medici Chapel, see fig. 552). Brunelleschi's sacristy was commissioned by Giovanni di Bicci de' Medici, founder of the family fortunes, as an addition to the medieval Basilica of San Lorenzo. With Giovanni's fortune supporting the work, it proceeded with rapidity, and when completed in 1428 (perhaps 1429, considering that the Florentine year began on March 25), the sacristy was the first Renaissance space that could actually be entered. In plan (fig. 137) the interior is an exact square, extended on one side by a square altar space flanked by two chambers. This principal side of the room (fig. 138) is articulated by fluted Corinthian pilasters, an entablature, and an arch framing the altar space. This arch is embraced by a larger arch, defined by moldings, that is supported on the pilasters that are folded into each corner of the room. Pendentives lead our eyes upward to the ribbed dome (fig. 139). The ribs divide the drum into twelve round-arched compartments, each containing an oculus. Since the circular base of the dome does not touch the four arches, its complex and luminous structure gives the impression of a vision—a kind of New Jerusalem (which had twelve gates) descending from Heaven. It may be significant that the four medallions that touch the arches and the circle contain Donatello's reliefs of scenes from the Life of St. John the Evangelist, who beheld the New Jerusalem.

Here again Brunelleschi maintained a simple system of proportions: the height of the lower story to the top of the architrave equals the distance from the architrave to the circular base of the dome; this in turn equals the height of the dome to the base of the lantern. Each story is related to the height of the entire building as one to three. On each side there are three arched windows and three medallions. The sacristy has four sides. Three times four equals the number of the ribs and oculi of the dome. Brunelleschi's numbers may have added significance, for three, of course, is the number of the Trinity and four is that of the evangelists, while the apostles number twelve.

The lightness and clarity of Brunelleschi's design are challenged by the powerful sculptures added by Donatello—bronze doors, reliefs filling the niches over the doorways, and medallions. Brunelleschi protested, and this is one of many occasions when artists of the Renaissance did not see eye to eye. Considering the gulf be-

measure is used for the width of the principal doors and the height of the second-story windows; halved, it governs the width of the smaller doors and windows, the height of the architrave, and the distance between the top of the architrave and the second-story windows.

These relationships—one to two, one to five, and two to five—are carried even into the proportions of capitals and bases and extended to the cubic proportions of the rooms in the interior. Surely it had escaped neither Brunelleschi nor his patrons that Christ, the supreme exemplar of the charity for which the hospital was founded, is the Second Person of the Trinity, that the wounds of Christ number five, or that the product of two and five is the number of the Commandments. This kind of measure is at the foundation of Renaissance art, which fuses faith and science, antiquity and Christian belief. The Divine Proportion was a goal of Renaissance theorists and artists, who were searching together for a new realm of experience in which a humanistic view of the universe could be justified on religious grounds.

Externally and internally the appearance of Brunelleschi's clear-cut, rational buildings is vastly different from that of Roman structures, even if these had provided many of the elements from which his new architecture is derived. Characteristically, he preferred the smooth shafts of Florentine Romanesque columns to the fluted ones he must have seen in Rome. He reserved fluting for pilasters, such as the ones that enframe the outer arches of the Innocenti loggia; it is no surprise to discover that the columns are three-fifths the height of these pilasters. Brunelleschi consistently simplified and

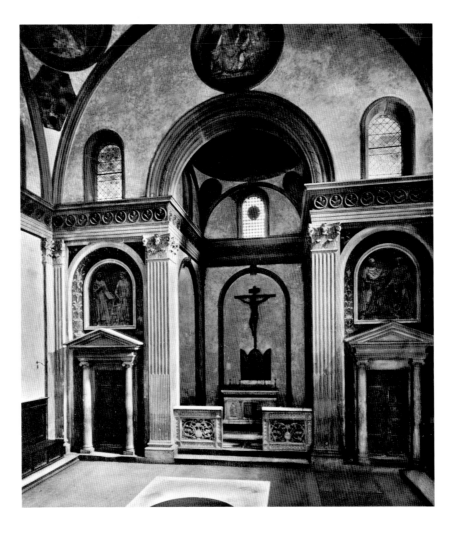

right: 138. FILIPPO BRUNELLESCHI. Sacristy, S. Lorenzo, Florence. 1421–28. Commissioned by Giovanni di Bicci de' Medici. Architectural sculpture by DONATELLO. After 1428–c. 1440. Probably commissioned by Cosimo de' Medici

below: 139. FILIPPO BRUNELLESCHI. Dome, Sacristy, S. Lorenzo, Florence. 1421–28. Stucco reliefs by DONATELLO. After 1428–c. 1440

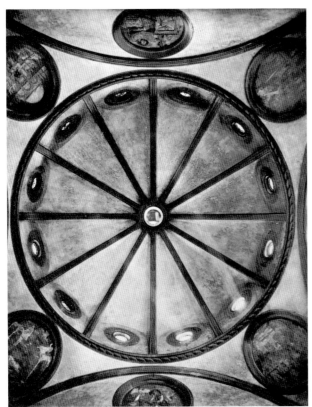

tween the serenity of Brunelleschi's ideas and the violence of Donatello's temperament, a clash between the two is hardly surprising.

SAN LORENZO AND SANTO SPIRITO

Brunelleschi was also responsible for a revolution in the plan of church interiors and in the relation between church buildings and the urban complexes surrounding them. He was commissioned to build two of the major churches of Florence, San Lorenzo and Santo Spirito, and in each case he also submitted a design for an adjacent piazza. He never saw either church completed, and the projects for their piazze were so altered that they retain nothing of his original plans. Nonetheless Brunelleschi's new ideas for church interiors and his vision of harmonious urban design remained influential for centuries.

The building history of neither church is clear, especially at the crucial planning stage, but it seems that both took shape in Brunelleschi's mind at about the same time. San Lorenzo had the advantage of Medici patronage, and consequently more expensive materials and elaborate detailing, but it was erected piecemeal and had to struggle with preexistent buildings, including Brunelleschi's own sacristy. Santo Spirito was designed from

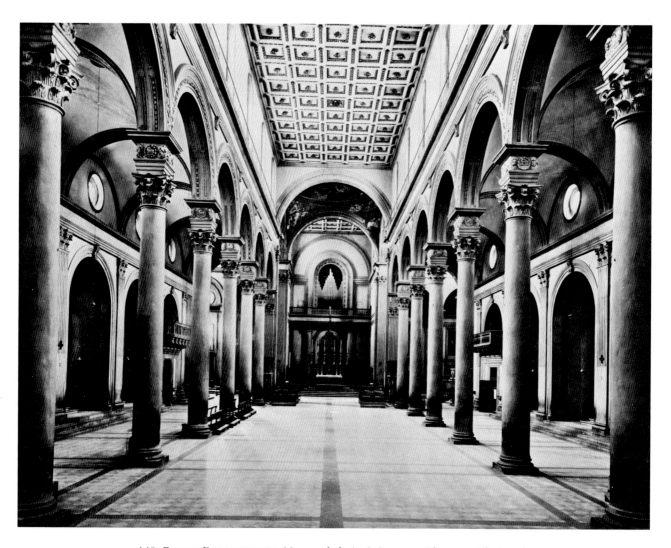

140. FILIPPO BRUNELLESCHI. Nave and choir, S. Lorenzo, Florence. Choir and transept begun c. 1425; nave designed 1434(?); construction 1442 to 1470s. Commissioned by Giovanni di Bicci de' Medici and Cosimo de' Medici

scratch and can be considered evidence of what Brunelleschi could do when given a free hand. In planning both churches he swept away the whole history of late medieval architecture—its complex vaulting systems, compound piers, and radiating chapels—and he even abandoned the openwork timber ceilings characteristic of Dominican and Franciscan churches in the Duecento and Trecento (see fig. 52). Clearly he wanted to return to the simple, three-aisled system of Early Christian basilicas in Rome, which he probably thought was also exemplified in the Romanesque Church of Santi Apostoli in Florence.

The lower stories of San Lorenzo (fig. 140) and Santo Spirito (figs. 141, 142) are nave arcades supported on monolithic Corinthian columns of great height, simplicity, and beauty. To achieve greater height, Brunelleschi has added impost blocks consisting of squared sections of Corinthian entablature, including the cornice, between the capital and the arch. The flat ceilings are supported on a clerestory wall that is unbroken save for round-arched windows. The interior details are simple and light, with delicate projections; the flat surfaces of the

masonry are covered with stucco and painted white, while the supporting elements and trim, including the columns, arches, and entablature, are made of a gray stone the Florentines call *pietra serena*. The result is a cool, harmonious, and austere alternation of gray and white that emphasizes the relationships between the parts of the structure. This new two-tone system, devised by Brunelleschi, is used to decorate the interiors of Florentine churches, palaces, and private dwellings into the eighteenth and nineteenth centuries. In contrast to the coffered ceiling of the nave—gray, with carved and gilded moldings and rosettes at San Lorenzo; merely painted in the cheaper ceiling of Santo Spirito—the side aisles are vaulted by the same pendentive domes used in the Innocenti loggia.

The combination of impost block and nave arch is half as high as a column with its capital; the impost blocks, therefore, are another of Brunelleschi's devices to make the π conform to his proportion system. If each square side-aisle bay is the module, then each nave bay is two modules and the crossing is four modules (see figs. 137–42). The bays of the aisles and ambulatory are four

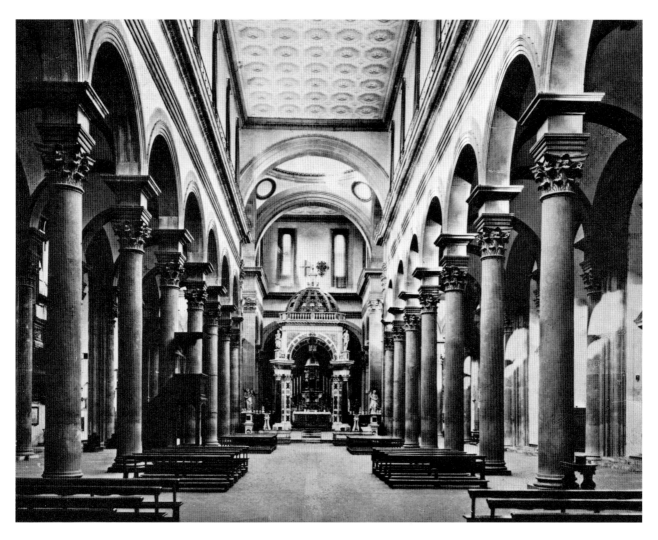

141. Filippo Brunelleschi. Nave and choir, Sto. Spirito, Florence.
Model submitted 1434–36 (?); construction 1446 to late 15th century

times as tall as they are wide, and the nave is twice as tall as the aisles and ambulatory. The width of the nave equals the height of the nave arcade. These relationships are emphasized in the floor pattern at San Lorenzo (never, unfortunately, carried out at Santo Spirito). Its double lines indicate the width of the plinths as well, establishing that the width of a plinth is one-fifth the distance between the plinths. At San Lorenzo there is a corbel in the middle of each spandrel, between pairs of nave arches; this may have been intended at Santo Spirito but never carried out. This structurally useless element helps us measure the procession of bays into the distance. The visitor is everywhere made aware of the grace of the individual shapes and of their function in the harmonic, Pythagorian structure of the church. Brunelleschi's membering also emphasizes the systematic diminution as the eye is led down the interior. No wonder Brunelleschi has been traditionally credited with the invention of one-point perspective—a system that, as we have seen, was developing long before his day, but for which he seems to have provided the first mathematical procedure.

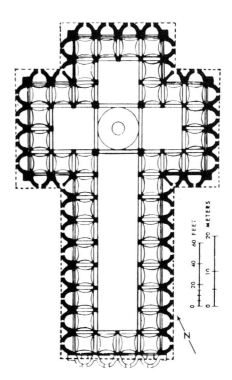

142. Filippo Brunelleschi. Plan of Sto. Spirito as originally intended; dotted lines indicate present exterior walls

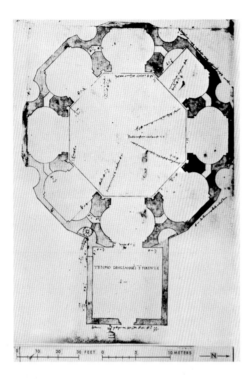

143. FILIPPO BRUNELLESCHI. Plan of Sta. Maria degli Angeli, Florence. Anonymous drawing after Brunelleschi's design. Construction begun 1434. Commissioned by the Arte di Calimala, executor for the heirs of Pippo Spano

A summary of the building history of both churches helps explain their striking differences. In 1418 it was decided to extend the medieval Church of San Lorenzo with a new choir and transept. Construction was started in 1421, but all the houses on the site were not demolished for two or three years. Only about 1425, when the foundations of the new choir and transept were already laid, was Brunelleschi—triumphant in the neighboring sacristy—called on the scene. He replaced the octagonal Gothic piers that were planned with square Renaissance piers faced by Corinthian pilasters, but it was no longer possible to make any changes in the plan. There was still no talk of tearing down the nave, for which the new constructions were still intended as an addition. It is not clear how much was completed before the expenses of the war with Milan forced abandonment of the work, but in 1434 houses flanking the church were torn down with the idea of creating a large piazza facing the Medici Palace. At this moment Brunelleschi seems to have conceived a plan for replacing the medieval sections of the church. This plan did not include the chapels that line the side aisles; they were added after 1470, and fit the structure poorly.

At the same time, Brunelleschi was involved in the project to build a new and grandiose basilica to replace a small thirteenth-century structure at Santo Spirito. Here lateral chapels were planned from the first, and Brunel-

leschi's design, probably datable in 1434–36, integrates the semicircular chapels into the total plan. Thus the entire plan becomes a succession and interrelation of circles and squares. Brunelleschi made the arms of the transepts and choir of equal length, and all are embraced by an ambulatory and chapels that continue the side aisles and their chapels to form a continuous belt surrounding the building. Originally this would even have included the façade. Brunelleschi intended that the apsidal shape of the chapels be visible on the exterior, establishing a play of curved forms against the flat clerestory walls and the roof lines that would demonstrate great plastic richness. Within the self-imposed limitations of Brunelleschi's style, there could scarcely have been a stronger departure from the "paper architecture" of his early work. Here he is concerned with solid rather than plane geometry. Unfortunately, the apses are now subsumed within flat walls, and the four chapels along the façade, which would have served as entrance porches, were never built.

At San Lorenzo, as at the Ospedale degli Innocenti, the nave arches coalesce before reaching the impost block. At Santo Spirito, however, each arch is complete and self-contained. As compared with the flatness, lightness, and grace of San Lorenzo, the interior of Santo Spirito produces an impression of mass, space, and majesty. The apsidal chapels in Santo Spirito are separated not by pilasters, as at San Lorenzo, but by half columns. Except for the long arched window, each apsidal chapel is smooth and unbroken and thus seems related to the pendentive vault above. Throughout the church we are presented with a rich alternation between massive, convex gray forms and elusive, elastic, concave white forms; this effect corresponds to the continuous shifting of spatial views through ever-changing relations of columns and arches. Unfortunately, the body of citizens responsible for carrying out the construction of the church from public funds after the Florentine victory at Anghiari in 1440 (see p. 447) did not accept the architect's idea of placing the church so that it faced the Arno across a wide piazza, which would have had a crucial effect on the plan, and indeed on the entire appearance, of the city of Florence.

San Lorenzo did not enjoy a state subsidy, and not until 1442 did Cosimo de' Medici agree to finance the continuation of the long-delayed building. Brunelleschi was destined to see his great architectural vistas only in imagination; when he died in February 1446, not one column for either of his basilicas had even been quarried. Under the supervision of Michelozzo di Bartolommeo, work dragged on at San Lorenzo (with many errors of judgment) until after 1470; at Santo Spirito it was even longer, and under a variety of masters. We have no idea how Brunelleschi intended either of the façades to appear; he seems to have been commissioned only to provide models for the body of each church. Santo Spirito has a simple plastered façade, while that of San Lorenzo, in spite of Michelangelo's great dream of

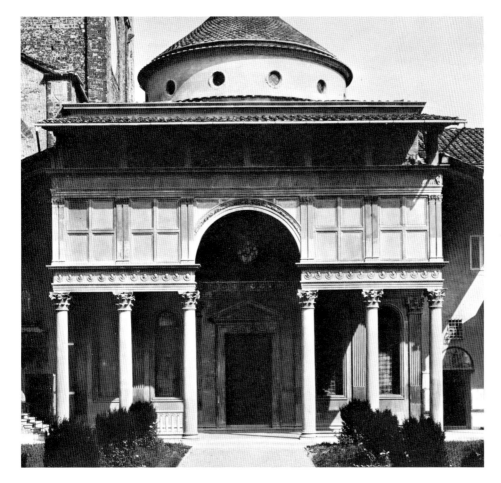

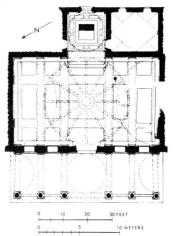

left: 144. FILIPPO BRUNELLESCHI
and GIULIANO DA MAIANO(?).
Pazzi Chapel, Sta. Croce,
Florence (see colorplate
37, p. 202). Begun c. 1433,
completed 1461. Commissioned
by Andrea dei Pazzi

below: 145. FILIPPO
BRUNELLESCHI. Plan of Pazzi
Chapel

completing it (see pp. 536–37 and fig. 551), remains rough and unfinished to this day. Despite these vicissitudes, San Lorenzo and Santo Spirito remain two of the most beautiful of Renaissance interiors.

SANTA MARIA DEGLI ANGELI

A little building that might have been one of Brunelleschi's masterpieces was the chapel of the Monastery of Santa Maria degli Angeli, the Florentine seat of the Camaldolite Order (see pp. 227–28), whose prior was then the celebrated and widely traveled scholar Ambrogio Traversari. The foundations were started in 1434 but the current structure dates almost entirely from 1937 and only the ground plan gives any hint of how Brunelleschi's building would have looked. It was intended for the community of about forty monks and would have had no space for public worship. Insofar as can be determined from early drawings (fig. 143), the plan was octagonal with each side opening into a rectangular chapel. The exterior, with sixteen sides, would certainly have been roofed by a dome—one is even shown in a fifteenth-century topographical map of the city. In this project we have the first step in the direction of the central plan, which was to reach its culmination later, in the High Renaissance projects for the new St. Peter's in Rome.

THE PAZZI CHAPEL

Brunelleschi's chapter house of Santa Croce was commissioned by the rich and powerful Pazzi family and is therefore known as the Pazzi Chapel (fig. 144). The documents date the beginning of construction to 1433, and by 1442 work had advanced sufficiently to permit the entertainment of Pope Eugenius IV in what was probably a temporary wooden pavilion. But inscriptions reveal that the dome and the cupola of the portico were finished in 1459 and 1461, long after Brunelleschi's death. The portico has been assigned to Brunelleschi, but in many places its masonry does not correspond with that of the building, suggesting that the architect did not leave a model for a portico. After the expulsion of the Pazzi in 1478, the architect Giuliano da Maiano submitted a bill for a considerable sum for work at the chapel, and the style of the portico corresponds to that of his known works (see p. 307). Certainly, the elaborate surface detail of the portico is alien to Brunelleschi's taste at any point in his career.

The plan and interior (colorplate 37, p. 202; fig. 145) represent an amplification and consolidation of the principles announced earlier in Brunelleschi's Sacristy of San Lorenzo (see figs. 137, 138); it is a rectangular structure of three stories, the second containing the arches and pendentives that support the third, a star-vaulted dome culminating in a lantern. Here the resemblance ceases. Probably because the Franciscan chapter of Santa Croce required a large meeting space, the central square is extended on either side by half the square. As a result, the building is twice as wide as it is deep; the center is roofed by the twelve-ribbed dome, the sides by barrel vaults.

The side walls are articulated by Corinthian pilasters upholding a nonstructural arch and embraced by the barrel vault; this, in turn, is supported by quarter-width pilasters, the remainder of which is folded onto the adjoining wall. The arched panels on the back and side walls match the size and shape of the windows on the entrance wall. The distance between the outer edge of a quarter-width pilaster and the inner edge of the next pilaster on the side walls is the basic module for the interior articulation—but not for the total proportions—of the chapel. The module is clearly indicated by the architect's use of corbels, and thus the space between the inner edges of the central pilasters is two modules wide. The area of the altar space is an exact square, two modules wide and two deep. The height of the order from its base (above the bench) to the top of the cornice is four modules; from above the bench to the bottom of the architrave, three and one-half. Each shaft is three modules high and one-third module wide, each capital one-third module high and one-half module wide at the abacus.

The proportions of the three stories—architectural order, arches, and dome—are not identical, as they were in the San Lorenzo Sacristy. Here they diminish as they rise. The amount by which these stories are decreased is in each case one-half module. The result of this controlled diminution is that the Corinthian order, used throughout the chapel, gains greatly in importance and dominates the interior to an extent impossible in the San Lorenzo Sacristy.

Brunelleschi's anonymous biographer tells us that his models showed structure alone, not ornament, and a certain fussiness in the detail of the Pazzi Chapel may be due to the intervention of Giuliano da Maiano after Filippo's death. But the structure is his, and as in his other works the clear-cut decorative details are set out in *pietra serena* against white stucco walls, vaults, and dome. The only color is provided by the stained-glass window and the glazed terra-cotta reliefs in the medallions— predominantly the sky blue of their backgrounds—and by the Pazzi coats of arms in the pendentives.

At this juncture one might bear in mind the admonition of the contemporary Florentine humanist Giannozzo Manetti, who states in his book *On the Dignity and Excellency of Man* that the truths of the Christian religion are as clear and self-evident as the axioms of mathematics. The rational, ordered clarity of Brunelleschi's religious buildings may disappoint those who, like Ruskin, the nineteenth-century British critic, are fascinated and moved by Gothic architecture. Yet Brunelleschi's churches are religious structures of the highest order. The Florentine humanists thought that geometric principles could unlock mysteries at the heart of the universe and reveal the intentions of a God who was, if one only knew how to go about it, eminently understandable and had created the universe for our enjoyment. Alas, Brunelleschi's vision of architectural harmony and perfection, reflecting the sublime order of the cosmos, was doomed to incompletion. The only work Brunelleschi ever saw finished, the sacristy at San Lorenzo, was spoiled in his estimation by the encroachments of others. Despite the incomprehension of those who continued it, his truncated lifework remained to inspire the architects of the Renaissance.

THE MEDICI PALACE

According to Vasari and certain of his sources, Brunelleschi submitted a model for a new house to Cosimo de' Medici, generally known as Cosimo il Vecchio (to distinguish him from Cosimo I, the sixteenth-century grand duke of Tuscany). It has been suggested that this house would have been situated on the Piazza San Lorenzo, its portal opposite that of the church, and that both would have enjoyed a large piazza extending as far as the site of the present Medici Palace on the Via Larga (today Via Cavour). This location was outside the old city of Florence, where the older families lived, but within the third circle of walls. Vasari reports that when Cosimo rejected Brunelleschi's proposal as too sumptuous, Brunelleschi smashed the model. The story suggests that Cosimo, who had been exiled in 1433–34, did not wish his residence to be so splendid that it would make him appear what, in fact, he was—the ruler of Florence. By 1445, when the Medici Palace was begun, Cosimo had reinforced his power by political maneuvers designed to secure the family from future exiles; in consequence, the Republic, although its machinery remained superficially intact, was directed by Cosimo.

The designation of the Medici house as a palace does not indicate any special status, for the Italian word *palazzo* (palace) is used to refer to any large building, and town houses of Florentine merchants, even modest ones, are called *palazzi*. But the dimensions of the Medici Palace (fig. 146) are by no means modest. Each story is more than twenty feet high, and the entire structure, to the top of the cornice, rises more than seventy feet above the street.

It is usually presumed that the architect of this palace was Michelozzo di Bartolommeo (1396–1472), but at least one scholar has recently reattributed it to Brunelleschi. After the palace was bought by the Riccardi family in the mid-seventeenth century, it was extended by seven bays of windows and a second portal; these later additions must be thought away to understand the original proportions of the palace. We must also imagine the building without the pedimented windows of the ground floor, which were added in the Cinquecento by Michelangelo at the request of Pope Leo X, then head of the Medici family. Originally the arches were open and the corner was an open loggia.

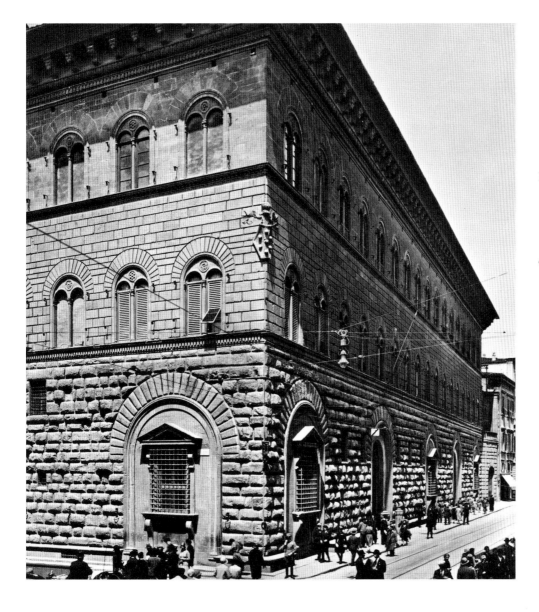

146. MICHELOZZO DI BARTOLOMMEO (attributed to). Palazzo Medici (now known as the Palazzo Medici-Riccardi), Florence. Begun 1445. Commissioned by Cosimo de' Medici. Ground floor pedimented windows by MICHELANGELO. c. 1517. Commissioned by Pope Leo X

To modern eyes the most striking aspect of the Medici Palace is its unpalatial appearance. The rough-cut stones of the ground floor seem more appropriate for a fortress, and something of the grimness of Florentine medieval house-towers seems to linger in this design. It is not that the rustication looks like that of medieval buildings; these blocks, haphazardly projecting, were imitated from the rustication of such ancient Roman monuments as the Forum of Augustus, which in the Renaissance was believed to have been the Palace of Caesar. Even in the turbulent civil existence of Florence, such rustication can have had no defensive nature. The rustication may have been intended to convey to the Florentine passerby a moral quality—the Tuscan dignity and antique fortitude of the House of Medici. The lucidity of the plan and the regularity of the basic shape of the palace are new to Florentine palace architecture and may have been inspired by the description of ancient Roman houses given by Vitruvius, the first century B.C. architect and theorist. The interior has been so remodeled that it is hard to reconstruct its original na-

ture and decoration; today we miss especially the inlaid wooden wainscoting of the bedroom with the battle scenes by Paolo Uccello (see colorplate 47, p. 257; fig. 263), and Piero de' Medici's study, which had an enameled terra-cotta ceiling by Luca della Robbia. An inventory made after the death of Lorenzo the Magnificent in 1492 shows that the palace housed a treasury of Quattrocento painting, sculpture, and minor arts, as well as a collection of ancient coins and gems.

Narrow horizontal moldings called stringcourses separate the three stories, and the progressive diminution in height from the lower to the upper story is accompanied by correspondingly smoother surface treatments. The powerful blocks of the ground story are replaced on the second by trimmed blocks with deep joints, while the blocks of the third story are completely smoothed, their joints almost invisible. The windows of the upper story are mullioned, as is characteristic of Florentine Quattrocento palaces. These windows, derived from such Gothic structures as the Palazzo dei Priori (see fig. 54), utilize round arches supported on slender Corinthian

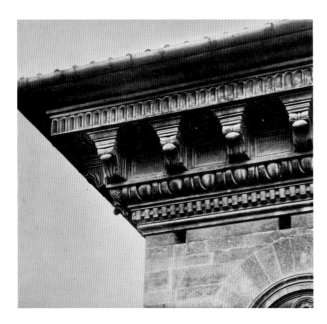

147. MICHELOZZO DI BARTOLOMMEO.
Detail of cornice, Palazzo Medici, Florence

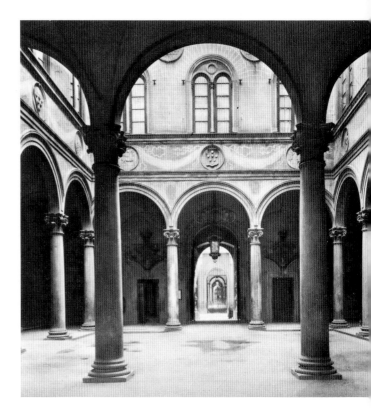

148. MICHELOZZO DI BARTOLOMMEO (attributed to).
Courtyard with *sgraffito* decoration, Palazzo Medici,
Florence. Begun 1446

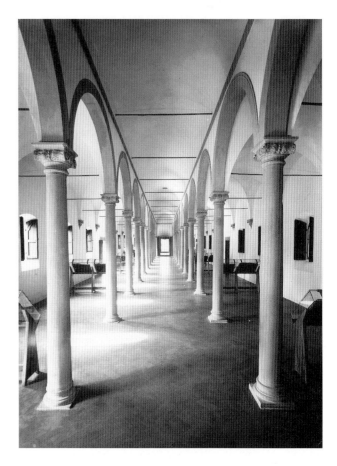

149. MICHELOZZO DI BARTOLOMMEO.
Library, Monastery of S. Marco, Florence. After 1436.
Commissioned by Cosimo de' Medici

colonnettes; the lunettes are decorated with Medici arms and symbols, and there is a large Medici coat of arms on the corner. The cornice (fig. 147), although its many elements are directly imitated from Roman models, echoes the traditional sharply projecting eaves that give Florence and its subject towns so distinctive an appearance.

Like the largest medieval palaces, the Medici Palace was built around a central courtyard (fig. 148). Its lower story is a continuous arcade, the second has mullioned windows resembling those of the exterior, and the third was originally an open loggia. The columns of the ground story at first sight resemble those of Brunelleschi's buildings, but they are heavier in their proportions, only seven and a half capitals high. These proportions are appropriate for columns that functionally and visually must support an enclosed second story. The Medici Palace served as the model for Florentine palazzi for almost a century.

Among all the churches, chapels, palaces, villas, and monasteries carried out by Michelozzo, either alone or in collaboration with other architects, one of his most charming creations is the library of the Monastery of San Marco (fig. 149), part of an extensive rebuilding project supervised by Michelozzo and financed by Cosimo de' Medici in the years immediately following 1436. The library has three aisles of equal height, the outer ones groin-vaulted, the central one roofed by a barrel vault and supported on an airy arcade of Ionic columns. The slenderness of the elements gives a lightness to the interior, an effect that reappears in the architectural backgrounds of paintings by Fra Angelico (see fig. 210), who lived and worked in this monastery.

7

Gothic and Renaissance in Tuscan Sculpture

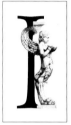f architecture is the art in which the new principles of the Renaissance—especially the use and transformation of classical elements and the evolution of a mathematical proportion system—are most clearly evident, sculpture can dispute with architecture the leading place in the first decades of the Quattrocento. In the creations of an astonishing group of sculptors, new concepts of the dignity and autonomy of the individual profoundly affect modes of representation.

THE COMPETITION PANELS

Among the most ambitious sculptural projects of the Early Renaissance was the continuation of the series of doors for the Florentine Baptistery, one pair of which, showing the Life of John the Baptist, had been made by Andrea Pisano in the 1330s (see fig. 86). Two more sets, to illustrate the Old and New Testaments, were needed. In 1401 the Opera del Duomo of the Baptistery announced a competition for the second set of doors. The competition was under the supervision of the Arte di Calimala, the refiners of imported woolen cloth and the oldest of the Florentine guilds. The seven sculptors who competed, all Tuscans, included the Sienese Jacopo della Quercia (c. 1380–1438), Filippo Brunelleschi, and Lorenzo Ghiberti (1381?–1455). When the models were submitted, sometime during 1402 and not later than March 24, 1403 (the Florentine new year was celebrated on March 25), the victor was Ghiberti, who was scarcely more than twenty at the time and trained as a painter, rather than the slightly older Brunelleschi or the middle-aged and more experienced sculptors.

The subject selected for competition was the story of how the faith of the patriarch Abraham was tested by God, who asked him to sacrifice his only son, Isaac, born in his old age. Abraham, accompanied by two servants and a donkey, took Isaac into the wilderness to enact the sacrifice, but at the last moment God sent an angel, who told Abraham that God would be satisfied with the offering of a ram that was caught in a nearby thicket. The story was interpreted as foreshadowing the sacrifice of Christ, but the officials of the Opera, as we shall see, may also have had a more immediate reason for selecting it. The two preserved competition panels, by Brunelleschi and Ghiberti, represent the same moments in the story: the angel intervenes as the boy kneels on the altar, his father about to put a knife to his throat. The two servants, the ram caught in the thicket, and the ass drinking from a stream are all represented. Perhaps these elements were required by the competition.

The theme in both reliefs is divine intervention that delivers the chosen people from impending doom, including even the substitute victim and the miraculous appearance of water. We must remember that the Florentines credited the sudden death of Giangaleazzo in September 1402 to divine intervention. The exact date of the assignment of the reliefs is not known; it may have been after September, or the choice of subject may have mirrored Florentine hopes for such a solution.

Brunelleschi's relief (fig. 150) is a brilliantly original creation, full of daring poses and naturalistic observation. Surprisingly, the harmony and balance of Brunelleschi's architecture are absent from this dramatic interpretation. Abraham has twisted Isaac's head to expose his neck, and the angel has to rush in and physically restrain him to prevent the sacrifice from occurring. Brunelleschi suggests that Abraham could only have carried out the sacrifice if he focused so completely on God's demand that he blocked out the knowledge that it is his son who will be sacrificed. The carefully observed body of the boy is scrawny, the poses of all the figures tense, the rhythms of both drapery and figures sharp and broken.

The young Ghiberti, who was trained as a painter but had not yet matriculated in any guild, least of all the Arte della Seta to which metalworkers belonged, nonetheless displays extraordinary accomplishment in handling bronze (fig. 151). In his interpretation the boy looks upward for deliverance from death. Abraham, his left arm embracing the boy's shoulder, is poised with his knife pointed toward—but not touching—his son. With a single gesture the floating, foreshortened angel stops the sacrifice. The ram rests quietly before his thicket. The servants converse gently. The physical contact and corporeal strain of Brunelleschi's relief are avoided, and Brunelleschi's harsh and jagged movements are replaced by poses as graceful as those of dancers. Throughout Ghiberti's composition—in every figure and drapery form and even in the rocks of the landscape—curving rhythms create a continuous melody as satisfying as the harmony of Brunelleschi's later architectural creations.

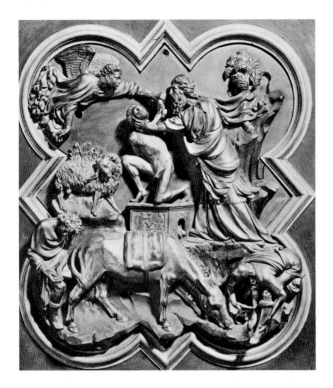

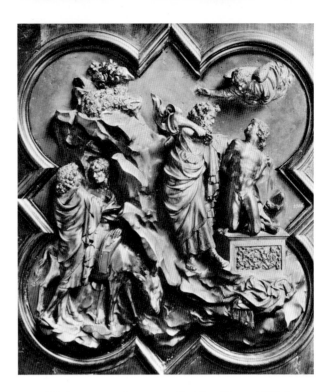

150. FILIPPO BRUNELLESCHI. *Sacrifice of Isaac.* 1402–3. Bronze with gilding, 21 x 17½" inside molding. Bargello, Florence. Competition panel for the second set of bronze doors for the Florentine Baptistery, sponsored by the Opera of the Baptistery and the Arte di Calimala

151. LORENZO GHIBERTI. *Sacrifice of Isaac.* 1402–3. Bronze with gilding, 21 x 17½" inside molding. Bargello, Florence. Competition panel for the second set of bronze doors for the Florentine Baptistery, sponsored by the Opera of the Baptistery and the Arte di Calimala

Ghiberti's melody comes to its climax in the body of Isaac (fig. 152). Brunelleschi had, it is true, analyzed the human body with unprecedented understanding of naturalistic detail, but his end result is ungraceful. Ghiberti's linearism has been called Gothic, but this is debatable. Ghiberti's line suggests, and is often derived from, that of classical antiquity. In the figure of Isaac, made in 1402–3, he created the first truly Renaissance nude figure; here naturalism and classicism are blended and sublimated by a new vision of what a human being can be. The body displays the strength and resiliency of a perfectly proportioned youth, overflowing with energy yet remarkably graceful. Not since the last Roman sculptor capable of doing so had imitated a Greek or Hellenistic original had such a nude been created. Ghiberti, without special study of anatomy as far as we know, understood how to represent the difference between bony and muscular tissue, the dynamic possibilities of muscles, and the softening quality of skin. Most beautiful of all, perhaps, is the expression of the boy—not only on his face but in the spring and lightness of his pose—which seems to convey his faith and joy at redemption from a terrible death.

Ghiberti's Isaac was certainly inspired by a study of ancient Roman nude figures, and other references to classical antiquity are evident in both reliefs. The head of Abraham in each relief shows the inspiration of ancient Roman heads of Jupiter. The servant plucking a thorn from his foot in Brunelleschi's relief is based on a Roman sculpture or statuette called the *Spinario* that is known in many copies, the second servant is also taken from an ancient model, and the relief on the front of Brunelleschi's altar seems to be derived from an Etruscan

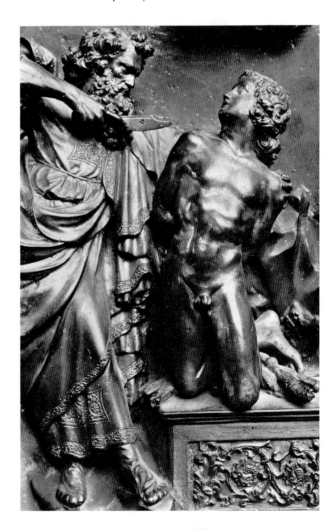

152. Isaac, detail of fig. 151

or other ancient model. In Ghiberti's relief the altar is decorated with an ancient Roman rinceau pattern, and antique models have been deduced for both servants and the ram. There are so many references to antiquity in the two competition reliefs and so few in the reliefs that Ghiberti subsequently created for his first set of Baptistery doors that one wonders if allusions to classical art were required by the competition.

Some important technical differences between the two reliefs should be noted. Brunelleschi's is composed of a flat bronze sheet to which individually cast figures are attached, while Ghiberti's background and figures are cast in a single, continuous piece, with the exception of the figure of Isaac, which was attached. Ghiberti's relief is, therefore, stronger, and because his figures are hollow, his relief is only two-thirds as heavy as Brunelleschi's. Doors made following Ghiberti's technique would endure better and require less bronze. For the practically minded members of the Arte di Calimala, such differences may have helped make Ghiberti the obvious winner in the competition.

Ghiberti was the author of a lengthy work titled, in classical style, the *Commentaries*. Much of the text deals with the relative merits of artists of classical antiquity whose works could have been known to Ghiberti only from literary sources. But the third Commentary discusses many scientific subjects and is especially devoted to an analysis of the eye, its structure and its functions, and the relation of sight to the behavior of light. Given these interests, it seems appropriate to note how Ghiberti treats the eye in his sculpture. Before his time the eye was generally modeled as a blank surface, whether or not the cornea was painted on later (as in the case of a marble statue) or sculpted away so that colored inlay of ivory or glass paste could be inserted. Ghiberti makes Isaac's gaze infinitely more expressive by delicately incising the line of the cornea and dot of the pupil. This treatment of the eye underscores other new optical qualities evident in Ghiberti's sculpture. Near the beginning of the second Commentary he says, "*Nessuna cosa si vede senza la luce*" ("Nothing can be seen without light"), and in his relief gilded surfaces send light flowing across delicate textures or reflect it into shadows. And in almost all of Ghiberti's sculpture the eye is delineated in this new way, conferring vividness and sparkle to the expressions.

GHIBERTI TO 1425

The Opera acquired the competition relief in 1403 and paid Ghiberti a sizable sum for gilding the figures and landscape. He then worked on the set of doors (which are today known as the North Doors) for twenty-one years, until 1424; such a long time was required by the scale of the project, by the complex bronze casting technique, which required modeling in wax, casting in bronze, chasing, gilding, and burnishing, and by Ghiberti's meticulousness in executing the work.

Between the competition and the commission, the subject for the doors was changed, and Ghiberti was confronted with illustrating the New Testament instead of the Old, and his panel of Abraham was set aside with the intent to use it for the third set of doors. The second doors (fig. 153) were designed to match the Trecento doors of Andrea Pisano, which were organized in twenty-eight quatrefoils in square panels arranged in seven rows of four. The borders that define Ghiberti's quatrefoils, however, provide a richer enframement than Andrea's relatively austere design of alternating diamonds and stylized flowers. Through Ghiberti's margins flows a tide of vegetable and animal life—branches, foliage, fruit, birds, lizards, and even insects—and there is a head in a quatrefoil at each intersection of the border strips. These forty-eight heads, with the exception of Ghiberti's self-portrait, apparently represent Old Testament prophets and prophetesses and all are different: some are young, some old, some male, some female, some calm, some agitated. Several show the influence of Ghiberti's study of antique sculpture.

The lowest two rows represent the four evangelists and the four Early Christian theologians known as the Fathers of the Church. Above these begin the New Testament scenes; the first is the *Annunciation* (fig. 154). Ghiberti's version is related to a number of Late Gothic Annunciations in Florentine art, particularly those by Lorenzo Monaco. In these Gabriel flies into the scene— a visionary angel with clouds streaming from his feet, his wings beating, still airborne at the command of God the Father, who in Ghiberti's panel sends down the dove of the Holy Spirit. Ghiberti's composition has grace, elegance of line, and economy of detail. Throughout the doors, Ghiberti is both attracted to the compelling rhythms of the quatrefoil format established by Andrea Pisano's doors and frustrated by its emphasis on surface patterning. He keeps the flat bronze background, but turns the portico before which the Virgin stands and deploys the supporting pier to indicate depth, thereby penetrating the flatness of the plaque. The foreshortened figure of God seems to emerge through the background rather than being placed against it, as were Andrea's figures. Here Ghiberti struggles against the limitations of the frame, trying to suggest the illusion of a deeper space. The drapery forms contribute to this illusion; Gabriel's cloak envelops his body in revolving drapery that enhances the effect of mass, and Mary's beltless tunic—perhaps a hint at conception—flows about her limbs to reveal their fullness and grace.

The *Flagellation* (fig. 155) takes place before a partly classical portico. One would like to know more about the dating of these reliefs: presumably this is among the later ones, for it seems to have been designed near the time when Brunelleschi was meditating on his new classical architecture for the Ospedale degli Innocenti and San Lorenzo (see figs. 136, 140) or perhaps the relief precedes these buildings. A search of the backgrounds in Florentine art of the early 1400s discloses symptoms of

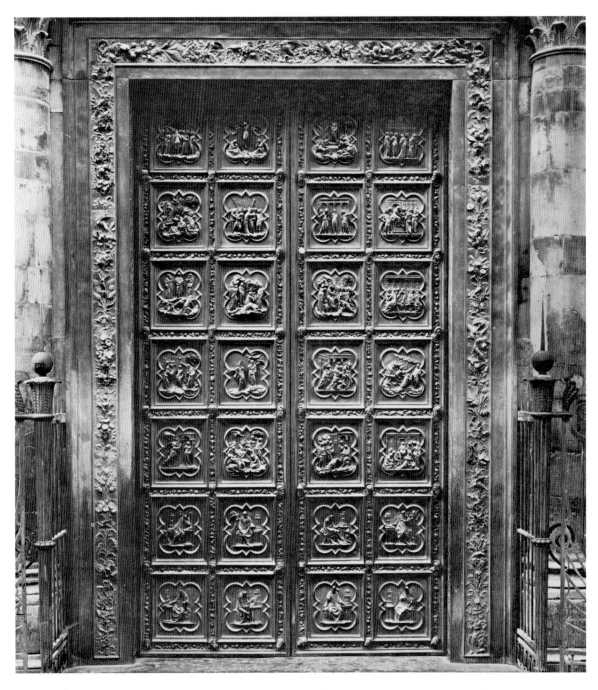

153. LORENZO GHIBERTI. North Doors. 1403–24. Bronze with gilding, height c. 15'. 🏛 Baptistery, Florence.
Commissioned by the Opera of the Baptistery and the Arte di Calimala

the oncoming Renaissance, and Ghiberti's Roman Composite capitals take an important place among these. The colonnade, however, is only a background for the coordinated interaction of the figures. Christ is tied to the central column, and his supple body continues the new classical tradition Ghiberti had established in his Isaac, while his face suggests patience. With twisting movements the men whipping Christ raise their now-missing weapons and carry the eye backward and up into the lobes of the quatrefoil. Among the few drawings that survive by early Quattrocento artists, several examples can be attributed to sculptors; in a pen sketch (fig. 156), Ghiberti worked out possibilities for the figures whip-ping Christ before he arrived at the final solution that identifies them with the forces of the frame. Interestingly, he also toyed with the idea of a deeper building with a coffered ceiling done in a remarkable approach to one-point perspective.

The *Crucifixion* (fig. 157) is shorn of all elements of pain and terror save for the grief of the angels. The curves of the bodies of Mary and John follow those of the quatrefoil and are echoed by those of the angels. This typical Ghibertian composition shows a counterpoise between the compositional elements and the directional flow of rhythms that produces a sense of abstract unity.

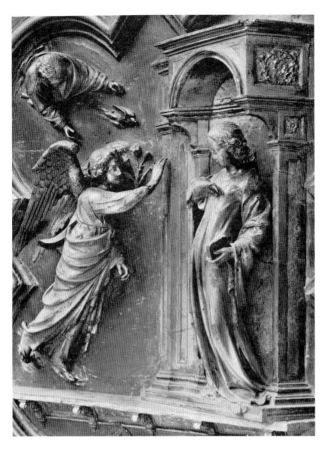

154. LORENZO GHIBERTI. *Annunciation*, panel on the 🏛 North Doors, Baptistery, Florence. Before 1407. Bronze with gilding, 20¹⁄₂ x 17³⁄₄" inside molding

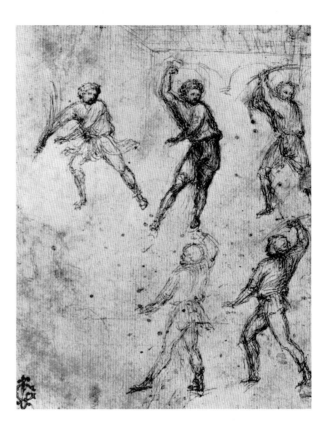

156. LORENZO GHIBERTI. *Flagellation*. c. 1416–19(?). Pen and bister, 8¹⁄₈ x 6¹⁄₂". Albertina, Vienna

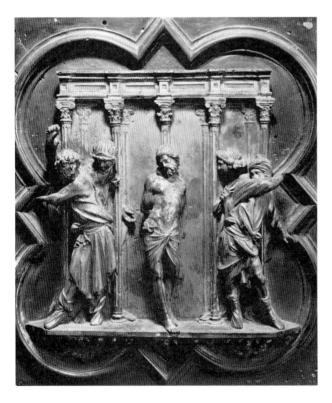

155. LORENZO GHIBERTI. *Flagellation*, panel on the 🏛 North Doors, Baptistery, Florence. c. 1416–19. Bronze with gilding, 20¹⁄₂ x 17³⁄₄" inside molding

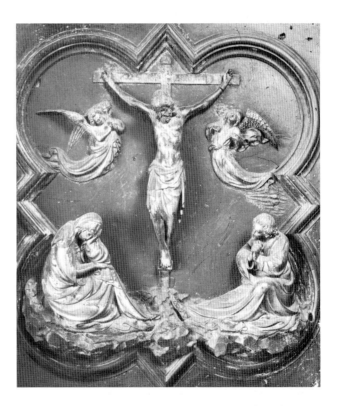

157. LORENZO GHIBERTI. *Crucifixion*, panel on the 🏛 North Doors, Baptistery, Florence. 1407–c. 1413. Bronze with gilding, 20¹⁄₂ x 17³⁄₄" inside molding

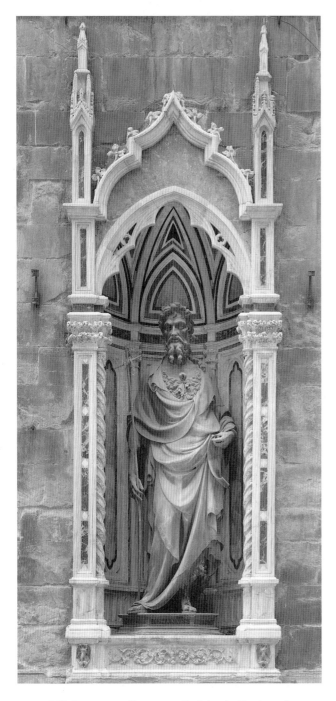

158. LORENZO GHIBERTI. *St. John the Baptist* and tabernacle. 1405–17. Bronze figure, originally with gilded decoration, and marble and mosaic niche; height of figure 8' 4". ⛪ Orsanmichele, Florence. Commissioned by the Arte di Calimala

While he was working on the doors, the Calimala guild commissioned Ghiberti to execute a bronze statue of St. John the Baptist (fig. 158) for the guild's niche at Orsanmichele (see fig. 6). This structure, originally a loggia, was rebuilt by the Commune in 1337 as a combined shrine, wheat exchange, and granary; its enormous size may have been intended to convince citizens of the vast amounts of grain the Commune kept available in case of seige or famine. In 1339 the fourteen niches on the ground floor level were assigned to the leading guilds of Florence, who had the obligation of

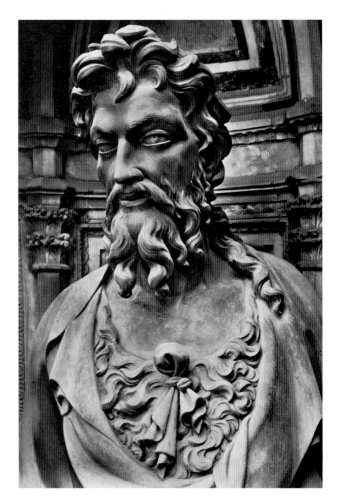

159. Head of St. John the Baptist, detail of fig. 158

filling them with statues of their patron saints. By 1400 only two of these statues had been set up. But under the stress of the attacks on Florence, first from Milan and then from Naples, pressure on the guilds was revived, and they were given a brief period to fulfill their obligations. All the statues were completed between 1411 and 1429, and thus a group of monumental heroic statues appeared in Florence that were easily visible from the street, since their feet were barely above the eye level of the passerby. Once it had begun, the march of Florentine statues did not stop for twenty years or so. At Orsanmichele and at the Cathedral, two centers of civic and spiritual life in the Florentine Republic, no fewer than thirty-four larger-than-life statues were set up; still more were planned. It is striking that the new figurative style of the Renaissance is seen first in sculpture and only later in painting.

Ghiberti's monumental bronze *St. John* was an ambitious undertaking. No bronze figure on this scale—more than eight feet in height—had been cast for centuries in Italy, and it seems clear that the idea of the statue must have come from the self-confident Ghiberti. The guild's uncertainty about his ability to complete a bronze figure on this scale is clear in the contract, which states that the guild would owe him nothing if he did not succeed. Ghiberti successfully cast this monumental figure in a single piece, thereby reviving the tradition of bronze figural sculpture known from antiquity.

Although what have been called the "sword-blade" rhythms of Ghiberti's drapery appear in Lorenzo Monaco's paintings, there is a naturalism and an intent of purpose about Ghiberti's *St. John* that is missing from the monk's painted fantasies. The statue shows us a saint who has lived long in the wilderness, whose hair and beard fall in disordered locks, whose eyes in their deep sockets seem to gaze intently into the future (fig. 159). But all the apparent wildness is governed by Ghiberti's sense of unity through linear movement. The curves of hair and beard are stylish and contrast elegantly with the large, strong folds of the saint's cloak.

The *St. John*, with its bursting curves and deliberate exaggerations of shape, is still imbued with the ideas of the International Gothic, as indeed are the earlier panels from the North Doors; Ghiberti's bronze *St. Matthew* (fig. 160), however, commissioned for Orsanmichele in 1419 by the Arte del Cambio, the guild of the bankers, represents the culmination of the new classical style. The only Gothic elements are the pointed arch and florid gable of the tabernacle. Otherwise, the grand figure, moving with poise and balance before its semicircle of Corinthian pilasters, suggests the dignity and ease of a classical philosopher portrait. In ancient style, St. Matthew places his weight on one leg, leaving the other relaxed and suggesting the figure's potential for movement. His right hand points toward his breast, his left holds an open book in which we read, in an early example of the grand Roman capitals that will soon become fashionable, the opening chapter of his Gospel. Such a figure is unthinkable without the intervening statues for Orsanmichele by Donatello and Nanni di Banco (see figs. 164, 168), in which, as we shall see, manifestoes of a new classicism were launched. But Ghiberti's version of the classical style is his own; flowing through it are the same linear ease, freedom, and harmony that are visible in his most "Gothic" works. The head, with its mountain of vigorous curls, epitomizes the meditative intellectuality of Ghiberti's art.

DONATELLO TO 1417

Ghiberti's contemporary Donato di Niccolo Bardi (c. 1386/90–1466), known as Donatello, seems to have been as tense and impulsive as Ghiberti was serene and shrewd. Donatello was a member of the Arte di Pietra e Legname, the guild of the workers in stone and wood, and although he made many works in bronze, he certainly did not think as a metalworker does. Neither can it be said that he was bound by the conventions of stoneworkers. He saw things in his own vivid and often revolutionary way. He shared neither Brunelleschi's concern for strict proportional relationships nor Ghiberti's interest in graceful line. He worked directly with his materials, seeing their possibilities almost as if he were painting in them. More than any of the contemporary innovators, he was fascinated by the inner life of his sub-

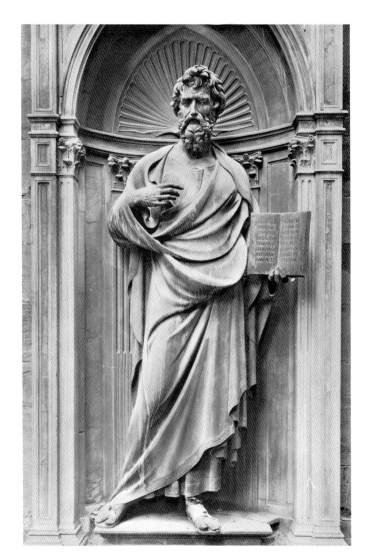

160. LORENZO GHIBERTI. *St. Matthew* and tabernacle. 1419–22. Bronze figure, originally with gilded decoration, and marble and mosaic niche; height of figure 8' 10". 🏛 Orsanmichele, Florence. Commissioned by the Arte del Cambio

jects and the naturalistic optical effects he observed in the world around him. The result is an art disturbing in its immediacy and careless of surface refinements, but able to reach a high level of force and drama.

One of Donatello's earliest known works is the marble *David* (fig. 161), which was originally commissioned to be placed high on a buttress of Florence Cathedral. Its fate was, in some respects, similar to that of another statue carved for this same position and also not put in place, the *David* created almost a century later by Michelangelo (see fig. 477); in 1416, the Priori of the Republic called for Donatello's statue to be set up in the Palazzo dei Priori as a symbol of the Florentine Republic. The right hand originally held a leather or bronze strap for the slingshot (only the marble portion enclosing the stone now remains, on Goliath's brow), and the statue was inscribed: "To those who bravely fight for the fatherland, the gods will lend aid even against the most terrible foes." David wears a crown of amaranth, a plant that in classical antiquity symbolized the undying fame of heroes.

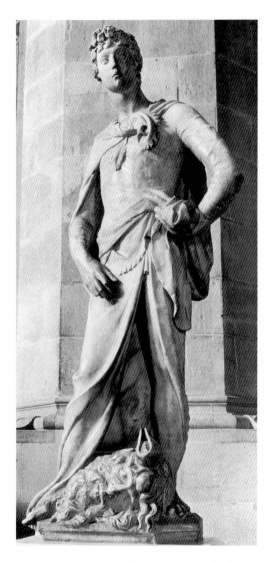

161. DONATELLO. *David*. 1408–9; reworked 1416.
Marble, height 6' 3" (including base). Bargello, Florence.
Commissioned by the Opera del Duomo for one
of the buttresses of the Duomo; later displayed at the
Palazzo dei Priori

In the pose and drapery, echoes of the Late Gothic
may be discerned, but the folds do not flow easily, as in
the work of Ghiberti. Nothing flows easily in Donatello—his work is often tense and sometimes deliberately harsh. The boy stands proudly yet awkwardly, with
his left hand bent upward on his hip and his head tilted.
The lines of the drapery oscillate back and forth in
curves, from his right foot upward toward the head. The
youth's elevated chin and self-confident posing assert his
awareness of his triumph, and he seems completely self-
centered.

The sculptor is fascinated by textures; although a hint
of Late Gothic serpentine line flows through the hair
and beard, they also form unkempt masses that contrast
to David's smooth cloak and smoother neck and cheeks.
Even at this early stage in Donatello's style, curious
sculptural effects are being investigated. Projections and
hollows in the marble no longer correspond to projections and hollows in the represented object, and Donatello has begun to flatten contrasts in form and to utilize
projections and hollows to attract light and cast shadows.

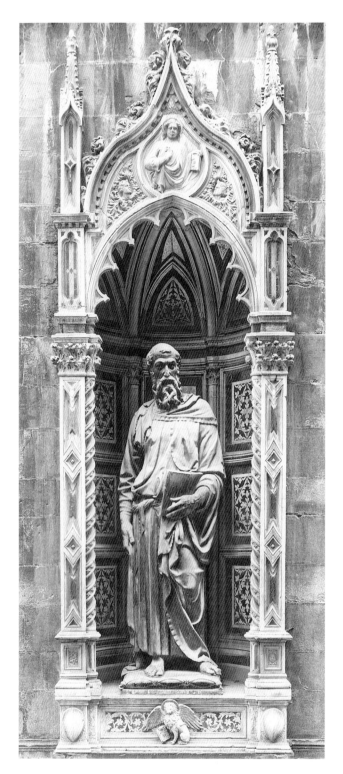

162. DONATELLO. *St. Mark*. 1411–15.
Marble figure, originally with gilded decoration and metal
additions; height 7' 10". Removed from niche on
Orsanmichele and now in storage. Commissioned by the Arte
dei Linaioli e Rigattieri for their niche on Orsanmichele,
Florence. Niche by Perfetto di Giovanni and Albizzi di Pietro

These tendencies toward suggestion rather than description will gradually increase in Donatello's work
over time. His earliest contribution to fill the niches of
Orsanmichele was probably a marble *St. Mark* (fig. 162)
for the Arte dei Linaioli e Rigattieri, the linen weavers
and peddlers. Shortly after the statue was commissioned

from Donatello, the guild approved the drawing submitted by two stonecarvers for the figure's elaborate inlaid marble tabernacle and commissioned them to execute the tabernacle. Donatello, then, did not design the niche in which his figure of Mark would be displayed. The contract set the tabernacle's price at 200 florins, but Donatello's statue was only to be appraised at the completion of the work, revealing that whereas decorative work could be evaluated in advance, a more creative project such as a figure could only be judged upon completion. Since Donatello was usually paid between 90 and 100 florins for a figure like the Mark, it is clear that the tabernacle would cost approximately twice as much as the figure.

A greater contrast could hardly be imagined than that between this statue and Ghiberti's *St. John the Baptist* (see fig. 158). Late Gothic drapery forms have completely disappeared. The feet of the figure seem to sink into his cushion (cushions were sold by the Rigattieri), a device that heightens the effect of reality, while the drapery seems to pulsate and subside over the underlying torso and limbs. Donatello seems to be demonstrating how cloth, the product of the patron guild, behaves. Why, one wonders, had the Florentines, whose fortunes were largely founded on the manufacture, processing, and sale of cloth, not paid more attention to its properties before, instead of being seduced by abstract formulas, whether Byzantine, Giottesque, or Late Gothic?

St. Mark's mantle, like David's, is tied about the shoulders, and pouches and folds of cloth fall around the hips without concealing their structure. The figure stands in the *contrapposto* pose derived from antiquity: the left knee comes forward through the folds to emphasize that this is the relaxed leg, while the straight folds over the weight-bearing leg reinforce its role in the figure's pose. In these areas the Mark bears a striking resemblance to the caryatids from the ancient Greek Erechtheum in Athens, a monument Donatello could not have seen but copies of which he may have known. If Donatello's figure suggests the potential for movement more strongly than do the Greek maidens, it is in large part because of the way the axes of Mark's body twist in space.

It has been rightly claimed that this statue represents so abrupt a break with tradition that it should be considered a mutation—a fundamental declaration of the new Renaissance position with respect to the visible world. Yet it has not been emphasized that this new position is stated with simple, practical means. Vasari tells us that a sculptor should first model a clay figure in the nude. The next step is to dip sheets of cloth in what potters today call "slip" (a very thin paste of water and clay), hang these masses of cloth on the clay figure until the drapery falls in a convincingly naturalistic manner, and let them harden. Then a full-scale statue in marble or bronze can be made on the basis of this draped model. In one of Donatello's later works, *Judith and Holofernes* (see fig. 292), we can see in the cloth over the forehead

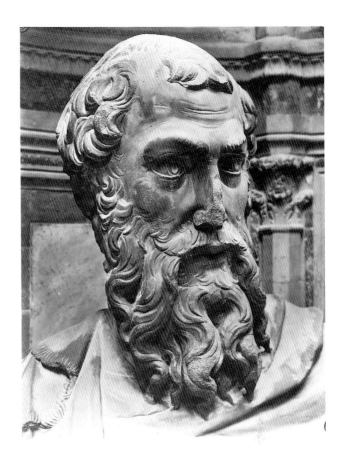

163. Head of St. Mark, detail of fig. 162

where the slip broke away during casting and the cloth itself was cast into bronze.

According to Vasari, the officials of the guild objected to the figure of St. Mark when they saw it in Donatello's studio and refused to allow it to be set up in their tabernacle. The sculptor asked them to let him work on it in its final position and, after it was placed on Orsanmichele, he pretended to continue carving behind a screen. He then called in the officials, who enthusiastically approved of the work they had previously rejected. Presumably, Donatello had from the beginning calculated how much he should lengthen the torso and shorten the legs to make the figure seem naturalistic when seen from street level.

Donatello's statue is formidable not only in the conviction and naturalism of its rendering but also in the concentrated power of the face. St. Mark seems, on the one hand, to assess the outer world and its dangers and, on the other, to summon up the inner resources of the self, which must be marshaled against them. This noble face with its expression of severe determination—the Italian term *terribile* is how the Renaissance would describe it—can be thought of as a symbolic portrait of the ideal Florentine under stress, so stirringly described at that time by the humanist propagandists for the Republic. It is a summation of the virtues demanded in an age of crisis. The eyes flare, the brow knits, the head lifts, the figure draws back in pride and a new moral grandeur. At this same time, the styles of Florence's opponents, Milan and Naples, remained flamboyantly Gothic.

In the details of the *St. Mark*, Donatello's optical suggestions show an important increase (fig. 163). Curls of

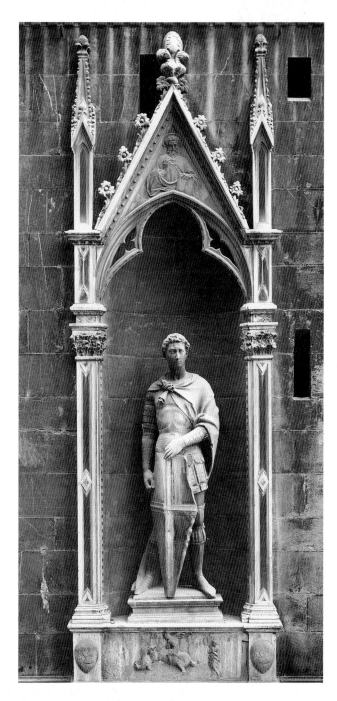

164. DONATELLO. *St. George* (historic photograph of the statue in its original location on Orsanmichele). c. 1415–17. Marble, height 6' 5". The figure is now in the Bargello, Florence. Commissioned by the Arte dei Corazzai e Spadai for their niche on Orsanmichele, Florence

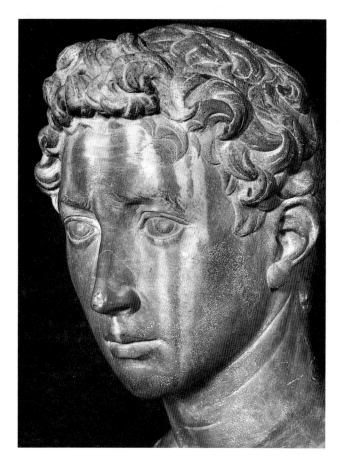

165. Head of St. George, detail of fig. 164

hair and beard are not modeled in the round as the Pisano family or Ghiberti would have done; grooves and scratches suggest reality as it is revealed in light and shade. Donatello's interest in optical effects leads him to abandon Ghiberti's incised cornea edge and drilled pupil, which set out to preserve the external shape of the eyeball; in Donatello's *St. Mark* the pupil is dilated, becoming a deep hole, so that shadows, equated to the tonal values within the transparent cornea, substitute for the external shape.

Donatello's new style is celebrated in his *St. George* (fig. 164), also for Orsanmichele. Like the *St. Mark*, this statue was made for a medium-sized guild that could not afford a work in bronze. The marble original, removed from its niche at the end of the nineteenth century to protect it from the elements, was replaced, ironically, by a cast in bronze. St. George was the patron saint of the Arte dei Corazzai e Spadai, the guild of armorers and sword makers, whose stock must have gone up sharply in the hectic days when Florence was threatened by Ladislaus. We can no longer see the *St. George* as Donatello intended him to look. A socket hole in his right hand, still bearing traces of corroded metal, and drill holes at various points indicate that the figure once sported the products of the guild he protected—a helmet, a jutting sword or spear, and a belt and sheath. These have long since disappeared. The helmet would probably have covered most of the curly locks, and the sword or spear would have protruded menacingly into the street. The taut lines of Donatello's figures, already evident in the marble *David*, are clarified here in the shield poised on its pointed tip, in the pointed shapes of the drapery, and in the sharply pointed, steel-clad feet.

The face comes as a surprise (fig. 165). It is not the face of an ideal hero but of an individual who knows what fear is. The history of human crises is studded with individuals who never did a brave thing until an emergency called forth a burst of action. Donatello's *St. George* shows us a sensitive, reflective face, with delicate features—a pointed nose, a slightly receding chin, dilated eyes looking outward as if fearful of the approaching combat, and a brow puckered with nervous tension. His stance, balanced on both feet, expresses resilient preparedness. His entire being seems to be marshaling resources against danger from without. "In times of safety anyone can behave well," said Niccolò da Uzzano, one of the humanist leaders of the Florentine Republic; "it is in adversity that real courage is shown." This passage and others written by the humanists reveal the same qualities of thought and feeling seen in the *St. George* and in many of the monumental statues of the new age.

The most startling innovation of the St. George tabernacle at Orsanmichele is the marble relief on the base (fig. 166) representing the story of the young hero's victory over a dragon. The marble for this relief, an especially fine piece, was ordered in 1417, a year that should be regarded as a crucial date in artistic history. Until this moment, sculptors had conceived of the background of a relief sculpture as a plane in front of which the figures were placed or from which they seemed to emerge. Even Ghiberti, although apparently wanting to penetrate the inert background, did so only by means of spatial implication. In traditional relief sculpture, figures were carved almost in the round, barely adhering to the background slab, or in a kind of half-round; only rarely were they systematically reduced in projection in the manner of low relief. A cross section of an ancient or medieval relief would show the background slab as a straight line and rising from it would be projections corresponding to cross sections of the figures. But a cross section of Donatello's *St. George and the Dragon* would be illegible, a mere series of shapeless bumps and shallow hollows. These projections and depressions are subtly manipulated to attract light and cast shadow.

Donatello's relief sculpture no longer corresponds to the idea of the object, nor to the object as we know it, but to the image of that object which light casts upon the retina. This is a crucial distinction that marks an end to medieval art. The eye is now supreme. The new technique is so subtle that Donatello dissolves the barrier between represented object and background. He turns the marble into air, showing us distant hills, trees, and even convincingly naturalistic clouds—not the visionary appendages seen in the Trecento and early Ghiberti. The little arcade to the right comes remarkably close to one-point perspective, and the forms are progressively altered in their precision of statement by an intervening veil of atmosphere. While the horse rears from the shock of George's lance plunged in the dragon's breast, the princess clasps her hands, the arcade and rocky ground carry the eye back into misty distance, and the intervening air even seems stirred by breezes. All this is done in a sketchy, remarkably unsculptural manner, with Donatello employing the chisel as if it were a drawing instrument. The Italian expression for Donatello's new invention is *rilievo schiacciato* (flattened relief). This useful term is inaccurate, for the forms are not created by flattening. Here Donatello has abandoned the traditional notion of relief in favor of optical suggestion.

Clearly, Donatello's effects were calculated for the position of the relief on the north side of the building, where it was exposed to a soft, diffused, unchanging light reflected from the buildings across the street. The relief depends on the autonomy of a single pair of eyes at a single point in space. Implicit in this approach is a new concept of the individual wholly alien to the medieval notion of corporate society. It may not be coincidental that the new idea should first appear in a relief of the victory of St. George over the dragon, which can be seen as symbolically reenacting the triumph of Florence against Ladislaus. There were imperfections in Floren-

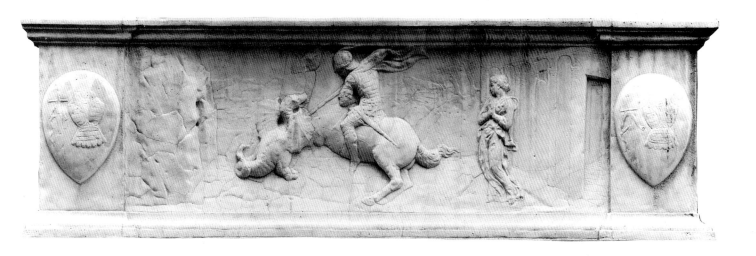

166. Donatello. *St. George and the Dragon*, relief now removed from the St. George tabernacle, Orsanmichele, Florence. c. 1417. Marble, 15 3/8 x 47 1/4". Bargello, Florence

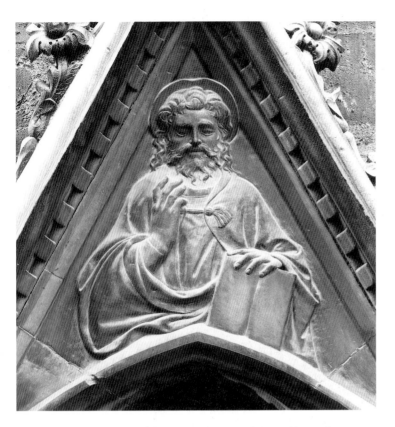

167. DONATELLO. *God the Father*, gable on the
St. George tabernacle, 🏛 Orsanmichele, Florence.
c. 1415–17. Marble, height 27"

tine democracy, but the declarations of her humanists
and, from the other side, the denunciations of liberty by
apologists for the dictatorships leave no doubt that to
contemporaries the freedom of the individual was at
stake. This concept of freedom is often exalted as one of
the wellsprings of the new style.

In Northern Europe a similar interest in naturalism
was taking place in the art of the Netherlandish minia-
turists and panel painters; their enthusiasm for the visible
world and every object that it contained resulted in a
technique of breathtaking accuracy of representation.
But the illustrations of the *Turin-Milan Hours*, the earliest
works by Jan van Eyck that show a stage comparable
to the new point of view revealed in Donatello's relief,
are datable probably in the 1420s. Paradoxically, then,
Donatello's sculptural relief could be called the most
advanced *pictorial* composition of its time. Lorenzo
Monaco and his Late Gothic contemporaries give no
hint that they knew what Donatello was about. In the
gable at the top of the St. George tabernacle, God the
Father (fig. 167) blesses and protects the patron saint
and, by extension, the guilds, the Republic, and freedom itself. He is depicted in *rilievo schiacciato,* and his
head appears to be leaning down, foreshortened, as he
lifts his right hand in benediction.

NANNI DI BANCO

A contemporary of Ghiberti and Donatello in the program at Orsanmichele was a short-lived sculptor, Nanni
di Banco (1385?–1421). Brought up by his sculptor father who worked in the Cathedral workshop, Nanni
was responsible for several important sculptures for the
Cathedral and for the statues in three niches at Orsanmichele. The most striking of these is certainly the *Four
Crowned Martyrs* (fig. 168). According to legend, these
martyrs were Christian sculptors working in ancient
Rome who, when commanded to carve a statue of a
pagan god by the emperor Diocletian, refused to betray

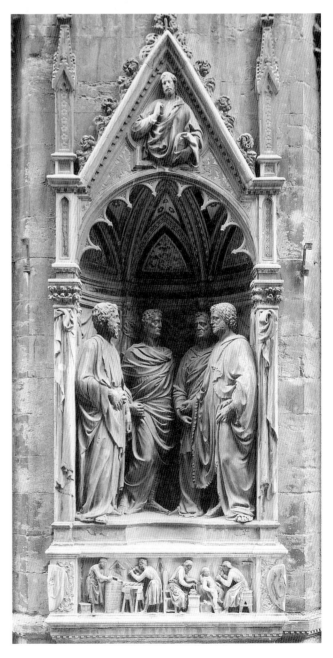

168. NANNI DI BANCO. *Four Crowned Martyrs* and tabernacle.
1410s. Marble, height of figures 6'. 🏛 Orsanmichele,
Florence. Commissioned by the Arte di Pietra e Legname

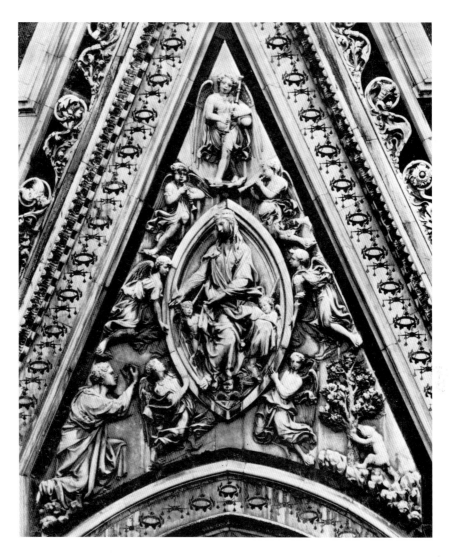

169. NANNI DI BANCO. *Assumption of the Virgin*, gable on the ⬚ Porta della Mandorla, Cathedral, Florence. 1414–21. Marble. Commissioned by the Opera del Duomo

their religious principles and were executed. The niche still has some Gothic details, but the sculptors themselves, enveloped in togalike cloaks, could hardly look more Roman, and their grand bearing is also inspired by Roman statuary. Their heads, strikingly reminiscent of Roman portraiture in some details, also have the vitality of living figures, and some scholars believe that two of them show Nanni's self-portrait and the portrait of his sculptor brother Antonio.

The propagandists for the Milanese and Neapolitan autocrats had recourse to examples drawn from Imperial Rome; the apologists for the Florentine Republic cited in rebuttal the virtues of Republican Rome and the Roman people, whose true heirs they felt themselves to be. And it is Republican models that these statues call to mind. Even the Tuscan version of Italian known as the *volgare* (vulgar) was defended by the humanists as the true successor to Latin. The intense Roman nature of Nanni's *Four Crowned Martyrs* may be the sculptor's attempt to be historically accurate—to represent these sculptors as a part of the ancient Roman world in which they lived, worked, and died. Such an attitude would coincide with the new interest in accurate, researched history evident in the work of contemporary humanists.

There is something conspiratorial about these four men who are united in a resolve to die for their principles. The patrons were the Arte di Pietra e Legname—the guild of workers in stone and wood—in which Nanni had been inscribed since 1405. By depicting the guild's patrons in this manner, Nanni has apotheosized the guild, as Donatello was shortly to do for the armorers in the *St. George*. The four standing figures grouped in a semicircle are an unprecedented composition in Italian sculpture, and they were to exercise a profound effect on the humanistic art of the Quattrocento, especially on the painters Masaccio and Andrea del Castagno.

The figure to the right seems to be speaking, while the others listen, contemplating their decision and assessing the consequences of their resolution. The movements of the drapery folds seem in some cases to sweep the four together, in others to hold them hesitantly apart. But the figures are united by two simple devices. First, the pedestal is carved in an arc that roughly follows the pattern of the feet. Second, the tabernacle is draped in broad folds, a motif taken from ancient sarcophagi that reinforces the semicircular grouping. Details of features, hair, and beards either long or stubbly (the decision not to shave was, in certain periods of Roman history, a penitential resolve) demonstrate both a strong Latinism and many survivals of the Gothic, natural enough in a sculptor educated in a fairly conservative tradition. Nanni is apparently not interested in the optical suggestions of Donatello; his drapery masses and details, locks of hair and beard, stubble, wrinkles, and veins are modeled as in the long tradition of *sculptural* sculpture and not flattened or sketched in Donatello's illusionistic method.

To enhance the naturalism of the group, the feet of the two outer figures overlap the base and, because the molding on which the white marble figures stand is a distinctive gray-veined marble the suggestion is that there is no base whatsoever. Like the malleable pillow below the feet of Donatello's *St. Mark,* which heightens the sense of reality, Nanni proposes that these figures could step out of their tabernacle. In the gable above, leaning out of the quatrefoil as from a window, Nanni shows us God the Father, fully modeled and without a halo; in the relief below, four stoneworkers representing the four branches of the guild build a wall, carve a column, measure a capital, and finish a statue of a nude putto.

It is, of course, idle to speculate on what might have been the achievements of an artist who died young. But the single-minded force of Nanni's art makes us wonder whether the course of the Quattrocento might not have been different had he lived to midcentury or even beyond, as did Donatello and Ghiberti. The culminating work of Nanni's brief career is his *Assumption of the Virgin* (fig. 169) above the Porta della Mandorla, a doorway on Florence Cathedral that takes its name from the mandorla (almond-shaped glory) surrounding the Virgin. The work, commissioned in 1414, was said to have been incomplete at Nanni's death in 1421, but this may refer only to the setting up of the ensemble.

In contrast to the gravity of Nanni's work at Orsanmichele, his *Assumption* is turbulent. Four sturdy, adolescent angels lift the strongly molded mandorla, and from within it the Virgin, supported by seraphim, hands down her belt to the kneeling St. Thomas as proof of her assumption (it was believed that this belt was preserved as a relic in the nearby Tuscan town of Prato). In Nanni's sculpture the belt was originally a length of golden-edged silk, but it was later replaced with a metal version; the spikes that held it in place can still be seen in Mary's hands. The usual witnesses are absent, and the scene acquires the character of a private revelation to St. Thomas, the most famous of doubters. The only other being who is present, except for the angels (three more, making music, fill the point of the gable), is a bear cub trying to shake acorns from an oak tree, a creature that must have some symbolic significance. Perhaps Nanni intended to contrast the impossibility of gaining bounty through force, exemplified by the animal's greed and rage, with the golden gift received by St. Thomas through divine grace.

The flying folds, agitated by the upward movement of Mary's mandorla, envelop figures of an insistent corporeality. The faces are full of the individuality, energy, and beauty that are hallmarks of Renaissance style. Nanni was in the forefront of the Florentine Renaissance, in full control of its naturalistic and classical resources.

DONATELLO c. 1417 TO c. 1435

Donatello was involved repeatedly in work for the Cathedral of Florence, even contributing two small heads to the Porta della Mandorla after Nanni's death. During the twenty years from 1415 to 1435, the master, sometimes in partnership with Nanni di Bartolo, carved for the Campanile (see fig. 77) seven marble prophets that complete a series of sixteen begun in the Trecento. These statues have now been transferred to the Museo dell' Opera del Duomo, where they have lost an essential element of their former effect—the tension between statue and niche evident in works by Donatello, Ghiberti, and Jacopo della Quercia. At Orsanmichele the statues could address the citizen in the street from not far from eye level, but the Campanile niches are so high above the ground that the figures can only be viewed from a distance of about sixty feet. Donatello, who had been relatively conservative in his treatment of the earlier statues in the cycle, began to realize as they were installed that he would have to adopt more drastic methods. The most dramatic of the group are certainly the so-called *Zuccone* ("Big Squash," i.e., "Baldy"), now often identified as *Habakkuk,* and *Jeremiah* (figs. 170, 172).

The psychological tension in these figures surpasses in intensity anything that Donatello had previously created. In Gothic cathedrals and throughout Italian Trecento art, Old Testament prophets and New Testament saints—with the obvious exception of John the Baptist—are dignified characters with flowing robes and well-combed hair. Not so these emaciated creatures, who seem to be throbbing with the import of their divinely inspired messages and the devastation of their rejection. Their stances and unforgettable expressions convey the fiery intensity of the Prophetic books of the Old Testament. They are deliberately ugly, but in their ugliness Donatello's conviction has found a strange beauty. The *Zuccone* (fig. 170) draws his chin in, gazes bitterly down, and seems to open his mouth in condemnation of humanity's iniquities. The figure is skin and bone under the rough heaps of cloth that suggest a toga. The hand clutches convulsively at the strap and the rolled top of the scroll. The bald head is carved with brutal strokes, left roughly finished (fig. 171), and the few marks that represent the stubble on the chin, the flare of the lips, and the eyebrows are exaggerated by the effects of weathering. Donatello has calculated the effect of the statue on an observer at least sixty feet away.

Jeremiah (fig. 172) is equally terrifying, and one wonders where Donatello found the models for these statues. Denunciatory types still roam the streets of Florence; per-

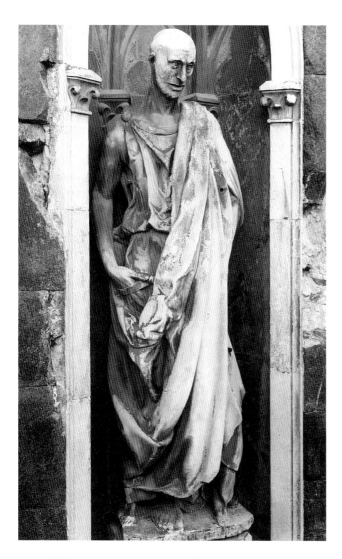

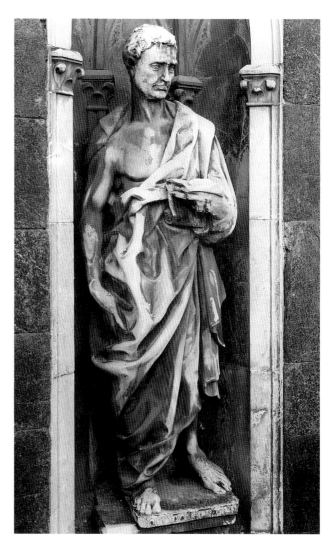

170. DONATELLO. *Zuccone (Habakkuk)*, seen here on the Campanile, Florence (now in Museo dell'Opera del Duomo, Florence). c. 1427–36. Marble, height 6' 5". Commissioned by the Opera del Duomo

172. DONATELLO. *Jeremiah*, seen here on the Campanile, Florence (now in Museo dell'Opera del Duomo, Florence). c. 1423–25. Marble, height 6' 3"

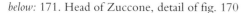

below: 171. Head of Zuccone, detail of fig. 170

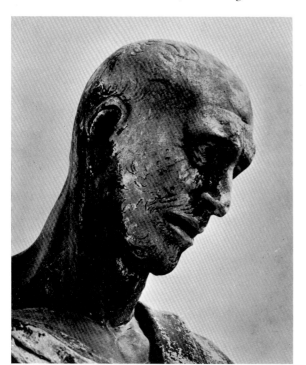

haps in Donatello's day there were even more of them. Certain features in Donatello's heads suggest that he was inspired by the realism found in Roman portrait busts, but these sources have been transfigured by Donatello's imaginative powers. The pulsating structure of folds, disordered locks, tense poses, and searing glances here become a modern equivalent for the Christian conflict between the Virtues and Vices. This theme, which is often represented symbolically in Gothic sculpture and painting (see Giotto's grisaille frescoes at Padua; figs. 69–71), has since Early Christian times been called the Psychomachia, or "warfare in the soul."

Donatello's optical interests and the vitality of his dramatic style reach a climax in the *Feast of Herod* (fig. 173) for the baptismal font of the Cathedral of Siena, a project in which he was involved with other sculptors, including Ghiberti and the Sienese Jacopo della Quercia. Donatello's contribution, executed between 1423 and 1427, is certainly closer to a consistent statement of one-point perspective than any earlier work in Western art. The invention of perspective was credited to Bru-

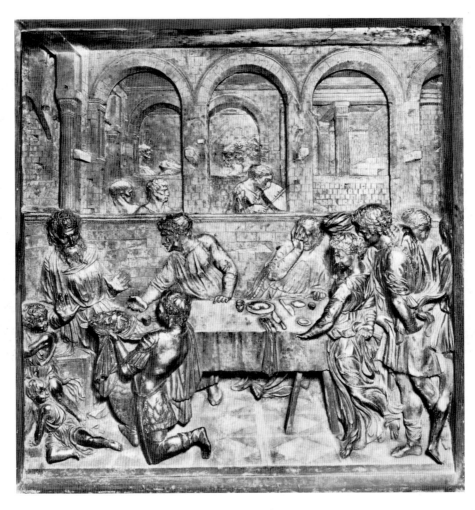

173. DONATELLO. *Feast of Herod*, panel on the 🜨 Baptismal Font, Baptistery, Siena. 1423–27. Gilded bronze, 23½" square

nelleschi by his anonymous biographer and by Vasari, although the question remains one of the most vexing in the history of ideas. The biographer describes in detail two paintings by Brunelleschi, one of which represented the Baptistery of Florence and the surrounding buildings as seen from just inside the door of the Cathedral. The sky was in burnished silver, to reflect the real sky and passing clouds and thus complete the sense of reality. The observer was required to look through a peephole in the back of the painting that was coordinated with the vanishing point of Brunelleschi's perspective view on the front; through this hole the observer saw the scene reflected in a mirror that was held an exact cubit (the distance from the elbow to the end of the middle finger, approximately eighteen inches) in front of the painted surface. The observer was thus assumed to be standing about three cubits inside the Cathedral door and sixty cubits from the front of the Baptistery. Measurements taken of the buildings were reduced in a 1:60 proportion and set forth on a plan that was then projected onto the panel.

Such a graph of space was derived from Brunelleschi's technique of producing measured drawings of architecture, for which the observer's actual position in space was a prime determinant. By forcing the observer to view the painting in the mirror, Brunelleschi was also able to guarantee that the observer's eye was exactly opposite the vanishing point. The device of the mirror also meant that the observer could see only the illusion and none of the distracting reality that surrounds a painting and reduces its illusionistic effect. Brunelleschi's perspective method seems to have been used in the early Quattrocento, in a somewhat reduced form, by a few adventurous souls, notably Donatello and, as we shall see, the painter Masaccio. For Alberti's later formulation of perspective, see pp. 238–39.

Donatello's *Feast of Herod* is not a painting, of course, but a three-dimensional relief that was to be placed on the base of a baptismal font and would, therefore, be seen from above at a rather sharp angle. To use a perspective scheme that coordinated with the observer's high viewpoint would have demanded architecture that was sharply distorted. Instead, Donatello has placed his vanishing point, established by floor lines, moldings, and

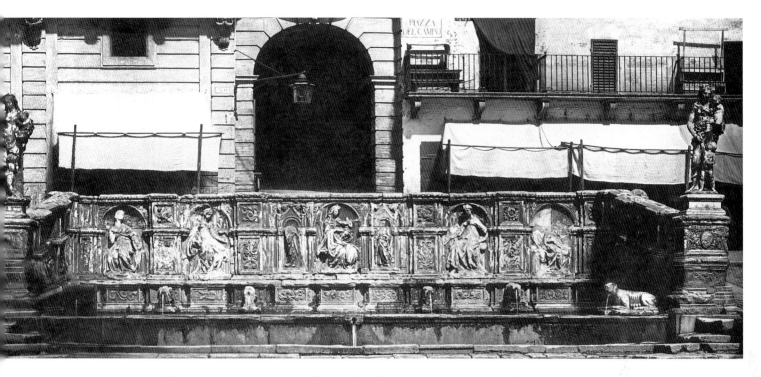

174. JACOPO DELLA QUERCIA. Fonte Gaia (historic photograph, before dismantling), Piazza del Campo, Siena. 1414–19. Marble, overall 4' 8" x 33' 4" x 18' 3". Fragments now in the Palazzo Pubblico, Siena. Commissioned by the Commune of Siena

the recession of capitals and lintels, in the exact center of the relief. But Donatello, always an enemy of regularity, has introduced so many different levels and architectural features that do not correspond from one side to the other that it is impossible to trace all the recessions accurately. He also created two curious recesses in the wall behind the figures that recede at angles counter to that of the perspective scheme and that do not even coordinate with one another. But he has also interrelated the square slabs of the inlaid floor diagonally, so that the extended diagonal of one becomes the diagonal of the square in the next row, and so on. As a result, he imposes on the basic system of orthogonals, which meet at a vanishing point within the frame, secondary systems of diagonals that meet at other vanishing points to either side, outside the frame. This produces an external control for establishing a systematic diminution of the distance between the transversals in depth. This secondary system is also a part of Alberti's perspective theory. Whether this was an original part of Brunelleschi's perspective demonstrations or Donatello hit on it ten years or so before Alberti published its formulation is uncertain.

Nothing in Donatello's architectural perspective, with its views through three successive levels separated by arches and piers, prepares us for what is happening in the foreground space. There the scheme is disrupted by the event—the presentation of St. John's severed head on a platter to Herod. The moment Donatello has chosen is the explosion of an emotional grenade that produces a wave of shock reactions among the spectators. Herod shrinks back; a guest expostulates; another recoils, covering his face with his hand; two children scramble away only to stop short and look back. At the right Salome continues her dance but two attendants stare, one with his arm about another's shoulder. It is in his composition that Donatello incorporates us and our position into his work, for when viewed from above it becomes clear that the figures are grouped in a semicircle, the center left open to express the drama of the event. The perspective network of interlocking grids is half submerged in the rush of conflicting drapery folds. Donatello's dramatic scene was to influence later artists, including Leonardo da Vinci, whose *Last Supper* (see colorplate 83, p. 452) adopts and refines the dramatic principle on which this history-making relief was based.

JACOPO DELLA QUERCIA

A fourth decisive sculptor of the Early Renaissance was a Sienese—Jacopo della Quercia (c. 1380–1438). If Vasari's accounts of Jacopo's early life are accurate, he must already have enjoyed a considerable career as a sculptor before taking part in the competition for the doors of the Florentine Baptistery in 1401, but little is preserved that can be attributed with certainty to Jacopo's early period. The major sculptural cycle dating from Jacopo's middle period is the Fonte Gaia in Siena (fig. 174), a fountain in the Piazza del Campo in front of the Palazzo

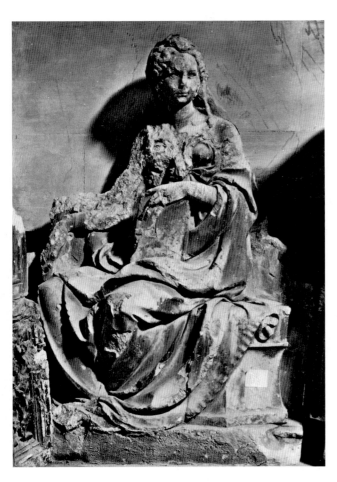

175. JACOPO DELLA QUERCIA. *Wisdom*, from the Fonte Gaia. 1418–19. Marble, 43 3/8 x 35 1/2"

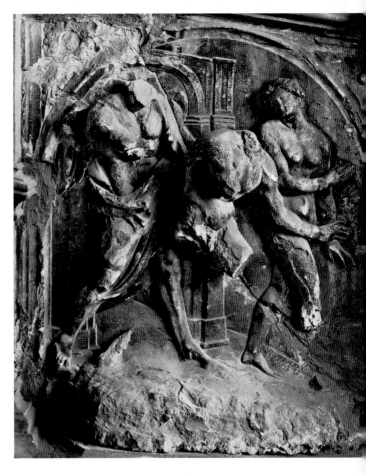

176. JACOPO DELLA QUERCIA. *Expulsion*, relief from the Fonte Gaia. 1418–19. Marble, 45 11/16 x 39 3/4". Palazzo Pubblico, Siena

Pubblico that was called "gay" because of the public celebrations that attended the opening of this first reliable water supply brought to the center of the hilly city. The fountain, commissioned in 1409, was not begun until 1414 and was finished late in 1419.

The water poured into a central rectangular basin from spigots fixed in the base of a parapet sculptured in high relief. The central niche contained the Virgin and Child, the Virgin being the patron saint of Siena. Wisdom, Hope, Fortitude, Prudence, Justice, Humility, Temperance, and Faith were represented in niches on either side of the Virgin. The reliefs at either end represented the *Creation of Adam* and the *Expulsion from Eden*, indications of the curse of Original Sin from which Mary and Christ had redeemed humankind and which is liberated by Baptism, the sacrament of water. On the terminals of the flanks stood statues of women with children that have recently been identified as Divine and Earthly Charity; previously they had been thought to represent Acca Larentia and Rea Silvia, the foster and real mothers of Romulus and Remus (Remus was considered to be the father of Senus, founder of the city of Siena). By the nineteenth century the fountain had fallen into such ruin that it was dismantled and replaced by a copy.

From *Wisdom* (fig. 175), we can see that Jacopo was well aware of the Renaissance movement in Florence. Within their low niches, the masses of these figures exert great power. The bodies twist and turn in powerful angles that counter the embracing arches. The drapery, surging in independent motion over the limbs, overflows the niches. The badly battered *Expulsion* (fig. 176) remains a work of immense power despite its condition. Adam and Eve, their muscular bodies strongly projected, are expelled from the gate of Eden by an athletic angel. The spiritual conflict evident in Donatello's art is translated by Jacopo into terms of physical action.

In many respects the art of Jacopo della Quercia is a curious phenomenon. He had little interest in the architectural achievements of the Florentine Renaissance and

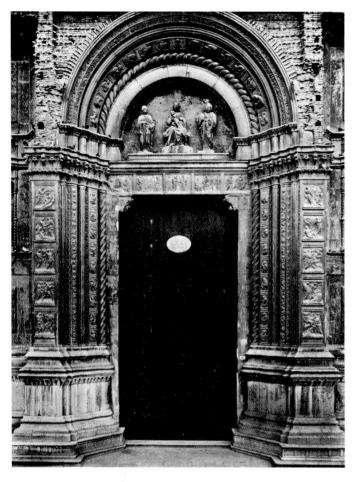

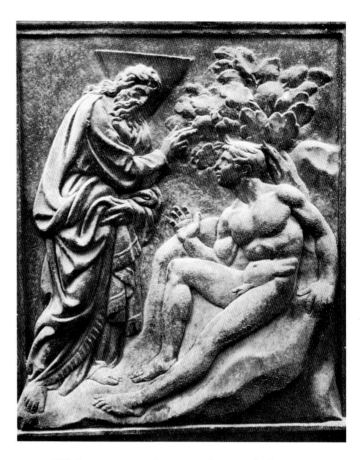

177. Jacopo della Quercia. Main Portal,
S. Petronio, Bologna. 1425–38. Commissioned by
Louis Aleman, Archbishop of Arles and Papal
Legate to Bologna

178. Jacopo della Quercia. *Creation of Adam*,
panel on Main Portal, S. Petronio, Bologna. c. 1429–34.
Marble, 39 x 36¼" with frame

paid no attention to its spatial harmonies, and his rare landscape elements remained Giottesque to the end of his days. Yet in his reliefs for the portal of San Petronio at Bologna (fig. 177) he raised the representation of the human body to a high level of dignity, beauty, and power. He projected a world of action in which figures of superhuman strength struggle and collide. Despite Jacopo's characteristic distortions (heads, hands, and feet are sometimes too large) and occasionally crude execution, his reliefs at San Petronio are immensely impressive. Fortunately, the projections are not high, and the panels have survived in better condition than the Fonte Gaia fragments.

In the *Creation of Adam* (fig. 178), a solemn, long-bearded Creator with a triangular nimbus gathers about him an enormous mantle whose sweeping folds contain all the power of Donatello's and Nanni's drapery yet none of their feeling for real cloth; with his right hand he confers on Adam a living soul. The figure of Adam, whose name in Hebrew means "earth," is read together with the ground from which he is about to rise. In contradistinction to Ghiberti's delicately constructed nudes (see fig. 237), this is a figure of athletic power, broadly built and smoothly modeled. Jacopo may have patterned the pose and treatment of the figure after the strongly classical Adam in a Byzantine ivory relief now in the Bargello in Florence that may have been available to him. Jacopo's noble figure, in turn, exercised a strong influence on the pose used by Michelangelo in the *Creation of Adam* on the Sistine Ceiling (see colorplate 97, p. 494). Of the garden itself, only the Tree of Knowledge, represented as a fig tree, is visible.

The evil effects of this tree are represented in the *Temptation* (fig. 179), a generally static scene that Jacopo has turned into a throbbing drama. To demonstrate supernatural qualities, the serpent slides right through the tree trunk to emerge on the other side. With one hand, a sinuous and sensuous Eve repulses the serpent's advance while with the other she already holds the fruit. Eve's body, one of the first voluptuous female nudes

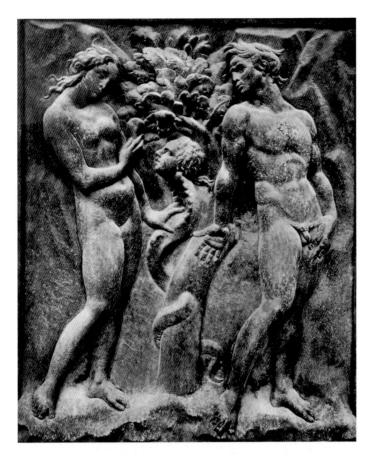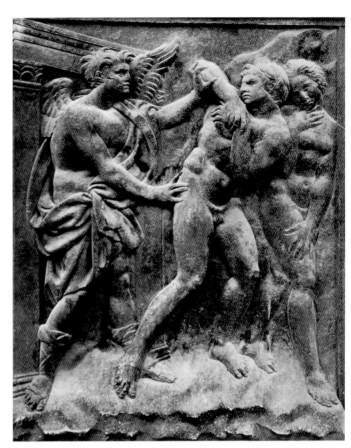

179, 180. JACOPO DELLA QUERCIA. *Temptation* (left) and *Expulsion* (right), panels on Main Portal, S. Petronio, Bologna. c. 1429–34. Marble, each 39 x 36¼" with frame

since classical antiquity, must have been influenced by an ancient statue of Venus. With a gesture of fury Adam turns away from Eve, expostulating with his head turned back toward his right shoulder, his eyes glaring. It is not hard to see why this heroic style appealed to the youthful—even the mature—Michelangelo, who must have studied Jacopo's works during his two visits to Bologna.

Most intense of all is Jacopo's *Expulsion* (fig. 180), its composition roughly the same as that of the relief on the Fonte Gaia. At San Petronio, however, the figures are well enough preserved to exhibit the full interplay of muscular forces. Adam attempts to resist, but he is powerless against the angel's touch. Eve's pose is based on that of a *Venus pudica*, the modest Venus type favored by Greek sculptors and their Roman copyists. Although occasionally there are superficial resemblances between Jacopo and Nanni, especially in facial types, the barren action-world inhabited by Jacopo's titanic figures was, at least in the Quattrocento, available only to his own tormented imagination.

8

Gothic and Renaissance
in Florentine Painting

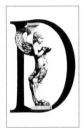

During the first two decades of the Quattrocento, the sculptors carried the banner for the new Renaissance style in the figurative arts in Florence. The painters were occupied in the execution of numerous altarpieces for Florentine churches and chapels and an occasional fresco cycle, all in variants of the Gothic style. They were not concerned with the problems that inspired the sculptors, and their works seem to belong to another era. In their midst there emerged, about 1420 or 1421, a non-Tuscan master of extraordinary originality, who, judging from the importance of his commissions, must have created a sensation.

GENTILE DA FABRIANO

Gentile da Fabriano (c. 1385?–1427) has suffered from two contradictory misconceptions at the hands of art historians. First, it was generally thought that he was born about 1370, long before the earliest probable date, and his undated works were therefore placed too early; second, he was thought to have been a conservative master. Our earliest documentary reference concerning Gentile shows him to have been living in Venice in 1408, far from his native town of Fabriano in the Marches. In the Doges' Palace in Venice, Gentile painted a fresco, now lost, of a naval battle between the Venetians and Emperor Otto III that took place in the midst of a great storm. Gentile's depiction of the storm clouds, the waves, and the battle was said to have been so realistic that those who saw it were filled with terror.

From 1414 to 1419 Gentile was in Brescia, painting a now-lost chapel at the command of Pandolfo Malatesta. There he met Pope Martin V, who, in 1417, had been elected at the Council of Constance to end the Great Schism that had divided the Church. Gentile was to follow the pope to Rome, but he only arrived there in 1426, after stopping to work in Florence, Siena, and Orvieto. In Rome he began a now-lost series of frescoes in San Giovanni in Laterano for the pope, but this work was interrupted by his death, perhaps as a consequence of the malaria that felled many visitors to the Eternal City.

Gentile's *Coronation of the Virgin* (fig. 181) from the Valle Romita altarpiece (c. 1410–14) is in some ways

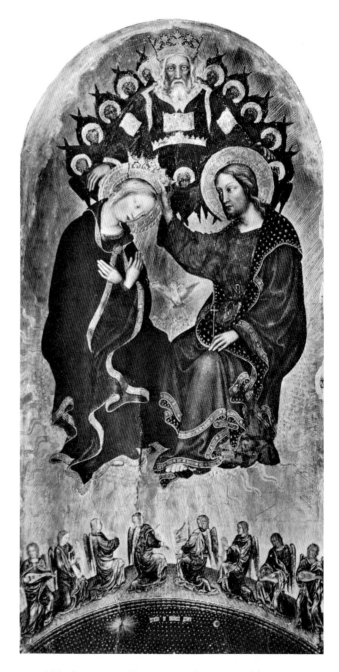

181. GENTILE DA FABRIANO. *Coronation of the Virgin*, from the Valle Romita polyptych. c. 1410–14. Panel, 70 1/8 x 31 1/8". Brera Gallery, Milan. Commissioned as the high altarpiece for Sta. Maria di Valdisasso outside Fabriano, probably by Chiavello Chiavelli, Lord of Fabriano

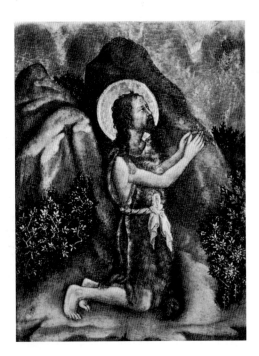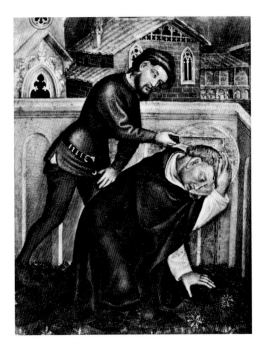

182, 183. GENTILE DA
FABRIANO. *St. John the
Baptist in the Desert* (left)
and *Assassination of
St. Peter Martyr* (right),
panels from the
Valle Romita polyptych.
c. 1410–14. Each
23½ x 15¾". Brera
Gallery, Milan

more naturalistic and less schematic than Lorenzo Monaco's representation of this same subject (see colorplate 35, p. 201). Christ and Mary sit suspended in the light of the gold background, the dove of the Holy Spirit floats between them, and God the Father above, surrounded by seraphim, extends his arms. From this empyrean height we look down on the top of the dome of Heaven, presented as if it were an architectural model bisected to show the interior, studded with stars, and hung with sun and moon. Music-making angels kneel on the outer surface of the dome, which is paved with gold and marble tiles.

The soft, full faces, heavy-lidded eyes, languorous expressions, and gentle flow of silky drapery folds are typical of Gentile's style, and the rich coloring and many details suggest his knowledge of Venetian painting. Mary's blond hair may be seen under her veil, and Christ's reddish-brown locks stream over his neck. Mary's azure mantle is lined with muted crimson lighted with tiny strokes of gold, while the mantles of God the Father and God the Son are vermilion. A brighter blue, starred with gold, lines Christ's mantle and contrasts with the vermilion of the seraphim. The gold background is tooled in conventionalized flames around the sacred pair, and incised rays surround the entire group. The effect is that of some natural celestial apparition, like the Aurora Borealis. Although the exuberant draperies of the saints in the lateral panels—not illustrated—are closely related to the International Style, their surface has a softness that is Gentile's own, as is the naturalism of the flowered carpet on which they tread. The rocky backgrounds of two of the predella panels (fig. 182) hardly differ from their Trecento forebears, but the architectural elements in the other two (fig. 183) are new and full of Venetian Gothic windows and chimneys.

Palla Strozzi, the richest man in Florence, commis-

sioned Gentile to paint the *Adoration of the Magi* (colorplate 38, p. 203) for his chapel in the sacristy of Santa Trinita. This narrative subject was unusual for a Florentine altarpiece and the splendor of its treatment unprecedented: both were justified by the destined location of the panel, for the Adoration of the Magi marks the moment when the infant Christ was first shown to the Gentiles. The theme and gorgeous garments were thus appropriate to a sacristy where the clergy vested themselves to carry the Host (the Corpus Christi) to the altar. The frame recalls the earlier Strozzi altarpiece for Santa Maria Novella by Orcagna (see colorplate 33, p. 119), but the forms are now swept together by a vitality so exuberant that it is difficult to follow the linear rhythms, as one more easily does in Lorenzo Monaco's clear-cut shapes. Lorenzo's polyphony is, as it were, replaced by a burst from a full orchestra. The left and right gables embrace roundels of the Annunciation, while in the central gable a youthful God blesses the scene and prophets recline in the spandrels. In the predella, the *Nativity*, the *Flight into Egypt*, and the *Presentation in the Temple* appear almost as one continuous strip. The life that proliferates in the ornamentation comes to a climax in the painted flowers and fruits that burst from Gothic openings in the frame and even seem to grow out over the gold itself.

Three small scenes in the arches of the main panel emphasize the journey of the Magi and their retinue to Bethlehem. In the left arch the Magi gaze at the star from the top of a mountain, while before them stretches a wavy sea, with ships awaiting at the shore. In the center the kings ride up a curving road toward the open gate of Jerusalem. To the right they are about to enter the walled town of Bethlehem; only in the foreground do they arrive at their destination—the cave of Bethlehem, with ox, ass, and manger, the ruined shed, and the modest family. Dressed in splendid garments, the oldest Magus prostrates himself before the Christ Child, his crown beside him on the ground; the second kneels and lifts his crown; the youngest, waiting his turn, still wears his crown. Attendants crowd the stage: some restrain horses (the animals shown, as becomes customary in Italian art, from the front and back), others toy with monkeys and hunting leopards, or release falcons to attack game birds.

The panoramic views and the rendering of farms, distant houses, and vineyards suggest that Gentile had seen Ambrogio Lorenzetti's *Good Government* series in Siena (see figs. 108, 109). He was also deeply influenced by the art of northern Italy, both the wild landscape backgrounds and the wonderful animals of the *ouvraige lombarde* (see pp. 150, 378). Gentile has been classified as an exponent of the International Gothic, but if this is true, his art is a phase that is remote from the Late Gothic painters in Florence. Gentile is uninterested in profiles, for example, and throughout his work, line is understood as part of a directional flow within the tissue of matter and space, whether the flow of the processions in the background, or the flow of a horse's proud body, or the flow of silks, velvets, and brocades.

The birds and animals are represented with scrupulous delicacy and also with a new psychological realism. Irreverent attendants exchange glances and, it seems, jokes as their royal masters are caught up in worship, or they look upward in suspense at a pair of fighting birds (fig. 184). The two midwives, like guests at a bridal shower, examine one of the gifts as if to assess its value. While chained monkeys chatter happily, the ox looks patiently down toward the Christ Child, and over the rim of a king's halo the ass stares with enormous eyes, his ears lifted to catch unaccustomed sounds. In the background, dogs chase hares, horses prance and rear, one horse kicks another who then complains, and two soldiers seem to be mugging a wayfarer. Gentile seems intent on re-creating in paint the whole fabric of the visible world. His rendering, however, is not merely encyclopedic, for he is satisfied only with surfaces whose vibrancy is achieved by coloristic means. As compared

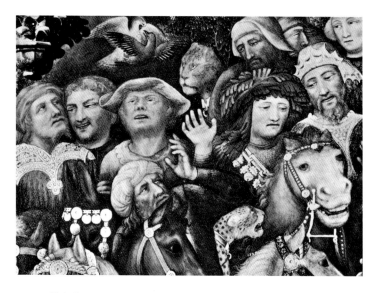

184. GENTILE DA FABRIANO. Attendants, detail of *Adoration of the Magi* (see colorplate 38, p. 203). Dated May 1423. Panel. Uffizi Gallery, Florence. Commissioned by Palla Strozzi for his burial chapel in the sacristy of Sta. Trinita, Florence

to the brilliance of Lorenzo Monaco, Gentile's color is subdued and rich, full of subtle hints and reflections. There may even be signs that Gentile had studied Florentine sculpture and Masaccio's paintings in the modeling of some of the heads and in the sharply foreshortened figure who is removing the spurs from the youngest king. Nonetheless, with all this display of visual richness and naturalism, certain basic archaisms remain. In the main panel of the altarpiece Gentile seems unaware of the new investigations of space and illusionism: his double scale for figures and setting is still Trecentesque, gold leaf over molded gesso is used for the gold damasks and gilded ornaments, and the landscape distances carry us to the distant horizons only to end in a gold background.

In the predella scenes, however, Gentile abandons, for the first time as far as we know in Italian painting, the abstract flat gold or blue background in favor of representing a sky with atmospheric and luminary effects. Gentile's *Nativity* (fig. 185), like that of Lorenzo Mona-

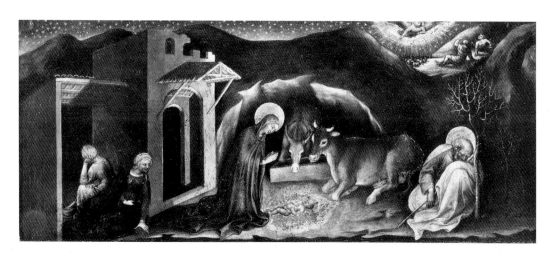

185. GENTILE DA FABRIANO. *Nativity*, on the predella of the Strozzi altarpiece (see colorplate 38, p. 203). Dated May 1423. Panel, 12¼ x 29½". Uffizi Gallery, Florence

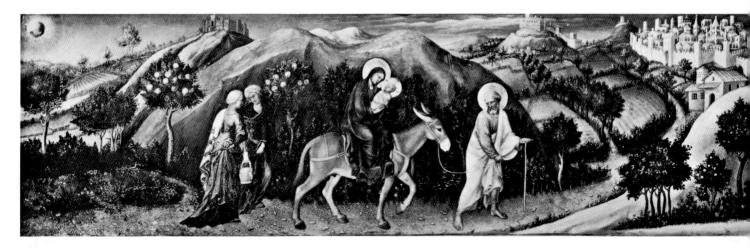

186. GENTILE DA FABRIANO. *Flight into Egypt*, on the predella of the Strozzi altarpiece (see colorplate 38, p. 203).
Dated May 1423. Panel, 12¼ x 43¼". Uffizi Gallery, Florence

co (see fig. 125), is founded on the vision of St. Bridget, but now the light effects are real rather than conventional. Although the pool of light that emanates from the Christ Child is still a surface of gold leaf with incised rays, Gentile has painted a believable light that shines upon the ceiling of the cave and the faces of the kneeling ox and ass. Illuminating the Virgin, this light casts her shadow on the shed and then casts the shadow of the shed itself upon the underside of the lean-to where the midwives have taken shelter—one curious, the other napping. This light even picks out the branches of the tree under which Joseph sleeps, making a tracery of light against the dark hills. While one portion of the hills is illuminated by a flood of gold from the angel who descends to bring the glad tidings to the shepherds, the remainder billows softly against a night sky dotted with shining stars.

The exquisite nature poetry of this scene is, to be sure, still partly Trecentesque, for it is miraculous rather than natural light that illuminates the scene and casts the shadows. Yet this is the first painting we know that contains the source of illumination within the picture and maintains its effect consistently on the represented objects. The supernatural is treated as if it were natural—so natural that one wonders if Gentile made a model of a stage set with figures and put a candle inside it before painting the scene. The little ruined structure is, of course, the same one he painted in the principal panel above; the only difference is that between December 25, in the predella, and January 6, in the main panel, the barren ground has brought forth flowering and fruit-laden trees. Apart from the religious meaning of the scene, the effect is naturalistic, convincing, and deeply poetic—especially the dark, distant hills and starry sky.

Equally convincing is the *Flight into Egypt* (fig. 186). The little family, still attended by the midwives, moves along a pebbly road that curves through a rich Tuscan landscape toward a distant city. The farms and hillsides are lighted by a sun raised in gesso and gilded, and the naturalistic light that washes over the fields, giving the effect of grain ripe for harvesting, is also gold leaf. The distant hills and towers rise against a soft, blue sky, the first naturalistic sky we know in Italian art. Darker toward the zenith, lighter toward the horizon, it is clearly represented with atmospheric perspective. One fortified villa is partly hidden by drifting clouds. So velvety is the landscape, so natural the light on rocks, pebbles, foliage, and people, and so free the brushwork that we easily accept the scene as a natural account, in spite of the persisting medieval double scale.

Gentile's stay in Florence was short, but his influence there was incalculable. To him belongs, as far as can be determined, the credit for being the first Italian painter to carry out the atmospheric discoveries Donatello had made and those realized in the North in the miniatures of the Limbourg brothers. He is also, as far as we now know, the first Italian painter to depict shadows cast consistently by light from an identifiable source, and the originator of an almost endless series of night scenes, a rarity in the Quattrocento but later a commonplace. Gentile has put into practice Ghiberti's maxim "Nothing can be seen without light."

MASOLINO AND MASACCIO

No artists in Florence in the early 1420s understood more clearly Gentile's innovations than two painters who, strange opposites, were conjoined by their collaboration in several works as well as by their sharing of the name Tommaso (Thomas). One, however, was known as Masolino ("Little Tom"), the other as Masaccio (untranslatable but certainly no compliment, since the suffix "accio" in Italian usually means "ugly" or "bad"). Perhaps these nicknames were coined to distinguish the painters according to their appearance, character, or style. Masolino, little concerned with the problems and ideals that inspired the great sculptors of the time, creates an artificial world of refined shapes and elegant manners, flow-

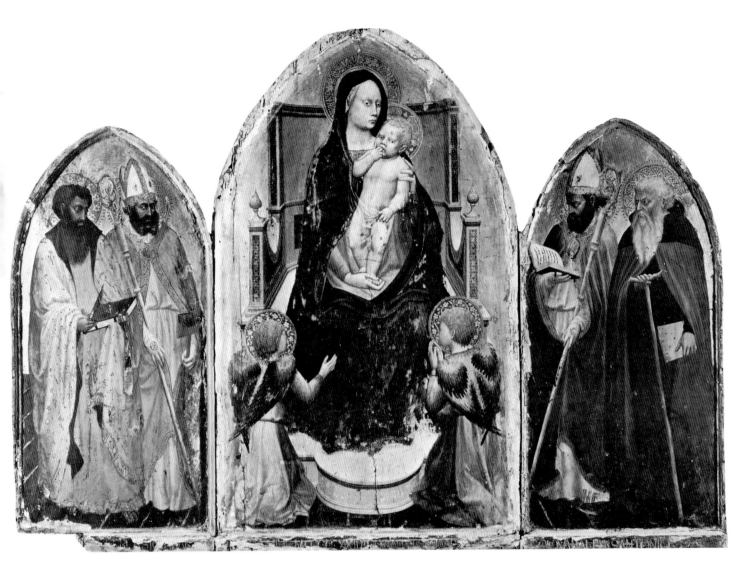

187. MASACCIO. *Madonna and Child with Saints*. Dated April 1422. Panel, 42¹/₂ x 60¹/₂".
S. Giovenale, Cascia di Reggello

erlike colors, and unreal distances. In the stream of Renaissance art, Masolino makes hardly a ripple. But Masaccio is one of the revolutionary painters of the Western tradition and as careless of "beauty" in his works as he was, apparently, neglectful of appearances in real life; he leads us into the world of space, emotion, and action that the sculptors had discovered. And yet the two managed to work together.

Maso di Cristofano Fini—Masolino—was probably born about 1400 in Panicale, a small group of houses in the upper Valdarno (Arno Valley). He joined the Arte dei Medici e Speziali in 1423. Much of his life was spent away from Florence; his most adventurous trip took him to Hungary in the service of the Florentine condottiere Pippo Spano, from September 1425 to July 1427. Later he worked in Rome and then, about 1435, in the Lombard village of Castiglione Olona. He died in either 1440 or 1447.

Masaccio—Maso di Ser Giovanni di Mone Cassai—was born December 21, 1401, in what is today San Giovanni Valdarno, not far from Panicale. He joined the guild in Florence in January 1422 and worked there and,

in 1426, in Pisa. In the summer or autumn of 1428 he went to Rome, where he died. If, as is generally claimed, this event took place in November 1428, he did not even reach his twenty-seventh birthday. Proof of this date has never been brought forward, however, and it is possible that Masaccio succumbed during the malaria season of 1429.

The old tradition that Masolino was Masaccio's teacher was laid to rest in 1961 by the discovery of an early work by Masaccio, a *Madonna and Child with Saints* (fig. 187) in the little Church of San Giovenale at Cascia di Reggello on the slopes of the Pratomagno, the mountain mass that dominates Masaccio's native town. The roughness, impulsiveness, and freedom of this triptych, dated April 23, 1422, justify Vasari's account of Masaccio as an artist who cared nothing about material considerations, neither the clothes he wore, the food he ate, the lodgings he inhabited, nor the money he received, so completely was he on fire with "*le cose dell'arte*" (literally, "the things of art"). The twenty-year-old master painted a stiff Madonna, with high forehead, staring eyes, and weak chin on a traditional inlaid mar-

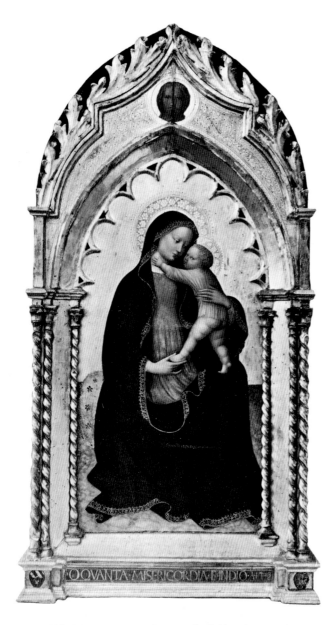

of, for example, the wings of the angels and the hair and beards of the saints. But already Masaccio has gone farther than Gentile. He needs no night illumination to prove the existence of form. The hands and limbs and, above all, the folds of the angels' tunics exist as ordinary daylight reveals them. At twenty Masaccio has assimilated the lesson of Donatello's *St. George and the Dragon* (see fig. 166), carved scarcely five years before.

One year later, in 1423, Masolino signed a dainty *Madonna and Child* (fig. 188) whose style, closely related to those of Lorenzo Monaco and Ghiberti, shows not a trace of the brutal naturalism of his fellow *valdarnese*. The delicately modeled head of the Virgin is typical of Masolino's female faces throughout his career, while the sweetness of the Christ Child, the tenderness with which he touches the Virgin's neck, and the easy curvilinear flow of the drapery are within the conventions of conservative Florentine style. Only the roundness of the modeling in light and shade betrays that Masolino, too, had attempted to learn some new lessons.

In the same year, if this author's currently unpopular view is correct, the two young artists collaborated in a

188. MASOLINO. *Madonna and Child*. 1423. Panel, 37³/₄ x 20¹/₂". Kunsthalle, Bremen

ble throne. The Christ Child, homely and stiff-limbed, holds a bunch of grapes and a veil in one hand and stuffs two fingers of the other into his mouth. Two angels kneel before the throne, and while their wings preserve the traditional rainbow gradations, the feathers are as disheveled as those of street sparrows. On either side stand pairs of morose saints. But under the guise of this workaday naturalism, the triptych still discloses its religious content, for the grapes Christ holds are those of the Eucharist.

In the triptych, no trace remains of the Late Gothic nor of Ghiberti's mellifluous folds (see fig. 158), and at first sight there appears no influence of Gentile either. But Gentile must already have been in Florence for several months at the time Masaccio's triptych was completed, and it may have been his style that offered the young painter the liberation from the precision of Gothic brushwork seen in the freedom and sketchiness

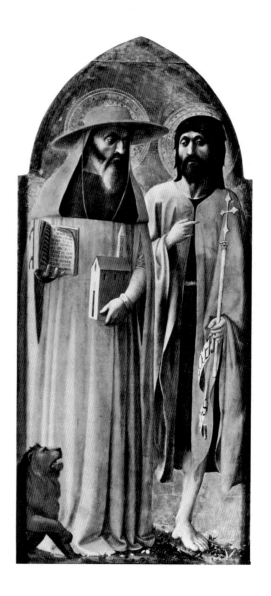

opposite below: 189. MASACCIO. *St. Jerome and St. John the Baptist*, from the Sta. Maria Maggiore triptych. c. 1423(?). Panel, 45¼ x 21½". National Gallery, London. Commissioned by Pope Martin V for Sta. Maria Maggiore, Rome

below left: 190. MASOLINO (and MASACCIO?). *Founding of Sta. Maria Maggiore*, from the Sta. Maria Maggiore triptych. c. 1423(?). Panel, 56¾ x 30". Museo di Capodimonte, Naples. Commissioned by Pope Martin V for Sta. Maria Maggiore, Rome

below right: 191. MASOLINO. *St. John the Evangelist and St. Martin of Tours*, from the Sta. Maria Maggiore triptych. c. 1423(?); reworked 1427 or 1428(?). Panel, 39⅝ x 20½". John G. Johnson Collection, Philadelphia

major joint undertaking, a two-sided altarpiece ordered by Pope Martin V for the Church of Santa Maria Maggiore at Rome that has been reconstructed from its scattered pieces. Although the lawless conditions still prevailing in the Eternal City after Martin V arrived in 1420 might have made painting difficult, the pope nevertheless embarked at once on a program of restoration of the major Roman churches. Nothing prevents the supposition that he ordered the altarpiece from Rome and that the artists painted it in Florence. The central panel of the front represents the *Founding of Santa Maria Maggiore* (fig. 190), whose plan, legend held, was quickly traced on the ground by Pope Liberius after it had been outlined by a miraculous snowfall in August. The program was altered later, and Masolino had to repaint the saints on the back of the altarpiece (not illustrated) and, on the front, to transform a figure of Pope Liberius into St. John the Evangelist and St. Matthias into St. Martin of Tours. The flanking panels of the front now represent St. Jerome with John the Baptist (fig. 189) and John the Evangelist with St. Martin of Tours (fig. 191). The latter is a likeness of Pope Martin V wearing a cope bordered with little columns, a play on his family name, Colonna. The changes may have been requested by the pope when

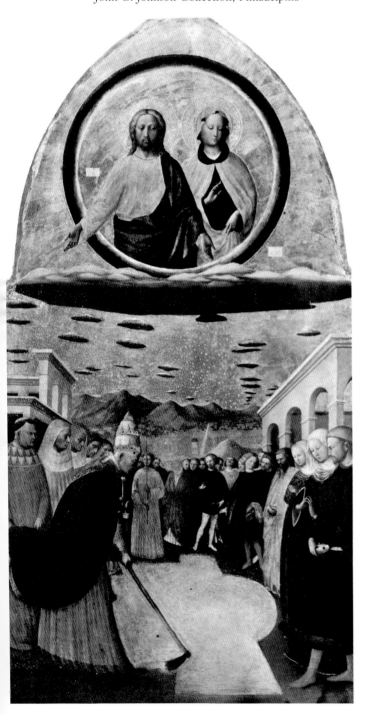

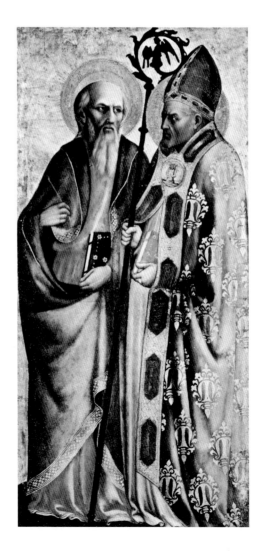

Masolino arrived in Rome, presumably in 1427 or 1428, in order to augment the importance of papal power in the principal image in the center.

Most scholars now agree that the panel of *St. Jerome and St. John the Baptist* (fig. 189) is by Masaccio and shows the depth and power of his new style. All other panels are accepted as the work of Masolino. But the immense distance of the central panel is daring, however unconvincing it may be in its details. The arcades repeat the characteristic motives found in the backgrounds of panels on Ghiberti's North Doors (see fig. 154), and the arches are not projected in perspective. The background is still gold. Above a bank of clouds Christ and the Virgin float side by side within a blue circle representing the heavens, while smaller clouds recede into the distance. Falling flakes of snow form the shape of the new basilica. Even though the pyramid of Gaius Cestius and the Roman mound known as the Testaccio are seen in the background, and the composition is derived from a mosaic on the façade of Santa Maria Maggiore, the painters need not have gone to Rome in order to represent these elements, which the pope may have specified. On the other hand, no one familiar with Rome would have inserted a background of Florentine hills or would have painted the Esquiline Hill, on which Santa Maria Maggiore stands, as flat.

Under the guise of the miracle of the snow, the altarpiece must have represented for the pope his mission to reunite the Holy Roman Church, which had been devastated by generations of schism. St. Jerome (fig. 189), one of the four church fathers, holds a model of a church in one hand and an open Bible in the other, in which can be read the first verses of Genesis: "In the beginning God created the heavens and the earth. And the earth was without form, and void; . . . And the Spirit of God moved upon the face of the waters." St. Antonine of Florence, who was in Florence at the time the altarpiece was painted, traces the conception of Mary mystically to this passage in Genesis, in which *maria*, the Latin word for "seas," later appears. He discusses the Miracle of the Snow a little farther on, right after the Assumption of the Virgin, the subject on the back of the altarpiece (not illustrated). In these first moments of the creation, in which God floated over the water, St. Jerome appears to be finding a prophecy of the planning of Santa Maria Maggiore by means of the congealed water falling from Heaven. Next to St. Jerome stands another saint connected with water, John the Baptist, his cross perched on a slender column to remind us that Florence, whose patron is the Baptist, had sheltered the Colonna pope.

Though there are earlier altarpieces with central scenes flanked by standing saints, no composition like this one had been seen before. And the rapidly receding space of the central panel, at times imperfectly controlled, is closer to Donatello's *St. George* relief of 1417 (see fig. 166) than to the careful perspectives of Masolino's paintings in the late 1420s and 1430s (see fig. 195

and colorplate 42, p. 206). The idea of the space may have come from the young Masaccio, but the figures in their curvilinear primness are typical of Masolino, as are the faces, whose surfaces remind us of smooth, hard porcelain or polished metal.

The *St. Jerome and St. John the Baptist*, by Masaccio (fig. 189), is more advanced than the rough statements of form in the San Giovenale altarpiece, the earliest known manifesto of the young man's new naturalism, but they are still far from the balanced harmonies of mass and space so impressive in the Brancacci Chapel (see colorplates 3, 39, pp. 12, 204) and the *Trinity* (see colorplate 41, p. 205). As sullen as the San Giovenale saints, these two figures are also compressed into a single panel, against a gold background with only a patch of earth providing a suggestion of recession. The brushwork is no longer so free, and firm and unified surfaces that turn in depth exert a strong sense of plasticity. The heavy features of the two men, the shoulders and ankle of St. John, the little cubic church model, and the open book with its pages turning in depth, all show a new study of how to use light to represent forms in space. The power and simplicity of the fold structure disclose the painter's knowledge of Nanni di Banco's and Donatello's achievements at Orsanmichele (see figs. 168, 164). Yet Masaccio refines and simplifies the sculptors' statements, making them if anything more sculptural, according to the paradox often seen in the early Quattrocento, when painters and sculptors seem to be trying to beat each other at their own game.

In expression these saints are close to Donatello, but they lack the fiery urgency of his heroes. They seem depressed, moody, as if crushed by the impossibility of realizing their mission. The fatalism of these faces will reappear when least expected in Masaccio's art, at the most exalted moments of his mature new style (see figs. 198, 200). And they are homely, as often in his work, with big noses, low and heavy cheekbones, and eye sockets sloping outward and downward from the bridge of the nose.

THE BRANCACCI CHAPEL. The most important manifesto of the new pictorial style was the decoration of the chapel of the Brancacci family in the Church of Santa Maria del Carmine in Florence, a cycle that was to become a model for Florentine artists, including Michelangelo, who came to draw from the frescoes and learn the new art of *chiaroscuro* (light and shade). In the cloister alongside the church Masaccio had painted a celebrated fresco of the *Sagra* (consecration) of the new church, in which he had represented, with all the vivacity of his art and according to his new principles of *chiaroscuro*, a procession of contemporary, recognizable Florentines. This influential work is long since destroyed, and we have only a few drawings—some by Michelangelo—showing how certain figures or groups of figures once looked. The Brancacci Chapel has also suffered losses. In the mideighteenth century the frescoes of the vault and lunettes were destroyed and replaced with a dome frescoed in the contemporary style. A disastrous fire in 1771 devastated much of the church, but the Brancacci Chapel frescoes suffered only some small areas of loss and the transformation of certain colors.

The chapel was founded as a result of the will of Pietro di Piuvichese Brancacci, who died in 1367; the head of the family during the period when the frescoes were painted was his nephew Felice. Felice may have commissioned the chapel when he returned from serving as the Florentine ambassador to Cairo in 1423. Because the lost vault and lunette frescoes were attributed to Masolino, it is now thought that Masolino alone received the original commission and that he was later joined by Masaccio. The dating of the chapel frescoes is uncertain, with some scholars placing the frescoes before Masolino's trip to Hungary (1425–27) and Masaccio's stay in Pisa in 1426, and others suggesting that work was continued on the cycle in 1427–28. Whether Brunelleschi also played a role in the chapel is uncertain, but the frescoes are enframed with Brunelleschian pilasters and entablatures. It is also unclear how much of the cycle was left unfinished and whether sections with portraits of the Brancacci family were destroyed after the Brancacci were exiled in 1435. In the early 1480s, Filippino Lippi finished the frescoes in the chapel. The decade-long restoration, completed in 1990, removed layers of grime, revealing high, clear color that represents a return to Giotto and undreamed-of delicacies of pictorial surface, muscular contour, and landscape detail.

The chapel frescoes, with two exceptions, represented scenes from the Life of St. Peter, the first pope. This was an important subject in Florence, for the dominant Guelph party had an alliance with the papacy, Pope Martin V was himself in Florence for two years, and the Florentines were making constant attempts to secure papal support in their struggles with Milan.

Masaccio's *Tribute Money* (colorplates 3, 39, pp. 12 and 204) dominates the chapel. The subject (Matthew 17:24–27), seemingly trivial, is seldom represented. When Christ and the apostles arrived at Capernaum, Peter was confronted by a Roman tax-gatherer who demanded the usual half-drachma tribute. Peter, returning to Christ for instructions, was told that he would find the money in the mouth of a fish near the shore of Lake Galilee. He paid the tax-gatherer, who then departed. Out of this episode Masaccio has built a scene of the utmost grandeur. He has also revised the story. The tax-gatherer comes directly before Christ and the apostles, who are not represented "at home," as in the text, but before a wide Arno Valley landscape culminating in the mass of the Pratomagno; the house is relegated to one side. On the left Peter finds the fish in shallow water and on the right he pays off the tax-gatherer, but the center of the stage is occupied by the confrontation of temporal and spiritual power and the instructions of Christ to the apostles, whose faces betray surprise, indignation, and concern.

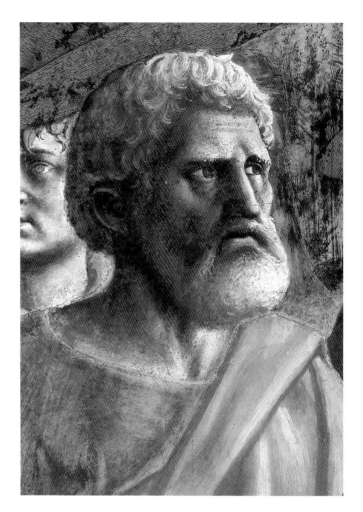

192. MASACCIO. Head of St. Peter, detail of *Tribute Money* (see colorplates 3, 39, pp. 12, 204). Probably 1425. Fresco. Brancacci Chapel, Sta. Maria del Carmine, Florence. Perhaps commissioned by Felice Brancacci

The year in which the fresco must have been painted was one of the most dangerous in the history of the Florentine Republic, which had just suffered crushing defeats at the hands of Filippo Maria Visconti, duke of Milan. In order to distribute equitably the financial burden of the war, the Florentines were debating the new tax called the *catasto*, based on ability to pay and provided with a system of exemptions and deductions (see p. 153), which was apparently a welcome substitute for previous taxation procedures. In his writings, St. Antonine of Florence interpreted the incident of the Tribute Money as Christ's instruction that all men, including ecclesiastics, must pay taxes to earthly rulers for the support of defense measures, and the subject is probably connected with the efforts of the Florentine Republic to tax Church holdings and the clergy, some of whom were jailed for nonpayment.

Apparently the Lord's blessing of taxation in Florence is what Masaccio was called upon to represent in 1425, and that is why he placed the scene on the banks of the

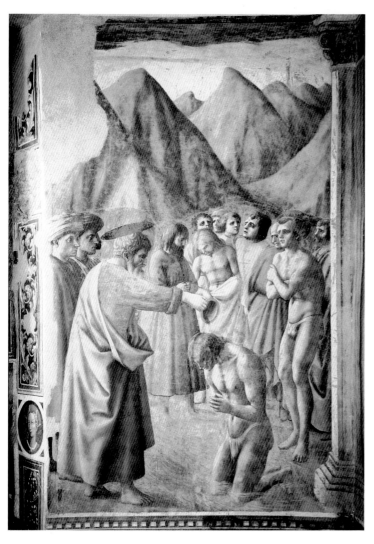

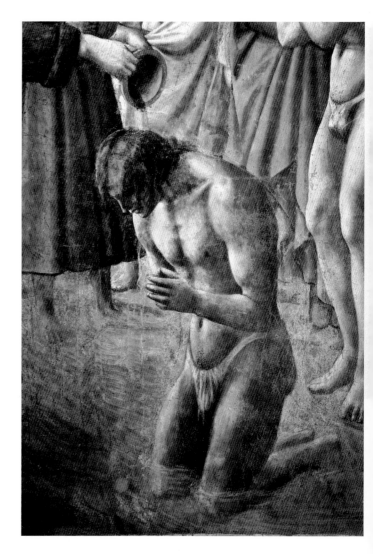

193. MASACCIO. *St. Peter Baptizing the Neophytes.*
Probably 1425. Fresco, 8' 1" x 5' 8". Brancacci Chapel

194. Kneeling man, detail of fig. 193

Arno and endowed it with such solemnity. A similar semicircular arrangement of heavily cloaked figures is to be seen in Nanni di Banco's *Four Crowned Martyrs* (see fig. 168); the young Masaccio may even have been watching when the group was set up in its niche at Orsanmichele. Certainly he studied the behavior of light on the powerful figures, faces, and drapery masses created by contemporary Florentine sculptors. In his landscape, however, he has surpassed sculptors and painters alike. The vast distances of Ambrogio Lorenzetti and Andrea da Firenze had been depicted partly from above and always ended at the abstract background, as if they were extensions before an impenetrable wall. Masaccio, adopting Donatello's low point of view and atmospheric distance and Gentile's complexity of construction (if not his surface richness), has produced a landscape of a grandeur unknown before his time. The impenetrable wall is dissolved, as was the predella panel in Gentile's Strozzi altarpiece (see fig. 186). The eye is taken inward harmoniously, with none of Gentile's still-medieval leaps

in scale, past the plain and the riverbanks, over ridges and distant mountains, some snow-capped, to the sky and the clouds. In this setting Masaccio's rugged figures stand and move at their ease. They and the landscape are represented with the full power of the new style that Masaccio had developed. He has abandoned Trecento linearism and analysis of detail. Objects, forms, faces, figures, and masses of heavy drapery all exist in light that models them and sets them forth in space.

The background is filled with soft atmosphere. Misty patches of woodland are sketched near the banks. Masaccio's brush moves with a new ease and freedom, representing not hairs but hair, not leaves but foliage, not waves but water, not physical entities but optical impressions. At times the brush must even have administered jabs at the *intonaco* in a manner suggesting the touch of nineteenth-century Impressionism. Each stroke of Masaccio's brush, in fact, is equivalent to a separate reflection of light on the retina. The equation of one stroke with a single particle of reflected light over both smooth

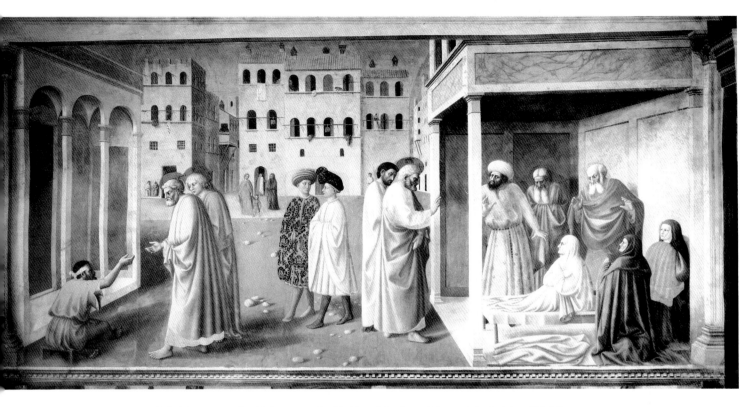

195. MASOLINO (and MASACCIO?). *Healing of the Lame Man and the Raising of Tabitha.*
Probably 1425. Fresco, 8' 1" x 19' 3". Brancacci Chapel. Perhaps commissioned by Felice Brancacci

and broken surfaces may also be found in Northern European art, in the works of Jan van Eyck. Yet most of these were painted five or more years later than the probable date of the *Tribute Money*.

The celebration of individual responsibility joins with the individual point of view in Masaccio's fresco, which depicts the apostles not as the officials of the oligarchy but as "men in the street," like the artisans and peasants on whose support the Republic depended (fig. 192). They are presented with conviction and sympathy—sturdy youths and bearded older men, rough-featured, each an induplicable human personality, each endowed with the fortitude that can still be counted on, as modern events like the bombing of the city's bridges in World War II and the 1966 Arno flood have shown, when the Florentine people face adversity. As if to symbolize both the spatial existence of the figures and the individuality of the personalities, the haloes are projected in perspective and touch or overlap at random angles. Even the tax-gatherer, as astonished as the apostles at the message of Christ, seems to participate with them in the ritual act that embodies the new revelation.

On the same upper tier, just to the right of the altar, Masaccio painted *St. Peter Baptizing the Neophytes* (fig. 193), the scene set high in the Apennine headwaters of the Arno. Here the artist shows himself the equal of Ghiberti and Jacopo della Quercia (see figs. 155, 178) in the representation of the nude figure; subsequent generations were impressed by the realism of the shivering

figure awaiting his turn at the bone-chilling ritual, the man drying himself with a towel, and the muscular youth kneeling in the foreground, over whose head St. Peter pours water (fig. 194). The nude is handled broadly, perhaps not with the subtlety of surface we find in Ghiberti, but conveying a real sense of being cold and naked in the presence of inhospitable nature. The volumes of the figures are defined by Masaccio's new *chiaroscuro* technique—smooth and consistent in the surfaces of legs, chests, and shoulders, strikingly sketchy and free in the loosely indicated heads in the background. The two young men at the extreme left, wearing the typical Florentine *cappuccio* wrapped around an underlying *mazzocchio* (wire or wicker framework; see p. 253 and fig. 260), appear to be portraits.

Masolino's principal contribution to the upper tier is the fresco opposite the *Tribute Money*—the *Healing of the Lame Man and the Raising of Tabitha* (fig. 195), miracles performed by St. Peter in Lydda and Joppa. Although it would have been difficult for Masolino, given his dual subject, to create a composition as close-knit and unified as that of the *Tribute Money*, the two frescoes were constructed using exactly the same perspective scheme, with the vanishing point at the same height within the fresco. Masolino represented two separate scenes, telescoping the space between them with a continuous Florentine city background whose simple houses, projected in perspective, are now sometimes attributed to Masaccio. On the left St. Peter and St. John, with typical Masolino

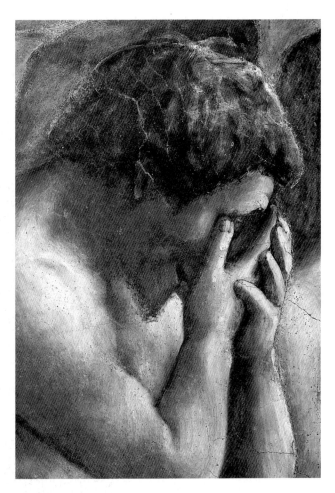

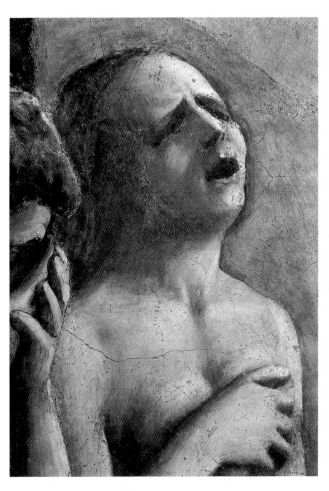

196. MASACCIO. Head of Adam, from the *Expulsion*
(see colorplate 5, p. 13). Probably 1425.
Fresco. Brancacci Chapel

197. MASACCIO. Head of Eve, from the
Expulsion (see colorplate 5, p. 13).
Probably 1425. Fresco. Brancacci Chapel

faces and haloes still parallel to the picture plane, command the lame man to rise and walk; on the right they appear in the home of Tabitha (on the ground floor, not the upper story mentioned in the text) and raise the fortunate woman from the dead. The two foppish young men in the center are the messengers sent from Joppa to fetch St. Peter and St. John with the greatest speed, although their doll-like faces betray little sense of urgency.

Masolino's drapery lacks the fullness and suppleness of Masaccio's, and there is little sense of the underlying figure. Expressions seem forced, the drama unconvincing, and even the shapes at times unfortunate, as for instance the manner in which the vertical cleavage between the houses in the background is carried down into the line of St. John's back. The rocks scattered on the ground plane, which cast long shadows that are directly related to the placement of the actual window in the chapel, help create a sense of illusionistic depth.

To modern eyes the styles of the two friends collide abruptly in the narrow scenes representing the *Temptation* (colorplate 4, p. 13) and *Expulsion* (colorplate 5, p. 13) that face each other across the entrance to the chapel. Masolino and Masaccio may well have found the

division of labor reasonable—to Masolino the less dramatic scene, to Masaccio the moment of universal tragedy. The two subjects signify the Original Sin from which Baptism frees believers, and they are therefore related to the general message of the cycle. Recent restoration has removed leaves that were added to cover the figures' genitals; now they are completely and unexpectedly naked.

Masolino painted a gentle Adam and an equally mild Eve, undisturbed by the trouble she is about to cause. She throws one arm lightly around the tree trunk while, from the bough above, the serpent's human head tries to attract her attention. The surfaces of nude flesh appear soft, but the feet hang instead of stand, and the masses do not turn in space.

Masaccio's *Expulsion* was influenced by Jacopo della Quercia's relief on the Fonte Gaia, but the painter projected the scene with even greater intensity. He abandoned the physical contest between the angel and Adam; a calm, celestial messenger hovers above the gate, holding a sword in one hand and pointing with the other to the barren world outside Eden. Adam moves forth at the angel's bidding as if driven by his shame. He

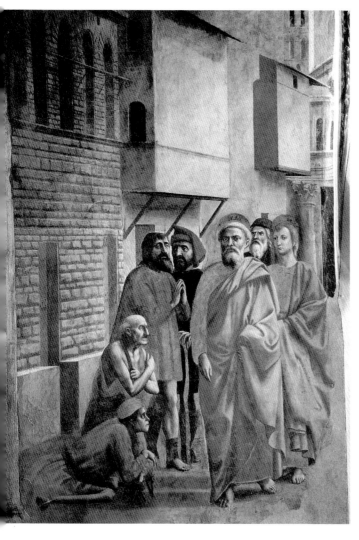

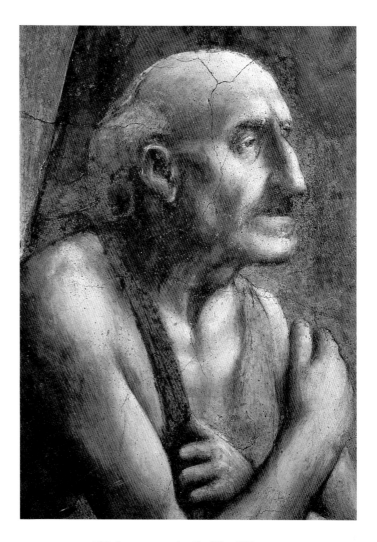

198. MASACCIO. *St. Peter Healing with His Shadow.*
Probably 1425. Fresco, 7' 7" x 5' 4". Brancacci Chapel

199. Lame man, detail of fig. 198

ignores his nakedness and uses his hands to hide his face (fig. 196). His mouth is contorted and the muscles of his abdomen are convulsed. Eve, her hands covering her nakedness, throws her head back, her mouth open in a cry of despair (fig. 197). Superficially, the drama has been reduced to its essential elements—two naked, suffering humans forced out into the cold. No more is necessary.

The scenes in the lower register flanking the altar, both by Masaccio, share a common perspective that converges behind the altarpiece. On the left is *St. Peter Healing with His Shadow* (fig. 198), a subject as rare as the *Tribute Money* and one that would, of course, be difficult to represent in the era before cast shadows had entered the artistic repertory. The setting is a narrow Florentine street bordered by one rusticated house and by other houses whose projecting rooms are supported on struts. As the architecture recedes, St. Peter walks toward us, not even looking at the sick who crowd before him and across whom his miraculous shadow is passing. The bearded man in a short blue stonecutter's smock may be a portrait of Donatello, and it has been suggested that

the beardless youth is Masaccio himself. The vivid faces of the two lame men at the lower left (see fig. 199) are unforgettable.

On the right-hand side of the altar, the *Distribution of the Goods of the Community and the Death of Ananias* (fig. 200) seems to be set in the middle of any village in the Florentine countryside. St. Peter and four other apostles, enveloped in majestic cloaks, distribute alms to the poor, who are at once as rough and as noble as they—the peasant woman holding her child comes from the same stock as any of Masaccio's Madonnas. In front of this evocation of the concern of the Christian community for its members is stretched the corpse of Ananias, the Christian who held back part of the price of a farm and was struck down at St. Peter's feet—a grim reminder of the fate of a tax delinquent. (Masaccio's tax declaration of 1427, written in his own hand, is still preserved, and the words and phrases are set forth with the simple dignity one would expect from him.) The houses frame a view over the freely painted Florentine landscape dominated by a towered villa.

In these paired frescoes a change has taken place in

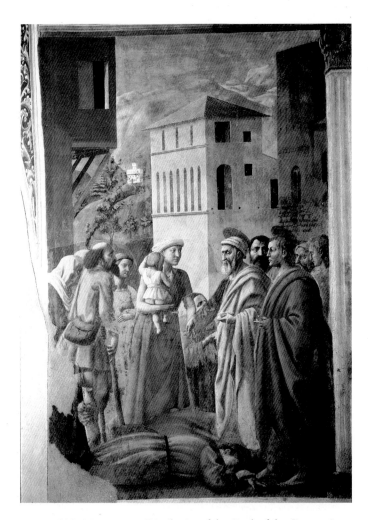

200. MASACCIO. *Distribution of the Goods of the Community and the Death of Ananias*. Probably 1425. Fresco, 7' 7" x 5' 2". Brancacci Chapel

Masaccio's style and mood. The masses are more densely packed than in the frescoes in the upper tier and the space less open and free, while the forms, when approached closely, are less consistent in structure and the surfaces more loosely sketched. One might even say that the expressions are more tense and even world-weary. In the *Raising of the Son of Theophilus* (fig. 201), one of the two broad frescoes of the lower tier, the artist has adopted an **S**-shaped plan in depth (as compared to the circle of the *Tribute Money*) with one center revolving around the miracle at the left, the other around St. Peter adored by Carmelites at the right. Both curves of the **S**, one moving toward us, the other away, are locked in a rectilinear architectural enclosure, formed partly by the palace of Theophilus, partly by the austere architectural block before which St. Peter is enthroned.

The architectural setting is by Masaccio, as are most of the figures except for the five at the extreme left, eight in the central section, and the delicate kneeling boy, which are by Filippino. The palace of Theophilus resembles no structure known in Quattrocento Florence, but the lower story has a fine series of Brunelleschian Corinthian pilasters, and the pedimented windows strongly resemble those of the Ospedale degli Innocenti (see fig. 136). A wall divided into panels of inlaid colored marble runs across the back of the scene. Its appearance so strongly suggests that of Quattrocento tombs, such as those of Lionardo Bruni and Carlo Marsuppini (see figs. 256, 296), and the backgrounds of paintings containing the symbolism of death, such as Castagno's *Last Supper* (see colorplate 50, p. 260) and Baldovinetti's *Annunciation* (see fig. 317), that one wonders if a similar meaning was intended in this case.

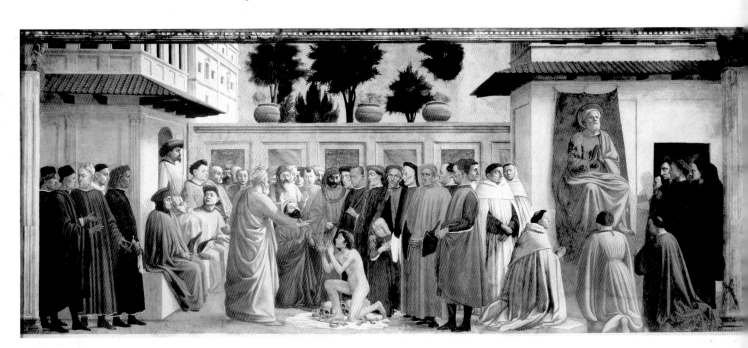

201. MASACCIO (completed by FILIPPINO LIPPI). *Raising of the Son of Theophilus*. Probably 1425; completed early 1480s. Fresco, 7' 7" x 19' 7". Brancacci Chapel

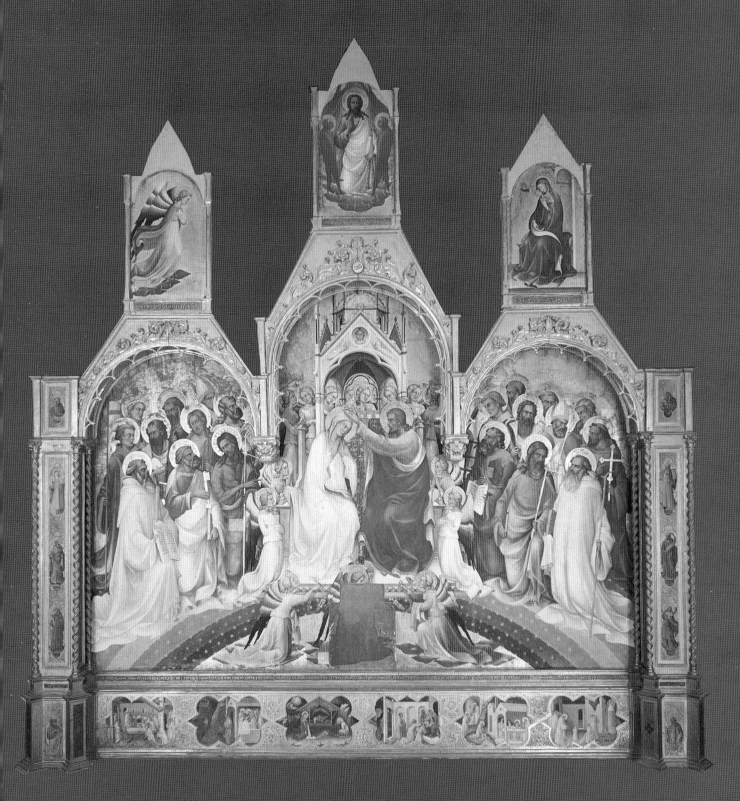

Colorplate 35. Lorenzo Monaco. *Coronation of the Virgin*. Dated February 1414. Panel, 8' x 12' 3".
Uffizi Gallery, Florence. Commissioned for the high altar of Sta. Maria degli Angeli, Florence

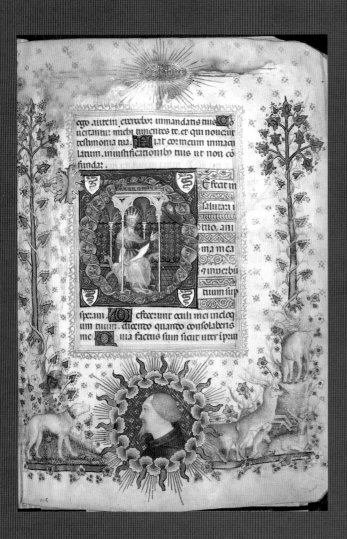

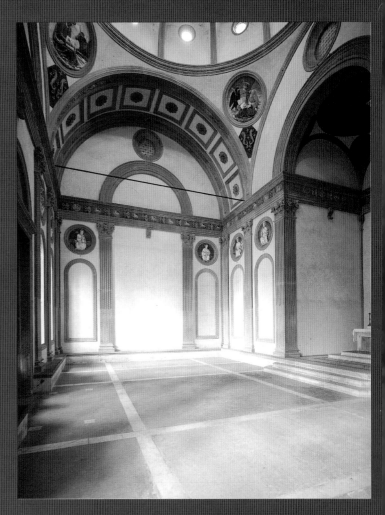

Colorplate 36. GIOVANNINO DE' GRASSI. Psalm 118:81. *Page from Visconti Hours*. Before 1395. Tempera and gold on parchment, 9¾ x 6⅞". Biblioteca Nazionale, Florence. Commissioned by Giangaleazzo Visconti

Colorplate 37. FILIPPO BRUNELLESCHI. Interior, Pazzi Chapel, Sta. Croce, Florence. Begun c. 1433; completed 1461. (Enameled terra-cotta medallions by BRUNELLESCHI [attributed to] and LUCA DELLA ROBBIA.) Commissioned by Andrea dei Pazzi

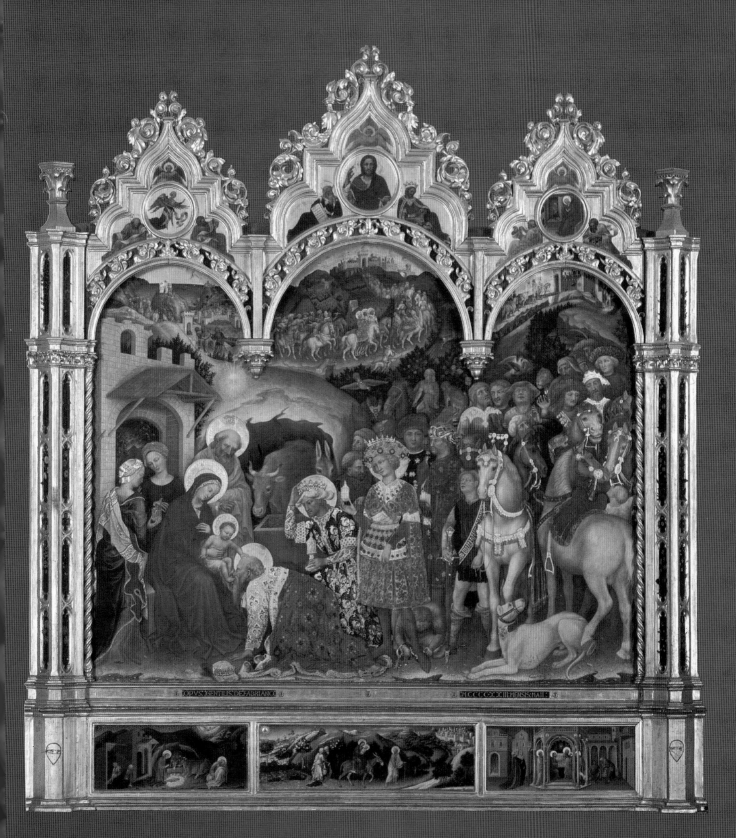

Colorplate 38. GENTILE DA FABRIANO. *Adoration of the Magi* (Strozzi altarpiece). Dated May 1423.
Panel, 9' 10" x 9' 3". Uffizi Gallery, Florence. Commissioned by Palla Strozzi for his burial chapel in the
sacristy of Sta. Trinita, Florence (the right predella, the *Presentation in the Temple*, is a copy;
the original is in the Louvre, Paris)

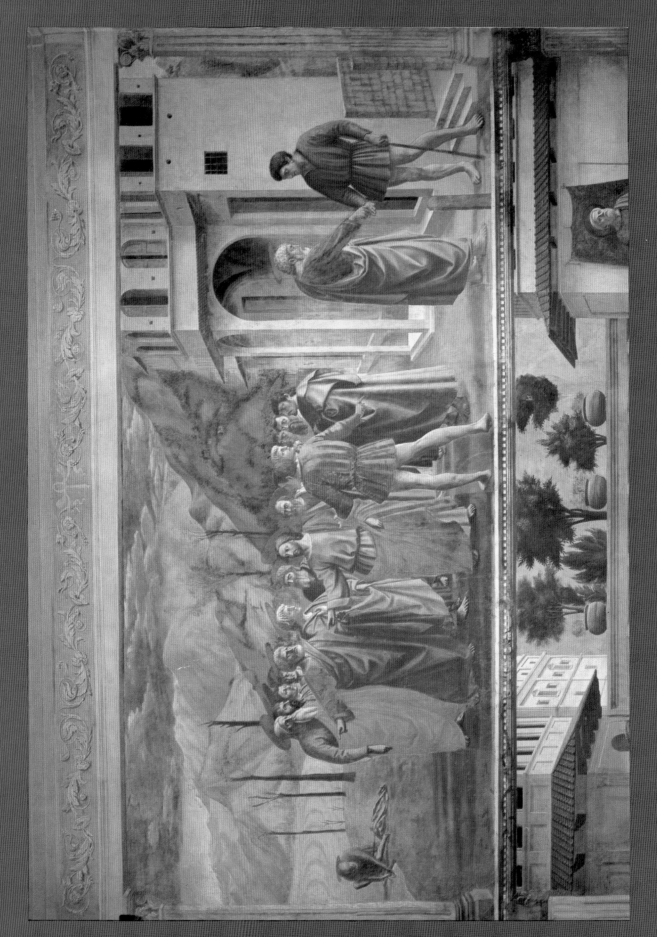

Colorplate 39. MASACCIO. *Tribute Money*. Probably 1425. Fresco. 8' 1" x 19' 7". Brancacci Chapel,
Sta. Maria del Carmine, Florence. Perhaps commissioned by Felice Brancacci

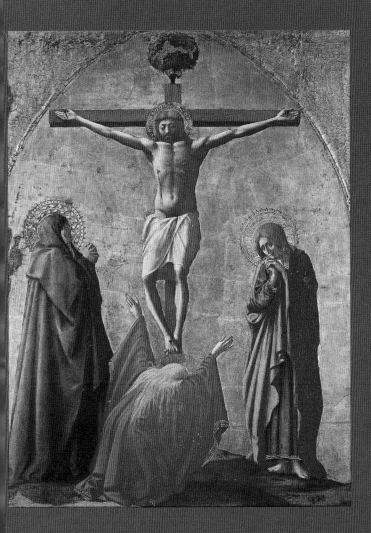

Colorplate 40. MASACCIO. *Crucifixion*, from the summit
of the Pisa polyptych. 1426. Panel, 30¹/4 x 25¹/4".
Museo di Capodimonte, Naples. Commissioned by Giuliano
di Ser Colino degli Scarsi for Sta. Maria del Carmine, Pisa

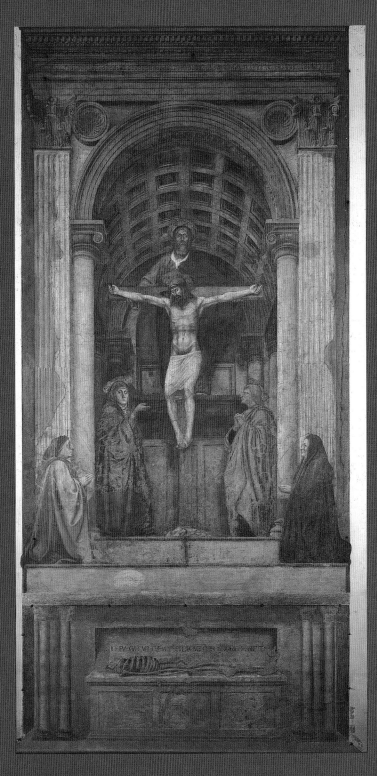

Colorplate 41. MASACCIO. *Trinity with Mary, John the Evangelist,
and Two Donors*. Probably 1427 or 1428. Fresco,
21' x 10' 5" (including base). Sta. Maria Novella, Florence

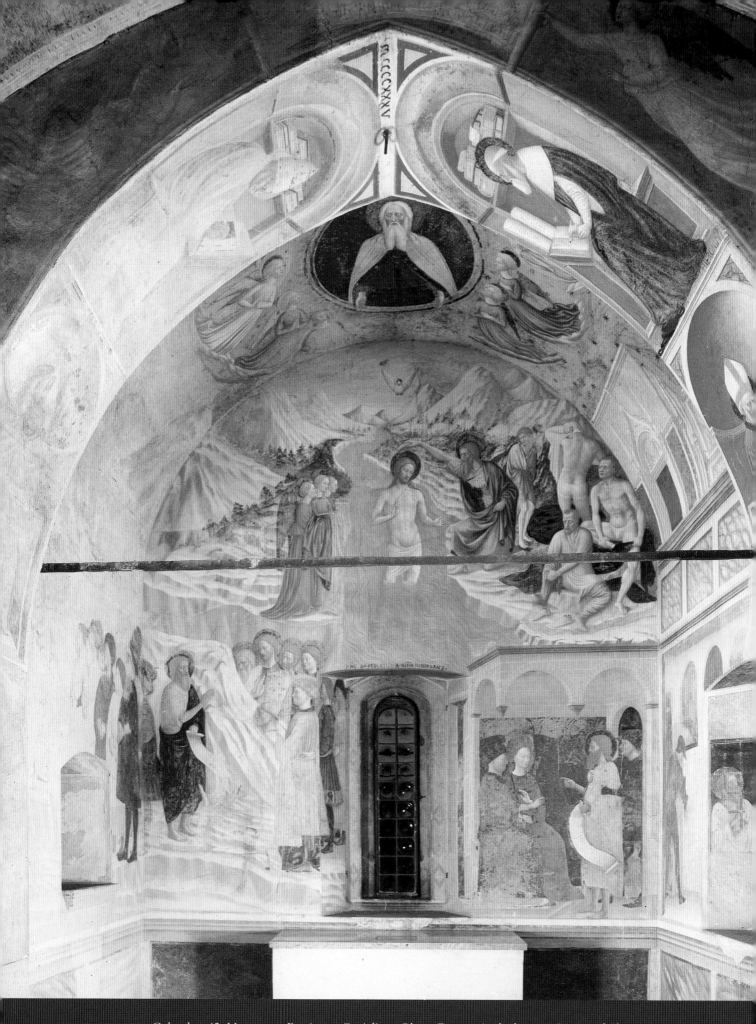

Colorplate 42. MASOLINO. Baptistery, Castiglione Olona. Frescoes in the lunette: *Baptism of Christ*;
lower register: *St. John the Baptist Preaching* and *St. John the Baptist Brought Before Herod*. 1435. Width of back
wall 15' 6". Commissioned by Cardinal Branda Castiglione

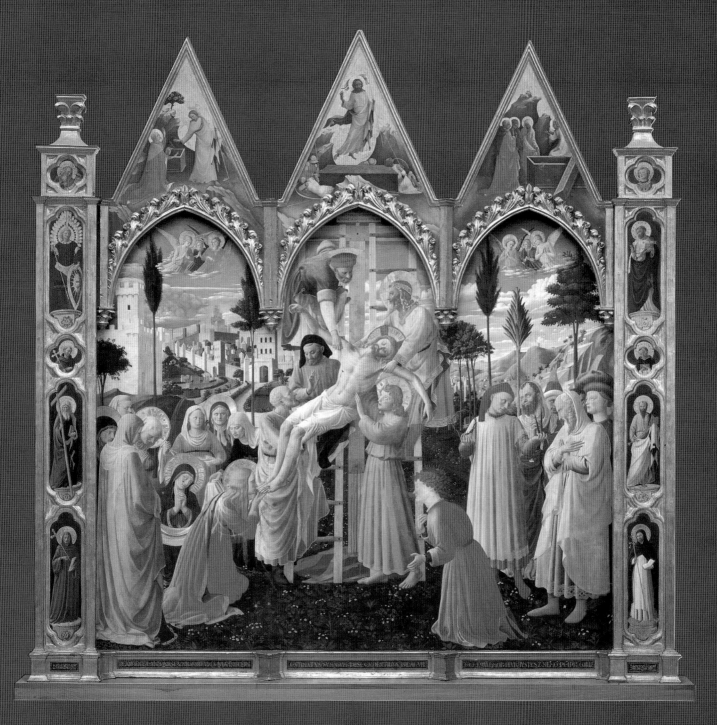

Colorplate 43. FRA ANGELICO. *Descent from the Cross*. Probably completed 1434. Panel, 9' x 9' 4".
Museum of S. Marco, Florence. Frame and pinnacles by LORENZO MONACO. c. 1420–22. Commissioned
by Palla Strozzi for his burial chapel in the sacristy of Sta. Trinita, Florence

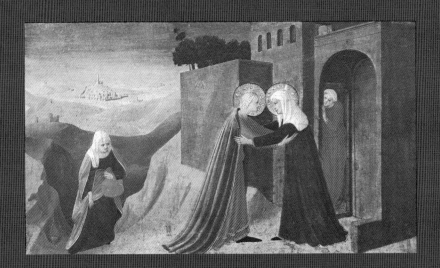

Colorplate 44. FRA ANGELICO. *Visitation*, from the predella of the Annunciation altarpiece (see fig. 206). c. 1434. Panel, c. 9 x 15". Museo Diocesano, Cortona

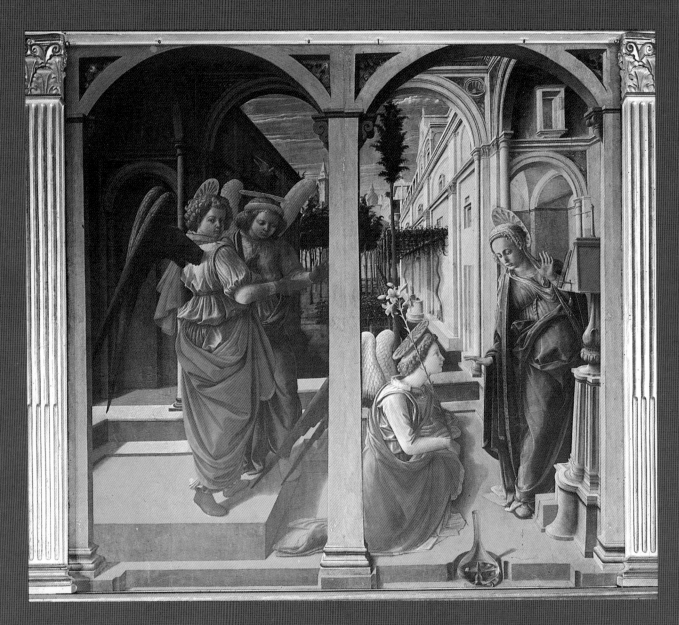

Colorplate 45. FRA FILIPPO LIPPI. *Annunciation*. c. 1440. Panel, 69 x 72". S. Lorenzo, Florence. Commissioned by a member of the Martelli family

Above the wall new life arises in the trees and potted plants, placed in asymmetrical sequence against the sky and so freely painted that they were once assumed to be an addition by Filippino.

More strongly than elsewhere in the chapel, one senses in this fresco a strict submission of the human individual to geometric law. The columnar or conical masses of the figures, projected so convincingly in depth and in light, adhere to the patterns of the embracing curvilinear and rectilinear ground plans within which they are set. Only the central St. Peter (by Masaccio, with the exception of the outstretched hand) is free to act and move. The conversion of the wicked Theophilus through the saving of his son's life has been explained as an allegory of papal—and by extension, Florentine—power against the Milanese. The head of Theophilus, in fact, with its particular style of beard and moustache, approaches an actual portrait of Giangaleazzo Visconti. The meaning of the fresco is reduced to simple and compelling terms in its composition: St. Peter appears twice, at the two foci of the S-plan; other mortals, including Theophilus, are only incidental elements in the structures that revolve around the Church.

THE PISA POLYPTYCH. Masaccio worked in Pisa from February to December of 1426 on a polyptych commissioned by Giuliano di Ser Colino degli Scarsi, a notary, for the Pisan Church of Santa Maria del Carmine. At an unknown date it was dismembered, the panels scattered and some lost. The effect of the surviving central panel, the *Enthroned Madonna and Child* (fig. 202), is so overwhelming that it is a surprise to discover its modest dimensions. That the Virgin's monumentality makes her resemble the giantesses of Picasso is a tribute to Masaccio's ability to elevate human figures, with all their physical defects, to a level of grandeur and power.

Some of the majesty of the figure doubtless derives from the fact that we read the two-story throne with its Corinthian columns as a work of architecture, imagining gigantic proportions for its occupant by analogy. She towers above the cornice, her blue cloak falling in heavy folds about the masses of her shoulders and knees. It is not impossible that Masaccio made a model throne and a clay figure with cloth arranged over it to chart the behavior of light and shade, as Verrocchio and his pupils did later. This could explain how Masaccio produced with such accuracy the shadows cast on the throne by its projecting wings or by the Virgin herself. The plain faces conform to a type seen over and over again in Masaccio's work. The Child, now totally nude, is again eating the Eucharistic grapes (see fig. 187).

The panel is damaged; here and there considerable passages of paint have broken away, but worse is the overcleaning, which has reduced the face of the Virgin to its underpaint. The architectural details of the *pietra serena* throne, including the rosettes and the strigil ornament (imitated from ancient and medieval sarcophagi still in Pisa; see Nicola Pisano's manger, fig. 37), are so

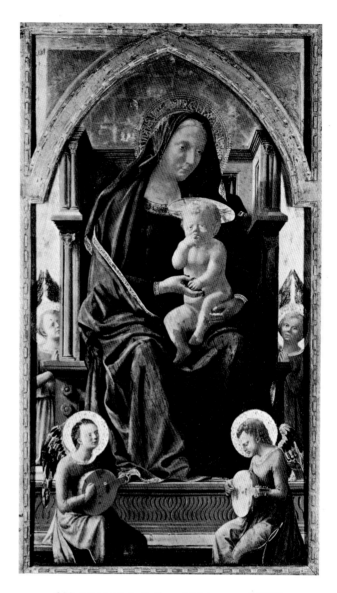

202. MASACCIO. *Enthroned Madonna and Child*, from the Pisa polyptych. 1426. Panel, 53¼ x 28¾". National Gallery, London. Commissioned by Giuliano di Ser Colino degli Scarsi for Sta. Maria del Carmine, Pisa

strongly projected as to seem magically three-dimensional, as are the lutes in the hands of the two little angels. The haloes are set parallel to the picture plane with the exception of that of the Christ Child, which is foreshortened in depth.

In the *Crucifixion* (colorplate 40, p. 205) intended for the summit of the altarpiece, Masaccio has determined the spot where the observer must stand to see all the forms correctly. The cross, for example, is seen from below, and the body of Christ is foreshortened upward, with the collarbones projecting in silhouette. The face inclines forward, looking down into the upturned face of the spectator like the figure of God the Father above Donatello's *St. George* niche (fig. 167). The gold background used throughout the polyptych may have been

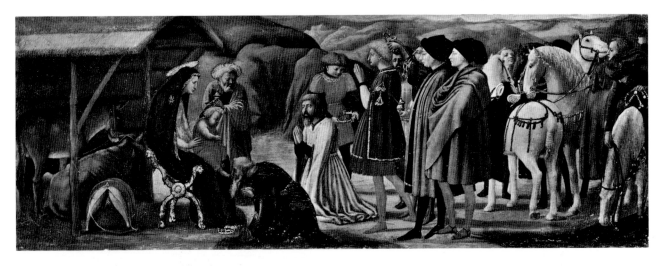

203. MASACCIO. *Adoration of the Magi*, from the predella of the Pisa polyptych. 1426. Panel, 8¼ x 24".
Picture Gallery, Dahlem Museum, Berlin

specified by the patron, but so convincing is the sense of mass and space created by Masaccio that the gold no longer seems flat; rather it sinks into the distance to become an illusion of golden air behind the figures on Calvary. The bush that grows from the top of the cross must once have contained the pelican striking her breast to feed her young, a medieval symbol for the sacrifice of Christ.

The sacrifice is Masaccio's theme, rather than the historical incident, which is here reduced to four figures. The Magdalen prostrates herself before the cross, her arms thrown wide so that the cross seems to rise upward from her gesture of despairing guilt to culminate in the arms of Christ stretched in pitying self-immolation. "For he shall grow up before him as a tender plant, and as a root out of a dry ground," said the prophet Isaiah (53:2), and the comparison is carried out by the tender plants that grow here and there in the "place of the skull," as they will before the infant Baptist in Michelangelo's *Doni Madonna* (see colorplate 85, p. 454). The yellow hair and red mantle of the Magdalen are in jarring contrast with the soft rose tone of the evangelist's cloak. St. John, wrapped in his own grief, seems to shrink into himself under the cross. Mary expands, a noble presence in her blue mantle whose voluminous folds are set forth with all the conviction of Masaccio's style at its best. No longer is she the swooning Virgin common in Trecento art. At the Crucifixion, St. Antonine writes, the Virgin Mary is "erect, not fainting on the ground . . . afflicted, but not tearing her hair or scratching her cheeks or complaining to the Lord." She stands firm under the cross, her hands folded in prayer. Christ, pale in death, his eyes closed and the crown of thorns low upon his brow, seems to be suffering still. The *Christus triumphans* of the twelfth century, the *Christus patiens* of the Duecento, and the *Christus mortuus* of Giotto and his followers are fused and transfigured

by Masaccio's new humanity. And in these four small figures, Masaccio achieved a drama of Aeschylean simplicity and power. All the grandeur of the Brancacci frescoes is here in miniature—all the beauty of light on the gradations of the fold structures revolving in space, all the consistency and breadth of anatomical masses, all the strength and sweetness of color. And nowhere more than in this panel did Masaccio's style deserve the characterization given it in the later Quattrocento: *puro, senza ornato* (pure, without ornament).

The epic breadth of Masaccio's art is maintained even in the predellas. The central *Adoration of the Magi* (fig. 203) may represent Masaccio's comment on the profusion of Gentile's Strozzi altarpiece (see colorplate 38, p. 203), painted only three years before, although the interval seems more like fifty. Masaccio has here adopted an eye-level point of view. He fills the foreground with figures and then discloses, between or just above them, a landscape of simple masses that recedes with more spatial conviction than the splendid miscellany in Gentile's world. The distant bay and promontories suggest the seacoast near Pisa; the barren land masses may be based on the eroded region called Le Balze, near the Pisan fortress-city of Volterra. His low viewpoint allows him to compose a magnificent pattern of masses and spaces using legs, both human and equine, and the flat shadows cast by these legs on the ground. Masaccio's soberly clad kings enjoy the services of only six attendants as they arrive before the humble shed. The vividly portrayed Giuliano di Ser Colino and his son stand in contemporary costume just behind the kings, the patterns of their cloaks worked into the structure of the composition. Everywhere one finds new delicacies of foreshortening: ox, ass, and saddle, all turned at various angles to the eye and therefore differently foreshortened; the white horse who lifts one hind hoof gently and turns his head so

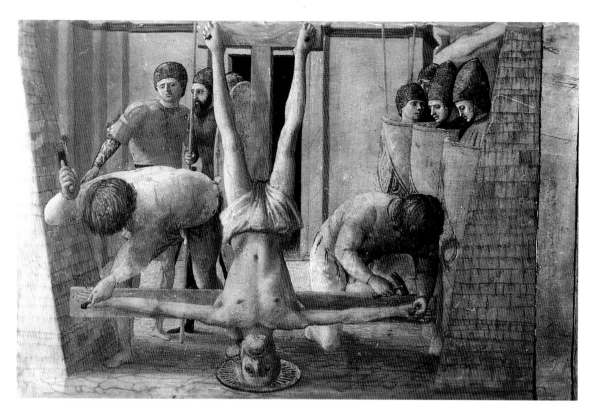

204. MASACCIO. *Crucifixion of St. Peter*, from the predella of the Pisa polyptych.
1426. Panel, 8½ x 12". Picture Gallery, Dahlem Museum, Berlin

that we can just discern his beautiful right eye; the groom at the extreme right who leans over toward us.

The same spatial principle compressed into minuscular scope is turned to dramatic effect in the *Crucifixion of St. Peter* (fig. 204). This subject had presented difficulties for artists because St. Peter had insisted that, to avoid irreverent comparison with Christ, he be crucified upside down. Masaccio meets the problem by underscoring it; the diagonals of Peter's legs are repeated in the shapes of the two pylons, which are based on the pyramid of Gaius Cestius in Rome. Between the pyramids the cross is locked into the composition. Within the small remaining space the executioners loom toward us with tremendous force as they hammer in the nails. Peter's halo, upside-down, is shown in perfect foreshortening.

THE TRINITY FRESCO. What may be Masaccio's most mature work is the fresco representing the central mystery of Christian doctrine, the *Trinity* (colorplate 41, p. 205), in Santa Maria Novella in Florence. Various dates have been proposed for it, but it is perhaps best dated after the Pisa altarpiece and the Brancacci Chapel, and therefore in 1427 or 1428, shortly before the artist's departure for Rome. When the detached fresco was returned to its original position in the left side aisle, a curious feature, mentioned by pre-Vasarian sources but long hidden from sight, was rediscovered—a skeleton

bearing the epitaph "IO FU GIA QUEL CHE VOI SIETE E QUEL CHIO SON VOI ANCO SARETE" ("I was once what you are, and what I am, you also will be"). The configuration of corpse and religious image is related to tomb iconography, and in the floor in front of the fresco was once visible the tomb of a member of the Lenzi family, who had served as *gonfaloniere* (standard-bearer) of the Florentine Republic and who died in 1426.

The setting of the *Trinity* is a magnificent Renaissance chapel. Its Corinthian pilasters flanking a coffered barrel vault conform so closely to the architecture of Brunelleschi and are projected so accurately in terms of his perspective principles that he is sometimes held responsible for the actual painting, but this correspondence could also be merely another example of the interchange of ideas between the masters of the new style. Vasari comments eloquently upon the effect of the illusionistic architecture in dissolving the wall to establish an apparently real chapel.

In the narrow space before the chapel kneel a man in the garments of *gonfaloniere* and his wife; he is possibly the occupant of the tomb in front. While they are placed in front of the enframing architecture to suggest that they exist within our space, the illusion of the tomb enclosing the skeleton suggests that it exists partly in our space and is partly recessed into the wall, a spatial equivalent for its inscription. Within the illusionistic chapel,

Masaccio has shown Golgotha reduced to symbolic terms—the sacrifice of Christ through the will of the Father, who stands on a kind of shelf toward the back of the chapel, gazing fixedly outward and steadying the cross with his hands. The figure of Christ is a *Christus mortuus* who seems to have endured pain and is no longer suffering. The dove of the Holy Spirit flies between the heads of Father and Son. Below the cross, Mary does not look at her Son but raises her hand to recommend him to us. St. John, no longer grief-stricken, is lost in adoration before the mystery. The portraits of the kneeling man and woman are stoically calm. Calvary has been stripped of its terrors. The kneeling Florentines pray to Mary and John, who in turn intercede with Christ, who, in terms of his sacrifice, atones with the Father for the sins of the departed and of all humanity.

The pyramidal composition of figures ascends from the mortals in our sphere, outside the arch, to God at its apex. The perspective, on the other hand, converges behind the lightly painted mound of Golgotha—at exactly eye level. Ascending and descending pyramids intersect in the body of the sacrificed Son. In its reduction to geometrical essentials that unite figures and architecture, forms and spaces, the composition could hardly be more closely knit. Its power embodies Giannozzo Manetti's contention that the truths of the Christian religion are as clear as the axioms of mathematics. The composition suggests that the Trinity is the root of all being, and that the principle of sacrifice dwells at the heart of the universe.

Within the imposing structure, the individual parts are powerfully projected to suggest three-dimensionality and a sense of mass. Details of arms, hands, and architecture show startling sculptural reality. Even the nails that hold Christ's hands are set forth in accordance with the perspective scheme. Yet the surface is rendered with a new breadth and freedom, even for Masaccio. This work prompts speculation about what he might have accomplished had he lived longer. When informed of Masaccio's death, Brunelleschi said, "*Noi abbiamo fatto una gran perdita*" ("We have had a great loss").

THE CASTIGLIONE OLONA FRESCOES. What of Masolino meanwhile? He, too, came to Rome. For a brief time the two friends collaborated there, although there is little trace of Masaccio's style in the surviving frescoes by the two artists in San Clemente. A few years later—in 1435, if the date of the inscription can be believed—Masolino was working in the Lombard village of Castiglione Olona, where he carried out two delightful series of frescoes for Cardinal Branda. The *Baptism of Christ* (colorplate 42, p. 206) emphasizes grace and charm, but it also contains an echo of Masaccio (see figs. 193, 194) in the figures undressing or drying themselves at the right. But Masolino apparently was not interested in re-creating Masaccio's rugged heroes, and his dainty Christ seems almost to dance in the ornamental patterns of the water. Masolino has learned how to construct one-point perspective, with strings and a nail, but he delights more in the fantastic nature of his landscape, in which hills, rocks, water, and drapery flow delicately together. What is new in Masolino is the quality of the infinite, luminous extent of earth; this will be helpful for the new generation, laden as it is with the burden of forms and emotions left to them by the young giant Masaccio.

9

The Heritage of Masaccio and the Second Renaissance Style

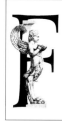rom our present vantage point, Florence at the time of Masaccio's death seems the undisputed leader of the new style in painting. But in 1428 Masaccio's influence was neither as immediate nor as far-reaching as Giotto's had been or as that of Masaccio's sculptural contemporaries already was. The Florentine situation was unlike that in contemporary America, where artists must compete for timeliness in a market that has no mercy for yesterday's ideas. It would be more fitting to compare Florence with Paris of the 1880s, when the paintings by the Impressionists and their successors were only bought by a few, and historical, classicistic, and genre painters still ran the Salons. The Gothic, for example, continued in Florentine painting through the 1430s and into the 1440s and 1450s. Altarpieces with gold backgrounds, pointed arches, tracery, and pinnacles continued to be commissioned and executed in quantity, as if Masaccio had never lived. He had no close followers, but his ideas bore fruit in the work of two painters who seem younger only because they survived him by decades—Fra Angelico and Fra Filippo Lippi—and in that of other masters born before Masaccio or a decade or so later. In the work of these painters, and in the mature creations of Ghiberti and Donatello, we can watch the transformation of the early Quattrocento stylistic heritage into something approaching a common style.

The artists of this second Renaissance style, which flourished in the 1430s, 1440s, and 1450s, lived in and worked for a society that was rapidly changing from the defensively republican Florence of the first third of the Quattrocento. Although hostilities continued until 1454, when the Peace of Lodi put an end to serious external warfare for forty years, the political and territorial independence of Florence was no longer threatened. But its republican integrity was, and by midcentury the oligarchic state, in whose government the artisan class was permitted at least token participation, persisted in name only. Political and economic rivalry had led to the expulsion of Cosimo de' Medici from Florence in 1433. He left as a private citizen, but he returned in 1434 as, to all intents and purposes, lord of Florence. Cosimo and his descendants seldom held office, but they maintained themselves in power by manipulating the lotteries that governed the "election" of officials. Until the second expulsion of the Medici, in 1494, the Florentine Republic was in effect a Medici principality, and the Medici related to foreign sovereigns as equals.

Paradoxically, this period comprised the decline of all the great Florentine banking houses, beginning with that of the Medici, but it also saw the establishment of a new social and intellectual aristocracy among the Medici and their supporters. These humanistically oriented patrons commissioned buildings, statues, portraits, and altarpieces in the new classical taste. The elegance of ancient Augustan Rome replaced the rougher republican virtues predominant in the art of Masaccio, Nanni di Banco, and the early Donatello. Although sumptuary laws still forbade luxury and display in personal adornment, the palace and villas of the Medici set the tone for a new existence of ease and grace.

At this juncture it is convenient to treat Fra Filippo Lippi (c. 1406–69) and Fra Angelico (c. 1400?–1455) together. Their names were mentioned in a letter written from Perugia in 1438 to Piero the Gouty, son and eventual successor of Cosimo de' Medici, by the painter Domenico Veneziano, who was trying to obtain a commission in Florence. Domenico lists Fra Filippo and Fra Angelico as the most important painters of the day and says that both are overwhelmed with commissions. In their roughly parallel development we can see the emergence of the new Renaissance style. One must remember, however, that both were, by and large, contemporaries of the masters we shall treat in Chapter 10 and absorbed in solving many of the same artistic problems.

Fra Giovanni da Fiesole, known to us as Fra Angelico, has long been called Beato (Blessed) Angelico by the Italians, though he was not actually beatified until 1983. His pious life and the devotion and sincerity of his religious work rendered the title appropriate. Fra Filippo Lippi, on the other hand, was a monk who fathered two children by a nun. Although Fra Filippo had a personal and visible connection with Masaccio, we know nothing for certain about his early style. We discuss Fra Angelico first because he was, according to all surviving evidence, the leading painter of Florence in the 1430s, and it was he who interpreted the conquests of Masaccio in a form that exercised a profound and lasting influence on Renaissance art.

FRA ANGELICO

In 1417 the artist we know as Fra Angelico was a painter named Guido di Pietro. In 1423 he is first mentioned as Fra Giovanni da Fiesole. Depending on his age at the time he entered the monastery, he was probably born between 1400 and 1402 and was in his mid-fifties when he died in 1455. For the span of more than a generation, he worked as an artist in the service of the Dominican Order, first at San Domenico in Fiesole and then at San Marco in Florence under the priorate of Antonino Pierozzi, who later became archbishop of Florence and was canonized in the sixteenth century as St. Antonine of Florence. Eventually, Fra Angelico succeeded St. Antonine as prior of San Marco. Even before his death, Fra Giovanni was being extolled as "the angelic painter."

The earliest fully Renaissance painting by Fra Angelico is his *Descent from the Cross* (colorplate 43, p. 207). This work had been commissioned by Palla Strozzi from Lorenzo Monaco for the sacristy of the Church of Santa Trinita, where its subject, the sacrifice of the adult Christ, would complement and fulfill that of the exhibition of the Christ Child in Gentile's *Adoration of the Magi* (see colorplate 38, p. 203) in the same chapel. Lorenzo completed only the pinnacles before his death in 1425, and at some later date the unfinished work was given over to Fra Angelico. The painting of the central panel may have been started in the late 1420s or early 1430s and was almost certainly finished by November 1434, when Cosimo de' Medici returned to Florence and members of the opposition party, including Palla Strozzi, were exiled. If this dating is correct (other scholars have placed the work in the 1440s), Fra Angelico's *Descent from the Cross* represents the first known successful Italian attempt to set a group of figures into a harmoniously receding landscape space rather than on the foreground stage used by Masaccio.

At first sight the artist seems hampered by the preexistent frame, but then we realize that Fra Angelico has exploited the Gothic arches for the purpose of his Renaissance composition, utilizing the central panel for the cross and the ladders and anchoring the bases of the arches to the gates of the city of Jerusalem on one side and to a grove of trees on the other. This monastic painter presents us with a world in which every shape is clear, every color bright and sparkling. Christ, gently lowered from the cross, is received by John, Mary Magdalen, and others and mourned by the kneeling Virgin and the Marys. On the right stand a group of men in contemporary Florentine dress. The young man kneeling in adoration and the older man wearing a red *cappuccio* and exhibiting the crown of thorns and the nails are characterized as *beati* (blessed) by gold rays emanating from their heads.

The figures, grouped on a flowering lawn, are united by their adoration of the sacred body, which is depicted with Fra Angelico's characteristic reticence and grace.

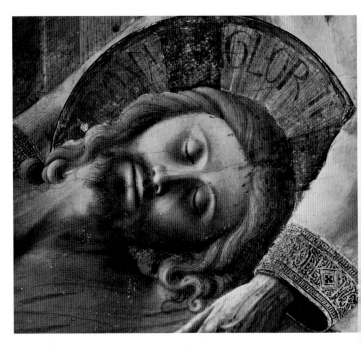

205. FRA ANGELICO. Head of Christ, detail of *Descent from the Cross* (see colorplate 43, p. 207). Probably completed 1434. Panel. Museum of S. Marco, Florence. Commissioned by Palla Strozzi for his chapel in the sacristy of Sta. Trinita, Florence

His superior, St. Antonine, was to preach and write in horrifying detail about the agony of Christ, but in Fra Angelico's rendering one barely notices the bruises on Christ's torso or the blood on his forehead. Instead, attention is concentrated on the quiet face (fig. 205) and on the light that dwells on the lips, eyelids, arching brows, and silky surfaces of hair and beard.

Fra Angelico's method of stylization presents the distant Jerusalem as an array of multicolored geometrical shapes crowned by a zigguratlike castle. The storm cloud that darkened the sky during the Crucifixion still casts a shadow over some of the city. On the right-hand side of the panel, a palm, a cypress, and other trees provide a loose screen through which one looks into a hilly Tuscan landscape punctuated by towns, villages, farmhouses, castles, and villas under a sky filled with soft clouds. Fra Angelico's *Descent from the Cross* was a milestone; at this time, no painter in Europe save Jan van Eyck could surpass his control of the resources of the new naturalism, and none could match his harmony of figures and landscape.

Fra Angelico's splendid *Annunciation* (fig. 206) was painted for San Domenico in Cortona, an ancient Tuscan town on a promontory high above the Chiana Valley. Evidence favors a dating of about 1432–33. Fra Angelico has set the scene in a portico of slender Corinthian columns that divide his panel into thirds—two occupied by the arches of his portico, the third by three receding arches and a garden. The angel enters the portico, bowing and genuflecting before Mary as he delivers

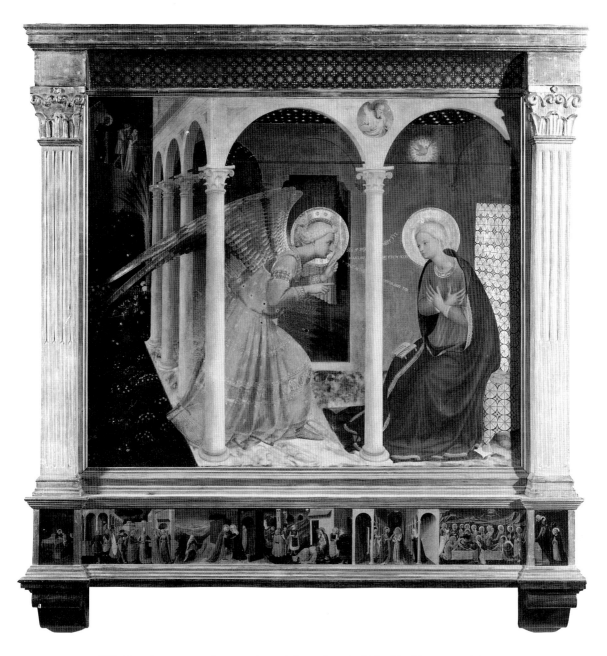

206. FRA ANGELICO. *Annunciation and Scenes from the Life of the Virgin*. c. 1432–33.
Panel with original frame, 63 x 71". Museo Diocesano, Cortona

his greeting. Mary, seated on a chair draped with gold brocade, abandons the book on her lap to cross her hands on her breast in acceptance of her destiny. Gabriel's words run from left to right, but Mary's reply, "Behold the handmaid of the Lord; be it unto me according to thy word" (Luke 1:38), must be read from Mary to the angel and is written upside down and in reverse. The angel replies: "The Holy Ghost shall come upon thee, and the power of the Highest shall overshadow thee" (Luke 1:35), and directly above Mary's head, in the shadow under the star-studded ceiling, the dove of the Holy Spirit emits golden light. A sculpted representation of the prophet Isaiah looks down from the spandrel. Behind the angel's head, through a doorway and past a

partially drawn curtain, we can see Mary's bedchamber.

The garden at the left, a symbol of Mary's virginity that will reappear in many Quattrocento Annunciations, illustrates the words of the Song of Songs, "A garden inclosed is my sister, my spouse" (4:12). St. Antonine had been connected with the Dominican community in Cortona, and here Fra Angelico follows Antonine's doctrine of the "garden of the soul," a set of meditations for penitents written in Italian. Fra Angelico also identifies the garden with Eden, for at the upper left the weeping Adam and Eve are being gently but firmly expelled. This association is natural since, according to St. Paul, Christ is the second Adam, Mary the second Eve. Angelico avoids the drama seen in Masaccio's *Expulsion* in the Brancacci Chapel (see colorplate 5, p. 13), and also the nudity, and instead clothes Adam and Eve in the coats of skins God made for them, according to Genesis.

Fra Angelico is aware of Masaccio's method of constructing forms and spaces, but he restrains *chiaroscuro* as firmly as he does emotion. His figures seem barely corporeal—slender and refined, their limbs are only just discernible under their enveloping garments. Their faces are drawn with the utmost simplicity and purity, and they have exquisitely tended blond hair. The poised shapes, the subtle rhythms of contour, and the harmonies of space and light are enhanced by the freshness of Fra Angelico's color. The angel, supplied with wings that seem made of beaten gold, is dressed in a tunic of clear, bright vermilion with bands of golden embroidery. Mary's blue mantle contrasts with the sparkling folds of the cloth of honor that hangs behind her, as do the snowy columns with the richly veined marble of the floor, or the white steps with the flowered lawn. As remote from the world as the imagination of a sensitive child, Fra Angelico's altarpiece admits us to a realm of unmarred celestial beauty.

In the predella scenes, however, the real world reappears. In the *Visitation* (colorplate 44, p. 208), we look past the two cousins to where an old woman labors up the hill toward us and then beyond her to a broad landscape, its distance enhanced by shadows of clouds. Mary "went into the hill country with haste" writes Luke (1:39), and St. Antonine's *Summa* stresses that a hilly background is important for this first recognition of the divinity of Christ—the prenatal joy of John the Baptist in the womb of Elizabeth. The background elements are identifiable as the town of Castiglion Fiorentino, the tower of Montecchi (still visible to travelers between Florence and Rome), and the wide lake (see fig. 446) that then filled the Chiana Valley—this may well be the earliest recognizable portrait of a known place in the Renaissance. Beyond the sun-drenched town, the plain fuses with the sky in imperceptible gradations of summer sunlight and dusty haze. The spatial experience of landscape is realized more fully in this tiny panel than in any previous Italian work.

In 1436 the decaying buildings of San Marco in Florence were taken from a negligent order of Sylvestrine monks and given to the Dominicans of Fiesole. Beginning in 1438, the Dominicans, supported by contributions from Cosimo de' Medici, employed Michelozzo to build a new church and monastery on the site (see fig. 149). Pope Eugenius IV was present at the consecration of the church in 1442 under its new prior, St. Antonine. Fra Angelico painted the high altarpiece, which was probably installed by 1440 (fig. 207). In this work the artist, too often considered a conservative or even a reactionary, showed himself to be abreast of the latest artistic developments.

In spite of overcleaning, the principal panel is still impressive. Gold curtains, their loops continued across the top of the picture by festoons of pink and white roses, are parted to show the court of Heaven. At the center, where the perspective lines converge, the Virgin is enthroned in a Renaissance niche whose Corinthian order is so closely related to Michelozzo's architecture at San Marco that he may have shown Fra Angelico how such things should be designed. Gold brocades decorate the throne and provide a barrier over which one looks into a grove of fruit trees, cedars and cypresses, palms and roses; these choices are not merely decorative, for Christ is the fruit of the Tree of Life, and Mary, according to symbolism derived from the apocryphal Book of Wisdom, is a cedar of Lebanon, a cypress on Zion, a palm in Cades, and a rose tree in Jericho. A circle of angels and saints gathers on the steps and on the Turkish carpet whose divisions provide the converging orthogonals of the perspective construction. In the foreground the circle is continued by the kneeling Medici patron saints, Cosmas and Damian, and completed by what seems to be a small panel of the *Crucifixion*, a picture within a picture. This device, which establishes the picture plane on which the construction is projected, reminded viewers that only through the cross can believers be admitted to Paradise, a point on which St. Antonine is explicit.

This type of composition of the Madonna with a group of conversing saints is known as the *Sacra Conversazione* (sacred conversation). With its perspective construction, lofty central arch, and pyramidal grouping of figures within a circle in depth, the altarpiece establishes an impressive and satisfying precedent that may well have influenced other centralized, multifigural compositions. Fra Angelico may have witnessed solemn group conversations on exalted themes, for in 1439, when this picture was being painted, the Council of Ferrara moved to Florence, where, under Brunelleschi's recently completed dome, the Eastern and Western Churches attempted to heal their division.

More completely than any work of Fra Filippo Lippi, Fra Angelico's San Marco altarpiece embodies the ideals of the new phase of the Florentine Renaissance. The pictorial space, measured by systematic perspective from the foreground plane to the horizon beyond the trees, provides a place and dimension for every person and thing. The space is projected by dividing the lower edge using the squares in the carpet, then drawing orthogonals from these segments to the vanishing point. One of the foreground saints looks outward as he points with his right hand, directing our eye into the center of the picture. These devices correspond, as we shall see, to the doctrines of Leonbattista Alberti, who had arrived in Florence a few years before and only two or three years before this picture was painted had circulated *Della pittura,* the Italian version of his treatise *De pictura (On Painting)*. In spite of the ruinous condition of the panel, the broad, harmonious drapery masses may still be made out. Details such as the luminous pearls that adorn the vestments of St. Lawrence at the far left show Fra Angelico's awareness of the mystical meaning of jewels as embodiments of divine light in the works of the Van

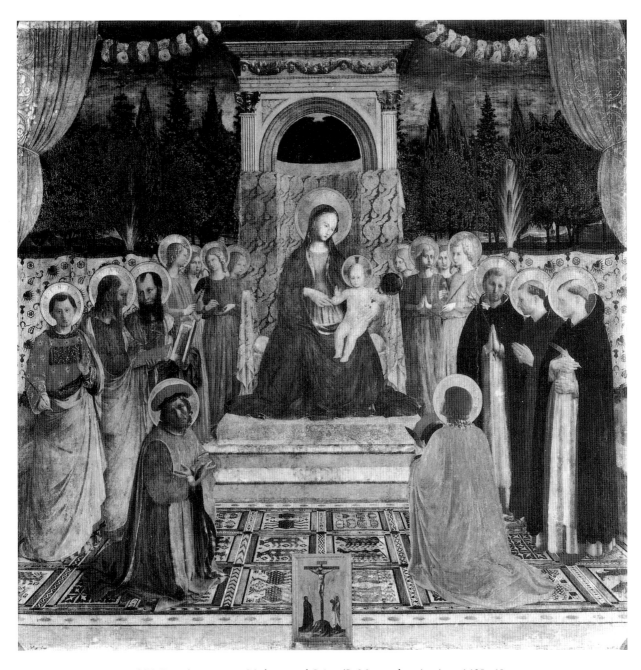

207. Fra Angelico. *Madonna and Saints* (S. Marco altarpiece). c. 1438–40.
Panel, 86⅝ x 89⅜". Museum of S. Marco, Florence. Commissioned by Cosimo de' Medici
for the high altar of S. Marco, Florence

Eycks, some of which may have been known in Florence by the late 1430s.

Fra Angelico displayed his versatility in handling both figures and the natural world, with its luminous and atmospheric effects, in the panels of the legend of Sts. Cosmas and Damian from the predella of the San Marco altarpiece. At first sight the interiors seem to be standard Trecento boxes. The *Miracle of the Deacon Justinian* (fig. 208) shows the two saints, who float in trailing soft clouds, exchanging the deacon's gangrenous leg for a healthy one amputated from a Moor. The space is illuminated naturalistically by light coming in from the front and slightly left, so that a shadow is cast across the right wall. A second source of light is the tiny window on the left wall, through whose bottle-bottom panes light filters onto the embrasure. A third is the light reflected upward from the floor, and there is a fourth source in the corridor that is visible through the open door at the right. In the separate effects of light from four different sources; in their interplay on walls, furniture, curtains, figures, and still life; and in the delicacy with which light suffuses the shadows, Fra Angelico has produced a triumph of observation.

Fra Angelico's landscapes are even more original than his interiors. The predella panels include scenes representing the several thwarted attempts to martyr Sts. Cos-

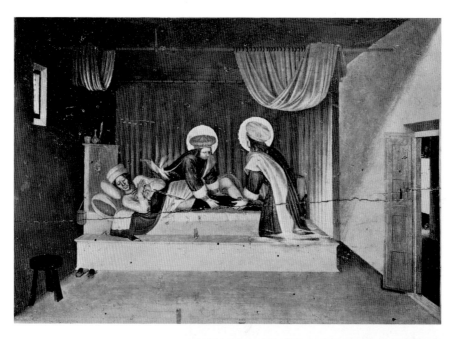

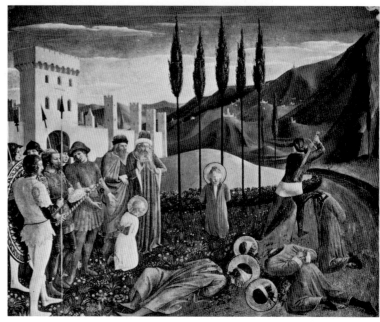

above: 208. FRA ANGELICO. *Miracle of the Deacon Justinian,* from the predella of the S. Marco altarpiece. Panel, 14½ x 18¾ ". Museum of S. Marco, Florence

right: 209. FRA ANGELICO. *Beheading of Sts. Cosmas and Damian,* from the predella of the S. Marco altarpiece. Panel, 14¾ x 18". The Louvre, Paris

mas and Damian that culminated in their beheading (fig. 209), which is set in a Tuscan landscape of crystalline beauty. In the foreground, on a road bordering a flowery meadow, the bodies of the two saints and their severed heads, still bearing haloes, tumble on the ground. One of their three younger brothers still kneels, his neck spouting blood, his head rolling beside the others. The other two, blindfolded, await the executioner's sword. The poses of the figures and their facial expressions, which range from the remorse of the officer to the calm brutality of the soldiers, display the artist's interest in physical and psychological activity. The execution, the like of which could doubtless be witnessed in the Florence of Fra Angelico's day, takes place, with all the ghastly irrelevancy of a modern traffic accident, among the sunlit spaces and cubic or curving forms of the walled city. The Tuscan hills, crowned by castles and vil-

las, rise range on range in the distance. The five cypresses, their lower branches pruned to reveal long, slender trunks, may symbolize the five martyrs, but their aesthetic function, as in the *Descent from the Cross* (see colorplate 43, p. 207), is as an indicator against which to measure the extent of the landscape.

Between the end of 1438 and late 1445, when he left for Rome, Fra Angelico and his assistants, probably also monks, provided paintings for the monastery of San Marco's chapter house, corridors, overdoors, and for forty-four individual monks' cells. They were certainly under the direction of the prior, St. Antonine. Their style differs sharply from that of the altarpieces for public view, and there is even a distinction between the frescoes destined for the monastic community as a whole and those in the individual cells. At the head of the staircase, which every monk used many times a day, Fra

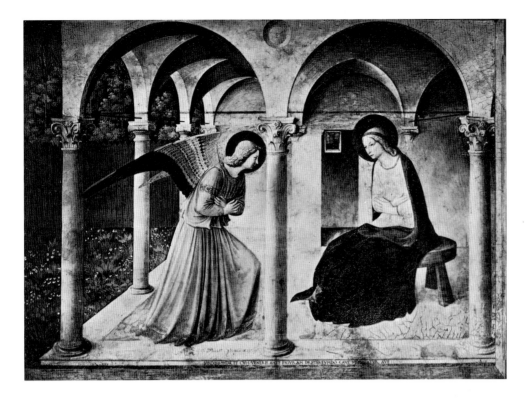

Angelico painted an *Annunciation* (fig. 210) that is supplied with the inscription, "As you venerate, while passing before it, this figure of the intact Virgin, beware lest you omit to say a Hail Mary." As befitted not only the fresco medium but also the monastic setting, the bright colors and gold of the Cortona altarpiece give way to pale, chaste tints. Moreover, the architecture is now seen directly from the front, so that the lateral columns recede toward a single vanishing point placed slightly to the right of center in the visual field. The greater weight of the columns and the care with which the capitals are rendered probably witness the painter's interest in Michelozzo's architecture, then in construction all about him. It is doubtful, however, that Michelozzo would have approved of the use of Corinthian and Ionic capitals in the same portico.

The mood here is calmer and more contemplative than in the ecstatic Cortona *Annunciation*. Mary holds no book and she sits on a rough-hewn, three-legged wooden stool. Her chamber, stripped of furniture, looks on the world through a barred window. The fence around her Antonine "garden of the soul" is higher and stronger, and one is reminded of St. Antonine's admonition to sweep clean the room of one's mind and to distrust the eye, the window of the soul. "The death of sin comes in at the windows, if they are not closed as they ought to be," says Antonine in analyzing the theme of the Annunciation. Fra Angelico has made the window the eye of his fresco, the center of perspective lines.

Within the monks' cells, the observer penetrates into deeper regions of the soul. Each arched fresco is about six feet high and, like an image from a projector, seems to float on the wall under the vault of the cell. Every-

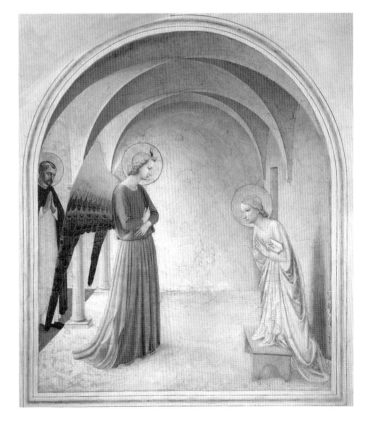

thing in these images is pure, clean, and disembodied. The world seems to retreat, leaving the single meditative subject suspended in the cell. The *Annunciation* (colorplate 6, p. 14; fig. 211) shows a standing angel and a kneeling Virgin who holds her open book to her breast. The angel has entered with the light, which falls on the Virgin; they are united by the rhythms in the painted

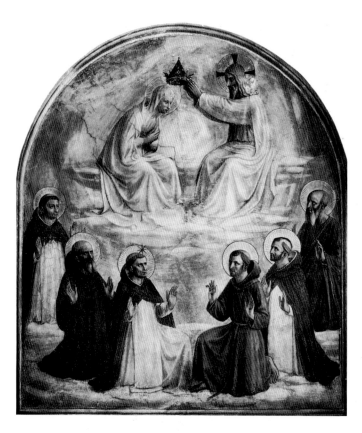

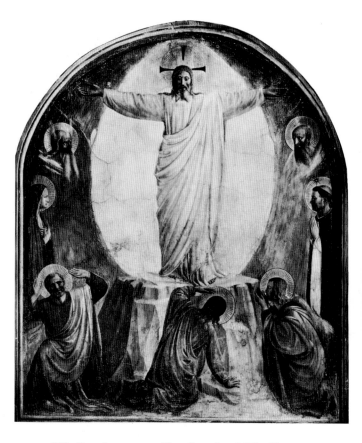

212. FRA ANGELICO. *Coronation of the Virgin.*
1438–45. Fresco, 6' 2¹/2" x 5' 2¹/2". Monk's cell,
Monastery of S. Marco, Florence.
Probably commissioned by Cosimo de' Medici

213. FRA ANGELICO. *Transfiguration.* 1438–45.
Fresco, 6' 2¹/2 " x 5' 2¹/2 ". Monk's cell, Monastery of
S. Marco, Florence. Probably commissioned by
Cosimo de' Medici

architecture, which is arched like the cell. There is no
garden, and outside the arcade St. Peter Martyr witnesses the event; he serves as an example for the monk,
who, under the hypnotic influence of the luminous pale
colors, clear shapes, and harmonious spaces, is expected
to experience mystically the miracle of the Incarnation.

The *Coronation of the Virgin* (fig. 212), a sublime oc-
currence in an icy Heaven, glitters with the colors of
snow-reflected light in the lilacs and greens that vibrate
softly throughout the cloudy throne and the glowing
white of the garments. Christ places a crown on the
head of the reverent Virgin while Franciscan and
Dominican saints, knowing the miracle without having
to see it, kneel in adoration in an arc on the floor of
clouds. The *Transfiguration* (fig. 213) becomes at once a
revelation of Christ's divinity and a prophecy of his
Crucifixion and Resurrection. He stands, arms spread,
enveloped as in the Gospel account by raiment "shining,
exceeding white as snow" (Mark 9:3), its shapes as severe as the folds of a Roman toga. He is surrounded by
a mandorla composed of the unpainted white *intonaco*.
The apostles below are represented in smaller scale.

The cell frescoes were painted *after* those affirmations
of Renaissance style that we have seen in Angelico's altarpieces, and these meditative images may seem to be
regressions to medieval ideals. True, in the visions of the
San Marco cells, through austere color and purified

shape, no worldly concerns trouble the spirit. In each
painting, however, Fra Angelico probes the sensibilities
of the individual observer, as Donatello had done in his
psychological sculpture (see figs. 162, 170); in these frescoes the individual is the center, as is also true in the
Renaissance perspective system. In this sense these
paintings are fully Renaissance works.

In 1445 Fra Angelico was called to Rome. Pope
Eugenius IV, who had been expelled from Rome in
1433 by the rebellious populace, had been in residence
in Florence, and after the consecration of San Marco in
1443, the pope slept there in the cell of Cosimo de'
Medici, already frescoed by Fra Angelico, and became
acquainted with his work. After he returned to Rome,
the pope called for Fra Angelico, who for five years
worked there under Eugenius and, in 1447, his successor, the humanist Pope Nicholas V. We read of an altarpiece for the high altar of Santa Maria sopra Minerva, a
large frescoed chapel at St. Peter's, and a study and two
chapels in the Vatican. Today the private chapel of
Nicholas V is the only witness to Fra Angelico's achievements in the Eternal City.

The chapel is frescoed with scenes from the lives of
two deacon martyrs, St. Lawrence and St. Stephen,
painted with the help of assistants. Despite the modest
scale of the chapel, the subject matter of the individual
scenes apparently encouraged him to endow them with

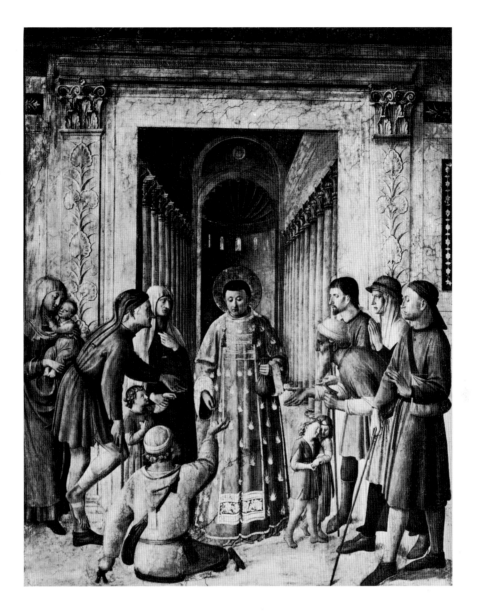

214. FRA ANGELICO.
*St. Lawrence
Distributing the
Treasures of the Church.*
1448. Fresco.
Chapel of Nicholas V,
Vatican, Rome.
Commissioned by
Pope Nicholas V

a new and very Roman grandeur. In *St. Lawrence Distributing the Treasures of the Church* (fig. 214), the saint, whose dalmatic is decorated with golden flames referring to the fire of his martyrdom, stands before the open Renaissance portal of a basilica probably intended to suggest St. Peter's as Nicholas planned to restore it. The monolithic ancient columns taken from pagan monuments had, for more than a millennium, been part of the common experience of Christianity; they are represented in all their solemnity. From there on the details are invented—a vaulted ceiling painted blue and decorated with gold stars, impossible to set on the fragile and tottering Constantinian structure; a groin-vaulted crossing; and an apse with a conched semidome—all representing the current architectural taste at the papal court.

The illusion of space is so persuasive that one notes with surprise that Fra Angelico has retained the Trecento double scale for figures and architecture. His strict sense of form and the simplicity and strength of his patterns endow the assembly of paupers and cripples with a majesty equal to that of the great colonnade behind

them. And as age, misery, weariness, and disease are represented without sentimentality, so is the delight of the children in the charity they have received. In the Chapel of Nicholas V, Fra Angelico proved himself one of the great Florentine masters of form and space. At the papal court he was considered "famous beyond all other Italian painters."

FRA FILIPPO LIPPI

Filippo was born about 1406 into the large family of an impoverished butcher in the poor quarter that surrounded the monastery of the Carmine in Florence. Together with an equally unwanted brother, he entered that monastery at an early age and took his vows in 1421. Vasari reports that he decided to become a painter while watching Masaccio at work in the Brancacci Chapel. The mistake of Filippo becoming a monk was compounded by his appointment to the chaplaincy of a convent in Prato where, according to Vasari, his attention was deflected while he was saying Mass by a young

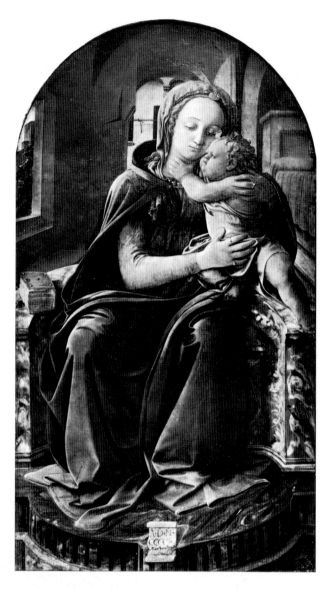

215. FRA FILIPPO LIPPI. *Madonna and Child*
(Tarquinia *Madonna*). 1437. Panel, 45 x 25½".
National Gallery, Rome

can city of Tarquinia, shows the profound influence of Masaccio. The heavy-featured, plebian type chosen for the Madonna and the simplicity of the domestic interior, complete with a bed and a view into a courtyard, are as reminiscent of Masaccio as are the heavy shadows throughout the painting. Only the marble throne and pearled diadem seem out of place. A touch of naturalism is the absence of a halo for either of the sacred figures. But a closer look reveals that Filippo is not interested in the consistency of Masaccio's style. The powerfully lighted drapery masses in the foreground project erratically, and the interior space seems throttled around the center. The homely gestures and attitudes natural in Masaccio here seem somewhat forced. The most striking feature of the style is the reappearance of contour. Apparently, Masaccio's *chiaroscuro* did not seem sufficient to Filippo, for around every form he supplied hard, drawn edges, accenting them by gradation of tone to give them the look of sharp lines. Yet for all its uncertainties the painting is a compelling work, filled with the wistful melancholy that characterizes many of Filippo's compositions.

Also in 1437, Filippo began a large altarpiece for the chapel of the Barbadori family in the Church of Santo Spirito in Florence (fig. 216). It is this work that Domenico Veneziano, in his letter of 1438, said would take Filippo at least five years to complete. The panel shows the Virgin standing before her throne in a kind of courtyard beyond which blue sky is visible. The architecture is Renaissance in every detail, however capricious, and the pointed arches of a Gothic triptych have been discarded in favor of round ones. The Virgin uses a sling to hold Christ on one hip, as Italian mothers still do. Sts. Fredianus and Augustine kneel before her and youthful, blond angels gather about them. The picture is suffused with Massaccesque shadow that is softer and richer than in the Tarquinia *Madonna*. The coloring, smoldering and subdued, is typical of Filippo's early work: soft deep greens, sonorous metallic reds, and smoky plum tones predominate. Here and there a clear yellow or a surprising orange-red enliven this chromatic scheme, as do occasional touches of gold. While Trecento artists seemed content with the traditional metallic halo, Quattrocento artists began to search for new, more naturalistic devices to suggest the glowing light of divinity. Here, apparently for the first time in Italian painting, the haloes of Mother and Child appear to be made of transparent crystal flecked with gold.

As in the Tarquinia *Madonna*, the proportions of figures and faces are full and heavy, and the masses are strongly projected by means of *chiaroscuro* that is now more successfully integrated. The pyramidal composition of the central figures is imposing, but we are distracted by the child-angels, who look like neighborhood youngsters dressed up with wings and lilies, as we know they were for festival occasions. At the Carmine each year, for example, Filippo could witness the Ascension of Christ reenacted for the pleasure of the local popula-

nun named Lucrezia Buti. We know from an anonymous denunciation, made to the Office of the Monasteries and of the Night, that from 1456 to 1458 Lucrezia, her sister Spinetta, and five other nuns were living in Filippo's house. During this period a son, who became the painter Filippino Lippi, was born to Lucrezia; later a daughter was born. There was other trouble: patrons claimed that Filippo did not fulfill his contracts; an assistant, Giovanni di Francesco, claimed that he was not paid; Filippo found himself in difficulty with ecclesiastical and secular authorities, and he was tried and tortured on the rack. It is said that Cosimo de' Medici persuaded Pope Pius II to release Filippo and Lucrezia from their vows and that they married and their children were legitimized.

The first dated painting by Filippo that we know, a *Madonna and Child* (fig. 215) done in 1437 for the Etrus-

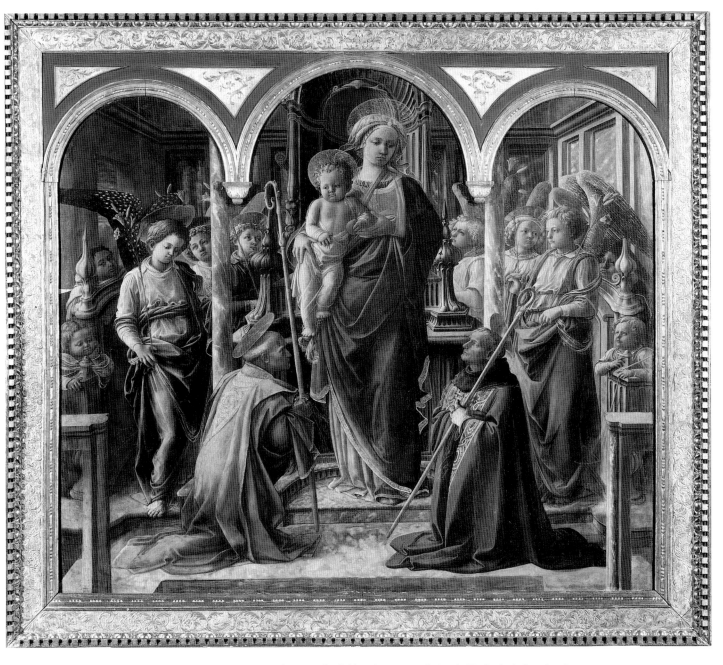

216. Fra Filippo Lippi. *Madonna and Child with Saints and Angels* (Barbadori altarpiece).
Begun 1437. Panel, 7' 1¹/2" x 8'. The Louvre, Paris. Commissioned by a member of the Barbadori
family for their chapel at Sto. Spirito, Florence (fig. 141)

tion: a hole cut in the vault made it possible for "Messer Domenedio" (as the documents call Christ) to sail right up through the crossing vault in front of the Brancacci Chapel. And the nearby Church of San Felice put on a similar annual show, designed by Brunelleschi himself, dramatizing the Annunciation. The angel Gabriel was lowered in a copper mandorla in the midst of the church, ran across a stage in front of the altar, and delivered the salutation to Mary, who was waiting in her little habitation. After listening to her reply, he ascended into a blue dome lined with lighted lamps for stars and with child-angels standing on clouds of carded wool and held in by

iron bars so that they could not fall "even if they wanted to," according to Vasari. The flavor of these popular festivals animates Filippo's paintings. At the extreme left, chin on balustrade, we see Filippo himself, in Carmelite habit, looking out at the observer.

One of Filippo's finest early paintings is the *Annunciation* (colorplate 45, p. 208) that is still in San Lorenzo in its original Brunelleschian frame. The painted arches are a bit surprising, as if Filippo or his patrons were unwilling to relinquish the Gothic division of an altarpiece into separate panels. But he gives us as a background a deep perspective into a monastery garden, at once the

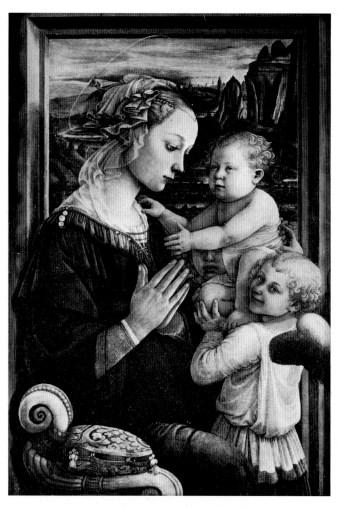

217. FRA FILIPPO LIPPI. *Madonna and Child.* c. 1455.
Panel, 35½ x 24". Uffizi Gallery, Florence

garden, with its flowers, trees, arbor, and blue sky beyond. It is the kind of effect one would expect from a Netherlandish rather than an Italian master, but perhaps Filippo had seen paintings by Jan van Eyck.

Fra Filippo's *Madonna and Child* in the Uffizi (fig. 217) is in keeping with the taste of the new age. Mary, more fashionable than Filippo's earlier Madonnas, is seated at an opening that affords a view over a rich landscape of plains, distant mountains, a city, and a bay. With her eyes modestly downcast, she lifts her folded hands in prayer before the Christ Child, who is held up by two angels, one of whom, far from angelic in appearance, grins out at the spectator. The elegance of mid-Quattrocento taste is seen in the new delicacy of figural proportion and in the refinement of the costume, especially the headdress with its artfully pleated design and gigantic pearl. Above the combed-back blond hair, its plaits mingled with the transparent linen veil, a string of graduated pearls makes a peak on the forehead. In Renaissance fashion, a high forehead was an object of special beauty, to be achieved, if necessary, by plucking or even shaving, in extreme cases, as far back as the top of the skull. The whole head thus resembles a glowing pearl. St. Antonine of Florence, confessor to the Medici family, explains the "pearl of great price" mentioned in Matthew 13:46 as the Incarnation of Christ; this idea probably explains the wondrous natural treasure poised on the Virgin's head, on the line between earth and sky.

Behind the Virgin's head we look off to the sea, while over that of the Christ Child tower lofty rocks, one of which seems about to fall. In the same chapter Antonine refers to Mary as the sea (see p. 194) and expounds the prophecy of the Virgin Birth in a vision of the prophet Daniel (2:31–35), who saw a stone cut without hands that fell from a mountain, smashing an idol with feet of clay before growing to become a mountain that filled the whole earth. But religious symbolism is subordinated to Filippo's enthusiasm for the beauties of light and atmosphere, rocks and fruitful plains, cities and soft cloud masses, lovely young women and healthy babies, tasteful garments and splendid furnishings. Masaccio's *chiaroscuro* has vanished along with the solemnity of a bygone way of life. Now the figures are illuminated by a soft, all-over glow without harsh shadows, and the sense of mass so striking in Filippo's earlier works is considerably reduced.

The delightful tondo (circular picture) of the *Madonna and Child with the Birth of the Virgin* is probably the one on which Filippo was working in 1452 for the prosperous merchant Leonardo Bartolini (fig. 218). The tondo eventually became the most popular shape for domestic religious images in the Florentine Quattrocento, but its origin and precise meaning remain obscure. It may have been derived from the mirror, characteristically circular in the Middle Ages and an age-old symbol of the Virgin, but it is more likely related to the Florentine tradition of painted birth-salvers, wooden trays presented to women from important families when they gave birth

garden of the Temple with which Mary was connected and the symbolic closed garden of the Song of Songs. Mary's agitated pose is derived from Donatello's *Annunciation* (see fig. 245), but the mood of the picture has little to do with that stern sculptured monument to classicism. As yet unexplained are the two curly-haired, puffy-faced angels to the left, who are not mentioned in any text. One looks downward, the other gazes out at the observer and points to the Annunciation—a device to lead the observer's eye into the painting that was authorized by the theorist Leonbattista Alberti, who had recently arrived in Florence.

The tones of the drapery of the foreground figures contrast surprisingly with the brilliant orange building at the end of the garden. A captivating feature of the picture is the glass vase in the foreground, from which Gabriel has apparently just plucked the lily he holds. Filippo has even painted a niche to suggest that the vase rests on the frame—or perhaps on the altar itself—and he thereby unites the real space of the chapel with his splendid illusion. With its shining water and soft shadow, the vase contrasts with the expanse of the softly painted

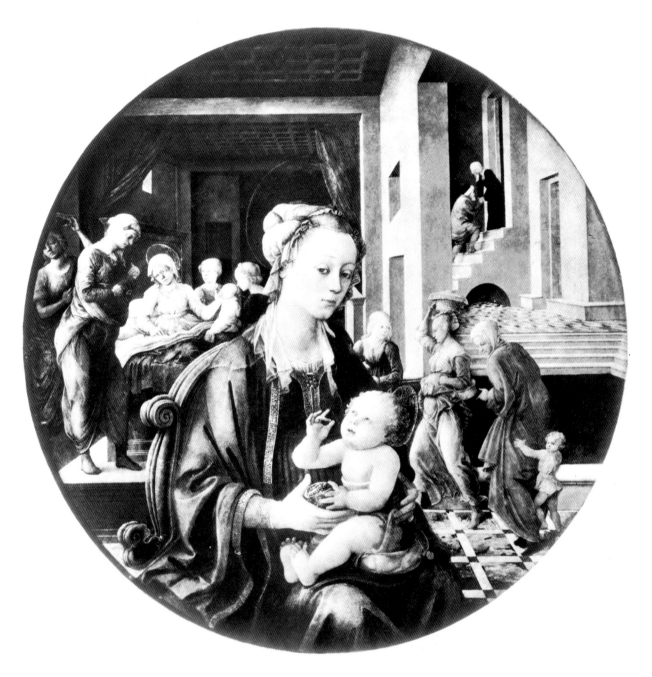

218. FRA FILIPPO LIPPI. *Madonna and Child with the Birth of the Virgin.* c. 1452. Panel, diameter 53".
Pitti Gallery, Florence. Perhaps commissioned by Leonardo Bartolini

to a male child. In the present instance the architectural background consists of a Quattrocento interior, and the subject emphasizes genealogy. On the left side the birth of the Virgin is depicted as if it had occurred in the Renaissance house of a well-to-do Florentine family, attended by maidservants carrying gifts. At the upper right there is a staircase on which St. Anne, mother of the Virgin Mary, receives the returning Joachim, perhaps a reference to their kiss of meeting when the Virgin was conceived. The planes and volumes resulting from the severe wall surfaces, the inlaid marble squares of the floor, the coffered ceilings, and the steps of varying breadth and pitch create an exceptionally complex spatial composition. The Virgin and Child sit at the focal point of the perspective—which conforms to the usual rules—but off-center in the tondo. A delicate creature who looks shyly out at the observer, she was certainly drawn from the same model as the Uffizi *Madonna.* The Christ Child holds a pomegranate and is about to pop a seed into his mouth. Like Masaccio's grapes (see figs. 187, 202), this realistic motive has a religious meaning; the pomegranate is red like the blood of Christ, and its numerous seeds are held within the skin like individual souls within the encompassing Church. In the elegance and wistfulness of this painting, we can already discern the sources of Botticelli's art.

Fra Filippo's frescoes in the chancel of Prato Cathedral were executed over a considerable period, from

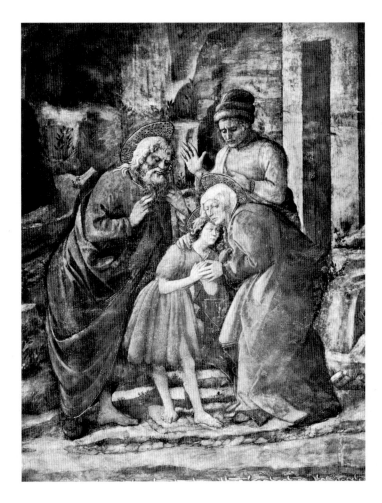

219. FRA FILIPPO LIPPI.
*St. John the Baptist Bids
Farewell to His Family*. 1452–66.
Fresco. Cathedral,
Prato. Commissioned by the
Datini family

their inception in 1452, through the date of 1460 found on one of the frescoes, into 1464, when officials complained to Carlo de' Medici that Filippo had not completed the job, and up to at least 1466, when the painter left for his final undertaking at Spoleto. Much of the work was done from Filippo's designs by his pupil, Fra Diamante, but everywhere the cycle overflows with details that show the human sweetness and warmth of Filippo's art. The Life of St. John the Baptist, for example, that unrolls in many episodes through an uncoordinated landscape, contains the moving scene (fig. 219) where the boy says farewell to his family before going off into the wilderness—a composition that still contains echoes of Masaccio's grand style.

The *Feast of Herod* (fig. 220) is a work of great originality. A splendid garden courtyard, floored with inlaid marble in a strong perspective pattern, is the setting for the celebration. The bordering walls are constricted toward the rear, somewhat like the throttled space in the Tarquinia *Madonna* (see fig. 215), and shrubs and trees appear above balustrades or are set in front of walls. The perspective lines shoot inward past the central table of Herod himself, seated directly below the arms of the Datini family, to windows opening on a view of a rocky landscape with a distant city. On this stage the action moves in three episodes. At the left, cut off from the festivities by a gigantic man-at-arms, Salome receives on a platter the head of St. John the Baptist, from which she looks away. The decapitation itself is painted on the adjoining wall, and the executioner has to reach around the corner to place the head on her platter; his elbow is bent the requisite ninety degrees to conform to the angle at which the walls meet. In the center Salome does her dance, poised in an oddly unsteady fashion on her left foot, while her right foot, hand, and assorted ribbons saw the air. This figure is the direct ancestor of the figures in motion painted by Fra Filippo's pupil Botticelli (see colorplate 61, p. 302). At the right Salome kneels, still not looking at the head she presents to Herodias, but at the extreme right two servants clutch each other as one surreptitiously captures a glimpse of the grisly trophy.

Fra Filippo was scarcely the artist for the Medici to select to paint a series of penitential pictures, but possibly in the late 1450s he was in no position to refuse. The flourishing world of the Renaissance had taken, at this time, a disagreeable turn. In 1448 the Black Death struck again, and it returned annually for three

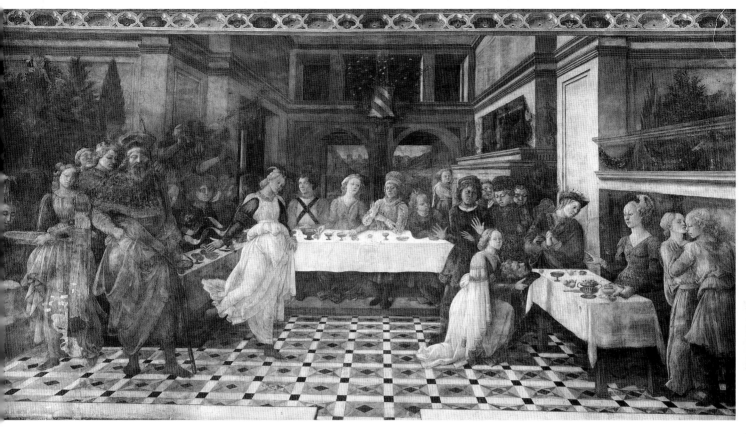

220. FRA FILIPPO LIPPI. *Feast of Herod.* 1452–66. Fresco. Cathedral, Prato

summers; thousands of Florentines succumbed, and the hordes of Northern pilgrims, passing through Tuscany on their way to the papal jubilee of 1450 in Rome, carried the plague with them and died miserably in the streets there. The archbishop of Florence at this time was St. Antonine, who had been prior of San Marco when Fra Angelico lived and worked there. A man of blameless personal life, Antonine allowed the revenues of his archdiocese to accumulate and lived in a simplicity unexpected in the mid-Quattrocento. Except on ceremonial occasions, he wore a threadbare Dominican habit. He may well have been responsible for the content of two similar works painted by Fra Filippo for Lucrezia Tornabuoni, wife of Piero de' Medici—one work was for her penitential cell at the monastery of Camaldoli, high in the Apennines, the other for the altar of the chapel in the Medici Palace (fig. 221). St. Antonine originally wrote his moral treatise "on the art of living well" for Lucrezia's sister, and he made a copy of it in his own hand for Lucrezia.

The Virgin kneels and adores the naked Christ Child, following, in part, the description of St. Bridget of Sweden of her vision of the Nativity (see p. 144); this suggests that these images represent Nativities even if there is no cave, no shed, no Joseph, angels, ox, or ass. The setting is the middle of a forest in which many chopped-down trees can be seen. In the picture painted for the Medici Palace, God the Father appears and the dove of the Holy Spirit descends from the clouds to join the Christ Child in forming the Trinity. Nearby stands St. John the Baptist as a boy of five or six although he was actually only six months older than his cousin Jesus. In the lower left-hand corner an ax jammed into a tree trunk has FRATER PHILIPPUS P (for *pinxit*—painted) on its handle. This is a penitential image derived from the Baptist's own words: "And now also the axe is laid unto the root of the trees: therefore every tree which bringeth not forth good fruit is hewn down, and cast into the fire" (Matthew 3:10).

Since the painting seems to date about the time of the Lucrezia Buti scandal, Filippo's signature on the axe handle may record his penance. But logging was also an essential daily activity of the monks at Camaldoli, who lived a rigorous existence in clearings they made in the forest, each monk in a separate hut, where he celebrated solitary Mass and lived on what he could raise in his garden plot. Taking the Camaldolites as his theme, St. Antonine recommends to penitents a life of religious

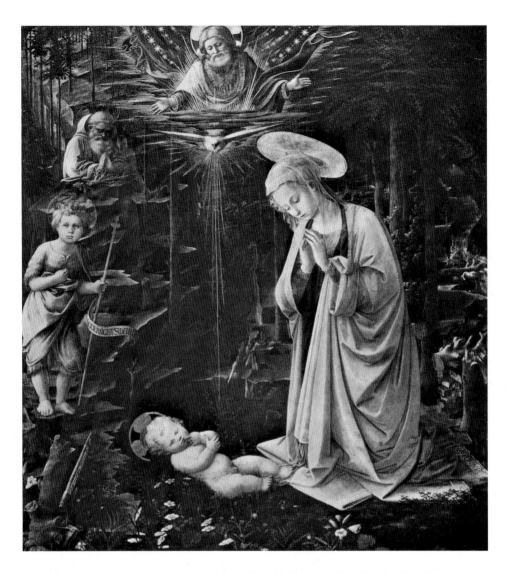

221. FRA FILIPPO LIPPI. *Madonna Adoring Her Child*. Late 1450s. Panel, 50 x 45 5/8".
Picture Gallery, Dahlem Museum, Berlin. Commissioned by a member
of the Medici family (Cosimo or Piero de' Medici or perhaps Lucrezia Tornabuoni)
for the chapel in the Medici Palace (see fig. 146)

meditation in what he called "the little garden of the soul," very like the garden plot in which we see Mary kneeling to adore Christ. First one should cut down the trees, he says, then uproot the stumps and brambles, then fence in the garden and appoint a guardian for the gate, and only then will the flowers of a good life spring up. He also offers for admiration St. John the Baptist—the last of the prophets and the first of the martyrs, who went into the wilderness before the age of seven. Most important, he quotes Christ's saying: "For whosoever shall do the will of my Father which is in heaven, the same is my brother, and sister, and mother" (Matthew 12:50).

St. Antonine claims that the true penitent will identify with the Virgin, and that through creating the "gar-den of the soul," the Christ Child can be born again in one's heart. Antonine had derived this doctrine from the teaching of his mentor and predecessor as prior of San Domenico in Fiesole, Giovanni Dominici. Around Christ, flowers spring up to form a garden protected by saints, while cut-down and uprooted trees fill the background. Fire comes down from Heaven—the fire of the Holy Spirit with which St. John said Christ would baptize (Matthew 3:11). In the deep blue-green gloom of the forest, Mary and the praying saint—Romuald, the founder of the Camaldolite Order—adore Christ. The new subject of the Adoration of the Christ Child, based on St. Bridget's vision of the Nativity, is appropriate to a new phase of Quattrocento thought and feeling, about which more will be said in Chapter 12.

10

The Second Renaissance Style in Architecture and Sculpture

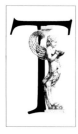he new stylistic concerns of the mid-Quattrocento are clearly focused in the life, thought, and artistic activity of Leonbattista Alberti (1404–72), whose shadow has been cast so often across the preceding four chapters. Alberti was immersed in the theory of architecture, sculpture, and painting, and on all of them had a lasting influence.

ALBERTI

Alberti authored a series of Latin works, ranging from poems and comedies to treatises on law, the horse, the family, and the tranquillity of the soul. In 1435 he circulated in manuscript form his Latin treatise *De pictura* (*On Painting*), following in 1436 with *Della pittura*, an abridged and less erudite version in Italian. He knew the treatise *De architectura* by the ancient Roman architect and engineer Vitruvius and before 1450 produced his own counterpart, *De re aedificatoria libri X* (*Ten Books on Architecture*). It is now thought that he wrote *De statua* (*On the Statue*) about 1433. His writings express the doctrine that *virtus* is the quality to be sought in human life; by this he meant not "virtue" in the Christian sense, but what we might call "humanity"—the quality that distinguishes us from the lower animals, comprising intelligence, reason, knowledge, control, balance, perception, harmony, and dignity. Alberti's was not a democratic theory, and it was intended for the same elite who, in the Florence of the mid-1430s, were gaining the political and economic power they were to hold until nearly the end of the century.

Without exception, the Florentine humanists came from the dominant social and economic class, and Alberti was a member of one of the grand Florentine families. But it had been expelled from the Republic in 1402 and Leonbattista was born in exile, in Genoa, in 1404. He received a humanistic education at the University of Bologna, where he took his doctorate in canon law at the age of twenty-four and became acquainted with the humanist scholar Tommaso Parentucelli, who later became Pope Nicholas V. He derived no steady income from family sources and was dependent on stipends from his patrons, who included princes both secular and ecclesiastical—the Este of Ferrara, the Malatesta of Rimini, the Gonzaga of Mantua, several

cardinals, and at least two popes, as well as the Florentine merchant prince Giovanni Rucellai. As a young man Alberti traveled widely in Germany and the Low Countries, eventually became a papal *abbreviatore* (briefwriter), and for more than thirty years enjoyed the benefice, or revenue, of the Church of San Martino a Gangalandi, in the Arno Valley. He seems to have made up for his habitual absence from San Martino by a bequest to build a handsome Renaissance apse—still standing—apparently from his own design. Alberti's role at the courts of his princely patrons was that of adviser, and his artistic influence, especially in the realm of architecture and city planning, extended far beyond the buildings that, in one way or another, he designed himself.

A style and almost a way of life are associated with Alberti's personality. His first appearance in Florence was in 1434, the year of Cosimo de' Medici's return from exile. But Alberti, in his own words, "went to Florence seldom and remained there little." His two great architectural creations in his ancestral city were not imitated by Florentine patrons or architects, although his architectural ideas had an enormous effect on other Italian centers, and the Roman High Renaissance is inconceivable without his inventions. His notions about the construction and organization of pictorial space and the compositional and narrative methods that painters should follow help explain the developments we have already observed in the works of Fra Angelico and Fra Filippo Lippi. They also clarify the pictorial sculpture of the mature Ghiberti and Donatello and the pictorial styles of Paolo Uccello, Domenico Veneziano, Andrea del Castagno, and Piero della Francesca.

THE MALATESTA TEMPLE. At midcentury Alberti was given an opportunity to put his classical ideas into visible form in an ambitious structure that, still unfinished today, endures as a beautiful fragment. The Adriatic city of Rimini was at that time under the rule of one of the least scrupulous yet most erudite of Renaissance tyrants, Sigismondo Malatesta, beside whose crimes and cruelties the worst excesses of twentieth-century gangsters pale into insignificance. Sigismondo enjoys, in fact, the distinction of being the only person in history publicly consigned to Hell while still alive; the ceremony was performed with due solemnity by the humanist pope Pius II in front of St. Peter's. In the

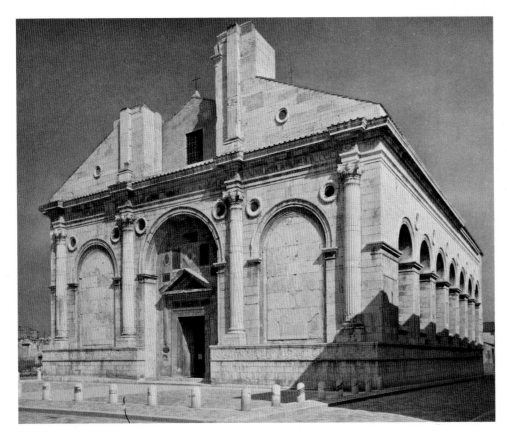

left:
222. LEONBATTISTA ALBERTI.
Malatesta Temple
(S. Francesco), Rimini.
Exterior designed 1450.
Commissioned by
Sigismondo Malatesta

below:
223. LEONBATTISTA ALBERTI.
West flank,
Malatesta Temple

pope's eyes, one of Sigismondo's most irritating offenses was the conversion of the monastic Church of San Francesco at Rimini into a sort of temple to Sigismondo and Isotta degli Atti, the mistress for whom he had caused his wife to be suffocated. The desecration of the Christian building had started unobtrusively. In the original Gothic church, funerary chapels were erected for Sigismondo and Isotta that were decorated by the sculptor Agostino di Duccio and the painter Piero della Francesca (see p. 282). Matteo de' Pasti, the Veronese architect who was responsible for the remodeling, continued to clothe the Gothic arches of the interior in Renaissance dress, destroying earlier works, including frescoes by Giotto. At the jubilee of Pope Nicholas V in Rome in 1450, Sigismondo seems to have made the acquaintance of Alberti, who was then advising the pope on redesigning the papal city. For Sigismondo, Alberti envisioned a splendid new exterior that would enclose and conceal the work of Matteo de' Pasti, which Alberti sharply criticized in a letter of 1454.

Only the exterior of Alberti's plan was brought anywhere near completion, and the beauty of the lower story of the façade (fig. 222) makes one doubly regret the mutilated, unfinished upper story. The dominant motif of the façade was to have been a triple arch based on Roman triumphal arches. The shapes and proportions of the elements, however, were borrowed from the Arch of Augustus in Rimini, which is only a few hundred yards from the Malatesta Temple. Early in the con-

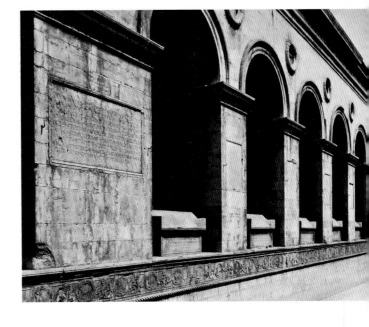

struction, Alberti was forced to convert the lateral arches into shallow niches and to continue the plinth underneath them. In other respects the lower story was carried out substantially as he desired. On the façade, four fluted, engaged columns uphold the entablature, and on the flanks (fig. 223) arches enframe sarcophagi for the humanists of Sigismondo's court. The three arches between the columns and the seven deep arches—Alberti

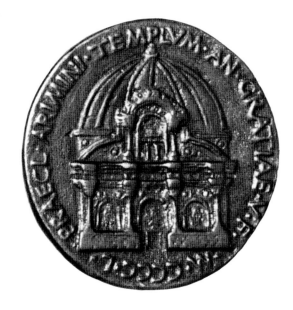

224. LEONBATTISTA ALBERTI. Malatesta Temple. Design for exterior, on a bronze medal after MATTEO DE' PASTI. 1450. Diameter 1⁹⁄₁₆". National Gallery of Art, Washington, D.C. (Kress Collection). Commissioned by Sigismondo Malatesta

and half-barrel vaults in wood over the side aisles. These vaults were to have been decorated to look like stone in order to confer an effect of simple grandeur onto a structure cluttered by Matteo's revetment. Alberti demolished the Gothic chancel and sanctuary to make way for what was to be the crowning feature of the building, the never-constructed dome visible in the medal.

Alberti's own words lend substance to conjectures about the appearance of the dome, which the medal shows as a hemisphere divided by ribs that spring from a cylindrical drum. Although Alberti admired Brunelleschi's dome for the Cathedral of Florence (see fig. 132), he insisted that its proportions were incorrect because they did not correspond to those invented by the Romans and demonstrated in the Pantheon, his ultimate authority. In all probability, therefore, we must imagine a rotunda surmounted by a hemisphere, as in the Pantheon, where the total height is equal to the diameter. If Sigismondo's own disastrous fortunes had not prevented completion of the Malatesta Temple, the subsequent history of ecclesiastical architecture might well have been different.

THE PALAZZO RUCELLAI. A strikingly original contribution to the history of Renaissance palace design was the façade of the Palazzo Rucellai in Florence (fig. 225), which Vasari attributed to Alberti. The palace belonged to a wealthy Florentine merchant, Giovanni Rucellai, who wrote an informative journal called the *Zibaldone*. The façade's general principles were followed in many other buildings, some actually built, others merely designed (see figs. 231, 386).

The harmonious and classical design of the façade of the Palazzo Rucellai may be taken as an answer to the rough-hewn Palazzo Medici (see fig. 146), started a decade earlier. The basic elements of the Palazzo Rucellai are the same as those used at the Medici Palace—a rusticated three-story building with an entrance portal and high, square windows on the ground floor, mullioned windows on the second and third, and a massive cornice. But in the Palazzo Rucellai these features have been absorbed into a new system of proportions. The three stories are of equal height, and the rustication, consisting of smooth pseudoblocks of stone (the real joints do not always correspond to the apparent ones), is identical in all three stories. Most important of all, the rustication is not allowed to assert itself as the dominant element of the structure but is held in check by a grid of pilasters supporting entablatures, an idea probably inspired by the engaged columns and pilasters of the Colosseum at Rome. The main purpose of Alberti's classical screen architecture, which is without structural function, is to convey to the Renaissance observer the humanistic erudition of architect and patron.

In the Palazzo Rucellai, articulation and details are stated with the utmost elegance. Roman practice placed the Ionic order above Doric or Tuscan, Corinthian above Ionic; Alberti maintained that if one knew the

preferred an uneven number of openings—on the flanks are supported not by columns, as in a Brunelleschian building, but by piers.

Alberti once defined beauty as "the harmony and concord of all the parts, achieved in such a manner that nothing could be added, taken away, or altered." In keeping with this basic statement, he explained that arches, as openings in a wall, should be sustained by sections of the wall; columns, in contrast, belong not to beauty but to decoration and should be treated as applied elements, not supporting members. The resultant emphasis on the block of the building itself is alien to Brunelleschi's architecture of plane, space, and line and represents a fundamental change in the conception of a Renaissance structure. The effect of massive grandeur is enhanced by the projection of arches, cornices, triumphal wreaths (enclosing slices of porphyry columns taken from Sant'Apollinare Nuovo in Ravenna), and capitals. What at first seem to be Roman Composite capitals have been invented by Alberti out of volutes, egg-and-dart moldings, acanthus leaves, and winged cherub heads. Matteo de' Pasti described Alberti's extraordinary designs for the capitals as "*bellissimi*" ("most beautiful"), and so they are.

Matteo's medal (fig. 224), struck for the laying of the cornerstone in 1450, shows a façade that culminates on the second story in a central bay with a triple mullioned window that is enclosed by an arch supported on two columns. Pilasters were substituted for columns in the execution, and only one was completed. According to the medal and to a number of buildings in Venice and Dalmatia that reflect Alberti's design, the sloping roofs were to have been half-arches. The central arch and flanking quarter-circles were intended as external reflections of a wooden barrel vault to be built over the nave

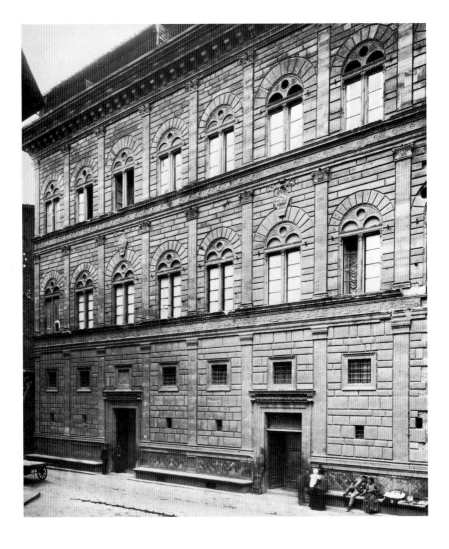

225. LEONBATTISTA ALBERTI.
Palazzo Rucellai, Florence.
Façade (left five bays). 1455–58.
Later extended by BERNARDO
ROSSELLINO. Commissioned by
Giovanni Rucellai

grammar of ancient architecture well enough, one could at times devise one's own vocabulary. Thus the ground story is Tuscan and the third Corinthian, but the second story displays graceful capitals of new invention composed of a single layer of acanthus leaves grouped about a central palmette—a fitting intermediate stage between the Tuscan and the Corinthian. The rectangular portals and square windows are bordered by frames scaled to harmonize with their respective dimensions. Within this tightly knit structure the only random element is the joints in the rustication, and even here the intersections are as delicate and austere as those in an abstract painting by Mondrian. Against this rectilinear system, projecting so slightly that the pilasters are nearly flush with the masonry, the modeled ornament of the portal cornices and the friezes containing Rucellai family symbols, including the beautiful motif of the billowing sail, provide the only enrichment.

The foregoing indicates a designer of brilliant originality, supporting Vasari's attribution of the façade to Alberti, which is sustained by at least two other sources. But others mention a "model" of the building made by the architect and sculptor Bernardo Rossellino (see pp. 236, 251), and some writers have contended that it was he, not Alberti, who designed and built the façade. Gio-

vanni Rucellai, writing about 1464, mentions the palace as his chief achievement in building but does not identify the architect or the builder. Neither does Filarete (see pp. 422–23), who was in Florence in 1461 and described the façade of the Palazzo Rucellai as "all made in the antique style."

The most persuasive solution is that the design by Alberti consisted of only five bays, reading from the left, and would therefore have been centralized. A five-bay façade would agree with the design principles stated by Alberti in his *De re aedificatoria*, where he recommends that, as a reflection of the natural bodies of humans and animals, a building should be centralized and have an equal number of supports. This should be combined with an odd number of openings, an idea based on the eyes, ears, nostrils, and mouth of the head. It follows that a five-bay design should have six pilasters combined with four windows and a central doorway. In fact, documents indicate that just such a five-bay façade was actually built, starting about 1455 and completed in 1458, over a core of remodeled earlier structures, to which the portal does not exactly correspond. Later, the sixth and seventh bays were added, as Giovanni Rucellai acquired more land, and the eighth bay remains fragmentary because the owner of the next house refused to sell.

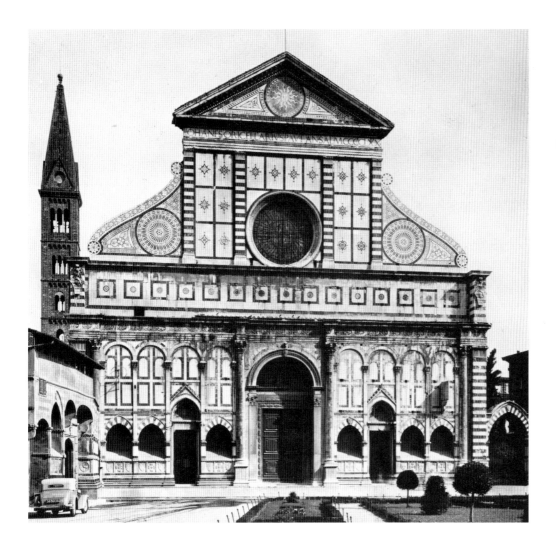

226. LEONBATTISTA
ALBERTI. Façade,
Sta. Maria Novella,
Florence. c. 1456–70.
Commissioned by
Giovanni Rucellai

Moreover, the quality of the carving in the sixth and seventh bays is not up to the level of that in the first five. All this suggests that Giovanni called in Bernardo to extend his palace, and that Alberti deserves credit for the original design.

SANTA MARIA NOVELLA. Alberti also furnished the designs for other projects commissioned by Giovanni Rucellai, including the façade of Santa Maria Novella (fig. 226), which has little in common with the Trecento church behind it (see fig. 50) save the harmony of its design. The white-and-green marble structure is the only Florentine church façade on a grand scale to be built during the Renaissance. In its design Alberti followed the Romanesque but classicizing façade of San Miniato al Monte, a church overlooking Florence, and divided the structure into an arcade below a second-story temple crowned by a pediment. Between the two stories he inserted a handsome mezzanine that serves as an attic for one and a base for the other. It is here that we see the name of the patron in huge Roman capitals and his motif of the billowing sail. Alberti framed the second-story temple on either side by large volutes, an ingenious solution to a problem that had perplexed designers of basilica façades for a millennium: how to unite

a narrow upper story with a wider lower story and at the same time mask the sloping roofs of the side aisles. In France and England the roofs were hidden behind towers; in medieval Italy, massive screens were commonly used. But Alberti's volutes make a virtue of necessity by turning the straight slopes of the roof lines into a delightful double curve.

Alberti's solution is so successful that we hardly notice how easily he has resolved the integration of the pre-existing Gothic tomb niches (*avelli*) and the side portals on the lower level of the façade. These he has absorbed into his Renaissance design by enclosing them within a round-arched blind arcade and by repeating their horizontal green-and-white banding in the pilasters on both levels. The result is one of the most impressive church façades in the history of Renaissance architecture.

SANT'ANDREA. Alberti's triumph as a church architect was his design for Sant'Andrea at Mantua (fig. 227), although it was only built after his death, and the present eighteenth-century dome has nothing to do with his intentions. Christian priest or no, Alberti never abandoned his humanist attitude long enough to write the word "church"; one always reads "temple." His innovations at Sant'Andrea are in part based on his criticism of

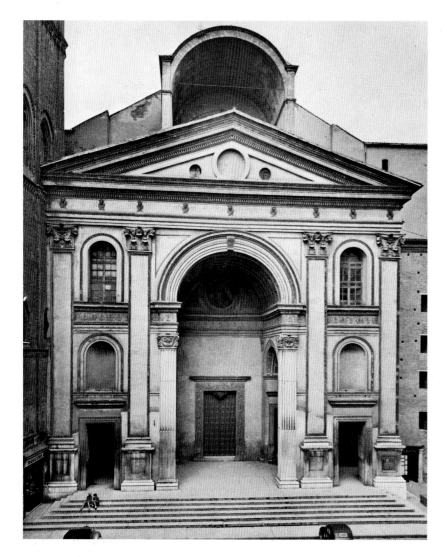

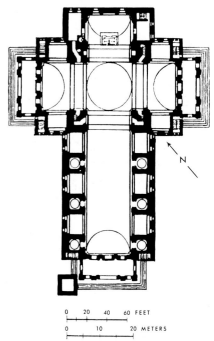

left: 227. LEONBATTISTA ALBERTI.
Sant'Andrea, Mantua. Designed 1470.
Commissioned by Ludovico Gonzaga

below: 228. Plan of Sant'Andrea, Mantua

the use of the ancient Roman basilican plan for church architecture. For the ancient Romans the basilica was used for courts of law, with proceedings taking place in twin apses, one at each end, while the nave accommodated litigants and spectators and clients conferred with their attorneys in the side aisles. The basilica's three-aisled plan had been adopted for the Early Christian church by changing the axis and focusing on a single apse, and this plan remained standard for church design throughout the Middle Ages. But Alberti maintains that the three-aisled plan was unsuited to the worship of "the gods" (never "God"), for the columns could conceal ceremonies at the altar. So out went eleven hundred years of Christian architecture. Illumination, moreover, should be calculated so as to inspire awe and reverence for the mystery of "the gods."

Ludovico Gonzaga, marquis of Mantua (see fig. 410; colorplate 8, p. 16), had commissioned Sant'Andrea in order to exhibit to pilgrims the relic of the blood of Christ, which St. Longinus was supposed to have brought to Mantua. In fact, at least nine major churches owe their existence to the wave of popular religiosity that, in the late Quattrocento and early Cinquecento, took the form of the adoration of relics; five are treated in this book (see figs. 313–15, 375–77, 506, 600–602), and none utilized the basilican plan. For Sant'Andrea, Alberti invented a new plan (fig. 228) based on the barrel-vaulted chambers of the ancient Roman Temple of Venus and Rome. The gigantic barrel vault of Sant'Andrea (fig. 229) produces a unified spatial effect concentrating on the high altar, which Alberti doubtless intended for a central position under the dome. Nothing hides the ceremony. The lateral arches admit worshipers not to side aisles but to secluded chapels, each crowned with a barrel vault at right angles to the nave. The single-aisle plan is matched by a single-story elevation, for the barrel vault rests, without clerestory, on the nave entablature; this in turn rests upon piers that are articulated by pilasters framing the arched entrances to the chapels.

Alberti's new barrel-vaulted church interior was repeated throughout Europe, from the St. Peter's of Bramante and Michelangelo to the churches of the Baroque. For illumination Alberti depended on the dome, the huge oculus of the façade, and the smaller oculi in the chapels; all of these showed only the sky, wherein

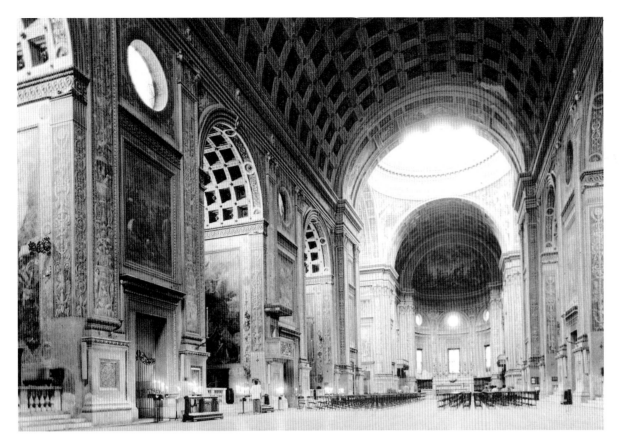

229. LEONBATTISTA ALBERTI. Nave, Sant'Andrea, Mantua. Designed 1470

dwelt "the gods." In the façade, whose unexpected scale depends on its relation to the small piazza in front of the church, Alberti establishes the motif of coupled giant pilasters that flank arches and are interlocked with a smaller order of pilasters supporting transverse barrel vaults. This motif is repeated throughout the interior of the church.

ARCHITECTURE AFTER ALBERTI. All over Italy the influence of Alberti's ideas was felt. Nicholas V's plans for a new papal Rome, centered for the first time on St. Peter's and the Vatican, were developed by Alberti. Many Roman buildings are derived from his inventions and link him with the more grandiose Rome of the High Renaissance and the Baroque. Interestingly enough, none of the architects of these Roman buildings has been securely identified. The courtyard of the Palazzo Venezia in Rome (fig. 230), built after 1455, at a time when Alberti was still connected with the papal court, imitates the arcades and engaged columns of such nearby Roman buildings as the Colosseum and the Theater of Marcellus (see the drawing by Giuliano da Sangallo, fig. 310). Several church façades built in the 1470s and 1480s, after Alberti's death, are variants of Santa Maria Novella. It seems unlikely, however, that Alberti would have approved the colossal Cancelleria (fig. 231)—its

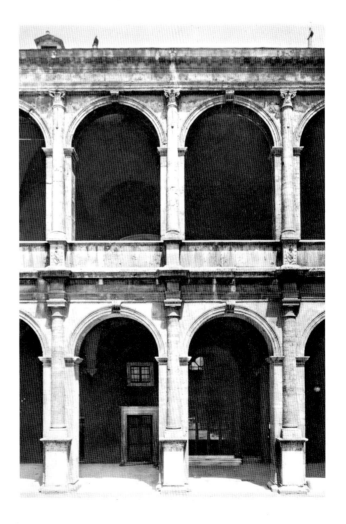

230. Circle of LEONBATTISTA ALBERTI. Courtyard, Palazzo Venezia, Rome. After 1455. Commissioned by Pietro and Marco Barbo

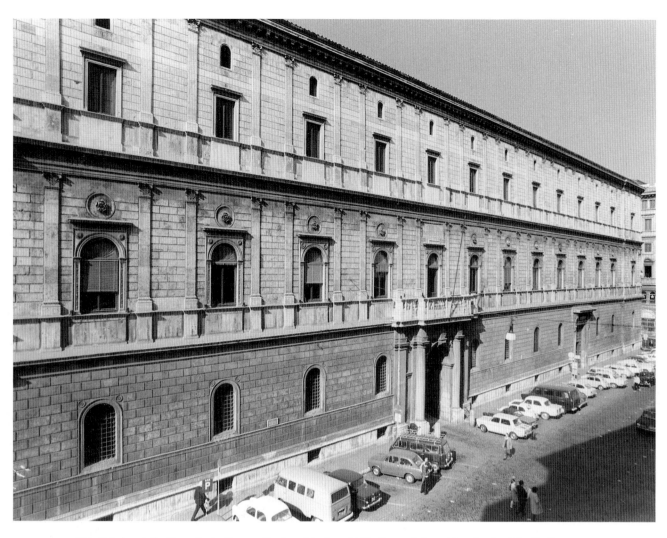

231. Palazzo della Cancelleria, Rome. Designed before 1489. Commissioned by Cardinal Raffaello Riario

principal façade is nearly 300 feet long—which dilutes the scheme of the Palazzo Rucellai over vast areas of masonry, intermingled with single-arch windows, heavy cornices, and ornamental motifs. The use of pilasters as a screen architecture here suggests the ideal cities of Luciano Laurana's panels (see fig. 386) and reappears in several other Roman palaces. Originally designed for Cardinal Raffaello Riario before 1489 (he is seen at the right hand of his uncle Sixtus IV in the fresco by Melozzo da Forlì, fig. 382), the building is impressive enough to have been attributed to Bramante—who did not arrive in Rome until ten years after it was started.

Pius II's plans for converting his native village of Corsignano into the papal city of Pienza (Pius and Pienza were both plays on the pope's family name of Piccolomini) were carried out by Bernardo Rossellino, the same master who probably extended the Palazzo Rucellai and who commenced, under Pope Nicholas V, the projected reconstruction of St. Peter's in Rome, doubtless under the supervision of Alberti. At Pienza he imitated the system of the Palazzo Rucellai in the Palazzo Piccolomini (one bay is visible at the right of fig. 233). The piazza at Pienza is the first of the new Renaissance town designs that was actually built (fig.

232). Although its details might well have offended Alberti, especially the irrational superimposition of arcade on colonnade in the façade of the cathedral, the supremacy of the building block in the design of the confronting church and palaces (fig. 233), to which pilasters, columns, and arches are added as decoration, conforms to Alberti's notions.

Plans and façades of churches built in Florence in the mid- and late Quattrocento show strong Albertian influences. The imposing Palazzo Pitti in Florence, commenced for Luca Pitti, a wealthy merchant, was attributed to Brunelleschi until the discovery that construction did not begin until 1458, twelve years after his death. As the official residence of the Medici grand dukes, it was extended during the late sixteenth (see fig. 696) and seventeenth centuries; in the nineteenth century it served as the first residence of the newly established Italian monarchy. The Quattrocento structure (fig. 234) was originally limited to the central seven bays, as shown here, and it is not known whether there was to have been a courtyard. The powerful rustication and the grandeur of the three superimposed arcades, obviously based on the ancient aqueducts whose ruins can still be found in the countryside around Rome, are alien

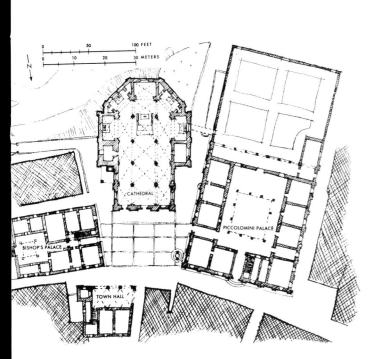

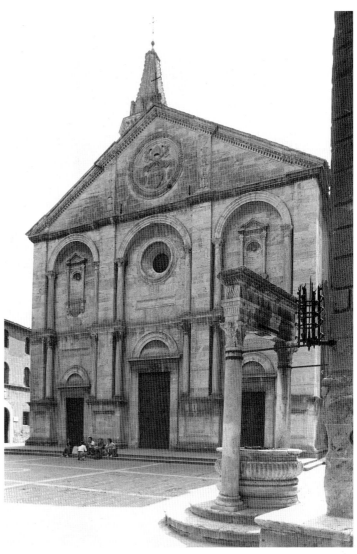

above: 232. BERNARDO ROSSELLINO. Plan of Piazza Pio II, Pienza. 1459–62. Commissioned by Pope Pius II

right: 233. BERNARDO ROSSELLINO. Cathedral, Pienza. 1459–62. Commissioned by Pope Pius II

below: 234. LUCA FANCELLI(?). Façade, central portion, Palazzo Pitti, Florence. Begun 1458. Commissioned by Luca Pitti

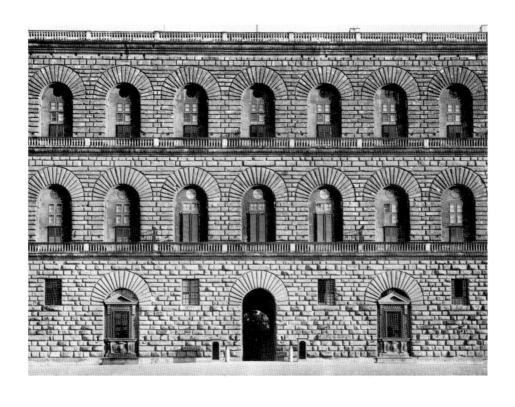

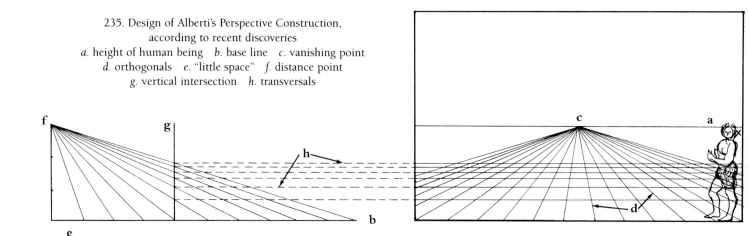

235. Design of Alberti's Perspective Construction,
according to recent discoveries
a. height of human being   *b.* base line   *c.* vanishing point
d. orthogonals   *e.* "little space"   *f.* distance point
g. vertical intersection   *h.* transversals

to the taste and practice of Brunelleschi, but believable for a follower of Alberti. The most likely candidate seems to be the Florentine architect Luca Fancelli, who was deeply imbued with Albertian ideas, was in Florence at the time, and built much of Sant'Andrea in Mantua after Alberti's designs.

Most important of all, Alberti's ideas on city planning, expounded in *De re aedificatoria*, were read and pondered by other architects and resulted in projects far more ambitious and comprehensive than Brunelleschi's piazze, such as the dreams of Filarete for Sforzinda (see fig. 436) and the urbanistic harmonies of Luciano Laurana (see fig. 386).

ALBERTI AND THE ART OF PAINTING. Alberti's relation to the pictorial art of his time is striking, but difficult to assess. It is still a moot point among scholars whether some of his ideas on perspective are a codification of what the painters and sculptors about him had long been doing on their own. Alberti's perspective theory is derived in great part from medieval studies on optics in the Aristotelian tradition. In any case, his Latin treatise on painting, *De pictura*, of 1435 (and its Italian version, *Della pittura,* of 1436), is the first known treatise on painting, as distinguished from handbooks of shop practice, such as Cennino Cennini's *Libro dell'arte.*

We do not know if Brunelleschi's perspective theory provided a system for projecting imaginary spaces and their contents within a pictorial field. It is clear, however, that Alberti's formula produced a result that was aesthetically attractive and visually convincing (fig. 235). Alberti required the artist first to establish the height of a human being in the foreground of the field (a in fig. 235), then to divide the base line (b) of the field into segments corresponding to one-third of this height, each segment called a *braccio* (or cubit). At the height of the figure above the base line (a), the artist was to set the vanishing point (c) and connect it with diagonal lines to the divisions of the base line. These lines are called orthogonals (d).

Then the question arose, how were the parallel hori-zontal lines crossing the ground plane—the transversals (h)—to be established? A passage missing in the Italian text but present in some of the Latin manuscripts, including one annotated by Alberti himself, shows that on a separate surface (e, called "little space" by Alberti), which could be another piece of paper or another part of the wall surface, the artist was to draw another horizontal base line divided into segments in the manner of the original line, and to set the distance point (f) perpendicularly above it at the same height as the vanishing point in the first construction, again drawing a set of diagonal lines from point to base. The viewer's distance from the picture was then expressed in terms of a vertical (g) intersecting the new diagonals at whatever point the artist wished. Then, setting the two constructions on the same level at any convenient distance, the artist could draw horizontal lines from these intersections in the second construction across to the first. These horizontal lines would become the transversals (h) in the first construction and, in conjunction with its orthogonals, would form trapezoids. The results can be easily counterproved by making sure that diagonals drawn through the corners of the trapezoids in the foreground squares always pass through the centers and corners of all diagonally related trapezoids in the first construction. Alberti's perspective was, quite simply, a graph of space. It provided a single, harmonious system for calculating the relative proportions of every figure, object, and spatial division within a pictorial field.

The remainder of Alberti's treatise is devoted to what he calls *istoria* (history, story, narrative) and how it should be represented, and to a discussion of the education of the painter. His three principles of pictorial art are circumscription, composition, and reception of light. These include his notions on drawing, division of the pictorial surface, light and shade, and color, to which he was extremely sensitive. His recommendations for balanced color chords constitute a direct attack on the often aggressive coloristic arrangements of the Trecento. Alberti is concerned with consistency and propriety in the representation of persons of various ages and various physical and social types, with their reactions to the dramatic situations in which the *istoria* places them, and with the delicacies of anatomical rendering of bodies and features. He wishes the narrative to unfold with copiousness and with a variety of humans and animals in poses and movements full of grace and beauty—all these in opposition to the figural alignments common not only in the Trecento but even in the compositions of Masaccio.

Above all, Alberti is profoundly aware of the magical qualities in pictorial art, which he says are the foundation of religion and the noblest gift of "the gods." "Painting," he tells us, "contains a divine force that not only makes absent men present, as friendship is said to do, but moreover makes the dead seem almost alive." Alberti views the artist as a person whose education demanded the intellectual activity of the Liberal Arts, as well as technical training. *Della pittura* gave a new dignity to the art of painting and to the artist; it established a foundation that would change our understanding of the visual arts. The last words of *Della pittura* sum up what Alberti desired: "absolute and perfect painting."

In many respects Alberti's ideals harmonize with the art of Masaccio, the only painter he mentions in the preface to *Della pittura*, but they are even closer to the painting of Fra Filippo Lippi and Fra Angelico, whom Alberti must have known personally. The new perspective governs Fra Angelico's *Annunciation* in the San Marco corridor (see fig. 210)—as distinguished from his pre-Albertian treatment of this subject at Cortona (see fig. 206)—and his San Marco altarpiece (see fig. 207). Fra Filippo's and Fra Angelico's frequent use of a foreground figure who looks out at the spectator, the copiousness and variety of their compositions, and their analysis of the reception of light all correspond to Alberti's principles. By the end of the century some of the classical subjects he recommended were re-created by such painters as Botticelli and Mantegna.

In the 1430s and 1440s the two surviving giants of early Quattrocento Florentine sculpture, Ghiberti and Donatello, underwent changes of style that are in keeping with Alberti's new doctrine if not always in accordance with its details. Both masters may have become acquainted with Alberti during visits to Rome prior to Alberti's return to Florence in 1434, for the tone of the dedication in his *Della pittura* of 1436 suggests long friendship. These relationships must have become close once Alberti was established in Florence.

GHIBERTI AFTER 1425

Ghiberti's *Gates of Paradise* (fig. 236) were so profoundly influenced by Alberti's ideas that they constitute, in a sense, a programmatic exposition of his theory. When given the commission for the third and final set of doors for the Florentine Baptistery in 1425, Ghiberti was in his late forties. The humanist chancellor of Florence Lionardo Bruni proposed a scheme of twenty-eight scenes

that would have matched the two previous sets (see figs. 85, 153). A second proposal reduced the number of scenes to twenty-four, judging from the divisions still visible on the backs, but the final scheme has only ten square fields, each a complete picture. This meant, of course, that Ghiberti's competition panel could not be incorporated into the final set of doors. In these doors the constricting Gothic quatrefoils are abandoned, and so is the notion of gilded figures and forms set out against a dark bronze background; now each square is totally gilded, background and all. Donatello had pioneered this idea in his *St. George* relief (see fig. 166).

The present title of the doors derives from the fact that they open on the *paradiso*, the Italian term for the area between a baptistery and the entrance to its cathedral. Michelangelo, playing on this word, is reported to have said that the doors were worthy to be the Gates of Paradise, and the nickname stuck. The modeling in wax of all ten scenes and the surrounding sections of frieze has been dated between 1429 and 1437, when all were cast in bronze. Finishing, gilding, and other time-consuming processes meant that the doors were not set in place until 1452.

Each panel deals with one or more incidents from the Old Testament arranged within a consistent space that stretches from the foreground into the remote distance. Although the individual scenes were each cast in a single piece, the foreground figures are so highly projected that they are almost in the round. The projection gradually decreases as the figures diminish in size and recede into the background, and the most remote are scarcely raised above the surface. The illusion of depth is enhanced by the use of gold over the entire relief, giving the feeling that the space is pervaded by a kind of golden atmosphere.

The first scene, the story of Adam and Eve (fig. 237), shows the Creation of Adam at the lower left, that of Eve in the center, the Temptation in the distance at the extreme left, and the Expulsion from the Garden at the extreme right. Emphasis is placed on the Creation of Eve in the center of the panel; the explanation lies in the doctrine that her creation from the side of Adam foretold the creation of the Church that issued, in the form of blood and water, from the wounded side of Christ upon the cross. This parallel, represented in medieval manuscripts and stained glass, was also set forth in a chapter of the *Summa* of St. Antonine. It is possible that Antonine was responsible for the programs of numerous important works of art (see pp. 216, 218. 292), and at the time the program for the *Gates of Paradise* was under discussion, in 1424–25, he was nearby at San Domenico in Fiesole and his presence has been recorded in Florence. When the doors were installed in the Baptistery, he was archbishop, and in a sense it was *his* Baptistery. The chapter noted above is a sermon on St. John the Baptist, to whom the Baptistery is dedicated, and St. Antonine compares the Baptist to a lantern whose light, thrown upon the Old Testament, brings

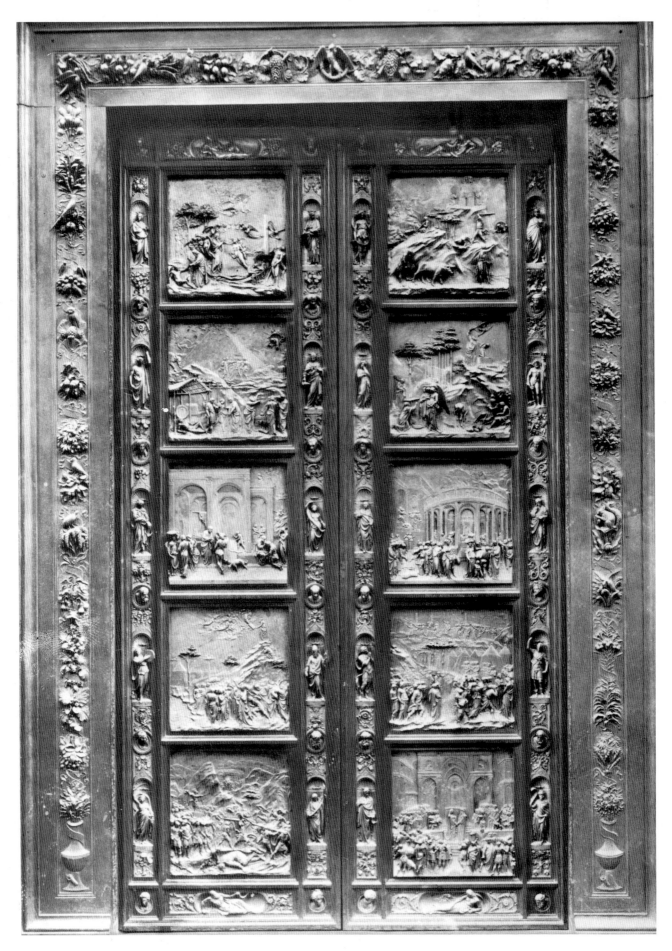

236. LORENZO GHIBERTI. *Gates of Paradise* (East Doors), Baptistery, Florence. 1425–52.
Gilded bronze, height c. 15'. Museo dell'Opera del Duomo, Florence. Commissioned by the Opera
of the Baptistery and the Arte di Calimala for the Florentine Baptistery

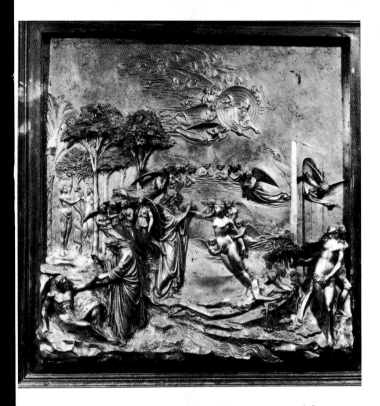

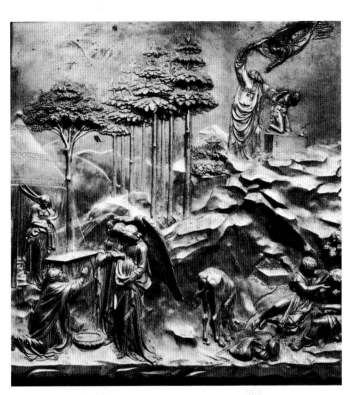

237. Lorenzo Ghiberti. *The Creation*, panel from
the *Gates of Paradise*. 1425–37. Gilded bronze, 31¼" square.
Museo dell'Opera del Duomo, Florence

238. Lorenzo Ghiberti. *Story of Abraham*, panel from
the *Gates of Paradise*. 1425–37. Gilded bronze, 31¼" square.
Museo dell'Opera del Duomo, Florence

forth the New. The ten specific stories discussed by St. Antonine are contained in nine of the ten panels of the doors, which vary only occasionally from Antonine's text.

Ghiberti represented the ideal male nude in the competition relief (see fig. 151) and in the North Doors of the Baptistery (see fig. 155); the female nudes in the *Creation* relief are among the first sensuous female nudes of the Renaissance. Although they are not classical in their proportions, they are nonetheless akin to the frank voluptuousness of the ancient nude sculptures Ghiberti had seen in Rome. In this relief the nude male and female figures contrast gracefully with the long, parallel folds of drapery and with the airy wedge-shaped striations of the clouds that create a shimmer of golden light around the angels and the crowned figure of God in the circles of Heaven. Still, Ghiberti has pierced the background only to the extent necessary to stage the Temptation a few yards off, and there is no distant view or horizon line.

By the time he made the *Abraham* scene in the second row, however (fig. 238), Ghiberti had dissolved the background to permit the eye to see beyond the slender trunks of trees to the profiles of distant hills against the sky, as Fra Angelico had done in his contemporary *Descent from the Cross* (see colorplate 43, p. 207). Here again the Old Testament scene prefigures the New, for the Sacrifice of Isaac, the subject of the 1402 competition, reappears in the background as a foreshadowing of the Sacrifice of Christ, the three angels appearing to

Abraham are a revelation of the Trinity, and the meal prepared for them by Sarah prophesies the perpetual banquet of the Eucharist; all are expounded in the same text by St. Antonine. The prominence given to the fountain flowing from a spring in the side of the cliff is in accordance with St. Antonine's emphasis on the water of Baptism.

In the *Jacob and Esau* relief in the third row (colorplate 46, p. 257), Ghiberti has adopted the perspective construction formulated by Alberti in *De pictura*. Presumably the relief was composed shortly after Alberti's arrival in Florence in 1434. The protruding apron that Ghiberti had used in the North Doors here becomes a base line, divided into cubits as Alberti indicated, and from these divisions he projected his receding orthogonals to the central vanishing point that also serves for the recession of the walls and ceilings of the soaring loggia. The pavement squares in the patch of terrace at the extreme right do not recede to this vanishing point, and therefore apparently do not correspond to the Albertian construction. But Ghiberti must have realized that these squares, if drawn in rigid conformity to Alberti's scheme, would have been compressed into absurdly distorted shapes, as the reader can easily verify by drawing out the construction. This Achilles' heel of one-point perspective becomes evident at the sides of an extended view, which expose the necessity, avoided by Alberti, of making the transversals curve away from the picture plane.

On the rooftop Rebecca, feeling her sons struggling within her, receives God's explanation of the two hostile

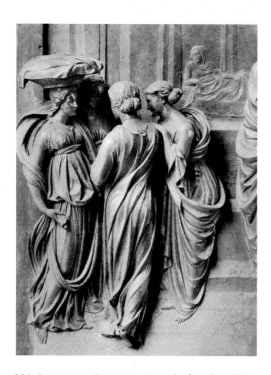

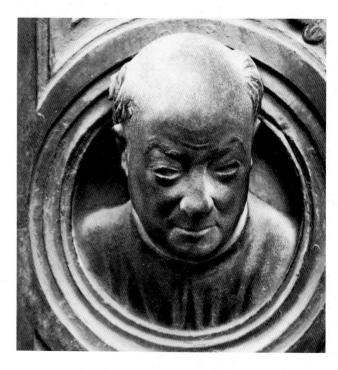

239. LORENZO GHIBERTI. Detail of *Jacob and Esau*,
panel from the *Gates of Paradise* (see colorplate 46, p. 257).
c. 1435. Museo dell'Opera del Duomo, Florence

240. LORENZO GHIBERTI. *Self-Portrait*
in frame of the *Gates of Paradise*. Museo dell'Opera
del Duomo, Florence

peoples who will spring from her womb. Under the left arch she appears in childbed; in the center, partly concealed by the foreground figures, Esau sells his birthright. On the right, "taught by God" according to St. Antonine, Rebecca rehearses Jacob in his "pious fraud," which will be accomplished by the meat and skin of the kid he holds. St. Antonine's interpretation culminates in the foreground, where Jacob, symbolizing the Christians, receives the blessing on the step, which foretells his approaching vision of a ladder to Heaven. The shocked and disappointed Esau signifies the Jews.

The very architecture of the scene is Albertian. First of all, the arches are supported by piers, not columns, and the Corinthian order, in the form of applied pilasters, is used as decoration (see pp. 230–31); presumably Alberti entertained such ideas long before he wrote them down in *De re aedificatoria*. Despite the airy beauty of the building, Ghiberti did not fully understand its details. He did not know what to do when he reached the corner capitals, which remain lopsided. But the architecture is Albertian in a deeper sense, for *Jacob and Esau* is an early example of a space construction that abandons the double scale of the Middle Ages in favor of Alberti's doctrine of visual unity. A single scale for figures and architecture that could still preserve the legibility of the narrative is achieved by setting the buildings a measurable distance behind the foreground figures and allowing some of the incidents to move back into it. The figures, too, demonstrate Alberti's contention that the artist should represent bodies in such a way that the drapery should move around them to reveal the beauty

of the limbs beneath. Ghiberti has done this with matchless grace in the four figures at the extreme left (fig. 239). Every motion is harmonious, whether within each figure, between one figure and the next, or among groups of figures within the perfectly coordinated space. Running across both doors just above eye level, Ghiberti's conspicuous signature reminds us who was responsible for this "marvelous art" (partially visible at the bottom of colorplate 46, p. 257). Nearby is his self-portrait in a medallion of the frame (fig. 240); wise, cultivated, shrewd, sensitive, it is an unforgettable self-assessment. In Alberti's phrase, Ghiberti has made "the dead seem almost alive."

LUCA DELLA ROBBIA

Alberti's introductory note to *Della pittura* contains one name that is surprising, since Luca della Robbia does not seem to belong in the same league as Brunelleschi, Ghiberti, Donatello, and Masaccio, the other artists mentioned. To posterity, the name Della Robbia has become associated with works in enameled terra-cotta with white figures against a blue background that were made according to a technical formula invented by Luca. The style was continued by Luca's nephew and successor, Andrea della Robbia, and by a host of assistants who prolonged the activities of the workshop well into the sixteenth century. But in the 1430s Alberti could believe that Luca would remain on the high plane occupied by the other four great masters. Alberti's confidence was doubtless based on the splendid marble *Cantoria* (choir gallery) being carved by Luca in

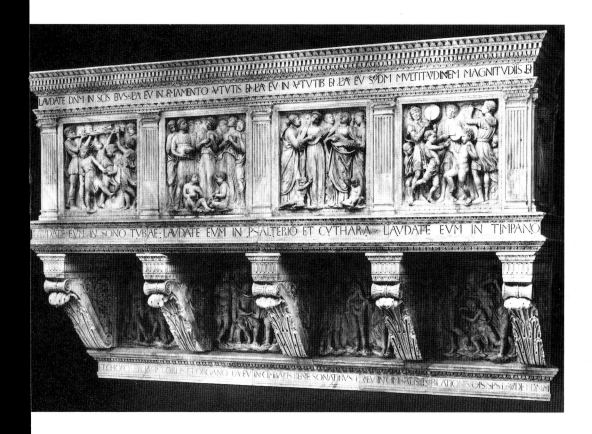

241. LUCA DELLA ROBBIA. *Cantoria*. 1431–38. Marble, length 17'. Removed from the Duomo; now in the Museo dell'Opera del Duomo, Florence. Commissioned by the Opera of the Opera del Duomo

1431–38 to be placed over the door of the left sacristy of Florence Cathedral. Luca's gallery (fig. 241), as well as that by Donatello over the door of the right sacristy (see fig. 243), was removed when the musical requirements for a grand-ducal wedding in the seventeenth century rendered them obsolete. In the documents, Luca's is mentioned as the organ loft, but that by no means excludes the presence of singers and perhaps instrumentalists as well, for whom the seventeen-foot length of the gallery would have provided sufficient room in those days of small choirs and portable organs.

Luca's gallery, supported on five beautiful acanthus consoles, consists of a parapet divided by paired pilasters. The enframed marble panels are carved with music-making children and adolescents illustrating Psalm 150, which is inscribed in its entirety on the *Cantoria*. The children praise the Lord "with the sound of the trumpet . . . with the psaltery and harp . . . with the timbrel and dance . . . with stringed instruments and organs . . . upon the high sounding cymbals." They are beautifully grouped in compositions that are centralized or balanced—moving, playing, singing in relaxed happiness, yet so arranged and projected as to recall the Augustan frieze on the Ara Pacis, that elegant Roman monument to early Imperial taste and erudition. These young people who stand so harmoniously, whose clothing falls so naturally into shapes reminiscent of Roman togas, nevertheless have youthful faces as winsomely commonplace as those by Fra Filippo Lippi (see fig. 217). Luca's smooth surfaces and sometimes inert modeling diminish the tension characteristic of much Florentine art, but his

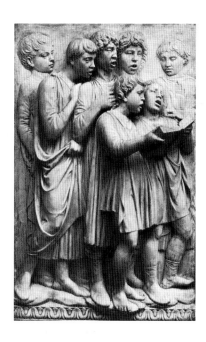

242. LUCA DELLA ROBBIA. *Singing Boys*, end panel on the *Cantoria*. Marble, c. 38 x 24"

youths and maidens, especially the famous singing boys—some treble, some bass (fig. 242)—retain a high place in popular imagination.

DONATELLO c. 1433 TO c. 1455

What a contrast there is between Luca's serenity and the energy of Donatello's *Cantoria*! Donatello seems to have sacked ancient art during his stay in the Eternal City in 1432–33 so that he could creatively reassemble his loot upon returning to Florence. All the elements of his

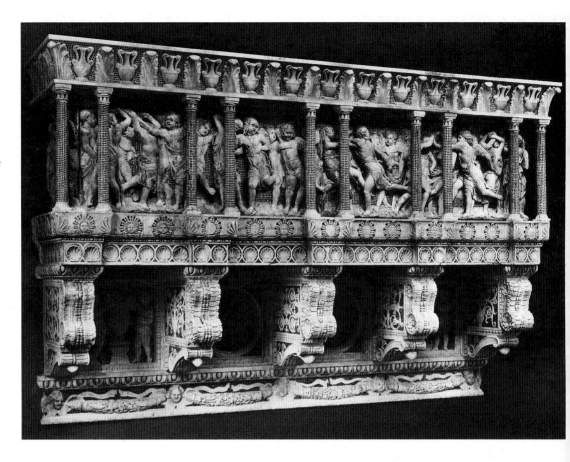

243. DONATELLO. *Cantoria*. 1433–39. Marble and mosaic, length 18' 8". Removed from the Duomo; now in the Museo dell'Opera del Duomo, Florence. Commissioned by the Opera of the Opera del Duomo

Cantoria (fig. 243) are found in classical art—the egg-and-dart molding, the acanthus, the palmette, the shell, the urn, and the mask—but they never appear in such combinations or with such proportions. Even the most basic architectural elements are unconventional and un-expected. Donatello's consoles, for example, have double volutes, one horizontal and the other vertical, in near collision. Every surface of every architectural member is heavily ornamented. The very substance of the colonnettes and backgrounds is disintegrated by rows of inlaid, colored marble disks.

Behind the colonnade and completely disregarding it surges a torrent of energetic activity (fig. 244). Donatello's children refuse to be constricted by the neat frames of Luca della Robbia and seem to rush wildly through the space in a paean of jubilation. Transparent tunics cling to their chubby limbs, and feathery wings erupt unexpectedly from their shoulders. The result is a work of intense dynamism. Subsequent generations ranked Donatello's *Cantoria* higher than Luca's smooth and somewhat static work; Vasari, for example, wrote with enthusiasm of the sketchy freedom of Donatello's surfaces, which from a distance produces an effect of far greater vigor.

The undated but probably almost contemporary *Annunciation* (fig. 245) shows another aspect of Donatello's new classicism. The enframing architecture is almost as unconventional as that of the *Cantoria*: note the colossal egg-and-dart molding that invades the frieze, the masks

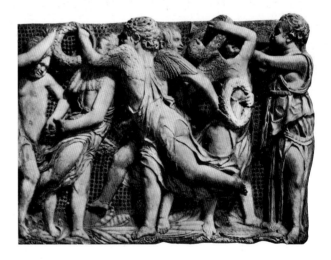

244. DONATELLO. Putti, detail of the *Cantoria*. Marble and mosaic, height 38½"

forming the capitals. The terra-cotta putti balanced on the corners or perched on the pediment may be a refer-ence to Vitruvius's report that Etruscan temples had terra-cotta figures decorating their roofs. Mary is shown gently recoiling in fear from the message of the kneeling angel and then, in the same moment, turning toward him with her hand on her heart to indicate her accep-tance of his message.

The beautiful faces of Mary and the angel, with their Greek noses and low, straight foreheads from which the

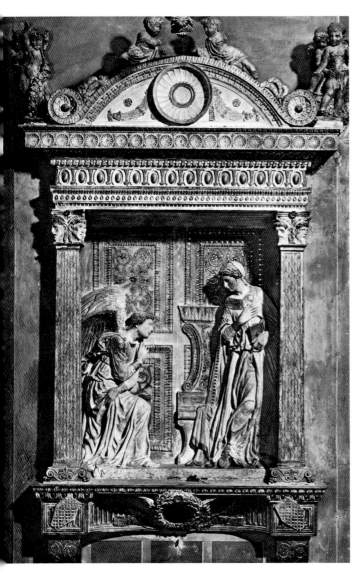

245. DONATELLO. *Annunciation*. 1430s. Limestone and terra-cotta with gilding, 13' 9" x 9'. ⛪ Sta. Croce, Florence. Commissioned by a member of the Cavalcanti family

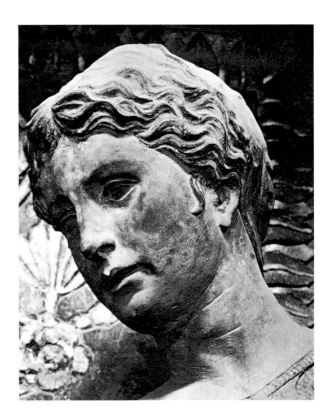

246. Head of the Virgin, detail of fig. 245

hair is drawn rippling back on either side, are among the most classicistic passages in Donatello's work (fig. 246). But neither these nor the evident classicism of the drapery can submerge the emotional tension evident in the momentary poses and the complexity of the surfaces. The richly ornamented and gilded panels of the background suggest the *porta clausa* (closed door) of Ezekiel's vision, the prophecy of the virginity of Mary. The lack of the usual hardware associated with doors should trouble no one, as a similar *porta clausa* in Piero della Francesca's *Annunciation* in San Francesco in Arezzo (see fig. 285) possesses neither handle, lock, nor hinges. The closed gate of Ezekiel needs none.

The least expected work of this period in any medium is Donatello's nude *David* in bronze (fig. 247), the earliest known nude freestanding statue in the round since antiquity. (It is noteworthy, however, that when

Andrea Pisano and Nanni di Banco wished to represent a sculptor, they showed him carving a male nude—see figs. 16, 168.) After Donatello's heroic marble *David* of 1408–9 (see fig. 161), we hardly expect a work of this sort. A slight boy of twelve or thirteen, clothed only in richly ornamented leather boots and a large brimmed hat crowned with laurel, stands with his left hand on his hip and a great sword in his right. His right foot rests upon a wreath, while his left foot toys idly with the severed head of Goliath, one huge wing of whose helmet caresses the inside of the boy's thigh. The boy's face, which seems to express a cold detachment, is largely shaded by the hat (fig. 248). In the *Speculum humanae salvationis* (a fourteenth-century compendium of imagery connecting personages and events of the Old and New Testaments, widely reprinted in the fifteenth), David's victory over Goliath symbolizes Christ triumphant over Satan. The laurel crown on the hat and the laurel wreath on which David stands are probably allusions to the Medici family, in whose palace the work is first documented in 1469.

Donatello's sculptural activity in Florence was interrupted by his departure for Padua in the early 1440s. He remained there for more than a decade, a fact that changed the entire course of sculpture and painting in northern Italy. A whole school of painting grew up in Padua around the personality of Donatello—during his presence, as he himself put it, among the Paduan "fogs and frogs." Vasari tells us that Donatello disliked the adulation he received in Padua and was relieved to re-

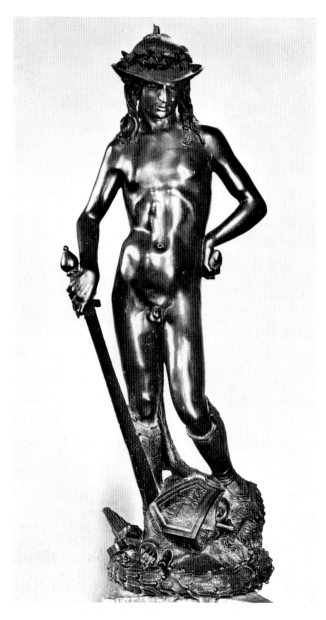

247. DONATELLO. *David.* c. 1446–60(?). Bronze,
height 62¼". Bargello, Florence. Perhaps commissioned
by Cosimo de' Medici for the courtyard of the
Palazzo Medici (see fig. 148)

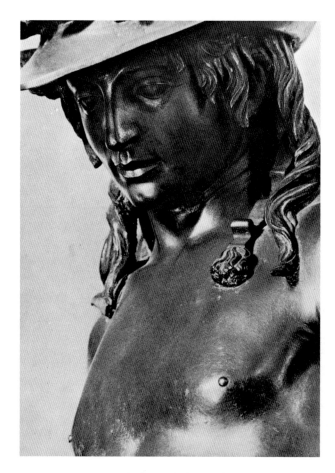

248. Head of David, detail of fig. 247

turn to Florence, where he knew he would receive from
the carping Florentines nothing but criticism, which
would spur him on to greater achievements. Whether or
not Vasari records Donatello's actual words, his comment admits us to an essential aspect of the Florentine
Renaissance, in which conflict of wills was a determinant of style.

The great Florentine sculptor was probably called to
Padua to execute the colossal equestrian statue in bronze
of the Venetian condottiere Erasmo da Narni, whose
nickname was Gattamelata ("Honeyed Cat" or "Calico
Cat"). The monument still stands in the square in front
of the Basilica of Sant'Antonio where Donatello placed
it after its completion in 1453 (fig. 249). Although the
funds were provided by the dead general's family according to a stipulation in his will, this kind of monu-

ment, previously reserved for rulers, must have been authorized by a decree of the Venetian Senate. The *Gattamelata* is by no means the first equestrian monument of
the Late Middle Ages and Renaissance in Italy. In Florence Donatello had an immediate pictorial forerunner
in Paolo Uccello's *Sir John Hawkwood* (see fig. 259). The
Tuscan examples, however, had been intended for interiors. In the Trecento, the ruling Scala family of Verona
built outdoor tombs surmounted by equestrian statues,
and Bonino da Campione had created an amazing monument to Bernabò Visconti (see fig. 131). In 1441 Niccolò d'Este was commemorated by an equestrian statue
by two otherwise unknown Florentine sculptors, which
stood in front of the Cathedral of Ferrara until it was
destroyed in 1796.

Donatello was influenced somewhat by ancient Roman examples, two of which were extant in Italy in his
day: the *Marcus Aurelius* in Rome, then thought to represent Constantine, and the so-called *Regisole* in Pavia,
an Imperial statue now lost. But Donatello's sculpture
surpasses the *Marcus Aurelius* in majesty and, above all, in
determination. Realizing the effect of the high base and
the vast space in which the *Gattamelata* was to be placed,
Donatello restricted his design to bold masses and powerful tensions. Any minor shapes that might compete
with the broad curves of the battle charger's anatomy are
suppressed. The horse's tail, tied at the end, is held to

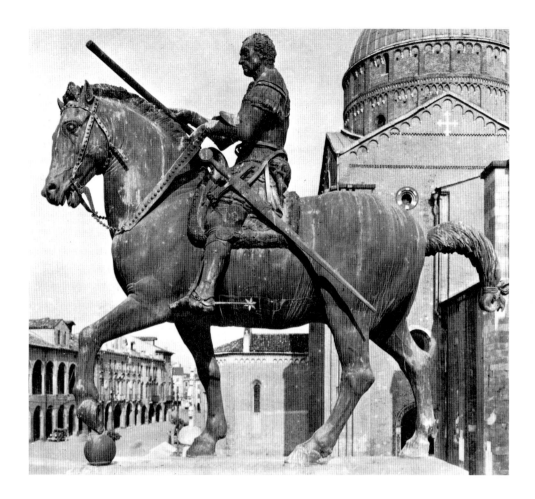

left: 249. DONATELLO.
*Equestrian Monument
of Gattamelata.*
c. 1445–53. Bronze,
height 12' 2". 🏛 Piazza
del Santo, Padua.
Commissioned by the
Venetian Senate

below: 250. Head
of Gattamelata, detail
of fig. 249

form a taut arc, while his left forehoof, poised on a cannonball, forms another. From above the horse's head down to his hind leg, a powerful diagonal formed by the general's baton and sword ties the composition together. Donatello may well have seen the famous general in Florence or in Rome, and it is likely that the head reproduces his features. The compressed lips, the firmly set jaw under pulsating facial muscles, the heavy, arched brows and close-cropped curls, and especially the wide eyes used to gazing into distances, all suggest a powerful personality in the prime of life (fig. 250). The horse, with his swelling veins, open jaws, and flaring eyes and nostrils, is under the general's control. Seldom in the history of portraiture can one point to so majestic an image of command. The later Quattrocento historian Vespasiano da Bisticci was so devoted to the contemporary cult of personality that he wrote a book on the "singular men" of the fifteenth century, but he never set before his public a character more imposing than this one.

The details play their part in the total picture. The general is dressed in fifteenth-century armor, complete with giant broadsword and greaves, but there are also references in the costume to the grandeur and glory of antiquity. From ancient Roman military costume Donatello borrowed the kilt and short sleeves made of leather thongs. Victory masks and winged genii, flying or on

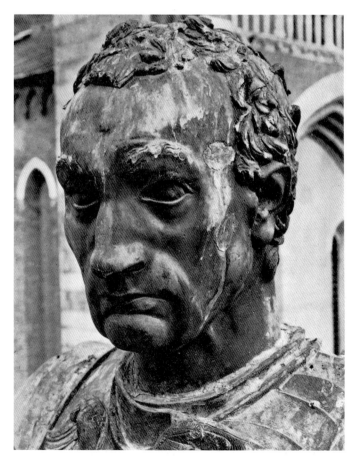

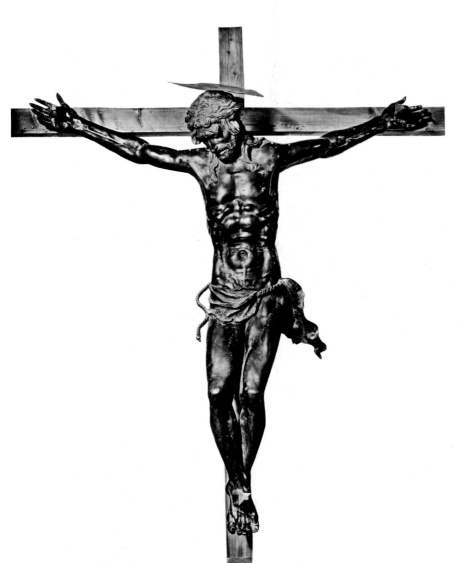

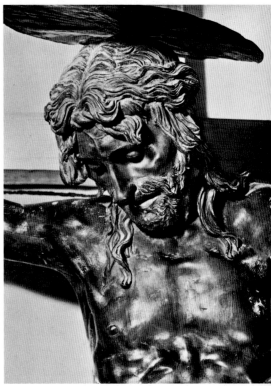

horseback, populate the surfaces of the armor and saddle. On the breastplate, a winged victory crying out in fury enhances by contrast the composure of the general. Virtually every element contributes to the impression of great emotional and physical forces held under stern control. This is the ideal man of the Renaissance, the exemplar of Albertian *virtus.*

While he was at work on the equestrian statue, dealing in absolutes on a colossal scale, Donatello was concerned with very different matters in another major commission, the high altar of Sant'Antonio, a grand architectural construction decorated with four large narrative reliefs, a number of smaller ones, and seven life-sized statues in bronze. The altar, repeatedly remodeled in the sixteenth and seventeenth centuries and erroneously restored at the end of the nineteenth, no longer looks at all as Donatello intended. The reliefs and statues are unchanged, but their original ambience is completely lost. The bronze *Crucifix* that now stands above the altar (fig. 251), which was originally to be placed elsewhere in the church, is the first work Donatello completed in Padua. Christ is depicted as a muscular man whose face (fig. 252) seems to display the ability to en-

dure pain calmly, in the manner of an ancient Stoic. Light glides across the strong arms, extended hands, sturdy rib cage, and firm thighs. If one may speak of a classical Crucifixion, this is it.

In Florence, Donatello had made remarkable experiments with relief narration and illusionistic space in his large-scale stucco medallions for the spandrels of the Old Sacristy of San Lorenzo (see fig. 139). But the stories that unfold in the large bronze reliefs of the Padua altar (figs. 253, 254) are so much more elaborate in their representation of architectural backgrounds that they seem Donatello's answer to Ghiberti's *Gates of Paradise* (see fig. 236). Not only are they, as we might expect, deliberately less harmonious than the graceful compositions of Ghiberti, but they also present a new and explosive conception of space, an alternative to Ghiberti's adherence to Albertian principles.

In the *Miracle of the Believing Donkey* (fig. 253), Donatello has illustrated simply and directly a tale from the legend of St. Anthony of Padua that tells how a skeptic refused to believe in the presence of the body of Christ in the Eucharist unless his donkey would kneel down and worship it, which the animal promptly did.

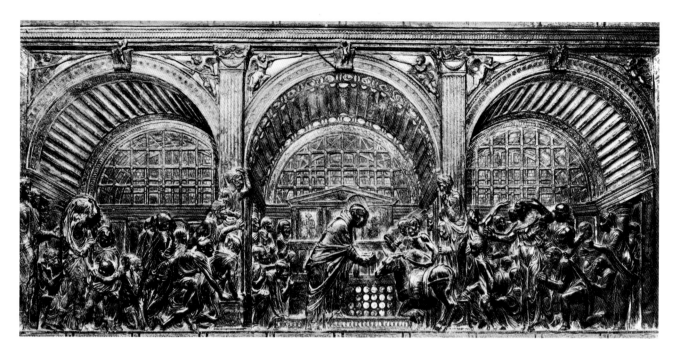

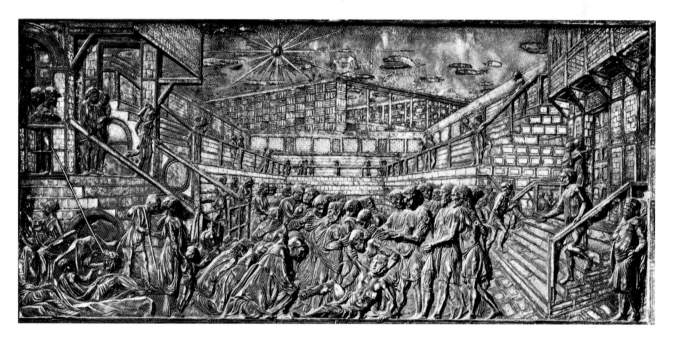

253, 254. DONATELLO. *Miracle of the Believing Donkey* (above) and
St. Anthony of Padua Healing the Wrathful Son (below), reliefs on the high altar, 🏛 Sant'Antonio, Padua. 1444–49.
Bronze, each 22¹/₂ x 48¹/₂". Commissioned by the Arca del Santo for Sant'Antonio, Padua

Donatello has shown the saint turning from the altar with the consecrated bread in his hands as the beast kneels on the top step. The excited crowds of the faithful who peer out from behind the altar and around columns and piers are swept by a wave of astonishment at the miracle. The energetic poses and the sketchily rendered, agitated drapery masses create an exciting surface pattern. The low viewpoint excludes any Albertian floor construction of receding transversals and converging orthogonals. The figures are dwarfed by a vast construction with barrel vaults recalling those of the ancient Roman Basilica of Maxentius and Constantine, known in the Renaissance as the Temple of Peace. Donatello has altered their appearance, substituting a horizontal grid for the original octagonal coffering and filling the windows with metal grilles through which one sees other barrel vaults and other grilles. Between the arches, pilasters with modified Corinthian capitals uphold an entablature. The resultant spatial formulation tends to break forward and outward rather than to recede smoothly into the distance, as in the *Gates of Paradise*. It is this kind of space, among many other aspects of Donatello's art, that fascinated the youthful Mantegna when he was working and studying in Padua during the period of Donatello's sojourn (see pp. 384–85).

St. Anthony of Padua Healing the Wrathful Son (fig. 254)

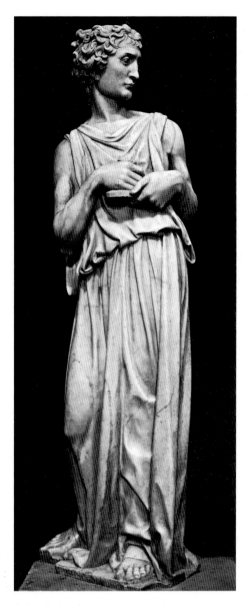

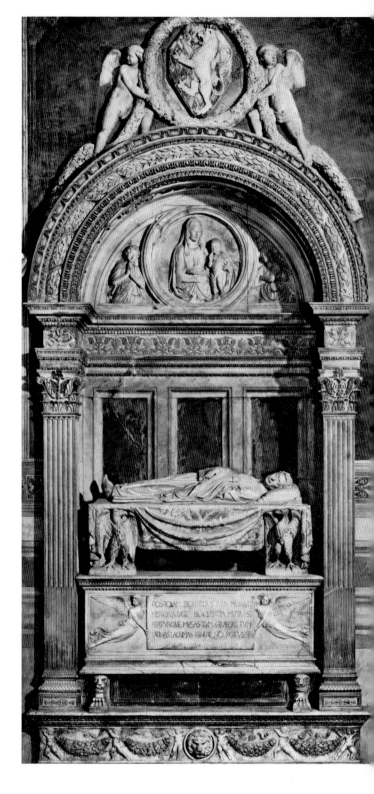

above: 255. MICHELOZZO DI BARTOLOMMEO.
Faith from the Tomb of Bartolommeo Aragazzi,
🏛 Cathedral, Montepulciano. c. 1427–37. Marble, life-sized.
Commissioned by Bartolommeo Aragazzi

right: 256. BERNARDO ROSSELLINO. Tomb of
Lionardo Bruni. c. 1445. White and colored
marbles, 20' x 10' 4¹/₂". 🏛 Sta. Croce, Florence.
Commissioned by the Signoria
of Florence or the College and Council of Arezzo

is even more surprising. Here St. Anthony heals the leg of a young man who had cut off his foot in remorse for kicking his mother. The setting is a stadiumlike structure that has been identified as an outdoor ball court, ancestor of the modern football field—somewhat too grimly appropriate to the incident. Most of the elements recede properly, but a fantastic building in the background and a structure with a flight of steps in the right foreground are set at angles to the main axis and refuse to conform, as if to provide a spatial fracturing appropriate to the theme. Clouds float in Donatello's sculptured sky, and a great sun throws out clustered sword-shaped rays. Donatello's dramatic compositions must have been a revelation for the north Italian painters of his day, and their influence continued to make an impact for the next century and a half.

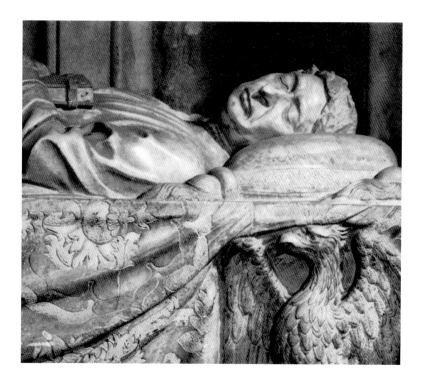

FLORENTINE TOMB SCULPTURE. Throughout the Late Middle Ages and the Renaissance a major field for sculpture in Italy was the funerary monument, not only the simple floor slabs carved or cast by Donatello, Ghiberti, and many others but also splendid sepulchers placed against a church wall and displaying the effigy of the deceased in a setting of architectural magnificence sanctified by the presence of Christian images, notably the Madonna and Child. Donatello and Michelozzo together made such a tomb for the deposed antipope John XXIII (Cardinal Baldassare Cossa) in the Baptistery in Florence, and Michelozzo made one, now dismembered, for the Aragazzi family in the Tuscan hill town of Montepulciano. The vigor and forthrightness of Michelozzo's sculptural style (fig. 255), as well as its strong classicism, place him in the second Renaissance style, and especially close to Luca della Robbia, if somewhat more energetic and tormented.

Another master of tomb sculpture was Bernardo Rossellino (1409–64), the fourth of five brothers who were all stonecutters from Settignano (Antonio, the youngest, will be discussed later). As an architect Bernardo had worked at the Palazzo Rucellai, in connection with Alberti (see p. 232), and on his own, he remodeled the papal city of Pienza for Pius II (see p. 236). His most conspicuous sculptural work was the tomb of Lionardo Bruni, the chancellor of the Florentine Republic and an eminent humanist scholar (fig. 256). Bruni died in 1444, and his tomb, paid for by the Republic, must have been built and carved shortly thereafter.

Bernardo, possibly under Albertian direction, devised a background of colored marble paneling that was followed in other tombs and imitated by painters of the second Renaissance style. In front of the white and deep-red marble panels lies the effigy of the chancellor, holding one of his own books, on a bier upheld by eagles. Angels in low relief, posed like winged victories, support a tablet with a Latin inscription: "After Leonardo departed from life, history is in mourning and eloquence is dumb, and it is said that the Muses, Greek and Latin alike, cannot restrain their tears." Above, the Virgin and Child are flanked by praying angels; high above, youthful nude angels steady a shield with the *marzocco* (lion) of the Florentine Republic. With forthright realism Bernardo shows the rugged features of the old statesman turned toward us, his brow crowned with laurel (fig. 257). In the clear-cut, simple arrangement and the emphasis on the dignity of the individual, Bernardo established the standard type of the Florentine wall tomb.

11
Absolute and Perfect Painting: The Second Renaissance Style

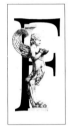our painters, each more or less closely associated with the others and with Alberti, sum up the possibilities and embody the ideals of the second Renaissance style: Paolo Uccello, Domenico Veneziano, Andrea del Castagno, and Piero della Francesca. We must bear in mind that, while they were painting, Fra Angelico and Fra Filippo Lippi were still at work, that the age gap between these six masters was insignificant, and that there must have been considerable interchange among them. In the works of their imitators, after midcentury, the styles of all six tend to fuse.

PAOLO UCCELLO

Paolo di Dono, known as Paolo Uccello (Paul "Bird," 1397–1475), is an odd and appealing figure. His life was long, but he seems to have painted little, and although he occasionally received an important commission, he was never responsible for a major altarpiece or large fresco cycle. At least twice his patrons complained of the unconventionality of his work. In his tax declaration of 1469, he laments that he is old and infirm, has no means of livelihood, and that his wife is sick. Scholars have complained that he spent too much time studying perspective; Vasari tells us that Uccello could use perspective theory to project a polyhedron with seventy-two sides from each of which projected a stick bearing a scroll; and also that he once refused to follow his wife into the bedchamber with the classic rejoinder, "What a sweet mistress is this perspective." He viewed perspective as a challenge and probably also as a game (fig. 258); he certainly did not approach it with the solemnity recommended by Alberti.

Little remains to give us an idea of Uccello's artistic achievements before his fortieth year. Unless certain decorative mosaic designs in San Marco can be attributed to him, the work he did in Venice in 1425–31 is lost. His earliest dated painting is a fresco in the Cathedral of Florence, an equestrian monument to the English condottiere Sir John Hawkwood (fig. 259), who was known to the Italians as Giovanni Acuto. Before his death in 1394, Hawkwood had been promised a monument sculpted in marble, an obligation that the city eventually fulfilled with Uccello's illusionistic painting, which suggests aged bronze. Donatello had seven years

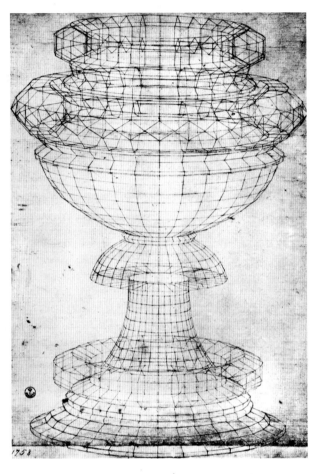

258. PAOLO UCCELLO. *Perspective Study.*
1430–40. Pen and ink, 13 3/8 x 9 1/2". Gabinetto dei Disegni e Stampe, Uffizi, Florence

to assess the painting before departing for Padua in 1443. There are numerous points of resemblance between Uccello's Hawkwood and Donatello's later *Gattamelata* (see fig. 249), including the pose of the rider's legs, the raised baton, and, of course, the horse's stride, with both legs on one side advanced, both on the other retracted. Although both works express the rider's control of the horse, the *Hawkwood* monument is less tense: the baton is lifted lightly, the forehoof paws the air, the tail flows free. And, unlike the Roman trappings of Gattemaleta, Uccello's general wears contemporary armor, cloak, and cap.

The pedestal rests on a base supported by three consoles, not unlike those of Luca della Robbia's *Cantoria*, also in the cathedral (see fig. 241). The consoles and base were originally projected in perspective to coincide with the eye level of a person standing in the side aisle, but this aspect is spoiled because the fresco has been detached and is now hung too low on the wall. This does not matter for the horse and rider, who are seen as if our eye level were slightly above the horse's knees. If Uccello had projected the horse and rider in conformity with the pedestal, the observer would have looked up at the horse's belly and seen little of the rider except for the bottoms of his feet and the underside of his chin and nose. Perhaps Uccello, who seems to have been a lifelong practical joker, did exactly that, for it is documented that the officials of the Opera objected to his first horse and rider, and he was compelled to destroy that section of the fresco and repaint it. Surprisingly, the discrepancy in viewpoints does not destroy the illusionistic quality of the monument. When seen from its original viewpoint and against a broad background of cathedral wall, Uccello's monument may well have tricked viewers into believing that Hawkwood had been granted a bronze monument and thus received even more than he had been promised. Today the deception is reduced because the fresco is enclosed in a later frame and hangs on the wall like an easel painting.

Uccello's fresco representing the *Deluge* in the Chiostro Verde (Green Cloister) of Santa Maria Novella (fig. 260) is part of a series started earlier by various Quattrocento painters, including Uccello himself, that was damaged (ironically enough, considering Uccello's subject) by the 1966 and earlier floods. The cloister acquired its name because the frescoes were largely painted in a *terra verde* (green earth) monochrome. The *Deluge* also employs ocher, but no other color. The style of the painting, with its emphasis on monumentality and spatial unity, is consistent with what other Florentine painters were doing about 1450.

Despite the damage the work has sustained, it is still a majestic creation. Uccello has shown us two scenes within the same lunette, thus giving two views of Noah's pyramidal ark, one from the side and another from one end, and creating a strong perspective recession in the center. As there is no border dividing the episodes, the figures in one scene tend to overlap those in the other to the detriment of legibility. On the left the ark is afloat, beset by thunder, lightning, wind, and rain. A bolt of lightning (fig. 262) strikes in the distance, casting onto the planking the shadow of a tree that is being blown away by a little wind-god, whose representation is recommended to painters by Alberti. Doomed humans attack the ark: one brandishes a sword as he rides a swimming horse, another threatens him with a club, a third clutches at the ark with his fingers (fig. 261). Others attempt to stay afloat on wreckage or in barrels. The club-bearer wears around his neck one of the favorite subjects of Uccello's perspective investiga-

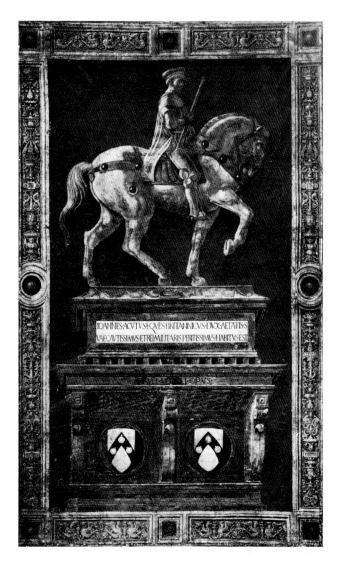

259. PAOLO UCCELLO. *Sir John Hawkwood*. 1436. Fresco, transferred to canvas; 26' 10" x 16' 10". Cathedral, Florence. Commissioned by the Opera of Florence Cathedral

tions, the *mazzocchio*, a faceted construction of wire or wicker around which the turban-shaped headdress of the Florentine citizen was draped. The hair on one side of his head remains neatly combed, but the wind has disheveled the other and it streams before him. A ladder floats parallel to the ark, providing two more Albertian orthogonals.

On the right the ark has come to rest, and Noah leans from its window as the dove, sent forth to discover dry land, is returning. Below the ark is the corpse of a drowned child, and a raven picks out the eyes of another. No one has yet successfully identified the cloaked man standing in the right foreground with one hand raised, while two mysterious hands clutch his ankles from the water below. The power of the drapery masses, the intensity of the facial characterizations, the sense of high tragedy in the individual figures and groups and of cataclysm in the entire scene are compelling enough to make us overlook the riddles Uccello seems to impose.

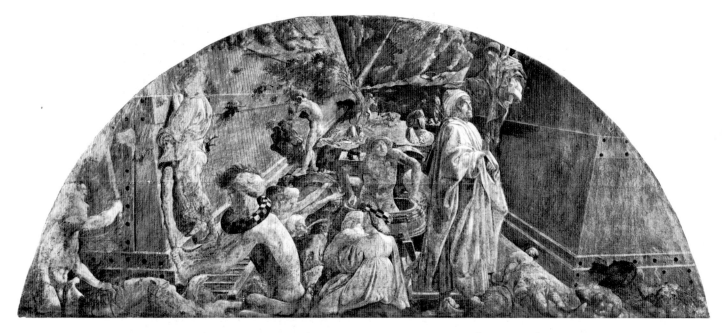

260. PAOLO UCCELLO. *Deluge.* c. 1450. Fresco, 7' x 16' 9". Chiostro Verde,
Sta. Maria Novella, Florence

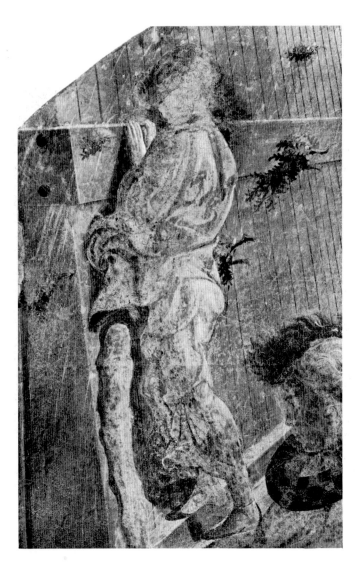

261. Detail of fig. 260

Despite its spatial and narrative disconnections, the *Deluge* is a grand painting in the tradition of Masaccio, but charged throughout with the intellectuality of the second Renaissance style.

More artificial in effect are Uccello's panels representing the *Battle of San Romano* (colorplate 47, p. 257; fig. 263), which once decorated a bedchamber in the Medici Palace that was later occupied by Lorenzo the Magnificent. The three panels are now divided among London, Florence, and Paris, and recent scholarship has asserted that the London and Florence panels were executed for an earlier Medici residence and that the Paris panel was added when a large space became available in the new Medici Palace (see fig. 146). A technical examination has shown that the upper corners have been cut in a manner that suggests that the panels may originally have been arched and that the tops were later cut off; this would explain why there is no horizon line or sky visible in any of the panels today. End to end, the whole series measures more than thirty feet. The panels form a continuing interlace of horses, horsemen, and weapons on a narrow foreground stage that is separated from the landscape background by a screen of fantastic fruit trees. United with the architecture of a vaulted room, the panels must have combined the coloristic brilliance of painting with the grandeur of a sculptural frieze. This effect would have been enhanced by the silvering of the armor, which has now darkened.

The events represented happened in 1432, and scholars have dated the London and Florence panels to the 1430s and the Paris panel to the 1450s, when the new Medici Palace was nearing completion. As a whole the

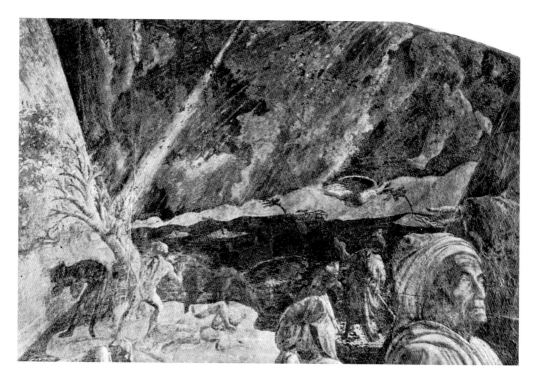

262. Detail of fig. 260

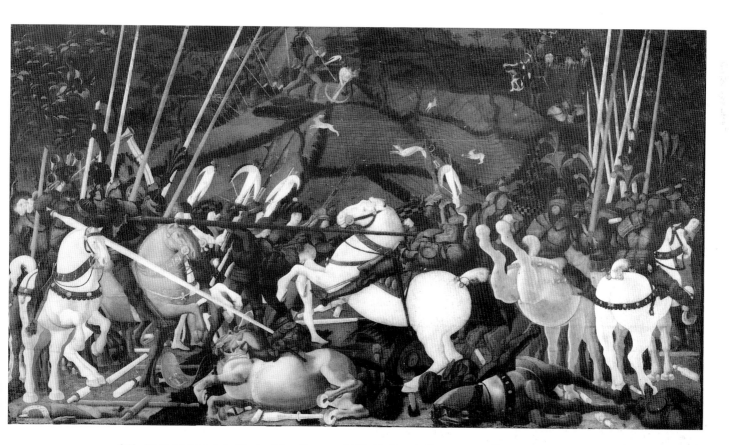

263. PAOLO UCCELLO. *Battle of San Romano.* 1430s(?). Panel, 6' x 10' 7". Uffizi Gallery, Florence.
Commissioned by a member of the Medici family for the first Medici palace on Via Larga

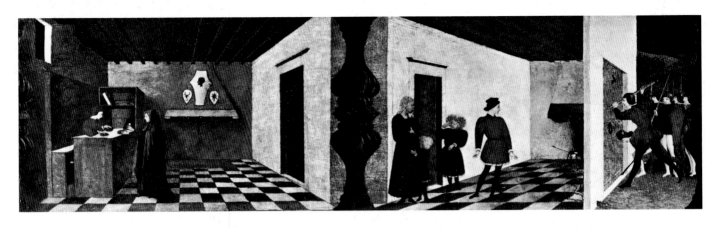

264. PAOLO UCCELLO. *Miracle of the Host*, first two episodes of a predella. 1468. Panel,
dimensions of whole predella 1' 4¹/₂" x 11' 6". Galleria Nazionale delle Marche,
Palazzo Ducale, Urbino. Commissioned by the Compagni del Corpus Domini for the Church
of the Corpus Domini, Urbino

battle panels lack the intensity felt in the *Deluge*. The rearing horses seem transplanted from a carousel, and the impression is one of a tournament rather than a military engagement. This is partly due, of course, to Uccello's stylization of contour and modeling and his emphasis on brilliant ornament rather than grim reality.

The unreality of the scene derives in part from the perspective construction. Most of the broken lances, like the floating ladder in the *Deluge*, have fallen in conformity with Albertian orthogonals. So have the pieces of armor, including, in the lower left-hand corner of the Florence panel, a shield around which is wrapped a scroll bearing Uccello's signature in perspective. Horses and horsemen are seen in profile or in foreshortening so that they recede into depth or plunge toward the spectator, often at right angles to the orthogonals formed by the lances. In one instance, at the lower left of the London panel, a soldier has managed to die in perspective. It is as if perspective were not a phenomenon of vision but a magical process, implicit in the air, that can force acquiescence on persons and objects.

In the midst of such a web of interwoven geometric compulsions, practical jokes, and abstract beauty, the humanity of certain faces comes as a surprise, especially the searching portrait in the London panel of Niccolò da Tolentino, captain of the Florentine forces. The landscape looks stylized but it resembles the rippling hills divided into fields of narrow strips still visible near San Romano in the Arno Valley, not far from Pisa. All sorts of things go on in this background: hand-to-hand combat, soldiers in hot pursuit of the enemy, a dog in equally hot pursuit of a rabbit, and unconcerned peasants serenely bringing baskets of grapes to the wine press—all in the midst of trees and hedgerows that are so patterned and ornamentalized that they look almost Japanese.

Uccello's last work is perhaps the predella (fig. 264) that was all he ever finished for an altarpiece for the Church of Corpus Domini in Urbino. Apparently he was offered the commission in 1468, painted the predella, and then started on the altarpiece itself. Records suggest that the work did not satisfy the Compagnia del Corpus Domini, who dismissed Uccello and tried unsuccessfully to persuade Piero della Francesca to take over the job in 1469. In 1473 the commission was given to the Netherlandish painter Justus of Ghent, who painted his famous *Institution of the Eucharist*.

The subject of Uccello's predella is an anti-Semitic legend of the kind circulated throughout history with appalling consequences. It concerns a Jewish pawnbroker who forced a poor Christian woman to redeem her cloak at the price of a consecrated Host, which the pawnbroker then roasted on a trivet in the fireplace. Streams of blood poured from the Host, arousing the attention of bailiffs, who battered down the door, burned the Jew and his family at the stake, and hanged the repentant woman after the Host had been returned to its altar by the pope himself. Uccello's treatment of the story is simple and direct. In the first scene, the interior of the shop, he gives us an exemplary statement of Albertian perspective construction. But in the next scene, beyond the intervening spiral baluster (projected in perspective, of course), he displays the Achilles' heel of Alberti's system. The interior of the pawnbroker's living room is shown from a point of view slightly to the right of its outer wall, so that the street is visible at the same time. As a result, the floor tiles become flattened at the extreme left into trapezoids that bear no relation to the actual phenomena of vision. Uccello has prolonged the perspective construction laterally to the point where, as we have seen in discussing Alberti's perspective theory (see p. 238), the transversals begin to draw away from the foreground plane in the form of a curve in order to recede to their own vanishing points. There can be little doubt that Uccello made this construction with tongue in cheek.

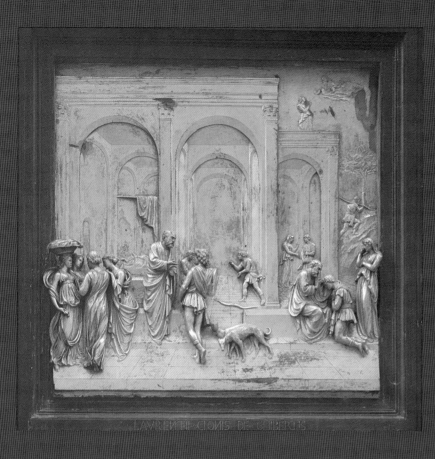

Colorplate 46. LORENZO GHIBERTI. *Jacob and Esau*, panel from the *Gates of Paradise*, formerly on the Baptistery, Florence. c. 1435. Gilded bronze, 31¼" square. Museo dell'Opera del Duomo, Florence. Commissioned by the Opera of the Baptistery and the Arte di Calimala for the Florentine Baptistery

Colorplate 47. PAOLO UCCELLO. *Battle of San Romano*. 1430s(?) Panel, 6' x 10' 7". National Gallery, London. Commissioned by a member of the Medici family for the first Medici palace on Via Larga

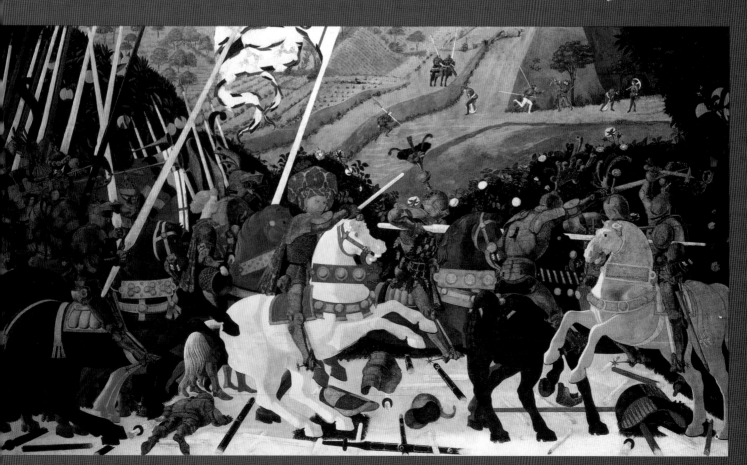

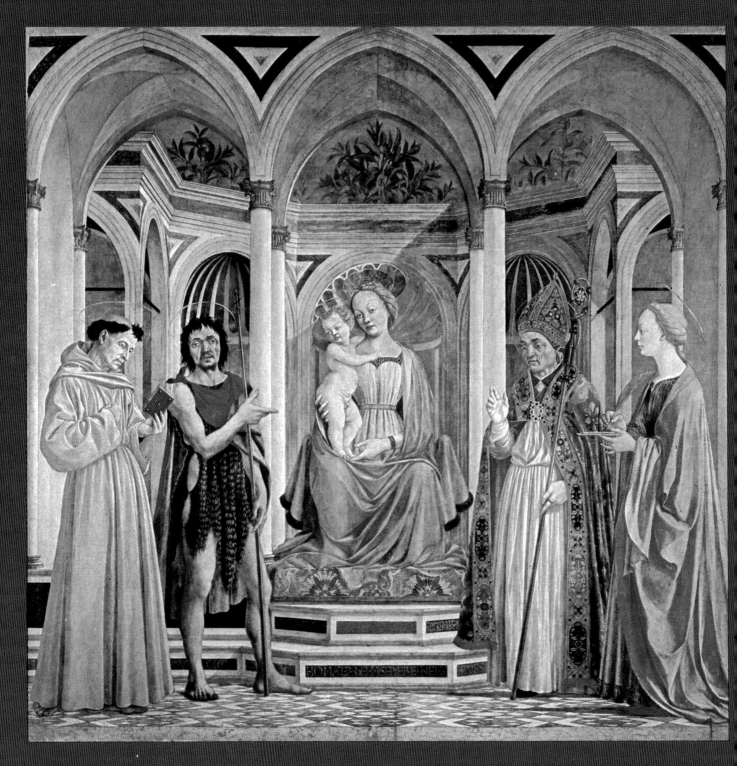

Colorplate 48. DOMENICO VENEZIANO. *Madonna and Child with Sts. Francis, John the Baptist, Zenobius, and Lucy* (St. Lucy altarpiece). c. 1445–47. Panel, 82 x 84". Uffizi Gallery, Florence. Commissioned for the high altar of Sta. Lucia de' Magnoli, Florence

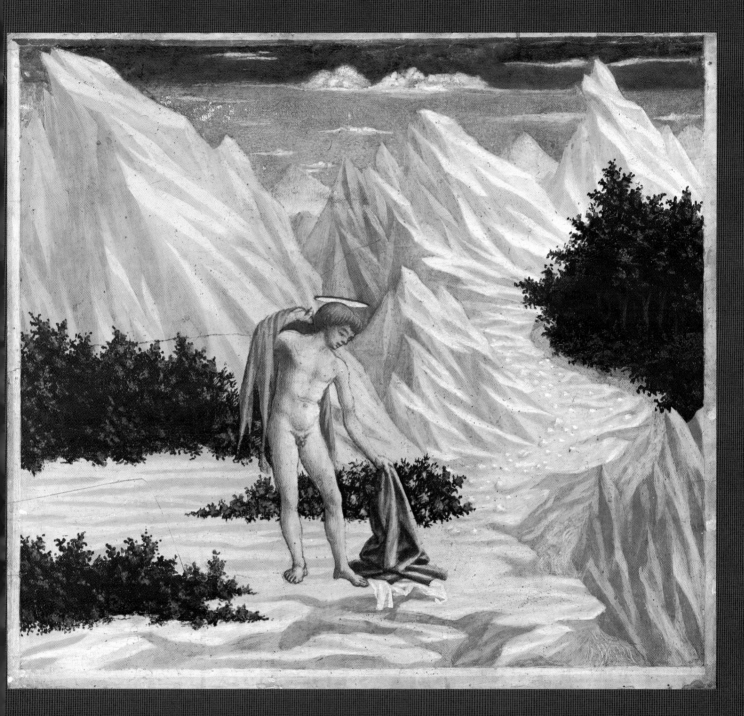

Colorplate 49. DOMENICO VENEZIANO. *St. John the Baptist in the Desert*, from the predella of the St. Lucy altarpiece. c. 1445–47. Panel, 11 x 12¾". National Gallery of Art, Washington, D.C. (Kress Collection)

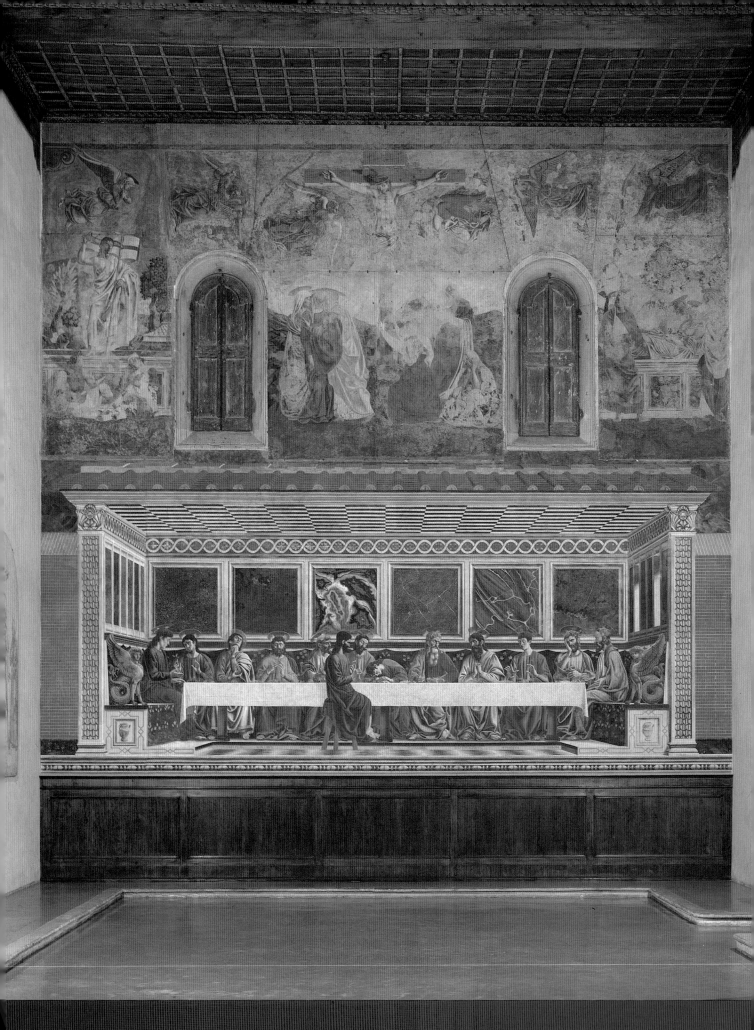

Colorplate 50. ANDREA DEL CASTAGNO. Cenacolo of Sant'Apollonia, Florence. Refectory wall showing frescoes of *Last Supper* and, above, *Resurrection*, *Crucifixion*, and *Entombment*. 1447. Width of wall 32'

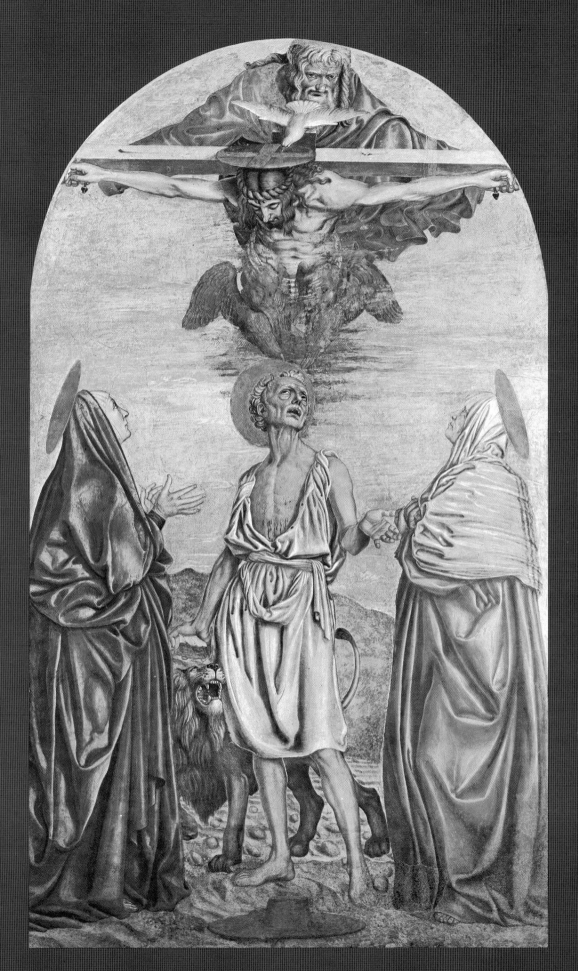

Colorplate 51.
ANDREA DEL
CASTAGNO (and
DOMENICO
VENEZIANO?).
Vision of St. Jerome.
c. 1454–55. Fresco,
9' 9" x 5' 10".
SS. Annunziata,
Florence.
Commissioned by
Girolamo Corboli

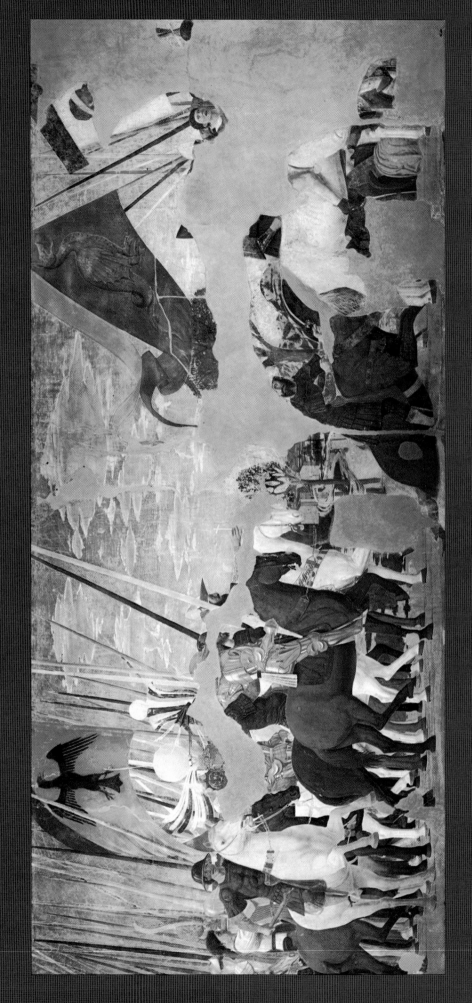

Colorplate 52. PIERO DELLA FRANCESCA. *Battle of Constantine and Maxentius*, from the Legend of the True Cross. c. 1454–58. Fresco, 10' 9" x 25' 1". S. Francesco, Arezzo. Commissioned by members of the Bacci family

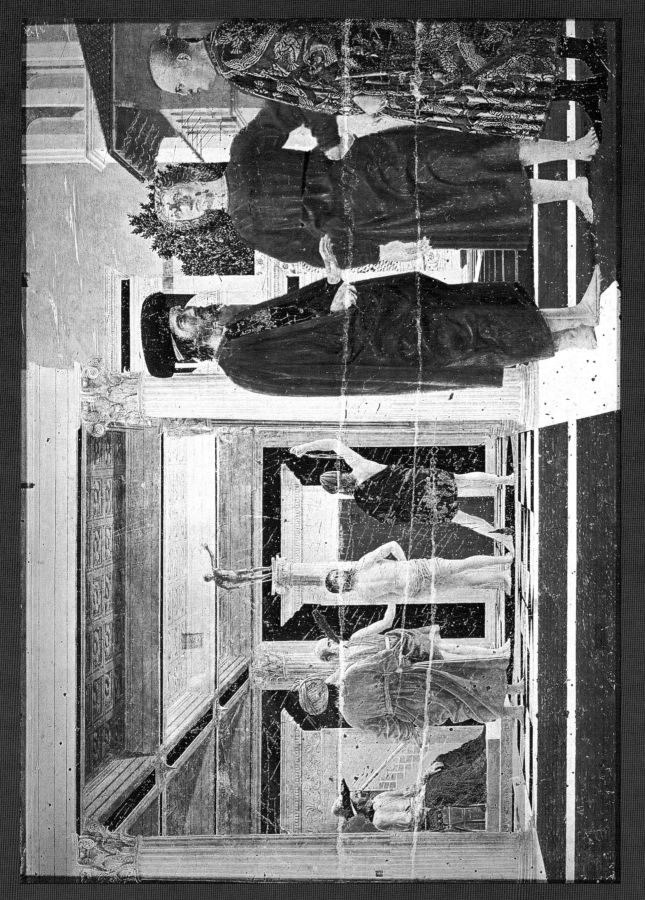

Colorplate 53. PIERO DELLA FRANCESCA. *Flagellation of Christ*. Late 1440s or 1460s(?). Panel, 23¼ x 32". Galleria Nazionale delle Marche, Palazzo Ducale, Urbino

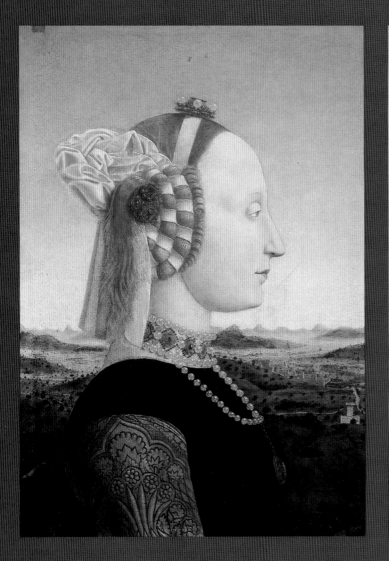

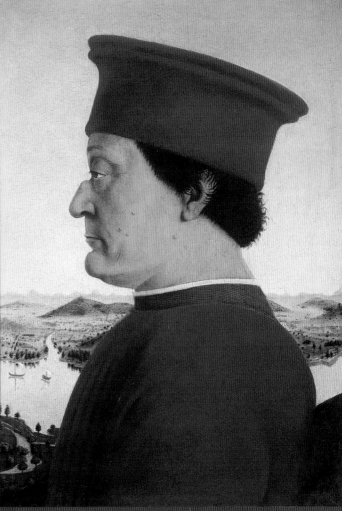

Colorplate 54. PIERO DELLA FRANCESCA.
Battista Sforza. 1472–73. Panel, 18½ x 13".
Uffizi Gallery, Florence. Probably commissioned
by Federico da Montefeltro

Colorplate 55. PIERO DELLA FRANCESCA.
Federico da Montefeltro. 1472–73. Panel, 18½ x 13".
Uffizi Gallery, Florence. Probably commissioned
by Federico da Montefeltro

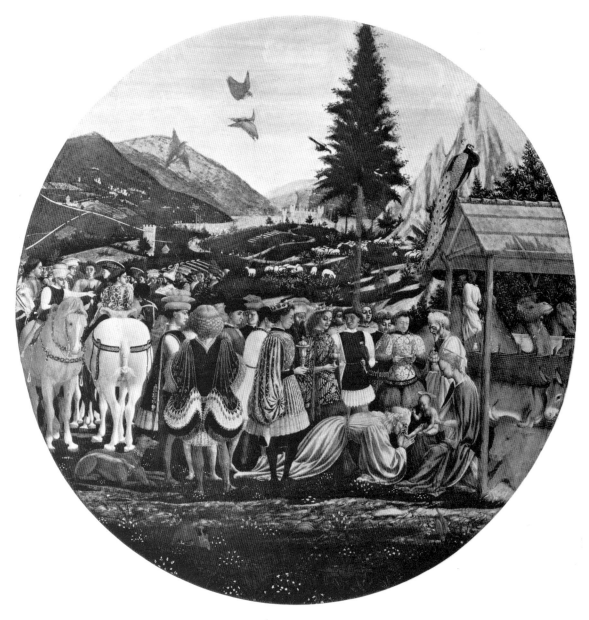

265. DOMENICO VENEZIANO. *Adoration of the Magi.* c. 1439–41. Panel, diameter 33". Picture Gallery, Dahlem Museum, Berlin. Perhaps commissioned by Piero de' Medici for the Medici Palace

DOMENICO VENEZIANO

Domenico Veneziano (c. 1410–61), as his name discloses, came from Venice. His artistic origins and the dates of many of his works are as uncertain as the date of his birth. Presumably he was influenced in his early paintings by the legacy of Gentile da Fabriano in Venice and by the early Quattrocento art of Lombardy, especially by Pisanello (see pp. 378–80), with whose paintings those of Domenico have sometimes been confused. He may even have studied the manuscript paintings of the Franco-Flemish school, such as the works of the Limbourg brothers. It has been suggested that he visited Rome and assisted Gentile da Fabriano and Pisanello. Domenico may have worked in Florence before he came there to stay in 1439.

A splendid, large tondo of the *Adoration of the Magi* (fig. 265) reveals that Domenico was familiar with the works of Masaccio and Fra Angelico. Like Fra Angelico's *Descent from the Cross* (see colorplate 43, p. 207), the painting sets a many-figured composition deep in a naturalistic space. The tondo shape itself was an innovation rapidly being taken up in both sculpture and painting by Quattrocento masters. The arrangement of Mary, the Christ Child, and the first Magus is similar to that in Masaccio's *Adoration of the Magi* (see fig. 203), but in reverse. The costumes, like those of Gentile da Fabriano's Magi and their retinue (see colorplate 38, p. 203), would have been illegal in Florence because of sumptuary laws, but that did not prevent the Florentines from enjoying the representation of forbidden fruits. After all, the Magi came from afar and were therefore not subject to Florentine law. Foreigners in Florence must have looked strange in this respect, as witness the two messengers in Masolino's *Raising of Tabitha* (see fig. 195). Domenico has endowed two of his figures with the towering hats of Greek courtiers, others with costumes bearing French and Italian mottoes inscribed in Gothic letters.

The forms are projected in space and light in a manner that reveals Domenico's study of Masaccio and Fra Angelico. The heads and headgear or masses of curled hair, the swinging sleeves of velvet, brocade, and fur, the stockinged legs—all are painted flawlessly in light and shade, and they overlap and diminish as they recede into the distance. But no one in Florence could have taught Domenico to paint the landscape background, a souvenir of northern Italy that is reminiscent of the shores and sub-Alpine surroundings of Lake Garda, with sailboats speeding before the breeze, castles, a road and travelers, and even a corpse swinging on a roadside gibbet. It may have been familiarity with works by Netherlandish painters that prompted such attention to nature. The rocky promontory at the right is inherited from traditional medieval landscape forms. Masaccio had developed a loose, suggestive brushwork in his landscape backgrounds that might almost be termed proto-Impressionist, and Domenico has developed this even further in the little touches that do duty for foliage or people in his expansive countryside.

In 1438, as we have seen (see p. 213), Domenico wrote from Perugia to Piero the Gouty, son and heir of Cosimo de' Medici: "I have hope in God to be able to show you marvelous things." Perhaps this tondo was one of them, as it was in the Medici Palace in 1492; the mottoes have been identified as Medicean, and it has been suggested that the standing figure to the right of the second Magus is a portrait of Piero de' Medici. By 1439 Domenico was at work in Florence on a cycle of frescoes, now lost except for a few fragments, for the Church of Sant'Egidio in the Hospital of Santa Maria Nuova. He was assisted by the youthful Piero della Francesca, Baldovinetti, and others. Probably about 1445–47, Domenico painted his principal surviving work, the St. Lucy altarpiece (colorplate 48, p. 258). The central panel admits us to a courtyard in which the enthroned Virgin and Child are flanked by Saints Francis, John the Baptist, Zenobius, and Lucy. The triptych format, which survived in the three-arched frame of Filippo Lippi's Barbadori altarpiece (see fig. 216), is still echoed in the pointed arches of the loggia.

Color seems to be the artist's major concern. The entire panel glows with a kind of color so foreign to Florentine experience as to account for Vasari's belief that Domenico painted in oil. The architecture itself—its arches, spandrels, steps, and elaborate pavement inlaid in rose, white, and green marbles like the Florentine campanile—is conceived in color and all its shadows are illuminated by reflections from the sunbathed surfaces. "Marvelous things" do indeed take place in the softly colored shadows of the shell niches, in the groin vaults,

and especially on the fabrics—the gold damask below the Virgin's feet, the blue cloth of her cloak, the green velvet of the sable-trimmed mantle thrown over her chair, the vestments of St. Zenobius, the rose-colored cloak of St. Lucy, and the pearls that shine at the neckline of her tunic and that of the Virgin. In St. Zenobius's miter, Domenico has even distinguished between the dull tone of seed pearls in the embroidery and the luster of larger pearls.

This does not mean that the Venetian was unaware of Florentine conquests in the realm of form. The wrinkled faces of the male saints indicate that Domenico had studied the works of Donatello and Ghiberti. The firm muscular forms of St. John's limbs would have been approved by Alberti, and the easy flow of the drapery folds is in harmony with passages in the *Gates of Paradise* (see fig. 236). Yet these forms have been created less by the traditional Florentine means of drawing in line, followed by shading, than by the changing play of color in light. Nowhere is Domenico's colorism more apparent than in the figure of St. Lucy, who extends the palm of martyrdom and the platter with her eyes, which she plucked out and sent to a young man who had admired them excessively (the Virgin rewarded her with a new pair). Light is especially appropriate to Lucy, patron saint of vision. The light dwells in the shadows of the cloak and projects its forms, all in tones of glowing rose. This calm, poised figure seems to typify the new aristocratic ideal of the Florentine upper middle class. St. Lucy's blond hair, its swept-back masses contrasting with wispy locks that have escaped, brings out the pallor of the face and forehead. The head is like one of Domenico's giant pearls, so gently does the light glide across it and across the silken surface of the neck. The haloes are transformed into disks of crystal rimmed with gold.

The setting of the *Annunciation* (fig. 266), once the central predella, is a court whose elegant forms contrast with Mary's rough bench and the simple rush chair, which is almost identical with those still used in Italian farmhouses. The angel kneels, bearing the lily, while Mary crosses her hands upon her chest. We look through an arch into the closed garden, symbol of Mary's virginity, as already seen in the *Annunciation*s of Fra Angelico (see figs. 206, 210). The garden walk ends in a *porta clausa*, a gateway studded with nails and secured with a huge wooden bolt. The rose beds and the vine clambering over the trellis are painted in small, separate touches of the brush in a manner recalling the foliage in Masaccio's frescoes (see p. 196), but more striking here since it was intended to be seen at close range. For Domenico the individual touch of the brush is equated with the individual ray of sunlight reflected from a leaf or petal.

An even more intense rendering of sunlight is given in the predella representing the youthful *St. John the Baptist in the Desert* (colorplate 49, p. 259). In the Trecento, St. John had been shown trudging cheerfully off, cross-staff in hand. Domenico's picture depicts the boy

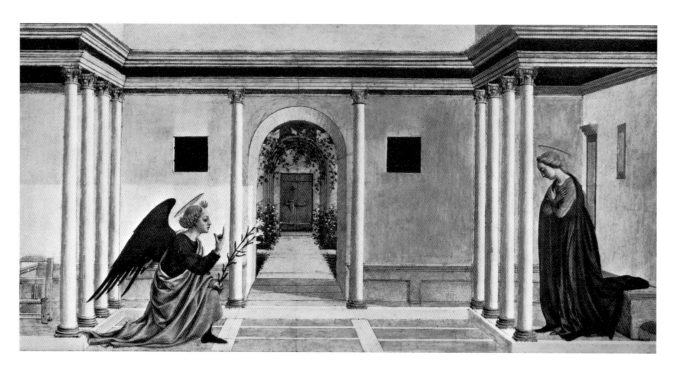

266. DOMENICO VENEZIANO. *Annunciation,* from the predella of the St. Lucy altarpiece (see colorplate 48, p. 258). c. 1445–47. Panel, 10⅝ x 21¼". Fitzwilliam Museum, Cambridge, England. Commissioned for the high altar of Sta. Lucia de' Magnoli, Florence

dropping his clothes on the rocky ground as he prepares to don the camel's skin that he will wear in the desert. With a sensuous grace typical of the new Renaissance delight in the body, the youth is exposed to the glare of the sun. The almost Greek rendering of the nude figure is in keeping with Ghiberti's Isaac of the competition relief and the Christ of the *Flagellation* (see figs. 151, 155). The unreal, still somewhat Byzantine forms of the surrounding mountains are made believable by the wild contours and the fierce sunlight, which changes their white facets to blue-white and yellow-white. The same light reflects from the rounded forms of the boy's body and dwells on every pearly stone.

ANDREA DEL CASTAGNO

Domenico's contemporary in Florence, and perhaps his friend as well, was Andrea del Castagno (1417/19–57), a man of such different temperament and artistic ideas that the association of the two is unexpected. According to Vasari, Castagno was a man of coarse and violent nature who became so jealous of his friend Domenico's skill at painting in oil in the Venetian manner (although, as we shall see, oil was not generally adopted in Venice until about 1475) that he murdered Domenico, and no one would have known who killed him if Castagno had not, on his deathbed, confessed. This story, which blackened Castagno's reputation for three hundred years, met with an obstacle a century ago, when the archivist Gaetano Milanesi unearthed the artists' dates and discovered that Castagno died four years before his supposed victim. Yet with that much smoke there is usually some flame, and

Castagno may well have been a difficult and irascible individual. Certainly, the human dilemma he presents in his works contrasts vividly with the serene, sunlit world painted by Domenico. Andrea came from a hamlet called Castagno (Chestnut Tree) at the head of a steep-walled valley near the crest of the Apennines, yet nature seldom appears in his work. His interest is in the human figure and human character, and the types he prefers are based on the peasants and mountaineers of his Tuscan surroundings.

When Andrea del Castagno was in his mid-twenties, he was already at work in Venice; Paolo Uccello and Fra Filippo Lippi had preceded him in bringing the ideas of the Florentine Renaissance to the city of the lagoons. The *Death of the Virgin* mosaic in San Marco (fig. 267) is now generally accepted as having been made largely from Castagno's designs in 1443. The Florentine Renaissance is here in all its most recognizable elements. The standing apostles flank an arch recalling Brunelleschi's architecture (see fig. 138) and Masaccio's *Trinity* (see colorplate 41, p. 205). The arcaded street in the background is close to those in Donatello's reliefs in the San Lorenzo Sacristy (see fig. 139). The Virgin on her bier is influenced by effigies in Florentine tomb sculpture. The two grand apostles at the left, clad in voluminous folds, recall the statues on Orsanmichele, particularly Donatello's *St. Mark* (see fig. 162). The ornament of the frieze above the arch resembles the portal decorations of the Cathedral of Florence, for whose construction the sawmill run by Castagno's father produced some of the timber. Accompanied by turbulent clouds, and placed so as to violate the keystone of the arch, the mandorla of

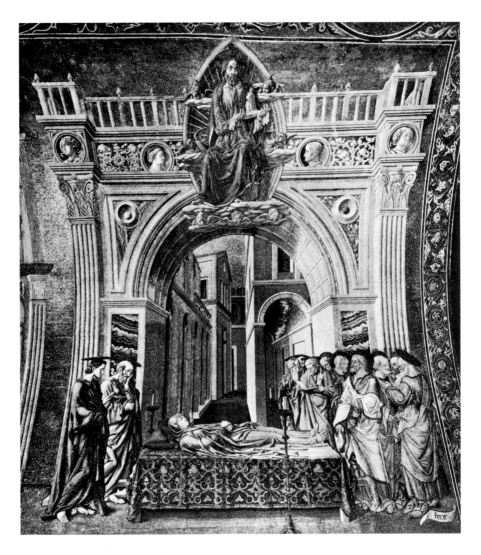

267. ANDREA DEL CASTAGNO and MICHELE GIAMBONO. *Death of the Virgin.* 1443. Mosaic, width 42' 7"; height of figures 5' 9". Mascoli Chapel, S. Marco, Venice. The six apostles at the extreme right were added by the Venetian painter MICHELE GIAMBONO

Christ moves upward with explosive power while the colossal Christ holds a cloth on which the weightless soul of his mother is kneeling. The rugged features of Christ and the apostles and the plain face of the Virgin are characteristic of Castagno's figure types. His *Death of the Virgin*, with its simple, triangle-within-a-square composition, its large arch embracing a grand perspective, and its majestic alignment of sculptural figures, must have been a revelation in Venice. The influence of the composition was incalculable in Venice and throughout northern Italy.

Castagno's fresco of the *Crucifixion* (fig. 268) was painted for a cloister of Santa Maria degli Angeli in Florence, where Lorenzo Monaco had worked only twenty years earlier. Imperfectly transferred from its original site several decades ago, the fresco is now installed in the refectory, or *cenacolo*, of the former convent of Sant'Apollonia. The muscular Christ is nailed to a cross whose grain is depicted with the care and knowledge of a sawyer's son. Mary is a weeping, toothless peasant woman and St. John is a stalwart, square-jawed youth. To the sides are St. Benedict and St. Romuald, as in Lorenzo Monaco's *Coronation of the Virgin* (see colorplate 35, p. 201). The shape of the flattened arch must have been determined by the architectural setting.

The proletarian figures in their sculptural drapery, rapidly painted (a single day for a full-length figure), stand in dignified sorrow before a dark blue background that probably depicts the darkness that fell over the land during the Crucifixion. Although, as we shall see, Castagno was capable of mocking Albertian perspective, he was well aware of its principal elements and has placed the viewpoint of the observer slightly to the left, so that St. Benedict's head is partly cropped by the arch, an unusual treatment that may be related to the viewpoint imposed by the cloister setting. The stoic Christ, bigboned and heavy-muscled, is one of Castagno's most original inventions. In every shape he seems obsessed by sculpture and impervious to the atmospheric style of Domenico Veneziano. His powerfully modeled forms are surrounded by an incisive contour, but they are never freely brushed or veiled in atmosphere. Yet, paradoxically enough, one could argue that his volumes do not revolve in space as successfully as do Domenico's more pictorial shapes.

THE CONVENT OF SANT'APOLLONIA. Castagno's surviving masterpiece is his fresco of the *Last Supper and Scenes of the Passion* for the convent of Sant'Apollonia (colorplate 50, p. 260, and fig. 269). Because the con-

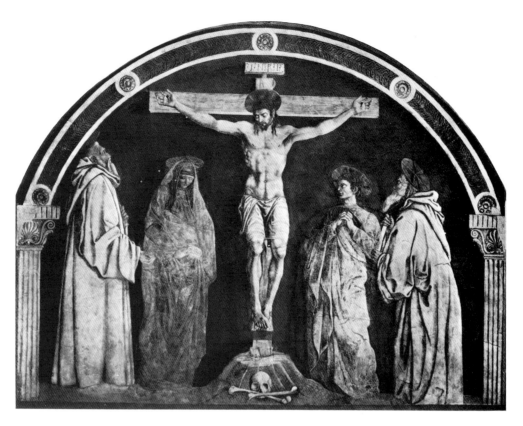

268. ANDREA DEL CASTAGNO. *Crucifixion with Four Saints.*
Detached from the cloister of the Monastery of Sta. Maria degli Angeli, Florence. c. 1453–55.
Fresco transferred to canvas, 8' 10" x 11' 5". Cenacolo of Sant'Apollonia, Florence

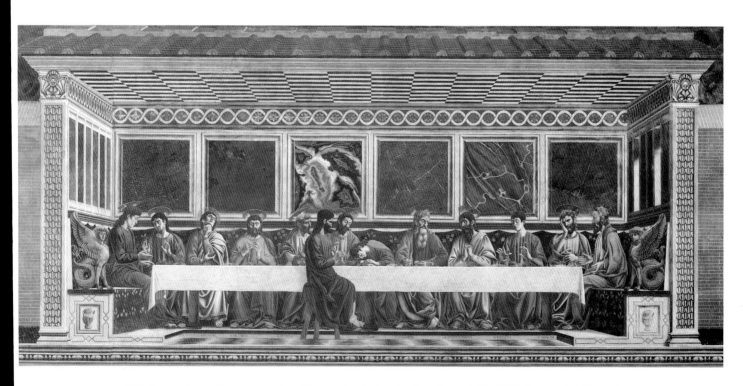

269. ANDREA DEL CASTAGNO. *Last Supper* (detail of colorplate 50, p. 260). 1447. Fresco, 15' 5" x 32'.
Cenacolo of Sant'Apollonia, Florence

Absolute and Perfect Painting: The Second Renaissance Style

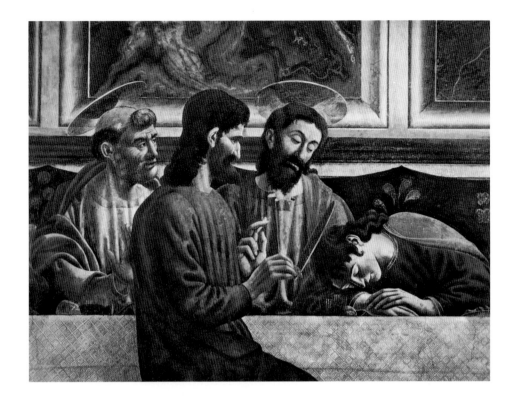

270. ANDREA DEL
CASTAGNO.
Detail of *Last Supper*
(see colorplate 50,
p. 260). 1447.
Fresco. Cenacolo
of Sant'Apollonia,
Florence

vent was under *clausura*, the frescoes probably became inaccessible to Castagno's contemporaries as soon as they were finished, and they escaped notice until the Kingdom of Italy expropriated the monasteries in the late nineteenth century. As we saw in the case of Taddeo Gaddi (see p. 98), the Last Supper was chosen for monumental representation in refectories to remind the religious at every meal of Christ's sacrificial self-perpetuation in the form of bread and wine. Castagno has set the scene in a paneled chamber, hardly intended to represent the upper room of a house in Jerusalem. In fact, it seems to be an independent construction, one story high and roofed with Tuscan tiles, with its front wall removed in the convention of a stage. The paneling of veined marble and porphyry squares is identical with that used for the sepulcher of Christ in Castagno's damaged frescoes of the *Entombment* and *Resurrection*; these are above the *Last Supper* on the same wall flanking the *Crucifixion*. Similar paneling was used in Florentine tombs of the period, especially that of Lionardo Bruni (see fig. 256). In his *Life of Christ*, the fourteenth-century German Carthusian monk Ludolph of Saxony reminds his readers that the monastic life is a kind of entombment, for the religious are entombed in their monastic buildings as was Christ in the sepulcher.

According to well-established tradition, Judas is seated on our side of the table (fig. 270) but he does not dip his hand into the dish with Christ, as described by St. Matthew and St. Mark; this was how most earlier artists, including Giotto and Taddeo Gaddi, represented the scene. Here, however, Judas takes the sop in wine to signify his betrayal, as recounted by St. John: "He it is, to whom I shall give a sop, when I have dipped it" (13:26).

Here, too, Ludolph of Saxony seems to have been Castagno's source: he tells us that this sop had not been blessed by Christ and therefore was not true Eucharist. Castagno carefully contrasts Christ's hand blessing the bread and wine with that of Judas already holding his sop. The Gospel of St. John, Ludolph reminds us, states that it is at this moment that the Devil entered Judas; this has clearly happened, for the betrayer has assumed a diabolical aspect, with hooked nose, jutting beard, and hornlike ears. Christ gazes down toward John while Peter looks at Christ with alarm, as if with foreknowledge of his own approaching denial of Christ.

Castagno suggests that the revelation of the betrayal, which Ludolph says entered the heart of each apostle like a knife, caused them to reflect on their inner life and their eventual martyrdom. In an unprecedented manner clearly dependent on Ludolph, Andrew holds up a knife to the praying Bartholomew, who was to be flayed alive. Next to Peter, James, who would be beheaded, gazes fixedly at the glass of wine he holds to his lips, as the locks of his hair seem to start upward from his head. Thomas, who was to receive the Virgin's golden belt as she was assumed into Heaven (see fig. 169), looks sharply upward, in a daring if not wholly successful attempt at foreshortening. Turning to one another and searching their individual souls, the apostles express their consternation at the disclosure. They hold their hands over the consecrated bread, or to each other in expostulation. So Castagno, doubtless under theological direction, visually unfolded the import of the Last Supper, the Betrayal, and the Eucharist for the nuns.

By surprising formal paradoxes Castagno has reinforced the dramatic intensity of the scene. He arranged the twelve figures so that they neither correspond numerically to the six panels behind them nor in any instance repeat the same relation of figure or figures to panel. We want to read the room as square because each of the three sides has six panels. But at the same time the friezes to left and right count seventeen guilloches—seventeen is still the unluckiest of numbers in Italy—and in the back frieze there are thirty-three and a half (Christ at the time of this event was a few months more than thirty-three years of age). Is the room oblong, with side panels that are only half as wide as those at the back? If so, what is the shape of the ceiling panels, which number sixteen in depth and fourteen across? The floor level is painted as if it is just below our eye level and as a result the flickering patterns of the receding floor lozenges are difficult to unravel. The illusion of the floor is convincing from a distance, but the blocks cannot be counted and the floor turns into a blur at close range. It is an amazing performance.

An observer standing in the refectory of Sant'Apollonia receives a striking impression of three-dimensional reality and tends to attribute it to Castagno's mastery of perspective, even if it is deliberately inaccurate. He did establish a consistent vanishing point for the ceiling in the middle of the tablecloth, directly below the hands of St. John, but the orthogonals of the footrest do not recede to this point nor, for that matter, to any common vanishing point. The orthogonals of the frieze remain nearly parallel, and the depth of the ceiling panels is identical from front to back, with no diminution.

There may have been a reason for such departures from Alberti's rational perspective system on the part of an artist who was familiar with Albertian theory. If Castagno had used a consistent one-point perspective, he would have restricted the observer to a single point in the refectory, yet he wanted the illusion to be valid to every nun in the room. He did his best, therefore, to achieve a visually and emotionally convincing reality by other means. One of these is the remarkable lighting, which seems to come from two windows substituted for marble panels on the same side of the painted room as the real windows of the refectory; it dwells on the broadly modeled features, sends reflected lights into shadows, and models the tubular fingers and massive drapery. Together with this clear light, Castagno's vigorous contours help to establish a sense of pictorial relief that seems a conscious emulation of sculptural prototypes made twenty or thirty years earlier at Orsanmichele or on the Campanile. Then, unpredictably, the tensions inherent in the marble itself erupt convulsively in the panel behind the group comprising the Prince of Peace, the Prince of Apostles, the Prince of Evil, and the Beloved Disciple. The surge and flow of this veining, if photographed by itself, could be mistaken for an Abstract Expressionist painting of the 1950s.

For Castagno the ultimate reality is direct emotional experience, and his art sometimes seems to foreshadow that of Caravaggio in the late sixteenth and early seventeenth centuries. The inner dramas of betrayal, self-searching, resignation, fear of death, crushing grief, and hope of salvation that seem to be going on within the souls of these apostles are revealed on their faces—old and bearded, young and strong, handsome or ugly, tormented or secure. With simplicity and dignity, Castagno presents the silent dialogue of their hands among the bread, the glasses of wine, the plates of salt. He worked with great speed. The *Last Supper* was painted in thirty-two sections, and perhaps within even fewer working days. Castagno began the figures with Andrew, at the right of center, and worked toward the right, each day painting one figure from table to halo. Then, in a single day, he painted Christ and the head and hands of Judas. In another day he painted John. He then worked even more rapidly, for James and Peter were painted in a single day, as were Thomas and Philip. Only after the tablecloth was painted did he insert the body of Judas from neckline to foot. The harsh grandeur of this fresco, its astringent colorism, and its penetration of the human dilemma remained hidden for more than four centuries, but perhaps it was briefly seen and admired by Castagno's contemporaries before the convent doors closed upon it.

LATER WORKS. A sharp contrast to the *Last Supper*, in content and style, is provided by Castagno's frescoes of famous men and women, commissioned in 1448 to decorate the loggia, or garden portico, of a villa at Legnaia, outside Florence. There were a number of such series in Quattrocento villas and palaces in various areas of Italy, although few survive today. These images were intended to awaken emotions ranging from civic pride to delight in the erudition of observer and patron. The nine figures from the long wall have been detached and are currently exhibited, hung on the wall as if they were independent easel paintings, at the Uffizi. Frescoes representing Adam and Eve and the Virgin and Child on one end wall of the loggia have been rediscovered in bad condition in the villa; no one knows what was to have gone on the other end wall; nothing is there now. The detached sections show three Florentine military leaders (Pippo Spano, Farinata degli Uberti, and Niccolò Acciaioli), three historical women (the Cumaean Sibyl, Queen Esther, and Queen Tomyris), and three Florentine literary figures (Dante, Petrarch, and Boccaccio). When they were detached, the frescoes were divided into separate panels, destroying Castagno's illusion of a continuous portico in which the figures stood against varied backgrounds of simulated marble, granite, or porphyry.

Pippo Spano (fig. 271), whose real name was Filippo Scolari, was a Florentine soldier of fortune in the service of the king of Hungary, and as we have seen, Masolino went to Hungary with him. His will endowed the Church of Santa Maria degli Angeli in Florence (see fig. 143). Since Pippo died in Hungary shortly after Castagno's birth, it is unlikely that this is a portrait, unless Castagno was supplied with a death mask or another

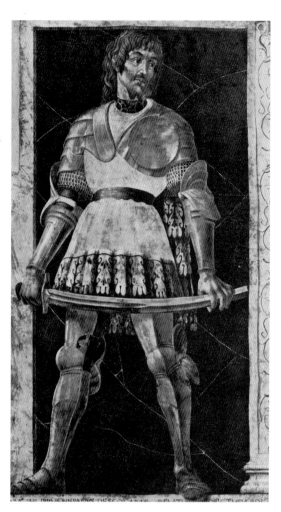
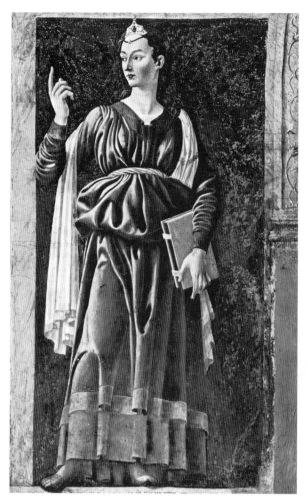

271, 272. ANDREA DEL CASTAGNO. *Pippo Spano* (left) and *Cumaean Sibyl* (right), from a series of Famous Men and Women, detached from loggia of Villa Carducci, Legnaia. 1448. Frescoes, each fragment 8' x 5' 5". Uffizi, Florence. Commissioned by Filippo Carducci

likeness of the soldier. In any case, it is a vivid image of a swashbuckling condottiere standing with feet apart, grasping a huge scimitar in both hands, and glaring at potential enemies. Only the underpainting of the short tunic was in true fresco; the final layer of blue shadows, added *a secco*, has peeled off, leaving the white plaster and causing an apparent reversal of lights and darks. The Cumaean Sibyl (fig. 272), a tall, athletic, and elegant woman holding a book and pointing heavenward, is robed in an iridescent tunic with powder-blue highlights and rust-colored shadows.

In the brief period since Castagno painted the *Last Supper*, his style has been transformed. The figures are still strong and wiry, but more diffused lighting replaces the earlier strong shadows and harsh modeling, and now a system of minute lines indicates contours, details of garments and ornament, locks of hair, and even individual hairs in the beard and eyelashes. Doubtless the new linear style was to please a different type of patron and, perhaps, to harmonize with the villa setting. The perspective—not visible in the illustrations but easily reconstructed from surviving fragments—could not possibly be unified, any more than that of the *Last Supper*, and for the same reason. A consistent one-point perspective would have looked incorrect save from a single spot in the loggia. But Castagno made every effort to suggest

reality. The feet, for example, overlap the ledge on which the figures stand and seem to project into the space of the room. And the folds of the skirts, seen from below, recede convincingly into depth.

Castagno's *David* (fig. 273), from the same period, owes its shape to its purpose as a shield, presumably for ceremonial use in pageants. As contrasted to Donatello's static *David*s, Castagno's lithe and wiry youth runs, swinging his sling in one hand and extending his other to help guide the trajectory of the stone, despite the fact that Goliath's decapitated head is at his feet. The movement causes his garments to flutter in the air above the tense muscles of his legs. This is one of the first great action figures of the Renaissance, and so impressive is the naturalism of this pose that it may come as a surprise to learn that the stance was probably suggested by a Hellenistic statue of a horrified pedagogue, part of a group representing Niobe and her slaughtered children, now in the Uffizi. The sculptors of the opening decades of the Quattrocento had turned to the authority of classical antiquity for their philosopher-saints and for their relatively quiet male and female nudes. Castagno now finds inspiration in ancient art for a pose that enlists the total resources of the body. Despite the deliberate archaisms of the linear shapes, the closely patterned hair, the stylized clouds, and the still-Gothic landscape forms, Castagno has taken a giant step along the road later taken by Antonio del Pollaiuolo, Leonardo, Michelangelo, and, eventually, the sculptors and painters of the Baroque. At the same time, however, it is clear that he has not forgotten Donatello, whose works provided models for Goliath's severed head.

The unhappy events described in Chapter 9, which darkened Florence at midcentury, may have prompted Castagno to open up new regions of inner experience in two altar frescoes for Santissima Annunziata. *St. Julian* (fig. 274) projects with intensity the guilt that must have been felt in Florence during the years of the plague and of the ascetic archbishop St. Antonine. According to legend, Julian killed what he thought were his wife and a lover in a dark bedroom, only to discover that he had murdered his parents. Tormented by his deed, he crosses his hands upon his breast and looks downward and inward. At one side is a farmhouse, scene of the double

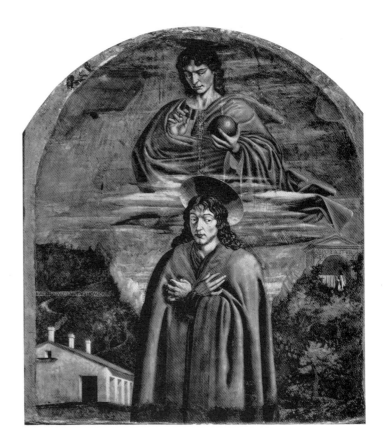

274. ANDREA DEL CASTAGNO (and DOMENICO VENEZIANO?). *St. Julian.* 1455. Fresco fragment, 6' 10" x 5' 10". SS. Annunziata, Florence. Commissioned by Piero da Gagliano

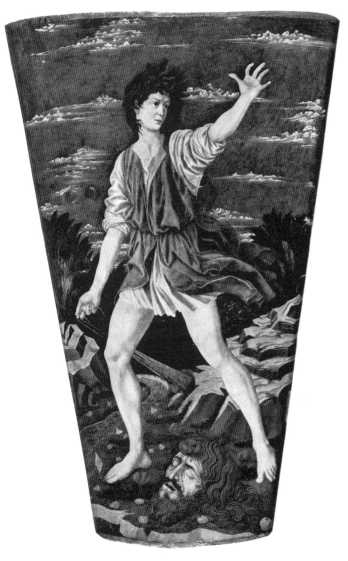

273. ANDREA DEL CASTAGNO. *David.* c. 1451. Leather on wood, height 45½". National Gallery of Art, Washington, D.C. (Widener Collection)

murder, and on the other, in the distance, the saint kneels in penance in a little country chapel. Above, yet invisible to him, hovers a bust-length vision of Christ as *Salvator Mundi* (Savior of the World), holding the orb and cross in his left hand while absolving the sinner with his right. Small inscriptions spell out the meaning of the scene, but they are hardly necessary in view of the wordless communion between the two figures. Both are young—Christ is beardless and St. Julian shows the beginning of a youthful beard. The broad, sculptural handling of the features and the delicate reflected light recall the apostles in the *Last Supper*, but the subtle contours and fine linear patterns, especially the gold pigment lighting the hair, set this work apart from the artist's more rugged earlier style. One can only regret the loss of the lower portion of the figure (especially a hunting dog admired by Vasari), which was destroyed when a higher altar was added in the sixteenth century.

At the next altar is Castagno's *Vision of St. Jerome* (colorplate 51, p. 261). St. Jerome was often represented as a theologian in a study, deep at work on his translation of the Scriptures. Instead Castagno places him among the rocks of the Egyptian desert—looking like any barren hill to the north of Florence—where, stripped to his undergarment, he has been beating his breast with a jagged rock in self-punishment. St. Antonine describes the torments St. Jerome endured in the desert, quoting a letter by Jerome himself. Perhaps this

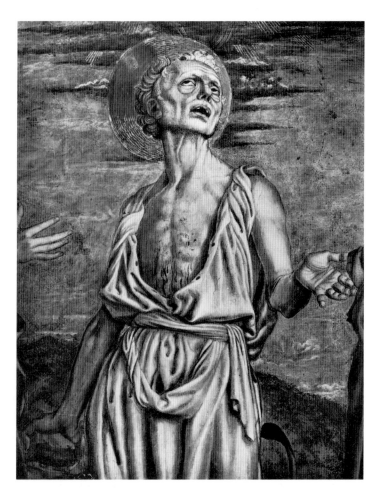

275. ANDREA DEL CASTAGNO
(and DOMENICO VENEZIANO?). St. Jerome,
detail of *Vision of St. Jerome* (see colorplate 51, p. 261).
1455. Fresco. SS. Annunziata, Florence

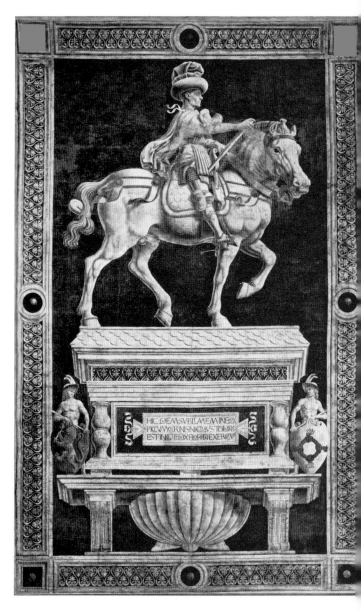

276. ANDREA DEL CASTAGNO. *Niccolò da Tolentino.*
1455–56. Fresco transferred to canvas; 27' 4" x 16' 9".
Cathedral, Florence. Commissioned by the Opera of Florence
Cathedral. The later border is by LORENZO DI CREDI

new penitential image of the saint, which, like the image of the Adoration of the Child, lasted throughout the Renaissance in Florence and Venice, owes its origin to the Florentine archbishop.

Flanking Jerome are St. Paola and her daughter St. Eustochium, followers of St. Jerome. The Trinity above—the Father holding the Son, and the Holy Ghost in the form of a dove—are so sharply foreshortened that they seem to glide out of the picture toward the observer. The seraphim that cover the lower part of Christ's body were added later *a secco* and have partially peeled away. Possibly the clergy or patron were offended by Castagno's assertively foreshortened Trinity and demanded this correction. Yet we still look down on the top of the crossbar, down on Christ's head crowned with the rope of flagellation, rather than with thorns, down even on his gold halo. The rope may have been included because the patron, Girolamo (Jerome) dei Corboli, was a member of the Girolamite community of flagellants. One hardly knows whether to be more astonished by the tortured face of the saint, his features and neck muscles twisted like a rope (fig. 275), or by the intensity of his inner convulsion, or by the gloomy appearance of the Eternal Father, staring fixedly over pendulous lower lids

as if despairing of the fate of his own creation. The color of the picture seems drowned in blood, which runs from the gashes in St. Jerome's bony chest, drips from the rock he holds, and oozes from the pierced side of Christ.

A curious sidelight on Castagno was furnished by the flood of 1966, which so threatened the *Vision of St. Jerome* that it was detached from the wall. Beneath appeared a *sinopia* that has been attributed by some scholars to Domenico Veneziano; others assign it to Castagno. And a comparison of the landscape backgrounds of the *Julian* and *Jerome* frescoes with the schematic landscape of the *David* (see fig. 273) has led scholars to suggest that the former may demonstrate the intervention of Domenico's light brush and divisionistic handling of color. If the *sinopia* is by Domenico, perhaps he received the commission and then relinquished it to Castagno as unsuited to his genius, only to have Castagno appeal to him to paint the landscape.

Castagno's equestrian *Niccolò da Tolentino* (fig. 276) was commissioned in 1456 as a pendant to Uccello's *Hawkwood* (see fig. 259). Uccello had painted Niccolò in the *Battle of San Romano* (see colorplate 47, p. 257), and it is perhaps significant that Uccello was not chosen to paint the second simulated statue for the cathedral. A comparison between the two is inevitable. The simple harmony of Uccello's earlier image is gone; perhaps such qualities were no longer accessible in the 1450s, not even to Uccello. Characteristically for Castagno, the perspective scheme has no single point of view. The harsh light throws into relief the simulated marble of the tomb, its giant balusters, inscriptions, and shell, and the nude youths who hold shields bearing the devices of Niccolò and of the Florentine Republic. The convoluted shapes of the horse's muscles, head, and tail, and of the rider's cloak produce an effect utterly different from that of Uccello's work. So, too, does the coloring, for Castagno's illusion of marble means that he has substituted earth tones and black for Uccello's shimmering violet and green.

The recurrent plague, whose effects Castagno must often have witnessed, carried off his wife in August 1457 and, eleven days later, the artist himself died. They were buried, apparently in a mass grave, at Santa Maria Nuova. Castagno's life was short and his achievement seems incomplete. He was ranked by his contemporaries among the leading masters of a period whose classical ideals and inner tensions he embodied almost to the full. His art was concerned with humanity's terrible dilemmas and tragic destiny. Nature was very nearly excluded from it, and painting for him rivaled sculpture in the conquest of form.

PIERO DELLA FRANCESCA

The artist who seems to us today to fulfill the Albertian ideal of absolute and perfect painting in every respect save that of motion is Piero della Francesca (c. 1406/12–1492). He was not a Florentine; perhaps by choice, perhaps through necessity—we shall never know—he stayed remote from the Tuscan metropolis. Except for occasional visits to Florence, he lived in Borgo Sansepolcro (Borough of the Holy Sepulcher), a Tuscan market town then still a possession of the Papal States. Apart from recent construction outside its walls, the town, now know simply as Sansepolcro, seems to have changed little since Piero's day. The name della Francesca, formerly believed to refer in some way to Piero's mother, is a feminine variant of the family name dei Franceschi. Both versions appear in early documents, which reveal the family as the prosperous owners of a wholesale leather business, a dyeing establishment, houses, and farms.

Before the beginning of the present century, Piero's art was thought an oddity, familiar only to a few erudites who found in it little merit and saw the artist as standing apart from the mainstream of the Renaissance. Even Vasari, to whom we are indebted for much information about Piero, was more concerned with the painter as a regional celebrity (Vasari's native Arezzo is the provincial center to which Borgo Sansepolcro turned) than as an important artist. Only the new appreciation of form, aroused by the art of Cézanne and his immediate successors in painting and sculpture, has raised Piero to his present pinnacle of admiration.

Our first reference to Piero is in 1439, when he was a modestly paid assistant of Domenico Veneziano working on now-lost frescoes in Sant'Egidio in Florence. In 1442 Piero became a member of the Priori (town council) of Borgo Sansepolcro, an office he retained for the rest of his life. His rustic town, set in the upper Tiber Valley among the massive, largely barren foothills of the Apennines, provides the atmosphere of simple dignity and calm that prevails throughout Piero's "noneloquent" art (the phrase is borrowed from Bernard Berenson). His three years or so in the Florence of Alberti, Luca della Robbia, Ghiberti, Fra Angelico, and Domenico Veneziano provided him with the technical resources, the knowledge of perspective theory, and the form, light, and color on which he proceeded. He certainly studied the works of Masaccio, and he may have returned to Florence from time to time and become acquainted with the work of Castagno. He may also have worked with Domenico again, at Loreto. But in the isolation of Borgo Sansepolcro, often compared to Cézanne's isolation at Aix, he set himself a lifelong series of problems bearing on the subject that seems to have concerned him most—the visual unity of the picture. He seems also to have meditated long and deeply on ultimate questions regarding our relation to the universe.

Piero's earliest known work is a polyptych commissioned in 1445 for the Compagnia della Misericordia (Company of Mercy) in Borgo Sansepolcro, which was painted slowly during the next few years and finished by assistants or other painters much later (fig. 277). The Misericordia, which still flourishes in Tuscan towns, is an organization of volunteers, similar to American rescue squads, who dedicate a portion of their time to works of mercy, especially the bringing of the sick to hospitals and the dead to burial. Piero's family had long been members of that confraternity. In order to replace an earlier polyptych, the Misericordia stipulated the antiquated format of Piero's altarpiece, which, with its several stories and standing saints in three sizes, reflects the towering Sienese structures that would have been familiar to the members (see fig. 101). The altarpiece has been damaged by fire and its elaborate Gothic frame is lost, but Piero may even have been constrained to emulate the moldings and decorations of the Trecento. The resulting proliferation of tiny compartments must have pained him, but perhaps no more than the gold background, which he never used willingly.

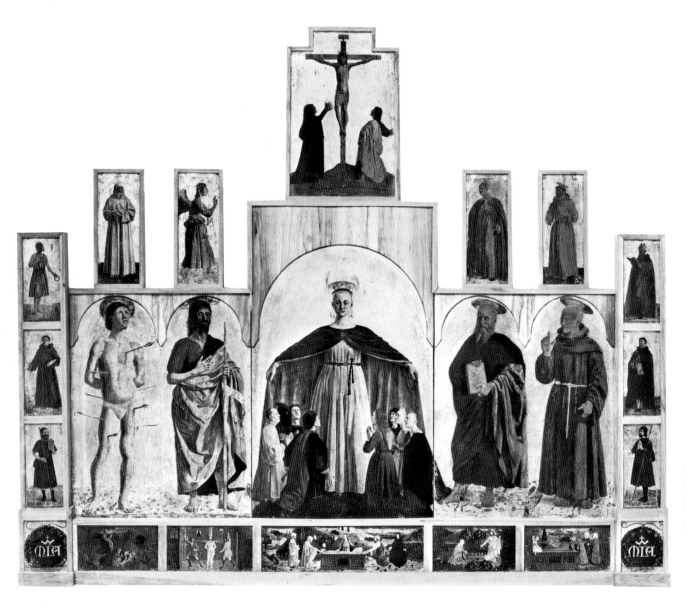

277. PIERO DELLA FRANCESCA and others. Misericordia altarpiece. Commissioned 1445; still incomplete 1454. Panel, 8' 8" x 10' 6". Museo Civico, Sansepolcro. Commissioned by the Compagnia della Misericordia

The central panel (fig. 278) represents the Madonna of Mercy, patroness of the Misericordia and a familiar figure in Tuscan art; the flanking saints are Sebastian, John the Baptist, John the Evangelist, and Bernardino of Siena. The Madonna towers as grandly and as rigidly as an Egyptian statue, calmly stretching out her blue mantle, symbol of Heaven, over the kneeling townspeople. One man, second from the left, wears the black habit of the Misericordia, with the hood pulled over his face so that his eyes look through slits, as it is still worn today when the Misericordia carry the dead. In this way the members' service to God and their fellow citizens was anonymous. The mortals appear in small scale compared with the Virgin, who seems as vast as the heavens whose protection she symbolizes. Her columnar form, its regularity only slightly interrupted by her extended knee, is the central axis of the domelike space created by her mantle. Vasari tells us that Piero generally made models, clothed them in drapery, and studied for hours the be-

havior of light on these folds. Here he seems to have done exactly that, setting a strong side light on the hanging or bunched folds of cloth and on the smoothly sculptured faces. Yet this light operates without recourse to the deep shadows of Masaccio and the early work of Filippo Lippi. Filled with color, it produces soft variations of light, direct and reflected, suffusing shadows in the manner invented by Fra Angelico and developed by Domenico Veneziano. Line is almost absent, and light is the true creator of form. The soft textures of cloth, hair, and skin possess a velvety bloom that helps establish convincing projections, recessions, and enclosures. Characteristically, the glances of the figures are calm, and their lips are closed. Piero permits himself to represent only an occasional gesture of deep emotion, only an infrequent dalliance with a delicately waved mass of blond hair, a sparkling jewel, or a gold-embroidered sleeve.

The *Crucifixion* (fig. 279) at the apex of the altarpiece is, like Castagno's (see fig. 268), a commentary on Ma-

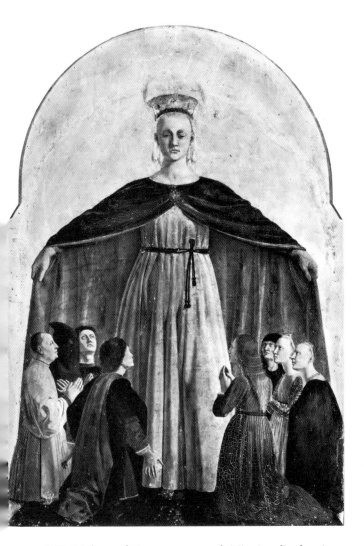

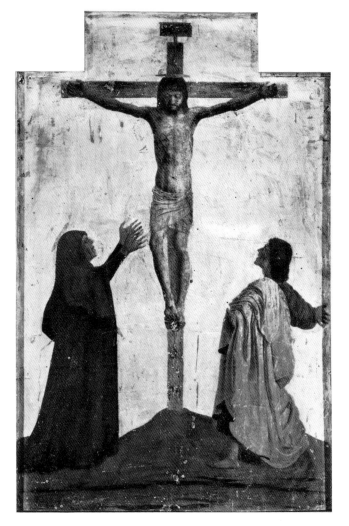

278. *Madonna of Mercy*, center panel, Misericordia altarpiece

279. *Crucifixion*, top panel, Misericordia altarpiece

saccio's Pisan *Crucifixion* (see colorplate 40, p. 205). Piero, however, has locked the cross to the frame and shows Christ as unresponsive to the grief expressed in the gestures of Mary and John. The figures below the cross are devastating precisely because such demonstrations are so rare in Piero's art. The sharply foreshortened left arm of St. John is one of the most impressive demonstrations of this sort before Michelangelo's drastic foreshortenings on the ceiling of the Sistine Chapel (see colorplate 99, p. 495).

Piero's *Baptism of Christ* (fig. 280) was painted in the 1450s as the central panel for an altarpiece for the Pieve of San Giovanni; the other panels were painted later by a Sienese, Matteo di Giovanni. The beauty of the airy landscape setting reveals Piero's command of the naturalistic conquests of the second Renaissance style—one is reminded of Fra Angelico's *Descent from the Cross* (see colorplate 43, p. 207). Christ stands in a glassy stream under a well-pruned tree in a Tuscan landscape with tan and olive hills. In the photograph the line is not visible, but he is up to his ankles in clear water, through which we can still see the stones on the bottom.

St. John steps from the bank to pour the water over Christ's head in a sparkling mass from a simple earthen-

ware bowl. Three blond angels, who might be peasant children supplied with wings and garlands for the occasion, attend the ceremony. Clearly Piero admired the classicism and naturalism of Luca della Robbia's *Cantoria* (see fig. 241), whose singing boys these figures recall. The homely face of Piero's Christ is unprecedented in the Italian tradition, which is dominated—with the sole exception of Castagno—by the Gothic conception of a handsome Christ with fine, clear-cut features. Piero seems to have painted a Tuscan farmer, with heavy cheekbones, thick lips, large ears, lank hair, and wiry beard.

Piero develops a visual relation between the legs of Christ—towering cylinders of light—and the cylindrical white trunk of the tree. The legs, as still as the trunk, are equally rooted in the earth, equally responsive to the light of the sky. In the same way he relates the dove of the Holy Spirit to the white clouds so that we have to look a second time to distinguish them. There is no representation of God the Father, not even the hand of God; apparently the blue sky will do. Piero is a nature poet who sees revelations or relationships in the simplest things—the Son in a tree, the Holy Spirit in a cloud, the Father in the sky. Piero's color is slightly bleached, similar to the color in his own countryside, where the in-

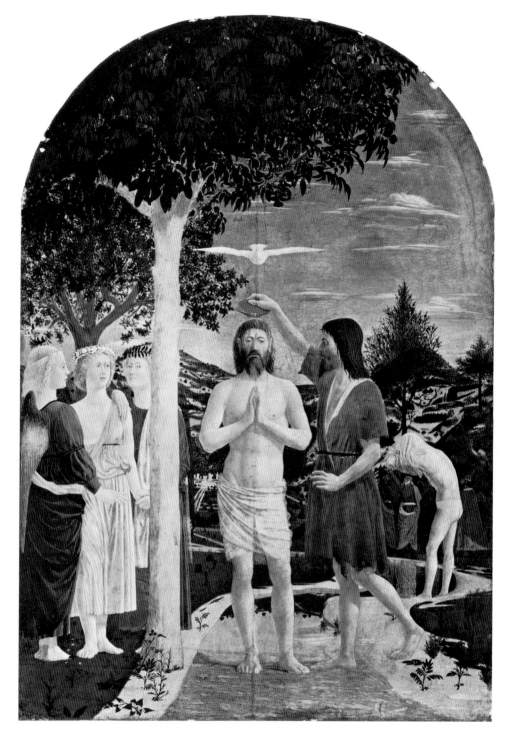

280. Piero della Francesca. *Baptism of Christ.* 1450s. Panel, 66 x 45³/₄". National Gallery, London. Commissioned by a member of the Graziani family and by the Opera of the Pieve of San Giovanni, Borgo Sansepolcro

tense light will not permit bright colors to survive. Shadowless, this white glare models the smooth forms of Christ's torso, reveals the thighs through the translucent loincloth, and models the figure of a man in the middle distance. Pulling his garment over his head as he prepares for Baptism, his arms are visible through the white linen.

Beyond the second curve of the stream stand bearded figures wearing bright robes and towering headdresses; they are reflected in the crystal water, which is as clear as it is bright. So is the terraced slope of the hill above, hanging upside down in this natural mirror. Piero must have studied such phenomena during country walks,

and he must have painted slowly. Neither his analysis of nature nor his vision of humanity could be set down at Castagno's impulsive speed. To our surprise, for example, just between Christ's hip and the tree trunk we get a view of Sansepolcro, its towers touched by light, and of the straight road running toward Anghiari. Background details are painted freely, without a line, for Piero has mastered Domenico Veneziano's doctrine of light and his equation of a single brushstroke with a separate sparkle of light from a facet of the visible object.

Piero's *Resurrection* (fig. 281) was painted for the Town Hall of Sansepolcro and moved from an adjoining

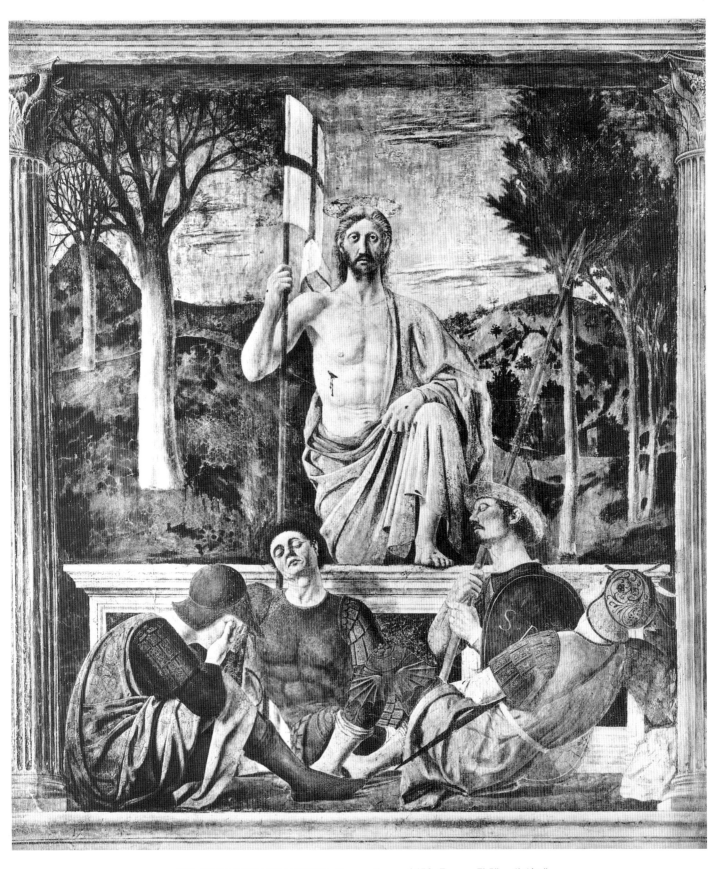

281. PIERO DELLA FRANCESCA. *Resurrection*. c. 1458. Fresco, 7' 5" x 6' 6½".
Museo Civico (originally the Town Hall), Sansepolcro. Commissioned by the chief magistrates
of Sansepolcro for their state chamber

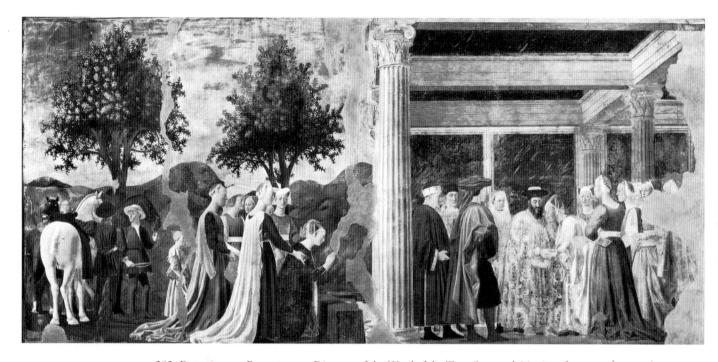

282. PIERO DELLA FRANCESCA. *Discovery of the Wood of the True Cross* and *Meeting of
Solomon and the Queen of Sheba*, from the Legend of the True Cross. c. 1454–58. Fresco, 11' 8" x 24' 6".
S. Francesco, Arezzo. Commissioned by members of the Bacci family

room to its present position in the early sixteenth century; the *di sotto in su* (looking up from below) viewpoint of the enframing columns suggests that it was originally rather high on the wall. The Holy Sepulcher was the symbol of Sansepolcro and appeared on its coat of arms. Piero compressed the scene to its essentials and represented the Resurrection not as a historical event—it is nowhere described in the Gospels—but as a timeless truth upon which one can meditate on any rocky hillside above Sansepolcro, in any gray dawn. The fresh light that pervades the picture is that of dawn on these barren slopes.

Christ stands with one foot in the sarcophagus, the other on the molding. One hand rests on his knee and the other grasps the red-cross banner of triumph, whose folds float behind him. A pinkish-red cloak with majestic folds leaves the right side bare to reveal the spear wound. The classical forms of the muscular torso are modeled by the dawn light coming from the left. Above the pillarlike throat, the powerful face, as frontal as that of the Virgin in the Misericordia altarpiece, is nobly projected. The smooth, curving lips seem to have been carved in pale stone. The wide-open eyes disclose no secrets of death but seem rather to stare into the innermost consciousness of the observer. Before the tomb the watchers sleep fitfully. According to Vasari, the soldier into whose face we look is Piero's self-portrait. The large eye sockets, broad cheekbones, square jaws, and firm chin recall those seen in Etruscan sculpture, features that are still visible in the inhabitants of many Tuscan villages.

The trees on the left are barren, on the right in full leaf. In a picture so densely organized, such a circumstance can hardly be devoid of meaning. On his way to Calvary, Christ had said, "If they do these things in a green tree, what shall be done in the dry?" (Luke 23:31), meaning, "If they do this to me while I am still alive, what will they do when I am dead?" The idea of green trees and withered trees was connected with the Tree of the Knowledge of Good and Evil and the Tree of Life, standing together in the Garden of Eden. In this case the trees doubtless symbolize the world before and after the Crucifixion and Resurrection.

SAN FRANCESCO, AREZZO. The *Resurrection* contains abundant evidence of Piero's slow technical procedures. Unlike Castagno, he took a working day for each face and a day for the torso, neck, and right arm of Christ. He must have proceeded with all deliberate speed in his only major fresco cycle, at San Francesco in Arezzo (figs. 282–86; colorplates 7, 52, pp. 15, 262), but perhaps not as slowly as has generally been assumed. The commission had been given to one of the last surviving painters in the Gothic tradition, Bicci di Lorenzo, who died in 1452 after almost completing the vault decoration. Plotting of the *giornate* in the chancel (Piero often applied wet cloths to the plaster at night so that he could work two days on a single section) has shown that the painting need have occupied him no more than two years. The preliminary calculations and working drawings and cartoons, however, are another matter, and they may have required more time than the actual painting. The most logical assumption is that the project was

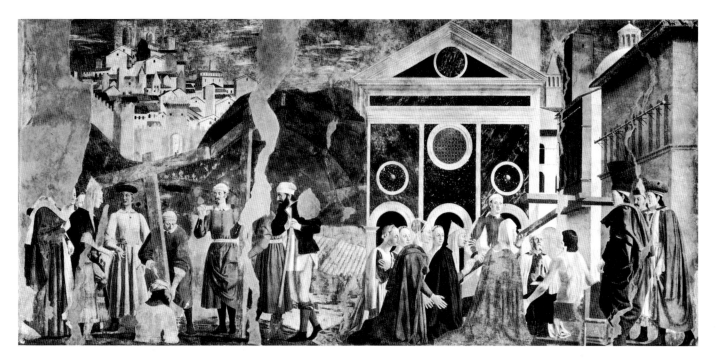

283. Piero della Francesca. *Invention of the True Cross* and *Recognition of the True Cross*, from the Legend of the True Cross
(see colorplate 7, p. 15). c. 1454–58. Fresco, 11' 8" x 24' 6". S. Francesco, Arezzo

planned at once and proceeded steadily until completion in 1458. The master had at least two assistants, but the designs and the principal figures are from his own hand. The entire chancel has been damaged by water, and sections of *intonaco* have fallen away, but the frescoes have recently been restored.

The subject, the Legend of the True Cross, was a medieval fabrication of fantastic complexity, and Piero was certainly familiar with the series on the same theme by Agnolo Gaddi at Santa Croce in Florence (see fig. 124). The tale begins with the final illness of Adam, who, an angel tells his son, can be cured only by a branch from the Tree of the Knowledge of Good and Evil from which Eve took the apple. Seth returns from Eden to find Adam already dead, but the branch is planted on his grave, where it takes root and flourishes. Later, King Solomon desires to use a beam from the new tree in the construction of his palace. It proves too large and is placed across a brook, where the queen of Sheba discovers it on her trip to Solomon's court. Gifted with prophecy, she recognizes that this beam will serve to produce a cross on which the greatest of kings will hang, and she kneels to worship it before proceeding onward to tell King Solomon, who has it buried deep in the earth.

The legend then shifts to the period after the Crucifixion, to the struggle between the rival emperors Constantine and Maxentius. An angel appears to Constantine in a dream, saying, "In this sign thou shalt conquer." Protected by faith in the cross, Constantine vanquishes Maxentius at the Milvian Bridge outside Rome. Helena, Constantine's mother, sets out to find

the True Cross which, along with those of the two thieves, was buried after the Crucifixion. The person who knows the location reveals it only after he has been lowered into a dry well and starved. When the three crosses are dug up, they show no external differences and the True Cross cannot be identified. Luckily a funeral procession is passing by, and when the crosses are held over the corpse, the True Cross revives him. Later, this falls into the hands of the Persian emperor Chosroes, who attaches it to his throne, but the Byzantine emperor Heraclius defeats Chosroes in battle and brings the cross back in triumph to Jerusalem.

The legend is complex, but Piero's sense of order was equal to the occasion, and he retold the story in his own way. Several episodes are rearranged to make analogous scenes face each other, and the final structure forms a visual harmony rather than a temporal sequence. Among the six scenes illustrated here, for example, he paired on facing walls the scenes dominated by women (the queen of Sheba and the empress Helena) and those of battles won by emperors, and on either side of the window he placed visions of the cross.

The story of the queen of Sheba (fig. 282) is divided into two episodes: at the left, the queen worships the wood of the cross, and at the right she is received at Solomon's palace. In the first episode the horses are shown foreshortened from front and rear in the manner of Gentile da Fabriano and Masaccio (see colorplate 38, p. 203; fig. 203). In the foreground the giant beam is placed across a tiny brook that runs past the bases of the palace columns. The shadow of the kneeling queen falls across the beam in accordance with the light from the window of the chancel. Piero avoids conventional beauty in the queen and ladies-in-waiting; their features are large and plain. Their garments are not elaborate, compared with those of Fra Filippo's Madonnas (see figs. 217, 218); their hair is simply dressed, and they wear few jewels. Yet these stately women make their Florentine contemporaries look overdressed. This is due partly to the carriage of their heads, the coolness of their gaze, and the authority of their gestures, but even more to the simplicity of Piero's forms and lines. The heads with their plucked foreheads and the long necks resemble perfect geometric forms, while the grand folds of the cloaks descend in parabolic curves. Small wonder that reproductions of these heads were so widely circulated when the post-Cubist styles of Braque and Picasso were first acclaimed.

The second episode takes place in the classical architecture of Solomon's palace, and here we are faced for the first time with the relation of Piero della Francesca to Leonbattista Alberti. The massive proportions of the Composite order of Piero's portico recall those of Alberti's Malatesta Temple at Rimini (see fig. 222), and it is no surprise to discover that in 1451 Piero had been in Rimini, where he painted a portrait of Sigismondo Malatesta with St. Sigismond, in a fresco in a chapel of Alberti's temple. He may also have absorbed Alberti's perspective doctrine in Florence, and many years later Piero himself wrote the first Renaissance treatise on perspective (see p. 289).

Piero's ceiling is an unbuildable set of veined marble slabs like those of the wall incrustation, but laid on white marble beams that run from column to column. The cool white columns and green and red marble panels make a splendid enclosure for the meeting of the two monarchs. Piero has set his vanishing point low, on a level with the eyes of the kneeling queen, and it is centered just outside the portico, so that some of the capitals are visible along the profile of the first column. Within the portico, we see the same queen and ladies, their heads drawn from the same cartoons reversed, a technique employed by Piero to achieve his effects of balance and regularity. They are received by a sumptuously dressed Solomon, whose gold-brocaded ceremonial robe was painted *a secco* and has largely peeled away. The second face from the left—bony, detached, calm, and staring directly at the spectator as faces rarely do in Piero's work—corresponds feature by feature, allowing for the foreshortening, to Piero's supposed self-portrait in the *Resurrection*.

In the companion piece on the opposite wall (fig. 283), there are again two episodes: at the left is the *Invention of the True Cross* (as the discovery is generally entitled), in which Empress Helena—her face line for line the same as that of the queen of Sheba—directs the excavation of the crosses. This takes place outside the gates of Jerusalem, which is still recognizable as a portrait of Arezzo; the cathedral can be made out and, at the extreme right, the flank of San Francesco itself. The almost

cubistic simplification of the architectural masses recalls Fra Angelico's treatment of the same subject in his *Descent from the Cross* (see colorplate 43, p. 207), which Piero may well have studied. The semicircle in which the figures are disposed around the cross is made easier to grasp by the low point of view, which increases the apparent diminution of figures more distant from the eye. When we look at the other half of the scene, we find that the height of this eye level is again that of a kneeling figure, the empress adoring the True Cross. The same point of view is adopted in both scenes for the same iconographic reason—reverence before the cross.

The episode at the right, the *Recognition of the True Cross*, is dominated by one of the most beautiful façades in Renaissance architecture. This is the more astonishing when we realize that Piero could not at this time have seen a single Renaissance church façade, for none had yet been built. The simple masses of his structure, divided into balanced rectangular, circular, and semicircular areas, the arches supported on piers, the clear-cut distinction between the beauty of the main design and the additive nature of the ornamentation (restricted here to an incrustation of enormous marble slabs within which the veins move like ocean waves) all point to a knowledge of Alberti's ideas. Piero is also keenly aware of the distinctions between historical styles, for above a street bordered with Tuscan houses are a Romanesque campanile, two medieval house-towers, and a dome culminating in a circular temple-lantern based on Brunelleschi's lantern for his Sacristy at San Lorenzo in Florence. Before these disparate yet harmonious architectural forms, Piero has disposed his kneeling, waiting figures, while the True Cross, its planes clearly defined in light, is projected toward us, above the beautiful torso of the man suddenly brought back to life.

Then come the two battles, facing each other across the chancel. Many scholars feel that Piero had seen Uccello's battle scenes (see colorplate 47, p. 257; fig. 263) in Florence, but they seem toylike compared with the solemn events that Piero depicts, scenes in which the realities of conflict, defeat, and death are deeply felt. Piero has contrasted the two battle scenes more sharply than the two scenes of discoveries. This was inevitable because Constantine defeated Maxentius through the cross alone, while Heraclius defeated Chosroes in massive, hand-to-hand combat. In the damaged *Battle of Constantine and Maxentius* (colorplate 52, p. 262), Piero depicted the army of Constantine advancing from the left. At the right Maxentius and his troops are in rout. If Piero had painted the Tiber at its proper scale, he would have had to reduce the figures to miniature size. Piero inserted a symbolic Tiber and, having done so, painted it as the narrow upper Tiber that flows by Sansepolcro, mirroring trees and farmhouses and providing a haven for three white ducks. His stony horses approach the edge, stare at the water, and paw the air, while against the blue morning sky Constantine holds forth a small white cross. Patterns are created by the cylindrical forms

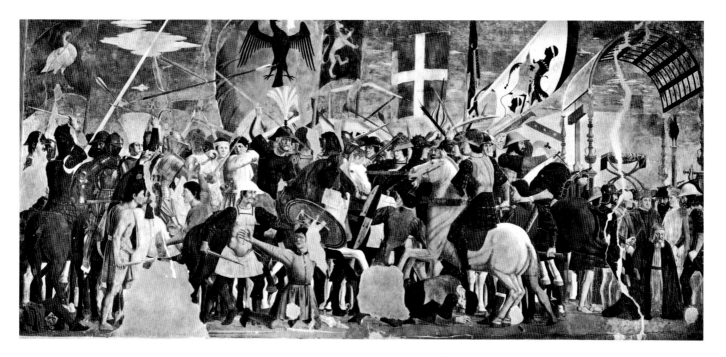

284. PIERO DELLA FRANCESCA. *Battle of Heraclius and Chosroes*, from the Legend of the True Cross.
c. 1454–58. Fresco, 10' 9" x 24' 6". S. Francesco, Arezzo

of the horses' legs and by the lances against the sky. While the dragon and Moor's-head banners of the defeated army totter in disarray, the black Imperial eagle on its yellow banner floats in triumph over Constantine's army.

Constantine wears the characteristic sharp-visored hat and bears the features of the Byzantine emperor John Palaeologus, the penultimate successor of Constantine, whom Piero must have seen in Florence in 1439. The emperor on his white horse is overlapped by a figure in armor so that we see only his head in profile and his outstretched hand. But seldom has armor been painted so magnificently. To Uccello, armor presented a series of forms that he could fit into ingenious patterns. To Piero, these surfaces of polished steel capture the morning light and break it up, reflecting it into the observer's eye. And it is this light, all silver and blue, that makes us catch our breath when first we walk into the chancel of San Francesco in Arezzo.

For the battle scenes Piero chose a point of view level with the feet of the riders, so that we look slightly upward to the belly of the rearing horse at the left. The horse is foreshortened toward us and seems to look at us as his rider tries to control him. This device, coupled with the roundness of the modeling, creates an illusion of depth that breaks up the flat procession of equestrian figures across the wall.

The *Battle of Heraclius and Chosroes* (fig. 284) has little of the luminary magic of the *Battle of Constantine and Maxentius*, for such a display would have been lost on the particular wall it occupies. The chapel's window wall faces west, and the *Battle of Heraclius and Chosroes* on the south wall never receives direct light. Piero in-

cludes no landscape, concentrating instead on the battle. He was guided in part by Roman battle sarcophagi, which could be seen in Florence or Pisa. The relief plane of the composition and such motives as the horse rearing over a fallen enemy recall Roman sculpture. One of the most celebrated military encounters of Piero's day, the battle of Anghiari (see p. 447), took place within sight of Borgo Sansepolcro in 1440. By that year Piero may have returned to his birthplace, and he could hardly have avoided hearing eyewitness accounts of the struggle.

His battlefield is a stretch of ground on which the two forces have gathered, and Piero has represented with care the grim mechanics of the slaughter. There are no beautiful patterns here, no lovely light; the shining armor has little allure. The legs of horses and people block and defeat the eye, while masses of steel and flesh collide. Occasionally, one makes out an incident of utter brutality, as when a soldier near the throne jabs his dagger into the throat of another, or one of pathos, as we watch the dying figure below the rearing horse, or look into the eyes of the severed head at the extreme left. The dethroned monarch on the far right awaits the executioner's sword. His ignominy is underscored by the kicking hooves that just miss him. Above him the True Cross is blasphemously incorporated into his throne.

Some have tried to show that the *Annunciation* (fig. 285), at the lower left of the chancel window, is not an Annunciation at all but a vision of Empress Helena; others have claimed that the scene is out of place in the Legend of the True Cross and was inserted later. Certain curious aspects of the subject, as well as its relevance to the legend, are clarified by St. Antonine. The Virgin

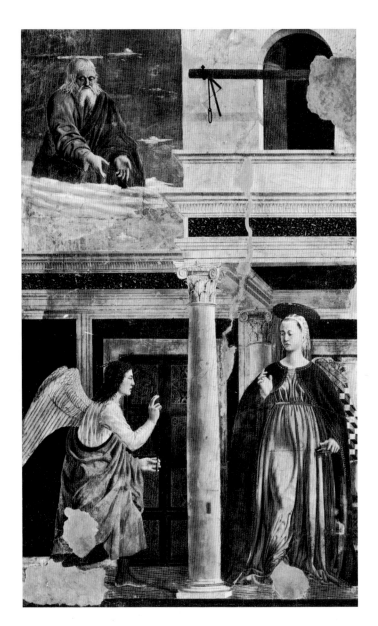

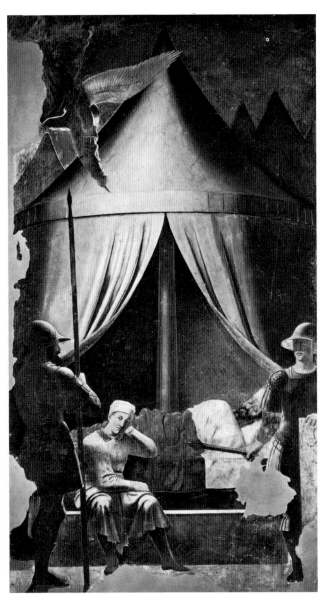

285, 286. PIERO DELLA FRANCESCA. *Annunciation* (left) and *Vision of Constantine* (right), from the Legend of the True Cross. c. 1454–58. Frescoes, 10' 9" x 4' and 10' 9" x 6' 3". S. Francesco, Arezzo

looks down toward Gabriel, while in the sky appears God the Father, his hands outstretched as if sending down the dove of the Holy Spirit. If so, it must have been painted *a secco* and since peeled off, for no trace of it remains. The loggia is formed by splendid columns similar to those of Solomon's palace. To the right is the open door of Mary's bedchamber, complete with a bed decorated with complex intarsia; to the left is probably the *porta clausa*, symbol of Mary's virginity. St. Antonine declared that the *porta clausa* is the way to salvation and that Christ said, "Narrow is the gate and strait the way that leads unto salvation," by which he meant the cross. St. Antonine suggests that the cross can be mystically identified with the *porta clausa*, and that it was therefore symbolically present at the Annunciation.

Of this Piero has given a strong hint. The entire pic-

ture has a cruciform scheme. Instead of the customary lily, Gabriel holds a palm, symbol of eternal life. As the miracle of conception takes place within Mary, the light from the real window of the chancel falls upon her womb. The light also pierces the open window above her, a symbol of divine revelation, and throws the shadow of the portico upon the *porta clausa*, the closed door of her virginity. Into this simple, massive composition, all in rose, blue, white, and the rich dark colors of the veined marble, Piero has compressed—in the outward guise of three figures, two doors, a column, and a window—the deepest mysteries of Christianity, all revealed by the miracle of light.

To the left of the window Mary becomes the greatest of queens by virtue of the cross, and to its right the same cross makes Constantine emperor, also through light. The *Vision of Constantine* (fig. 286) has its ancestry in the luminary revelations of Taddeo Gaddi, Pietro Lorenzetti, and Gentile da Fabriano (see figs. 82, 103, 185). Constantine's tent fills the scene almost from window to wall, and behind it stand other tents, two of which are touched by moonlight. The parted curtains show the emperor asleep in bed, on the base of which sits a sleepy servant. A guard armed with a lance looks toward Constantine, another looks outward. No waking figure is aware that an angel has appeared over the group, flying into the picture downward, in a manner invented by Uccello. The right shoulder of the angel obscures his head, and the extended right arm holds a tiny golden cross. And suddenly the light is there, although from no recognizable source, illuminating the figures and the tent, shining even through the feathers of the angel's wing. No one seems to notice this miraculous radiance. As in the *Annunciation* on the other side of the window, the cross is implicit in the picture's construction, and the shapes of the two scenes subtly correspond, pillar for pillar, horizontal for horizontal. Male and female, day and night, the cycle comes in these last two scenes to its fulfillment.

Piero's palette in the Arezzo cycle is limited to the subdued colors of the central Italian landscape and its light, vegetation, architecture, and people. The colors are so exactly studied that when one stands in the chapel, the objects and people seem almost to be real, despite the damage. Then reality itself becomes miraculous. Piero may have found the majestic order and harmony of his compositions in nature, but this order, as his intellect displays it, is beyond and above nature and transfigures the walls of the chancel with the illusion of a higher reality, the more convincing in that it idealizes nothing.

URBINO. Piero's reluctance to stay in Florence should not lead us to conclude that he did not travel. He seems to have worked in Ferrara at the court of the Este dukes, and he certainly left a mark on the Ferrarese school. In 1459 he painted a fresco, now lost, in the Vatican. He may have visited Rome earlier, for his handling of figures in architectural and landscape settings at San Francesco owes much to Fra Angelico's frescoes in the Chapel of Nicholas V (see fig. 214). But Piero's strongest ties outside Sansepolcro were with the neighboring mountain principality of Urbino, then ruled by Count Federico da Montefeltro, who was elevated to duke in 1474. Urbino's territory was largely unproductive and the count's revenues small, but he came from a family of long military traditions. His talents were valued by the popes, who made him captain general of the Church and relied on his aid in warfare against rebels, including Sigismondo Malatesta. Young men came from as far away as England to Federico's palace to study the art of war and to acquaint themselves with the principles of noble conduct and gentlemanly behavior. Under his rule Urbino became less a second Sparta, as might have been expected, than a tiny Athens. Federico was a wise

and learned man, scholar and bibliophile, who surrounded himself with humanists, philosophers, poets, and artists, and under his successors the cultural preeminence of Urbino lasted well into the seventeenth century. Federico's palace, a brilliant example of Renaissance architecture (see colorplate 70, p. 359), contained many important works of art. His Studiolo (study; see colorplate 9, p. 17, and fig. 387), center of his intellectual life, may have been the original location for Piero's *Flagellation of Christ* (colorplate 53, p. 263). It is by no means certain that Federico was the patron, however, and there is little scholarly agreement on the dating of the painting.

The setting is the portico of Pontius Pilate's palace; recent scholarship suggests that Piero based many details of the setting on descriptions of the palace and surrounding structures in Jerusalem. What has perplexed all observers is the placing of Christ and his tormentors deep at the left of the picture, while in the right foreground stand three figures who seem to have nothing to do with the subject and do not even look at what is going on. There have been many different interpretations of this work, including those that appeared in previous editions of this book. Most of these contain elements of value; the interpretation offered here borrows from them and tries to bring them into a coherent and intelligible focus that is consistent with the historical situation at the time.

Crucial is the vanished inscription *Convenerunt in unum* (They gathered together), which was recorded in the early nineteenth century as being near the group of three figures; it was perhaps removed during a later restoration. The words appear in Psalms 2:2 and are quoted in a slight variation in Acts 4:26: "The kings of the earth stood up, and the rulers were gathered together against the Lord, and against his Christ." In fifteenth-century breviaries this verse appears in the Antiphon for the First Nocturn of Good Friday; it is followed by a passage from Acts 4:27 that refers to the trial of Jesus and names both Herod and Pilate. It has often been suggested that Piero's picture refers allegorically to the capture of Constantinople by the Turks in 1453 or to the threat of that capture in the years preceding the fall of the city; torments then inflicted on the Church, which is still known today as the mystical body of Christ, could easily be symbolized by the Flagellation.

An old tradition in Urbino identified the youthful, barefoot figure in the group on the right, clothed only in a plain red garment, as Duke Oddantonio, Federico's half-brother (Federico, though older, was illegitimate), who was murdered in his nightshirt; more recently the figure has been identified as a wingless angel (see fig. 290). The splendidly robed figure at the right has the red mantle of a nobleman thrown over his right shoulder, barely visible, and may be a portrait of Duke Guidantonio, father of both Federico and Oddantonio; a more recent interpretation identifies him as Francesco Sforza. An identification for a third portrait has been suggested: Pilate, who superintends the torture from a throne, is thought to be the Turkish usurper Mahomet II. In all likelihood, then, the remaining man in the foreground is a portrait as well. Dark-eyed, bearded in the Byzantine fashion, he also wears a Byzantine hat. He gazes earnestly outward, and his mouth is open in speech as he gestures to his two companions. We are led to conclude that the suffering of Christ, placed deep in space as the Flagellation is remote in time, and the contemporary events it symbolizes are the subject of his discourse. It is here suggested that the speaker is a Greek scholar at the court of Urbino who expounds the meaning of the event taking place behind him.

Deep in the portico Christ stands calmly, awaiting the blows about to fall upon him from men in Turkish dress. He is bound to a column surmounted by a golden figure of a nude man that one scholar has identified with a statue of the Sun that was a principal monument of Constantinople; it indicates the idolatry of those who are persecuting Christ. In his left hand the figure holds a colossal pearl, whose significance as the Incarnate Word we have already seen (see p. 224), and the entire ceiling panel above the statue is illuminated by a strong light from this pearl as if from an electric bulb. If Federico was the patron, the picture may have been intended to embody Federico's own ideals for his mission as captain general of the Church involving the liberation of the Holy Land and Constantinople, the holy city of the East, and his own eventual reward, the ducal mantle of his predecessors.

The architectural setting of the portico, as well as the buildings surrounding the square, has been constructed with such accuracy that modern scholars have been able to play Piero's perspective backward, so to speak, and reconstruct the plan of the inlaid marble floor. This turns out to have been put together according to precise mathematical principles. The orthogonals are projected from divisions in the base line, as Alberti says they should be, but Piero has placed the point of view slightly below the figures' hips rather than at eye level, as Alberti recommends. In consequence, the foreground figures loom grandly and their colloquy becomes all the more important. The architectural details are studied with even greater refinement than at Arezzo, and the ceiling is coffered rather than filled with impossible monolithic marble panels. Presumably, we are not asked to believe that a single unsupported beam could span the entire width of the portico, but merely that some columns have been removed for our convenience, according to a stage convention quite common in Quattrocento painting, so that we may see Pilate sitting impassively upon his throne. The steps visible behind Pilate surely represent the staircase used by Christ in Pilate's palace; later it was brought to Rome for veneration and it is now known as the Scala Santa.

Outside and inside the portico Piero's sunlight works its usual magic, reflecting from the snowy marbles, penetrating the deep-toned slabs of onyx and porphyry, and

creating tones of blue and rose, red and gold, that suffuse the whites in the indirect illumination of the portico. Lavenders and blues make up the shadows in the white garments of the turbaned man who stands with his back to us. All in all, the interlocking web of form, space, light, and color represents Piero's most nearly perfect single achievement. If the Albertian ideal of absolute and perfect painting could be embodied in a single picture, this is it. Piero seems to have thought so, too, for he signed the panel conspicuously. Through what compensatory modesty, then, did he choose the lowest step of Pilate's throne for the signature? The enigma of this unusual painting, with its combination of a subordinate narrative scene with a dialogue in the foreground, will undoubtedly continue to perplex scholars. Among the many alternative interpretations and identifications, none has found universal favor among them.

In July 1472, Federico's wife, Battista Sforza, who had governed Urbino capably during his frequent absences, died in her twenty-sixth year, six months after the birth of her ninth child and first son, Federico's long-expected heir, Guidobaldo. Federico stopped all work on his palace and began the construction of a new church of San Bernardino across the valley from Urbino that is visible in the background of Raphael's *Small Cowper Madonna* (see fig. 483). For this church he commissioned Piero to paint the *Madonna and Child with Saints* (fig. 287). This Albertian setting is brilliantly projected, and the picture was probably intended to have a marble frame with matching architectural membering. The Virgin sits with her hands folded in prayer, and on her lap sleeps the Christ Child. Grouped around them are saints and angels. On the right kneels Federico, wearing a suit of shining steel armor from which he has removed helmet and gauntlets. The rose and gold brocade of the Virgin's tunic is repeated in Federico's cape, and her blue mantle is decorated with pearls that are painted with almost Flemish detail. From the shell of the apse, divided half in shadow and half in light, hangs an egg suspended by a silver cord. Throughout the picture stillness reigns.

Behind Federico stands his patron saint, John the Evangelist, but the spot before St. John the Baptist, where Battista (Baptist) Sforza should be kneeling, is vacant. So exact is Piero's perspective that the size of the egg can be measured, revealing that it is an ostrich egg. Such eggs often hung over altars dedicated to the Virgin—one still hangs in the Baptistery of Florence, and others appear in works by Mantegna and Giovanni Bellini (see colorplates 73, 79, pp. 410, 416)—for it was believed that the ostrich let her egg hatch in the sunlight, without the intervention of the bird itself, and the ostrich egg was thus, according to medieval logic, a symbol of the Virgin Birth. It was also believed that the ostrich subsisted on a diet of nails, nuts, bolts, screws, and other hardware, appropriate for the soldier Federico, whose need for iron and steel was considerable, and it

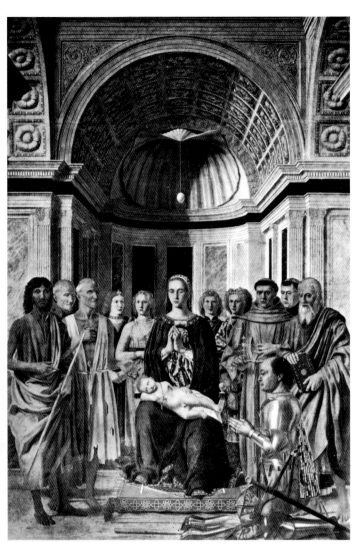

287. PIERO DELLA FRANCESCA. *Madonna and Child with Saints.*
Mid-1470s. Panel, 98 x 79". Brera Gallery,
Milan. Commissioned by Federico da Montefeltro for
S. Bernardino, Urbino

ta, therefore, appears as a countess and her husband as a duke. Federico's profile, disfigured by a sword blow in a tournament that cost him his right eye and the bridge of his nose, was done from the same cartoon as the portrait in the *Madonna*. Both figures are in absolute profile, set against immense, continuous landscapes that surely refer to the extent of their realm. These views are not those visible from the Palazzo Ducale of Urbino; the Urbino landscape is quite different, cut off by lofty ranges with some jagged peaks, and devoid of water. The little city in Battista's portrait is probably Gubbio, second city of the Montefeltro dominions, where Battista had taken her children during the construction of the palace in Urbino, where she gave birth to Guidobaldo, and where she died.

The portraits are typical of Piero in their combination of unsparing realism with inner nobility. Motionless as pharaonic statues and with heads held so high that their chins are silhouetted against the sky above the horizon, these heads create an effect of utmost grandeur. No more convincing symbol could be found of the Renaissance ideal of the dominance over nature. Piero's cool light plays full on the face of Battista, leaving that of Federico somewhat in shadow. His olive skin is set against her pallor, his low-set red hat and tunic against her fashionably high forehead, blond hair, and splendid jewels. Every element of luxury in the veil and jewels has been submitted to the sense of order that dominates both portraits. The headdress conforms to the architecture of the head, and the pearl-studded jewels against the sky seem like a lantern crowning a dome. The extraordinary pearls concentrate the cool radiance of the landscape and sky in their chain of lucent globes, deliberately joined with and contrasted with the chain of square, gray towers of Gubbio.

In the landscapes behind the figures, Piero has set himself new problems—first, that of atmospheric perspective. He makes us aware of the intervening veil of atmosphere that even in a Tuscan summer contains some moisture, inevitably softening contours as the elements recede. But these hills, so strangely formed, have a second, more important, purpose. Piero was in touch with the major intellectual and especially scientific currents of his time and must have known his Tuscan contemporary Paolo del Pozzo Toscanelli, who believed the world was round and made the map that started Columbus on his voyage. Piero has set out to prove this proposition visually, by establishing a continuous plain of a kind rarely to be found in central Italy. He then studded the plain at recurrent intervals with conical hills that have the texture and atmosphere of Tuscan hills but are not connected in ranges.

For some reason the atmosphere is somewhat thinner, the contours harder and clearer, in the two allegorical triumphs on the reverse. Below (not shown) are Latin inscriptions in fine Roman capitals. Federico's refers to the "fame of his virtues" and asserts that he is the equal of the greatest leaders. In the inscription below Battista's

appeared on his coat of arms. Finally, the ostrich was an absent mother, and therefore a symbol of the deceased Battista. The flawless Albertian architecture, the soft interior light penetrating into it and reflected from porphyry and onyx, the delicacy of the subdued color, and the silvery blond of the angels' hair all enhance the unexpected blend of harmony and suspense.

Piero's portraits of Federico and Battista (colorplates 54, 55, p. 264) must originally have been hinged; the backs of the panels are painted with allegories of their triumphs (figs. 288, 289). The ducal mantle worn by Federico in the triumph scene dates the panels after September 1474, when he was elevated to his long-desired rank (he does not wear the mantle in the *Madonna and Child with Saints*); Battista had been dead for more than two years. Probably Piero worked from the still-extant death mask; the features also correspond to those shown in Francesco Laurana's bust (see fig. 385). Battis-

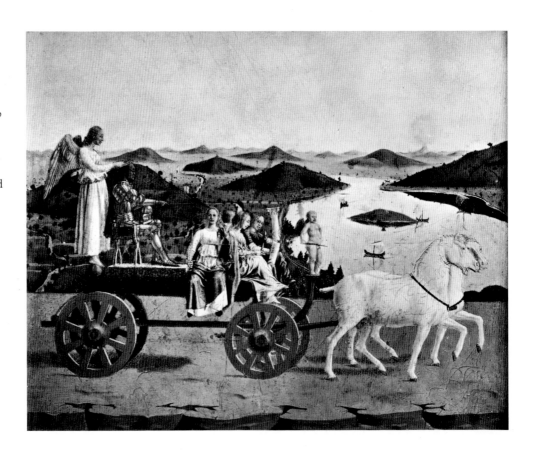

288. PIERO DELLA
FRANCESCA. *Triumph
of Federico da Montefeltro*
(detail, reverse of
colorplate 55, p. 264).
1472–73. Panel. Uffizi
Gallery, Florence.
Probably commissioned
by Federico
da Montefeltro

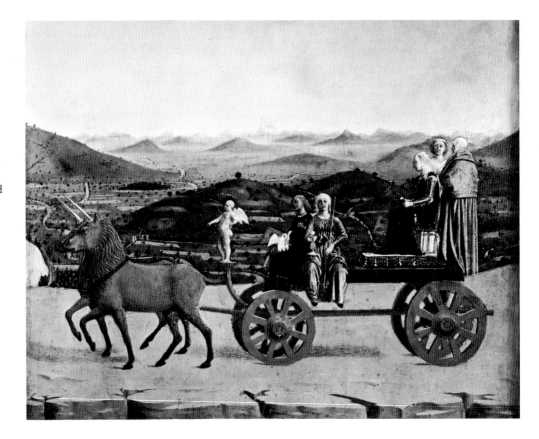

289. PIERO DELLA
FRANCESCA. *Triumph
of Battista Sforza*
(detail, reverse of
colorplate 54, p. 264).
1472–73. Panel. Uffizi
Gallery, Florence.
Probably commissioned
by Federico
da Montefeltro

triumph she is mentioned in the past tense; her fame is never mentioned, but she is "honored by the praise of the accomplishments of her great husband." In the allegories, triumphal cars driven by winged love gods approach each other before the landscape, the car of Federico drawn by horses, that of Battista by unicorns, symbols of chastity and fidelity. Fortune holds the ducal coronet above the head of Federico. On his car sit Justice, Prudence, Fortitude, and Temperance. Standing by Battista are figures that have been identified as Chastity and Pudicitia (Modesty); seated on the front of the car are Charity and Faith. The clear colors of the costumes and armor resonate against the vastness of the landscape, into whose olive-colored hills and valleys a lake brings the sky by reflection. The luminosity of the pictures is so great and the color tones so softly painted that the pictorial possibilities of tempera as a medium seem almost to have been exceeded. Here for the first time one senses that Piero had knowledge of the art of Jan van Eyck and Rogier van der Weyden. Although research has yet to clarify such problems, it would seem unlikely that Piero's luminary effects could have been achieved in tempera or been done without oil glazes in Netherlandish style.

In Piero's later work, his interest in the most subtle manifestations of color and light—and correspondingly in the art of the Netherlands (see fig. 357), which had won such conspicuous conquests in this field—deepens and intensifies. The *Adoration of the Child* (fig. 290) takes place on a sunny day in the Tiber Valley. Before a ruined wall, hastily converted into a shed by means of a lean-to roof, Mary kneels to adore Christ, who stretches out his arms to her. Behind Mary a weary Joseph sits on a saddle, not even looking at the two shepherds who point upward toward the star, outside the picture. Behind the Child stand five angels. Three of them, dressed in tunics and playing lutes and a viol, could have stepped out of Luca della Robbia's *Cantoria* (see fig. 241); the other two, apparently vested as deacon and subdeacon at the first Mass, sing joyously.

Piero's color is pure and lyrical, especially in the passage of blues through the garments of the foreground figures—deep blue, light blue, blue-gray, violet-blue, blue-white, like the tones found in a gigantic bluejay. All around flows Piero's silvery air, but it is especially enchanting about the face of the calm Virgin, with her pearl-studded hair and tunic. In the distance the Tiber Valley opens to the left; the river reflects the sky and the bordering rocky bluffs and scattered trees. On the right the principal church of Borgo Sansepolcro, which then contained Piero's *Baptism*, can be seen above the roofs and streets of the town, its campanile competing with the neighboring house-towers. The figures of the shep-

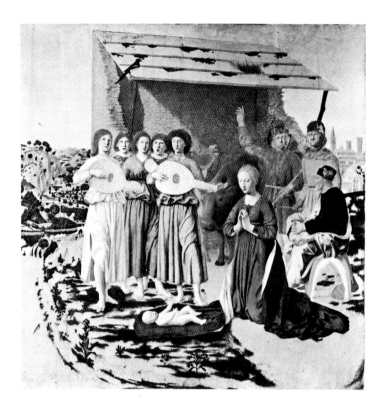

290. PIERO DELLA FRANCESCA. *Adoration of the Child*. c. 1483–84. Panel, 49 x 48½". National Gallery, London. Perhaps painted by Piero as a wedding gift for his nephew Francesco when he married Madonna Laudomia

herds were apparently never finished; the linear underdrawing in perspective is clearly visible.

Piero lived on for about a decade more but seems to have given up painting for his studies on perspective and mathematics. His principal theoretical works are preserved in his own handwriting and include *De prospectiva pingendi* (*On Painting in Perspective*), in which he treats a series of problems in perspective as propositions in Euclidean style, and *De quinque corporibus regolaribus* (*On the Five Regular Bodies*), a study of geometry. According to Vasari, the aged Piero was blind, and in the mid-sixteenth century a man still lived who claimed that, as a boy, he had led Piero about Borgo Sansepolcro by the hand. This story has been doubted, but it may well contain more than a grain of truth even though in 1490, two years before his death, Piero still wrote a clear and beautiful hand. Writing with the aid of a magnifying glass might have been possible for an artist who could not see well enough to paint panels and frescoes.

So the second Renaissance style ends in the contemplation of mathematical harmonies that, for the Quattrocento humanists, contained the secrets of the universe and served to admit humanity to the workings of the mind of God.

12
Crisis and Crosscurrents

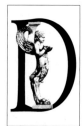uring the first half of the Quattrocento, there were variations of manner, taste, and content but no basic stylistic conflicts between the revolutionary Florentine artists. In our imaginations these architects, sculptors, and painters present the appearance of a band of hardy conspirators—let us say the heroic artists of Nanni di Banco's *Four Crowned Martyrs* (see fig. 168)—united against the entrenched Gothic style. By the 1430s the outcome of the struggle was no longer in doubt. The major commissions were going to the innovators, and their Gothic opponents and even some of their weaker supporters were banished to the villages or constrained to seek their fortunes in such still-Gothic centers as Milan or Venice. The triumph of the Renaissance masters was absolute, and by the middle of the Quattrocento, furniture, textiles, metalwork, and ceramics had all been transformed by Renaissance taste. Workshops of painters turned out birth salvers, painted chests, processional banners, shields, and bridles in the new taste. They also colored reliefs made by sculptors and painted outdoor tabernacles and altarpieces for village churches, using ideas and motifs—sometimes even by means of stencils—borrowed from the revolutionary painters.

In the 1450s, just when the Renaissance style was beginning to seem as standard as Giotto's had in the 1320s, there appeared a rift that widened rapidly within a few years. Soon there was no longer a single dominant style but several, almost equally important, in sharp contrast to each other and, in general, to the previously dominant second Renaissance style (see pp. 213, 252). For the next fifty years these contrasting, sometimes conflicting, currents characterize Florentine art.

Consider the dramatis personae: Brunelleschi, Masaccio, Nanni di Banco, and Jacopo della Quercia were all dead. After the installation of the *Gates of Paradise* in 1452, Ghiberti had retired to his moated grange to live the life of a country squire. Fra Angelico was at work on a series of small panels that emphasize personal religious and artistic introspection. Alberti, Fra Filippo Lippi, and Piero della Francesca were largely or entirely active outside Florence and so, until 1454, was Donatello. We do not know much about Domenico Veneziano in the 1450s, but he seems to have fallen under the spell of Castagno, whose style had taken a strange and shocking turn. So did that of Donatello, on his return to Flor-

ence. Yet along with these two great masters, so deeply affected by the terrible events of the time, comes a group of sculptors and painters who depict a life of unshadowed delight.

We have already seen that the plague of 1448, a century after the Black Death, had serious consequences for Florence and Rome (see pp. 226–27). Moreover, it kept coming back. The humanist pope, Nicholas V, who once had been a university companion of Alberti, fled the Eternal City to the remote safety of Fabriano, to which papal soldiers then forbade further access. In Florence, St. Antonine, the ascetic archbishop, remained in the city and organized house-to-house efforts to aid the sick, bring the last comforts of the Church to the dying, and bury the dead. Events succeeded each other with frightening rapidity. Stefano Porcari, a Roman noble, led a conspiracy to assassinate the pope at High Mass on Easter Sunday. Halley's comet, considered a harbinger of disaster, hung over Europe in the summer of 1453. Repeated earthquakes shook central Italy, especially Florence, many of whose inhabitants slept outdoors for a month. Also in 1453 Constantinople, the last citadel of the Greek Orthodox Church, fell to the Turks.

In due time Florence recovered and in 1454 the Peace of Lodi put an end to most armed conflict in northern Italy and in Tuscany for forty years and brought the illusion of restored tranquillity. But something seems to have happened to the energies of the Florentines. On the surface the government of Cosimo de' Medici, although it suffered some serious challenges, worked well enough. He and his sons controlled politics from behind the scenes by ensuring that only names approved by the Medici party went into the leather purses from which were drawn those who held public office. Cosimo also tried to guarantee that his chief enemies, or those of whom for one reason or another he disapproved, were so heavily taxed that they fled the Florentine state rather than submit; one conspicuous victim of this practice was the humanist Giannozzo Manetti.

Under such circumstances it might be assumed that the Medici bank and allied commercial establishments would flourish, but exactly the opposite was the case. Cosimo gave less attention to banking, his sons Piero and Giovanni received little training in finance, and Piero's sons Lorenzo and Giuliano even less. Perhaps as a result, perhaps as part of a European-wide business decline in the second half of the fifteenth century, the

Medici bank closed one after another of its European branches, and its volume of transactions declined precipitously. The fiscal corrosion was contagious, and by 1495 almost every bank in Florence had closed its doors.

Yet the splendor of the Medici family, emulated by those who sought their favor, took little account of the weakening of its financial base. Architects, sculptors, painters, and artisans were kept busy designing, building, and decorating the palaces that now interrupted with increasing frequency the severity of the medieval streets, or the villas (often converted farmhouses) that rose in the nearby countryside, surrounded by formal gardens.

Cosimo, an amateur architect in his own right, was succeeded in 1464 by his sickly son, Piero the Gouty, whose tastes for refinement and luxury were, it seems, rapidly satisfied by the artists. Piero's successor in 1469 was Lorenzo the Magnificent, who managed adroitly to keep up the fiction of republican liberties at home while freely relating as an equal with kings and princes abroad. In a conspiracy headed by the Pazzi family that involved the archbishop of Pisa and even Pope Sixtus IV, an attempt was made in 1478 to assassinate Lorenzo and his brother Giuliano. Again the time chosen was High Mass on Easter Sunday—in the Cathedral of Florence, under Brunelleschi's dome—and the signal was the moment when the priest raised the sacrament. Giuliano was murdered, but Lorenzo escaped behind Luca della Robbia's bronze sacristy doors. Many of the conspirators were brought to trial and executed. The anti-Medicean party, largely of popular origin, grew during the last years of what can only be known as Lorenzo's reign, the flames of their anger fanned by the sermons of Girolamo Savonarola, a Ferrarese monk who succeeded St. Antonine and Fra Angelico as prior of San Marco.

After Lorenzo's death in 1492, his incompetent son, Piero the Unlucky, was unable to continue the family's control of the city. In 1494 Piero and his brothers—Cardinal Giovanni, later Pope Leo X, and Giuliano, later duke of Nemours—were forced to flee the city. Some of the works of art from the Medici Palace were moved to the Palazzo dei Priori; the rest of the contents were sold at auction. Small wonder that the humanistic premises of the second Renaissance style—intellectuality, order, harmony—had lost their relevance. Whatever styles succeed each other, or coexist, in the third and fourth quarters of the Quattrocento in Florence, the second Renaissance style is not one of them.

DONATELLO AFTER 1453

Donatello's harrowing figure of *The Penitent Magdalen* (colorplate 56, p. 297), carved in poplar wood and polychromed and gilded, is often dated after his return to Florence from Padua in the early 1450s, but the rediscovered date of 1438 on a similar statue renders this uncertain. Its original location and patronage are likewise unknown. Emaciated from thirty years of penitence in the wilderness at the end of her life and clothed only in

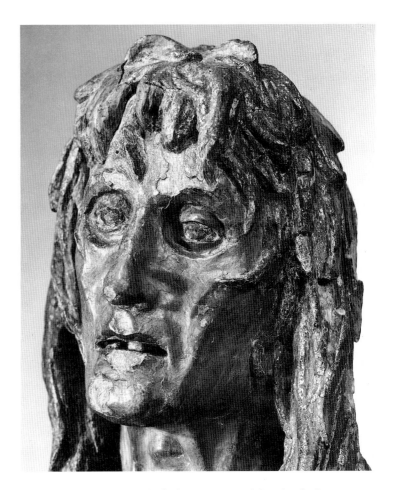

291. DONATELLO. Head of *The Penitent Magdalen*, detail of colorplate 56, p. 297. 1430s–1450s(?). Wood with polychromy and gold. Museo dell'Opera del Duomo, Florence

her own hair, this skeletal, even spectral, apparition with shrunken cheeks and almost toothless mouth seems the antithesis of the noble figures created by Florentine masters only a few years before. But a careful study of the figure reveals that she stands in a beautiful, subtle *contrapposto*, while the exquisitely refined bone structure of her cheeks, eye sockets, and nose, not to mention her long fine fingers and delicately formed ankles and feet, remind us of her former beauty. Her eyes are focused on some inner reality (fig. 291), and her mouth seems to be muttering a prayer as her hands are raised.

The flood of 1966 immersed the lower part of the statue in water mixed with mud and oil and necessitated a cleaning of the surface. A coat of brown paint added in the seventeenth century was removed, disclosing that Donatello had originally painted the flesh to indicate the tan produced by the desert sun and had gilded the hair. Like the late works of Castagno (see colorplate 51, p. 261), those of the much older Donatello admit us to an inner world of emotional stress, and study with fascination the ravages of time and decay on the human body, whose youthful beauty a happier generation had discovered with joy.

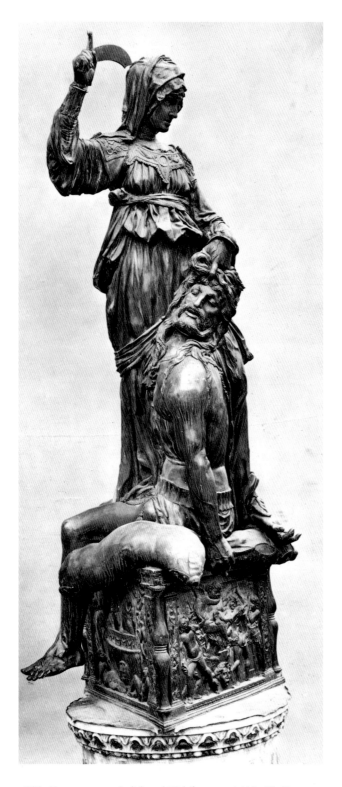

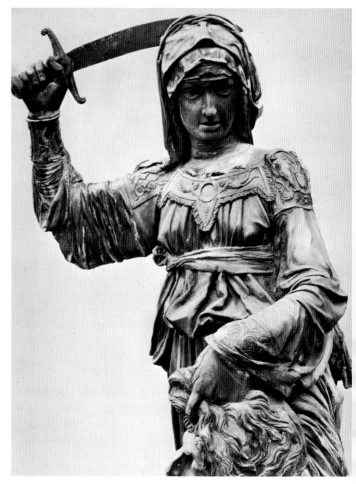

293. Judith, detail of fig. 292

292. DONATELLO. *Judith and Holofernes*. c. 1446–60. Bronze, height 7' 9" (including base). Palazzo Vecchio, Florence. Perhaps commissioned by a member of the Medici family for the garden of the Medici Palace

Donatello's bronze group of Judith cutting off the head of Holofernes (fig. 292) was probably originally commissioned for the garden of the Medici Palace, where it is later documented. After the second expulsion of the Medici, in 1494, the statue was set up in front of the Palazzo dei Priori as a symbol of revolt against tyranny. But when it belonged to the Medici, the group had

another meaning, indicated by an inscription describing how the head of Pride was cut off by the hand of Humility. St. Antonine may have provided the Medici with a written program for the statue; in his *Summa* he compares Judith's victory over Holofernes with that of Mary over sensuality (*luxuria*), which derives from pride (*superbia*), the first sin and source of all the others. Judith's purity under the blandishments of the pagan general awaiting her in his tent is compared to the virginity of Mary; she, like Mary (in a simile borrowed from the Song of Songs), is a camp of armed steel, an army terrible with banners. Donatello's *Judith* stands transfixed at the moment of victory. She has already struck Holofernes once and cut deeply into his neck. The sword is raised for the second blow as she gazes outward with unfocused eyes (fig. 293). One foot is planted on Holofernes' hand, the other on his genitals.

The tense shapes and halting movements of the *Judith* are intensified by the convulsed masses of cloth that cover the figure. In making the mold, Donatello apparently applied cloth soaked in a thin paste of clay to the clay figure, modeling it in place. In the band over Judith's forehead some of the clay broke off before the figure was cast in bronze, revealing the underlying cloth. Donatello did not repair the break, perhaps because he liked the accidental effect, and so his method is preserved for us beyond question.

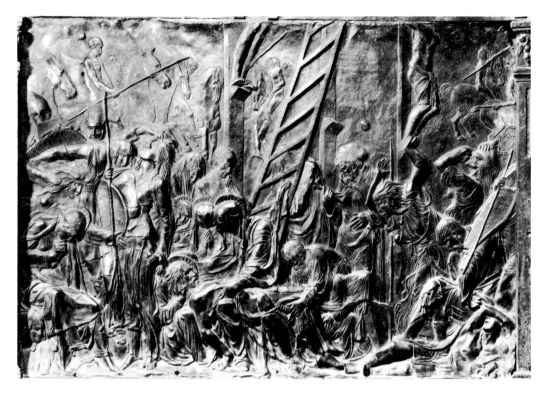

294. DONATELLO. *Lamentation.* 1460s; completed by students of Donatello at a later date. Bronze, height c. 40". 🏛 S. Lorenzo, Florence. Commissioned by a member of the Medici family

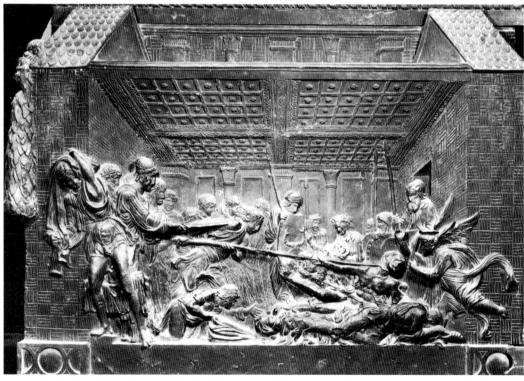

295. DONATELLO. *Martyrdom of St. Lawrence.* 1460s. Bronze, height c. 26". 🏛 S. Lorenzo, Florence. Commissioned by a member of the Medici family

Even more startling than the *Magdalen* and *Judith* are the reliefs by Donatello, finished in part by his students, that are now on two pulpits in San Lorenzo. These pulpits were not set up in Donatello's lifetime, and it has been proposed that the reliefs were originally intended for a single pulpit, an altar table, and a tomb monument for Cosimo de' Medici. The reliefs are done in a style whose freedom and sketchiness, even brutality at times, are extraordinary even for Donatello and do not recur until the twentieth century. The scenes on one of the pulpits are framed by fluted pilasters, although they fre-

quently negate the implications of their supposed frames. The *Lamentation* (fig. 294) takes place below the three crosses, which are placed diagonally in the pictorial space and are cut off by the frame. The thieves are still attached, but we see only the knees, calves, and feet of the penitent thief. To make the spatial relations even more disturbing, a ladder leaning against the central cross recedes diagonally in the opposite direction. Christ, his flowing hair and beard mingling in a torrent, lies across the knees of the Virgin, his head upheld by Mary and an unidentified figure whose own head it totally conceals. There are insoluble mysteries. Four screaming, maenad-like women rush about, but which one is the Magdalen? Who is the seminude figure reclining at the lower right corner? Why are the soldiers on horseback completely nude? Some of the surface finish, particularly the hammering of the bronze, is attributable to students, but they have left Donatello's angular draperies, especially the sleeve of the apostle holding Christ's legs, intact.

The panels on the second pulpit are framed in an unprecedented illusionistic configuration: the architecture—low brick walls roofed with tiles—projects outward at disconcerting speed from the scenes within, whose figures seem to erupt into the space of the church where we are standing. The *Martyrdom of St. Lawrence* (fig. 295), inscribed 1465, is the last dated work of the aged master. The explosive architectural setting enhances the frightful event; with a huge, forked stick the executioners force the saint not onto the traditional grill but directly onto the blazing logs. One blows the flames with bellows, another is felled by the heat, another rushes away, while an angel floats in to receive the soul of the dying martyr. As if in total disregard of the tumult and horror below, the elements of a noble architecture carry the ceiling into strikingly deep space.

In his last works the aged sculptor, one of the founders of the Renaissance and a prime mover of every change in its evolution, abjured his own ideals in order to emphasize drama and emotion and to involve the observer in his work. In the 1450s, only Donatello and Castagno possessed the insight into suffering that enabled them to explore the darker regions of human experience.

DESIDERIO DA SETTIGNANO

Desiderio da Settignano (c. 1430–64), one of the most skillful masters of the age, chose a different direction and style. He was born and trained in Settignano, a village of stonecutters and also home of the Rossellino family. Few sculptors have understood the possibilities and limitations of marble with such intimacy as Desiderio.

In 1453 he received the commission for the tomb of the Florentine humanist-chancellor Carlo Marsuppini (fig. 296) as a pendant to Lionardo Bruni's tomb by Bernardo Rossellino (see fig. 256). The general proportions of the monuments are similar, but the Marsuppini tomb produces an impression of greater lightness and grace. The sarcophagus and bier are lower, the moldings narrower, and Desiderio has divided the paneling into four narrower, higher slabs that accent verticality and openness. Desiderio crowns his design with a lampstand and frame imitated from Roman art, in keeping with the classical nature of the epitaph: "Stay and see the marbles which enshrine a great sage, one for whose mind there was not world enough. Carlo, the great glory of his age, knew all that nature, the heavens and human conduct have to tell. O Roman and Greek muses, now unloose your hair. Alas, the fame and splendour of your choir is dead." Adolescent figures, probably wingless an-

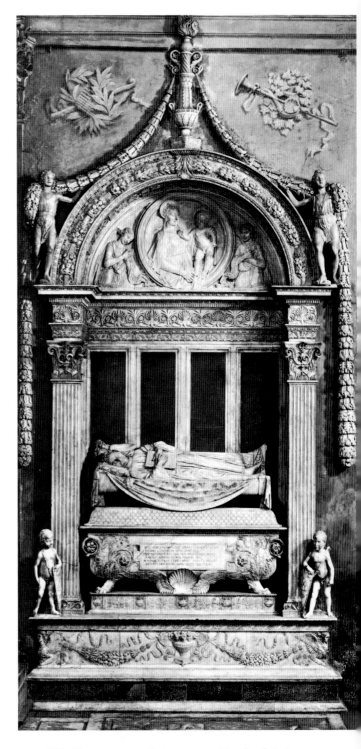

296. DESIDERIO DA SETTIGNANO. Tomb of Carlo Marsuppini. After 1453. White and colored marbles, 20' x 11' 9". ⬛ Sta. Croce, Florence

gels, seem to come running around the top of the cornice to lift up the garlands. The garlands repeat the curve of the pall over Marsuppini's bier and the sweep of garlands on the plinth. At the base of the pilasters two putti hold shields with the Marsuppini arms (fig. 297). The sarcophagus is curved rather than block-shaped—a kind of expanded Roman funerary urn—and beautiful Roman vine-scroll ornament animates its surfaces and dissolves its angles. Even the sacred figures in the tympanum are more lively than Bernardo's: the angels bend

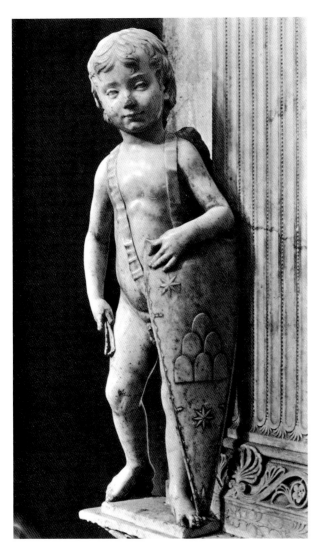

297. Putto, detail of fig. 296

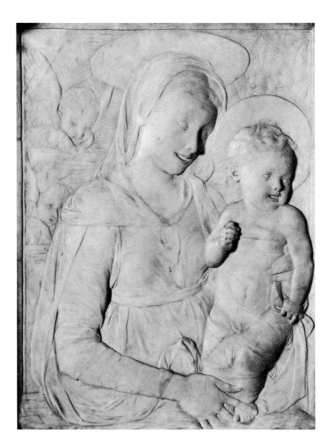

298. DESIDERIO DA SETTIGNANO.
Madonna and Child. c. 1460. Marble relief, 23¼ x 17¾".
Philadelphia Museum of Art (Wilstach Collection)

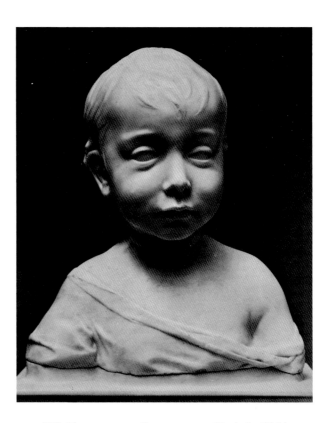

299. DESIDERIO DA SETTIGNANO. *Head of a Child.*
c. 1460. Marble, height 10½". National Gallery of Art,
Washington, D.C. (Mellon Collection)

forward as they pray while the smiling Virgin leans back slightly, the better to contemplate her Child as he blesses.

Desiderio was a great sculptor of children; his earnest little putti are bewitching, as are the children in his low-relief *Madonna*s, like the one in Philadelphia (fig. 298). Desiderio employed techniques to take advantage of the luminosity in marble. Aware of how light sinks into the marble crystals, is held there, and then given back to the delighted eye, Desiderio aimed at achieving in marble the light effects created in paint by Fra Angelico and Domenico Veneziano and in gilded bronze by Ghiberti. He knew that the crystalline structure and brilliant whiteness of marble meant that any shadow would be partly dissolved by the light from the crystals, partly radiated by reflections from surrounding illuminated surfaces. The *schiacciato* technique, by means of which Donatello established form, space, and atmosphere, was further refined by Desiderio to suggest how light is diffused through the atmosphere. In the figures on the Marsuppini tomb these effects are obtained by broad surfaces, understated cutting, and a delicate polish. But at the end of his brief career, in the *Madonna*s and in the child's head (fig. 299) in Washington, D.C. (which may

Crisis and Crosscurrents

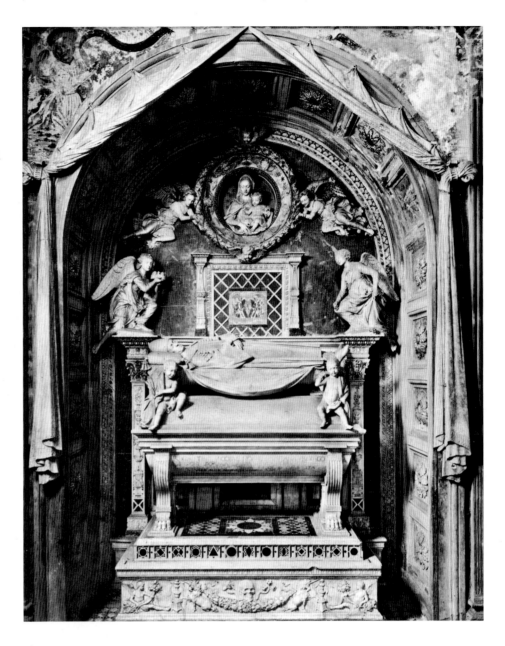

300. ANTONIO ROSSELLINO.
Tomb of the Cardinal
of Portugal. 1460–66.
White and colored marbles
with traces of polychromy and
gold, width of chapel
wall 15' 9". ⬛ Chapel of the
Cardinal of Portugal,
S. Miniato, Florence (see
also fig. 319). Commissioned
by the executors of
the will of the Cardinal
of Portugal

be the portrait of a contemporary boy intended to appear as the Christ Child), Desiderio renounces polish and lets the marble crystals speak for themselves by suppressing surface definition—apparently by filing the surface to blur lines and soften the junction of shape with shape, as if all were seen through a luminous haze. Bernini in the seventeenth century and Rodin in the nineteenth may well have studied Desiderio's transitory effects of expression and the fluid luminosity of his sculptures. Desiderio, apparently disinterested in representing the deeper human emotions, is the personification of the ideal of elegance and refinement, sensitivity and grace, of the new Florentine aristocracy of the midcentury.

ANTONIO ROSSELLINO

Antonio Rossellino (1427–79) was the youngest of the five Rossellino brothers, and it was by his nickname—

Rossellino means little redhead—that the whole family became known. Antonio's tomb of the Cardinal of Portugal at San Miniato in Florence (fig. 300) is the central jewel in the cardinal's burial chapel—a complex of architecture, sculpture, painting, and other arts that achieves, as never again in the Quattrocento, a real decorative unity (see also fig. 319). James, a prince of the Portuguese royal family who had been made a cardinal at the age of twenty-two, died of tuberculosis in Florence three years later, after expressing a desire to be entombed at San Miniato. Immense sums were forthcoming for the funerary chapel, for one cousin was king of Portugal, another was Holy Roman Empress, and the cardinal's aunt was duchess of Burgundy, then the richest state in Europe. The chapel was designed by Antonio Manetti, a pupil of Brunelleschi, and the architectural detail was carved by Giovanni Rossellino, third of the five brothers. Work started in 1460 and was carried out with rapidity, as is shown in documents that clock the work on the chapel almost from day to day.

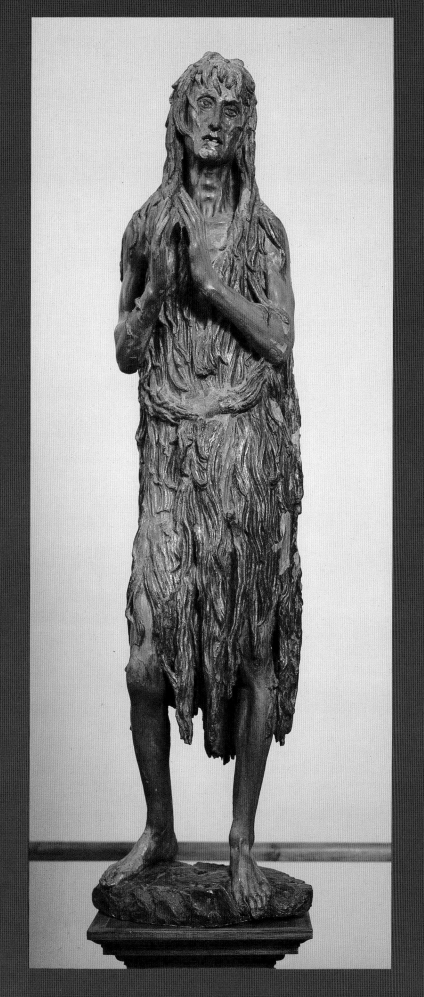

Colorplate 56. DONATELLO. *The Penitent Magdalen.* 1430s–1450s(?). Wood with polychromy and gold, height 6' 2". Museo dell'Opera del Duomo, Florence

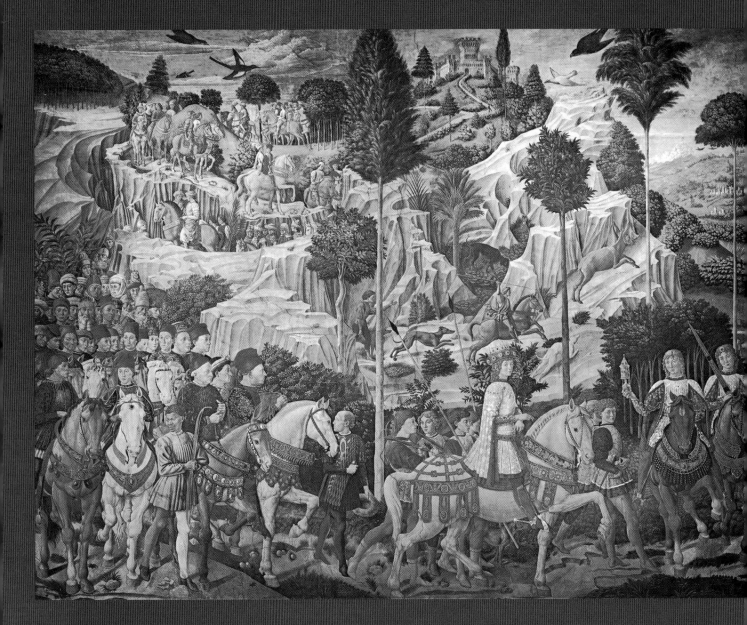

Colorplate 57. Benozzo Gozzoli. *Procession of the Magi*. c. 1459. Fresco. Chapel, Palazzo Medici-Riccardi, Florence. Probably commissioned by Piero de' Medici

opposite: Colorplate 58. Alesso Baldovinetti. *Madonna and Child*. c. 1460. Canvas, 41 x 30". The Louvre, Paris

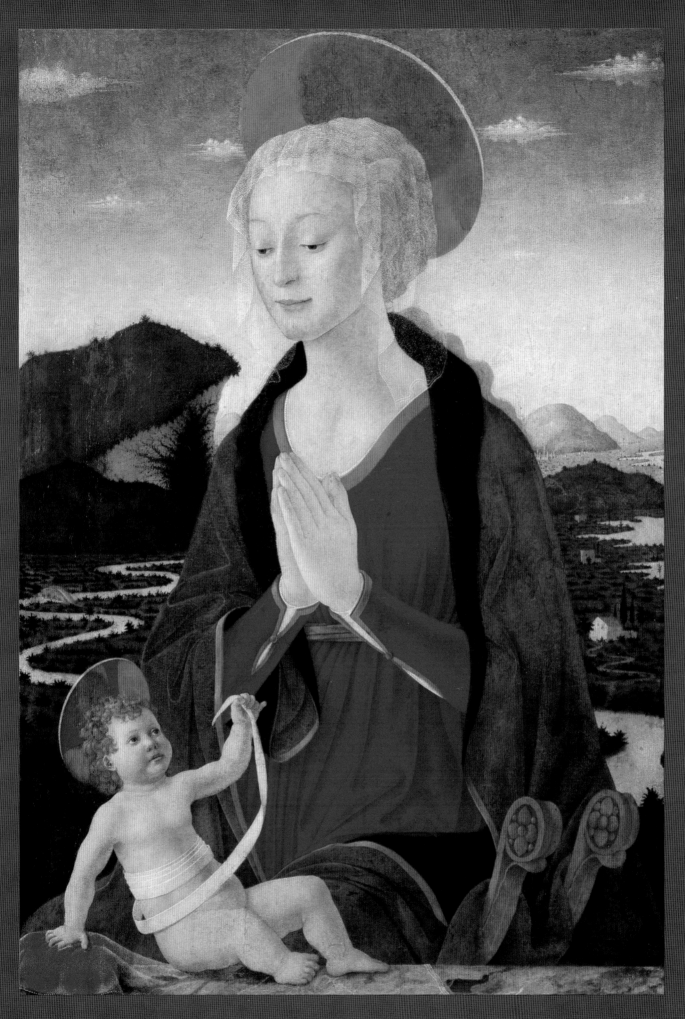

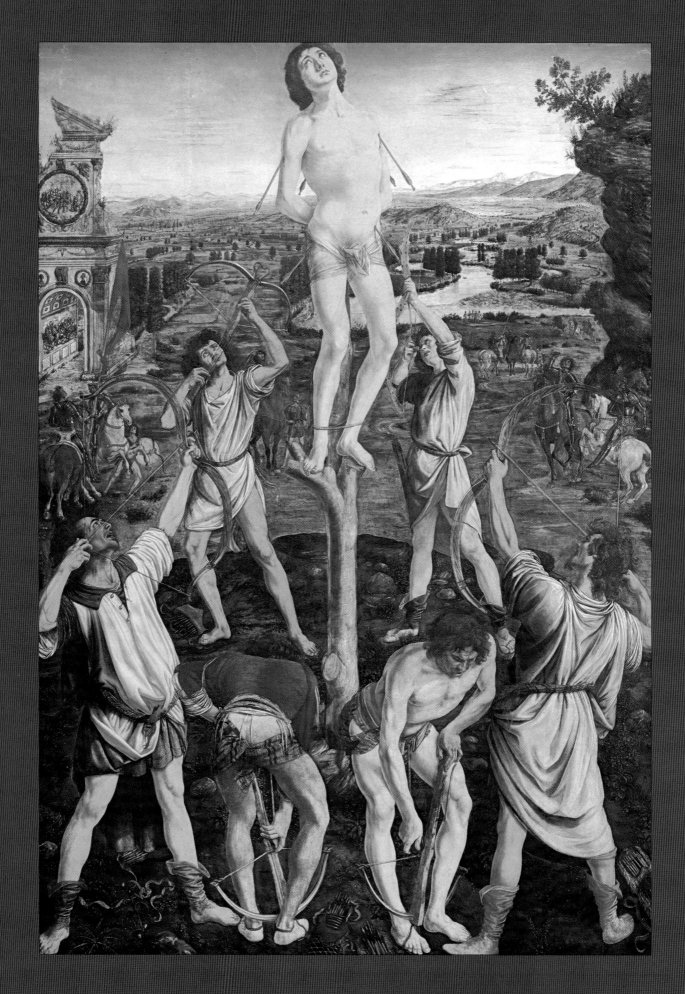

opposite: Colorplate 59. ANTONIO DEL POLLAIUOLO
(and PIERO DEL POLLAIUOLO?). *St. Sebastian.* Finished 1475.
Panel, 9' 7" x 6' 8". National Gallery, London. Commissioned
by the Pucci family (perhaps Antonio Pucci) for the Oratory
of S. Sebastiano at SS. Annunziata, Florence

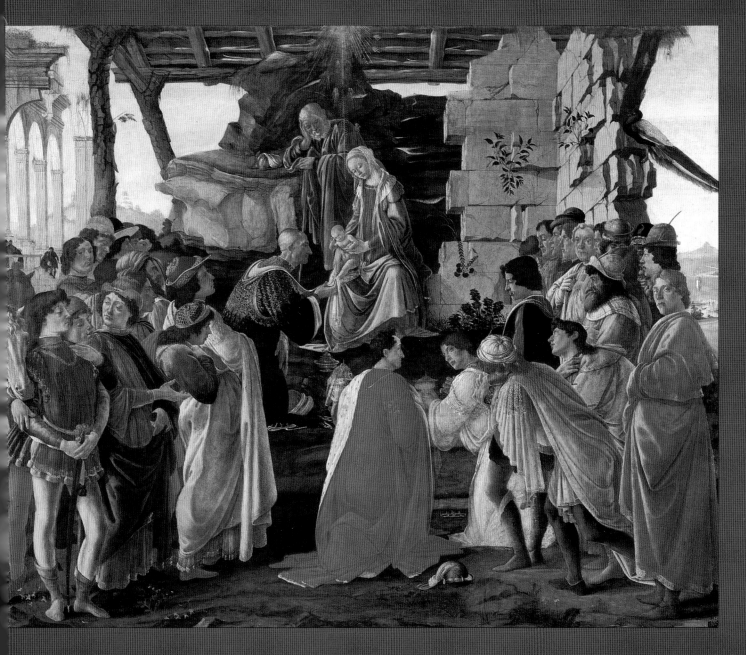

Colorplate 60. SANDRO BOTTICELLI. *Adoration of the Magi.* Probably early 1470s.
Panel, 43³/₄ x 52³/₄". Uffizi Gallery, Florence. Commissioned by Guasparre dal Lama for
Sta. Maria Novella, Florence

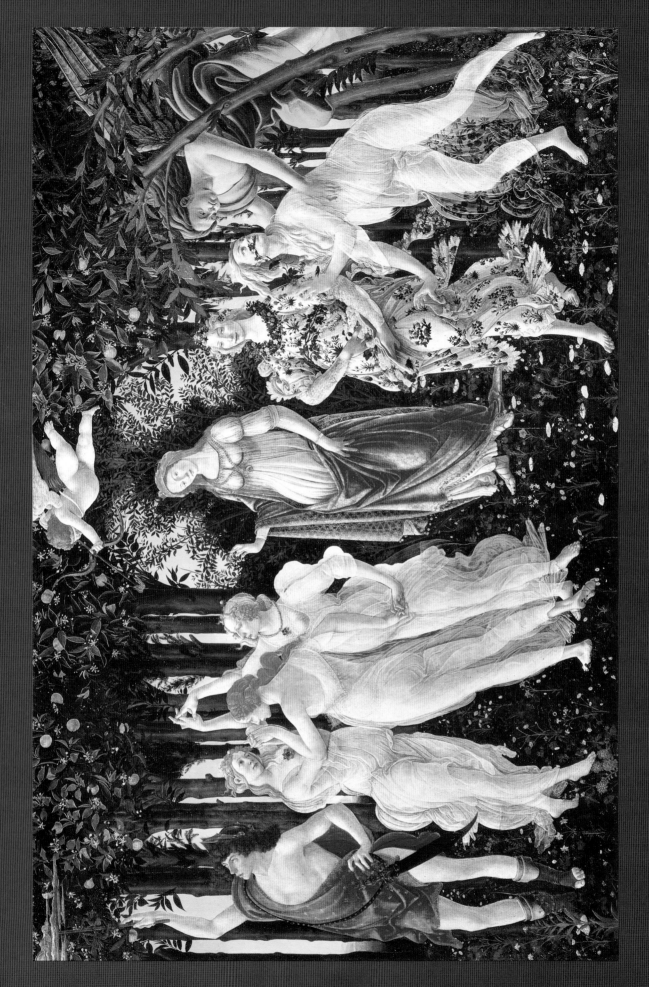

Colorplate 61. SANDRO BOTTICELLI. *Primavera. c.* 1482(?). Panel, 6' 8" x 10' 4". Uffizi Gallery, Florence.
Probably commissioned by Lorenzo di Pierfrancesco de' Medici for his Florentine palace at the time of his wedding

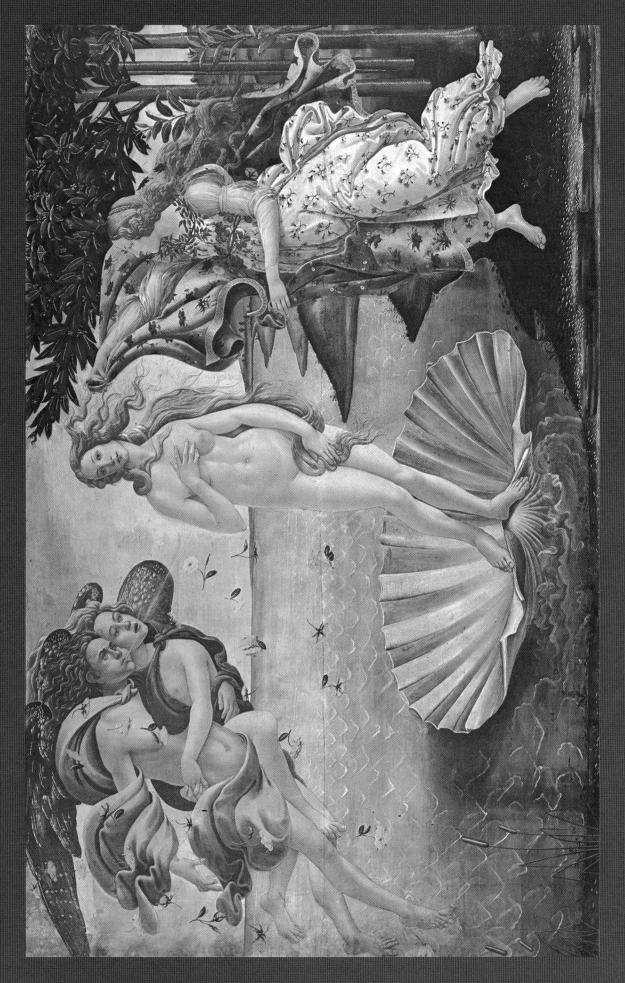

Colorplate 62. SANDRO BOTTICELLI. *Birth of Venus*. c. 1484–86. Canvas. 5' 9" x 9' 2". Uffizi Gallery, Florence. Probably commissioned by a member of the Medici family

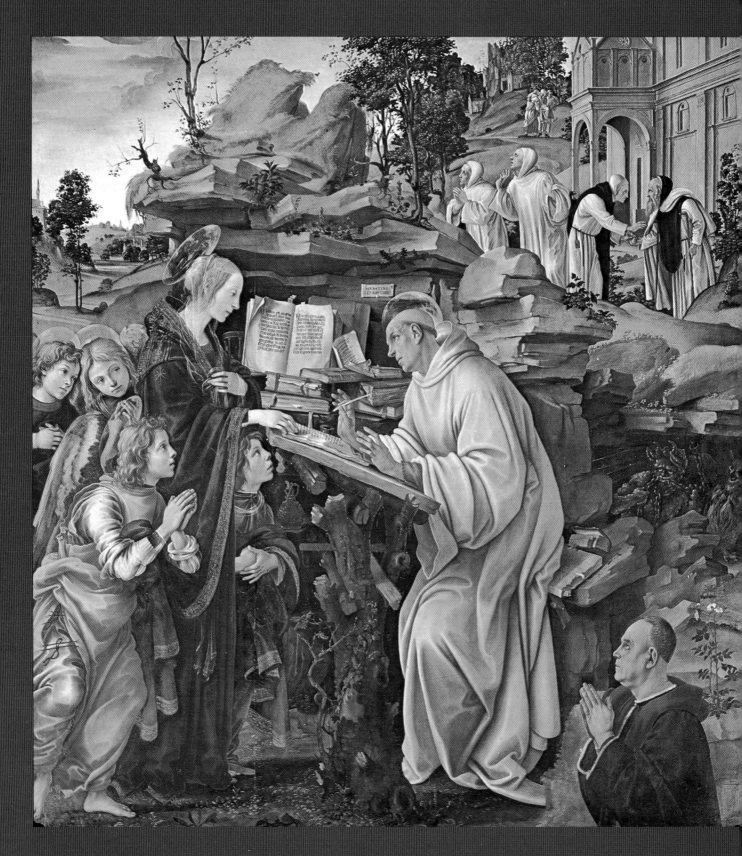

Colorplate 63. FILIPPINO LIPPI. *Vision of St. Bernard.* c. 1485—90. Panel, 82 x 77".
Church of the Badia, Florence. Commissioned by Francesco del Pugliese for the monastic
Church of Le Campora at Marignolle, near Florence

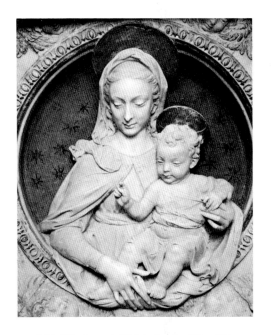

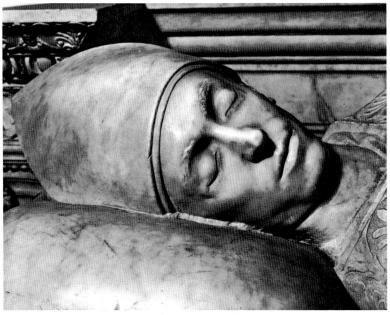

301. Virgin and Child, detail of fig. 300

302. Head of the Cardinal of Portugal, detail of fig. 300

Although it is documented that Antonio was helped by several assistants, as well as by his brother Bernardo, the monument leaves us in no doubt as to the identity of the designer and leading master. As compared with earlier tombs, a tremendous change has taken place. To use an overworked polarity, up to that moment the Renaissance tomb was a static monument; Antonio has made it dynamic. There is no closed architectural structure, the outer frame of the tomb being provided by the arch of the chapel wall. Marble curtains, common in Gothic tombs and used by Donatello and Michelozzo in their monument to the antipope John XXIII, are reintroduced, but—as earlier—they have been drawn aside as if to disclose a vision. On the tomb, the cardinal, vested as a deacon and wearing a bishop's miter, lies on a bier above a marble coffin that Antonio imitated—at the cardinal's request—from an ancient Roman porphyry sarcophagus that then stood in the portico of the Pantheon. On the richly ornamented pilasters that embrace the sarcophagus, two angels who seem to have just alighted are genuflecting. One bears the crown of eternal life, the other originally carried the palm of victory. No panels divide the background, which, save for an ornamental structure in the center, is a continuous surface of deep red-veined marble that was once covered with gilded designs to resemble a red velvet brocaded cloth of honor. Against this background two angels seem to fly in, holding a circular marble wreath. Here, against a ground of blue with gold stars, the Virgin and Child bless the departed cardinal (fig. 301). This heavenly vision seems to be resting here just for an instant, poised against the architecture by the efforts of the winged cherub heads, and in a moment it might move on.

The angel with the crown can be attributed to the conservative Bernardo, but the angel who once held the

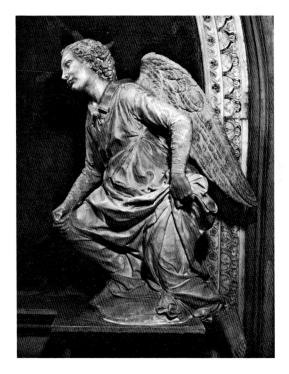

303. Angel, detail of fig. 300

palm (fig. 303) shows the lightness and dynamism of Antonio's style in its delicately crumpled drapery surfaces and the gossamer shimmer of light over features and hair. Antonio was as aware as Desiderio of the luminous possibilities of marble, but found other means of exploiting it. The Madonna and Child, who are placed so that the light in the chapel never leaves their features, show that Antonio enhanced and unified his sculpture through light that flowed over the surfaces of flesh and drapery.

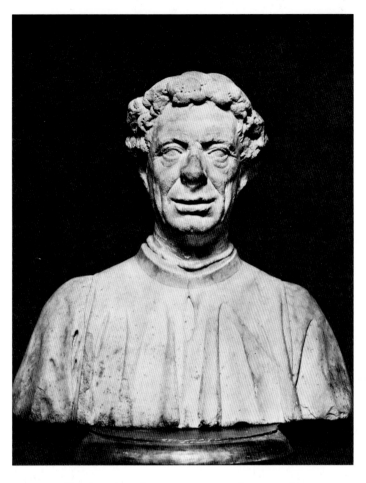

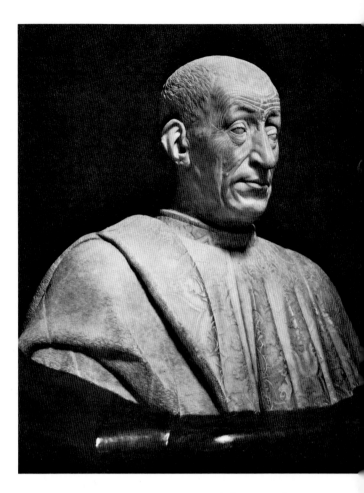

304. ANTONIO ROSSELLINO. *Bust of Matteo Palmieri.*
1468. Marble, height 21". Bargello, Florence. Probably
commissioned by Matteo Palmieri

305. BENEDETTO DA MAIANO. *Bust of Pietro Mellini.*
1474. Marble, height 21". Bargello, Florence. Probably
commissioned by Pietro Mellini

Most touching of all is the young cardinal himself, who seems to dream of the Paradise to which the sacred figures promise him entrance—although it lies around us as we stand in this most perfect of Quattrocento chapels. Desiderio, so the documents tell us, supplied a head of the cardinal, doubtless a death mask, since the cardinal was in no condition to pose for a sculptor during his final agony. From this, Antonio worked out a portrait at once persuasive in its reliance on reality and flawlessly organized as a work of art (fig. 302). The same sense of soft gradation of luminous surfaces, the same harmonious control of masses, the same subtle modeling is carried into the smallest details of the tomb, especially the plinth, which was designed by Antonio and executed by Antonio and Bernardo. Youthful genii hold cornucopias on the ends, and in the center a garland, held by unicorns, enframes a smiling death's head, as if the tomb were a portal to a life of gladness.

The liveliness, vigor, and harmony of form that mark Antonio's style are evident even in his portrait of the humanist Matteo Palmieri (fig. 304). Despite damage to the surface, Antonio's representation of Matteo is a striking example of the bust portraits of men that became popular in Florence in the middle and later Quat-

trocento. The subject seems to radiate intelligence and good will; it is indeed a "speaking likeness." Yet beyond this realism lies Antonio's instinctive sense of how to control the masses so that they harmonize, fold against fold, wrinkle against wrinkle; and a surprising nobility of form emerges from what could have been, in the hands of another artist, a caricature.

BENEDETTO AND GIULIANO DA MAIANO

A host of marble sculptors were at work in the later Quattrocento; one of the most vigorous was Benedetto da Maiano (c. 1442–97), who also came from a family of stonecutters. Maiano is still a perfect Quattrocento village because it lies within the boundaries of a Florentine estate under severe legal restrictions against change. It is close to the still-operating quarries where the *pietra serena* for the columns, arches, and decorative trim of Florentine Renaissance churches and palaces was extracted. Benedetto's portrait of Pietro Mellini (fig. 305) presents a topographic survey of the wrinkled features of the elderly subject with an exhaustive accuracy possibly inspired by Netherlandish art. Yet even if Benedetto has observed his subject with Flemish precision, he has also endowed him with Roman majesty. More than any other portrait bust of its time, Benedetto's Mellini approaches the honesty of Republican and early Imperial Roman portraiture.

Benedetto and his brother Giuliano da Maiano were architects as well as sculptors. Giuliano (1432–90) is best known as a woodworker and executor of architectural ornament, but since his name turns up so often in documents connected with the Pazzi family, he has been credited with the design of two major works of architecture long attributed to Brunelleschi, the façade of the Pazzi Chapel (see fig. 144) and the Palazzo Pazzi, now known as the Pazzi-Quaratesi (fig. 306). Although both attributions are tentative, the delicacy of the designs are in keeping with what we know about Giuliano. The façade of the Pazzi Chapel was not completed until 1461, fifteen years after Brunelleschi's death, and there is no bond between the building itself and the portico, which was clearly an afterthought. This evidence reinforces the sharp contrast between the sometimes trifling detail of the upper story and the simplicity of Brunelleschi's geometrical architecture. The tiny paired pilasters behind which the central arch seems to be disappearing, the molded panels of *pietra serena*, and the entablature with its strigil motif seem more appropriate to wood than to stone architecture.

A similar taste is at work, and with similar results, in the façade of the Palazzo Pazzi (fig. 306). The rustication of the ground story and the round-arched, mullioned windows of the upper two stories are obviously derived from the Palazzo Medici (see fig. 146). But above the ground story the rustication disappears and the walls are covered with smooth *intonaco* that may have been intended for fresco painting or for the scratched and tinted ornamental designs known as *sgraffiti* that were common on house façades in Florence and its subject cities. The floral ornament of the window arches resembles that on the central arch of the Pazzi Chapel façade. No crowning cornice was constructed, and perhaps none was intended. Its absence, coupled with the row of delicate oculi that light an attic story, completes the effect of decorative charm that is in strong contrast with the power of the Palazzo Medici or the harmony of the Palazzo Rucellai. Nonetheless, the Palazzo Pazzi is typical of many smaller palaces that were built in Florence in the second half of the century.

The Palazzo Strozzi is an exception (fig. 307). Of such gigantic scale and massive bulk that it dwarfs any other residence in Florence, the Palazzo Strozzi represents the culmination of the Florentine palace type and the direct origin of the huge, blocky palaces that would ornament Cinquecento Rome. The design (fig. 308) is probably to be attributed to Benedetto da Maiano, Giuliano's younger brother, whom we have seen as a sculptor, but a still-extant wooden model was made by another Giuliano, Giuliano da Sangallo, whose work will be treated shortly. Furthermore, the colossal cornice, so necessary a feature of the design, was added

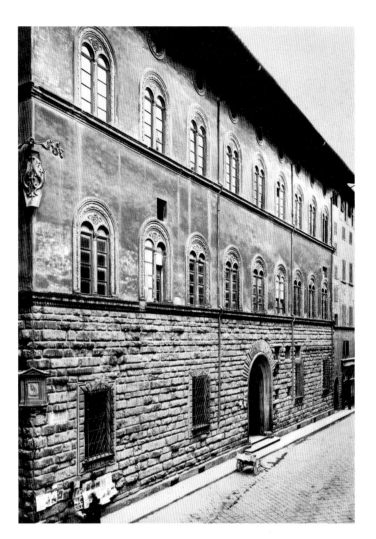

306. GIULIANO DA MAIANO. Palazzo Pazzi (now known as Palazzo Pazzi-Quaratesi), Florence. 1460s. Commissioned by Jacopo de' Pazzi

many years later by Simone del Pollaiuolo, called Il Cronaca, who succeeded Benedetto as architect. Unfortunately, the cornice stops halfway along the Via Strozzi façade, and it is still uncertain if it conforms to Benedetto's original design.

Sources tell us that the Florentine banker Filippo Strozzi wanted to build a palace that would outshine any other in Florence. Mindful of the fate of his exiled ancestor Palla, however, Filippo slyly showed designs for a more modest structure to Lorenzo de' Medici. Lorenzo thought them insignificant and urged Filippo to build something more imposing, as befitted the magnificence of the Strozzi family and of Lorenzo's Florence. This gave Filippo the green light to do what he had intended to do all along. He and his architects succeeded, not only in the noble exterior but also in the superb courtyard. The finished building differs from all other Florentine palaces of the Medici type, including Giuliano da Sangallo's model, in its unification of the stories by means of a rustication whose projection is so slightly graduated from one story to the next as to seem uniform throughout. Within the confines of the three-story type, doubtless required by the patron, Benedetto won a

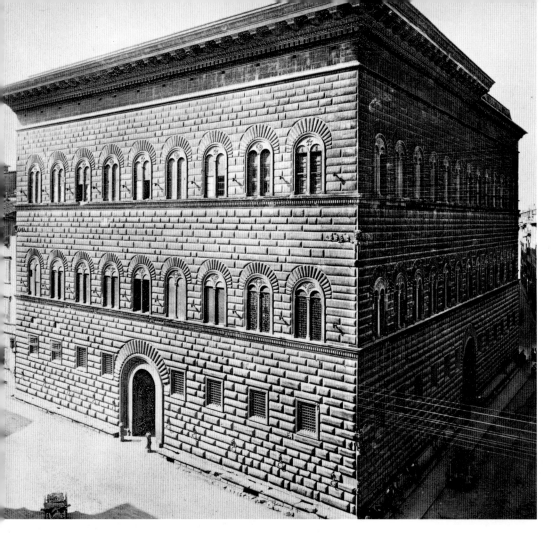

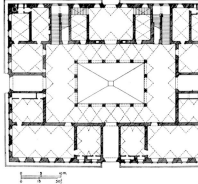

308. Plan of Palazzo Strozzi, Florence

signal victory in the battle for the harmony of all the parts, an Albertian ideal less honored than it might have been by Florentine architects after Alberti's departure. When Filippo Strozzi died in 1494, his palace reached only partway up the lowest story, to the height of the iron rings to which the reins of horses were to be tied.

Giuliano da Sangallo, in both his wooden model and his Palazzo Gondi, substituted smoothly rounded blocks of masonry for the rugged masses of the lower story of the Palazzo Medici. Benedetto further domesticated the rustication in the Palazzo Strozzi, creating a design in which each arch springs from unbroken horizontals and each keystone touches the bottom joint of a new course. The small square windows cut here and there in Michelozzo's building are brought to heel by Benedetto and given independent frames. They rest upon and are crowned by unbroken masses of stone so that they are anchored into the fenestration of the palace. Nonetheless, Benedetto, afraid of too rigid an application of his principle of harmony, varied the width of the courses and set up currents of verticals within the horizontals; in the lower story verticals multiply sharply toward the corner of the block and decrease just as sharply in the second and third stories.

The oblong courtyard (fig. 309) is, in the opinion of many scholars, the finest Quattrocento courtyard in Florence, partly because of the greater space at Benedetto's command and the greater height of his columns and arches, as compared with Michelozzo's heavier propor-

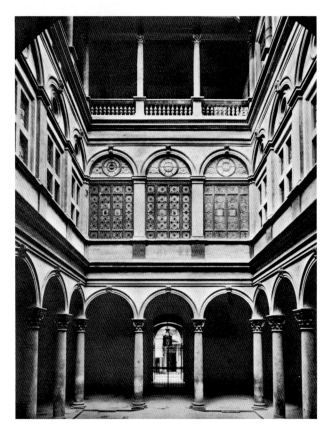

309. BENEDETTO DA MAIANO. Courtyard, Palazzo Strozzi, Florence

tions at the Palazzo Medici (see fig. 148). But there are further refinements. Mullioned windows were abandoned in favor of arches supported on piers; those on one side of the court were open (since filled with glass), and on the other sides the arches enclose cruciform windows surmounted by oculi in the lunettes. The third story is an open loggia of delicate Corinthian columns on podia united by an open balustrade. Since these columns support, as often in such Florentine galleries, a wooden beam shadowed in the eaves, they seem almost freestanding. Thus the courtyard opens not only outward in its expanded plan but also upward through the use of superimposed verticals.

GIULIANO DA SANGALLO

Giuliano da Sangallo (1443?–1516) was the first eminent member of a dynasty of architects that included Giuliano's brother Antonio the Elder and their nephew Antonio the Younger. Giuliano, perhaps the most imaginative Florentine architect of the later Quattrocento, was deeply imbued with the rarified classicism of the age, and his buildings provide a setting for the refined life that we know from the writings of contemporary historians and philosophers. His vast knowledge of Roman antiquity was derived from careful study of the monuments of the Eternal City and its surroundings,

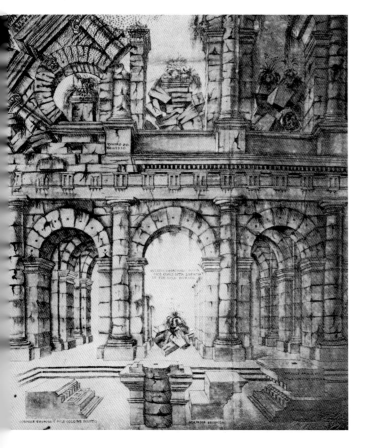

310. GIULIANO DA SANGALLO. *Theater of Marcellus.* 1480s. Drawing, 18¼ x 15½". Biblioteca Apostolica Vaticana, Vatican, Rome

and because his drawings often document buildings that no longer exist (fig. 310), they provide important information for archaeologists. At the same time, however, Giuliano never forgot his Tuscan, specifically Brunelleschian, heritage. Although he was probably only a year older than Bramante, founder of High Renaissance architecture, Giuliano did not produce any convincing work in the new, grand style.

But his Florentine buildings of the 1480s are delightful, especially the villa at Poggio a Caiano (fig. 311), about five miles west of Florence, built for Lorenzo de' Medici. Poggio a Caiano is on a modest eminence (*poggio* is Italian for hill) near the southern edge of the plain of Prato. The site was chosen to command views of the plain and the Apennines to the north and Monte Albano to the south. Giuliano's structure, a simple block with plain walls and sharply projecting eaves, is set in the center of an extensive terrace that was remodeled when the double staircase and crowning clock were added in the eighteenth century. But the temple portico is original (fig. 312), and in more than one sense. It was apparently the first in a long line of such temple porticoes, so characteristic of Renaissance and Baroque villas, and doubtless was the fruit of Giuliano's studies of Roman art and architecture. The low, broad, open proportions are unexpected, but they find their justification in the function of the portico in the unrelieved *intonaco* of the villa wall. This cream-colored plane is used again and again in Florentine villas as a ground on which windows, doors, and porticoes in *pietra serena* are grouped or scattered. Visually only the quoins at the corners support the eaves, and there is no attempt to organize the entire façade as northern Italian architects were later to do. Quite likely Giuliano was familiar with Etruscan temple pediments, which had similar proportions. In any event, an Augustan Roman temple, with its closely grouped columns and vertical emphasis, would have been out of keeping with the broad villa wall.

Having established his principle of horizontality, Giuliano enhanced it by the pedimental moldings and the ribbons that stretch out from the Medici arms and fill the pediment with continuous S-shapes. The columns are Ionic, but with a broad, fluted necking band that diminishes their apparent height and increases the importance of the capitals, in keeping with the weight of the pediment. Behind the pediment, a barrel vault roofs a loggia where, in the early morning or late afternoon, the Medici and their guests could walk or sit in the shade. A similar barrel vault, much larger, roofs the central hall of the villa, which was later decorated with a fresco by Pontormo (see fig. 579). The cream color of the *intonaco* and the gray of the *pietra serena* are relieved by a enameled terra-cotta frieze of white figures against a blue ground that unfolds legends of the ancient gods, who were very much present at the court of Lorenzo. Neither the sculptor of the frieze nor all the subjects have yet been identified. With the delights of Poggio a Caiano in our memories, we can only imagine what a

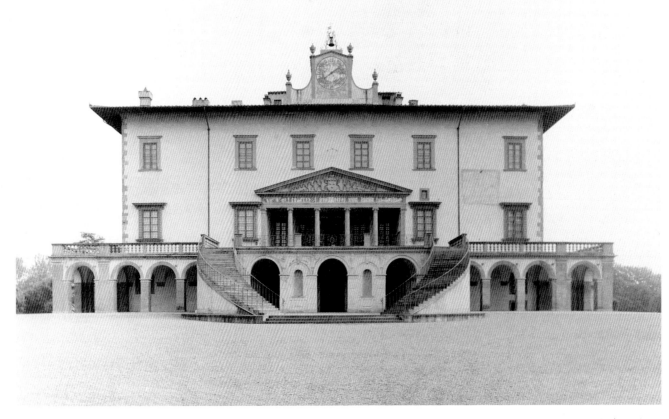

311. GIULIANO DA SANGALLO. Villa Medici, Poggio a Caiano. 1480s. Commissioned by Lorenzo de' Medici

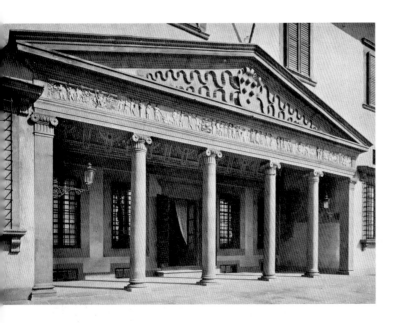

312. Portico of Villa Medici, Poggio a Caiano

paradise Giuliano would have created in Naples, if its king had built the vast palace Giuliano wished to design for him.

Giuliano's other principal extant structure is the Church of Santa Maria delle Carceri at Prato (fig. 313), built, like so many of the important churches of the later Quattrocento and early Cinquecento, to enshrine a miraculous image. The plan of Santa Maria delle Carceri (fig. 314) is a Greek cross, like that of Alberti's San Sebastiano in Mantua. It is surmounted by a dome with twelve ribs, twelve oculi, and a lantern (fig. 315) that closely follows Brunelleschi's domes for the Sacristy of San Lorenzo and for the Pazzi Chapel (see fig. 139; colorplate 37, p. 202). But Giuliano's forms are more richly modeled, in accordance with the taste of the time, and on the interior he has inserted a balustrade between the pendentives and the base of the dome. The blue-and-white terra-cotta frieze is rich with lampstands, garlands, and ribbons; and the capitals, probably carved by Giuliano himself, are figured and all different. The exterior, unfortunately left unfinished, has marble incrustation in the Albertian tradition, as seen in the Urbino panel (see fig. 386). A Doric lower story is surmounted by an Ionic story two-thirds its height; both have pilasters clustered at the corners. The proportions of the stories are brought into harmony with each other by paneling off the upper third of the lower story with the green marble bands (the same Prato marble used for the green incrustations of buildings in Florence) that surround all the panels.

BENOZZO GOZZOLI

The painter who seems to typify the luxurious proclivities of the 1450s was Benozzo Gozzoli (1420–97), and his career, like that of many another fashionable decorator, went up and down with the fortunes of his patrons.

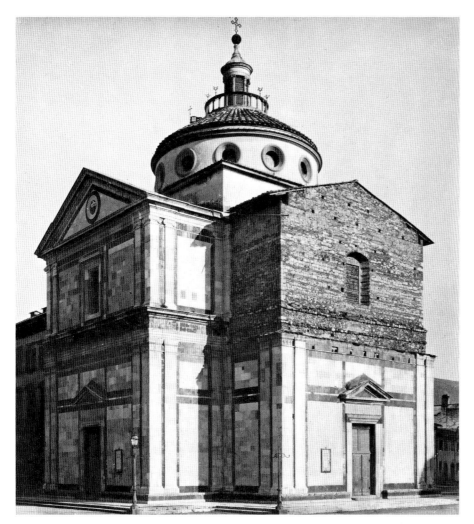

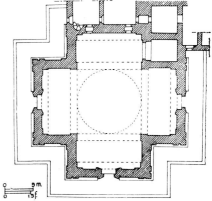

left: 313. GIULIANO DA SANGALLO. Sta. Maria delle Carceri, Prato. 1485–92. Commissioned by the Opera of Sta. Maria delle Carceri

314. Plan of Sta. Maria delle Carceri, Prato

Benozzo's long artistic activity commences in the studio of Fra Angelico, whose chief assistant he was in painting the Chapel of Nicholas V in the Vatican (see fig. 214). At the close of that commission he worked independently in Umbria, but why the Medici chose Benozzo to paint the frescoes in their chapel in the Palazzo Medici in Florence (colorplate 57, p. 298) is uncertain. Perhaps there was no one else at that moment in Florence competent to do the job; perhaps Fra Angelico had established Gozzoli's reputation. It was an inspired choice, yet never again was Benozzo able to obtain a commission of such importance, and he wandered from one lesser center to another, ending up in his seventies as a painter of country tabernacles.

The Medici belonged to the Company of the Magi, a Florentine religious organization that flourished in the Renaissance, and that may explain their choice of the Journey of the Magi as the subject for the chapel decorations. Certainly, the bright frescoes of Benozzo had nothing to do with the penitential mood of the St. Antonine-dominated *Madonna Adoring Her Child* painted by Fra Filippo Lippi for the altar of the chapel only a few years before (see fig. 221). Perhaps in 1459, after the archbishop's death, the Medici may have felt like children let out of school.

The theme is the same one that fills the background of Gentile da Fabriano's Strozzi altarpiece (see colorplate 38, p. 203), but it has been updated, and the landscape is derived from the surroundings of Florence,

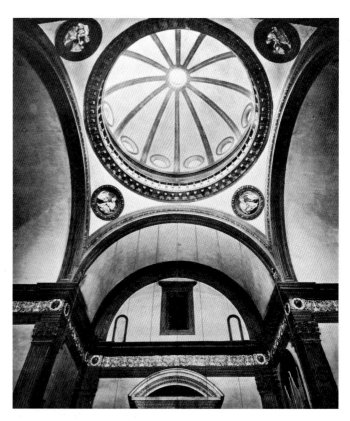

315. GIULIANO DA SANGALLO. Dome, Sta. Maria delle Carceri, Prato. 1485–92

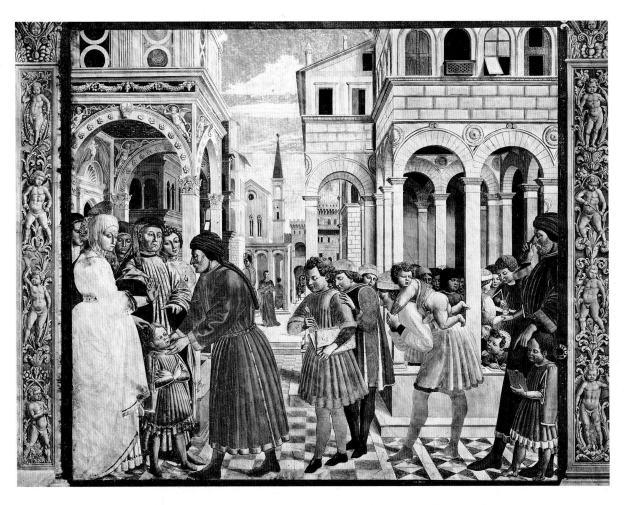

316. BENOZZO GOZZOLI. *St. Augustine Given to the Grammar Master.* 1465.
Fresco. Sant'Agostino, San Gimignano

including castles and villas in Medici possession. There is no proof for the assertion that the Magi are portraits of Cosimo de' Medici, John Palaeologus (neither is visible in the illustration), and the young Lorenzo, but the last two identifications are not impossible to accept. The second Magus does resemble the Byzantine emperor who had visited Florence twenty years earlier, and the crowned youth is shown against a laurel plant (Lorenzo is Laurentius, or laurel-growing, in Latin). The man on the white horse leading the cavalcade at the left has been identified as Piero the Gouty. In the mass of figures to the left in our colorplate, Benozzo appears, with the signature OPUS BENOTII (The work of Benozzo) on his hat. The retinue is studded with contemporary personages, a number of whom eye the spectator. The array of ceremonial costumes and horse trappings, studded with gold and blazing with red, blue, and yellow against the green of the foliage and the blue-green of the distance, is further strengthened by the red of the Florentine costume worn by all but foreigners. The composition is held together by the verticals of the trees and the curves of the roads. The walls of the small chapel are painted away with a continuous panorama that covers every wall.

Benozzo demonstrates his familiarity with the repertory of the Florentine masters. He can give us distance, set horses in perspective, and draw figures in action. Yet there is something archaistic in his insistence on line. Not so much in the rock shapes—anyone who has gone up the Via di Vincigliata above the Berenson villa I Tatti will recall similar cliffs and jagged rocks everywhere among the cypresses—but in the sharp insistence on detail throughout. The figures, for all their vivacity and motion, seem almost like polychromed wood carvings. In the Medici Chapel this effect is delightful because it harmonizes with the overall decorative nature of the frescoes, but it did not enable Benozzo to compete with his contemporaries during the ensuing years of ferment and change.

Among Benozzo's later works are the frescoes of the life of St. Augustine in Sant'Agostino in San Gimignano (fig. 316). Benozzo's faces and expressions are more wooden than ever, but the loggie, streets, and churches of the setting present a disarming picture of life in a Florentine subject town. Gothic windows and battlements compete with the newest Renaissance inventions, all neatly drawn and daintily colored, while doll-like people dressed in the tubular folds of Fra Angelico act

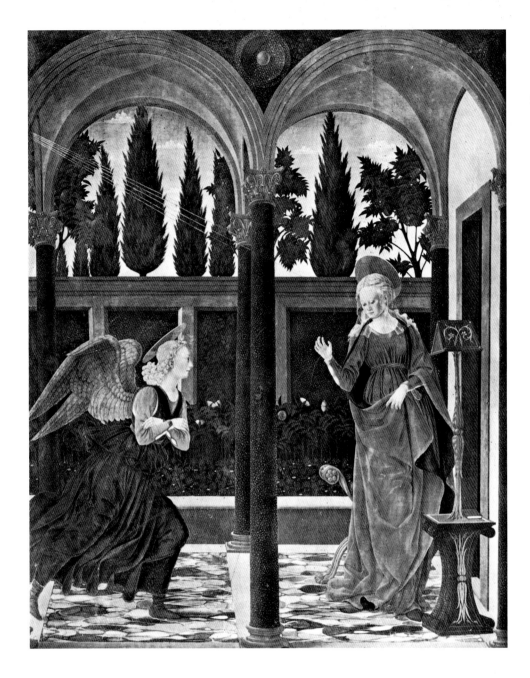

317. ALESSO BALDOVINETTI. *Annunciation*. Before 1460. Panel, 65³/4 x 54". Uffizi Gallery, Florence. Commissioned by the Salvestrini Fathers, perhaps with the intervention of the Medici, for S. Giorgio alla Costa, Florence

out the stories. Benozzo surely knew Albertian perspective, and his combinations of figures in the foreground with architectural spaces are based on works by Fra Angelico and Ghiberti. Benozzo's chief charm to us, and probably his chief drawback to the Florentines, was his naïveté. Augustine's mother, St. Monica, primly pushes her slightly distrustful son into the hands of the grammar master, whose pupils follow obediently, but the most striking detail in the picture, to modern eyes, may be the exposed backside of a baby at the right, who is being dragged off over the father's shoulder.

ALESSO BALDOVINETTI

Among the artists of the Florentine Renaissance, Alesso Baldovinetti (1425–99) was the only one to have been brought up in comfortable, patrician surroundings. The Baldovinetti were among the oldest families in Florence, and their house-tower, visible from the Ponte Vecchio,

still stands in Florence. Alesso was apprenticed to Domenico Veneziano at Sant'Egidio, and he completed the frescoes there on his own many years later for the cost of the materials alone. He soon came under the influence of Andrea del Castagno, and in his journal he records having painted, more or less from Castagno's dictation when the latter was ill, a Hell scene "with many infernal furies." But the gentleness of Alesso's art had little in common with that of Castagno, from whom he seems to have absorbed chiefly a devotion to line and pattern. It is a different kind of pattern, though, filled with Domenico Veneziano's light and spun out to delightfully improbable conclusions. Whimsical, witty, charming, unsentimental, and eventually so conservative that he seems to have cut himself off from the mainstream of Florentine ideas, Baldovinetti was nonetheless capable of creating images of enduring beauty and refinement.

In Baldovinetti's lovely *Annunciation* (fig. 317), painted before 1460, Mary receives Gabriel in a little loggia

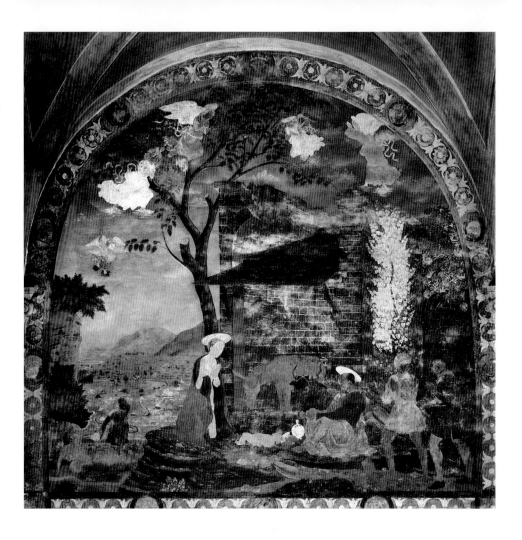

318. ALESSO BALDOVINETTI. *Nativity*. 1460–62. Fresco, 13' 4" x 14'. Atrium, SS. Annunziata, Florence. Commissioned by Arrigo Arrigucci

whose colonnettes recall those of Domenico Veneziano in the St. Lucy altarpiece (see colorplate 48, p. 258). Beyond a low parapet one looks into Mary's closed garden, with its fruit trees (perhaps the *cedro*, the huge Italian lemon) and cypresses. According to the Book of Wisdom, Mary is a cedar of Lebanon (also *cedro* in Italian) and a cypress on Mount Zion. Mary and Gabriel, with their small heads and long, slender bodies, represent the utmost in patrician refinement. Gabriel, his blond tresses as elegantly curled as those of the pages in Gozzoli's frescoes, trips in to bear the news to Mary. In a pose derived from Donatello's *Annunciation* (see fig. 245), she turns from her reading, draws her cloak about her, and lifts her right hand in a gesture of combined wonder and docility.

The color is as refined as the content and form, and as unexpected, especially in the dull red of the arches. The rose and powder blue of Mary's tunic and mantle are reversed in the garments of the angel. Brighter tones, including pinks and yellows, are picked up in the flowers and in the haphazard pattern of the marble scraps that compose the pavement. Capitals, ornament, and haloes are painted—not real—gold, to show Alesso's command of the new rendering of light. Although some colors are highly saturated, the effect is delicate and restrained.

The same grace and wit are visible in Baldovinetti's *Madonna and Child* (colorplate 58, p. 299), a work of about 1460. The Virgin is seated on a backless chair

above a vista of the Arno Valley—a winding stream, farms, roads, cypresses, and the hills diminishing under a few sunny summer clouds. Mary folds her hands in adoration of the Christ Child on the parapet, who appeals to her to finish swaddling his body. Baldovinetti records subtle gradations of tone (learned from Domenico Veneziano) that pass over the face of his shy young Mary. The flow of blond locks seen through Mary's veil, which escapes in a ponytail down her back, and the shadow of her head on the golden disk of her halo are delightful touches.

The delicacies of Alesso's Arno Valley landscape should be kept in mind as we examine a mural at the Annunziata (fig. 318) that occupied him off and on from 1460 to 1462. This very length of time should indicate that he did not follow the traditional piecemeal method, by means of which Andrea del Castagno, let us say, could have knocked out a fresco this size in a month. That method was all right for Castagno, who cared little about the subtleties of diffused light or Alberti's total visual unity. Baldovinetti seems to have concluded that he could not obtain such unity, and more especially the subtleties of light gradations, by traditional means. He therefore painted only a few portions of the picture in true fresco, and then waited until the plaster had dried so that he could paint *a secco* as if working on an altarpiece. Such a procedure would have been dangerous even in an interior, but the *Nativity* in the atrium of the church was exposed to winter fogs and even rain. In

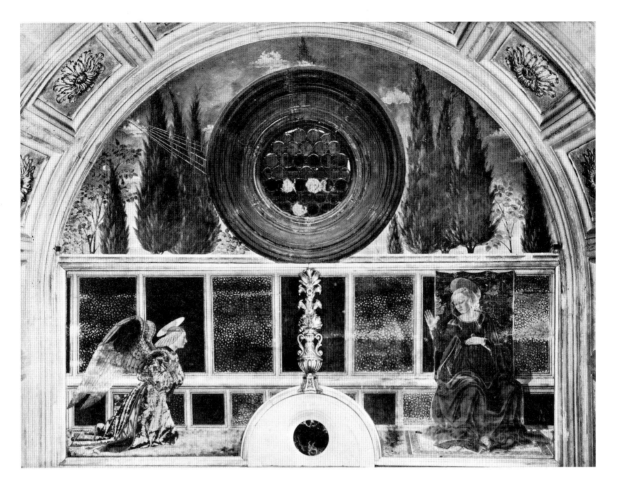

319. ALESSO BALDOVINETTI. *Annunciation*. 1466–67. Fresco and panel, width of chapel wall 15' 9". Chapel of the Cardinal of Portugal, S. Miniato, Florence. Commissioned by the executors of the will of the Cardinal of Portugal

time the *a secco* faces, hands, and drapery have peeled off, and Alesso's underdrawing is now visible. Even so, the painting is beautiful in the airy openness of its setting, with the small figures, the lofty ruin and shed, the trees, the angels, and the view over the expansive plain of Prato to the foothills of the Apennines. The details are wonderfully accurate, and the unprecedented vast plain is filled with the light of a clear winter day.

Baldovinetti was the choice when, in 1466, the executors of the Cardinal of Portugal wanted a painter to decorate the walls, lunettes, and spandrels of the Chapel of the Cardinal of Portugal in San Miniato (see p. 296). The tomb (see fig. 300) had been completed that very year. Baldovinetti's *Annunciation* (fig. 319) is placed over the empty cardinal's throne that faces the Rossellino tomb. Again Baldovinetti had to experiment, possibly because of pressure to finish the paintings rapidly. While the background, with its cypresses and cedars, is painted in fresco, the wall, bench, and figures of the foreground are painted on an unprimed oak panel, doubtless in the artist's studio in the winter months of 1466–67. Here and there the color has peeled away to show the grain.

Baldovinetti must have been impressed by the beauty and youth of the cardinal and by Antonio Rossellino's exquisite tomb across the chapel, for a new solemnity enters his work. The model for the Virgin (fig. 320) also

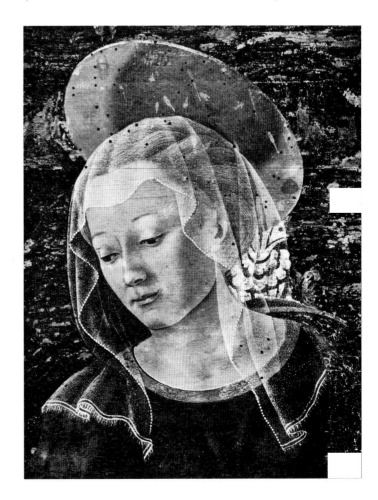

320. Head of the Virgin, detail of fig. 319

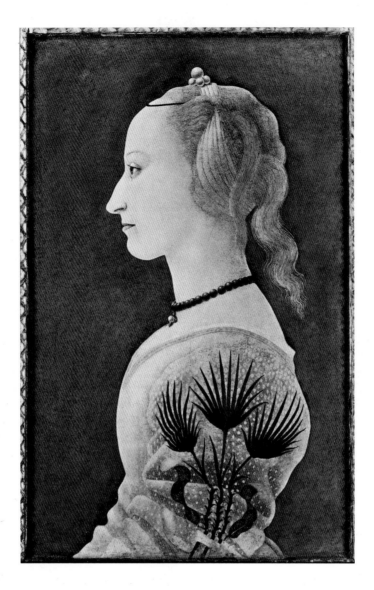

posed for the Louvre *Madonna and Child* (see colorplate 58, p. 299); here the Virgin accepts her new role seriously, lifting her right hand as she places her left on her body, within which she seems to feel the conception taking place. The angel who kneels before her is dressed in a deacon's dalmatic, as is the cardinal on his tomb; a circle of coral beads crowns his head, a ruby carved into the shape of a strawberry rests on his brow, and peacock eyes flash from his wings. There are seven marble and porphyry panels behind, like the seven Gifts of the Holy Spirit or the seven Joys and seven Sorrows of the Virgin (these and many more were listed in a special paragraph on the mystical significance of the number seven by St. Antonine of Florence). The twelve panels of the bench probably refer to the twelve apostles, and the lily that in the Rossellino tomb symbolizes the cardinal's purity enters the composition, carved and gilded, to become the lily of Mary's virginity. The choice of the Annunciation, a strange subject for a tomb chapel, is appropriate to the symbolism of the pictorial decoration of the chapel, built around the theme of the closed gate of Ezekiel, which is connected with the Annunciation by long tradition (see p. 81 and figs. 245 and 285).

Baldovinetti's profile portrait of an unknown Florence woman (fig. 321) represents the ultimate in patrician Florentine Quattrocento elegance; her slender features can still be seen in the Florentine aristocracy today. She is posed in the conventional profile view that persists in female portraits until almost the end of the century, long after male sitters are shown turned toward the observer (see fig. 350). Baldovinetti emphasizes the crisp lines of her profile and the dainty flow of her ponytail against the blue-gray of the background, which can be read as sky or as an abstract blue ground.

13
Science, Poetry, and Prose

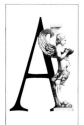t the beginning of the final third of the Quattrocento, few of the founders of Renaissance art were still alive. Uccello was not working at all, Luca della Robbia was old and his style had deteriorated. Piero della Francesca was painting in Urbino and Borgo Sansepolcro, Alberti designing for Florence and Mantua. The new generation of painters and painter-sculptors was encouraged by what appears, in view of the general economic decline, as extravagant patronage on the part of the great Florentine families, providing an enormous demand for their art. The period was dominated by five artists—Antonio del Pollaiuolo, Andrea del Verrocchio, Sandro Botticelli, Filippino Lippi, and Domenico del Ghirlandaio. Toward the middle of the period, new courses for art were laid out by Leonardo da Vinci and by two visitors to Florence, Luca Signorelli and Pietro Perugino, but none of the three were in Florence for very long at this time, and for various reasons their activity, like that of the Florentine Piero di Cosimo, belongs to other chapters.

Despite their relative freedom, our five artists were to a certain extent limited by the discoveries of their predecessors. The methods of depiction of space, form, and light were well known, and there seemed little point in merely repeating them. But many new fields remained for exploration, and the five leading masters set out to investigate them, in three different directions. Doubtless each direction appealed to a somewhat different sector of Florentine society. None of the three can be labeled conservative. All were basically new, and all were destined to have a strong influence on future developments.

The first of these later Quattrocento tendencies begins with the premise that all nature is one: that there is no essential difference between humans and other animals; that plant, animal, and human physiology are as worthy of study as the principles of form, space, and light; and that motion, growth, decay, and dissolution are more truly characteristic of our world than are mathematical relationships or, indeed, any other apparently enduring verity. The greatest exponent of this vitalistic, animistic, dynamic, scientific trend (these are epithets, not names) is Pollaiuolo, but similar concerns motivated Verrocchio as well, if to a less marked degree. These two masters, to whom form is a by-product of motion, are the only two painter-sculptors of the period, and they are also the most original sculptors. Pollaiuolo seems to have appealed especially to the elite of the circle of Lorenzo de' Medici.

The second current is concerned less with the outer world, from which, indeed, it seeks to withdraw, than with the life of the spirit. This lyrical, poetic, romantic current (again these are mere characterizations) often ignores tangible reality in favor of abstract values of line and tone and chooses subjects that express emotional yearnings. The unchallenged leader in this movement is Botticelli, but Filippino Lippi at times keeps pace with him and at times goes beyond him into the realms of the unreal. This second current seems to have pleased less the Medici themselves than those in their circle, and especially the Neoplatonic philosophers.

The third trend emphasizes the here and now. The foregrounds of their scriptural narratives and scenes from saints' legends are filled with contemporary Florentines, while the backgrounds show how Florence looked or how the painters thought it should look. Prose, not poetry, is the aim of the artist; their representations are not only exact and descriptive, but also well balanced, measured, composed, and intelligible. Underneath an exterior of admirable craftsmanship, this naturalistic current (again, not a title) can also on occasion express an interest in psychological relationships. Ghirlandaio was the master of this style, and because he appealed to the well-to-do citizen without intellectual pretenses, the successful merchant and banker, his shop was the most heavily patronized in Florence.

ANTONIO DEL POLLAIUOLO

Antonio del Pollaiuolo (1431/32–98) excels in subjects of action, especially mythologies, in which his naturalism can be allowed free rein; when he treats scriptural themes, they sometimes take on a fierce air that has little to do with any religious purpose. His name means "poultry-keeper," apparently a reference to his father's occupation. Piero, Antonio's older brother and assistant, was a painter—a dull one, judging from his one signed work. Antonio began as a goldsmith and designer of embroideries with gold and silver thread. One would expect to find him a master of linear precision, and so he is, but his fascination with the human figure in mo-

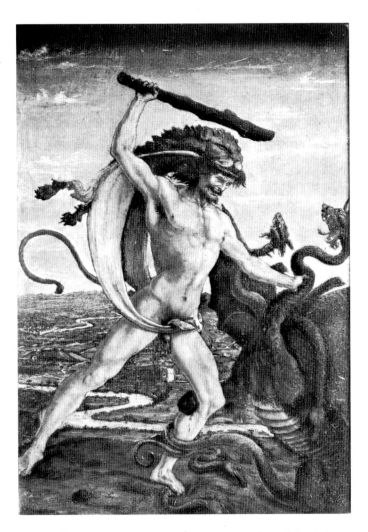

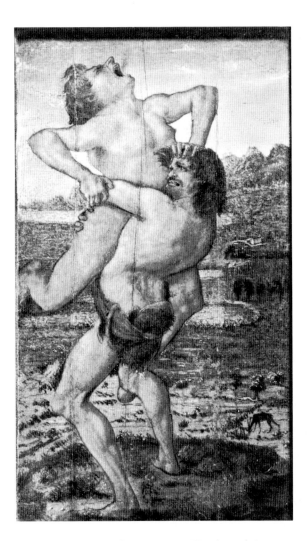

322. ANTONIO DEL POLLAIUOLO. *Hercules and the Hydra.*
c. 1460. Panel, 6³/₄ x 4³/₄". Uffizi Gallery, Florence. Probably
commissioned for the Medici Palace

323. ANTONIO DEL POLLAIUOLO. *Hercules and Antaeus.*
c. 1460. Panel, 6¹/₄ x 3³/₄". Uffizi Gallery, Florence. Probably
commissioned for the Medici Palace

tion is a surprise. No artist in any medium since Hellenistic times had treated this theme with anything approaching his ability. Castagno, who greatly influenced Pollaiuolo, had tried, in his *David* shield (see fig. 273), but his attempt seems stiff when compared with the violent movement of Pollaiuolo's figures.

About 1460 Antonio painted three large pictures representing the Labors of Hercules that are listed in the 1492 inventory of the Medici Palace. Hercules, a favorite Florentine hero, appeared on the seal of the Republic in the late Duecento and was represented in monumental art as early as the reliefs by Andrea Pisano on the Campanile. Pollaiuolo's three paintings were among the works moved to the Palazzo dei Priori after the expulsion of the Medici, which suggests that they probably had a political content. The paintings are among the first large-scale mythological works known to us and because they were painted on canvas, it is possible that their original function was as banners for a festival or tournament. The originals are lost, but Pollaiuolo's two tiny panels of *Hercules and the Hydra* and *Hercules and Antaeus* (figs. 322, 323) probably preserve two of the larger compositions.

As in Piero della Francesca's Montefeltro portraits (see

colorplates 54, 55, p. 264), the figures are silhouetted against earth and sky. But while Piero's figures project a serene control over nature, Antonio's erupt from nature and seem pitted against it in mortal combat. Compositionally, the necks and tail of the hydra are counterparts of the winding river. Hercules seems almost as feral as the lion whose skin he wears and no less cruel than Antaeus, whose strength derives from his mother, the Earth. Antonio chooses not to represent Hercules as a glorious hero, superior to the forces of evil that he is vanquishing. In rendering the human figure, he avoids its potential nobility or the play of light upon its surfaces, emphasizing instead the strain imposed on muscles and even bones by its activity. His bodies seem pushed to the limits of their capability. He must have studied carefully the behavior of bodies in motion, and evidence suggests that he dissected corpses to understand how muscles, tendons, and bones are interrelated. Like Baldovinetti, Pollaiuolo lets our eyes wander over the rich tapestry of the earth in the backgrounds: the Arno Valley in *Hercules and the Hydra*, with a microscopic Florence at the extreme left, and the seacoast in *Hercules and Antaeus*, with a little city at the right and the Apuan Alps above.

Probably during the 1470s, Antonio repeated the

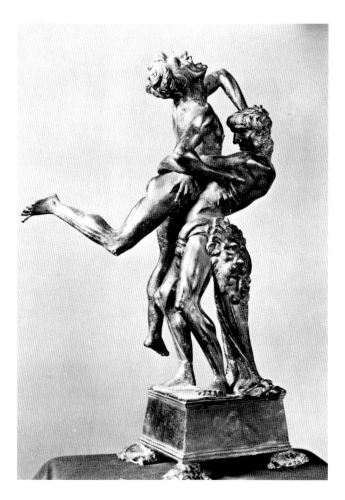

Antaeus composition in a small bronze group (fig. 324) that broke the rules that earlier sculptors had followed. The contours of medieval and previous Renaissance statues and groups had been limited by the ideal contours of the mass, even when the bronze medium theoretically allowed a free rein. In Pollaiuolo's revolution—and, indeed, that of Verrocchio as well—figures can move in any direction necessitated by their actions. To be sure, Antonio Rossellino had led the way, in the dynamism of the soaring angels and floating Madonna tondo above the tomb of the Cardinal of Portugal. But his figures were constrained by the overall composition of the monument. Pollaiuolo's figures do not seem to be posed; their actions seem to determine the composition, and its contours are defined by flying legs and arms, clutching toes, noses, open mouths, even unruly curls. For one of the first times since antiquity, surrounding space is electrified by the energies developed within a sculptural group.

In his engraved *Battle of the Nudes* (fig. 325), the largest Florentine print of the fifteenth century, Pollaiuolo's control of naturalistic anatomy at first seems somewhat less secure. This impression is due in part to the shading, which may be intentionally exaggerated because of the print's probable use as a demonstration of anatomy for other artists. If the print had a narrative subject, it has eluded identification by scholars. The unifying themes appear to be struggle and death. At the lower left a nude is about to dispatch a prostrate foe, but his intended victim plants a foot in his groin and aims a dagger at his eyes. Two swordsmen in the foreground are equally matched and may well dispose of each other,

324. ANTONIO DEL POLLAIUOLO. *Hercules and Antaeus.* Probably 1470s. Bronze, height 18" (including base). Bargello, Florence. Probably commissioned by a member of the Medici family for the Medici Palace

325. ANTONIO DEL POLLAIUOLO. *Battle of the Nudes.* c. 1465. Engraving, 15¹⁄₈ x 23¹⁄₄". The Metropolitan Museum of Art, New York (Joseph Pulitzer Bequest, 1917)

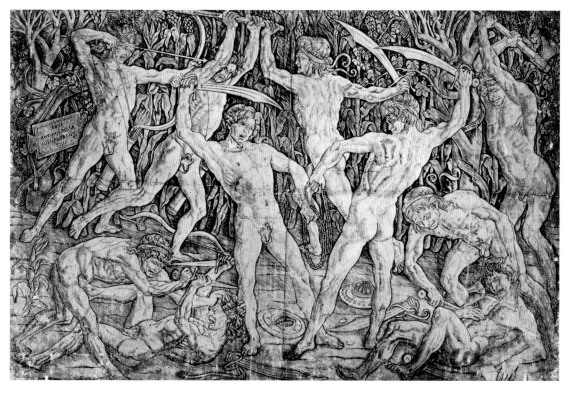

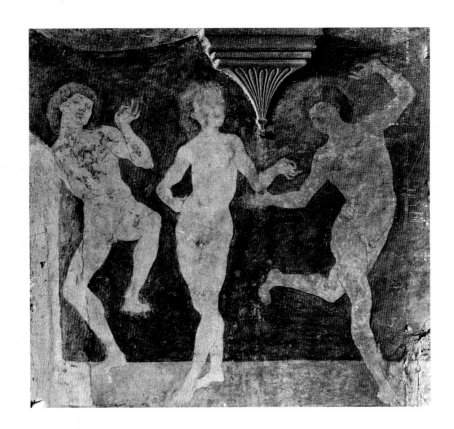

326. ANTONIO DEL POLLAIUOLO. *Dance of the Nudes* (portion). Presumably 1470s. Fresco underdrawing. Villa La Gallina, Florence. Probably commissioned by a member of the Lanfredini family

as will the figures just behind them, armed with sword and ax. At the right a man withdraws his sword from the side of his dying enemy, unaware that he is about to be slaughtered by the uplifted ax of a man behind him, who in turn does not notice the arrow aimed at him by the archer at the upper left. The composition of intertwined figures in superimposed registers to indicate depth may have been suggested by ancient Roman sarcophagi, especially those dealing with the story of Hercules, which Antonio may have studied as he worked on his paintings of that legend. He sets his figures against a background of dense vegetation of corn, olive trees, and grapevines. As much as the actions, the expressions of pain or cruelty on the faces of Antonio's figures convey the horror of a scene that has its only medieval counterpart in the torments of Hell in representations of the Last Judgment (see fig. 116).

Equally unrestrained is the dance of nude figures painted by Antonio on a wall in the Villa La Gallina, near Florence (fig. 326). Their present appearance is deceptively like the red figures of Greek vase painting, since the painted surface has completely fallen away and the surviving underdrawing has been enhanced by a repainted dark background. Originally, the figures must have been carefully modeled. One figure, at the extreme left, moves in a pose frequently seen in ancient sculpture, but the other poses seem derived from direct observation. They are so uninhibited, in fact, that one wonders if Antonio had models dancing about his studio, as Rodin was later to do. The subject of the *Dance of the Nudes* is no more easily resolved than that of the *Battle of the Nudes.*

Christian subjects seem to have interested Antonio little, and he generally turned over such commissions in whole or in part to his brother. But the order for a

monumental altarpiece of St. Sebastian for the Pucci family chapel at Santissima Annunziata, where it would be seen in competition with frescoes by Andrea del Castagno (see colorplate 51, p. 261; fig. 274), apparently could not be resisted. The painting (colorplate 59, p. 300), Antonio's most ambitious extant work, is a milestone in Renaissance art. For the first time, it might be argued, a large-scale composition is produced by the actions of the figures rather than by their mere disposition. The triangle is hardly a new idea in pictorial composition, but Antonio's triangle is the product of the figures and their movements: the minute the last arrow is discharged and the bowmen leave, the triangle will dissolve. The painting was still the object of great admiration in Vasari's time, even after all that Leonardo and Michelangelo had achieved in the intervening period. Antonio may have left the face of the saint to Piero, but the longbowmen and crossbowmen became a showcase to demonstrate Antonio's skill. The positions of strain seen in the two crossbowmen who wind their bows seem to display everything Antonio knew about muscular tension.

In reality there are only three poses among the six archers. Antonio has reversed each figure, as if he had turned around a clay model rather than following the common painter's practice of reversing the cartoon. Sculptor that he was, he may have done exactly that, although the flesh is so convincing that it looks as if living men posed for him in the final stages; the effect of vivacity is increased by the scale, for the figures in the foreground are nearly life-sized. Michelangelo used the pose of the nude crossbowman for one of the nude youths on the Sistine Ceiling and, much later, for an angel hauling two souls into Heaven in the *Last Judgment.* Antonio's incisive contour, a new kind of analytic

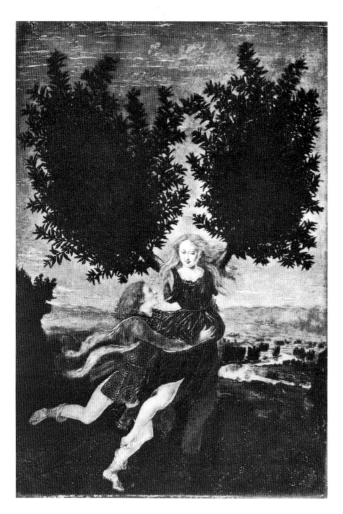

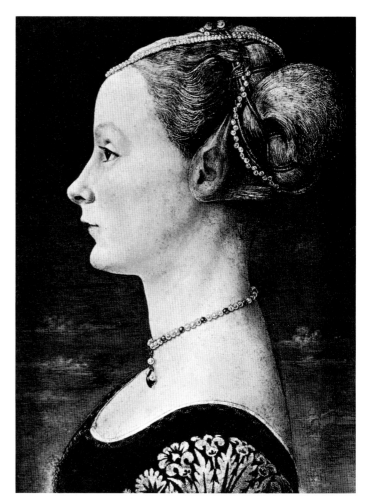

327. ANTONIO DEL POLLAIUOLO. *Apollo and Daphne.* Undated. Panel, 11⁵/₈ x 7⁷/₈". National Gallery, London

328. ANTONIO DEL POLLAIUOLO. *Portrait of a Young Woman.* 1460s. Panel, 18¹/₈ x 13³/₈". Museo Poldi Pezzoli, Milan

line that describes shapes with such delicacy that we sense how they revolve in depth, leads directly to Michelangelo.

The Arno Valley landscape in the background gave Antonio an opportunity to exercise his skill in the rendering of nature. But he must have done this to please himself, because at a height of eight feet above the altar, this landscape would have been virtually invisible. Even in the National Gallery today much of the delicacy of observation is imperceptible. The triumphal arch is adorned with battle reliefs and looks more like a ruined Renaissance façade than like anything in Rome. In the distance, enveloped in nature, should lie Rome—which Antonio had not yet visited. He substituted Florence, with an occasional hint of a Roman theater, dome, or obelisk. The shapes of the hills are taken from those near Florence, and so is the point of view. To study this landscape Antonio may have stood on Monte Albano near Carmignano, above Poggio a Caiano. From here the city becomes a speck in the luminous, blue-green valley. Antonio was interested not in the abstract shapes that Baldovinetti found in nature, but in the spontaneity of growth and the sense of atmosphere over hills and farms and among the trees. The Arno sweeps into view, moving too rapidly to offer reflections in the manner of

Piero della Francesca's still waters. Then the water hits a dam and a shoal, and the surface breaks into rapids. We know that Antonio used oil as a medium in his altarpiece for the Chapel of the Cardinal of Portugal in San Miniato; perhaps he used it here as well, or at least oil glazes, to convey the soft effects of light, distant haze, soft foliage, and rushing water.

Antonio's ability to render the transitory effects of nature is also displayed in the tiny *Apollo and Daphne* (fig. 327). Before the curves of the Arno, touched in with an almost Impressionist softness of brushwork, the god, a long-haired adolescent in a short tunic, rushes across the meadow in pursuit of the unwilling Daphne. At the point of embracing her, he finds only defeat; her father, a river-god, has answered her prayer for salvation. Daphne's left leg has taken root, her arms have become branches, and she looks down smiling, for in another minute she will become a laurel tree. Perhaps this picture was intended as an allegory of the invincibility of Lorenzo de' Medici's government, for the laurel was his plant and also that of his second cousin and neighbor, Lorenzo di Pierfrancesco de' Medici. Two branches might even refer to both.

Antonio's *Portrait of a Young Woman* (fig. 328) is one of the last profile portraits of a woman, for the type was

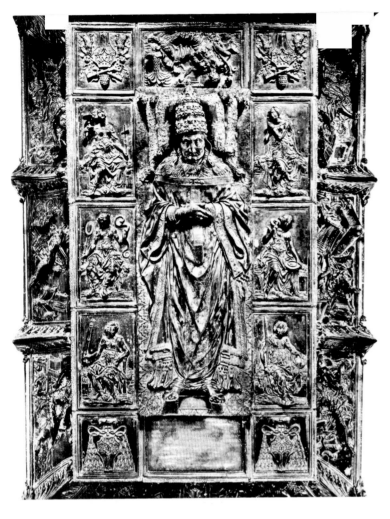

soon to give way to the three-quarter or full-face view already commonly in use for male portraits. But Antonio delights in the profile, whose rigidity yields to vibrant life in his hands. His analytic line responds to every nuance of shape in the face of this young woman. We can follow the line with delight as it models her delicate features almost without the aid of variations of light.

By the last decade of the Quattrocento, Antonio's influence in Florence and elsewhere was enormous. In 1489 Lorenzo de' Medici described him as the leading master of the city: "Perhaps, by the opinion of every intelligent person, there was never a better one." Antonio's final commissions were the papal tombs of Sixtus IV and his successor Innocent VIII. The bronze tomb of Sixtus IV (figs. 329, 330) occupied the artist and his shop for nine years after the pope's death in 1484. The recumbent pope, wearing tiara and pontifical vestments, is surrounded by reliefs representing the seven Virtues (Charity, Hope, Prudence, Fortitude, Faith, Temperance, and Justice). Below these, on the sides of the tomb, separated by acanthus consoles, are ten Liberal Arts: Philosophy, Theology, Rhetoric, Grammar, Arithmetic, Astrology, Dialectic, Geometry, Music, and Perspective. It is noteworthy that Perspective has entered this august company (fig. 331); she holds a book with a quotation paraphrased from the medieval philosopher Peckham, an oak branch (the pope came from the Della Rovere family, whose name means oak), and an astrolabe. The astrolabe suggests that during the Renaissance navigation and exploration were considered part of perspective, the definition of space.

The harshly honest portrait of Sixtus dwells with fascination on the hawklike features and sagging flesh. The

above and below: 329, 330. ANTONIO DEL POLLAIUOLO. Tomb of Pope Sixtus IV. 1484–93. Bronze, length 14' 7". Museo Storico Artistico, St. Peter's, Rome. Commissioned by Cardinal Giuliano delle Rovere for Sixtus IV's burial chapel in Old St. Peter's, Rome

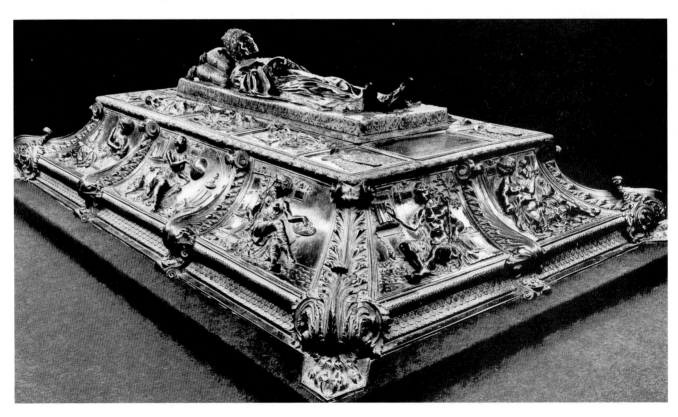

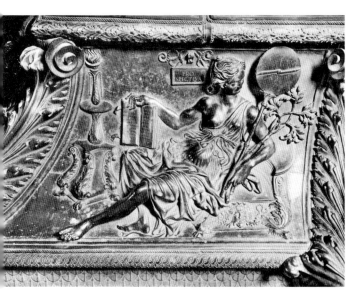

331. Perspective, detail of fig. 330

crumpled folds of the pope's vestments and the drapery of the allegorical figures suggest the latest style of Donatello, but they are, in actuality, the sculptural counterpart of the drapery shown in the paintings of Antonio and Piero del Pollaiuolo.

ANDREA DEL VERROCCHIO

Verrocchio, the nickname of Andrea di Michele Cioni (1435–88), means "true eye," but it refers not to any exceptional powers of vision but to a Florentine family who were his early patrons. His most notable painting is the *Baptism of Christ* (fig. 332); when his workshop was assisting in the creation of this work, Verrocchio's young pupil Leonardo da Vinci painted some remarkable passages that are distinctive of his new style. Forgetting Leonardo for the moment (for his contributions, see p. 436), Verrocchio's composition in itself is simple and grand. The figures are aligned across the foreground, but

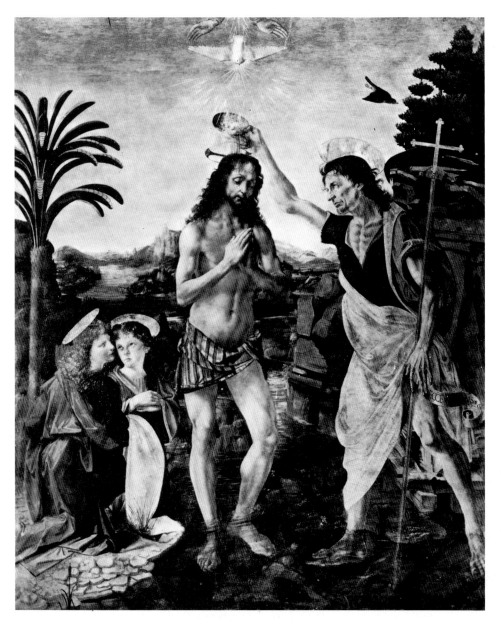

332. ANDREA DEL VERROCCHIO and LEONARDO DA VINCI. *Baptism of Christ.* c. 1470. Panel, 69 1/2 x 59 1/2". Uffizi Gallery, Florence. Commissioned for S. Salvi, Florence

so loosely as to afford wide views into a distant land-scape. Between the palm tree of eternal life on one side, its fronds studied in perspective, Uccello-style, and the pine-crowned bluff on the other, the figures are spread out almost like anatomical charts. Bony masses, the in-sertion of muscles and tendons, and the play of light over torsos, limbs, and hands are analyzed with the care of Pollaiuolo but without his interest in movement. The picture is impressive in its directness. The Baptist looks at Christ with devotion, and in the cavernous eyes and pale features of Christ we can almost perceive fore-knowledge of the Passion.

The *Baptism* is closely related to a sculptural group on which Verrocchio lavished his skill in composition, his knowledge of anatomy, and his depth of feeling—the *Doubting of Thomas* at Orsanmichele (fig. 333). The marble tabernacle had been commissioned in the early 1420s by the Parte Guelfa, then the dominant force in Florentine political and economic life, for their niche on Orsanmichele; it was designed by Donatello to enclose his gilded bronze statue of St. Louis of Toulouse. With the rise of the Medici, the Parte Guelfa was eclipsed, and in 1460 their niche was sold to the magistrates of the Mercanzia, or merchants' guild, and Donatello's stat-ue was moved to Santa Croce. The subject of the new group may have been chosen because of the magistrates' own insistence that in all their deliberations they re-quired, as did Thomas, tangible evidence.

Verrocchio could have squeezed two figures into Donatello's niche, but the principles of composition prevailing in the later Quattrocento suggested another solution. Verrocchio clearly wanted to bring out the emotional intensity of the moment when, to prove his identity, Christ invites the apostle to touch the wound in his side. The composition overflows the niche, and Thomas stands on the ledge below. Thus the figures had to be smaller in scale than Donatello's *St. Louis*, and it was discovered when the group was removed for safe-keeping during World War II, that the statues have no backs, but are hollow shells of bronze.

Drama is centered less in the individuals (both faces are quiet, even reserved) than in the pregnant space be-tween them—the wound revealed by one hand, ap-proached by another (fig. 334). Nowhere does drapery unite the figure in the manner of the Early Renaissance. Rather, in its countless pockets, it shatters the forms into facets of light and dark, the sculptural counterpart of Pollaiuolo's free brushwork, within which the rhythm of the figures is felt, but not their mass. Donatello's de-vice of using cloth soaked in hardened slip was, accord-ing to the sources, emulated by Verrocchio, who sub-stituted plaster for clay. But here it is employed for dif-ferent ends. The restless activity of the drapery, like the quivering of the fingers and the rippling descent of the curls, helps to communicate emotion. The Christ is the same as in the *Baptism*, with the same haunting expres-sion. On the border of his mantle are written his words, "Because thou hast seen me, thou hast believed: blessed

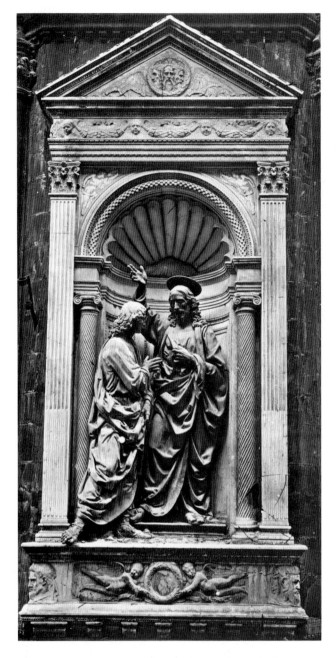

333. ANDREA DEL VERROCCHIO. *Doubting of Thomas.* 1465–83. Bronze, height of Christ 7' 6½". Orsanmichele, Florence. (Marble niche by DONATELLO, c. 1422–25; commissioned by the Parte Guelfa.) Verrocchio's group was commissioned by the Mercanzia

are they that have not seen, and yet have believed" (John 20:29). The work is so impressive and its content so profound that the question of the participation of the young Leonardo has been raised, but perhaps this is only because Verrocchio has been persistently underrated. When the group was placed in its niche in 1483, the di-arist Landucci described the head of Christ as "the most beautiful head of the Savior that has yet been made."

Verrocchio's *Bust of a Young Woman* has been often identified, but without proof, as Lucrezia Donati, mis-tress of Lorenzo de' Medici (fig. 335). We note at once how sharply the style of fashionable appearance has changed since the days of Filippo Lippi and Piero della Francesca: gone are the plucked, domelike forehead, the penciled eyebrows, and the tresses intermingled with veils

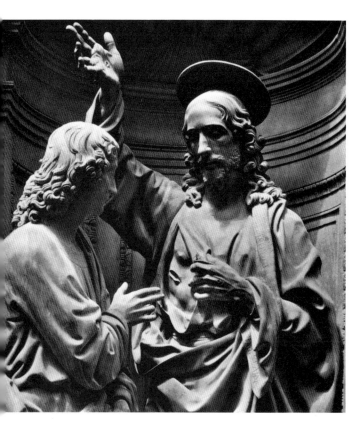

334. Christ and St. Thomas, detail of fig. 333

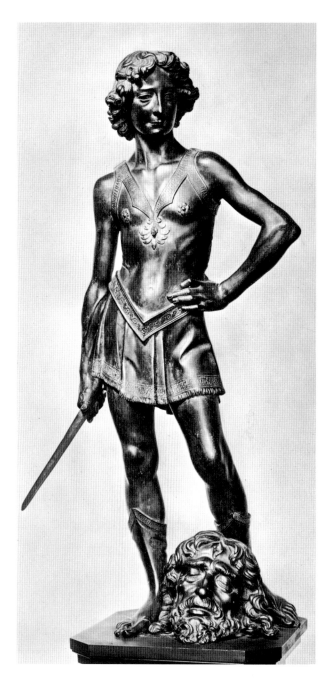

336. ANDREA DEL VERROCCHIO. *David*. Probably early 1470s. Bronze, height 49⅝". Bargello, Florence. Commissioned by Lorenzo de' Medici for the Medici Palace

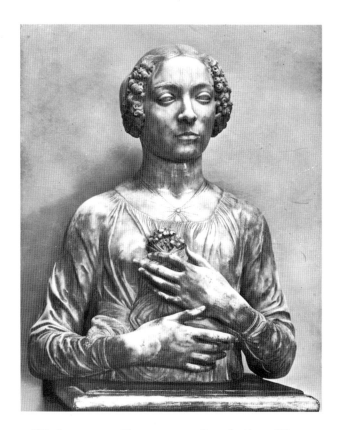

335. ANDREA DEL VERROCCHIO. *Bust of a Young Woman*. 1480s. Marble, height 24". Bargello, Florence

and pearls. Now the subject's hair, parted in the middle to reveal a natural brow, is drawn to the sides and then allowed to escape in clustered curls. The eyebrows are broad and full, the costume is an unadorned tunic, and there is not a pearl to be seen. With her graceful hands the woman holds to her chest a small bouquet of flowers. This is the new honesty and naturalism of the advanced 1480s, and Verrocchio has carried it out in every detail, suggesting in marble the fullness and richness of flesh even where it is covered by the suggestion of a translucent garment.

When commissioned by Lorenzo de' Medici to make a bronze *David*, Verrocchio clothed the angular boyish figure in leather jerkin and skirt (fig. 336), in contrast to the nudity of Donatello's earlier figure (see fig. 247), and

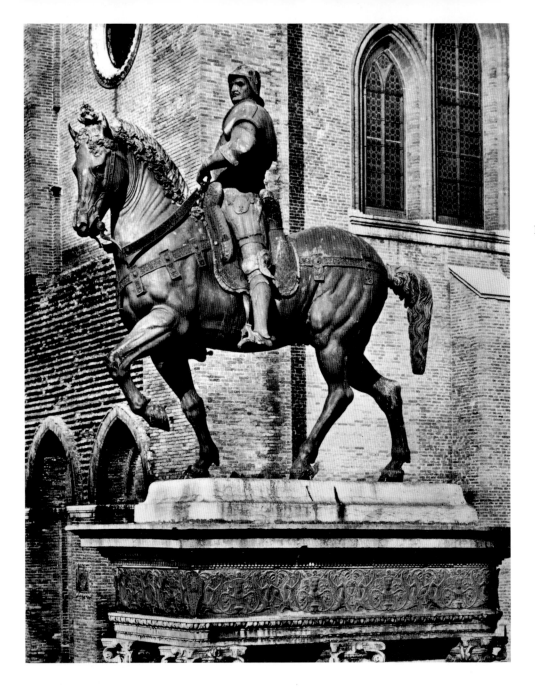

armed him with a dagger suitable to his stature rather than with Goliath's enormous sword grasped by Donatello's *David.* The expression of Verrocchio's *David* seems far from triumphant—he is pensive and gentle in the moment of victory.

Verrocchio's final work is also his grandest. The condottiere Bartolommeo Colleoni (d. 1475) left to the Venetian Republic a considerable sum of money, providing that a bronze equestrian monument to him be set up in the Piazza San Marco, nerve center of Venetian life. The authorities hedged and destined the statue for a less important square, in front of the Scuola di San Marco, and thus, in a sense, conforming to the letter of Colleoni's stipulation. When and how Verrocchio came into the picture is far from clear, but in 1483 a wandering monk recorded seeing on exhibition in Venice three colossal horses by three competing masters. Verrocchio died before he could cast his clay model, and the bronze was carried out by a Venetian bronze founder, Alessandro Leopardi, who also designed the base (figs. 337,

338). Leopardi deprived many details, particularly the ornament and the mane and tail, of the vitality that Andrea would probably have given them had he been able to do the chasing himself. But the total effect of the statue as one comes upon it, crossing the little bridge into the Campo San Zanipolo, is stupendous.

In keeping with the new interests of his period and the stylistic current to which he belonged, Verrocchio has abandoned Donatello's static concept of the equestrian monument (see fig. 249). Now the general, helmeted and armed with a mace, seems to be riding his charger into battle. In mass and silhouette the group commands the surrounding space. The horse's left foreleg steps freely, his veins and muscles swell, his head is turned, and his muzzle is drawn in. The rider stands in the stirrups, his torso twisted against the movement of the horse's head, his dilated eyes staring, his jaw clenched (fig. 339). Seldom has concern with the moment of drama been expressed more powerfully in sculpture than in Verrocchio's last work.

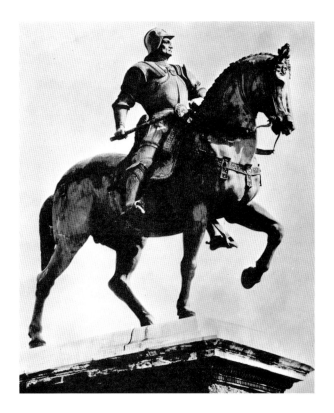

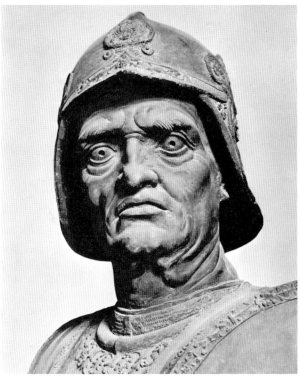

339. Head of Colleoni, detail of fig. 337

SANDRO BOTTICELLI

The leader of our second, or poetic, current in later Quattrocento Florentine art is Sandro Botticelli (1445–1510). In a twentieth-century list of the great painters Italy produced, Botticelli has a place, but he never emulated the monumentality and humanity of Giotto, Masaccio, and Michelangelo, the spatial harmony of Piero and Raphael, the inventiveness of Leonardo, the natural beauty of Giovanni Bellini, the free colorism of Titian and Veronese. Lorenzo de' Medici, who patronized Botticelli little and Pollaiuolo much, seems to have preferred the latter. Then what accounts for Botticelli's present standing, which has endured for at least a century and seems unlikely to diminish? The answer is complex, but no more so than Botticelli himself. Partly, he seems to be beloved because in his art he withdrew from the world around him, and withdrawal is natural under circumstances of stress. Partly, it is because Botticelli knew, more than any other Renaissance artist, what line could accomplish and wove linear compositions with such subtlety that sixteenth-century polyphonic music comes to mind as a parallel. Partly—and this is seldom admitted—it is because in his later works, with their barren, unmodeled architectural backgrounds, he achieved an unforgettable sense of fatality.

A number of Romantic misconceptions cloud our understanding of Botticelli, beginning with his name. The unromantic fact is that Alessandro di Mariano Filipepi had an older brother, Giovanni, who was a successful broker and who was nicknamed "il Botticello" (the keg). Sandro appears to have been cared for by this brother, and it was therefore natural to call him "del Botticello," which in time became Botticelli. Next we might consider the proverbial flatness of Botticelli's style, out of which critics have made so much. Fra Luca Pacioli, assistant and follower of Piero della Francesca, wrote that Botticelli was one of the great masters of perspective! Botticelli's perspective and form may run counter to the tradition of Alberti and Piero della Francesca, but both elements are prominent nonetheless and significant for the understanding of his art. Finally, to dispel the illusion of Botticelli's gentleness, we might glance at some of the events in his Sistine Chapel frescoes, especially Moses killing the Egyptian taskmaster (see fig. 342) or the fate of Korah, Dathan, and Abiram (see fig. 344).

Botticelli had his start as an assistant to Fra Filippo Lippi, and they became so close that before Filippo died he entrusted Botticelli with the guidance of his son Filippino, who was only twelve years younger. The shadow of Masaccio's mantle, therefore, descends on Botticelli; certainly he knew the tradition, and from a man who had watched Masaccio paint. Later, Botticelli was active in the shop of Verrocchio, along with the young Leonardo da Vinci, and his knowledge of the scientific tendency was completed by association with the Pollaiuolo brothers, with whom he collaborated on one project. But his own style, despite echoes of Fra Filippo and Verrocchio, takes on the character of a personal revolt. It is antiatmospheric, antioptical, and antiscientific almost from the start.

Botticelli's *Adoration of the Magi* in the Uffizi (colorplate 60, p. 301), painted for an eccentric Florentine merchant, Guasparre dal Lama, was placed on an altar in Santa Maria Novella. The subject is common in the later Quattrocento, and Botticelli painted it at least seven times. As has been mentioned in connection with Benozzo Gozzoli's frescoes (see p. 311), the Medici belonged to a Company of the Magi, and traditionally, the Medici are supposed to be represented as the Magi in this panel. The aged Cosimo, who had died in 1464, before the picture was painted, is identifiable as the first and oldest Magus, kneeling before the Christ Child. This Magus holds the Christ Child's feet, which he covers with a veil that goes over his shoulders. This is similar to the humeral veil, of ancient origin, that is worn by the priest at the more recent ceremony of the Benediction of the Sacrament; the priest covers his hands with it when holding the foot of the monstrance containing the Eucharist, the body of Christ, for the adoration of the faithful. The Adoration of the Magi was the first occasion when the body of Christ was shown to the Gentiles. At the feast of Corpus Christi, the Sacrament was carried in solemn procession from Santa Maria Novella, past the very altar on which Botticelli's painting was placed, to the Duomo. Botticelli's picture is thus, apparently, a perpetuation of this annual event in which the Medici took part, and to its religious significance a certain political ingredient must be added.

A further detail connects Botticelli's paintings of the Adoration of the Magi with the Passion. In most of these works by Botticelli (see also fig. 346) and others, there are conspicuous remains of a vast structure with arches and columns, presumably a temple, that houses a rapidly erected shed that shelters the Holy Family. Christ said to the Jews: "'Destroy this temple, and in three days I will raise it up.' . . . But he spake of the temple of his body. When therefore he was risen from the dead, his disciples remembered that he had said this" (John 2:19–22). Usually, the ruins have been explained as examples of the interest of Botticelli and others in classical antiquity, but this does not tell us why ancient ruins turn up in Bethlehem, and why they first appear in Adorations of the Magi and not in other subjects and only after Botticelli's painting for Santa Maria Novella. The simple shed is indeed a structure that could be built in three days, and the Corpus Domini procession explains its use as a contrast between the Old Law, ruined at Christ's coming, and the New, a contrast often met with in Quattrocento painting.

Botticelli's ghostly arches move in flawless perspective and the massive corner at the right is projected with hallucinatory three-dimensionality. Yet the two perspectives are never permitted to connect into one Albertian visual cone. Unlike that of Piero, Botticelli's perspective space is fragmentary and dreamlike, and even when it seems real, its reality becomes the surreality that torments us in dreams.

The Star of Bethlehem hovers over the Virgin and Child, who are enthroned upon a rock that hints at Calvary. A gentle Joseph stands behind and slightly above them. Below the first Magus the two other Magi kneel in intense conversation—apparently Giovanni (d. 1463)

and Piero the Gouty (d. 1469), Cosimo's sons. The youth at the extreme left, embraced by a friend as he listens to the words of a somewhat older mentor, may be Lorenzo. At the right (fig. 340), a dark-haired youth in profile, gazing downward, resembles the portraits of Giuliano, Lorenzo's brother. The faces are delicately illuminated and foreshortened from above, below, and behind. All, down to the most distant, are projected with equal sharpness by means of sculptural contours and incisive light. From some radiates a surprising fervor, from others a haunting languor.

The young man in the gold-colored cloak at the extreme right (fig. 341), gazing directly at the spectator in the characteristic manner of a self-portrait, has generally been accepted as one. The heavy-lidded eyes, the large nose, the slightly pouting mouth with open lips, and the heavy chin are pervaded by an expression that can be read as keen intelligence and deliberate withdrawal. It is not hard to believe that the sensitive and melancholic Botticelli looked like this at about twenty-seven.

Botticelli's first monumental fresco commission was to depict the rebels of the Pazzi conspiracy of 1478, hanged and writhing, on the walls of the Florentine Customs House. These frescoes were destroyed after the expulsion of the Medici in 1494, but possibly their success (certainly not their subject, as Pope Sixtus IV was implicated in the conspiracy) suggested that Botticelli be called to Rome in 1481, together with his fellow Florentines Cosimo Rosselli and Domenico del Ghirlandaio and Perugino, from Perugia, to decorate the chapel newly constructed by Pope Sixtus and known today as the Sistine Chapel (Sixtus is Sisto in Italian, and the chapel was soon called the Cappella Sistina). The Sistine Chapel was intended to accommodate not only the Masses and other services of the papal court, but also the meetings of cardinals. Today only unusual tourists can detach themselves from Michelangelo's frescoes on the ceiling to contemplate the Quattrocento paintings on the broad, unbroken wall surfaces below the windows (see colorplate 11, p. 19). Studies have shown that the scenes from the Lives of Moses and Christ on opposite walls were chosen to represent crucial episodes in the history of spiritual leadership in the Old and New Testaments that prefigured and justified the traditional claims of the papacy to universality. Vasari believed that Botticelli was placed in charge of the entire decorative program; more recently an attempt has been made to place Perugino in this role.

If anyone exercised a commanding position, it must have been the pope. Moreover, some credit ought to be given to the common sense and good taste of the artists, none of whom were likely to wish their paintings in so important a place to appear out of harmony with the others. In the Chapel of the Cardinal of Portugal, for example, every visitor is struck by the decorative beauty of the ensemble, yet the architect died before the project got under way, the sculptors and painters represented conflicting tendencies, the paintings were an after-

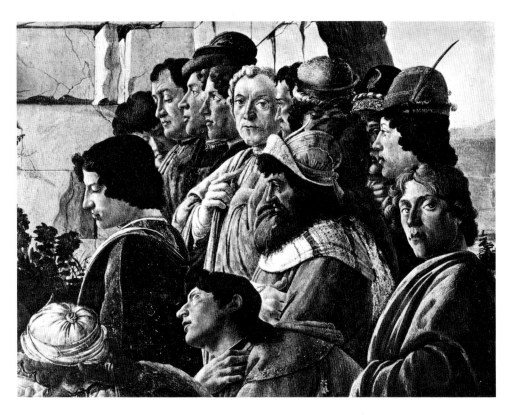

340. SANDRO BOTTICELLI. Group of figures, detail of *Adoration of the Magi* (see colorplate 60, p. 301). Probably early 1470s. Panel. Uffizi Gallery, Florence

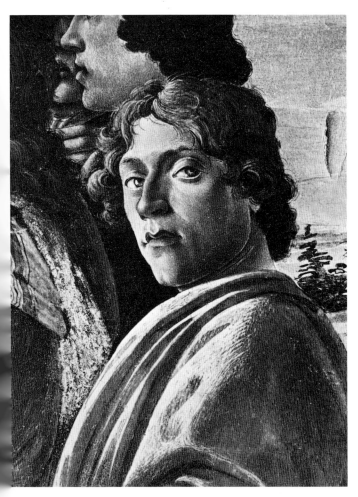

341. SANDRO BOTTICELLI. Self-Portrait, detail of *Adoration of the Magi* (see colorplate 60, p. 301)

thought, and no one artist stayed on the job from beginning to end. In the case of the Sistine Chapel, it is safe to suppose that the pope and his advisers determined the subjects and gave the artists general guidelines as to unity, and that they left the artists to work out in conference the consistency of scale, horizon line, palette, and the like. On closer examination it becomes evident that none of the original four artists—or Pintoricchio or Signorelli, who were later brought into the project—were willing to sacrifice their artistic identity. Sharp discrepancies of feeling and even of compositional principles are found throughout the series, and none of the masters went home with even a trace of any of the others recognizable in his style.

In each of the surviving frescoes of the Quattrocento cycle (two were torn down to make way for Michelangelo's *Last Judgment* in the Cinquecento and two were completely repainted), the foreground is almost filled with figures that narrate the principal incidents and are scaled at roughly two-fifths the total height of the scene. The vanishing point for the landscape—which ought to govern the recession of the foreground architecture as well, but does not always do so—is placed one-fifth above their heads. This two-fifths, one-fifth, two-fifths horizontal division of the scenes, crossed by a vertical division into thirds, is respected but never insistent, save in the three scenes by Botticelli. With typical Florentine rigor, he treats each scene as a triptych, grouping the foreground figures and vertical masses such as architecture and trees into a central block flanked by two supporting wings.

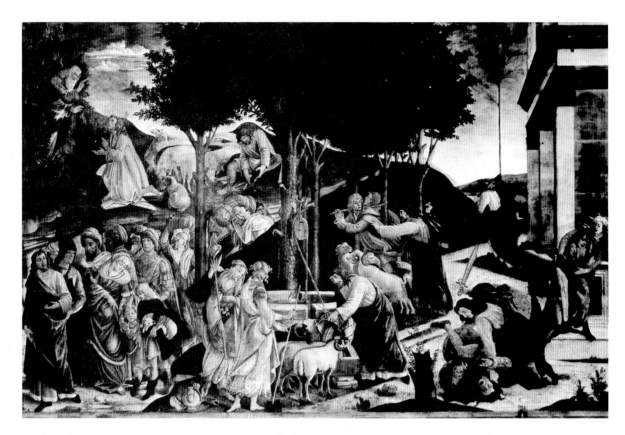

342. SANDRO BOTTICELLI. *Youth of Moses*. 1481–82. Fresco, 11' 5" x 18' 3½".
Sistine Chapel, Vatican, Rome. Commissioned by Pope Sixtus IV

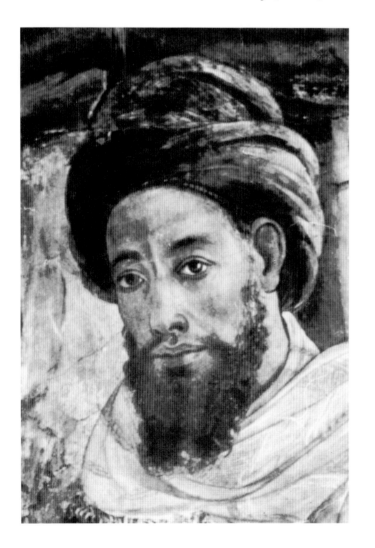

The *Youth of Moses* (fig. 342) shows Moses at the right killing the Egyptian taskmaster. In the center Moses drives away the Midianites who were molesting Jethro's daughters and then, lower down, he draws water at a well for the women. At the left, bearing a rod, he leads the Israelites out of Egypt. In the background Moses is represented three more times, first fleeing the scene of the slaying, then removing his sandals before he comes into the presence of God, then kneeling before the Burning Bush in which God appears to him. In general, the frescoes, which had to be painted rapidly to satisfy the pope, are executed more coarsely than Botticelli's panels. Yet this one abounds in beautifully conceived figures (fig. 343) and groups, from the scene of terror at the right, to the delicate idyll in the center (in which the long-haired daughters of Jethro anticipate the Three Graces in the *Primavera*; see colorplate 61, p. 302), to the gentle group at the left, with its vivid contemporary likenesses.

The *Punishment of Korah, Dathan, and Abiram* (fig. 344) narrates how these three men challenged Aaron's right to the high priesthood; when they inappropriately assumed his role by offering incense to the Lord, they were swallowed up by the earth (Numbers 16:1–35). In Botticelli's fresco, the story is narrated from left to right and fused with other incidents concerning Moses. At

left: 343. Head of an Israelite, detail of fig. 342

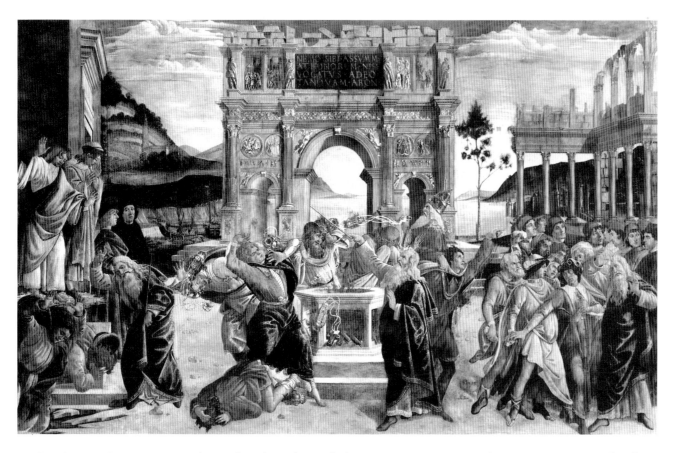

344. SANDRO BOTTICELLI. *Punishment of Korah, Dathan, and Abiram*. 1481–82. Fresco, 11' 5½" x 18' 8½". Sistine Chapel, Vatican, Rome. Commissioned by Pope Sixtus IV

the left the earth opens up; only two figures are shown—one must already have vanished into Hell—and flames arise to consume them. In the center six figures who are offering false fire to the Lord are consumed by fire from Heaven. On the right Moses seeks refuge from the seditious Israelites who tried to stone him. Botticelli has added an inscription from St. Paul to the otherwise accurate representation of the Arch of Constantine: "And no man taketh this honor unto himself, but he that is called of God, as was Aaron" (Hebrews 5:4). Read together with the altar and punishment, the arch prefigures the mission of the Roman Church, especially as Aaron wears a papal tiara. Botticelli's linear patterns and sharply lighted forms appear throughout the densely packed groups. Moses is older here (fig. 345), with long white hair and beard, and his countenance has a mystic intensity that prefigures the *Moses* of Michelangelo (see fig. 516). The two clusters of rays issuing from Moses' forehead have a curious history. When Moses came down from Mount Sinai the second time, rays of light shone from his face. In translating the Bible into Latin, St. Jerome balked at attributing light to anyone who antedated Christ. The Hebrew word could also be rendered "horns," so Moses is often represented with horns. In St. Paul's Epistle, however, the word "rays" was allowed to stand. Botticelli's Moses is a compromise, with two horns made up of rays.

More formal and classical than the Uffizi version (see colorplate 60, p. 301), the *Adoration of the Magi* in Wash-

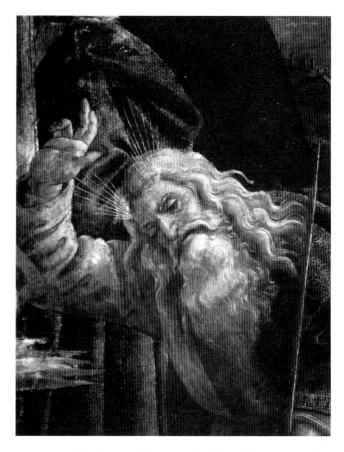

345. Head of Moses, detail of fig. 344

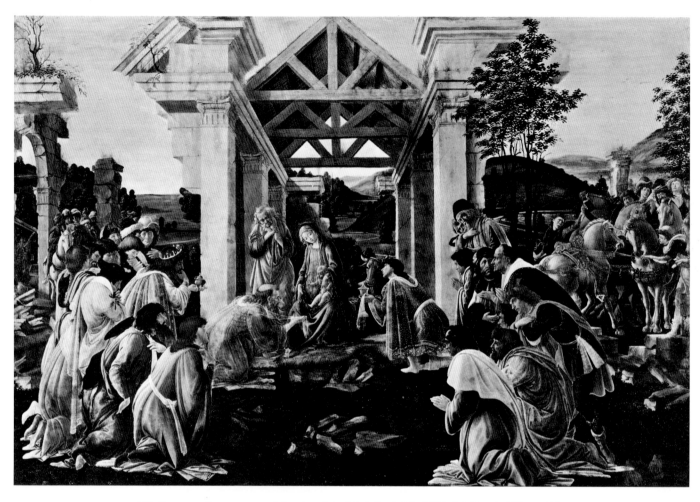

346. SANDRO BOTTICELLI. *Adoration of the Magi*. Probably 1481–82. Panel, 27⅝ x 41".
National Gallery of Art, Washington, D.C. (Mellon Collection)

ington, D.C. (fig. 346), may reflect Botticelli's stay in Rome. The free figural arrangements of the earlier picture have given way to a circle in depth that is broken in the foreground to give the spectator a view of the Virgin and Child. Now the ruins suggest a once imposing Roman monument. The shed roof substitutes fresh, firm lines for the angle formed by an entablature stone about to topple at the left. Its beams recall the open timber ceilings of the Early Christian basilicas Botticelli saw in Rome, particularly Old St. Peter's.

Botticelli has chosen the point of view of a hypothetical spectator standing at the center and well within the picture, on a line with the two Magi nearest the Madonna. All the other worshipers, therefore, and we along with them, are excluded from the scene by the entire width of the grassy lawn, which we instinctively attempt to traverse in order to make the architectural perspective come right. We are caught up involuntarily in the yearning of the worshipers toward the sacred figures. As will shortly be seen, Botticelli must have been aware of the beliefs and teachings of the Platonic Academy formed within the court of Lorenzo de' Medici. One of these doctrines was the principle of *desío* (desire, long-

ing, yearning), by which the soul, in its earthly exile, could traverse mystically the gulf separating it from its true home in God. It is such *desío*, nascent in the Uffizi picture, that in the Washington version assumes the power of a natural force, activating the figures in the composition, and us along with them.

In this case none of the faces can be identified as portraits, but in many of them Botticelli has achieved subtle psychological effects. Considering the difficulty of dating most of Botticelli's works, it is hypothetical whether the picture was conceived before or after the unfinished *Adoration of the Magi* by Leonardo da Vinci (see fig. 455). In any event, the two paintings cannot be separated by more than months, and the two Verrocchio pupils almost certainly knew each other's compositions. They may even have quarreled about them, as we know they did over perspective and landscape. The background scene at the upper right, in which the grooms are having difficulty restraining unruly horses, is common to both pictures, although it is more tempestuous in the work by Leonardo. In his writings, Leonardo tells us that Botticelli claimed it was possible to paint a landscape by throwing a sponge filled with paint at the panel and turning the smears into landscape forms. Leonardo added that Botticelli painted bad landscapes. From Leonardo's scientific, or quasi-scientific, point of view, they were bad landscapes—but they are still beautiful. In its broad contours the landscape here enhances the movement of the figures, while its blue-green color provides a foil for the strong reds, blues, and yellows of the costumes. And in their soft shapes and great spaces they echo sympathetically the *desío* that runs through the group of worshipers.

Like Pollaiuolo, Botticelli was called upon to paint the mythological subjects fashionable at the court of Lorenzo and in the elegant society of the Florentine patriciate. Throughout these paintings the graceful figures, nude or draped, stand, recline, or move always in the foreground, filling the frame, from top to bottom, with the gravity and dignity of the figures Botticelli had seen in profusion in classical marble reliefs in Rome. Botticelli's mythologies have been explained through the writings of the Florentine Neoplatonists, notably Marsilio Ficino, but the interpretations are complicated by the kaleidoscopic nature of the Neoplatonic writings, which often demonstrate how humanists can derive a host of different meanings from the same classical legend. In the following discussions, some persuasive elements have been here selected from still-controversial interpretations, and new elements added; someday perhaps a "lucky find," as Gombrich puts it, will reveal just what these tantalizing images were intended to mean.

Let us start with *Camilla and the Centaur* (fig. 347). The subject, which was previously thought to be Pallas and the Centaur, has been identified from a 1499 inventory, which revealed that a painting of *Camilla* was hanging outside the nuptial chamber of Lorenzo di Pierfrancesco de' Medici in his Florentine palace. Camilla, who appears in Virgil's *Aeneid*, is a Latian princess and chaste huntress dedicated to the service of Minerva, whose olive branches she wears. Camilla, who holds a halberd, the weapon of guards, grasps a cringing centaur by the hair. Her diaphanous tunic is profusely ornamented with the Medici symbol of three interlocked rings. The centaur is a typical personification of lust; the picture suggests that Camilla is preventing him from breaking into the fence. Semiramide d'Appiano, Lorenzo di Pierfrancesco's bride, was herself a princess from Latium, and the picture should probably be read as an allegory of marital chastity, an appropriate subject for its position outside Lorenzo's nuptial chamber.

Jagged rocks are the realm of the centaur, but behind Camilla lies an open landscape containing a tranquil sea and a ship full of people. The jagged rocks contrast, in their brilliantly illuminated bulk, with the weightlessness of the bodies. These have now assumed proportions characteristic of Botticelli's mature style, with necks and torsos prolonged and arms and legs of the same length. Once one has entered Botticelli's imaginary realm, however, the conventions of the real world

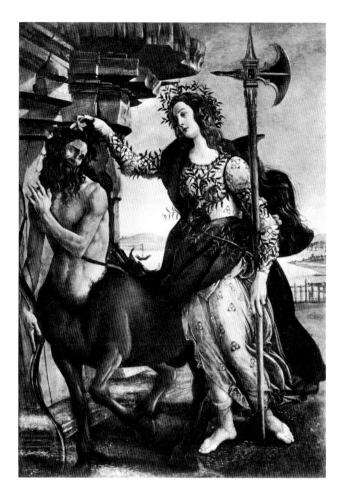

347. SANDRO BOTTICELLI. *Camilla and the Centaur.* After 1482. Canvas, 81½ x 58¼". Uffizi Gallery, Florence. Probably commissioned by Lorenzo di Pierfrancesco de' Medici for his Florentine palace at the time of his wedding

can be forgotten, and one readily accepts the new race of beings he invented.

Whoever was responsible for them, the conceits behind Botticelli's mythologies are, of course, highly artificial, but hardly more so than the way of life prevailing in the society for which Botticelli painted, or the style of the master himself. Regardless of Christian disapproval, the ancient gods had survived in one form or another throughout the Middle Ages, especially as planetary personifications that were believed to exercise power over human life and destiny. But in their vicissitudes they had lost their ancient appearance; with Botticelli they reenter Quattrocento life on a grand scale, without much visual resemblance to classical representations, and with an allegorical meaning closely paralleling that of Christian subjects. Botticelli's *Venus and Mars* (fig. 348), for example, is not intelligible in terms of the naked Venuses of antiquity. Here we behold a lovely creature, barefoot but clothed in a garment with double sleeves and voluminous folds that conceal her waist. Mars, a slender youth, lies on the ground, naked save for a strip of white cloth. While he sleeps, four impudent baby satyrs—among the first, if not the first, satyrs to make an appearance in

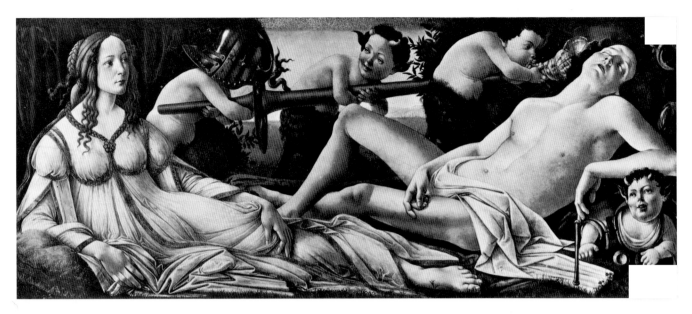

348. SANDRO BOTTICELLI. *Venus and Mars*. c. 1483. Panel, 27¼ x 68¼". National Gallery, London.
Perhaps commissioned by a member of the Vespucci family

Renaissance painting—make sport with his armor and spear, and one of them blows through a conch shell into his ear, demonstrating how soundly he sleeps.

Like many of Botticelli's mythologies, this one has been often connected, on slight evidence, with the tournament of 1475, which was celebrated in Poliziano's poem *La giostra*, in which Giuliano de' Medici received the victor's crown from Simonetta Vespucci. But the picture must have some connection with the Vespucci family, Botticelli's neighbors: the wasps buzzing about the head of Mars come from the Vespucci coat of arms (*vespucci* in Italian means little wasps). More than one passage from classical literature was doubtless used by whatever humanist devised the program for the painting. Especially relevant is Marsilio Ficino's astrological characterization of Mars as "outstanding in strength among the planets because he makes men stronger, but Venus masters him. . . . Venus, when in conjunction with Mars, in opposition to him, . . . often checks his malignance . . . she seems to master Mars, but Mars never masters Venus."

The laurel branches behind both Mars and Venus suggest that its meaning, in the days when, due to Lorenzo's adroit politics, peace seemed eternal, was the conquering power of love, even over war, and the subjugation of violence by the higher powers of culture and the intellect. The overpowering languor of the *Venus and Mars* is induced as much by the painting's long, low shape as by the subtly depicted sleep of Mars. One scholar has enticingly suggested that both the defeat and the slumber of Mars were occasioned by lovemaking with Venus. Her appearance opposes this idea, especially her long, white, opaque garment, which subdues her charms even if it does not entirely conceal them, and her high girdle, symbol of chastity. It might be remem-

bered that Mars was considered in Florence a hostile antitype of St. John the Baptist, who took over his temple and made it into the Baptistery.

In the *Primavera* (colorplate 61, p. 302), we cross the portals of sleep and enter the very dream. The scene is a grove of dark orange trees, thickly massed. Their intertwined branches and golden fruit fill the upper portion of the picture. Between the trunks one glimpses the sky and, at one point, a hint of a distant landscape. Just off center stands a maidenly figure, one hand raised as if in benediction. At the extreme right Zephyrus, the wind god, enters the scene in pursuit of the virgin nymph Chloris, from whose mouth issue flowers; Zephyrus will rape and then marry her. As a happy wife she became Flora, goddess of Spring, and this is the figure who is strewing flowers from her flower-embroidered garment. Because the picture represents the eternal spring that flourished in Venus's garden, Flora is one of the key figure in decoding the meaning. On the left Mercury pokes his caduceus up among storm clouds that are trying to enter the garden. Next to him the Three Graces dance in a ring; above, the blindfolded Cupid shoots a blazing golden arrow in their direction. The figure in the center, so much like one of Botticelli's Madonnas, is Venus. In studying this picture, it is important to remember that, in addition to being the goddess of love, Venus was also the goddess of marriage.

The picture, like *Camilla and the Centaur*, is first documented in the private apartments of Lorenzo di Pierfrancesco de' Medici in his town house near the Palazzo Medici; when Vasari saw it half a century later it was in his villa at Castello. Probably in 1478, Marsilio Ficino wrote to Lorenzo, then only fourteen or fifteen years old, a letter in which Ficino recommended to the youth the espousal of Venus:

Venus, that is to say, Humanitas, . . . is a nymph of excellent comeliness, born of heaven and more than others beloved by God all highest. Her soul and mind are Love and Charity, her eyes Dignity and Magnanimity, the hands Liberality and Magnificence, the feet Comeliness and Modesty. The whole, then, is Temperance and Honesty, Charm and Splendor. Oh, what exquisite beauty! . . . My dear Lorenzo, a nymph of such nobility has been wholly given into your hands! If you were to unite with her in wedlock and claim her as yours, she would make all your years sweet.

Ficino's Venus is an allegory of all those moral qualities that, it was thought, a cultivated Florentine patrician should possess.

The Graces are harder to interpret; Ficino himself supplies a number of shifting explanations, but we cannot go wrong if we regard the Graces as emanations of Venus, embodying the beauties she creates. Alberti, moreover, had recommended that Renaissance painters try to re-create Seneca's description of a painting of the Three Graces, to be shown nude or in transparent garments, dancing together with intertwined hands. Botticelli may also have been inspired by a surviving sculptural composition from antiquity that shows three nude Graces, their hands joined; in one view, one of the figures is seen from the rear and the other two from the front. One of the Graces gives forth the benefits of Venus, the second receives, the third gives forth again. Their long, loose, flowing hair indicates that they are unmarried virgins.

A treasury of classical sources has been amassed for most of the elements in the painting, drawn from the ancient writers Horace, Ovid, Lucretius, and Columella. The Roman poet Claudian, who was believed in the Renaissance to have been a Florentine, wrote that all clouds were excluded from Venus's Garden of the Hesperides, where her "golden apples" (i.e., oranges) grew. Mercury is brushing away the clouds with his caduceus; armed and helmeted, he stands guard in a pose derived from those of the *David*s by Donatello and Verrocchio (see figs. 247, 336). Venus, moreover, in addition to being decorously clothed, wears the headdress of a Florentine married woman. Sensuality in the depiction of female anatomy is exquisitely modulated by transparent garments. And thanks to a cleaning, we can now see the delicate lines of breath from Zephyrus' mouth instilling new life in the nymph Chloris, so that her mouth in turn may sprout flowers and that she may be reborn as Flora. Lovers of English poetry will think at once of Chaucer's lines:

Whan Zephirus eke with his swete breeth
Inspired hath in every holt and heeth
The tendre croppes . . .

This painting was appropriately placed outside the nuptial chamber of Lorenzo di Pierfrancesco, whose wedding was planned for May 1482. Botticelli's garden boasts no fewer than forty-two varieties of mostly flowering plants, all common to a Tuscan spring.

Recent scholarship has raised new issues about the painting, particularly in reference to the intended meaning that the imagery may have had for Lorenzo di Pierfrancesco's bride, Semiramide d'Appiano. The chaste, modest, and submissive Venus in the image may have been meant as a behavioral model for the new bride. These qualities are emphasized in humanist writings by Alberti and Bruni as appropriate for the ideal woman and the ideal wife. Bruni wrote that women should especially study the Roman poets, for "in no other writers can be found so many examples of womanly modesty and goodness . . . the finest pattern of the wifely arts."

The last word about this perpetually alluring allegory has yet to be written. For example, the orange grove, so strikingly similar to the one that separates foreground from background in Uccello's *San Romano* panels (see fig. 263), may have other connotations. Oranges cannot be raised outdoors in the Arno Valley, and to a Florentine Quattrocento eye these golden balls could hardly have failed to suggest the Medici arms, borne by Lorenzo di Pierfrancesco as well as by Lorenzo the Magnificent. Also, Mercury's beautiful rose-colored chlamys is strewn with golden flames, and while these are a proper attribute of Mercury, they also belong to St. Lawrence (Lorenzo). They decorate his vestments in Fra Angelico's San Marco altarpiece (see fig. 207), made for Cosimo de' Medici, and many other representations; the meteor showers that descend on the earth in August each year are known in Italy as "fires of St. Lawrence" because they occur at the time of his feast. Nor is this attribute of both Lorenzos limited to Mercury: Venus's white gown is bordered at the neckline with a continuous row of golden flames, and loops composed of these flames encircle her breasts. Finally, Mercury also bore the responsibility for doctors, whose symbol he bears. Medici means "doctors," and the Medici patron saints were doctors. The metaphor was standard in any eulogy of the Medici family.

The entanglements of Botticelli's mythologies typify the learning and social graces of a society bent on reviving antiquity on a new scale, less for the moral lessons that interested Alberti than for private delight. Botticelli's painting has given this rarefied ideal its perfect embodiment, and at the same time raised it to the level of poetry. Before the dark green leaves and giant golden fruit of the grove that shuts out the world, the pale, long-limbed figures move with a solemn and melodious grace, their golden tresses and diaphanous garments rippling about them. The circumstances of real existence no longer apply. These lovely creatures seem almost weightless, and the composition wavers as the winds of spring blow through it. Cupid's arrows are intended to inflame the hearts of the Graces with love, and yearning streams from their eyes.

Yet there is nothing weak or hesitant about Bot-

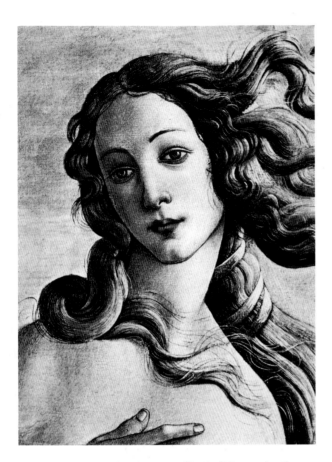

349. SANDRO BOTTICELLI. Head of Venus, detail
of *Birth of Venus* (see colorplate 62, p. 303). c. 1484–86.
Canvas. Uffizi Gallery, Florence

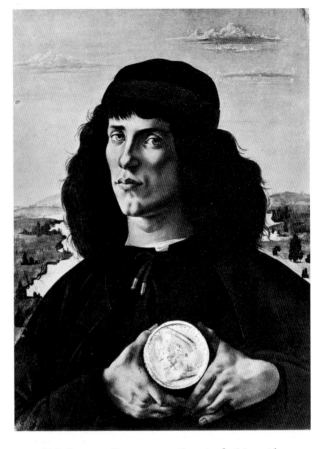

350. SANDRO BOTTICELLI. *Portrait of a Man with a
Medal of Cosimo de' Medici.* c. 1465–69. Panel, 22 5/8 x 17 3/8".
Uffizi Gallery, Florence

ticelli's style. In his hands line is a penetrating instrument, flexible but unflagging, uniting with a characteristic lighting from the side to pick out in sculptural relief every feature, every long tress, every jewel. All surfaces are smooth, all masses firm, no edge is veiled in atmosphere, no brushwork visible. In Botticelli's developed style most faces are tilted sharply to one side, and the axis of the eyes slopes at a stronger rate than the rest of the face, as though the lower eye were sliding downward. Although this may be more of a persistent mannerism than a conscious device, its effect increases the unreality of the style.

Slightly smaller than the *Primavera*, painted on canvas (a surface usually reserved for ceremonial banners), and recorded in no inventory, the *Birth of Venus* (colorplate 62, p. 303; fig. 349) was seen together with the *Primavera* in Lorenzo di Pierfrancesco's villa at Castello by Vasari in the mid-sixteenth century. Although this picture corresponds to a passage in Poliziano's *La giostra*, Gombrich successfully adduced Ficino's interpretation of the mythical birth of Venus from the sea, which had been fertilized by the severed genitals of Uranus, as an allegory of the birth of beauty in the mind of humanity through the fertilization of matter by divinity. Botticelli has turned the myth into an image of grace and beauty, likened to the traditional composition of the Baptism.

Venus, arisen from the sea, stands on—rather than in—a shell, while the Zephyr and a nymph waft her to shore, where she will be robed by a waiting Hour, one of the attendants of Venus. Even this nude Venus, deriving from classical statues of the *Venus pudica* (modest Venus) type, hides her nakedness with her hands and with her long golden hair, which is sweeping about her. The waiting Hour has her neckline wreathed in laurel. The sea itself is almost flat, with V-shapes that suggest waves. Flowers drift through the air and Venus's unearthly beauty is heightened by the use of gold pigment to highlight her hair. The atmospheric and voluminous qualities which so interested Renaissance artists are ruled out in this picture, which is dependent on the delicacy of Botticelli's line. His proportions show here their greatest exaggeration, yet the flow of the long neck and the sloping shoulders and the torrent of honeyed hair about the cool body are entrancing.

One of Botticelli's most striking portraits is the *Man with a Medal of Cosimo de' Medici* (fig. 350), now in the Uffizi. The raised and gilded gesso medal represents Cosimo de' Medici, but the sitter who displays his support for Cosimo so ostentatiously has never been identified. Could he be Lorenzo di Pierfrancesco? The two portraits we have of him, both profiles on medals, do not noticeably resemble each other. But one shows the

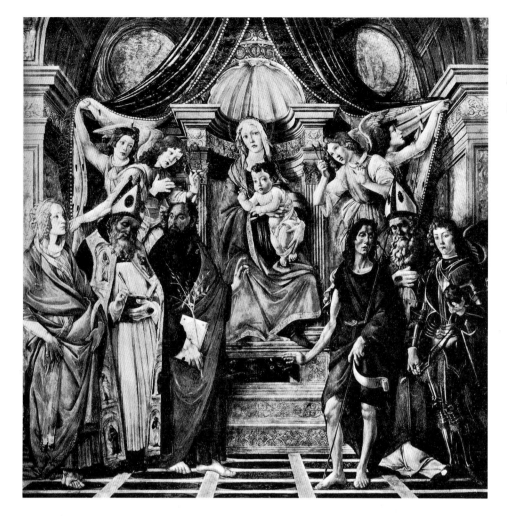

351. SANDRO BOTTICELLI. *Enthroned Madonna with Saints*. Mid-1480s. Panel, 11' 2" x 8' 10". Uffizi Gallery, Florence. Commissioned for S. Barnaba, Florence, by the Arte dei Medici e Speziali

flaring eyebrows, bulbous nose, heavy, broad cheekbones, full lips, and long, slightly receding chin of the Uffizi portrait. The placing of the head in three-quarter view against the sky is unusual in Quattrocento portraits. The characteristic discrepancy in the level of the subject's eyes is accented by the off-center placing of the hands holding the medal, the twist of his left hand, the tilt of the medal opposite to that of the axis of the eyes, and the angle of the hat. The sculptural modeling of the hands and face contrasts with the flattened landscape and its maplike riverbank.

Some of the transformations that take place in Botticelli's style in the later 1480s make themselves felt as early as the *Enthroned Madonna with Saints* (fig. 351) for San Barnaba. Angels part a crimson and ermine curtain before the throne of the Queen of Heaven, while others uphold the crown of thorns and the nails. On the steps are carved the words, "Virgin Mother, daughter of thy Son," from Dante's *Paradiso*. To the Virgin's right stand Saints Catherine, Ambrose, and Barnabas, to her left Saints John the Baptist, Augustine, and Michael. This most monumental of Botticelli's large-scale panels is so massive in its grouping of figures and architecture and so dense in its richly colored simulation of metal, marble, and textiles that it suggests a carved and polychromed relief. Delicate variations from exact symmetry

are the only factors that disturb the almost Byzantine rigidity of the composition, yet the faces are as sensitive as ever, especially that of the gaunt St. John the Baptist, who is an unexpected apparition in Botticelli's art—a haunting figure who looks outward through unfocused eyes glazed with pain.

The *Annunciation* for Santa Maria Maddalena dei Pazzi (fig. 352) shows the gathering intensity of Botticelli's religious fervor. The event takes place in a room furnished only by Mary's lectern, but through the open door we can look into her closed garden. The barrenness of the architecture, which is more like a draftsman's rendering than a painting of a real room, provides a foil for the emotional figures. Mary, whose pose is ultimately derived from Donatello's *Annunciation* (see fig. 245), sways as if caught in a rushing wind. The biblical text says only that "her heart was disturbed within her," but here she seems almost to swoon. Her eyes are almost closed, her features deadly pale. The flow of Botticelli's line is the vehicle not of beauty but of a new and passionate emotional expression that points toward the Florentine Mannerism of the Cinquecento and even the mysticism of El Greco.

The strong emotions, severe architectural lines, and clashing colors of Botticelli's late style suggest that he was a willing listener to the fiery sermons of the Fer-

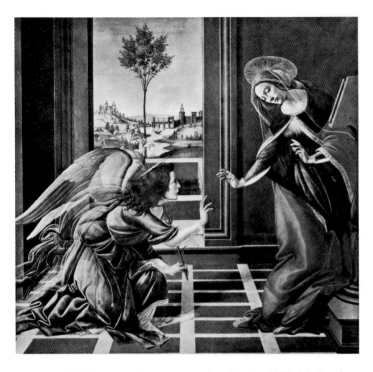

352. SANDRO BOTTICELLI. *Annunciation.* 1489–90. Panel, 59 x 61¾". Uffizi Gallery, Florence. Commissioned by Benedetto di Ser Francesco Guardi del Cane for Sta. Maria Maddalena dei Pazzi, Florence

rarese monk Girolamo Savonarola, who arrived at San Marco in 1482, an heir to the asceticism of St. Antonine. He remained until 1487, returned in 1490, and was appointed vicar general of the Tuscan congregations of Dominicans in 1493. Unlike his younger brother Simone, Sandro never became a partisan of the political

movement Savonarola set in motion. The adherents of the Dominican preacher—known as *piagnoni* (weepers, from *piangere*, to weep)—mobilized popular resentment against the Medici supporters, or *palleschi*. Savonarola preached sermons in the Duomo, the only building in Florence large enough to hold his enormous audiences, that denounced the sins of Florence and the worldliness of the Renaissance with such force that his listeners wept openly and bitterly. Sometimes we are in doubt as to exactly what he said, because the *piagnoni* were weeping so fitfully they could not take accurate notes. His prophecies of the destruction to be visited on Florence began to come true with the arrival of the armies of King Charles VIII of France in 1494, after the expulsion of Piero the Unlucky. The peace that had reigned with few interruptions in central and northern Italy for forty years was over, and it became evident that the Italian states could not stave off domination by the rising centralized monarchies of France and Spain, not to mention the Holy Roman Empire. Eventually, Savonarola took over the government of the Republic, but problems in Florence and his attacks on Pope Alexander VI turned both the Florentines and the papacy against him. In 1498 Savonarola, under torture, admitted to charges of heresy that had been leveled against him. He and two of his chief monastic assistants were hanged in front of the Palazzo dei Priori and their bodies burned on the gallows; the ashes were thrown in the Arno.

Botticelli's moralistic fervor during this period is illustrated by the *Calumny of Apelles* (fig. 353), which he may have painted for his own pleasure. The work carries out a suggestion by Alberti, who had encouraged artists to re-create a lost painting by the ancient Greek master

353. SANDRO BOTTICELLI. *Calumny of Apelles.* 1497–98(?). Panel, 24⅝ x 36". Uffizi Gallery, Florence

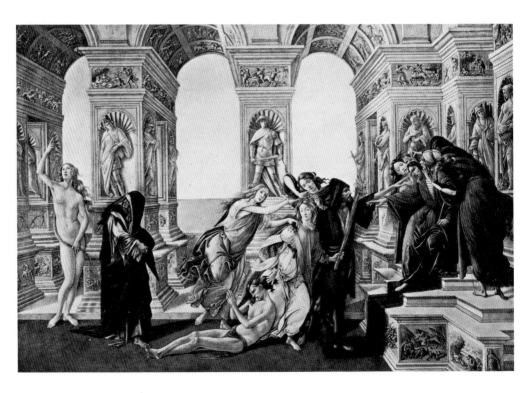

Apelles that was described by the ancient author Lucian. Botticelli has followed the letter of Alberti's advice. Standing beside the throne of Midas, the unjust judge, allegories of Ignorance and Suspicion lift his donkey ears to whisper their advice. Led by the hooded, bearded Hatred, and attended by Deceit and Fraud who adjust her jewels, Calumny, bearing a torch, drags her victim, a nearly naked youth, for judgment. Penitence, an old woman, rends her garments while the naked Truth points to heaven.

The oppressive effect of the *Calumny* is in part produced by its illogical space. Most of the perspective lines vanish toward a common point, located behind the head of Fraud, but the central pier of Midas's judgment hall supports a cornice and two barrel vaults that are projected to a lower vanishing point. The composition is further complicated by the placing of the throne at the right, which creates an axis of interest that conflicts with the visual axis of the perspective.

The architecture presents a series of highly animated surfaces. The second story and the front arches of the first are cut off by the frame. Entablatures with simulated sculptural friezes representing classical subjects dwarf the supporting piers, which are pierced by transverse passages and decorated by niches. From these niches protrude statues, a Judith with the head of Holofernes at the extreme right, for example, and at the center a warrior in the pose of Castagno's *Pippo Spano* (see fig. 271). More reliefs adorn the double podia on which the piers rest, and even the coffers of the vault are filled with reliefs.

Within this active architecture, whose windows look out on a monotonous marine horizon, the frenzied figural composition is rendered with all Botticelli's formidable skill in draftsmanship. Echoes of earlier graceful figures occur here and there. The handmaidens of Calumny recall Jethro's daughters (see fig. 342), and Truth is an obvious reference to the *Birth of Venus* (see colorplate 62, p. 303). But the dreamlike quality of Botticelli's painted mythologies has turned into a nightmare. It can be argued that Mannerism, the dominant style in Florentine painting of the 1520s, is prefigured in this work, which even exceeds the most dramatic aspects of Donatello's late style. It has often been suggested that the iconography was prompted by a desire to defend the memory of Savonarola by suggesting that his accusers were wicked and his judge weak. This suggestion is rendered plausible by the tattered Dominican habit in which Penitence is dressed. Yet most scholars do not think that the picture can be as late as 1497 or 1498.

The style and content of the *Calumny* appear with resounding effect in contemporary religious works by Botticelli, such as the harrowing *Lamentation over the Dead Christ with Sts. Jerome, Paul, and Peter* (fig. 354). The painting is pervaded by the self-flagellating gloom of Savonarola's doctrines, and we seem almost to dwell in the tomb with Christ. Jagged rocks form the entrance to the tomb and enclose the mourning figures. Within is the sarcophagus—and blackness. The pose of Christ, with his long, hanging arm, was inspired by a window designed by Castagno for the dome of Florence Cathedral. Botticelli seems also to have been impressed by Pietro Lorenzetti's *Descent from the Cross* (see fig. 102), from which he adopted not only the appearance of rigor mortis but also the upside-down confrontation of the Magdalen's face (in Lorenzetti's fresco, it is the Virgin's) with that of Christ.

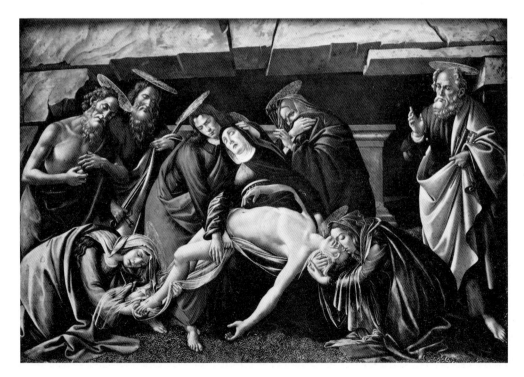

354. SANDRO BOTTICELLI. *Lamentation over the Dead Christ with Sts. Jerome, Paul, and Peter.* Late 1490s(?). Panel, 54 3/8 x 82". Alte Pinakothek, Munich. Commissioned for S. Paolino, Florence

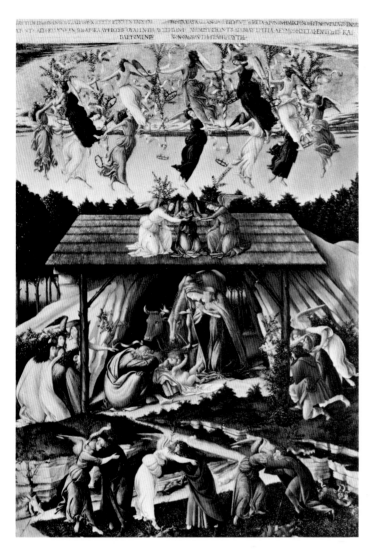

355. SANDRO BOTTICELLI. *Mystical Nativity*. 1500. Canvas,
42¼ x 29½". National Gallery, London

Botticelli's *Mystical Nativity* (fig. 355) of 1500 was probably painted for the artist's personal satisfaction. At the top is an inscription in Greek: "This picture I, Alessandro, painted at the end of the year 1500, during the trouble in Italy in the half time after the time which was prophesied in the 11th [chapter] of John and the second woe of the Apocalypse when the Devil was loosed upon the earth for three years and a half. Afterward he shall be put in chains according to the twelfth woe, and we shall see him trodden underfoot as in this picture." In spite of Botticelli's inscription, the picture has been difficult to interpret, as only a few elements from chapters 11 and 12 of the Book of Revelation are illustrated; some of his figures and groups are not in those chapters, and there is more than an echo of certain specific sermons by Savonarola. The second woe, describing the fiery prophecies of two "witnesses" and their death at the hands of the Antichrist, must surely refer to the deaths of Savonarola and his principal follower, Fra Domenico da Pescia. And the "half time after the time" can only refer to the half-

millennium after the millennium after the Nativity of Christ, the subject of the picture—in other words, the year 1500.

The "trouble in Italy" is not hard to identify, considering that the armies of Cesare Borgia were then loose in Tuscany. After all this passes—so Botticelli dreams—we will be brought to where the mystic woman of Revelation 12 has found refuge with her child in the wilderness, all devils will be chained under the rocks (we see this in the lowest foreground), angels will embrace us, and we may dwell in safety. Angels with olive branches draw shepherds to adore the Child. In the heavens above, angels dance in a ring, the age-old symbol of eternity, and crowns are suspended from the olive branches they carry. It might be said that this final regression assuages the longings of Botticelli's lifetime. The embrace of peace, the circling patterns, the sheltering wood, and the protecting mother are part of a ritual of surrender through which the painter's fever is stilled at last. Even the color is transformed: the jewellike blues, yellows, and reds are a release from the harsh tones that characterized the period of stress through which the artist had passed.

But he had made his choice. In renouncing the contemporary world he suffered the corollary penalty: the world renounced him. During the last ten years of his life—from about fifty-five to sixty-five, that is—Botticelli seems to have painted little. Although he was consulted with other masters about the placing of Michelangelo's *David* in 1504, the Florence of Leonardo, Michelangelo, and the young Raphael apparently had no work for him. Commissions went to artists who could emulate the new style of the High Renaissance. If we are to believe Vasari, Botticelli became prematurely old and walked with two canes.

FILIPPINO LIPPI

The fourth important Florentine painter of the end of the Quattrocento, Filippino Lippi (1457/58–1504), remains in Botticelli's shadow. This is unfair—Filippino was a splendid artist in his own right—but perhaps inevitable, since he entered Botticelli's shop at the moment when that master was enjoying his greatest success. Filippino received his early training from his father, Fra Filippo Lippi, accompanied him to Spoleto in 1466 (see p. 226), and remained there until Fra Filippo's death in 1469. Filippino's association with Botticelli lasted for a number of years, perhaps until the latter was called to Rome in 1481. In 1484 Filippino was asked to complete the frescoes by Masaccio and Masolino in the Brancacci Chapel (see p. 195; colorplate 3, p. 12).

Filippino's *Virgin and Child with Angels* (fig. 356) is the largest painted tondo of the Quattrocento, and it displays the artistic and poetic resources of Filippino's style. Nonetheless, the influence of the young Leonardo da Vinci, who had left Florence for Milan in 1483, can be felt in all Filippino's works of this period, in which

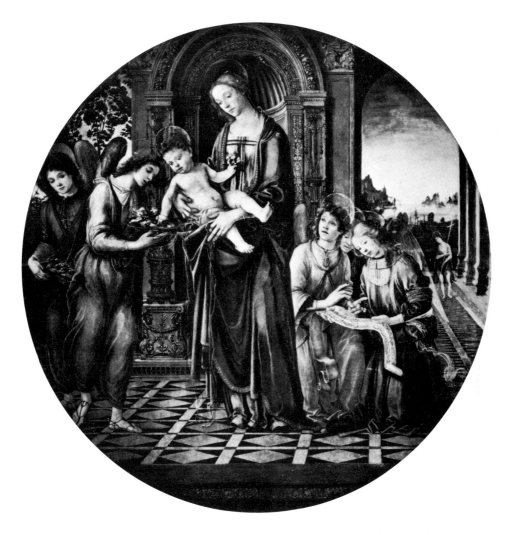

356. FILIPPINO LIPPI. *Virgin and Child with Angels.* c. 1485.
Panel, diameter 68¹/8". Corsini Gallery, Florence. Perhaps commissioned by
Lorenzo de' Medici for the Medici Villa at Careggi

he abandoned Botticelli's linear clarity for the soft *sfumato* (smoky) manner of Leonardo. Another element derived from Leonardo is the mysterious landscape in the background: a seaport with towers, breakwaters, and a lighthouse is enclosed by jagged mountains that suggest the Apuan Alps. A similarly fantastic port scene appears in the background of Leonardo's *Annunciation* (see fig. 453). On the left shoulder of Filippino's elegant Madonna shines the golden star seen in many representations of the Virgin; it is hers by virtue of the meaning of her name "Star of the Sea" (see p. 104), and the passages in theological writings from St. Augustine onward that call her "the port of the shipwrecked." St. Bernard combines both images, calling her "the star directing us to God, to the port of our salvation." The port scene appears in other representations of the Virgin, many with the star on her shoulder, datable in the 1480s. There may be some connection between Filippino's work and the Consoli di Mare (Consuls of the Sea), a special body of Florentine officials responsible for the administration

of the Florentine ports at Livorno and Pisa, especially since the youthful figure of St. John the Baptist, the patron saint of Florence, can be seen silhouetted against the harbor.

The richly decorated niche, which is gently pushed to the left of center so that the view of the distant sea may be more prominent, is hung on either side with rosaries. Graceful angels with pale faces and shadowy eyes present the Child with bowls of roses, from which he has culled a nosegay for his slender Mother. Such delicacy and sensitivity are traits that Filippino shares with Botticelli, but he has also understood Leonardo's *sfumato*, for the flow of tone veils exact statements and melts precise edges. The glowing color—blues, rose tones, greens, violets—in the often diaphanous drapery is characteristic of Filippino's style. And despite the elements derived from Leonardo, we recognize a new personal style in the elusive, poetic expressions of the faces.

Filippino's peculiar magic is at its strongest in the *Vision of St. Bernard* (colorplate 63, p. 304). Jacobus de

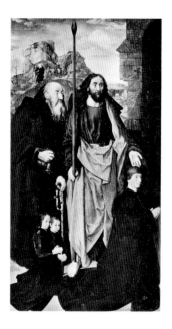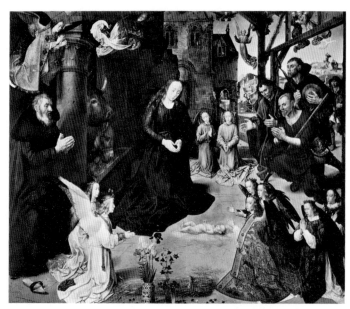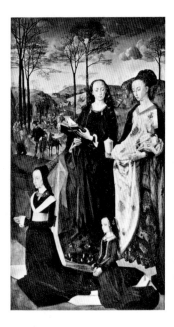

357. HUGO VAN DER GOES. *Adoration of the Shepherds* (Portinari altarpiece). Late 1470s.
Panels: center, 8' 4" x 10'; laterals, each 8' 4" x 4' 8". Uffizi Gallery, Florence. Commissioned by
Tommaso Portinari for Sant'Egidio, Florence

Voragine's *Golden Legend* tells us that one day when St. Bernard was feeling so tired and ill that he could scarcely hold his pen, the Blessed Virgin, for whose cult he had done so much, came to strengthen him. In Cinquecento representations of the vision, Mary and her accompanying angels float as a heavenly apparition (see fig. 486). Here she stands quietly before St. Bernard's outdoor desk, attended by wide-eyed child-angels who watch in wonder or genuflect and pray, as she lays a slender hand with infinite lightness on Bernard's rumpled page. He stops writing to look up in adoration, and between the pure profile of Mary and the face of the monk a Trecento manuscript stands open so that one can read St. Luke's account of the Annunciation. Filippino must have meant us to feel that Mary came to St. Bernard as the Angel Gabriel had come to her, and that in this vision the Christ Child is born a second time—as St. Antonine would have put it—in St. Bernard's heart. On the hillside monks look upward, astonished, at the golden glow through which Mary and her angels have descended. In the lower right-hand corner the donor, Francesco del Pugliese, a wealthy cloth merchant, folds his hands in prayer, and in a hole in the rocks just above his head a demon, gnawing his chains in defeat, can be seen.

The naturalism of faces and hands, rocks and trees, even the appearance of the angels recalls an artistic event of great importance for Florentine art. Filippino and other Florentine painters were profoundly impressed when a large altarpiece representing the *Adoration of the Shepherds* by the Netherlandish painter Hugo van der Goes (fig. 357) arrived in Florence, probably in 1483. Commissioned by Tommaso Portinari, a Florentine who worked in Flanders, it was placed on the high altar of Sant'Egidio between the now-vanished frescoes of Domenico Veneziano, his young assistant Piero della Francesca, and, later, Castagno and Baldovinetti. The Florentines had certainly seen small examples of Netherlandish painting, especially a *St. Jerome* by Jan van Eyck and Petrus Christus that belonged to Cosimo de' Medici, but the extensive realism of Northern painters had never before been spread before them on the scale of the Portinari altarpiece. It proved a revelation, and Filippino must have studied the melancholy faces of the Portinari children with care, as there is more than a reflection of them in his angels.

In his composition Filippino has achieved something similar to the broken quality of Verrocchio's sculptured drapery surfaces (see fig. 334). The forms seem to move restlessly, shimmering in small facets and pervaded by movement but with little sense of overall mass. In Filippino's Strozzi Chapel frescoes of the legends of Saints Philip and John the Evangelist, this antimonumental style comes to its climax. The frescoes were commissioned in 1487 by Filippo Strozzi, builder of the Strozzi Palace (see fig. 307), who gave Filippino permission to go first to Rome for an important commission in Santa Maria sopra Minerva. Strozzi died in 1494 without seeing the frescoes, which were only completed in 1502.

St. Philip Exorcising the Demon in the Temple of Mars (fig. 358) is one of the strangest pictures of the Florentine Renaissance. Apocryphal sources relate that when St. Philip entered the Temple of Mars in Hierapolis in Asia Minor, a demon in the shape of a dragon burst from the base of the statue of the god and emitted such poisonous fumes that the king's son fell dead. St. Philip's exorcism of the dragon greatly displeased the priest of

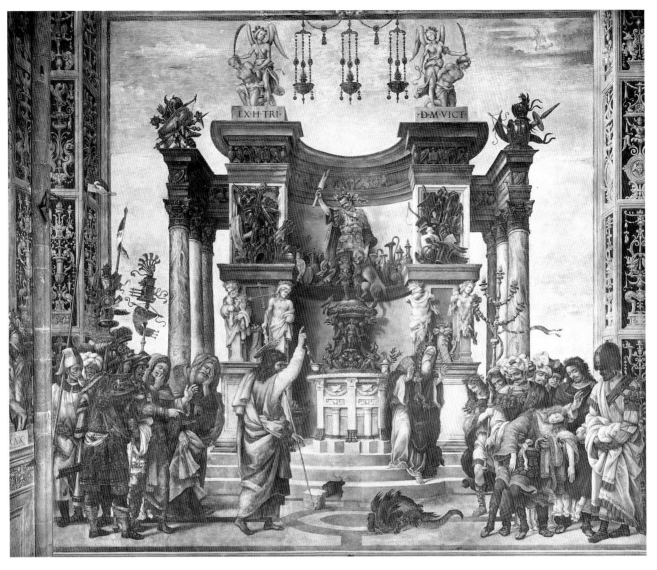

358. FILIPPINO LIPPI. *St. Philip Exorcising the Demon in the Temple of Mars*. 1487–1502. Fresco.
Strozzi Chapel, Sta. Maria Novella, Florence. Commissioned by Filippo Strozzi

Mars and led to the saint's crucifixion, which Filippino represents in the fresco above this one. Filippino has created a frame that is united with the brilliant painted architectural scheme in which he clothed the old Gothic chapel. The details are borrowed from the decorations he had seen in Rome in the Golden House of Nero, portions of which had just been unearthed. Since these decorations were found in what seemed to be a grotto, they became known as *grotteschi*, the origin of our word "grotesque." They generally consist of lamps, urns, consoles, masks, harpies, lions' feet, and other ancient Roman decorative elements that can be combined vertically on pilasters or woven into fantastic webs covering walls or vaults. Filippino's enframement is one of the first examples, if not the first, of *grotteschi* to reach Florence.

The altar is a huge exedra that encloses a statue of Mars, while below, to either side, herms, supposedly marble sculptures, twist as if alive. The ledges above are

crowded with trophies and, behind Mars, amphorae of various sizes and shapes. On the cornice, statues of kneeling, bound captives below winged Victories seem to mesh with the painted lamps that hang into the scene on chains from the mouths of three putti, from outside the frame. The intervening space is thus canceled out, and the illusion becomes even more contradictory through Filippino's placement of some figures in front of the frame at the sides. By such devices the hard-won perspective space of the Renaissance is renounced—even though individual elements are correctly projected—by an artist who, along with Botticelli, was classified by Fra Luca Pacioli in 1494 as a master of perspective.

Mars, looking more like a living person than like a statue, brandishes a shattered lance with one hand while with the other he caresses what is supposedly a wolf, however much it may look like a hyena. The priest cringes in terror at the power of St. Philip. On either side stand priests, courtiers, and soldiers wearing Filippino's idea of Near Eastern costume. Shape and consistency have been drained from their bodies, and they seem to be mere bundles of cloth. The dignity of the individual has vanished from Filippino's art along with the clarity of space. Despite differences of costume, age, hair, beards, and skin color, the faces are essentially the same; all are pervaded with the same look of incipient nausea, and they are painted with the utmost subtlety of surface and freedom of brushwork. It was hardly necessary for Filippino to show three of the bystanders holding their noses, for the emanations from the monster in the center of the stage seem to have attacked figures and setting. What a distance we have come since Masaccio! Filippino's fresco is, in the last analysis, the painting of a bad smell.

At the upper right-hand corner, so high and small that one hardly notices him, Christ appears in a rift in the clouds, carrying his cross and offering his blessing. One is reminded of the contemporary works of Hieronymus Bosch in the Netherlands, an artist who seemed obsessed with the worthlessness of man. This is an unexpected end for Filippino and for the poetic current in late Quattrocento art, but it is not dissimilar to what happened to Botticelli in the despairing *Calumny of Apelles* (see fig. 353). For the Florentines at the turn of the century, it seems that an affirmation of faith in humanity was no longer possible. It was to require a new political movement and younger artists to achieve a new vision of human destiny. Filippino died in 1504 at the age of forty-six, only three months after having submitted his judgment on the placing of Michelangelo's *David* (see fig. 477). We are told that all the workshops of Via dei Servi closed in respect as his body was carried from the Church of San Michele Visdomini to its final rest in Santissima Annunziata. Ironically, it was for San Michele Visdomini that Jacopo Pontormo, only thirteen years later, after the evaporation of the short-lived High Renaissance, was to paint an altarpiece that has been regarded as one of the first manifestations of Mannerism, a style that owes much to Filippino's introspection and interest in personal expression.

DOMENICO DEL GHIRLANDAIO

Our account of the Florentine Quattrocento ends with Domenico del Ghirlandaio (1449–94), who, in a career even briefer than that of Filippino, rose from still-unidentified artistic origins to become the leading personality in the Florentine School, if measured by the standard of worldly success. Domenico, together with his brother Davide and their brother-in-law Bastiano Mainardi, not to mention an army of assistants, captured the major commissions for public painting in Florence—frescoes and altarpieces—and many lucrative portrait commissions as well. Like Agnolo Gaddi at the end of the Trecento (see p. 140) and Giorgio Vasari in the third quarter of the Cinquecento (see p. 647),

Ghirlandaio and his school represented the official taste of the period. The scientific pursuits of Pollaiuolo and Verrocchio might appeal to Lorenzo the Magnificent, the arcane researches of Botticelli to Lorenzo di Pierfrancesco and his friends, but the ordinary Florentine businessman knew what he liked and may even have been irritated by so much fierce knowledge on the one hand and so much wild imagination on the other. Ghirlandaio's prose style suited the successful merchant perfectly.

Its subsequent fate is instructive. When Quattrocento art was rediscovered by nineteenth-century critics, Ghirlandaio's meticulous and convincing view of the life about him impressed a generation that never quite understood Masaccio and cast only a scornful glance in the direction of Uccello and Piero della Francesca. Then came the revolution of "Form" in the wake of Cézanne, Picasso, and the Cubists, and that of "Expression" after Van Gogh, Rouault, and Nolde, and Ghirlandaio fell from grace a second time. After all, he had made no discoveries about form or space, and he often demonstrated what little interest he had in drama. So Ghirlandaio—who to Ruskin was *the* master of painting in Quattrocento Florence—dwindled to minor significance in twentieth-century eyes. Gradually, in the last few decades, Ghirlandaio's merits have become appreciated again. His art shows at least three important qualities: he had the freshest and most consistent color sense of any Florentine painter of his day; he was familiar with the achievements of contemporary architecture and was thus able to compose figures and architectural spaces into a complex unity beyond that achieved by Quattrocento painters elsewhere in Italy; and, finally, in his rendering of human beings, his reserve sometimes veils his interest in representing character.

Domenico Bigordi, the son of a dealer in the golden garlands worn by wealthy women, acquired his father's nickname, Ghirlandaio (garland maker). He was trained as a metalworker, and we are not sure just how, when, or with whom he went into painting. His earliest works are somewhat clumsy, and a certain naïveté remains throughout his career. Eventually he absorbed some of the innovations of Pollaiuolo and Verrocchio, but he was apparently disinterested in the styles of Botticelli and Filippino. The last fourteen years of Ghirlandaio's life mark his rapid ascendancy as a painter, so rapid, in fact, that he could not work fast enough to satisfy the demand. His *Last Supper* for the refectory of the monastery of Ognissanti (fig. 359) was dependent on Castagno—probably not the work at Sant'Apollonia (see colorplate 50, p. 260), which Ghirlandaio may never have seen, but on a lost composition for Santa Maria Nuova. His table is situated in an upper room with a view over citron trees and cypresses into a sky with soaring falcons and pheasants. Nowhere is there a face as intense as those in Castagno's fresco, yet the subtle analysis of the inner life of the apostles is not to be underrated. Nor is the freshness of Ghirlandaio's color, the poised balance

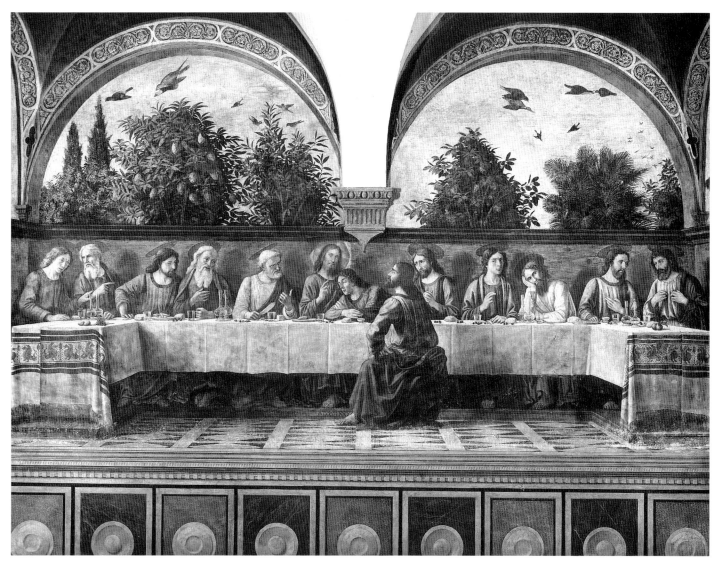

359. DOMENICO DEL GHIRLANDAIO. *Last Supper*. 1480. Fresco. Refectory, Ognissanti, Florence

of the composition, or the simple handling of the faces and drapery.

Domenico and his brother Davide were called to Rome in 1477. Domenico's contribution to the frescoes of the Sistine Chapel is the *Calling of Sts. Peter and Andrew* (fig. 360). The space of the fresco is formed by a glacial lake—suggestive of Lake Garda in northern Italy—stretching into the luminous distance, with cliffs, walled cities, and monasteries on its banks. In the middle ground, on the left shore, Christ calls Peter and Andrew from their nets; on the right he welcomes James and John. In the foreground Peter and Andrew kneel before Christ, who consecrates them in their mission, the foundation of the Church. The sides are filled with contemporary portraits, as in the Sistine frescoes of Botticelli (see figs. 342, 345). Ghirlandaio must have studied Masaccio's *Tribute Money* (see colorplate 39, p.

204), and, although he was apparently disinterested in the intensity of Masaccio's drama, he firmly controls the light on the drapery masses and endows the faces, especially that of Peter, with earnestness and calm.

The Sassetti Chapel in Santa Trinita in Florence, dedicated by the wealthy banker Francesco Sassetti to the Life of St. Francis, shows Ghirlandaio at the height of his achievement (colorplate 10, p. 18). In the background of the *Miracle of the Child of the French Notary* (fig. 361), the boy can be seen falling out of a window in the Palazzo Spini. In the center St. Francis blesses the child, who sits upright on his bier. The clarity of the narrative reminds us of folk art, especially the ex-voto scenes still painted today for Italian village churches to record the miraculous intervention of saints in the lives of the faithful. Moreover, Ghirlandaio has taken great pleasure in showing us the Piazza Santa Trinita, outside the church where the

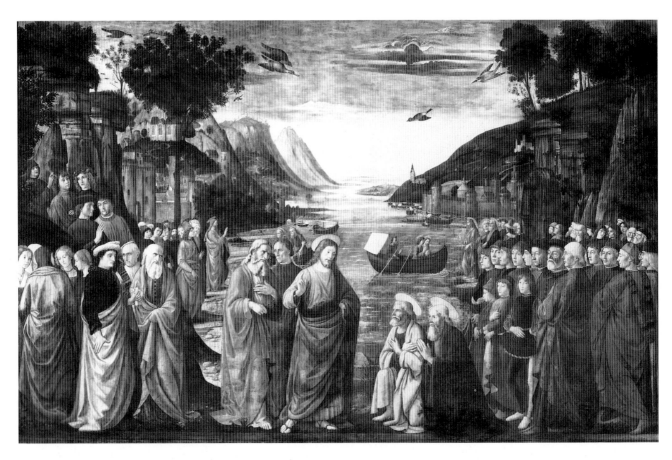

360. DOMENICO DEL GHIRLANDAIO. *Calling of Sts. Peter and Andrew.* 1481.
Fresco, c. 11' 5" x 18' 5". Sistine Chapel, Vatican, Rome. Commissioned by Pope Sixtus IV

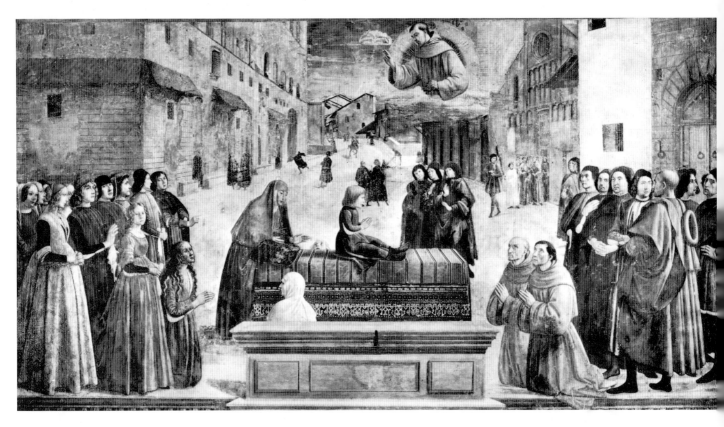

361. DOMENICO DEL GHIRLANDAIO. *Miracle of the Child of the French Notary* (see colorplate 10, p. 18). 1483–86.
Fresco, width 17' 2". Sassetti Chapel, Sta. Trinita, Florence. Commissioned by Francesco Sassetti

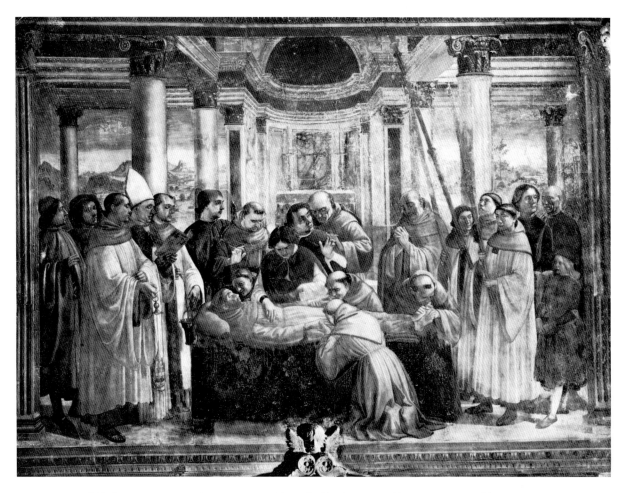

362. Domenico del Ghirlandaio. *Funeral of St. Francis*. 1483–86. Fresco, width 17' 2".
Sassetti Chapel, Sta. Trinita, Florence

chapel is situated. On the left rises the Palazzo Spini, on the right the Romanesque façade of Santa Trinita (replaced with a Mannerist structure by Bernardo Buontalenti in the late Cinquecento), and in the distance is the old Ponte Santa Trinita, lined with houses (this was replaced, after the flood of 1555, with the monumental bridge designed by Bartolommeo Ammanati with Michelangelo's intervention; see fig. 697). At the extreme right Ghirlandaio himself looks out toward us.

In the *Funeral of St. Francis* (fig. 362), Ghirlandaio has placed the scene in a colonnaded Renaissance loggia whose forms recall the architecture of Giuliano da Sangallo (see fig. 315). A poignant group gathers around St. Francis, whose emaciated face is certainly drawn from a corpse. Weeping monks kneel to kiss his hands and feet, while the knight of Assisi on the far side bends over to confirm the wound in the saint's side. The bishop of Assisi at the left, his glasses perched on his nose, calmly reads the service. His features and the youthful faces of the two monks are modeled by light with an unusual grace.

In the chapel's altarpiece, the *Nativity and Adoration of the Shepherds* (colorplate 64, p. 353), the Virgin adores

the Christ Child, who is pillowed by a bundle of hay. Classical elements witness Ghirlandaio's fascination with Roman antiquity. Two elegant square Corinthian piers, one bearing the date 1485, support the roof of the shed. The ox and ass look earnestly out and down over the manger, a Roman sarcophagus whose inscription records a divine promise of resurrection for the former occupant. The Roman triumphal arch in the background bears an inscription of Pompey the Great.

The train of the Magi passes through the triumphal arch and moves toward the foreground. The naturalism of the painting of the ox and ass, of Mary, and above all of the three shepherds shows devoted study of Van der Goes's Portinari altarpiece (see fig. 357). Ghirlandaio must have admired this work not for its disturbed emotional depths but for the honesty and completeness with which the tiniest detail was rendered. He even incorporates a vase of flowers into his foreground. Although the types and poses of his shepherds come straight out of the Portinari altarpiece, the differences are instructive. For all his absorption in Netherlandish naturalism, the artist is a Florentine, and he has assimilated the new detail

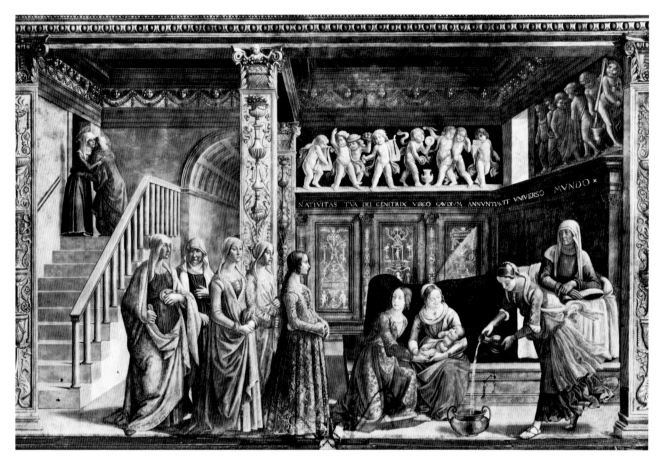

363. DOMENICO DEL GHIRLANDAIO. *Birth of the Virgin.* 1485–90. Fresco. Cappella Maggiore,
Sta. Maria Novella, Florence. Commissioned by Giovanni Tornabuoni

into the overall monumentality, compositional harmony, and tonal balance of an Italian Renaissance altarpiece.

One of Ghirlandaio's major commissions was the colossal series of frescoes of the Lives of Mary and John the Baptist that fills the Gothic chancel of Santa Maria Novella. The patron was the wealthy Giovanni Tornabuoni, a relative by marriage of the Medici, and Ghirlandaio was under such pressure that he enlisted his whole shop in the undertaking, including possibly a thirteen-year-old apprentice named Michelangelo Buonarroti. Although the execution, especially in some of the uppermost scenes, is occasionally hasty, the compositions are framed by a beautiful architecture closely connected, like that in the Sassetti Chapel, with the ideas of the architect Giuliano da Sangallo (see p. 309) and full of elaborate decorative detail. The *Birth of the Virgin* (fig. 363) takes place in a Giuliano da Sangallo interior. St. Anne reclines on a bed that is surrounded by paneling inlaid with ancient Roman designs, within which one can read both Ghirlandaio's family name and his nickname. The child is held by attendants, while an-

other pours water for her bath. Giovanni Tornabuoni's daughter Ludovica stands dispassionately with four attendants, dressed in splendor that surely violated the Florentine sumptuary laws. The details, including the frieze of putti, are painted with Ghirlandaio's precision of observation, smoothness of surface, and perspective consistency.

An unexpected side of Ghirlandaio's nature is seen in the *Massacre of the Innocents* (fig. 364), a dramatic scene that takes place in front of a Roman triumphal arch based on the Arch of Constantine. The foreground is filled with soldiers on galloping horses, an arrangement influenced by Roman battle scenes, especially the Trajanic reliefs on the Arch of Constantine. The mothers clutch their babies, and the ground is littered with the bodies and severed heads of little children. While the details are unequal in quality, some passages show great power, foretelling in their violent movements the battle scenes of the early Cinquecento.

Our farewell to Ghirlandaio might best be made with the portrait of an old man with a child, possibly his

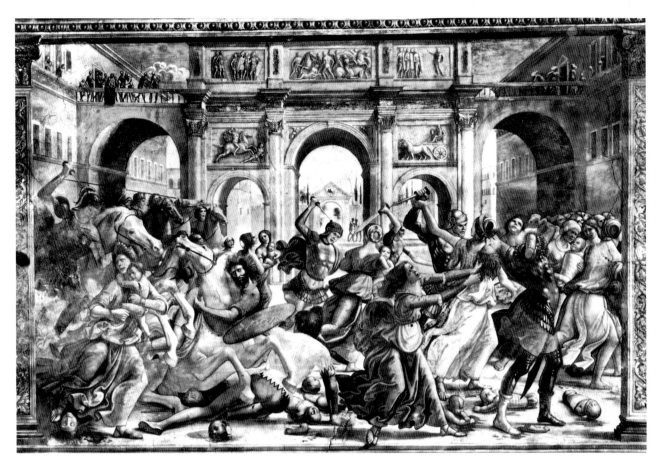

364. DOMENICO DEL GHIRLANDAIO. *Massacre of the Innocents*. 1485–90.
Fresco. Cappella Maggiore, Sta. Maria Novella, Florence

grandson (colorplate 65, p. 354). The subject has never been identified, although the deformed nose would seem to be easily traceable. A drawing by Ghirlandaio showing the old man on his deathbed was almost certainly a study for the painting. All the best qualities of his art appear here—the honesty of detail, studied with such respect that it loses its ugliness; the inner gentleness of expression; the delicate light on the smooth surfaces; the brilliance of the color; the beauty of the distant landscape; and the strange rigidity and inflexibility of composition, which combine a distinct archaism with all the studied naturalism of the artist's drawing.

Botticelli, Pollaiuolo, Verrocchio, Ghirlandaio, and Filippino Lippi, together with innumerable imitators, bring to its close a century of great artistic fertility. As we will see, the new century found it necessary to make a new beginning and to move in a sharply different direction.

14

The Renaissance in Central Italy

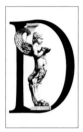espite the broad impact of Florentine artistic innovations, central Italian cities outside of Florence's political control felt no obligation to imitate the artistic ideals of the Florentine Renaissance. The problems of most central Italian towns had little in common with the civic tasks considered urgent by the Florentines; their trade was generally more limited, their horizons more personal. If these states escaped absorption by Florence—whose territorial ambitions were aimed largely at protecting the Arno Valley, from its headwaters to the sea—they fell under the sway of other powers, chief of which, in the second half of the century, was the papacy. The old communal form of government might linger on, but most towns owed their fealty to the States of the Church. This was true to a lesser extent of some of the independent sovereigns of the region, such as the counts (later dukes) of Urbino and the lords of Rimini. A number of local schools flourished in the southern portion of Tuscany and in the regions now known as Umbria, Latium, and the Marches. The most important schools developed in the two most populous centers, Siena and Perugia.

SIENA

By the early Quattrocento the bonds that formerly linked Siena with its Trecento confidante, Florence, had almost dissolved. Siena submitted to the temporary overlordship of Giangaleazzo Visconti of Milan, thereby outflanking Florence from the south. Against Guelph Florence, Siena supported the Holy Roman Empire and received visits from the emperors Sigismund and Frederick III. At the end of the Quattrocento, the city was under the rule of a dictator, Pandolfo Petrucci. It is perhaps no wonder that Siena could show no Masaccio or Brunelleschi, that for its artists, perspective was a plaything rather than an instrument, that antiquity made a tardy and fragmentary appearance in their work, and that they were little interested in the Early Renaissance and less in the High Renaissance.

One exception—the sculptor Jacopo della Quercia (see pp. 183–86)—proves the rule, but even Jacopo worked as much in Lucca and Bologna as in his native city, and in the 1402 competition for the Baptistery

doors, made an attempt to storm Florence (see p. 167). We may wonder what the Florentine artists thought of Siena. Occasionally one went there. The reliefs contributed by Donatello and Ghiberti to the baptismal font in the Cathedral of Siena (see fig. 173) were soon imitated by Sienese artists. Donatello returned in the 1450s, and a spark of his late style caught fire in the minds of local sculptors. Bernardo Rossellino was called to Siena by the Sienese humanist Aeneas Silvius Piccolomini, when he became Pope Pius II in 1458, for various architectural projects there and in the Piccolomini village of Corsignano, rechristened Pienza (see figs. 232, 233).

There are many other contacts as well, but Siena in the Quattrocento went in its own Gothic direction. The patrons seem to have kept right on requesting pointed arches and gold backgrounds, and there is no record that the painters protested. They idolized their Trecento predecessors and made exact copies of or variations on their works when commissioned to do so. Yet these same painters were very close to nature. Almost without the usual intermediary of villas and suburbs, the open country began, and in places still begins, at the walls of Siena, with low ranges of hills and spacious views, compared with which the steep slopes and greater heights that ring Florence seem constricting. Without the aid of Florentine science, the Sienese painters made certain discoveries about art, particularly about landscape, that were denied to the more systematic Florentines. In the tedium of his country town in southern Tuscany, even Piero della Francesca found much to learn from the Sienese.

SASSETTA

Before he left for Florence, Piero may have met Sassetta, who came to Sansepolcro in 1437 to produce an altarpiece for San Francesco. Sassetta's painting was in position by 1444, a year before Piero accepted the commission for his own early work, the Misericordia altarpiece (see fig. 277). Stefano di Giovanni (c. 1400–1450), called Sassetta for unknown reasons, may have come from Cortona. The Sansepolcro altarpiece, its original elements now scattered, is his major work (colorplate 66, p. 355; figs. 365, 366). It was doublesided; the front showed the *Enthroned Madonna and Child* between four saints in separate panels. Eight panels illustrating scenes

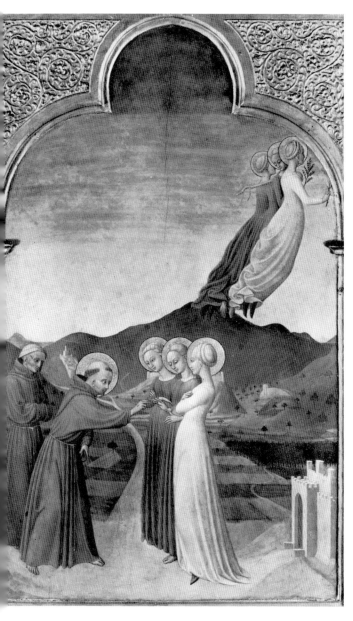

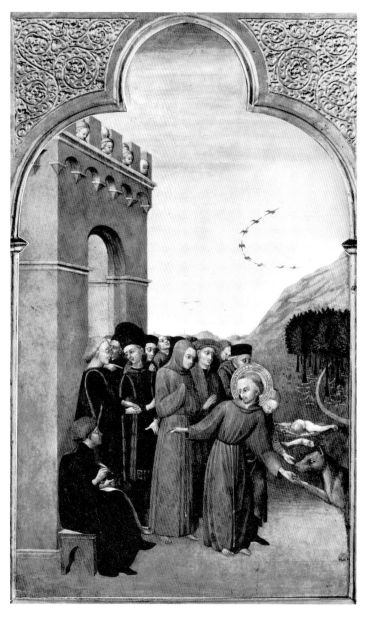

365. SASSETTA. *Marriage of St. Francis to Lady Poverty*, from the back of the Sansepolcro altarpiece (see colorplate 66, p. 355). 1437–44. Panel, 34⅝ x 20½". Musée Conde, Chantilly. Commissioned by the Franciscan community in Sansepolcro for the high altar of S. Francesco, Sansepolcro

366. SASSETTA. *Pact with the Wolf of Gubbio*, from the back of the Sansepolcro altarpiece. 1437–44. Panel, 34⅝ x 20½". National Gallery, London

from the Life of St. Francis originally accompanied the *St. Francis in Ecstasy* on the back. Smaller panels, about whose places in the polyptych there is little agreement, have turned up in different museums and collections.

Seen in its original position in the restricted space of a monks' choir, the *St. Francis in Ecstasy* must have exercised a commanding effect. St. Francis, extending his arms as he glides miraculously over the sea, stands like a statue from a cathedral portal upon Wrath, a crowned and bearded figure attended by a lion. To the left, a nicely dressed young woman leaning on a boar and looking in a mirror personifies Lust. On the right, Avarice, a shriveled old woman dressed in black and accompanied by a wolf, keeps her money bag in a rectangular press. Above the saint soar three dainty blond maidens

who represent the Franciscan Virtues: Chastity with her lily, Poverty dressed in rags, and, in the center, Obedience with her yoke. The inscription on St. Francis's halo identifies him as the patriarch of the poor.

In the saint's pose and expression, rapture and calm appear in perfect accord. The drapery and the limbs beneath are modeled in broad, clear-cut masses by a high light source. Their weight and thickness are emphasized to the point where we are tempted to suspect that Sassetta had studied the works of Giotto and even Masaccio. The features are equally sculptural, but the head is curiously constructed. Following Byzantine tradition, Sassetta has used the bridge of the nose for the center of the face. A circle described from this point corresponds only to the inner circle of the halo; the forehead and hair fall short, apparently to indicate that they are tilted back. When we approach more closely, we fall under the spell of the old Sienese linearism: what appear to be wrinkles in the saint's forehead, temples, and cheeks are drawn as artificially parallel curves, moving in elliptical, parabolic, or figure-eight patterns with dizzying effect.

Around the saint blazes a mandorla composed of red seraphim with interlocked wings, a traditional Trecento device. These have largely peeled away from the gold background, but originally their effect must have been striking. That the gold is intended to represent the sky is suggested by the distant shore with its bare hills and towers. There are echoes of Simone Martini and the Lorenzetti, and some aspects of the style even remind us of Chinese Buddhist sculpture. None of these resemblances, however, should blind us to the essential: that without reference to Florentine perspective, Sassetta has created distant space into which his landscape elements convincingly recede and has set a solid, reasonably illuminated figure within this space. These are Renaissance elements, and they place Sassetta in harmony with what was then going on in Florence.

In the smaller scenes Sassetta gives free rein to his imagination and his interest in space. The *Marriage of St. Francis to Lady Poverty* (fig. 365) first shows the saint stepping happily forward to place a ring on the finger of Poverty, who stands between Chastity and Obedience; as the three float off for celestial regions, Poverty glances back sweetly toward her bridegroom. The flattened curves of the three Virtues harmonize with the shapes of the cusped frame. At the lower right, Sassetta makes an obeisance to Duccio in the shape of a tiny city that might have come out of one of the panels of the *Maestà* (see fig. 92). Between Francis and the Virtues a long white road runs across the checkered valley floor to branch into curves among distant ranges that are not just a backdrop; these mountains loom before us, their contours rippling in the evening air. Sassetta has achieved a compelling sense of natural space.

The *Pact with the Wolf of Gubbio* (fig. 366) shows Francis taking the paw of a wolf who had been devouring the city's inhabitants. Francis has persuaded him to accept instead a steady and harmless diet that will be provided at public expense. Below the city gate a notary holds the pact ready for the wolf's signature. The authorities gather before the gate in wonder and thanksgiving, while the women and children peek less trustingly between the crenellations. The road leading into the forest is bordered by well-cleaned bones and the foreshortened fragments of the wolf's latest meal. Again Sassetta has given us an experience of deep landscape; we look past the rocky shoulder to the remote horizon, punctuated by the towers of two Sienese towns. Many a traveler along the Via Cassia has seen the towers of Montalcino and San Quirico d'Orcia rise like this. High above, a flight of cranes in formation is a further spatial indicator.

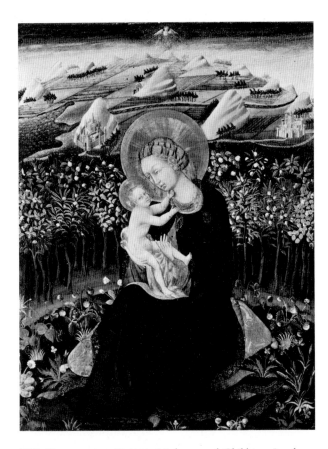

367. GIOVANNI DI PAOLO. *Madonna and Child in a Landscape* (*Madonna of Humility*). c. 1460s. Panel, 22 x 17". Museum of Fine Arts, Boston (Marie Antoinette Evans Fund)

GIOVANNI DI PAOLO

The slender bodies, delicate features, and small eyes of Sassetta's figures are further exaggerated in the works of his prolific contemporary Giovanni di Paolo (1403?–83). We do not know which of the two was the older. A Giovanni di Paolo was born in 1403, but many men may have shared the name, which translates literally as John, Son of Paul, in early Quattrocento Siena. Our artist was painting in 1420—not uncommon for a seventeen-year-old in the Renaissance, but unlikely. In the course of his long life he painted enough to fill two galleries in the Pinacoteca at Siena, not to mention altarpieces scattered throughout the town and the *contado* (countryside), and his paintings turn up in collections throughout the world. Giovanni copied Ambrogio Lorenzetti and Gentile da Fabriano and purloined from Ghiberti, Donatello, Lorenzo Monaco, and Fra Angelico, but his style is uniquely his own. In the *Madonna and Child in a Landscape* (fig. 367), Mary sits on a cushion in a flowered clearing surrounded by an orange grove. In the background a landscape, whose perspective orthogonals stubbornly refuse to converge, stretches off to the crack of doom. Its rippling waters and checkerboard fields alternate at intervals with sugarloaf hills.

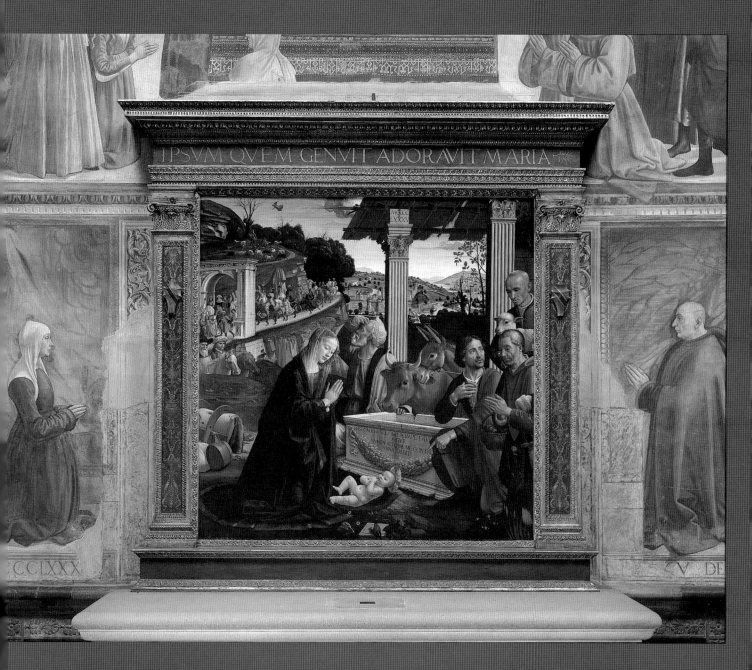

Colorplate 64. DOMENICO DEL GHIRLANDAIO. *Nativity and Adoration of the Shepherds*. 1485. Panel, 65¾" square.
⚱ Sassetti Chapel, Sta. Trinita, Florence (see colorplate 10, p. 18). The frame is original. The donors to the sides are
painted in fresco. Commissioned by Francesco Sassetti

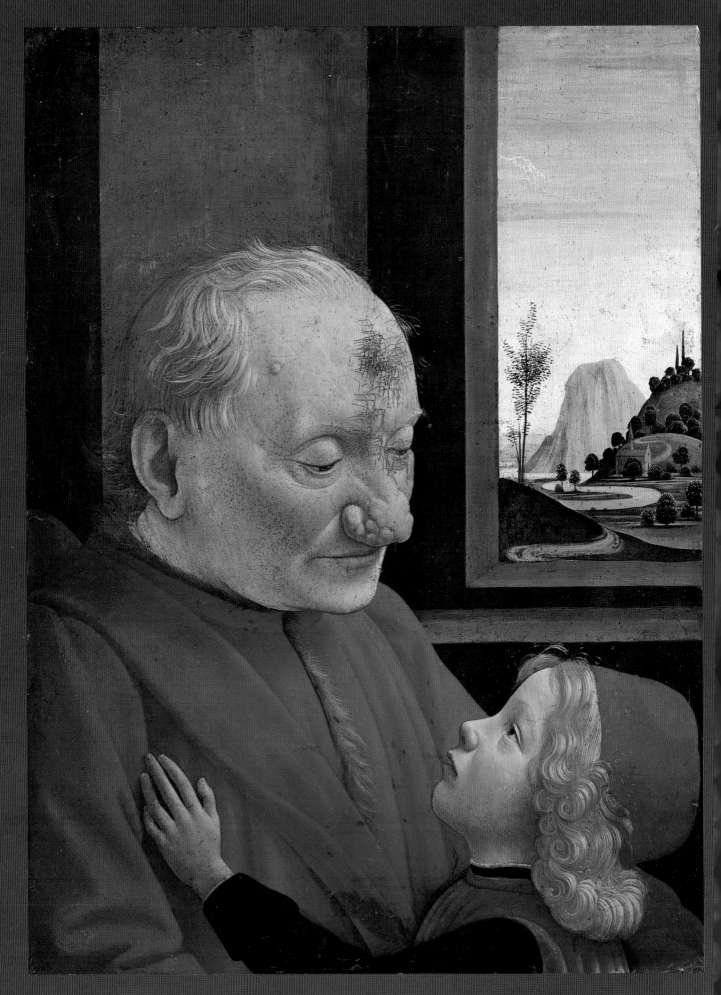

Colorplate 65. DOMENICO DEL GHIRLANDAIO. *Old Man with a Young Boy.* c. 1480. Panel, 24³/₈ x 18¹/₈". The Louvre, Paris

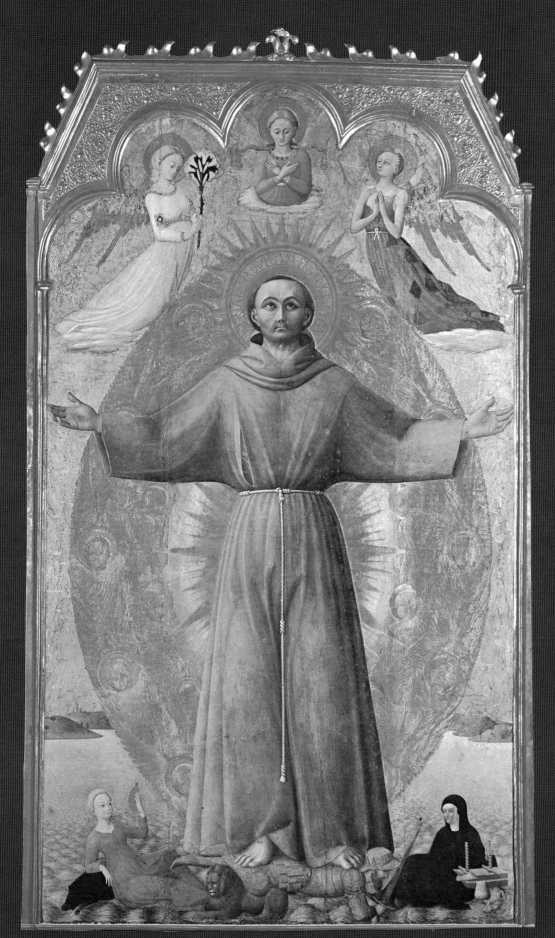

Colorplate 66. SASSETTA.
St. Francis in Ecstasy,
from the back of the
Sansepolcro altarpiece.
1437–44. Panel,
80¾ x 48". Berenson
Collection, Villa I Tatti,
Florence (reproduced by
Permission of the
President and Fellows
of Harvard College).
Commissioned by the
Franciscan community
in Sansepolcro for
the high altar of
S. Francesco, Sansepolcro

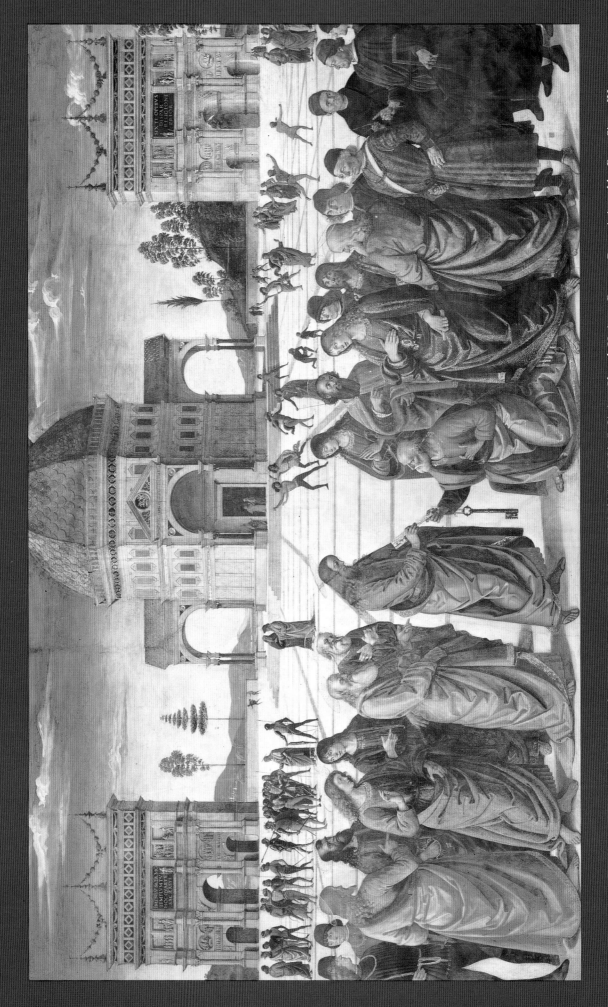

Colorplate 67. PERUGINO. *Christ Giving the Keys to St. Peter.* 1481. Fresco, 11' 5¹/₂" x 18' 8¹/₂". Sistine Chapel, Vatican, Rome. Commissioned by Pope Sixtus IV

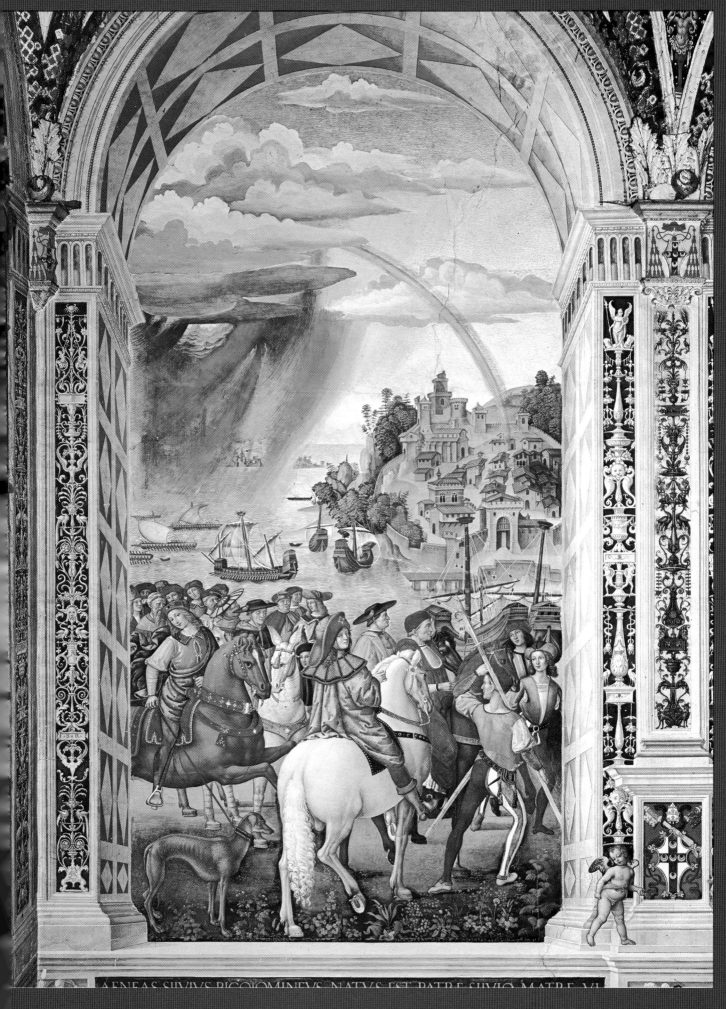

Colorplate 68. PINTORICCHIO. *Departure of Aeneas Silvius Piccolomini for Basel.* 1503–8. Fresco.
Piccolomini Library, Cathedral, Siena. Commissioned by Cardinal Francesco Piccolomini

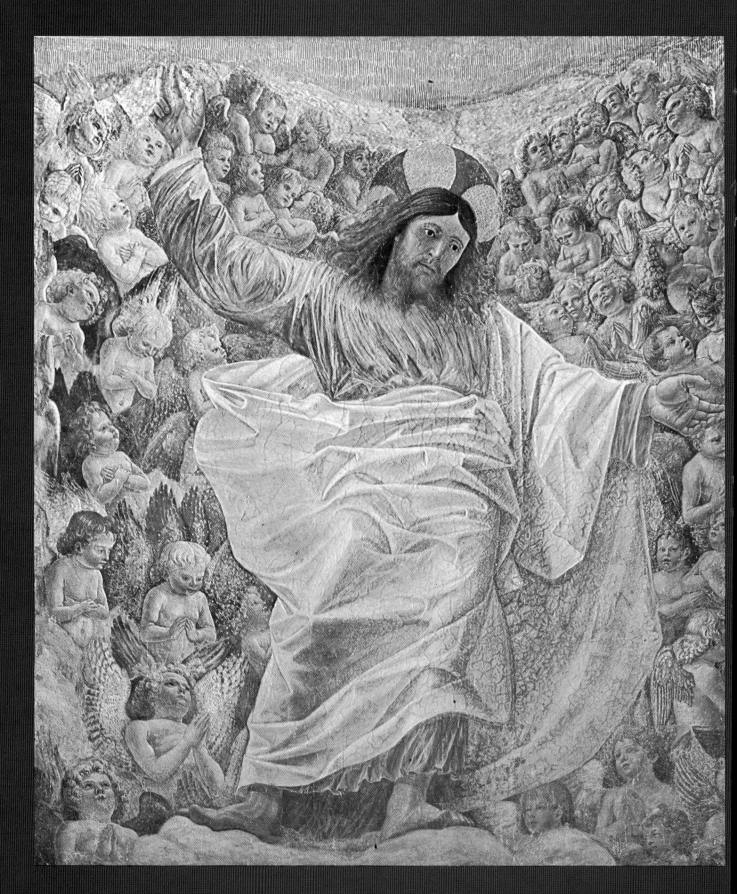

Colorplate 69. MELOZZO DA FORLÌ. *Christ in Glory*, from the *Ascension*. 1481–83.
Detached fresco from the Church of SS. Apostoli in Rome; now in the Quirinal Palace, Rome.
The patron may have been Cardinal Giuliano della Rovere or Pope Sixtus IV

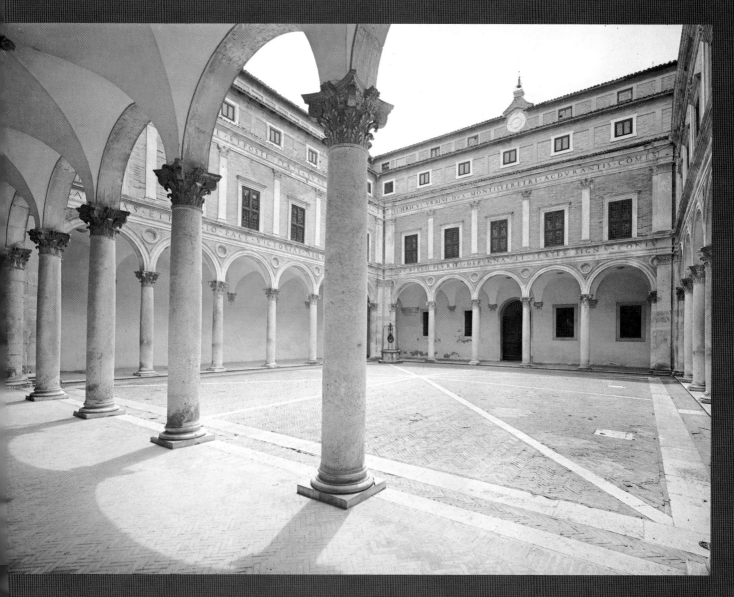

Colorplate 70. LUCIANO LAURANA. Courtyard, Palazzo Ducale, Urbino. c. 1465–after 1479.
Commissioned by Federico da Montefeltro

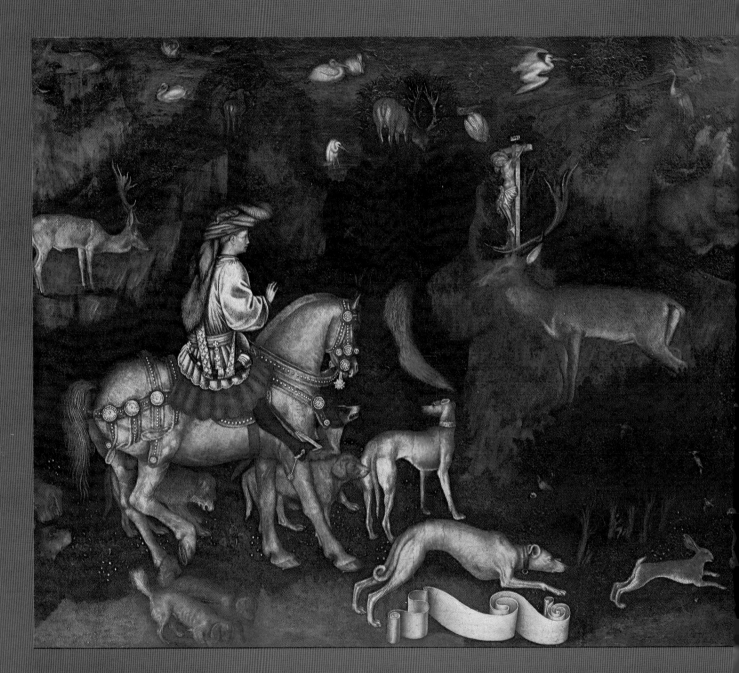

Colorplate 71. ANTONIO PISANELLO. *Vision of St. Eustace.* c. 1440(?).
Panel, 21½ x 25¾". National Gallery, London

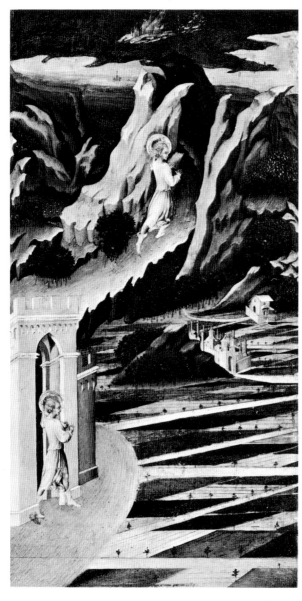

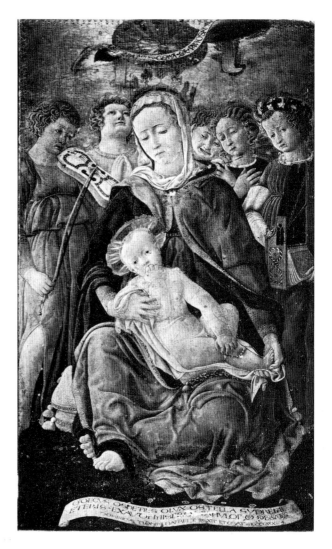

368. GIOVANNI DI PAOLO. *St. John Entering the Wilderness*, perhaps part of a reliquary cupboard (*custodia*). 1455–60. Panel, 27 x 14¼". The Art Institute of Chicago (Mr. and Mrs. Martin A. Ryerson Collection)

369. DOMENICO DI BARTOLO. *Madonna of Humility*. 1433. Panel, 36⅝ x 23¼". Pinacoteca, Siena

Both the archaistic charm of Giovanni di Paolo and his magpie borrowings are evident in a series of panels of the Life of John the Baptist. In the scene showing *St. John Entering the Wilderness* (fig. 368), two episodes are superimposed. First we see John stepping bravely out of a Sienese city gate that recalls Duccio and Simone Martini in the details of architecture and rendering. He gazes out on a cultivated plain made endless by Giovanni's characteristic device of what we might call one-legged perspective—orthogonals that never meet. Above, the world bursts into wild, flamelike mountains that are imitated from those depicted with vivid effect by Lorenzo Monaco in the opening years of the century (see fig. 125). The two episodes are separated by a tiny grove of distant trees, producing the effect of a sudden and disconcerting change in scale and in landscape character as the eye moves up the panel.

DOMENICO DI BARTOLO

The first Sienese painter whose relation to the Florentine Renaissance can be measured in terms of specific elements is Domenico di Bartolo (c. 1400–47). The influence of Masaccio is apparent in his *Madonna of Humility* (fig. 369), which, judging by its modest size, was probably painted for a private patron. The representation of the Madonna seated low upon a cushion is a Sienese invention that can probably be credited to Simone Martini; by the early Quattrocento it was widespread. Domenico has packed his picture tightly with figures of Masaccesque bulk that are projected in perspective. But Domenico's Sienese linearism requires that every shape be surrounded by a clear, unbroken contour, negating the Florentine modeling. The Christ Child stuffs fingers into his mouth, instead of grapes,

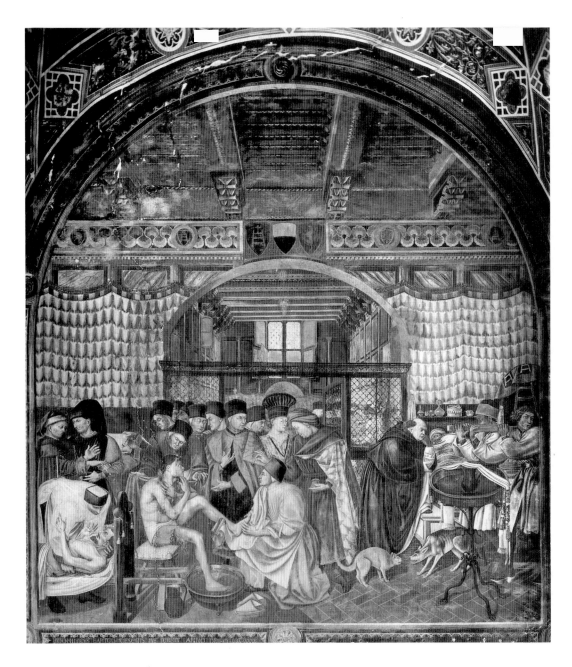

370. DOMENICO DI BARTOLO. *Care of the Sick.* 1440–47. Fresco. Pellegrinaio, Hospital of Sta. Maria della Scala, Siena

and the angels with their elaborate curls and solemn faces have nothing to do with Masaccio's ragamuffins. The *cartellino* (scroll) in the foreground, which antedates examples by Paolo Uccello (see fig. 263), tells us that Domenico "painted and prayed to" this Madonna. The pearly, silvery coloring is one of the most appealing traits in Sienese Quattrocento painting.

Domenico's major surviving achievement is his participation in a series of frescoes on the walls of the Pellegrinaio, a receiving ward still in use in the Sienese Hospital of Santa Maria della Scala (fig. 370). Our interest in Domenico's series is heightened by their secular subjects, which deal with the charitable, civic, and medical activities of the hospital. The arched frames are determined by the Gothic vaulting above, but through them we look, as through windows, straight into the fifteenth century. The perspectives are Albertian except for the tilted floors. The viewpoints are sometimes taken from within the rooms of the hospital and show decorations that are still in place today or even, in the case of the three-legged basin in figure 370, objects that still survive.

In their unabashed naturalism, the frescoes recall less the formally organized compositions of the early Florentine Renaissance than the more freely arranged paintings of the Netherlands, with their wealth of imagery drawn from contemporary life. In their suggestion of window views into space, Domenico's hospital frescoes are ancestors of Pintoricchio's fresco decoration in the Piccolomini Library, only a few hundred yards away in the Duomo (see colorplate 68, p. 357). In their naturalism and free disposition of figures, Domenico's frescoes are forerunners of the narrative method of Domenico del Ghirlandaio in the 1480s (see figs. 361–63). This may not be entirely accidental, as among Ghirlandaio's earliest commissions was a frescoed chapel in nearby San Gimignano. Domenico's figure style has shed its Florentine monumentality yet, interestingly enough, he has not reverted to the archaisms of Giovanni di Paolo or Sassetta. In the *Care of the Sick* (fig. 370), Domenico displays both a portrait realism and a sensitive treatment of

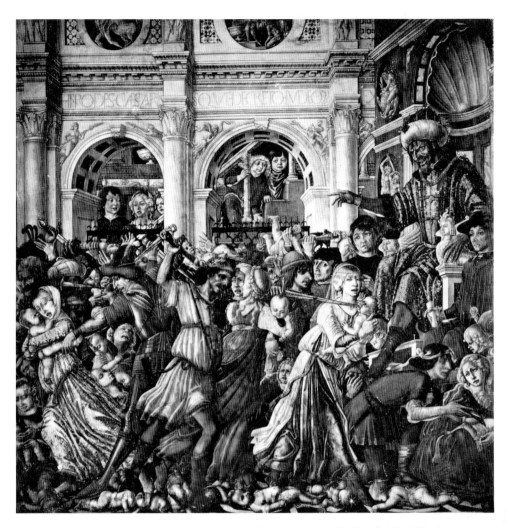

371. MATTEO DI GIOVANNI. *Massacre of the Innocents*. 1482. Panel, 95 x 94¹/₂".
Sant'Agostino, Siena

the nude figure. The sick man being placed in bed and the wounded man being washed are among the most naturalistic figures in Quattrocento painting.

MATTEO DI GIOVANNI

The Sienese painters of the next generation absorbed the details of Renaissance architectural backgrounds while ignoring the spirit of Renaissance architecture, and they transformed the linear grace of Botticelli to their own ends. In their isolation, they invert Florentine inventions to achieve the poetic purposes of their art. One of the most subjective of these late Quattrocento masters is Matteo di Giovanni (1435?–95), who may have been born in Sansepolcro. He was brought up in Siena, and by the 1470s he maintained a productive shop there. Matteo is best known for four monumental images of the Massacre of the Innocents, three for Sienese churches and one for the pavement of the

Duomo. It has been suggested that the popularity of this gory subject at just that moment is due to the massacre of Christian children by the Saracens at Otranto in southern Italy in 1480. Matteo's *Massacre of the Innocents* of 1482 (fig. 371) is fairly typical. The arches and columns of Herod's palace suggest that Matteo had been to Rome. Matteo has left no foreground space, and every inch of Herod's hall is occupied by screaming mothers, dead or dying babies, and bloodthirsty soldiers. The marble pavement is covered with infant corpses, among which the figures trample horribly. Impassive courtiers flank Herod's throne, but the gloating king is a monster: one hand is outstretched to order the butchery; the other, tense, clutches the marble sphinx on the arm of his throne. From the stair rail, children watch the slaughter with what seems to be fascination. Of all the lifelike faces in the group, the head of a soldier near the right-hand column is the most arresting because he pauses in his bloody task to look straight at the specta-

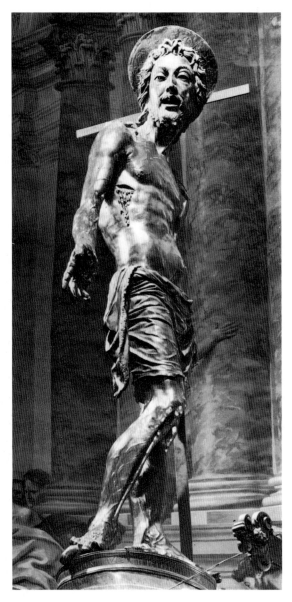

372. VECCHIETTA. *Risen Christ*. 1476. Bronze, height 6'.
⚱ Sta. Maria della Scala, Siena. Created by the artist for his
own tomb chapel

tor, with all the revelatory quality of a self-portrait. Can
this be Matteo himself, glorying in his holocaust?

VECCHIETTA

The visits of the Florentine sculptors Donatello and
Ghiberti and the intermittent presence of the Sienese
Jacopo della Quercia provided the impetus for a considerable school of Sienese sculptors. It is ironic that one of
the most memorable of these, Lorenzo di Pietro, called
Vecchietta (1412–80), was more prolific (if less exciting)
as a painter. He was involved at an early age in the work
on Masolino's frescoes at Castiglione Olona (see colorplate 42, p. 206), picked up elements from the Florentine painters at midcentury, and executed one of the

frescoes in the Hospital of Santa Maria della Scala.
However, he is most strongly remembered for a vivid
Risen Christ (fig. 372), made for his own tomb chapel at
Santa Maria della Scala. The bronze figure is harrowing
in its insistence on such realistic details as the network of
veins on the legs, arms, and torso; it betrays in exaggerated form the influence of the sinuous grace of Ghiberti
and the dramatic expression of the late Donatello. The
artist's personal involvement is evident from the touching petition he addressed to the hospital officials asking
that he be permitted to place the statue in his chapel.
Perhaps for this reason he was able to break the fetters of
stylistic archaisms and borrowings that generally bind
him and to produce a compelling witness of late Quattrocento religiosity.

FRANCESCO DI GIORGIO

Siena's equivalent of the multifarious Florentine artists,
who so often combined excellence in two arts, was Francesco di Giorgio (1439–1502), who did well at three.
He was, in fact, the only Sienese Quattrocento artist
save Jacopo della Quercia to acquire a reputation in
other areas of Italy; he worked at the courts of Urbino,
Naples, and even Milan, where he became acquainted
with and was influenced by Leonardo da Vinci. One of
his most impressive paintings is the huge *Coronation of
the Virgin* (fig. 373). The spatial composition of the towering altarpiece is difficult to unravel. A marble floor recedes to steps that end at a wall articulated by pilasters
and paneled in veined marble. The floor and the steps
are crowded with saints, and prophets sit atop the wall.
Angels and cherubs support a platform of cherub wings
and heads that floats in midair, and on this platform
Mary kneels to receive her crown from Christ. At the
top, one sees a foreshortened figure of God the Father,
feet first, surrounded by a spinning cloud that has been
identified with the *primum mobile* as described by Dante.
The concentric circles around God represent the seven
heavens; each has a planetary sign from the zodiac. At
the apex of the altarpiece, inside the highest circle, one is
taken aback to find a voluptuous array of female nudes,
but this must be based on Dante's statement that the final
heaven, or empyrean, was *pieno d'amore* (full of love).

However well Francesco may have been able to manage perspective, he has almost renounced it in this complex composition that represents a synopsis of the Christian universe, including nine hierarchies of angels and
eight of souls. In spite of the Renaissance treatment of
figures and drapery, the general effect is that of an abstract schema, like Duccio's *Maestà*, which nobody in
Siena ever quite forgot (see colorplate 28, p. 115). The
mournful faces and staring eyes are as characteristic of
Francesco's paintings as are the halting linear flow in
drapery and hair and the delicately awkward posing of
necks and hands. The dramatic and unexpected color
scheme is dominated by reds, orange-reds, and several
shades of bright blue.

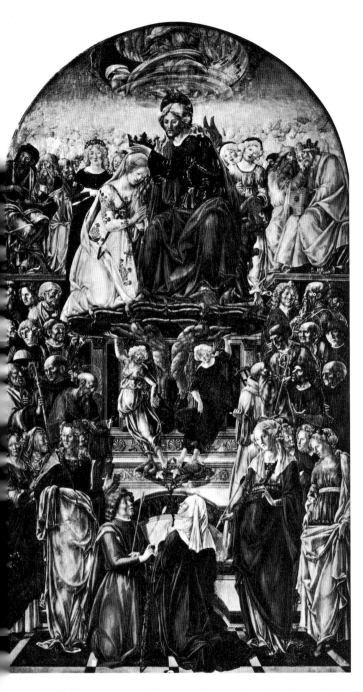

373. FRANCESCO DI GIORGIO. *Coronation of the Virgin*. 1471. Panel, 11' x 6' 6". Pinacoteca, Siena. Probably commissioned for the high altar of the Benedictine Monastery of Monte Oliveto Maggiore, near Siena

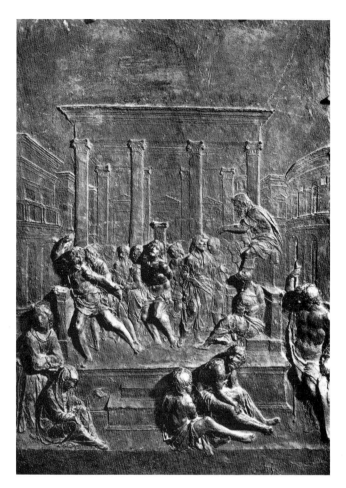

374. FRANCESCO DI GIORGIO. *Flagellation*. Late 1470s. Bronze, 22 x 16". Galleria Nazionale dell'Umbria, Perugia

Francesco's sculpture demonstrates a close acquaintance with the Florentine masters, not only Donatello and Ghiberti, who had intimate connections with Siena, but also Francesco's contemporary Antonio del Pollaiuolo. The *Flagellation* relief (fig. 374), which was probably modeled and cast in bronze during Francesco's stay in Urbino in the late 1470s, may have provided a model for the figure of Herod in Matteo di Giovanni's representations of the *Massacre of the Innocents*. The relief provides a striking contrast to the quiet *Flagellation* by Piero della Francesca (see colorplate 53, p. 263), also for Urbino.

The spatial impression created by the central portico and flanking architectural masses goes back to Ghiberti's reliefs on the *Gates of Paradise* (see colorplate 46, p. 257; fig. 236). But the handling of the clay, left rough and sketchy after its translation into bronze, is derived from Donatello's late style. The tormented pose of Christ, with his head thrown back, and the wild movement of the yelling man who beats him suggest the poses and expressions of Pollaiuolo. The almost nude figure at the right, in contrast, is extremely graceful.

The buildings Francesco portrays are new in style, and so were those he designed and built. The palaces in the background of the *Flagellation* are conceived as single-story structures, raised on ground stories treated like gigantic podia and crowned by deep entablatures. Francesco has emphasized what is later to be known as the *piano nobile* (story for the nobles), and on the left he has provided it with balconies. This new type, which contrasts to the three-story palaces common in Florence and other Italian cities, seems to have been Francesco's invention. Bramante, the most important architect of the Roman phase of the High Renaissance, was a citizen of Urbino and may have received the idea from Francesco. Second in importance is the emphasis given to the windows. No longer are they merely openings in

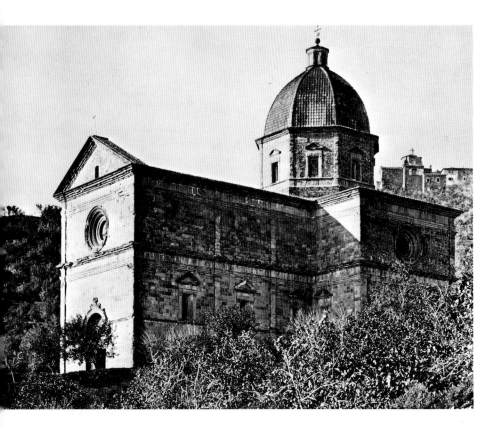

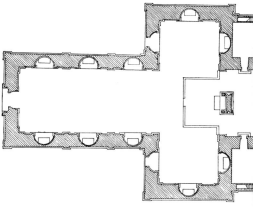

376. Plan of Sta. Maria del Calcinaio, Cortona

a rusticated wall—in fact, rustication itself is abandoned. Now the windows are independent tabernacles with sharply projecting frames; some are composed of pilasters supporting a pediment and resting upon a continuous cornice. These, too, were taken up by Bramante, Raphael, Antonio da Sangallo the Younger, and Michelangelo, and they become a constant feature of monumental architecture through the Baroque period.

Some of the grandest constructions of the late Quattrocento and early Cinquecento were sanctuaries to enshrine miracle-working images of the Virgin. Giuliano da Sangallo's Santa Maria delle Carceri in Prato (see figs. 313–15) was such a sanctuary, and so was Francesco di Giorgio's major building, Santa Maria del Calcinaio (fig. 375), on a slope leading up to Cortona. A miraculous image was found here in 1484, and the influx of pilgrims became so great that Francesco was called upon to design a large church to contain them. The church was completed in 1515, long after Francesco's death, but the initial phases of the construction seem to have proceeded rapidly, and there was already enough to dedicate in 1485. The shape is a Latin cross (fig. 376) whose nave is composed of three bays of diminishing depth in order to increase the apparent length of the church as seen from the entrance. The flexibility of proportions is made possible by Francesco's daring abandonment of the usual articulation of a church in terms of arcades or colonnades. His is a lofty two-storied hall, roofed by a barrel vault (fig. 377) and articulated by pilasters; the Corinthian order of the second floor, which is supported by the flat, unmolded strips of the

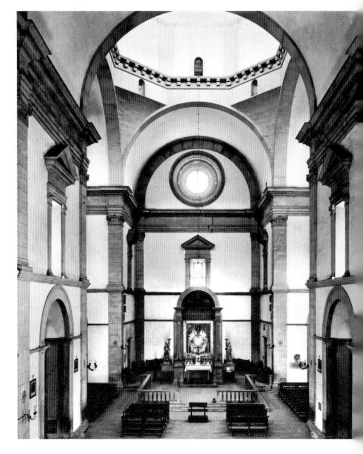

377. FRANCESCO DI GIORGIO. Interior, Sta. Maria del Calcinaio, Cortona

lower floor, supports the same kind of heavy entablature and cornice seen in the sculptured palaces of the *Flagellation.*

Although the ground-story niches suggest the arches of the characteristic nave arcade, their function seems to be to support the *piano nobile,* to which attention is directed. The tabernacle windows, with their sharply projecting pediments, are identical inside and out and are the direct ancestors of the tabernacles that play so important a role in the architecture of Michelangelo (see fig. 562). The four ends of the cross are flat, the entablature runs unbroken around the church, and the walls and barrel vaults, unrelieved in their plain white *intonaco,* suggest a space larger than the one they actually enclose. The tabernacles in *pietra serena,* therefore, seem to be independent sculptural entities within an apparently limitless expanse of white. The octagonal dome is supported on a peculiar compromise between pendentives and squinches, but even these are no stranger than the fact that the four arches rise into the octagonal drum, a device that increases the apparent height of the building.

In his paintings, more in his sculpture, and most of all in his archaeological drawings, theoretical investigations, and architectural creations, Francesco di Giorgio emerges from Siena into an all-Italian arena. A similar course, leading from provincial isolation to strong influence upon other centers, is followed by the Quattrocento School of Perugia.

Perugia

Since 1701 Perugia has been the capital of the region of Umbria, but in the Middle Ages and Renaissance the name "Umbria" was little known, having lapsed with the dissolution of the Roman Empire. In ancient times Perugia had been an important Etruscan center. In the Middle Ages the communal government asserted itself against the duchy of Spoleto, and in the Renaissance Perugia came under the control of the Baglioni family while owing ultimate allegiance to the papacy. In a chronicle of 1478 by Giovanni Santi, the father of Raphael, Perugia is said to be in Etruria (Tuscany). The designation "Umbrian" for Perugia is therefore avoided in this book.

Perugia stands on top of a near-mountain, dominating a considerable section of modern Umbria and southern Tuscany. Although the city embellished itself with a number of splendid buildings, and although the most important Roman, Florentine, and Sienese painters worked at nearby Assisi, Perugia did not produce an important school of painting in the Duecento or the Trecento. Its finest work of sculpture before the Quattrocento was the Fontana Maggiore, a fountain carved by Nicola Pisano and his assistants. But in the 1430s the presence of Domenico Veneziano in person and of a notable altarpiece by Fra Angelico (who may well have visited the town)—as well as the activity of Benozzo Gozzoli at nearby Montefalco in the early 1450s—

awakened local masters to the achievements of Florentine art.

Perugino

The leading painter of the Perugian School was Pietro Vannucci (c. 1445–1523), who may have been born in Città della Pieve but is known today simply as Perugino (Perugian). He brought the city from artistic obscurity to considerable influence and, as the teacher of Raphael, may be said to have had a hand in shaping the High Rennaissance. Where Perugino received his training is not known, but in 1472 he is listed as a member of the Company of St. Luke in Florence. He may have worked with Verrocchio for a period, and he certainly absorbed Florentine notions of perspective and figure drawing, but he rapidly developed a distinctive style. He had little or no feeling for religious subjects—Vasari said he was an atheist—and often reduced figure types to routine patterns. Nonetheless, Perugino became the master of a kind of spatial composition unknown before his day.

The principles of Perugino's spatial composition are evident in his first major work, *Christ Giving the Keys to St. Peter* (colorplate 67, p. 356), painted in the Sistine Chapel as part of the decorative program commissioned by Pope Sixtus IV. Perugino has been credited with the supervision of the cycle because he painted not only this subject, which is of primary importance to papal claims, but other crucial scenes and the altarpiece. In point of fact, none of the painters called to Rome had had much experience with monumental frescoes and all were relatively young; the impression of consistency among the frescoes may result partly from the overall supervision by the papal court and partly from the good taste and common sense of the artists, who seem to have been willing to work together to assure the success of the principal pictorial undertaking of the decade.

Perugino represents the moment when Christ gives St. Peter the keys to Heaven and Earth, and the structure in the center of the piazza is doubtless intended to represent the Church, founded on the "rock" of St. Peter. It is flanked by triumphal arches, modeled on Constantine's arch in Rome, that bear inscriptions comparing the building achievements of Sixtus to those of Solomon. In the middle ground the scene in which Christ says "render therefore unto Caesar the things which are Caesar's" (Matthew 22:21) is shown to the left; to the right is the stoning of Christ, who, according to the Gospel of St. John, hid himself, then passed through the midst of his assailants.

The perspective of the piazza is constructed according to Alberti's system, although with larger squares than Alberti recommended, probably to avoid the visual complexity that would have resulted from using Alberti's squares for a huge piazza. Perugino's scheme recalls the contemporary drawing by Leonardo da Vinci for the *Adoration of the Magi* (see fig. 456), a scheme that Leonardo eventually abandoned but which Perugino might

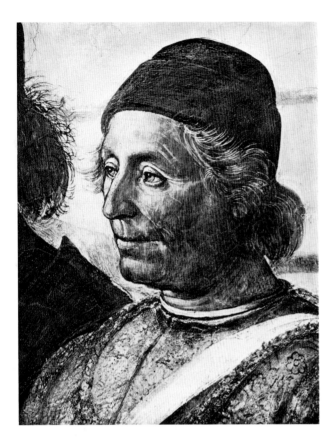

378. PERUGINO. Head of a Man, detail of *Christ Giving the Keys to St. Peter* (see colorplate 67, p. 356). 1481. Fresco. Sistine Chapel, Vatican, Rome

sees from Perugia, or in fact anywhere in present-day Umbria, may be debated. But that a painter with Perugino's sensitivity to space might be strongly influenced by the views that stretch from the heights of Perugia is more than possible. At any rate, an open space, intuitively perceived rather than rationally organized, is one hallmark of his style.

Perugino's figures, moreover, are only superficially Florentine. They stand with natural ease and an absence of tension not found in the works of Florentine Quattrocento artists. The weight is generally placed on one foot, the hip slightly shot, the knee bent, and the head tilted—the figure as a whole seems to unfold gently upward like the growth of a plant. Raphael was to adopt this S-shaped pose from Perugino, and it was to survive, in altered and spatially enriched form, to the final phases of his art. Perugino's main figures, like those of the other collaborators in the Sistine frescoes, occupy a shallow foreground plane, but they detach themselves more strongly from the distant space than do those of the other masters in the chapel. The grace of their stance is united with flowing drapery, and a looping motion carries the eye almost effortlessly across the foreground from one graceful figure to the next.

Perugino's *Crucifixion with Saints* (fig. 379), which probably dates from before his activity in Rome, shows considerable influence from the Netherlands and, in particular, the style of Hans Memlinc. The triptych differs from Florentine representations of the Crucifixion in the absence of strong emotion. Christ hangs calmly on the cross; Mary looks downward, St. John looks upward, and neither seems to betray a trace of grief, any more than does St. Jerome in the left panel or Mary Magdalen in the right. We are surprised, moreover, to notice that Mary Magdalen's pose is almost a carbon copy of John's: there is no difference between them, save for a slight change in the position of the clasped hands. Perugino seems to have made a pattern book of stock poses and to have repeated them even within the same picture, but this repetition of poses helps create the calm, lucid quality of Perugino's works. In the final analysis, the color of the painting is so cool and silvery, the finish so sensitive and exact, and the pervasive mood so poetic that we can accept the absence of emotion.

The fantastic rocks crowding the sky are characteristic of an eroded plateau in the upper Arno Valley, and Perugino must have studied these rock formations and the roads winding through them, one of which led from Florence toward Arezzo and Perugia. The jagged profiles and sparse foliage against the sky are exploited for sheer artistic effect, as are the floating S-curves of Christ's loincloth, a motif probably borrowed from the Flemish painter Rogier van der Weyden. Much of the picture's effect is gained from the precision of detail—leaves, twigs, wildflowers, a castle or two—against smooth surfaces of ground or sky.

Perugino was a remarkable portraitist, and in this also he seems to have been influenced by Memlinc. His por-

have seen. The figures and drapery masses are deeply indebted to Florentine doctrine, with echoes of painters and sculptors from Masaccio to Verrocchio, and the ideal church blends elements drawn from Brunelleschi's dome and the Florentine Baptistery (see figs. 132, 85). The cool precision of the contemporary portraits (fig. 378) is not excelled, even by Ghirlandaio.

Yet the fresco's effect of openness is strikingly un-Florentine and, for that matter, un-Sienese. Florentine spatial compositions are usually circumscribed by the frame, by figures, or by architecture. Perugino allows the eye to wander freely through his piazza, which is filled with little but sunlight and air and which is open at the sides so that we can imagine its continued indefinite extension. No such immense pavement was ever built in the Renaissance; it would have been useless, impractical, and in bad weather intolerable. But in Perugino's painting it provides a refreshing sense of liberation, as if the spectator could move freely in any direction. The perspective is truncated by the distant building so that the eye cannot follow it to the vanishing point. Its inward motion dissolves, rather, in the hills on the horizon, which substitute their gentle curves for the severe orthogonals of the piazza. The hills diminish and form the "bowl landscape" characteristic of the paintings of Perugino and his followers. That this is the landscape one

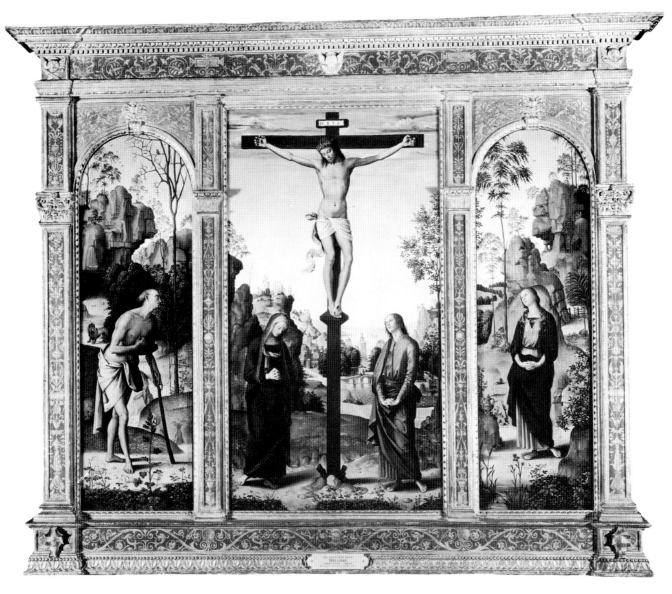

379. PERUGINO. *Crucifixion with Saints*. Before 1481. Panel, transferred to canvas:
center, 40 x 22¼"; laterals, each 37½ x 12". National Gallery of Art, Washington, D.C. (Mellon Collection).
Commissioned by Bartolommeo Bartoli, Bishop of Cagli and Confessor of Pope Alexander VI,
and presented to S. Domenico, San Gimignano

trait of *Francesco delle Opere* (fig. 380) is the direct ancestor of portraits by Raphael, such as those of *Angelo Doni* and *Maddalena Strozzi Doni* (see figs. 484, 485). The subject is placed behind a ledge—a typical Netherlandish device—on which he rests his hands, one of which holds a scroll bearing the motto TIMETE DEUM (Fear God). The landscape is half-filled with an expanse of sea forming a distant horizon, over which rises the carefully observed head, its hair streaming out against the sky. This is a typical Perugino sky, beautifully graduated in aerial perspective from milky blue at the horizon to a resoundingly clear and deep blue at the zenith. The balancing of mass and void, the harmonizing of the contours of the sitter with those of the sloping hills and feathery trees, and the sense of quiet and easy control

mark a new stage in the development of portraiture.

The culmination of Perugino's mature style, to a point where it is difficult to separate it from the youthful work of Raphael, is seen in his altarpiece for the Certosa at Pavia, commissioned about 1496 but still unfinished in 1499. Although the three central panels, representing the *Virgin Adoring the Child, St. Michael,* and *Tobias with the Archangel Raphael* (fig. 381), have lost several inches at the bottom—sacrificing a recumbent Satan in front of St. Michael, part of the sack on which the Christ Child sits, and the dog in front of Tobias— the effect is still one of calm repose. St. Michael is wearing glittering steel armor, and Tobias looks trustingly at the Archangel Raphael, who protected the boy during his lengthy quest to find the fish that would cure his fa-

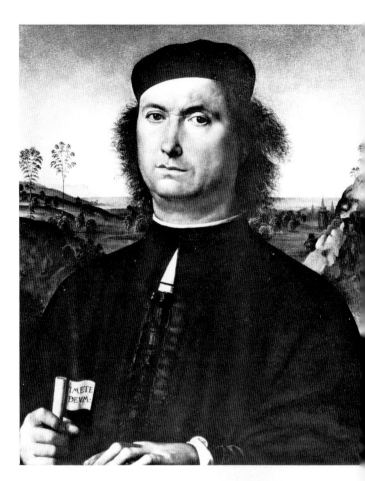

380. PERUGINO. *Francesco delle Opere*. 1494. Panel, 20⅛ x 16⅞". Uffizi Gallery, Florence

ther's blindness. Tobias was a favorite subject for altar-pieces commissioned by mercantile families sending a young son to work in a distant city. Though the facial types are standardized, the heads are drawn and painted with apparent spontaneity, as are the tranquil valley between its feathery trees and the three angels lightly dancing in the deep blue sky. It is no wonder that the question of Raphael's participation, quite possible if the work dragged on after 1500 when he began to work with Perugino, has arisen. The question can be answered no more easily than the analogous suspicions about the participation of the young Leonardo in the works of Verrocchio.

Like all central Italian painters who made their reputations in the 1470s—save only Leonardo da Vinci—Perugino arrived at the threshold of the High Renaissance but did not cross it. The grand style emerged in Florence and developed in Rome, while in Perugia Perugino continued to paint his oval-faced Madonnas and serene landscapes. He outlived Raphael by three years.

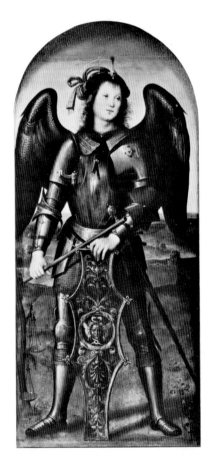
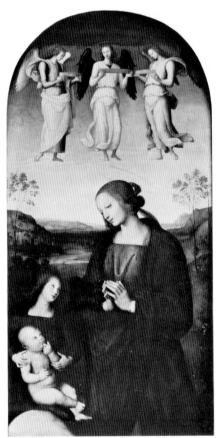
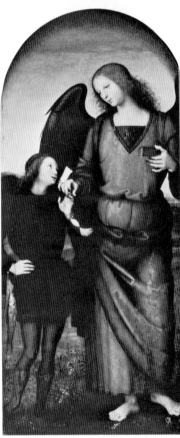

381. PERUGINO (and RAPHAEL?). *Virgin Adoring the Child, St. Michael,* and *Tobias with the Archangel Raphael.*
c. 1499. Panels: center (cut down), 50 x 25"; laterals (cut down), each 50 x 22 ¾". National Gallery, London.
Commissioned by Lodovico il Moro for the Certosa of Pavia

PINTORICCHIO

The works of the Perugian painter Bernardino di Betto (c. 1454–1513), who is known to posterity by the nickname Pintoricchio, are endearing because of their decorative and narrative charm—Pintoricchio is a kind of Perugian Benozzo Gozzoli. The success of his work cannot be gauged by reproductions, even in color, because so much of their appeal depends on the relation of the paintings to the space for which they were painted. A visit to the frescoed rooms and chapels of Pintoricchio is thus a rewarding but incommunicable experience. Pintoricchio emerged upon the Roman scene as Perugino's co-worker in the Sistine Chapel frescoes, and he returned to paint an entire apartment in the Vatican for Pope Alexander VI, as well as chapels and ceilings in various Roman churches. His largest work is the fresco cycle in the Piccolomini Library of the Cathedral of Siena (colorplate 68, p. 357), commissioned in 1502 by Cardinal Francesco Piccolomini to celebrate the life of his uncle, Pope Pius II. After the death of Alexander VI in 1503, Cardinal Piccolomini succeeded him as Pope Pius III, but lived to reign only ten days. Nevertheless, the fresco series financed by the Piccolomini heirs kept Pintoricchio busy until 1508.

The long, narrow room was built to house the illuminated manuscripts assembled by Pius II (Aeneas Silvius Piccolomini), who was one of the most learned humanists of his age. After his election as pope, he poured much of the revenues of the papacy into his library. The frescoes narrate an embellished version of the career of Aeneas Silvius before and after his election. Their stilted flattery contrasts with the salty memoirs of the pope, which, though long suppressed save in an expurgated version, have been preserved and furnish us with perhaps the single most vivid eyewitness account of mid-Quattrocento events. The frescoes fill ten lofty compartments that reach from the reading desks to the arches of the vault. The compartments are separated by painted pilasters and are framed by illusionistic arches whose jambs and soffits are decorated with marble incrustation (painted, of course); the pilasters have a continuous decoration in *grotteschi*. Each compartment allows us to look out, as if through the arch of a gigantic loggia, into a scene from Aeneas Silvius' life, painted in clear and brilliant colors. The pageantlike incidents of this mythologized biography display a gorgeous panoply of costumes against fanciful architectural or landscape backgrounds, except when a recognizable setting was required by the narrative.

In one scene (colorplate 68, p. 357) Aeneas Silvius, as secretary to a cardinal, starts off from Genoa to the Council of Basel (later declared an anticouncil), at which his performance was so disloyal to the papacy that he had to do penance before Pope Eugenius IV. In the distance we see two caravels at anchor in the port, and at sea is depicted an earlier incident in which the cardinal's galleys were lashed by a storm. The port of Genoa,

of course, never looked like this; Pintoricchio has represented an Italian hill town, with a Romanesque church and a castle on top of the hill. But if his Genoa is derived from local experience, so is his storm. One of the earliest naturalistic storm scenes preserved to us, it is made especially convincing by the way in which the artist shows the long, dark veils of rain bent by the force of the wind and the sharp contrasts in colors among the thunderclouds. It does not pay to look too closely at Pintoricchio's faces, which are often schematically drawn, and even less to examine the heads of his horses and mules, but his crowds of people appear relaxed and natural. As noted earlier, Pintoricchio owed a debt to the illusionistic and naturalistic frescoes of Domenico di Bartolo at the Hospital of Santa Maria della Scala, just across the piazza from the Duomo.

MELOZZO DA FORLÌ

Every now and then in Italian art, an innovative painter arises in a center that lacks a school of painting that could have formed and directed their early work. Gentile da Fabriano was such a case, as was Piero della Francesca, and so, a little later, was Melozzo da Forlì (1438–94). Perhaps their initial isolation helped to make these masters among the most original and self-reliant of Renaissance artists. Forlì, the city of his birth and early activity, is in the Romagna, a string of papal-dominated communes along and near the Adriatic, and not far from Ravenna, whose mosaics may have inspired the young Melozzo in the use of color and the combination of figures with architecture. His work was praised by Giovanni Santi, father of Raphael, before Melozzo's thirtieth year, as well as by other Quattrocento writers, but by the time Vasari published the first edition of his *Lives* in 1550, Melozzo had been so far forgotten that Vasari credited his Santi Apostoli frescoes to Benozzo Gozzoli. Today, Melozzo's detachment from the creative centers of Tuscany and central Italy and the limited number of his surviving works mean that he is often overlooked.

He began his visits to Rome as early as 1460, and a few years later was active at the court of Urbino, where he worked for Federico da Montefeltro and must have come into contact with Piero della Francesca. Although Piero was certainly the dominant influence on his art, Melozzo's perspective interests seem to have been well established even earlier. He must also have been impressed by Netherlandish art, particularly that of the Fleming Justus of Ghent, who was active at Federico's court. There is no record that Melozzo went to Florence or Siena—or even Mantua, where Mantegna was working—save for brief intervals. But Melozzo may have known about Mantegna's work through Ansuino da Forlì, who worked for a while with Mantegna in Padua. Melozzo probably encountered Alberti in Rome, and it is certain that he was familiar with his teachings.

In 1480–81, Melozzo was at work in the Vatican Library, which had been newly rebuilt and reorganized

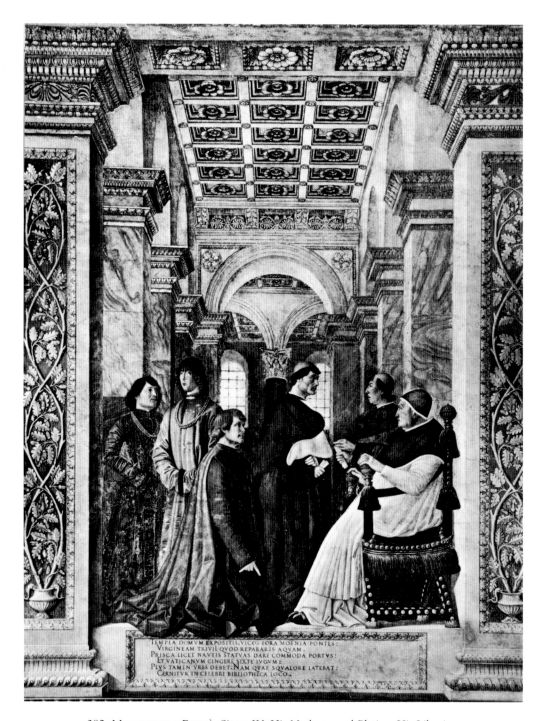

382. MELOZZO DA FORLÌ. *Sixtus IV, His Nephews, and Platina, His Librarian.*
1480–81. Detached fresco from the Vatican Library; transferred to canvas and now in the Pinacoteca,
Vatican, Rome. 13' 1" x 10' 4". Commissioned by Pope Sixtus IV

by Pope Sixtus IV. Most of his frescoes there have perished, since the room where he painted has long since been converted to other uses, but in 1821 Melozzo's fresco of *Sixtus IV, His Nephews, and Platina, His Librarian* was removed from the wall and transferred to canvas (fig. 382). It is the first surviving papal ceremonial portrait of the Renaissance (as distinguished from tomb effigies or from the portraits of popes disguised as their Early Christian predecessors in the paintings of Ma-

saccio, Masolino, and Fra Angelico). The fresco once adorned the end wall of the library and was undoubtedly integrated with the decoration carried out by Domenico del Ghirlandaio and his brother Davide. Two painted piers that cast convincing shadows admit us to an audience chamber in the Vatican, one no longer extant—if, indeed, it was not invented by Melozzo as a background for this painting. At the right sits the pope in a Renaissance armchair upholstered in velvet and studded with brass-headed nails. At his right stand his four nephews, including Cardinal Giuliano della Rovere, later to become Pope Julius II, in the center. Before him kneels the humanist Platina, the director of the library, pointing downward to a Latin inscription he composed to extol the pope's building achievements. To heighten the illusion, Melozzo allows the folds of Platina's cloak to overlap the frame.

The architecture is projected in perspective as if the eye of the observer were level with the pope's knee. The room, not large by Renaissance standards, is impressive in the simple bulk of its masses and the clarity of the ornamentation. Square, marble-encrusted piers, culminating in simple but heavily ornamented entablatures, support arches. Immediately above the arches rests the coffered ceiling. Through an arch at the end of the room we see a transverse chamber with an arcade and a similarly coffered ceiling. Rosettes, palmettes, acanthus, bead-and-reel, and other ornaments from ancient Roman architecture are picked out in gold. The entwined oak branches silhouetted against blue on the foremost piers refer to the coat of arms of the Della Rovere family, to which Sixtus IV belonged.

Melozzo avoids a ceremonial grouping, yet each person is motionless, each face firmly composed and staring directly ahead. Melozzo's substances are firm, his line definitive, his drapery forms crisp. These portraits relax only through the lyric beauty of Melozzo's color. The crimson of the papal cope, biretta, and chair contrasts with the vermilion of the cardinal's habit and with the violet, ultramarine, and blue-green in the other costumes. This coloristic display is intensified by the coolness of the pearly marble piers and the sparkle of the gilded ornament.

Melozzo's grandest commission was a huge apse fresco of the *Ascension* for the Early Christian Basilica of Santi Apostoli in Rome. The commission may have been given him by Cardinal Giuliano della Rovere, whose titular church, San Pietro in Vincoli, was not far away, but it has also been suggested that the project was paid for by Pope Sixtus IV. The remodeled basilica was consecrated by the pope in 1480, but there is no certainty that the decorations were complete at that time. In the early eighteenth century the church was remodeled again, and Melozzo's fresco was destroyed, save for the central section and a dozen or so fragments. From these it is possible to gain some notion of how the composition must have looked. At the base of the apse stood a row of apostles, looking up. Above, a semicircle of angels playing musical instruments surrounded the central figure of the ascending Christ (colorplate 69, p. 358), who appeared in the middle of clouds and putti, his arms extended, his hair and beard floating in the breeze, his eyes gazing calmly downward. All the figures were painted as if seen from below, in the sharp foreshortening painters had been using since the days of Castagno and Uccello. But, as far as we know, this is the first time that a large-scale, monumental composition was seen

from below in such a way that the mass of the building seemed to dissolve, creating the illusion that the figures exist in the air outside. Melozzo's composition was the inspiration of many ceiling painters, from Michelangelo, Raphael, and Correggio in the sixteenth century to the great decorators of the Roman Baroque and the Venetian Rococo.

Melozzo's idea was not wholly original. A vault is often termed *il cielo* (the sky) in Italian documents, and the association of the dome with Heaven is the subject of an immense literature. The small dome over the altar of Brunelleschi's Sacristy of San Lorenzo in Florence is frescoed with the constellations at a specific moment, somewhat on the order of a modern planetarium. Moreover, the Early Christian apse mosaic of Sts. Cosmas and Damian in Rome shows Christ walking toward us on sunrise-tinted clouds through an azure Heaven, and it is even possible that a similar mosaic originally decorated the apse of Santi Apostoli. But the crucial step—the treatment of the dome or half-dome as a vision into space—was taken by Melozzo alone.

The central figure of Christ hints at the openness of Melozzo's lost composition, but the full effect of even this fragment cannot be experienced unless you hold the illustration about thirty degrees above your head and tilt it slightly toward you. Then the figure will appear to float on the clouds, as Melozzo intended. His insistence on solid form is as strong here as in the *Sixtus IV*, yet the winds of Heaven themselves seem to blow through the composition.

As usual, the color is brilliant. The putti boast red and green wings, the white cloak and violet tunic of Christ glow against the sky, and the haloes are dotted with gold, achieving in fresco something of the sparkle of mosaic. As the official artist to Sixtus IV, Melozzo enjoyed the title of *pictor apostolicus* (apostolic painter). After his spectacular success as a painter of monumental frescoes, one wonders why his work is not to be found in the Sistine Chapel; none of the artists the pope called to Rome for that commission had as much experience.

In any event, Cardinal Girolamo Basso della Rovere, one of Sixtus' nephews who appears in the group portrait, called Melozzo to Loreto, on the Adriatic coast, to decorate the sacristy of St. Mark in the Basilica of the Santa Casa (fig. 383). This remarkable building, a favorite project of the Della Rovere family, was being constructed by Giuliano da Sangallo to enshrine the holy house (Santa Casa) of the Virgin Mary, which tradition held had been brought from the Holy Land to Loreto by angels in the thirteenth century. Although Melozzo never had a chance to complete the commission, which involved a series of wall paintings as well, it is his only cycle that survives in its original spot unaltered, since a bomb in World War II obliterated his ceiling decorations for San Biagio in Forlì.

Melozzo has painted each face of the dome with ornamental paneling composed of his favorite elements— guilloches, acanthus, bead-and-reel, palmettes, and dol-

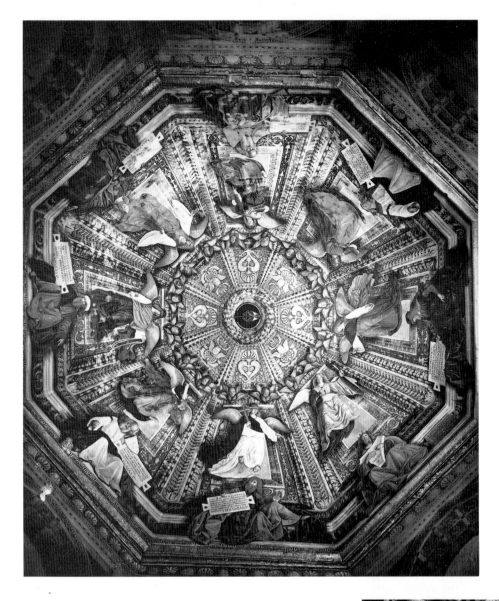

383. MELOZZO DA FORLÌ.
Dome, Sacristy of St. Mark,
Basilica of the Sta. Casa,
Loreto. 1477–80(?). Fresco.
Commissioned by Cardinal
Girolamo Basso della Rovere

below: 384. Angel, detail
of fig. 383

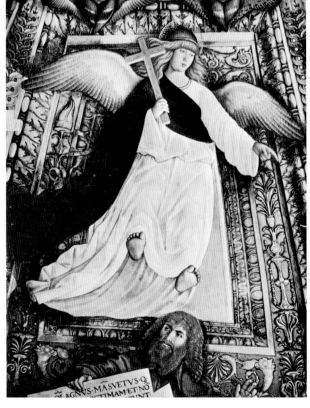

phins—converging on a central garland of Della Rovere oak leaves that embraces the cardinal's coat of arms. In front of this illusionistic structure Melozzo painted figures that seem to sit or float in the actual space of the sacristy. The painted cornice framing the dome is treated as a parapet, and on each segment sits a prophet holding a tablet with his name and a passage from his writings that prophesizes the Passion; the one exception is David, who holds his harp while his tablet is propped beside him on the ledge. Above each prophet hovers an angel holding one of the instruments of the Passion; above the angels, finally, as a kind of repetition of the garland of oak leaves, is a circle of six-winged seraph heads. Melozzo even exploits such details as the soles of the angels' feet, shod or unshod, seen from below, and makes the angels' wings cast shadows on the painted architecture of the dome (fig. 384). As a result, it is easy to believe that Melozzo's figures are sitting or floating above your head. The drapery glows with Melozzo's usual brilliance of color, and every face and lock of hair are painted with his customary firmness. In 1484 Melozzo returned to Forlì, possibly because of the death of Sixtus IV. His connection with Rome and with monumental painting on a grand scale was never resumed.

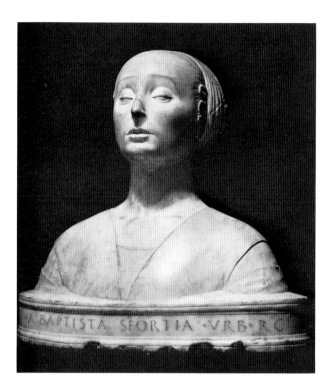

385. FRANCESCO LAURANA. *Battista Sforza.*
c. 1473. Marble, height c. 20". Bargello, Florence. Perhaps
commissioned by Federico da Montefeltro

THE LAURANA BROTHERS

In the late Quattrocento, Urbino was an important cultural center; this chapter closes with the work of two brothers whose achievements in sculpture and architecture played an important role in establishing the city's artistic significance. Both were born in Dalmatia, an area until recently part of Yugoslavia but which had been colonized by Venetians and was open to the influences of Italian culture. Francesco Laurana (c. 1420–1503), the sculptor, moved from one dynastic court to another and was responsible for the only Quattrocento triumphal arch—that of Ferdinand of Aragon in Naples—that is preserved. His best known achievements are his female portrait busts, and that of Battista Sforza, countess of Urbino (fig. 385), whom we have already met in Piero della Francesca's profile portrait (see colorplate 54, p. 264), may serve as typical of Francesco's ideals of elegance. These serene heads have much in common with those in Piero's Arezzo frescoes (see figs. 282, 283) in their insistence on geometric or quasi-geometric volumes and clear contours, and owe next to nothing to Florentine sculpture of the period (see fig. 305). The transitions from shape to shape, apparently so sharply simplified, are in reality rich and subtle, and repay careful study. Form flows into delicately distorted form with the same beauty that the twentieth-century sculptor Brancusi found in wave-worn pebbles.

After an extended search for a master "learned in the mysteries" of classical architecture, in 1468 Federico da Montefeltro announced that he could find no one in Tuscany, "fountainhead of architects," and appointed Francesco Laurana's brother Luciano (d. 1479) as chief architect of his unfinished palace, now the Palazzo Ducale of Urbino. Luciano had probably already been at work on the palace for two years. The chief glory of the Palazzo Ducale is its courtyard (colorplate 70, p. 359), whose construction can be dated during the years of Luciano's activity, and it is therefore generally assumed that he was its architect. After Luciano's death in 1479, Francesco di Giorgio was brought to Urbino to complete some of the decorative detail.

In contemplating the design of Luciano's courtyard, we must mentally strip away the two upper stories, added later, and finish it with the crowning cornice of the second story. Thus reduced, the courtyard emerges as one of the most harmonious constructions of the Renaissance. Luciano has adopted the simple arithmetical proportion scheme of Brunelleschi, for each bay of the lower floor is an exact square that is articulated by semicircular arches. The second-story windows are two-thirds the height and one-third the width of each bay. But Luciano avoided some major Florentine difficulties. First, he managed to unite both stories with a single scheme, rather than allowing a solid second story to weigh down upon an open arcade. Second, he turned each corner in a way that completes both corner arches instead of having them come to rest on the same capital, in the uncomfortable way we find in Florentine courtyards (see figs. 148, 309). The first problem he solved by giving the second story an order of Corinthian pilasters that harmonize with the Composite columns of the arcade and by setting these stone pilasters against a wall of tan brick that is continued in the spandrels of the arcade. The result is not quite the same as the screen architecture of the façade of the Palazzo Rucellai (see fig. 225). The columns, pilasters, entablatures, and windows against a darker background of shadow or of brick give the Palazzo Ducale the appearance of an open framework, an effect unprecedented in Renaissance architecture.

The second problem necessitated even greater ingenuity. Luciano decided to treat each face of the courtyard as if it were a separate facade, complete in itself. He therefore terminated each side of the arcade and *piano nobile* with pilasters, one above the other. At the corners of the arcade level the cornices of the intersecting façades touch, but above the second story they fuse, creating an unbroken cornice that originally crowned the entire courtyard. At arcade level each corner is composed of a compound pier combining two pilasters and two half-columns.

Whether or not Luciano's solutions are fully consistent with the doctrines of Alberti, they would probably have pleased him. Certainly he would have enjoyed—and possibly did—the two friezes ornamented with inscriptions extolling the virtues of Federico in handsome

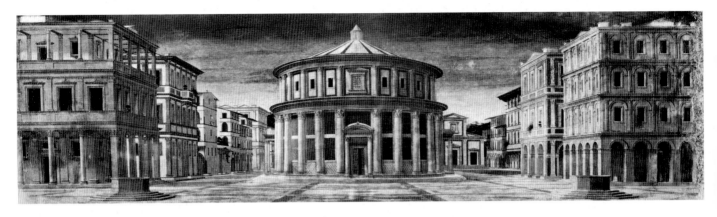

386. LUCIANO LAURANA (design attributed to; perhaps painted by PIERO DELLA FRANCESCA). *View of an Ideal City.*
Third quarter of 15th century. Panel, 23⅝ x 78¾". Galleria Nazionale delle Marche, Palazzo Ducale, Urbino

capital letters in a style derived from ancient Roman monuments. As compared with the verticality and density of Florentine Renaissance architecture, the columns, the pilasters, the windows, and even the letters of the inscriptions are widely spaced, so that the dominant direction of the courtyard is horizontal. The skill with which the intricate problems of form and space are solved, and the consequent effect of harmonious calm, mark a determined step in the direction of High Renaissance architecture. Bramante, born in Urbino in 1444 and therefore twenty-four years old at the time Luciano was appointed to his historic task, found his own artistic origins in this building, and the young Raphael also walked through these perfect arcades.

In all probability we should look to Urbino for the origin of two panels, one in Urbino (fig. 386) and the other in Baltimore (not illustrated), that show enormous piazze bordered by palaces and centering around monuments of a more-or-less classical nature. A number of ingenious solutions, none wholly convincing, have been suggested to explain the purpose of these panels. While the execution of the Urbino panel has been attributed to Piero della Francesca or a close follower, the designs of both panels have been assigned to Luciano Laurana. The architecture looks like that of the Palazzo Ducale at Urbino, but the best support for the theory is the characters in the ruined inscriptions at upper left and right in the Urbino panel, which are Slavic, and probably Old Church Slavonic, written in Cyrillic character, and doubtless by a Slav and not an Italian.

The three-story palaces are built on the same principle of open framework filled in by screen walls as the Palazzo Ducale, and the arcaded façades of both palaces at the right terminate, as in the courtyard of the Palazzo Ducale, before reaching the corner in order to avoid corner columns. The general feeling of breadth and openness in the proportions and spacing is like what we find in the Palazzo Ducale and quite opposed to the tensions of Florentine architecture in general and Giu-

liano da Sangallo's in particular. Some of the ideas are unprecedented, such as the rows of pediments crowning some of the palaces, and the entire cityscape clearly represents the kind of civic center that the Early Renaissance wanted to build but could never achieve save on the small scale of Pienza (see fig. 232).

The round building in the center is more beautiful than most of the centralized structures built during the Renaissance. The small upper-story windows correspond perfectly to Alberti's desired "temple" illumination (see pp. 229–31). The lantern is capped by a crystal orb surmounted by a faint cross. The building was surely intended to represent an Albertian "temple," which at the center of a city always dominates the law court, the three-aisled basilica with no religious insignia visible at the right. This ideal temple may have inspired the Tempietto by Bramante (see fig. 498).

A more stable society under autocratic rule was required for the realization of the kind of ideal city shown in the Urbino panel, which had to await the later sixteenth century and found its full fruition only in the Baroque. Architectural perspectives, however, were also characteristic of *intarsie*, the panels of inlaid wood that were the delight of the Quattrocento and Cinquecento for the decoration of small rooms and choir stalls. This chapter may well conclude, therefore, with the *intarsia* decoration of Federico da Montefeltro's study in Urbino (colorplate 9, p. 17; fig. 387), where his manuscripts were kept and where he read—standing—at a desk from which he could also look out through marble arches to the blue mountains of his domain. The unknown designer of the *intarsie* certainly worked in harmony with Luciano's architecture and possibly in part from his designs or suggestions. As in many *intarsia* schemes, the decoration simulates cabinets and niches; on the lower level, with its latticed compartments, one door appears to be open to show the contents. Then comes a zone of ornaments, including the symbols of the duke, then a framework of pilasters, between which one looks into

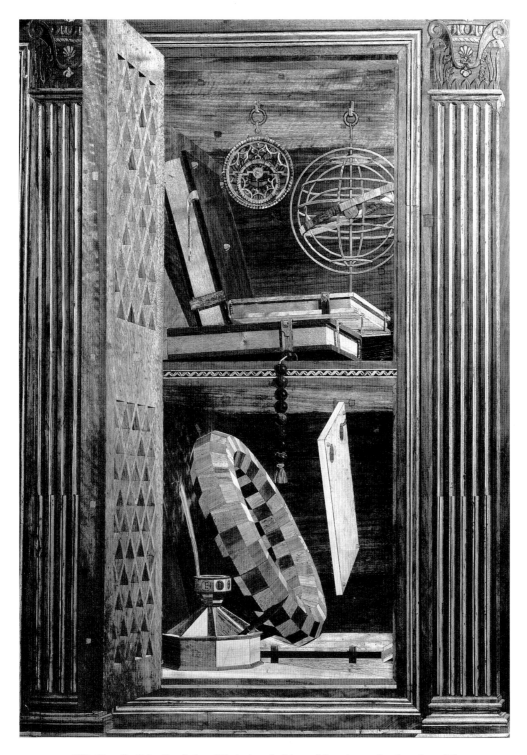

387. Detail of the Studiolo of Federico da Montefeltro (see colorplate 9, p. 17).
🏛 Palazzo Ducale, Urbino. 1470s. Intarsia

niches with statues, into cabinets with books, candle, and hourglass, into a cupboard filled with the duke's armor, and into an architectural perspective with a distant view of mountains and lakes. This decoration offers a glimpse of how the intellectual refinements of an ideal life were concentrated within the confines of a tiny chamber, in an exquisite decoration executed with consummate illusionistic skill to please a noble Renaissance prince.

15

Gothic and Renaissance
in Venice and Northern Italy

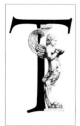he Po Valley, studded with magnificent cities—Bergamo, Brescia, Verona, Vicenza, Como, Cremona, Lodi, and Pavia, to mention only a few—had been transformed politically and socially during the Trecento by the rise of tyrannies (see p. 146). During the Quattrocento these despotisms were often the scene of flourishing court life and artistic activity. The most splendid of the smaller courts were those of Mantua, under the Gonzaga family, and Ferrara, ruled by the Este. But Milan, first under the Visconti dukes and then under their relatives the Sforza, became one of the richest and most powerful principalities in Europe, able to attract important and well-known artists. At the other side of the north Italian triangle, the Republic of St. Mark was beginning to turn its sights toward the Italian mainland, largely because the loss of remote outposts and commerce to the Ottoman Empire forced Venice to look toward Central and Northern Europe for trade. At this point it transferred its previous system of colonial government to the absorption and administration of inland bases, in part to protect new trade routes over the Alps. Padua, Treviso, Vicenza, and Verona became Venetian subject cities, and in 1498 the Lion of St. Mark appeared on the ramparts of Bergamo, from which, on clear days, Venetian soldiers could discern the distant Cathedral of Milan. There were conflicts with the French conquerors of Milan at the end of the Quattrocento, and in the early Cinquecento the League of Cambrai, which included every major power in Western Europe, arrayed itself against Venice, but the city survived, maintaining its land power and much of its maritime empire until Napoleon disbanded the Republic in 1794. Among the many smaller independent states of northern Italy, only Mantua and Ferrara were able to keep their independence throughout the Renaissance, probably because they were convenient buffer states for both Milan and Venice. The flowering of Venetian Renaissance art dates from the period of Venetian continental expansion.

In the early Quattrocento, Lombard naturalism had an electric effect in Florence when imported by Gentile da Fabriano (see p. 187). But in general it was Florentine artists who migrated northward. Padua and Venice were visited by Paolo Uccello in 1421, Fra Filippo Lippi in 1433–34, Andrea del Castagno in 1442–43, Dona-

tello from the early 1440s to the 1450s, and others. During the Quattrocento, the Renaissance was largely a Florentine import, and only in the works of Domenico Veneziano did Venetian ideas and inventions have any lasting effect in Florence. But before the end of the Quattrocento Venetian painters had begun to develop a style that would attain for the city a special importance in the history of painting.

PISANELLO

The tradition of north Italian naturalism went on, after Gentile's death, in the work of his associate and follower Antonio Pisanello (before 1395–1455). Although from a Pisan family, Pisanello was born in Verona. As a young man, he worked with Gentile on frescoes, now lost, in the Doges' Palace in Venice, and after the latter's death he continued his work in Rome. Pisanello seems never to have painted in Florence. He made medals for several north Italian princes and seems to have had a close relationship to the Este family, dukes of Ferrara.

Compared with contemporary Florentine art, or even with Pisanello's north Italian Trecento predecessors, the fresco of *St. George and the Princess* (fig. 388) is static; people and animals do not even look at each other. But the fresco—or what is left of it, since much of the splendid ornament was painted *a secco* and has peeled away—is a tour de force of naturalism. Pisanello's animals come out of this tradition; his sketchbooks record many different species in minute fidelity to the texture of fur and feathers and to details of animal structure (fig. 389). In *St. George and the Princess,* the more interesting figures are the hunting dogs and the horses pawing the earth. From Gentile Pisanello takes the combination of front and back views of horses (see colorplate 38, p. 203), but his horses are more powerful and are thus more in the tradition of Avanzo (see fig. 129).

The splendidly dressed people—especially the princess with her lofty forehead, towering headdress, and sleeves sweeping the ground—are reminiscent of Pisanello's watercolor designs for elaborate costumes, while beyond them there appears a row of low hills, and then the battlemented towers, Gothic gables, and domes, pinnacles, and spires of a north Italian city. At the left are uplands divided into fields and farms, then the sea with a ship under sail; before the city gates two partially de-

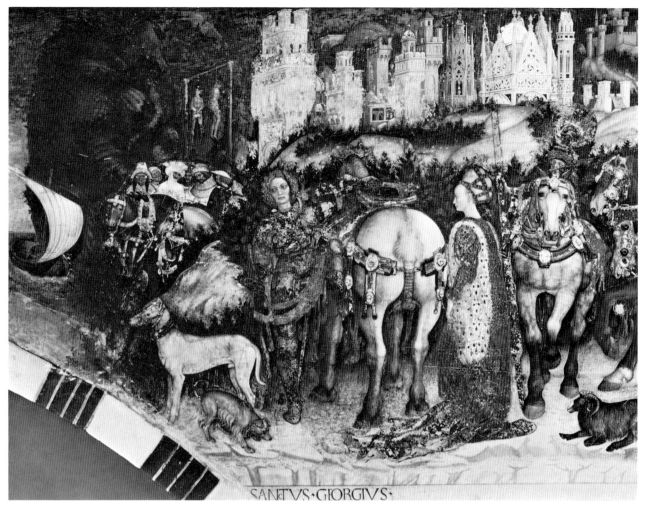

388. PISANELLO. *St. George and the Princess*. c. 1437–38. Fresco. Pellegrini Chapel, Sant'Anastasia, Verona

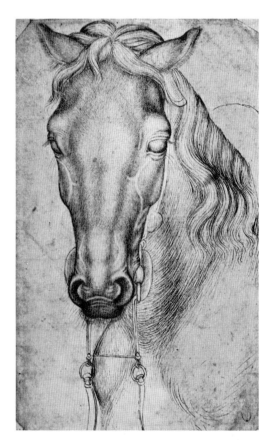

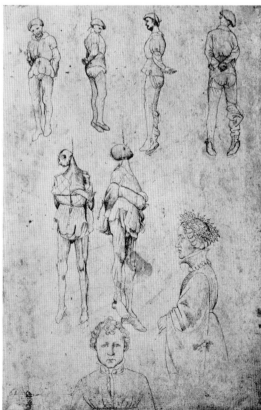

far left: 389. PISANELLO. *Study of the Head of a Horse*. c. 1437–38. Pen, 10⁷/8 x 7³/4". Cabinet des Dessins, The Louvre, Paris

left: 390. PISANELLO. *Study of Hanged Men*. c. 1433. Pen over metalpoint, 11¹/8 x 7⁵/8". British Museum, London

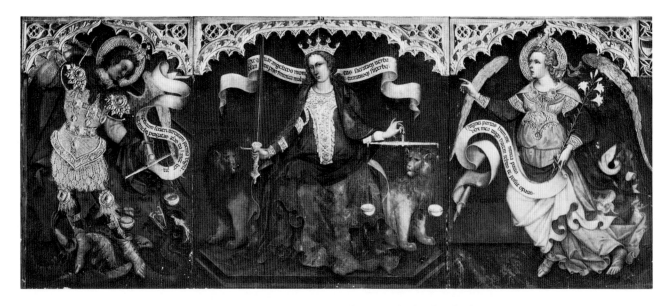

391. JACOBELLO DEL FIORE. *Justice with Sts. Michael and Gabriel.* 1421.
Panels: center, 82 x 76½"; left, 82 x 52½"; right, 82 x 64". Accademia, Venice

composed corpses hang from a gallows. The soldiers in the middle distance show Asian facial types that may have been observed from Mongol or Tartar slaves. Many of Pisanello's preparatory drawings for the fresco survive, including animal studies and exact renderings of the corpses (fig. 390). When the fresco was in good condition, the naturalistic effect of the animals and figures must have been overpowering, for they were precisely drawn, beautifully shaded, and perfectly projected in depth. Pisanello seems to show no interest in Florentine perspective, and here he seems to have made no effort to achieve a unified space or controlled recession. Yet a perspective drawing by Pisanello survives that demonstrates his control of the Albertian formula for spatial recession. It is Tuscan intellectuality that does not appeal to him, and he encourages the natural world to fill every possible space. Perhaps the only real difference between Pisanello and his Florentine contemporary Paolo Uccello is the former's unwillingness to make the world conform to patterns imposed upon it. In detail, their paintings are sometimes strikingly similar. This north Italian interest in nature is sometimes termed Gothic, but if it is Gothic, then so is Antonio del Pollaiuolo or Leonardo da Vinci, both of whom subordinated the human figure to nature and led the Florentines toward a new phase of the Renaissance.

Pisanello's animals take over the brilliantly painted but darkened panel (colorplate 71, p. 360) probably representing the *Vision of St. Eustace* (although a similar legend is told about St. Hubert). Once when Eustace was hunting deer, a stag bearing the crucified Christ between his antlers appeared before him, and Eustace was converted on the spot. The legend refers to Psalm 42, "As the hart panteth after the water brooks, so panteth my soul after thee, O God." No profound religious experience seems to be going on inside Pisanello's St.

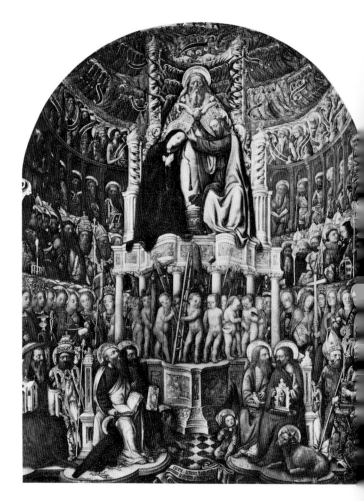

392. ANTONIO VIVARINI and GIOVANNI D'ALEMAGNA.
Coronation of the Virgin. 1444. Panel, 90 x 69½".
S. Pantaleone, Venice

Eustace, who, sporting the latest excesses of north Italian fashion, merely lifts one hand in mild astonishment. The horse, however, snorts, rears back, and paws the ground. Space continues on all sides and up—a deep forest that obeys no rules of perspective, but gives the artist a dark background against which to project the jewel-bright costume and the lively animals and birds. Besides the stag that bears the Crucifixion, another trembles in the dimness at the left, at the upper left a doe crouches, and at the center a stag drinks from a stream enjoyed by swans, cranes, and pelicans (a bird symbolic of Christ), one of whom is in flight. A bear inhabits the shadows toward the upper right, and at least three varieties of hunting dogs crowd around the saint's horse. One hound sniffs at an offended greyhound, while a second greyhound gives solemn chase to a hare, the taut curves of his body measured against the cramped ones of a scroll. This is now blank; either the inscription was never added or it was removed by a later owner. Whatever Pisanello intended—his signature, a religious text, a dedication from a patron—is unknown today.

EARLY QUATTROCENTO PAINTING IN VENICE

One of the first important Venetian painters of the early Quattrocento is Jacobello del Fiore (d. 1439), who signed the huge triptych representing *Justice with Sts. Michael and Gabriel* (fig. 391) for the Doges' Palace in 1421. His Gothic frame, with its flattened shapes derived from contemporary work in Austria, encloses a seated and crowned Justice, holding sword and balance and flanked by Venetian lions. In the left wing St. Michael slays a rather inoffensive dragon; in the right Gabriel bearing a lily appears as if on his way to the Annunciation. This is an unusual surviving example of a civic picture that would almost certainly have been located in a chamber where judgments and prison sentences would have been determined and/or announced. There are lingering elements of Gentile's art, especially in the raised stucco modeling of the gilded portions, but Jacobello seems to have had little interest in Gentile's naturalism.

In 1444 Antonio Vivarini (c. 1420–76/84), together with his still-mysterious brother-in-law Giovanni d' Alemagna ("from Germany," d. 1450), both from the island-city of Murano near Venice, dated a large altarpiece of the *Coronation of the Virgin* (fig. 392). Here Gothic, Byzantine, and Renaissance elements blend in a strange amalgam. Saints and prophets are seated in tiers like choir stalls, as if Heaven were the apse of a gigantic church. Rows of angels bring the altarpiece to a dome-like top. The entire center of the structure, from the checkered marble pavement to the apex of the living dome, is filled with a fantastic throne containing Late Gothic motifs and vaguely Byzantine columns with foliated capitals. Between the columns and around them, infants (probably the Holy Innocents, the babies killed at the command of Herod) carry the symbols of Christ's Passion, and between the spiral columns of the upper stories of the throne, whose back is also formed by angels, God the Father blesses Christ, who crowns his mother, while the dove of the Holy Spirit hovers between them. At the bottom right, St. Luke's doglike bull cuddles beside his master, who, with pride, exhibits his framed portrait of the Virgin, in a typical Venetian Gothic frame. The painting of individual faces and the handling of light and shade on the drapery show that Antonio and Giovanni had learned an occasional lesson from Florentine visitors to Venice. The Vivarini family and its pupils remain a conservative current in Venetian painting through two generations and even into the sixteenth century.

JACOPO BELLINI

The sequence of great north Italian masters starts with Jacopo Bellini (active before 1420–70/71) and continues with his son-in-law Andrea Mantegna (1431–1506) and his two sons, Gentile (1429–1507) and Giovanni Bellini (c. 1430–1516). Jacopo got his start under Gentile da Fabriano, which is probably why he named his oldest son Gentile. At first sight Jacopo's work may seem uninteresting. His Madonnas (fig. 393) show a lingering trace

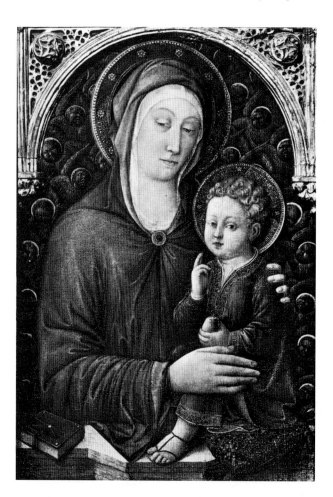

393. JACOPO BELLINI. *Madonna of the Cherubim.* 1450s. Panel, 37 x 26". Accademia, Venice

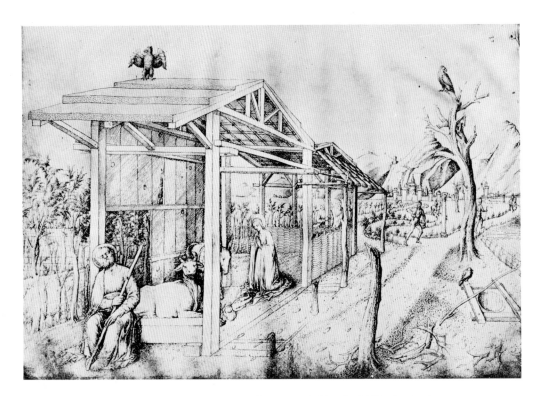

394. JACOPO BELLINI. *Nativity,* from a model book. 1440s. Leadpoint,
13¼ x 16¼". British Museum, London

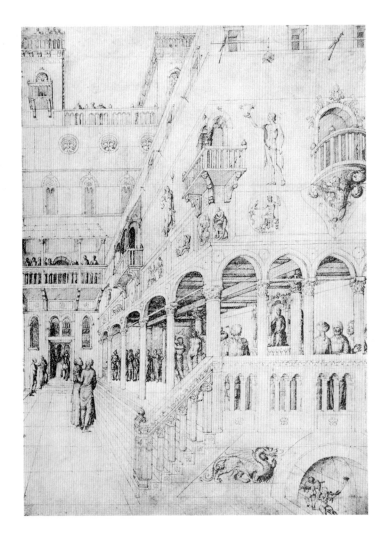

395. JACOPO BELLINI. *Flagellation,* from a model book.
c. 1450. Leadpoint on parchment, with later pen retouching,
16¾ x 11¼". The Louvre, Paris

of Byzantine remoteness and rigidity, but a closer look discloses that Jacopo had a clear understanding of Renaissance principles. The parapet on which he has placed the Christ Child's cushion, Mary's elbow, and a book is convincingly projected in space, and so is the book. There are Byzantine echoes in the gold pigment used for highlights—a last remnant of the old gold striations—but these do not muffle the artist's firm and consistent control of form. Under the drapery, bodies turn in depth and light shimmers on the folds, which behave like cloth. The short curls on the Christ Child's head are delicately rendered. All in all, the elements of the picture, even the mourning seraph heads in gold that compose the background, are treated with harmony and restraint.

Highly regarded by poets and writers of his time in north Italy, Jacopo was in Ferrara in 1441 working for Lionello d'Este, but the *Madonna of Humility with Donor (Lionello d'Este?)* (colorplate 72, p. 409) has been dated somewhat earlier. The Gentilesque elements in the picture are evident, if softened by Jacopo's ability to paint silken drapery folds. The scope of the landscape background extends beyond Gentile's development. This Virgin of Humility is seated low on a cushion like the examples by Giovanni di Paolo (see fig. 367), which show an immense view over the distant world. But Ja-

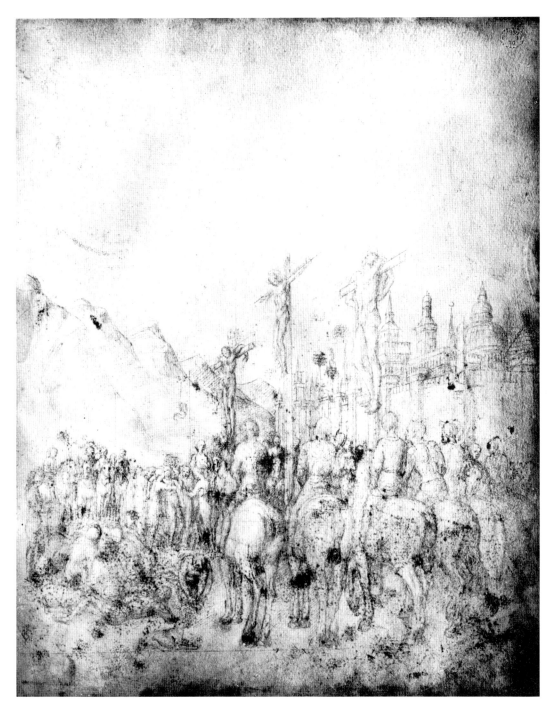

396. JACOPO BELLINI. *Crucifixion,* from a model book. 1440s. Leadpoint,
16¼ x 13¼". British Museum, London

copo's Madonna rises grandly against the sky, and the
words repeated on her halo, "Hail Mother, Queen of
the World," help explain her dominance of the landscape and may also hint at the donor's political aspirations. The tiny scale of the donor kneeling before her is
an archaism that recurs even in the Cinquecento. A
semicircle of trees, in whose shadow a deer grazes, separates the sacred figures from what is the most ambitious
landscape view of the decade. Jacopo's vision has taken
in farms, castles, cities, the Magi on horseback riding
toward a shed in which the Holy Family may be dimly

seen, and a range of mountains probably not done after
drawings from nature (they are conventionalized in their
shapes), but particularly convincing because of the way
in which their summits are touched with light. Even
more persuasive is the sky, with its low banks of clouds
illuminated from below by this same light, apparently
the last glow of afternoon. The soft, heavy atmosphere
common in northern Italy appears here for the first time
in painting. These clouds with gently glowing undersides will reappear again and again as a standard motif in
the art of Jacopo's son, Giovanni. Despite the fact that

Jacopo has attempted no perspective unity in the Florentine sense, his figures are convincingly projected in space, and so is the Christ Child's halo.

More than his paintings, it is Jacopo's drawings that testify to his extraordinary compositional imagination. These were made on separate sheets of parchment or paper and were then bound into drawing books; they were probably intended to be model books that could be used in his workshop and by his descendants—as indeed they were—and also as a record of his style and attainments. Two survive, one of drawings on paper in the British Museum, the other, of parchment, in the Louvre. Both are datable close to 1450 and both include an extraordinary array of subjects—scriptural, mythological, archaeological, and purely fantastic. The books were inherited by Gentile Bellini, who had his father's rubbed and faded leadpoint drawings in the Paris volume retouched in pen; those in London remain in leadpoint. The books appear to have been consulted as compositional models by Venetian painters, including Mantegna and Giovanni Bellini, until well into the sixteenth century. They show that Jacopo learned the principles of Albertian perspective without losing his north Italian interest in a broad, panoramic conception of nature. His adherence to Albertian rules occasionally constrains him to present us with absurdly rapid perspective recessions. But his adoption of the single point of view enables him to keep the horizon in its proper place, to exploit glimpses among and between foreground objects, and to dissolve the last vestiges of medieval double scale in favor of a single scale that places human figures in a reasonable relationship to architectural and natural space.

In his *Nativity* (fig. 394), for example, Joseph sleeps in the foreground. Mary is reduced to two-thirds his size because she kneels a little deeper into the space, while shepherds and wayfarers continue the diminution systematically to the point where distant Bethlehem, like a city on the northern edge of the Po River, rises with its walls and towers at the base of the mountains. While still betraying Byzantine mannerisms of landscape construction, these masses recede into even smaller hills, castles, and cities that are visible between the uprights of the shed. Renaissance order has been imposed on the miscellaneous world of north Italian art without weakening the dominance of nature. The figures are mere specks in this landscape world.

The same principle is exploited to a greater degree in Jacopo's *Flagellation* (fig. 395). We see an enormous Gothic palace, vaguely like the Doges' Palace in Venice, with an open loggia, balconies, classical reliefs, and statues adorning its walls, and an even larger distant building that culminates in two towers. In the foreground, a marble bridge arches over a waterway. Tiny figures appear here and there on the steps, on the balconies, and in distant courtyards. Only after examining the drawing for a while do we notice the nude Christ, who is tied to a column in the loggia, and Pilate, who sits in a niche while bystanders look on idly. Those nearest us are, of course, represented as larger than Christ. In these drawings, Jacopo shows that this is the way even important events happen, not neatly centered and aggrandized, but as part of a universal texture of experience in which many of the characters are uncaring. Jacopo's adoption of Albertian perspective gave him a powerful instrument to demonstrate his views and to prove, moreover, the basic contention of north Italian (as distinguished from Florentine) art: that nature is dominant over humanity.

Jacopo could also be a more traditional tragic dramatist. In his *Crucifixion* (fig. 396), he imagined a scene of epic breadth—Calvary set before the walls of Padua, with the three crosses seen diagonally (apparently for the first time) and the backs of the soldiers on horseback turned toward us, thus throwing the horses into sharp foreshortening and the crosses into the middle distance. Even in the much later art of Tintoretto and Veronese, Venetian historical painting never surpassed the spatial daring of Jacopo's extraordinary perspective compositions.

ANDREA MANTEGNA

Andrea Mantegna, who married Jacopo Bellini's daughter Nicolosia in 1453, was the leading Quattrocento painter of the north Italian mainland. Born, probably in 1431, near Padua, the boy was adopted and trained by Francesco Squarcione—part painter, part collector, part dealer, part entrepreneur—who seems to have employed several talented boys whose services he farmed out to prospective patrons. Eventually, Mantegna freed himself from Squarcione, but not without legal difficulties. When the artist was still only eighteen, so young that his contract had to be signed for him by his older brother, he was already engaged in a series of frescoes in the Ovetari Chapel in the Eremitani Church in Padua, together with such established masters as the Venetian team of Antonio Vivarini and Giovanni d'Alemagna and the Paduan painter Niccolò Pizzolo. Giovanni died in 1450, Vivarini withdrew in 1451, and in 1453 Pizzolo was killed in a quarrel. A new contract in 1454 assigned some of the subjects to Mantegna and others to such minor masters as Bono da Ferrara and Ansuino da Forlì. Eventually both withdrew, leaving the field to Mantegna, whose paintings in a remarkable new style were finished before February 1457, when the artist was only twenty-six.

In the second register above the floor, Mantegna painted two scenes from the Life of St. James, the *Baptism of Hermogenes* (fig. 397) and *St. James Before Herod Agrippa* (fig. 398), that are united by a common perspective scheme with a vanishing point concealed behind the frame between them. To enhance the illusionism, putti seem to be hanging garlands of fruits and flowers around the Ovetari and Capodilista arms in front of the narratives, as if in the very space of the chapel. In these first mature works, Mantegna shows his Squarcionesque training and also his interest in the compositional de-

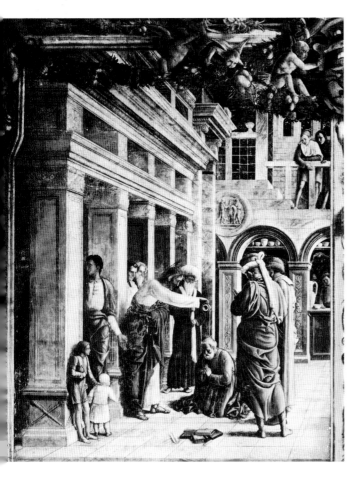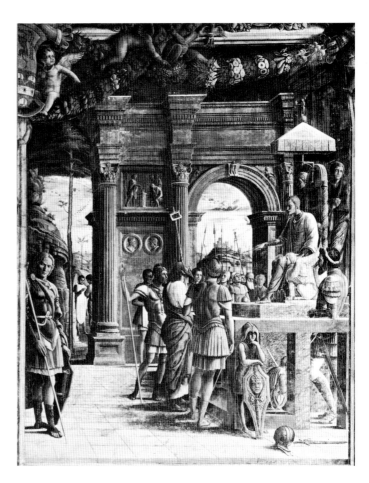

397, 398. ANDREA MANTEGNA. *Baptism of Hermogenes* (left) and *St. James Before Herod Agrippa*
(right). 1454–57 (destroyed 1944). Frescoes, width of each 10' 9". Ovetari Chapel, Eremitani Church, Padua.
Commissioned with monies from the will of Antonio di Biagio degli Ovetari;
the patron of the frescoes was his wife, Imperatrice Capodilista, and members of her family

signs of his father-in-law, his absorption of the principles
of Albertian perspective (which were to fascinate him
for the rest of his life), and above all the impression
made by the work of Donatello in the reliefs for the
high altar of Sant'Antonio (see figs. 253, 254). The marble pavement on which Hermogenes kneels, and which
seems continuous with that of the square before the
throne of Herod Agrippa, forms an Albertian perspective grid whose orthogonals and transversals establish the
relative sizes of the figures. At this moment not even
Piero della Francesca could produce so doctrinaire an
exposition of Albertian perspective as did Mantegna,
who has even marked off the foreground slabs in cubits.

This much of Tuscan rationalism and order made its
way into north Italian style, but it is still joined with
north Italian realism. The classicistic architecture of piers
and arches, decorated with an apparently invented "classical" relief with the familiar Renaissance detail of the
horse seen from the rear, leads up to a potter's shop in
which Mantegna has painted a variety of jars and cups
and even the wood grain of the rough counter. He even
shows how the water striking Hermogenes' bald crani-
um splashes outward into a fountain of separate drops,

like pellets of quicksilver. A typical detail of Mantegna's
naturalism is the infant at the left, who wants to take
part in the ceremony but is restrained by the older boy,
who leans against the pier.

On the right, St. James is brought before Herod
Agrippa in front of a Roman triumphal arch that is not
an imitation of a specific Roman example but a re-creation of Roman art in an Albertian manner, working
from a knowledge of its principles. Mantegna belonged
to a group of humanists in Verona who constituted
themselves into an academy; they went for boat rides on
Lake Garda, enlivening the trips with readings from classical authors, and also made some archaeological investigations on their own. Mantegna must have made a
repertory of drawings from classical remains that he
could use whenever he needed a specific detail.

The atmosphere is so clear that every element in the
fresco is visible with biting clarity, to the last tree and
castle on the farthest hill. The rocks are formed in accordance with the sweep of those in Jacopo Bellini's
drawings (see fig. 396), but without Jacopo's fluidity.
The experience of Donatello's sculpture, and perhaps
even his personal influence, seem to have made Man-

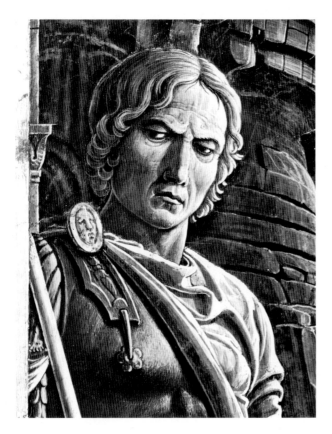

399. Head of a soldier, detail of fig. 398

tegna more sculptural in his paintings than was Donatello in his highly pictorial reliefs. The figures are so sharply projected by light, which is painted to match the light that enters the chapel from the windows, that they almost seem carved in stone. Cloth does not fall over the limbs in masses, as in the paintings of Masaccio and his followers, but clings like the clay-soaked cloth of Donatello's figures (see fig. 162). The soldier leaning against the frame at the left, whose expression suggests that he is ravaged by inner torment, has long been held to be a self-portrait (fig. 399). This formidable face corresponds to the difficult, domineering character we know Mantegna to have possessed and resembles the bust that appears in his tomb chapel in Mantua. It is so stony in its consistency and harsh in its details that the artist seems almost to have done it with a chisel instead of a brush. But in the midst of the solemnity of St. James's judgment, Mantegna still found room for naturalistic byplay. The boy who holds the soldier's shield and wears his enormous helmet looks right, while the eyes of the mask on the shield look just as sharply to the left. And the sword has been neatly placed parallel to the transversals of the pavement.

The lowest register of frescoes of the Life of St. James begins just above the eye level of a person of average height during the Renaissance; the scenes are planned as if we were seated before a stage filled with figures who naturalistically move downward as they recede from us. Only the feet of the figures nearest to the picture plane

appear (some, in fact, even break through the picture plane), while others are cut off by the edge of the stage. In *St. James Led to Execution* (fig. 400), we look up at buildings portrayed with a real effect that is intensified by the heads popping out of windows above us and by the random placing of medieval structures in a curving street—their arches and battlements rendered with the same scrupulous attention to detail as the classical elements. The coffering of the arched gateway is also seen from below. But a moment's reflection will disclose that if Mantegna had been consistent, he would also have made the verticals converge as they rise, in conformity to our viewpoint standing below. That he did not do this is doubtless due to his unwillingness to violate the verticality of the wall on which he was painting and, in consequence, the structure of the chapel itself.

Again Mantegna records, analyzes, and sets into its exact relationship in a universal mathematical structure virtually every facet of human experience. A penitent breaks from the crowd to receive the blessing of the saint while a soldier uses a staff to hold back a woman who wishes to follow. Mantegna's strict sense of form invests humble faces with an unexpected majesty. The sad countenance of the saint (fig. 401) is carved and compartmentalized with the same lapidary clarity as the masonry blocks in the buildings.

The final fresco, the *Martyrdom of St. James* (fig. 402), depicts the saint's beheading. Mantegna has developed a composition in which the saint lies prone, foreshortened toward us in depth, under a blade that slides in channels between two posts. An executioner is about to strike the blade with a gigantic mallet and when the blow falls, it seems that the severed head will roll into the chapel where we stand. Although this is difficult to see in the photographs, the illusion is increased by painting the rail of the sapling fence so that it overlaps the painted frame, and by having the soldier lean forward over the fence. A powerful tension in depth is established by the rise of the hill—its classical ruins illuminated against the slaty sky common to the chapel frescoes—to a castle on the hilltop. As we wait for the blow to fall, we note that a bough has snapped at the top of the tree in the foreground, that the executioner's sleeve is ripping with the strain, and that a gigantic crack cuts through the keep of the castle from the top almost to the foundation. The contrast between this tension and the calm of the soldiers idly watching the execution, together with the various illusionistic devices, encourages the observer to identify with the event through suspense and apprehension. We look directly up into the gentle features of the head that is about to be cut off and roll out upon us.

The blow fell, delivered by another executioner. On March 11, 1944, American bombs intended for the nearby railway yards of Padua rained wide of their mark and demolished the Ovetari Chapel, indeed the entire east end of the Eremitani Church. The shattered remains of Mantegna's frescoes that were recovered are mounted in the rebuilt chapel on photographs of the

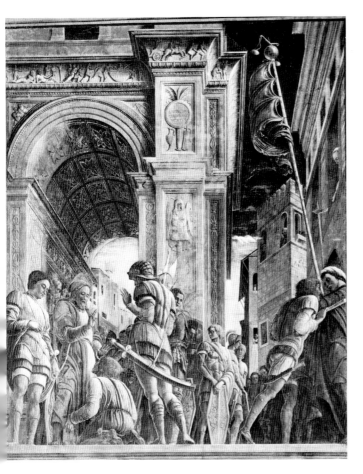

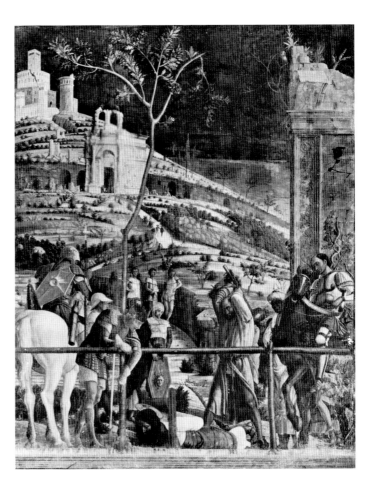

400, 402. ANDREA MANTEGNA. *St. James Led to Execution* (left) and *Martyrdom of St. James* (right).
1454–57 (destroyed 1944). Frescoes, width of each 10' 9". Ovetari Chapel, Eremitani Church, Padua

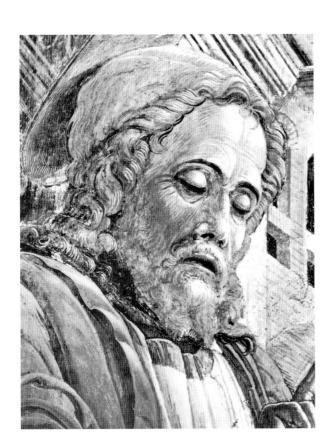

401. Head of St. James, detail of fig. 400

lost frescoes, together with a single, already badly damaged scene from the Life of St. Christopher that had been removed earlier from the walls for safekeeping.

Mantegna's first major altarpiece is in its original position on the high altar of the Romanesque Church of San Zeno in Verona (colorplates 73, 74, pp. 410, 411). The altarpiece has often been characterized as a pictorial version of Donatello's sculptural altarpiece for Sant' Antonio in Padua, and it probably does reflect some of the sculptor's architectural and figural arrangements. The wooden frame became a carved and gilded façade whose pediment and entablature are supported by four columns that seem to be attached to painted piers. Together the real half-columns and the painted piers seem to form one side of a square loggia that is completed by the other piers within the picture. In the center of this loggia, the Virgin sits on a classical marble throne that terminates in a large circle that enhances her halo, which Mantegna has sharply reduced in size. In the side panels eight saints, in meditation or conversation, diminish in size as they recede from us. Their costumes are painted in brilliant colors against the veined marble of the painted architecture, the blue sky, and the icy white clouds. Garlands of fruits and flowers, suspended from a ring above the Virgin's head, hang between the gilded columns and the painted piers. From the same ring hangs an egg, doubtless symbolizing the Virgin Birth, as in Piero's later

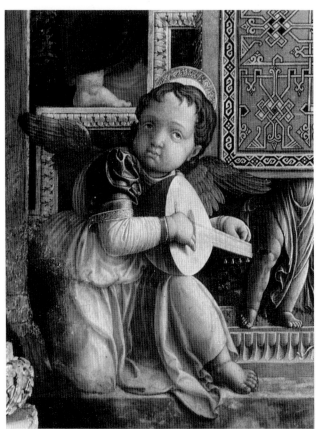

Madonna and Child (see fig. 287), and from the egg is suspended a burning oil lamp. The garlands are connected by a rosary. Around and below the throne, putti sing or strum on lutes (fig. 403). The Oriental rug under the Virgin's feet naturalistically conceals the putti sculpted on the pedestal of the throne.

Considering the brightness of the colors and the gold, the power of the architectural masses, the sharp definition of the forms, and the consistency of the spatial formulation, the illusion of reality—a higher reality—is overpowering. It is, of course, the sort of thing that had been initiated by Pietro Lorenzetti in his *Birth of the Virgin* (see fig. 105), although Mantegna probably had no knowledge of that picture. The illusionistic altarpieces of northern Italy start from Mantegna's grand formulation at San Zeno and continue in a rich series well into the Cinquecento.

The *Crucifixion* from the predella (fig. 404) is so majestic in composition and so intense in its tragic emotion that in reproduction it looks like a monumental fresco instead of a modest panel. The three crosses on Gol-

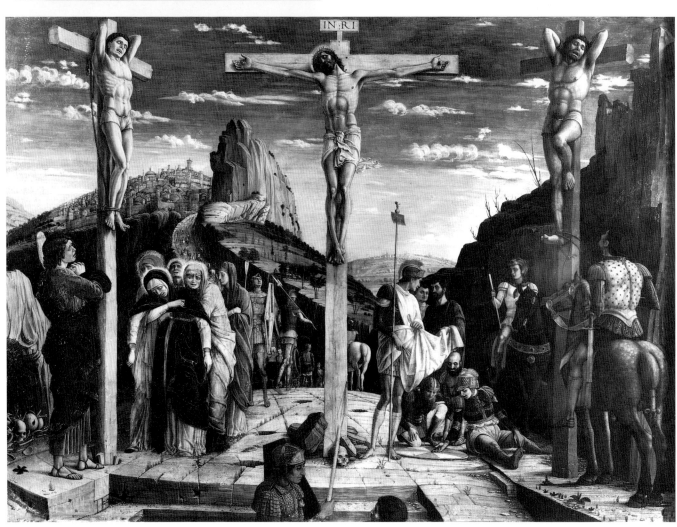

404. ANDREA MANTEGNA. *Crucifixion*, from the predella of the S. Zeno altarpiece
(see colorplate 73, p. 410). 1456–59. Panel, 26 x 35⅛". The Louvre, Paris

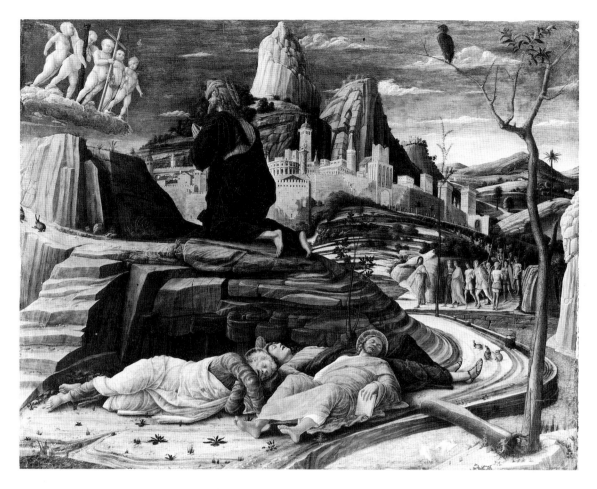

405. Andrea Mantegna. *Agony in the Garden.* c. mid-1450s. Panel, 24³/₄ x 31¹/₂". National Gallery, London

gotha—the place of the skull—are set in holes made in a rounded, skull-shaped stone outcropping and held in place by wedges and rocks. At first sight the cracks in the stone appear to conform to Albertian orthogonals, but they do not intersect rationally. In the foreground two soldiers emerge from steps cut in the rock. Behind the cross of Christ a road leads toward Jerusalem, whose roofs, domes, walls, and towers follow the curves of the hill. Beside the ascending road, filled with the crowds returning from the spectacle of the Crucifixion, towers a gigantic crag. The crosses of the thieves, as in one of Jacopo Bellini's drawings (see fig. 396), are turned inward and, following north Italian tradition, the thieves are not nailed to their crosses but tied. The cross of Christ is so placed that his toes, deprived of the usual footrest, match the junction point between two distant hills and his body is silhouetted against the sky. His arms are thrown wide in a heroic gesture of suffering, a pose that seems to bring together all the discordant elements of the landscape. The lines of the arms and turn of the head are related to the horizontal clouds in the cold sky. The tragic contrasts of the scene—the suffering women, whose haloes dissolve into soft-edged, gold clouds, the indifferent soldiers, and the beauty of the landscape and cityscape—make this small picture one of the grand Crucifixions in Italian art.

Closely related to the San Zeno altarpiece, indeed a second version of the same subject painted in the predella, is the *Agony in the Garden* (fig. 405). Here Mantegna repeats the hardness of sculptured form, the enameled brilliance of color, and the ringing clarity of atmosphere of the San Zeno altarpiece, and, as in all his early works, he drives perception to its utmost limits so that the last stone, the last mountain, the last rabbit in the road are projected with flawless precision. The compositions of both of Mantegna's versions of the *Agony in the Garden* derive from a Jacopo Bellini drawing, even to the ominous bird perched on a dead branch, but the rock masses and human forms have been subjected to Mantegna's relentless passion for definition and organization. Jerusalem appears as a mixture of the north Italian cities Mantegna had seen and the Rome he knew as yet only from drawings and descriptions. Mantegna's Christ kneels, contemplating not the chalice usually presented to him by an angel ("Father, . . . let this cup pass from me: nevertheless not as I will, but as thou wilt"; Matthew 26:39) but a phalanx of child-angels bearing symbols of the Passion. Particularly striking is the foreshortening of one of the sleeping apostles, which may have been suggested by some vanished work of Paolo Uccello in Padua or Venice. Down the road, in the middle distance, Judas is bringing the Roman soldiers to arrest Christ.

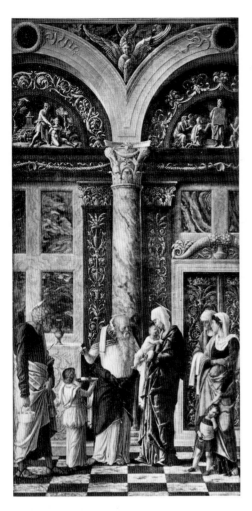

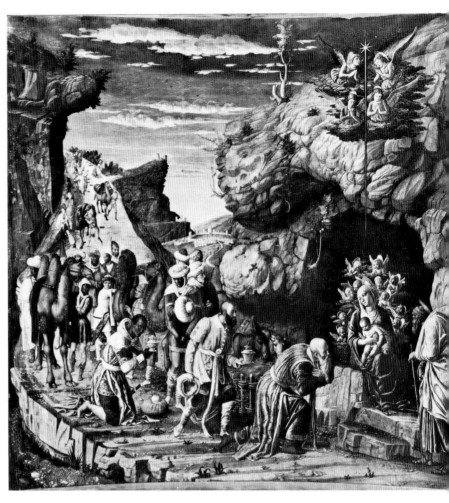

406. ANDREA MANTEGNA. *Circumcision and Presentation of Christ.* 1464(?). Panel, 34 x 17". Uffizi Gallery, Florence. Commissioned by Ludovico Gonzaga for the chapel of the Gonzaga castle in Mantua

407. ANDREA MANTEGNA. *Adoration of the Magi.* 1464(?). Panel, 30¼ x 29½". Uffizi Gallery, Florence. Commissioned by Ludovico Gonzaga for the chapel of the Gonzaga castle in Mantua

After years of negotiation, in 1459 the young artist went to Mantua as official painter to the court of Marquis Ludovico Gonzaga. He worked there for nearly half a century, becoming one of the first princely artists of the Renaissance. He painted altarpieces and frescoes for churches, chapels, and palaces, designed pageants, painted allegorical pictures, and performed the many official tasks that fell to the lot of a court artist. From this Mantuan period is to be dated a group of panels, including the *Circumcision and Presentation of Christ* (fig. 406), the *Adoration of the Magi* (fig. 407), and the *Ascension* (fig. 408), that originally lined the small chapel in the Gonzaga castle.

The panel on which the *Adoration* is painted is concave, a kind of shallow niche that is probably a perspective device. If you stand at the center of the circle of which this panel, in plan, is an arc, then the picture plane, equidistant from you at all points, will seem to disappear and the effect of illusion will be greatly enhanced. Mantegna always tries to lead us across the threshold of his pictures, and here he does it with great success. By 1464,

or thereabouts, he had discovered and put into practice the principle of the panoramic curved screen that in the twentieth century was used in cinemas.

The rock formations and stone road that sweep toward us in a flattened, reversed S-curve are again derived from Jacopo Bellini's drawings, but enhanced by every subtlety of Mantegna's perspective and naturalistic observation. The color is richer and somewhat softer than in the works of the 1450s, but no less intense, and he may already be using oil glazes to obtain the deep glow that characterizes this and other paintings of his mature and later years. Mantegna's camels are the first convincing ones we have seen, and to the best of our knowledge, this is the first time in Italian art that the third Magus is shown as black. One unexpected detail is the shape of the star, which has seven points for the Seven Joys of Mary (of which the Adoration is one). The long ray shaped like a sword may refer to the prophecy of Simeon, "A sword shall pierce through thy own soul also" (Luke 2:35). Thus the cave of the Nativity foretells the cave of the Entombment.

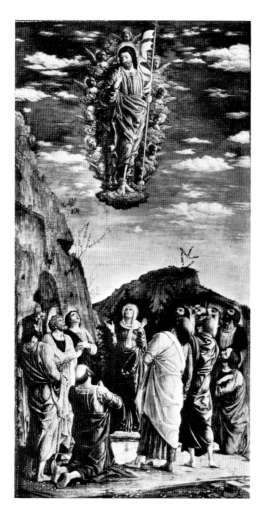

408. ANDREA MANTEGNA. *Ascension*. 1464(?).
Panel, 34 x 17". Uffizi Gallery, Florence. Commissioned
by Ludovico Gonzaga for the chapel of the Gonzaga
castle in Mantua

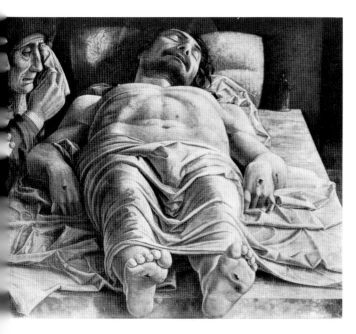

409. ANDREA MANTEGNA. *Foreshortened Christ*. After 1466.
Canvas, 26³/4 x 317/8". Brera Gallery, Milan

The *Circumcision and Presentation of Christ* is about to take place in the Temple. Someone from the sizable Jewish community in Mantua, which was protected by the Gonzaga family in return for substantial payments for their immunity, probably provided Mantegna with the necessary technical information. The architecture demonstrates Mantegna's understanding of the new classical forms of the Renaissance and his ability to paint glowing veined marble. Mantegna extends the space beyond the narrow limits of the panel by cutting two arches by the frame; the centralized column that results symbolizes both the Church and the column at which Christ's blood was next to be shed, in the Flagellation. The simulated reliefs in the lunettes make this allusion clear, for on one side Moses is shown holding the Tablets of the Law, on the other is the Sacrifice of Isaac, which foretold that of Christ. The *Circumcision* contains Mantegna's usual touching children—a boy who obediently holds the plate with the roll of bandages and bottle of water, and an infant who turns away to suck his finger.

The *Ascension* is yet another example of Mantegna's reliance on Jacopo Bellini's compositions. Here, however, the younger artist supplies a solid cloud mass for Christ to stand upon, rather than having him stand in thin air as in Jacopo's drawing. Haloes are again dissolved to become vaguely circular mists of gold around the heads. Coloristically, this panel is radiant with blues, yellows, and reds against a resoundingly blue sky.

In 1466 and 1467 Mantegna made two trips to Florence. This was probably the painter's initial contact with large numbers of Florentine works of art. He must have been impressed by the art of Castagno (whose earlier works he had been able to study in Venice), especially the *Vision of St. Jerome* in the Santissima Annunziata (see colorplate 51, p. 261) and the *Death of the Virgin*, destroyed in the seventeenth century but in Mantegna's time in Sant'Egidio. Mantegna emulated the sharp foreshortening of these pictures (Castagno's dead Virgin was seen feet foremost, as is the one in the drawing books of Jacopo Bellini) in his *Cristo in Scurto*, or *Foreshortened Christ* (fig. 409). This is the name by which the painting was known when it was listed among the works in Mantegna's house at the time of his death; it is more traditionally known as the *Lamentation* or the *Dead Christ*. The *Foreshortened Christ* is painted on canvas, and it may therefore have been intended as a processional banner for a society or confraternity dedicated to the Corpus Christi (the mystical "body of Christ"). Or it may have been painted as a private devotional image, perhaps for Mantegna himself, since it remained in his possession until his death.

The picture shows the body of Christ lying on a marble slab with a white cloth over his legs, his head raised on a pillow so that we look into the closed eyes and slightly parted lips. Strange as it may seem in an era in which the fact of death is glossed over and people "pass away," this grim reminder of mortality is probably the painting that Federigo Gonzaga, first duke of Man-

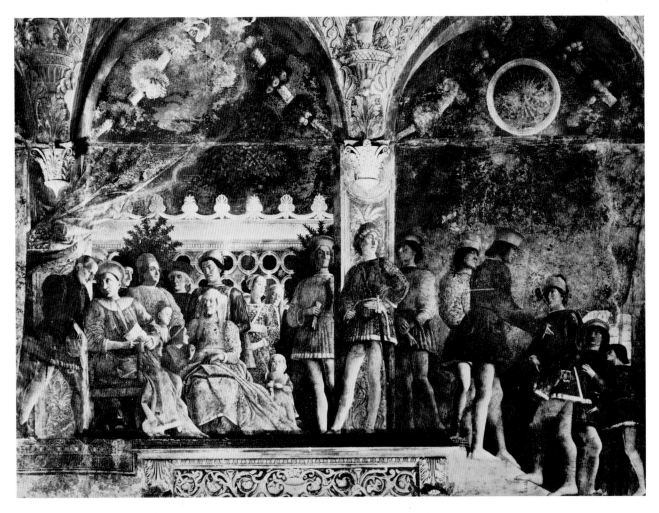

410. ANDREA MANTEGNA. *Ludovico Gonzaga, His Family, and Court* (see colorplate 8, p. 16). 1465–74.
Walnut oil on plaster, width c. 20'. Camera Picta, Palazzo Ducale, Mantua. Commissioned by Ludovico Gonzaga

tua, placed just outside his bride's chamber in 1537. In the Quattrocento the death of Christ was a matter for frequent personal meditation. In his *Imitation of Christ,* the fifteenth-century German mystic Thomas à Kempis exhorted his readers to "dwell in the wounds of Christ," and this is what Mantegna asks his observers to do. His sculptural form provides the body, and in consequence the open wounds, with convincing three-dimensionality. The perspective recession seems to catapult the body, wounds and all, out of the frame and into the observer's inner life. Nor can the viewer escape, for the feet, projected from our point of view, follow us wherever we stand in the gallery, and the wounds always lie open to our gaze.

If you compare the painting with a figure in this position, you will note that the head of Mantegna's Christ is unnaturalistically large and his feet are unrealistically small, but you will also immediately understand that a naturalistic painting of a figure in such a position would make the figure look ludicrous—gigantic feet would overwhelm the miniature head. Mantegna has painted a Christ that we recognize immediately and in which we

do not sense any inherent disproportion. At the same time, our position rivets attention on the body and the wounds of Christ. If the painting was originally meant as a processional banner, it would have appeared somewhat high overhead and perhaps at an angle; in this position it becomes an uncanny synthesis of Christ in the tomb and Christ on the cross as we might have seen him from below.

The happiest manifestation of Mantegna's art is the Camera Picta (Painted Chamber), which he painted over an extended period from 1465 to 1474 for Ludovico Gonzaga and his family in one of the towers of their castle (colorplate 8, p. 16). Over the fireplace Mantegna painted the marquis and marchioness, Barbara von Hohenzollern, together with their children, courtiers, and favorite dwarf (fig. 410). They are gathered on a terrace enclosed by a high parapet that is formed by linked circles of white marble filled with disks of veined marble and crowned with palmettes; this parapet motif is used as a unifying factor in the frescoes of the room. The real mantelpiece in the room, seen at the bottom of our illustration, becomes a platform for the figures. At

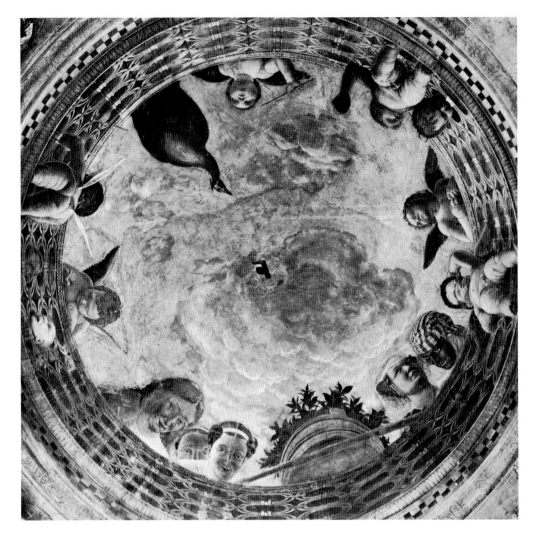

411. ANDREA
MANTEGNA. Ceiling
fresco, diameter 8' 9".
1465–74. Camera
Picta, Palazzo Ducale,
Mantua

the left a messenger, who has just brought the marquis a letter, listens intently to his instructions. The group portrait has often been compared to that of *Sixtus IV, His Nephews, and Palatina, His Librarian* (see fig. 382), painted later by Melozzo da Forlì.

Mantegna has grouped the figures with ease and simplicity, but within the apparent spontaneity of their attitudes are many carefully studied relationships of form and surface. The portraits, few of which can be securely identified, are rendered with Mantegna's customary precision, but his style has changed sharply since the early work. The forms are not so strongly projected, and the color is gentler and softer, without the harshness of the Eremitani frescoes or the brilliance of the San Zeno altarpiece.

The paintings are continuous on two of the four walls and over the vaulted ceiling. The main scene on the adjoining wall (colorplate 8, p. 16) takes place in the right section of the fresco; it has eluded identification with any known event and may be symbolic. At the left stands Ludovico, at the right his older son and successor, Federico, and in the center his second son, Cardinal Francesco, who in 1472 was made titular of the Church of Sant'Andrea in Mantua (see figs. 227–29). The background, possibly symbolic of Rome, has Roman ruins

and statues outside its walls and a castle above. In spite of large losses, made up by recent inpainting that is hatched so as not to be confused with the original, the glowing color is one of the chief delights of Mantegna's painted room. There is, however, a considerable coloristic difference between the ceiling, painted in fresco, and the walls, which Mantegna carried out with a vehicle of walnut oil.

Mantegna painted the vaulted ceiling to resemble marble relief sculpture and gold mosaic. Then in the center, unexpectedly, we look straight upward through a cylindrical parapet—also painted, and designed to match the one in the group portrait—into the sky above (fig. 411). Putti, foreshortened from below, stand inside the rim, others poke their faces through what turn out to be empty circles, and laughing servants look over the parapet at us. As a final prank, Mantegna has perched a heavy tub of plants on the edge of the parapet, propped only by a pole that might roll away at any moment.

In 1488 Mantegna at last went to Rome, where he was able to study classical antiquities in large numbers, as well as the frescoes recently painted for Sixtus IV in the Sistine Chapel (figs. 342, 344, 360; colorplate 67, p. 356). In 1489 and 1490 he painted a chapel for Pope

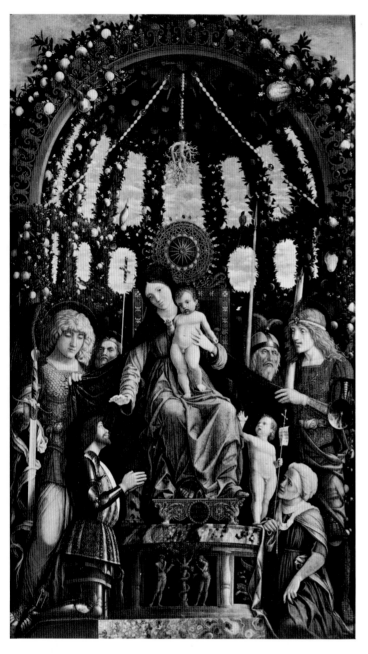

412. ANDREA MANTEGNA. *Madonna of the Victory*. 1493–96. Canvas, 9' 2" x 5' 10". The Louvre, Paris. Commissioned by Marquis Gianfrancesco Gonzaga of Mantua

mored marquis. The infant St. John the Baptist appears at the right, and kneeling next to him is an old woman, who in all probability is his mother, St. Elizabeth. On the pedestal a simulated relief shows the Temptation of Adam and Eve, from whose sin Christ and the Virgin have redeemed humanity. The figures are enclosed by the Virgin's bower, a charming construction of espaliered orange trees supported by a carved wooden arch with palmettes and a profusion of gourds and vines. From the apex of the bower a branch of rose-colored coral—efficacious in warding off demons and the evil eye—hangs from an early form of the rosary composed of coral and crystal beads. In the openings of the bower perch parrots and cockatoos.

The picture abounds in subtleties, such as the off-center placing of the Virgin's footstool to compensate for the fact that she extends her right hand to direct attention to Francesco. The details are painted with even greater refinement of linear accuracy than in Mantegna's earlier periods, but the form has lost some of its bite and the color is muted. It appears that in his old age the princely artist, working in isolation from other Italian schools and living in considerable splendor in the classical house he had designed for himself in Mantua, had become unmistakably if brilliantly reactionary.

Mantegna's classical proclivities endeared him to Isabella d'Este, who was married to Francesco Gonzaga in 1490. This learned princess took pleasure in her Studiolo, a combination study and treasure chamber that she had decorated in the Gonzaga castle at Mantua, not far from the Camera Picta, commissioned by her husband's grandfather Ludovico. The Gonzaga inventories disclose that she had an amazing collection of classical gems, coins, medals, precious and semiprecious stones, vases, manuscripts, gold and silver work, and other rarities, all stored and displayed in carved and gilded wooden cabinets. The ceiling was gilded and decorated with Isabella's private mottoes and emblems, and the walls were eventually filled with paintings, two of them by Mantegna. In the *Parnassus* (fig. 413), already in place in 1497, Mars embraces Venus in front of a bed perched on the kind of natural bridge Mantegna always enjoyed painting. Cupid blows a dart toward the genitals of Vulcan, Venus's deceived husband, who menaces the happy couple from a cavern illuminated by the soft glow from his forge. In front of the natural bridge, Apollo provides music on his lyre for a dance performed by the Muses, while Mercury at the right leans gently against Pegasus, the winged horse. It is a delightful classical fantasy, full of involved relationships of line and form and the muted colors of Mantegna's late style.

This painting, replete with references to ancient sculpture that Mantegna had studied, celebrates the wedding of Francesco and Isabella on February 11, 1490, when the planets Mercury, Mars, and Venus all stood within the sign of Aquarius, as did the westernmost bright star of the constellation Pegasus. The colors of Mars's garments, Venus's scarf, and the coverings of the

Innocent VIII, but this was destroyed in 1780 to make way for a new wing of the Vatican Museums.

On his return to Mantua, Mantegna's style suffered what has been described as desiccation, and his late paintings substitute a curiously dry intellectuality for the force of his youthful and mature styles. A fine example in his late style is the *Madonna of the Victory* (fig. 412). The picture was paid for with a penalty of 110 ducats that was extracted from a Jewish banker who had removed a fresco of the Madonna and Child from the wall of a house he had bought—even though he had received the bishop's permission to do so. The military saints Michael and George and Sts. Andrew and Longinus, patrons of Sant'Andrea in Mantua, protect the ar-

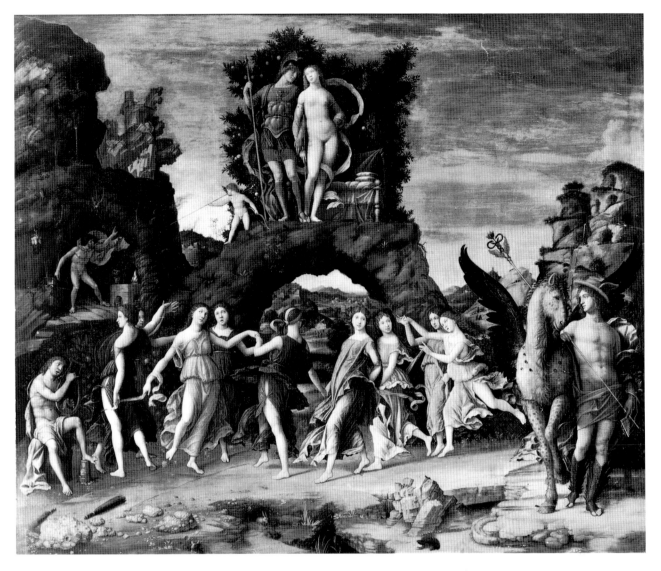

413. ANDREA MANTEGNA. *Parnassus*. 1490s. Canvas, 63 1/2 x 75 5/8". The Louvre, Paris.
Commissioned by Isabella d'Este for her Studiolo in the Gonzaga castle, Mantua

bed are the mingled colors of the Este and Gonzaga families. The painting, whose elements were doubtless specified by Isabella (we have her explicit instructions for other pictures done for the Studiolo), was clearly an allegory of marital harmony, under which the arts, led by music, would flourish. The smooth surface finish probably represented a concession to the tastes of Isabella and her desire to create a unity between her jewel-like treasure chamber and the jewels it contained. Mantegna's death in 1506 was felt as a personal tragedy by the Gonzaga family, for whom he had worked for nearly half a century. Albrecht Dürer, on his second visit to Italy, was on his way to visit this painter, to whom he owed so much, when death intervened.

GENTILE BELLINI

In Venice, meanwhile, the Bellini family was creating a new style. The older brother Gentile, who won a num-

ber of large, official commissions, painted for the same kind of public as Ghirlandaio, recording the Venetian scene as faithfully as Ghirlandaio did that of Florence. His *Procession of the Relic of the True Cross* (fig. 414) was painted in 1496 for the Scuola di San Giovanni Evangelista. The *scuole* (schools) of Venice were not educational institutions but confraternities, on the order of the Misericordia in Florence, dedicated to good works under ecclesiastical auspices. Their headquarters always included a large hall, used as a combined hospice for the poor and hospital ward, a chapel, and often a meeting room as well. In a climate inimical to frescoes, paintings on canvas formed suitable decorations for these public rooms, and series of huge framed narrative scenes for the various *scuole* comprise a large part of the production of some of the leading masters from the time of Gentile Bellini through the Cinquecento. The relic of the True Cross, the pride of the Scuola di San Giovanni Evangelista, is shown as it was carried in solemn procession

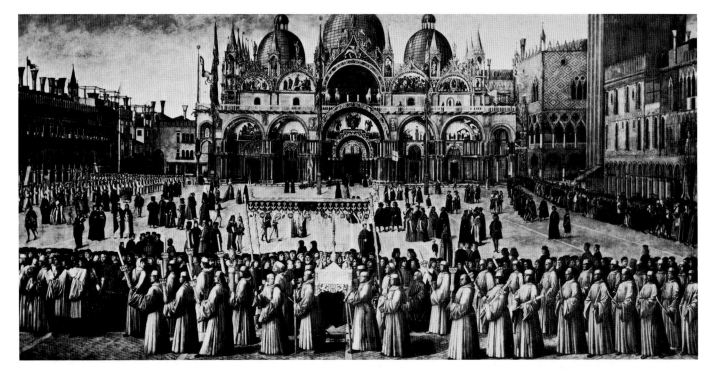

414. GENTILE BELLINI. *Procession of the Relic of the True Cross*. 1496. Canvas, 10' 7" x 14'. Accademia, Venice.
Commissioned by the Scuola di S. Giovanni Evangelista for their confraternity headquarters

on the feast day of St. Mark through the Piazza San
Marco. The painting records the procession of 1444,
when a miraculous healing took place that demonstated
the relic's efficacy. The brothers of the order, dressed in a
monkish habit, are doubtless portraits of Bellini's contemporaries, as are many spectators, but to us the principal interest of this work is its description of contemporary Venetian life and buildings. The Basilica of San
Marco and the Doges' Palace are now much as they
were then, although the original mosaics of San Marco
and Uccello's *St. Peter*, under the first pinnacle at the
left, have long since been replaced; we gain an idea of
their original appearance only from Gentile's painting.

The most colorful episode in the artist's otherwise
routine life was his stay at the court of Sultan Mahomet
II in Constantinople in 1479–80. Most of the paintings
he did for the sultan are lost, including, unfortunately,
his decorations for the imperial harem in the Topkapi
Palace. Despite its rubbed condition, his portrait of
Mahomet (fig. 415) evidences a combination of Eastern
and Renaissance elements. Even more charming is his
Portrait of a Turkish Boy (fig. 416), which reveals that, at
least for a Turkish public, Gentile showed an interest in
the kind of patterned surface composition that does not
emerge in Western art until the late nineteenth century,
and then only under the influence of Japanese wood-
block prints. Gentile's life in Constantinople provided
material for many anecdotes; one tells how he showed
the sultan a painting of the severed head of St. John the
Baptist, a subject intended for personal contemplation.
The sultan considered the picture quite unnaturalistic,

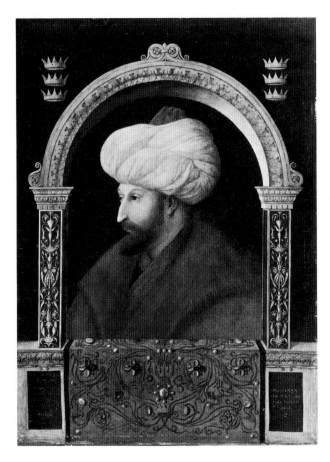

415. GENTILE BELLINI. *Sultan Mahomet II*. 1480.
Canvas, 27³/₄ x 20⁵/₈". National Gallery, London

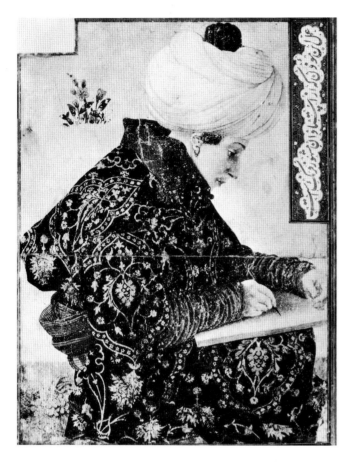

416. GENTILE BELLINI. *Portrait of a Turkish Boy.* 1479–80. Pen and gouache on parchment, 7¼ x 5½". Isabella Stewart Gardner Museum, Boston

and to prove his point called up two slaves, one with a sword. "This," said the sultan to Gentile, after the headsman had given one expert blow, "is how a freshly severed head should look!" Gentile, deciding that his life might be longer if less lucrative in Venice, soon left for home.

ANTONELLO DA MESSINA

At this juncture the orderly progress of Venetian art is interrupted by the appearance of one of those extraordinary figures who turn up every now and then, as if to refute theorists who like to relate history in terms of necessary developments from stage to stage. Real life provides an infinity of surprises for us—such as the peripatetic Gentile da Fabriano early in the Quattrocento or El Greco in the late Cinquecento. As his name suggests, Antonello da Messina (c. 1430–79) came from the Sicilian city of Messina, where there had been no artistic tradition since the days of the twelfth-century mosaicists. Active as master of his own shop in Messina in 1456, he nonetheless traveled widely, but always returned to his native city. He arrived in Venice in 1475, stayed a year and a half, and changed the course of Ve-

netian painting. Old sources credit Antonello with having introduced the Venetians to the technique of painting in oil. While this may not be strictly true (oil painting was known in Venice and Florence at a much earlier date, and both Antonio del Pollaiuolo and Piero della Francesca had experimented with it), Antonello seems to have shown the Venetians how oil could be used to give previously unknown atmospheric, luminary, and coloristic effects to landscapes, interiors, and figures. Venetian painting before and after Antonello is radically different, and it is impossible to escape the assumption that he was responsible for the change.

Antonello may have learned to paint in oil from a Flemish-influenced painter named Colantonio, with whom he could have been apprenticed in Naples. But as early as 1456 he was recorded at the court of Galeazzo Maria Sforza in Milan, where he was paid on the same basis as Petrus Christus, a pupil of Jan van Eyck. He certainly studied Jan van Eyck's paintings in Naples.

Antonello, son of a stonecutter, had a sculptor's sense of form, and one scholar has suggested that Antonello studied Archaic or Severe Style Greek sculpture in Sicily. Certainly he was able to blend a Netherlandish passion for the details of visual reality and the saturation of vision in light and shadow with a quintessentially Mediterranean purity and clarity of form. But neither these disparate influences nor their unexpected combination in a single artistic personality can account for the phenomenon of Antonello.

One of Antonello's earliest pictures is the *St. Jerome in His Study* (colorplate 75, p. 412), a work so Netherlandish in style that a Venetian who saw it in 1529 thought it might have been painted by Hans Memlinc or even by Jan van Eyck himself. St. Jerome reads quietly in a fantastic alcove within a monastic library. We are admitted to his study through an illusionistic stone arch similar in effect to those used by Rogier van der Weyden in a number of altarpieces although its shape is typical of Spanish Gothic forms in Sicily. On the step, beautifully lighted from the left, are a brass bowl, a peacock, and a quail. The same light throws the shadow of the arch on the interior and competes with the light from the distant windows on the other side. St. Jerome's desk and shelves are mounted in the brightest section, just below a clerestory window. Behind him, in the shadowy region between the two lights, his lion strolls across the elaborate majolica floor—a kind of pavement widely used in southern Italy, Sicily, and even, occasionally, in Tuscany. In true Van Eyck tradition, the picture is complete down to the tiniest detail of architecture and still life, including the characteristic Netherlandish motif of a towel hanging on a nail. The light effects on the stone, the floor, the atmosphere of the room, and the landscape visible through the windows suggest Van Eyck's techniques of oil painting and glazes. This little picture, like a painting by Jan van Eyck, is a microcosm of its own at the same time that it reflects, as in a sphere of crystal, the vastness of the outside world.

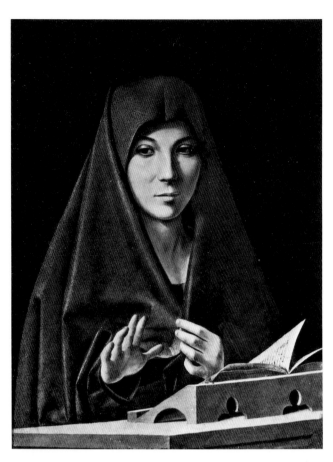

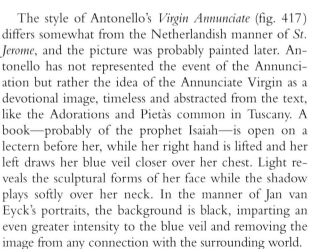

417. ANTONELLO DA MESSINA. *Virgin Annunciate*. c. 1465.
Panel, 17³/4 x 13³/8". Museo Nazionale, Palermo

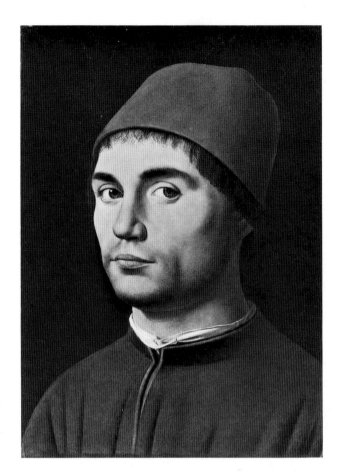

418. ANTONELLO DA MESSINA. *Portrait of a Man*. c. 1465.
Panel, 14 x 10". National Gallery, London

The style of Antonello's *Virgin Annunciate* (fig. 417) differs somewhat from the Netherlandish manner of *St. Jerome*, and the picture was probably painted later. Antonello has not represented the event of the Annunciation but rather the idea of the Annunciate Virgin as a devotional image, timeless and abstracted from the text, like the Adorations and Pietàs common in Tuscany. A book—probably of the prophet Isaiah—is open on a lectern before her, while her right hand is lifted and her left draws her blue veil closer over her chest. Light reveals the sculptural forms of her face while the shadow plays softly over her neck. In the manner of Jan van Eyck's portraits, the background is black, imparting an even greater intensity to the blue veil and removing the image from any connection with the surrounding world.

The serious face, with its grave, composed features, is the face of a Sicilian peasant girl, with the Greek nose still common among Sicilians. Under the arched dark brows, the brown eyes seem to show a realization of the meaning of the Incarnation. In the smoothly controlled and projected forms of the face, the influence of Greek sculpture seems probable. At the same time, the clarity of form, the brilliance of the illumination, the emphasis on inner psychological experience, and the absence of a background point ahead more than a century to the revolutionary works of Caravaggio.

An arresting example of Antonello da Messina's insight as a portraitist is his *Portrait of a Man* (fig. 418). An inscription at the bottom that is believed to have identified this as a self-portrait was cut off in the eighteenth century, but it may merely have been a signature. It is a portrait of astonishing psychological depth and great simplicity and dignity of form, a painting in which Antonello has exemplified both major tendencies blended in his style. He rivals Netherlandish painters in his observation of the movement of light across the textures of the skin, the faint stubble of the beard, the luminous clear eyes, and the dark hairs that escape from the red cap or compose the powerful eyebrows. The plastic force of the forms is in the sculptural tradition of the *Virgin Annunciate*.

The *Crucifixion* (fig. 419) exhibits, just below the cross, the illusionistic *cartellino* that appears in many north Italian paintings of the Quattrocento; here it bears Antonello's signature and the date 1475, and in all probability the picture was painted after his arrival in Venice. The composition, with the Virgin and St. John seated at either corner, is close to that of Ghiberti's *Crucifixion* on the Baptistery Doors of Florence (see fig. 157), a city Antonello may have visited on his way north. In the unearthly stillness of the broad, softly colored, tan and olive landscape, there is a suggestion of Piero della Fran-

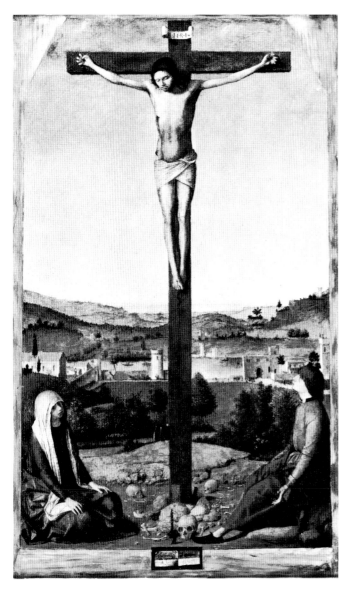

419. ANTONELLO DA MESSINA. *Crucifixion*. 1475.
Panel, 16½ x 10". National Gallery, London

76, p. 413), which is almost contemporary with Pollaiuolo's altarpiece on the same subject (see colorplate 59, p. 300), but as different as possible within the requirements of the subject. Antonello has chosen a late moment in the story: the attack is over and the soldiers have left. One sleeps in the sun, projected feet first, Mantegna-style, and two more chat before an arcade in the middle distance. The saint, pierced by arrows and tied to a tree, looks upward with calm trust. The beautifully drawn figure is at once commonplace and noble. In the reciprocal rhythms of the harmonious stance and the low viewpoint of the perspective construction, set just below the knees of the saint, Antonello shows himself the master of the classic style created by Mantegna. Figure and architecture tower above us as in the *St. James Led to Execution* (see fig. 400), but the only vestige of Mantegna's archaeological interests is the broken column. Instead of the usual loincloth, the saint wears fifteenth-century undershorts, and the buildings are contemporary Venetian houses, even to the flaring cylindrical chimneys. A dreamy afternoon sunlight unites and warms the entire scene—the buildings, the people watching from carpet-hung balconies, the flowers in the window boxes, the Greek priests in the middle distance, the landscape beyond, the smooth, glowing skin of the nude figure, and the clouds in the sky.

GIOVANNI BELLINI

Now we can turn to the work of the last and greatest member of the Bellini family, Giovanni Bellini or, in Venetian dialect, Giambellino, who brought Venetian painting to the threshold of the High Renaissance. His evolution is incomprehensible without Antonello for whom, in fact, Bellini had the deepest admiration and from whom he must have learned the new possibilities of oil painting. We know little about Bellini's character, and most of his paintings, especially the early ones, are undated. We have no evidence for the date of his birth save that he signed a document as a witness in 1459, when he was already living away from his father and brother, and that in 1506, when Albrecht Dürer visited Venice for the second time, he wrote that Bellini was very old but still the best painter in the city. Taken together these would seem to place Bellini's birth in the early 1430s, fairly close to the birth date of his brother-in-law, Andrea Mantegna. He is recorded as a painter before 1460, and he was painting up to the time of his death in 1516, so his pictorial career lasted for at least two generations, a record that in the Renaissance only Michelangelo and Titian would surpass. Although the same poetic temperament can be felt in all Bellini's paintings, the difference in style between the earliest and latest is so great as to make it hard at first to believe they were done by the same artist (compare fig. 420 with colorplate 79, p. 416, for example).

cesca, and in the harmony between the extended arms and the shape of the landscape there is a hint of Mantegna. But Antonello needs none of Mantegna's passionate violence (see fig. 404) to evoke the mystery of death and of Christ's sacrifice in the warmth of the sun-filled earth and cloudless sky. This, too, is Golgotha, the "place of the skull." Not only is Adam's skull visible below the cross, but other skulls, almost indistinguishable from the earth, fill the middle distance. Yet there is no gruesome emphasis on this detail. One notices it with surprise but can accept it with calm. Such is the meditative unity of the picture that life and death seem mysteriously one, regeneration and resorption part of the same process, a reconciliation to death so necessary a part of the law of life that grief is superfluous.

A final work by Antonello, dating probably from the end of his stay in Venice, is the *St. Sebastian* (colorplate

Bellini's earliest works show a strong affinity with Mantegna's style, but while the sculptural hardness of

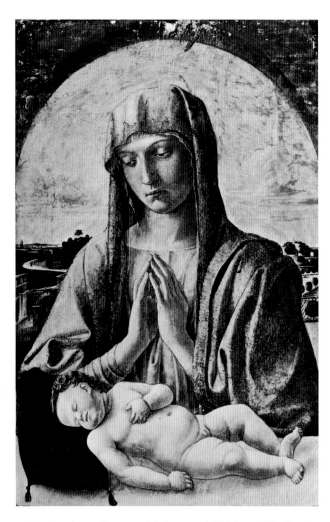

420. GIOVANNI BELLINI. *Madonna and Child*. c. 1455. Panel, 28¹/₂ x 18¹/₄". The Metropolitan Museum of Art, New York

to envelop the figures. Bellini is not interested in the enameled brilliance of color seen in the contemporary works of his brother-in-law. At the start he prefers a harmonious combination of pearly pale flesh tones, soft gray-blues, and roses as seen here; later with the use of oil, his color warms and deepens, and the sea light is strengthened by these new coloristic developments.

Bellini's *Agony in the Garden* (fig. 421), for example, which is probably not far from that by Mantegna (see fig. 405) in date, offers itself for comparison. Both derive compositionally from the inventions of Jacopo Bellini, but Mantegna's stoicism is missing from Giovanni's composition, as is the grandeur of the landscape and the classical reminiscences. We have only the dullness of the north Italian scene, where the Venetian plain meets the hills near Padua; a hill town on one side; a clustered village on the other; and in between a badly eroded valley through which flows the brook Hebron, not moving directly toward us as in Mantegna but disappearing behind rocks at the left. The river, the steps, the buildings, and the rocks cannot be followed at every stage, as one can follow the voices in Mantegna's polyphonies. The rosy dawn light of Good Friday has started to color the undersides of the clouds, as it does in Jacopo Bellini's *Madonna of Humility with Donor* (see colorplate 72, p. 409). The color scheme is dominated not by the reds, yellows, and blues of the garments, but by the tones of the still-shadowed earth. Bellini's Christ lifts his head just above the horizon against the first dawn as he contemplates a single transparent angel holding the chalice. Instead of Mantegna's Roman platoon, Bellini's Judas leads a ragtag of sleepy soldiers, and in the foreground Bellini is less interested in perspective projection than in the fitful slumber of the apostles, who seem to have experienced more than they can bear. Bellini suggests the sympathetic reaction of surrounding nature to human and divine experience. What he lacks in intellectual acumen he makes up in poetic intuition and spiritual depth.

Of all the early works, the most searching is the *Pietà* (colorplate 77, p. 414), which is again closely related to compositions originated by Jacopo Bellini. The tomb ledge suggests the parapet of Jacopo's Madonna compositions, while behind the ledge Mary and St. John the Evangelist hold up the dead Christ for meditation. His head, still crowned with thorns, falls toward that of the ashen Mary, who brings her cheek almost to his and searches the pale face and sunken eyes. Her eyes, and those of John, are red from weeping, and the inscription at the bottom reads, "When these swelling eyes evoke groans, this work of Giovanni Bellini could shed tears." The streams of blood that have congealed below the lance wound and along the left forearm are the brightest tones in the picture. The cold clear sky complements the subdued colors of the drapery, and the entire picture suggests the crisp clarity of a winter day. The colors of the flesh of Mary and John are a subtle contrast to the greenish tones of Christ's gently illuminated body, and

the masses, the firmness of contour, the crispness of detail, and the careful construction of the picture suggest Mantegna, never, even in his earliest paintings, does Bellini present us with the same consistency, the same rigor of organization, the same finality. Unlike that of Mantegna, his world is not always accessible to analysis and cannot always be rationally comprehended. Forms are often set next to each other with only a slight attempt at connection; they are united by a community of feeling.

A grave, pensive *Madonna and Child* (fig. 420) is typical of Bellini's early half-length Madonnas. Mantegna's steely intellect would probably have devised a more coherent design, and it is unlikely he would have imparted this kind of mood to the picture. Lifting her hands in prayer, Mary looks sadly down toward the sleeping Christ, whose slumber foreshadows his death. Her face is suffused by light from below—the sea light of Venice that was reflected from canals and palaces and which Bellini used even for Madonnas set in landscapes. In the early works these backgrounds offer easy roads and gentle slopes, but as Bellini's work develops they will grow

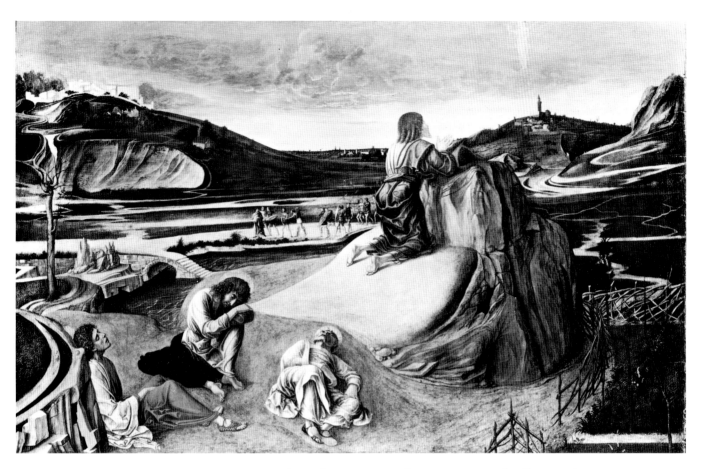

421. GIOVANNI BELLINI. *Agony in the Garden.* c. 1460. Panel, 32 x 50". National Gallery, London

the figures and the tan and olive landscape seem locked between the upper and lower blue-gray horizontals of marble and cloud.

Never again are Giovanni's dramas so intense or his appeal to emotion so explicit. As his style matures, the content of his pictures becomes warmer and richer along with his sun-drenched color. His first real triumph in the new style is the huge altarpiece of the *Coronation of the Virgin* (fig. 422), commissioned by Costanzo Sforza, lord of Pesaro. The altarpiece, with its original carved and gilded Renaissance frame, lacks only its culminating *Pietà*, now in the Vatican Pinacoteca. The altarpiece was probably painted in the early 1470s, before Antonello's arrival in Venice. The space of the central panel is almost filled by an elegant Renaissance throne in white marble, and we look through an opening in its back into a landscape that represents, certainly by direct order of Costanzo Sforza, his fortress of Gradara; it may still be seen only a few miles from Pesaro. The grouping of the saints in depth on either side of the throne is reminiscent of Mantegna's San Zeno altarpiece (see colorplate 73, p. 410), but what is startlingly new is the brilliant sunlight that plays upon the scene, sparing only the face of the Virgin, and even that is gently radiated by reflections from the marble pedestal. The saturated colors have lost the restrained quality of those in Giovanni's

earliest works. Intense reds and blues appear in the drapery, and there are passages of special splendor in the glowing white and gold damask of Christ's tunic, which sums up the warmth and beauty of the sunlight. The greens of the foliage and the rosy reflections on the clouds, not to mention the reds, whites, and blues of the cherubim above, carry this new joy in color throughout the landscape and the surrounding atmosphere. Giovanni must have been using a medium containing some oil; it is difficult to see how he could have obtained such effects in any other way. Investigations have disclosed that he was also using varnishes in which a certain amount of colored pigment was dissolved for glazing effects and also for some actual passages of painting. The new sonority of color in the Pesaro altarpiece has the unexpected effect of increasing the roundness of the forms, making them more sculpturally convincing and less linear than ever before in Bellini's work.

The small narratives in the sides of the frame and the predella are even more surprising in their increased freedom from Mantegnesque discipline, for the figures are surrounded, bathed, and warmed in a natural environment that seems to elude definition. In the *Adoration of the Child* (fig. 423), for example, hills, roads, and streams not only lose their palpable continuity—this had already taken place in the *Agony in the Garden* (see fig. 421) and

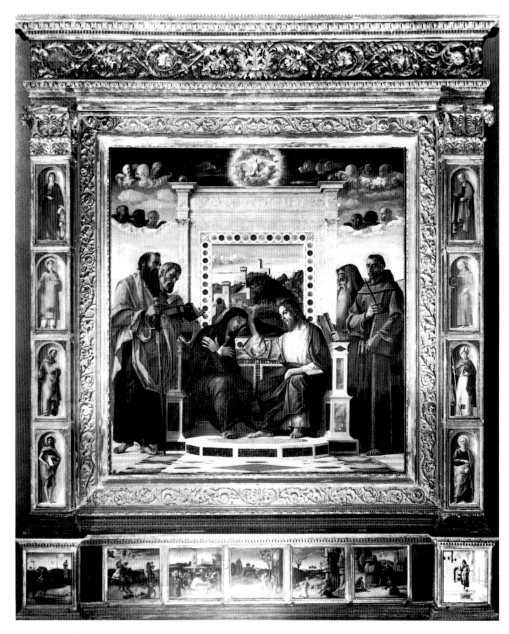

422. GIOVANNI BELLINI. *Coronation of the Virgin* (Pesaro altarpiece). Early 1470s. Panels: center, 8' 7" x 7' 10". Pinacoteca, Pesaro. Commissioned by Constanzo Sforza, lord of Pesaro, for the Church of S. Francesco, Pesaro

below: 423. GIOVANNI BELLINI. *Adoration of the Child*, on the predella of the Pesaro altarpiece. Early 1470s. Panel, 16³/4 x 14". Pinacoteca, Pesaro

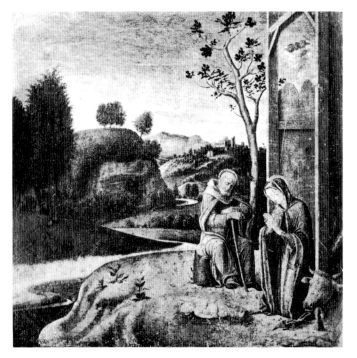

other early works—but even, along with trees and castles, merge their contours in the surrounding atmosphere. The real subject of Bellini's picture seems to be the light of early evening in an enchanted valley, and we look for a moment before we discover the Christ Child lying on the ground before the kneeling Virgin, or the three tiny cherub heads from which emerge golden rays and the Star of Bethlehem. This new feeling for the poetry of nature, which first began to appear in the works of Jacopo Bellini, assumes such importance in a long sequence of works by his younger son that it does not seem farfetched to wonder whether Giovanni, if he were given to verbal defense of his religious and philosophical position, might not have declared himself a pantheist.

Although nature is reduced to two brief echoes in the background, one at either side, Bellini's *Enthroned Madonna and Child with Sts. Peter, Nicholas, Benedict, and Mark* (fig. 424) shows a steady increase in the artist's en-

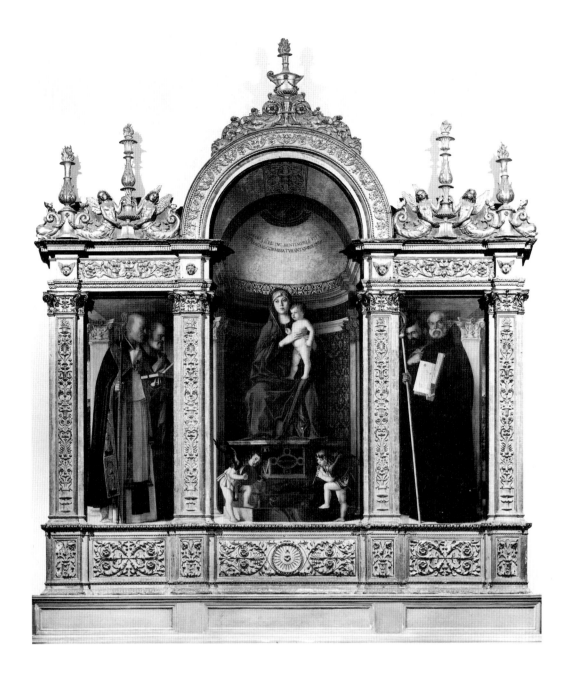

424. GIOVANNI
BELLINI. *Enthroned
Madonna and Child
with Sts. Peter,
Nicholas, Benedict,
and Mark*
(Frari altarpiece).
1488. Panel.
🏛 Sacristy,
Sta. Maria Gloriosa
dei Frari, Venice.
Commissioned
by the sons of Pietro
Pesaro and
Franceschina Tron
in memory of their
mother

joyment in depicting natural light. The altarpiece is still
in its original frame and in the position for which it was
painted in the Sacristy of Santa Maria Gloriosa dei Frari.
The painting was commissioned in memory of Franceschina Tron, who is buried in a tomb in front of the altar
that became the tomb of her descendants. Giovanni has
borrowed his brother-in-law Mantegna's device of the
architectural frame into which one looks as if into a
shrine (see colorplate 73, p. 410). In this case the illusion of reality is greater because the capitals inside the
picture are identical with those of the frame and because
the picture is painted in oil, enabling the artist to maintain a continuous atmosphere into whose shadows light
is dissolved. It is as if the marine magnificence of the
gilded Renaissance frame, with its dolphins and winged
tritons, were casting a golden light into the recesses of
Mary's shrine, to be given forth again in softer keys by
the painted gold mosaic of the apse—a typical Venetian
reference to the Church of San Marco—and still more

softly by the silk and gold brocade of the cloth of honor
behind the throne. The forms themselves are no longer
so clearly stated; the contours of faces and figures and
the boundaries between major masses merge with the
atmosphere as richly as in the small narratives from the
Pesaro altarpiece. Only oil medium and oil glaze can account for this transformation, and certainly it was prompted by Bellini's wonder—recorded by the sources—at
Antonello's work. But now he understands even better
than Antonello how to present the fluid fabric of light
and atmosphere that surrounds us. In this new delight in
optical beauty, however, some observers may feel that
certain precious qualities of Bellini's early works have
been lost. The poignancy and, at times, the somber
drama of those pictures are very different from the world
of opulence and ease that Bellini depicts in his years of
success. His Madonnas now seem untroubled by any premonition of the Passion.

Giovanni's altarpieces assumed tremendous scale. One

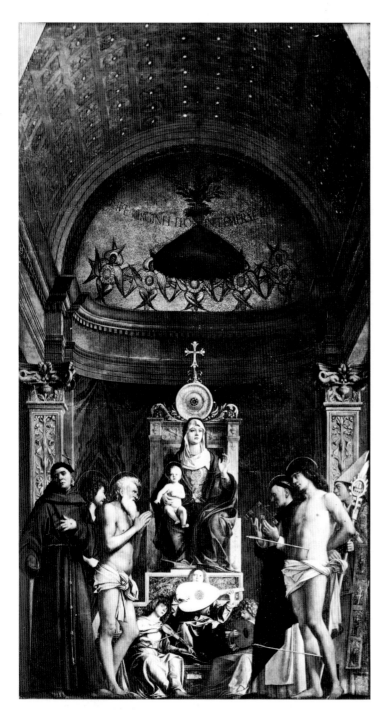

425. GIOVANNI BELLINI. *Enthroned Madonna and Child with Sts. Francis, John the Baptist, Job, Dominic, Sebastian, and Louis of Toulouse* (S. Giobbe altarpiece). Late 1470s. Panel, 15' 4" x 8' 4". Accademia, Venice. Commissioned for the chapel in the Hospital of S. Giobbe, Venice; perhaps the patron was the Scuola di S. Giobbe

of the most imposing is the *Enthroned Madonna and Child with Saints* (fig. 425), which is generally known as the San Giobbe altarpiece because it was painted for the chapel of the Venetian Hospital of San Giobbe (St. Job). Christian churches are seldom dedicated to Old Testament figures, but in Venice Job and Moses each has his own church. Probably the picture dates from the late

1470s. It is closely related to a large *Madonna Enthroned with Saints* painted by Antonello in 1476, which is now lost save for a few fragments, and also to the *Madonna and Child with Saints* by Piero (see fig. 287). Bellini has given the figures not only reasonable proportions in comparison with the architecture—Piero had already done that—but also reasonable positions *within* the illusionistic space instead of before it. As a result, the standing figures are less than one-third the height of the barrel vault above them, and even the Virgin's towering throne does not elevate her head as high as the mathematical center of the picture, which is occupied by the golden cross issuing from the marble disk above her head.

These proportions show that Bellini was accustomed to composing on a grand scale, placing life-sized figures in vast surroundings. We tend to forget this fact, because almost all of his historical compositions were destroyed in the 1577 fire that gutted the Doges' Palace in Venice. If all the compositions painted by Giovanni to fulfill commissions originally given to Gentile—left incomplete when the older brother went to Constantinople in 1479—were extant, we would have a more balanced picture of Giovanni's capabilities.

At any rate, the spatial effect of the shadowy Venetian Renaissance church interior that the softly lighted figures occupy is an essential element in the composition, and it would have been enhanced when the painting was in its still-surviving frame, whose marble pilasters and entablatures match those in the painting. On Mary's left, the beautiful figure of St. Sebastian, more classical in feeling than Antonello's representation of the same saint (see colorplate 76, p. 413), is here as protector of the sick. The old man with long white beard at Mary's right is Job, patron saint of the hospital because of his physical and mental sufferings. The lofty space of the picture creates an effect of grandeur, and the details show Giovanni's beauty of texture and sweetness of expression and also a new freedom and sketchiness in the use of the brush.

Two sublime examples of Bellini's pantheism seem to date from this period. The *Transfiguration of Christ* (colorplate 78, p. 415) differs from an earlier rendering of the same subject by the artist. The event is now shorn of its supernatural character, and Mount Tabor, traditionally represented as quite an eminence, is reduced to a slight rise. Broad meadows are interlocked along low, projecting escarpments. The afternoon is well advanced. At the left a farmer leads an ox and a goat past a monastery on a crag that is already darkening in the evening shadows; at the right, churches with cylindrical towers like those in Ravenna and partially ruined city walls still catch the light, which also dwells on the lower slopes of nearby mountain masses. In the center of this bleak yet mysteriously beautiful landscape stands Christ, his hands and head silhouetted against the shining white clouds, his eyes just avoiding our gaze. The text says that "his raiment became shining, exceeding white as snow" (Mark 9:3), and Bellini has shown him in a color that

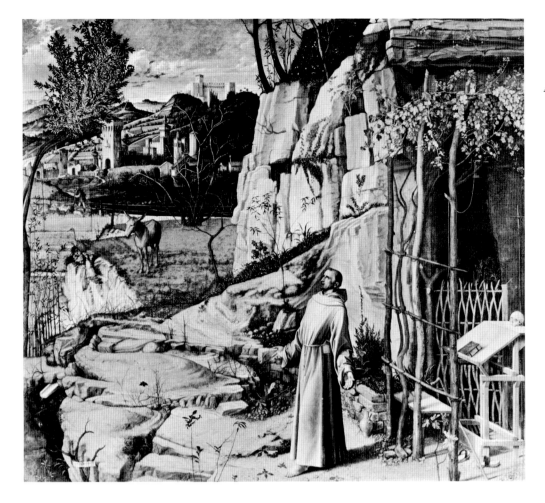

426. GIOVANNI BELLINI.
St. Francis in Ecstasy.
1470s. Oil and tempera
on panel, 49 x 557/8".
Copyright The Frick
Collection, New York

grows out of the land and unites it with the sky, for the shadows are tinged with tan and green, and the whites are those of the lower layer of clouds shining against the darker masses above. The broad, sculptural masses of the drapery of Moses and Elijah epitomize in their colors the meadows and the mountains, and these two figures appear with all the majesty of the Old Testament. Before this group, rather than below it, the three apostles have fallen to the ground. Bellini's *Transfiguration* is a revelation of God in nature, but he has cut us off from this revelation—and not only by the device of Christ's averted gaze. A sapling fence moves diagonally across the foreground, and immediately behind it opens a rocky chasm—suggestions, perhaps, of the barrier of death and the gulf of the grave that lie between the Christian and final understanding.

Even more explicit is the *St. Francis in Ecstasy* (fig. 426). It is not certain exactly what moment in the saint's life is represented in this unusually large narrative painting; it has been argued that this is not the stigmatization because we already see the wounds in the saint's hands. Whatever the exact moment, what we see here is the ecstatic communion of St. Francis with God in a beautiful natural setting. He stands before a cave supplied with a grape arbor (an obviously Christian symbol) that shades his rough desk, on which only a book and skull appear. With hands outstretched, he looks upward to-

ward a burst of golden light in the upper left corner. The slender sapling seems to bend toward him, and water flows from a stone spout attached to a little spring below. Both water and sapling are references to Moses—the burning bush and the water struck from the rock—in line with the attempts of Francis's followers to depict him as a second Moses. Beyond a standing crane and a motionless donkey, exemplar of patience, a shepherd watches over his flock. The sunlight seems to pour down on the fertile valley, the rich hillsides, the outcroppings of rock, the tranquil city, the humans, animals, and plants, and, above all, the saint. The magnificent clear deep blue of the sky helps to explain the crystalline nature of the detail throughout. Every object is represented with a Netherlandish fidelity to fact worthy of Antonello.

As the Quattrocento ended and the new century began, Bellini's art grew ever deeper and stronger. Sharing only with the youthful Leonardo da Vinci the honor of being the greatest European painter of his day, the aged Bellini seems to have experienced no slackening of observation or imagination, no dulling of sensitivity, no loss of skill. His sun-filled altarpieces and Madonna images, such as the *Virgin and Child Between St. John the Baptist and a Female Saint* (fig. 427), take us into a new world of liberated color. Bellini's favorite waning afternoon light plays on the fortifications of the distant port (probably a symbol of Mary), the distant crags of the

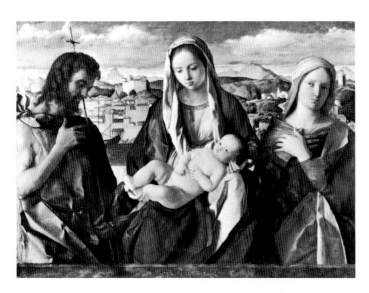

427. GIOVANNI BELLINI. *Virgin and Child Between St. John the Baptist and a Female Saint.* c. 1500. Panel, 21¼ x 29⅞". Accademia, Venice

Dolomites, and the clouds that gather about them. It sends blue and lemon-yellow lights from the landscape over the still faces whose outlines are softer than anything we have yet seen. There are astonishing passages of coloristic change, such as the wide range of hue within the orange satin lining of the female saint's cloak, or the rich interweaving of blues, roses, and violets in her brocaded tunic. The splendor of reflected color lightens even the ascetic garb and features of the Baptist. Here Bellini is carrying Venetian painting along the road that leads to Velázquez, to Vermeer, and eventually to Monet, Seurat, and Cézanne.

If he was not already a High Renaissance painter in the late altarpieces—such as the *Enthroned Madonna with Saints* (colorplate 79, p. 416)—it is hard to say why not. Certainly this was the kind of painting that deeply impressed Fra Bartolommeo when he visited Venice in 1507, that he emulated on his return to Florence, and that Raphael in turn derived from him. At first sight the general formulation seems almost identical with that of the San Giobbe altarpiece (see fig. 425), but there is a profound difference. The painted architecture is not related to our position as spectators nor to our angle of vision. The viewpoint proposed by the perspective scheme, as in Leonardo's *Last Supper* (see colorplate 83, p. 452), is on a level with the heads of the saints, which are nine or ten feet above the floor, given the height of the intervening altar and its steps. And of the seven figures in the painting, not one looks at another. As a result, the immediacy and intimacy of the altarpieces of Bellini's maturity are replaced by a certain remoteness that is increased by the meditative calm of the saints, each of whom is wrapped in a voluminous mantle, separated from the next by the enveloping light and atmosphere. The outlines, vaguer than ever, are almost completely dissolved in light or in shadow, but the master's control

of form remains absolute. Every mass is felt in its essence, every relation is harmonious and clear, brought out against the creamy marble and blue-green-gold mosaic of the shrine by the brilliance of the garments—the Virgin in bright blue, St. Peter in russet and gold, the angel in yellow with orange shadows, and St. Jerome in an astonishing red enlivened by crisp white. Even this noble altarpiece is by no means Giovanni Bellini's swan song, but for the next eleven years of his life he had to compete with, and was eventually influenced by, his gifted pupils and successors: Giorgione, whom he outlived, and Titian, who was to live almost beyond the chronological limits of the Renaissance.

To complete his innumerable commissions, Giovanni maintained a large staff of assistants, who painted many a Madonna that bears the Bellini signature from the master's sketches and directions. These followers and numerous other imitators of varying degrees of talent and fidelity popularized the Bellini manner in Venice and its subject cities, where it became the dominant style. But Giovanni Bellini's style was not the only one available for patrons; even at the moment of his triumph, Gentile Bellini's narrative style continued, as did the Mantegnesque manner of the Vivarini family.

VITTORE CARPACCIO

Vittore Carpaccio (originally Scarpaza, then Carpathius, c. 1460–1526) owes almost nothing to Giovanni Bellini and only the idea of the crowded, newsy, anecdotal narrative to Gentile. His style is his own, and it is a fanciful one, full of witty observation embodied in a new kind of composition.

Carpaccio was the perfect painter for the *scuole*, and he spent most of his artistic career decorating them with narrative canvases of considerable size; we have little evidence that he received many commissions for altarpieces and Madonnas. Most of his time in the 1490s was spent in carrying out an extensive cycle for the Scuola di Sant'Orsola. The legend of Ursula, as the saint is known in English, tells how Etherius, the pagan son of the king of Britain, sought the hand of the Christian Ursula, daughter of the king of Brittany, who exacted as her condition for the match Etherius's conversion to Christianity, as well as a three-year cooling-off period during which Ursula and her ten maids of honor, each accompanied by a thousand virgins, could make a pilgrimage to Rome. On the way back the eleven thousand and eleven virgins were waylaid by the Huns at Cologne and slaughtered. Carpaccio divided the story into eight large paintings to line the chapel of the now-destroyed *scuola*, and these are now displayed with the altarpiece in the Accademia in Venice.

One long canvas shows the departure of the young prince from Britain, his arrival in Brittany, and the departure of the betrothed couple for Rome (fig. 428). Although Britain at the left and Brittany at the right are separated by a flagpole, the same sunny Venetian sky

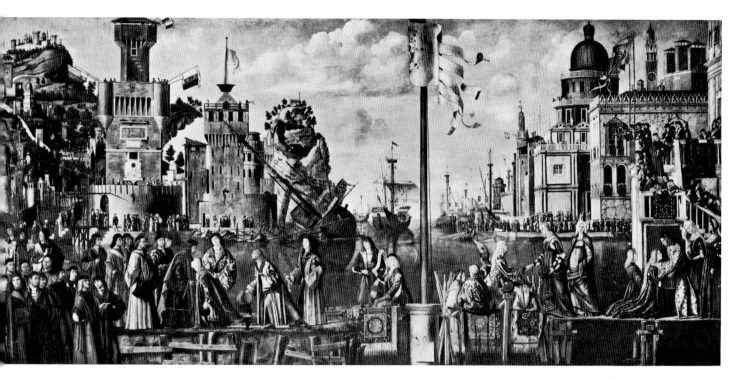

428. VITTORE CARPACCIO. *Departure of the Prince from Britain, His Arrival in Brittany, and Departure of the Betrothed Couple for Rome.* 1495. Canvas, 9' 20" x 20'. Accademia, Venice. Commissioned by the Scuola di Sant'Orsola for the confraternity headquarters, perhaps with the financial assistance of the Loredan family

with big, floating clouds unites them both. For Carpaccio they are merely two sides of the same ideal harbor, a background for the narrative sequence that allows a celebration of the naval power and palatial splendor of imperial Venice. Britain could be any Venetian port along the Dalmatian coast or in the Aegean islands, with a castle rising above the fortifications of a seaside city. The two fortresses by the water have been identified as the Venetian strongholds at Rhodes and Candia. Whether or not Carpaccio had seen these buildings is unknown, but he had certainly watched the careening of ships in the naval arsenal of Venice, and he represents this essential repair procedure of the pre-drydock era with concentration. Brittany is Carpaccio's fantasy on the theme of Quattrocento Venice, with marble-clad palaces, domes, and towers crowding to the sea. The verticals of towers, flagpoles, and masts and the diagonal of the careened galleon give him straight lines with which to bind the diffuse composition together—motives that traverse, organize, and contain the space and the figures.

The narrative moves gently from left to right along the wharves, as though these constituted a bridge across the English Channel from Britain to Brittany, although we are, of course, supposed to imagine a sea trip in between. First, the young prince kneels to take leave of his father; next we see him in a gorgeous brocaded costume meeting his bride; then, prince and princess kneel before the king of Brittany; finally, to the sound of trumpets, the young couple and the first contingent of virgins move in the distance toward the longboat that will take

them to waiting ships. Carpaccio's colors are generally subdued by a rich, all-over golden tonality, doubtless produced by glazes, so that even the occasional strong reds, blues, and greens are never obtrusive. The shapes are controlled by his preference for triangular areas, often balanced on their points—people, costumes, drapery passages, sails, banners, architectural shapes. The result is a Venetian web of space and tone in which the triangles are embedded almost like fragments of glass in a kaleidoscope. The subtly observed, delicately lighted, strongly individual faces seldom betray emotion. Many are surely contemporary portraits; perhaps the artist himself peers at us from the worldly crowds who throng his docksides and marble piazze. The figures and the details of the contemporary setting are rendered in a series of sure, parallel touches that owe nothing to the styles of Giovanni Bellini and Andrea Mantegna. In fact, Carpaccio abandons traditional linear drawing and shaded modeling in favor of definition by pure brushwork.

The *Arrival of the Ambassadors of Britain at the Court of Brittany* (colorplate 80, p. 449) depicts an earlier episode in the legend. In the center the ambassadors kneel before the enthroned monarch, flanked by four of his councillors. On the right, the king is seated at the edge of a bed, his crowned head propped on one hand, as he listens wearily while his daughter ticks off on her fingers the conditions she intends to impose for the marriage.

Here the composition is somewhat more tightly knit and the details, especially the architectural masses, more strongly projected. The painting offers many delightful

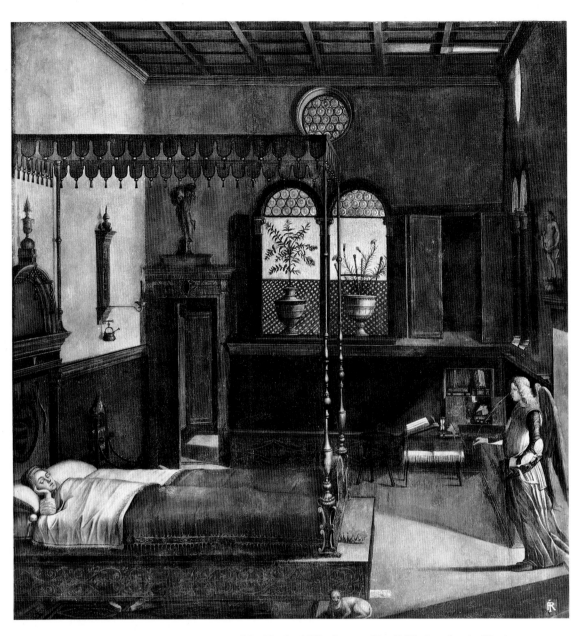

429. VITTORE CARPACCIO. *Dream of St. Ursula*. 1495. Canvas, 9' x 8' 9". Accademia, Venice

details, including the shrewd portraiture, the wittily drawn distant figures, and the intimate scene in the king's bedchamber, on whose wall hangs what appears to be an early *Madonna* by Giovanni Bellini. A flight of steps arches over a grated aperture, as if to afford us a special entry into the king's privacy, and at the foot of the steps sits an old woman with a cane, paying no attention to us or her sovereign. Carpaccio's rich golden tonality saturates the marble slabs and splendid fabrics with the glow of afternoon.

Carpaccio's warmly poetic style is evident in the *Dream of St. Ursula* (fig. 429). The saint is sleeping in a high-ceilinged bedroom when a golden-haired angel enters to bring her the palm of her approaching martyrdom. The angel is accompanied by a burst of powerful light that is based on Carpaccio's study of morning sunlight effects but which here may be intended to represent a burst of divine light accompanying a revelation in

the deep of night. Every detail is observed with almost Antonellesque fidelity, down to the three-legged stool, the reading table with lectern and portable library that accompanied the saint on her trip, the wooden clogs before her bed, and the crown carefully laid on the bench at its foot. The light effects that enhance the magic of the scene range from the flood of light accompanying the angel and the sharp ray running along the ceiling from the oculus window at the right to the softer effects in the anteroom and the diffused sparkle of the bottle-bottom windows. All are unified by the softened red and greenish-gray tones that predominate in the room, and they become part of the cubes of space created by the contours of the room and the delicate spindles of the bedposts and the lines of the canopy. Someday perhaps iconographers will discover why over one door there is a beautifully painted nude statue of a water carrier and over the other a provocative Venus on her shell.

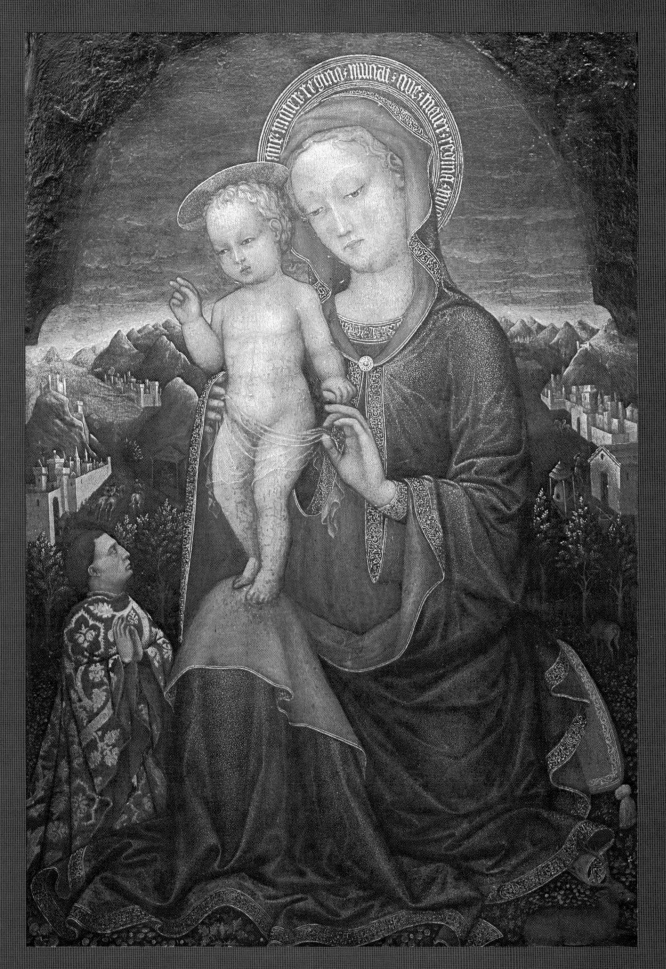

Colorplate 72. JACOPO BELLINI. *Madonna of Humility with Donor (Lionello d'Este?).* c. 1430. Panel, 23 x 16".
The Louvre, Paris. Perhaps commissioned by Lionello d'Este

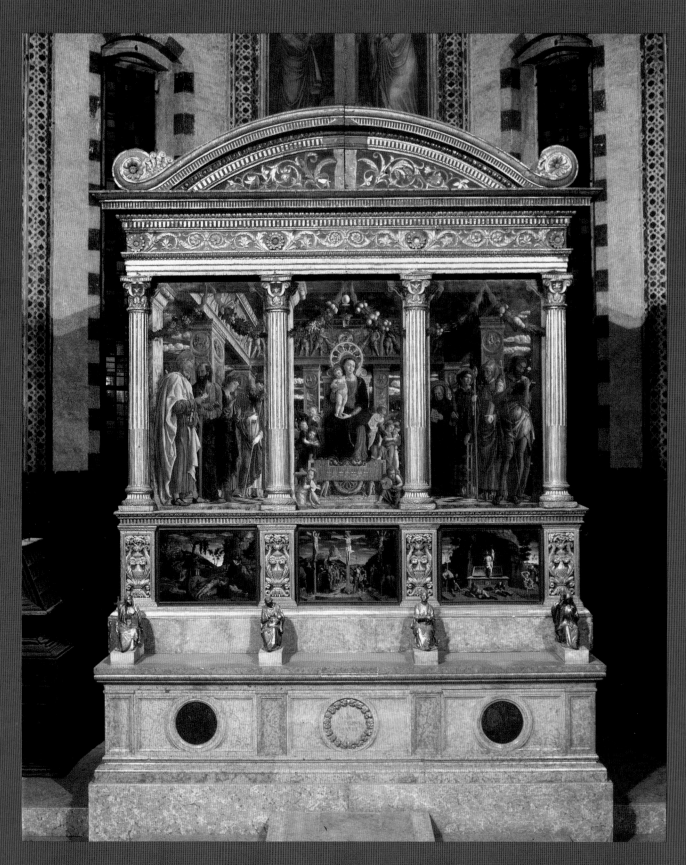

Colorplate 73. ANDREA MANTEGNA. *Enthroned Madonna and Child with Saints* (S. Zeno altarpiece). 1456–59.
Panel, height 86½". ⛪ S. Zeno, Verona. Commissioned by Gregorio Correr (the predellas shown here are copies;
the originals were taken by Napoleon and are now in French museums; see fig. 404)

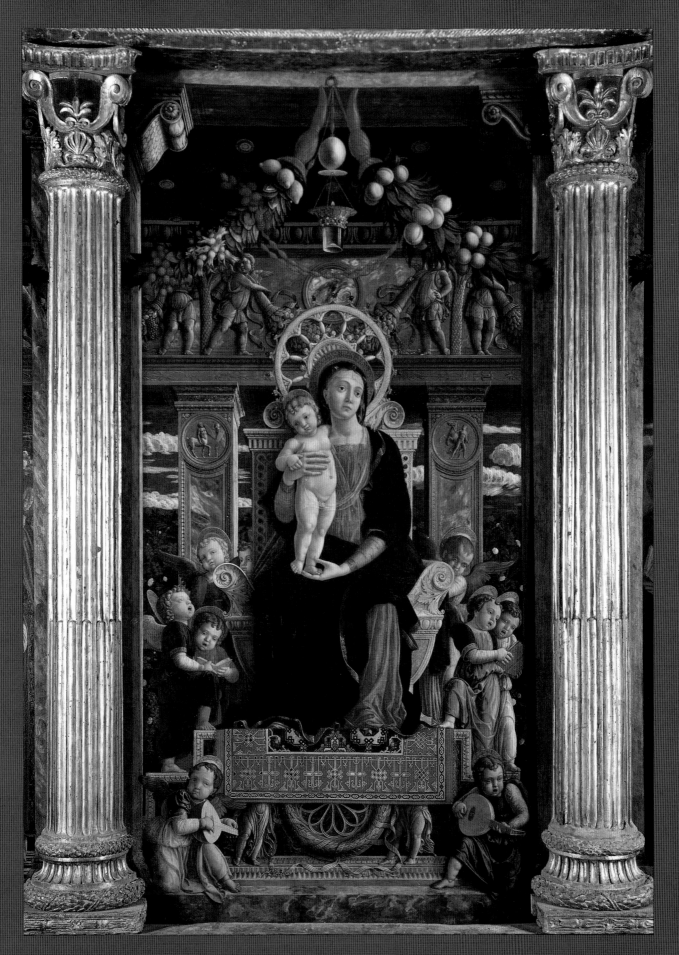

Colorplate 74. ANDREA MANTEGNA. *Enthroned Madonna*, detail of the
S. Zeno altarpiece (see colorplate 73, p. 410). ▯ S. Zeno, Verona

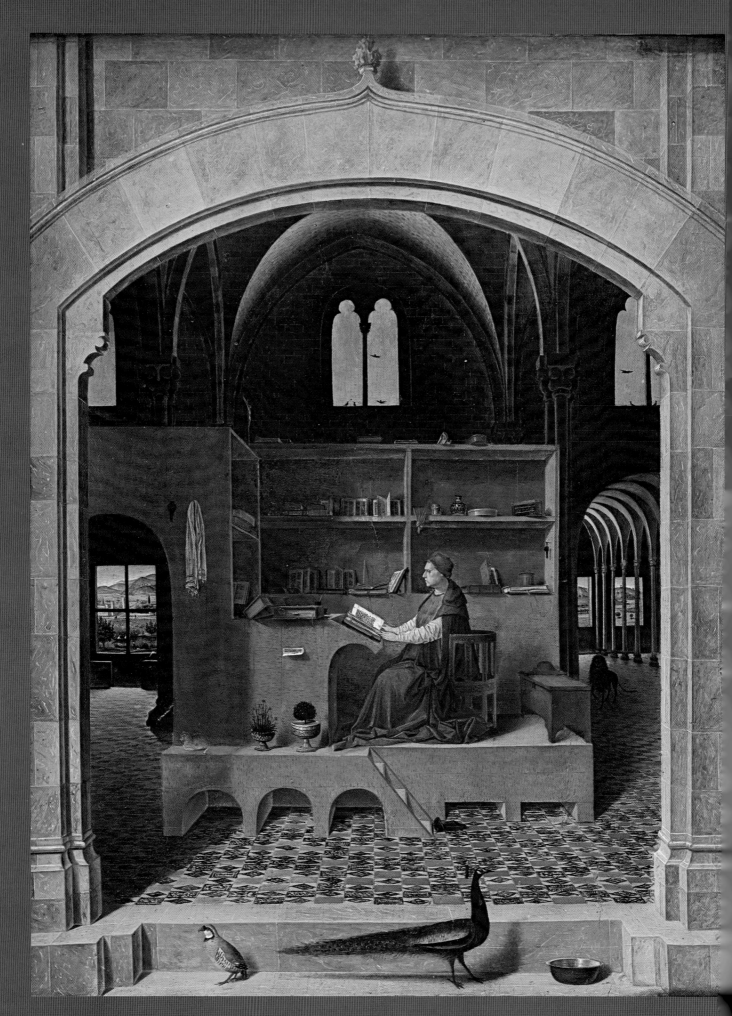

opposite: Colorplate 75.
ANTONELLO DA MESSINA.
St. Jerome in His Study. Possibly
c. 1450–55. Panel, 18 x 14⅛".
National Gallery, London

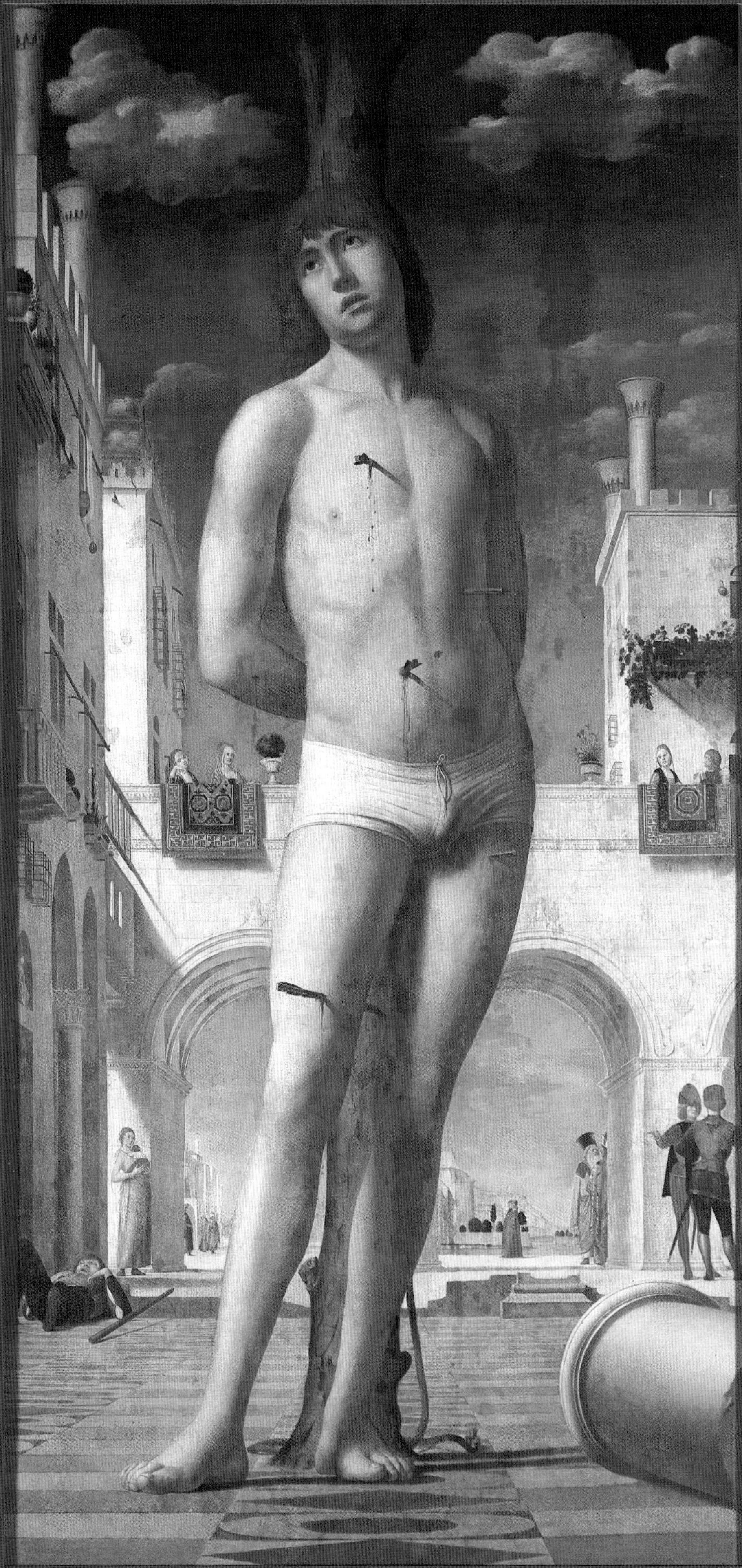

Colorplate 76. ANTONELLO
DA MESSINA. *St. Sebastian.*
c. 1475. Canvas, transferred
from panel, 67¼ x 33⅞".
Gemäldegalerie, Dresden.
Commissioned for the Scuola
dei SS. Rocco e Nicolò,
Venice

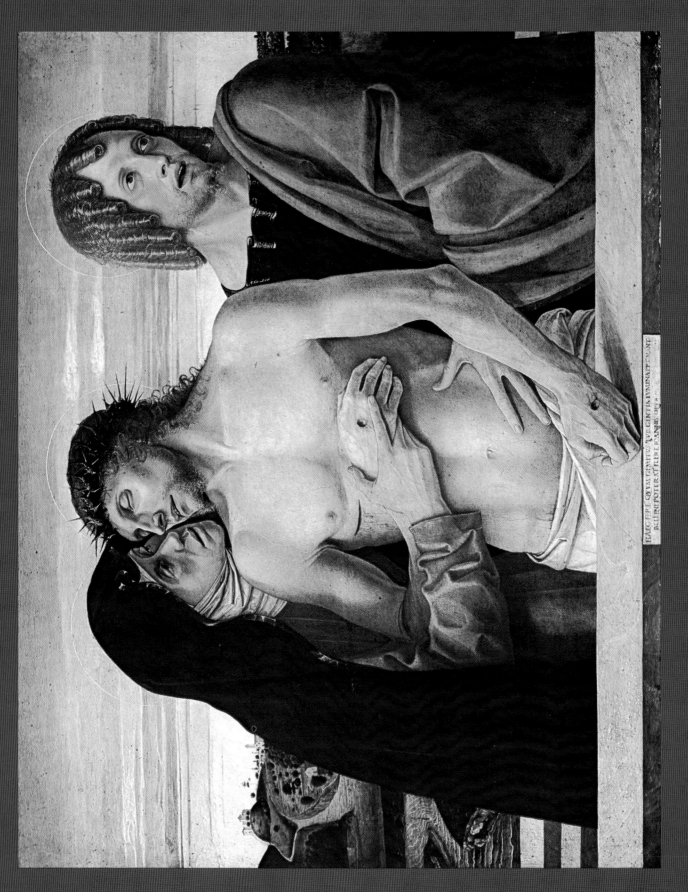

Colorplate 77. GIOVANNI BELLINI. *Pietà*. c. 1468–71. Panel, 33¼ x 42". Brera Gallery, Milan

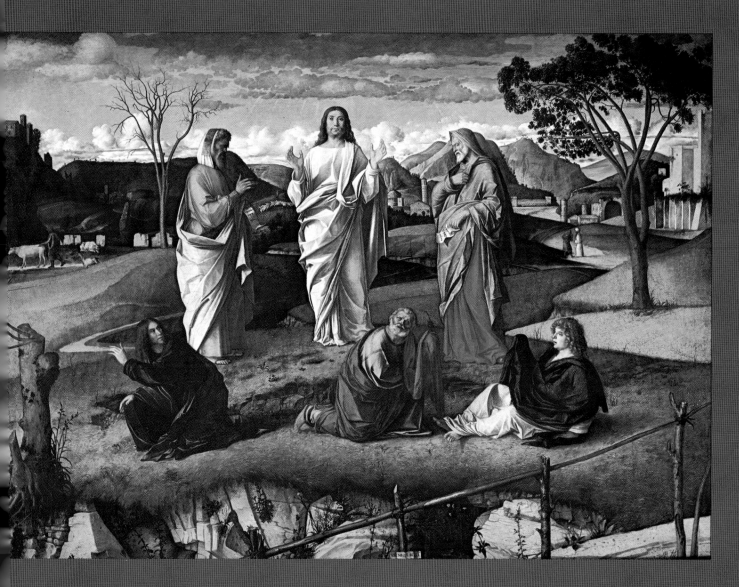

Colorplate 78. GIOVANNI BELLINI. *Transfiguration of Christ*. c. 1475–80. Panel, 45¼ x 59".
Museo di Capodimonte, Naples. Probably commissioned for the funerary chapel of Archdeacon
Alberto Fioccardo in the Cathedral of Vicenza

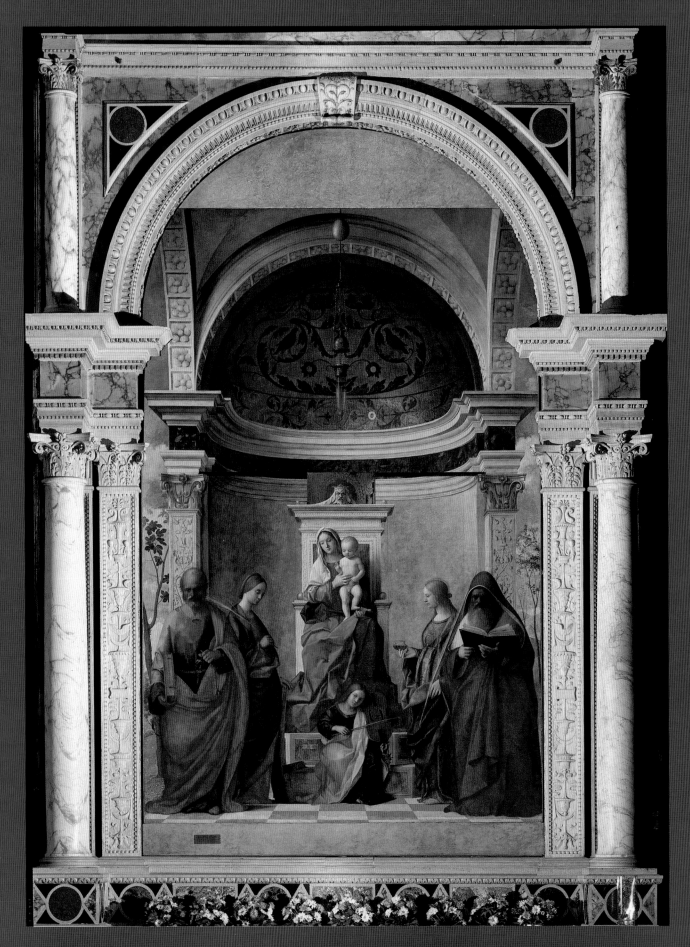

Colorplate 79. GIOVANNI BELLINI. *Enthroned Madonna with Saints* (S. Zaccaria altarpiece).
1505. Canvas, transferred from panel, 16' 5½" x 7' 9". 🛉 S. Zaccaria, Venice

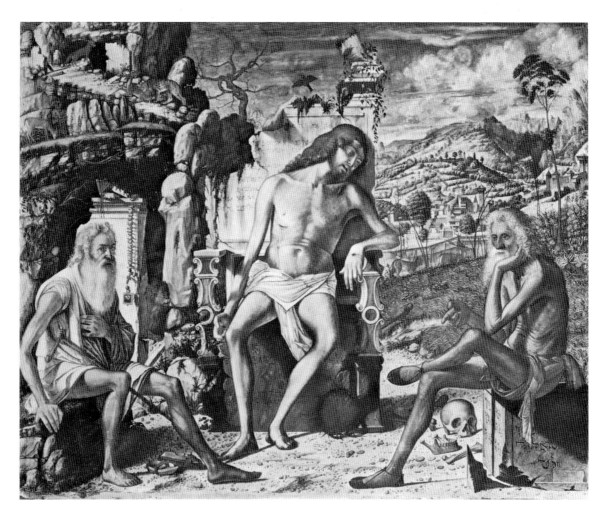

430. VITTORE CARPACCIO. *Meditation on the Passion*. Late 1490s. Panel,
27³/4 x 34¹/8". The Metropolitan Museum of Art, New York

Neither seems to have much to do with the chaste saint, sleeping so peacefully in her bed, or her legend.

Probably in the late 1490s Carpaccio painted his *Meditation on the Passion* (fig. 430). The body of the dead Christ is displayed on a ruined throne between two bearded hermit-saints. St. Jerome, on the left, is recognized by his lion in the background. The author unraveled the iconography of the picture in 1935, when he was a college senior, by demonstrating that Jerome's leathery companion is Job, an identification based in part on his similarity to Job as he appears in Bellini's San Giobbe altarpiece (see fig. 425). Reminders of death appear everywhere: a skull rests on the ground under Job's knees, the top of Jerome's staff is carved with a hand clutching a bone, and his rosary is a threaded set of vertebrae. Yet the dead Christ almost seems to be dreaming, and the warm afternoon sunlight that glows on the scene is reflected upward onto his features and closed eyes. St. Jerome wrote a commentary on the Book of Job in which he interpreted Job's words, "I know that my redeemer liveth, and that he shall stand at the latter day upon the earth" (19:25), as a prophecy of Christ's Resurrection and, through him, that of all humanity. In the preceding verse Job had asked that his words be

"graven with an iron pen and lead in the rock," and this is just what Carpaccio has done. Among the generally meaningless tracks on the block on which Job sits can be read, "My redeemer liveth. 19."

The landscape is doubtless symbolic. As in Piero della Francesca's *Resurrection* (see fig. 281), it is sharply divided. On the left, dominated by a withered tree, is a wild and rocky mountainside where a doe grazes, oblivious of the fate that has befallen her mate, who is borne to earth by a leopard. On the right, where a stag runs from a pursuing leopard, there is a rich landscape of farms, orchards, castles, a peaceful town, and green trees. The stag, symbolic of the human soul (Psalm 42: "As the hart panteth after the water brooks, so panteth my soul after thee, O God"), is torn by the leopard on one side and escapes on the other, just as Job, once tormented, was later blessed by God. A bird, symbolizing the Resurrection, flies up from behind Christ's throne.

In his later surviving works Carpaccio never surpassed the glowing landscape and the pearly clouds of this painting, nor did he equal the personal religious poetry that gives it meaning. His late work has been interpreted as a decline and, after 1510, he could not compete with the High Renaissance style of Titian; he

Gothic and Renaissance in Venice and Northern Italy

obtained commissions only in such places as the fishing town of Chioggia or the provincial centers of Istria and the Dalmatian coast.

CARLO CRIVELLI

The last Venetian Quattrocento master we shall consider, Carlo Crivelli (c. 1435–c. 1495), is even harder to place than Carpaccio. Although a Venetian by birth, he spent almost all his active life far from Venetian territory. He might logically be considered a central Italian painter if it were not for the fact that his early style was formed by the Paduan school. Our first information about him is a court judgment against him in 1457 for having "kept hidden for many months" the wife of an absent sailor, "knowing her carnally in contempt of God and of Holy Matrimony." Sentenced to six months in prison and a heavy fine, he is presumed to have left Venice soon after his release. Still signing himself proudly "Carolus Crivellus Venetus," he spent the rest of his life in the Marches, where his sharply individual style had considerable influence on the local masters.

Throughout Crivelli's known activity of about thirty

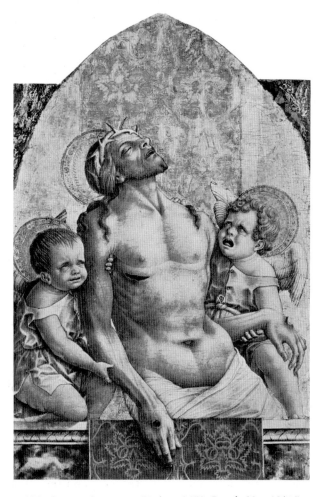

431. CARLO CRIVELLI. *Pietà*. c. 1470. Panel, 28 x 18½".
John G. Johnson Collection, Philadelphia

years, his style developed little. He left Venice before the flowering of Giovanni Bellini's atmospheric art, taking with him his own linear version of the Paduan manner. Hair, veins, and muscles are relentlessly outlined and forms are sharply projected. Sometimes the drops of Christ's blood, the tears of his mourners, and the attributes of saints are modeled in gesso before being painted or gilded. His color and form are dominated by metal and stone, which appear in profusion. In 1492 he was still using a gold background, although this may have been required by some of his patrons. Yet, paradoxically enough, the general effect of a Crivelli painting is not hard. The stone is colored marble, containing rich fluctuations of tone, while the metal is gold, silver, or both. The result is something like a tapestry with gold threads—sumptuous, russet, deeply glowing but subdued. This is Crivelli's own version of the Venetian web (see pp. 147–48).

A typical work, the *Pietà* (fig. 431), reveals the tragic intensity of Crivelli's rendering of the scenes of the Passion. Probably this panel was part of a polyptych with other, still-unidentified panels. Before a cloth of honor made by tooling and painting the gold background, Donatellesque child-angels, screaming with grief, uphold the dead Christ within an altarlike sarcophagus. Christ's head is thrown back, his mouth hangs open. A gigantic spear wound yawns in his side, and one huge nail wound in his left hand is shown in profile so that its depth may be assessed. The taut veins, tendons, and wrinkles are projected by Crivelli's sharp surface hatching to an almost unbearable degree. Yet his sense of pattern is so strong and his golden tonality so insistent that not even the strongest projections produce any sense of disunity.

In his latest works Crivelli achieved a harmony of form, color, and surface. In the *Madonna della Candelletta* (fig. 432), Crivelli signed himself as "eques" (knight), a slight inflation of the rank of "miles" (soldier) conferred upon him in 1490 by Prince Ferdinand of Capua, later King Ferdinand of Naples. The picture gets its title from the candle that burns at the lower left. The crowned Virgin sits upon a veined marble throne whose bench, pedestal, and base seem to continue out of the frame at either side so that they appear as richly variegated stripes of glowing fabric across the surface rather than as solid entities in depth. The garlands of fruit and leaves, which Crivelli had brought with him as part of his standard repertory from Padua and Venice, are here united into a little bower. Not even the dark blue and gold velvet brocade of Mary's mantle or the red and gold of her sleeves can compete with the magnificence of the apples, cucumbers, and pears. These great, rounded shapes with their metallic colors and rippling leaves dominate the picture with a kind of magical intensity. Even Mary's face, with its downcast eyes and solemn frontality, is likened in shape to the apples and the pears and shines as softly as they do. Again Crivelli projects his forms sharply and lets the light cast shadows on the marble,

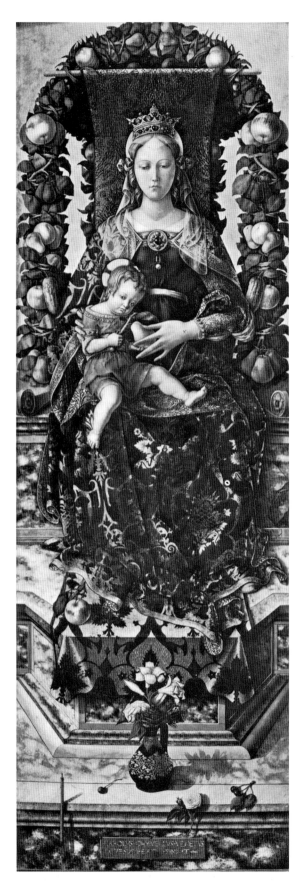

432. CARLO CRIVELLI. *Madonna della Candelletta*. Early 1490s.
Panel, 86 x 29¹/₂". Brera Gallery, Milan

and again the effect is that of a precious Renaissance
textile. Crivelli's was a strongly personal style of refinement and brilliance, hermetically sealed from the developments of his Venetian contemporaries, from whom
the artist exiled himself. Yet his work was certainly one
of the major achievements of Venetian and north Italian
art of the Quattrocento.

LATE QUATTROCENTO ARCHITECTURE IN VENICE

In its entire history, Venice produced few architects of
importance. Venetian builders, for the most part imported from other regions, fell heir on the one hand to the
splendors of the Byzantine tradition—inevitable, with
the Basilica of San Marco in their midst—and on the
other to the rich linear complexities of the Flamboyant
Gothic style brought from France and Germany. In Carpaccio's backgrounds (see colorplate 80, p. 449; fig.
428), the Byzantine and Gothic currents blend imper-
ceptibly, clothed with the same rich marble paneling
and impregnated by the same Venetian sunlight they
seem created to exploit. Only here and there are Carpaccio's hybrid buildings punctuated by arched windows
or delicate pilasters borrowed from the Florentine Renaissance. Such, indeed, was the first timid appearance of
the Renaissance in Venetian architecture in structures
built almost exclusively by Lombard masters; many examples survive throughout the city. During the last third
of the Quattrocento, a family of builders, stonecarvers,
and sculptors named Lombardo (they were from Ca-
rona, near Lugano, which is today in Switzerland but
was then in Lombardy) competed for dominance on the
Venetian stage with Mauro Codussi (c. 1440–1504), another Lombard, from Bergamo. Codussi (also spelled
Coducci) was in closer touch with the ideas of the central Italian Renaissance, and by the end of the century
he dominated the changing appearance of Venice and
was, more than any other single individual, responsible
for the appearance of a truly Venetian Renaissance style
in architecture.

The towering façade of the Quattrocento Gothic
Church of San Zaccaria in Venice was almost exclusively
the creation of Codussi (fig. 433). The preexisting lowest
story, a sort of pedestal with rectangular paneling and insistent—if unorthodox—moldings, established a mood of
complexity from which Codussi could hardly vary. He
added an astonishing series of superimposed stories in the
new classical style, exploiting by their projections and recessions, as well as by their ornamentation and veined
marble material, the play of light one expects from Venetian painting of the period. The buttresses are continued
upward, dividing into three segments the arcade of the
second story and assuming the form of paired, freestanding Corinthian columns in the third and fifth. The proliferation of windows of differing sizes and proportions, the
superimposition of orders utilizing different numerical
systems, and the oddly stumpy proportions of the final

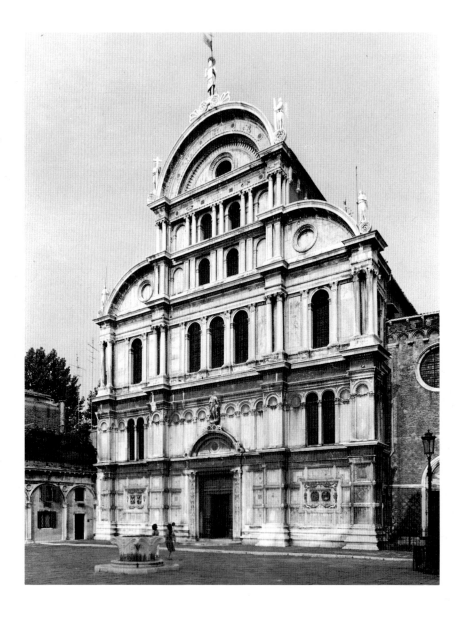

433. MAURO
CODUSSI. Façade,
S. Zaccaria, Venice.
Second half of 15th
century

Corinthian colonnade produce an effect of irregularity and improvisation alien to the Albertian tradition. Yet it is from Alberti's idea for the Malatesta Temple (see fig. 224) that Codussi derived the dominating shape of his great structure, the lofty central arched pediment, flanked by quarter-circles on either side.

Protected by their canals, Venetian palaces did not require the fortresslike construction of even the most princely dwellings of Florence, Siena, Rome, and other central Italian cities. Throughout the Late Middle Ages and into the most extreme manifestations of Venetian Gothic in the Quattrocento, Venetian builders constructed the façades of palaces along the main thoroughfare, the Grand Canal, according to a system devised as early as the eleventh century and characterized by long rows of arches and windows opening onto the canal. The lowest story was centered on a triple-arched entrance that provided admission from the private landing to the palace courtyard and stairways; this entrance was flanked by service rooms lighted by relatively small win-

dows. This tripartite division was maintained in the second and third stories, but here enormous windows ran throughout.

The culmination of the palace type of the Venetian Quattrocento, indeed the bridge to the masterpieces of the High Renaissance in Venice, was the marble façade designed and built by Codussi for the palazzo of the powerful Loredan family, which is now known as the Palazzo Vendramin-Calergi (fig. 434). Ironically enough, the work was completed, after Codussi's death, by the Lombardo family. But the work in all of its essentials is Codussi's, and in the relationship between columns and windows he achieves a balance and maturity of proportions that had eluded him at San Zaccaria. Florentine double-light windows appear, but in a wholly un-Florentine way are enlarged to the point where their jambs are contiguous with the embracing Corinthian columns and the wall disappears. Even the tympanum of each embracing arch is pierced by an open oculus, an echo of the lingering tradition of Gothic tracery. The entire

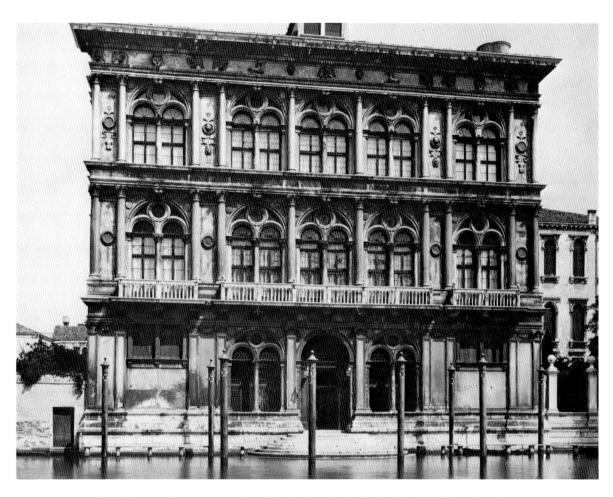

434. MAURO CODUSSI; completed by the Lombardo family. Façade, Palazzo Loredan
(now known as the Palazzo Vendramin-Calergi), Venice. Begun c. 1500; completed 1509.
Commissioned by the Loredan family

façade seems to consist of a framework around openings, a succession of clusters of columns and colonnettes, with brief intervening spaces of veined marble that are enlivened by sculptured ornament and porphyry disks. The stories are separated by balconies and rich entablatures, and the whole is crowned by a majestic cornice. There could be no more extreme contrast between pictorial architecture of this sort and the roughly contemporary Palazzo Strozzi in Florence (see fig. 307), where every effort seems to have been made to enhance the forbidding density of the *pietra serena* masonry. Yet in harmony and balance there is little to choose between them. Like the other great palace façades along the Grand Canal, the Palazzo Loredan (Vendramin-Calergi) enjoys the incomparable advantage of being reflected in the water, whose glittering light in turn softens all shadows and dematerializes all forms.

LATE QUATTROCENTO ART IN MILAN

Francesco I, the founder of the Sforza dynasty in Milan, was of low birth but a successful general; he married the illegitimate daughter of Filippo Maria Visconti; three years after the latter's death without male issue in 1447, Francesco managed to abolish the revived Milanese Republic and assume the hereditary dukedom. His son, Galeazzo Maria, duke from 1466 to 1476, was a tyrannical and cruel ruler and an insatiable patron of the arts. After his murder in 1476, when he left a son too young to govern, the reins of government were taken over by his brother, Ludovico il Moro, who was only declared duke in 1494. Ludovico became one of the most enlightened of Renaissance rulers and patrons of art, but unfortunately the magnificent structures he built are now largely transformed or destroyed and his art collections almost entirely dispersed. His expulsion from the dukedom by the French in 1499, in spite of his brief return in 1500, and his death in a French prison mark the end of a brilliant era.

VINCENZO FOPPA

Perhaps the most original Lombard painter of the Quattrocento was Vincenzo Foppa (c. 1428–1515) from

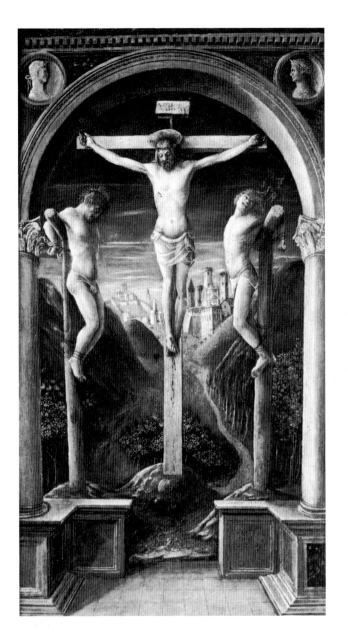

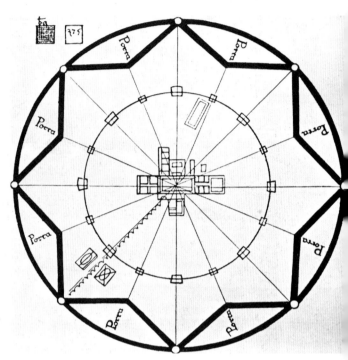

left: 435. VINCENZO FOPPA. *Crucifixion.*
1456. Panel, 26³/4 x 15". Galleria dell'Accademia
Carrara, Bergamo

436. ANTONIO FILARETE. Plan of Sforzinda.
c. 1457–64. Biblioteca Nazionale, Florence.
Commissioned by Francesco Sforza

Brescia who, in an unusually long career, left an impressive array of panels and fresco cycles. The relation of his earliest dated work, the *Crucifixion* of 1456 (fig. 435), to Quattrocento art in Padua and in Venice is clear. The embracing arch and imperial profile portraits in the spandrels have been borrowed from Castagno at the Basilica of San Marco (see fig. 267), and the pose of the impenitent thief, not to mention the treatment of the background landscape, betrays a knowledge of Jacopo Bellini (see fig. 396; colorplate 72, p. 409); there is even a suggestion of the predella of Mantegna's San Zeno altarpiece (see fig. 404). Nevertheless, the muscular vigor of the bodies, the violence of the expressions and poses, and the disregard for structure in order to obtain a tragic immediacy of action are Foppa's own, and very Lombard, as is the uncanonical way he treats the elements of classical architecture.

FILARETE

Antonio Averlino (c. 1400–after 1465) was a curious Florentine sculptor and architect who adopted the name Filarete (from the Greek, "love of virtue"). In 1445 his set of bronze and silver doors commissioned by Pope Eugenius IV were installed at Old St. Peter's; they are in use today on the new building. Filarete left Rome under a cloud and sought employment in Milan where, in the early 1450s, he began working for Francesco Sforza. His ideas, founded on what he could glean from Alberti in Rome, came into conflict with the entrenched conservatism of such local Gothic builders as the Solari family (see below), which doomed his projects from the start. But his treatise on architecture, under strong Albertian influence, was presented in duplicate manuscript form to Piero de' Medici in Florence, who could do little

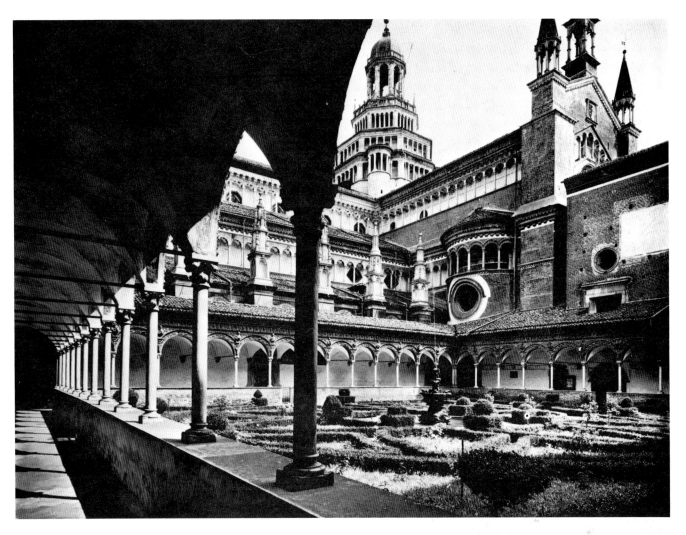

437. GIOVANNI and GUINIFORTE SOLARI. Certosa, Pavia. Begun 1396; finished after 1492.
View from the cloister. Commissioned by Giangaleazzo Visconti

save dream of such undertakings, and to Galeazzo Maria Sforza, who possessed the power to carry them out.

Filarete describes in detail the practical and theoretical aspects of a vast Ospedale Maggiore (Main Hospital) for Milan that would have been composed of two enormous cross-squared structures united on either side of a central piazza and including a lofty church. The basic plan was followed, and the building, in spite of later alterations and damage from aerial bombardments, still exists. Even more fascinating was Filarete's proposal for an island city to be built heaven knows where and named Sforzinda after the ruling family of Milan (fig. 436). The exterior walls were to be shaped like an eight-pointed star, with the palace of the prince and a nucleus of public buildings in the center, in true Albertian style. Such a centralized city, impossible even for despots such as the Sforza, was carried out at the close of the sixteenth century in the pentagonal plan for Livorno, designed by Bernardo Buontalenti for Grand Duke Ferdinand I de' Medici, and in the spiderweb of canals in Amsterdam. The imprint of Filarete's ideas is evident in the vast constructions of Ludovico il Moro,

including the villa, castle, scientific farms, and central square of Vigevano, built by Bramante, and in the system of canals—some of which are still in use—in Milan.

THE CERTOSA DI PAVIA

The vast monastic constructions of the Certosa (Carthusian monastery) in the flat country outside the old Lombard capital of Pavia were, aside from the Cathedral of Milan itself, the major architectural undertaking of the Visconti and Sforza dukes. Begun in 1396 under Giangaleazzo Visconti, the church, destined for the ducal tombs, was taken up by the Gothic architect Giovanni Solari; his son Guiniforte was associated with him in 1459. Basically a Gothic structure, the cruciform church was planned on a succession of squares—four for the nave, one each for the arms of the transept, and one for the apse—not unrelated to the plan of the Cathedral of Florence. From the exterior (fig. 437) the church is a picturesque agglomeration of superimposed external arcades of stone, set in the brick walls essential throughout much of Lombardy, but Renaissance details in capitals and arch-

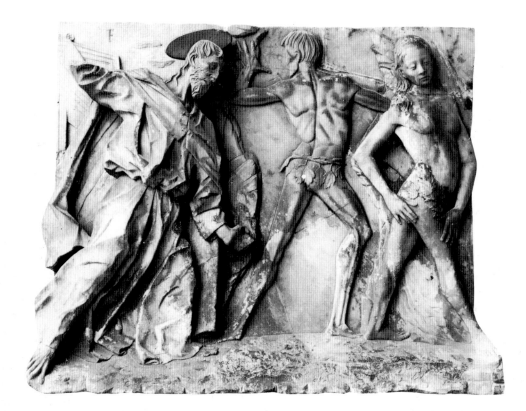

438. CRISTOFORO
MANTEGAZZA.
*Expulsion
from the Garden.*
c. 1480. Marble.
Certosa, Pavia

es have begun to permeate the basically Gothic building.

The original façade of the Certosa di Pavia was to have corresponded in shape to the typical cross section of a Christian basilica. Some of the sculptural decoration survives from this façade, which was commenced in 1473. Some expressionistic reliefs have been attributed to the Milanese sculptor Cristoforo Mantegazza (d. 1482); a violent *Expulsion from the Garden* (fig. 438), for example, shows God himself angrily driving Adam and Eve to their fate in a tremendous gesture of condemnation. Influences from Jacopo della Quercia are absorbed into the tradition of Lombard realism, transforming the supple musculature of the Sienese master into forms of striking angular tension. There may even be traces of the late expressionistic style of Donatello.

A wholly new façade, of overwhelming richness and splendor, was added by Ludovico il Moro, beginning in 1492, from the designs and under the supervision of the Pavian architect and sculptor Giovanni Antonio Amadeo (1447–1522). The fabric (fig. 439) was built entirely of marble, imported from Carrara on the other side of the Ligurian Alps at staggering cost. The enormous mass of marble is divided and subdivided into windows and other openings—rectangular, arched and round, single, double, quadruple, and quintuple—and enriched with sculptural reliefs and carved ornament of bewildering complexity. Despite the hints of a Flamboyant Gothic past that make the Certosa façade appear the utter opposite of Florentine rationality, a certain logic runs through it all; the elements are largely of classical deriva-

tion, the successions can be deduced, and the single statues and reliefs enjoyed, although none show the intensity of Mantegazza.

QUATTROCENTO PAINTING IN FERRARA

We cannot leave the north Italian Quattrocento without a mention of the vigorous school of painting that flourished at Ferrara. Although it could be argued that none of the Ferrarese masters reached the rank of Mantegna, Antonello, or Giovanni Bellini, collectively they maintained a high level of fantasy and skill. Ferrara is a flat city spread out over a considerable area of lowland a few miles south of the Po River, with which it is connected by waterways. In the middle of the thirteenth century, Ferrara came under the power of the Este family and was the seat of its cultivated ducal court until 1598. During this period of prosperity, the Este dukes, especially Niccolò III (1384–1441) and Lionello (1404–50), called foreign artists of first importance to Ferrara. These included Antonio Pisanello, Jacopo Bellini, Leonbattista Alberti, Rogier van der Weyden, Piero della Francesca, and Andrea Mantegna. The local school that began to emerge about 1450 absorbed a great deal from the visits of figures from abroad, but it was distinguished almost at once by some very special qualities. It may have been the flatness of Ferrara and its surroundings, the absence of anything that might be called landscape, the comparative dullness of the wide, straight streets and low houses that spurred the painters to great imaginative efforts.

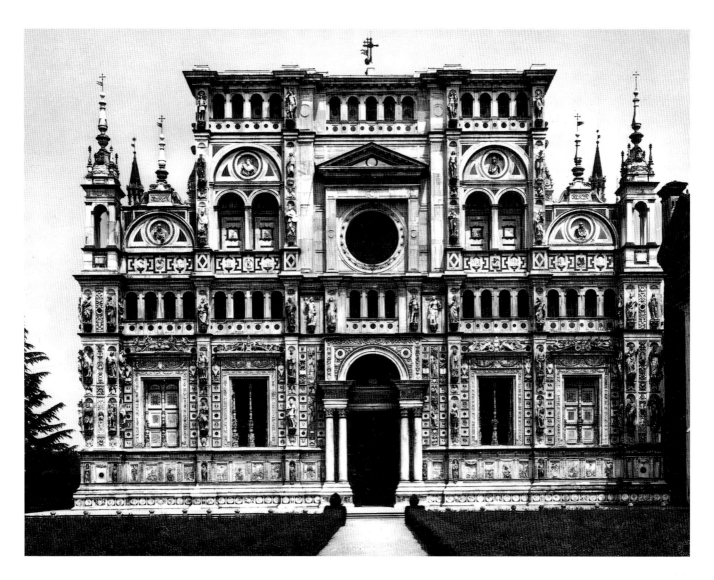

439. Giovanni Antonio Amadeo. Façade, Certosa, Pavia. 1473–first half of 16th century.
Marble. Commissioned by Ludovico il Moro

The oldest of the three important Ferrarese painters was Cosimo Tura (c. 1430–95), an artist in whose style sculptural elements from Piero della Francesca and Mantegna are twisted into shapes of tension and torment. His Roverella altarpiece, painted for the Church of San Giorgio Fuori in Ferrara, has been dismembered and the parts scattered among a number of museums. The central panel, a towering *Enthroned Madonna and Child with Angels* (colorplate 81, p. 450), is startling in its combination of plastic intensity with unexpected color combinations. Renaissance architectural elements, for example, alternate between green and pink. The shell above the Virgin's throne supports an upside-down shell, and at the top there are statues of the symbols of the four evangelists. Above, winged putti flank the arch, and from their cornucopias dangle bunches of grapes. Instead of pilasters, the throne bears the tablets of the Ten Commandments in abbreviated Hebrew. On the steps of this fantastic structure angels play treble viols and strum lutes. Below,

an angel plays an organ with spirally arranged pipes while another works its bellows. The crowded space is characteristic of Tura's work; even more so are the contorted shapes, which for all their wildness radiate a strange beauty. Tura has exaggerated the movement of incisive line, the modeling, and the play of reflected lights to produce effects that aim at sculptural hardness but almost seem to turn soft as we watch. This knotted, involved, elaborate style, for all its harshness, can also be poetic. It is, perhaps, the Ferrarese answer to Botticelli.

North Italian painters and sculptors were unrestrained in the expression of grief, as is revealed in Tura's *Pietà* from the summit of the Roverella altarpiece (fig. 440). We look upward at a barrel vault repeating that of the Madonna panel originally below, but with more coffers. The contorted body of Christ is spread across the Virgin's knees, his arms held out by lamenting figures. Yet however exaggerated, the emotion demands respect on account of its directness and sincerity,

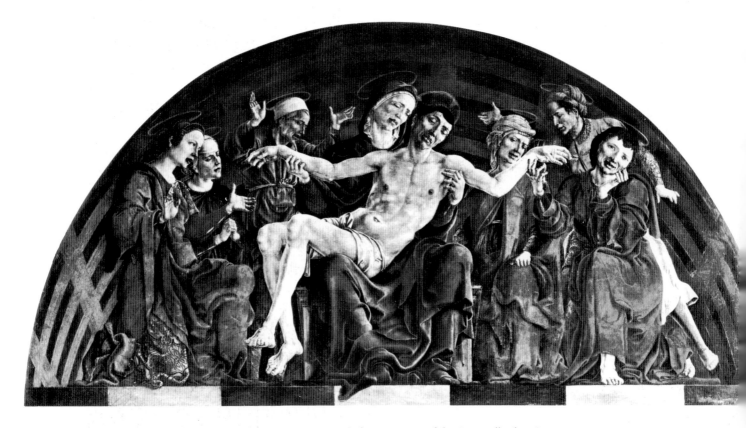

440. COSIMO TURA. *Pietà*, from summit of the Roverella altarpiece
(see colorplate 81, p. 450). c. 1480. Panel, 4' 4" x 8' 9". The Louvre, Paris. Commissioned
by a member of the Roverella family for S. Giorgio Fuori, Ferrara

and the tortured shapes achieve a certain nobility in their lofty position.

The second leading Ferrarese painter is Francesco del Cossa (c. 1435–c. 1477), whose Griffoni altarpiece was painted in 1473 for San Petronio at Bologna. The *St. John the Baptist* (fig. 441) is an excellent example of the style of this son of a stonemason, who shows in his pictures a special interest in architecture and in the stones, carved or otherwise, of which it is built. The fantastic landscape behind St. John offers a kind of natural dream architecture; perhaps such inventions delighted the Ferrarese because they were accustomed to nothing but plains. Handsome as Cossa's painting of the red-cloaked figure is, the eye is immediately struck by his rocky pinnacles, his Pelions piled on Ossas, his vast, open arcades and natural bridges supporting turreted castles and domed churches in impossible positions. Cossa's cloudless blue sky and brilliant light—another invention, because Ferrara, like all Po Valley towns, is humid and foggy much of the year—reveal with relentless clarity this stony world and all the objects in it, whether carved by nature or human fantasy. Such is the magical intensity of some of Cossa's projections—notably the rosary hanging from rings around a pole and the crumpled

scroll bearing St. John's words, "Behold, a voice crying in the wilderness"—that his art served as a model for some of the Surrealists of the 1930s.

The most remarkable surviving monumental project of the Ferrarese masters is the fresco cycle lining the Sala dei Mesi (Hall of the Months) in the Palazzo Schifanoia at Ferrara, a pleasure palace enlarged by Duke Borso d'Este in 1470 (fig. 442). The frescoes are related to the calendar illustrations that appear frequently in Northern European manuscripts. Each section originally showed the triumphal car of the deity who presided over that month, the pertinent signs of the zodiac, and a number of the activities and labors appropriate to the month. The frescoes show all the freshness and brilliance of Ferrarese coloring as well as the charm of Ferrarese imagination. There is as yet no agreement regarding the attribution of all the scenes. Tura may have been involved in the scheme, also Ercole de' Roberti (see below), but the leading master was apparently Cossa. In his *April* (fig. 442), the triumphal vehicle of Venus is a kind of barge drawn by swans. On either bank of this inlet elegantly dressed ladies and gentlemen in pleasant gardens indulge in amorous courtship that is parodied by omnipresent white rabbits. Presiding over the couples are the Three

441. FRANCESCO DEL COSSA. *St. John the Baptist*,
from the Griffoni altarpiece. 1473. Panel, 44¹⁄₈ x 21⁵⁄₈".
Brera Gallery, Milan. Commissioned by Floriano
Griffoni for S. Petronio, Bologna

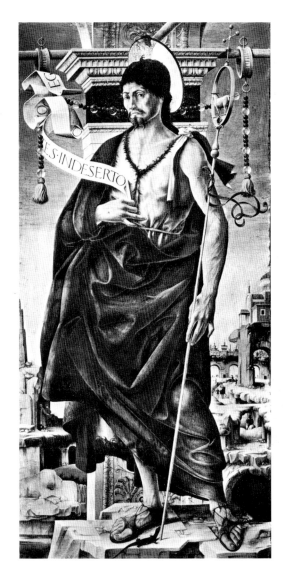

below: 442. FRANCESCO DEL COSSA. *April.* 1469–70.
Fresco, width 13' 2". Sala dei Mesi, Palazzo Schifanoia,
Ferrara. Commissioned by Duke Borso d'Este

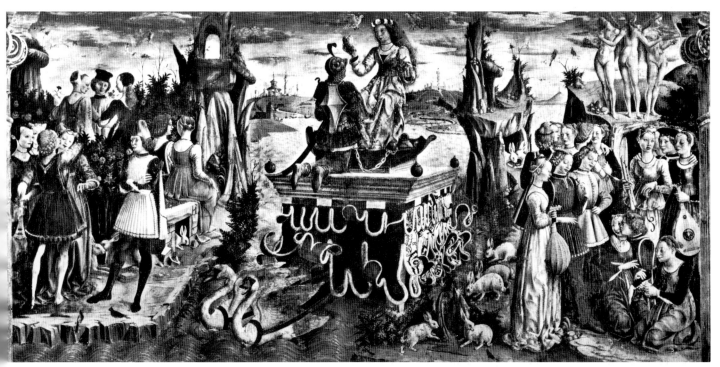

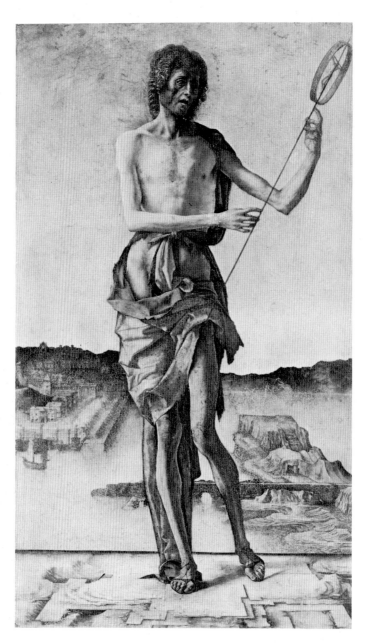

443. ERCOLE DE' ROBERTI. *St. John the Baptist.* c. 1478–80. Panel, 21¼ x 12¼". Picture Gallery, Dahlem Museum, Berlin

Graces at the upper right. Like the other frescoes, this scene resembles a continuous tapestry replete with fascinating details and an occasional penetration into depth.

Ercole de' Roberti (1456–96) is the youngest of the three major painters of Quattrocento Ferrara. His *St. John the Baptist* (fig. 443) is a haunting work that makes Cossa's rendition of the saint (see fig. 441) seem almost pedestrian. Roberti's emaciated and mystical figure, rising in skeletal gauntness above a distant horizon, seems a premonition of the towering saints of El Greco a century later. The rocks are those of Tura and Cossa, but their scale and substance have been reduced. The interlocking planes of the ledge on which St. John stands seem to melt as we watch, and the sea mists that rise around the promontory, the port, and the ship are suffused with a rosy Bellinesque glow. The anguished head of the saint recalls that of St. John the Evangelist in Bellini's Brera *Pietà* (see colorplate 77, p. 414). Roberti never resolves the relation between foreground and background, which is separated by a line that makes the latter look almost like a backdrop. Perhaps he intended to leave the relationship unresolved; perhaps this ambiguity is part of the mystery of the image, which leaves us in constant doubt as to the substance of reality. But that was the very question to which the activities of Leonardo were to provide unexpected answers in the last decades of the Quattrocento, thereby to transform the whole nature of Italian art in the Cinquecento.

PART THREE

THE CINQUECENTO

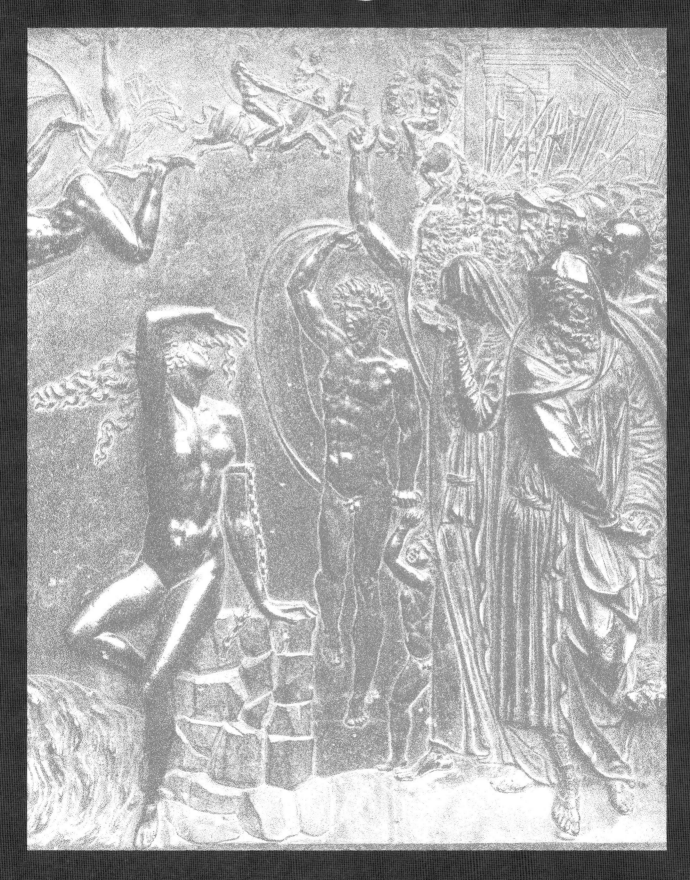

16

The High Renaissance in Florence

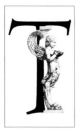

he period that we now call the High Renaissance has its origins in the works of Leonardo da Vinci (1452–1519). The artist was born seven years after Botticelli and Perugino, and five years before Filippino Lippi, all of whose styles belong indisputably to the Quattrocento. Moreover, all of Leonardo's most important artistic achievements were completed or well under way before the death of Filippino, the first of the three to die, in 1504. The fact that we tend to think of Leonardo as a Cinquecento artist, and to speak of him together with Michelangelo, born in 1475, or with Raphael, born in 1483, is an indication of his importance as the creator of the first, or Florentine, phase of the High Renaissance—even though he spent most of that period in Milan.

LEONARDO DA VINCI

The shopworn remark about personalities who seem to be "ahead of their time" is a statement of fact in the case of Leonardo. He was ahead of his time not only in painting, sculpture, and architecture, but also in engineering, military science, botany, anatomy, geology, geography, hydraulics, aerodynamics, and optics, to mention only some of the branches of human knowledge to which he made crucial original contributions. Leonardo was able to make innovations in both art and science by virtue of his conviction that the two were intimately interrelated. He did not consider them interchangeable, for science was to him an investigation of nature and art an expression of beauty. In both his artistic and scientific activities he rejected authority and explored the natural world independently and without traditional prejudices or the restrictions put on investigations by religious belief. In an era in which the revived authority of antiquity competed with that of Christianity, he had little respect for either source. Final authority to Leonardo emanated from a single source: the human eye. He maintained that no activity was nobler than that of sight. No text, no matter what its pretensions to divine revelation or philosophic authority, could block the evidence of sight or impede the process of induction based on sight. As he wrote in his notebooks:

Now do you not see that the eye embraces the beauty of the whole world? It is the lord of astronomy and the maker of cosmography; it counsels and corrects all the arts of humanity; it moves men to the different parts of the world; it is the prince of mathematics, its sciences are certain; it has measured the heights and sizes of the stars, it has found the elements and their locations . . . has generated architecture, perspective, and the divine art of painting. Oh most excellent thing above all others created, what peoples, what tongues shall be those that can fully describe your true operation? This is the window of the human body, through which it mirrors its way and brings to fruition the beauty of the world, by which the soul is content to stay in its human prison.

We know a great deal about what Leonardo thought and felt from his voluminous writings. The thousands of pages that survive on separate sheets or are gathered into notebooks range from quick jottings to careful and extended analyses. Although he never assembled them into any sort of order, Leonardo's notes crackle with new ideas and observations on nature and humanity. Some of these observations were not to be made again by others, much less systematized into a coherent body of theory, for decades or even centuries. Seldom in his pages do we encounter a classical name—in contrast to Alberti and Ghiberti, for example, who are always citing classical authors or artists. Only infrequently do we find references to God, and occasionally we meet with caustic comments on organized Christianity (e.g., "Why are we supposed to worship the Son when all the churches are dedicated to the Mother?"), but nature is mentioned reverently again and again, and his sketchy views of mountains (fig. 444) are among the earliest mountain studies known. If Leonardo had a religion, it was a kind of nature-mysticism, accessible through sight, and it was this only partly expressed conviction that united his art and his science.

The reverse of the coin is Leonardo's detachment from human beings and their ways. As greatly as he admired the human body as a work of nature, he felt that humans did not deserve so fine an instrument, and he called human beings "sacks for food" and "fillers-up of privies." In spite of Leonardo's charm of appearance and manner and his conversational gifts, in thousands of pages there is not a line to show that he ever cared deeply for any other human being. Florentine though

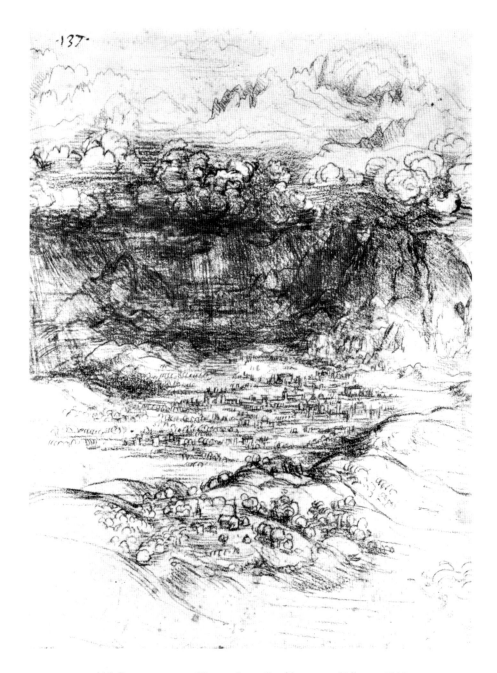

444. LEONARDO DA VINCI. *Storm Breaking over a Valley*. c. 1500.
Red chalk on white paper, 8 x 6". Royal Library, Windsor

he was, he could detach himself sufficiently from the concerns of his native republic to work for Ludovico Sforza, duke of the traditionally inimical Milan, or even for that evil genius of the late Quattrocento, Cesare Borgia, son of Pope Alexander VI, against whose armies the Florentines were trying to preserve their liberties.

Leonardo may have derived some of his Olympian aloofness from the circumstances of his birth. He was born the illegitimate child of a notary named Piero in the little town of Vinci, on a hillside overlooking the Arno Valley about twenty miles west of Florence, where the river enters a narrowing rocky gorge. At an early age the child was taken from his peasant mother, Caterina, about whom we know next to nothing, and brought up by his father and his father's wife. A notary in Italy verifies the legality of contracts, takes a percentage from both contracting parties, and can make himself prosperous, and this Piero seems to have done. But Leonardo's life was clouded by his illegitimacy, which brought with it legal disabilities. In addition, Leonardo was left-handed, and although the Italian expression for "left-handed" is the mild word *mancino*, this may be because "left" in Italian is *sinistro*, a word that comprised in the Renaissance, as it does today, a variety of unpleasant meanings, such as sinister, wicked-looking, unfavorable, or, as a noun, disaster. Leonardo drew and wrote with his left hand—from right to left, for his own benefit. To read his writings, in addition to the usual linguistic and paleo-

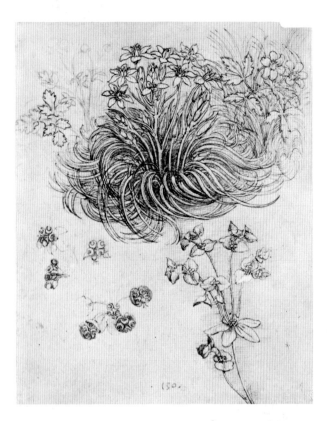

445. LEONARDO DA VINCI. *Star-of-Bethlehem and Other Plants*. c. 1505–8. Pen and red pencil, 7³/4 x 6¹/4". Royal Library, Windsor

graphic training, scholars must use a mirror. Possibly it was Leonardo's detachment that permitted him to soar intellectually above human preconceptions and rendered him attentive to much that escaped ordinary mortals.

Over and over in Leonardo's writings one encounters the lament, "Who will tell me if anything was ever finished?" and it is true that his pursuit of the mysterious and elusive aspects of nature was never finished; neither were a number of his works. Few of the finished ones survive in anything like what Leonardo intended. Sadder yet—so Leonardo's contemporaries complained—his scientific and mechanical interests kept him from his activities as an artist. A fuller picture of his interests and style can be gained from his drawings, both the studies intended for specific paintings and sculptures and the sketches that illustrate almost every page of his notes.

Not the smallest living thing is neglected in these drawings. A cat, an insect, or a flower—each is worthy of prolonged and sympathetic study. In his drawing of a star-of-Bethlehem and other plants (fig. 445), for instance, Leonardo analyzes the shapes of the leaves with accuracy but is also concerned with the rhythm of the plant's growth and the elusive quality of natural life and motion: the leaves seem to unfold before us, like the time-lapse photography of plants growing and blossoming shown in classroom instruction in botany. The organisms seem to grow and unfold, open, and blossom

before us. At the same time Leonardo can move from the microcosm to the macrocosm with the ease of the Netherlandish masters, such as Jan van Eyck, whose work he may well have studied. During his stay in Milan, within sight of the Alps, he climbed their slopes frequently and recorded what he saw. He noticed, for example, fossilized shells embedded in sedimentary rocks and, calculating the time required to produce such a phenomenon and carry the shells to such heights, concluded that the world could not have been created in 4004 B.C., as theologians maintained. Leonardo conveyed in his mountain drawings the elation of the climber on reaching a summit and beholding a view over mountains and plains. And he described triumphantly the painter's power to reproduce this:

> If the painter wishes to see beauties that charm him, it lies in his power to create them, and if he wishes to see monstrosities that are frightful, ridiculous, or truly pitiable, he is lord and God thereof; and if he wishes to generate sites and deserts, shady and cool places in hot weather he can do so, and also warm places in cold weather. If he wishes from the high summits of the mountains to uncover the great countrysides, and if he wishes after them to see the horizon of the sea, he is lord of it, and if from the low valleys he wishes to see the high mountains, or from the high mountains the low valleys and beaches, and in effect that which is in the universe for essence, presence, or imagination, he has it first in his mind and then in his hands, and these are of such excellence that in equal time they generate a proportionate harmony in a single glance, as does nature.

This is what Leonardo has done in a red chalk drawing (see fig. 444) that depicts a landscape that stretches from plains with a towered city up into the cloudy Alpine valley and above storms to snowcapped summits.

Aside from the satisfaction that such studies gave him, they served a distinct purpose in assisting Leonardo to advance one of his favorite causes—the superiority of the painter. God has often been called an artist and the process of creation compared to artistic activity. Leonardo reversed the metaphor and saw the artist's creativity as analogous to that of God: "The deity that invests the science of the painter functions in such a way that the mind of the painter is transformed into a copy of the divine mind, since it operates freely in creating many kinds of animals, plants, fruits, landscapes, countrysides, ruins, and awe-inspiring places."

In Leonardo's day, the listing of the Liberal Arts still rejected painting in spite of earlier efforts to include it (see p. 32). In the material for his *Treatise on Painting* (compiled after his death by his pupil Francesco Melzi), Leonardo argued at length not only for the inclusion of painting among the Liberal Arts but also for its precedence over poetry or music, since these depend on the

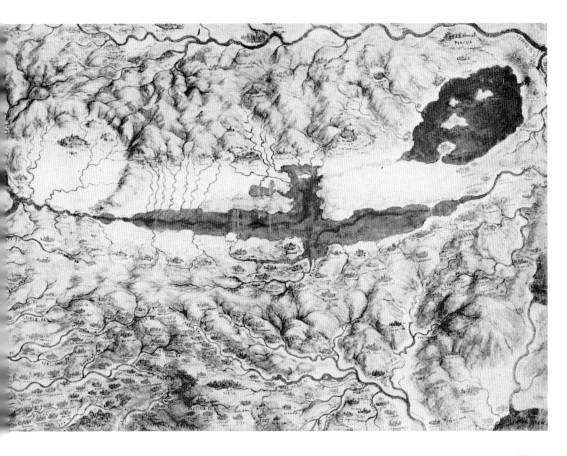

446. LEONARDO DA VINCI. *Bird's-eye View of Chiana Valley, Showing Arezzo, Cortona, Perugia, and Siena.* c. 1502–3. Pen and ink and color, 10³/₄ x 15¹/₄". Royal Library, Windsor

ear, and the eye is the superior organ. He had little trouble arguing that it is better to be deaf than blind, and he pointed out that when the last note of a song has died away, the music is over and must be played again to exist, while a picture is constantly there. He asks if anyone ever traveled a great distance to read a poem, while pictures are the goal of many pilgrimages.

After many similar arguments, Leonardo turned to sculpture, which he was bent on excluding from the Liberal Arts, or at least on maintaining in a rank below that of painting. The elegantly dressed painter can sit in a pleasant studio, with soft breezes entering from the gardens through the open windows, and listen to music while working without physical strain. The poor sculptor must attack the stone with hammer and chisel, sweating violently, being covering with marble dust, which mingles with sweat to form a gritty paste, and being deafened with the noise of hammer and chisel on stone.

Leonardo's interests were also practical, and many of his landscape drawings are studies of drainage, irrigation, water transportation, and military campaigns. He did a number of bird's-eye views showing a considerable area of central Italy. One map-like view (fig. 446) stretches from Arezzo at the left to Perugia at the extreme upper right, with Siena just to the left of lower center. This was apparently made as part of a project to divert water into the Arno from a lake in the center Chiana Valley, but it might also have had some purpose in Cesare Borgia's military campaigns. Leonardo also drew genuine relief maps in the modern sense, in which the forms are shaded according to their altitude, and this he accomplished without the benefit of surveying instruments.

Leonardo studied the human body as it had never been studied before. His drawings from the nude model—such as one done about 1503–7 (fig. 447) in red chalk, a medium that Leonardo was one of the first to use—show a new attentiveness to the structure of the body, the consistency of its layers, and their effect upon the surface as the light plays across it. In his writings he admonishes artists not to exaggerate the musculature, like those mistaken masters who make their figures look like "sacks of nuts" (he was most likely referring to Michelangelo), and in his drawings he emphasizes the grace and ease of the figure as a whole. Beginning with his initial anatomical studies in Milan in the mid-1480s, Leonardo carried anatomical dissection to remarkable lengths; it is recorded that he dissected more than thirty bodies. His anatomical drawings, made for purposes of scientific investigation and demonstration, are usually accompanied by a lengthy commentary that he made as he worked. All are part of Leonardo's exploration of the secrets of the natural world and of human life; only occasionally are they influenced by tradition at the expense of observation. His analyses of how muscles and tendons are connected to bones and how joints and muscles worked had an immediate bearing on the art of the High and Late Renaissance—but they had little effect on Leonardo's own, which had come almost to a stop at the time he embarked on his most extensive series of detailed anatomical studies. A drawing that shows how

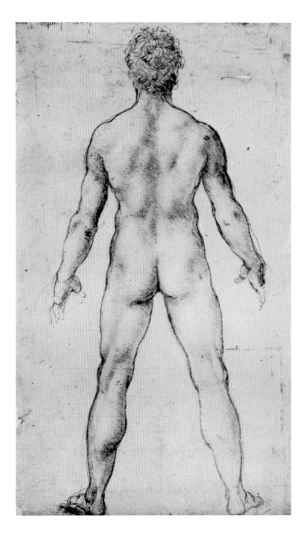

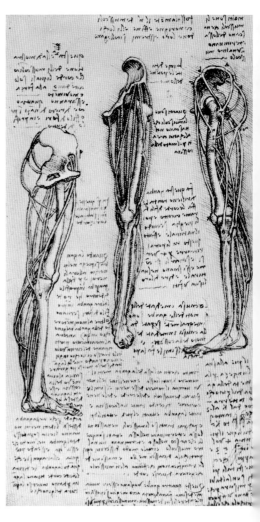

right: 447. LEONARDO DA VINCI. *Male Nude.* c. 1503–7. Red chalk, 10³/₄ x 6¹/₄". Royal Library, Windsor

far right: 448. LEONARDO DA VINCI. *Studies of a Left Leg, Showing Bones and Tendons.* c. 1508. Pen and ink, 8¹/₂ x 4¹/₄". Royal Library, Windsor

he compared the behavior of the muscles overlying the bones of the human leg to that of cords (fig. 448) demonstrates how Leonardo, spurred by observation and imagination, sought to record the complexity of human anatomy in a lucid manner.

Although they have little importance for his artistic work, the machines Leonardo designed are interesting in themselves, and the drawings are so accurate and the principles involved so well understood that a number have been built by an engineer and seen by many in traveling exhibitions. They include refinements on all sorts of known mechanical principles and improvements of pumps, dredges, pulleys, and tackles, as well as weapons ranging from crossbows to chariots equipped with rotating scythe blades for dismembering the enemy and improvements to artillery and to defenses against these innovations. Among his inventions are an automotive machine equipped with a differential transmission, a mobile fortress somewhat like a modern tank, and a flying machine—all of which, however, lacked an adequate source of power. Leonardo's optical studies and his invention of machines for grinding concave mirrors resulted in a telescope that was in existence by 1509, a century before Galileo.

Although as far as we know Leonardo never built a building, his architectural drawings promulgated new principles of design that had a far-reaching effect on buildings built by others, and it may be said that Leonardo founded the High Renaissance style in architecture just as he did in painting. For Leonbattista Alberti, whom the youthful Leonardo may have met and whose ideas he must have known, the best form of building was a centralized structure because architecture is founded on nature, and nature, in plants and the structure of animals, is centralized. Vasari said that Leonardo had wasted time covering sheets of paper with meaningless squares, triangles, circles, and so forth, but what he was probably doing was exploring permutations and combinations of geometrical figures as he developed ground plans for buildings.

In a number of architectural drawings, he starts, at the right of the sheet, of course, with plans composed of geometrical elements, and he then proceeds to erect churches in perspective upon these plans. The drawing in figure 449 shows an octagonal church surrounded by eight domed circular chapels, each with eight niches; a diamond plan with apses on the sides and towers on the points; and sketches for two more plans. But if these

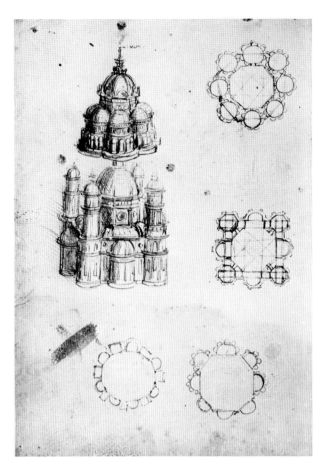

449. LEONARDO DA VINCI. *Plans and Perspective Views of Domed Churches*. c. 1490. Pen and ink. Institut de France, Paris

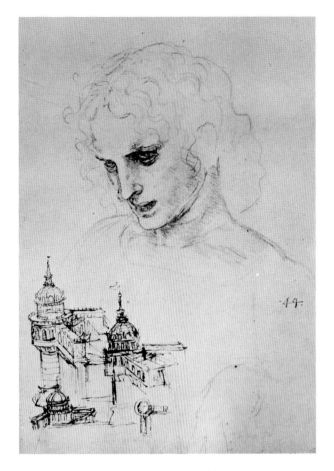

450. LEONARDO DA VINCI. *Head of the Apostle Matthew for Last Supper; Architectural Studies for Sforza Castle*. c. 1495. Red chalk, pen and ink, 9³/4 x 6³/4". Royal Library, Windsor

centralized plans follow Alberti's principles, the details recall Brunelleschi's dome for Santa Maria del Fiore and his plan for Santo Spirito (see figs. 132, 142). The end result, however, is something entirely new. The buildings are not juxtapositions of flat planes, as in Brunelleschi, or inert masses, as in Alberti. They are living organisms that radiate outward from a central core, like the petals of a flower, the legs of a crustacean, or the rays of a snow crystal. What Leonardo discovered—and this is the basis of High Renaissance composition in any artistic field—is a unified totality that is the product of the dynamic interrelationship of its components. Antonio del Pollaiuolo had hit on something similar in the ephemeral triangle of archers in his *St. Sebastian* (see colorplate 59, p. 300)—or perhaps the youthful Leonardo had already suggested the notion to him. In any case, Leonardo did not stop at individual buildings or parts of buildings, such as the turret for the Sforza Castle that he drew on the same page as a study for the *Last Supper* (fig. 450). He also designed solutions for the urban problems of his day, such as underground canals for the removal of refuse and streets for horse-drawn traffic below elevated walkways and pedestrian malls for human enjoyment. None of this came to reality at the

moment, any more than did his designs for a flying machine, but the ideas are typical of Leonardo's concern with discovering principles of order in the apparent disorder of life.

What fascinated him his whole life long, perhaps more consistently than any other natural phenomenon, was the behavior of water. His notebooks abound with schemes for providing it in abundance to cities, rendering it useful and free of obstruction in harbors, making it a safe means of transportation in rivers and canals. For such purposes one has to know how water works, and to this end Leonardo must have sat hour after hour studying the patterns produced by a stream striking a body of water (fig. 451), penetrating it in spiral eddies, emerging again on the surface in bubbling circles. Or he examined the configurations formed by a board suspended at various angles into a rushing stream. He notes that such shapes resemble curls of hair (fig. 452), and shows how the principles of spiral growth in the leaves of plants are found in water as well.

On a page where Leonardo drew the valves of the heart, he wrote, "Let no one who is not a mathematician read my principles." For Leonardo the perception of mathematical structures underlying nature was the

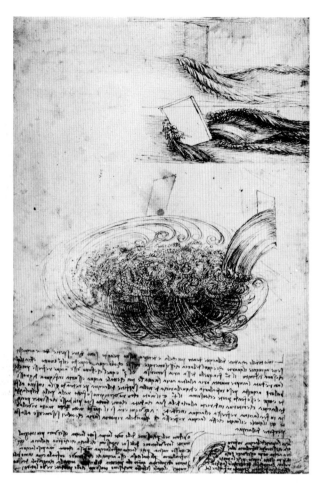

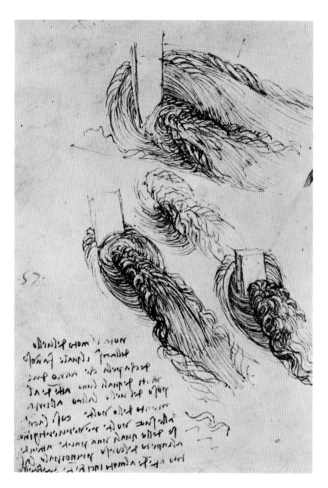

451. LEONARDO DA VINCI. *Studies of Water Movements.* c. 1505. Pen and ink, 11½ x 8". Royal Library, Windsor

452. LEONARDO DA VINCI. *Studies of Water* (portion of drawing). 1490–95. Pen and ink; area shown, 6 x 8½". Royal Library, Windsor

wellspring of his scientific investigation and creative imagination. Faith in the certainty of mathematical principles gave Leonardo the ability to correlate a broad yet diverse range of studies. The unified, pyramidal composition of the figures in his *Madonna of the Rocks* (colorplate 82, p. 451), for example, and the pyramidal form of the parachute he designed are both related to his understanding of the efficiency of operation demonstrated in a tri-cusped heart valve or an arrangement that used three ballbearings. Leonardo's use of the geometry of the triangle in painting is thus related to his investigations of nature and mechanics, demonstrating that art, as he wrote, "truly is a science."

Most of the problems connected with the interrelationship of Leonardo and his master, Andrea del Verrocchio, with whom he worked for several years after about 1470 in Florence, are unresolved, and we shall limit ourselves to a few words about his participation in Verrocchio's *Baptism of Christ* (see fig. 332). About most of the painting there can be little doubt, for Verrocchio's hand is everywhere apparent. But of the two kneeling angels, the curly-headed boy at the right, who still belongs to the world of Fra Filippo Lippi, is a sharp contrast to his companion at the left, who looks out from

deep, luminous eyes and whose hair streams from his forehead to his shoulders with the mysterious beauty of Leonardo's water patterns. The water above him, whose shimmering surface breaks into rapids over underlying shoals, whose juncture with the surrounding rocks is masked by mists, and whose very origins defeat our imaginations, this too is by the man who was to paint the elusive watercourses that irrigate the background landscape of the *Mona Lisa* (see fig. 463). Very possibly the clear and beautiful water in the foreground as well comes from the brush of the youthful Leonardo.

One of his few remaining works from this Florentine period is the *Annunciation* (fig. 453), datable somewhere in the late 1470s, from the Monastery of Monte Oliveto. The Virgin is seated on the threshold of a splendid villa with granite walls and perfectly projected corner quoins of *pietra serena*, a combination unknown to Florence. Her book rests on a lectern made from a Roman sepulchral urn that is rendered with remarkable fidelity. Mary acknowledges the angel's message by lifting her hand in a gesture of somewhat patrician surprise, but not a trace of emotion disturbs her features. Gabriel kneels before her on a carpet of grass and flowers, each of which is rendered with Leonardo's botanical accuracy and sense

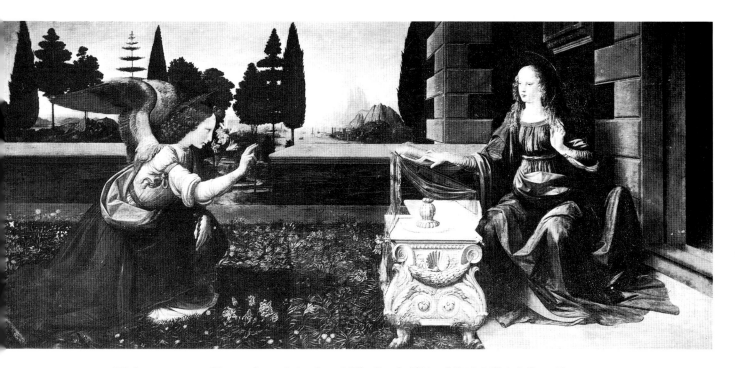

453. LEONARDO DA VINCI. *Annunciation.* Late 1470s. Panel, 38³/4 x 85¹/2". Uffizi Gallery, Florence. Commissioned by the monks for the Monastery of Monte Oliveto, outside Florence

of rhythmic growth. Over the garden wall, past cypresses and topiary cedars, is a distant port, with towers, lighthouses, and ships, much like that by Filippino in the Corsini *Virgin and Child with Angels* (see fig. 356) and probably painted for the same reason—Mary's titles of "Star of the Sea" and "Port of the Shipwrecked."

The picture seems decades later than Ghirlandaio's *Adoration* (colorplate 64, p. 353) rather than several years earlier. The atmospheric veil that Leonardo interposes between the object and our eye—and about which he discourses at length in his writings—is completely new. The blue air becomes denser as we look toward the shimmering mountains, which resemble the Apuan Alps seen in the afternoon light from Monte Oliveto. The figures' drapery, solid and sculptural, reveals Leonardo's method as recorded by Vasari (fig. 454): after soaking a piece of soft linen in gesso Leonardo would arrange it over a small figure and allow it to harden. He would then move this model into a satisfactory illumination and draw it with a brush on linen canvas before starting to paint the final picture.

The two faces are without shadow and show an unearthly softness and lightness, even though the light that has entered the picture with the angel casts a shadow on the grass and creates a strong play of shadows in the drapery over Mary's knees. At the same time, every nuance of shape in the faces is clear and firm. Leonardo speaks in his notebooks of how to use light in painting faces. He warns against drawing or painting faces in the harsh, direct light of the sun, reminding us of the beauty of faces passed in the street in the morning before sunlight has appeared, or in the early evening when the sun has

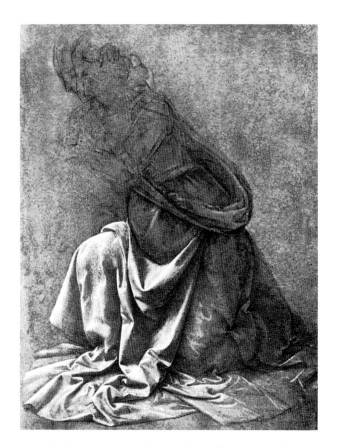

454. LEONARDO DA VINCI. *Study of Drapery.* 1470s. Silverpoint, ink, wash, and white on red prepared paper, 10 x 7³/4". National Gallery, Rome

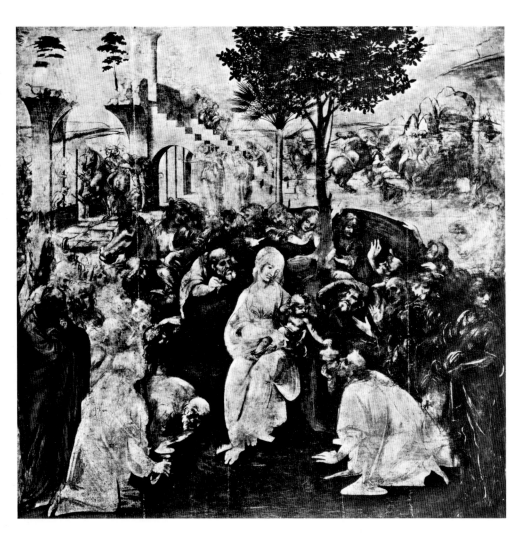

455. LEONARDO DA VINCI. *Adoration of the Magi.* Begun 1481. Panel, 8' x 8' 1". Uffizi Gallery, Florence. Commissioned by the monks of S. Donato a Scopeto for their monastery

just gone down. At that time, he writes, you see soft and mysterious expressions, forms that you cannot quite grasp, and the faces take on an inexplicable loveliness and grace. To produce such effects in the studio, he recommends painting all four walls of a courtyard black, stretching a sheet of linen over the courtyard, and then placing the model under this linen so that the diffused light will radiate the face without sharp reflections or shadows to break up the forms. This is exactly the effect he achieved in his *Annunciation.*

These procedures for studying and rendering light reveal that darkness precedes light in his thought (e.g., the black-walled courtyard, the darkness of the enclosure behind the cloth-and-gesso draped model). Light penetrates the darkness but cannot entirely replace it. In Leonardo's paintings, therefore, form and color must compete for their existence against the surrounding dark and against the overlying bluish atmosphere. As a result of this effort, color enjoys a new and deeper resonance, form has a more convincing three-dimensional existence, and the darkest shadows unite to give the picture a new kind of unity. In the artificially bright world inhabited by most of Leonardo's Florentine contemporaries, form is a shell and color an enamel.

Leonardo's *Adoration of the Magi* (fig. 455) was commissioned in March 1481 by the monks of San Donato a Scopeto, a now-vanished monastery formerly outside the Porta Romana of Florence. The picture was left unfinished when the artist departed for Milan some time late in 1481 or early in 1482. But unfinished is hardly the proper word for a picture in which there is not a touch of color. What we see is an incomplete underdrawing that has been reinforced with a dark wash to begin to establish the unifying structure of shadows. To understand the painting properly we should try to imagine how it would look if it were brought to the same state of completion as the *Annunciation.* Nonetheless, the methods used by the young artist in his underdrawing are exciting in themselves and offer visual proof of his attitude toward light that reinforces the ideas in his writings.

Again it is difficult to accept Leonardo's chronological position as a contemporary of the masters treated in Chapter 13. This revolutionary picture comes only a few years after Botticelli's altarpiece on the same subject for Santa Maria Novella (see colorplate 60, p. 301), and probably before his *Adoration* now in Washington, D.C. (see fig. 346). A perspective study for Leonardo's *Adoration* (fig. 456) shows that he originally intended to in-

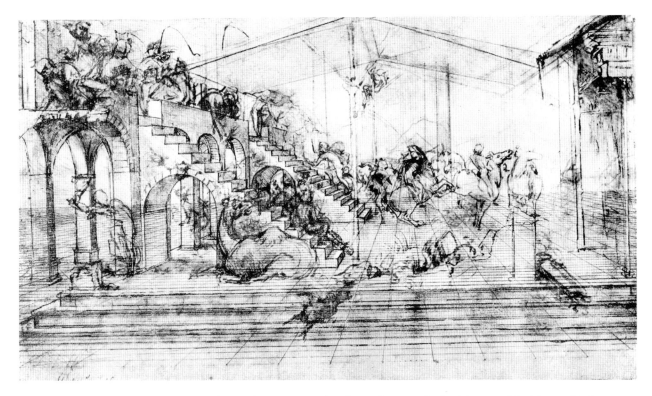

456. LEONARDO DA VINCI. *Architectural Perspective and Background Figures, for the Adoration of the Magi.* c. 1481.
Pen and ink, wash, and white, 6¹/₂ x 11¹/₂". Gabinetto dei Disegni e Stampe, Uffizi, Florence

clude the ruins and shed of the Botticelli tradition. The drawing is a celebrated example of Albertian one-point perspective, but it also discloses the Achilles' heel of this system—the distortion imposed on the squares at the extreme right and left of the construction.

In the perspective study, the principal groups of figures do not appear—Leonardo studied them separately in many other drawings—but on the steps and ruins are members of the train of the three Magi. A camel crouches below the steps, and in the background, at the vanishing point, a man tries to maintain his balance on a rearing horse, while another horse kicks backward with both legs, motifs Leonardo may have observed in Uccello's *Battle of San Romano* (see colorplate 47, p. 257). But these are far from Uccello's geometricized horses; they are as replete with uncontrollable energy as the water that fascinated Leonardo, and, like the rushing water, they reappear again and again in his imagination as symbols of the forces of nature.

In the painting Leonardo omits the shed and, therefore, its elaborate perspective construction, which is no longer relevant to the problems that concerned him. The ruins remain, abbreviated somewhat—and still in flawless perspective—but now they are relegated to a background position. The arches are broken and the figures and horses surge beneath them. The camel has vanished, and both horses rear on their hind legs, as if their riders were in combat.

In the *Adoration of the Magi*, Leonardo demonstrates his interest in studying the group psychology that results

when crowds are drawn together by the electric excitement of an event. Whatever their ostensible subject, in fact, Leonardo's compositions always seem to be systematic expositions of his psychological interests. The yearning that sends the Magi to their knees runs like a storm through the crowd of attendants, building up a pyramid composed of psychological relationships with the Virgin's head as its apex.

Earlier painters, when we are able to observe their technical procedures from unfinished or damaged works, or deduce them from pictorial surfaces, drew contours on white priming and applied color between them. Leonardo inundates the surface with a dark wash that creates the envelope of shadow so apparent in the *Annunciation*. The light areas—the figures—are the residue, but the darkness has invaded many of them. He then begins to define their edges with the brush. To Leonardo, therefore, the traditional roles of light and darkness are reversed. Darkness is universal and primal, and light must struggle against it. Light fascinated him, and his notes record luminary experiments and analyses, including even a projector powered by a candle. Once the basic light areas received definition, Leonardo sharpened the details, always as a movement of dark against light. A few touches can make a beautiful young head or a ravaged old one spring into being, full of life and emotion. At times ghostly in its softness, at times volcanic in its power, the fluid dark pours over figures, horses, and vegetation. The tree in the upper left corner shows the method clearly. A few horizontal strokes of the brush

The High Renaissance in Florence

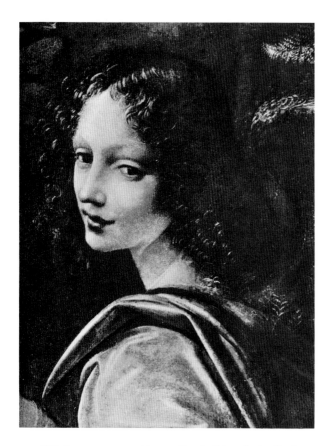

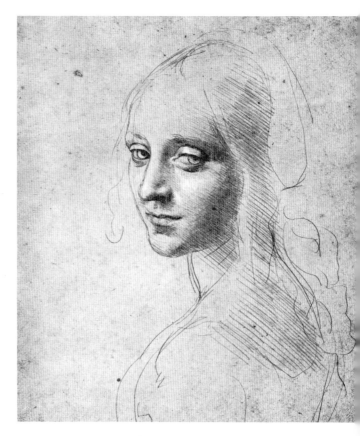

457. LEONARDO DA VINCI. Head of Angel, detail of
Madonna of the Rocks (see colorplate 82, p. 451). Begun 1483.
Panel, transferred to canvas. The Louvre, Paris

458. LEONARDO DA VINCI. *Study of the Head of the Angel,*
for the *Madonna of the Rocks.* c. 1483. Silverpoint
and white on rose-colored prepared paper, 7¼ x 6¼".
Royal Library, Turin

represent the foliage, and later he would have united these masses with a trunk and branches.

When Leonardo left Florence in 1481 or 1482 for a stay of nearly twenty years in Milan, he left the picture in its present state, and the monks eventually ordered another one from Filippino Lippi. In his letter of application to Duke Ludovico Sforza, the artist speaks eloquently about his abilities as a civil and military engineer, emphasizing how his inventions could further the duke's conquests and render life more agreeable in his capital. He suggests a sculptural project for an equestrian monument to the duke's late father, and only at the end does he mention his skills as a painter. Of these, however, he was to show splendid evidence shortly after his arrival in his painting of the *Madonna of the Rocks.* Two versions survive, an earlier one in the Louvre (colorplate 82, p. 451) and a later one in the National Gallery in London (not illustrated). One or both were painted for the Confraternity of the Immaculate Conception, which had a chapel in San Francesco Grande in Milan; according to a document of 1483, the painting was part of an elaborate altarpiece by Leonardo, two of his pupils, and an independent sculptor. The history of the London version can be traced continuously from the original altar until its sale to an English collector in 1785. Could it have been substituted at some time and for some un-

known reason for the Paris version? There is no general agreement, but the majority of scholars concede that the Louvre panel is earlier and entirely by Leonardo, whereas the London panel, even if designed by the master, shows passages of pupils' work consistent with the date of 1506, when there was a controversy between the artists and the confraternity.

The patron confraternity was devoted to the Immaculate Conception, the doctrine that Mary was conceived without sex and free from all stain of Original Sin. This belief, promulgated in papal bulls written by Pope Sixtus IV close to the date when Leonardo painted the picture, was represented in a sculptured image at the same altar (above or below the painting) and has infiltrated the meaning of Leonardo's painting. The artist has shown the youthful Virgin kneeling on the ground, her arm around the kneeling John the Baptist and her left hand extended protectively over the seated Christ Child, who is worshiped by John. A kneeling angel steadies the Christ Child and looks outward toward (but not direcly at) the spectator (fig. 457), while pointing at John. The composition of the figures creates the unified pyramid that will be the basis of High Renaissance compositional practice.

The most extraordinary aspect of the painting is its dark and gloomy background, a wilderness of jagged rocks rising almost to the apex of the arch. Through this arch, as through the mouths of caverns, we look into mysterious vistas flanked by rocky pinnacles that rise from dim watercourses until they lose themselves in the half-light of misty distances. According to tradition, the cave of the Nativity was mystically identified with the cave of the Sepulcher, and St. Antonine claimed that both are foretold in the Song of Songs: "O my dove, that art in the clefts of the rock, in the secret places [*caverna*] of the stairs, let me see thy countenance" (2:14). The dove may be identified with the Virgin, and perhaps the shadowy caves are intended to suggest humanity's dark mortality, into which Divine Light enters through the role of Mary as the immaculate vessel of God's purpose. Whatever importance Leonardo attached to the subject he was commissioned to paint, he saw it as a richly romantic vision and painted shadows of unprecedented depth and poetic beauty, within which the light picks out sweet faces and delicate hands, warm flesh and exquisite curls, while hinting at the shapes of geological formations and wild vegetation. This is the fulfillment of the new kind of light that Leonardo creates in the underdrawing of the *Adoration of the Magi*.

One of the most beautiful drawings for the picture is the silverpoint study for the head of the angel (fig. 458), made on rose-colored paper and delicately heightened with white. In order to make this drawing Leonardo may well have used the method recommended in his notebooks—setting the model in a black courtyard beneath a linen sheet—and he has reproduced the effect of this illumination with separate strokes of silverpoint that are so sensitive and close to each other that they almost blend into a gliding, all-over tone. The light that gives "a grace to faces," as Leonardo put it, strikes the luminous eyes, which truly seem to be the windows from which the soul of the figure looks toward us.

Leonardo's projects for the Duke of Milan ranged from military and civil engineering to richly costumed pageants enlivened by mechanical devices, but we know too little about the monument that was his major artistic undertaking for the duke. Judging from a fiery preparatory drawing (fig. 459), Francesco Sforza was to have been reining in a rearing horse while an enemy cowered below. The military leader who restrains a rearing steed has a long history in ancient art, not as an independent statue but in historical reliefs, many of them as accessible to Leonardo as they are to us. Piero della Francesca had used the motif in the *Battle of Heraclius and Chosroes* (see fig. 284), but it remained for Leonardo to translate the notion into a project for a colossal statue in the round.

The first example of such a statue to be erected was Bernini's *Louis XIV* in 1669, and we have no way of knowing why Leonardo ultimately renounced the dramatic idea in favor of a striding pose in the tradition of Donatello and Verrocchio (see figs. 249, 337). Drawings show he developed both ideas simultaneously, and it is possible that the duke objected to the unconventional idea, or perhaps Leonardo became discouraged by the

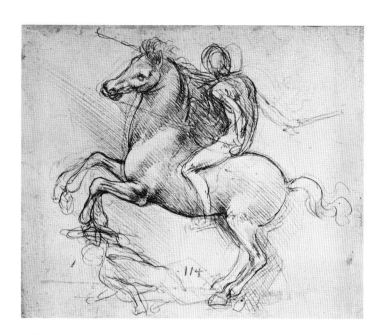

459. LEONARDO DA VINCI. *Horseman Trampling on Foe, study for an Equestrian Monument to Francesco Sforza.* c. 1485. Silverpoint on greenish ground, 6 x 7 1/4". Royal Library, Windsor. Commissioned by Ludovico Sforza

technical problems of casting and mounting such a large and precariously balanced group in bronze. For a while the duke considered taking on some other artist for the project, but in 1490 Leonardo set to work, on the basis of exhaustive anatomical studies of horses, and produced a full-scale model some twenty-four feet high in clay or plaster, as well as complete plans for casting it in bronze. Unhappily, the drawings are our only evidence for the monument. After Louis XII ascended the French throne, he laid claim, as a descendant of the expelled Visconti, to the duchy of Milan, and the duke found himself in a military crisis that made it impossible for Leonardo to obtain the necessary metal. The French invaders who chased out Ludovico Sforza in 1499 used Leonardo's colossus for target practice. What was left of it soon fell to pieces, and its grandeur can be revived in our imaginations only as we peruse the drawings.

Leonardo's *Last Supper* (colorplate 83, p. 452) in the refectory of Santa Maria delle Grazie in Milan is often known through prettified versions that conceal its poor condition, which is due to a disastrous technical experiment on Leonardo's part. An artist as sensitive as Leonardo to the slightest throb of light in atmosphere was bound to be impatient with the fresco method, which could not allow the time needed to establish his customary shadowy unity to the painting and his perfect luminous finish to the details. It will be remembered that, for similar reasons, Baldovinetti had combined underpaint in fresco with a finish in tempera at the Santissima Annunziata (see fig. 318). Leonardo painted directly on the dry *intonaco* with an oil tempera whose composition

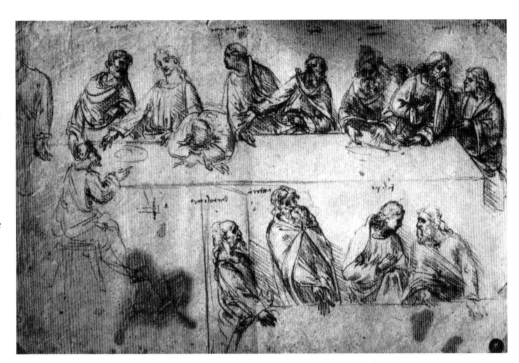

right: 460. LEONARDO DA VINCI. *Study of composition of Last Supper* (see colorplate 83, p. 452). c. 1495. Red chalk, 10¹/₄ x 15¹/₂". Accademia, Venice

below: 461. LEONARDO DA VINCI. Thomas, Matthew, and Philip, detail of *Last Supper* (see colorplate 83, p. 452). 1495–97/98. Fresco. Refectory, Sta. Maria delle Grazie, Milan

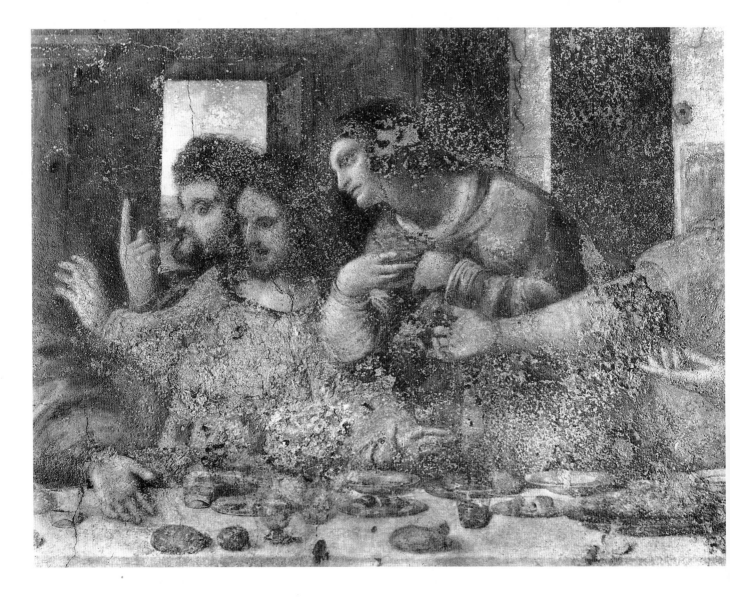

is not yet known. According to literary accounts, he would sometimes stand on the scaffolding an entire morning without picking up the brush, studying the relationships of tone. When completed, the painting inspired extravagant praise, but in 1517, while the artist was still alive, it had started to deteriorate, and when Vasari saw it a generation or so later, he found it almost indecipherable. It was repainted twice in the eighteenth century, it suffered from the brutality of Napoleonic soldiers and from the monks, who cut a door through it, and it was again repainted in the nineteenth century. In 1943 Allied bombs destroyed much of the rest of the refectory but the painting, protected by sandbags supported on steel tubing, survived. Extensive conservation efforts after World War II disclosed more of the original under the repaint than anyone had dared to hope, and the picture is currently undergoing a cautious, scientific restoration that has already revealed Leonardo's delicacy of touch and luminosity of color in the better-preserved areas.

The popular reproductions of the *Last Supper* have numbed us to the meaning of this powerful composition. In preliminary drawings (fig. 460), Leonardo toyed with the idea of placing Judas on our side of the table, as had Taddeo Gaddi, Castagno, and Ghirlandaio (see figs. 83, 270, 359). The Gospel of St. John (13:26) states that Judas is indicated as the betrayer by the sop in wine that Christ hands to him, while in the Gospels of Matthew and Mark, Christ says, "He who dippeth with me in the dish," and in Luke, "He whose hand is with me on the table." Leonardo refers to the text from Luke, for Judas's hand is on the table, stretching after the bread. Because Christ's hands gesture toward the bread and the wine, the picture also refers to the institution of the Eucharist. Leonardo has fused this episode with yet another moment—never before represented—as recounted by Matthew, Mark, and Luke: "Verily I say unto you, that one of you shall betray me. And they were exceeding sorrowful, and began every one to say unto him, Lord, is it I?" Instead of designating the betrayer, Leonardo has shown how the announcement sparked astonishment on the part of the apostles and intense searching of their own souls.

Donatello represented a similar effect in his *Feast of Herod* (see fig. 173), but Leonardo has gone further. He has, in fact, composed the apostles' reactions in accordance with his own mechanistic Renaissance view of psychology, thus revealing the underlying mathematical unity of all life. As if by inexorable law, the revelation of betrayal factors the number twelve into four groups of three each. This grouping about the axial figure of Christ establishes a symmetrical order that subsumes the figurative variety of the individual apostles. In addition, Leonardo was certainly aware of the symbolic meaning of these numbers in Christian tradition. Three, the number of the Trinity, is the most sacred number, while four conveys the essence of matter in the elements of earth, air, fire, and water. Leonardo thus joins the components of creation, spirit, and matter. More complex numerical

symbolism has also been seen here, for there are three Theological Virtues and four is the number of the Gospels, the Cardinal Virtues, the Rivers of Paradise, the seasons of the year, and the times of day. Three plus four make seven, the number of the Gifts of the Holy Spirit, the Joys of the Virgin, and the Sorrows of the Virgin. Three times four make twelve, not only the number of the apostles in the picture, but also of the gates of the New Jerusalem, the months of the year, the hours of the day, and the hours of the night. Christ, the divider, appears at the center of both light and space, the vanishing point of the perspective and the second window of a group of three, whether the group is read from the left or from the right. As we have seen, windows are symbols of revelation, and Christ is the Second Person of the Trinity. Numerical tradition is exploited by Leonardo to make the divisions of his composition significant to his audience, to create mathematical order out of dramatic confusion, and to emphasize the impact of the revelation of betrayal on the inner lives of the apostles by identifying their reactions with the underlying number system.

In preliminary sketches made before he resolved his composition, Leonardo labeled each apostle, and in one of his manuscripts he describes their respective attitudes and emotions. He later studied each from live models, some of whose names are known. Many drawings are preserved, including one in red chalk for the terror-struck apostle (see fig. 450) who recoils as from a blow, his eyes staring, his mouth open. In the painting, this horrified figure sinks back between St. Thomas, with his pointing, probing finger, and St. Philip, whose love for his Master seems to stream from his eyes, his hands pressed to his breast as he protests that he is not the betrayer (fig. 461).

Judas is the only apostle who need not protest; he knows. He is also the only apostle who reaches for food, bearing the implication of having received the sacrament unworthily. Judas is the only apostle who recoils from the Master and the only one whose face is not in the light. His dark bulk is contrasted in the same group with the lighted profile of St. Peter and the face of St. John, whom, in defiance of tradition, Leonardo has placed at Christ's right. Christ turns from Judas, and the resigned expression on his face suggests his words in the Gospels, "And the Son of man indeed goeth . . . but woe to that man by whom the Son of man shall be betrayed."

Here and there, especially in the pewter plates, the freshly unfolded tablecloth, the simple wineglasses, and the rolls set upon the table, we can catch an echo of the surface quality of the original painting. Every silken curl, every passage of flesh must once have been virtually perfect. Leonardo's forms have lost their definition but not their impact, his space its precision but not its depth. The psychological effect of the ruined masterpiece can still bring the observer to silence.

In the *Last Supper* Leonardo has taken a step as definitive as that taken by Donatello eighty years before in the *St. George and the Dragon* relief (see fig. 166), but in a totally different direction. He has broken with the Quattrocento tradition that culminated in the illusionistic systems of Mantegna and Melozzo, which decreed that represented space must be an extension of the room in which the spectator stands. Although Leonardo's perspective is consistent, there is no place in the refectory where spectators can stand so that their eyes are on the same level as the vanishing point. The walls of the upper chamber in Jerusalem cannot be read as continuations of the real walls of the refectory, and the Albertian role of the picture as a vertical intersection through the visual pyramid has been abandoned. The painting is now a projection on an ideal plane of experience in which lower realities are subdued and synthesized. This is a perfect perspective, which could be seen by no pair of human eyes, and within it are set forth larger-than-life human beings who exist and act and move on a grander plane, above our experience. Ideal masses inhabit ideal space to expound an idea. The delight of the Quattrocento in visual reality and vivid anecdote has been replaced by that wholly different satisfaction to be obtained from imagined grandeur and noble concepts. We are now truly in the High Renaissance, whose basic idea is Leonardo's single-handed creation and which will be adopted later by Michelangelo, Fra Bartolommeo, Raphael, and Andrea del Sarto.

It is noteworthy that this new and grander vision of ideal reality is expressed at just the moment when the reality of the Italian political situation was recognized as hopeless. After the French invasion of Italy and the Battle of the Taro in 1495, it was clear that no matter who claimed victory in that disastrous encounter, divided Italy was and would remain impotent in the face of the unified monarchies of Western Europe. Despite the appeals of Machiavelli and others, it was only a matter of time before the Italian states, with the exception of the Genoese and Venetian republics, would be overwhelmed by the forces of foreign tyranny, by whose courtesy, once the struggles had subsided, Florence and the papacy were allowed to maintain a shadowy independence. The High Renaissance in Florence and Rome can be understood as an extension into an ideal plane of those images of human grandeur and power that the Italians knew were in real life doomed. It is a valiant effort, and there is often something dreamlike about its noble productions, as compared with the pedestrian solidity of early Quattrocento images.

Save for a five-year stay in Milan from 1508 to 1513, Leonardo was never again to spend more than two or three years, sometimes only a few months, in the same city. We have records that he returned to Florence and Rome repeatedly, stayed in Venice and Parma, and traveled about with the army of Cesare Borgia. From this last association date many of the master's daring engineering and cartographic exploits.

In 1501 Fra Pietro da Novellara, acting as agent for Isabella d'Este, wrote to the marchioness from Florence about a cartoon that Leonardo had made depicting a Christ Child about one year old who, almost slipping from his mother's arms, grasps a lamb and seems to hug it. The mother, half rising from the lap of St. Anne, takes the Child as though to separate him from the lamb, which signifies the Passion. St. Anne, also appearing to rise from a sitting position, seems to wish to keep her daughter from separating the Child and the lamb, and perhaps is intended to represent the Church, which does not wish the Passion of Christ to be impeded. And these figures are life-sized, but they are in a small cartoon, because they are all either seated, or bending over, and one is placed in front of another, moving toward the left, and this study is not yet finished.

The cartoon, exhibited at the Monastery of the Santissima Annunziata, was intended for a picture for the high altar of the church. The cartoon is lost, but its composition is known from a surviving sketch. It excited admiration and wonder and influenced Florentine artists profoundly, especially Fra Bartolommeo, the young Michelangelo, and the still-younger Raphael. They must have been impressed by those very qualities that Fra Pietro sets forth—the compression and overlapping of figures that enabled the artist to fit three life-sized figures into a small cartoon. But the general public also thronged to see it, probably because in April 1501 they implored the intervention of St. Anne, traditionally a protector of the Florentine Republic, at a moment of danger from Cesare Borgia's armies. At least thirty-three reflections of Leonardo's composition survive, and almost all are devotional images for private patrons.

The *Madonna and Child with St. Anne* (colorplate 84, p. 453), deriving from the lost cartoon and painted for a still-unknown purpose, was imitated by Raphael in 1507, but the background landscape dates from much later, probably from the artist's stay in Milan between 1508 and 1513. It was one of three paintings—the others were the *Mona Lisa* (fig. 463) and a bust-length figure of *St. John the Baptist* (not illustrated here)—that Leonardo took to France and kept with him until his death. If the *Last Supper* is the first High Renaissance wall painting, then the *Madonna and Child with St. Anne* is the first example of the new principles of unity, scale, and compression in panel painting. In the *Last Supper* the composition is the product of the emotions and actions of the moment; in the *Madonna and Child with St. Anne* the figures that make up a single group are now intertwined, and the tendency toward a living, moving pyramid that began with Pollaiuolo's *St. Sebastian* (see colorplate 59, p. 300) has reached its climax. It is no accident that the pyramidal composition produced by the interaction of the figures is an essential of classic art; although Leonardo could not have known this, the same principle is exemplified in the pedimental sculptures of the Parthenon. For Leonardo the activating principle of his classic composition and the origin of form itself is

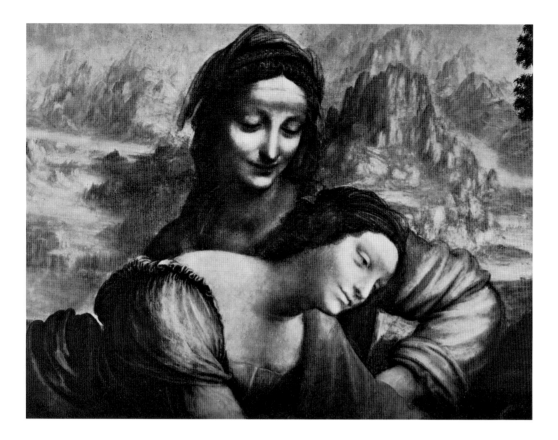

462. LEONARDO DA VINCI. Detail of *Madonna and Child with St. Anne* (see colorplate 84, p. 453). c. 1508–13(?). Panel. The Louvre, Paris. Painted for the high altar of SS. Annunziata, Florence

motion, which in his writings appears to be at the heart and core of his universe.

The summary appearance of the face of the Virgin is due to past overcleaning. We miss the veils of highlights and soft shadows that have been rubbed off, and here and there the underdrawing shows through the surface of the cheeks and neck (fig. 462). The Virgin's blue mantle has apparently lost much of its color, but in the other drapery and the sweetly sad face of St. Anne, as well as in the foreground with its rocky layers and rounded pebbles, Leonardo's surface is nearly intact, and it is even palpable where he wished it to be so, through his mysterious *sfumato*. Throughout the painting, the enameled brilliance of late Quattrocento coloring—Ghirlandaio's, for example—has been replaced by a subdued resonance reflecting the sobriety of the new era.

The figural pyramid divides the mountain landscape. This is not a poetic portrait of a natural landscape like those of Bellini, which evoke the mood of a time and place—any more than Leonardo's perspective can be related to a specific moment of vision—but a composite of observations and memories collected in his Alpine wanderings. The fantastic spires recall the Dolomites above Belluno so accurately that they make the rocky pinnacles of Leonardo's earlier backgrounds seem mere inventions. Escarpments, crags, lakes, rivers, and cascades recede and blend into the distance and are lost behind gossamer blue until neither observation nor imagination can distinguish solids in the pearly shimmer. Through this landscape and its watery and atmospheric envelope runs an unaccountable movement, a universal

upheaval, as if the elements harmoniously balanced in the foreground figures were now in conflict with each other, as doubtless in Leonardo's imagination they were—the conflict between rock and water, solidity and motion that can result only in chaos and dissolution.

There is still debate about the identity of the sitter in the painting that is universally known as the *Mona Lisa* (fig. 463). According to Vasari, she was Lisa di Antonio Maria Gherardini, the wife of the prominent Florentine Francesco del Giocondo. (Mona is a term of respect, a shortened version of the Italian phrase equivalent to "my lady.") Vasari also tells us that Leonardo worked on the painting for three full years. It was executed between the cartoon and the final painting of the *Madonna and Child with St. Anne* and, like it, was kept by the artist and taken by him to France. These factors, plus the presence of an imaginary mountain landscape, suggest that we might consider the paintings together. In the *Mona Lisa*, in fact, Leonardo treated the single figure much as he had the intertwined group in the *Madonna and Child with St. Anne*. Earlier full-face or three-quarter portraits such as Botticelli's *Man with a Medal* (see fig. 350) and Perugino's *Francesco delle Opere* (see fig. 380) concentrate on the head and shoulders, cutting the body at mid-chest and raising the hands so they are visible within the frame. Leonardo continues the figure well below the waist, and both arms appear complete. The left forearm lies along the arm of the chair, the right hand falls across it, the fingers sloping down. Both hands are utterly relaxed, completing in their unity the gentle spiral turn of the torso and head.

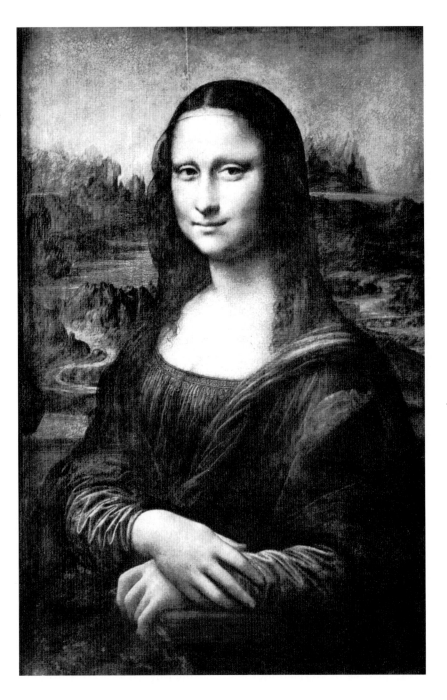

463. LEONARDO DA VINCI. *Mona Lisa.* 1503. Panel, 30¼ x 21". The Louvre, Paris

By implying a full-length portrait, Leonardo suggests that it is the whole person who is represented here. This new format was followed almost without exception in Italian portraiture—and indeed Northern European as well—through the nineteenth century. In Leonardo's invention the subject looks larger and grander than in Quattrocento portraits, in keeping with the new dignity of the High Renaissance. This effect would originally have been even more impressive, but the panel was at some later time cut down on either side, eliminating colonnettes that framed the figure and creating a more vertical format (the base of the colonnettes is still visible on the balustrade to either side).

The calm hint of a smile, about which so much has been written, and the composure of the hands were characteristic for a generation whose standards are summed up in the untranslatable word *sprezzatura*, from *disprezzo* (disdain). *Sprezzatura* is one of the norms of aristocratic behavior set out by Baldassare Castiglione in his book of dialogues called *Il libro del cortegiano* (*The Book of the Courtier*). Castiglione did not mean disdain for others, but the serene unconcern about economic realities or financial display that often denotes the inheritors of wealth and power. The sense of satisfied self-confidence is new, and it is especially remarkable that it is expressed by a woman. Renaissance books of etiquette stress that a woman should never look directly into a man's eyes, and one aspect of the painting's fame is surely the manner in which this woman challenges traditional cultural assumptions about appropriate female behavior.

This work has evoked a flood of literature, and whether or not Freud was correct in his interpretation of Leonardo's character, there is abundant evidence to suggest that his feelings toward women were ambivalent.

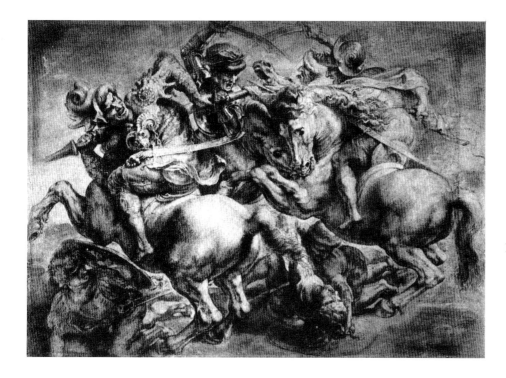

464. Copy after
LEONARDO DA VINCI.
Battle of Anghiari. 1503–6
(destroyed). Copy of
central section by PETER
PAUL RUBENS
(c. 1615). Pen and ink and
chalk, 17³/4 x 25¹/4".
The Louvre, Paris.
Leonardo's original was
commissioned by the
Florentine Republic for the
Salone del Cinquecento
in the Palazzo dei Priori

It seems unlikely that the sitter exercised a romantic attraction over the artist, even if her husband did permit a visible three-year tribute. Moreover, we cannot dissociate her personality from the surrounding landscape, with which it must have seemed even more intimately connected when the colonnettes were intact. As it is, motif after motif is continuous in figure and landscape. The locks of hair falling over her right shoulder blend with rocky outcroppings through which a road winds; the folds of the scarf over the left shoulder are continued in the line of a distant bridge. As one watches, this wife of a Florentine burgher assumes chameleonlike roles that become more poetic and perhaps even threatening.

But what a nature she dominates! It is the same world of roads, rocks, mists, and seas that constitutes Leonardo's backgrounds from the *Baptism of Christ* on (see figs. 332, 453); devoid of humans or animals, habitations, farms, fields, or even trees, it is dominated by Dolomitic crags like those in the *Madonna and Child with St. Anne*. The only human constructions, the roads and the bridge, lead to indistinguishable waters and unscalable rocks. As the levels rise to inaccessible heights, one is tempted to ask whether this is not what "woman" meant to Leonardo in his fifties. Most subtle of all is the placing of the highest level of mist so that it accentuates the expression of the eyes. The whole is covered with layers of darkened, yellowish varnish, and while the hands and garments still retain a veil of shadowy atmosphere, the face seems to have been stripped down to the underpaint by overcleaning.

In 1503 Leonardo was commissioned by the Florentine Republic under Piero Soderini to paint the *Battle of Anghiari* for the Palazzo dei Priori. The now-lost picture was never finished, and only the central section can be reconstructed with any degree of certainty, but dur-

ing the brief period when it was in existence and sections of the cartoon survived, they fundamentally changed the whole idea of battle painting, influencing the Late Renaissance, the Baroque, and even the heroic machines of the Napoleonic painters and the battle compositions of Delacroix. Leonardo's picture was intended to commemorate the 1440 victory of the Florentines over the forces of the Milanese duke Filippo Maria Visconti, who was abetted by the treachery of Rinaldo degli Albizzi and other Florentine exiles. In the days when the Republic still had to contend with the invading forces of Cesare Borgia, it is understandable that the government would wish to make reference to this triumph over an ancient enemy on the walls of the Sala del Cinquecento (Hall of the Five Hundred), which had been added to the Palazzo dei Priori to accommodate the Council of Five Hundred that ruled the new Republic. Apparently, Leonardo painted only the central section; for the rest, perhaps divided by windows, we have only vivid sketches. The work was executed in another of Leonardo's experimental techniques. The painting was abandoned by the artist in 1506, and its remains were apparently cleared away in 1557 by Vasari to make way for his murals glorifying the Medici principate under Grand Duke Cosimo I, the very opposite of the original purpose of the room and its decorations.

The Republican decorations were also to include, on the other half of the same wall or on the opposite side of the room, the *Battle of Cascina* by Michelangelo (see fig. 479), and briefly at least, in 1504–5, these two giants of the High Renaissance worked for, if not in, the same room. Our most detailed notion of the original effect of Leonardo's lost painting is furnished by a drawing by the seventeenth-century Flemish painter Peter Paul Rubens (fig. 464). Although Rubens had seen only infe-

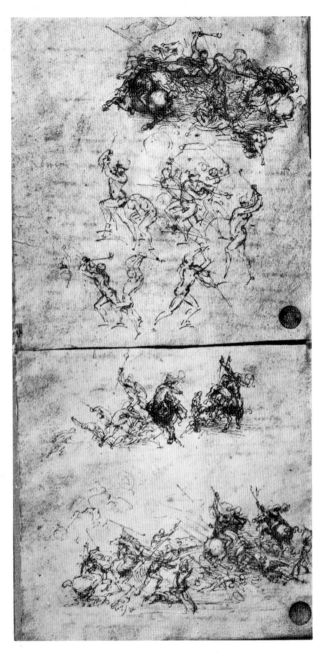

465. LEONARDO DA VINCI. *Two Sheets of Battle Studies.*
c. 1503. Pen and ink, each c. 6 x 6". Accademia, Venice

and those of the vanquished by pain and despair. To achieve this plane of cosmic struggle, Leonardo converted the horses and riders, whose ancestors we have seen in the *Adoration of the Magi* and the Sforza monument (see figs. 455, 459), into a tornado of intertwined figures. The High Renaissance figural composition, attained by the interaction of the forces of its component figures in the *Madonna and Child with St. Anne* (see colorplate 84, p. 453), here reaches an intensity so great that we are torn between the fascination of watching the beautiful interplay of rhythmic elements—the streaming manes and tails, for example—and the urge to turn in fear from the snarling ferocity of the horses, who almost outdo the riders in violence. Their hooves interlock and they fight with their teeth while the riders' swords clash in midair and the horses crush fallen warriors below. More encounters must have filled the remaining spaces, as they cover many sheets of Leonardo's sketchbooks (fig. 465), but their precise arrangement has eluded art historians despite a rich literature of controversy.

To the consternation of his contemporaries and the regret of posterity, Leonardo painted little or not at all during the last ten years of his life. He returned to Milan in 1506, where he was occupied for a while in the design of another never-executed equestrian monument, for Giangiacomo Trivulzio, marshal of the Italian armies of King Louis XII of France. He was appointed *Peintre et ingénieur ordinaire* to the king, which apparently involved little work and gave the artist a handsome stipend. Except for a brief sojourn in Florence in 1508, he remained in Milan, largely occupied with his scientific, and especially his anatomical, studies until 1513, when he went to Rome at the invitation of Pope Leo X. The Roman phase of the High Renaissance had largely passed, with the completion of the Sistine Ceiling by Michelangelo and the first two Vatican Stanze by Raphael, and Leonardo must have seemed like an apparition from another era. He had a suite of rooms at his disposal in the Vatican Belvedere, where he continued his studies and inventions, which are said to have included a pair of lizard-skin wings mounted on golden wires and attached to a tiny corset around the waist of a live lizard, which could thus march about like a little dragon, displaying its wings in the sunlight. The grandiosity of Michelangelo, then working in seclusion on the statues for the second version of the tomb of Julius II, can have held little appeal for Leonardo, and there is, surprisingly, no record that Leo X ever thought of entrusting him with actual commissions.

The old man's peripatetic existence between Florence, Rome, and Milan continued until 1517, when he accepted the invitation of King Francis I of France to spend his remaining years at the little château of Cloux, near Amboise, where his only duty was to talk to the king. According to accounts by contemporary witnesses, his conversation was charming, radiating his immense learning and imagination. But his artistic activity? Among the works attributed to these last years are draw-

rior copies of a painting that perished before he was born, he seems to have been able to re-create something of the furious dynamism of the original through the power of his own imagination.

The central scene depicted the contest of four horsemen for the possession of the standard of the Republic. Leonardo wrote that the superiority of painting over poetry was evident in the immediacy with which the painter could represent the smoke rising from the battlefield, the dust of the ground mingled with blood and turning into a red mud under the hooves of the horses, the faces of the victors distorted by rage and exultation

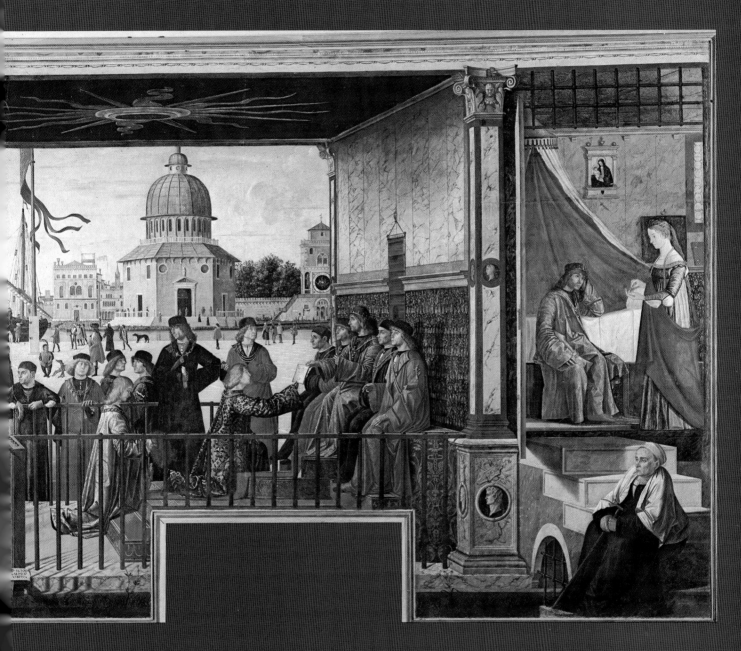

Colorplate 80. VITTORE CARPACCIO. *Arrival of the Ambassadors of Britain at the Court of Brittany.*
c. 1495—96. Canvas, 9' x 19' 4". Accademia, Venice. Commissioned by the Scuola di Sant'Orsola for
the confraternity headquarters, perhaps with the financial assistance of the Loredan family

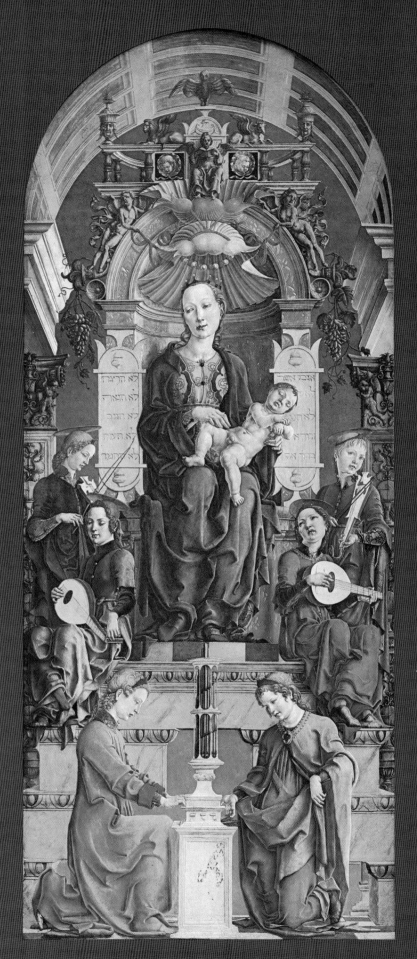

Colorplate 81.
COSIMO TURA.
Enthroned Madonna and Child with Angels, from the Roverella altarpiece. c. 1480. Panel, 94 x 40". National Gallery, London. Commissioned for S. Giorgio Fuori, Ferrara

opposite:
Colorplate 82.
LEONARDO DA VINCI.
Madonna of the Rocks. Begun 1483. Panel, transferred to canvas, 78¹/₂ x 48". The Louvre, Paris. Commissioned by the Confraternity of the Immaculate Conception for their chapel in S. Francesco Grande, Milan

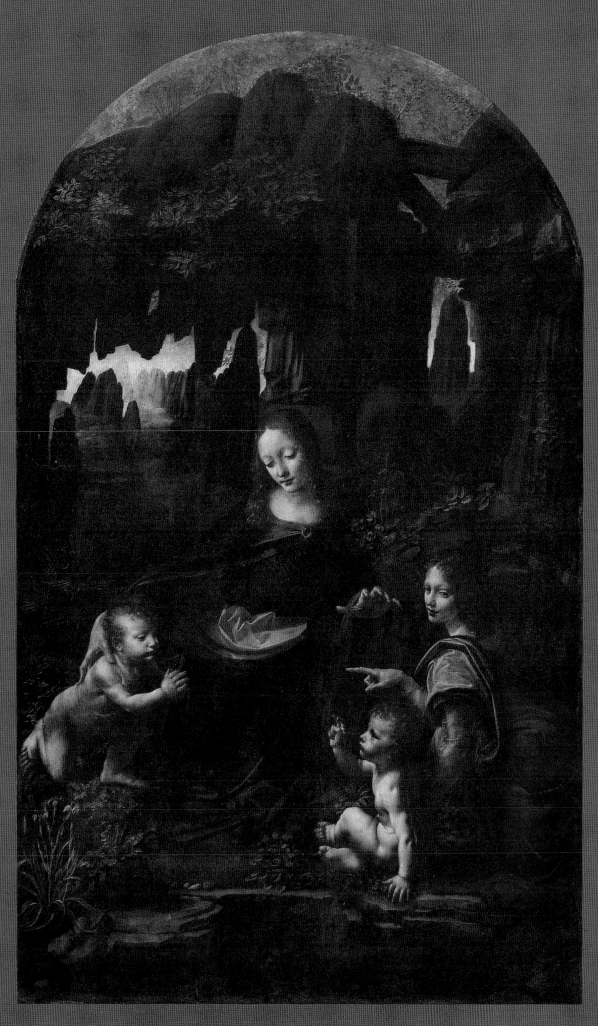

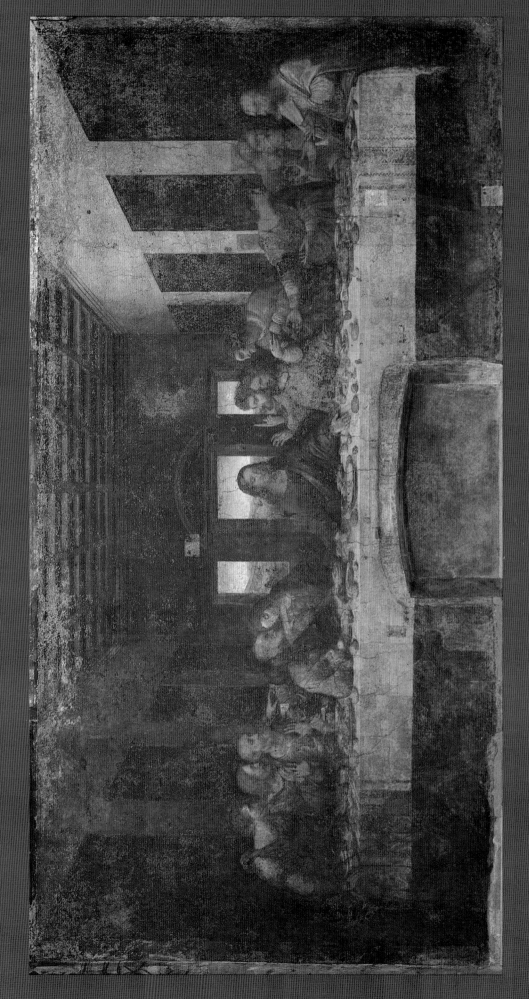

Colorplate 83. LEONARDO DA VINCI. *Last Supper*. 1495–97/98. Fresco, 13' 9" x 29' 10". Refectory, Sta. Maria delle Grazie, Milan. Commissioned by Ludovico il Moro

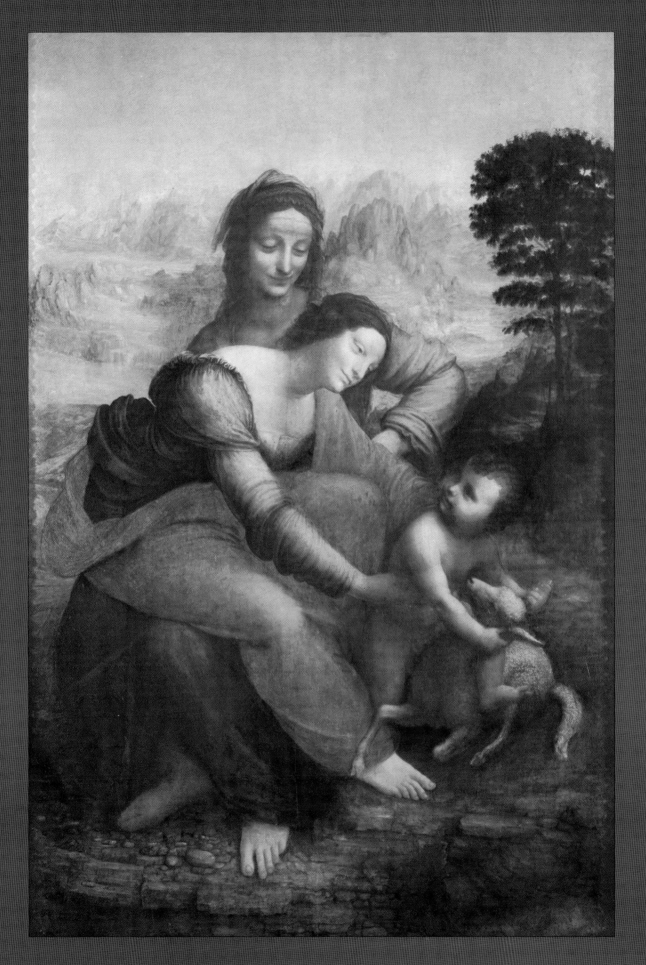

Colorplate 84. LEONARDO DA VINCI. *Madonna and Child with St. Anne*. c. 1508–13(?).
Panel, 66¼ x 51¼". The Louvre, Paris. Painted for the high altar of SS. Annunziata, Florence

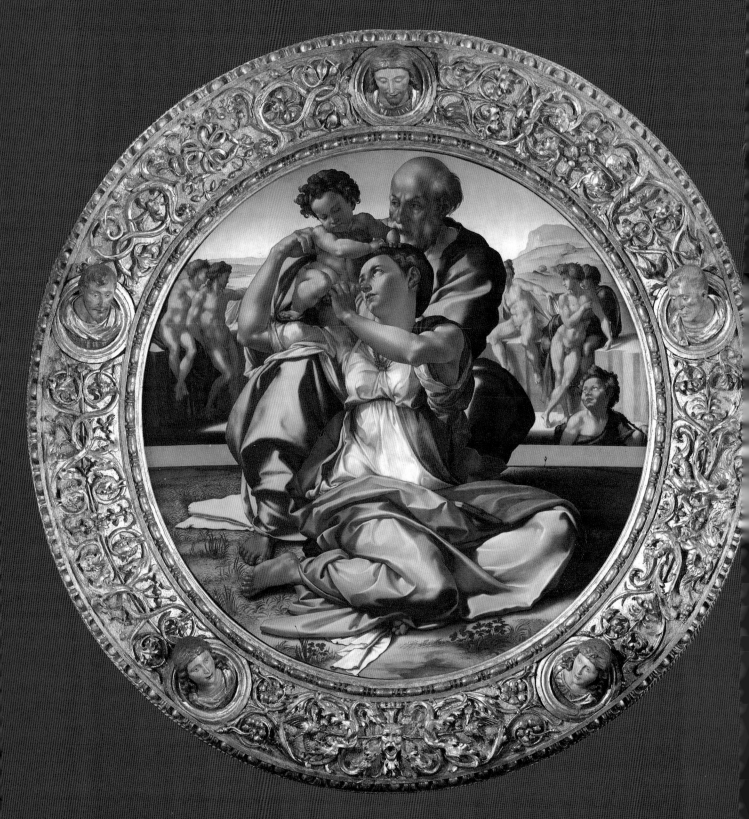

Colorplate 85. MICHELANGELO. *Doni Madonna*. c. 1503. Panel, diameter 47¼".
Uffizi Gallery, Florence. The frame was designed by the artist. Probably commissioned by Angelo Doni

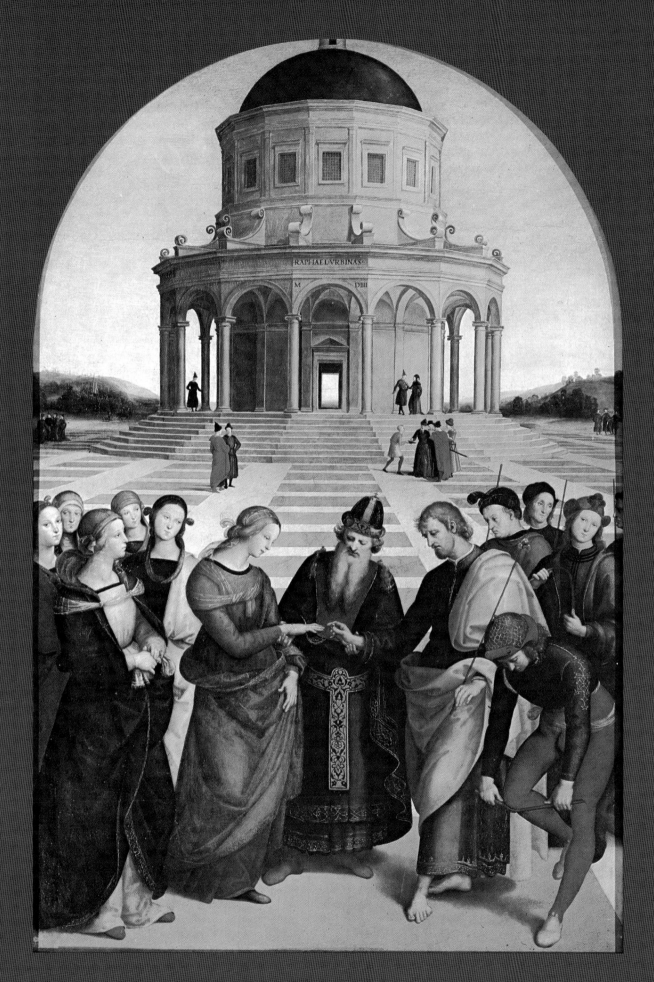

Colorplate 86. RAPHAEL. *Marriage of the Virgin*. 1504. Panel, 67 x 46½". Brera Gallery, Milan.
Commissioned by the Albizzini family for the Chapel of St. Joseph in the Church of S. Francesco, Città di Castello

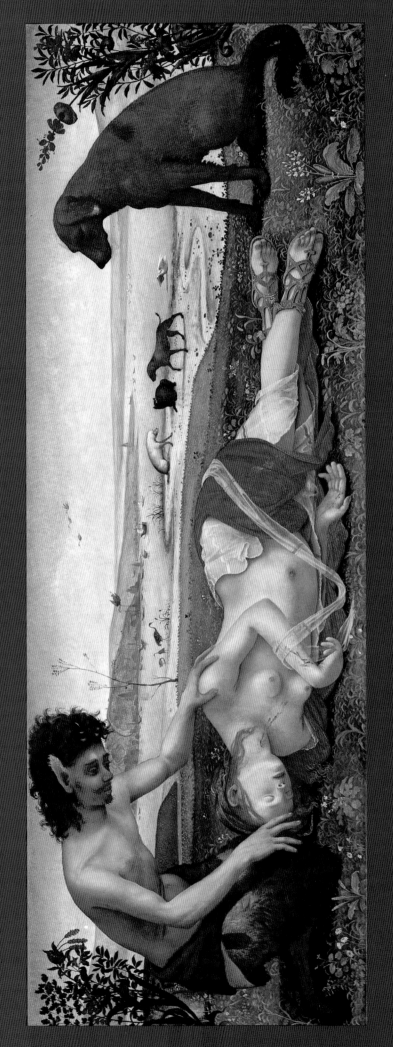

Colorplate 87. PIERO DI COSIMO. *Mythological Scene. c.* 1510. Panel, 25³/4 x 72¹/4". National Gallery, London

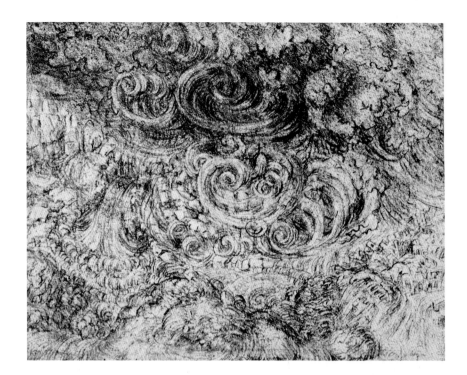

466. LEONARDO DA VINCI. *Deluge*. c. 1514–19. Black chalk, 6¼ x 8¼". Royal Library, Windsor

ings of water (fig. 466), whose limitless powers Leonardo had spent much of his life studying, utilizing, canalizing, and taming; now the waters are unchained, descending destructively upon the earth. Leonardo claimed that water was more dreadful than fire, which dies when it has consumed that which feeds it, while a river in flood continues its destructive course until it rests at last in the sea: "But in what terms am I to describe the abominable and awful evils against which no human resource avails? Which lay waste the high mountains with their swelling and exalted waves, cast down the strongest banks, tear up the deep-rooted trees, and with ravening waves laden with mud from crossing the ploughed fields carry with them the unendurable labors of the wretched tillers of the soil."

The force of water in these final drawings, engulfing barely visible human constructions, assumes beautiful and terrible spiral shapes that seem as prophetic of the abstract art of the twentieth century as were Leonardo's inventions of much of modern science. Mourn as we will all that he did not create, all the time spent on inventions that no one used and on the discovery of scientific principles that had to be rediscovered centuries later, we can console ourselves with the brief bursts of light that the drawings give us from one of the greatest imaginations known to history, and with the few faded and damaged paintings, still of remarkable beauty.

MICHELANGELO TO 1505

In the Florence that Leonardo abandoned for Milan in the early 1480s, another artist of precocity and longevity, Michelangelo Buonarroti (1475–1564), was, as he put it himself, drinking in a love of stonecutters' tools with his wet-nurse's milk. By the time Leonardo returned in 1500, the young sculptor was a formidable competitor to him in the art of painting as well. Mi-

chelangelo's fierce loyalty to the Florentine Republic meant that he became its chief protagonist in the production of a new kind of heroic imagery that would represent the Republic's challenge to history. Michelangelo, rather than Leonardo, became the dominant personality of the Florentine and later the Roman versions of the High Renaissance. In fact, he dominated the sixteenth century to such a degree that it was virtually impossible for artists to escape his influence. One could accept him—and succumb—or rebel against him, but not ignore him.

Michelangelo's character and stylistic credo place him in opposition to Leonardo. Where Leonardo was skeptical, Michelangelo believed; where Leonardo was apolitical, Michelangelo was, above all, a Florentine; where Leonardo looked on the world and humanity with detachment, Michelangelo was obsessed by guilt; where Leonardo was intellectually and physically charming but seems to have cared little for those he attracted, Michelangelo was spare, taciturn, and irascible, yet consumed with a deep love for others that only in his old age was requited by the adoring reverence of his pupils; where Leonardo was endlessly absorbed in the mysteries of nature, of which the human being was only a single facet, Michelangelo scorned landscape, which appears in his art only occasionally as a fragment of bleak rock or blasted tree; where Leonardo considered the eye the window through which the soul was enabled to assess the nature of the physical world, Michelangelo in his writings extolled the eye's spheroid beauty moving inside the head or shrank from the shattering emotional effect of the spiritual radiance from eyes he loved. Throughout the seventy-five years of Michelangelo's known artistic production his main interest was in the life of the human soul as expressed in the structure and movements of the human body, which he often called the "mortal veil" of divine intention.

Michelangelo was born in a wild and barren region of the Apennines, in the village of Caprese, which clings to the ruins of a medieval castle. His father, an impoverished but pretentious gentleman named Lodovico di Simone Buonarroti, was *podestà* (governor) of this Florentine outpost. Before the child was quite a month old, Lodovico's one-year term came to an end, and the family returned to Florence, but even in his old age the artist attached special importance to having seen the light of day in the rarefied air of this world of stone. He was set to nurse on a small family property at Settignano, a village of stonecutters that had been the home of Desiderio and the Rossellino family. His remark about the origin of his love of stonecutters' tools can scarcely be ignored in light of his fondness for representing the unusual theme of the Virgin nursing the Christ Child.

In 1549, when the artist was already old, he was subjected to a questionnaire on the relative merits of painting and sculpture that was circulated among artists by the humanist and historian Benedetto Varchi. We already know that Leonardo, who was long dead, would have argued the superiority of painting. Michelangelo's reply stated that "the nearer painting approaches sculpture the better it is, and that sculpture is worse the nearer it approaches painting. Therefore it has always seemed to me that sculpture was a lantern to painting and that the difference between them is that between the sun and the moon." By sculpture Michelangelo explained that he meant works that are produced "by force of taking away [i.e., by carving off]; sculpture that is done by adding on [i.e., by putting on pieces of clay one after another] resembles painting." He thus placed himself in opposition to such sculptors as Ghiberti and Donatello, who based their works, whether in bronze or marble, on preliminary studies in clay or wax, and who exploited optical and pictorial effects.

Michelangelo's theoretical opposition did not prevent him from making sketches and finished models for his marble sculptures out of clay, wax, and other soft materials. Vasari, who worked for a while as a sculptural assistant to Michelangelo, utilized what is probably the sculptor's metaphor when he compared the process of carving a statue from a block of marble to that of lowering the water from a figure in a bath. The sculptor would draw the contours on the faces of the block, especially the front, and then pursue the profiles inward until the process of removal of the stone liberated the indwelling figure. In one of his poems, Michelangelo compared this procedure to that of the Creator in liberating man from matter.

Michelangelo's youthful desire to become an artist was opposed by his family, especially his father and uncle. These brothers fancied themselves, as Michelangelo did later, as descendants of the counts of Canossa and therefore above mechanical labors. Eventually, they yielded and placed the lad in Domenico del Ghirlandaio's studio in 1488, at the age of thirteen. He must have been skillful already, for he drew an annual salary instead of having his father pay for his indenture, as was the custom with young apprentices. He could have found no better teacher in the Florence of his day from whom to absorb the traditions and techniques of the Quattrocento. In many a passage of the Sistine Ceiling one still feels the solidity of Ghirlandaio's form and spatial structure, and even fifty years after his apprenticeship, when he was occupied with the *Last Judgment*, Michelangelo was still contemptuous of the newfangled methods of painting in oil, preferring the traditional Tuscan fresco technique that he had learned in Ghirlandaio's shop. In none of his paintings does he admit the shadows and atmosphere of Leonardo, and he always insists, where the subject permits, on the clarity and brilliance of the Florentine tradition.

He may well have taken part in the execution of Ghirlandaio's fresco cycle in the chancel of Santa Maria Novella (see figs. 363, 364), although any attempt to identify figures by the thirteen-year-old painter seems doomed to futility. He did not serve out his three-year contract because after barely a year he was invited into the house of Lorenzo the Magnificent, and he stayed in the Palazzo Medici and worked in a kind of free art school about which we could wish we knew more. It was held in the now-vanished Medici gardens, farther up the same street, opposite the Church of San Marco. At the palace he would have been able to study works of ancient art—including marble sculpture, cameos, and medals—and Renaissance paintings and sculpture. He was under the tutelage of Bertoldo di Giovanni, a sculptor who had been Donatello's assistant in the master's old age, and thus the youth could absorb Donatello's doctrine at second hand. In expeditions to Santa Croce and the Carmine, he drew from the frescoes of Giotto and Masaccio. It was in the Brancacci Chapel, in fact, that Michelangelo's comment on the ineptitude of a drawing by the young sculptor Pietro Torrigiani earned him the blow that broke his nose and disfigured him for life.

At Lorenzo's table whoever arrived first sat closest to the Magnifico, and Michelangelo must sometimes have found himself sitting near Piero the Unlucky, Lorenzo's eldest son and eventual successor; Giuliano, later to be ruler of Florence; and Giovanni, later Pope Leo X. It was a heady atmosphere of political power and intellectual performance, for although Michelangelo in all probability never learned more than a few phrases of Latin, in Lorenzo's house he came into contact with the Neoplatonists in the Magnifico's circle. Much—in the opinion of the present writer too much—has been made of these youthful influences, which the determined Neoplatonist Varchi discovered in Michelangelo's poetry but which none of his contemporaries mentioned noticing in his art.

Probably from these years—and therefore before Michelangelo was eighteen—dates what is accepted as the artist's earliest extant work, the small marble relief known as the *Madonna of the Stairs* (fig. 467). It is done in a style that Michelangelo never utilized again and that

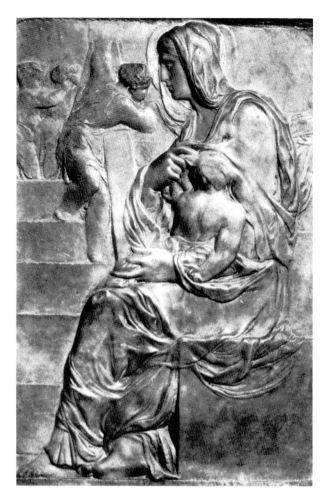

467. MICHELANGELO. *Madonna of the Stairs*. 1489–92. Marble, 21³/4 x 15³/4". Casa Buonarroti, Florence

is deeply influenced by the *rilievo schiacciato* of Donatello (see fig. 166), as well as, possibly, by some ancient relief, cameo, or coin then in the Medici collections. The classic dignity and harmony of the profile pose remind us of Greek fifth-century grave steles, but to the best of our knowledge such works were not known in Italy at this time. For the only time in the work of Michelangelo, we are not exactly sure what forms exist under the shimmering drapery that covers the Virgin's limbs (it was later said of him that his figures were nude even when clothed), and there is other evidence of his youth and immaturity. But the back and right arm of the Christ Child are extraordinary, already surpassing sculptures of the Early Renaissance in the fullness of muscular power. This same back was reused many years later in the figure of *Day* in the Medici Chapel (see fig. 557). It will be noted that in this first known work Michelangelo has chosen to represent the nursing Madonna, a theme that will reappear in grander dimensions in the *Medici Madonna* (see fig. 555). The mood of sadness that pervades the relief is probably due to Michelangelo's not-unusual attempt to suggest Christ's Passion and death at the time of his infancy. The stairs probably indicate Mary's role as Stairway to Heaven. The children in the background, who are probably angels—wingless as almost always in Michelangelo's work—are engaged

in spreading what seems less like a cloth of honor than a shroud. These background figures are unfinished, having yet to receive the final polish, while their heads are scarcely more than blocks. Already in the sculptor's adolescence, the artistic paralysis that prevented him from finishing all but a handful of his sculptural works and even some of his paintings is manifest.

Another relief from the Medici period is the *Battle of Lapiths and Centaurs* (fig. 468), whose powerful movement contrasts with the elegiac sweetness of the *Madonna of the Stairs*. Both strains coexisted in Michelangelo's complex and conflicting nature, and the dichotomy between them may be witnessed again and again, often within the same work. The battle between the Lapiths and centaurs was described by the ancient writer Ovid, and there have been attempts to identify the figures and even to question whether this is indeed the subject. What is more to the point is that Ovid's account of the mayhem between the centaurs (who attempted to carry off the Lapith women at a Lapith wedding feast) and the defenders has been reduced to symbolic and aesthetic terms. No blow connects with its intended victim, no stone strikes a human head, no club disfigures a human body. Occasionally, in this vibrant interlace of struggling figures, two actually wrestle, but this is as far as the artist will let himself go in depicting brutality.

And if the *Madonna of the Stairs* is the direct ancestor of the sibyls of the Sistine Chapel and of the *Medici Madonna*, the figures of the *Battle of Lapiths and Centaurs* are progenitors of the herculean nudes of the *Battle of Cascina* and the *Last Judgment*. The nudes are, for the most part, unfinished, and some heads in fact are still so rough that they can hardly be distinguished from the rocks wielded by the centaurs (fig. 469). With his characteristic abhorrence of the monstrous—indeed of any violence done to the human body—Michelangelo has so subordinated the horse parts of the centaurs that they are difficult to make out even in the original. The *Battle of Lapiths and Centaurs* may be characterized as among the most advanced figural compositions of its time. It is worth noting, however, that in Michelangelo the figural interlace does not, as in Pollaiuolo and Leonardo, add or multiply to construct a total geometrical shape, but produces a composition in which no clear-cut form can be deduced. It is difficult to imagine any classical work among the statuary fragments, sarcophagi, and relatively minor ancient objects available to him in Florence that this astonishing teenager had not already challenged in quality and depth of feeling.

With the death of Lorenzo in 1492, however, it was all over, and the boy found himself back in the modest house of his father in the stone street that follows the curves of the old Roman arena, near Santa Croce. If the sources are to be believed, Lorenzo's successor Piero the Unlucky did call the boy back to the Palazzo Medici for a few months but he had no more important work for him than a statue in snow. The wooden *Crucifix* (fig. 470) that many scholars identify as the one Michel-

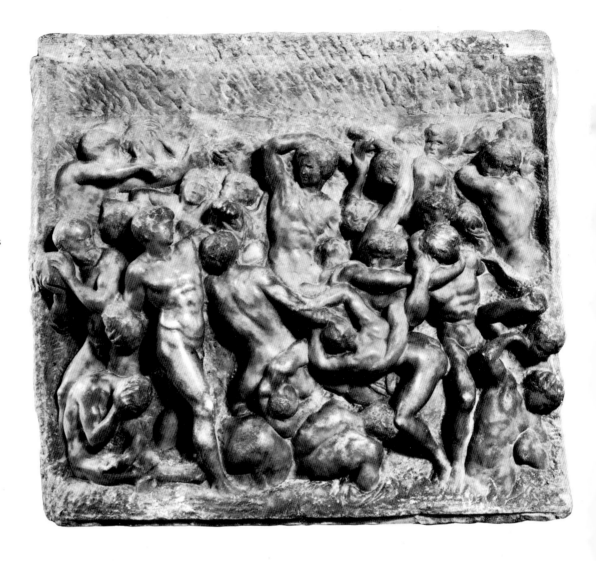

angelo made for the prior of Santo Spirito would, if it is
by Michelangelo, have been made at this time. It is in a
languorous style that contains more than an echo of
Botticellian grace, and the sculpted figure is absolutely
nude, in keeping with the artist's reverence for the human body as the mortal veil of divine intention, which
was most completely manifest in the Incarnation. Thus,
to the scandal even of his contemporaries, Michelangelo
repeatedly depicted Christ to be as gloriously nude as
any mythological Greek hero (when it was used for
public devotion the figure would certainly have had a
loincloth made of fabric). The sculpture, the only work
in wood that we know by Michelangelo, foreshadows
his later statues on a grander scale, especially the *Captive*
now known as the *Dying Slave* (see fig. 517), and the
face recalls some in the battle relief. Michelangelo is reported to have carved the *Crucifix* in gratitude for the
prior's permission to dissect corpses in the Hospital of
Santo Spirito. Unlike much of Leonardo's anatomical
study, which moved into the realm of physiology,
Michelangelo's anatomical investigations were geared toward understanding gestures and movements and how
they express spiritual life. Like Leonardo, he dissected
corpses well into his advanced years and hoped to author a treatise on anatomy for artists.

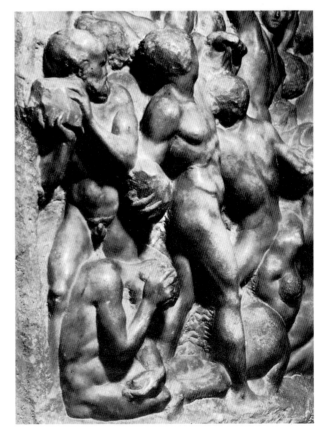

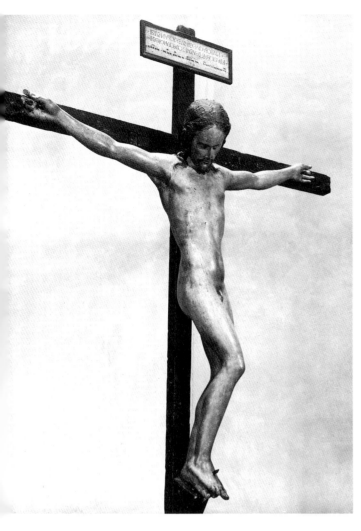

470. MICHELANGELO (attributed to). *Crucifix*. 1492.
Painted wood, height 53". Sto. Spirito, Florence. Made
as a gift for the prior of Sto. Spirito, Florence

inspiration for the twenty-one-year-old artist, it did provide contact with ancient Roman architecture, sculpture,
and painting, whose influence upon his art is incalculable. In the *Bacchus* (fig. 471), made for a rich Roman,
Michelangelo explored human flesh in a manner unprecedented since antiquity. The figure's sensuality bears
testimony to the extent to which pagan beauty fascinated the young Florentine. The god of wine, completely
nude and wreathed with vine leaves and bunches of
grapes, is shown as deeply affected by alcohol: his eyes
seem glazed and he lurches unsteadily. The grapes he
lets fall from his panther skin are caressed by a boy satyr.
There may be a hint of Christian content in the statue
for Christ, like Bacchus, was a god of wine (the Eucharist), and the mystery of drunkenness was considered to
be comparable to the mystery of death; representations

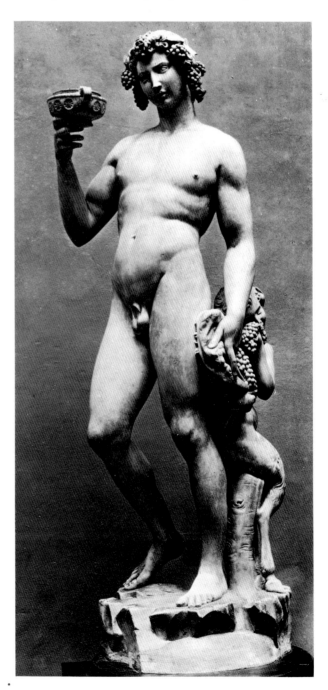

A brief visit to Venice in 1494 seems to have had little effect on either the guest or the host city, but during
Michelangelo's stay in Bologna during the winter of
1494–95 he executed three statuettes to complete the
tomb of St. Dominic. He also came into contact with
the works of Jacopo della Quercia (see figs. 178–80),
with their emphasis on the power and dignity of the
human body, whether heroically nude or enveloped by
surging waves of drapery. Jacopo's influence on Michelangelo's style was immediate and profound, and it played
an important role in the formation of some of the images on the Sistine Ceiling. Also, although its precise
connection with specific works has never been successfully demonstrated, Savonarola's preaching may well
have had an effect upon the young artist. In his old age
Michelangelo still read Savonarola's works and recalled
the sound of his voice.

Although the Rome of 1496, dominated by the Borgia pope Alexander VI, can have afforded little spiritual

471. MICHELANGELO. *Bacchus*. 1496–97. Marble,
height 79½". Bargello, Florence. Commissioned by
Jacopo Galli for the garden of his house in Rome

The High Renaissance in Florence

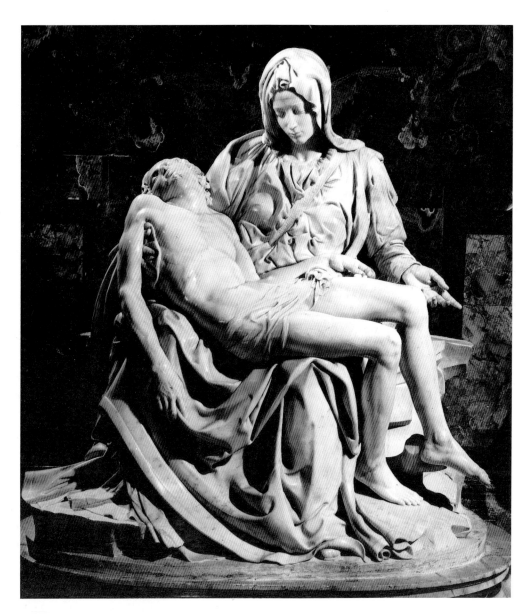

right: 472.
MICHELANGELO. *Pietà.*
1498/99–1500.
Marble, height 68½".
St. Peter's, Vatican,
Rome. Commissioned
by the French Cardinal
Jean de Bilhères
Lagraulas for the chapel
where he planned
to be buried at Old
St. Peter's

below: 473.
Head of Christ, detail
of fig. 472

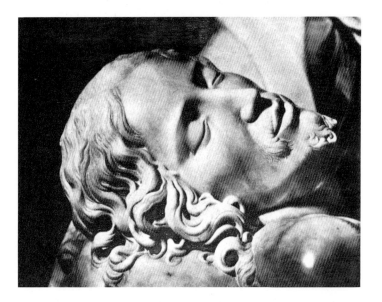

of the Drunkenness of Noah sometimes compared it to
the death of Christ. But it seems more probable that
Michelangelo's image is entirely pagan. The flat face of
the marble block, still maintained in part in the relieflike
character of the carving of the satyr and the grapes, contrasts with the unusual fullness and richness of the bodily
masses of the main figure.

In 1498 Michelangelo, then twenty-three, accepted a
commission for what became one of his most famous
works, the *Pietà* (fig. 472). This Northern subject—
common in France and Germany, it was virtually unknown in Italy—was ordered by a French cardinal who
did not survive to see the work completed. The sculptor
made a special trip to Carrara, the first of many, to find
marble of the highest quality for the group, which according to the contract was, following the typical
rhetoric of artistic contracts, expected to be "the most
beautiful work in marble which exists today in Rome."
Today one must view the work against a background of
multicolored marble whose opulence would certainly

have offended Michelangelo, and it is raised too high and has to be tilted forward by a prop of cement inserted at the back. Originally Michelangelo must have intended that the group be placed on or near the floor, so that the viewer had a clear view of the face of Christ.

After the muscular violence of the *Battle of Lapiths and Centaurs* and the sensuous richness of the *Bacchus*, it may seem strange that Michelangelo should return here to the Botticellian slenderness of the *Crucifix*, but these three apparently contrasting veins—and others besides—coexisted within the imaginative life of an artist too spontaneous and original ever to be reduced to a single stylistic formula or to submit to a single category of taste. Never did he carry refinement and delicacy to a higher pitch than in the complex rhythms of the drapery or the exquisitely finished torso and limbs of Christ. At crucial points line seems to cut into the marble flesh, especially in the features of Christ and Mary, setting up a conflict between form and contour that was to persist for several years in Michelangelo's style; the delicate curls of the moustache and beard of Christ (fig. 473), for example, are incised into the surface of the marble. No trace of pain remains in the face, and the wounds are barely noticeable.

In Michelangelo's lifetime there was speculation about the discrepancy between Mary's apparent age here and her actual years—she should be about eighteen years older than her Son, who was thirty-three at the time of his death—but if anything the artist has made her look younger than her Son. Michelangelo's answer, perhaps deliberately mystifying, was that a pure virgin will retain the appearance of youth much longer than a married woman. Michelangelo's friend Giovanni Strozzi provided a solution when, many years later, he composed a quatrain for a copy of the *Pietà*. His poem is based on the lines from Dante that appeared on Botticelli's *Enthroned Madonna with Saints* (see fig. 351): "Virgin Mother, daughter of thy Son." Michelangelo's representation, then, partakes of a timeless doctrine: the Virgin is shown as the mortal vessel of Divine Grace, the body through which divinity took on human flesh, and the question of age thus becomes irrelevant.

Vasari records that when the group was first placed in St. Peter's, an astonished crowd of Lombards thought it was by a fellow countryman, whereupon Michelangelo stole into St. Peter's at night and added his signature. It is the only genuine signature that appears on any of his sculptures. In view of the artist's remark that he drew in the love of stonecutters' tools with his wet-nurse's milk, it is noteworthy that the place he chose was a strap crossing the Virgin's chest. Neither to Michelangelo nor to the artists of his time would there have been the least suggestion of irreverence in such a fact, or any conflict between the universal and the personal levels of symbolism apparent in the group.

The only preserved panel picture Michelangelo painted entirely himself—and even this seems incomplete here and there in the background—is the *Doni*

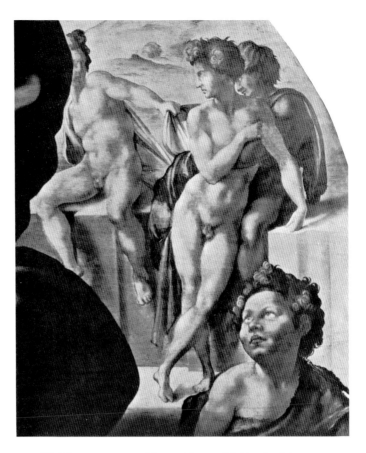

474. MICHELANGELO. Young Men and Infant St. John the Baptist, detail of *Doni Madonna* (see colorplate 85, p. 454). c. 1503. Panel. Uffizi Gallery, Florence. Probably commissioned by Angelo Doni

Madonna (colorplate 85, p. 454), so called because it was the property of Angelo Doni, a prosperous weaver, and it was probably painted in 1503 to celebrate his wedding to Maddalena Strozzi, of the famous banking family. This couple was immortalized a few years later in Raphael's portraits (see figs. 484, 485). The painting is a tondo, a form often associated with marriage in Renaissance art, but the composition is indebted to Leonardo's lost cartoon for the *Madonna and Child with St. Anne* (see p. 444), which Michelangelo must have seen in 1501, when he had returned to Florence from Rome and was at work on the *David*. The metallic orange of Joseph's mantle clashes with Mary's rose tunic in a manner that anticipates the astonishing colors of the Sistine Ceiling. The compressed grouping has the power of a spring coiled tightly within the frame, and this tension is increased by the sharp and brilliant modeling of the folds of the drapery masses and the color.

The composition is stabilized by the horizontal band of stone separating foreground and background. In the smoothly polished surfaces and brilliantly exact contours of the foreground figures, Michelangelo created the masses as if he were working with marble instead of pigment. The modeling of the nude youths in the background, however, is softer (fig. 474); possibly Michelangelo began all the figures in this fluid style and only gradually brought them to the almost obsessive finish seen in Mary and the Christ Child. The nudes, direct ancestors of the nudes of the Sistine Ceiling, show an attitude toward pulsating human flesh as a continuous substance that is different from the perfectly articulated and smoothly functioning human machines designed by Leonardo (see fig. 447).

The difficult meaning of the picture has provoked some farfetched explanations. Like so many of Michelangelo's abstruse visual symbols, the *Doni Madonna* may perpetually defy exact interpretation, but certain elements are clear. Mary and Joseph appear to be presenting or giving the Christ Child. A prayer for the Octave of Epiphany exhorts God to look down in mercy on the gifts of his Church, by which we offer "that which is signified, immolated, and received by these gifts, Jesus Christ"; *doni* is the Italian for "gifts," *dona* the Latin. The curious dry font or tank on whose edge the nude youths sit or lean is a half moon, a motif from the Strozzi arms, which appear in the frame of the painting. It was customary for family names to appear pictographically. Pebbles (*sassetti*) are evident in some of Ghirlandaio's Sassetti Chapel frescoes, and we have seen the importance of such symbols in works designed for the Medici. The symbols of the Della Rovere family in the Sistine Ceiling are even more strongly visible.

The Epistle for the Fifth Sunday after Epiphany is drawn from Colossians 3:12–17, and in the preceding chapter (2:17) St. Paul characterizes the new moon as a "shadow of things to come, but the body is of Christ." The Epistle deals with Baptism as a death to old life and a resurrection in Christ, and the infant Baptist appears in the font. (The first four sons of Angelo and Maddalena Doni, all of whom died shortly after birth, were named Giovanni Battista.) The Epistle urges the faithful to strip themselves of their old persons and deeds and to put on the new, and it lists two groups of five vices, each of which must be renounced. There are five nude youths (and five sculptured medallions in the frame Michelangelo designed for the picture). The five virtues that are to be put on are "mercy, kindness, humility, modesty, patience." The five youths have partly or entirely removed their colored garments and are stretching out white cloths that may symbolize a new purity. We are asked to forgive one another "if any have complaint against another," and the two youths at the left turn their attentions toward those at the right, as if to dissuade them from their quarrel.

Some symbols are traditional. The flower that rises near the edge of the font recalls Isaiah's prophecy of the Virgin Birth, "for he shall grow up before him as a tender plant, and as a root out of a dry ground." The bay of water in the background, which we have seen in Filippino Lippi, Giovanni Bellini, and Leonardo, recalls Mary's title as "Port of the Shipwrecked." The strange pose of the Christ Child, treading on the Virgin's arm, may refer to the prophecy of the Virgin Birth in Lamentations, "The Lord hath trodden the virgin, the daughter of Judah, as in a winepress" (1:15). The position of

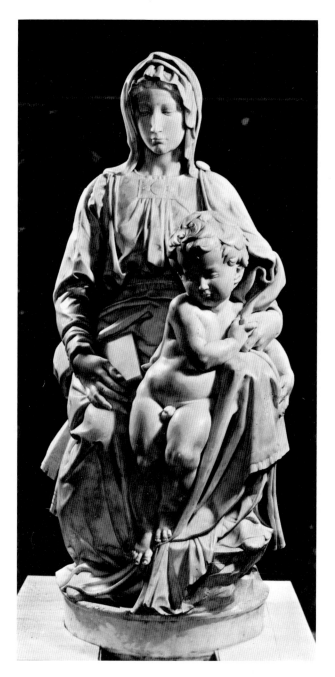

475. MICHELANGELO. *Bruges Madonna*. 1503–4. Marble, height 48". Church of Onze Lieve Vrouwe, Bruges

the Virgin, seated lower than her husband in spite of Mary's rank as Queen of Heaven, comes again from the Epistle to the Colossians, "Wives, submit yourselves unto your own husbands" (3:18), and the total configuration may come from the Epistle for the Sunday in the Octave of the Epiphany, repeated today in the Mass of the Holy Family: "[Jesus] went down with them . . .and was subject unto them" (Luke 2:51). In all probability the picture was intended to celebrate the virtues of Christian marriage for Angelo and Maddalena and to place their conjugal life under the protection of the Holy Family, although we should not exclude the possibility that the painting might allude to the death of their first child. If this is the case, the date of the painting would be later.

The *Doni Madonna* is inseparable from the *Bruges Madonna* (fig. 475), probably carved at about the same time and sold in 1506 to a Flemish wool merchant who took it to Bruges. The Christ Child, whose gravity and beauty shine so unexpectedly from his chubby features, must have been done from the same model used for the Doni Christ Child. The Virgin is seated upon rocks, with one knee elevated, like that of Joseph in the *Doni Madonna*. Christ, still holding her hand, ventures forth with one foot. The head of the pensive Virgin, derived from that of Mary in the *Pietà*, is more ample in proportion, with a new emphasis on the breadth of the forehead and the soft fullness of the eyebrows. The Virgin's arms, which emerge from slits in her mantle, were badly chipped when the statue was taken to Paris by Napoleon's troops.

As compared with the *Pietà*, the group is more compact, and both drapery and anatomical forms are simpler and grander, the masses already foretelling some of the majesty of the Sistine Ceiling. The statue is lovingly finished, although some passages at the back never received their final polish. Only occasionally in Michelangelo's mature work will we reencounter the haunting beauty of the Virgin's countenance or the sense of deep and sad repose found in this tranquil group.

In contrast is the dynamism of the *Taddei Madonna*, a tondo, also undated but probably contemporary, that Michelangelo blocked out for Francesco Taddei but never completed (fig. 476). The Christ Child is shown fleeing to the protection of his Mother's arms, away from a bird held out to him by John the Bapist. Under this apparently playful imagery is concealed a deeper meaning, for the bird is a symbol of the human soul, and the Baptist is here relinquishing to Christ the responsibility for cleansing the soul from sin—a responsibility that can only be discharged through Christ's Passion and death. A second level of meaning probably involves the protection of the Florentine Republic, in which Francesco held high office, and of which St. John is the patron saint. In the early Cinquecento, when the Republic was threatened by the armies of Cesare Borgia and the attempts of the Medici to return to power, images of the Virgin and Child with the Baptist in the open landscape are sufficiently numerous to form a special type (see p. 470). Once the Medici regained control of the Republic after 1512, the type to all intents and purposes died out. Michelangelo derived the pose of Christ from a Roman sarcophagus representing Medea about to slaughter her children, a parallel between the sacrificed children of the barbarian princess and the sacrifice of Christ that would not have offended the Renaissance.

The unfinished portions of the *Taddei Madonna* show the stages of Michelangelo's working practice. The hair of the Baptist and portions of the hair of Christ, like the whole of the background, are roughed out with the

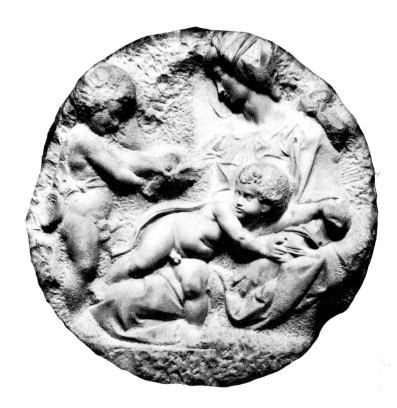

476. MICHELANGELO. *Taddei Madonna*. c. 1500–1502. Marble, diameter 43". Royal Academy of Fine Arts, London. The first owner was Taddeo Taddei

pointed cylindrical chisel. One can still observe the marks of the drill used to profile major elements. The Baptist has reached a somewhat higher state of completion under the strokes of the coarse, two-toothed chisel, while the face of the Virgin and almost all of the Christ Child are finished in all essentials with the three-toothed chisel, by whose manipulation Michelangelo achieved a breathing, pulsating surface much praised by Vasari. All that is missing is the finishing with a file and the polishing with pumice and straw pads. The passionate grouping within the circle, a variant on the problem of the *Doni Madonna*, results in a powerful composition, but despite the excitement offered by the unfinished surface, we would be mistaken to suppose that Michelangelo consciously intended the work to look as it now does. It is hard to believe that the *Taddei Madonna* would have lost any of its fire if it had been carried to the same pitch of completion as the *Pietà* or the *Bruges Madonna*.

During the opening years of the Cinquecento, when Michelangelo was creating these and other works for public and private patrons, he was also carrying out a far greater responsibility, the colossal *David* in marble (fig. 477) intended for one of the buttresses of the Cathedral of Florence, a commission that he accepted in 1501. The huge marble block had been languishing since the 1460s, when it had been partially blocked out by the sculptor Agostino di Duccio. Agostino was most likely executing a model designed by the aged Donatello, and the latter's death probably caused the officials of the

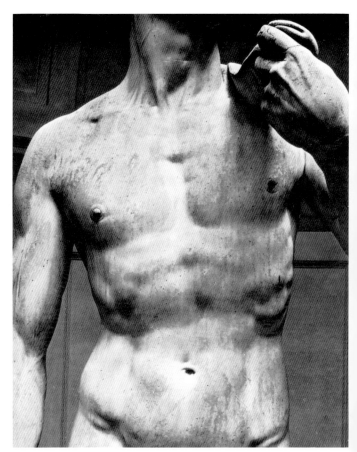

478. Torso of David, detail of fig. 477

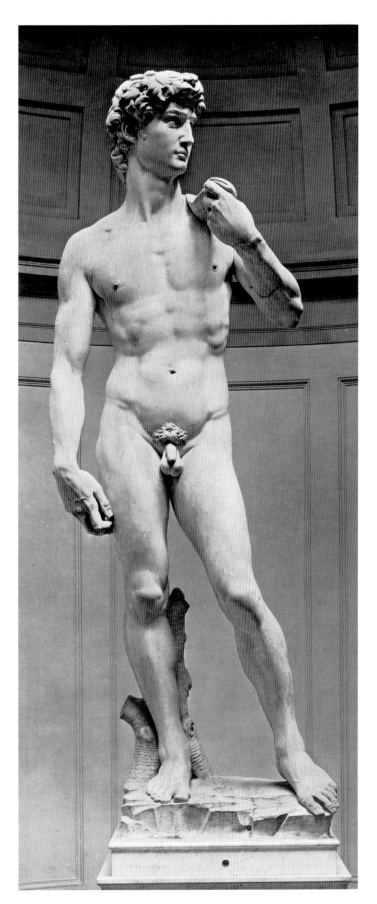

477. MICHELANGELO. *David*. 1501–4. Marble, height 14' 3". Accademia, Florence. Commissioned by the Opera of the Cathedral to be placed on a buttress below the dome, but originally placed in front of the Palazzo dei Priori (see colorplate 16, p. 24)

Opera del Duomo to abandon the project. Donatello's colossal *Joshua*, in terra-cotta painted to resemble stone, had long been in position on one of the buttresses, where it survived into the seventeenth century, and Donatello and Brunelleschi had made a model for a huge *Hercules* for the same program.

Such was the magnificence of the *David* when Michelangelo completed it in 1504 that the Florentines were reluctant to have it placed so high and, as in the case of Donatello's marble *David* nearly a century earlier, the Republic took over. A commission was formed to decide where the statue should go, and it heard testimony from Filippino Lippi, Botticelli, Leonardo, Giuliano and Antonio da Sangallo, Piero di Cosimo, and other artists, as well as artisans and other citizens. Many of the opinions are recorded, very nearly verbatim. Leonardo wanted the colossus to be in the Loggia dei Priori, the great three-arched portico for public ceremonies to the west of the Palazzo dei Priori that was later renamed the Loggia dei Lanzi (colorplate 16, p. 24). The Sangallo brothers insisted that it be kept out of the rain because the marble was soft and had already suffered from exposure. Piero di Cosimo suggested that the commission ask Michelangelo. There is no record that it ever did, and no one knows what his opinion would have been. But it is unlikely that he would have favored a position in the

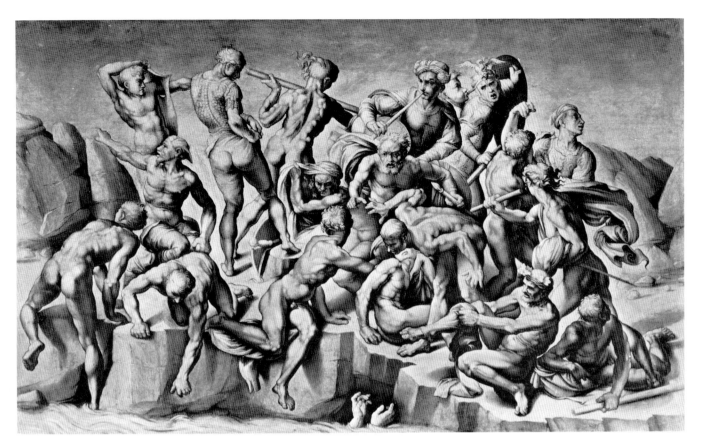

479. Copy after MICHELANGELO. *Battle of Cascina*. 1504–6 (destroyed).
Early 16th-century copy of central section, by ARISTOTILE DA SANGALLO. Grisaille on panel, 30 x 52".
Collection the Earl of Leicester, Nolkham Mall (Courtesy Courtauld Institute of Art, London).
Michelangelo's original was commissioned by the Florentine Republic for the Salone del Cinquecento
at the Palazzo dei Priori, Florence

Loggia dei Priori, which would have condemned the statue's back to permanent shadow, not to mention dwarfing the colossus by contrast with the huge, open arches of the Loggia. In any case, the statue went where the herald of the Republic wanted it—in front of the principal entrance to the Palazzo dei Priori as a symbol of the valiant Republic, which had elected Piero Soderini *gonfaloniere* for life and was staking everything on the Republic's continued freedom from the Medici. It took four days to haul the statue on rollers to its final position, and one night it was attacked with stones by a band of youths, probably Medici supporters.

The political symbolism of the work, recognized by the officials of the Republic in 1504, had been present from the start in all the colossi planned for the Duomo, a building of the highest civic as well as religious importance. The *David* differs from its Florentine predecessors in its total and triumphant nudity, in keeping with Michelangelo's views on the divinity of the human body, and in its emphatic muscularity. The prudery of Soderini's Republic kept the statue hidden from public gaze for two months until a brass girdle with twenty-eight hammered copper leaves could be devised and hung about the young hero's waist!

Michelangelo's hero is a boy of perhaps sixteen, not fully grown, but with the powerful muscles of a child of the people, rather than an effete aristocrat like Verrocchio's *David* (see fig. 336). Michelangelo chose an unusual moment to represent, for he shows David before the battle. The sling is over his shoulder and the stone rests in his right hand, but his muscles are taut and a defiant scowl seizes his face. The figure pulls powerfully to the left, away from the implied enemy, and David's apprehension is further indicated by the swelling veins in the hand and the sucking in of breath revealed in the tense muscles of the abdomen. Michelangelo's *David*, his first adventure in the new realm of the colossal, is also intended as a symbol, not only of the Republic, but also of all humanity raised to a new power—a plane of superhuman grandeur and beauty.

At the time of the third expulsion of the Medici from Florence, in 1527, a bench thrown from a window of the Palazzo dei Priori shattered the *David*'s left arm and hand. The pieces were rescued by Vasari and Francesco Salviati, in their teens at the time, and kept until they could be reattached many years later. Just as the Sangallo brothers predicted, the soft marble of the statue eventually suffered from exposure, and the fine finish on the top of the head and the upper surfaces of the shoulders is gone and in several other places it is damaged. In the nineteenth century the statue was removed to a sky-lighted rotunda built especially for it at the Accademia.

The pose, which was partly conditioned by the shallow shape of the block and Agostino di Duccio's efforts to carve a figure, must also be understood in terms of the intended position of the statue on the Duomo. Placed on one of the buttress pedestals (see fig. 132), the young hero would have looked defiantly out over the city, seeming to emerge from the very forces of the architecture. The knotty muscles and heaving rib cage (fig. 478), the heavy projections of the hair, the sharp undercutting of the eyes, and the frowning brow were all intended to register from a distance. In the forms of the face, the conflict of mass and line, which we have seen as early as the *Pietà*, reaches a climax of intensity.

Shortly after the *David* was set in place, the sculptor received his first commission for a colossal work of painting, a fresco of the *Battle of Cascina* for the Sala del Cinquecento in the Palazzo dei Priori, the same room where Leonardo had already been working for a year on the cartoon for the *Battle of Anghiari* (see p. 447). There is no evidence that Michelangelo objected or that he declared that he was a sculptor, not a painter. The moment chosen for his subject may seem trivial—the Florentine soldiers, cooling off in the Arno, are called out by a sudden alarm and caught in the act of struggling into their clothes and armor. Yet, like its predecessor, the *Battle of Lapiths and Centaurs* (see fig. 468), the *Battle of Cascina* gave Michelangelo the opportunity to demonstrate his mastery of the nude body. Working in secret in the Hospital of Sant'Onofrio, he produced a composition of interlocking figures, turning, twisting, crouching, climbing, tugging boots over wet legs, blowing trumpets, reaching to help comrades. Michelangelo probably derived much of his knowledge of figures climbing out of the water and pulling on clothes from visits to a Florentine public bath, which Leonardo frequented every Saturday for the same purpose. According to Vasari, some of the figures were drawn with crosshatching, others with shading and lighted with white.

Although Michelangelo probably commenced painting on the huge fresco after his return to Florence from Bologna in 1506, neither the unfinished painting nor a scrap of the cartoon remains. The latter, during its brief existence, became something of an art school in its own right and was widely imitated by Florentine masters of the High Renaissance and the Mannerist period as an example of how nude figures in action ought to be drawn. The best evidence we have for the original appearance of the cartoon is Michelangelo's drawings for the figures in the foreground, as well as for the battles of mounted warriors taking place in the background at either side. A copy (fig. 479) shows only the central part of the composition, which must have been an awesome thing, bursting with a new vision of the powers of the human body.

RAPHAEL IN PERUGIA AND FLORENCE

After Leonardo and Michelangelo, the third and youngest member of the trio of High Renaissance masters, Raffaello Santi (or Sanzio; 1483–1520), known to us as Raphael, comes almost as an anticlimax. He was not an innovator in the same sense as were Leonardo and Michelangelo. He seldom attempted to push his paintings to the same point of completeness as did his older contemporaries, and he sometimes glossed over imperfect observation or handed grand ideas to more or less gifted pupils for execution. Yet for four centuries Raphael has stood as the perfect High Renaissance painter, probably because of his idealism. In his art, noble individuals move with dignity and grace through a calm, intelligible, and ordered world. His pictures mirror Renaissance aspirations for human conduct and Renaissance goals for the human mind. He synthesized the movements of his figures and the spaces of his compositions into ideal structures that are integrated and harmonized from the picture plane to the point of infinity. But Raphael's order is not merely intellectual or contrived. His figures seem to be impelled by an energy that causes them to twist and turn gracefully and to assume oval and spherical forms and compositions. So easy is this motion, so harmonious the relations of the figures, that even at moments of high drama his pictures seem to radiate a superhuman calm.

Born in Urbino, Raphael was brought up in its extraordinary atmosphere of literary, philosophic, and artistic culture and cosmopolitan elegance. His father was Giovanni Santi, a mediocre painter and versifier on whose rhymed chronicle we depend for much of our information about the reputation of Quattrocento painters. Both father and son seem to have had access to the Montefeltro court and to the Palazzo Ducale (see colorplate 70, p. 359). There, in spaces of the utmost harmony and beauty, the young Raphael could absorb influences from the art of Piero della Francesca, Botticelli, the Laurana brothers, Uccello, Melozzo da Forlì, the Spaniard Alonso Berruguete, and the Netherlander Justus of Ghent. From its windows and from the steep streets of the city lined with austerely simple brick houses, Raphael looked out over a magnificent landscape filled with color and light.

When Raphael was eleven, his father died. We are not certain at what age the boy went to Perugia to be apprenticed to Perugino, but according to Vasari he was brought to Perugino's studio by his father, who had said that the artistic dictator of Perugia was "equal in age and endeavor" to Leonardo. Raphael absorbed with facility the virtues and clichés of Perugino's style and rapidly became the outstanding member of a busy workshop; by the age of sixteen he was already influencing other artists. At the same time he was learning how to manage the atelier system, which during his maturity in Rome would help him maintain a massive production schedule. Often it is nearly impossible to separate the style of Raphael from that of his master. The young artist's hand must have been at work in many of Perugino's major commissions. And even in the *Marriage of the Virgin* (colorplate 86, p. 455), which Raphael proudly signed and dated in 1504, his debt is obvious when we make a comparison with Perugino's *Christ Giving the Keys to St. Peter* (see colorplate 67, p. 356). There is the same array of foreground figures, the same polygonal background temple, the same intervening piazza. Even the clear, simple colors of the painting—the cloudless blue sky, the strong, deep blues, roses, and yellows of the drapery, the sun-warmed tan of the stone, and the blue-green hills—are derived from Perugino.

A second glance will disclose how the twenty-one-year-old painter improved on his master. The serenity of this altarpiece, which is the crowning achievement of Raphael's earliest period, results from a High Renaissance integration of form and space. It was commissioned for an altar dedicated to the Virgin's wedding ring in a church in Città di Castello, where Raphael painted several other pictures. According to the *Golden Legend*, the suitors for Mary, a virgin in the Temple, were to present rods to the high priest and Mary's hand would be granted to the one whose rod bloomed. The fortunate Joseph is shown with his flowering rod in one hand, while the other, bearing a ring, is joined to Mary's by the high priest. On the left stand the other Temple virgins, on the right the rejected suitors, one of whom breaks his barren rod over his knees. The graceful figures are woven into a closely knit unity unknown in Perugino's art. The perspective orthogonals lead past the steps into the Temple, and we look directly through it to the horizon, while hills embrace the structure, whose dome is identified with the arch of the frame.

The architecture of the Temple reflects the ideas of Raphael's fellow townsman, the much older Bramante, who two years earlier had been authorized to create the Tempietto (see fig. 498); it was not completed until after 1511, and this painted structure appears to be a precursor. One wonders, however, what Bramante or any other practicing architect would have thought of the scrolls treated like metal springs in which Raphael's characteristic spirals discharge against the sky. Despite its radial character, reflecting the architectural ideas of Leonardo (see fig. 449) even more than those of Bramante, Raphael's design—a multifaceted building, each of whose sides is treated as a separate plane—still belongs stylistically to the Quattrocento. Its lofty shape also contains more than a hint of the Dome of the Rock (on the site of Solomon's Temple in Jerusalem and often identified with it by travelers), some knowledge of whose shape may well have reached Raphael's inquiring mind.

In gratitude for the Order of the Garter conferred upon him by Henry VII of England, the duke of Urbino commissioned Raphael to paint a picture of England's patron, St. George, as a Knight of the Garter slaying the dragon (fig. 480). It was presented to the king by Raphael's friend Baldassare Castiglione, author of *Il libro del cortegiano*, whom the artist later immortal-

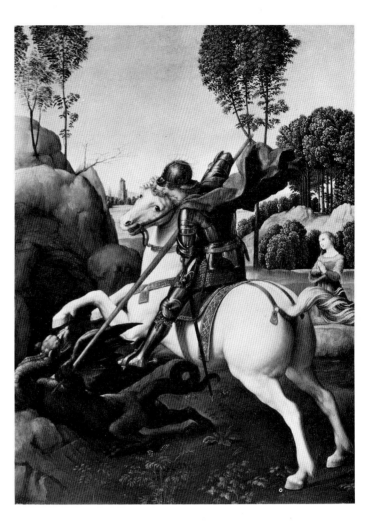

480. RAPHAEL. *St. George and the Dragon*. 1504–5. Panel, 11⅛ x 8½". National Gallery of Art, Washington, D.C. (Mellon Collection). Commissioned by Guidobaldo da Montefeltro, Duke of Urbino, as a gift for King Henry VII of England

ized in a portrait (see fig. 529). The combat between St. George and the dragon had already been represented by Raphael in another small picture, but this version betrays the influence of Florentine art, especially Leonardo's *Battle of Anghiari*, to such a degree that we suspect that the painter must have visited the Tuscan metropolis. He also must have visited Rome, as the Torre della Milizia, a medieval structure still standing in the ancient Imperial Forums, is portrayed just above the muzzle of the horse. Now the broad, curving rhythms of Raphael's forms are integrated in a new way. The warrior saint on his rearing white charger is crossed with the masses of the landscape in an X-shape, so that the downward thrust of the lance discharges into the monster's breast all the gathered-up energies of the picture. From the painter's proud signature on the bridle to the spiraling curves of the horse's tail and the clarity of the foliage, the forms have taken on a metallic tension and precision. Such luminous effects as the gleaming armor and the reflection of the princess in the water are rendered with almost Netherlandish delicacy.

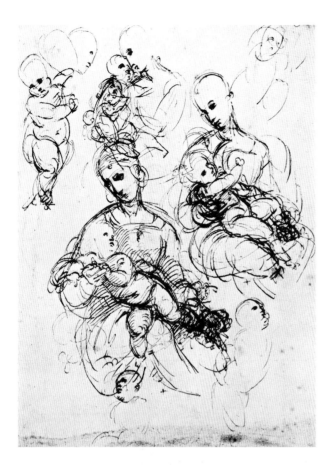

481. RAPHAEL. *Studies of the Madonna and Child.* c. 1505–8. Pen and ink, 10 x 7¼". British Museum, London

and foot. Most of the series belong to this new type, which we might call the Madonna of the Land because an open expanse of Florentine countryside seems to be placed under the protection of the Virgin and Child and of the infant Baptist, patron of the city. The background often shows, as here, the body of water that appears in the *Doni Madonna* and its many Florentine predecessors and probably has the same meaning (see pp. 463–64). Here Raphael has, as throughout the series, let the Virgin's neckline dip to follow the curves of the horizon and built up her shoulders to make them as high as the hills. The clear, simple coloring and the easy upward movement of reciprocally balancing forms are Raphael's own, as is the return of energy from the downcast eyes of the Virgin to the group below. But the astonishing purity of form, particularly in the head of the Virgin, suggests that even in this High Renaissance painting he had been studying the unearthly beauty of Fra Angelico's shapes and lines (see fig. 210). The halo, now reduced to a simple circle of gold seen in depth, enhances the grace of the linear movement and completes the balance between the ovoid forms and the distant landscape spaces.

One could argue that to Leonardo or Michelangelo, Raphael's Florentine Madonnas might have looked less complete than their own works, because Raphael was not interested in the problems of anatomy and expression that were important to them. To Raphael a picture was complete once its main masses were posed in a satisfying relationship, and line, color, and surface had a fluid interrelationship; at this point in his career he was not interested in defining shapes further. Nonetheless, in these Florentine Madonna compositions Raphael presents a noble and serene existence in which pictorial harmonies seem less a human creation than a natural emanation from the divine figures he portrays. These gentle, blond Virgins and gravely sweet children are gracefully poised against the answering background of hills and deep-blue sky.

In the *Small Cowper Madonna* (fig. 483), one of the most intimate of the series, the Virgin is seated upon a low bench before a landscape of open, road-traversed meadows and clumps of trees, reflected in a still lake on one side, on the other climbing the rounded slopes of a hill. On its summit stands a church that closely resembles the sanctuary of San Bernardino outside Urbino. The asymmetry of the hills is related to the pose of Christ's figure, and the smooth, gliding forms of the Virgin's hair are continued in the veils that descend from her head and course lightly about her shoulders and bust. Christ's head moves slightly away as his arms complete the circling motion of the veils. And the two divergent yet harmonious shapes are echoed in the haloes, delicate lines of gold against the blue. It was the beautiful and deceptively easy example of Raphael's Madonnas, not the unattainable ideals of Leonardo and Michelangelo, that was repeated continuously by the secondary painters of Florence for the next fifteen years.

Probably sometime in 1505 Raphael decided to settle in Florence, where Perugino had painted so many frescoes and altarpieces. He fell into an avid market. It seems that appetites excited by the unattainable Leonardo and Michelangelo could be satisfied rapidly by Raphael; in three years, he painted no fewer than seventeen surviving Madonnas and Holy Families plus other major works for Florentine patrons. Unaffected by the conflicts and problems that tormented Leonardo and Michelangelo, Raphael glided from one harmonious creation to another as serenely as a figure skater. Pen drawings (fig. 481) show how he worked: even before he had decided just where the features were to go, Raphael let his hand revolve in a series of spontaneous curving motions, not unlike the flourishes of old-fashioned penmanship. The resultant ovoid and spiral forms convey the energies of the figures at a moment prior to the determination of form and underlie the smoothly finished shapes of the completed paintings.

Once the relationship of masses was decided, Raphael condensed them into a Leonardesque pyramid. Probably the first of the series, dated 1505 by the inscription on the border of the Virgin's garment, is the *Madonna of the Meadows* (fig. 482), which still contains echoes of Leonardo's *Madonna and Child with St. Anne* (see colorplate 84, p. 453), especially in the placing of the Virgin's leg

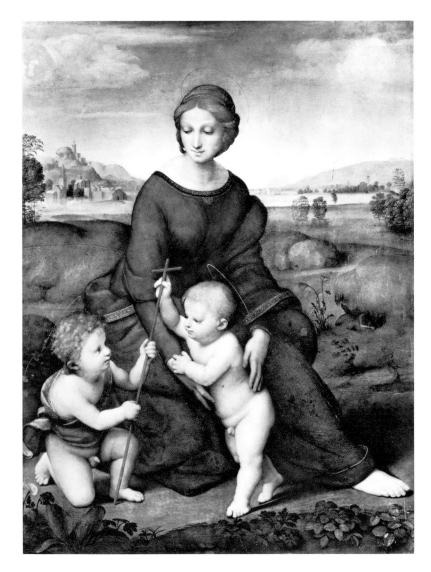

482. RAPHAEL. *Madonna of the Meadows.* 1505. Panel, 44½ x 34¼". Kunsthistorisches Museum, Vienna. Perhaps commissioned by Taddeo Taddei

It is a curious fact that some of the most convincing and accurate portraitists—Raphael, Holbein, Poussin, Ingres—sharply separated this vein of their production from the idealism of their more formal work. Raphael, cool and detached by nature, did not interpose his own feelings between the sitter and the observer, with the result that the subject's character is suggested as never before in Italian portraiture. Even here, it should be noted, he did not dwell on the individual idiosyncrasies in the manner of the Netherlandish realists. He set his Florentine patrons, like his Madonnas, against a background of landscape and sky delicately adjusted to the shapes of their bodies and the forces of their personalities.

Angelo Doni, for example (fig. 484), relaxes outdoors with one arm on a balustrade, the shaggy masses of his hair reflected in the trees at the lower right, the bulky shapes of his arms and hands in the low hills of the background. The matronly forms of his wife, Maddalena Strozzi Doni (fig. 485), are also integrated with the landscape, to the point that the artist repeated the pattern of the beaded border of her transparent shoulder veil in the foliage of the slender tree. As in Perugino's

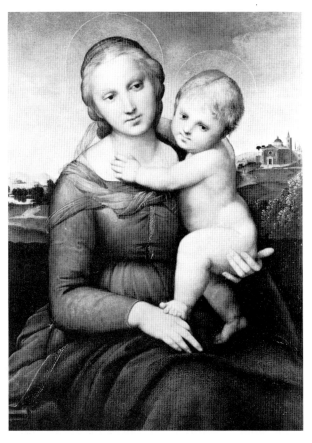

483. RAPHAEL. *Small Cowper Madonna.* c. 1505. Panel, 23½ x 17⅜". National Gallery of Art, Washington, D.C.

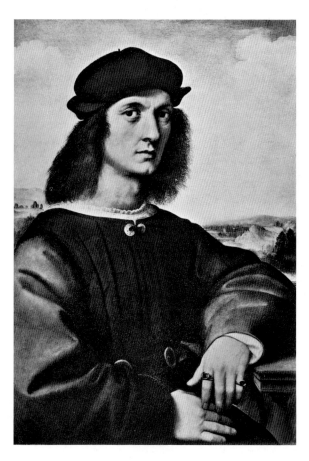

484. RAPHAEL. *Angelo Doni*. c. 1505. Panel,
24½ x 17¼". Pitti Gallery, Florence. Probably
commissioned by Angelo Doni

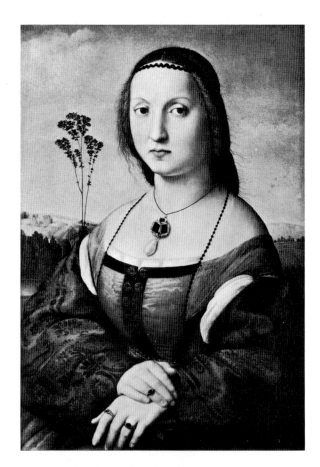

485. RAPHAEL. *Maddalena Strozzi Doni*. c. 1505.
Panel, 24½ x 17¼". Pitti Gallery, Florence. Probably
commissioned by Angelo Doni

Francesco delle Opere (see fig. 380), an effect of energy is obtained by individual wisps of hair silhouetted against the sky. The wealthy young wool merchant is impressive—cool, self-contained, firm. The portrait of his wife, however, has to compete with her obvious prototype, the *Mona Lisa* (see fig. 463). There are no mysteries concealed by this young woman—but neither, at this juncture, are there many in Raphael's art, save for his uncanny sense of proportion and balance. To the successful young painter, in command of the resources of the new style, the unknowable of Leonardo may not have seemed worth knowing. He seems to have been satisfied with his compositional perfection and, in these portraits as never in his Madonnas, he devoted some overtime to the careful modeling of the features and hands of the husband and wife, even to their rings, to the damask and moiré of Maddalena's dress, and to the careful approximation of her shoulders and chest to the shape and texture of the pearl that hangs from her pendant. Like Michelangelo, Raphael was destined to enter a new dimension once he left Florence for papal Rome, a crowning phase of his activities that belongs to the following chapter.

FRA BARTOLOMMEO

From his Florentine drawings, we know that Raphael was familiar with the works of Leonardo and Michelangelo. He also learned and adapted a great deal from, and may as well have imparted much to, a generally underrated Florentine named Baccio della Porta (1472–1517), who is known to us as Fra Bartolommeo after his assumption of the monastic habit and his temporary retirement to San Marco in 1500. By the time Raphael arrived in Florence, Fra Bartolommeo was at work on his lyrical *Vision of St. Bernard* (fig. 486), an obvious attempt to update Filippino Lippi's painting of the same subject (see colorplate 63, p. 304) in terms of the new High Renaissance style. Everything immediate, personal, and introspective and all references to daily existence have been discarded in the search for a new idealism. The saint kneels before a classical pedestal on which books are open, but we are not asked to imagine that this is, as in Filippino, his outdoor study. He is where he is for compositional and symbolic purposes, and he is backed up by two other saints (apparently Anthony Abbot and John the Evangelist) from other eras.

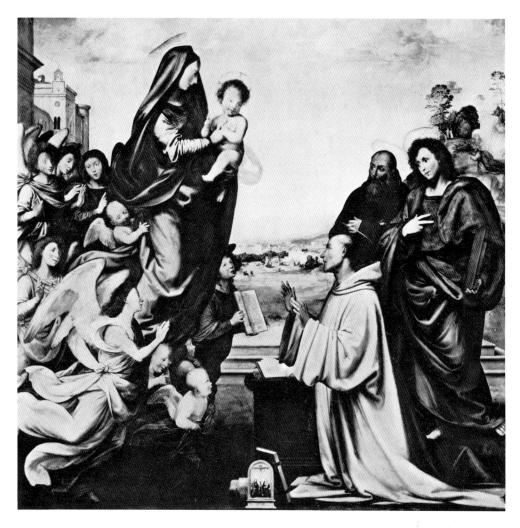

486. FRA BARTOLOMMEO. *Vision of St. Bernard.* 1504–7. Panel, 84 x 86¼".
Accademia, Florence. Commissioned for the Badia, Florence

In contrast to Filippino's version, Mary is a completely heavenly vision, touching nothing earthly with her feet or hands, and is borne by angels as she carries her smiling Child, while one of the angels holds before the saint an open book at which he does not even glance, so lost is he in the ecstatic realization of a transcendent superreality. The picture is in poor condition—much of the upper surface is lost—but the atmospheric landscape is intact, and the elements of figures and drapery move with a grace that must have struck the young Raphael with the force of revelation. Fra Bartolommeo did not entirely invent, but merely modernized, this kind of broad curvilinear movement. Although his forms possess the gravity and amplitude of the High Renaissance, he had certainly been admiring the linear sweep of his great monastic forebears such as Lorenzo Monaco, whose *Annunciation*, with a similarly floating Angel Gabriel, was already in place on an altar of the Badia, the church for which Fra Bartolommeo's painting was intended. And the unusual device of a little picture-within-a-picture of the *Crucifixion* is probably borrowed from Fra Angelico's altarpiece for Fra Bartolommeo's home monastery of

San Marco (see fig. 207), but Fra Bartolommeo has extended the illusion by leaning a book against it. For him, as for Fra Angelico, the device serves as a foreground counterpart for the vanishing point of perspective, in an attempt to achieve spatial harmony. His is probably the first of a series of High Renaissance visionary Madonnas, and it is the ancestor of Michelangelo's floating Virgin for the 1513 version of the tomb of Julius II (see pp. 503–4) and of Raphael's *Sistine Madonna* (see fig. 527). The purity of Fra Bartolommeo's lines and volumes was a major source of inspiration for Raphael well into his Roman period.

LUCA SIGNORELLI

Two masters, Luca Signorelli and Piero di Cosimo, who are generally discussed in the context of the Quattrocento, are discussed here because their major works are incomprehensible without prior consideration of the early achievements of Leonardo and Michelangelo. One would have to strain a point to consider either painter a representative of the High Renaissance, and neither was

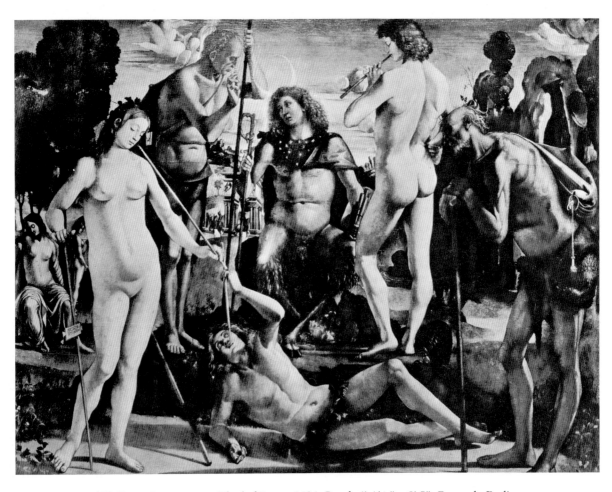

487. LUCA SIGNORELLI. *School of Pan*. c. 1496. Panel, 6' 4¹/2" x 8' 5". Formerly Berlin, destroyed 1945. Probably painted for Lorenzo de' Medici

much of a worldly success after about 1505, in competition with the developed Cinquecento style of Michelangelo, Raphael, and their many imitators.

Signorelli (after 1444–1523) was born in Cortona, a Florentine subject town in southern Tuscany. He was trained initially, according to Vasari, by Piero della Francesca, and he later went to Florence, where he worked for many years and was deeply influenced by the works of Antonio del Pollaiuolo. He was called to Rome to complete the cycle of frescoes on the walls of the Sistine Chapel (see p. 328), which had apparently been left incomplete by the group of painters assembled by Pope Sixtus IV. He painted for the Medici during the late 1480s and early 1490s, and his *School of Pan* (fig. 487) was influenced by the classicism of the circle surrounding Lorenzo the Magnificent, who greatly revered this sylvan deity.

The *School of Pan* has never been adequately interpreted. Apparently, it represented the mythological god Pan instructing a group of largely nude divinities and aged shepherds in the rudiments of the art of music, using flutes cut from reeds. In this idyllic re-creation of

classical antiquity, the crescent moon hangs over Pan's streaming tresses, and the low light of late afternoon models the figures like so many statues in the Medici gardens. The hips, legs, and feet of the nude at the left were probably taken from Botticelli's *Birth of Venus* (see colorplate 62, p. 303), and Signorelli seems to have had access to Michelangelo's *Bacchus* (see fig. 471) or to the sculptor's preliminary drawings, for the nude figure at the right reproduces the Bacchus from the back in almost every respect, down to the tension of the calf of the bent leg.

Like Leonardo and Michelangelo, Signorelli was fascinated by the human body in movement, and he was able to demonstrate this interest on a grand scale in the frescoes in the San Brixio Chapel in the Cathedral of Orvieto, painted from 1499 to 1504. Fra Angelico had commenced a fresco cycle illustrating the Last Judgment in the chapel in 1447, but he had finished only two of the compartments of the vaults before being called to Rome by Pope Nicholas V. Signorelli was originally employed to finish the vaults, but in 1500 he won the assignment to paint the walls as well. Here he created

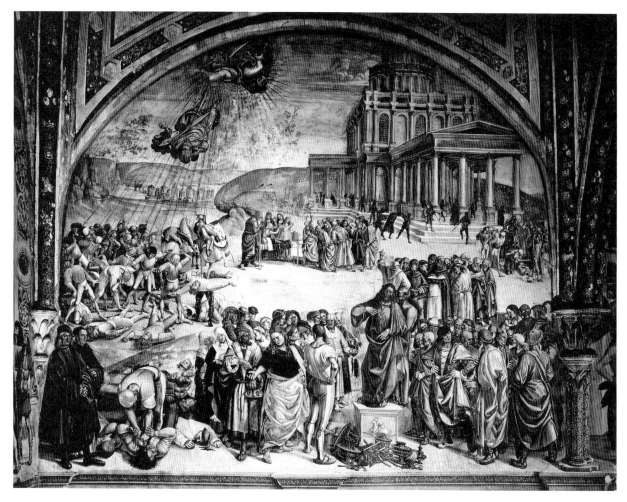

488. LUCA SIGNORELLI. *Preaching of the Antichrist*. 1499–1504. Fresco, width c. 23'. S. Brizio Chapel, Cathedral, Orvieto. Commissioned by the Opera of Orvieto Cathedral

the first colossal dramatic paintings of the Cinquecento.

One step into the interior, and we are caught up in a world of terrible action. Three of the six episodes of the end of the world are shown. In the first we see the *Preaching of the Antichrist* (fig. 488) as described in Matthew 24:5–31. Christlike in his garments, hair, and beard but terrible in his expression, the Antichrist repeats the words whispered into his ear by a demon. Around him stand people of all ages, many of whom are portraits (Dante is recognizable in the second row, to our right). In the background rises the Temple, a Renaissance structure more ambitious than carefully articulated, its porches filled with soldiers who have stripped it of its vessels, now piled as gifts before the Antichrist, and who are beheading innocent people at the right. In the middle, the Antichrist is represented raising a dead person, but finally an angel casts him down in a shower of golden rays at the left. The foreshortened figures tumble even into the foreground, in front of Signorelli, who has depicted himself full-length in contemporary costume and included Fra Angelico at his side. The somewhat disordered composition seems to be based

partly on Perugino's *Christ Giving the Keys to St. Peter* (see colorplate 67, p. 356).

The *Resurrection of the Dead* (fig. 489) was the most ambitious nude composition of its day, yet it would have been unthinkable without Michelangelo's *Battle of Lapiths and Centaurs* (see fig. 468), and in almost no time it was to be superseded by the *Battle of Cascina* (see fig. 479). Responding to the trumpets' call, the bulging nudes, which seem to be made of stone or wood, crawl out of the stony plain before us—a plain that is self-sealing, apparently—and strut or even dance about, sometimes embracing amiably, sometimes in conversation with skeletons who have yet to get their flesh back. The gold of Heaven is pitted with little cup-shaped depressions to produce a glittering reflection (this device will be adopted by Raphael in the *Disputà*; see fig. 519).

The wildest scene is the *Damned Consigned to Hell* (fig. 490). Heaven is guarded by the armored archangels Michael, Raphael, and Uriel, while demons with batlike wings carry off protesting mortals through the air. The foreground is filled with a wild, howling tangle of devils and mortals, on whom highly specific torments are

The High Renaissance in Florence

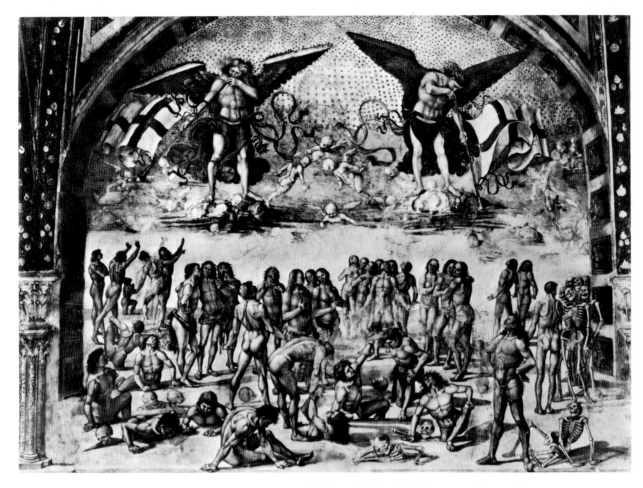

489. LUCA SIGNORELLI. *Resurrection of the Dead*. 1499–1504. Fresco, width c. 23'.
S. Brizio Chapel, Cathedral, Orvieto

being inflicted. One woman lies on her stomach, while a demon lifts her foot and tears her toes apart. Other demons rip off the ears or sink their teeth into their victims. Signorelli's wild imagination and rude vigor are enhanced by the unexpected brilliance of the coloring. The tan and white flesh tones themselves are vivid enough, but the skin of the demons is often parti-colored like the garments of contemporary German soldiery, varying from orange to lavender and green on the same figure. After a while things begin to look a bit mechanized, partly because Signorelli employed several assistants, and as a result the details are sometimes clumsy. But the entire effect is beyond anything that had been seen in Italy before, and it is still overwhelming.

PIERO DI COSIMO

We know a great deal about Piero di Cosimo (1462–1521). He hated thunderstorms and fire, the latter to such an extent that he was afraid to cook, and he lived on hard-boiled eggs, which he prepared fifty at a time.

He never allowed anyone to prune his fruit trees or weed his flowers. He represents a deviation from the orderly development of Italian art as he took quite literally and lived to the full the naturalism of the Pollaiuolo-Verrocchio-Leonardo current. His Madonnas, Holy Families, and Adorations provide a welcome relief from the wholesale imitation of Raphael in early Cinquecento Florence.

Piero's painting that is often identified as a *Portrait of Simonetta Vespucci* (fig. 491) may not represent this Florentine woman—the inscription was added later—and it may not even be a portrait. The female figure is shown as Cleopatra, with the asp coiled about her bosom. The picture may be somehow related to Lorenzo di Pierfrancesco de' Medici, whose device was the serpent biting its tail. Piero seems to have enjoyed setting up the shapes of the profile against the white and black thunderclouds and the breasts against the shapes of the hills. The whole picture is as unweeded and unpruned as Piero's garden.

His long panel representing a *Mythological Scene* (colorplate 87, p. 456) is often believed to represent the

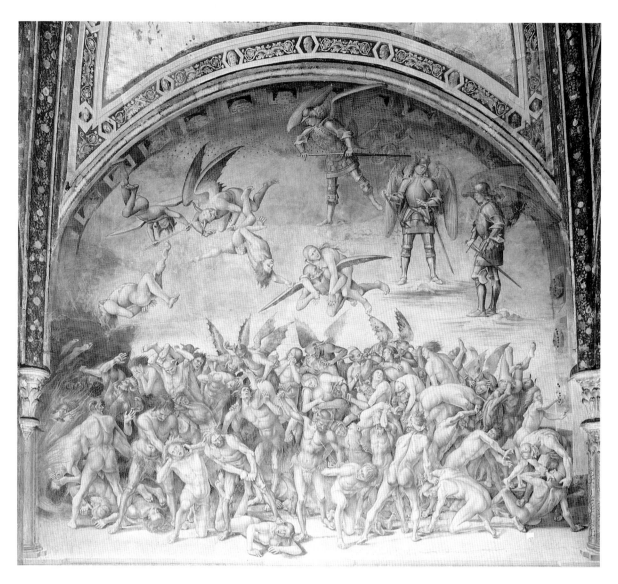

490. LUCA SIGNORELLI. *Damned Consigned to Hell.*
1499–1504. Fresco, width c. 23'. S. Brizio Chapel,
Cathedral, Orvieto

death of Procris, daughter of Erectheus, king of Athens.
According to Ovid, Procris was pierced in the chest by a
javelin thrown by her husband, Cephalus, who mistook
her for an animal concealed in the forest. Here an al-
most-nude woman, wounded in the throat, is mourned
by a half-comprehending satyr, whose grief is as touch-
ingly represented as is the wordless sympathy of the dog.
Piero must have felt a deep kinship with animals. His
simple, descriptive style is a far cry from the elaborate
technique and observation of Leonardo, but it seems absolutely appropriate for his unique and personal interpretation of his subjects.

It may have been Francesco del Pugliese, the wealthy
cloth merchant who had commissioned Filippino Lippi's
Vision of St. Bernard (see colorplate 63, p. 304), who
asked Piero to paint a series of panels representing the
early history of humanity that would have been installed

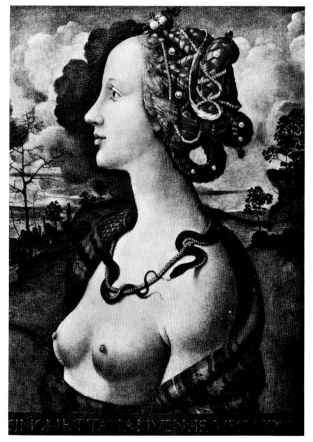

491. PIERO DI COSIMO. *Portrait of Simonetta Vespucci(?).*
c. 1501. Panel, 22½ x 16½". Musée Condé, Chantilly

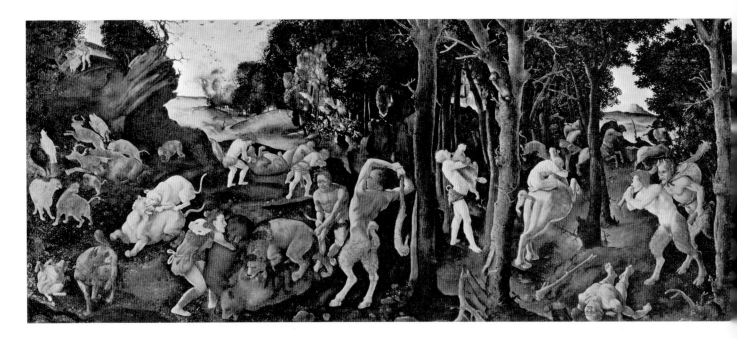

492. PIERO DI COSIMO. *Hunting Scene*. 1490s. Panel,
27³/4 x 66³/4". The Metropolitan Museum of Art, New York
(Gift of Robert Gordon, 1875).
Perhaps commissioned by Francesco del Pugliese

above wooden wainscoting to decorate a room; such panels are known as *spalliere*. The series illustrates an account from *De rerum natura* by the ancient Roman author Lucretius. One panel (fig. 492) depicts a battle between humans, a great variety of animals, and such half-human creatures as centaurs and satyrs. The forest setting is typically unpruned and at the mercy of Piero's hated fire, which breaks out here and there in wild gusts that seem to be brushed on quickly with bold brushstrokes. Piero pulls us into prehistory through a combination of distant landscape and foreshortened figures: a dead dog at the far left, a horse to the right of center,

and a rotting corpse in the right foreground. How this evolutionistic view of mankind was reconciled with the account in Genesis we can only guess. Certainly, Piero's panels are related to, and probably in their muscular vigor even influenced by, Michelangelo's *Battle of Lapiths and Centaurs* (see fig. 468). But, like Signorelli in his Orvieto frescoes, Piero depicts what was most repugnant to Michelangelo—humanity in a subhuman stage and subject to the depredations of antihuman creatures and forces. In the following chapter we will see how, with impassioned energy, Michelangelo and other artists attempted to raise humanity again to a divine level.

17

The High Renaissance in Rome

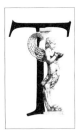he next phase of Italian art and history is dominated, at the outset at least, by a single figure, Pope Julius II. As Cardinal Giuliano della Rovere, this forceful Ligurian exercised great power during the pontificate of his uncle, Sixtus IV, and the following reign of Innocent VIII. When Rodrigo Borgia ascended the papal throne as Alexander VI, Giuliano left Rome. His election as pope in 1503, following the ten-day pontificate of Pius III, was the beginning of what might be called a revolution, starting in the Vatican and expanding to Rome, to central Italy, to the entire peninsula, and eventually to all of Europe. Julius II loathed the Borgias and refused to use the rooms decorated by Pintoricchio in which Alexander VI had once lived. He immediately set about a program of reform in the Church, while in the secular sphere this was matched by his reestablishment of law and order in the crime-ridden streets of Rome and by the subjugation of the rebellious Roman nobles. Next he set out to reconquer the lost provinces of the papacy. Then he began campaigns to drive foreign invaders out of Italy, beginning with the French in the north. His success there would doubtless have been followed by an expulsion of the Spaniards in the south and the unification of the peninsula under papal leadership if death had not stopped the pope's meteoric career after ten years. Nonetheless, Julius II succeeded not only in establishing the borders of the Papal States but he is also credited with inspiring a new confidence and vitality in Renaissance Catholicism.

The last decade of the pope's life—his sixties—treated Europe to the spectacle of the pontiff standing in armor beside his blazing cannons, censuring his enemies in language both coarse and violent, beating his cardinals over the shoulders with his cane when they hesitated to follow him through snow breast-high on the horses, growing a great beard in defiance of all custom and tradition, and acting in general like an unchained giant loose on the map of Italy. The unsystematic attempts of Quattrocento popes to convert the picturesque agglomerations of medieval Rome into a classical city were immediately superseded by Julius's determination to rebuild whole sections, to drive broad avenues, bordered with palaces, through hovels and ruins alike, and to replace the Basilica of St. Peter's, now more than

a thousand years old, with a new structure that would embody the imperial splendor and spiritual drive of his regime. Intellectually and artistically, Julian Rome was an exciting place to live. It was also dusty and noisy from incessant demolitions and reconstructions, and it was repeatedly threatened by the collapse of the pope's political schemes and invasion by his enemies.

It has been said Julius chose the High Renaissance as the artistic style that would best embody his new ideals, and one can hardly imagine him calling upon Botticelli or Perugino to create the visual symbols for his new militancy. High Renaissance style, forged in the crisis of republican Florence, was a perfect instrument for him, and Michelangelo an ideal artist. Later these two were joined by Raphael and by Bramante, who was to become the most important of High Renaissance architects and also a close friend and confidant of the pope. The painters summoned by Sixtus IV for his first program in the Sistine Chapel had returned to their cities without having created a common style (see pp. 328, 371). But, whether or not they knew it was happening, the three artists who carried out Julius's mighty projects did, to an extent, submerge their individual personalities as they were fired by the example and inspiration of their patron.

The Roman period of the High Renaissance is distinct from its Florentine predecessor—grander in scope, freer in its dynamism—and it developed with rapidity from phase to more majestic phase. Pope Julius II, as patron, exercised a formative influence on High Renaissance style and should be considered one of its creators, just as in an earlier period Pericles influenced the classical style in ancient Athens. Julius determined what was to be built, carved, or painted, and by whom; what were to be the subjects; how they were to be treated; and which among several alternate projects was to be executed. Such was the grandeur of Julius's undertakings that Italian art, even in Venice, could never again return to its former, more modest, self.

BRAMANTE

Donato di Pascuccio (1444–1514), known as Bramante, from Urbino, started as a painter of considerable creativity and first appears as an architect in Milan in 1485, when, already over forty, he undertook the rebuilding of

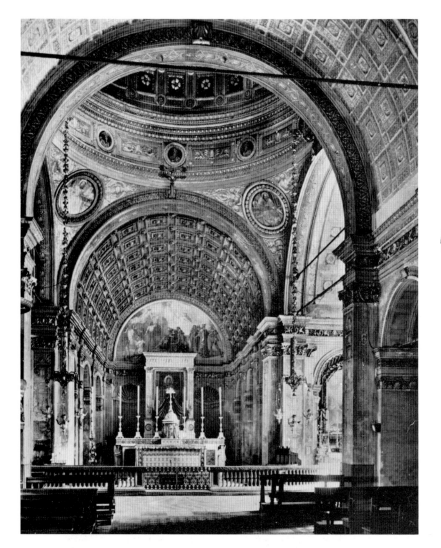

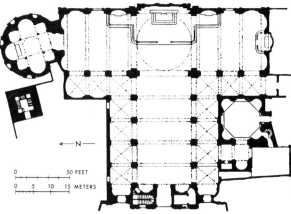

Santa Maria presso San Satiro (fig. 493). Basically Albertian in its single-story, barrel-vaulted nave, whose round arches are supported by piers divided by Corinthian pilasters, the church culminates in a crossing crowned by a Pantheon-like dome that gives us a hint of how Alberti's domes for the Malatesta Temple (see fig. 224) and Sant'Andrea at Mantua might have appeared. The most startling element of the interior, however, is the choir, which appears to stretch for three bays beyond the crossing, under a barrel vault matching that of the nave. But while our eyes can see this distance, we cannot enter it, for the choir does not exist. It is a triumph of the Renaissance art of deceit on a grand scale (fig. 494). Where we think we see a choir, there is the street outside; the illusion is created by stucco relief on a flat wall, and the actual depth is only a matter of a few feet. The false choir of Santa Maria presso San Satiro is an indication of Bramante's lifelong preoccupation with space, and a remarkable premonition, in miniature, of how the interior of Julius II's St. Peter's (figs. 501–4) would have looked if it had been completed and decorated according to his plans.

The Church of Santa Maria delle Grazie in Milan had been started in Gothic style in 1463, but in 1492

Duke Ludovico Sforza ordered the newly built choir torn down and replaced by a Renaissance structure to house the tombs of the Sforza dynasty; Leonardo's numerous drawings for a central-plan church (see fig. 449) may be related to this project. Although no document connects his name with its construction, the present apse, transept, crossing, and dome are attributed to Bramante under the influence of Leonardo da Vinci, whose ideas on radial architecture they clearly reflect. This architecture, whether or not all its surface decorations were designed by Bramante himself, is composed, like the architecture in Leonardo's drawings, of various permutations and combinations of cubes, hemispheres, half-cylinders, and so on (figs. 495, 496). Bramante transformed the oculi of the preexistent Gothic church into circles that move throughout the exterior design as ornament. In the spacious interior (fig. 497), from which apses open outward like the membranes of inflated balloons, the circles rotate around the arches upholding the dome like cars on some gigantic Ferris wheel.

The fall of the Sforza dynasty in 1499 left Bramante without work at what was, for the Renaissance, the fairly advanced age of fifty-four. He moved to Rome and immediately commenced a rich architectural activity in

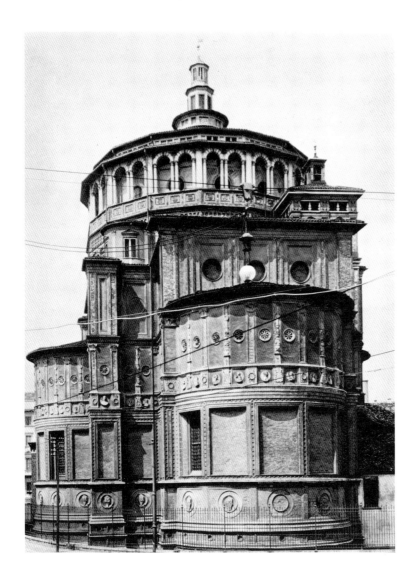

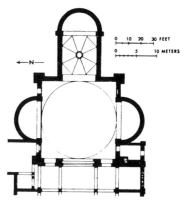

left: 495. DONATO BRAMANTE. Sta. Maria delle Grazie, Milan. Begun 1492. Commissioned by Ludovico Sforza

496. DONATO BRAMANTE. Plan of Sta. Maria delle Grazie

the last years of the pontificate of Alexander VI. Under Julius II, Bramante developed at extraordinary speed and with unexpected originality and power to became the leading architect of the High Renaissance.

The Tempietto (little temple; fig. 498) was commissioned in 1502 by Ferdinand and Isabella of Spain to be erected on the spot where it was believed St. Peter had been crucified, but it was probably not built immediately. The building is not mentioned in Albertini's guide to Rome of 1511, which describes the less important nearby church, and the style of the Tempietto is incompatible with that of Bramante's first works in Rome, and the date remains uncertain. Instead of the Corinthian and Ionic orders preferred by Quattrocento architects, Bramante chose the Roman Doric, which is severe and regular because of the prescribed alternation of triglyphs and metopes. The circular shape, however, whose effectiveness he could observe in ancient round temples in Rome and Tivoli, allowed him to abandon the planimetric quality of Quattrocento architecture, which had already been challenged by Leonardo's radial schemes. The Tempietto has no single elevation; it exists in space like a work of sculpture, and, as we move about it, its

497. DONATO BRAMANTE. Interior view toward choir, Sta. Maria delle Grazie, Milan

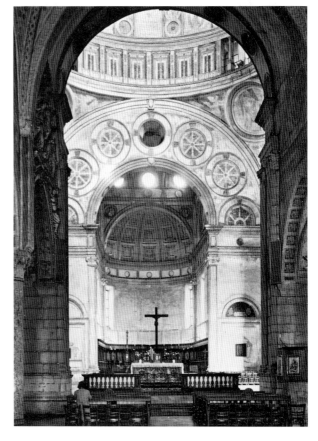

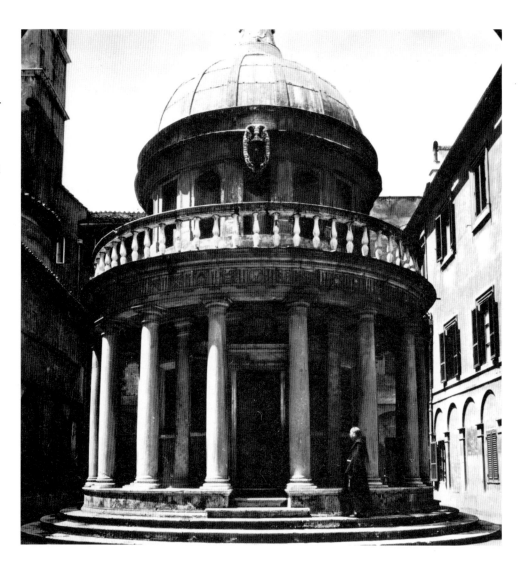

498. DONATO BRAMANTE. Tempietto, S. Pietro in Montorio, Rome. Authorized 1502; completed after 1511. Height 47'. Commissioned by King Ferdinand and Queen Isabella of Spain

peristyle and steps revolve around the central cylinder.

The full spatial effect Bramante intended can be realized today only if we attempt to re-create the surrounding circular courtyard, whose plan and elevation were preserved in Serlio's mid-Cinquecento architectural treatise (figs. 499, 500). Each widely spaced column of the outer peristyle is related radially to a column of the Tempietto, tying the inner structure to its frame by an imagined web of relationships that cut across the surrounding space. The resultant interrelationship of forms and spaces, brought into a simple unity that is the product rather than the sum of its parts, makes the Tempietto the architectural equivalent of Leonardo's lost cartoon for the *Madonna and Child with St. Anne* (see p. 444), even if it may not be the first High Renaissance structure preserved today. It may thus be said that, through Bramante, Leonardo's ideas founded not only the Florentine but also the Roman phase of the High Renaissance. The intellectual order and inherent majesty of this building, whose solids and spaces are so perfectly harmonized, justify the choice of Bramante as papal architect by Julius II, even if they can no longer be used to explain it.

In 1506, with the excuse that it was in danger of imminent collapse, the pope commissioned Bramante to rebuild the Basilica of St. Peter's, archetype of Early Christian church architecture in the West, sanctified by more than eleven hundred years of ritual, and filled with monuments of sculpture and painting. Nicholas V had already transferred the seat of the papacy from the Lateran Palace to the Vatican, and a new apse had been begun that was intended to replace the Early Christian apse; Bernardo Rossellino was the builder, but it may have been designed by Alberti. Julius II decided to sweep aside both the traditional basilica and the new apse. To Michelangelo's anger, he even destroyed the monolithic ancient columns that lined the nave, which were brought down with such violence that they shattered on the pavement. This gesture of negation and affirmation was to launch the greatest constructional dream of the Renaissance on its perilous course. Twelve architects and twenty-two popes later, the building Bramante began was completed but, with its Michelangelesque shell and Baroque extensions, it is barely recognizable.

The very grandiosity of the Julius-Bramante project is

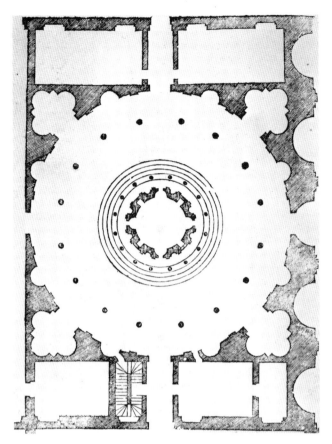

499. DONATO BRAMANTE. Plan of Tempietto, S. Pietro in Montorio, Rome (from SEBASTIANO SERLIO, *Il terzo libro d'architettura*, Venice, 1551)

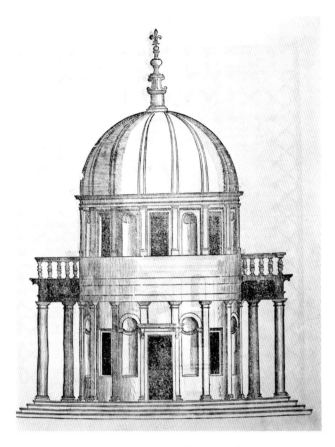

500. DONATO BRAMANTE. Elevation of Tempietto, S. Pietro in Montorio, Rome (from SEBASTIANO SERLIO, *Il terzo libro d'architettura*, Venice, 1551)

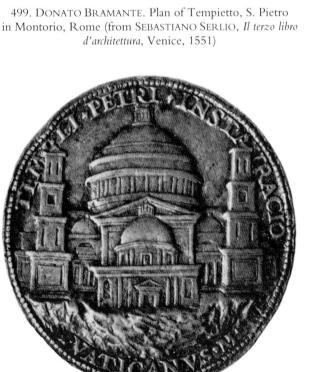

501. DONATO BRAMANTE. Design of exterior, St. Peter's, Vatican, Rome, on bronze medal by CARADOSSO. 1506. British Museum, London. Commissioned by Pope Julius II

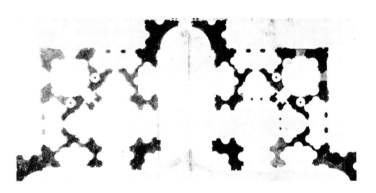

502. DONATO BRAMANTE. Plan of St. Peter's. 1506. Pen and wash. Gabinetto dei Disegni e Stampe, Uffizi, Florence

perhaps a symptom of the weaknesses of the High Renaissance as well as a symbol of its ideals and aspirations. The immense structure could not possibly have been completed during the reign of the aging pope, but it was commenced with surprising speed considering the conditions of disorder and attack that Julius and his papacy were facing. Although there is more of Bramante's construction in the present interior than is often realized, we can reconstruct the exterior appearance only through drawings by others and through a medal (fig. 501) struck by Caradosso, Bramante's collaborator for architectural ornament in Milan. Bramante's drawing (fig. 502) has generally been interpreted as showing one-half of a Greek-cross plan, with four equal arms

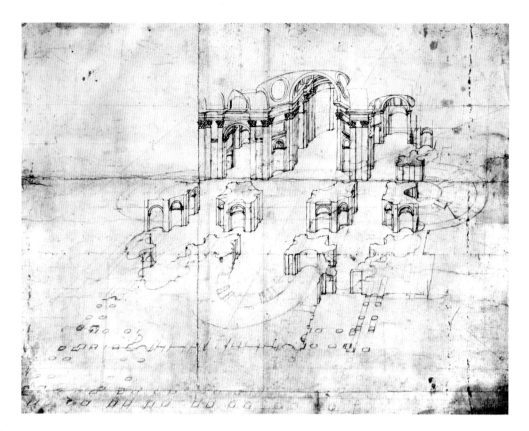

ending in apses. At the corners are four smaller Greek crosses with two of their four apses dissolved into the arms of the larger cross, and in the outer angles are four towers. On each side the towers and the central entrance are connected by three-bay loggie. An observer entering at one of the principal portals would have looked through relatively simple spaces straight through the building and toward the opposite portal, but the view from one of the loggia entrances would have offered a more complex succession of spaces, culminating in the central area again, and then repeated in reverse. There is no certainty, however, that this half plan was to have been doubled; the missing section might have comprised a nave, making a Latin cross. In any case it was never carried out.

The church whose construction Bramante commenced was to have had an apse of three bays, and the apse and apsidal transepts were to have been surrounded by ambulatories (fig. 503). The tomb of St. Peter was to remain at the crossing, where it is today. The single-story, barrel-vaulted structure, recalling the interior of Santa Maria presso San Satiro, would have been crowned by a colossal dome on pendentives—not the vertical-ribbed dome of the Tempietto, but the dome of the Pantheon, set on a peristyle of columns on the exterior that repeats a similar but smaller columned gallery on the inside (fig. 504). The hemispherical dome, with its horizontal elements, would have created an impression of masses at rest, deliberately contrasting with the soaring towers, which from most vantage points would partially have concealed its outline.

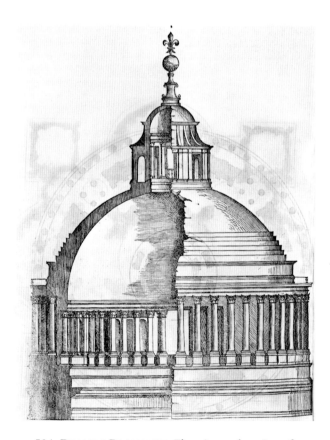

504. DONATO BRAMANTE. Elevation and section of dome, St. Peter's, Vatican, Rome (from SEBASTIANO SERLIO, *Il terzo libro d'architettura*, Venice, 1551)

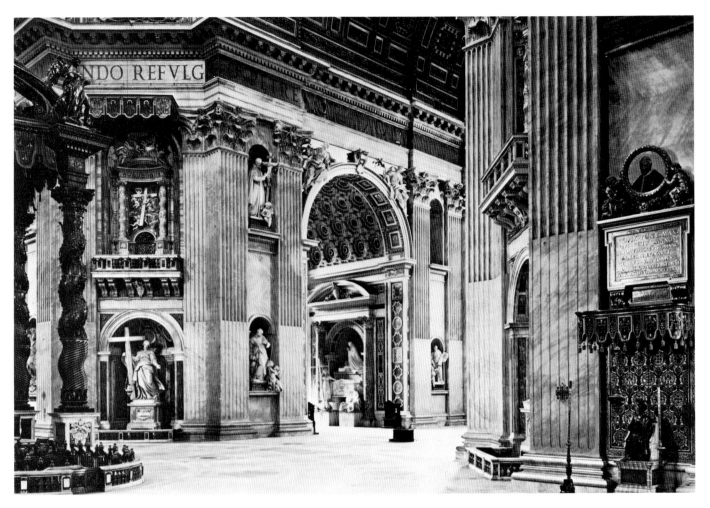

505. DONATO BRAMANTE, MICHELANGELO, and others. Interior view at crossing,
St. Peter's, Vatican, Rome

Except for the raised level of the floor, the interior was built substantially as Bramante planned it (fig. 505). By 1514 the architect, then seventy years old, was able to see the four arches of the dome, the Corinthian order including marble shafts, capitals, and entablatures, and the four pendentives in place, as well as the foundations of three of the arms of the cross and of some of the chapels. The four arches and piers are built on such a scale that they could not be changed and, in fact, are visible from the inside today, in spite of the marble and gold ornament that cover them. In 1514, however, much of the nave of Old St. Peter's still stood, and a temporary construction sheltered the tomb of the Prince of the Apostles. Bramante's dome was not even commenced according to his plans, and from the outside the building belongs to Michelangelo and to the subsequent Baroque period.

Some insight into the sensation of unity and harmony that Bramante devised for St. Peter's is offered by the pilgrimage church of Santa Maria della Consolazione at Todi, in Umbria. Begun in 1508, the church was long believed to have been based on a model by Bramante

himself, although the only architect's name recorded is that of the otherwise obscure Cola da Caprarola (fig. 506). Four apses roofed by semidomes radiate outward from a central square in a plan that strikes many visitors as perfection itself, although there was apparently some question at first as to whether tradition might not necessitate a nave, as at Santa Maria del Calcinaio at Cortona (see fig. 375). The delicacy of the window frames, entablatures, and corner pilasters contrasts with the broad wall surfaces to create an effect of fragility and lightness unique among central-plan churches of the Renaissance. The Consolazione was not completed until the following century, and the entrance, balustrade, and dome show Roman taste of a later era.

Another vast project designed in 1505 by Bramante for Julius II that was, like St. Peter's, left truncated at the architect's death, was the rebuilding of the Vatican Palace. The palace was to be united to the earlier country house of the Belvedere, nearly a thousand feet away at the top of a hill. Bramante's plan proposed two enormous corridors that, enclosing garden terraces, staircases, and fountains, followed the slopes of the hill (fig. 507).

The High Renaissance in Rome

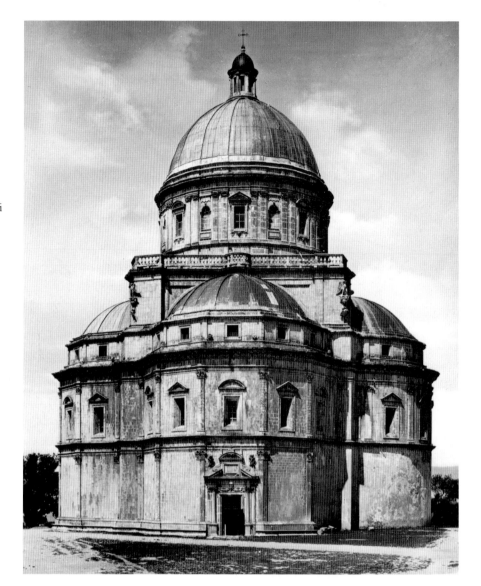

506. Cola da
Caprarola
and others.
Sta. Maria della
Consolazione.
Begun 1508. Todi

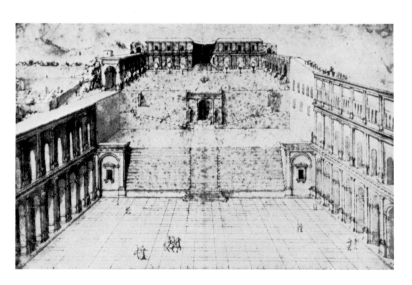

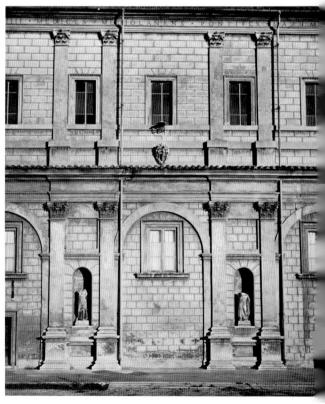

507. Donato Bramante. Belvedere, Vatican, Rome,
as seen in an anonymous 16th-century drawing. Begun 1505.
Collection Edmonde Patio, Geneva. Commissioned
by Pope Julius II

right: 508. Donato Bramante and others. Portion of
north façade, Belvedere Court, Vatican, Rome. Begun 1505.
Commissioned by Pope Julius II

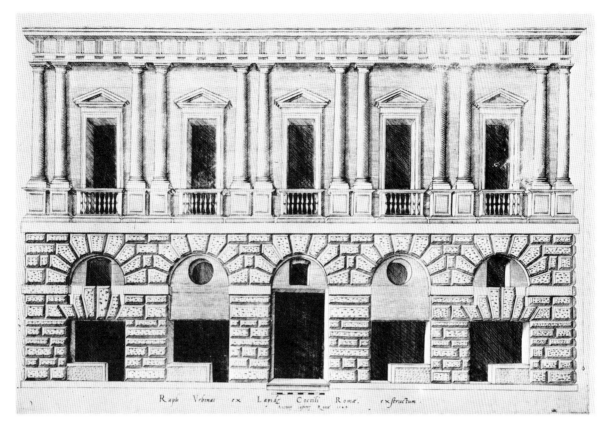

509. DONATO BRAMANTE. Façade, Palazzo Caprini, Rome. c. 1510. Engraving by LAFRERI, 1519. Commissioned by Adriano Caprini

For articulation Bramante designed a flexible system of coupled Corinthian pilasters enclosing niches, and flanking arches set into the masonry of the wall (fig. 508). While the huge barrel vaults of St. Peter's echo Alberti's Sant'Andrea (see fig. 229), the screen architecture of the Belvedere reflects Alberti's Palazzo Rucellai (see fig. 225) and the Albertian panels by Laurana (see fig. 386), as well as the Cancelleria (see fig. 231) and other Roman palaces. But the ambition of the scheme transcends anything ever attempted in the Quattrocento. Together the pope and the architect, who read Dante to him in the evenings, created in their imaginations a plan more extensive than any other palace built between the days of Emperor Hadrian and those of Louis XIV. Time itself was against them, and their vision was doomed to incompletion. Later, Bramante's palace suffered insensitive additions and an amputation of the vista by an arm connecting the two sides.

Little remains of the other official buildings designed and in some cases built for the grand new Rome of Julius II. Although long since destroyed, Bramante's Palazzo Caprini—also known as the House of Raphael because the artist bought it in 1517—cannot be overlooked (fig. 509) because it provided a new model for patrician town houses that replaced the three-story structure with screen architecture of superimposed orders that had been so widespread after Alberti's Palazzo Rucellai (fig. 225). In the Palazzo Caprini, Bramante followed the typical Roman custom of devoting the ground floor to shops and setting above it a *piano nobile*

destined for the owner. The heavily rusticated ground floor provided a base for engaged pairs of half-round columns that offer a rich alternation between flat and grouped cylindrical masses. This idea was so successful that it was repeated a number of times in Roman palaces and in northern Italy as well.

MICHELANGELO 1505 TO 1516

In 1505, the second year of Julius's pontificate and one year before he commissioned Bramante to rebuild St. Peter's, the pope called Michelangelo from Florence to design and carve for him a tomb of unexampled formal richness and dramatic intensity to be placed in Old St. Peter's. We are not sure of the intended location in the old basilica, but it is possible that Julius, engaged in rejuvenating and rebuilding the Church, intended his tomb to confront that of Peter, the Prince of the Apostles, the first pope, and the man on whose rock the Church was founded. To carry out his commission, Michelangelo abandoned his many undertakings in Florence, including the cartoon of the *Battle of Cascina*. We have today nothing but verbal accounts, written much later, a few drawings, and the carved decorations of the lower story with which to reconstruct the three-story mausoleum that Julius and Michelangelo originally planned. Scholars disagree on many elements, but agree on what follows: Michelangelo made a number of preliminary designs, one of which was selected by the pope. This was for a freestanding structure containing an oval burial chamber

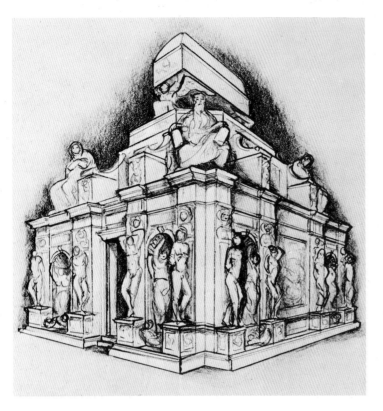

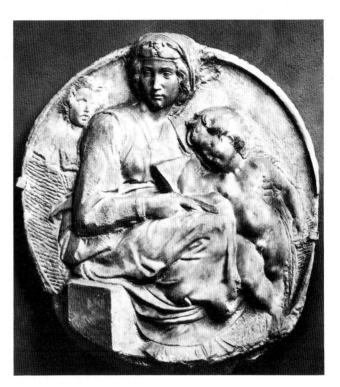

510. MICHELANGELO. Tomb of Pope Julius II. Proposed reconstruction drawing of project of 1505. Commissioned by Pope Julius II for Old St. Peter's, Rome

511. MICHELANGELO. *Pitti Madonna*. c. 1506. Marble, diameter 33½". Bargello, Florence. Commissioned by Bartolommeo Pitti

in which the sarcophagus was to have been placed. The lower story of the exterior was to be decorated by niches containing statues of Victories flanked by herms, to which were to be attached bound and struggling male Captives. There were to be at least eight Victories and sixteen Captives; one theory calls for ten Victories and twenty Captives. On the second story were to be placed statues of Moses, St. Paul, the Active Life, and the Contemplative Life.

The principal dispute arises over the appearance of the top story. Vasari wrote: "The work rose above the cornice in diminishing steps, with a frieze of scenes in bronze, and with other figures and putti and ornaments in turn; and above there were finally two figures, of which one was the Heavens, who smiling held on his shoulder a bier together with Cybele, goddess of the earth, who seemed that she was grieving that she must remain in a world deprived of every virtue by the death of this man; and the Heavens appeared to be smiling that his soul had passed to celestial glory." Despite the fact that no text mentions any statue of the pope, two theories hold that the bier supported his effigy. One claims that the pope was recumbent (which would have made him almost invisible from the floor), another points out that the explicit word used for bier really meant the *sella gestatoria*, or portable papal throne, and that Julius II was to have been shown carried live into the next world, blessing as he went. Documents tell us that the marble block for a papal effigy was actually delivered. In all probability this was to have been a recumbent figure but destined for the only logical place, the sarcophagus in the burial chamber. A suggested recon-

struction of the 1505 design, culminating in a bier that follows Vasari, is offered here (fig. 510).

After Michelangelo had spent a year of labor bringing marble blocks from Carrara to the Piazza San Pietro and had started the carving, the pope suddenly interrupted the commission. Although the circumstances were narrated several times by Michelangelo himself, with always richer and more picturesque detail, it is still not clear why the work was stopped. Presumably funds had to be diverted to the rebuilding of St. Peter's by Bramante. In any case the magnificent dream, which was destined to become a nightmare for Michelangelo during the next forty years, was the first instance in which he combined figures and architecture and was, therefore, the germ of his major pictorial work, the Sistine Ceiling. Element after element designed for the 1505 version of the tomb came to fruition on the ceiling, and the ceiling in turn was to act as a crucible for new sculptural ideas to be utilized in later versions of the tomb.

Of the architecture and the more than forty over-life-sized statues that were to have adorned the tomb, Michelangelo had completed only the niches with their rich decorations before he left in anger for Florence in 1506. There is evidence to show, however, that the poses of the two *Captives* now in the Louvre (see figs. 517, 518) and the *Moses* (see fig. 516) were determined and already blocked out at this time.

In Florence, Michelangelo returned to the *Battle of Cascina*, and according to a letter from Piero Soderini, leader of the Republic, the artist was at work painting the fresco. This same moment is the most likely date for the *Pitti Madonna* (fig. 511), whose compact masses and

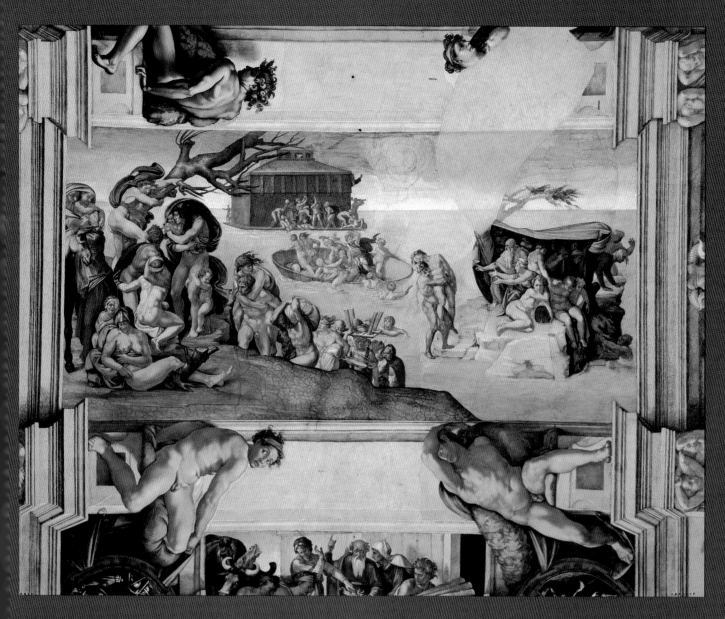

above: Colorplate 88. MICHELANGELO. *Deluge.* 1509. Fresco, 9' 2" x 18' 8". Sistine Ceiling, Vatican, Rome

right: Colorplate 89. Father Carrying Son, detail of colorplate 88

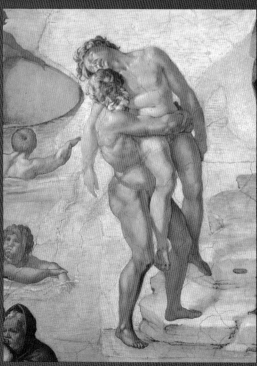

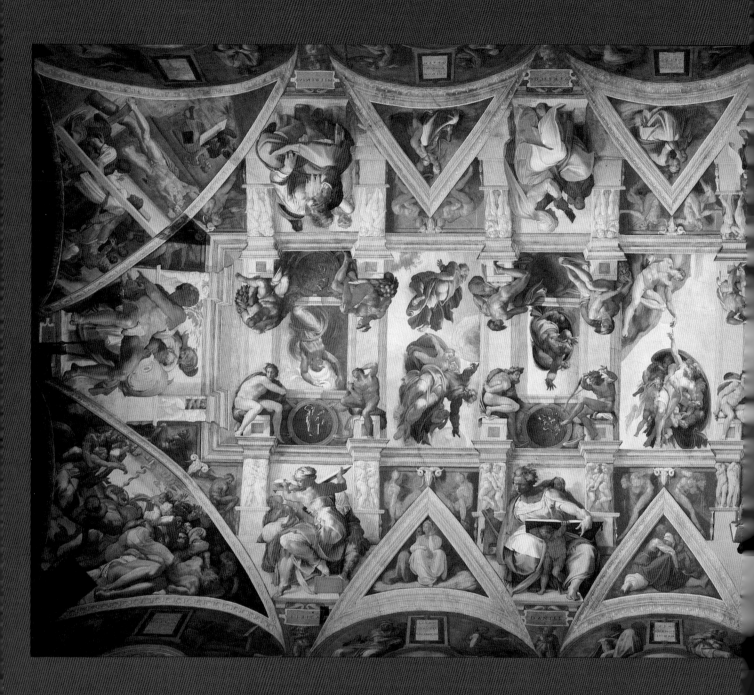

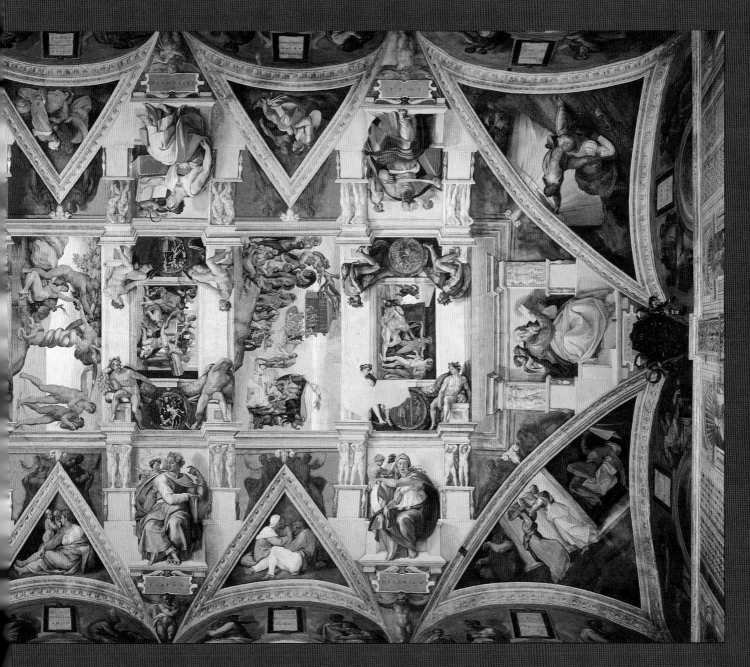

Colorplate 90. MICHELANGELO. View of the restored Sistine Ceiling frescoes, Vatican, Rome.
1508–12. 45 x 128'. Commissioned by Pope Julius II

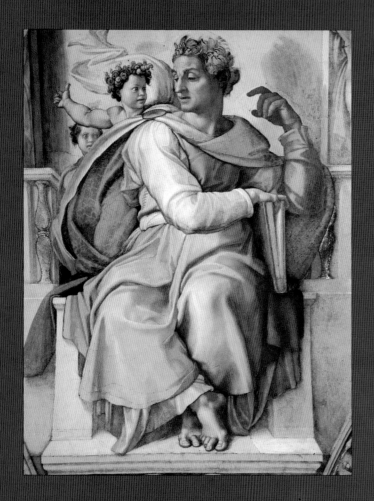

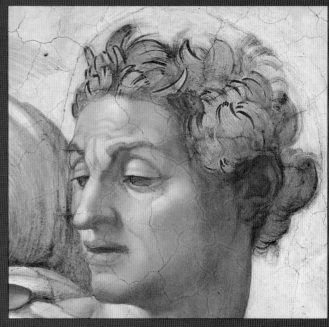

left: Colorplate 91. MICHELANGELO. *Prophet Isaiah.*
1509–10. Fresco. Sistine Ceiling

above: Colorplate 92. Head of Prophet Isaiah,
detail of colorplate 91

below: Colorplate 93. MICHELANGELO. *Fall of Adam and Eve*
and *Expulsion.* 1510. Fresco, 9' 2" x 18' 8". Sistine Ceiling

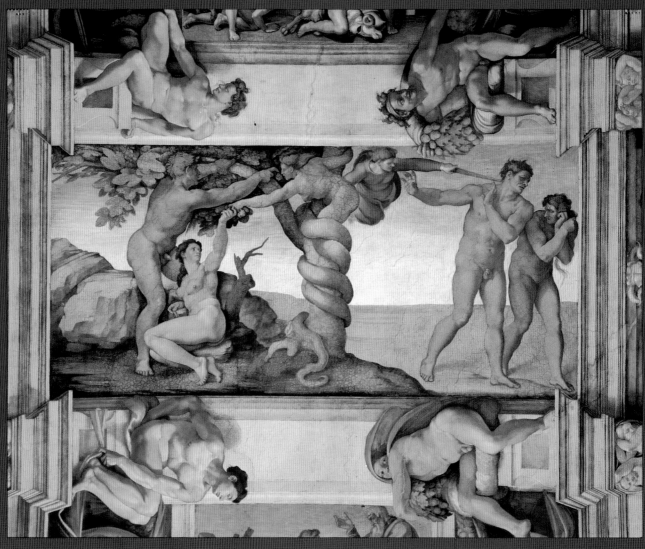

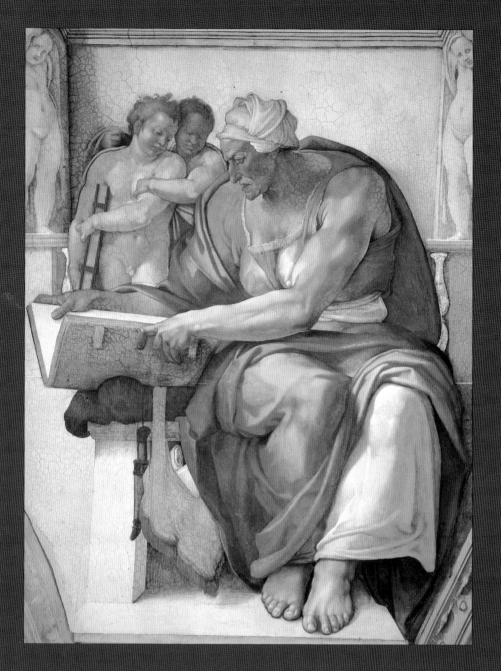

above: Colorplate 94. MICHELANGELO. *Cumaean Sibyl.*
1510. Fresco. Sistine Ceiling

right: Colorplate 95. Head of Cumaean Sibyl, detail
of colorplate 94

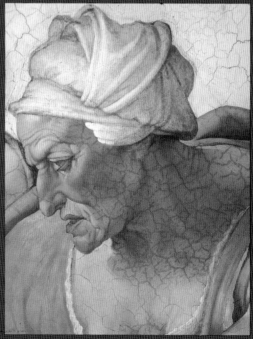

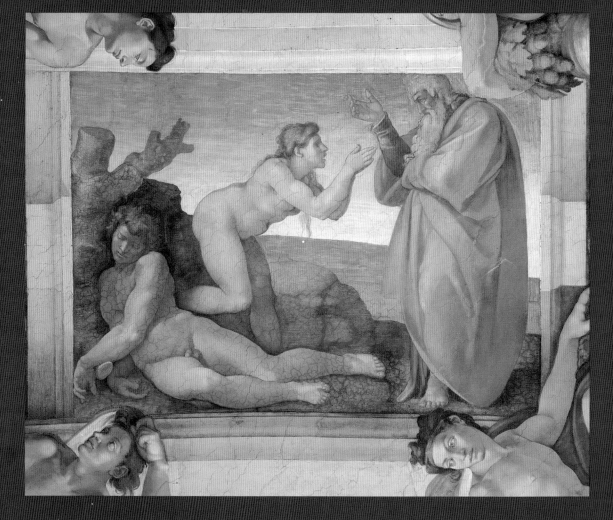

Colorplate 96.
MICHELANGELO.
Creation of Eve.
1510. Fresco,
5' 7" x 8' 6¹/2".
Sistine Ceiling

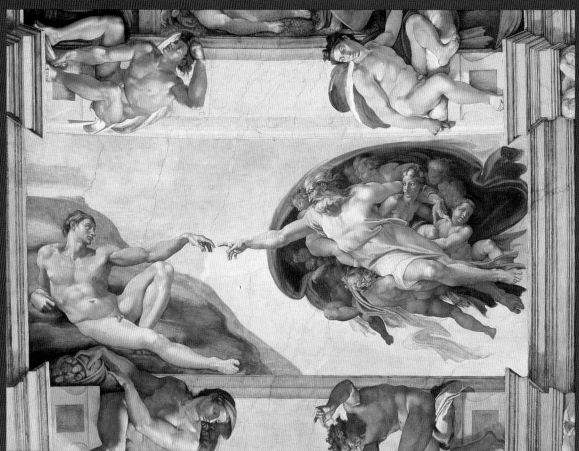

Colorplate 97.
MICHELANGELO.
Creation of Adam.
1511–12. Fresco,
9' 2" x 18' 8".
Sistine Ceiling

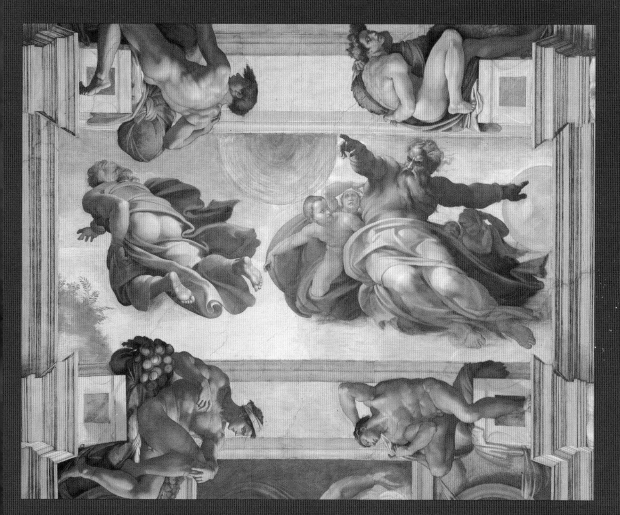

Colorplate 99.
MICHELANGELO.
*Creation of Sun,
Moon, and Plants.*
1511–12. Fresco,
9' 2" x 18' 8".
Sistine Ceiling

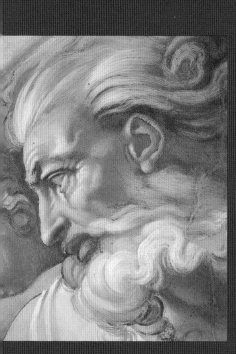

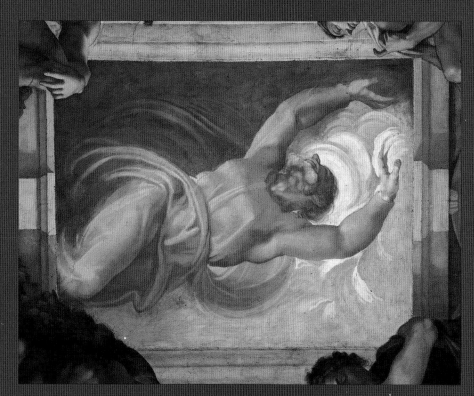

Colorplate 98. Head of God, detail
of colorplate 97

Colorplate 100. MICHELANGELO. *Separation of Light from Darkness.*
1511–12. Fresco. Sistine Ceiling

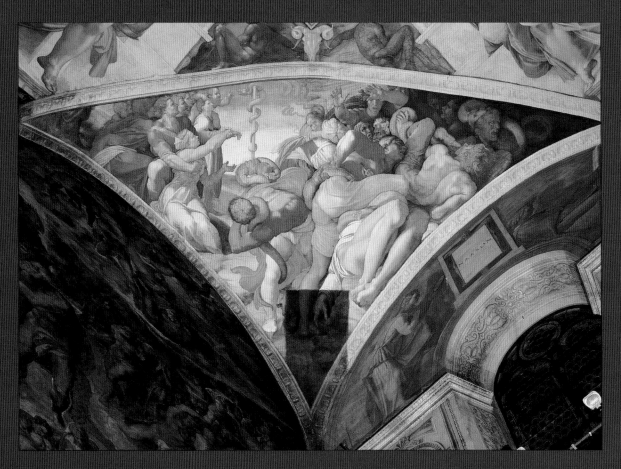

Colorplate 101. MICHELANGELO. *Brazen Serpent*. 1512. Fresco. Spandrel of Sistine Ceiling

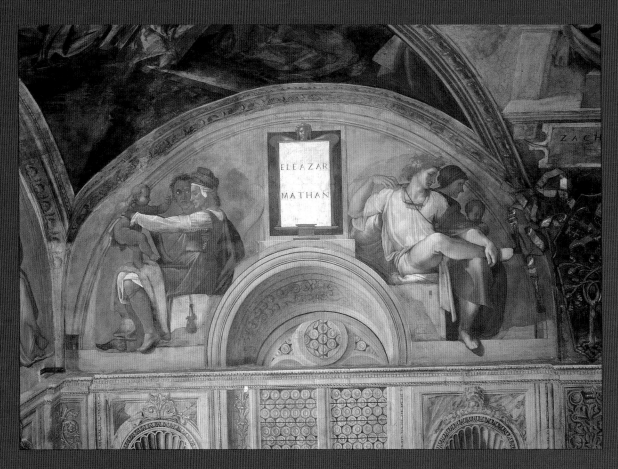

Colorplate 102. MICHELANGELO. *Eleazar and Matthan*. 1508–10. Fresco. Lunette of Sistine Ceiling

blocklike shapes forcefully protrude from the tondo form and mark a stage well beyond the delicacy of the *Bruges Madonna* or the relatively open composition of the *Taddei Madonna* (see figs. 475, 476). In the complex, *contrapposto* pose and prophetic gaze of the *Pitti Madonna*, it is possible to discern something of the new grandeur and monumentality of the style Michelangelo had evolved in the project for the tomb of Julius; the figure may even reveal the pose of one of the never-executed figures for the second story.

Although the pope had already envisioned inviting Michelangelo to paint the ceiling of the Sistine Chapel, Julius instead marched to Bologna in 1506, recaptured the city, and from that vantage point requested the outflanked Florentines to send Michelangelo to him. The sculptor spent the next eighteen months modeling and casting in bronze a colossal portrait of the pope. The finished work enjoyed an existence of little more than three years before antipapal forces, again in control of Bologna, pushed it from its pedestal on the façade of San Petronio, melted it down, and cast the bronze into a cannon, mockingly called La Giulia, to fire at the pope. The life of the colossus was so short and its content so despised by the Bolognese that no reliable evidence, not even a sketch or description, has come down to us. We have nothing but our imaginations with which to reconstruct what must have been a vividly dramatic statue. Perhaps some hint of its vanished grandeur is embodied in the prophets of the Sistine Ceiling.

Scarcely back in Florence in the spring of 1508, Michelangelo was called again to Rome when the idea of painting the Sistine Chapel became a definite commission. The program of Sixtus IV (colorplate 11, p. 19) stopped with images of the popes at the window level, and the vault had been painted blue with gold stars. Here, according to Michelangelo's own later account, the pope wanted him to paint the twelve apostles, one in each of the spandrels between the arches. The central part of the ceiling was to be filled by "ornaments according to custom," apparently an elaborate network of painted ornamental motifs and geometrical fields. Michelangelo objected that the design would be "a poor thing." "Why?" asked the pope. "Because they [the apostles] were poor too," replied Michelangelo. And then, still according to the artist's own version (written much later, at a time when he was threatened with lawsuits over the nondelivery of the tomb), the pope told him he could paint anything he liked. There is no reason to doubt that the expansion of the original program was due to Michelangelo's dissatisfaction. But despite the aura of romantic independence with which Michelangelo has been enveloped since the nineteenth century, it is hard to accept the idea that so determined a pope would have entrusted a complex theological program at the nerve center of Western Christendom to an artist who, in all probability, could not read Latin.

It is believed by many that Michelangelo had a theological adviser, and this person has been identified as Marco Vigerio della Rovere, Julius's fellow Franciscan, fellow townsman, and first cousin once removed; he was on the pope's first list of cardinals, elevated in 1503. The *Christian Decachord*, published by Vigerio in Rome in 1507 and dedicated to the pope, contains indications that it was Vigerio who advised Michelangelo in the preparation of the subjects for the second program for the Sistine Ceiling.

Now the twelve apostles gave way to Old Testament prophets and sibyls from classical antiquity, all seated on gigantic thrones. They are arranged so that prophets alternate with sibyls around the ceiling and prophets face sibyls across the ceiling, with the exception of the prophets at each end of the chapel (colorplate 90, pp. 490–91). The thrones are niches with massive cornices upheld by pairs of putti painted to resemble marble sculpture, and they become part of the simulated architecture of the ceiling when their verticals extend into bands that reach across the chapel to merge with the thrones on the opposite side and which define the frame of the smaller narrative scenes. At left and right above each throne along the side walls sit two nude youths (twenty in all), holding lengths of cloth that pass through slits in the rims of ten medallions painted to resemble bronze.

Nine scenes from Genesis, alternating between large and small, fill the center of the ceiling. This central spine of narratives is framed by continuous cornices that run above the thrones of the prophets and sibyls; at the corners of this frame and above the triangular areas that surmount the windows, the cornice seems to be supported by the horns of twelve rams' skulls, a motif taken from the vocabulary of ancient Roman decorative motifs. The spaces between the triangular areas above the windows, the cornice, and the thrones are filled by bronze-colored nudes. The footstools of the thrones are wedged between the frames of the triangular areas. The four corner spandrels contain four more scenes from the Old Testament, and the eight triangular areas and the lunettes above the windows contain figures representing the forty generations of the ancestry of Christ. Two of these lunettes were later destroyed by Michelangelo himself to make way for the *Last Judgment*, which fills the end wall of the chapel. The prophets, sibyls, nudes, and scenes are painted in naturalistic colors, and the nudes and their accessories are often permitted to overlap the scenes. The bands simulate marble architecture; some figures simulate bronze sculpture, others marble.

The scenes have no spatial relation to the surrounding figures, and the whole structure cannot be seen from a single viewpoint. In order to see the scenes right side up, one must start at the entrance to the chapel and move toward the altar; the sequence must, therefore, be read backward in time, from the story of Noah overhead to the Creation at the far end. The ceiling demands four conflicting directions of vision, and although at key points it is tangent to the architecture of the chapel, it is not derived from the preexistent shapes and spaces but is almost wholly autonomous. In the last analysis, a vision is incommensurate with the material world, and the Sistine Ceiling is, above all, a colossal vision.

The meaning of this vision has been the subject of much controversy, and the solution suggested here is that of the author. The prophets and sibyls can hardly be considered as prophesying the events shown on the spine of the ceiling, for these took place before they lived. According to a basic principle of Christian theology, prophets and sibyls see in these Old Testament events the revelation of the New Testament, the coming of Christ. For this reason the ancestors of Christ in the lunettes around the windows represent the physical origins of what the prophets and sibyls see in spirit. The meanings of their Hebrew names, as understood by medieval theologians, tally with the content that the prophets see in the central narratives.

Another level of symbolism is provided by the garlands of oak leaves held by a number of the nudes. Rovere, the family name of Sixtus IV and Julius II, means oak; the oak tree of the family arms decorates the marble barrier that divides the chapel at floor level; and oak leaves turn up in innumerable other places in the original Quattrocento decorations. Six of the seven prophets are concerned with the vision of the Tree of Life, which also figures in the poetic account of the writings of the sibyls. The Tree of Life, a Franciscan doctrine from the days of St. Bonaventura (see Taddeo Gaddi's fresco; fig. 83), was a natural parallel to the Della Rovere oak. Six of the nine Genesis scenes prominently display trees or wood, and two others are invaded by masses of oak leaves and acorns held by the neighboring nudes.

The symbolic structure of the ceiling can be interpreted in terms of the prophetic allusions seen by the pope in the tree on his own coat of arms, at the moment when he considered himself divinely chosen to lead the battle for the survival and renewal of the Church. We have no way of knowing how readily Michelangelo accepted this complex structure of interlocking allusions, but he provided it with a visual equivalent in the intricate design relationships of the ceiling. Moreover, he was able to find in each scene and figure a content so deep and a formal grandeur so compelling that it is generally difficult to think of these subjects in any other way. Inspired by the message and starting with his own vision of human beauty, Michelangelo rose to heights from which he alone, among all Renaissance artists, saw the Creator face-to-face.

He set to work at once, producing the hundreds of preliminary drawings that had to be made before the large cartoons could be started. Some of the drawings survive (fig. 512), suggesting the labor that went into every detail, but the cartoons have perished. They were laid up against the surface of the moist *intonaco*, and their outlines traced through with a stylus. The stylus marks in the plaster can even be seen in photographs. Michelangelo designed a new kind of scaffolding that could bring him up to the proper level, without support from

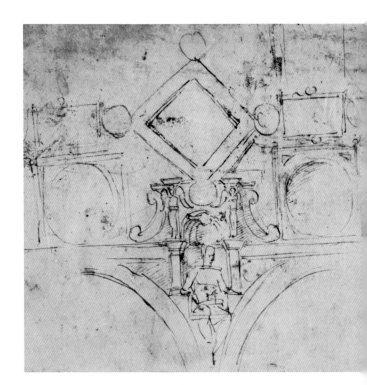

512. MICHELANGELO. *Study for Sistine Ceiling* (portion of sheet). c. 1508. Ink and black chalk. British Museum, London

either the ceiling or the floor. This scaffolding was based on beams that project like brackets from holes in the walls. Recently these holes were unblocked to become a base for rails for the mobile steel scaffolding used in restoring the ceiling. Michelangelo's scaffolding was shaped like a vault and, except for periodic removal and replacement of the boards so that the work could be seen from the floor, it was in place for the entire four and a half years of his undertaking. It permitted the artist to walk about as he wished and to paint from a standing position—and not lying down, as is still popularly believed. In a sonnet he described the physical discomfort he experienced while painting continuously from a standing position:

I've got myself a goiter from this strain . . .
My beard toward Heaven, I feel the back of my brain
Upon my neck, I grow the breast of a Harpy;
My brush, above my face continually,
Makes it a splendid floor by dripping down. . . .
Pointless the unseeing steps I go.
In front of me, my skin is being stretched
While it folds up behind and forms a knot,
And I am bending like a Syrian bow.

The scaffolding also aided Michelangelo in creating the measured framework of illusionistic architecture, a delicate procedure since the chapel narrows toward the altar. By September 1508 Michelangelo was already painting, and by January 1509 he was already in difficulties. Apparently he did not know enough about the recipe for *intonaco*, despite advice from his friend Giuliano da Sangallo, then also at the papal court, and the *Deluge* became moldy and had to be scraped off and redone.

The course of his work paralleled dramatic events in the pontificate of Julius II. When Michelangelo ran out of money, which happened twice, he had to go up to Bologna and beg from the pope, who was in the midst of the crucial phase of his war against the French. At the time of Michelangelo's second trip, in December 1510, the pope had already grown the long beard that gives him such a prophetic appearance in his late portraits. Quite possibly, the artist was moved by the spectacle of the old man's heroism, as well as by his vision of a unified Italy. Whatever the source of his inspiration, the artist seems to have became more deeply involved as the work proceeded. The first section of the ceiling to be undertaken—populated by relatively small-scale, neatly drawn figures and comprising the Noah scenes and flanking prophets, sibyls, and spandrels—is relatively timid in handling. The grandeur of the ideas and the heroic postures of the figures seem held in check by the precision of the sculptor's drawing. The *Deluge* (colorplate 88, p. 489), first of the larger scenes, probably gives some suggestion of the *Battle of Cascina* (see fig. 479) in its panoramic view filled with tightly drawn figures resembling sculptural groups. Despite the powerful figures and the dramatic conception, the composition seems scattered when compared with the unity of later scenes.

The deluge is depicted at a moment when only two rocks remain above the rising waters. On one stands a withered tree, on the other a green tree (largely destroyed in an explosion in 1797), which recall Christ's words when led to Calvary: "If they do these things in a green tree, what shall be done in the dry?" and are an implied reference to the Tree of Life and the Tree of Knowledge (see p. 280). Groups of helpless men, women, and children struggle to save themselves and their household goods from the waters. In the center the ark, which prefigures the cross as an instrument of salvation, moves rapidly into the distance. One of the most moving details is the father who holds in his arms the body of his drowned son (colorplate 89, p. 489). Michelangelo's precision extends even to the representation of homely benches and pots in the midst of this cosmic disaster.

One of the earlier prophets is *Isaiah* (colorplate 91, p. 492), who is seen as relatively youthful though he is gray-haired, with a poet's face ravaged by profound thought (colorplate 92, p. 492). Wrapped in meditation, Isaiah closes his book and turns in a majestic movement. He is about to drop his left hand—on which his head had apparently been propped—as he listens to one of his accompanying putti (each of the prophets and sibyls has two attendant figures, who exhort or inspire). He turns his face from the *Deluge* (above and to his left); the Lord had promised him, "For as I have sworn that the waters of Noah should no more go over the earth; so have I sworn that I would not be wroth with thee."

After the first section of the ceiling was completed in September 1510, the planks of the scaffolding were removed, and Michelangelo had his first chance to see how the work looked from the floor. Even within the first section, we can see that his style was changing as he worked and that the figures were growing in size and breadth. His response to the 1510 viewing was immediate, and the figures in the second section are dramatically expanded in scale.

The Temptation and Expulsion had always been depicted separately, as by Masolino and Masaccio in the Brancacci Chapel (see colorplates 4, 5, p. 13), but Michelangelo has united the subjects (colorplate 93, p. 492) by means of the huge tree that almost fills the scene from side to side, echoing the shape of the Della Rovere tree on the marble barrier. In a single overarching shape, the crime leads to its punishment. The tempting Satan and the avenging angel almost function as branches. Vigerio described the Temptation as an antitype of the Last Supper, and the fruit of the Tree of Knowledge as an opposite to the Eucharist, fruit of the Tree of Life. He tells us how Adam "turned his eyes from the morning light which is God, and gave himself over to the fickle and dark desires of woman," which is what seems to be happening in the fresco.

For the first time Michelangelo's figures fill the entire foreground space and are scaled to harmonize with the surrounding nudes. Foreshortened masses and features appear in a manner that will be more fully exploited in the later scenes. The expressive depth has also increased, and in no earlier works do we find any face approaching in anguished intensity of feeling that of the expelled Adam. The right half of the scene is a deliberate commentary on Masaccio and Jacopo della Quercia (see colorplate 5, p. 13, and fig. 180)—their scenes are here brought within the concept of High Renaissance harmony and compositional logic.

The Sibyl Cumaea (colorplate 94, p. 493), immensely old and incredibly muscular, is enthroned directly above the spot where the marble barrier originally stood that separated the section of the chapel reserved for the papal court, ambassadors, and other favored political and religious figures from that to which outsiders were admitted. Turning her wrinkled face toward the altar (colorplate 95, p. 493), she reads a book while her attendants hold another. In her youth when she was beautiful she was loved by Apollo, who promised to grant her as many years as the grains of sand she held in her hand; when she refused him, he doomed her to look her age. She is the sibyl of the Roman Mysteries because her *Sibylline Books* were believed to be preserved on the Capitoline Hill, and she therefore symbolizes the age and strength of the Roman Church. Her attendants, recalling the Child of the *Bruges Madonna*, look gently down on the weather-beaten buttresses of the aged face and the herculean left arm, which foretells in its superhuman might the arm of the *Moses* (fig. 516).

Michelangelo placed the *Cumaean Sibyl* next to the

scene of the creation of Eve from Adam's side (color-plate 96, p. 494), which Vigerio, following long tradition, compared to the creation of the Church from the side of Christ. God, who appears here for the first time in the Sistine Ceiling, stands on the ground, his eyes averted, his mantle wrapped about him. In all five representations of the Lord, this mantle is violet, the color of priestly vestments and altar decorations during the penitential seasons of Advent and Lent. Adam sleeps below a tree whose form suggests a cross. These massive volumes, recalling Masaccio in their bulk and even in their freely painted surface, hardly prepare us for the sudden flight into the heavens once the marble barrier is passed. It appears that these two scenes and their attendant prophet and sibyl must date between the autumn of 1510 and the return of the pope to Rome the following summer, his armies routed, and the city awaiting the attack of the French that never materialized. On August 14, 1511, the eve of the Assumption of the Virgin, the pope attended the first Mass in the chapel after the planking had been removed for the second time.

In the final section of the ceiling, concomitant with the revival of papal hopes and the triumph of Julius's armies, both form and spirit change beyond recognition. The first thing we notice is another increase in the scale of the figures. The prophets and sibyls, who have empty space around them in the first section of the ceiling and fill their thrones in the second, now overflow them. The footstools have to sink and the surrounding ornament give way before these figures, who are now nearly half again larger than their predecessors. In the narrative scenes, fewer, more colossal figures move within frames now too small to hold them. God himself, who was absent from the first four scenes and who stood on the earth in the *Creation of Eve*, moves through the heavens in the last four scenes.

Of all the images that crowd the ceiling, the *Creation of Adam* (colorplate 97, p. 494) is the one that has most deeply impressed posterity. Here we are given an unprecedented vision of the sublimity of God and the potential nobility of humanity. Borne aloft in his wide-floating mantle, which is bursting with wingless angels, God moves before us, his calm gaze accompanying and reinforcing the movement of his powerful arm (colorplate 98, p. 495). He extends his forefinger, about to touch that of Adam, whose name means earth and who reclines on the barren ground, his arm supported on his knee. The divine form is convex and explosive; the human is concave, receptive, and conspicuously impotent. All the dignified pomp of customary depictions of the Almighty has vanished, and he is garbed in a short tunic that reveals the strength of his body and limbs. Even Michelangelo's precise depiction of muscles, veins, wrinkles, fingernails, and gray hair does not reduce the power radiated by this celestial apparition.

Love and longing seem to stream from the face of Adam toward the Omnipotent, who is about to give him life, strength, and responsibility. The beauty of God's creation is evident in the breadth and nobility of the proportions and in the pulsation of the forms and the flow of their contours. A century of Early Renaissance research into the nature and possibilities of human anatomy seems in retrospect to lead to this single moment, in which all the pride of pagan antiquity in the glory of the body and all the yearning of Christianity for the spirit have reached a mysterious and perfect harmony.

The contact about to take place between the two index fingers has been described as a current, an electrical metaphor foreign to the sixteenth century but natural enough considering the river of celestial life surrounding the Lord that is ready to flow into the waiting body of Adam. At the same time, Michelangelo's new image symbolizes the instillation of divine power in humanity, which took place at the Incarnation. Given Vigerio's repeated insistence on the doctrine of Christ as the new Adam and the position of the scene immediately after the barrier to the sanctuary, a spot customarily reserved for the Annunciation, we can recall Isaiah's prophecy of the Incarnation: "Who hath believed our report? and to whom is the arm of the Lord revealed? For he shall grow up before him as a tender plant, and as a root out of a dry ground."

The mighty right arm of the Lord is revealed, naked as in no earlier representation. And directly below Adam, the arm of the veiled youth above the *Persian Sibyl* projects into the scene. This hand holds a cornucopia bursting with Della Rovere leaves and acorns that appear to grow from the dry ground. But the final explanation of the content of the *Creation of Adam* may lie in the third and fourth stanzas of the hymn *Veni Creator Spiritus* (Come, Holy Spirit); this is the hymn that was sung before each afternoon vote when the Sistine Chapel was used for a conclave to elect a new pope. A literal translation discloses the relation of text to image:

> Thou, sevenfold in thy gifts,
> Finger of the paternal right hand,
> Thou, duly promised of the Father
> Enriching our throats with the word,
> Let thy light inflame our senses,
> Pour thy love into our hearts,
> Strengthen us infirm of body
> Forever with thy manly vigor.

So is explained in terms of divine guidance not only the outpouring of love into the heart of Adam but the impotence of his body until the Lord fills it with "manly vigor." It could even be argued that the Della Rovere acorns (*glandes*) are related visually to the genitals of the nudes. In High Renaissance Rome such explicit symbolism was considered neither indecent nor irreverent, in contrast to the Florence of Soderini, which required a girdle to cover the genitals of the *David*.

Never was the "melodious line" of Michelangelo more beautiful than in this scene, for which a number of life studies survive. These splendid drawings show that the power and perfection of Michelangelo's figures were derived from his own imagination. Muscles that in the live model were knotted and awkward are transfigured in the fresco by the force that flows through them, as well as by the inner logic of the lines, which relates profiles on opposite sides of a single limb to each other like intertwined themes in a polyphonic composition.

The final large scene depicts two incidents in one, the *Creation of Sun, Moon, and Plants* (colorplate 99, p. 495). In a simple cruciform gesture, the Lord, sweeping through the heavens attended by angels, thunders the sun out from one hand and, apparently simultaneously, the moon from the other. According to the account in Genesis, this event occurred on the fourth day. At the left Michelangelo shows us the Lord from the back, stretching forth his hand on the third day to call plant life from the earth. In an Augustinian interpretation of the ceiling, one scholar has called attention to St. Augustine's quotation of the words of the Lord to Moses: "While my glory passeth by, that I will put thee in a clift of the rock, and will cover thee with my hand while I pass by: And I will take away mine hand, and thou shalt see my back parts: but my face shall not be seen" (Exodus 33:22–23). Michelangelo has represented the Creator exactly according to these lines, hidden face, back parts, and all. The scene is directly over Botticelli's fresco of the *Youth of Moses* (fig. 342) and the throne of the Della Rovere pope.

After the relative restraint of the preceding scenes, the violent movement of the *Creation of Sun, Moon, and Plants* comes as a shock. On the right the Lord hurtles toward us in space, then turns as swiftly to move away again. His awesome expression and the powerful masses in full movement combine to raise the image to a new plane of grandeur. The sun and moon are whirling out of the space of the picture. All the forms are foreshortened in depth; Vasari expressed his wonder at how the Lord's right arm could be inscribed within a square and still seem completely projected in depth. And the figures are so huge that, if brought to the foreground plane, they could not be contained within the frame. A new pictorial freedom accompanies this new expressive depth. Broad sweeps of the brush indicate torrents of beard and hair, from which a few wisps escape and seem to dissolve into air. Line is still operative, as always in Michelangelo, and very powerful, but it has lost much of its precision and is no longer the sole means for creating volume.

The last scene, the first in time, places the *Separation of Light from Darkness* (colorplate 100, p. 495) directly over the altar on which Mass was celebrated, and now even the point of view changes. For the only time in the ceiling, one of the scenes is presented as if viewed from below. With his arms raised like those of the priest at the consecration of the Host, the Lord shows that his plan for human salvation was preexistent from the moment when he first separated light from darkness. This idea is illuminated in Vigerio's *Christian Decachord* by a

dialogue across the ages between Moses and St. John the Evangelist, the Alpha and Omega of the Scriptures:

> *Moses*: In the beginning God created the heavens and the earth.
> *John*: In the beginning was the Word.
> *Moses*: The earth was without form and void.
> *John*: The Word was with God and the Word was God.
> *Moses*: Darkness was on the face of the abyss.
> *John*: In Him was life and the life was the light of men, and the light shineth in darkness.
> *Moses*: The Spirit of God floated over the waters.
> *John*: And the Word was made flesh.

In the words of the Gospel of St. John, the scenes of Moses on the left wall of the chapel are united with those of Christ on the right through the Christian revelation of the meaning of Moses' words. The message of the entire pictorial cycle of the chapel, ceiling and walls, culminates as it should above the altar, where the sacrifice of the Eucharist, fruit of the Tree of Life, takes place. Above us the Creator moves beyond the frame, his face turned from us so that it is seen only from below, his shape still obscure, upholding like Atlas the very weight of the heavens as he floats.

The *Libyan Sibyl* (fig. 513), last of her line, has stripped off her outer garments, which lie against the back of her throne, and turns in a *contrapposto* movement to close her book and replace it on its desk while she looks downward at the altar, ready to step from her throne. Scroll under arm, one of her attendant putti points to her as both putti depart. She has no need of book or scroll; her whole being is absorbed in the ultimate reality, the body of Christ in the Eucharist, celebrated on the altar below. The red chalk drawing for this figure (fig. 514) shows that, like all the female figures on the ceiling, the Libyan Sibyl was done from a male model. In the painting, Michelangelo has softened the harsh rack of male bone and muscle with a smooth veil of overlying tissue. At the lower left-hand corner of the study, he repeated the face, apparently in an effort to transform the commonplace features of his male model into the Hellenic beauty of a sibyl. In addition he has repeatedly analyzed the structure of the foot and hand, both of which bear an enormous weight. In the fresco these vital fulcra are defined and illuminated, as the masses of book, drapery, and body are brought to bear upon them.

The twenty nude youths, glorying in their beauty and power, may appear at first sight out of place in a Christian chapel, the more so in that most of their poses are drawn from pagan prototypes. There is, however, a long tradition for nudity in Christian art: all souls are naked before God and are so depicted in the Last Judgment (see figs. 489, 490). The youths are descendants of those who appeared a few years earlier in the background of Michelangelo's *Doni Madonna* (see color-

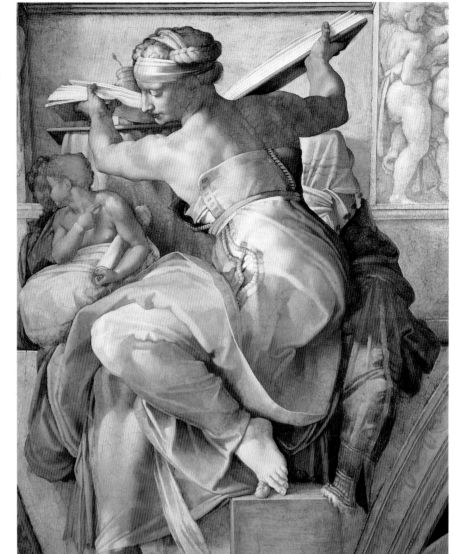

513. MICHELANGELO.
Libyan Sibyl.
1511–12. Fresco.
Sistine Ceiling

plate 85, p. 454). They uphold not only the medallions, most of which depict biblical scenes from the Book of Kings, but also garlands of Della Rovere leaves. Whether or not the nudes can ever be fully "explained," surely they represented in Michelangelo's mind a vision of a new and transfigured humanity.

Throughout the twenty nudes runs a surprising variety of types, movements, poses, and expressions, often responding to the scenes they flank. The nobility of their forms, the melodious course of their contours, and the light shining on youthful skin reflect in smaller scale the quality of Adam in the *Creation of Adam*. One of the finest is the heroic youth above Jeremiah (visible at the lower left in colorplate 99, p. 495), his right hand gently touching his breast. While the broad masses of his

frame balance each other in perfect equilibrium, his wide-open eyes gaze calmly into the abyss where the Lord divides the light from the darkness.

The four spandrels at the corners of the chapel were painted with the adjacent sections of the ceiling and there is, therefore, a strong discrepancy in style between the first two, which are fairly timid in composition, and the powerful masses and drastic foreshortenings of the second two, which date from the final campaign. All four represent scenes from the Old Testament that prefigure the coming of the Savior through violence and death. Through the words of Christ himself, the scene of the *Brazen Serpent* (colorplate 101, p. 496) was thought to foreshadow the Crucifixion: "Even as Moses lifted up the brazen serpent in the wilderness, so shall

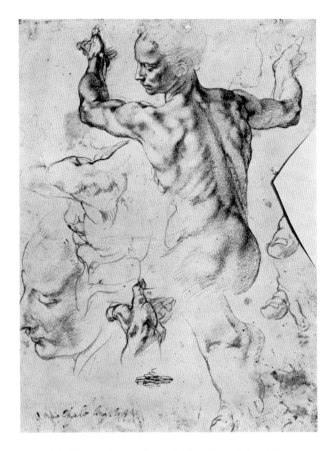

514. MICHELANGELO. *Study for Libyan Sibyl*. 1511.
Red chalk, 11 3/8 x 8 1/2". The Metropolitan Museum of Art,
New York

the Son of man be lifted up." At the left of the spandrel the young Moses lifts a woman's hand to the miracle-working image, strongly suggestive of the serpent that winds around the tree in the *Fall* (see colorplate 93, p. 492), much as Adam's hand is extended toward the life-giving Creator. On the right those who have not yet beheld the serpent of brass that will heal them writhe in a fantastic tangle of arms, legs, and pain-racked bodies, seen from below in unheard-of foreshortenings. Never had figures been so treated, not even at the most extreme moment of the ancient Hellenistic style. The Mannerist painters of the late sixteenth century and the Venetian Tintoretto (see figs. 702, 706, and colorplate 126, p. 615) were to draw continuing lessons from the extraordinary freedom of this composition, in which ground and background, up and down, in fact all the relationships of everyday existence are dissolved by the storm of shapes.

It is now clear that Michelangelo painted the sixteen lunettes containing the forty generations of the ancestry of Christ in groups corresponding to the campaigns of 1508–10, 1510–11, and 1511–12, once that entire section of the vault had been completed. He devised a special scaffolding for the purpose, a design for which is found on one of the sketches for the *Creation of Adam*. Probably this scaffolding hung from the central scaffold-

ing and could be moved from bay to bay as the artist worked. Michelangelo painted the lunettes at breakneck speed and apparently without the aid of cartoons. The earlier ones were done in two days apiece, one day for each group of figures (if the adults stood erect they would be nine feet high!). Those in the second half of the chapel, beyond the barrier, Michelangelo painted each in a single day, omitting the ornamentation seen in the earlier groups.

Restoration has freed Michelangelo's surfaces from layers of lamp, candle, and incense smoke, a coating of animal glue, and even the application of Greek wine in the eighteenth century to brighten things up; when this layer darkened with time, another campaign resorted to extensive repainting. The astonishing results have banished forever the old conceptions of a grayed-down, marbly Michelangelo that were based entirely on the layers of smoke, dust, and glue through which one had to look. The colors are as brilliant as those of the *Doni Madonna* (see colorplate 85, p. 454). The nudes glow with strong flesh colors and are more delicately modeled than was realized previously. The drapery vibrates with electric contrasts of hue and with iridescence, creating effects of startling vivacity. *Isaiah*, for example (see colorplate 91, p. 492), wears a tunic of a clear rose color, a blue cloak with a green lining, and an underskirt and sleeves of changing tones of gray, yellow, and lavender.

In the *Eleazar and Matthan* lunette (colorplate 102, p. 496) the cinnamon-red cloak of the graceful, pensive young Matthan is scarcely more surprising than the brilliant orange and green iridescence of the tight-fitting hose that clothe his smoothly contoured legs. Cinnamon and green compete in the garments of Eleazar's wife, and it is now evident that the formerly monochromatic architectural enframement has at least three different hues—pale gray with a faint admixture of green for the moldings and cornices, creamy white for the pedestals and the flat slabs behind the prophets and sibyls, and soft lilac for the background and trim of the lunettes; only the latter was faintly perceptible before restoration. These new revelations have necessitated some rethinking of our attitude to the coloring of the painters of the following decade.

After the death of Julius in February 1513, Michelangelo returned to the abandoned project of the tomb, now a necessity. Many of the stones, deserted all this time in the Piazza San Pietro, had "gone bad," as Michelangelo described it, and some had even been stolen. Julius's heirs no longer wanted a freestanding tomb, probably because they were not sure if it would be possible, under a new pope, to place it in St. Peter's. One of the original rejected designs was revived, and about this we know a good deal from drawings and from the contract. The tomb was to be connected with the wall of the church on one side (fig. 515). The burial chamber was gone; the pope was to be interred in a sarcophagus on the second story and was to be shown either being lifted from it or lowered into it by angels. Doubtless this

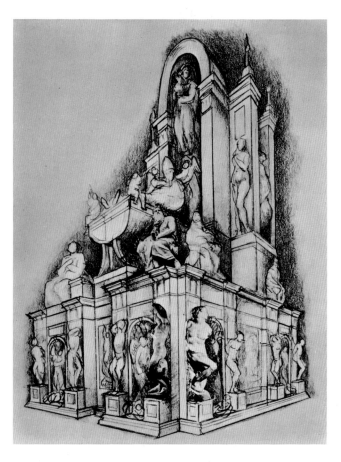

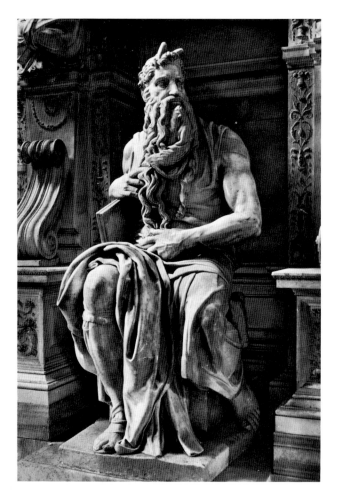

515. MICHELANGELO. Tomb of Pope Julius II. Proposed reconstruction drawing of project of 1513. Commissioned by Pope Julius II for Old St. Peter's, Rome

516. MICHELANGELO. *Moses*. 1513–16; 1542–45. Marble, height 7' 8½". 🏛 S. Pietro in Vincoli, Rome. Commissioned by Pope Julius II for his tomb

was to utilize the same block ordered earlier and possibly even the pose designed earlier for the recumbent statue in the burial chamber. Above, in a lofty niche, was to stand the Virgin, floating as if in a vision, holding the Christ Child. There were to be standing saints in other niches, but the rest was to have followed the 1505 project, save that the Victories would be reduced to six and the Captives to twelve, and the space intended for the door to the burial chamber would be filled with a relief.

Although Michelangelo worked at great speed for three years to advance the tomb, only three of the statues were brought even close to completion. The *Moses* (fig. 516) is now in place on the reduced version of the project dedicated in 1545 (see fig. 676), but two *Captives* (figs. 517, 518), for which there was no room in the final version, were, in consequence, given away by Michelangelo. Originally *Moses* was intended to occupy a corner position on the second story and therefore was intended to be seen sharply from below and as a transitional figure between two faces of the monument. The reader fortunate enough to see the original should attempt to view it from a crouching position opposite the right front corner. In its position on the revised monu-

ment of 1545 and in virtually all photographs, the torso seems unusually long. Moses has not just come down from Mount Sinai, as the tourist is often told, nor is he angry at the Israelites for worshiping the Golden Calf. Moses holds the Tablets of the Law and looks outward, not in anger but with prophetic inspiration, as the man who on Sinai saw and talked with God. Like the *David* (see fig. 477), the statue is symbolic rather than merely anecdotal. The horns on Moses' head are the horns generally shown there in Christian art, through a possibly deliberate mistranslation of the original Hebrew word for "shining," used in Exodus to describe Moses' face the second time he came down from Sinai (see p. 331).

The figure is closely related to some of the prophets and sibyls on the Sistine Ceiling. The left arm repeats almost exactly the muscular left arm of the *Cumaean Sibyl* (see colorplate 94, p. 493). The face, whose expression is disturbed by the fire and thunder of the mountaintop revelation, seems to be related to Michelangelo's own face-to-face colloquies with the Almighty as he painted the Sistine Ceiling, as in the *Creation of Sun, Moon, and Plants* (see colorplate 99, p. 495). The immense vitality of Moses is expressed in the mantle surging over the right knee, and in what may be the most spectacular

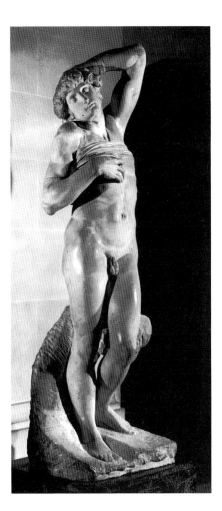

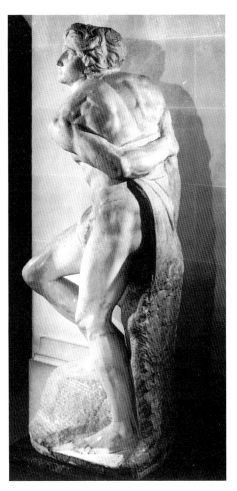

right: 517. MICHELANGELO.
Captive now known as the
Dying Slave. 1505–6; 1513–16.
Marble, height 7' 6". The
Louvre, Paris. Commissioned
by Pope Julius II for his tomb

far right: 518. MICHELANGELO.
Captive now known as
the *Rebellious Slave.* 1513–16.
Marble, height 7'⁵/₈". The
Louvre, Paris. Commissioned
by Pope Julius II for his tomb

beard in the history of human imagination. This cataract tumbles in waves, billows, and freshets from the prophet's cheeks and chin down over his deep chest. The bulk of the locks, pulled aside by the right hand, continue down to the gigantic lap, where the rest is hidden behind the left hand.

Michelangelo made detailed scale models for his earlier statues, and one of these for the *Moses* was surely seen by Raphael as early as 1511 (see p. 509), but the bulk of the carving must have been done in 1513–16. In a letter of 1542, Michelangelo mentions that the *Moses* is almost finished, although he may have done more work on the face just before the statue was placed on the final tomb. Certainly, the subtle shifting of planes and the new softness of surfaces are unlike the hard precision of Michelangelo's earlier sculptural style; perhaps this was due to his intervening experience as a painter.

The two *Captives* in the Louvre may have been intended for positions flanking the corner that culminated in the *Moses* on the second story, as indicated in the reconstruction (fig. 515). The *Captive* known as the *Dying Slave* (fig. 517) is not dying but is overpowered by the bonds against which he plucks idly, as if he were drowsy, overcome by the stupefying effects of a potion. His tall figure seems ready to collapse, or rather to sink slowly downward. During the period when this statue was being worked on, and during the ensuing decade or so, Michelangelo often drew figures almost or even entirely without contours, resorting to shading in leadpoint to indicate the rhythmic swelling and subsidence of the muscular surface of the figure. Here, throughout the back and left arm, and in the abdomen and beautifully rendered thigh, this pulsation reaches a new peak of intensity. The legs and feet are delicately handled, down to the last silken passage of skin around a thigh or calf, or the faintest change in the pressure of toes and tension of ligaments. Contour still operates throughout the body, sweeping along with the rolling surfaces of the intervening volumes. One wonders, in view of the contrast between the absolute finish of the legs and the rough stone next to them, if the artist intended to carve jagged rocks, as in the *Bruges Madonna* and the *David* (see figs. 475, 477).

Seething with rage, the *Captive* known as the *Rebellious Slave* (fig. 518) struggles against the slender bands that tie back the immense torso, the powerful arm, and the heaving masses of bone and muscle that comprise the back. Although in one sense he is prefigured by some of the massive nudes in the latest section of the Sistine Ceiling, this being seems to come from another race. He seems crushed, tormented, and anguished, and at the same time his forms have lost the resiliency of youth. The face, unfinished and also badly cracked, seems to have held less interest for the artist than the body. With its backward twist and rolling eyes, it suggests the agonized ancient sculpture of the *Laocoön*, but the mouth is closed. Drill marks are visible at the roots of the hair and among the locks. The crisscrossing sweeps of the three-toothed chisel, employed almost like a brush, are worlds apart from the neat, engraverlike hatching of the *Taddei Madonna* (see fig. 476). The muscles are no longer individually defined and separated, but flow together in a tide that even obliterates the boundaries between leg and torso, or torso and arm. It is as if the figure were formed from some primal bioplasm, pulsating with human life, but not yet functionally differentiated.

Previous interpretations of the meaning of the 1505 project for the tomb of Julius II (see fig. 510) present it as an ascension from a life of struggle on earth through a succession of Neoplatonic realms to the ultimate perfection of the pope's translation to a heavenly existence at the summit. This view would seem to suffer if no statue were to have been placed at the top and, as we have seen, there is no evidence that one was to go there. A worse blow is the probability that the 1513 project (see fig. 515), culminating in the vision of the Virgin and Child flanked by saints, is based on an alternative design presented by Michelangelo in 1505. Insofar as we know, Julius II never showed much interest in either Neoplatonism or its advocates but was passionately concerned about the papacy and his own messianic role.

During his thirty-two years as cardinal of San Pietro in Vincoli (St. Peter in Bonds, or Chains), Julius had been known by the name of this church, as contemporary panegyrics and lampoons constantly remind us. His tomb was eventually erected in San Pietro in Vincoli, and, as we will see, Raphael made St. Peter in his *Liberation of St. Peter from Prison* (see colorplate 104, p. 514) a recognizable portrait of Julius. The Introit of the Mass of St. Peter in Bonds contains the verse from Psalm 138 in the Douai version of the Bible: "Lord, thou hast proved me, and known me: Thou hast known my sitting down and my rising up." The Latin sentence concludes with "my resurrection," and that is what we were intended to see—dimly through the tomb's chamber door in 1505, triumphant on the second story in 1513: the resurrection of the pope, like St. Peter, from the earthly prison to eternity.

In 1550 Vasari wrote that the *Captives* were to be identified with the provinces captured by the pope, but Michelangelo's pupil Ascanio Condivi said they were the Liberal Arts captive at the pope's death. In his 1568 edition Vasari tried to combine both ideas. But in 1505 Julius's captive provinces and his patronage of the arts were both still in the future. Actually, the Mass of St.

Peter in Bonds provides an explanation: "O God, Who made the blessed Apostle Peter to go from his bonds absolutely unharmed, absolve us, we pray, from the bonds of our sins, and graciously keep all evil from us."

The *Captives*, then, twisting and writhing in their bonds, are held by sin, and by the example of St. Peter they can appeal for deliverance, which is represented by the Victories in the niches. The herms (*termini* is the word usually used) are symbols of death, and to these *termini* the *Captives* were bound by narrow bands of cloth. The Latin word *vincula* has been translated as "bands." It is hard to think of any other explanation for the bands that in Michelangelo's *Captives* has excited wonderment on the part of spectators but little interest from scholars.

In the unfinished marble behind the *Captives* in the Louvre, apes can be seen—only lightly roughed in behind the *Captive* known as the *Rebellious Slave* and more clearly visible and holding a small object alongside the left knee of the other. The rival interpretations of these animals as the subhuman tendencies in mankind, characterizing as evil the matter to which the Captives are fettered, or as the figurative arts (art as the "ape of nature") may both contain an element of truth. The Christian interpretation of the Captives in the bonds of sin and death is not incompatible with the Neoplatonic doctrine of how the lower soul is tied to matter. And Michelangelo may really have meant the apes to suggest—impishly rather than seriously—that the visual arts had died with Julius II, perhaps in part because the new pope, Leo X, had for the moment given him no commissions. But if the figures had been entirely finished, it seems that the apes would have to have vanished, as there is no room for them on the pedestals.

In both the 1505 and the 1513 versions, the tomb would have been an unprecedented combination of architecture and sculpture, rich in its surfaces, powerful in its vertical motifs made of struggling figures, imposing in its presentation of apostle and prophet, compelling in its suggestions of the torment of earthly existence and the heavenly release, transparently simple in its message.

RAPHAEL IN ROME

While Michelangelo was at work on the first campaign of the Sistine Ceiling, the young Raphael arrived in Rome, exactly when or why we are not sure. His style appealed to the pope, who stopped the work of the more conservative Sodoma and turned over the official decorations of his Vatican apartments (the *Stanze*, or rooms) to this new representative of High Renaissance classicism. The first room to be painted, from 1509 to 1511, was the Stanza della Segnatura (Signature), named after the highest papal tribunal, held under the presidency of the pope and requiring his signature. Leaving Sodoma's ceiling ornamentation largely intact, Raphael set up walls of brick in front of the preexisting and perhaps unfinished frescoes of the walls, thereby slicing off

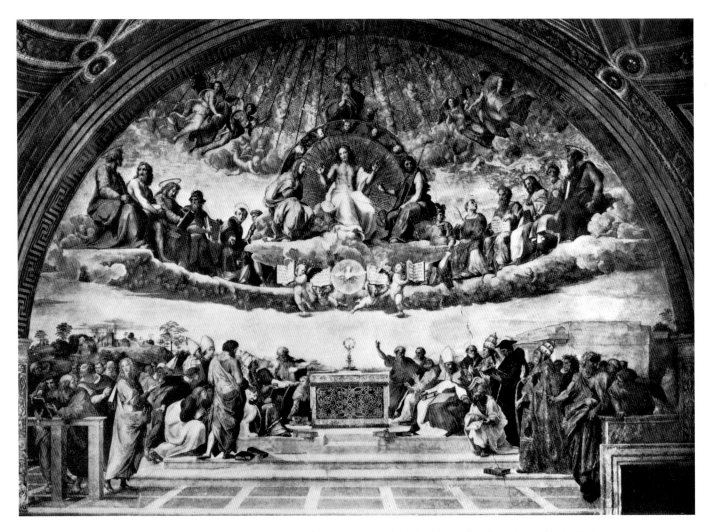

519. RAPHAEL. *Disputà (Disputation over the Sacrament)* or *Theology* (see colorplate 12, p. 20). 1510–11. Fresco, 19 x 27'. Stanza della Segnatura, Vatican, Rome. Commissioned by Pope Julius II

some of the decorations of the embracing arches. On the new walls he painted his own frescoes, which set forth the new ideals of Julius's reign and provided a new amplitude and harmony of space and form. The first of the wall frescoes to be carried out was the scene that is popularly known as the *Disputà* (fig. 519 and colorplate 12, p. 20), or *Disputation over the Sacrament*, in which Raphael created an airy apse composed of clouds and figures. The subject is an exposition of the doctrine of the Eucharist. The sacrament is traced from its origin in Heaven, where God the Father, Christ, the Virgin, and St. John the Baptist are enthroned among saints alternating with patriarchs and prophets from the Old Testament in a majestic semicircle of clouds, while angels fill the golden sky above. Overshadowed by the dove of the Holy Spirit between child-angels carrying the Four Gospels, the Host appears on an altar below, at the center of the perspective scheme, displayed in a shining monstrance.

The rapt tranquillity of the heavenly figures is contrasted with the active theologians on earth, coming from all ages to vie in discussions on the nature of the sacrament. At the left St. Jerome, his head bowed, con-

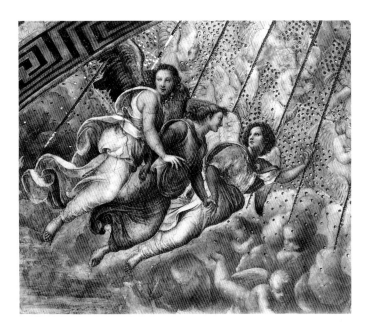

520. Angels, detail of fig. 519

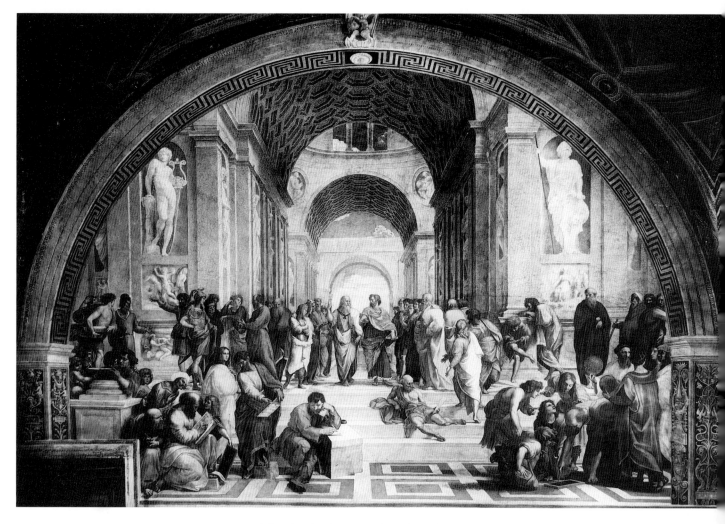

521. RAPHAEL. *Philosophy*, also known as the *School of Athens*. 1510–11. Fresco,
19 x 27'. Stanza della Segnatura, Vatican, Rome

templates the Vulgate, his translation of the Bible, while St. Gregory, a portrait of Julius II before he grew the famous beard, gazes at the revelation upon the altar. Among the figures at the right can be made out the standing Sixtus IV and, with a laurel crown, Dante. Raphael has endowed the earthly figures with a new sculptural quality and a new gravity of bearing, as if inspired by the grandeur of the Eternal City. He has set them in an ideal perspective which, as in Leonardo's *Last Supper* (see colorplate 83, p. 452), is no longer the point of view of an actual person standing in front of the fresco but that of a colossus. As a student once noted, such High Renaissance paintings depict not another room but another realm.

While Raphael was painting the *Disputà*, Michelangelo, only a few score yards away across an intervening court, but behind locked doors, continued work on the Sistine Ceiling. Raphael's new monumental figures are his own independent response to the demands of the High Renaissance. At the apex of the celestial dome (fig. 520), still covered with gold leaf and pitted with little cup-shaped depressions as in Signorelli's Orvieto

frescoes (see fig. 489), cloudy angelic shapes take on substance along glittering, incised rays, and before them soar archangels, their hands linked, their drapery billowing in the golden light. In these, as in the statuesque mortals below, the eye easily follows the spiral axis characteristic of Raphael's figures throughout his career. Their garments continue the spirals in broad airy curves that envelop the angels in a melodic motion, still faintly Botticellian but more ample and serene.

The medallions inserted by Raphael into Sodoma's ceiling decorations project a system of knowledge related to the frescoes of the four walls below. An allegorical figure of Theology is enthroned above the *Disputà*. Facing the *Disputà* is *Philosophy*, which is popularly known as the *School of Athens* (fig. 521), a misleading title that dates back only to the eighteenth century. The picture, recognized as a culmination of the High Renaissance ideal of formal and spatial harmony, was intended to confront the *Disputà's* theologians with an imposing group of philosophers of classical antiquity, likewise engaged in solemn discussion. As in the *Disputà*, the figures are arranged in groups, but now in a circle in depth, like that used by Ghiberti in his *Solomon and the Queen of Sheba* (see fig. 236) and by Fra Angelico in the San Marco altarpiece (see fig. 207). The perspective scheme converges at the far edge of the floor of the imagined building.

This is a noble structure, a single story in the Roman Doric order preferred by Bramante, and its grand barrel-vaulted spaces suggest less the obvious prototype in Alberti's Sant'Andrea, which Raphael probably had not seen, than Bramante's designs for St. Peter's (see fig. 503). At left and right are niches in which statues of Apollo and Minerva preside over the assemblage. Raphael's setting is not meant to suggest a real building; it is a pictorial invention intended to establish a grand classicized setting for his debators.

In the center stand Plato and Aristotle, who still are recognized as the two greatest philosophers of antiquity. Plato holds the *Timaeus* in his left hand and points with his right to heaven, the realm from which his ideas radiate to their embodiment in earthly forms; Aristotle holds the *Nichomachean Ethics* and points downward to earth as his source for the observation of reality. At the left Socrates can be seen engaging some of the youth of Athens in argument, enumerating points on his fingers. The old man sprawling on the steps is Diogenes. Others, surrounded by youthful pupils, are recognizable: at the lower left Pythagoras demonstrates his proportion system on a slate, while at the extreme right Ptolemy contemplates a celestial globe held before him, and just to the left Euclid bends down to describe a circle on another slate. Euclid is a portrait of Bramante—an appropriate choice considering the latter's concern with geometry. Just behind Ptolemy, Raphael and Sodoma can be seen side by side, but one wonders how much Sodoma, whose frescoes were being covered up, appreciated the compliment.

A single, lonely, mysterious man sits in the foreground, his left elbow on a marble block, his head propped on his hand. Oblivious of the others, wrapped in his own thoughts, he holds a pen over a piece of paper. Instead of the flowing mantles of the other philosophers and their attendants, this bearded, burly man wears the short, hooded smock and soft boots of a sixteenth-century stonecutter. He is absent from the cartoon for the figures and is, therefore, an addition inserted during the process of painting. His features are clearly those of Michelangelo. Apparently Raphael went into the Sistine Chapel with the rest of Rome in August 1511, experienced the new style, and returned to pay this prominent tribute to the older master. Perhaps he had actually seen the sculptor sitting dejectedly in the Piazza San Pietro, alongside one of the blocks for the tomb of Julius II. At any rate, his own style was never again to be quite the same. This single figure shows a mass and power not found elsewhere in the *School of Athens*, nor indeed in Raphael's entire earlier production. The impact of Michelangelo is also documented in the Apollo sculpture, whose head, torso, and legs are so

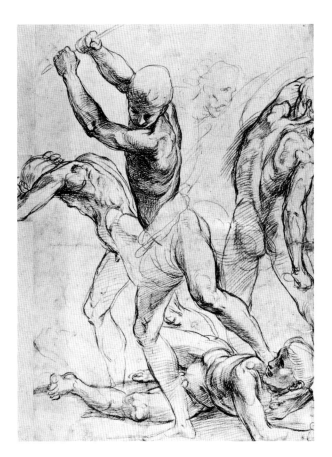

522. RAPHAEL. *Fighting Men* (study for relief sculpture in *School of Athens*). 1510–11. Red chalk over leadpoint, 15 x 11". Ashmolean Museum, Oxford

obviously based on the *Captive* known as the *Dying Slave* that Raphael must at least have been able to draw from Michelangelo's model. In addition, the study of fighting men for the relief below Apollo (fig. 522) shows a knowledge of anatomy and action learned from the Florentine sculptor.

Raphael at once put his discovery of Michelangelo to work in the lunette representing three of the four Cardinal Virtues: *Fortitude, Prudence,* and *Temperance* (fig. 523, and colorplate 12, p. 20)—the fourth, *Justice,* is in the ceiling roundel above. All the amplitude and monumentality of the last phase of the Sistine Ceiling are here, but Raphael avoids the tension of Michelangelo's work and infuses his own grace into the grand manner. Form and line sweep with ease from figure to figure, and all the surfaces glow with the fresh, blond tones and silvery light seen throughout the room. *Fortitude* holds a Della Rovere oak tree, and her legs and drapery are derived directly from those of the *Moses. Prudence,* as in Piero's Urbino portrait (see fig. 288), has two faces, one young, looking into a mirror, one old and bearded, looking backward. The long loops of *Temperance*'s bridle continue the curves of the composition.

The classic poise and precision of Raphael's Roman style are already showing signs of giving way to a new, almost Baroque manner in this lunette. This dramatic

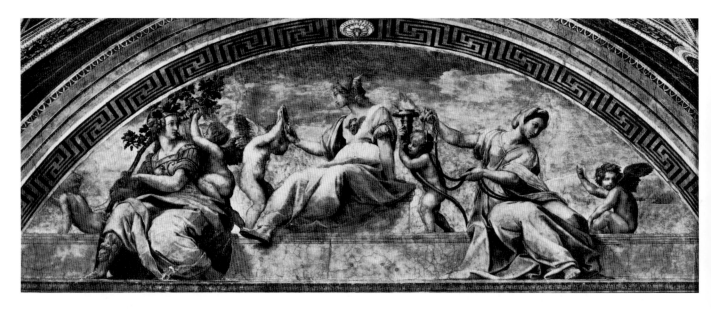

523. RAPHAEL. *Three Cardinal Virtues: Fortitude, Prudence, and Temperance.* 1511. Fresco,
base line c. 15'. Stanza della Segnatura, Vatican, Rome

phase comes to its climax in the second of the chambers, the Stanza d'Eliodoro, apparently commissioned by Julius II in August 1511, when he still wore the beard he had grown the preceding winter. As early as February 1512, the pope removed his beard because things were "at a good point." An early study by Raphael for one of the wall compositions, in fact, shows him without it. After the news of the battle of Ravenna, which seemed at first to be a defeat, reached Rome on April 14, 1512, the pope apparently grew his beard again, and he is shown wearing it in three wall frescoes of the Stanza d'Eliodoro, which could not have been painted between August and cold weather (there is no fireplace in the room), and he is still wearing the beard on Michelangelo's final version of the tomb (see fig. 676).

Over one of the windows Raphael painted the *Mass of Bolsena* (fig. 524), recounting a miracle that took place in 1263 (see p. 131). A Bohemian priest who could not bring himself to believe in the presence of Christ in the Eucharist was celebrating Mass when, to his astonishment, the consecrated bread shed drops of real blood in the form of a cross on a cloth (the corporal used in the Mass) on which it was resting. The blood-stained corporal, preserved as a relic in the Cathedral of Orvieto, was adored by Julius II for a full day during his first conquering march northward in 1506. Apparently, he attributed his victories then, and his triumph over the French after Ravenna—the news of which reached him on June 29, 1512—to the intervention of the relic, and in Raphael's representation he had himself represented as if he had been present at the original event.

The compositional movement, skillfully arranged around the off-center window, lifts gracefully through the group of mothers at the lower left to the torch-bearing acolytes, the amazed priests, and the calm pope,

now seen in profile with a full beard. Heavier and fuller architecture with powerful Ionic columns is glimpsed beyond the curve of the wooden niche behind the altar. Below, at the right, kneel the officers of the Swiss troops who spearheaded Julius's triumph in 1512. In these figures Raphael achieved superb portraits of forthright military men, whose splendid black-and-yellow uniforms are painted with the full coloristic richness of the artist's mature style. There is a greater breadth of handling than in the Stanza della Segnatura and a sonority of tone new in Raphael's style that is dominated by the black and gold of the chasuble, decorated with Della Rovere oak leaves, and the crimson of the papal cape.

The second stanza is named after the fresco that depicts the *Expulsion of Heliodorus* (colorplate 103, p. 513), an incident from the Book of Maccabees. One of the Seleucid monarchs, successors of Alexander the Great, sent his general Heliodorus to carry off the treasure of the Temple in Jerusalem. In the midst of the raid a heavenly rider in gold armor appeared upon a white charger accompanied by two youths "notable in their strength and beautiful in their glory." They beat the pagan general, who dropped the treasure and fell blinded before them. As in the *Mass of Bolsena*, the pope saw a parallel between this event and his own battle to expel rebellious cardinals who had followed the command of the king of France in attacking the papacy. The fully bearded pontiff enters the scene on his *sella gestatoria*; the bearer in the foreground with the square beard is Marcantonio Raimondi (1487–1534), whose engravings of Raphael's compositions gave them wide currency and popularity. Raphael himself, displaying an incipient beard, is seen partially hidden behind the chair.

Raphael's spiraling figures (see fig. 522) have entered on a new phase of heroic action in the whirlwind group

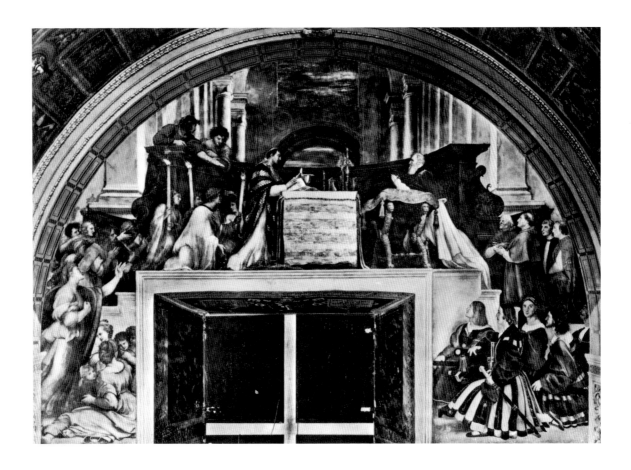

524. RAPHAEL. *Mass of Bolsena.* 1512. Fresco,
base line 21' 8". Stanza d'Eliodoro, Vatican, Rome.
Commissioned by Pope Julius II

at the right (fig. 525) and have been invested with the
weight and muscular power of Michelangelo. The dis-
grace of the despoiler and the howling rage of his attendants are contrasted with the inspired anger of the
celestial messengers, who float just above the pavement
and cast shadows on the marble. Like virtually all riders
on rearing horses for the next three centuries, the celestial warrior exhibits the influence of Leonardo's *Battle of
Anghiari* (see fig. 464). The architecture has changed
sharply since the *School of Athens* (see fig. 521); the
masses are heavier and more compact and the space
more restricted. The colors offer greater depth and resonance—the vaults of the Temple shine with a deep
golden light; in harmony with the *Mass of Bolsena,* the
color chord is dominated by the reds and blacks of the
pope and his entourage, against which the paler tones of
the kneeling women form delicate contrasts.

Facing the *Mass of Bolsena,* Raphael painted the *Liberation of St. Peter from Prison* (colorplate 104, p. 514), illustrating a passage from the Acts of the Apostles: "The
same night Peter was sleeping between two soldiers,
bound with two chains: and the keepers before the door
kept the prison. And, behold, the angel of the Lord
came upon him, and a light shined in the prison: and he
smote Peter on the side, and raised him up, saying, Arise

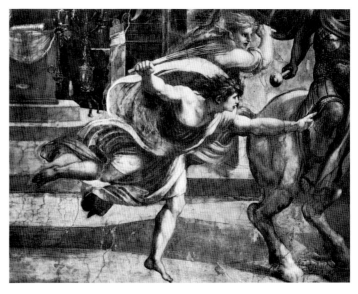

525. RAPHAEL. Angelic Messengers, detail of
Expulsion of Heliodorus (see colorplate 103, p. 513). 1512.
Fresco. Stanza d'Eliodoro, Vatican, Rome

up quickly. And his chains fell off from his hands. . . .
And he went out, and followed him, and wist not that it
was true which was done by the angel, but thought he
saw a vision" (12:6–9). Peter's salvation refers to the deliverance of the papacy from the French invader, for
when Julius II received the news of his unexpected vic-

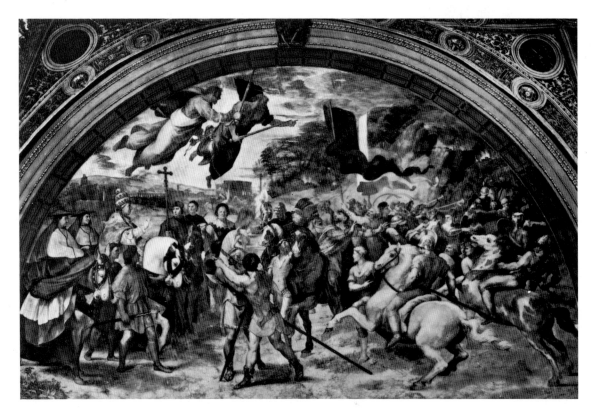

526. RAPHAEL. *Expulsion of Attila.* 1513–14. Fresco, base line 21' 8". Stanza d'Eliodoro, Vatican, Rome

tory in 1512, he was praying at the Church of San Pietro in Vincoli (St. Peter in Bonds). That night, in a reenactment of the liberation of Peter by the angel of light, Julius led to the Castel Sant'Angelo a procession that carried more torches than Rome had ever seen. But not long after, in 1513, probably while Raphael was painting this fresco, the pope died, and the work took on an additional meaning—the liberation of the old warrior from the earthly prison into eternal light.

Raphael's prison is a single massive arch built of rusticated blocks like those Bramante was using at the time for the new palaces (still unfinished today) for the papal administration. The grate through which we look into the dungeon was derived from ltalo-Byzantine representations of John the Baptist in prison, but there is a spectacular effect due to Raphael's new understanding of light. And the light effects are everywhere. Clouds drift in front of a waning moon and torches gleam on the armor of the guards, but the light from the angel transcends them all, fills the prison, and shines in the dark streets through which the spellbound Peter walks.

The room is completed by a final, dramatic fresco, the *Expulsion of Attila* (fig. 526). This event took place in the fifth century, when the unarmed Pope Leo I routed the king of the Huns outside Ravenna through the miraculous intervention of Sts. Peter and Paul. Raphael has set the event before the gates of Rome as an allusion to Julius's expulsion of the French invaders, and perhaps even to the deliverance of the papal city from Louis XII, who, in the summer of 1511, could have taken it easily and did not. The familiar shapes of

the constructions on the Palatine Hill, the half of the Colosseum that was still standing, and a Roman aqueduct can be seen in the distance at the left, while, at the right, the advance of the barbarians is marked by flames in the forest. The seemingly wild confusion of the foreground resolves itself rapidly into a collision between the calm might of Heaven at the upper left and the impotent fury of paganism at the right. Riding a mule, the pope extends one hand, the two saints float above holding their swords, and Attila turns away terrified. The other warriors rear back on their steeds, a wind sweeps over them, the flags fly, and the trumpets sound, but the shock of spirit on matter has stalled the advance.

The movement not only of the figures but also of the forms and colors in this work has been described as "Baroque" or "proto-Baroque," and at times we seem almost to be looking at a work by Rubens, who could not have done what he did in the way of battle scenes had it not been for this example. It should not be forgotten, however, that this kind of dynamic battle composition had been invented by Leonardo in his *Battle of Anghiari* (see fig. 464). Raphael had already expressed his admiration for Leonardo's rearing horses in his *St. George and the Dragon* (see fig. 480). Perhaps his interest in Leonardo's art was revived by the appearance of the master himself in Rome in 1513, while this fresco was being painted. It was completed after the death of Julius II, who should have been seated on the mule; instead, Giovanni de' Medici appears twice, as a cardinal at the extreme left and as Pope Leo X, claiming for himself the miracle of Leo I.

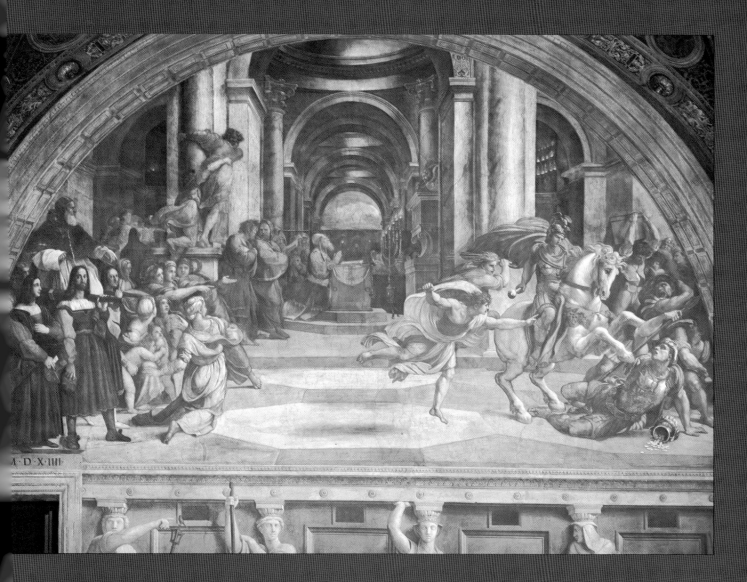

Colorplate 103. RAPHAEL. *Expulsion of Heliodorus*. 1512. Fresco, base line 21' 8". Stanza d'Eliodoro,
Vatican, Rome. Commissioned by Pope Julius II

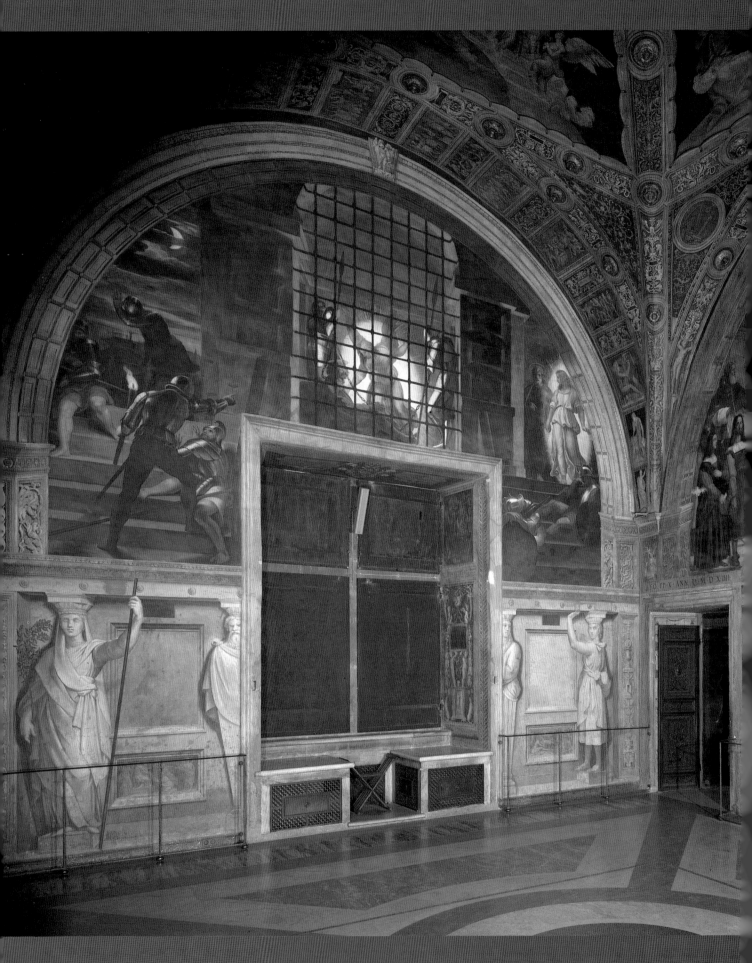

Colorplate 104. RAPHAEL. *Liberation of St. Peter from Prison*. 1513. Fresco, base line 21' 8".
Stanza d'Eliodoro, Vatican, Rome

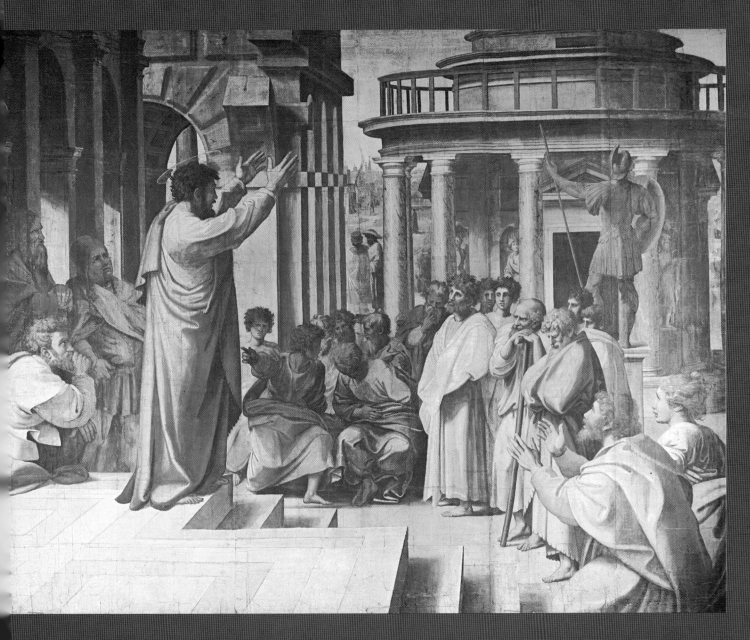

Colorplate 105. RAPHAEL. *St. Paul Preaching at Athens*. 1515–16. Cartoon,
watercolor on paper, 11' 3" x 14' 6". Victoria and Albert Museum, London. Commissioned by
Pope Leo X for the tapestries for the Sistine Chapel

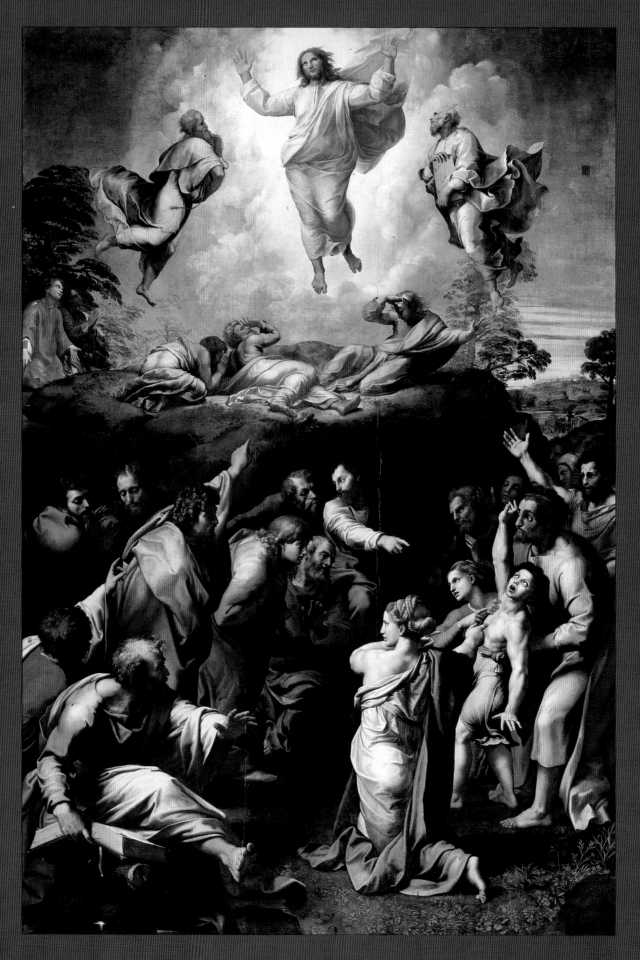

Colorplate 106. RAPHAEL. *Transfiguration of Christ*. 1517. Panel, 13' 4" x 9' 2". Pinacoteca, Vatican, Rome.
Commissioned by Cardinal Giulio de' Medici for the Cathedral of Narbonne

Colorplates 103–110

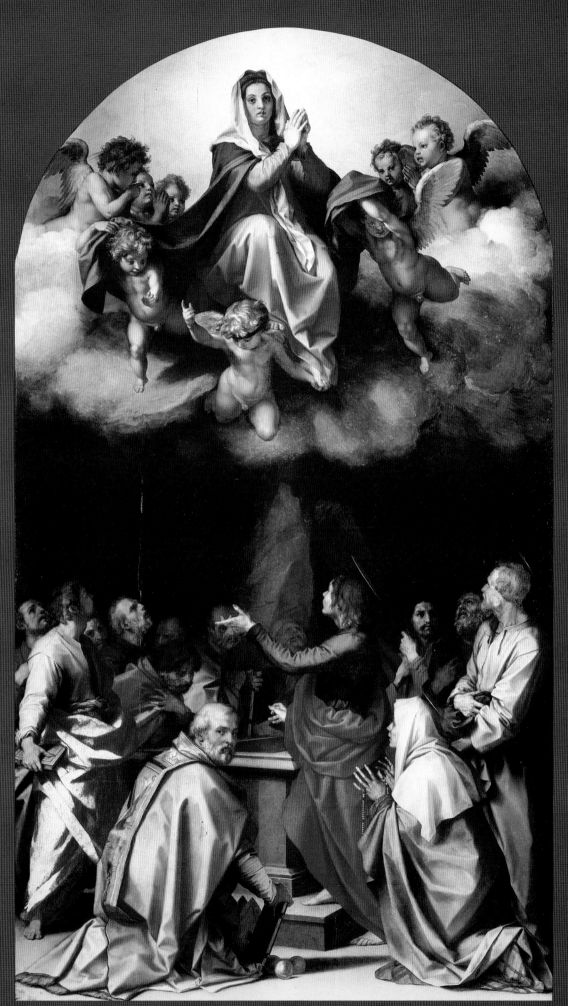

Colorplate 107.
ANDREA
DEL SARTO.
*Assumption
of the Virgin.*
1526–29.
Panel, 93 x 81".
Pitti Gallery,
Florence.
Commissioned
by Margherita
Passerini for
Sant'Antonio
dei Servi,
Cortona

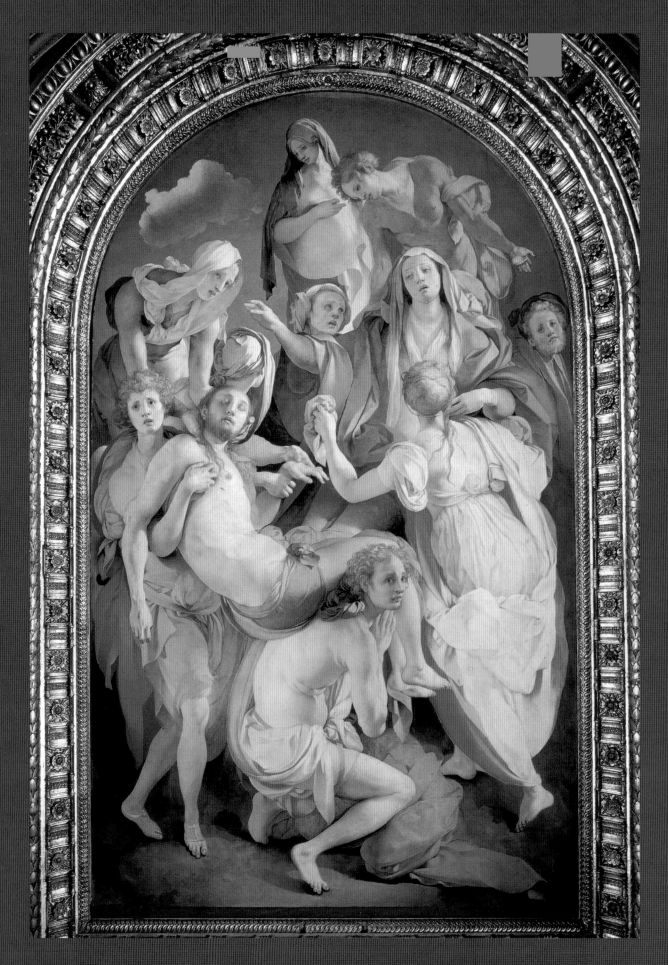

Colorplate 108. PONTORMO. *Entombment*. 1525–28. Panel, 10' 3" x 6' 4".
🏛 Capponi Chapel, Sta. Felicita, Florence. Commissioned by the Capponi family

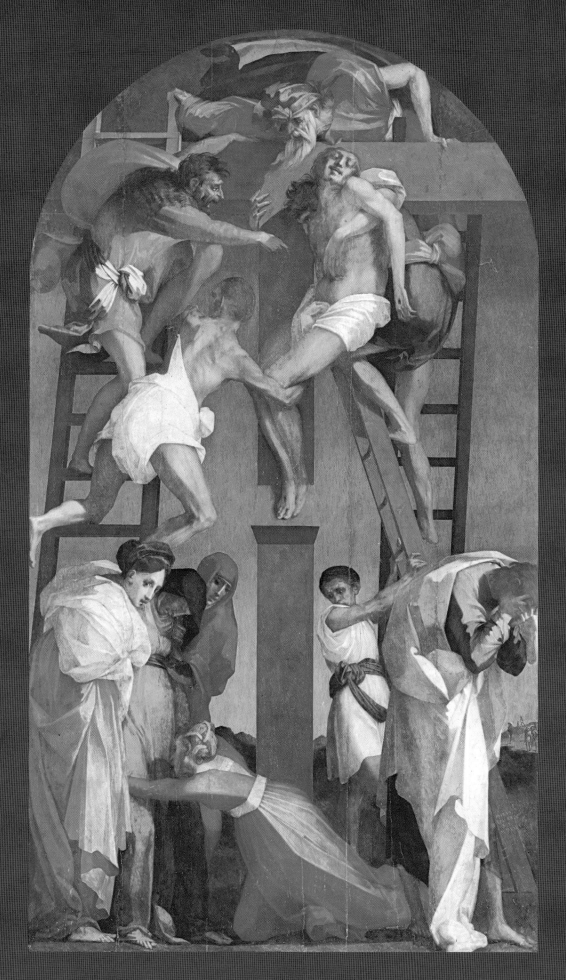

Colorplate 109. ROSSO FIORENTINO. *Descent from the Cross*. 1521. Panel, 11' x 6' 6". Pinacoteca, Volterra

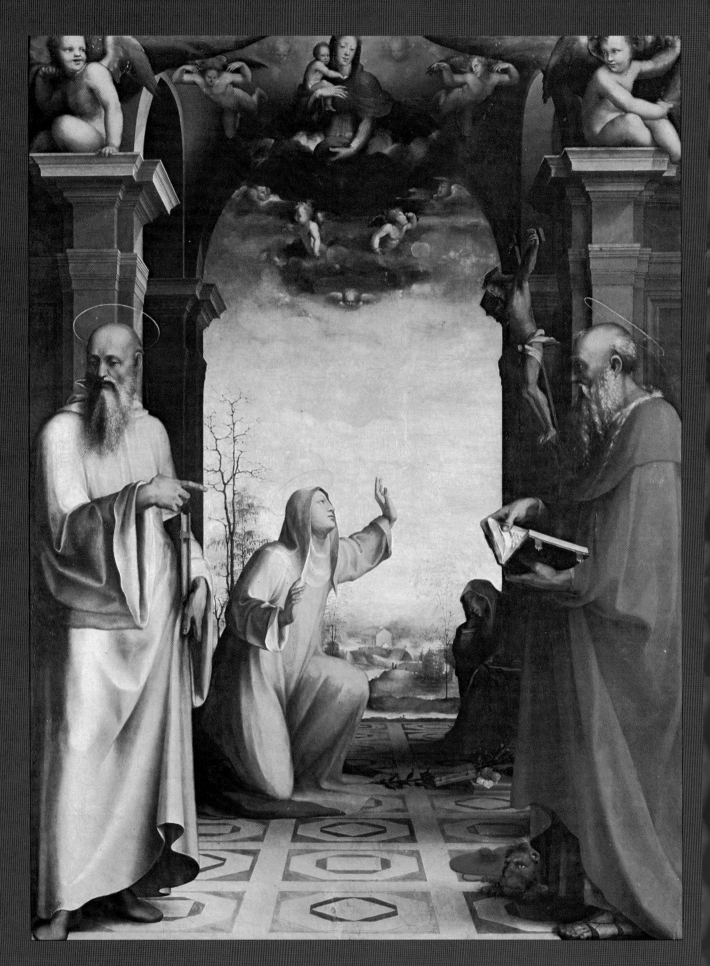

Colorplate 110. DOMENICO BECCAFUMI. *Stigmatization of St. Catherine.* c. 1518. Panel, 80³/4 x 61¹/2".
Pinacoteca, Siena. Commissioned for the Benedictine Convent of Monte Oliveto, near Siena

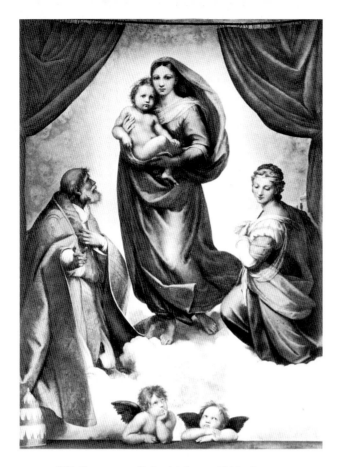

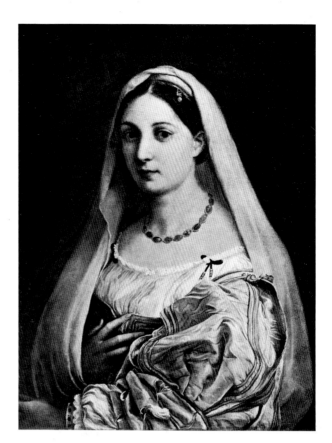

527. RAPHAEL. *Sistine Madonna.* 1513. Canvas, 8' 8½" x 6' 5". Gemäldegalerie, Dresden. Commissioned by Pope Julius II for S. Sisto, Piacenza

528. RAPHAEL. *Donna Velata (Veiled Woman).* c. 1513. Canvas, 33½ x 23½". Pitti Gallery, Florence

The old pope was gone, yet Raphael had one more chance to immortalize him. The *Sistine Madonna* (fig. 527), which hung for centuries in San Sisto at Piacenza, in northern Italy, may have earlier fulfilled another purpose. It was once suggested that this painting, the most celebrated of all Raphael's Madonnas and the first to be painted on canvas, was originally intended to hang above the bier of Julius II and that it was then sent to Piacenza because the principal church dedicated to St. Sixtus, patron saint of the Della Rovere family, was situated there. It has been pointed out, however, that the pope had promised the painting to Piacenza in appreciation for the assistance given him by that city in his war against the French. Nonetheless, the picture assumed a commemorative role. As can be verified by comparison with medals and other portraits (see fig. 382), Sixtus is a portrait of Julius II, his beard and moustache shaggy and unkempt as in his last, illness-ridden days, just as we see him in the *Liberation of St. Peter.* The ornament of his cope is made up largely of oak leaves, and an acorn crowns his tiara, which is laid on a brown strip of wood on which two disarming putti lean their elbows as they gaze upward.

This wood has been identified as the lid of Julius's coffin, with the papal tiara placed above his head, as the crown still is today in royal funerals. At the right kneels St. Barbara, gazing downward; as the patron saint of men-at-arms, she is an appropriate pendant for Julius II. Because she was liberated from a tower (its battlements can be glimpsed between her back and the curtain), she

is the patron saint of the hour of death and of liberation from the earthly prison. Finally, the suddenly parted curtains reveal a vision, as one of Raphael's loveliest Virgins walks toward us, holding up the Christ Child. Mother and Child look upon us with eyes of unusual size, depth, and luminosity, of calm and perfect understanding. Mary's pose is identical with that imagined by Michelangelo, probably as one of the alternates for the design of the tomb of Julius II accepted in 1505 and certainly for the definitive version in 1513 (see fig. 515). Either the idea of the floating Virgin arose in the pope's mind and was communicated to both artists, or it was developed by Michelangelo in 1505, not long after the completion of Fra Bartolommeo's *Vision of St. Bernard* (see fig. 486) and, like many of Michelangelo's ideas, reached Raphael later.

The Virgin Mary in this allegory of the pope's entry into Paradise is revered as a representation of ideal motherhood. In its broad rising and descending curves, its subtle balance of masses, its rich tonalities of gold and green, gray and blue, its air of peace and fulfillment, the *Sistine Madonna* is one of Raphael's most memorable creations. No one could have predicted at the time of the arrival in Rome of Perugino's pupil, fresh from absorbing what he could understand of Leonardo and Michelangelo in Florence, that in a few years Raphael of Urbino would earn the rank of a great master, speaking with the full authority of High Renaissance utterance.

Whoever she may have been, the sitter for the so-called *Donna Velata (Veiled Woman;* fig. 528) is probably

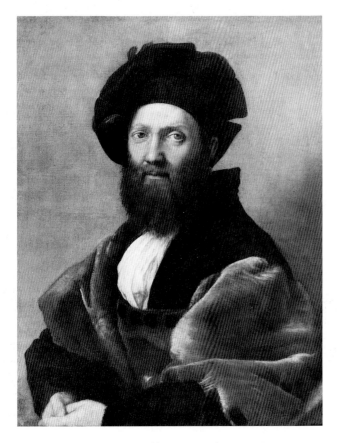

529. RAPHAEL. *Baldassare Castiglione*. c. 1515.
Canvas, 32¼ x 26½". The Louvre, Paris

friend of the painter, exemplifies the *riposo*, or inner calm, he recommends as essential of gentlemanly character. The picture has been cut at the bottom, but old copies show it with the folded hands in their entirety. If it were complete, the appearance of closed harmony and poise would be even more impressive.

The black, white, and soft gray of the costume embody the sobriety and restraint preached by Castiglione to a society reacting to the flamboyant colors of late Quattrocento dress. Raphael develops this monochromatic scheme with surprising resonance against the golden gray of the background, which is warmly reflected in the lights on the richly painted sleeves. Rembrandt once tried to acquire this painting at auction; forced to retire when the bidding went out of his reach, he never forgot the composition, and twice did his own self-portrait in the pose and style of the *Castiglione*. Even in the midst of Raphael's maturity and his new-found colorism, the spiral principles of his earliest compositions are still at work and can be easily followed in the masses of the costume and hat and the tilt of the head.

The death of Julius II brought a boyhood acquaintance of Michelangelo's, Cardinal Giovanni de' Medici, second son of Lorenzo the Magnificent, to the papal throne as Leo X. Perhaps based on memories of the young sculptor's behavior in the Palazzo Medici, the new pope, an easy-going, luxury-loving, corpulent man only thirty-eight years old at the time of his election, had little interest in a close association with Michelangelo: "*É troppo terribile*," said the pope; "*non si puol pratichare chon lui*" ("He is too violent; one can't deal with him"). The commissions in the Vatican, therefore, went to others, chiefly to Raphael and his increasing entourage. Leo provided a relaxed atmosphere, and the Vatican was filled not only with artists, poets, philosophers, and musicians, but also with dancers, animal-tamers, and clowns, to whom almost equal importance was attached. Pious pilgrims from Northern Europe were shocked by the appearance of the pope and his cardinals in hunting dress and would have been even more outraged if they could have attended Vatican ceremonies, including funerals and beatifications, at which the Olympian deities were extolled. The pontiff, who immediately dropped the aggressive political policy of his predecessor, seems to have had no comprehension of his spiritual mission, and no inkling of what effects the challenges led by Martin Luther were bound to wreak. His learned and well-composed bulls were not enough to stop the Reformation.

A few years after his accession, the pope sat for a group portrait in which Raphael established a new level for searching analysis of character (fig. 530). The pope is not occupied with affairs of state but with antiquarian erudition and the delight of possession. He sits before a table where he has been perusing a splendid Trecento illuminated manuscript that is so accurately represented that the original, still preserved, has been identified. Beside the manuscript rests a silver bell, with gold top

the same woman Raphael used as a model for the *Sistine Madonna*. In color this is the richest of Raphael's portraits, so fresh and glowing as to suggest that the artist had absorbed still another achievement of a school to which he was not born—the colorism of Venice. No trip to the lagoons is recorded for Raphael, but in 1511 Sebastiano del Piombo had brought to Rome a repertory founded on the achievements of Giovanni Bellini, Giorgione, and Titian. Only by assuming a measure of Venetian influence is it possible to understand the rich color chords of the frescoes in the second stanza and the dazzling white-and-gold drapery of this portrait, the depth of the dark eyes and chestnut hair, the brilliance of the pale flesh, the soft glow of the stones in the necklace, and the luminous pearl hanging from the woman's veil. In its asymmetrical placing, this jewel brings all the other ellipses of the composition into relation with each other.

The portrait of *Baldassare Castiglione* (fig. 529), painted about 1515, is also typical of the moment of balance that Raphael achieved in Rome. As we have seen, Castiglione's *Il libro del cortegiano* expounded and established the qualities expected of an ideal gentleman in the High Renaissance. In his cool composure the count, a close

and gold borders, covered with classical vine scrolls. Both manuscript and bell are rendered with such precision that we wonder if Raphael has not used a magnifying glass like the one held by the pope. At the pope's right stands his cousin, Cardinal Giulio de' Medici, son of the murdered Giuliano and subsequently Pope Clement VII; on Leo's left stands his nephew Cardinal Luigi de' Rossi. The manner in which the three gazes cross is disconcerting. The composition is an **X**-shape, or would be if it did not lack a diagonal at the lower right. The diagonal movement of the architecture into depth lends a strange quality of baselessness to the painting.

The unease created by the unresolved composition is increased by the dissonance of the orange reds of the cardinals' attire and tablecloth with the purplish crimson of the pope's cape and hat. The pope's puffy countenance is rendered, like his shapely hands, with a striking fidelity to nuances of skin and flesh. In this atmosphere of tension, irresolution, and gloom, only the surge of crimson in the cape and the blizzard of whites in the rich damask sleeve provide any release. The polished brass sphere on the chair contains a distorted reflection of the room, like the convex mirror in the background of the *Arnolfini Wedding* portrait by Jan van Eyck, and although one can clearly make out the window at the right that is the source of illumination, Raphael's own figure is reduced to a few vague vibrations by the glare.

Under Pope Leo X, Raphael rose to a scale of power and wealth not previously enjoyed by any Italian artist. At Bramante's death in 1514, Raphael became papal architect and was charged with continuing the construction of St. Peter's. He was showered with commissions for Madonnas, portraits, frescoes, and mosaics. He was asked to paint a third stanza (the Stanza dell'Incendio) and to design the decorations of other rooms in the Vatican, including the loggie built by Bramante and a loggetta and bathroom for Cardinal Bibbiena, one of the cronies of Leo X. Raphael directed new buildings, including at least one church and one palace, and a villa for Cardinal Giulio de' Medici (see fig. 533). Raphael was also appointed as superintendent of antiquities—the first that we know anything about—and given power over excavations in the papal dominions. One of his major projects was a map of ancient Rome with its monuments traced and identified.

To keep up with this massive and manifold commitment, Raphael had to employ a number of assistants, probably not the "army" so often referred to, but including at least two skilled artists, Giulio Romano and Perino del Vaga. On occasion, independent painters were called in to aid in special assignments. As a result, the execution is at times uneven and the work of the less skilled pupils painfully evident. Even some of Raphael's contemporaries, in an era indulgent to the workshop system, deplored these lapses. There is evidence that Raphael sometimes asked his pupils to turn out scale models of pictures on the basis of his small sketches or verbal directions. When preserved, these models are in-

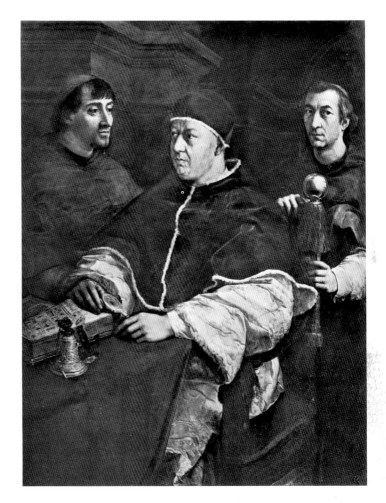

530. RAPHAEL. *Pope Leo X with Cardinals Giulio de' Medici and Luigi de' Rossi.* c. 1517. Panel, 60½ x 47". Uffizi Gallery, Florence. Originally owned by Pope Leo X

variably by the pupils, with an occasional possible correction from Raphael. However, they seldom correspond exactly to the finished compositions, which would indicate that the master then stepped in and somewhat reset the stage. It is surprising that under the pressures exerted upon Raphael in these seven years any substantial proportion of the finished paintings could have come from his brush, and yet, all in all, more than half the surface is surely by him in the most important commissions. Most of the detailed life studies, however, are by the pupils, who then presumably enlarged the approved model into a full-scale cartoon and carried out the preliminary procedures of the actual painting. Only by this system of preplanning the design and execution of the paintings was it possible for Raphael to carry out so much himself, on such a grand scale, and with the freshness of original creation.

The grandest of the pictorial projects assigned to Raphael in this hectic period was a series of ten tapestries, for which he produced ten full-scale cartoons in

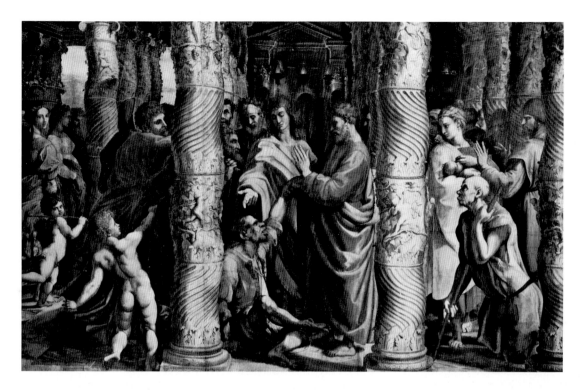

left: 531. RAPHAEL. *Healing of the Lame Man.* 1515–16. Cartoon, watercolor on paper, 11' 3" x 17' 7". Victoria and Albert Museum, London. Commissioned by Pope Leo X

below: 532. Male Heads, detail of fig. 531

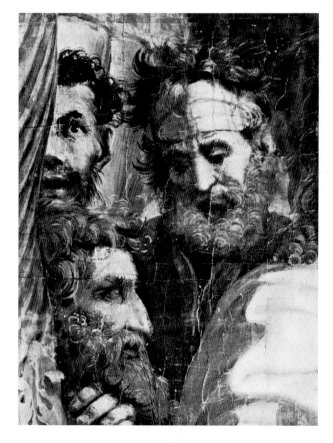

color (colorplate 105, p. 515; figs. 531, 532). These he painted in approximately eighteen months during 1515–16 as guides for tapestry weavers in Flanders. The finished tapestries, representing scenes from the Acts of the Apostles, were for the lower walls of the Sistine Chapel; covering approximately twelve hundred square feet, they completed the iconographic cycle that depicted the Life of Christ and the Life of Moses, the ancestry of Christ, the prophets and sibyls who foretold the coming of Christ, and scenes from Genesis. Raphael must have been aware not only that his compositions were to be on display at the center of papal power, but also that he was invading the sanctuary of Renaissance painting consecrated to Botticelli, Perugino, Signorelli, Ghirlandaio, and Michelangelo himself. While so exalted a destination probably did not cause him to alter his style, it did inspire him to devote all his energies—and probably those of the whole shop as well—to these figural compositions.

The resulting combination of grand-scale figures with the new architecture of the High Renaissance and with landscape backgrounds produced compositions that were exciting in their dense packing of elements and in their dramatic power. Moreover, since the cartoons were reproduced in many new series of tapestries throughout the sixteenth, seventeenth, and eighteenth centuries, and in numerous engraved copies as well, they ultimately became the most influential of Raphael's compositions. They provided inspiration for such later masters as Poussin, Domenichino, David, and Ingres. The original cartoons had to be cut in strips for the convenience of the weavers, and eventually three cartoons were lost. The other seven were acquired by King Charles I of England in 1630, but they were not remounted and ex-hibited as works of art until 1699. Today they are shown at the Victoria and Albert Museum under near-ideal circumstances of space and light. In spite of the numerous retouches to hide the joints, the majestic forms and brilliant color upset the traditional notions of the serene gentleness of Raphael's art, which is largely based on his early Florentine Madonnas.

The cartoons were painted in a glue-based watercolor over often-visible charcoal preparation that was probably drawn by the pupils, especially Giulio Romano, under Raphael's supervision. But by far the greater part of the color seems to have been laid on by Raphael himself, and there are passages in which the beauty and emotional fire of his mature style come through to us unaltered. Heads, drapery, landscape, and even, at times, architecture are painted with a new sketchy openness and freedom that may be related to ancient illusionist painting technique. Perhaps Raphael's own immersion in antiquity—deeper, more prolonged, and more lasting in its effects than that of any other Renaissance artist until this time—had familiarized him with Roman first-century painting.

But there are other sources as well. It has been noted how closely Raphael had studied Masaccio's frescoes in Santa Maria del Carmine (see colorplate 3, p. 12) and how he revived in the cartoons Masaccio's method of enhancing the physical bulk and psychological presence of his figures by enveloping them in voluminous mantles. It has been pointed out that Raphael may have revisited Florence briefly in 1515, just before his embarkation on this cycle. To an artist with Raphael's sense of history, it may have seemed appropriate to return to Masaccio's images, in which the barefoot apostles had been invested with such dignity and power. To keep the figures large in comparison with their setting, they are set in front of massive architecture that is cut off at the top by the frame yet breaks here and there to allow us to see, in the middle distance, the full extent and proportions of a classical order.

Raphael was able to contrast the largely decorative effect of the late Quattrocento wall frescoes, in which one must often search for the subjects, with the power of Michelangelo's scenes on the ceiling, especially those simplified subjects with which his tapestries would be placed in instant comparison. He therefore set the average height of a standing foreground figure at approximately eight feet, more than two-thirds the total height of the scene within the border. The effect of these heroic proportions against the restricted space, combined with the reality of Raphael's physical types, gives a new turn to the Renaissance vision of an ennobled humanity. For this is no longer, as in the ceiling, a nude, predominantly male, ideal race: through study of Masaccio, the man and woman in the street are raised to heroic stature and are framed—rough garments, bare feet, and all—by the richness of classical architecture.

In the *Healing of the Lame Man* (fig. 531), for example, the group is centralized at the Gate of the Temple, the Porch of Solomon (Acts 3:1–11). In the cartoon St. Peter lifts the lame man by the left hand, instead of the right, as in the text, because Raphael knew that in the tapestry the composition would be reversed; for the same reason St. Peter blesses with his left. The setting is surprising and even proto-Baroque in its vibrancy of form, light, and color. Apostles, mothers, children, and cripples move between spiral columns that reveal Raphael's interest in historical correctness. The screen before the chancel of Old St. Peter's had been formed by Late Antique spiral columns, probably brought to Rome in the fourth century A.D. from Syria, and it was believed that these had come from the Temple of Solomon. It was thought that Christ had often leaned against one of them to rest while teaching, and in the Cinquecento those obsessed by demons used to tie themselves to it to effect a cure. The columns, temporarily removed during the construction of Bramante's St. Peter's, were gradually relocated in various parts of the new building.

The original alternation of spiral fluting with vine scrolls and putti has been retained by Raphael, who apparently found plastic and pictorial excitement in the contrasting motifs. The columns, multiplied in depth, enshadow the porch and provide richly colored shadows against which the figures are fitfully illuminated. Their pulsating contours contrast with the other forms, and especially the broad outlines of St. Peter's cloak. The light seems to flash in eyes filled with wonder, and the shaggy hair and beards have even been compared to landscape masses (fig. 532). They may remind us of wild crags and forests, but control is provided by the spiral harmonies of Raphael's glittering brushstrokes.

Because of its classic balance of figural and architectural masses, *St. Paul Preaching at Athens* (colorplate 105, p. 515) became the most widely imitated of the cartoons. It was to be placed alone, just outside the marble barrier, as a symbol of the preaching mission of the apostles, which accounts for the device of the steps jutting down into the area where the Athenians, with whom Cinquecento visitors to the chapel could identify themselves, sit or stand. St. Paul, raising his hands, reminds his hearers of their altar to the unknown God: "Whom therefore ye ignorantly worship, him declare I unto you" (Acts 17:23). The statue of Mars is seen from the back (he carries his shield on his right arm and his spear in his left hand for subsequent reversal), while the Athenians listen, some with quiet conviction, others greatly disturbed. In the heavyset soldier directly behind the preaching apostle the features of Leo X can be recognized. The commanding figure of St. Paul is derived from Masaccio's St. Peter in the *Tribute Money*, *St. Peter Baptizing the Neophytes*, and the *Raising of the Son of Theophilus* (see colorplate 3, p. 12; figs. 193, 201). The dramatic central group, their bodies twisted, the folds of their draperies agitated as by a storm, is one of the finest passages from Raphael's later period. The man and woman at the lower right, however, like the two putti at the left of the *Healing of the Lame Man*, show the style of Giulio Romano.

The architecture is noteworthy. The round temple is a recognizable tribute to Bramante, as are the unfinished rusticated buildings, recalling his structures for the papal tribunal. The patterns of the receding arcade produce a kind of checkerboard of light and dark, an unexpected

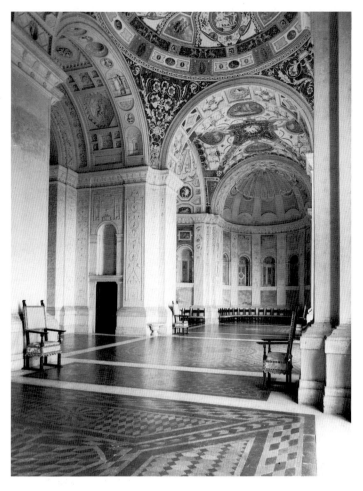

533. RAPHAEL. Interior of Medici Villa, now know as
Villa Madama, Rome. c. 1515–21 (decorations by GIULIO
ROMANO, GIOVANNI DA UDINE, and BALDASSARE PERUZZI).
Commissioned by Cardinal Giulio de' Medici

The great hall, with its single-story arches, groin vaults, and central dome, all looking out through arches to the garden, was a new invention that gracefully harmonized the architectural space with nature outside. The delicate decoration of stucco *grotteschi* and little paintings that clothes Raphael's simple forms was carried out after his death by his pupils Giulio Romano and Giovanni da Udine and his associate, the Sienese painter-architect Baldassare Peruzzi. The cardinal instructed the painters that he did not care what the subjects were, so long as they were recognizable and one would not have to add explanatory inscriptions, like the painter who wrote, "This is a horse." Ovid would do as well as anything else, the cardinal said, but the Old Testament was only good enough for the loggia of the pope. The present illustration was taken after Fascist renovations, which include a polished marble floor more appropriate to a luxury hotel.

Cardinal Giulio also gave Raphael the opportunity to express a new phase of his art, which, had he lived, might have had repercussions for Italy and perhaps all of Europe. For in 1517 the cardinal commissioned Raphael to paint a large panel representing the *Transfiguration* (colorplate 106, p. 516) for his cathedral at Narbonne, in France. The completed picture was so impressive that the cardinal kept it at San Pietro in Montorio in Rome rather than sending it to France. The story tells how Christ went with the apostles Peter, James, and John to the top of a high mountain, and there suddenly Moses and Elijah appeared, and Jesus' countenance shone with light, and his raiment was "white and glistening." Then a bright cloud came upon them, and the voice of the Father could be heard saying, "This is my beloved Son in Whom I am well pleased." They feared greatly when the prophets entered into the cloud, but when it passed away Jesus was again alone with the apostles. This is the scene that is represented by Fra Angelico (see fig. 213) and Giovanni Bellini (see colorplate 78, p. 415), but the sequel is rarely shown—the demoniac boy whom the apostles could not cure by their own efforts in Christ's absence, but whom he was able to heal immediately on his return.

Darkness deeper than any known to Leonardo and lighted only by fitful flashes reigns over the tormented world below. In the upper section the radiance of divinity and the wind of the spirit pull Christ upward, illumine and sustain the prophets in widening circles of rapturous contemplation, and blind the apostles in an unbearable intensity of revelation. Raphael's characteristic spiral movement sweeps through these figures: St. James struck to the ground as if by lightning, St. Peter writhing in torment, and St. John traversed by divine energy as if by electric current (fig. 534), one hand groping in the air, the other hiding his eyes from the omnipotent light.

The picture is designed in a giant figure eight and was intended to show the powerlessness of humanity when we are separated from the source of all energy in

instance of Raphael's interest in geometry. The grandeur of the severe classical architecture is contrasted with the remote, dimly seen background of shaggy, ivy-covered towers that tells us more about Cinquecento Rome than about ancient Athens.

Raphael's most ambitious architectural undertaking—save for St. Peter's itself, on which little was accomplished—was a villa designed for Cardinal Giulio de' Medici and known today as the Villa Madama (fig. 533). Originally, it was intended to have a two-towered façade facing St. Peter's, a circular courtyard, domed and porticoed rooms, gardens exploiting the slope of the hillside in descending levels, and many delightful fantasies and inventions. The project continued after Raphael died in 1520, but the death of Pope Leo X in 1521 diverted Cardinal Giulio's attention to the problem of hanging onto Medicean control of Florence. Even after his accession to the papacy as Clement VII in 1523, little more was done. The existing fragment, however, is enchanting, even though the spacious landscape that once opened before it is now a barren expanse of apartment houses and squatters' shanties.

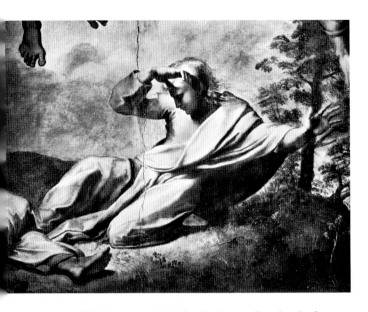

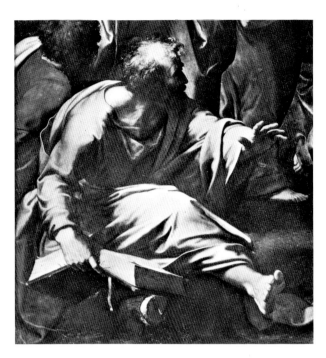

534. RAPHAEL. St. John the Evangelist, detail of
Transfiguration of Christ (see colorplate 106, p. 516). 1517.
Panel. Pinacoteca, Vatican, Rome. Commissioned by
Cardinal Giulio de' Medici for the Cathedral of Narbonne

535. RAPHAEL. St. Andrew, detail of *Transfiguration
of Christ* (see colorplate 106, p. 516). 1517. Panel.
Pinacoteca, Vatican, Rome

God. The lower portion was partly executed by pupils, especially Giulio Romano, who did all the preliminary figure drawings. The possessed boy and his family are typical of Giulio's style, but the St. Andrew at the lower left (fig. 535), turning from his book in amazement as the others argue hopelessly or point to the summit, is not Giulio's. This group is surely by Raphael himself, and St. Andrew, with his outstretched hand and his foot projecting through the picture plane, not to mention the intense contrasts of light and dark around him, would provide a vital model for certain arresting productions of the young Caravaggio in Rome seventy years later.

Cleaning has revealed astonishing coloristic brilliance. The lower half of the picture displays intense reds, blues, yellows, greens, and pinks against the encompassing dark. In contrast, the color of the upper portion testifies, perhaps, to Raphael's interest in Venetian art, but since every new influence he absorbed became rapidly his own, the blending blue and gold that shift through Christ's glistening raiment shine with a new radiance that is transfiguring.

How was it that so serene and successful an individual as Raphael could imagine so mystical a subject and convey it with such power? One scholar has suggested that in his later years Raphael frequented the meetings of a group of priests and laymen called the Oratory of Divine Love, an organization about which far too little is known. The goal of the movement was the reform of the Church from within, not by means of a monastic order, but through the parishes. The program was simple: common prayer and preaching, frequent Communion

(Communion was a rarity in those days), and works of neighborly love. One of the founders, Giovanni Carafa, eventually became Pope Paul IV. Together with another co-founder, Gaetano da Thiene, later canonized as St. Cajetan, Carafa spread the doctrines of the group into northern Italy. By March 1517, perhaps even earlier, the society had Leo's grudging approval; thus, at least seven months before Martin Luther nailed his ninety-five theses to the door of Wittenberg Cathedral, the reform of the Catholic church was quietly under way.

Although the Oratory was dissolved in 1524, its members expanded its original work in that of the newly founded Theatine Order. It may well be that we should look in the activities of this self-effacing, quietist group for the sources of Raphael's mysticism. It is worth remembering that Gaetano was often prostrate in ecstasy for hours before the Eucharist, like Raphael's three apostles, and that he preferred to celebrate Mass at an altar where the sacrament was already reserved, so as to obtain, as he put it, "greater light and heat."

On Good Friday, April 6, 1520, after a brief illness, Raphael died at the age of thirty-seven. At his own request, his funeral was held in the Pantheon in Rome, with the unfinished *Transfiguration* hung above his bier, and he was buried there. Raphael's death was widely mourned, and with him passed an unrecapturable moment when the noble ideals of classical antiquity and the high aspirations of Christianity coexisted in harmony.

Raphael participated in one of the most delightful artistic undertaking of the Roman High Renaissance, an enchanting palace known to us today as the Villa Farne-

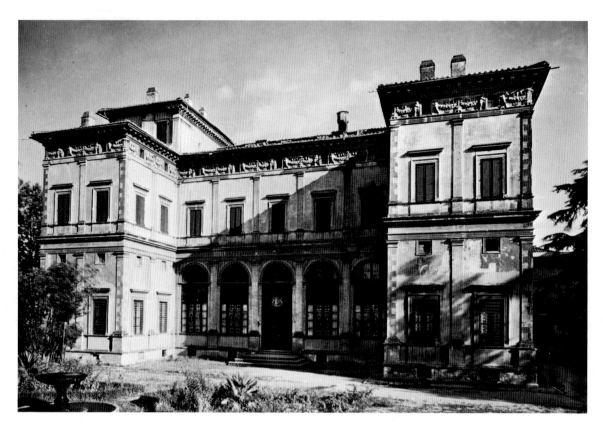

536. BALDASSARE PERUZZI. Garden façade, Villa Farnesina (originally Palazzo Chigi),
Rome. 1509–11. Commissioned by Agostino Chigi

sina (fig. 536) because at a later date it was bought by
the Farnese family and added to their possessions in
Rome—connected, in fact, by means of a bridge across
the Tiber to the Palazzo Farnese on the opposite bank
(see fig. 604). In use by autumn 1511, the palace was
built for Agostino Chigi, a Sienese banker who established the headquarters of his far-flung financial empire
in Rome and who underwrote the conquests of Alexander VI and Cesare Borgia, the ambitious projects of
Julius II, and the pleasures of Leo X. From its very purpose—a retreat for Chigi's beloved Imperia, the most
celebrated courtesan in Rome—down to the details of
the decoration and imagery, the palace is thoroughly
and exquisitely pagan. Although the outbuildings and
gardens overhanging the Tiber have largely perished and
the pastoral quiet this paradise once enjoyed is now replaced by the thunder of Roman traffic, there is still
nothing like the Farnesina anywhere on earth. It is a delicious venture into Olympus or Elysium, or both.

The Farnesina ensemble was coordinated by Raphael's Sienese associate, the architect and painter Baldassare Peruzzi (see pp. 578–79). The palace is a rectangle
with projecting wings, a plan known in ancient Roman
villas, that opens onto the gardens by means of an
arched loggia (fig. 537). Its two stories are articulated
with Tuscan pilasters that flank windows about half their
height. No balustrades or balconies alter the severity of
the general disposition, but the walls were once decorated with delicate ornament incised in the *intonaco*. Today
only the modeled terra-cotta frieze crowning the second
story remains to hint at the filigree of decoration that
once covered the villa.

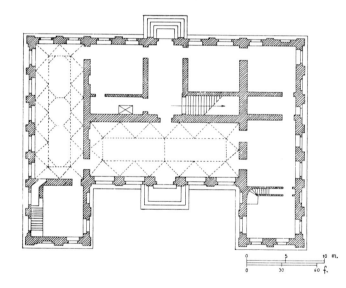

537. BALDASSARE PERUZZI. Plan of Villa Farnesina

The frescoes that embellish the interior are by the
finest painters then working in Rome, save only the increasingly withdrawn Michelangelo. Peruzzi himself carried out the cycles for two major rooms and most of a
third, but he was joined by Sebastiano del Piombo,
Sodoma, and even Raphael, who brought several pupils,
including Giulio Romano. Imperia died before she
could enjoy many of the splendors of her villa, but
Chigi consoled himself with Andreosia, by whom he
eventually had four children (whom Leo X baptized)
before he finally married her (Leo officiating, of course).

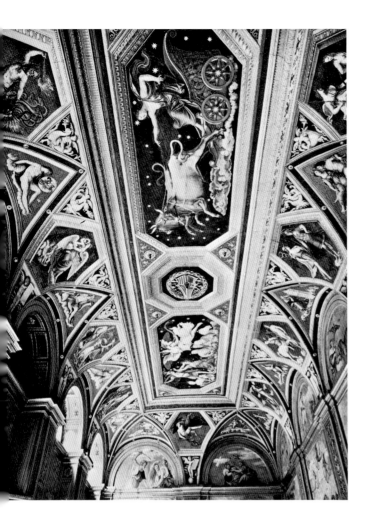

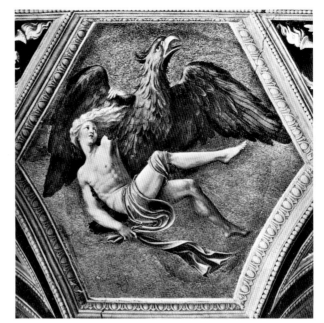

540. BALDASSARE PERUZZI. *Aquarius,*
compartment of ceiling, Sala di Galatea (see fig. 538)

The great hall of the Farnesina, the Sala di Galatea (fig. 538), is lined by a cycle of frescoes unprecedented in the completeness of their pagan imagery. We move from one group of ancient deities to another, reveling in the revival of a mythology that, though it never fully succumbed to the attacks of Christian theologians, lived a half-life of shadows and disguises in the Middle Ages and was only now and then fully lighted during the Early Renaissance. But the gods and heroes who throng the vault compartments turn up in surprising relationships. These have been explained by translating the deities back into their stellar and planetary equivalents.

Careful plotting of the positions of these equivalents on the ceiling of the Sala di Galatea produced the configuration of the heavens above central Italy on the night of December 1, 1466, the presumed birth date of Agostino Chigi, whose horoscope, complete down to the last detail, is thus represented in the ceiling panels.

To embody this intellectual conceit, Peruzzi produced a pictorial style that is at once artificial, elegant, and beguiling. One of the two long central panels shows the constellation Perseus (fig. 539), with the hero himself about to decapitate Medusa, while the winged Fame blows her trumpet in the direction of the Chigi arms, modeled in stucco in the center of the ceiling. The arrangement of figures, strictly adhering to the foreground plane and silhouetted singly or in groups against a background that, for all its stars, remains inert, displays the restrained luxury and mannered tastefulness of a giant Augustan cameo; possibly it was inspired by one.

Aquarius (fig. 540), clearly further identified as Gany-

above: 538.
BALDASSARE PERUZZI.
Ceiling frescoes.
c. 1511. Sala di Galatea,
Villa Farnesina, Rome.
Commissioned
by Agostino Chigi

right: 539.
BALDASSARE PERUZZI.
Perseus and Medusa,
ceiling of Sala di Galatea
(see fig. 538)

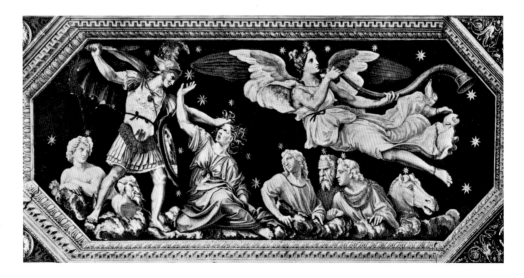

The High Renaissance in Rome

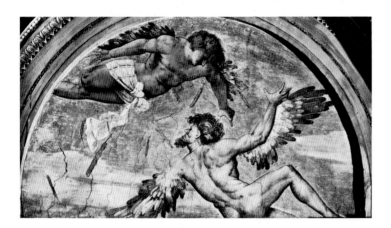

541. SEBASTIANO DEL PIOMBO. *Fall of Icarus*. c. 1511.
Fresco. Lunette of Sala di Galatea, Villa Farnesina, Rome.
Commissioned by Agostino Chigi

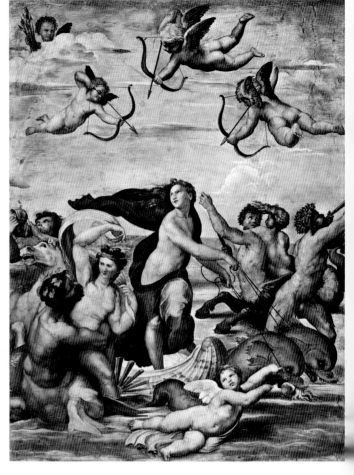

542. RAPHAEL. *Galatea*. 1513. Fresco,
9' 8" x 7' 5". Sala di Galatea, Villa Farnesina, Rome.
Commissioned by Agostino Chigi

mede, demonstrates Peruzzi's figure style. Although contemporary with the achievements of his friend Raphael in the Stanza della Segnatura, Peruzzi's slender, supple figure with its streaming hair, and the gigantic eagle, which seems to have flown off the lectern of some Gothic pulpit, owe remarkably little to the High Renaissance style. His is an individual style, rejoicing in subtleties of line and in restrained color. As an architect, Peruzzi was insistent on painting architectural detail so that it is projected accurately in perspective when seen from the center of the room.

The lunettes, which are not directly connected with Chigi's horoscope, represent mythological events that took place in the airy regions below the heavens. They were assigned to the Venetian Sebastiano del Piombo (c. 1485–1547), who brought a new colorism to the predominantly sculpturesque pictorial style of early Cinquecento Rome. A continuous blue sky with drifting clouds runs through Sebastiano's lunettes; the *Fall of Icarus* (fig. 541) is typical in that we seem to be looking through half-moon windows into the air outside. The contrast between Sebastiano's openness and Peruzzi's flatness is sharp and was probably deliberate. Sebastiano's large figures, who float in and out of these pseudo-windows, seem remarkably weightless. They are painted with a broad, easy flow of the brush directly dependent on the early Titian and more suitable to oil on canvas than to fresco. But Sebastiano's anatomical constructions leave a good deal to be desired. It is not hard to see why a few years later we find him writing letters to Michelangelo, asking for drawings of arms, legs, and torsos.

The walls of the Sala di Galatea were to be decorated by a variety of painters with frescoes representing divinities of earth and sea, but only Sebastiano's *Polyphemus* and Raphael's *Galatea* (fig. 542) were ever painted. Ironically enough, after all the delicate calculations of Peruzzi and the labors of Sebastiano, Raphael contributed a single painting and walked off with the honors. According to his own account, he based his image of the sea nymph not on any single beautiful woman but on an idea he had of female perfection, combining elements he had seen in various women. The graceful *contrapposto* pose is similar to that of the philosopher to the left of the figure portraying Michelangelo in the *School of Athens* (see fig. 521), with raised left knee, twisted torso, lowered right shoulder, and right arm crossing the body. Galatea is more compactly arranged and her head is turned upward so that her glance unites with the motion of the cupids above her. As a result, she concentrates within her own voluptuous figure all the energies of the figure-of-eight composition, an idea Raphael was to retain and redevelop subsequently in the *Transfiguration* (see colorplate 106, p. 516).

Very little of Ovid's text on Galatea seems to have interested Raphael. He has omitted Galatea's sixteen-year-old lover, Acis, whom Polyphemus was soon to destroy, and has shown the Nereid in triumphant control of her own beauty, oblivious of the amorous gaze of the monster Polyphemus from the adjoining bay. Raphael had

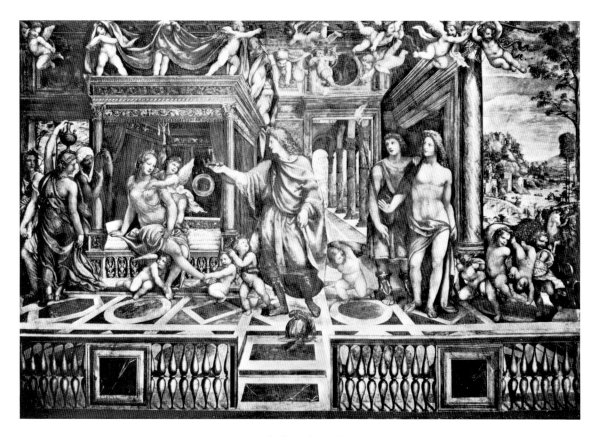

543. SODOMA. *Marriage of Alexander and Roxana.* c. 1517. Fresco,
12' 1" x 21' 9". Bedroom, Villa Farnesina, Rome. Commissioned by Agostino Chigi

toyed with the idea of a Birth of Venus in an earlier drawing and retained from this subject the shell-chariot as seen by Botticelli, to which, however, he added curious paddle wheels, apparently as stabilizers. Drawn by dolphins, the chariot is accompanied by a procession including tritons blowing a conch and a trumpet, sea horses, Nereids, and sirens. Although the composition is centralized, the movement of the chariot from left to right is accented by the movement of the Eros in the foreground.

The picture is suffused by a sunny, broad light that emphasizes the soft flesh tones of the female figures and the tanned musculature of the male torsos against the green water. The deep red cloak and golden hair of Galatea float in a wide rhythm around and behind her. Raphael's *Galatea* inspired some of the most beautiful compositions of classicistic art in the seventeenth century, especially several by Nicolas Poussin.

After the nobility of the Farnesina *Galatea*, the intrusion of Sodoma (1477?–1549)—of Lombard origin, but a resident of Siena—comes as something of a shock. His *Marriage of Alexander and Roxana* (fig. 543) in the bedroom of the Farnesina was—despite some shortcomings of composition, perspective, and anatomy—based on a Raphaelesque drawing that may have followed suggestions from Raphael himself. The relaxed Roxana sits on the edge of a gorgeous bed whose posts are gilded Corinthian columns, while three putti disrobe her. An-

other tugs Alexander in her direction; serving maids depart; and on the right the almost nude god of marriage, accompanied by a torchbearer, presides over the occasion. Luxurious in its surfaces, overripe in its coloring, this frankly voluptuary fresco is the opposite of the moralized mythologies of Botticelli. Yet it seems mild compared with the erotica soon to follow, popularized after Raphael's death by Giulio Romano and Marcantonio Raimondi.

In the Sala delle Prospettive (fig. 544) on the upper story, Peruzzi revived the perspective of Melozzo da Forlì and Mantegna, possibly under the influence of both, for their illusionistic works in the Vatican and the Church of Santi Apostoli were in place and intact. The perspective was planned to function correctly when the observer is standing toward the left of the room. Peruzzi has designed a splendid architecture of dark, veined marble piers and columns with gilded capitals that incorporates an actual architecture of veined marble door frames. The frescoed architecture is so precisely painted that it is almost impossible to distinguish where the real marble ends and the illusion begins. Through the lofty columns one looks out to a painted terrace that opens onto a continuous landscape—country facing what was then country.

The decoration of the Farnesina culminates in the series of frescoes painted by Raphael's pupils from his sketches, under his direction, and occasionally with his

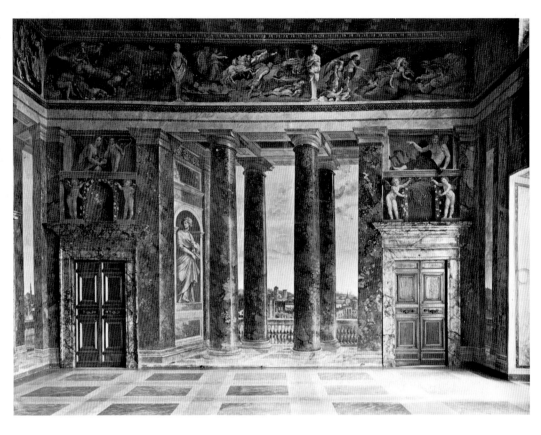

544. BALDASSARE PERUZZI. Perspective view. 1515–17. Fresco. Sala delle Prospettive, Villa Farnesina, Rome. Commissioned by Agostino Chigi

direct intervention, in the garden loggia, the Loggia di Psiche (figs. 545–47). Raphael's garlands of leaves, fruits, and flowers along the groins of the vaults and around the center of the ceiling transform solid architecture into an open bower. The episodes of the story of Cupid and Psyche are seen against the blue sky, as if the figures are appearing in the openings of the bower, and the two culminating scenes fill two enormous simulated tapestries or painted awnings overhead. The appearance of the interior, therefore, is all air and tension—the tension of the bower and the light tug of the awnings. Within this graceful illusion only those incidents of the legend of Cupid and Psyche that took place in heaven are represented. Perhaps the others were to go on the walls, now filled by simulated architecture, or perhaps the cycle was restricted to the airy episodes.

Although the noble female figures of Raphael's mature imagination are sometimes hampered by the pupils' inadequate execution, those carried out by Giulio Romano, as in the *Cupid Pointing Out Psyche to the Three Graces* (fig. 548), can be quite grand. The figures are less supple than the *Galatea*, certainly, but full of a new sense of statuesque volume, heavy and hard as marble, and characteristic of Giulio as we have seen his style in the *Transfiguration*. The unusual coloristic passages in the back of one of the Graces must come from Raphael's brush, which doubtless intervened at crucial moments again and again in works being painted by his pupils.

Within eight years after the completion of the last paintings in the Farnesina, Raphael, Chigi, and Leo X

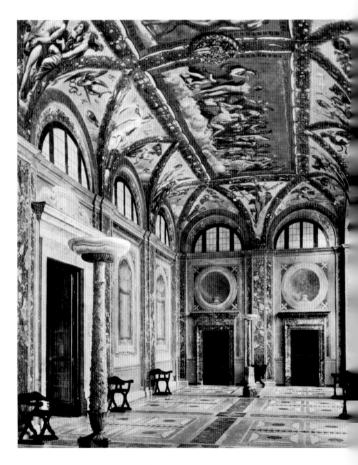

545. RAPHAEL and assistants. Frescoes, Loggia di Psiche, Villa Farnesina, Rome. 1518–19. Commissioned by Agostino Chigi

THE CINQUECENTO

532

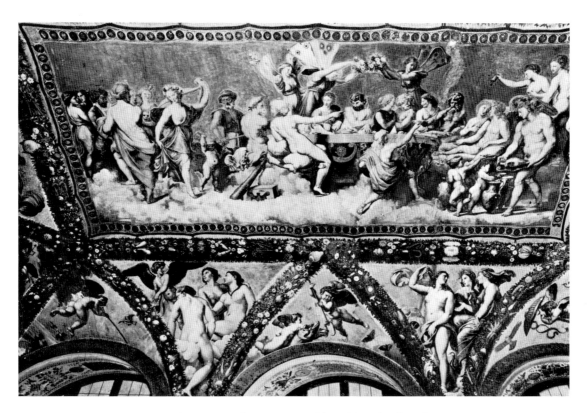

546. RAPHAEL and assistants. *Wedding of Cupid and Psyche*,
western half of ceiling, Loggia di Psiche

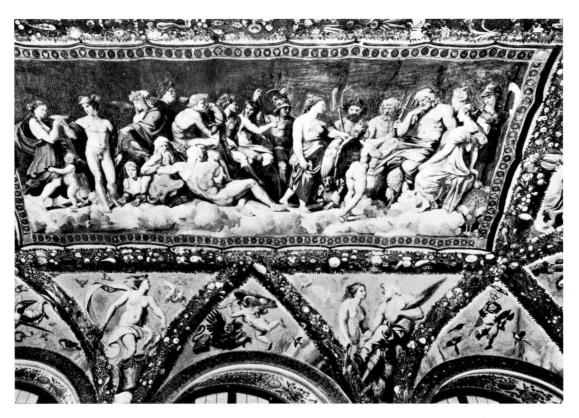

547. RAPHAEL and assistants. *Psyche Received on Olympus*,
eastern half of ceiling, Loggia di Psiche

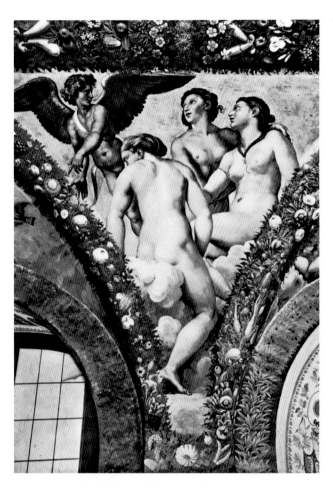

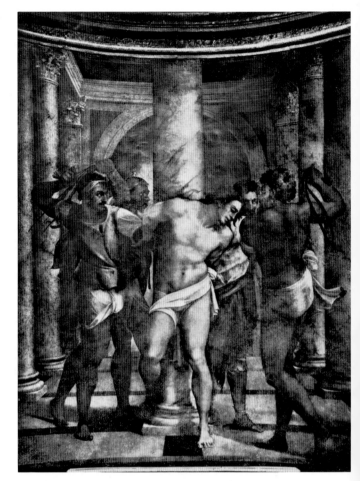

548. RAPHAEL and GIULIO ROMANO. *Cupid Pointing Out Psyche to the Three Graces*, compartment of ceiling, Loggia di Psiche. Commissioned by Agostino Chigi

549. SEBASTIANO DEL PIOMBO. *Flagellation*. 1516–21. Fresco. Borgherini Chapel, S. Pietro in Montorio, Rome. Commissioned by Pierfrancesco Borgherini

were in their tombs and, as we shall see, the world in which they moved had been swept out of existence. Sensitive ears could discern many a rumble of the approaching earthquake, and doubtless Raphael heard them; one might conclude that his heart was not in the myths of the Loggia di Psiche but in the message of the *Transfiguration*. It is perhaps fitting to close our account of the Roman High Renaissance on a prophetic note. Sebastiano del Piombo's *Flagellation* in San Pietro in Montorio (fig. 549), begun in 1516, admits us to a darker world of experience to which we will soon become accustomed, as it was to be the scene of daily existence for most of central Italy for decades. Christ, based on a drawing by Michelangelo given to Sebastiano in response to his request, is tied to a column that stretches outside the limits of the picture and that ap-

pears to grow from the actual altar below. Since the mural exploits the curve of the chapel wall, on the principle of Mantegna's *Adoration of the Magi* (see fig. 407), the wall disappears, leaving the marmoreal figure, painted with a mastery of anatomy, to be assailed by figures who appear to have sprung from the columns. This powerful conceit, which converts a painting into a work of sculpture and projects Christ's suffering in three dimensions, returns us to the personality of Michelangelo, then absent in Florence. After Raphael's death, about which his contemporaries wrote as if it were the death of a saint, no one in Rome could continue in his vein. Other tendencies and ideals replaced the harmonies of Raphael, while impressive developments were taking place in the Florence of Michelangelo or the Venice of Giorgione and Titian.

18

High Renaissance
and Mannerism

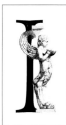n the entire history of writings on Italian art, no development has caused so much confusion as the fluctuating critical fortunes of the artists at work in central Italy following the High Renaissance. No other phase of Italian art is so difficult to fit into accounts of historical evolution. It is possible that the changes in art reflect the difficulties of Italian Cinquecento history. In keeping with the policy followed throughout this book, an attempt will be made to interpret intellectual concepts and artistic events in terms of history, but first it will be necessary to examine the nature and origin of the much-discussed expression "Mannerism."

A glance at many of the illustrations in this chapter as compared with those in the two preceding ones should persuade the reader that something strange has happened. These pictures, statues, and buildings no longer fit the ideals of the High Renaissance. When artists and writers of the seventeenth and eighteenth centuries examined the tensions and distortions, the visual and emotional surprises of the years around 1520, they characterized these developments as a decline and referred contemptuously to what they called *maniera* (manner). This is derived from the Italian word *mano* (hand) that signifies the ascendancy of manual practice—and especially the art of drawing—over visual observation and intellectual clarity. The assertion of a post–High Renaissance decline in central Italian art persisted throughout the nineteenth century; the decline was generally attributed to the excessive imitation of Michelangelo, to the pernicious influence of Giulio Romano, or to both.

Shortly before World War I, in an artistic atmosphere charged with the revolutionary developments of twentieth-century art, works of artists of this period that had been condemned or ignored for more than three hundred years began to excite sympathetic interest. The phenomenon was not unlike the revival in the 1880s of such once-forgotten artists as Botticelli, or of Piero della Francesca about 1900, but it was complicated by the difficult and contradictory nature of the material.

The first twentieth-century scholars who discussed the period found a parallel to the antiacademic manifestoes of the early twentieth century in the position taken by such artists as Pontormo or Rosso Fiorentino against the principles of Michelangelo and, especially, Raphael. This phenomenon was named "Mannerism,"

translated from *maniera,* and the post–High Renaissance generation of artists was dubbed Mannerists. The expression was fraught with danger, since "mannerist" and "mannerism" describe something quite different from the often startlingly original works of art under discussion. Some writers thought that in Mannerism they had found a new period to be set between the High Renaissance and the Baroque, forming a Hegelian succession of thesis, antithesis, and synthesis.

Like all intellectual abstractions imposed upon the events of history, the concept of Mannerism has had an effect beyond the history of art. As a result of the attempt to define the principles of Mannerist style and apply them to the analysis of literature and music, even of life and behavior, Shakespeare became a Mannerist, and Hamlet and Queen Elizabeth I became Mannerist characters. Recent critics have become increasingly disturbed by such ideological excesses and have drawn attention to the coexistence of High Renaissance and Mannerist artists in the same artistic center at the same moment, to the difficulty of forcing the painting of the Venetians or the architecture of Palladio into the Mannerist mold, and to the sharp discrepancy between the artistic generation of about 1520 and the masters of the second half of the Cinquecento in Florence and Rome, who were indeed mannerists (with a small "m") in the traditional sense. Some writers have preferred to restrict the word "Mannerist" to the later artists, who will be treated in Chapter 20, and there is much to justify this point of view, etymologically and historically. Others have recommended complete abandonment of the word "Mannerism," a losing battle considering all the ink that has been spilled in the past sixty years.

One sensible course might be to recall that diametrically opposed styles, sometimes as many as three at once, coexisted at other periods in Italian art, as was the case, for example, during the period treated in Chapters 13 and 14, or even, for that matter, the Early Renaissance itself. The expression "Mannerist" will be used in the following pages, not because it is any more accurate than "Gothic," let us say, as an artistic term, but because it has become so deeply embedded in our experience that we cannot just forget about it. Misnomer though it may be, the term "Mannerism" is doubtless here to stay. Although they are included here under the broadly defined category of Mannerism, those court artists of the second half of the Cinquecento whose style is indeed mannered (see Chapter 20) are referred to in this book as representatives of a particular subcategory called the *maniera*.

As we look back on the history of Italian art, we note that its chief sources of power were found in the republics and the Church, not solely because these were the patrons who could commission the most ambitious works of art, but also because they constituted the social forces that sustained and, to a degree, inspired the artists. Throughout the Renaissance both Church and republics came under intermittent but sometimes fierce attack. Nonetheless, they resisted and survived, and some of the crucial manifestations of Italian art (the Early Renaissance in Florence, the High Renaissance in Florence and Rome) derive much of their conviction and even essential traits of their style from the artists' debt to these sources.

In Chapter 17 we have already had some insight into the dangers posed to the papacy during Leo X's tenure as pope. The state of affairs in Florence, meanwhile, was no less unfortunate and was bound in time to grow worse. Since their expulsion in 1494, the Medici had been scheming to return, and their reinstatement in 1512 followed the sack of nearby Prato by Spanish troops under Julius II and the expulsion of Piero Soderini, who fled into exile. While Julius II lived, the Medici ruled Florence again in the mild government of Giuliano, youngest brother of Cardinal Giovanni. Giuliano believed in control from behind the scenes, in the traditional manner of the Medici, leaving the framework of the Republic externally intact, but Giovanni's elevation to the papacy as Leo X in 1513 brought about a sharp change. He replaced Giuliano with their nephew Lorenzo, who entertained sterner ideas. In 1516 the pope, having driven out the rightful duke of Urbino, invested Lorenzo with the duchy. To the great distaste of the Florentines, Lorenzo maintained a ducal splendor in their midst and behaved as if he were duke of Florence. Leo X used Lorenzo as a pawn in his dynastic ambitions and married him off to a French royal princess, but the princess died in childbirth in April 1519, and six days later Lorenzo followed her to an early grave. The direct male line of Cosimo de' Medici was thus extinct.

For four years, power in the Florentine state was exercised by Leo's cousin, Cardinal Giulio de' Medici, still without disturbing the now-sham Republic. Leo X's death in 1521 brought a non-Italian pope to the chair of St. Peter, a pious and learned Dutchman who, as Adrian VI, made a sincere effort at internal reform. He ejected the entourage of Leo X, including the artists, and all artistic projects in the Vatican came to a halt. After less than two years, Adrian died suddenly, under general suspicion of poison. Giulio de' Medici was elected Pope Clement VII and continued to control the Florentine Republic. It was not long before the Florentines realized that, under the Medici popes, they had lost not only their internal liberties but also their external independence. From a position as one of the proudest of the medieval republics and the founder of the idea of liberty

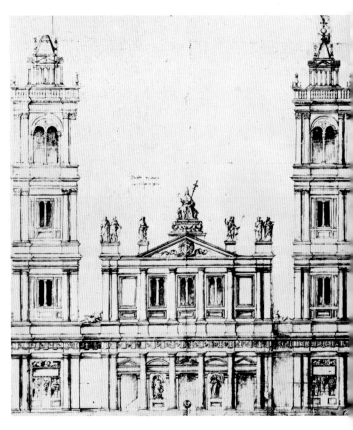

550. GIULIANO DA SANGALLO. Design for the façade of S. Lorenzo, Florence. 1516. Drawing. Gabinetto dei Disegni e Stampe, Uffizi, Florence. Commissioned by Pope Leo X

in modern times, Florence had sunk to the status of a captive province of the papacy. Commercial activity stagnated, and so did morale. Money and power were centered in Rome.

MICHELANGELO 1516 TO 1533

In the midst of this discouraging picture, Michelangelo reappeared in Florence at the end of 1516 to carry out an important commission, Pope Leo's project for a façade for San Lorenzo. This Medicean church had become more important than ever as a symbol of dynastic power now that the head of the family was a duke, and still more once he was allied with the royal family of France. In the year of his death, Giuliano da Sangallo, now well over seventy, submitted several drawings of alternative projects for the façade. One remarkable design (fig. 550) masked Brunelleschi's clerestory and the lateral chapels along the side aisles with a two-story temple, flanked by freestanding campanili topped by tiny cruciform temples ending in pyramids, crosses, and orbs. The central pediment would have bristled with sculpture, notably a statue of the seated Leo X flanked by saints, as if in an altarpiece. In both the central façade and the corner towers, the superimposed engaged colonnades would have culminated in square piers at the corners.

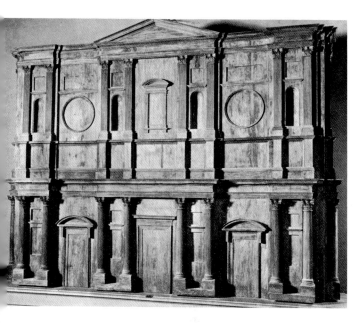

551. MICHELANGELO. Model for the façade of S. Lorenzo, Florence. 1517. Wood, 7' x 9' 4". Casa Buonarroti, Florence. Commissioned by Pope Leo X

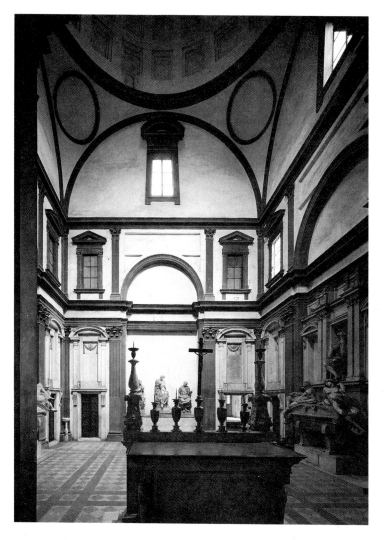

552. MICHELANGELO. Medici Chapel, S. Lorenzo, Florence. 1519–34. Commissioned by Cardinal Giulio de' Medici, who later became Pope Clement VII

Although the campanili recall those designed for St. Peter's by Bramante (see fig. 501), Giuliano's do not taper upward. Moreover, his Doric order is imitated almost exactly from one he had drawn from the ancient Roman Basilica Emilia. In all these respects, his drawing was followed by his younger brother Antonio in the campanili and interior of the Madonna di San Biagio at Montepulciano (see figs. 600, 602) only a few years later. But Giuliano's grand design misses the point of High Renaissance composition not only because the mullioned windows are an anachronism recalling the Palazzo Medici and its successors, but also because the effect is a cumulative one, derived from multiple, superimposed elements, rather than from the principle of unified dynamic growth that infuses the architecture of Leonardo and Bramante.

The commission instead went to Michelangelo, who for three years worked on plans for the façade, which he intended, in his own words, to be a "mirror of architecture and sculpture of all Italy." His planned two-story structure, almost freestanding, was to have included twelve standing statues in marble, six seated ones in bronze, and fifteen reliefs. Michelangelo spent many months quarrying the marble, first at Carrara, then at Seravezza, within the boundaries of the Florentine Republic; to reach the new quarries of the latter, he had to build a road through the mountains. Although we know too little about the final projected appearance of the façade, the wooden model built to Michelangelo's specifications still exists (fig. 551). Within its dense and compact structure of interlocking elements, the statues and reliefs must have been intended to jut forth from the niches and frames, imparting a passionate interplay of masses and of lights and darks to a scheme that otherwise

looks prophetic of the classicism of seventeenth-century France. Michelangelo's sculptural ideas, expressed in drawings and in lost models for the statues, must have had an overwhelming effect on his Florentine contemporaries.

Suddenly, in March 1520, the contract for the façade of San Lorenzo was annulled and the marbles abandoned, to Michelangelo's violent indignation. The reason, however, is not hard to find. The death of Lorenzo in May of 1519 had deprived the façade of its principal *raison d'être*, and the money was needed for another project, the tomb chapel for the two dukes, Lorenzo and Giuliano (who had died in 1516), as well as for the two brothers who may conveniently be called the Magnifici, Lorenzo the Magnificent (died 1492) and Giuliano (murdered in 1478). According to a document, plans for the funerary chapel (fig. 552) were divulged in secrecy by Cardinal Giulio to a canon of San Lorenzo in June 1519, less than a month after Lorenzo's death. Construction began in November 1519, and Michelangelo was the architect from the start. He was apparently asked to build on a plan that would be a twin to Brunelleschi's sacristy on the left side of the transept (see figs. 137, 138). The windows on the exterior of the Medici Chapel, however, which harmonize with those of the sacristy, do not always correspond to those on the interior, for Michelangelo arranged the lighting to produce a subdued, all-over illumination essential for the prevailing mood of his architectural and sculptural compositions.

The work progressed irregularly and was never completed. Some of the sculptures were never finished, others and the still-hypothetical paintings never started. Nevertheless, the Medici Chapel is the only one of Michelangelo's architectural-sculptural fantasies to be realized in anything approaching entirety. The tombs and their sculptures must have been designed rapidly, because by April 1521 Michelangelo was in Carrara with measured drawings, ready to order the marble blocks. Letters and sketches indicate that at first a freestanding monument was planned, with the four tombs on four faces, and that the wall tombs are a later development. The final arrangement placed the two dukes in their present wall tombs and relegated the Magnifici to a third wall (fig. 552), under the statues of the Madonna and Sts. Cosmas and Damian, between the entrances and facing the altar. This wall was never completed: the *Medici Madonna* (see fig. 555) was left unfinished, and the statues of the patron saints were eventually relegated to pupils.

During the pontificate of Adrian VI no marble was shipped, but early in 1524, a few months after the accession of Clement VII, the blocks began to arrive in Florence. By March 1526 four statues were almost finished, and in June two more were begun and one was ready to start; the only other important figures that were planned were the four river-gods to go in front of the tombs; these were never started but are known from drawings and a model. By June 1526 Clement's political machinations had involved the papacy beyond rescue, and hostilities broke out between the pope and Emperor Charles V. In September the Vatican and St. Peter's were attacked and plundered by the Colonna party, and in January 1527 the pope ordered the fortification of Rome against the imperial forces. Early in the morning of May 7, 1527, began the terrible sack that seems to have put an end to the High Renaissance, or what was left of it, in Rome. After months of unspeakable horror—looting, burning, rapine, torture, murder, desecration—the pope, a prisoner in Castel Sant'Angelo since June, escaped and fled to Orvieto on December 7. Many statesmen, scholars, and members of the general populace felt that this humiliation was the judgment of God for the paganism of Medicean Rome.

In the contemporary sources, four intertwined themes can be distinguished: a deep sense of collective guilt, a desire for punishment, a need for healing the wounds inflicted by punishment, and a longing for a restoration of order in which individuals would no longer be free to seek their own destruction. Nor do these themes date only from the Sack of Rome. Itinerant preachers had long predicted the ruin of the Church, and years earlier Machiavelli had declared in Florence that "the nearer people are to the Church of Rome . . . the less religious are they. And whoever examines the principles upon which that religion is founded and sees how widely different . . . its present practices and application are, will judge that her ruin or chastisement is at hand. . . . The evil example of the court of Rome has destroyed all religion and piety in Italy."

Not until October 1528 was the pope able to return, poverty-stricken, to his burned-out and half-depopulated capital. Florence, meanwhile, had thrown off the Medici yoke for the third time and reestablished the Republic. But in 1530 Florence was captured by an unexpected combination of papal and imperial forces, in an alliance that would force despotism on most of Italy, and the new Medici governor of the city gave orders for Michelangelo's assassination because the artist had aided the Republic in fortifying itself against invasion. The canon of San Lorenzo hid the artist until the pope issued an order sparing Michelangelo so that he might continue work on the Medici Chapel. This proceeded in a desultory fashion, interrupted by the artist's trips to Rome. Aided by Emperor Charles V, Clement installed Alessandro, probably the illegitimate son of Lorenzo, but widely believed to be the son of the pope himself, and known for his vices and his cruelty, as the first hereditary duke of Florence. When the pope died in 1534, Michelangelo was in Rome and was unwilling to risk his life to the limited mercies of Alessandro. Not even after the duke's assassination in 1537 would he return to Florence, and not until 1545 were the statues placed on the tombs by Michelangelo's pupils. Only those of the dukes were completed to the penultimate details, and the four statues of the Times of Day still show passages of rough marble.

In his architectural formulation Michelangelo added an extra story to the Brunelleschian scheme, perhaps in part to raise the windows, the principal sources of illumination, above the neighboring housetops. In his *pietra serena* pilasters, however, he maintained a close correspondence to Brunelleschi's norms. The coffering of the Pantheon-like dome, bare and white today, was originally ornamented in color by Giovanni da Udine, Raphael's specialist in decoration, but Clement had the decorations whitewashed. The traditional two-tone architecture of *pietra serena* and white *intonaco* is set in opposition to a second marble architecture, richly carved and polished; this is ostensibly enclosed by the first yet it refuses to remain within its enclosures. Incommensurate in style, character, substance, proportion, and scale with the first architecture, the second consists not only of the tombs with their statues but also of the flanking tabernacles, which are of unprecedented shape and still-enigmatic purpose. These protrude so far beyond the pilasters that they nearly meet at the corners, in front of the imprisoned Corinthian capitals of the primary scheme.

The sarcophagi of the dukes (figs. 553, 554) are

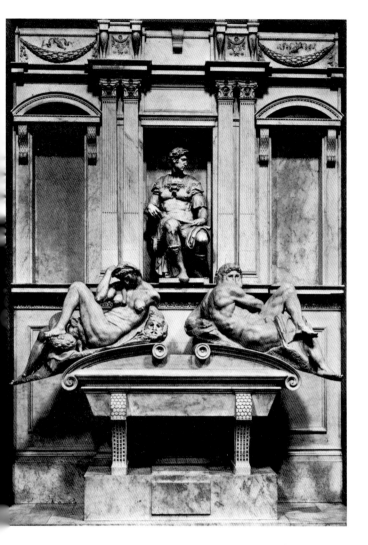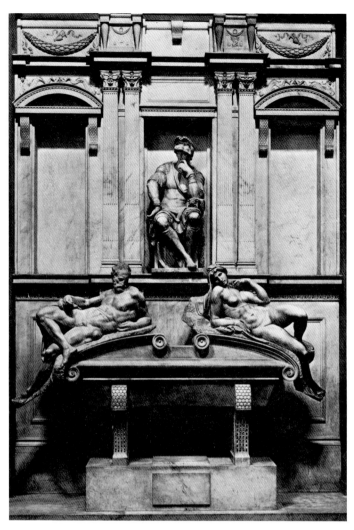

553, 554. MICHELANGELO. Tomb of Giuliano de' Medici (left), with allegorical figures of *Night* and *Day*.
Tomb of Lorenzo de' Medici (right), with allegorical figures of *Dusk* and *Dawn*.
Marble, height of seated figures 5' 10" and 5' 8". Medici Chapel, S. Lorenzo, Florence. 1519–34

crowned by consoles in the shape of flattened elliptic arcs, on which recline male and female figures representing Night and Day, Dawn and Dusk. The dukes, shown as young men in Roman armor, sit in niches in the second story. The often-heard criticism that the Times of Day appear to be slipping off the sarcophagi would be less justified if the river-gods, intended to lie on a platform just off the floor, had been executed, for they would have completed a roughly circular composition of figures. There is less excuse for the old theory that the Times of Day protrude because they do not fit and were therefore intended for some other project in the chapel. Michelangelo's figures always tend to outgrow their enclosures (think of the steady expansion in size of the figures of the Sistine Ceiling), and one can watch the continuous increase in size of the Times of Day throughout the sketches for the ducal tombs.

The meaning of the chapel has long been obscured by the contention that every complex by Michelangelo should be interpreted as a synopsis of the Neoplatonic cosmogony, on the grounds that in his boyhood Michelangelo was acquainted with Neoplatonists at the court of Lorenzo the Magnificent, and that in Michelangelo's old age some of his poems (not, it should be noted, his works of visual art) were analyzed by a Neoplatonist, Benedetto Varchi, and found to contain Neoplatonic concepts. There is no other evidence. On the face of it a papal chapel, intended for the perpetual celebration of Mass and the saying of prayers for the salvation of departed Christians, would seem to require a Catholic content. But the Neoplatonic hypothesis has become, to some scholars, an article of faith.

On a sheet of studies for architectural details in the chapel, Michelangelo wrote the following: "The heavens and the earth Night and Day are speaking and saying, We have with our swift course brought to death the Duke Giuliano; it is just that he take vengeance upon us as he does, and the vengeance is this: that we having slain him, he thus dead has taken the light from us and with closed eyes has fastened ours so that they may shine

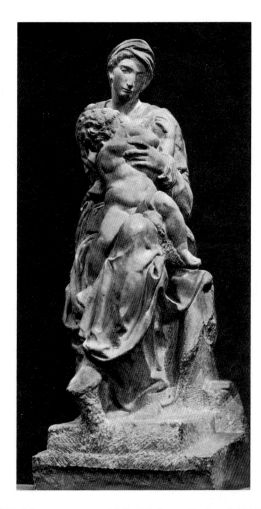

555. MICHELANGELO *Medici Madonna*. Designed 1521; carved 1524–34. Marble, height 99½". Medici Chapel, S. Lorenzo, Florence

In the chapel the statues of the dukes, as well as the priest behind the altar, gaze toward the *Medici Madonna* (fig. 555), the *Virgo lactans,* or nursing Virgin, the oldest and one of the most persistent motifs in Michelangelo's imagination (see fig. 467). *Day* (fig. 557) and *Dusk,* both male, face the life-giving mother and her Son; *Dawn* and *Night,* both female, turn from her. *Dawn* is characterized as a virgin, with firm, high breasts and the symbolic belt, or "zone"; *Night* (fig. 556), whose abdomen and breasts are distorted by childbirth and lactation, as a mother. In the Virgin Mary these two states are united.

The celebration of the Mass of the Dead (which in the late seventeenth century was still being celebrated in the chapel four times daily) is the central energizing principle of the chapel. Even the pearly radiance so carefully calculated by Michelangelo suggests the light perpetual that was to shine upon the departed dukes. The celebrant was probably to have looked up from the *Virgo lactans* to a fresco of the *Resurrection* in the now-blank lunette. Such an image would have been required by the dedication of the chapel to the Resurrection, and the theme of the Epistle for the Mass of the Dead is the Resurrection. One drawing on the subject by Michelangelo (fig. 558) corresponds to the shape of the lunette and can be connected with no other commission. After the darkness of his Passion and death, Christ leaps from the tomb. He is totally nude, as always in Michelangelo's Resurrection drawings.

Suggestions locate frescoes of the Attack of the Fiery Serpents and the Delivery by the Brazen Serpent, for which an otherwise unexplained Michelangelo drawing survives, over the ducal tombs. But in neither sketch does the Brazen Serpent itself appear, probably because it foretold the cross, and the crucifix on the altar would have fulfilled that function. The papal bull *Exsurge, Deus,* launched against the Lutherans by Leo X on June 15, 1520, while Michelangelo was at work on the plans for the Medici Chapel and its imagery, may shed light on this aspect of the chapel's meaning: "Arise, O God, and judge Thine own cause . . . rise up, O Peter . . . defend the cause of the Holy Roman Church, mother of all Churches . . . there rise up lying teachers, introducing sects of perdition . . . whose tongue is fire, restless evil, full of deadly venom . . . they begin with the tongue to spread the poison of serpents." Leo's appeal to the Resurrection was personal, for he was crowned on Easter Saturday, a day marked in Florence by the festival of the Explosion of the Chariot, at which moment Christ was, according to Florentine tradition, officially resurrected.

The never-completed river-gods may represent the rivers of Paradise or their significance may have been geographical, since Vasari, who was one of Michelangelo's assistants in the chapel, remembered that he "wished all the parts of the world were there." Tiber and Arno, present at the Medici ceremony of 1513 in Rome, are possible candidates, but there may have been no intention to identify any of them precisely.

forth no more upon the earth. What would he have done with us then while he lived?"

Michelangelo did not follow his own notes literally, because the eyes of all the figures save those of *Night* are wide open. Under a sketch for the third wall, then planned to contain the tombs of the Magnifici and the *Medici Madonna,* he wrote: "Fame holds the epitaphs in position; it goes neither forward nor backward for they are dead and their working is finished." That the beautiful ducal statues were not intended to be recognizable portraits of the bearded Medici dukes is again shown by Michelangelo's words, recorded by a contemporary: "He did not take from the Duke Lorenzo nor from the Lord Giuliano the model just as nature had drawn and composed them, but he gave them a greatness, a proportion, a dignity . . . which seemed to him would have brought them more praise, saying that a thousand years hence no one would be able to know that they were otherwise." Roman armor was appropriate to captains of the Roman Church, which the dukes were, and even more so to Roman patricians, a rank conferred on Lorenzo and Giuliano in a ceremony on the Capitoline Hill in 1513 that was complete with Roman trophies, Medici symbols, personifications of the rivers Tiber and Arno, and an altar at which Mass was celebrated.

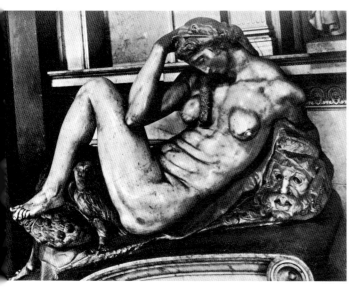

556. MICHELANGELO. *Night*, on the Tomb of Giuliano de' Medici, Medici Chapel. Designed 1521; carved 1524–34. Marble, length 76½"

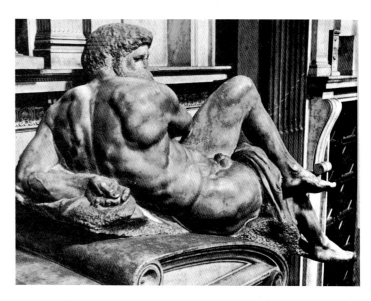

557. MICHELANGELO. *Day*, on the Tomb of Giuliano de' Medici, Medici Chapel. Designed 1521; carved 1524–34. Marble, length 80¾"

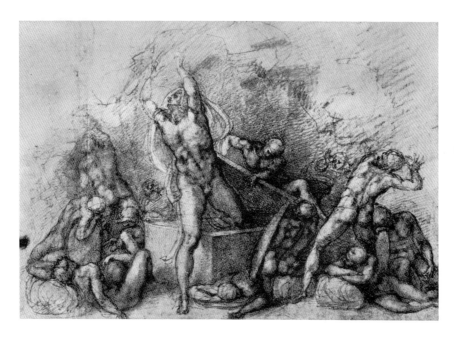

558. MICHELANGELO. *Resurrection*. 1520–25(?). Black chalk, 9½ x 13⅝". Royal Library, Windsor

Seated in the power of their office and the glory of their eternal aspect, the dukes are liberated from the remorseless circle of the Times of Day and the Parts of the World by faith in the resurrected Christ and the nourishment of Holy Mother Church. The imagery of the chapel is also, of course, connected with the growing appeal of absolutism to many Italians in the Cinquecento, as the sole release from the chaos to which centuries of republican civil strife had brought them. In *Il principe* (*The Prince*), Machiavelli had appealed to Duke Lorenzo to liberate and unify Italy. The idea of the magically charged and supernaturally justified Prince, successor to the discredited ideal man of the High Renaissance, was the collective fantasy with which Late

Renaissance Italy tried to assuage its sense of its own inadequacy to unite before the threats from the north. That the dukes themselves, especially Lorenzo, were so openly recognized as worthless could, under such circumstances, only lend the legend stronger wings. The symbolism of the chapel, which in other hands would have become mere pomp, was transfigured by Michelangelo into a view of human destiny that is both tragic and heroic.

The compositions of the two ducal tombs are opposites in subtle and significant ways. While *Giuliano* is characterized as open and cheerful, *Lorenzo* is closed, moody, self-contained, and deserving of his nickname, *Il Pensieroso* (The Thinker). The contrast may have sug-

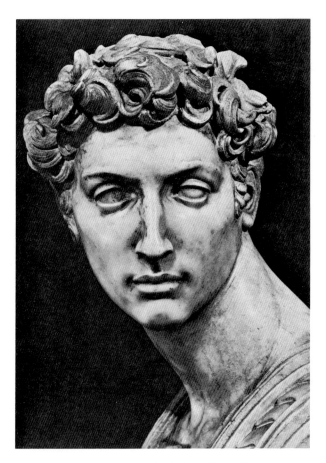

559. MICHELANGELO. Head of Giuliano de' Medici
(see fig. 553)

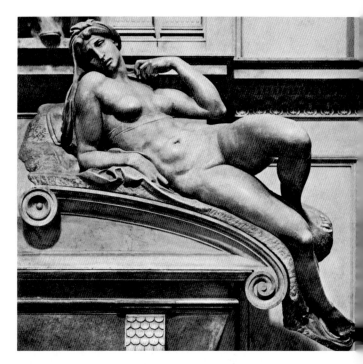

560. MICHELANGELO. *Dawn*, on the Tomb of
Lorenzo de' Medici, Medici Chapel. Designed 1521;
carved 1524–34. Marble, length 81"

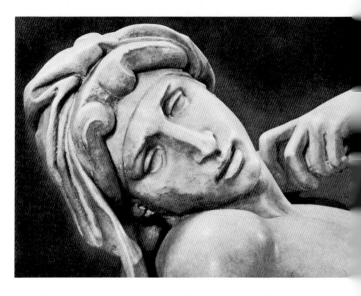

561. MICHELANGELO. Head of Dawn, detail of fig. 560

gested the opposition in John Milton's famous poems *L'Allegro* and *Il Penseroso*. Giuliano idly holds several coins, as if in intended largesse; Lorenzo plants his elbow on a closed money box, decorated with the fierce mask of a bat or lynx. Light plays freely on the face of *Giuliano*, but *Lorenzo*'s is enshadowed by his helmet and half-hidden by his hand. *Night* and *Day*, arranged at angles counter to the shape of the volutes, toe sharply out; *Dawn* and *Dusk*, weighed down by the prevailing gloom, conform to the volutes and toe downward.

Giuliano and *Lorenzo*, while related to some of the types and poses of the Sistine Ceiling, are less massive and energetic. A strange lassitude overcomes both, and it is perhaps worth remembering that while at work on the statues, Michelangelo, then only in his late forties, wrote that he was already old, and that if he worked one day he had to rest four. Their shoulders slope, muscles sag, hands hang heavily. The drowsy face of *Giuliano* (fig. 559) is drained of the fire and conviction of the *David*, let us say, or the prophets of the Sistine Ceiling. In both ducal figures the lines are longer, the proportions slighter, the angles smoother, the execution less crisp than might have been expected. Although the Times of Day are extremely muscular—the pulsating masses of *Day*'s gigantic back surpass anything that

Michelangelo had achieved in the projection of male musculature—they either writhe in helpless involvement with their own limbs or droop in painful weariness. The male faces are unfinished. *Day*'s is merely blocked out, but in the rough surfaces of *Dusk*'s sad head many have discerned Michelangelo's own disfigured face. The finished—or almost finished—female faces are strangely ornamental and, although superficially unreal, nonetheless deeply poetic. *Night*, with her strongly Hellenic nose and not quite closed eyes, a great star caught in the crescent of her diadem, dreams fitfully of her lost

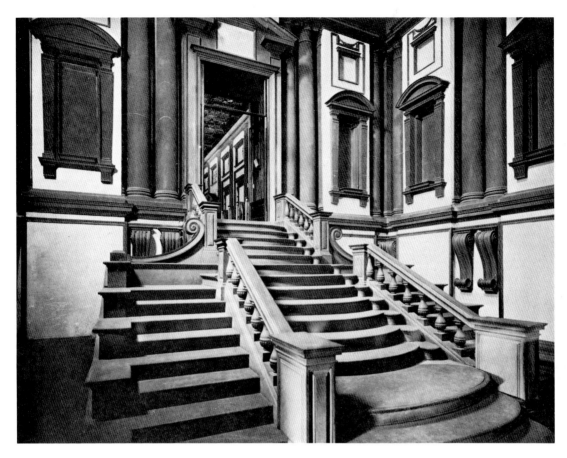

562. MICHELANGELO. Entrance Hall, Laurentian Library, S. Lorenzo,
Florence. 1524–34; staircase completed 1559. Commissioned by Pope Clement VII

children. The tragic *Dawn* (figs. 560, 561), her brows
knitted in a shape recalling the facial structure of the
Italo-Byzantine Madonnas of the Duecento, seems to be
grieving over her childlessness.

Michelangelo's mighty female forms were done from
male models, and many male studies for the *Night* are
preserved. Breasts were attached later. The ornamental
shapes of thighs, shins, and ankles carry the taut arcs of
the sarcophagi into the figural masses. The *Medici Madonna* (fig. 555) was reshaped many times and cut down
in the process; the lower portions reveal the original
scale of the group. Although the deeply meditative face
of the Virgin and the body of the Child never received
their final polish, Michelangelo's sensitive use of the
three-toothed chisel gives these passages an atmospheric
quality, as if seen through a veil of haze.

The total effect of the sculpture is disturbing, and so
are the details of the ornament. The leering mask, symbol of false dreams—for which Michelangelo cut away
the original left arm of *Night* and started a new one
twisted behind her shoulder—brings into larger focus
the steady procession of tiny, snarling masks that compose the frieze running behind all the Times of Day,
suggesting that death is a nightmare from which we will
awaken. The architecture of the chapel, the mood of its
statues, and the new, artificial ideals for the human body

and face had an immediate and profound effect on contemporary artists at work in Florence. In what has come
to be known as the crisis of Mannerism, the Medici
Chapel is a central monument.

While engaged in the carving of the statues for the
Medici Chapel, Michelangelo was taking a radical step
in the development of new architectural forms. A new library for San Lorenzo, to house the Medicean collection
of books and manuscripts, had been on Cardinal Giulio
de' Medici's mind as early as June 1519, but the commission for the structure was only given to Michelangelo
after Giulio became Pope Clement VII in November of
1523. The Laurentian Library had to be constructed as a
third story on top of the monastic buildings connected
with San Lorenzo. Construction began in 1524, was
halted in 1526, recommenced along with the Medici
Chapel after 1530 and abandoned in 1534, when Michelangelo took up residence in Rome. In 1557 he sent
a model for the staircase, but he never saw the building
in its present form.

The entrance hall is startling (fig. 562). Its two stories
are composed of superimposed orders of coupled Tuscan
columns that ostensibly support the abbreviated entablatures but in reality are recessed into niches in the wall,
where they are flanked by pilasters. This extraordinary
idea, which seems to have been developed from the

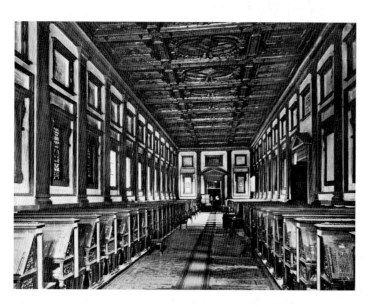

563. MICHELANGELO. Reading Room, Laurentian Library,
S. Lorenzo, Florence. 1524–33

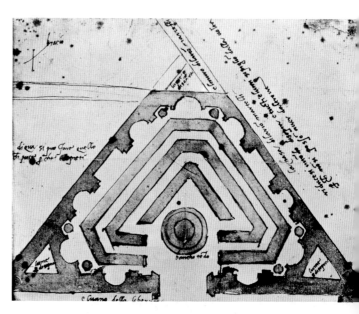

564. MICHELANGELO. *Plan for Triangular Rare-Book Room
of the Laurentian Library*. 1525–26. Pen and ink, 8³/4 x 11".
Casa Buonarroti, Florence

walled-in pilasters in the corners of the Medici Chapel, produces an apparent reversal of the functions of wall and column. What is revived, on a grand scale and in architectural terms, is nothing less than the conflict between line and mass that we saw in Michelangelo's early sculpture. Mass protrudes into the space of the room, line cuts against it. Locked in conflict, the opposed forces produce a strange, cold, and tragic beauty of shape and line that is painfully elaborated in the finespun motives of the ornamental panels and reduced in the weird tabernacles to forms of mortuary chill and utter unreality. Not since Minoan times had supports tapered downward as these pilasters do, and never had they been cut into three unequal segments by variation in surface fluting. The staircase, whose design, we are told, came to Michelangelo in a dream, freezes the principle of conflict by opposing ascending lateral flights with a descending central stair with bow-shaped steps pushing downward.

At first sight the long reading room looks more conventional (fig. 563). The pilasters support, the walls do not move inward, and there are no floating consoles. And then, as we analyze the structure and space, we come to realize that the battle is still on, and we are caught in it. Pilasters, ceiling beams, and floor patterns unite to produce a continuous cage of space in which the reading desks (also designed by Michelangelo) are trapped, two to a bay, and the observer with them. Similar linear refinements are elaborated in the windows and tabernacles, but the precision of ornament serves only to underscore the most disturbing aspect of the room—it has no reasonable focus or terminus. Since all the bays are identical, like cars in a train, the succession could contain two more or three less with no effect on the purely additive composition.

Today we see the Laurentian Library without its crowning feature, which would have completed the procession of painful spatial configurations with a climax

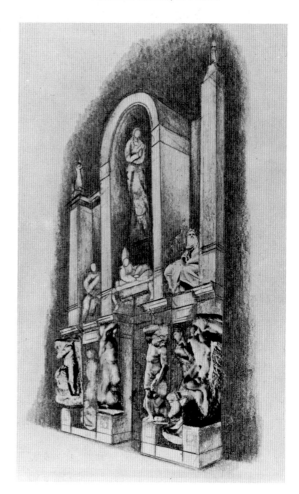

565. MICHELANGELO. Tomb of Pope Julius II. Proposed
reconstruction drawing of project of 1532

that might even be compared to the effect of Poe's *The Pit and the Pendulum*. The parade of identical bays was to have led to one of the strangest spatial ideas of the entire Renaissance (fig. 564), a triangular rare-book room enclosing a maze of reading desks lit from concealed

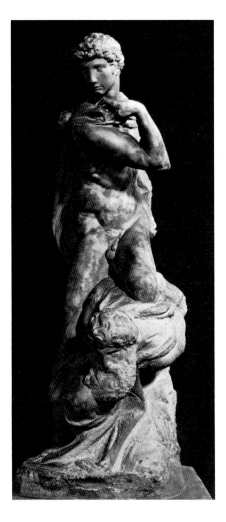

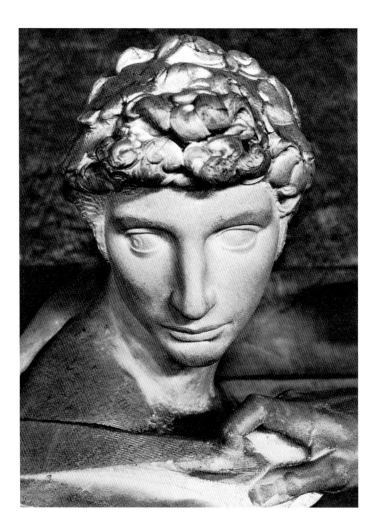

right: 566. MICHELANGELO. *Victory.* 1527–28. Marble, height 8' 6¾". Palazzo Vecchio, Florence. Commissioned for the Tomb of Pope Julius II

far right: 567. Head of Victory, detail of fig. 566

sources. In point of fact, the space available to Michelangelo between preexistent buildings outside was triangular, but another artist would probably have tried to cut the corners and fit a rectangle, or at most a circle, into the triangular shape. Michelangelo made a virtue of necessity. Alas, his rare-book room was never built.

Four more *Captives* and one *Victory* (see figs. 566–71) for the tomb of Julius II are preserved in Florence, and the most reasonable assumption is that Michelangelo set to work on them in Florence after all Medicean operations were suspended late in 1526. The most troublesome of the heirs of Julius II, Francesco Maria della Rovere, duke of Urbino, had recaptured his duchy after the death of Leo X in 1521 and was an implacable enemy of the Medici. As ally of the Florentine Republic, he passed through Florence twice during this period, at the head of a powerful force, and it can be assumed that he used his presence there to bring pressure on Michelangelo to complete the tomb. The Florence *Captives* are larger than those in the Louvre (see figs. 517, 518), but would certainly have been carved down, as was Michelangelo's practice with all statues.

The fourth project for Julius's tomb was formalized in a written contract in 1532. It calls for a wall tomb (fig. 565) with the *Moses* still on the upper story and the pope reclining on a sarcophagus. The meaning of the tomb has changed since the earlier projects, for the idea of resurrection has been discarded; the *Captives*, like Atlas figures, support the cornice, straining under its enormous weight. The *Victory*, too, has changed its meaning. The youthful figure is engaged in subduing rather than liberating a captive, yet withdraws at the moment of triumph. A revival of the old Psychomachia theme (see p. 181) takes place not only in the *Victory* but also in the newly liberated Florence. Niccolò Capponi, *gonfaloniere* of the Republic, asked the Florentines in 1527: "Do you hold dear the conquering of your enemies, or that your enemies do not conquer you? Then conquer yourselves, put down wrath, let hatred go, put aside bitterness." Speaking of the miserable state of the Medici pope, prisoner in Castel Sant'Angelo, he warned: "Not the words that are said, ignominiously or injuriously, against enemies, but the deeds that are done, prudently or valorously, give, won or lost, the victory." These words were delivered in the great hall of the Palazzo dei Priori, which still may have held the beginnings of the *Battle of Cascina* (see fig. 479) and certainly showed the unfinished *Battle of Anghiari* (see fig. 464). The following year, in the same place, Capponi pointed out that the Florentines had won their victory without bloodshed, through the intervention of God: "To his divine Majesty, therefore, we have to lift the eyes of our mind, recognizing God alone as our King and Lord, hoping firmly in him, who has undertaken the protection of this city and state."

The twisted *Victory* group (fig. 566), one of Michelangelo's most original conceptions, is now tilted somewhat forward. Originally, the young hero stopped his

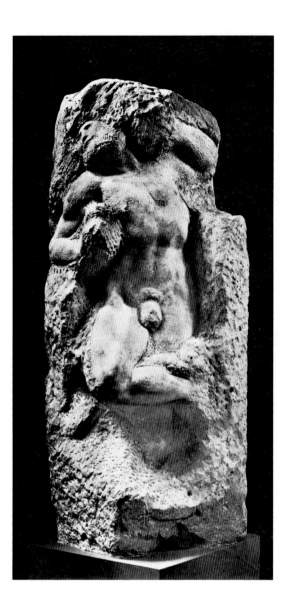

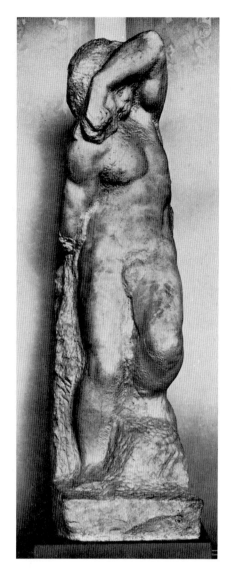

struggle to look upward toward Heaven, drawing with one hand the mantle, age-old symbol of heavenly protection, around him. It is to Donatello's marble *David* (see fig. 161) and *St. George* (see fig. 164), both of which express passionate civic conviction, that we must look for certain aspects of the style of Michelangelo's tense and haunting group. Seen upright, the group loses its strained appearance and harmonizes with the architecture of the tomb for which it was designed (see fig. 565). Quite as important, it regains its lofty dignity—a kind of soaring quality, intended not only for its aesthetic result but also for its moral significance. The taut effect of the lanky victor is communicated to his muscles and to his expression, for he is intent on communication with divinity, like an Abraham or a David. While the beard of the vanquished is largely uncut marble, elsewhere almost all the work with the toothed chisel has been completed. Here and there the splendidly muscled torso, alive with shifting tensions, has even received its finish. Only the right eye, strangely enough, was given an incised iris; this treatment of the eye had been used previously by Michelangelo, but he will renounce it altogether in finishing the statues for the Medici Chapel.

As in the related face of the *Medici Madonna* (see fig. 555), one sees the countenance of the *Victory* (see fig. 567) as through a haze of chisel strokes. This figure, beautiful as a Hellenic warrior, sensitive as Donatello's *St. George*, remains one of Michelangelo's least understood creations.

It is unrealistic to guess at the order planned for the four *Captives* (figs. 568–71) on the lower story of the tomb formalized in the 1532 contract. Some of the motifs may go back as far as the 1505 project (see fig. 510), notably the classical pose with legs crossed (fig. 568). When Michelangelo came to carve the statue, however, he made it writhe and twist in a new manner, transmitting the weight from the upraised left elbow through the body to the unaided left foot. To support this weight the torso arches, the chest lifts as though in pain, and the bearded head is tilted back. The beardless *Captive* (fig. 569) supports the weight in an axis running from left elbow to right foot, but in a languorous, almost dreamy way. The titanic, bearded *Captive* (fig. 570), whose anguished face and expanding chest carry memories of the ancient *Laocoön*, loses somewhat in the execution because of the clumsy cutting of the legs, probably the result of

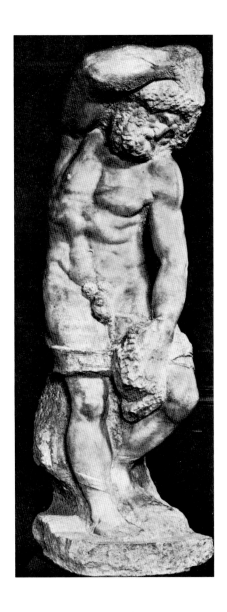

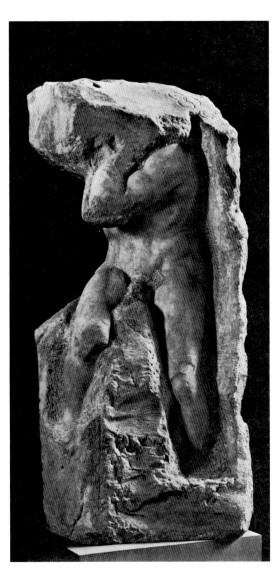

an ill-fated later attempt to finish what Michelangelo had left unfinished.

In all four statues Michelangelo's chief interest lay in the torsos, which are, from the front at least, fully developed with the toothed chisel and lack only surface finish. Sometimes an arm or a leg is brought to a similar condition, but never a head. The heads remain either roughed in or, as in one striking instance (fig. 571), still encased in the block, save for features faintly visible on one side as through a dense cloud of marble. Sometimes the statues have been started from two sides at once, sometimes from three, but in each case the back is still concealed within the block. One can usually follow the contours around the torso with considerable clarity up to the point where the shape suddenly disappears. For all their mass, not to speak of their superhuman strength, the figures are oddly soft. The vast areas of muscle and skin heave, swell, subside, or shine silkily against the drilled blocks of stone. Whatever might have been Michelangelo's conscious intent—and he must have thought he would finish the statues—their present condition reveals essential aspects of his nature as well as the turmoil of the years during which he worked on them. To watch these giants struggle to free themselves from the surrounding marble has for four centuries been a strongly empathetic experience for viewers. If the great artist could miraculously return and carve away the rough marble, we would probably miss it.

ANDREA DEL SARTO

The absence of Leonardo, Michelangelo, and Raphael from Florence after 1508–9 left a clear field for other masters. One of these, Andrea del Sarto (1486–1530), sailed through Mannerism untouched by the disorders of the era. One finds yearning and melancholy in his style, but never the neurosis that seems to have infected some of his fellow artists. One senses in Andrea's early work echoes of Leonardo, Raphael, and Fra Bartolommeo, but it is the naturalism of Andrea's teacher Piero di Cosimo, in whose shop he remained from about 1498 to 1508, that is most evident in his frescoes of the Life of St. Philip Benizzi in the atrium of the Santissima Annunziata, which had long been resplendent with Baldovinetti's *Nativity* (see fig. 318). Throughout the series, Andrea retained the outdoor light and atmospheric

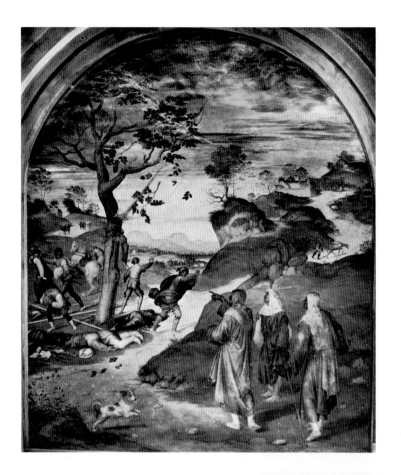

amplitude of Baldovinetti, which was in fact suggested by the site itself, which was filled with sunlight. The fantastic landscape masses, jutting rocks, and trees in the *Punishment of the Gamblers* (fig. 572) obviously derive from Piero di Cosimo. One can imagine how much more Piero, whose eccentricities, by the way, finally drove Andrea from his studio, would have made of the bolt of lightning that severs the tree and kills the gamblers. At any rate, the shapes and spaces of Andrea's landscape move with the ease of a lowland river, full, swollen, and deep, submerging the well-drawn but somehow less-than-significant figures. His fresco surface, lightly and freely brushed, glows with flower tones against the blue-greens in the ascending landscape.

In the grave *Annunciation* of 1512 (fig. 573), he adopts something of the measured dignity of the High Renaissance style, already practiced for several years by Fra Bartolommeo. The large-scale figures almost fill the foreground and are united with the remote distance by a well-constructed perspective. Mary stands before the Temple, and Gabriel unexpectedly approaches from the right. The broad, graceful figures and grand heads turn beautifully in relation to the distant perspective, whose apex is placed behind the head of a seated, almost nude figure. Could this be Isaiah, whose prophecy Mary was

572. ANDREA DEL SARTO.
Punishment of the Gamblers,
from the Life of St. Philip Benizzi.
1510. Fresco, 11' 9" x 10'.
Atrium, SS. Annunziata, Florence.
Commissioned by
Fra Mariano, the church's
sacristan

573. ANDREA DEL SARTO.
Annunciation. 1512. Panel,
71 1/2 x 71 1/2". Pitti Gallery,
Florence. Commissioned
for the Monastery of S. Gallo,
Florence

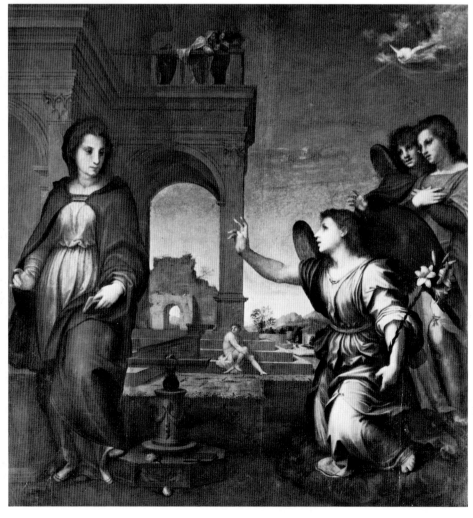

reading as she sat by the closed fountain, symbol of her virginity? The deep, blue sky, of almost Peruginesque clarity, harbors only an occasional cloud; from one of these descends the dove of the Holy Spirit. The color scheme of smothered reds, blues, and oranges accords with the new seriousness of Andrea's art.

In 1514 he returned to the Annunziata to paint the *Birth of the Virgin* (fig. 574), which might be interpreted as a High Renaissance commentary on the diffuse miscellany of Domenico del Ghirlandaio's fresco on the same subject (see fig. 363). The patrician interior reflects the architectural ideals of Giuliano da Sangallo (see pp. 309–10), and the massive figures, echoing Raphael's Stanza d'Eliodoro and Michelangelo's Sistine Chapel, are united by the same kind of curving rhythm that in the St. Philip Benizzi series flowed through the landscape. The deep shadows of the mature Raphael have also made their way to Florence, which had generally remained impervious to Leonardo's mysterious *chiaroscuro.* The angels on their clouds above the bed canopy, joining the dancelike movement of the foreground figures, were derived from an engraving by the German artist Albrecht Dürer, while Joseph, in the center toward the back, is lifted in reverse from Raphael's portrait of Michelangelo in the *School of Athens* (see fig. 521).

In the *Madonna of the Harpies* (fig. 575), Andrea has arrived at a noble statement of the Florentine version of Roman grandeur, again not without a conspicuous borrowing. Vasari tells us that Andrea painted the St. John the Evangelist on the Virgin's left from a clay model by Jacopo Sansovino that the sculptor had submitted in competition with Baccio da Montelupo for the statue of the saint at Orsanmichele. It has not, apparently, been noted that the real inventor of the figure was Raphael; Sansovino had merely reversed the philosopher holding a book, between Pythagoras and the portrait of Michelangelo, in the *School of Athens.* Since Raphael himself reused the figure in the *Galatea* (see fig. 542), these borrowings demonstrate the lack of any sense of personal ownership of a figural motif among High Renaissance artists, and their interest, on the contrary, in extracting the maximum effect from a handsome invention. The influence of Michelangelo is evident in the increased dignity, even majesty, of Andrea's forms, the severity of his architectural background, the force and dominance of his figures as well as their sculptural roundness and integrity, and his splitting of the drapery surface into facets like the planes of marble carving.

These various elements are assimilated by Andrea, whose noble altarpiece is, in the last analysis, wholly

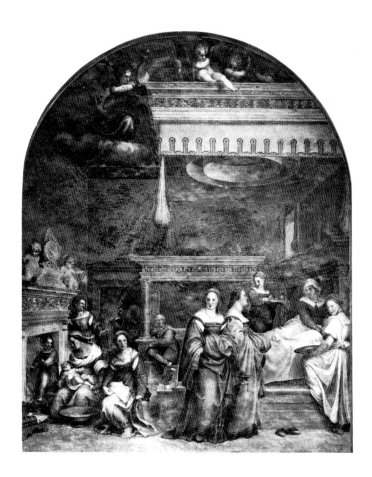

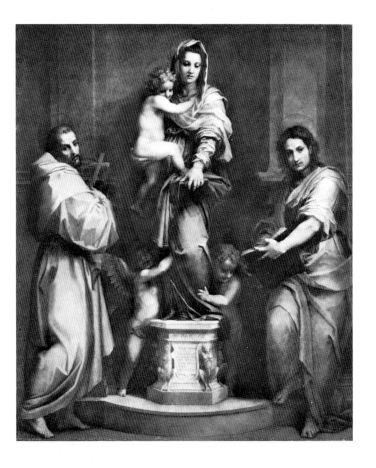

575. ANDREA DEL SARTO. *Madonna of the Harpies.*
1517. Panel, 81¹/₂ x 70". Uffizi Gallery, Florence.
Commissioned for the high altar of S. Francesco in Via
Pentolini, Florence, by the abbess

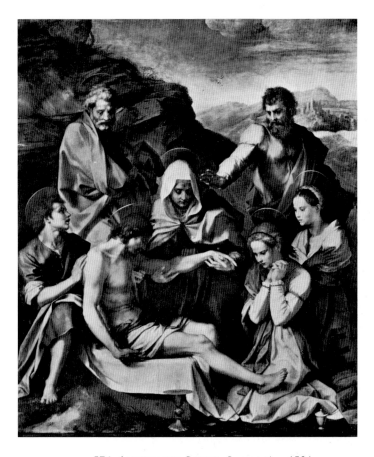

576. ANDREA DEL SARTO. *Lamentation*. 1524.
Panel, 94 x 80". Pitti Gallery, Florence.
Commissioned by Abbess Caterina di Tedaldo for the
high altar of S. Pietro in Luco, near Florence

historical scene, for Sts. Peter and Paul appear at the sides, and St. Catherine looks quietly from her kneeling position, her hands crossed on her chest.

Although the dedication of the church in Luco to St. Peter and the fact that its abbess was called Catherine account for the presence of these two saints, we need more than that to elucidate the warm, personal character of the picture. No more are we invited, as in the Quattrocento, to dwell on the wounds of Christ. Rather his body is presented mystically in the form of the sacrament, and the chalice stands in the center foreground, covered by the paten on which the Host appears, mysteriously erect. It is the Eucharist that draws the gaze of all the saints save John, who looks, as he was bidden, toward Christ's mother. Andrea's wife, stepdaughter, and sister-in-law posed for the Virgin, the Magdalen, and Catherine; the town of Luco appears in the background in the evening light, against the hills of the Mugello. It is hard to explain the intimacy of this family-style *Lamentation* by any other supposition than the arrival in Florentine territory of the quietist doctrines of the Oratory of Divine Love. The sacrament, "source of light and heat," draws all to itself, and we are to forget the pathos of the darkened face of Christ as we contemplate his perpetuation in the shining wafer.

Andrea's huge *Assumption of the Virgin* (colorplate 107, p. 517) was painted for the Church of Sant'Antonio dei Servi in Cortona; commissioned in 1526, it may not have been finished until the year before his death. Although, like so many of Andrea's Madonnas, this one is a portrait of his wife, there is an air of unreality about the whole picture. Mary, seated on clouds, her hands folded in prayer, is surrounded by sturdy putti. The light shines on the circle of saints, but then darkness closes in, the golden light fails, and we can discern the rocky cliffs of the background in massive shadow. In its combination of clarity and dimness, substance and dissolution, reality and vision, the picture seems to belong more to the seventeenth century than to the sixteenth. Or is that because we still do not fully understand the complexity and richness of the Cinquecento?

PONTORMO

Andrea del Sarto remained a High Renaissance painter even in his most mystical phase, but his pupil Jacopo Carucci da Pontormo (1494–1557) is often identified as a Mannerist. Pontormo opens up for us a world of fantasy, poetry, and torment that is unprecedented in the history of Italian Renaissance art.

As a youth of eighteen, according to Vasari, Pontormo studied with Leonardo da Vinci, Piero di Cosimo, and Andrea del Sarto in succession. Temperamentally, he was certainly closest to Piero, and indeed in his later years Pontormo was also to become a recluse, shutting himself away from the world in a studio accessible only by means of a ladder, which he could draw up after him. But even in his early works the strangeness of his style is

original. It is unified by his own sense of formal harmony and deep-toned color, as well as by his characteristic melancholy sweetness, which may seem unconvincing in the expression of St. Francis but is compelling in the face of the Virgin. The harpies who guard her throne are doubtless there to fulfill their role as leaders of souls to another world. The strong, simplified composition, the poise and counterpoise of masses, and the eloquence of figural style achieved by Andrea in this and other contemporary pictures gave him the leadership of Florentine painting toward the end of the second decade of the Cinquecento.

In 1523, with his wife, her daughter, and her sister, Andrea fled the plague, which had returned to Florence, for the healthful air of the Mugello, the valley that separates the first range of hills to the north of Florence from the major rampart of the Apennines. There, in 1524, in the village of Luco, he painted a *Lamentation* (fig. 576) that transforms grief into lyric exaltation. In deliberate reminiscence of a well-known composition by Perugino, the dead Christ is upheld in a seated position by John the Evangelist, while the Virgin holds his left hand and looks downward. Mary Magdalen, kneeling in prayer before the feet she once washed with her tears and dried with her hair, withdraws into meditation. This is not a

THE CINQUECENTO

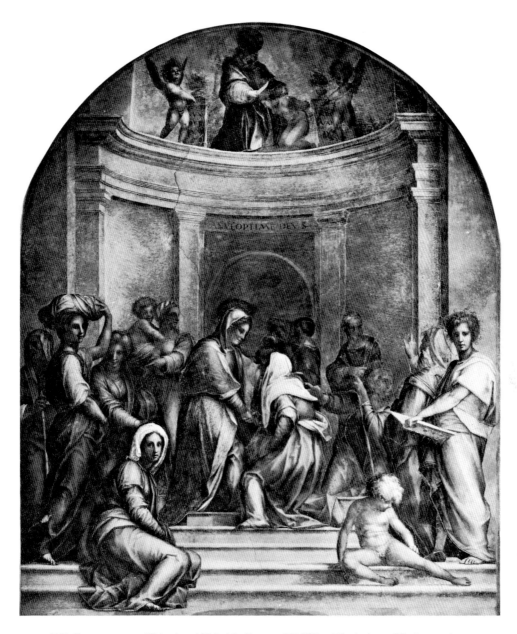

577. PONTORMO. *Visitation*. 1514–16. Fresco, 12' 10" x 11'. Atrium, SS. Annunziata, Florence. Commissioned by the Servites of SS. Annunziata

evident. In his *Visitation* (fig. 577) in the atrium of the Santissima Annunziata, for example, Pontormo already transforms High Renaissance structure. At first sight his composition looks like an exaggeration of High Renaissance symmetry, for the main incident is centralized and the figures are neatly arranged within the architectural setting. But then, instead of balancing the woman seated on the stairs at the left with a similar motif at the right, Pontormo breaks the symmetry by introducing a naked boy who looks down at his left leg and seems to scratch it gently. This figure initiates a strong and unexpected lateral surge inward and upward along lines continued by the kneeling St. Elizabeth. The bright and sometimes jarring color combinations, based on those established in Michelangelo's Sistine frescoes—Elizabeth wears a golden-yellow tunic with a sea-green outer sleeve and a violet inner sleeve—heighten the unconventional figural composition.

One wonders why the Visitation, which took place in front of Elizabeth's house, should be staged in a monumental exedra at the apex of a pyramid of steps; there appears to be a ritual intention, for the setting draws attention to the apex of the arch where, instead of the expected semidome, we see the Sacrifice of Isaac between chanting putti holding urns of flowers. The Sacrifice of Isaac was traditionally held to foretell that of Christ, and its juxtaposition with the Visitation converts the prenatal meeting of Christ and St. John the Baptist into a prophecy of their martyrdoms that is expressed sacramentally rather than dramatically. This would fulfill the will of God, which is extolled in the inscription over the arch. In view of the works painted by Pontormo at this time

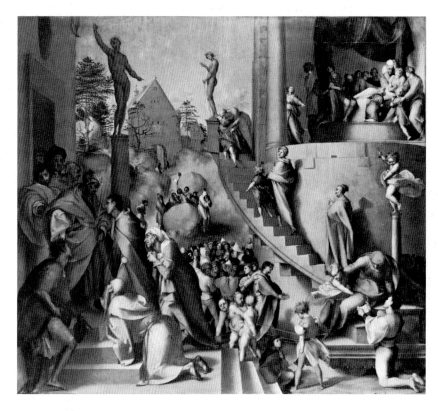

578. PONTORMO. *Joseph in Egypt.* c. 1518. Panel, 38 x 43¹/₈".
National Gallery, London. Painted for the nuptial chamber of Pier Francesco
Borgherini in the Palazzo Borgherini, Florence

for the new pope, Leo X, it is possible to find in Elizabeth's obeisance to her cousin, amid general rejoicing, a reference to the new submission of Florence to the Church. How to explain Pontormo's inclusion of the naked sunbather remains uncertain.

A fuller expression of Mannerism is seen in Pontormo's contributions to the nuptial chamber of Pierfrancesco Borgherini in the Palazzo Borgherini (now Palazzo Rosselli del Turco), a splendid example of Florentine High Renaissance architecture that still stands in Borgo Santi Apostoli. Pierfrancesco, a close friend of Michelangelo and by all accounts a delightful person, ordered a series of paintings of the Story of Joseph from Andrea del Sarto (suggested by Michelangelo), Pontormo, and two other leading Florentine painters that was to be incorporated in the wainscoting. Pontormo's *Joseph in Egypt* (fig. 578) makes a total break with the High Renaissance in its crowds of nervous figures, statues pulsating on the tops of slender columns, uncertain and unprotected staircases spiraling into nowhere, broken and spasmodic rhythms, irrational light and space, and avoidance of centrality, symmetry, or any other form of unifying compositional device. The picture splits up into little vignettes, some very close to us, some far away, yet without apparent connection, exploiting irrational jumps in scale, from Pharaoh's dream at the upper right, to the discovery of the cup in the center, to the reconciliation of Joseph and his brethren at the left.

Through the whole picture, with its rubbery surfaces and brassy colors, runs a strange terror that results in an almost physical tremor, like chills and fever. A center-background group of figures, clinging about a gigantic boulder, seems transfixed, as one is in dreams, by a power beyond comprehension or control; they have been interpreted in terms of the brethren's lament: "Wherefore shall we die before thine eyes, both we and our land?" (Genesis 47:19). The relevance of the verse for contemporary Florentines, well aware that they had lost both freedom and independence, may not be accidental. The Germanic buildings in the background are derived from the engravings of Albrecht Dürer. Vasari, indeed, blamed Pontormo for having sacrificed Italian grace to Northern strangeness in his figures as well. Incidentally, the anxious boy in contemporary costume seated on the step in the foreground was later identified by Vasari as Pontormo's pupil and adopted son, Agnolo Tori, called Bronzino (see Chapter 20).

A different mood is celebrated in the bucolic fresco Pontormo painted, probably in 1520–21, for the Villa Medici at Poggio a Caiano (fig. 579), built some forty years earlier for Lorenzo the Magnificent (see fig. 311). Leo X wanted the great hall decorated with classical subjects, and placed Cardinal Giulio in charge of the project at the same time that the cardinal was watching over the progress of Michelangelo's designs for the Medici Chapel. Andrea del Sarto and others were com-

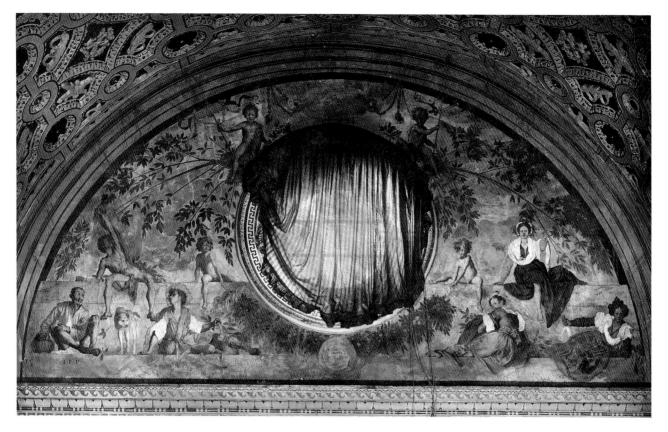

579. PONTORMO. *Vertumnus and Pomona*. Probably 1520–21. Fresco, 15' x 33'. Villa Medici,
Poggio a Caiano. Commissioned by Cardinal Giulio de' Medici

missioned to paint the side walls and Pontormo the end walls, but at the death of Leo in 1521 the work was interrupted, not to be resumed until much later in the century. Of Pontormo's share, only one lunette was ever completed. Vasari tells us that the subject—Vertumnus, Roman god of harvests, and Pomona, goddess of fruit trees—was provided by the humanist Paolo Giovio.

The motto "GLOVIS" below the oculus was that of Lorenzo de' Medici, duke of Urbino, who died in 1519. Read backward, it comes out "*si volge*," or "it turns," a reference to the reversals of fate that characterized the history of the Medici. Another inscription, above the oculus and not shown here, comes from Virgil's *Georgics* (I, 21), in which the gods are depicted in bucolic activities. Vertumnus and Pomona are united by the garland of fruits and vegetables under the window and by the laurel branches, symbols of Lorenzo, which seem to grow from its frame, and with which Pomona has filled her lap. While old Faunus, god of the woods, crouches in the left corner, Vertumnus turns to gaze at the beautiful Apollo seated on the low wall in a strikingly natural pose and reaching up to the laurel branches. Opposite him is a clothed and chaste Diana who holds a laurel branch. The content of Pontormo's lunette is remarkably close to that of an elegy that the poet Ariosto composed for Lorenzo, "*Ne la stagion. . . .*"

The sunlit scene of this enchanted terrace is deceptive, for within the bucolic spontaneity of the lunette lurks compositional principles that challenge the unity and logic of the High Renaissance. The oculus window (covered by a curtain in our illustration), for example, is treated as if it were a solid disk, the low walls as if they were golden air, the ground is nonexistent, space is nowhere defined, the figures are poised on the horizontals as if balanced on wires, and the whole composition, on three levels, is delicately laced together by the spreading laurel branches. Every seemingly relaxed pose is in reality tense when compared with the poses in Michelangelo's Sistine Ceiling or Raphael's Stanze, which, no matter how active, always harbor a reserve of latent energy. Pontormo's poses are calculated to bring out unexpected, sometimes unconventional aspects of the figures and arrestingly new and beautiful linear rhythms. Where in Renaissance art have we seen, or will we see again, a front view of a stretching nude youth (a god, no less!) with his legs spread wide, above a dog with its back arched, also stretching itself? While the animal naturalism of such poses negates the idealism of the High Renaissance, it should be noted that these poses also preclude the possibility of easy motion. Figures and vegetation are fixed within a web of delicate color and endless line.

Pontormo's *Entombment* (colorplate 108, p. 518), the nucleus of the cycle of paintings for the Capponi family in their tiny chapel in Santa Felicita, is a work of poignancy and beauty, but is this an Entombment or a Deposition? There is no tomb, there are no crosses. Stranger yet, no clear demarcation separates earth from

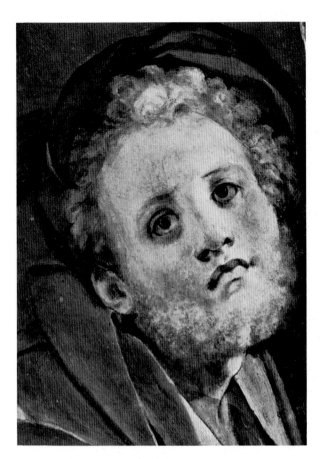

580. PONTORMO. Head of Young Man,
detail of *Entombment* (see colorplate 108, p. 518). 1525–28.
Panel. ⛪ Capponi Chapel, Sta. Felicita, Florence

581. PONTORMO. *Study for Deluge Fresco for
San Lorenzo* (portion of sheet). c. 1546. Red chalk,
whole sheet 16½ x 8½". Gabinetto dei
Disegni e Stampe, Uffizi, Florence. Commissioned
by Cosimo de' Medici

sky, and the only identifiable object in the background is a floating cloud. Like Andrea del Sarto's *Lamentation* (see fig. 576), this is a meditative picture and its real subject is the Eucharist. Two unidentifiable youths carry the lifeless body of Christ while two women tend to Mary, who stretches out one hand above the shining body. The wounds, already washed, are barely visible. The figures ascend in the mysterious space like a fountain in a Renaissance garden, the spray wafted by the wind. Every motion is slow, dreamlike, and unreal. At the top St. John, the Beloved Disciple, bends over not through his own volition but as if carried by the now descending waters of the fountain and the arch of the frame, stretching out his hands toward the body. No one weeps. The faces betray either an intense yearning, answered by the ghost of an expression on the closed eyes and parted lips of Christ, or a look of surprise, as if the observer is intruding upon the common act of love that unites them.

The colors, deriving in part from the Sistine Ceiling, pass all belief—pinks, sharp greens, pale but intense blues—and appear in improbable places, including what looks like the nude flesh of the two youths but on inspection turns out to be tight-fitting leather jerkins. The effect is like colored lights playing over a fountain of figures. At the upper right, the young man with blond curls and beard, full lips, and wide-staring, hypnotized eyes (fig. 580) is Pontormo himself. In looking at that face one can understand why, as Vasari relates, Pontormo walled up the chapel for three years and let no one enter while he painted so private a testament. As we seek to understand the painting, we would do well to remember that close to the year in which it was painted the Theatines under St. Cajetan had instituted the perpetual adoration of the Blessed Sacrament.

After the Capponi chapel Pontormo seems to have become morose and warped, ingrown and strange. His

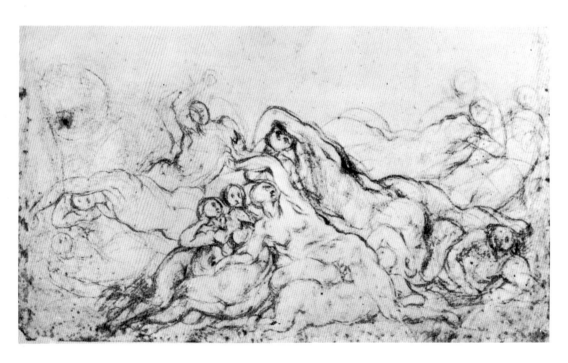

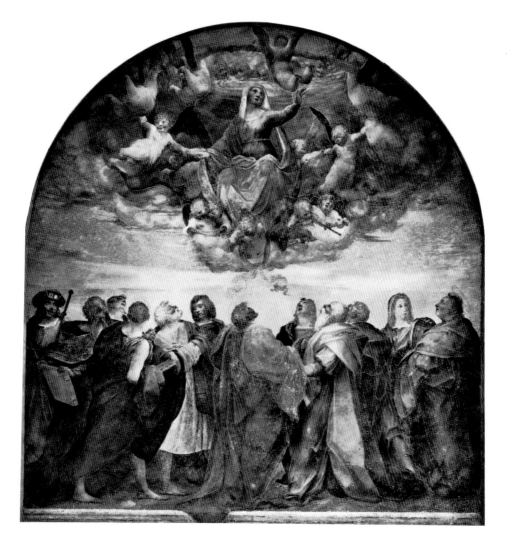

582. ROSSO
FIORENTINO.
*Assumption
of the Virgin*. 1517.
Fresco. Atrium, SS.
Annunziata,
Florence.
Commissioned by
the Servites of SS.
Annunziata

Last Judgment frescoes (1546–51) for the chancel of San Lorenzo were destroyed in a later remodeling of the building. What we see in the drawings (fig. 581) is how the autonomy and even the beauty of the human figure are now swept away by the movement of the linear composition.

ROSSO FIORENTINO

Pontormo's contemporary, Giovanni Battista di Jacopo, is known to us by his nickname of Rosso Fiorentino (the red-headed Florentine; 1495–1540). Rosso's entry in the competition of early Cinquecento painting in the atrium of Santissima Annunziata is an *Assumption of the Virgin* (fig. 582). The foreground is crowded with the twelve apostles, wall-to-wall with no landscape background. Their massive cloaks collide alarmingly and at one point project over the lower edge of the frame and drop into the spectator's space. In the upper portion the Virgin is shown ascending so quickly that she will soon be snapped out of the picture altogether. She is enclosed within a ring of smiling putti, whose arms and clasped hands make a continuous circle in depth, their feet flying out as the ring revolves. All this takes place to the music of a lute and a flute played by angels below the Virgin's feet. To cap the climax, the putti who hold the girdle

that Mary customarily drops to St. Thomas tie it in knots and tease him by dangling it in front of his nose! Not even Piero di Cosimo ever got away with quite such a trick, which is in tune with the rough surfaces and the strange, even disturbing expressions of the apostles.

Vasari is eloquent about the pranks played by this impish redhead, notably the torments inflicted by his pampered and mischievous monkey on the monks of Santa Croce. Rosso did not abandon his practical jokes even when treating the most serious subjects, as in the *Descent from the Cross*, originally painted for the Cathedral of Volterra (colorplate 109, p. 519), but he also showed that he could raise these devices to the level of high tragedy. The cross and ladders, powerfully projected in a low side light, carry the figures against a leaden sky, below which a few distant hills appear. There is no center; as in the contemporary Poggio a Caiano lunette by Pontormo (see fig. 579), the composition weaves a fabric of shapes that seeks the frame rather than the central axis. Again as in Pontormo, the figures assume poses of the utmost extension or are cramped in postures from which they cannot move freely. But there the resemblance stops. Rosso's muscle-bound figures are hard, as if carved from wood, and their bodies and faces are formed of cubic shapes related to the bleak planes of the cross and ladders. In the kneeling, stretching Magdalen

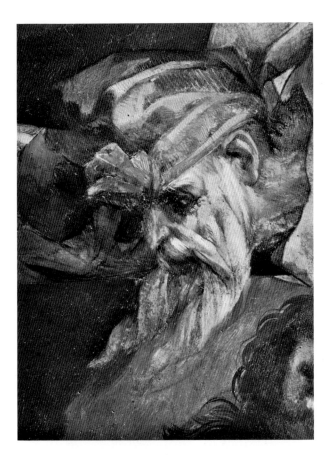

583. ROSSO FIORENTINO. Head of Joseph of Arimathea, detail of *Descent from the Cross* (see colorplate 109, p. 519). 1521. Panel. Pinacoteca, Volterra

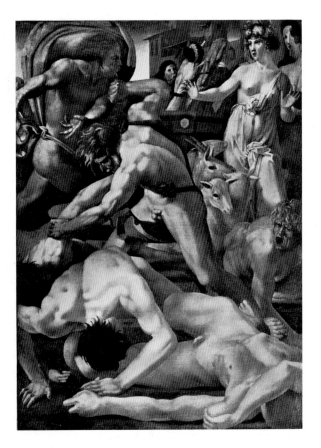

584. ROSSO FIORENTINO. *Moses Defending the Daughters of Jethro*. c. 1523. Canvas, 63 x 46½". Uffizi Gallery, Florence

under the cross, a knife-edge crease splits the figure into light and dark halves, and to show that this is no accident, her belt is bent as it goes around the crease.

Other figures, however, are treated on a different principle. The head of the weird Joseph of Arimathea, leaning over the top of the cross, seems to be composed of twisted rags (fig. 583). John the Evangelist, turning away from the cross and covering his face with his hands, collapses into a bundle of cloth caught pitilessly in the raking light. In Rosso's devastating picture we turn from the wooden blocks and crumpled cloth that represent man, once the measure of all things, to the face of Christ, and find nothing but a smile that suggests a detached and secret satisfaction. Rosso seems to be denouncing God and man, and we sense not only the deadly emptiness of the chronic jokester but also the dilemma of a lost generation.

Rosso went to Rome and was there in 1527, right through the Sack, and suffered severely. His *Moses Defending the Daughters of Jethro* (fig. 584), whose color scheme of pink and blue contrasts grimly with its brutal subject matter, makes sense only as a comment on the foreshortened figural heap developed by Michelangelo in the *Brazen Serpent* spandrel (see colorplate 101, p. 496). Moses, flailing away with his fists, creates the apex of an apparently conventional High Renaissance pyramid based on the prostrate Midianites. But the pyramid is dissolved and tied to the frame by a ferocious, oncoming Midianite at the upper left and a provocative daughter of Jethro at the upper right, whose body is partially covered by filmy drapery that reveals more than it hides. The construction of the figures in terms of light and dark patches is based on Michelangelo's practice of laying on underpaint. But the lack of the naturally resilient contours characteristic of the human body results in artificial edges that separate the foreshortened figures into almost abstract planes of tone, subdivided by the patches. Rosso's flight from the horrors of the Sack of Rome, his subsequent wanderings in Umbria and Tuscany, and his move to France, where he and other Italian émigrés created a French version of the Mannerist style, lie outside the province of this book.

PERINO DEL VAGA

The style of a third Florentine Mannerist, Piero Bonaccorsi, known as Perino del Vaga (1500/1–1547), differs sharply from that of Pontormo and Rosso, possibly because of his association with Raphael in Rome. Perino bridges, in fact, the historical gap between the Roman High Renaissance and the *maniera*, the dominant style of the middle and late Cinquecento, of which he was one of the founders. After the Sack, he took refuge in Genoa. His *Adoration of the Child* (fig. 585) is a variant on the Nativity, although neither shed, manger, ox, ass, nor shepherds are represented. Signed and dated 1534 on the foreshortened tablet in the foreground—a device borrowed from Albrecht Dürer—the lofty altarpiece

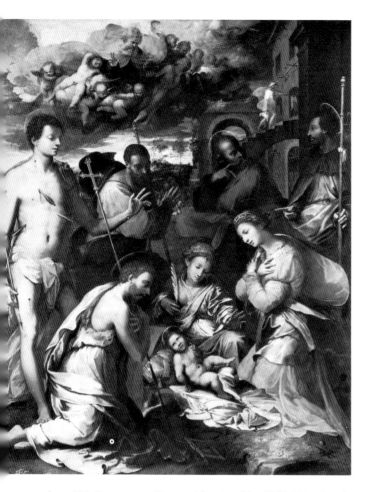

was commissioned by the Basadonne family for the Church of Santa Maria della Consolazione. The Christ Child, whose pose is derived from one of Michelangelo's nudes in the Sistine Ceiling, looks and points toward John the Baptist. The cloud-borne God the Father at the top of the picture is accompanied by child-angels, and around the Child and Mary stand or kneel six saints, only one of whom, Joseph, was present at his birth. Sebastian on the left and Roch on the right were protectors against the plague; John the Baptist (adult here, but believed to have been only three months older than the Christ Child), Catherine of Alexandria, and James the Greater were possibly required by the Basadonne family. The languid grace and sensuous flesh of Sebastian, who toys with an arrow, and the smooth shoulder of John the Baptist contrast with the density of crinkled and shimmering draperies that conceal the female bodies. Acute preciosity and metallic brilliance of color are combined with *chiaroscuro* derived from Raphael's latest works. A shaft of light at the upper right strikes a male figure from whose right hand dangles a slaughtered lamb, symbol of Christ's sacrifice.

Perino's cycle of frescoes for the Palazzo del Principe in Genoa was painted somewhat earlier than the Basadonne altarpiece. The most surprising is the *Fall of the Giants* (fig. 586), an enormous ceiling painting, al-

above: 585. PERINO DEL VAGA. *Adoration of the Child.* 1534. Panel, transferred to canvas, 9' 1/4" x 7' 3 1/8". National Gallery of Art, Washington, D.C. (Kress Collection). Commissioned by the Basadonne family for Sta. Maria della Consolazione, Genoa

below: 586. PERINO DEL VAGA. *Fall of the Giants.* Begun c. 1529. Fresco, c. 21 x 30'. Palazzo del Principe, Genoa. Commissioned by the Doria family

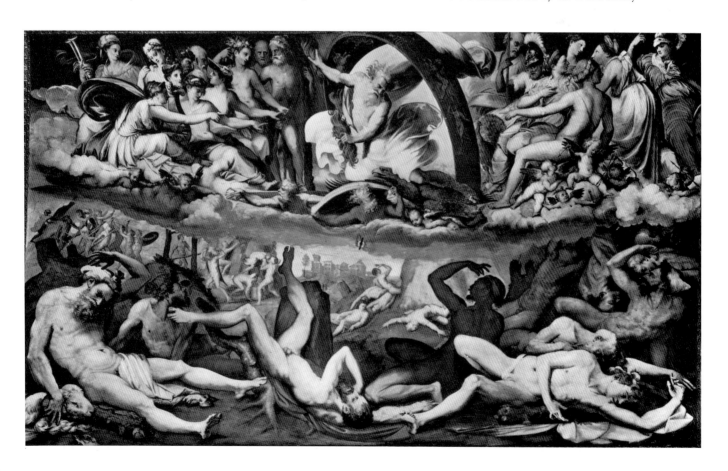

though, like those by Michelangelo and Raphael, it does not indulge in illusionistic views from below. The subject, a typical Mannerist invocation of authority, invites comparison with Giulio Romano's bombastic and illusionistic treatment of the same theme (see figs. 611, 612). Both may have been suggested by the arrival of Charles V in Italy in 1530 to bring order out of chaos. Significantly enough, he landed in Genoa, where he was greeted with cries of "Long live the emperor of the world!" Jupiter, whose face is almost identical with that of God the Father in the Basadonne altarpiece, brandishes his thunderbolt from the foreshortened circle of the zodiac, surrounded by Perino's typically sensuous deities. Meanwhile, the giants, who are oddly flaccid in musculature, pile up on the ground in dreamlike attitudes, nerveless before the thundering king of the gods.

DOMENICO BECCAFUMI

The Sienese Domenico Beccafumi (1485–1551) can be compared to Pontormo in the imaginative breadth, sensitivity, poetry, and consummate craftsmanship of their pictures. The traditional Sienese grace of line and surface and delicacy of color function at high intensity in Beccafumi's paintings. His *Stigmatization of St. Catherine* (colorplate 110, p. 520), painted for the Convent of Monte Oliveto in the desolate, eroded countryside to the east of Siena, might at first glance be taken for a High Renaissance work, but it shows many traits that we are accustomed to call Manneristic. Its symmetrical format goes back to Perugino, but the inlaid floor is projected from the foreground plane, through an arch, to the outer edge of a terrace in a manner suggesting Raphael's *School of Athens* (see fig. 521). The grand simplicity of the architecture is in keeping with Bramante's noble style, while the softening effects of the *chiaroscuro* recall Leonardo's *sfumato*. And then differences appear. The floor patterns, apparently based on systematic alternations of formal elements and color schemes, are so pervaded by shifting lights as to offer no rational successions. The two foreground piers are so closely associated with the flanking St. Benedict and St. Jerome that at a certain point the piers and figures seem to merge. The bases of the piers are replaced by the feet of the saints; the folds of the saints' habits flow in a manner that suggests less the shapes of their bodies than the rigid verticals of the piers. The arches, pendentives, and vaults (in Italian *vele*, or veils) become veils or curtains upheld by putti, then dissolve to admit the apparition of the Virgin and Child. The clouds fade off into the haze that conceals the sky, and this, in turn, blends into the exquisite ground mists floating upward from the hillocks and valleys of the landscape.

A High Renaissance master would probably have placed the central figure in the center, but Beccafumi shows St. Catherine kneeling on the left. Awaiting the stigmata, she raised her hands in a manner that continues the orthogonals of the cornices and the arms of

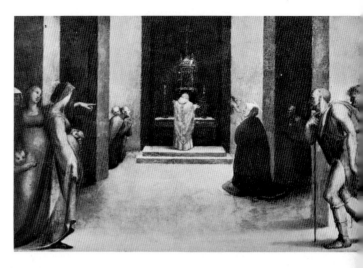

587. DOMENICO BECCAFUMI. *Communion of St. Catherine*, on the predella of the St. Catherine altarpiece (see colorplate 110, p. 520). c. 1518. Panel, 12 x 17¼". Pinacoteca, Siena

the cross, and what we expect to be orthogonals receding in space become a diagonal in a single plane. At the same time the orthogonals of the floor, instead of carrying our eye, as Raphael's do, to a clearly seen horizon, lead us into impenetrable mist, and that mist, rather than any person or object, occupies the center of the composition.

Features are brilliantly modeled, but their shadows are murky. Drapery masses shine like flames, but while the edges are clear enough, the exact shape of any fold eludes our baffled perceptions. Things and beings lurk in the shadows—St. Catherine's lily and book, St. Jerome's lion. In this language of diaphanous color and tremulous line, Beccafumi seems to be telling us that all substance is an illusion, that earthly reality will vanish into the shadows and luminous mist. Not only does he transform substance, he also annihilates space. The predella (fig. 587) shows St. Catherine, like the contemporary St. Cajetan, unwilling to approach the altar because of her sense of unworthiness. Yet she is miraculously given Communion by an angel who traverses in a single reach the intervening space of the church. Once again, the space is pervaded by an otherworldly light that is as substantial as the figures.

Beccafumi's huge *Fall of the Rebel Angels* (fig. 588) was intended for the Church of the Carmine in Siena. It was refused by the monks, perhaps because it was too extreme, and Beccafumi was required to paint another picture, not completed until much later; in the second version (not illustrated) God the Father plays a more assuring and authoritative role. In this original version, all is chaos. St. Michael, his spread wings flickering with peacock eyes, brandishes his sword while in the clouds about him other angels flail away at the rebels. At the bottom of the picture, near the observer, Hell opens. Pale, nude fallen angels, mostly wingless now, twist and turn in agony, gesticulate and cry out, and fall to the ground writhing as the heat torments them. In a manner unprecedented in Italy, Beccafumi allows us to look into

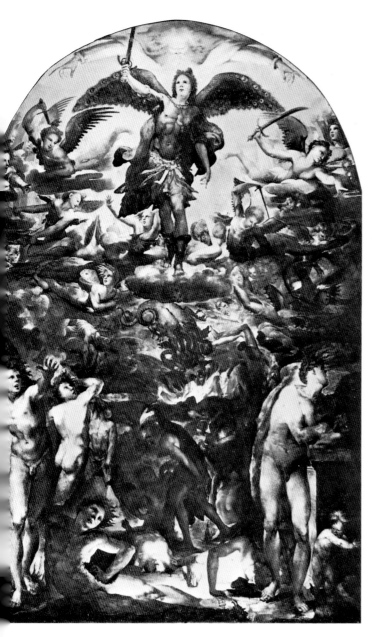

588. DOMENICO BECCAFUMI. *Fall of the Rebel Angels*.
c. 1524. Panel, 11' 4¹/₂" x 7' 4". Pinacoteca, Siena.
Commissioned for the Church of the Carmine, Siena

the phosphorescent lights of Hell: "No light, but rather darkness visible / Served only to discover sights of woe." (One wonders if John Milton in his travels might even have seen this picture.) When we look for God, we find him above St. Michael, half lost in the mist. His head is foreshortened toward us, his arms spread along the inside of the arch. How far from the paternal majesty and mighty arms of a High Renaissance image of the Deity is this remote and even menacing phantasm!

CORREGGIO

The contrast between High Renaissance and Mannerist tendencies that characterizes Florence and Siena in the early Cinquecento separates in a similar way Correggio and Parmigianino, two masters of the Po Valley city of Parma, which had not heretofore produced a painter

worthy of note. Antonio Allegri, known as Correggio (1494–1534) from the north Italian town of his birth, would have been of merely art-historical interest if he had remained on the level of his provincial, youthful works, deeply influenced by Leonardo, whose ideas he generally absorbed at second hand. But in 1518 Correggio arrived in Parma, where he appears to have fallen under the spell of the Roman High Renaissance, again not from originals but from drawings and engravings. He may also have seen paintings by Raphael in Bologna and in Piacenza (the *Sistine Madonna* was then in Piacenza; see fig. 527). Sixteenth-century writers agree that he never went to Rome, but modern writers are far from certain, and the question may never be settled. The weight of evidence seems to favor such a visit, but if it did not take place, Correggio's would not be the only instance of High Renaissance influence from a distance; the same thing happened in the case of Titian in Venice, as we shall shortly see. Regardless of how Correggio absorbed his knowledge of what was going on in Rome, he creatively transformed the Roman heritage into his own personal style, becoming in a few years a leading master of northern Italy.

From the start of Correggio's mature period, he seems to have been intent on substituting emotional for formal principles in the unification of his compositions, religious and secular alike. No longer are the components of a *Sacra Conversazione* sedately balanced around a central Madonna figure, as in works by Giovanni Bellini and Raphael. Rather they are drawn together in unconventional, diagonal, and changing compositions by emotional relationships. In the bewitching *Madonna and Child with Sts. Jerome and Mary Magdalen* (fig. 589), Mary holds the Christ Child in the crook of her left arm. The Magdalen presses her cheek against his thigh, bringing one foot toward her lips. He caresses her mass of silken hair but seems to concentrate his attention on the book lifted up by the aged St. Jerome as a youthful angel turns the pages. Behind this apparently spontaneous burst of mutual affection is a deeper message. The Magdalen's angel displays her ointment jar, and the Magdalen herself was destined to wash the feet of the adult Christ with her tears and dry them with her hair. Christ, meanwhile, for all his babyish expression is conferring divine blessing and authority on Jerome's Latin translation of the Bible from its ancient sources, which are represented by the scroll in the saint's right hand.

Human emotion and sacred purpose are inextricably blended in Correggio's art. His tumultuous shapes, whether of cloth that flows like melting marble, or of tanned male and white female and infantile flesh, or of torrential, honeyed hair, are swept together by these two organizing principles into a sweet climax that seems to be half erotic, half religious. One might say that it is love that makes Correggio's world go round. Sometimes his imagery remains on a level of delightful sweetness, unquestioning and childlike. He never seems to have been perplexed by the inherent conflict between the two realms he so happily united. But his forms are so soft, his light and shade so melting, his surfaces so delicious, his people so well-nigh irresistible, that it would be a harsh Puritan indeed who could take him to task. As far as we know, his religious paintings never fell victim to the strictures of the Council of Trent, which sternly forbade nudity in religious works. Moreover, Correggio's principle of emotional composition, as well as his actual shapes and surfaces, became an essential ingredient of religious art in the Baroque period, inspiring such masters as Rubens and Bernini.

In 1522 Correggio accepted the commission for his most familiar *Adoration of the Shepherds* or, as it is more generally called, *Holy Night* (fig. 590), but it was not placed in the Church of San Prospero in Reggio Emilia until 1530. Now the "light and heat" that St. Cajetan

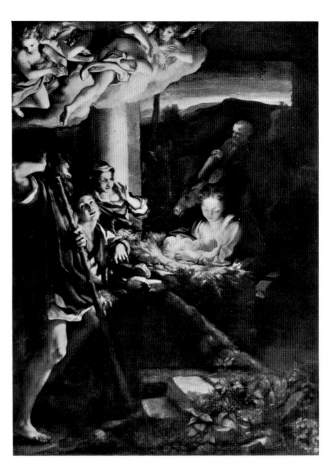

590. CORREGGIO. *Adoration of the Shepherds* (*Holy Night*). 1522. Panel, 8' 5" x 6' 2". Gemäldegalerie, Dresden. Commissioned by Alberto Pratoneri for S. Prospero, Reggio Emilia

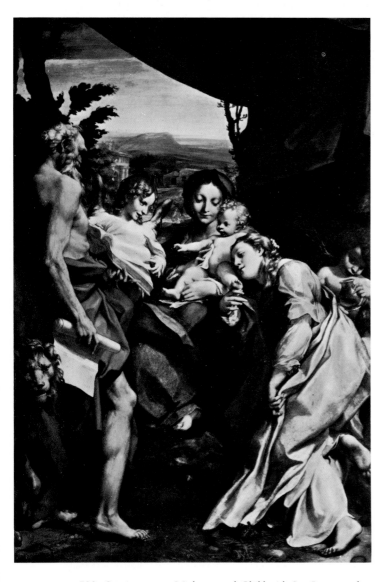

589. CORREGGIO. *Madonna and Child with Sts. Jerome and Mary Magdalen*. After 1523. Panel, 7' 8½" x 4' 7½". Pinacoteca, Parma. Commissioned by Briseide Colla, widow of Orazio Bergonzi, for Sant'Antonio, Parma

had sought in the Eucharist are fused with St. Bridget's vision of the glowing Christ Child and identified with Correggio's own energizing principle of love. A believable if incandescent baby, beautifully foreshortened and lying on a bundle of wheat in a reference to the Eucharist, is the source of light for the entire painting, as in Gentile da Fabriano's predella a century earlier (see fig. 185). Christ illuminates Mary's sweetly smiling face, while the midwife draws back and raises her hand, as if to protect herself from the intensity of the radiance. In addition, the light falls on two shepherds, the young one looking up rapturously at his companion, and on the angels who sweep in on a cloud in brilliantly foreshortened poses. The same light touches the faces of Joseph and the ox and ass, leaving in darkness the hills, over which can be seen the first glimmer of dawn.

In 1640 the Este family, then dukes of Modena, took possession of the painting and carried it off to their palace, to the infinite sorrow of the inhabitants of Reggio Emilia; the parish priest inscribed its loss in San Prospero's register of the dead. Either this picture or one of its many descendants inspired, in 1646, Richard Crashaw's *Hymn in the Nativity*, with its recurrent refrain:

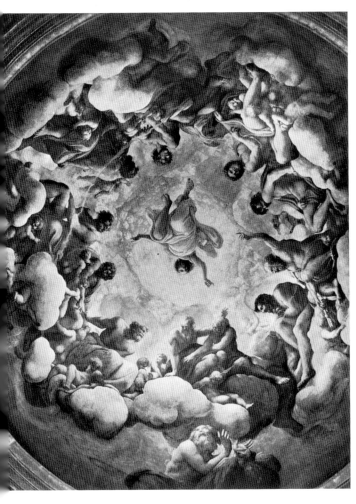

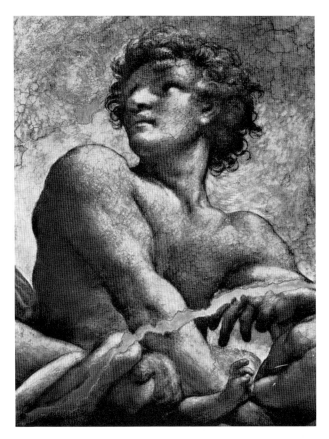

591. CORREGGIO. *Vision of St. John the Evangelist.*
1520–24. Fresco in dome, greatest width 31' 8". S. Giovanni
Evangelista, Parma

592. An Apostle, detail of fig. 591

We saw thee in thy baulmy Nest,
Young dawn of our aeternall DAY!
We saw thine eyes break from their EASTE
And chase the trembling shades away.
We saw thee; and we blest the sight,
We saw thee by thine own sweet light.

Historically, Correggio's major triumphs were his dome compositions, which opened up a whole new field for religious painting, particularly in the seventeenth and eighteenth centuries. The earliest of these represents the *Vision of St. John the Evangelist* (figs. 591, 592). Correggio took as his point of departure Mantegna's ceiling in the Camera Picta (see fig. 411), and the drum of the dome serves as a frame through which we look into the open sky. On clouds banked round the cornice, the apostles are seated in pairs, their poses recalling Michelangelo's nudes on the Sistine Ceiling, while in the center Christ ascends into Heaven. There are other suggestions of the Sistine Ceiling in the Michelangelesque grandeur and muscular power of the figures, who are supported by putti like those who surround Michelangelo's Deity on his flights through space.

The foreshortenings betray a knowledge of the *Brazen Serpent* (see colorplate 101, p. 496), and the idea of looking through an opening across which a divine figure is floating must have been suggested by the *Separation of Light from Darkness* (see colorplate 100, p. 495). But the handling of the forms shows Correggio's own melting style, without any of Michelangelo's tension or linear definition. Correggio has given us a surprising view of the ascending Christ from below—partly wrapped in a floating cloak, to be sure, but sharply foreshortened from a most unconventional angle. To view the scene correctly you must hold the illustration overhead and look up.

Such views are abundantly visible in the dome of the Cathedral of Parma, which Correggio painted in 1526–30 (colorplate 111, p. 569; figs. 593, 594) as part of an extensive series of frescoes. The damaged composition, prototype of innumerable Baroque domes, shows the *Assumption of the Virgin* in the center, surrounded by a ring of ascending figures who are for the most part nude. As we watch, this ring seems to ascend, leaving the apostles behind. Correggio has carefully masked the transition between the octagonal drum and the circular central composition by means of enormous balusters,

High Renaissance and Mannerism

561

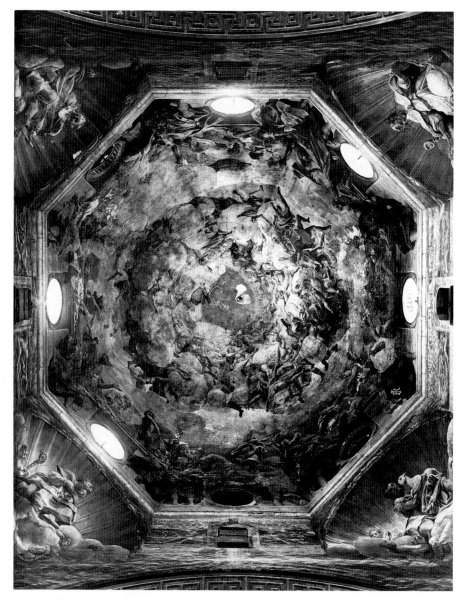

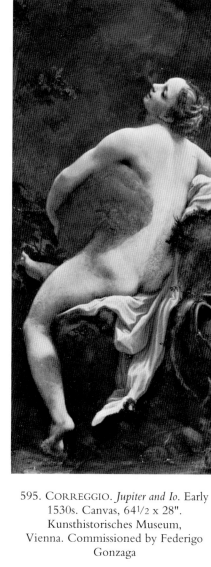

left: 593. CORREGGIO. *Assumption of the Virgin* (see also colorplate 111, p. 569). 1526–30. Fresco in dome. Cathedral, Parma

below left: 594. CORREGGIO. Apostles and Angels, detail of fig. 593

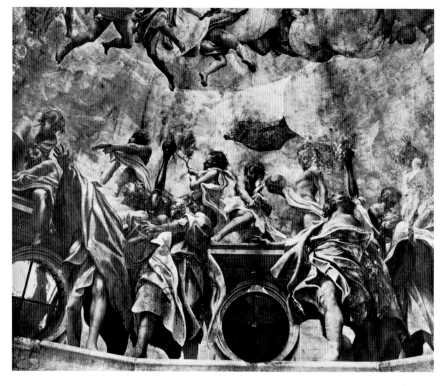

595. CORREGGIO. *Jupiter and Io.* Early 1530s. Canvas, 64½ x 28". Kunsthistorisches Museum, Vienna. Commissioned by Federigo Gonzaga

which, with boy-angels in between, carry our eye effortlessly up the angles until these disappear in the central composition.

In Correggio's dome compositions we are dealing with rapture in the strict etymological sense of the word. The central figure is rapt—torn loose from earthly moorings—and carried upward as the spectator is intended to be, vicariously at least. No wonder, therefore, that some of the artist's most alluring compositions deal with classical abduction scenes, especially the series made for Federigo Gonzaga, first duke of Mantua, but never delivered. The duke's penchant for such subjects was to be satisfied by lining a room in the palace with the Loves of Jupiter—a far cry from Mantegna's chaste frescoes nearby (see fig. 410). Jupiter was a mythical ancestor of the Gonzaga family and, in his amorous exploits, not unlike Federigo. In Correggio's *Jupiter and Ganymede* (colorplate 112, p. 569), a favorite High Renaissance and Mannerist subject, Ganymede swings in the grip of Jupiter's fierce eagle, whose wings darken the air. Dazzlingly foreshortened, the boy looks back toward the spectator with an expression that seems to combine fear and pleasure. Below the floating figure, mountains, slopes, and valleys lead to the horizon. The boy's leave-taking is dramatized by the leap of his beautiful white dog, desperate at his master's disappearance.

No such picture had ever been painted in earlier Italian art, nor had anything like the daring *Jupiter and Io* (fig. 595) been seen before. The jealousy of hawk-eyed Juno forced her promiscuous husband to seduce Io, a mortal maiden, in the guise of a cloud. Io sits in a pose familiar to us from Raphael's frescoes in the Farnesina (see figs. 542, 548). Her head thrown back, she accepts the embrace of one huge, cloudy paw, as the face of Jupiter surfaces from the cloud to plant a kiss on her lips. The contrast between the soft, trembling warmth of Io's flesh and the mystery of the attack by the cold yet divine cloud increases the startling intensity of what is clearly a representation of sexual climax. In an astonishing conflation of Christian and pagan traditions, Correggio has painted at the lower right the head of a stag drinking from the water, a traditional symbol of the human soul drawn from Psalm 42: "As the hart panteth after the water brooks, so panteth my soul after thee, O God." At his death, Correggio stood alone, save for his contemporary Titian, in the completeness of his acceptance of human sexuality as a subject for art, on a level with and interchangeable with religion.

PARMIGIANINO

Correggio's slightly younger contemporary in Parma, Francesco Mazzola, called Parmigianino (1503–40), stands in the strongest contrast to Correggio's High Renaissance, even proto-Baroque style. Parmigianino, unmistakably a Mannerist, introduces himself to us in his startling *Self-Portrait in a Convex Mirror* (fig. 596). Vasari, who knew the picture when it belonged to the letter

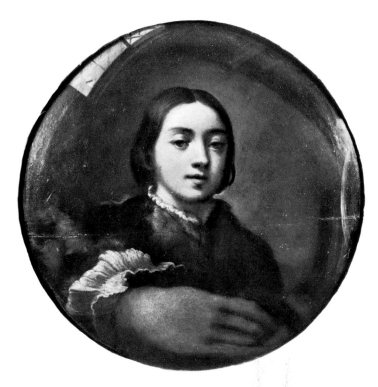

596. PARMIGIANINO. *Self-Portrait in a Convex Mirror*. 1524. Panel, diameter 9¹/₂". Kunsthistorisches Museum, Vienna

writer and lampooner Pietro Aretino, tells us that Parmigianino painted it just before his departure for Rome in 1524, when he was twenty-one, to show his skill in "the subtleties of art." Fascinated by his own reflection in a barber's convex mirror, he decided to reproduce it exactly. He had a carpenter turn a wooden sphere on a lathe and then saw off a section similar in size to a convex mirror. On this surface he painted himself looking outward with an air of utter detachment, "so beautiful," Vasari says, "that he seemed an angel rather than a man." His face is far enough back from the surface not to suffer distortion, but his hand and sleeve are enormously enlarged, and the skylight of his studio and the opposite wall are sharply curved.

In the High Renaissance, self-portraits are rare, and they generally appear in lieu of signatures, looking out from a lower corner. In Mannerist art they become more numerous, and they are generally revealing and disturbing. Leonardo had called the mirror the master of painters, and he asserted that painters' minds should resemble it insofar as it "transforms itself into the color of that which it has as object, and is filled with as many likenesses as there are things before it." But he is not referring to a curved mirror, which he compares to the distortion moving water wrecks on objects seen through it. Parmigianino, however, has delighted in these distortions. The curved surface, which to Jan van Eyck and Raphael was a fascinating distortion fit only for a small position in the background, now becomes the whole image.

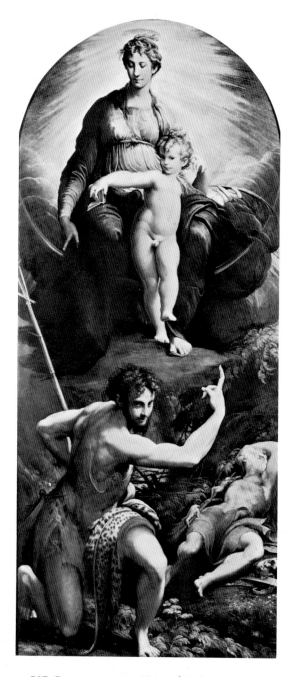

597. PARMIGIANINO. *Vision of St. Jerome*. 1527.
Panel, 11' 6" x 5'. National Gallery, London.
Commissioned by Maria Bufolina for S. Salvatore in
Lauro, Città di Castello

constricted painting, and Jerome is almost reduced to an afterthought. St. John's right arm, pointing into the picture in Albertian style, seems tremendously enlarged in contrast to his foreshortened and partially enshadowed right leg. The Virgin and Child are attenuated in a manner not seen since Lorenzo Monaco (see colorplate 35, p. 201) and have the sloping shoulders and long arms of Botticelli's figures (see fig. 351). Not one figure looks at the observer or at another; even the gaze of the Child seems to glide just past us. In the darkness that veils any possibility of establishing spatial relationships, rays of light flash from the Madonna's head and shoulders like shards of ice.

Every surface is as cold as the unsmiling figures, who are porcelain-hard and at times almost glassy. Seldom does Parmigianino let his brushwork show. The picture has all the preternatural clarity of a dream, but in contrast to the eroticism of Correggio, this dream seems lascivious and perverse. Parmigianino has emphasized the Child's genitals and with unprecedented daring has shown the Virgin's nipples erect against the tight, sheer fabric of her tunic.

Parmigianino's *Madonna dal Collo Lungo* (*Madonna of the Long Neck*) was commissioned in 1534 but was never fully completed (colorplate 113, p. 570). Here the elongated proportions, sloping shoulders, preciosity of surface, and chill eroticism of the *Vision of St. Jerome* are refined to produce shapes of startling ornamental beauty. The Christ Child is asleep in a pose suggestive of death, his left arm hanging as in Michelangelo's Rome *Pietà* (see fig. 472). At the left, five graceful and sexually ambiguous figures appear in varying stages of undress; one holds a huge urn and looks up at the Virgin, another, possibly a self-portrait, gazes past us. The Virgin's body and neck are dramatically attenuated, and her marmoreal forehead and glossy curls are adorned with ropes of pearls and an enormous ruby. Even more astonishing than her long neck, perhaps, is the fantastic length of her fingers.

Whether or not the Child's head was to remain bald is uncertain. It might be recalled that Joseph was shaved while in prison and a tradition insists that Christ was also. But even more disturbing than any of the figural representations is the towering column, smooth and polished but without a capital, that stands in nightmarish incompleteness in the background. Its base reveals that the artist intended to represent a complete temple portico, and preserved drawings show that it was to be Corinthian. Perhaps Parmigianino realized that the row of capitals would detract from the soaring unreality of the Madonna. Thus, unsatisfied with the picture, as Vasari tells us, he limited himself to caressing with Brancusi-like tenderness the infinitely subtle entasis of the column, leaving it perfect in its very truncation against the unfinished surface of the panel. But if Parmigianino had painted himself into a corner with the column, he had nonetheless created one of the most remarkable pictures of the Cinquecento, whose mood of despair be-

Parmigianino's bravura *Vision of St. Jerome* (fig. 597) was painted for the chapel of the Bufalini family in San Salvatore in Lauro in Rome. Abandoned by the artist after the Sack of Rome, it was later taken by the Bufalini to their palace in Città di Castello. It is as tormented as Correggio's *Holy Night* is peaceful, and its space is as distorted as that of the *Holy Night* is convincing. Such purposeful ambiguity of space is a typical attribute of Mannerist art. In a sharply foreshortened pose at an unexplained depth in the picture, St. Jerome lies sleeping fitfully. The entire painting, foreground and background (if we may call them that), is his dream. The visionary figures towering before us form the vertical axis of the

THE CINQUECENTO

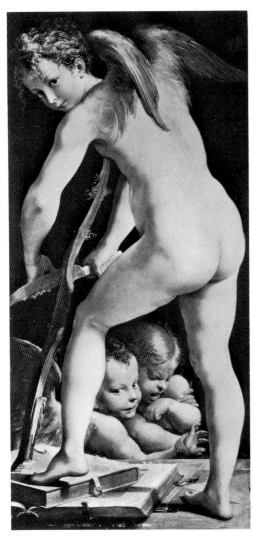

598. PARMIGIANINO. *Cupid Carving His Bow*. 1535.
Panel, 53 x 25³/₄". Kunsthistorisches Museum, Vienna.
Commissioned by Cavalier Baiardo

neath its jeweled surface is epitomized in the tiny distant figure with a scroll. Is it Isaiah prophesying the Passion?

About contemporary with the *Madonna dal Collo Lungo* is *Cupid Carving His Bow* (fig. 598), which was ordered by a private patron. The epicene youth turns his naked back to us yet twists his head about for one arch glance at our discomfiture. With one foot braced on books, apparently symbolic of love's triumph over knowledge, he carves his bow from a freshly cut sapling. One putto in the background screams in pain while his companion mischievously twists his chubby arm, trying to force his already burned hand back against Cupid's hot leg. The figure, drawn with fantastic linear precision in the contours, shimmering with reflected lights, is painted with a mother-of-pearl surface that dazzled the young Peter Paul Rubens, who made a copy of this picture. Cupid is parallel to the picture plane, but he is pushed so far forward and his flesh is so minutely observed that he is propelled toward us with a force like that of Mantegna's *Foreshortened Christ* (see fig. 409), but with what a difference! For all the brilliance of his tech-

nical and psychological achievement, Parmigianino's *Cupid* represents the epitome of the hidden sensuality of the mid-sixteenth century, to be gloated over by aristocrats and princes.

PORDENONE

A shocking contrast to the refined sensuality of the two painters of Parma is furnished by Giovanni Antonio de Sacchis (1483/84–1539), called Pordenone from the town of his birth in Friuli, a sub-Alpine region northeast of Venice. Among the early Cinquecento painters of northern Italy, Pordenone is surely the most startling. In his life, as well as in his art, he seems to have been a person of unbridled energy and ambition—and few scruples. According to charges made in court, he hired a band of cutthroats to murder his brother Baldassare so that he could lay hands on the entire paternal inheritance. He shuttled back and forth throughout northern Italy and even to far-off Genoa, turning out altarpieces, organ panels, and especially frescoes, at amazing velocity. In 1516 he journeyed to Umbria for some fresco commissions and must have visited Rome, although no visit is documented.

Brought up under diluted Venetian influence in the provinces, he lost no time in absorbing the latest in Rome, without benefit of the study of the figure and of *disegno* that made the Roman High Renaissance possible, and he brought to the north vivid and simplified memories, and perhaps sketches, of the achievements of Michelangelo and Raphael. Pordenone never fully detached himself from Friuli, though from 1528 on he was active in Venice and its environs, where he was esteemed for his frescoes on the outer walls of palaces and cloisters—exposed to the weather and thus foredoomed to ruin—and for his works in the Doges' Palace, destroyed in fires in 1574 and 1577. It is difficult to assess the effect of these lost works on Titian (see Chapter 19) and, more probably, on Tintoretto, of whose dramatic style Pordenone was a precursor. We must judge him now mostly by his surviving fresco cycles in Emilia, Lombardy, and the Veneto, which are painted with speed, vigor, and coarseness of expression and execution; these are works intended to shock.

His most powerful cycle is the Passion series in the Cathedral of Cremona. A cycle of the Life of Christ had been begun by local Cremonese painters and continued by Romanino of Brescia, whom Pordenone apparently contrived to have dismissed so that he could complete the series himself. Characteristically, it is Pordenone's frescoes that one remembers. A typical example is the *Nailing of Christ to the Cross* (fig. 599), which, like Pordenone's other episodes in the nave arcade, are seen from below in Mantegnesque illusionistic style; they exploit as never before the actual space in which the observer stands. Demonic faces glower from the dimness at the left, above a soldier who has felled one of his own comrades and holds him by the hair so that he may termi-

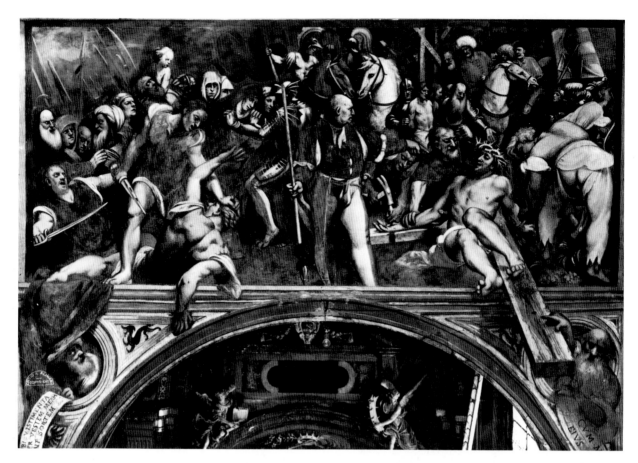

599. PORDENONE. *Nailing of Christ to the Cross*. 1521–22. Fresco. Cathedral, Cremona

nate their private quarrel with a thrust from his short sword. Scrabbling helplessly for a handhold in the painted architecture *outside* the scene, the victim seems about to fall over the edge onto our heads. The pose and the muscular back suggest several in the works of Michelangelo, as does the dense concentration of foreshortened *contrapposto* figures throughout the scene.

Center stage is occupied by a bald Lanzknecht (lancer) whose bestiality is underscored by his beer belly, loosely tied breeches, and pendulous codpiece. On the extreme right, the foreshortened cross is being shoved into the scene from outside the painted frame by one of the prophets. Christ is crowned with thorns, his eyes closed, and his legs so sharply bent that the thighs disappear from view. He writhes as a gigantic hammer drives the spike into his right hand, which gushes blood, while a foreshortened and twisted executioner holds ready another claw hammer. The tumult of figures surging into the scene and spilling out of it is delineated by broad, rough strokes and a violence seldom repeated in Italian art. In spite of his brilliance and daring, violence to Pordenone is its own message; he seems to have little to say of a spiritual nature, in contrast to his successor Tintoretto (see pp. 604–8; 617–18).

Up to this point it has been possible to avoid a "definition" of Mannerism. Now that we have seen the style in operation, we are at least in a position to make a few generalizations. Whereas the content of High Renais-

sance art is often ideal, Mannerist art often chooses subjects that are abnormal or anormal, and the strange and unexpected aspect of a subject may be emphasized. Mannerist interpretations sometimes stress uncontrolled emotion or withdrawal. In High Renaissance art the narrative will usually be direct, compact, and comprehensible; in Mannerist art it is often elaborate, involved, and abtruse. While space in a High Renaissance work will be measured, harmonious, and ideal, Mannerist space can be disjointed, spasmodic, and/or limited to the foreground plane. High Renaissance compositions are harmonious and integrated, they are often centralized, and they may assume a pyramidal or conical form; Mannerist compositions may be conflicting, and forms often seek the frame or violate it. While High Renaissance proportions are normative and idealized, Mannerist proportions can be uncanonical, usually attenuated. The figures in a High Renaissance work are easily posed and often suggest the possibility of movement, while Mannerist figures are tensely posed, overextended, or confined or appear in an exaggerated or excessive *contrapposto*. While High Renaissance color is balanced, controlled, and harmonious, Mannerist color is contrasting and surprising.

Leonardo, Fra Bartolommeo, Raphael, and to a great extent the mature Michelangelo belong in the High Renaissance category, as do Andrea del Sarto and Correggio. To Mannerism we can assign Pontormo, Rosso, Perino del Vaga, Beccafumi, Parmigianino, Pordenone,

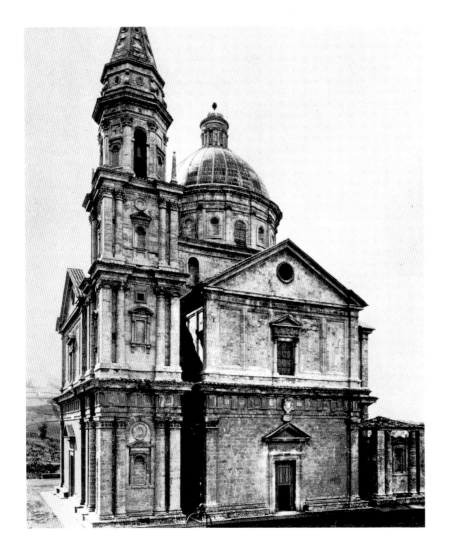

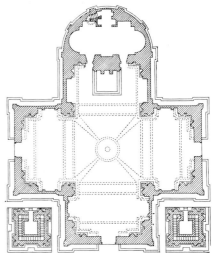

left: 600. ANTONIO DA SANGALLO THE ELDER. Madonna di S. Biagio, Montepulciano. 1518–34

601. ANTONIO DA SANGALLO THE ELDER. Plan of Madonna di S. Biagio

and, to a great extent, the Michelangelo of the Medici Chapel. The two categories, or schools, overlap chronologically, so they cannot be considered separate periods. Mannerism seems to appear by 1517, and we must think of the period from about 1517 to the early 1530s as one sharply divided between opposing tendencies. During the 1530s a related style that will be called the *maniera* takes over almost entirely in central Italy (discussed in Chapter 20).

ANTONIO DA SANGALLO THE ELDER

Many of the formal qualities discussed above are applicable to architecture, and some are abundantly visible in Michelangelo's buildings. He had, nonetheless, architectural rivals in Florence who maintained independence from his ideas and theories. One of these was Antonio da Sangallo the Elder (1455–1534), younger brother of Giuliano. During his youth, Antonio was active chiefly as a military architect, and he designed religious and civil structures for minor centers. He was engaged to complete the Church of Santa Maria del Calcinaio at Cortona, left unfinished at the death of Francesco di Giorgio (see fig. 375). When Giuliano died in 1516, Antonio was left in a position of prominence and, two years later, accepted one of the major architectural commissions of the period, the pilgrimage church of the Madonna di San Biagio at Montepulciano (figs. 600,

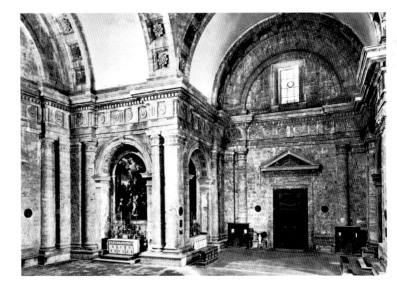

602. ANTONIO DA SANGALLO THE ELDER. Interior, Madonna di S. Biagio

601). The church was built to commemorate a miracle that took place on one of the slopes surrounding the city, and thus Antonio had an enviable site in the midst of a magnificent landscape unencumbered by preexisting constructions.

The structure, on which he worked from 1518 until his death in 1534, was the most ambitious church building of the period with the exception of St. Peter's in Rome, whose construction was dormant after the death of Bramante in spite of designs submitted by Raphael, Peruzzi, and others. Antonio chose a Greek-cross plan crowned with a dome, similar to that of his brother Giuliano's Santa Maria delle Carceri at Prato, an unfinished commission he also inherited (see figs. 313–15). Antonio eschewed the typical Florentine marble incrustation, however, and constructed his church inside and out, except for the barrel vaults, of blocks of travertine that confer upon the building a clifflike massiveness that is surprising after the surface elegance of the Florentine tradition. The main façade was to be flanked by two lofty, freestanding towers, but only one was built. While these towers may have been suggested by those Bramante designed for St. Peter's, it should be recalled that such towers reappear constantly in Leonardo's architectural fantasies (see fig. 449).

Antonio set up the three cubic stories of the towers in a canonical succession of Doric, Ionic, and Corinthian orders. The octagonal fourth story was not built until 1564, and it may or may not follow the original plans. Because only one tower was completed, much of the effect Antonio intended is dissipated, but if we complete the tower mentally, it is not hard to imagine the tension that would have existed between these massive verticals and the planar, less energetic façades. The façades, in fact, continue the Doric order of the first story only in pilaster form. The second story is divided into recessed panels, the center one penetrated by a window enclosed in a pedimented tabernacle.

In contrast, the towers are richly articulated, with square corner piers composed of engaged columns, so that the intervening wall spaces are sharply recessed and the entablatures broken. Giuliano had drawn a Roman Doric order almost exactly similar to this one, including the square corner piers and the ornamented necking band, from the ruins of the Basilica Emilia in Rome, and utilized these motifs in a design for the façade of San Lorenzo in Florence (see fig. 550).

Wherein, then, lies the originality of the younger brother, who merely adapted two years later what was, after all, company property? Perhaps it is the wholly new sense of drama, never present in Giuliano's work and never absent from that of Antonio. A real fight seems to be going on between the clustered column-and-pier and the massive wall. The latter is enlivened not by the gracious windows favored by Giuliano, but by tabernacles capped on the second story with segmental pediments whose lower cornices are broken, a motif later used in profusion by Michelangelo. The jagged effect of the entablatures is heightened on the third story by corner obelisks. And even the raking cornices of the pediments of the three façades are broken against the sky. The dome, so impressive a feature of the building when seen from behind the apse, carries only a slight effect from the main façade, where it would have been outflanked by the towers. It is worth noting that An-

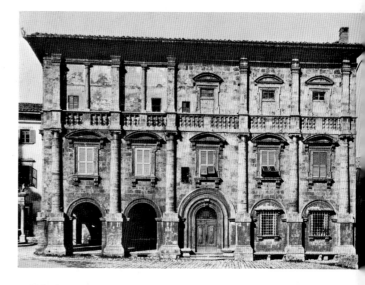

603. ANTONIO DA SANGALLO THE ELDER. Palazzo Tarugi, Montepulciano. c. 1515

tonio sticks to the traditional Florentine vertical dome with ribs, placing it on a round drum divided by pilasters in imitation of a peristyle.

The effect of the interior is overwhelming (fig. 602)—not in terms of space, which one would expect in the Brunelleschi-Alberti-Bramante tradition, but of brute mass. The accent is not on the walls but on the jutting, reentrant corners, as if these were the inner walls of the ground stories of the towers. The squat Roman Doric order is identical, inside and out, but these strong projections appear pugnacious and bull-like when moved indoors; the piers carry arches that are just as heavy. The inside walls are travertine throughout, so the supports do not detach themselves from the walls in the traditional Florentine fashion. The barrel vaults, however, are white *intonaco*, with the result that the ground floor seems to sustain independent arches of gigantic force against a white expanse of sky.

Montepulciano, a Cinquecento cultural center in spite of its small size, is lined with palaces by major architects, including several by or attributed to Antonio da Sangallo the Elder. The most original of these is the Palazzo Tarugi (fig. 603), which has two façades fronting on the principal piazza opposite the cathedral. Antonio made each façade roughly symmetrical, but he varied the articulation so as to introduce an open corner arcade on the ground floor and an open loggia, now walled in, on the top floor. Convenient and delightful as these corner porches must have been for the inhabitants, they violate the symmetry of the façades in spite of the ponderous, central arch, which seeks to maintain its dominance. And in a reversal of the accepted succession, the first story is Ionic, the second Doric. Finally, the Ionic columns of the ground story, perched on lofty podia, rise to embrace the *piano nobile* as well, an early example of the giant order Michelangelo was soon to employ. No stringcourse separates the two first floors;

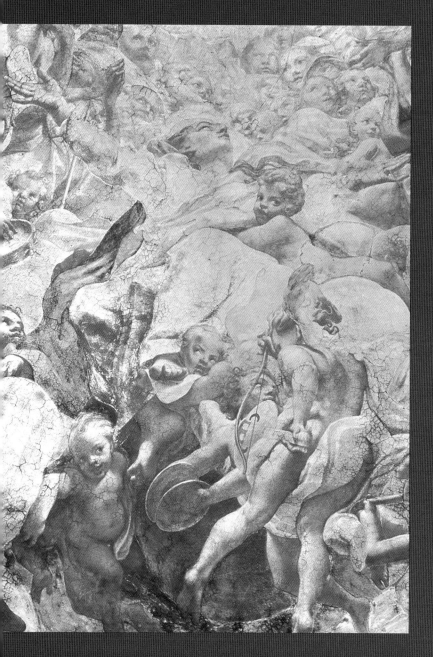

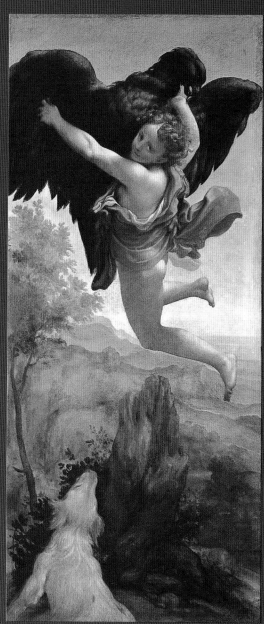

Colorplate 111. CORREGGIO. *Assumption of the Virgin.* 1526–30.
Fresco in dome (portion), diameter of base of dome
35' 10" x 37' 11". Cathedral, Parma. Commissioned by the
authorities of Parma Cathedral

Colorplate 112. CORREGGIO. *Jupiter and Ganymede.*
Early 1530s. Canvas, 64¹/₂ x 28". Kunsthistorisches
Museum, Vienna. Commissioned by Federigo
Gonzaga

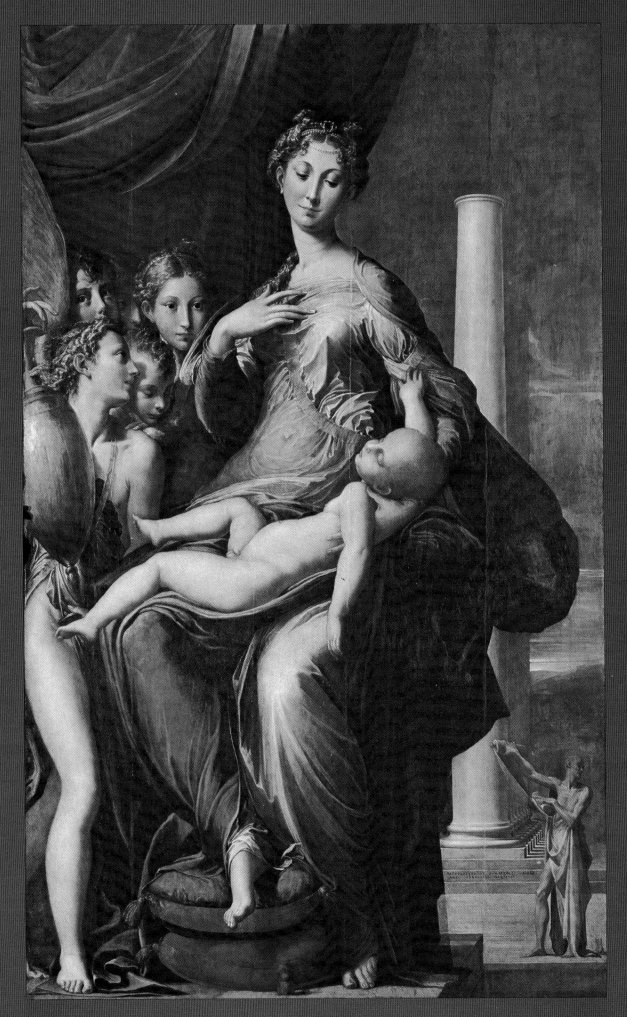

opposite: Colorplate 113. PARMIGIANINO. *Madonna and Child with Angels,* now known as the *Madonna of the Long Neck.* 1534–40. Panel, 85 x 52". Uffizi Gallery, Florence. Commissioned by Elena Baiardi for the Church of the Servites, Parma

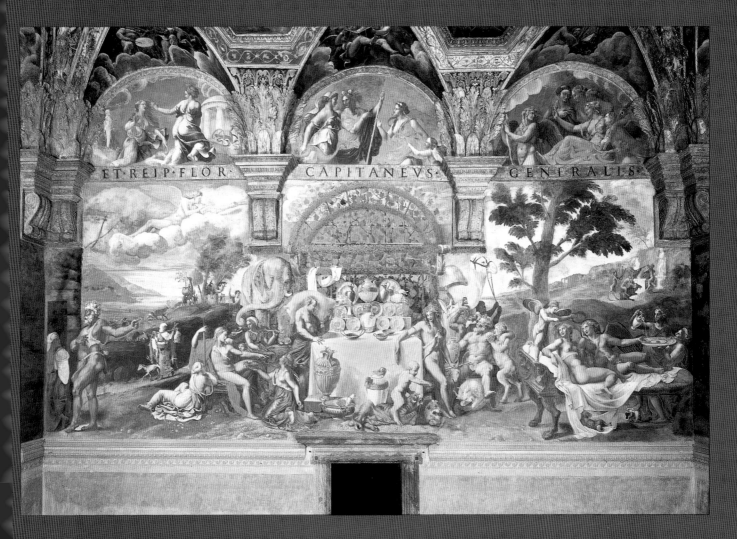

Colorplate 114. GIULIO ROMANO. *Wedding Feast of Cupid and Psyche* (portion). 1527–30. Fresco. Sala di Psiche, Palazzo del Te, Mantua. Commissioned by Federigo Gonzaga

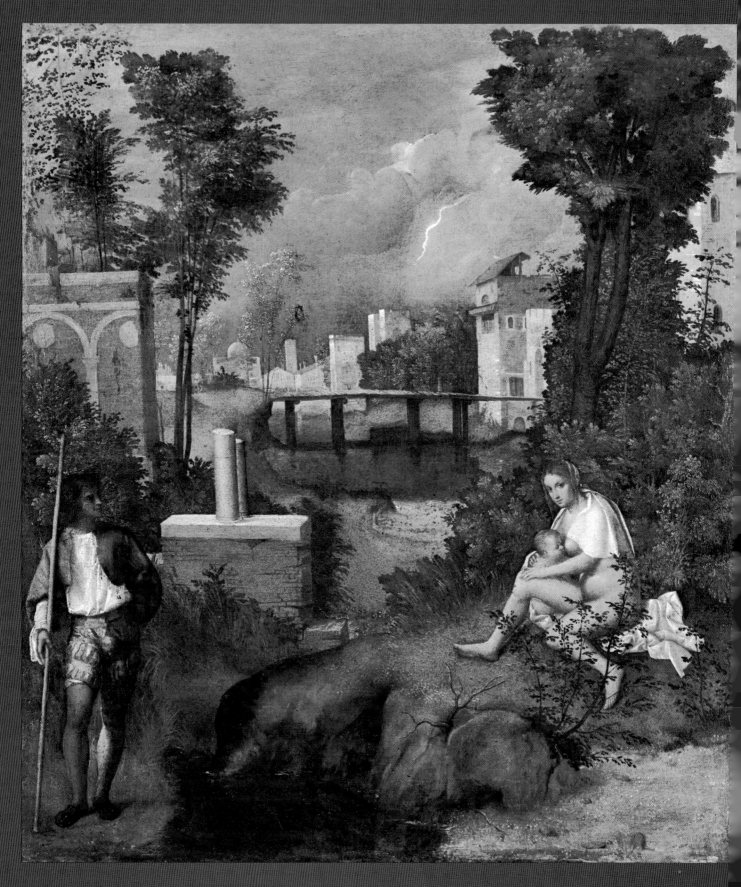

Colorplate 115. GIORGIONE. *Tempestuous Landscape with the Soldier and the Gypsy.*
1505–10. Canvas, 30¼ x 28¾". Accademia, Venice

opposite: Colorplate 116. GIORGIONE. *Pastoral Scene,* now
known as the *Fête Champêtre.* c. 1510. Canvas, 43¼ x 54¼".
The Louvre, Paris

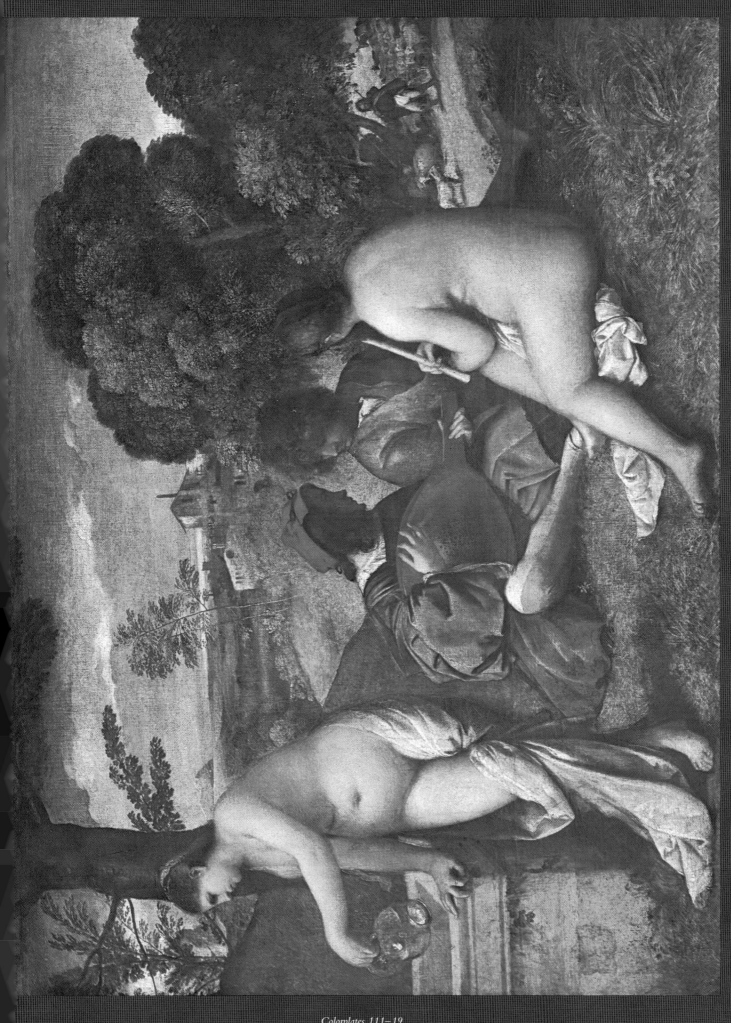

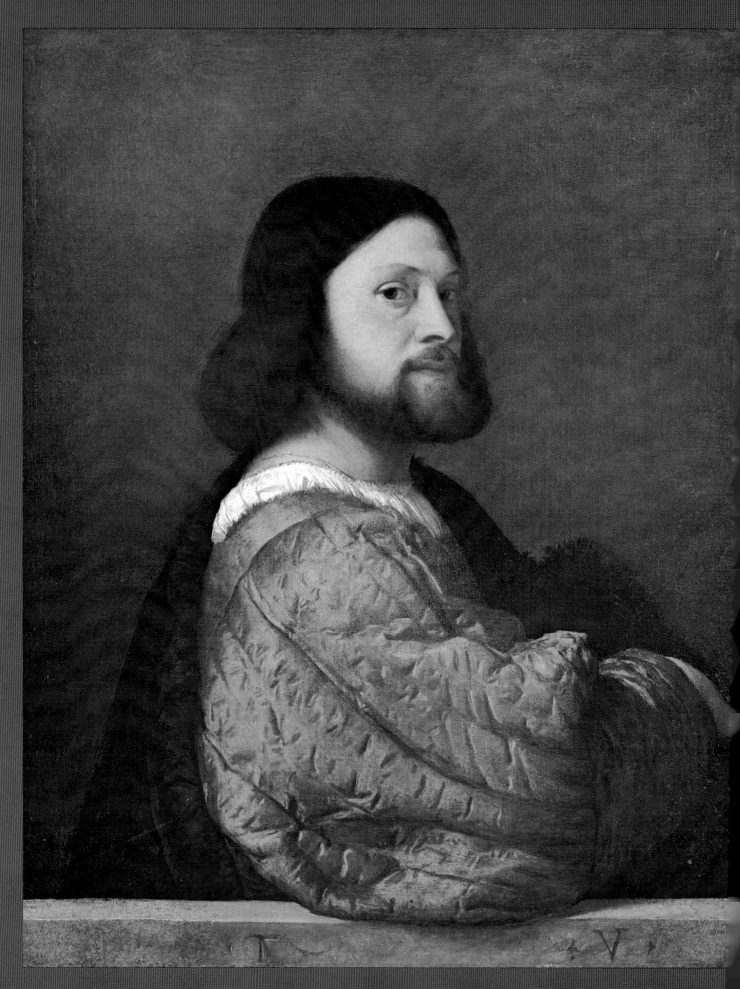

Colorplate 117. TITIAN. *Portrait of a Bearded Man (Self-Portrait? Ludovico Ariosto?)*.
c. 1511–15. Canvas, 32 x 26". National Gallery, London

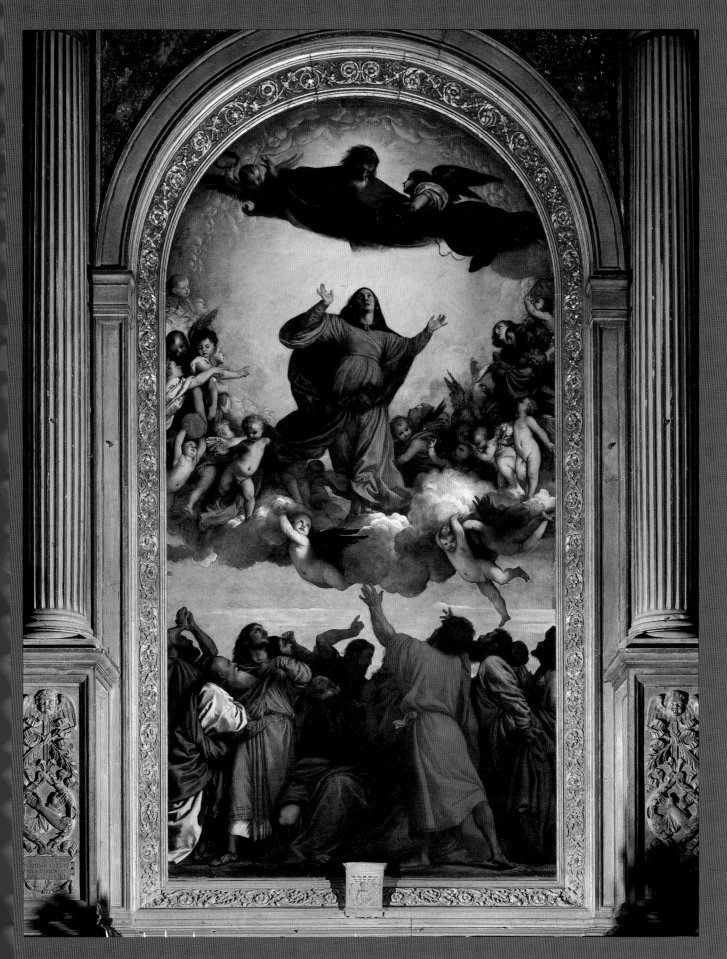

Colorplate 118. TITIAN. *Assumption of the Virgin*. 1516–18. Panel, 22' 6" x 11' 10". ▮ Sta. Maria Gloriosa dei Frari,
Venice. Commissioned by Germano da Caiole, the Abbot of the Monastery of the Frari

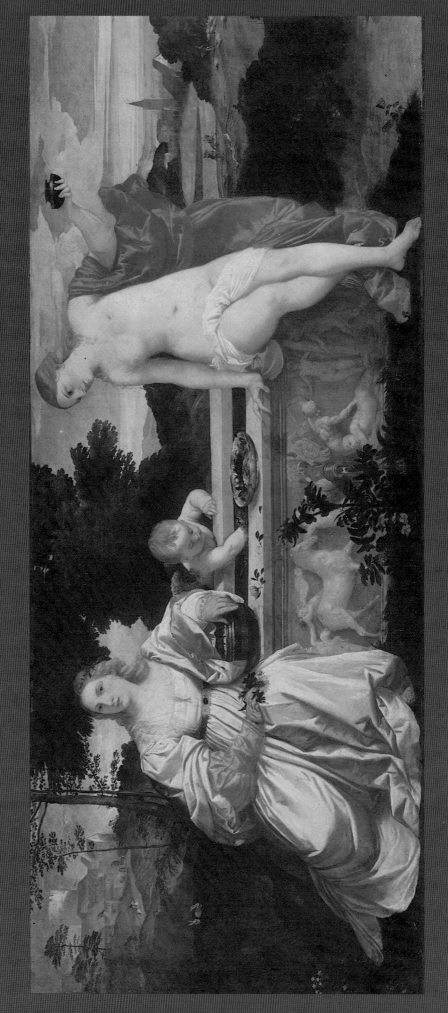

Colorplate 119. TITIAN. *Sacred and Profane Love*. 1514. Canvas, 3' 11" x 9' 2". Borghese Gallery, Rome. Probably commissioned by Niccolò Aurelio in celebration of his wedding to Laura Bagarotto in 1514

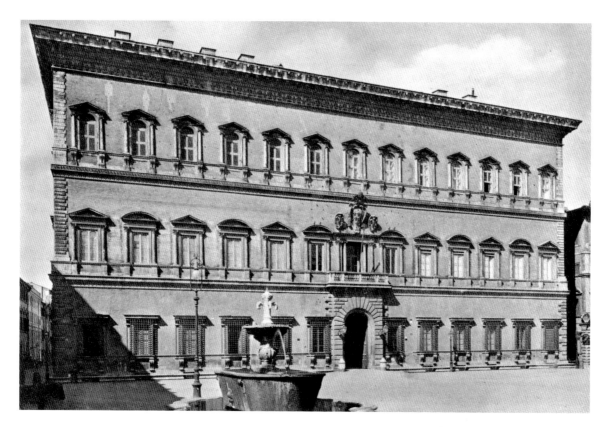

604. ANTONIO DA SANGALLO THE YOUNGER and MICHELANGELO. Palazzo Farnese, Rome. 1517–50. Commissioned by Cardinal Alessandro Farnese

thus the windows of the *piano nobile* seem to be floating upward, beating against the balustrade that runs across the second floor.

ANTONIO DA SANGALLO THE YOUNGER

The last member of the numerous Sangallo family to concern us is Antonio da Sangallo the Younger (1485–1546), nephew of Giuliano and Antonio the Elder. He was an imaginative architect whose two major undertakings came to grief at the hands of Michelangelo. Originally a carpenter who was responsible for the colossal centering for Bramante's four great arches to uphold the dome of St. Peter's, Antonio soon became an architect in his own right. His star went into the ascendant in 1517 when the powerful Cardinal Alessandro Farnese acquired a palace in the center of Rome and decided to rebuild it from Antonio's designs. That it is the most majestic and influential of all Roman Renaissance palaces is due to the combined efforts of Antonio and Michelangelo. Antonio's design was ambitious from the start—an immense rectangle (figs. 604, 605) whose façade is a towering block of masonry recalling the Palazzo Strozzi (see fig. 307), but with rustication restricted to its quoins.

Both the screen orders of the Alberti-Laurana tradition and Bramante's engaged colonnade are abandoned in favor of aedicula windows. On the ground floor

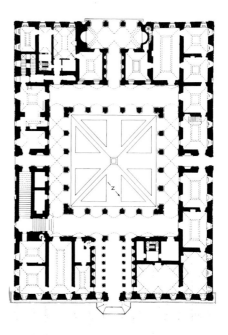

605. ANTONIO DA SANGALLO THE YOUNGER and MICHELANGELO. Plan of Palazzo Farnese

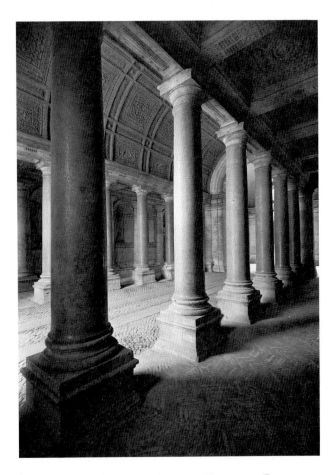

606. ANTONIO DA SANGALLO THE YOUNGER. Entrance loggia, Palazzo Farnese, Rome. Begun before 1524

Antonio adopted the "kneeling window" type (used by Michelangelo in 1517 at the Palazzo Medici in Florence; see fig. 146); here they seem suspended along a string-course that continues their sills. For the second-floor aediculae he used a Corinthian order, supported on high bases resting on a stringcourse and unified by a smaller stringcourse at sill level, as on the ground story. The windows have alternating triangular and arched pediments, save for the central window, which was originally a large arch, repeating the motif of the entrance portal below. The third story is a combination of both lower ones, for now columned aediculae rest on consoles like those of the first floor. Arched windows break upward into the triangular pediments. All the architectural trim, including the massive quoins at the corners, is in stone set off against the flat surface of tan brick walls.

The rich and restrained, severe and grand effect of this façade depends largely on a single change made by Michelangelo. Antonio's cornice would probably have been narrow, more or less on the scale of the stringcourses between the stories, and the whole would have created a rather diffuse impression. Only the front wing of the palace had been carried out before the Sack of Rome in 1527, and only, irregularly, through the level of the *piano nobile*. Not until 1539–40 did Alessandro, now Pope Paul III, resume the original design, with some in-ternal changes, under the original architect. But in 1546 the pope, dissatisfied with Antonio's design for the cornice, called in Sebastiano del Piombo, Perino del Vaga, Giorgio Vasari, and Michelangelo to provide competing designs. He accepted the colossal cornice by Michelangelo, which is even heavier than that of the Palazzo Strozzi; it combines elements from various orders and was so heavy that in some places Antonio's walls had to be rebuilt to provide an adequate foundation.

It is Michelangelo's cornice that imparts unity to the structure. According to Vasari's probably exaggerated account, such was Antonio's displeasure that he died of shock and grief. A second alteration by Michelangelo drew the elements of the building to a central focus: he filled the arch of the centralized opening on the second story and flanked it with a Corinthian order that moves outward in a cluster of column-pilaster-column. This gave a new unity to the second story and allowed space for Michelangelo to insert the Farnese arms on enormous cartouches.

Antonio's three-aisled entrance loggia (fig. 606) is a little basilica in itself, for the central aisle is barrel-vaulted, the side aisles flat-roofed, and both are supported by a Roman Doric order of polished granite columns with heavy capitals. The low, almost cavernous effect is increased by the narrow entablature, which makes the ribs of the coffered vault seem to rise directly from the columns. It must have been designed before Giulio Romano left for Mantua in 1524 because Giulio adapted the idea on a tiny scale in one of the entrances to his Palazzo del Te. Antonio's courtyard would have been conventional—a grand reproduction of the three superimposed orders of the Colosseum, along the lines of such Quattrocento archaeological courtyards as that of the Palazzo Venezia (see fig. 230)—but, as we shall see, Michelangelo added a third story that transformed this design as well (see fig. 680). For Antonio's projects for St. Peter's, we must again turn to the later work of Michelangelo (see pp. 635–37).

BALDASSARE PERUZZI

Meanwhile in Rome, Baldassare Peruzzi (1481–1536), one of the leaders of the High Renaissance (see pp. 528–29), seems to have succumbed to Mannerism in an extraordinary building now named, on account of its ground-floor columns, the Palazzo Massimo alle Colonne (fig. 607). The present fantastic view was not possible until the late nineteenth century, when the then narrow street was widened; at the time the Massimo family commissioned the building, the irregular curve of the façade would have seemed less illogical because it followed the curve of the street. From no single point of view would the entire façade have been visible, and Peruzzi's design, like that of Vasari a generation later for the Uffizi in Florence (see fig. 705), must have been an experience in time as well as in space. His supports—successively pilasters, single columns, paired columns—

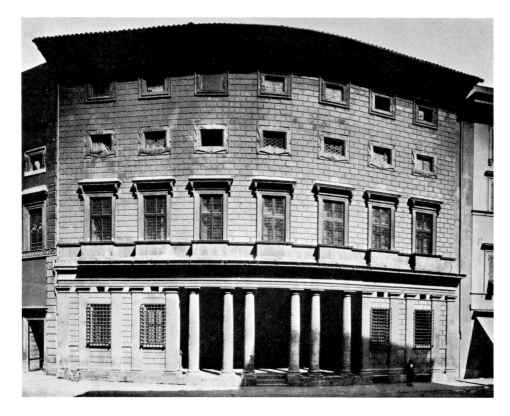

607. BALDASSARE PERUZZI. Palazzo Massimo alle Colonne, Rome. Begun 1532. Commissioned by Pietro, Luca, and Angelo Massimo

and the wide central opening, placed just where the bend in the road became most acute and least tolerable, would certainly have provided welcome relief to the passerby.

Peruzzi could have unified the building by vertical motifs, but instead he chose a Tuscan order deprived even of triglyphs so that the eye is led around the bend without interruption. From street level, the windows of the *piano nobile*, each on its broad podium, must have seemed to move around the bend in a solemn, regular rhythm. There are no other monumental motives. The third and fourth stories are afloat in the rustication, with their window frames decorated with moldings and scrolls.

GIULIO ROMANO

It is fitting to close with a fantastic structure, the Palazzo del Te in Mantua, which Giulio Romano (c. 1499–1546), Raphael's pupil and heir, constructed and decorated from 1527 to 1534 for the insatiable Federigo Gonzaga, then a marquis but made first duke of Mantua while the building was under way. The palace (figs. 608, 609) is known from the region in which it is situated; the Te is the name, of unknown origin, applied to a peaceful island that connected the fortified city of Mantua, then surrounded entirely by lakes, with the mainland. The meadows of the Te had been the scene of Federigo's horse-breeding ventures, and the first plan, possibly executed in 1526, involved only the addition of a frescoed banqueting hall to the stables. This soon expanded into a palace that is smaller than its appearance suggests.

Giulio treated the exterior façades in a sequence of distinct rhythmic groups of forms, all within the general scheme of a Roman Doric order that was probably derived from the Basilica Emilia. This order embraces the ground story and a mezzanine for servants and storerooms. A feeling of tension and compression is created by the peculiar rustication. While the second story is rusticated in flat, Albertian blocks like those of Peruzzi's Palazzo Massimo alle Colonne, the windows and arches of the first story are so heavily rusticated that their quoins and archivolts expand as if to devour the elegant architecture surrounding them, in what has been aptly described as a struggle of formlessness against form.

The courtyard goes to even greater extremes (fig. 610). The pilasters have become engaged columns of great nobility. The stringcourse separating ground floor and mezzanine has vanished, the Albertian blocks have increased in size and projection, and some are roughened, as if the conflict between form and formlessness in the outer façades had ended in the fusion of extremes. But the war has entered a new phase. The windows are capped by massive pediments whose raking angles do not quite meet, while at the same time the rusticated keystones below them have crept upward from the lintels, as if forced out of line. And then the climax: between every pair of columns, and between every two columns, one triglyph drops down, out of place, leaving a blank hole above it!

Nothing like this had ever been seen in Renaissance architecture, but Giulio must have noticed this alarming phenomenon in the tottering ruins that surrounded his house in Rome (he was brought up next door to the

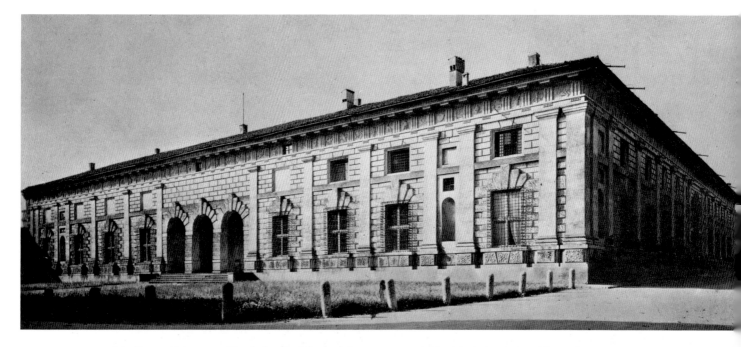

608. GIULIO ROMANO. North façade, Palazzo del Te, Mantua. 1527–34. Commissioned by Federigo Gonzaga

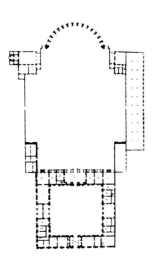

609. GIULIO ROMANO. Plan of Palazzo del Te

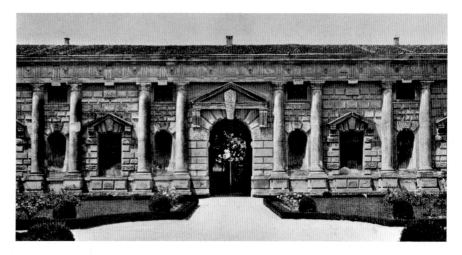

610. GIULIO ROMANO. Courtyard, Palazzo del Te, Mantua. 1527–34

Forum of Trajan). He did not use this motif, however, in an attempt to create an imitation ruin. It is too systematic for that, for it reoccurs at regular intervals, and on only two of the inner façades of the courtyard. The effect on the observer is a fascinated horror at watching what can only be described, in contemporary aerospace jargon, as a self-destruct device.

The interior, in which Emperor Charles V was entertained, comprises a series of rooms unmatched in their time for luxury and splendor; now, alas, they are stripped of all the beautiful furnishings mentioned in old inventories. But the pictorial decoration, which Giulio and his pupils executed at breakneck speed, still survives. The Sala di Psiche (colorplate 114, p. 571) tells in detail

the story of Cupid and Psyche, which in the Farnesina had been limited to its airy episodes (see figs. 545–48). Most gorgeous of all is the wedding feast, which covers two entire walls in a panorama of gods, nymphs, satyrs, and animals in an endless fabric of fleshy, hot-colored figures against peacock-green foliage that is heightened by the silver and gold table service.

In sharpest contrast to this idyllic—at times orgiastic—scene of sensuous indulgence is the Sala dei Giganti (figs. 611, 612), a room of the same size and shape as the Sala di Psiche at the opposite corner of the palace. When the door closes upon us, we realize that the entire room, doors and all, has been painted in one continuous scene. The event represented is the destruction, by

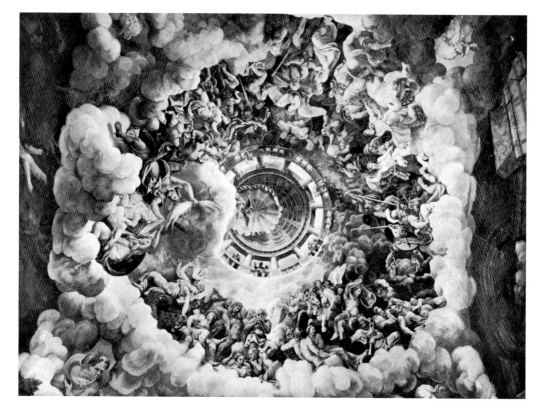

611, 612.
GIULIO
ROMANO. *The
Gods on Mount
Olympus and
the Fall of the
Giants.* 1530–32.
Fresco. Sala
dei Giganti,
Palazzo del Te,
Mantua.
Commissioned
by Federigo
Gonzaga

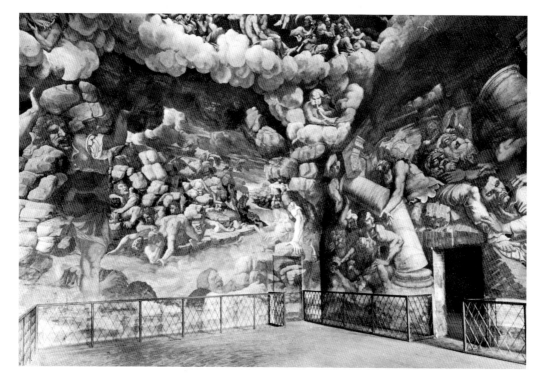

thunderbolts from the hand of Jupiter, of the rebellious giants who had attempted to assault Mount Olympus. The palaces and caves of the colossal giants seem to collapse upon them—and upon us as we watch. This paean of destruction and slaughter, painted in a hurry after the emperor's first visit in 1530 so that he could see it completed when he came again two years later, is an eloquent if somewhat coarse expression of feelings then quite widespread among Italians; after the annihilation of so many values that had seemed permanent until the Sack of Rome and its aftermath, many welcomed the new order of absolutism. And even if the Sala dei Giganti seldom rises above the level of dramatic scene painting, it provides images and literary associations that make explicit the conflict we have found in all the arts during the period of Mannerism.

19

High and Late Renaissance in Venice and on the Mainland

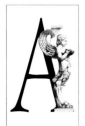t the opening of the sixteenth century, the Venetian school of painting had reached the height of its power and influence, a position that it maintained until the last years of the century.

VENICE

The passing of the High Renaissance and Mannerist artists of central Italy, almost all of whom were either dead or in decline before 1540, eventually left the Venetian painters in a position of supremacy in Europe, challenged only by Michelangelo. As in Quattrocento Florence, the general level of production in Cinquecento Venice was high, and many derivative works by minor artists seem at first to be more original than they are because they partake of the quality radiated by the innovators.

Several Venetian painters survived from the Quattrocento: one member of the Vivarini family lingered on; Carpaccio was still painting, although past his most impressive period; and Giovanni Bellini, in spite of extreme old age, continued doing paintings of depth and beauty until his death in 1516. Two innovative masters emerged on this crowded stage: Giorgione, briefly, and Titian, with longevity second only to that of Michelangelo. He remained in control of Venetian painting until the last quarter of the century. About the middle of the century, two more painters, Tintoretto and Veronese, made their appearance. Lotto carried the Venetian style from Lombardy to the Marches, the School of Ferrara fell under the spell of Venice, and after an important work by Titian arrived in Brescia, a new school arose in that Lombard city under Venetian influence.

It is difficult to convince ourselves at this distance that the Republic of St. Mark, whose artistic production in the early Cinquecento suggests a position of security and splendor, was in fact in a precarious situation. Perhaps only its virtually impregnable location in the lagoons saved the Serenissima from the peril of dynastic rule, which eventually extinguished the liberties of its sister republic, Florence. Venice was, in fact, involved in the warfare between France and the Holy Roman Empire that devastated so much of Italy. Moreover, it had profited from the fall of the Borgia family in 1503 by annexing many papal dominions in the Romagna. Julius II, not satisfied with recapturing these in 1506, in

1508 organized the League of Cambrai, which in the ensuing months stripped from Venice, temporarily at least, almost all its possessions on the Italian mainland. Although most were eventually regained, throughout the sixteenth century Venice was compelled to adopt a defensive position with regard to the European monarchies, and especially the Empire, which under Charles V had assumed mastery over much of Europe.

It is a curious fact that, at the moment when the aged Bellini and the young Giorgione were bringing landscape and the beauties of nature closer to us than ever before in the history of the Renaissance, Venice itself possessed little nature to enjoy. It may well be that an important ingredient of the interest in landscape is the absence of landscape from daily experience. The Romantic movement in England—nature poetry and nature painting—went hand in hand with the Industrial Revolution, which was rapidly devouring the landscape around major urban centers, and the explosion of landscape painting in France in the middle of the nineteenth century accompanied the triumph of industrialism and the resulting expansion of Paris and the industrialization of its suburbs.

GIORGIONE

Be that as it may, the landscapes of the late Bellini and the art of Giorgione explore the moods of nature in a new way. Bellini, as we have seen previously, may be credited with the invention of the Venetian landscape, which envelops the sacred figures and seems to reach out toward the observer. Giorgione, traditionally and observably his pupil, is more of a mystery. Giorgio (in Venetian dialect, Zorzi) was born in Castelfranco, a small town on the Venetian mainland, probably about 1475–77, and came to Venice at an early age. A few documents record his activities in 1507–8, and in 1510 he died, still young, of the plague. According to a tradition retold by Vasari, Giorgione ("-one" is the Italian suffix for "big") was given to worldly delights, was a good conversationalist and therefore good company at parties, and a great lover. He also sang beautifully and accompanied himself on the lute. It seems that Giorgione enjoyed nature and loved life.

About the works of no other Italian painter save Giotto is there so little agreement. Expansionist scholars

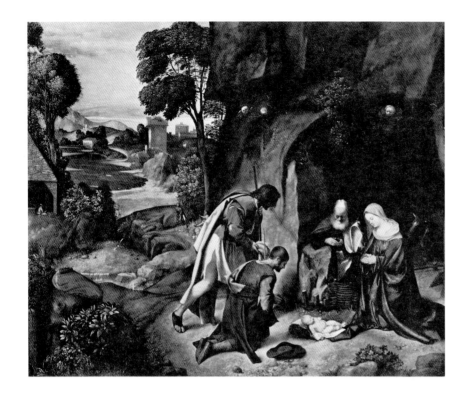

613. GIORGIONE. *Nativity and Adoration of the Shepherds* (*Allendale Nativity*). c. 1505(?). Panel, 35³/4 x 43¹/2". National Gallery of Art, Washington, D.C. (Kress Collection)

give Giorgione credit for dozens of paintings in a variety of styles; contractionists reduce the list to a bare half-dozen. Whatever the truth, all but the first of the five paintings here discussed as works of Giorgione are now universally accepted. Even that one, the *Nativity and Adoration of the Shepherds* (fig. 613), ought to be accepted, save for a few figures, disproportionately small, that a later hand added in an attempt to enliven the landscape at the left (these figures are absent from a contemporary replica of the picture, now in Vienna).

Despite these minor additions, the painting is a thrilling work, luminous and rich in its combination of red, blue, and yellow draperies with the sonorous depth of the landscape's greens and tans. The natural elements dominate the figures to such a degree that we seem almost to be looking at a Landscape with a Nativity rather than the reverse. And at first sight it is a convincing landscape—wild, rocky, and unsentimental as compared with the transfigured nature of Bellini. But a moment's analysis reveals that in the proportion established between rocks and distant space, in the configuration of the group, and in the shape of the cave and its surrounding rocks, Giorgione has relied on Mantegna's *Adoration of the Magi* (see fig. 407). In his observation of rocks, however, Giorgione has pushed naturalism no further than did Mantegna some four decades earlier. Nor has he studied vegetation with the scientific care bestowed upon it by Leonardo: Giorgione stands his branches on edge and his leaves are not arranged as in nature. They grow in bunches reminiscent of the schematic trees of Giotto, and they are lighted in Trecento fashion, with the leaves nearest the observer in strong light, those most distant in shadow.

It is the artist's love of wildness for wildness' sake that gives Giorgione's studio landscapes their special quality. The rocks are gloomy and frightening, the cave suitably dark. No road winds through the landscape; the shepherds clearly had to scramble for it, over ledges and across streams. And the few buildings seem in danger of being reabsorbed into the generally hostile—or at least not friendly—world Giorgione imagines. One might even argue that fatalism, not religion, is the motivating force in his art. But for his human figure he entertains warm emotions communicated through illumination derived from the late work of Giovanni Bellini. Each head, simplified to spherical or cubic essentials, exists in a radiant envelope of light and shadow with which the forms themselves seem at every point to be imbued. Probably the work is to be dated after 1505 and, significantly enough, it shows no hint that the artist knew or cared about the Florentine High Renaissance.

Two or three years later, perhaps, the young painter produced his only surviving altarpiece, the noble and gracious *Enthroned Madonna with Sts. Liberalis and Francis* (fig. 614), still in the Cathedral of Castelfranco, for which he painted it. Even this symmetrical composition is not without its surprises. Ordinarily, a Renaissance artist provides some means of access to the Virgin, no matter how regally she is installed, but Giorgione's Mary is seated on a throne that rises beyond the limits of the frame and is completely without visible steps. His heavenly Queen is, for all her gentle beauty, as remote as Cimabue's.

The armored St. Liberalis (fig. 615), patron of the Cathedral, carries a lance with a cross banner. St. Francis addresses the worshiper in a gesture that points to his

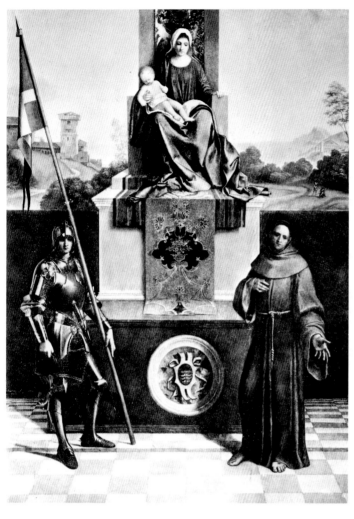

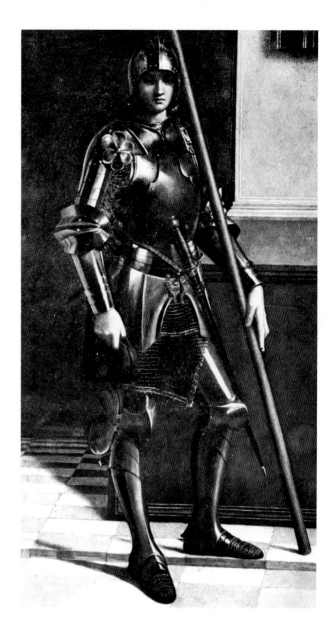

614. GIORGIONE. *Enthroned Madonna with Sts. Liberalis and Francis.* c. 1500–1505. Panel, 78³/4 x 60". ⛪ Cathedral, Castelfranco. Commissioned by Tuzio Costanzo, perhaps to commemorate the death of his son Matteo in 1504

615. St. Liberalis, detail of fig. 614

wounded side. Behind Mary's throne and over a draped wall, our gaze moves out freely over land and sea. We recognize Mary's port scene, a detail seldom seen in the background of non-Marian pictures, above St. Francis; a mountain village above St. Liberalis is protected by an enormous tower. Both landscapes show signs of warfare. Two men-at-arms, one standing, one seated, have stopped by a bend in the road at the right, and at the left the wooden parapet and roof of the guard tower are shattered as if by artillery.

These explicit allusions, coupled with the melancholy mood of the picture, permit us to interpret the lofty placing of the Virgin as an appeal for her intercession, in the manner of the Florentine "Madonnas of the Land" (see p. 470), and for similar reasons and under similar circumstances of military occupation. The high point of view and the pyramidal composition suggest a familiarity with the Florentine High Renaissance, which Giorgione could have acquired through the visit of Fra Bartolommeo to Venice in 1508. This may well be the date of the

altarpiece. But within the imported pyramid, Giorgione plays with characteristically Venetian diagonals: the slanting spear and the parallel motion of the drapery over the Virgin's right knee are answered by a whole fabric of counterdiagonals in the smaller folds of her mantle.

Giorgione's *Tempestuous Landscape with the Soldier and the Gypsy* (colorplate 115, p. 572) has been the subject of endless scholarly controversy. Who is the nude woman? Why is she nursing her child outdoors? Why is the soldier standing nearby and watching? Many efforts have been made to find a credible subject for the painting in ancient literature or in the Bible, and it has been suggested that perhaps the picture has no literary subject. In 1530, twenty years after Giorgione's death, the Venetian Marcantonio Michiel saw it in the house of Gabriel Vendramin and referred to it in his journal: "The little landscape on canvas with the tempest, with the gypsy and the soldier, was from the hand of Zorzi da Castelfranco." Furthermore, an X-ray has shown that where the soldier now stands Giorgione had originally painted a

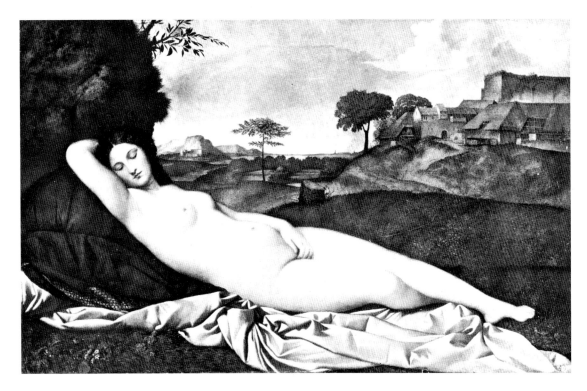

616.
GIORGIONE
(finished by
TITIAN).
Sleeping Venus.
c. 1510.
Canvas,
42³/4 x 69".
Gemäldegalerie,
Dresden

nude woman bathing. A change in the dramatis person-ae from nude woman to clothed soldier spells disaster for any story one can imagine, and the picture may well be a caprice on Giorgione's part—a nonsubject. From our distance it seems that he has given us the spare parts of a story, which we can utilize as we wish.

Again, he shows us an unfriendly nature. The woman seems almost trapped in the unkempt, weedy world around her. The trees are unpruned, the bushes shaggy, the columns ruined, the bridge precarious. And the scene is threatened by an immense, low storm cloud that casts the shadow of the bridge on the river and by a bolt of lightning that illuminates the scene with a sudden glare. Lightning we have seen before (Uccello's *Deluge*, for instance; see fig. 260), but never has it been so believable. A high level of humidity is suggested, and there is a crackling tension in the air. When the picture hung in the Accademia in a room by itself, with its own light, one could watch it for hours with inexhaustible fascination.

Another unconventional picture ruled by savage na-ture, the so-called *Fête Champêtre* (colorplate 116, p. 573), has been interpreted as an allegory of Poetry. Two young gentlemen, one fashionably dressed and playing a lute, are seated on the ground in conversation, paying no attention to two women who are, by and large, un-clothed. One of these women seems about to give voice to a recorder, while the other pours water back into a well from a pitcher. The stocky proportions of the women represent a Venetian ideal that will reappear in Titian's Venuses. The women's rounded masses are played off majestically against the masses of the tree in the middle distance.

The artist takes us into a landscape without clear-cut shapes or edges. Line exists even less than in Giovanni Bellini's later works. Form is drowned in shadow, and there is almost more shadow than light. The face of the young man on the left, for instance, seems full of ex-pression, but it is so deeply shaded that we can see little more than the profile and the position of one eyebrow. Here Giorgione begins to move his brush with greater speed and freedom, animating his opulent shadow world with the motion of his hand as well as with the saturation of color.

One of his last paintings, or so we are led to believe because it was finished by Titian after Giorgione's death, is the *Sleeping Venus* (fig. 616), the first of a series of re-cumbent Venuses by later masters, starting with Titian. Far removed from Botticelli's Christianized goddess (see colorplate 62, p. 303), who stands nude for a brief time at birth, Giorgione's Venus is sleeping nude, and her body is associated with the curves of the earth. The face in its present state is suspect and was probably repainted in Dresden in the early nineteenth century. X-rays reveal a kneeling cupid at the Virgin's feet who was overpainted when this area of the painting was damaged. The land-scape was completed by the young Titian, who rapidly replaced Giorgione as the leading master among the new painters of Venice and who soon acquired a dominance over his Venetian contemporaries almost equal in author-ity to that exerted by Michelangelo in central Italy.

TITIAN

Tiziano Vecellio, known in English as Titian, was not Venetian born. He came to the city of lagoons from the town of Cadore, high in the mountains at the beginning of the most spectacular ranges of the Dolomites. No one knows when he was born, but he survived in astonishing health until 1576 and attempted to give the impression of immense age. The tradition that he lived to the age of ninety-nine, and was therefore born about 1477, is no longer taken seriously. When Vasari visited Titian in 1566, he recorded the master's age as seventy-six, which would place the date of his birth in 1489 or 1490. No independent artistic activity on Titian's part is recorded before 1508 when, barely twenty years old according to his friend Ludovico Dolce, he assisted Giorgione in painting frescoes on the exterior of the Fondaco dei Tedeschi, the German commercial headquarters in Venice. No dated works by him before 1511 survive, and contemporary sources describe him as still young when, in 1516–18, he painted the *Assumption of the Virgin* (see colorplate 118, p. 575). The most probable date for his birth would therefore be about 1488.

His documented career still spans sixty-eight years, in a period when life was generally short. During this career, in fact toward the beginning of it, Titian is to be credited with one of the crucial discoveries in the history of Western art. He was the first painter in modern times to free the brush from the task of exactly describing tactile surfaces, volumes, and details, and to convert it into a vehicle for the direct perception of light through color and for the unimpeded expression of feeling. Others—notably Masaccio, the Van Eycks, Domenico Veneziano, and Giovanni Bellini—had taken steps on this road, but it was Titian who found and crossed the bridge. As early as the *Assumption of the Virgin*, Titian demonstrated his knowledge and mastery of the new type of brushwork, but he restricted its use to portions relatively remote from the observer. Long before the end of his life he was painting entire pictures by this method, as were the majority of painters in Venice.

Brushwork was, however, only the beginning of Titian's style. Contemporaries tell how he used to build up his pictures in oil over a reddish ground to establish a warm base for all the colors, and how he would turn his paintings face to the wall for months and then study them anew as if they were his worst enemies. New layers of paint might then be applied, especially glazes (the Italian word *velatura*, or "veiling," expresses well the role these glazes play) that tone down colors that might stand out too much and that create a deep, rich tone in which colors, shadows, and highlights seem miraculously suspended. "*Trenta, quaranta velature!*" ("Thirty, forty glazes!") he is said to have cried, and possibly there are that many, except where zealous restorers have cleaned them off, stripping Titian's paintings down to the brilliant colors he was at pains to tone down and unite.

Ludovico Dolce, whose *Dialogue on Painting* was published when Titian still had nineteen years to live, and who knew the master well, tells us that Titian arrived in Venice at the age of eight with his older brother Francesco and was at first set to work with the mosaicist Zuccato. Dissatisfied, he was taken on by the aged Gentile Bellini, whose manner he doubtless found old-fashioned, and then by Giovanni Bellini. Even in this authoritative shop he did not stay long, but moved on to study with Giorgione. By 1510 he seems to have become independent. The young man, whose exuberant strength fills a majestic series of canvases with form, light, and color, was also a shrewd businessman who invested his earnings in lumber in Cadore. By 1531 he was able to buy a palatial residence in Venice, looking out across the lagoons to Murano and, on clear days, to the summits of his Alpine homeland. In 1533, already wealthy and famous, Titian was summoned to Bologna to meet Emperor Charles V, who made him a count and his children hereditary nobles. In 1545 and 1546 he was in Rome, where he was awarded Roman citizenship on the Capitoline Hill. Twice the emperor called him to Augsburg as court painter. There is even a famous tale that one day, when Charles V was visiting his studio, Titian chanced to drop his brush and the emperor of most of the known world stooped to pick it up. Leonardo da Vinci, who had striven hard to see that painters received the honors and material rewards he considered due them above all other artists, would have been pleased indeed at the princely state this painter was able to maintain.

From the start of his career, Titian showed a sovereign impatience with the cliché. Every motive, every convention had to be seen afresh. In his beautiful early *Madonna and Child* (fig. 617), nicknamed the *Gypsy Madonna* because of the unusual dark hair and eyes of Mary, he takes the theme of the parapet, standing Child, and hanging cloth of honor, all familiar to us from the works of Giovanni Bellini, and pushes them off center. The Virgin stands slightly to the right of center, but she overlaps only one edge of the cloth of honor, which has been moved to leave a single landscape view instead of the customary two. The parapet runs less than halfway across the lower edge, and the diagonal, rising relationship between parapet and cloth of honor corresponds to the direction our glance follows over a second parapet and off to the hills of the middle distance and the mountains of the horizon. The diagonals are carried off with such authority that the off-center composition is satisfactorily balanced.

Throughout Titian's career, diagonal placings and diagonal views will be used in increasing intensity to break up the traditional symmetry of High Renaissance pictures. But another of Titian's lifelong compositional principles is already visible in the *Gypsy Madonna*—the Virgin forms an equilateral triangle—and the two principles are related. The triangle and the diagonal are for Titian's art what the spiral is for Raphael and the block for Michelangelo.

In the *Gypsy Madonna*, the sweetness of Bellini's Madonnas is replaced by a sturdy healthiness. The sun shines full on her round face with its large, wide-set eyes, and a half-shadow lingers on her neck. Her cheeks

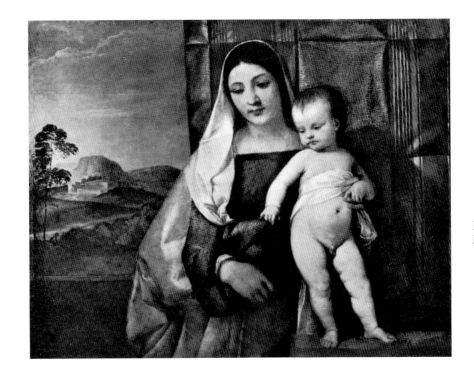

617. TITIAN. *Madonna and Child*, known popularly as the *Gypsy Madonna*. c. 1510–15(?). Panel, 26 x 32½". Kunsthistorisches Museum, Vienna

and lips glow in the light. Her quiet grace of bearing replaces the linear harmonies of Quattrocento female figures. She is splendid and opulent, warm and fertile, and her Child, whose classical pose shows a knowledge of Mantegna (see fig. 412), is a sturdy boy of whom she may be justly proud. Although Titian's ideal of womanhood reaches full expression only in his later works, it is already present here.

Among his early half-length portraits and figures, one of the most striking is the *Portrait of a Bearded Man* (colorplate 117, p. 574), whom some have identified as the Venetian poet Ludovico Ariosto and others have felt was a self-portrait. It was probably painted a year or so after the *Gypsy Madonna*. Titian has placed his sitter behind a parapet, in the manner introduced in Jan van Eyck's portraits. But with his usual ease, he rests the man's right elbow full on the parapet, so that the sleeve somewhat overlaps the edge. Although the body is almost at right angles to the picture plane, the head turns and the eyes look calmly toward us. The broad, spiral motion, in depth, of the arm and head suggests that Titian already knew, at a distance and perhaps from Fra Bartolommeo, something about what was going on in Florence. But he handled the motif entirely in his own way. The manner in which the hand suddenly turns out of sight, into shadow, is surprising and un-Florentine. The high side light illuminates the near side of the face, emphasizing the cheek, forehead, and strong, straight nose. The composed, dignified face holds its own against the beauty of the sleeve, in which an indefinable blue with a strong violet component catches and holds our eye against the softer tones of the warm stone and the gray background. A lesser master might have allowed this color to eclipse the sitter; in Titian's painting it seems a proud emanation of his inner nature.

Titian's *Assumption of the Virgin* (colorplate 118, p. 575; fig. 618) is well over twenty feet high, but the composition seems even larger because of Titian's handling of the figures, who are heroic not only in their proportions but also in their deportment. So grand is the picture that it competes successfully with the vast Gothic interior of the Church of Santa Maria Gloriosa dei Frari, on whose high altar it still stands. There may or may not be some relation to the *Sistine Madonna* of Raphael (see fig. 527), which was probably painted in 1513, three years before Titian began the *Assumption*. Titian was not to visit Florence and Rome until 1545, but some notion of the grandeur and scale of the central Italian High Renaissance could have been brought to Venice by Fra Bartolommeo and others, and possibly he came to know certain aspects of the style through drawings and prints. Most likely it was through such sources that Titian was inspired to create his own Venetian version of the High Renaissance style.

He has imagined the moment of the Assumption—the physical ascent into Heaven of the Virgin's body miraculously reunited with her soul after burial—as a scene of cosmic jubilation. Nature, so fascinating to Giorgione, has vanished. The foreground is filled with healthy, sturdy apostles who gesticulate wildly. One is seated on what may be the sarcophagus, or perhaps it is just a stone. Their movements converge to form a triangle from whose apex "Santa Maria Gloriosa" ascends on a curving cloud populated by countless putti (fig. 618). These are not the sometimes cute, sometimes impish babies of Quattrocento tradition, but robust children who sail upward with Mary into the golden light, which warms their bodies and flashes from their curly hair. In the midst of the ascending throng, Mary sways in the winds of Heaven and her mantle billows about her, creating more diagonals and triangles. Even God the Father floats diagonally toward us in space.

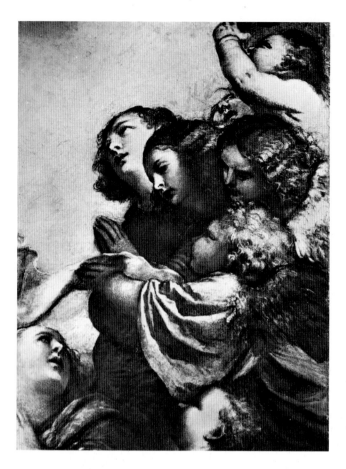

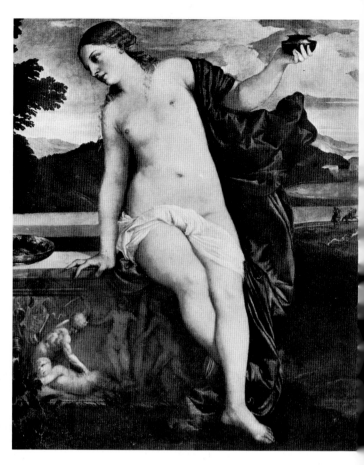

618. TITIAN. Angels, detail of *Assumption of the Virgin* (see colorplate 118, p. 575). 1516–18. Panel. ⛪ Sta. Maria Gloriosa dei Frari, Venice. Commissioned by Germano da Caiole, the Abbot of the Monastery of the Frari

619. TITIAN. Nude Woman, detail of *Sacred and Profane Love* (see colorplate 119, p. 576). 1514. Canvas. Borghese Gallery, Rome. Probably commissioned by Niccolò Aurelio in celebration of his wedding to Laura Bagarotto in 1514

Activated by an irresistible upward drive, humanity conquers Heaven in the person of Titian's Mary, her entire being yearning for this final realization, like Michelangelo's Adam. It is not without significance for the understanding of Titian as compared with Michelangelo (or, for that matter, Venice as compared with Florence) that the latter found the perfect expression of ideal humanity in the nude male, the former in beautifully robed women. Certainly, Titian's rapt Virgin, in the fullness of her physical and emotional powers, has as beautiful a face as one can imagine, but significantly enough it does not differ essentially from the faces of Titian's nude goddesses or allegorical figures. Like Correggio, he places no barrier between the physical and the spiritual.

And finally there is the color, which is unforgettable to anyone who has seen the painting in the Frari. Perhaps the necessity for broad effects that would be visible from a distance persuaded Titian to restrict himself to a few dominant hues—reds, blues, and greens in the garments of the apostles and the traditional blue and red for Mary's mantle and tunic, set off against blue sky below and the gold of Heaven above. The result is a composition of grand simplicity, within which the blood-warmed flesh tones and splendid hair operate freely, a symphonic structure in massive chords reaching the observer immediately and directly.

Probably a year or so earlier than the *Assumption*, and possibly using the model who later posed for Mary, Titian painted the so-called *Sacred and Profane Love* (colorplate 119, p. 576), about whose interpretation much has been written. The appeal of this picture is so strong—due to the harmonious composition, the contrast between splendid materials and glowing flesh, and the beauty of the women—that the simplest explanation is probably nearest the truth. The following combines elements drawn from several interpretations. Two women, so similar in form and coloring that they look like sisters, sit at either end of a fountain in the light of late afternoon. One is clothed, girdled with a locked belt, gloved, and holds a closed jar; she is seen against a fortified hill town to which a huntsman returns, while in the countryside two rabbits, symbols of love, converse in peace; as she looks past us intently, seeming to be listening, she toys with a cut rose, one of several on her side of the fountain.

The other figure is nude (fig. 619), save for a white scarf and a rose-colored cloak, and she holds aloft an urn from which a flame rises. Behind her stretches a more open and luminous landscape in which, before a lake, huntsmen catch up with a rabbit, shepherds tend their flocks, and a church steeple rises above the horizon. The fountain has the shape of a sarcophagus, and its lid is thrust aside so that Cupid may stir its waters. A golden

THE CINQUECENTO

588

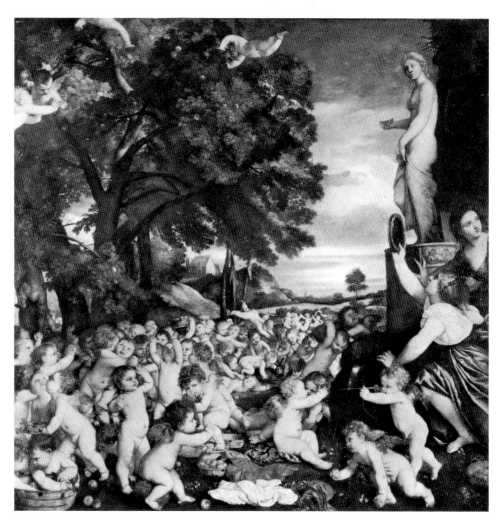

620. TITIAN. *Festival of Venus*. 1518–19. Canvas, 68 x 68". Prado, Madrid. Commissioned by Alfonso d'Este for his Studiolo in the Castle at Ferrara

bowl half filled with clear water rests upon the edge. On the sarcophagus-fountain are carved the arms of Niccolò Aurelio, vice-chancellor of the Venetian Republic; to the left, in emulation rather than imitation of ancient sculpture, a horse is led by its mane by one groom while others flee, and to the right a man is beaten and a woman is led by her hair.

That the nude woman in the picture is exhorting her listening "sister" is evident. What, then, is the nature of that exhortation? Through an analogy with Carpaccio's *Meditation on the Passion* (see fig. 430), also an allegorical arrangement of figures and carved stone with an upland scene on the left and a peaceful lowland on the right, a mystical transition between two states of being appears to be indicated, and this takes place through suffering and death. The image of the horse on the sarcophagus, it has been suggested, is derived from a Platonic metaphor for the control of the lower senses, and those of torment from ancient initiations into the rites of love. Through the water in the tomb and the cup, a parallel can be drawn to baptism, according to St. Paul a death to the old life and a rebirth in the new; and this baptism into the mysteries of love, requiring control and purification, is what the silent nude is recommending with her earnest gaze. The fortress must be abandoned, the garments shed, the roses dropped, the jar opened, the quarry caught. But that the new life of love is sacred is

indicated by the ritual lamp held to Heaven and the church steeple rising against the sky.

Titian has composed this apotheosis of human well-being in terms of his characteristic triangles in a simple harmony based on whites and silver-grays, blues, roses, and deep greens that already show the warmth and depth of his glazing technique. Setting this picture against Raphael's *Galatea* (see fig. 542), the palm for the painting of feminine beauty probably goes to Titian, but the two pictures stand together as symbols of an ennobled humanity. *Sacred and Profane Love*, which would be more appropriately renamed something such as the *Persuasion to Love* or the *Baptism in Love*, would have been as much at home in Agostino Chigi's villa as in Niccolò Aurelio's house.

Another aspect of Renaissance paganism can be seen in three pictures that Titian painted for Alfonso d'Este, duke of Ferrara, the foe of Julius II. Alfonso commissioned pictures to adorn an alabaster pleasure chamber (let us recall the efforts made by his aunt Isabella d'Este and his cousin Federigo Gonzaga to assemble similar painted rooms; see figs. 413, 595; colorplate 112, p. 569). Two of Titian's works were painted from literary descriptions by Philostratus, the third-century Roman author, of pictures he said he had seen in a villa near Naples. First is the *Festival of Venus* (fig. 620), representing Cupids before a statue of Venus; they romp through

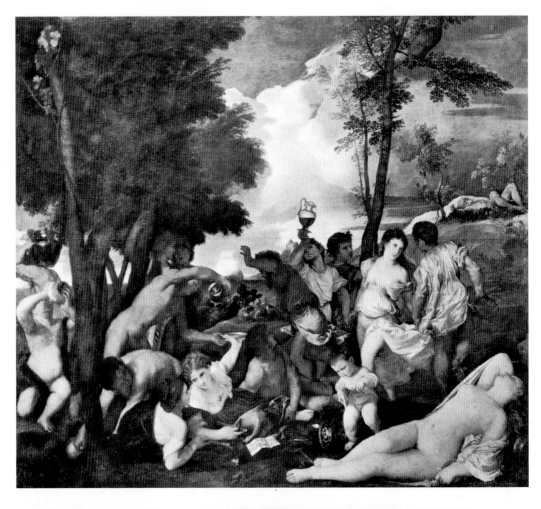

621. TITIAN. *Bacchanal of the Andrians.* c. 1522–23. Canvas, 69 x 76". Prado, Madrid. Commissioned by Alfonso d'Este for his Studiolo in the Castle at Ferrara

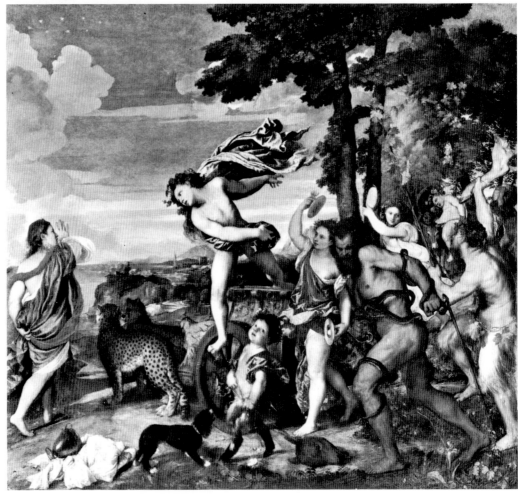

622. TITIAN. *Bacchus and Ariadne.* 1522–23. Canvas, 69 x 75". National Gallery, London. Commissioned by Alfonso d'Este for his Studiolo in the Castle at Ferrara

a meadow devouring baskets of her golden apples and even fly into the trees to pick more fruit. In the second, the *Bacchanal of the Andrians* (fig. 621), the inhabitants of the island of Andros, where a river of wine gushes from the ground, are shown in various stages of abandon as a result of the wine they pour and drink from amphorae, vases, pitchers, and cups. Inflamed with wine and love, the Andrians dance, gather in couples, or sleep, like the nude Ariadne, below right, who lies in a pose that would be imitated by Poussin and Goya. One little boy unashamedly urinates, while at the top of the hill the god of the river of wine, caught in a shaft of sun, lies in a torpor. The final painting of the series, *Bacchus and Ariadne*, whose subject is drawn from a variety of classical sources, shows Bacchus leaping from his chariot to rescue Ariadne, abandoned on the island of Naxos by the faithless Theseus (fig. 622). The god is attended by drunken maenads clashing cymbals and satyrs brandishing sticks and even the hindquarter of a goat they have torn apart for their feast.

In these three paintings Titian reaches a new freedom of figural composition and brilliance of coloristic expression. The richness of the flesh tones and the sparkle of the blues and roses were clearly designed to stand out against the alabaster architecture. But the eloquence of color in the shadows is almost more surprising than its beauty in the light. Such effects as the dull red of the wine that no light touches, and the soft sheen of its crystal pitcher against the cloud, are unexpected, as is the deep glow of the coats of Bacchus's leopards within the shadow he casts upon them as he leaps.

Meanwhile, in his religious works Titian was exploiting the implications of his diagonal-triangular principle for monumental composition. An example is the *Madonna of the Pesaro Family* (fig. 623), commissioned in 1519 for a side aisle altar in the Franciscan Church of Santa Maria Gloriosa dei Frari and completed in 1526. Like Correggio's contemporary *Madonna and Child with Sts. Jerome and Mary Magdalen* (see fig. 589), the scene is laid outdoors in full sunlight. But Titian has chosen as his setting a portico of the Virgin's heavenly palace. An armored warrior holding an olive-crowned flag with the arms of the Pesaro family presents Saint Peter, in the middle, with a captured Turk. This is a reference to the battle of Santa Maura, which was won in 1502 by Jacopo Pesaro, bishop of Paphos and commander of the papal galleys. Jacopo himself kneels at the left, and at the right kneel five male members of his family.

An artist in the conservative Venetian tradition would have given us a purely symmetrical composition, but Titian deployed his diagonals and triangles in depth and height. First, he has turned the palace at a sharp angle to the picture plane, then set the Virgin so far to one side that her head forms one corner of an equilateral triangle whose other two points are provided by the kneeling chiefs of the Pesaro clan. Similar triangles in smaller scale reappear throughout the picture in figures and drapery patterns. The columns seem to soar beyond the arched

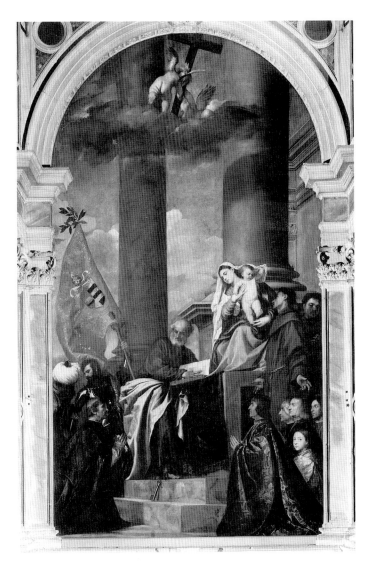

623. TITIAN. *Madonna of the Pesaro Family*. 1519–26. Canvas, 16' x 8' 10". 🏛 Sta. Maria Gloriosa dei Frari, Venice. Commissioned by Jacopo Pesaro, Bishop of Paphos, and his brothers

frame, and at the top of the arch a cloud floats in bearing two putti holding a cross. The result is noble and dramatic. Titian's pictures of the 1520s have all the harmony of the High Renaissance, but with a new power of shapes rather than muscular action. Now Titian's color has quieted down; the *Pesaro Madonna* is darker and richer than the work of the preceding decade, doubtless softened by multiple glazes.

When, at some time in the mid-1520s, Titian took up the subject of the *Entombment* (fig. 624), he did so in a measured and controlled fashion. The pose of Christ is borrowed from that of the dead Meleager carried from the boar hunt in a well-known group of Roman sarcophagus reliefs. Titian has fitted his central group— Christ, Nicodemus, Joseph of Arimathea, and John—

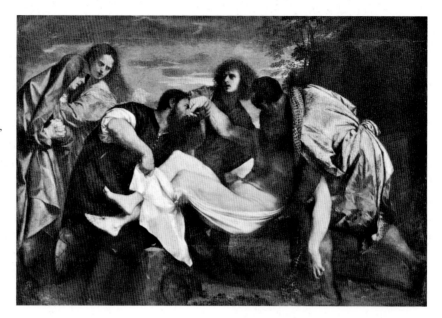

624. TITIAN. *Entombment*. Mid-1520s. Canvas, 58 x 81". The Louvre, Paris. Probably commissioned by a member of the Gonzaga family

into an isosceles triangle, but the diagonals of Christ's thighs form one side of another isosceles triangle that has its apex at the head of the Virgin; the other two sides correspond to those of the lower left corner of the frame. These intersecting triangles are enriched by numerous curving shapes, such as the back of Nicodemus or the arms of Christ. Within the compact composition the heads, simplified to geometrical essentials as in the *Pesaro Madonna*, shoot glances of tragic intensity.

Titian's portraiture in the 1520s enters a similar phase of dignity and reserve. No expression crosses the face of the *Man with the Glove* (fig. 625), and the triangular relationship of hands and face functions within a color scheme restricted to black, white, and flesh tones. Yet the effect of the painting is intense. One cannot escape the solemnity of the gaze, and it seems that not even black-and-white reproduction can fully suppress the richness of Titian's color.

In the 1530s a conservative phase of Titian's work begins, epitomized by the *Presentation of the Virgin* (figs. 626, 627) for the Scuola della Carità in Venice. Here Titian coped with two preexisting doors by reviving the traditional motif of a staircase for the Virgin to ascend. One door he incorporated into the painted masonry of the staircase by painting archivolts for it; the other he ignored. The architecture of the background reflects and rationalizes a number of inequalities of proportion and spacing in the wooden paneling below and the carved and gilded wooden ceiling above, producing a setting that has at the same time the accidentality of a city street and a satisfying harmony with both its component parts and the random organization of the room.

There is a suggestion of the Trecento about this, and Titian may have looked with interest on the subtle organization of architectural space and crowds of standing figures in the murals of Jacopo Avanzo and Altichiero in Padua (see figs. 129, 130)—where he had painted a major fresco series as a young man—and adapted their ideas to

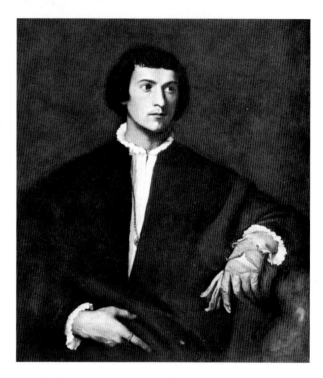

625. TITIAN. *Man with the Glove*. c. 1520–21. Canvas, 39³/8 x 35". The Louvre, Paris

large-scale narrative composition. The details of the architecture are resolutely Renaissance, save for the pink-and-white lozenge patterns in the marble wall, borrowed from the Doges' Palace. On the left appears Titian's idea of the Pyramid of Gaius Cestius in Rome and in the distance—a nostalgic touch—the summits of the mountains above Cadore. In this tapestrylike mural, depending for its effect more on areas of bright costumes and rich marbles than on form or movement, Titian has returned to the web of color and line that often seems to underlie Venetian painting. The details

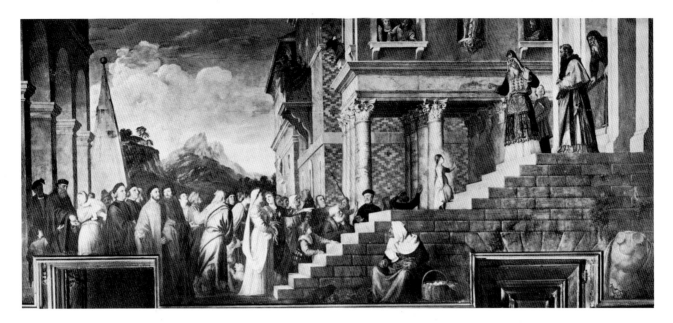

626. TITLE. *Presentation of the Virgin*. 1534–38. Canvas, 11' 4" x 25' 5". ⌂ Scuola della Carità, Venice (now part of the Accademia, Venice)

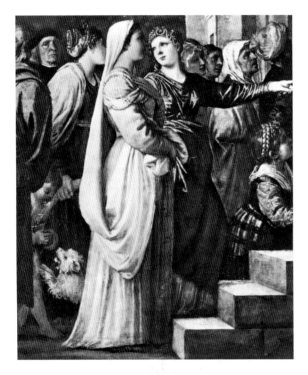

627. Women, detail of fig. 626

are impressive in richness of color, but the figures are withdrawn in expression and austere in form. The three-year-old Virgin, center of a soft radiance of light, is a touching figure as she pauses on the first step of the second flight, and the high priest is very grand, dressed with some attention to the biblical description of his vestments, including the jeweled breastplate. The old market woman seated below the stairs to direct our gaze inward, along with hers, is a tribute to Carpaccio's rendering of St. Ursula's nurse (see colorplate 80, p. 449) in a similar position.

In this same vein of quiet luxury and emotional reserve, Titian painted the so-called *Venus of Urbino* (fig. 628), finished in 1538 for Guidobaldo della Rovere, then duke of Camerino. In this, the earliest of the long series of recumbent Venuses, he returned with such fidelity to the pose of Giorgione's *Sleeping Venus* (see fig. 616) that one can only suspect that the patron requested it. But now the sleeper has awakened and looks at us with a calculating stare. She lies upon a couch, her dog asleep at her feet; one hand idly holds a nosegay of flowers; and her rich, silky, delicately waved golden-brown hair floods over one white shoulder in a contrast of textures and colors that Titian used and reused from his youth to old age. Instead of Giorgione's natural setting, Titian has divided his background between the curtains and wall of the cubicle in which the nude reclines and an adjoining chamber, paved with marble, hung with brocades, and lit by an opening onto treetops. In this palatial environment a splendidly dressed woman looks on while a girl in white, presumably a servant, searches for something in one of a pair of carved and gilded *cassoni*, the chests in which clothes were kept in the Renaissance.

Is this Venus at all? Guidobaldo's correspondence, which betrays his impatience to receive this picture, refers to the subject simply as a nude woman. Only her connection with Giorgione's earlier and Titian's later Venuses suggests otherwise. If this is Venus, then Titian has gone to considerable pains to demythologize her, to represent her as a prince's mistress who basks in the warmth of her own flesh, while her lady-in-waiting and maidservant find a garment splendid enough to clothe her. Titian's fascination with the surfaces of marble and brocade in the background—regularly subdivided areas of rich and various texture, uniformly maintained—is indicative of his own attitude toward painting at that time.

Titian painted an uninterrupted sequence of dramatic, passionate works from the early 1540s until he was

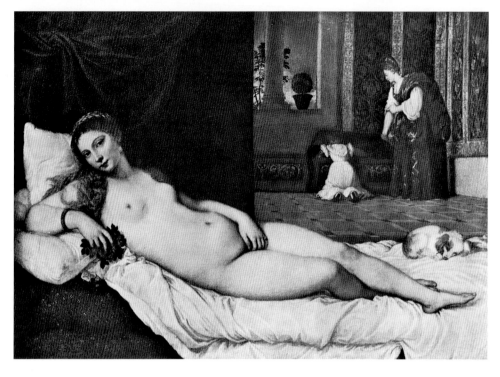

628. TITIAN. *"Venus of Urbino."* Finished in 1538. Canvas, 47 x 65". Uffizi Gallery, Florence. Commissioned by Guidobaldo della Rovere

stopped by death. In 1542 he accepted a commission, offered originally to Vasari when he visited Venice, for three scenes of violent action for the ceiling of the Church of Santo Spirito in Isola in Venice; these were later removed to a similar position in the Sacristy of Santa Maria della Salute (figs. 629–31). For the first time Titian, who still had not visited Rome, showed a sustained interest in the heroic poses and powerful muscula-

ture of the Roman High Renaissance. It would be easy to attribute this to the influence of Michelangelo, but the Venetian painter seems to have known of the innovations of his Florentine rival before 1520, and the question arises why he resisted influence from him for so long.

Titian's first contact with the Roman artistic vocabulary was at second hand, through the person of Giulio Romano, who was still working in Mantua; if we are

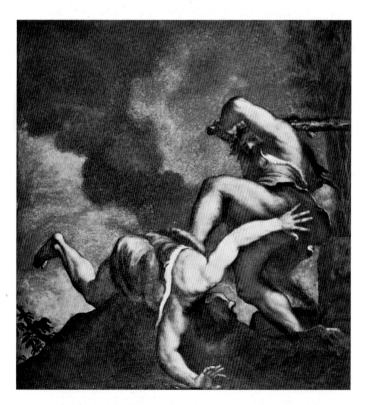

629. TITIAN. *Cain Killing Abel.* 1542. Canvas, 9' 2" square. Sacristy, Sta. Maria della Salute, Venice. Commissioned for Sto. Spirito in Isola, Venice

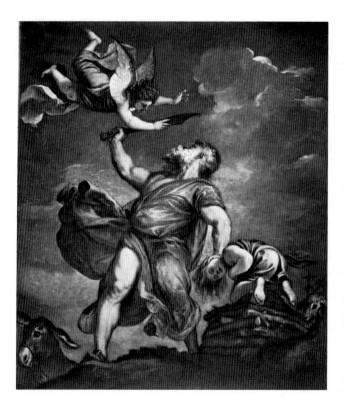

630. TITIAN. *Sacrifice of Isaac.* 1542. Canvas, 10' 6" x 9' 2". Sacristy, Sta. Maria della Salute, Venice. Commissioned for Sto. Spirito in Isola, Venice

to believe Pietro Aretino, Titian wanted Giulio to come to live in Venice after the death of Federigo Gonzaga in 1540. In the huge, heavily muscled figures who battle and tumble through and seem almost to fall out of Titian's *Cain Killing Abel, Sacrifice of Isaac,* and *David and Goliath,* there is more than an echo of Giulio's giants (see figs. 611, 612). Titian's poses are sometimes derived from Giulio, and so is the startling viewpoint from below. But Titian's figures, like the clouds that tower in the background, are interpenetrated by light and color, and they too weave, twist, and turn. The emotional stasis of the 1530s is shattered, and from their shadows the half-seen faces launch glances of a surprising depth of passion.

Among the earliest in a series of portraits in the new, emotionally charged style is *Pope Paul III* (fig. 632), which Titian painted when the pope visited Bologna in 1543. The unwilling supporter of the Counter-Reformation was at heart a Renaissance prince, and he is shown in a restless pose, twisted in his velvet chair, one hand on his purse, his head jutting forward, his gaze glinting in our direction. The insightful characterization of the shrewd face and the powerful drawing of the features, hands, hair, and beard, painted with the relatively fine brushes traditionally in use in Venice, are combined with an electrifying display of reds and flashes of light on the velvet mozzetta. In a technique that recalls the gold striations of Byzantine painting (see fig. 128), Titian beat these strokes rapidly on the canvas with a broad and heavy brush. His lights crackle from the picture with a new freedom, living a life of their own to such an extent that they dominate the composition.

As Titian's lifework culminates in a final quarter-century of intensive activity, the new freedom of light and brushwork increases, often at the expense of solid form. Tactile reality is softened, dissolved, even shattered by bursts of brushwork that record luminary visions. Generally, these are connected with erotic imagery or with scenes of religious experience. Three times Titian repeated, for various patrons, his composition showing how the mortal Danaë was seduced by Jupiter, who descended upon her as a shower of golden coins. In the pose of Danaë, Titian utilized a pose he took from Michelangelo. Michelangelo, who had derived the motif from an ancient Roman relief, had used it for his now-lost picture of Leda—a woman seduced by Jupiter in the form of a swan—and for the *Night* (see fig. 556) of the Medici Chapel.

In Titian's earliest version (not illustrated), he balanced the recumbent Danaë with a standing Eros, but in the version painted for King Philip II of Spain (fig. 633), he substituted a greedy maidservant stretching out her apron to try to catch some of the coins. Her gnarled ugliness and avarice contrast with the beauty and rapture of Danaë; one woman looks for material gain, the other waits for a love that, for all the fullness of its physical expression, is divine in origin and expressed in light. The

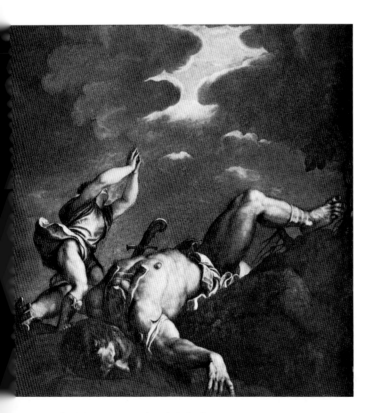

631. TITIAN. *David and Goliath*. 1542. Canvas, 9' 2" square. Sacristy of Sta. Maria della Salute, Venice. Commissioned for Sto. Spirito in Isola, Venice

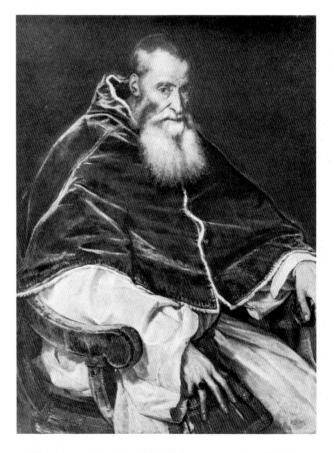

632. TITIAN. *Pope Paul III*. 1543. Canvas, 45 x 35". Museo di Capodimonte, Naples. Commissioned by Pope Paul III

High and Late Renaissance in Venice and on the Mainland

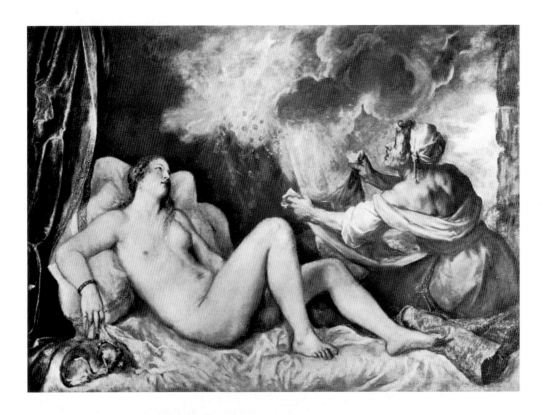

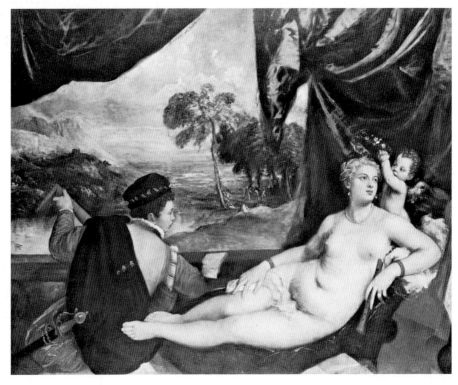

above: 633. TITIAN. *Danaë.* 1554.
Canvas, 50¼ x 70". Prado, Madrid.
Commissioned by Philip II of Spain

right: 634. TITIAN (completed by
another artist). *Venus and the Lute
Player.* Probably late 1550s. Canvas,
65 x 82½". The Metropolitan
Museum of Art, New York
(Purchase, Munsey Fund, 1936)

Danaë resembles the nude figure in the *Sacred and Profane Love*, painted some forty years earlier, and the glance
that of the yearning Mary in the *Assumption of the Virgin*.
The broken brushwork of Titian's late style releases
Danaë's warm, glowing body from any trace of Michelangelesque muscular tension, shatters the drapery folds
into luminary reflections, and culminates in the glorious
burst of golden, copper, silver, and turquoise rays flood-
ing from the cloud.

In his last years, Titian painted a series of Venuses
who in pose recall the *Venus of Urbino*. In the last of this
series, *Venus and the Lute Player* in New York (fig. 634),
the goddess is about to be crowned by Cupid. She sets
aside her recorder, but a curly-headed youth in Cinquecento costume plays music for her and stares boldly at
her body. The subject is almost certainly related to the
Neoplatonic debate over whether beauty was better perceived through the ear or the eye; the rapturous gaze of

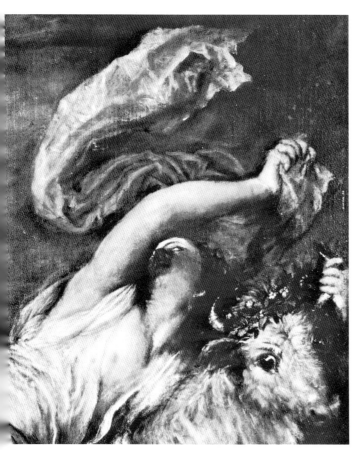

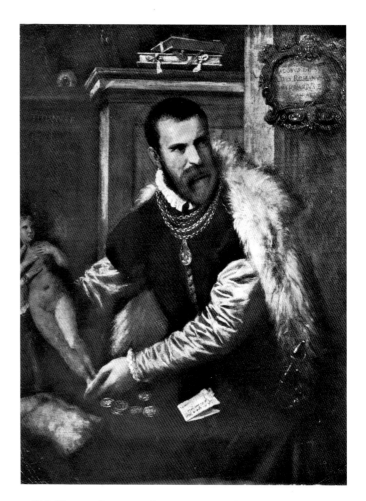

635. TITIAN. Europa and the Bull,
detail of *Rape of Europa* (see colorplate 120, p. 609).
1559–62. Canvas. Isabella Stewart
Gardner Museum, Boston. Commissioned
by Philip II of Spain

636. TITIAN. *Jacopo Strada.* 1567–68. Canvas, 49 x 37½".
Kunsthistorisches Museum, Vienna. Probably commissioned
by Jacopo Strada

the musician may give us Titian's answer to this question.

In boldly asymmetrical diagonals, a red curtain is parted to reveal a luminous landscape that is painted with the freedom, speed, and authority of Titian's late style. Shimmering water, castled hills, and blue-tinged mountains surround a glade where nymphs dance to a shepherd's pipe. The reader should ignore the uninteresting handling of such details as the face and ornaments of Venus. These were probably completed by others to make the work salable when it was left unfinished at Titian's death. But they do not detract from the breezy freshness of the landscape, which inspired later painters from Rubens to Turner.

In the same rhapsodic style is the *Rape of Europa* (colorplate 120, p. 609), begun in 1559 and shipped to Spain in 1562. The nymph Europa had been playing on the seashore with her companions when Jupiter appeared as a beautiful white bull. Europa innocently wove garlands of flowers for the bull, but he suddenly swept off with her across the waters, leaving her alarmed companions on the beach. Europa clings to one of the bull's horns and tries to maintain her balance. The wind and the bull's speed lift her garment to expose her legs and carry her rose-colored mantle in a spiral into the

blue (fig. 635). The picture's direction from left to right is accelerated by cupids, one riding behind the bull on a fish and two others, with bows and arrows, swooping in the air. As Correggio does in his *Jupiter and Ganymede* (see colorplate 112, p. 569), Titian expresses the departure from earth in terms of spatial separation between the foreground figures, with whom we identify, and a distant landscape. But Titian exaggerates the distance between foreground and background by diminishing the mountains and the figures reflected in the sea to tiny proportions. The landscape, which in the *Venus and the Lute Player* is like a sudden burst of orchestral music, is here treated with sustained symphonic breadth. The flashing brushwork of the mountain ranges blends the mountains, sea, clouds, and sky into indistinguishable fluctuations of blue, silver, and apricot. Chords of deeper blue and silver play through the water, and the foam around the bull's forelegs parts to reveal a spiny fish. Blue and silver lights fluctuate through the bull's shaggy coat and Europa's filmy garments.

In the last decades of Titian's life, he developed a new type of action portrait, as seen in the portrait of the Mantuan painter and art dealer Jacopo Strada (fig. 636). To indicate his profession, he holds a marble statuette of

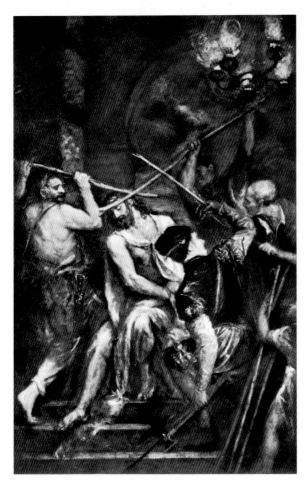

637. TITIAN. *Crowning with Thorns*. c. 1570. Canvas,
9' 2" x 5' 11½". Alte Pinakothek, Munich

a nude Venus, and ancient coins, a fragmentary torso, and a bronze figurine lie on the table. Strada's success is shown by his rich costume, fur cape, and massive gold chain, his gentlemanly status by the sword and dagger, and his scholarship by the books. The diagonals of the arms, the marble statuette, and the sidelong glance communicate to the customary sixteenth-century portrait-with-attributes the excitement of a moment of drama. This apotheosis of antiquarian commerce could almost be mistaken for a detail from a larger narrative picture. Finished as far as the aged Titian ever finished anything, *Jacopo Strada* shows a controlled version of his rich brushwork and luminous glazes.

At the close of Titian's life, his thoughts, like those of Michelangelo at a similar age, turned with intensity toward religious subjects, especially the Passion of Christ. Contemplating the inevitable approach of his own death, he meditated on Christ's suffering in pictures for which no patron is known. In the 1540s Titian had painted the *Crowning with Thorns* in a vigorous style similar to that of the Salute ceiling (see figs. 629–31); he took up this subject again about 1570 (fig. 637) in a more personal and even violent manner in a picture found in his studio

after his death. In this later picture, which was acquired by Domenico Tintoretto, son of the painter, the violence is communicated by color and brushwork, not by form. The blows strike the wounded head from staves wielded by figures that seem to be virtually weightless. The drama of shadows and lights acquires its ferocity through the vibrancy of the brushwork and what might be called the slow burn of the coloring. Thick impasti rain upon the canvas. The blues, reds, and yellows of Titian's early style are still there, operating through a nocturnal depth of glazes. The compositional triangles clash and interlock, increasing the storm of pain that surrounds the suffering Christ.

The frequent motives of torment and chaos that recur in Titian's last years are resolved in the *Pietà* (fig. 638). We are drawn into the painting by the Magdalen, who rushes toward us, her hair streaming, her arm outstretched, her mouth open in a cry of grief. In a rusticated niche, Mary holds the dead Christ. Statues of the Hellespontine sibyl and of Moses stand on bases formed by snarling lions' heads, symbols of devouring death. Moses carries the tablets with the Ten Commandments and the rod with which he struck water from the rock, prefiguring the stream from the side of Christ at the Crucifixion. St. Jerome kneels before Christ, holding one of his hands and looking up into his face. The motive of the rushing Magdalen is repeated, diagonally, at the upper right by a soaring putto who carries an immense torch. Below the statue of Moses, another putto holds the Magdalen's jar of ointment; below that of the Hellespontine sibyl the little votive picture leaning against the pedestal shows Titian and his son Orazio in prayer before the Virgin for delivery from the plague of 1561.

The drama of human redemption through Christ's sacrifice is summarized in the niche, for above it appear the fig leaves of the Fall of Adam and Eve and on the raking cornices burn six of the seven lamps, the Seven Spirits of God (Revelation 4:5). The seventh is perched above the central block of the triple keystone, which is Christ, the Second Person of the Trinity. Within the niche above Christ, a golden apse mosaic appears as a final reminder, in Titian's own memorial, of his place in a Venetian tradition that encompasses both the real mosaic domes and apses of San Marco and those that appear in the paintings of his teacher, Giovanni Bellini, and others (figs. 424, 425). Shimmering in the luminous glow, we can make out a pelican striking her breast, a traditional symbol of Christ's blood shed for humanity.

The *Pietà* was painted by Titian for his tomb in Santa Maria Gloriosa dei Frari, the church that already contained two of his masterpieces. He was not able to complete it, for both he and Orazio died in the plague of 1576. He represented himself as the kneeling St. Jerome (fig. 639), with whose self-inflicted torments in the desert he seems to have felt some form of mystical identification. After Titian's death, the picture was finished, in a manner of speaking, by his assistant Palma Giovane, but it is by no means easy to discover just what he did to

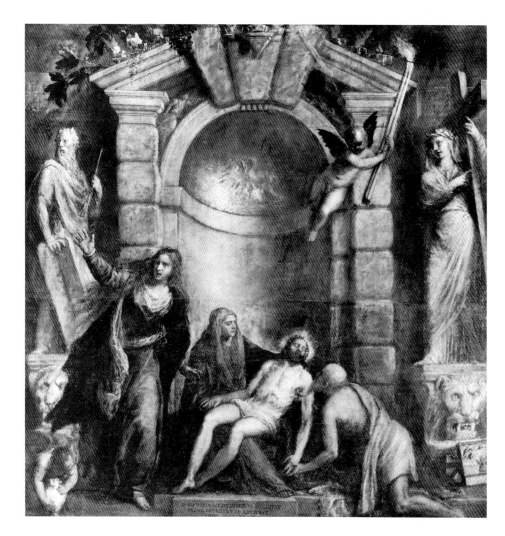

it. Certainly, he spared it the tight detail that was added to other unfinished works. In general, the broken brushwork seems to be Titian's, and the painting contains glorious passages, especially in the green tunic of the Magdalen and the masses of her light-brown hair. Echoes of form seem to vibrate about the faces of Christ and the Virgin and light to break from the thorn-crowned head. The closed eyes are barely indicated. But the tremulous disorder of the surface is locked into the massive triangles of the composition, crossing in depth as they emanate from or converge upon Christ and Mary. The hypotenuse of Titian's last triangle, by his own careful design, is formed by his own body and by the direction of his gaze as, in the semblance of St. Jerome, he concentrates all his being on that of Christ.

LORENZO LOTTO

A strikingly original and almost equally long-lived contemporary of Titian was the somewhat older Lorenzo Lotto (1480–1556), who spent most of his active years far from the city of the lagoons. Most of Lotto's works were produced for centers on the Venetian mainland and

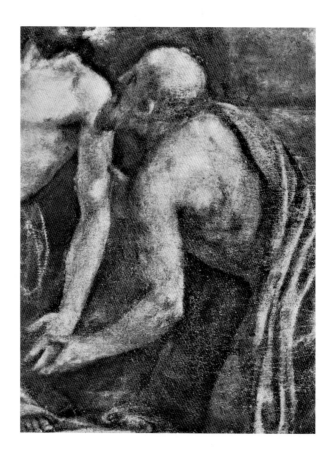

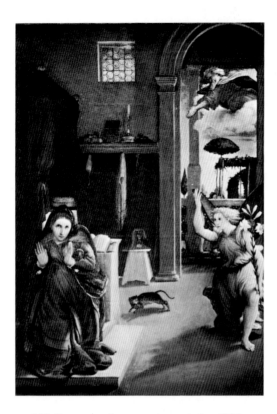

640. LORENZO LOTTO. *Annunciation*. 1520s.
Canvas, 66³/8 x 44⁷/8". 🏛 Church of Sta. Maria
sopra Mercanti, Recanati

ing in an expression that is half awe, half trance. A cat scurries away in terror, casting a shadow on the floor like that of the rushing angel.

The very oddness of the scene and its peculiar lighting suggest a familiarity with Parmigianino and Beccafumi, and the dense, often marblelike surfaces have little to do with the coloristic dissolution of Titian. The upstage properties include, in addition to the prie-dieu and the bed, a shelf with books, a candle, and an inkstand, a towel hanging from a nail, and, strangest of all, an hourglass with the sands half run out, partly covered with a cloth—at first glance these look like a chalice and paten from an altar. Exactly what inspiration motivated this novel painting will probably never be known; perhaps Lotto set out to create an Annunciation that was distinctly different from any of the hundreds that had previously been painted.

Worlds apart from the riddles of this painting is Lotto's *Sacra Conversazione* (colorplate 121, p. 610), in which the blue of Mary's tunic and mantle fills the whole picture as if with the distilled quintessence of the sky and distant hills. The picture is a hymn to youth, health, and beauty, yet the figures are self-contained. The partly shadowed countenance of Lotto's Virgin seems almost Praxitelean in the breadth, harmony, and calm of her soft features. Lotto's brushwork, rich yet restrained, recalls that of Correggio rather than the free strokes of Titian, which Lotto never emulated.

PARIS BORDONE

A somewhat more prosaic painter than Lotto, but a master at his own interpretation of Venetian material splendor, was Paris Bordone (1500–1571), from Treviso on the Venetian mainland. At an early age he studied with Titian who, by Bordone's account, treated him badly. On his own, he developed a special sort of vision, as if his world of rich foliage, grand architecture, glowing flesh, and sparkling silks were seen in a glass darkly. His unmistakable personal style floats a shimmer of light over resonant color that can only be suggested in black-and-white reproductions. One aspect of Titian's art that Bordone did absorb was his glazing technique, which he adapted to his own purposes. One always feels that a Paris Bordone has been staged, seldom that it was felt.

He can be credited with the invention of a new type of architectural painting, evident in his painting of *A Fisherman Delivering the Ring* (fig. 641), which shows a loyal citizen bringing back to the doge the ring with which Venice annually wed the sea in a splendid ceremony. The portrait figures (doubtless all once recognizable) are easily grouped, in the tradition of Carpaccio but with a touch more grandiloquence, in and before High Renaissance loggie and galleries of white and colored marble, sometimes embellished with mosaic panels. If the accepted dating of 1534 or 1535 is correct, the painting is prophetic, for at this moment no such structures existed in Venice. Bordone must have made the

in what is now Lombardy, and he was active in one town after another in the hilly regions of the Marches, near the Adriatic coast. Only relatively late in his life did he settle in Venice, and even then he did not break his ties with the mainland. Throughout his career Lotto retained his own individuality, and he could ring a surprising number of changes on his personal inventions, running from extreme naturalism, through attempts at the bizarre that may reflect an interest in the Mannerism of central Italy, to an exultant lyricism of mood and color.

An *Annunciation* in the Marchigian city of Recanati (fig. 640) shows many of Lotto's delightful qualities. Datable somewhere in the 1520s, the picture is at first hard to take quite seriously. We are in Mary's chamber, represented with Carpaccio-like fidelity to detail yet lighted in surprising ways, often from below. Mary has been reading or praying at a prie-dieu. God the Father, enveloped below the waist in clouds, pops through the loggia, stretching forth his hands as if sending down the dove of the Holy Spirit, although no dove is seen. Perhaps we are meant to believe that the Holy Spirit descended invisibly upon Mary. The angel runs in through the door bearing a huge lily. He drops suddenly to one knee, leaving the other bare, and raises his arm in a theatrical gesture, staring with wide-open eyes under flying yellow locks of hair. Mary turns toward us, away from her book, and opens her hands in wonder, yet at the same time she seems to shrink into herself, her eyes star-

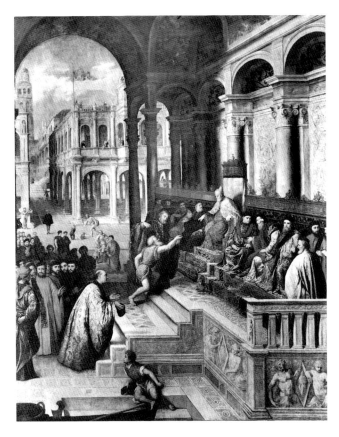

641. PARIS BORDONE. *A Fisherman Delivering the Ring.*
c. 1534–35. Canvas, 12' 1⅝" x 9' 10⅛". Accademia, Venice.
Commissioned for the Sala dell'Albergo of the Scuola
Grande di S. Marco, Venice

acquaintance of Jacopo Sansovino, who had arrived in the city of the lagoons in 1527, but as yet was known chiefly as a sculptor. The noble architectural setting, therefore, may reflect Jacopo's dreams for the civic center of Venice, to be realized in the construction of the Library of San Marco (see colorplate 130, p. 651), the Zecca (see fig. 663), and other public buildings. It may even have enjoyed the benefit of his specific ideas and his draftsmanly expertise in the projection of these perspectives. In the second half of the century, the new type of ideal setting proclaimed here inspired Veronese and Tintoretto.

THE MAINLAND

During the first two decades of the Cinquecento, as we have seen, the plain of the Po, with its wealthy and beautiful cities, was the victim of prolonged dynastic strife between the Venetian Republic, the Sforza dukes, the French kings, the Habsburg emperors (who were also kings of Spain), and the papacy. Louis XII of France, who had dethroned and imprisoned Ludovico Sforza in 1500, was himself ejected by Swiss troops in the service of Julius II in 1512. Nonetheless King Francis I of France returned to the duchy of Milan in 1515, only to lose it for good to Charles V in 1521; Milan, once a brilliant creative center, became a Spanish province, ill-governed and economically depressed. Par-

ma, under the papacy, and Mantua and Ferrara, independent duchies, fared better. So did the flourishing cities of Bergamo, Brescia, Verona, and Vicenza, all enjoying the enlightened government of the Serenissima, which quickly recovered its political and economic fortunes. Artistically, the heritage of Mantegna remained a force to be reckoned with in Milan, although less powerful than the physical presence, activity, and teaching of Leonardo da Vinci. Parma, as we have seen, had strong ties to Rome. Ferrara had its own artistic tradition, but Brescia and Cremona did not. All three were inevitably submerged in the tide of colorism flowing from Venice.

BRAMANTINO

At the turn of the century, the Milanese scene was dominated by clones of Leonardo, sometimes so close to the master that attribution problems plague specialists to this day. These imitators are seldom original. One of the few holdouts was Bartolommeo Suardi (c. 1465–1530), known as Bramantino because he studied painting with Bramante. Bramantino was the most original painter of the Milanese School, and his *Adoration of the Magi* (colorplate 122, p. 611) shows the characteristic style from which he never wavered, despite a sojourn in Rome just before the arrival of Raphael. If one has to look for influences, one might find them in the spatial construction of Mantegna and the coloring of Giovanni Bellini, but both have been assimilated into Bramantino's personal vision. The painting, whose small size and symmetrical disposition suggest it was made for private devotion, breathes the serenity, clarity, and calm typical of this artist.

Seated on a block of stone in a ruined classical building whose symbolic nature we can surmise from other such representations (see pp. 328, 331–32), the Virgin is flanked by Isaiah on her right and Daniel on her left. The latter is shown as a wayfarer, disheveled in appearance and carrying a staff, pointing toward Christ and looking out to the spectator. On either side in the foreground and in bright light stand two bareheaded Magi, the older carrying what looks like an ancient gold vase, the younger a rose quartz bowl. The third Magus is barely visible behind the youngest, and Joseph is relegated to the extreme left. The identification of the figure to Mary's left as Daniel is reinforced by the "stone cut out without hands" of Daniel's prophecy (see p. 224). The intricate linear construction of Mantegna is transformed into a broad handling of masses, disposed, however, with exquisite asymmetrical balances between the circular turban, the circular basin, the rectangular basins, and the architecture, which was perfect until it was suddenly shattered. The broad handling of anatomical forms and drapery is as typical of Bramantino as is the harmony of the colors, which is dominated by his own special sonorous blue in the Virgin's mantle, the rose of her tunic, the red lining of the left-hand Magus's cloak, and the unexpected and magnificent olive-green of the cloak of the youngest Magus. In spite of the Leonardo followers, Bramantino was able to achieve his personal version of the High Renaissance style.

Dosso Dossi

The occasional elements from Giorgione in Lotto's style become so prevalent in certain north Italian centers as to constitute a real Giorgionism, depending for its effect on a combination of figures at ease in a romantic landscape. There were scores of practitioners of the Giorgionesque manner on the mainland, and many achieved a high level of poetic charm. The prolific Ferrarese School fell under the Giorgionesque spell. The Dossi brothers, especially Dosso Dossi (Giovanni de Lutero; c. 1490–1542), who came originally from Trento, dominated the school, which was now freed from the tensions of the Quattrocento Ferrarese masters (see pp. 424–28) but not from their artificiality.

Dosso's *Melissa* (colorplate 123, p. 612) represents the benign character in Ariosto's *Orlando Furioso* who frees humans that have been turned into animals or plants by the sorceress Alcina. Melissa burns Alcina's seals, erases her spells, and we watch as two men begin to emerge from the trunks of trees. Men-at-arms, presumably just liberated, relax in the background, while a very convincing dog (in whom surely lurks a person) gazes longingly at the suit of armor he will soon be allowed to resume. Dosso tames the hostile nature of Giorgione; his trees are an array of standardized landscape elements that provide a perfect setting for this magical scene. There is an echo of early Titian in Melissa's facial type and proportions, and the rather wooden drawing characteristic of the Ferrarese painters is enriched by Titianesque glazes. The glow of the crimson-and-gold brocade of Melissa's fringed robe is alluring against the gold-and-green sparkle of trees and meadows.

Savoldo and Moretto

In Venetian territory since 1426, the Lombard city of Brescia had been subject to influences from Leonardesque Milan and Bellinesque Venice. Nonetheless its painters generally maintained a tradition of sober everyday realism that is often considered characteristic of Lombardy as a whole. The Brescian Girolamo Savoldo (c. 1480–after 1548) was working in Florence in 1508, where he absorbed something from the Florentine anatomical and draftsmanly tradition, but in 1520 he settled in Venice and is often included among the Venetian School. Of the same generation as Giorgione and Lotto, Savoldo generally uses figure and landscape arrangements from the Giorgionesque tradition. His deep coloristic resonance emanates from glazes similar to those of the younger Paris Bordone, but his poetry is deeper and more intense, possibly because it is firmly based in fact. The two figures in *Tobias and the Angel* (colorplate 124, p. 613) were painted from models posed

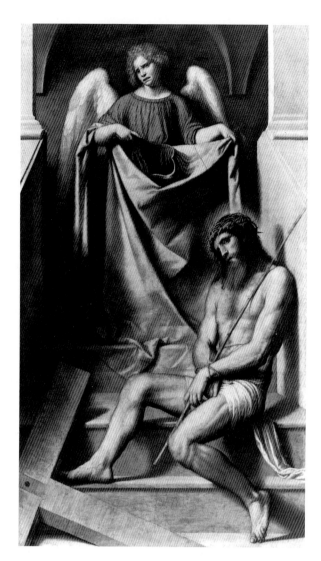

642. Moretto. *Ecce Homo with Angel*. c. 1550–54. Canvas, 84¼ x 49¼". Pinacoteca Tosio Martinengo, Brescia

in a strong crosslight. It is not hard to imagine Savoldo picking up wings for the Archangel at the poultry market, and the fish—the oil from whose liver will restore the sight of Tobias's father—looks fresh. The colors are lovely and the picture is irresistible, perhaps because of our pleasure at seeing miracles achieved by figures who seem as if they are a natural part of everyday life.

Alessandro Bonvicino, called Moretto (1498–1544), is a sturdy realist who grew to maturity in Brescia during Savoldo's absence and came to dominate the local scene. Like Savoldo, he began under the spell of Giorgione, but Moretto's dogged devotion to fact soon took over, even in the realization of religious visions. His figures and facial types are derived from Venice, but Moretto's sobriety inclined him to a dry, carefully modeled, often grayish surface in broad and uniform light rather than the broad range of Venetian colorism, *chiaroscuro*, and brushwork.

Moretto's realism is evident in the *Ecce Homo with Angel* (fig. 642), which is not the customary representation of the tormented Jesus in his mock royal robe, crowned with thorns, sceptered with a reed, and displayed by Pilate to the people of Jerusalem. Deriving from the relief sculptures on the doors of Venetian tabernacles where the consecrated Host was reserved, the painting, doubtless an altarpiece, shows Christ presented to us by a grieving angel who holds the seamless garment woven by Mary that is perpetuated in the chasuble worn by the priest at Mass. Modeled with a combination of Michelangelesque grandeur and earthy literalism, Christ, a burly carpenter with hairy legs and chest, sits across a step in a narrow staircase leading to a transverse corridor above the carefully morticed, pegged, and planed cross. We are reminded, with all the forcefulness and reliance on fact recommended by the *Spiritual Exercises* of St. Ignatius Loyola, of Christ's physical torture and mental humiliation. Through the position of Christ across the steps, the stairway to Pilate's palace becomes the stairway to Heaven ("No man cometh unto the Father, but by me"; John 14:6). And thus the literalism of Moretto's art is raised to the level of spirituality. In contemplating such works as this, the appearance of Caravaggio toward the end of the century, scarcely thirty miles from Brescia, seems somewhat less surprising.

SOFONISBA ANGUISSOLA

During the Middle Ages women played a considerable role in the art of manuscript illumination, much of which was done in convents. Although lists of women illuminators are preserved, no surviving Italian manuscript can be specifically connected with a female artist. But when panel and fresco painting began to flourish on the Italian peninsula, the secular *bottega* within which these works were created became part of the strictly controlled world of male activity. The exclusionary nature of the guilds meant that women were prevented from practicing in the crafts and professions. The growing necessity of study from the nude as Renaissance art developed reinforced the exclusion of women. But with the transformation of painting from a Mechanical to a Liberal Art in the course of the Cinquecento, women artists began to emerge. At first they were considered something between a freak and a miracle, but soon success won them respect in their own right. Most were their father's assistants; in fact, the only successful woman painter not trained at home was Sofonisba Anguissola (1528–1625).

She was born to a learned gentleman in Cremona called Amilcare, who named his only son Asdrubale. (Hamilcar and Hasdrubal were brothers of Hannibal, leader of the Carthaginians against Rome.) Sophonisba was named after the queen of ancient Tyre, and three of her five sisters were named Minerva, Europa, and Elena (after Helen of Troy). Amilcare brought two of his daughters to study the art of painting with Bernardino Campi, youngest of a dynasty of competent painters who controlled artistic life in Cremona, then part of the Spanish-ruled duchy of Milan. Since Amilcare never traveled, it is unlikely that the young women had any

other artistic contacts, and under such circumstances the inventiveness and originality of Sofonisba are even more impressive. The sisters were also taught musical performance, languages, and literature, but Amilcare's concern with painting may not have been limited to its cachet as a cultural pursuit. He complained to Michelangelo of the difficulty of supporting six daughters in their appropriate station in life. Sofonisba's career is slowly being reconstructed, but at the present moment we know of only four nonportraits, including two Holy Families and a Pietà, by her. Many of her portraits appear to have been commissioned, and they must have provided a welcome addition to the family income. They deserve a high rank in the history of Italian portraiture for their directness, penetration of character, and pictorial skill.

The Campi are today studied mainly by specialists, but Sofonisba Anguissola has become a hero for those who are reexamining the role of women in art. Amilcare wrote to Michelangelo in 1557 in an attempt to establish Sofonisba's professional position on the highest authority. He even offered to have her "color in oil" a drawing by the master, if he would so favor her. Amilcare apparently knew that in his last years Michelangelo made a practice of giving drawings to others to paint from, and judging from Amilcare's next letter, Michelangelo complied. Neither the drawing, the painting, nor Michelangelo's response to Sofonisba's work is preserved, but the reply must have been complimentary, as Amilcare thanked him profusely.

Sofonisba Anguissola is acknowledged to have invented a new type of group portraiture in which the sitters are not merely aligned and accompanied by conventional props, as was customary, but shown in lively activity. An impressive example is the *Portrait of the Artist's Three Sisters with Their Governess* (colorplate 125, p. 614). Sensitive to the interplay of intimacy and rivalry in a large household, Sofonisba has concentrated on a single moment during a game of chess—a recognized intellectual pastime. An older sister has made her move and turns for admiration to the artist and to us. The next oldest, planning a coup, searches her sister's unsuspecting face and raises her right hand for the devastating move. The youngest sister sees what is coming and laughs, while a gentle governess looks on. All this takes place without breaking the format of a half-length group portrait.

Apparently Bernardino Campi was able to substitute for life drawing from the nude some other form of anatomical study, probably from mid-sixteenth-century anatomical drawings and engravings, for in Anguissola's painting the masses of the figures are convincing and correct, and everything that propriety allows to emerge from the armor plate of sixteenth-century Spanish costume is exquisitely constructed. Anguissola's delicate brushwork delineates every nuance of the faces and detail of the fabrics. Her subdued coloring is relieved by the soft rose of the older sister's sleeve and by the blue and silver of the north Italian landscape of distant lake and castle and still more distant mountain ranges.

In 1558 Anguissola went on a voyage to Sicily, and the next year she was appointed lady-in-waiting to the queen of Spain, to whose territories both Cremona and Sicily belonged. She seems to have painted little for the next sixty years or so. Perhaps in conservative Spain painting was not considered an appropriate activity for a gentlewoman. She eventually returned to Sicily, and in Palermo in 1623 this renowned Renaissance painter, mentioned by Vasari, sat for a portrait to the Baroque master Anthony van Dyck. Sofonisba Anguissola died in Palermo in 1625 at the age of ninety-seven, the second oldest Italian artist on record, and the first internationally recognized woman artist of whom we have any certain knowledge.

TINTORETTO

In the middle and late Cinquecento, Tintoretto and Veronese disputed the leadership of the Venetian School with Titian. The older and more dramatic of these younger artists is Jacopo Robusti (1518–94), called Tintoretto after his father's trade as a dyer. Tintoretto's long life takes us, in a sense, beyond the Renaissance, yet not into the Baroque, whose earliest masters preferred to emulate others. Fruitless attempts have been made to identify Tintoretto's teacher, a matter perhaps of slight importance considering the originality of his style from the beginning of his career to its end. But Carlo Ridolfi, who wrote about Tintoretto in the seventeenth century and had access to local traditions, records that he worked in the studio of Titian until the great man saw one of the boy's drawings, inquired who did it, and ejected him from his house. To the end of his days, however, Tintoretto had an unrequited admiration for the master, whom he considered his true teacher. Titian's contrary opinion of Tintoretto may have arisen partly from fear, for, as we shall see, this daring young man offered formidable competition to all artists desiring public commissions. But more likely his distaste is attributable to fundamental incompatibilities of personality, stylistic aims, and methods. The careful craftsman, with his endless succession of glazes and his distrust of his own unfinished paintings, may well have been offended by Tintoretto's impetuosity.

We are told that in 1564, when the artists competing for the commission of a ceiling painting in the Scuola di San Rocco in Venice arrived with their scale models, according to instructions, they were outraged to find that during the night Tintoretto had installed his full-sized, completed painting on the ceiling. This and other infractions of union rules aroused hostility from the artists and also from conservative elements of the Venetian citizenry. Nevertheless, Tintoretto's strategy worked, and he obtained many commissions that he executed at hitherto unimagined speed. This speed also made enemies for him, but it is an essential aspect of his style. Tintoretto's art is one of rapid action and passionate emotion, and it is supported by the velocity of his execution.

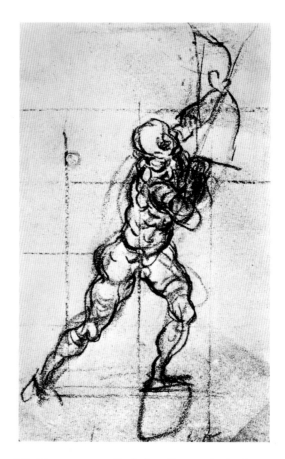

643. TINTORETTO. *Study for a Bowman in the Capture of Zara.* Before 1585. Black chalk, 14 3/8 x 8 5/8". Gabinetto del Disegni e Stampe, Uffizi, Florence

This was attainable first by shorthand drawing methods. A story is told about two Flemish masters, the scrupulous realism of whose detailed and polished drawings astonished the Venetian public. Tintoretto's response was to pick up a piece of unsharpened charcoal and in a matter of minutes, with a few rough, hooklike strokes, knock an action figure into abundant and astonishing life, whereupon he commented, "We poor Venetians can only draw like this." Tintoretto's preserved drawings (fig. 643) are almost exclusively in this hasty style, yet he considered them accurate enough to serve for his pictorial compositions. Although, according to Ridolfi, an inscription on the wall of Tintoretto's studio proudly proclaimed "the Color of Titian and the Drawing of Michelangelo," suggesting that his art was a combination of these two forces, we never encounter detailed Tintoretto life studies in Michelangelo's manner.

Tintoretto apparently had little patience with the drawn-out methods of Titian. He must have felt an overpowering urge to cover vast areas of canvas with rapidity. Financial rewards, incidentally, seem to have had little to do with this desire, as he often underbid his competitors and is reported to have painted certain works for the cost of the materials alone. In order to speed up his production, Tintoretto primed his canvases with dark tones—gray-green, brown, or slate-gray—and some-times even divided the priming into different color areas to correspond to the tonal divisions of the finished painting. Figures from the sketches were then outlined on the priming, which served as the basic tone for the shadows. Once the lights were painted in with bright colors, creating an effect rather like drawing on a black-board with colored chalks, the picture was virtually complete and needed only a few tonal refinements in crucial areas. As a result, the underlying darks dominate Tintoretto's pictures, which often look as if the action were taking place in the middle of a thunderstorm, illu-minated by sudden flashes of lightning. Unfortunately, in many canvases the dark underpainting has begun to show through, dimming the overlying colors.

A further increase in the speed of execution was af-forded by Tintoretto's use of the wide, square-ended brush introduced by Titian, but Tintoretto's strokes were so wide that the nineteenth-century critic John Ruskin accused him of painting with a broom. Today the vigor of Tintoretto's brushwork is a source of enjoy-ment, but there is evidence that in the late 1540s, when he introduced his new style at full intensity, his tech-nique was considered by some of his contemporaries to be an indication of deplorably hasty execution.

In order to draw and paint not only with rapidity but with conviction, Tintoretto prearranged his composi-tions by posing little wax figures in wooden box-stages, sometimes even hanging them from wires and turning them at angles to the foreground plane to study the striking foreshortenings that play so important a role in his dramatic technique. He even moved little lamps about to achieve vivid *chiaroscuro* contrasts. By means of a grid of horizontal and vertical threads or wires across the stage—like the veil invented by Alberti that became standard in sixteenth-century "drawing machines"— Tintoretto could record his composition on squared paper in a relatively short time, and, using another grid, his pupils could enlarge it on the dark-primed canvas in a matter of hours, ready for the master to paint in the lighted areas. A high rank in the brigade of pupils was occupied by the painter's daughter. Although no certain pictures by her are known, it is probable that many square yards of her father's canvases, including important figures, were painted by Marietta Robusti.

Tintoretto's own life, insofar as we can reconstruct it from the meager documentary evidence, was quiet. He left Venice just once, to supervise the installation of a cycle of canvases in Mantua, and then only on the con-dition that his wife accompany him. He seems to have lived the simple existence of a successful craftsman, pros-perous enough, but without the aristocratic and literary acquaintances that enlivened the household of the prince-ly Titian. He is thought to have been a pious, even mys-tical, Christian. It might be said that he lived not only for but in his paintings, and that their fiery brushwork, rushing movement, hurtling bodies, and expressive faces provide witness to the pilgrimage of a poetic soul.

If Tintoretto had died at an early age, like Masaccio, he would have remained a charming art-historical cu-riosity. His first serious threat to the Titianesque estab-lishment was his *St. Mark Freeing a Christian Slave*, painted for the Scuola Grande di San Marco (colorplate 126, p. 615). According to legend, the slave of a knight of Provence left without permission to go to Alexandria to venerate the relics of St. Mark. On his return, his master decided to punish him by having his eyes gouged out and his legs broken with hammers, but St. Mark himself came down from Heaven to liberate the slave. At the right the knight is about to fall off his throne with surprise, while on the ground the foreshortened figure of the slave is surrounded by broken ropes and smashed hardware. A wave of astonished servants, exe-cutioners, and bystanders, at once moving away and looking backward and down, flank the saint. At the top St. Mark zooms downward into the picture. In combi-nation with the turbaned servant lifting a broken ham-mer, St. Mark forms a kind of pinwheel composition in depth; this twisted, turning vortex appears in many of Tintoretto's paintings as the inner form of his cyclonic compositions.

In *St. Mark Freeing a Christian Slave*, the colors blaze against the dark, and the brushwork of the drapery, glit-tering armor, sparkling curls, and faces throbbing with emotion is fresh and vital. Restoration has revealed that it was originally intended as a ceiling painting in a roughly octagonal shape, and that the artist arranged di-agonal figures to run parallel with, or at right angles to, the corners cut off by the frame.

When the picture was unveiled in 1548, the adverse criticism, emanating largely from the studio of Titian (in spite of the support given Tintoretto by Pietro Aretino), caused the artist to take his picture back. For several years he kept it in his studio, but eventually he returned it to the scuola, and in 1562 the wealthy guardian of the scuola, Tommaso Rangone of Ravenna, offered to pay for three more pictures to continue the narration of the Legend of St. Mark. One of the three represents the *Transport of the Body of St. Mark* (fig. 644). Captured by the pagans, the saint was dragged by a halter around his neck through the streets of Alexandria for two days until he died. As the pagans were about to burn his body, a great storm broke, they fled, and the Christians were able to carry the body reverently to burial.

Tintoretto has set the scene in a long paved square not unlike the Piazza San Marco in Venice. The orthog-onals formed by the paving stones and the arcades re-cede rapidly into the distance, while the little band of devoted Christians, about to load the body onto a camel, emerge toward us at the right. The resultant ten-sion in depth, appearing here for the first time in Tin-toretto's art, became a standard compositional device in his mature and late works, as frequent as the pinwheel and often combined with it. The perspective is accurate enough as far as the orthogonals go, but the arches, pos-sibly painted by pupils, do not coordinate with the rest

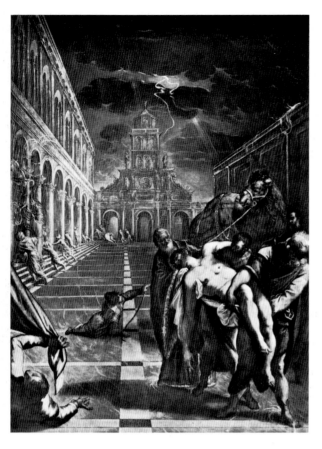

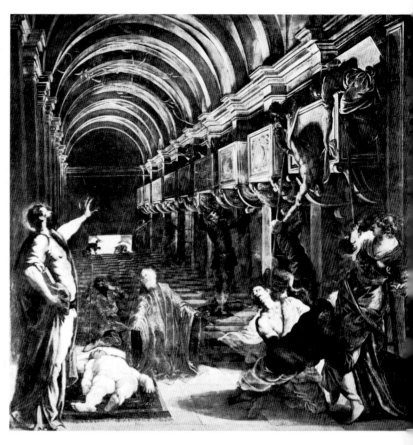

644. TINTORETTO. *Transport of the Body of St. Mark*. 1562–66. Canvas, 13' 10" x 10'. Accademia, Venice. Commissioned by Tommaso Rangone for the Scuola Grande di S. Marco

645. TINTORETTO. *Discovery of the Body of St. Mark*. 1562–66. Canvas, 13' 1 1/2" square. Brera Gallery, Milan. Commissioned by Tommaso Rangone for the Scuola Grande di S. Marco

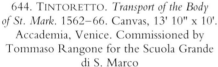

of the setting. This is the kind of detail that Tintoretto allowed to pass and that must have infuriated other artists. But his foreshortening of the figures, the rapidity of their action, and the rush of the pagans for shelter under the arcade show all the power of Tintoretto's hand. Such effects could not have been attained by conventional methods: perhaps if Tintoretto had tried to paint them slowly, he would have stifled the volcanic activity that is the wellspring of his art. And if the lightning is a trifle stagy (Giorgione did it better), the rush of water across the stones of the piazza is a sight all too familiar to contemporary as well as Cinquecento Venetians and very convincing. Rangone, in the gown of a Venetian patrician, is shown gently supporting the head of the saint on his chest, while Tintoretto has painted his own bearded features just to the right of the camel's hairy neck.

The third canvas from the series (fig. 645) is equally dramatic. Centuries have passed, and a group of Venetians has come to Alexandria to rescue the saint's body from the Saracens. As they search the crypt of the cathedral, taking bodies down from sarcophagi and opening up a trap door in the floor (with a wonderful light effect), St. Mark emerges, shows them his true body, and puts a stop to the despoiling of the tombs. Again the

power of the composition is achieved by the tension between the succession of arches moving rapidly inward in perspective (correct, this time), and the figures moving out at the right. An added element is the placing of the hand of the saint at the vanishing point of the perspective, bringing its motion to a sudden halt, as he arrests also the well-meaning sacrilege of the Venetians. As is generally the case with Tintoretto, the architecture is thinly painted, so that large areas of dark priming are not even covered, while the occasional passages of careful modeling are reserved for the most important figures. Again Rangone appears just to the left of center, kneeling in reverence as he contemplates the body of Venice's patron saint.

The crowning achievement of Tintoretto's life is the cycle of paintings—fifty-odd pictures, large and small—for the Scuola di San Rocco and its neighboring church. The three principal scuola rooms are filled with Tintoretto paintings carried out in several stages: the Sala dell'Albergo in 1564–67, the ceiling of the Sala Grande in 1575–77 and the walls in 1577–81, and the wall paintings in the ground-floor room in 1583–87. The *Crucifixion* in the Sala dell'Albergo (colorplate 127, p. 616) reaches a new peak of religious feeling. Approximately forty feet in length, the painting presents a

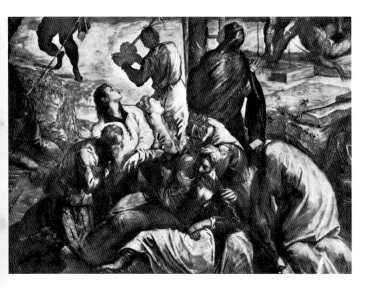

646. TINTORETTO. Virgin, St. Joseph of Arimathea, and others, detail of *Crucifixion* (see colorplate 127, p. 616). 1565. Canvas. Scuola di S. Rocco, Venice. Commissioned by the Brotherhood of S. Rocco

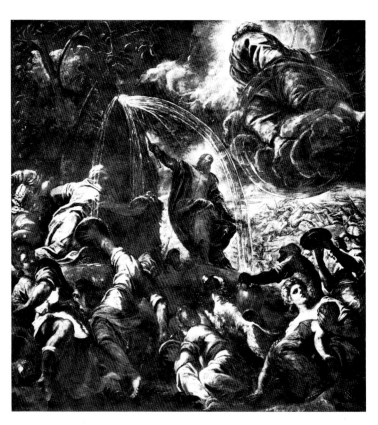

647. TINTORETTO. *Moses Striking Water from the Rock.* 1575–77. Canvas, 18' 2¹/₂" x 17' 2³/₄". Ceiling of Sala Grande, Scuola di S. Rocco, Venice. Commissioned by the Brotherhood of S. Rocco

panorama of Golgotha populated by an immense crowd of soldiers, executioners, horsemen, and apostles. The scene is divided by the cross, whose bar almost reaches the frame; the top is cut off, the titulus is barely visible, and the shadowed head of Christ leans down almost as if from Heaven. At the left the cross of the penitent thief is being partly lifted, partly tugged into place by ropes; at the right the impenitent thief is about to be tied to his cross. A soldier on a ladder behind Christ reaches down to take the reed with the sponge soaked in vinegar from another soldier on the ground.

At the left the diagonals of the ropes continue the direction of the rays emanating from the glory of light around the head of Christ. The axis of the ladder on the ground is prolonged by the upward glance of St. John the Evangelist and the reed. On the other side, occupied by the impenitent thief, these lines are absent, but their function is fulfilled by the gaze of the bearded figure on horseback (not the Roman centurion, who must be the rider in armor at the extreme left). The radial principles of the composition correspond to Christ's prophecy of his death: "And I, if I be lifted up from the earth, will draw all men to me. This he said, signifying what death he should die" (John 12:32–33). The tumult of the crowd, the grief of the apostles, and the yearning of the penitent thief seem to come to a focus in the head of Christ.

Due to Tintoretto's light-on-dark technique, his figures sometimes have a tendency to look a bit ghostly, especially in marginal areas and backgrounds, but the foreground figures in the *Crucifixion* (fig. 646), grouped in a massive pyramid at the base of the cross, are modeled with plastic force in bold planes of light and dark and defined by vigorous contours. Here, as throughout his work, Tintoretto's expressive sensitivity is abundantly

visible, and especially in the head of the aged Joseph of Arimathea, who, holding his hands crossed on his breast, looks downward with intense sympathy at the Virgin swooning under the cross. The little group, huddled as if for protection against the massive hostility of the surrounding crowds, forms the base of the composition.

For the Sala Grande on the upper story, Tintoretto's theological advisers developed a scheme relating Old and New Testament subjects to each other and to the scuola's charitable purposes. Although each scene, like those of Michelangelo on the Sistine Ceiling, is best viewed as a component element in a vast iconographic and formal totality, they also function as individual images. Because *Moses Striking Water from the Rock* (fig. 647) is a ceiling painting, the reproduction should be held overhead to appreciate Tintoretto's purpose and method. We look up along the diagonals of the square, past a series of drastically foreshortened, rapidly moving figures holding bowls and jars, to the miracle on which all the figures converge—water pouring in clear arcs of light at the touch of Moses' rod. The illusion suggests that the water would fall on our heads were it not for the intervening receptacles. At the upper right corner, God the Father floats into the picture, partly enclosed in a circle of light that is intended to symbolize the circles of Heaven. The composition is largely built on the opposition of the arcs, the heavenly circle, and the smaller circles of the

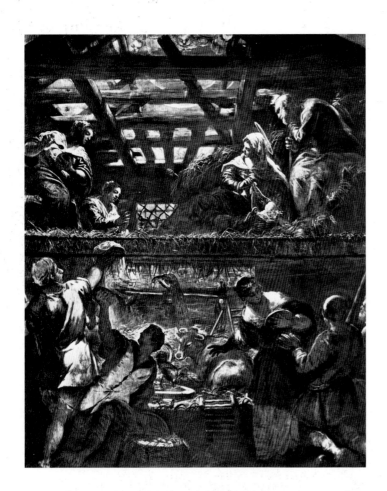

bowls to the tumultuous movement of the active figures.

In the scenes of the Sala Grande, Tintoretto's light-on-dark technique imparts a shadowy and diaphanous appearance to the figures, even when he devoted some modeling to an occasional important face or limb. The light areas surrounding silhouetted dark heads often seem more solid than the heads themselves. Generally, the principal figures are lifted to an upper level. In the *Nativity* (fig. 648), the adoring shepherds, a woman, and some animals are below, while the Holy Family and two more women huddle in the hayloft above, illuminated by the light coming through the rafters and the ruined roof. Here, as in other San Rocco compositions, figural diagonals complement and continue those established for the space as a whole by the perspective orthogonals.

In the *Temptation of Christ* (fig. 649), Christ has taken refuge in a ruined shed on a rocky eminence while a beautiful Satan holds out stones, tempting him to change them into bread. The *Last Supper* (fig. 650) is

648, 649, 650. TINTORETTO. *Nativity* (left), *Temptation of Christ* (below left), *Last Supper* (below right). 1577–81. Canvas, height of each 17' 9". 🏛 Walls of Sala Grande, Scuola di S. Rocco, Venice. Commissioned by the Brotherhood of S. Rocco

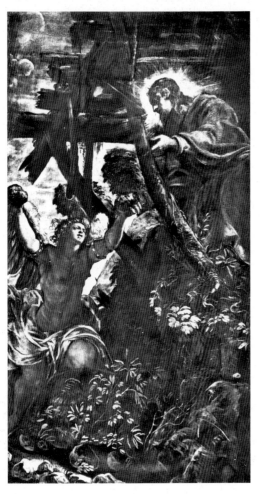

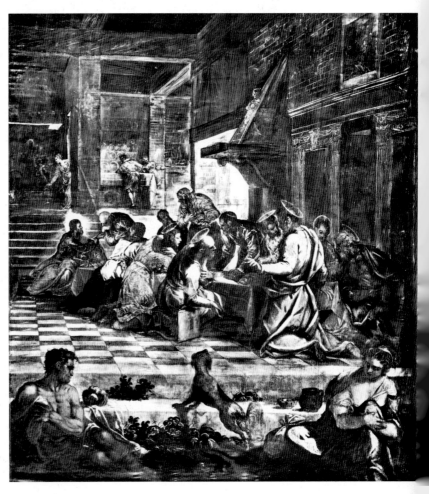

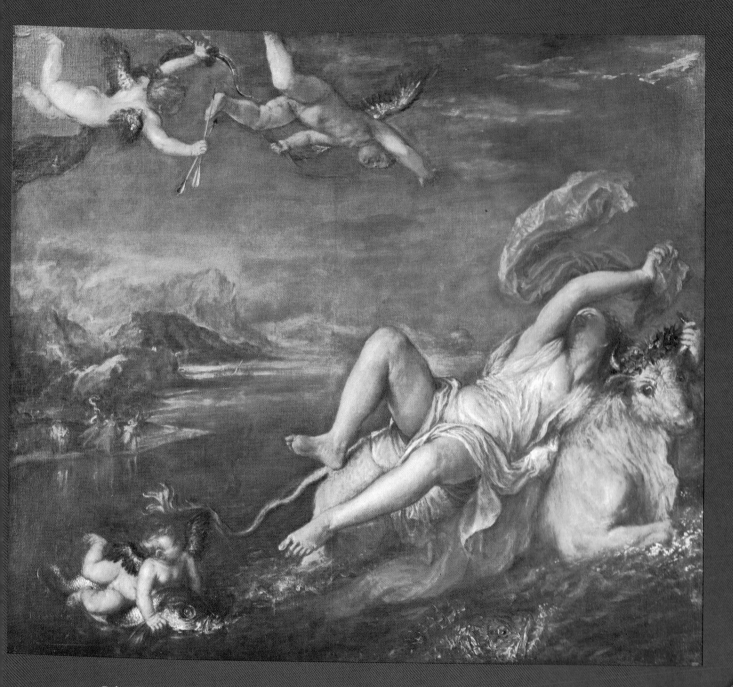

Colorplate 120. TITIAN. *Rape of Europa*. 1559–62. Canvas, 73 x 81". Isabella Stewart Gardner Museum, Boston. Commissioned by Philip II of Spain

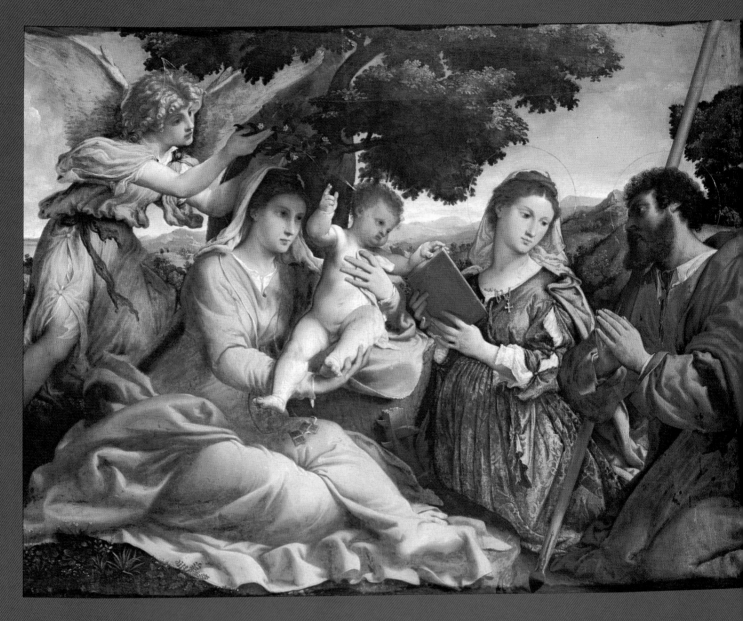

Colorplate 121. LORENZO LOTTO. *Sacra Conversazione*. c. 1520s. Canvas, 44³/4 x 60".
Kunsthistorisches Museum, Vienna

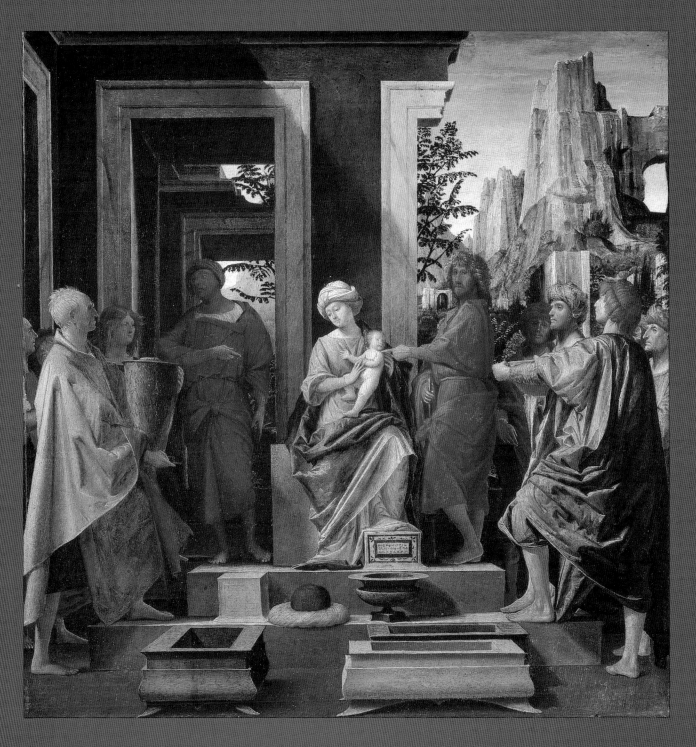

Colorplate 122. BRAMANTINO. *Adoration of the Magi*. c. 1500. Panel,
22³/₈ x 21⁵/₈". National Gallery, London

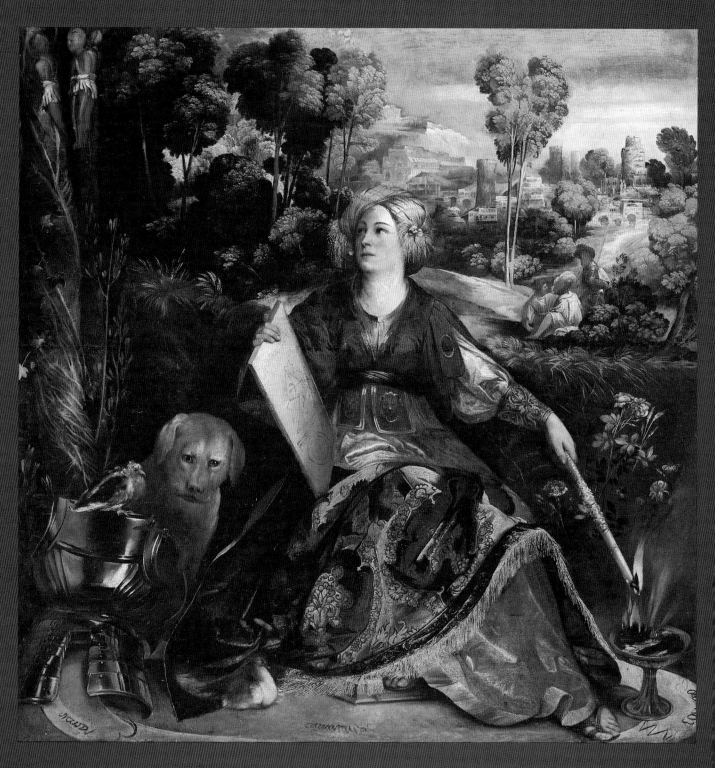

Colorplate 123. DOSSO DOSSI. *Melissa.* 1520s. Canvas, 69¼ x 68½".
Borghese Gallery, Rome

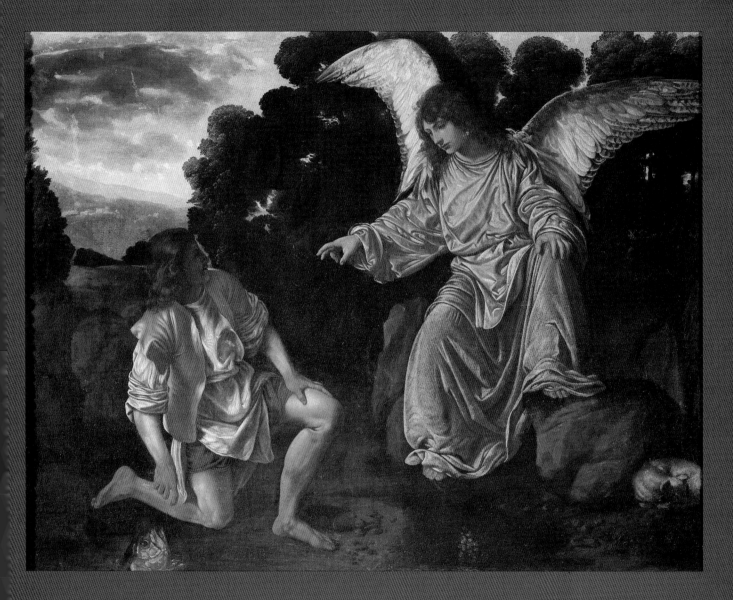

Colorplate 124. GIROLAMO SAVOLDO. *Tobias and the Angel.* Early 1530s. Canvas,
37³/4 x 49¹/2". Borghese Gallery, Rome

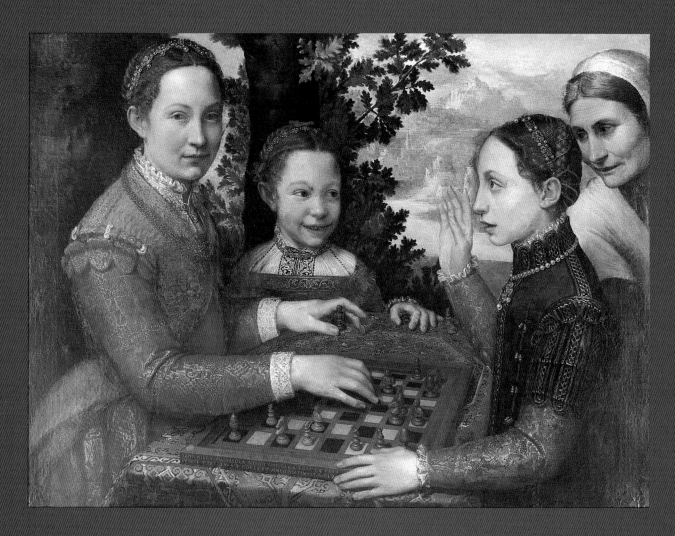

Colorplate 125. SOFONISBA ANGUISSOLA. *Portrait of the Artist's Three Sisters with Their Governess*. 1555.
Oil on canvas, 27⁹⁄₁₆ x 37". Narodowe Museum, Poznan

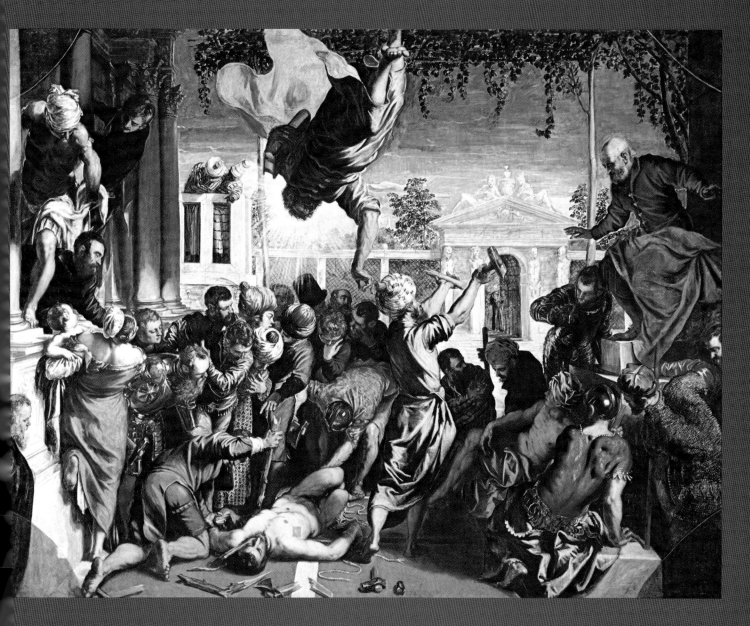

Colorplate 126. TINTORETTO. *St. Mark Freeing a Christian Slave*. 1548. Canvas, 13' 8" x 11' 7". Accademia, Venice.
Commissioned by the head of the Confraternity of S. Marco for the Scuola Grande di S. Marco

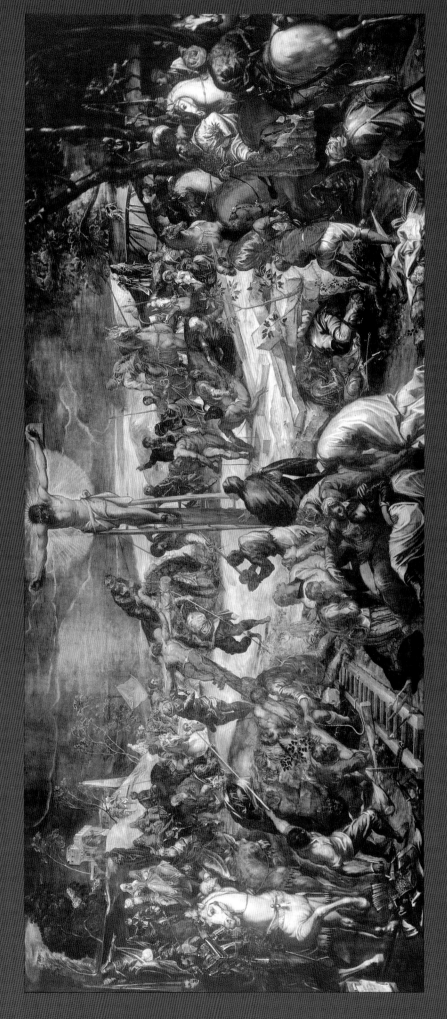

Colorplate 127. TINTORETTO. *Crucifixion*. 1565. Canvas, 17' 7" x 40' 2". ▥ End wall of Sala dell'Albergo, Scuola di S. Rocco, Venice. Commissioned by the Brotherhood of S. Rocco

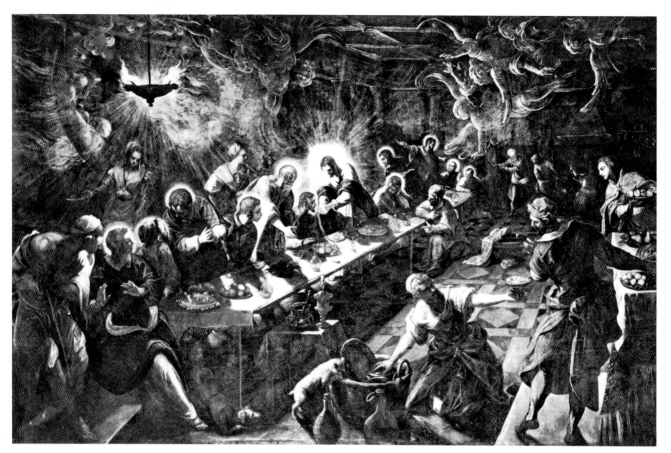

651. TINTORETTO. *Last Supper*. 1592–94. Canvas, 12' x 18' 8". 🏛 S. Giorgio Maggiore, Venice.
Probably commissioned by Michele Alabardi, Prior of S. Giorgio Maggiore

transformed from the announcement of the betrayal seen in Leonardo into the older Byzantine subject of the Institution of the Eucharist. We must look past two servants and a dog in the foreground to where Christ gives the wafer of the Eucharist to St. Peter. Only eleven apostles can be counted; Judas has already left. As in several of Tintoretto's paintings of the Last Supper, the chief figures are deep in the receding perspective construction. At the top of a flight of steps, we look into the kitchen, where food is being prepared and dishes arrayed—a deliberate contrast, as in Pietro Lorenzetti (see fig. 103), of spiritual and material food.

Tintoretto was responsible for several hundred surviving works, as well as for a considerable number that, with paintings by Giovanni Bellini, Titian, and others, perished in a fire that gutted the Doges' Palace in Venice in 1577, and it is impossible to give more than a summary of his style and a suggestion of his vast artistic activity. In his last years material substance and worldly concerns both seem to dissolve before our eyes, and in the darkness of his paintings a transcendent light shines. This is evident in the huge representation of *Paradise* that Tintoretto, his son Domenico, and his assistants created to replace an earlier fresco of this subject in the Hall of the Great Council at the Doges' Palace (colorplate 14, p. 22).

One of Tintoretto's last works, finished in the year of his death, is the *Last Supper* in San Giorgio Maggiore (fig. 651), where its otherworldliness contrasts with the architectural setting by Palladio (see fig. 668). The painting is placed on the side wall to the right of the freestanding high altar, and to understand the dynamism of Tintoretto's composition, you need to hold the illustration on your right so that it is receding away from you. The long table, set on a diagonal in depth, divides the material from the spiritual. To the right of the diagonal, powerfully modeled servants gather up the remains of the feast and stack the dishes in a basket, where they attract the interest of a marauding cat. A dog crunches a bone at the foot of the table. Another servant (distinguished as such by his clothing and his cap, although it has also been suggested that the figure might be Judas) sits on the floor with his elbow on the table, trying to understand what he sees. But behind the table the emphasis is on the light of the spirit. Starting from the heads of the eleven apostles like the corona in a solar eclipse, it bursts in rays from the head of the gentle Christ, who stands to give Communion with both hands to a waiting apostle, streams from the flames of the hanging lamp, and floats in disembodied wisps that assume the shapes of angels—heavenly ministers who contrast with the worldly servants. At the end of his life,

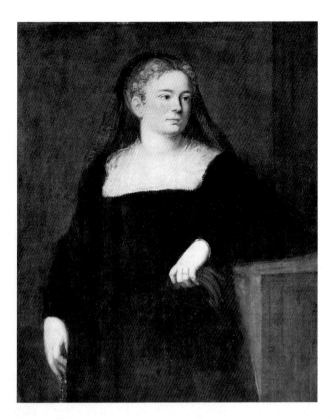

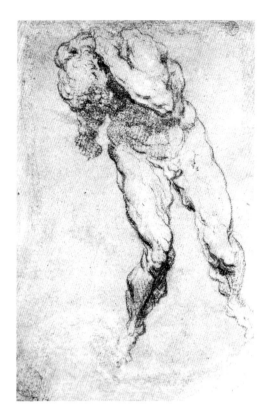

652. TINTORETTO. *Portrait of a Woman in Mourning.*
c. 1550. Canvas, 41 x 34¾". Gemäldegalerie, Dresden

653. TINTORETTO. *Study of Nude after a Statuette
by Michelangelo.* Black and white chalk on blue paper.
Gabinetto del Disegni e Stampe, Uffizi, Florence

Tintoretto's light-on-dark technique, invented to lend speed to his brush, becomes a vehicle for revelation.

We cannot leave Tintoretto without a word about his portraits, of which more than 150 are known. Even if we could imagine this impetuous artist buckling down to a minute transcription of his sitters' features, costumes, and background settings in the Lombard manner, numbers alone would preclude such treatment. The most important sitters have columns, curtains, or appropriate battle scenes as props, but generally there is no accompaniment. Features and costumes are broadly painted with no concern for details of attire, but Tintoretto's pictorial shorthand can suggest that his sitters are capable of deep emotion and decisive action. Perhaps it was this reservoir of latent feeling, often enhanced by the rich coloring of the costumes as a foil for the faces, that made such portraiture attractive to the Venetian patriciate that were Tintoretto's clientele.

In *Portrait of a Woman in Mourning* (fig. 652), he had only deep black to rely on for the costume. Still Tintoretto played the pale face of the sitter and her blond hair and white scarf against the black with resounding effect, heightened by the dramatic pose and powerful side lighting. In consequence, this portrait takes on some of the emotional depth of the master's religious narra-

tives. Tintoretto wants the viewer to share her grief and admire her noble demeanor.

Is Tintoretto, as some say, a Mannerist? If Pontormo, Rosso, Perino del Vaga, Beccafumi, Parmigianino, and Pordenone are Mannerists, then he is not. Tintoretto's style, no matter how feverish, is devoid of the conflicts of the central Italian Mannerists of the 1520s and 1530s. His studies of central Italian art—and he worked long and lovingly to assimilate Michelangelo's style to his own needs from drawings and especially from small models of Michelangelo's figures (fig. 653)—were intended to liberate him from the stereotypes of his youth. The elements he paints are firmly based on visual reality. Insubstantial though his compositions may seem, they are based on rigorous, consistent logic. The violent activity is disciplined and ordered to produce a clear, often mathematically formulated expression of channeled velocity. His figures, however violently they may throb with emotion, are not tormented but deeply, freely expressive. While their bodies move at angles to the picture plane or in alarming trajectories through space, their limbs convey the forces of the composition as a whole. Often surprising, Tintoretto is never bizarre. He speaks in parables, but not in riddles. He aims to express the harmony of physical and spiritual reality, and in this he is a creation of the Renaissance.

PAOLO VERONESE

The second of the aged Titian's competitors, and the last of the Renaissance masters in Venice, was Paolo Caliari (1528–88), called Paolo Veronese because of his birth and training in Verona. He came to Venice in 1553, and for the next thirty-five years delighted the Venetians with his style, which in some ways seems to be diametrically opposed to that of Tintoretto. Veronese, too, painted biblical suppers, but his concern was with the material splendor of the setting and the sumptuous costumes of the actors. In his canvases, contemporary Venice passes before our eyes in a parade of marble palaces and healthy people, dressed in velvets, satins, and brocades, eating, drinking, and making love with a stolid conviction that this was all they were meant to do in this world. In his festivals and pageants, Veronese offers a banquet of delicious hues that are almost always high and clear, dominated by the pale tones of marble columns and by lemon-yellows, light blues, silvery whites, bright orange, and delicate salmon colors. His colors are neither subdued with glazes down to Titian's smoldering embers nor shadowed like the nocturnal visions of Tintoretto. Among sixteenth-century composers, Tintoretto's rhythms, darkness, and religious intensity recall the masses and motets of Palestrina, while Veronese makes us think of the bright brass music of Giovanni Gabrieli.

Looking a little more deeply into Veronese, however, one encounters two surprises. First, as Carlo Ridolfi, writing sixty years after the artist's death, tells us, he was a model of rectitude and piety who brought up his sons according to severe religious and moral principles. Though he "wore expensive clothes and velvet shoes," he lived "far from luxury: was parsimonious in his expenses, whereby he had the money to acquire many farms and to accumulate riches and furnishings." Second—and this is seldom noted—Veronese was as impatient as Tintoretto with Titian's time-consuming methods and, like Tintoretto, invented a shorthand for his pictorial statements.

The principal purpose of Veronese's art was to achieve a kind of intoxication with intense color, not unlike Lorenzo Lotto's earlier experiments. But Veronese went beyond Lotto in the subtlety of the relationship he developed between color areas. Having established the basic masses of his architectural settings, he subdivided the remaining fields into areas. Each area would be covered with a layer of bright underpaint, giving Veronese his ground color and allowing him to see exactly its relationship to the adjoining hue. Once these layers dried, he could rapidly paint in a system of simplified and precalculated lights in a slightly modified version of the same hue or in a contrasting hue to give a hint of iridescence while avoiding shadows. This method enabled Veronese to paint drapery and architecture rapidly, and yet with a seeming accuracy of detail derived from his precise placing of the lights but which vanishes at close

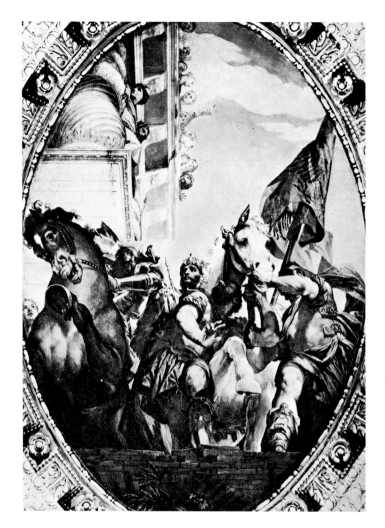

654. VERONESE. *Triumph of Mordecai.* 1556. Canvas, 24 x 18'. 🏛 Ceiling, S. Sebastiano, Venice. Commissioned by Bernardo Torlioni, Prior of S. Sebastiano

range. He maintains, as it were, a threshold of visual observation that keeps the observer standing a certain distance from his canvases and subject always, therefore, to the total decorative effect. By these means, Veronese was able to cover an acreage of canvas not inferior to that painted by Tintoretto, yet without any appearance of haste.

Two years after his arrival in Venice, Veronese began the series of frescoes, altarpiece, ceiling paintings, and organ shutters that transforms the little Church of San Sebastiano into a dazzling display of Venetian painting by a single artist. In the central ceiling oval he painted the *Triumph of Mordecai* (fig. 654), envisioning the biblical scene (Esther 8:15) as if it were happening in a Renaissance city: "And Mordecai went out from the presence of the king in royal apparel of blue and white, and with a great crown of gold, and with a garment of fine linen and purple: and the city . . . rejoiced and was glad." Veronese must already have visited Mantua, where Giulio Romano had built colossal spiral columns mod-

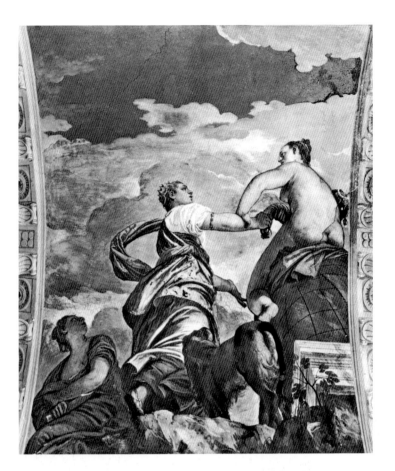

655. VERONESE. *Abundance, Fortitude, and Envy*. c. 1561. Fresco. Ceiling, Villa Barbaro, Maser. Commissioned by Marcantonio and Daniele Barbaro

eled on those thought to be from Solomon's Temple that Raphael had painted in one of his tapestry cartoons for the Sistine Chapel (see fig. 531).

In the same year as Veronese's ceiling, Giulio's colonnade was being extended on three sides to become a courtyard for exhibiting Duke Federigo Gonzaga's special breed of horses. Thus Veronese's ceiling painting of mighty steeds with clashing hooves, below spiral columns and balconies with lords and ladies shown against the blue, was not only a daring bit of *di sotto in sù* illusionism, but also a reference to a project in the latest style. Like Mantegna (see fig. 411), whose murals in Mantua he must have studied in detail, Veronese plays tricks on the spectator: we instinctively duck from the threatening hooves. According to the story, Mordecai will soon fall from power and be executed; by showing the crowned Mordecai and his attendants arriving full tilt at the crumbling brickwork on the edge of an abyss, Veronese seems to be making a reference to the transitory nature of his triumph.

Veronese went to Rome in 1560, but his trip had little effect on the fundamental nature of his style. He was a Veronese and an adopted Venetian before he went, and

he returned not at all Romanized. But he must have made some drawings, and he did adopt an occasional motive that pleased him. It is not hard to imagine that he walked critically through the Farnesina (see figs. 538–48), which may well have impressed him as a bit old-fashioned. In his own utterly different frescoes, which line the walls and vaults in several rooms of the Villa Barbaro at Maser, Veronese not only accommodated his illusionistic designs to Palladio's architecture, but seems to pay tribute to Raphael's *Cupid Pointing Out Psyche to the Three Graces* (see fig. 548) in his ceiling fresco of *Abundance, Fortitude, and Envy* (fig. 655) by adopting the figure seen from the rear and adapting it to a *di sotto in sù* view. Fortitude, with her lion, steadies the cornucopia in the hand of Abundance, and nobody pays any attention to Envy with her ugly knife. The high, silvery clouds recall those of the early Titian.

The largest of all Veronese's scenes of feasting is the *Marriage at Cana* (fig. 656). The huge canvas was painted in 1563 for the refectory of San Giorgio Maggiore, and perhaps Tintoretto's spiritualized *Last Supper* (see fig. 651), painted for the chancel of the same church a generation later, contains an element of reaction to the material splendor of Veronese. The table is laid on an open terrace, with flanking Roman Doric colonnades and a higher terrace at the back, set off by a powerful balustrade beyond which one looks past Corinthian and Composite porticoes to a campanile and cumulus clouds against the sky.

One hardly notices Christ and Mary in the midst of so much architecture, so many brocaded costumes, and all the good things to eat and drink on the table. The guests are well fed gentlemen and ladies who, by the expressions in their eyes—and, at times, the lack of expression—have reached a state of saturation. No one is eating any more, and one somnolent woman is picking her teeth (fig. 657). Some men are interested in the newly created wine, others in the women. The master of the feast directs operations at the left; a black boy hands a glass of wine to a guest and a cat at the right rolls over to scratch a mask on the amphora. The group of musicians in the center (fig. 658) includes portraits of the painter Jacopo Bassano with a viol, Veronese with a viola da braccio, and Titian with a bass viol. If anybody is concerned about the miracle that has just taken place, the spectator would never know it.

Ten years later, another refectory painting landed Veronese in serious trouble (colorplate 128, p. 649). He was brought before the Inquisition and asked to account for the presence of "buffoons, drunkards, dwarfs, Germans, and similar vulgarities" in a trial whose fascinating record is still preserved. With transparent naïveté, Veronese replied that there is a kind of license observed by poets, painters, and madmen, and to this he appealed. He had apparently been commissioned to paint a Last Supper, and the Holy Office presumed this is what they were looking at. Veronese agreed to call the painting the *Feast in the House of Levi*, a subject which would give him

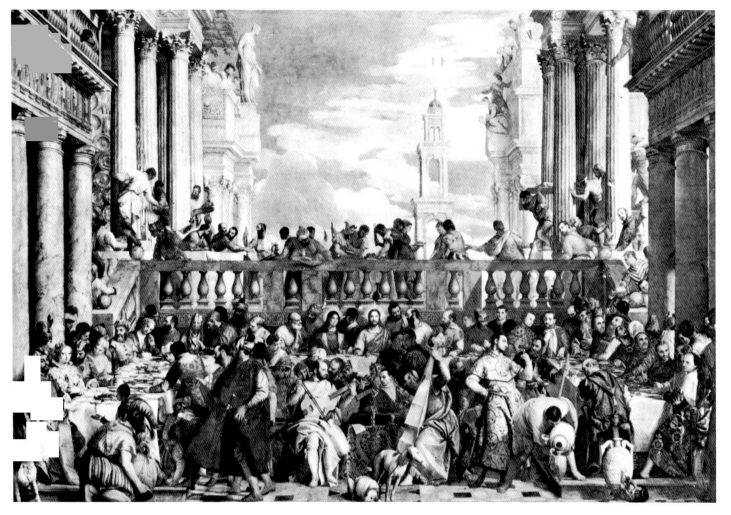

656. VERONESE. *Marriage at Cana.* 1563. Canvas, 21' 10" x 32' 6". The Louvre, Paris. Commissioned for the refectory of the Benedictine Monastery of S. Giorgio Maggiore, Venice

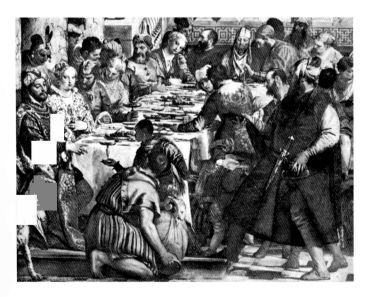

657. Guests, detail of fig. 656

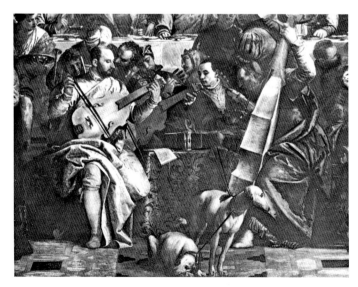

658. Musicians, detail of fig. 656

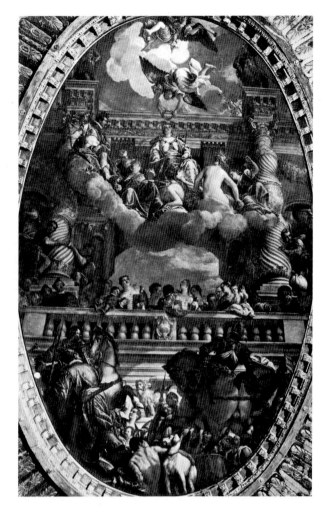

659. VERONESE and pupils. *Triumph of Venice* (see also colorplate 14, p. 22). Probably 1585. Canvas, 29' 8" x 19'. ⚜ Ceiling of Hall of the Great Council, Doges' Palace, Venice. Commissioned by the city government of Venice

uses veined marble for the Corinthian columns of the smaller order and gilds the sculptured Victories in the spandrels. The background architecture is more restrained, allowing the principal role to be played by the loggia, which outweighs the figures at the table. Aside from the usual classical buildings, we are surprised to see a window with Gothic tracery at the right, as if Paolo were introducing a note of historical distance into his ideal classical setting.

Veronese's instinct for composing figures and architecture was as sure as that of Mantegna, the festival aspects of whose art he re-created using Cinquecento pictorial methods and Cinquecento scale. His *Mystical Marriage of St. Catherine* (colorplate 129, p. 650) is such a festival picture, and there is little mysticism about it. The Virgin is seated at the top of three steps, between massive Composite columns seen diagonally, somewhat in the manner of those Titian introduced into his *Madonna of the Pesaro Family* (see fig. 623). The sun warms the columns and the splendid fabrics, as well as the angel heads and the two swooping putti (recalling those in Titian's *Rape of Europa*; see colorplate 120, p. 609), who hold the Virgin's crown and the saint's palm. St. Catherine was, after all, a princess, and Veronese has represented her crowned and dressed in blue-and-white damask. Veronese's juxtaposed hues are at their best in the pair of angels seated at the lower left-hand corner. Instead of paying attention to the divine favor bestowed on St. Catherine, they seem to be arguing over a piece of music and are not quite ready for the festival. Few passages in Venetian painting are more seductive than the white-and-gold brocade, green silk, and heavy orange taffeta of their garments.

Probably in 1585 Veronese and his workshop painted the *Triumph of Venice* (fig. 659; colorplate 14, p. 22) on the ceiling of the Hall of the Great Council in the Doges' Palace. The picture contains many elements seen in his earlier works, such as the prancing steeds and the Solomonic columns that he had introduced at San Sebastiano thirty years earlier, the seated nude from the Farnesina, which he had used at Maser and repeated again and again, and two winged figures lifted from Giulio Romano's ceiling frescoes in the cathedral of Paolo's native Verona, one holding a crown over the head of Venice, the other—clearly Fame—brandishing a trumpet.

Yet the idea of the picture is essentially new. The massive architecture recedes upward with the solemnity of organ music, and clouds carry with it the sceptered Venice, flanked by allegorical figures and enthroned between the towers of the Arsenal, from which Venetian galleys sailed forth to dominate the seas. Tintoretto's late *Last Supper* (see fig. 651) takes us into a world of personal mysticism that offers no exit for the forces of history; Veronese's composition leads to the Baroque, and specifically to the ceiling decorators of the seventeenth century, who studied its principles and experimented with the implications of its daring flight.

the freedom to leave in the offending figures, including a soldier getting drunk on the stairs at the right.

To clarify this new meaning, Paolo inscribed "LUCAE CAP. V" on the balustrade, which includes this passage: "And Levi made him a great feast in his own house: and there was a great company of publicans and of others that sat down with them. But their scribes and Pharisees murmured against his disciples, saying, Why do ye eat and drink with publicans and sinners? And Jesus answering said unto them, They that are whole need not a physician; but they that are sick" (Luke 5:29–31). Christ sits in the center, chatting with the publicans and their attendants, who combine to weave a changing fabric of rose, yellow, blue, green, and silver against the pale stone and the blue of the sky with its sultry clouds.

Veronese's architectural setting is reminiscent of the opulent version of classical architecture developed by Jacopo Sansovino (see colorplate 130, p. 651). Veronese

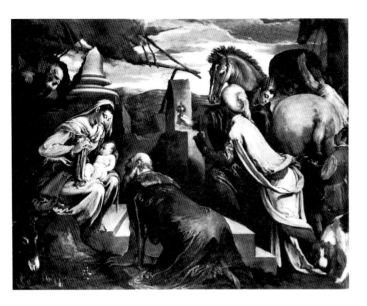

660. JACOPO BASSANO. *Adoration of the Magi.* c. 1563–64.
Canvas, 37 x 46". Kunsthistorisches Museum, Vienna

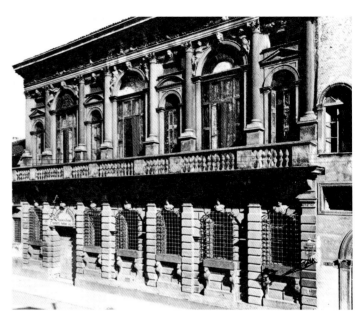

661. MICHELE SANMICHELI. Palazzo Bevilacqua,
Verona. c. 1532–33

JACOPO BASSANO

No one familiar with Bassano's youthful work, which is
at best a dull reflection of the style of Bonifazio de'
Pitati, a Veronese master who influenced him at the
start, could predict the sophistication of his mature art.
Jacopo dal Ponte, called Bassano (c. 1517/18–92), belonged to the second generation of a dynasty of painters
that would later include his four sons. Jacopo's best work
was achieved by close observation and careful study. After escaping from the limited possibilities of picturesque
Bassano, on the banks of the Brenta and in the shadow
of Monte Grappa, he seems to have fallen under the influence of the Florentine Francesco Salviati, who visited
Venice in 1536 and must have acquainted Jacopo with
some of the inventions of the central Italian *maniera*.

Although of unequal quality, Bassano's work can be
dazzling in its unexpected combination of rustic naturalism with a daring freshness of invention and color.
The dogs, horses, and donkey of the *Adoration of the
Magi* (fig. 660) are astonishingly alive, while the elegantly attenuated Virgin and Magi radiate the princely
splendor of the Venetian society Bassano painted for, as
well as something of the artificiality of the *maniera*.
Coloristically, the picture is dominated by the resonant
green of the mantles of the kneeling and the youngest
Magi and the dissonant pink of the Virgin's tunic,
which is repeated in the mantle of the turbaned Magus.
The long lines of the torsos and their silky drapery form
a web of shuttling shapes that are ultimately released in
the blue hills of the background. Unfortunately, the formal and compositional inventions of Jacopo Bassano became quickly standardized in the work of his sons and
even in his own.

MICHELE SANMICHELI

Bramante's rich classical tradition had been continued
throughout the cities of northern Italy by a host of talented architects, but the Roman version of the High
Renaissance style was imported to the north only by
masters who had experienced the new grand manner in
full operation in the Rome of Julius II and Leo X. One
of these was Michele Sanmicheli (1484–1559), an architect from Verona who worked from 1509 to 1521 at the
Cathedral of Orvieto and who, in 1526, collaborated
with Antonio da Sangallo the Younger in a survey of
papal fortifications. On his return to Verona, after the
Sack of Rome in 1527, Sanmicheli began constructing
fortifications, ornamented with splendid Renaissance
gates, and Renaissance places and churches that transformed this Gothic city into one of the richest centers
of Renaissance architecture in northern Italy, to be
ranked only after Venice itself (where Sanmicheli later
built two palazzi on the Grand Canal) and the Vicenza
of Palladio. While based on the general principles of
Bramante's Palazzo Caprini (see fig. 509), with a rusticated lower story and a columned *piano nobile*, such
Sanmicheli palaces as the Palazzo Bevilacqua (fig. 661)
are strikingly original and often reflect aspects of the
Roman monuments still standing in Verona.

As in the Roman palaces by Giulio Romano and
other followers of Raphael that Sanmicheli studied, the
ground floor pilasters of the Palazzo Bevilacqua are rusticated, but now they are so encased in heavy blocks that
only the capitals can escape. The three huge, arched
windows of the *piano nobile* alternate with a complex
arrangement of smaller arched windows that are surmounted by pediments and rectangular attic windows.

This combination of interlocked architectural motifs contrasts with sculpted figures, heads, and garlands across the top of the structure. While four of the eight columns are fluted normally, the other four have spiral fluting—a device derived from Late Roman architecture, but unusual in the Renaissance. Two run clockwise, two counterclockwise, and they are arranged so that every pair of columns is made up of incompatible members. Coupled with the rich ornamentation of the frieze, the effect is one of disturbing complexity.

JACOPO SANSOVINO

It is a curious and perhaps significant fact that although the Grand Canal in Venice is, by virtue of its succession of palaces, one of the most beautiful thoroughfares in the world, not one of its Renaissance palaces was built by an architect born in Venice. The tradition began with Early Renaissance palaces, which are largely by such Lombard architects as the Lombardo family and Mauro Codussi, but not until well into the Cinquecento did the masterpieces of Venetian palace architecture begin to appear. Their style, which was definitive for the subsequent history of Venetian architecture, was the invention of a Florentine, Jacopo Tatti (1486–1570), who was called Sansovino after his master, Andrea Sansovino. He was known chiefly as a sculptor before he came to Venice, and had he remained one, it is doubtful that Jacopo would have commanded our attention, in spite of the charm of such works as the bronze *Venus Anadyomene* (fig. 662), which is probably the *Venus* ordered by Duke Federigo Gonzaga for the Sala di Psiche in the Palazzo del Te at Mantua. Pietro Aretino wrote to Federigo in 1527 that this statue was "so true and so live that it fills with desire everyone who beholds it."

The magnificence and authority of Jacopo's classical style establish him as the most original architectural thinker in Venice. As we have seen, he influenced the architectural backgrounds of the works of the Venetian painters (see colorplate 128, p. 649) and laid down the principles on which Venetian architecture was to proceed for the next two centuries.

Sansovino's arrival in Venice in 1527, after the Sack of Rome, must have been liberating for him, trained as he was in the High Renaissance environment of Bramante, Raphael, and Peruzzi. Florence, with its narrow streets and its tradition of fortress-palaces, could offer only limited opportunities to an architect brought up on Roman columns, arches, and balconies; Venice, on the other hand, suffered from no such physical restrictions. The lagoons protected the city, and its public and private buildings could exploit the advantages of light and air; Venetian palaces, from the Romanesque-Byzantine through the Gothic and Early Renaissance, present to the Grand Canal a series of wide windows and superimposed open arcades built of white Istrian limestone whose luminosity imparts a special brilliance to the Venetian scene. Sansovino's Roman architectural her-

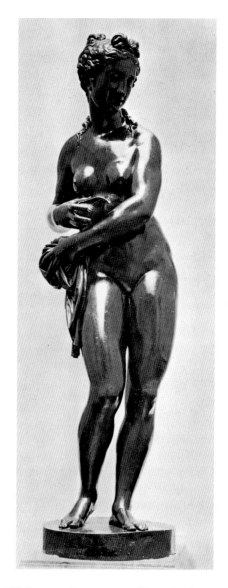

662. JACOPO SANSOVINO. *Venus Anadyomene.*
Before 1527(?). Bronze, height 66". National Gallery
of Art, Washington, D.C. (Mellon Collection).
Probably commissioned by Federigo Gonzaga for the
Sala di Psiche, Palazzo del Te, Mantua

itage could therefore be allowed an almost ideal freedom of expression.

His Library of San Marco (colorplate 130, p. 651) was commenced in 1537 to shelter the manuscripts left to the Republic of St. Mark by Cardinal Bessarion, the Greek humanist and patriarch of Constantinople turned Latin prelate. As was so often the case with Renaissance architectural works, the architect was not privileged to see his finest building completed. In 1554 its construction was interrupted; it was resumed only after the master's death in 1570 by his pupil Vincenzo Scamozzi. Nonetheless, the work was continued with fidelity to Jacopo's designs, and the library stands as a unified monument.

An ancient prototype has been adduced—the Roman Emperor Hadrian's marble library, whose columns and

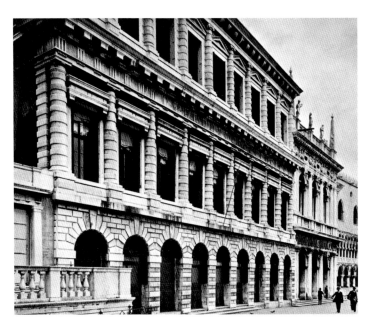

663. JACOPO SANSOVINO. Zecca (Mint), Venice.
1536–45. Third story added in 1558–66. Commissioned
by the Council of Ten

gilded ceiling were described by Pausanias—and it has
been suggested that the writings of Vitruvius, whose architectural treatise was widely known in Fra Giocondo's
Venetian edition of 1511, might have influenced the decision to situate the reading room to face the morning
light. It was placed in a commanding position, safe from
high tides, on the upper story. Sansovino's two-story
structure has three bays facing the Canale San Marco
and twenty-one facing the Doges' Palace. The ground-
story arcade is in the Roman Doric order, based on that
of the Colosseum, with keystones carved into alternating masks and lions' heads and with recumbent figures
in the spandrels. In the higher second story, which is
Ionic with elaborate decoration in high relief, Sansovino
shows his originality. The engaged columns on high
bases, like the second-story columns of Bramante's Palazzo Caprini (see fig. 509), support an entablature whose
frieze of putti and garlands encloses a half-story of mezzanine windows hidden in the ornamentation. Each
arch is flanked by pairs of fluted columns that are two-
thirds the height of the smooth, larger columns. The
pairing of these smaller columns in depth creates an effect of extraordinary plastic richness that is increased by
the sculptured figures of the spandrels and friezes.

The verticals are accented at the corners of both
stories by piers articulated by pilasters, and the crowning
balustrade is divided at each bay by high bases that support statues and obelisks. All traditional boundaries are
thus dissolved. No walls appear on either story, only
clusters of columns, large and small, and the piers to
which they are engaged or around which they are deployed. The upper contour of the structure, until this
moment in Renaissance architectural history invariably

marked by an unbroken cornice, is here dissolved against
the Venetian sky. Verticals are prolonged from the
ground to the heads of the statues, with an effect comparable to that of the pinnacles marking the divisions of
Gothic buildings.

The mass of the building encloses the shadows of the
ground-story portico and upper-story windows; the balustrade and statues incorporate the sky. The structure,
whose columns, piers, arches, balustrades, and statues in
white Istrian stone cast dark shadows and glitter against
the sky, partakes of the ordered insubstantiality of a
painting by Titian. Palladio called the building "probably the richest ever built from the days of the ancients
up to now," and Pietro Aretino pronounced it "superor
to envy." It is hard to dispute their judgment.

Next to the library, along the quayside facing the
Canale San Marco, Sansovino built the Zecca (mint; fig.
663 and colorplate 130, p. 651), for which he invented a
new order of columns interrupted by rusticated bands to
give an effect of impregnability. This idea was derived
from the Porta Maggiore, one of the ancient city gates
of Rome. The building was originally erected as a two-
story structure, but the heat of the foundries necessitated
a protective third story, added in 1558. The effect is imposing, and although some of the horizontals continue
those of the neighboring Library of San Marco, the proportions of the severe Zecca are deliberately kept separate from the library's luxurious beauty.

ANDREA PALLADIO

Andrea di Pietro (1508–80) is known by the classical
name Palladio—derived from Pallas Athena, goddess of
wisdom—that was bestowed by his first patron, the humanist Giangiorgio Trissino. Whether Palladio was born
in Padua or Vicenza is still a matter of controversy, but
there is no doubt that he was brought up in Vicenza,
which he and his pupils turned into one of the most
beautiful cities in Italy through their public and private
buildings designed in a new, more strongly archaeological version of the Renaissance style. Trissino took Palladio to Rome with him, and on that and subsequent trips
the young architect studied in detail the works of the
High Renaissance architects and the ruins of antiquity.
Palladio also mastered the writings of Vitruvius and
Alberti, and made influential literary contributions of
his own, including *L'antichità di Roma*, printed in 1554,
and *I quattro libri dell'architettura*, which appeared in 1570.
In the latter, the *virtus* of Roman architecture, so important a principle to Alberti, is developed in terms of its
application to the architectural problems—domestic,
public, and religious—of Palladio's own day.

In 1549 Palladio commenced a two-story structure
of open loggie wrapped around the fourteenth-century
Palazzo della Ragione (fig. 664), which had been a typical example of the large public halls built in a number
of north Italian cities at the close of the Middle Ages.
Palladio himself called it his Basilica, justifying the term

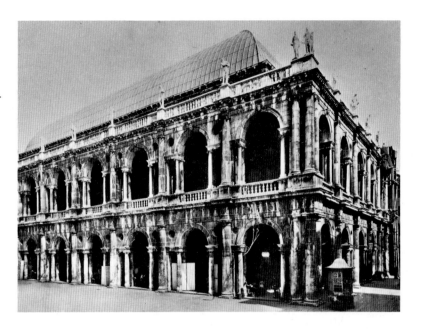

right: 664. PALLADIO. Basilica
(Palazzo della Ragione), Vicenza.
Begun 1549; completed
1614. Commissioned by the
city council

below: 665. PALLADIO. Palazzo
Chiericati, Vicenza. Begun
1551, completed in the
17th century after Palladio's
design. Commissioned
by Girolamo Chiericati

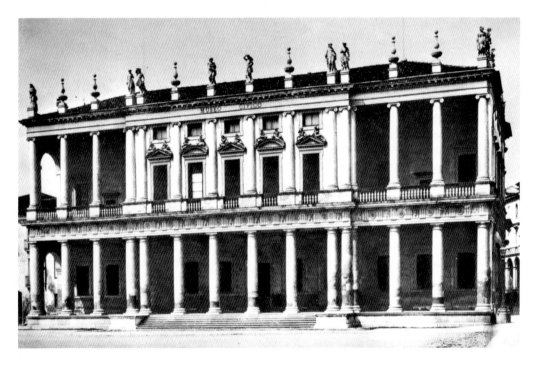

by the structure's use as a law court, the original function of Roman basilicas. He did "not doubt that this building may be compared with the ancient edifices, and ranked among the most noble and most beautiful fabrics that have been made since the ancient times, not only for its grandeur and its ornaments, but also for the materials."

Derived from Sansovino's Library of San Marco (see colorplate 130, p. 651), Palladio's Basilica is more severely architectonic, less reliant on sculpture, and at the same time more flexible. What we know today as the "Palladian motive or window"—an arched opening supported by columns and flanked by narrow compartments—is anticipated in Sansovino's second story and had probably originated in the circle of Bramante in

Rome. In the Renaissance it is virtually always enframed by a giant order supporting an entablature. Palladio uses it for both stories of the Basilica and demonstrates on a grand scale how the motive made it possible to vary the proportions of bays. Here the corner bays are narrower than the others because the intervals between the small and the embracing orders are less, while the arches maintain the same radius throughout the building.

There are some curious aberrations. On both stories the spandrels are pierced by unmolded oculi, but those of the corner bays remain unbroken. The columns of the large order are doubled on the corners, creating a bundle of three columns when seen from both sides. Sansovino's device of coupling the columns in depth is

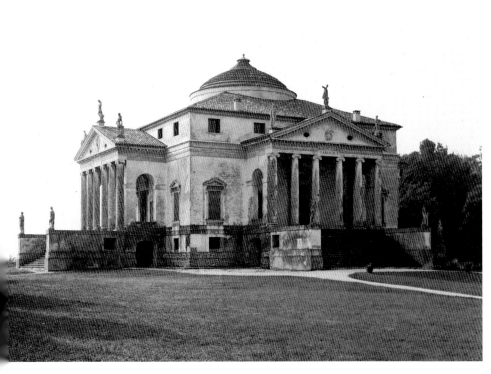

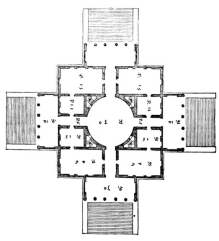

left: 666. PALLADIO. Villa Almerico,
now known as Villa Rotonda or
Villa Capra, Vicenza. Begun 1550.
Finished by VINCENZO SCAMOZZI.
Commissioned by Paolo Almerico

above: 667. PALLADIO. Plan of Villa
Almerico/Rotonda, Vicenza

used by Palladio for both stories, but in neither do the shafts rest on conventional bases. Palladio has substituted unmolded cylinders, apparently so the columns will not detract from the bases of the giant order. The high medieval convex roof is still visible, but Palladio has deployed his arcades in such a manner that the old walls are invisible, and the roof seems moored to his building almost like a tent.

The most original of Palladio's private residences in Vicenza is probably the Palazzo Chiericati (fig. 665). In other urban dwellings the architect was restricted by the narrow streets, which he confronted with classical façades in many variations of the Bramante tradition. But here his loggie look out on a piazza, and he was able to give free rein to his architectural imagination. The ground story is a Bramantesque loggia reminiscent of the Tempietto (see fig. 498), and the second story is a loftier Ionic loggia, but he interpenetrated the horizontal floors by a vertical division into three. The central section of the building advances somewhat, its corner columns are doubled, and the outermost of these columns fuses in a peculiar Siamese-twin relationship with its neighbor in the slightly recessed wings. The second story is quite unexpectedly filled in by a wall fenestrated as a story-and-a-half, with the result that a solid block of masonry appears suspended among the columns. The effect has been compared to the architecture on stilts developed in the twentieth century by Le Corbusier. Palladio manages it with the utmost severity, as if this caprice were the most natural thing in the world, never relaxing the clarity and dignity of his classical style. On the top of the building, the internal divisions are suggested by the alternation of clustered statues with fantastic balusters.

Palladio's most influential building for the history of domestic architecture is the Villa Rotonda (fig. 666), which was built for Paolo Almerico and is also sometimes known as Villa Capra. Its site is an eminence that projects from the flank of a ridge overlooking the city of Vicenza. Like most of the villas designed by Palladio for wealthy citizens of Vicenza and Venice, the building is organized around the idea of a classical temple portico, but the Villa Rotonda is unique in having four porticoes, one for each cardinal point of the compass, that radiate outward from a central dome (fig. 667). Each portico, therefore, commands a different view of mountains, hills, valleys, city, and suburbs, and enjoys different atmospheric qualities and is appropriate to varying times of the day. Each portico is protected on the sides by a diaphragm wall that wards off the sun but which is pierced by an arch to admit ventilation, and the inhabitants could thus profit from an almost endless variety of sun and shade, breeze and shelter. It is no wonder that Palladio's ideas were adopted with special enthusiasm in the architecture of plantation mansions in the American South, where it is natural to live in large measure out-of-doors for much of the year, and yet protection against the sun is essential.

Each portico is reached by a flight of steps flanked by projecting walls that suggest the sides of a spatial cube with the stairs forming a diagonal. On the outer corner of each of these walls and on the corners of each pediment, statues—twenty in all—extend the axes of the villa. Yet despite the atmospheric principles inherent in the structure, the villa is also austerely simple in its flat walls, severe Ionic columns, and undecorated frieze. It has been demonstrated that Palladio used the numerical ratios of the harmonic relationships within the Greek

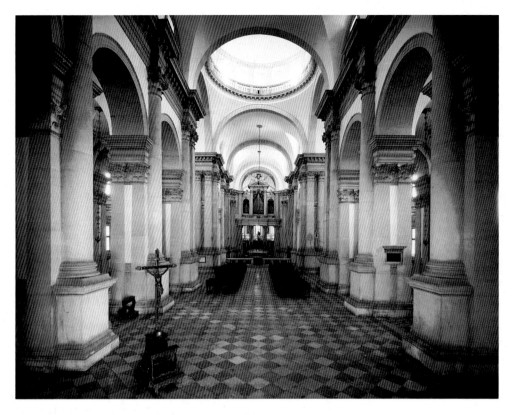

668. PALLADIO. Interior, S. Giorgio Maggiore, Venice (for the façade see colorplate 15, p. 23).
Begun 1566. Commissioned by the monastery's abbot, Andrea Pampuro da Asolo

musical scales, which were known in theory in the Renaissance, to calculate the proportional relationships between the rooms in his villas, between the length and breadth of each room, and between the height and width of any wall. Palladio's ratios are more elaborate than those utilized by Brunelleschi or those used and discussed by Alberti, and although they are not consciously discerned by the observer, they are doubtless responsible for the effect of harmony and balance so evident in Palladio's buildings.

His few churches also set out some milestones in architectural history. His grandest interior is that of San Giorgio Maggiore (figs. 668, 669), on its island facing Venice across the Canale San Marco. The design is Albertian in the sense that it is conceived in terms of a single giant order flanking arches supported by a smaller order, but unlike Alberti's Sant'Andrea in Mantua (see figs. 228, 229), San Giorgio Maggiore retains the traditional side aisles of a basilica. The sculptural quality of the interior is based on a sustained opposition between engaged columns and pilasters. The inner order consists of smaller pilasters, coupled in depth like the paired columns of Sansovino's Library of San Marco (see colorplate 130, p. 651); the giant order consists of single engaged columns, and at the corners of the crossing the columns are paired with giant pilasters. The effect of the interior is predicated on combinations of flat and rounded forms, and decoration is almost totally eliminated. The frieze, for example, is convex but devoid of orna-

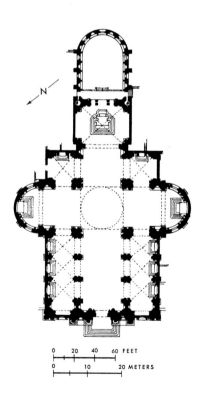

669. PALLADIO. Plan of S. Giorgio
Maggiore, Venice

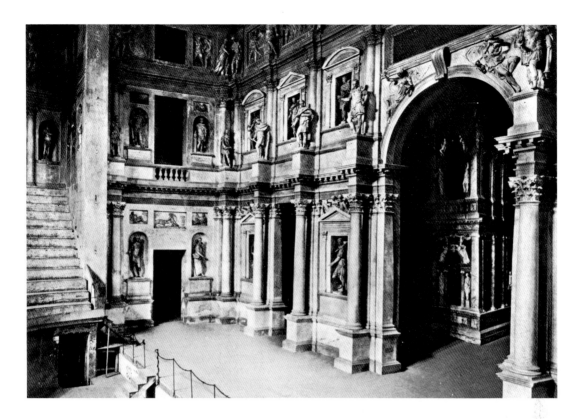

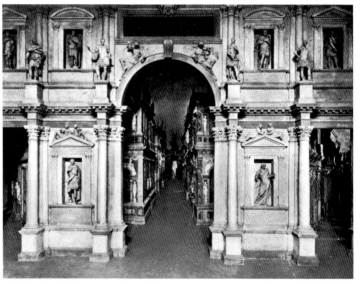

above: 670. PALLADIO. Interior, Olympian Theater, Vicenza. 1580–84. Executed by VINCENZO SCAMOZZI. Commissioned by the Accademia Olimpica

right: 671. PALLADIO. View of stage, Olympian Theater, Vicenza. 1580–84. Executed by VINCENZO SCAMOZZI

ment; the columns and pilasters are unfluted; and even the acanthus leaves lack the customary indentations and look more like petals than thistles.

San Giorgio Maggiore was commenced in 1566, but Palladio did not live to see the façade, which was erected from his designs by Scamozzi (colorplate 15, p. 23). In this and other church façades, Palladio presented a perfect solution to the age-old dilemma of the architect confronted with devising a classical façade for the difficult shape of the Christian basilica. At Santa Maria Novella (see fig. 226), Alberti had bridged the gap between the side-aisle roofs and the central temple shape by means of giant consoles, but this was a mere screen. At Sant'Andrea in Mantua (see fig. 227)—not actually a basilica—he applied a small façade to a large church. Palladio adopted Alberti's notion of two interpenetrating orders seen on the Sant'Andrea façade and amplified it into two intersecting temples—one low and broad and articulated by pilasters to accommodate the side-aisle roofs, the other tall and slender with engaged columns to embrace the lofty nave. This solution—ingenious, harmonious, and definitive—was never used again, perhaps because any further use could only appear to be an imitation. The major architects of the seventeenth century, influenced as they were by Palladio's ideas, had their own special problems and devised their own solutions. But Palladio's interlocking temples have a dense and perfect beauty of their own and are unforgettable.

Like all the leading architects of the Renaissance, Palladio was destined never to see his major designs completed. After his death Scamozzi executed the Olympian Theater at Vicenza (figs. 670, 671), one of several

Cinquecento attempts to re-create, usually in temporary materials such as wood and stucco, the shape and appearance of an ancient Roman theater. The building, intended for the production of classical drama, is typical of the classicizing ideals of the society for which Palladio built and in which he moved. The stage is provided with fixed scenery, on the principle of the ancient Roman *scenae frons*, of which a number of examples, especially that at Orange in southern France, were known to the Renaissance. But Palladio's arrangement of columns, statues, tabernacles, and reliefs, on two stories and an attic, follows no exact model. The three central openings lead into radiating streets that seemingly terminate at a vast distance from the stage, but this illusion is created by a rising pavement and the rapidly diminishing height of the buildings that line these avenues. If you penetrate as far as the stage, you will discover that these Renaissance palaces are only a few feet in depth, and if you try to walk up the street, it will rise up as the rooftops descend. You have, of course, violated the basic principle of Renaissance perspective by retaining your proper height when, according to its laws, you should have shrunk.

ALESSANDRO VITTORIA

With its predominantly pictorial interests, Venice does not seem to have encouraged sculptors. Every important Italian Renaissance sculptor working in Venice came from Tuscany, and all but two of them were Florentines, native or adopted. Nonetheless, sculpture was needed in Venice, as elsewhere, for tombs, altars, and exterior decoration, and the best of it managed to partake of the pictorial quality of the architecture into which it fitted or the paintings that surrounded it.

Alessandro Vittoria (1525–1608), who came from Trento, in the Adige Valley north of the plain of the Po, is clearly related to the innovators in painting. His *St. Jerome* (fig. 672), originally for the Scuola di San Fantin, demonstrates that he has studied the lessons of central Italian anatomy, but the figure is now caught up in the current of Counter-Reformation religiosity that is also seen in the late works of Titian and Tintoretto. The work is in itself more pictorial than sculptural. The penitent saint, withdrawn from the world in a state of self-lac-

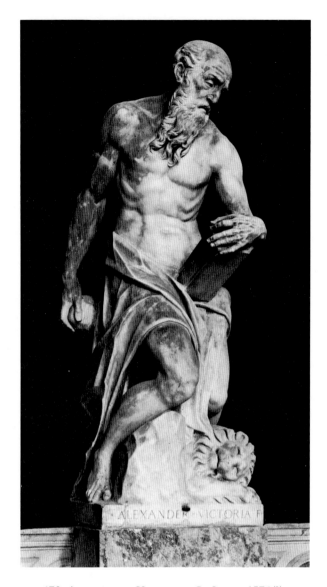

672. ALESSANDRO VITTORIA. *St. Jerome*. 1576(?). Marble, height 66½". SS. Giovanni e Paolo, Venice. Commissioned for the Scuola di S. Fantin, Venice

erating catatonia, seems almost to be floating over his rock rather than kneeling on it. His lion is reduced to a symbol and the sculptor concentrates on the swollen veins in arms and hands and, above all, on the shuddering muscles and the look of terror at the emptiness within.

20
Michelangelo and the Maniera

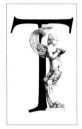he final paradox in the history of Italian Renaissance art is the coexistence during the middle and late Cinquecento of the late style of Michelangelo and of the later phase of Mannerism that here will be called the *maniera*. While the artists of the *maniera* placed Michelangelo at the summit of greatness in their writings and borrowed figures, groups, and compositional ideas from his works, the art of the *maniera* is characterized by standardization, artificiality, and elaboration. These ideals were institutionalized with the founding of the Florentine Academy in 1563. The prime movers of the *maniera* were about thirty-five years younger than Michelangelo and, although Michelangelo had been one of the founders of High Renaissance style, this had not prevented him from devising inventions of a strikingly different sort in Florence between 1516 and 1534. It should be kept in mind that Michelangelo never relaxed his republican principles, although briefly toward the end of his life he entertained the possibility of returning to Florence to work for Duke Cosimo I. He kept aloof from dynastic patrons save when they promised the liberation of Florence, and he worked for the Church—at times without pay—and for himself. The leaders of the *maniera*, on the other hand, were court artists and their art, whose linear and formal complexities matched the allegorical conceits of its content, was chiefly intended to glorify dynastic rule, court society, and a formalized version of religion. Despite the almost universal veneration in which Michelangelo was held, in his old age he became both an anachronism and, in architecture at least, a prophet of the Baroque.

MICHELANGELO AFTER 1534

The central monument of mid-Cinquecento painting in Rome is Michelangelo's *Last Judgment* (colorplate 131, p. 652), painted in 1536–41. Early in 1534, when Pope Clement VII first discussed with Michelangelo the fresco he wished for the altar wall of the Sistine Chapel, to replace the *Assumption of the Virgin* by Perugino, the subject was to be the Resurrection, to which the Medici Chapel in Florence had been dedicated. But Clement died that year, and the new pope, Paul III, commissioned Michelangelo to paint the Last Judgment, which must have seemed more appropriate to the situation of Rome and the papacy. Images of justice and punish-

ment, sacred and secular, had already appeared on a grand scale in Italy—Beccafumi's *Fall of the Rebel Angels* (fig. 588) and Giulio Romano's and Perino del Vaga's frescoes of the *Fall of the Giants* (figs. 586, 611, 612) are only three of the numerous examples.

The new subject was to fill the entire wall, from the altar to the edge of the vaulting. Certainly, the idea captured the imagination of the aging master, who devoted a series of studies to the development of the huge composition, with its torrents of figures, and to the definition of individual figures. The project meant that he had to destroy two more frescoes by Perugino, the *Nativity* and the *Finding of Moses,* that were part of the fifteenth-century narrative program lining the side walls of the chapel, as well as the end windows, the figures of popes, and his own lunettes over the windows, which represented the first seven generations of the ancestry of Christ. In his new composition, he retained the autonomy of the lunettes by separating them from the rest of the wall by the edges of the clouds that envelop them. He emphasized the axes of the spandrels above (the cross on which Haman is crucified, and the staff around which the Brazen Serpent is wrapped; see colorplate 101, p. 496) in the diagonals of the cross and the column in the lunettes below.

Michelangelo's gigantic fresco dissolves the altar wall of the chapel. Medieval Last Judgments (generally inside the entrance wall of churches) are solid hierarchical and compartmentalized structures in which all figures, including sometimes even the resurrected dead, are dressed according to their social position, and Christ, the Virgin, and the apostles are enthroned in Heaven; instead, Michelangelo has represented a unified scene without any break, without thrones, without insignia of rank, generally even without clothes. In a huge clockwise motion that has been compared to a wheel of fortune, figures rise from their graves, gather round the central Christ, and sink downward toward Hell.

What gives the fresco its special character is the vision of the Second Coming in Matthew 24:30–31: "And then shall appear the sign of the Son of man in heaven: and then shall all the tribes of the earth mourn, and they shall see the Son of man coming in the clouds of heaven with power and great glory. And he shall send his angels with a great sound of a trumpet, and they shall gather together his elect from the four winds, from one end of heaven to the other." The open background of the fres-

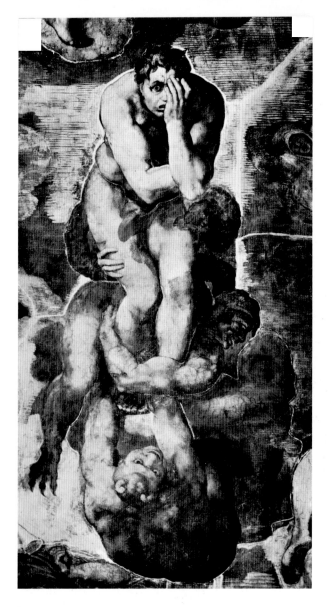

673. MICHELANGELO. Damned Soul Descending to Hell, detail of *Last Judgment* (see colorplate 131, p. 652). Fresco. Sistine Chapel, Vatican, Rome. Commissioned by Pope Paul III

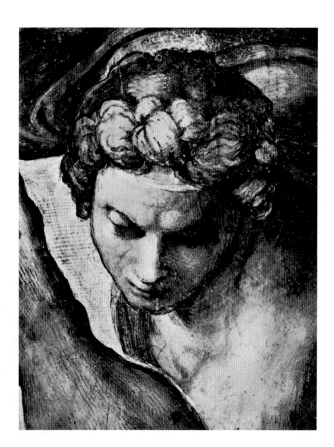

674. MICHELANGELO. Angel, detail of *Last Judgment* (see colorplate 131, p. 652). Fresco. Sistine Chapel, Vatican, Rome

co, of course, should not be construed as infinity; the notion of infinite space had occurred to nobody in the 1530s. It is the fulfillment of Christ's words a few verses later: "Heaven and earth shall pass away." In fact, only enough of the earth is shown to provide graves from which the dead can crawl. Some corpses are well preserved, some skeletons, in conformity with a tradition appearing in monumental form in Signorelli's Orvieto frescoes (see fig. 489). The dead show no joy in resurrection or in the recognition of those they knew in life, only dread of the judgment taking place around and above them. Some are still dazed, others hopeless; some look upward in awe and wonder. Some soar as if drawn upward by magnetic attraction; others are fought over by angels who lift them, or by demons who drag them down (fig. 673).

The nudity of most of the figures—so shocking to the prudery of the Counter-Reformation that Michelangelo's pupil Daniele da Volterra was later commissioned to paint drapery over some of the offending portions—is in harmony with Michelangelo's lifelong concern with the human figure in its most elemental aspect. Thus not only the dead rising from their graves but also the elect in Heaven were shown naked before Christ. To help unify the composition, Michelangelo arbitrarily increased the scale of the figures in the upper part of the fresco. In addition, the figures are broader and fuller than those of the Sistine Ceiling—the proportions heavier, the heads smaller, and the modeling even more vigorous. As the resurrected dead float upward, compassionate angels help them into Heaven. Michelangelo generally omits wings and haloes as hindrances to the expression of bodily perfection. Only their greater power and often startling beauty (fig. 674) distinguish the angels from ordinary mortals. The grace of these figures derives from their motion, which is communicated by a fluid pulsation that is new. Throughout the *Last Judgment*, the dominant color was that of human flesh against a vivid ultramarine blue sky—revealed in the ongoing restoration of the fresco—with a few touches of brilliant drapery to echo the splendors of the ceiling. The dead rising from their graves still preserve the colors of the earth—dun, ocher, drab. A few patches of red appear in the angels' cloaks.

Around Christ the Judge, the elect are gathered in ranks that recede into the clouds until only the heads can be numbered. Christ is placed in the zone best lighted by the windows on either side and given a scale greater than that of the gigantic apostles who surround

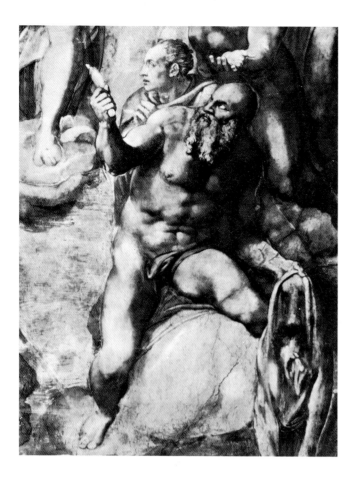

675. MICHELANGELO. St. Bartholomew, detail of *Last Judgment* (see colorplate 131, p. 652). Fresco. Sistine Chapel, Vatican, Rome

him and the Virgin at his side. Although his attention is largely occupied with the gesture of damnation—his right hand held on high as he turns in this direction—his left is extended gently, as if summoning the blessed up toward him. Instead of the traditional mandorla surrounding his body, a subtle radiance seems to extend from the figure. In spite of some repaint, Michelangelo's beardless and almost nude Christ shows much of what must have been the artist's original heroic intention, a summation of the new, more massive canon of proportion on which all the male figures of the fresco are constructed. Among the apostles before the Judge, St. Bartholomew, who was flayed alive, holds his empty skin; the face is an anguished self-portrait of Michelangelo (fig. 675), revealing, as do the artist's letters and poems, the intensity of his sense of guilt and inadequacy:

I live for sin, dying to myself I live;
It is no longer my life, but that of sin:
My good by Heaven, my evil by myself was given me,
By my free will, of which I am deprived.

As the damned descend to their fate, a few struggle against the angels who drive them from Heaven, but most seem resigned to the overpowering force of divine will. As a child, Michelangelo must have contemplated the torments of Hell as depicted in colossal works in Florence: the mosaic of the *Last Judgment* (see colorplate 19, p. 59) in the Baptistery; Orcagna's frescoes (now largely destroyed) in Santa Croce, Michelangelo's own parish church; and the *Hell* by Nardo di Cione in Santa Maria Novella (see fig. 116). He read Dante's *Inferno* (which Nardo illustrated), and most likely knew Giotto's *Last Judgment* in Padua (see colorplate 1, p. 10). It is surprising how little these works of literature and art affected him. His interests moved in a realm far beyond that of physical torment, indeed physical experience of any sort. Charon drives the damned from his boat into Hell with an oar as Dante says he should, but the oar never touches a body. The only torments shown are spiritual, and only a glimmer of fire appears on the horizon. But a Hell mouth opens up directly above the altar, as a reminder that the celebrant at Mass, often the pope himself, is in the same mortal danger as all humanity. It has been suggested that for a number of reasons, including the surprisingly gentle expression of Christ and the presence of a broad expanse of water separating the shore from the mouth of Hell, that Michelangelo and others in his circle in Rome may not have believed that punishment for sin was irrevocable. Although seemingly heretical, this view may have been tolerated before the Council of Trent.

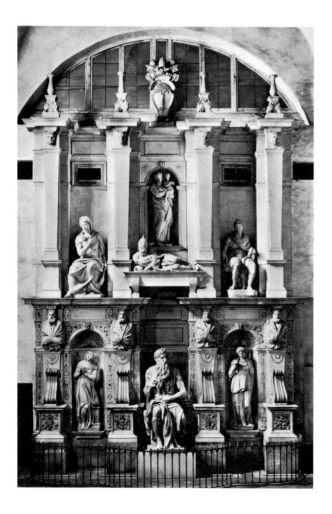

676. MICHELANGELO. Tomb of Julius II. Completed 1545. Marble. 🏛 S. Pietro in Vincoli, Rome. Upper figures by other artists. Commissioned by Pope Julius II and his heirs

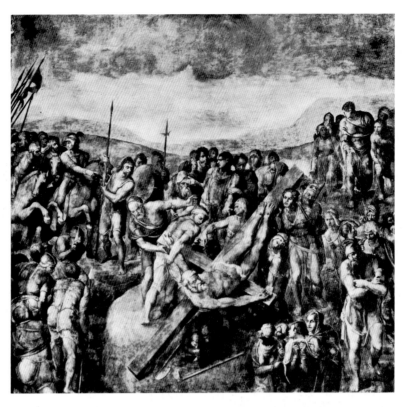

677. MICHELANGELO. *Crucifixion of St. Peter.* 1545–50. Fresco, 20' 4" x 22'. Pauline Chapel, Vatican, Rome. Commissioned by Pope Paul III

In 1542, still hounded by the heirs of Julius II to finish the tomb (the reduced version was not dedicated until 1545; fig. 676), the sixty-seven-year-old artist took up his brushes and climbed still another scaffold to paint two frescoes in a chapel constructed for Pope Paul III just outside the entrance to the Sistine Chapel. Interrupted by illness and other commissions, he worked spasmodically on these frescoes of the *Crucifixion of St. Peter* and the *Conversion of St. Paul* (figs. 677, 678). The Pauline Chapel, as it has been named, was not completed until the spring of 1550, several months after Pope Paul's death. In spite of passages now in poor condition, the Pauline paintings are among Michelangelo's most powerful works. True, a kind of rigidity has set in that is disturbing after the freedom of the Sistine Ceiling or even the *Last Judgment*, but the artist's powers of expression and drawing have in no way diminished, and the color shows a new freedom as well.

Against barren landscapes whose buttes and ridges recall the desolation of the mountains around Caprese, where Michelangelo was born, the two scenes are staged with cataclysmic violence. Saul, on the road to Damascus to persecute Christians, is struck down by a ray from the heavenly apparition and falls from his horse: "And suddenly there shined round about him a light from heaven: And he fell to the earth, and heard a voice saying unto him, Saul, Saul, why persecutest thou me?" (Acts 9:3–4).

The vision is here fully corporeal. A sharply foreshortened Christ, shorn of the luminary display customary in representations of this subject, appears in the sky among angelic platoons whose figures, reminiscent of many in the *Last Judgment*, have been compressed into

blocks, their curves flattened into planes. As Christ moves downward and outward, the equally foreshortened horse leaps upward and inward, splitting Saul's attendants also into blocks of figures. The dramatic figure of the blinded Saul (fig. 679)—shortly to become the apostle Paul—was clearly suggested by Raphael's blinded Heliodorus (see colorplate 103, p. 513). He falls forward as if struck by a force emanating from the floating Christ, and his face reflects both the blindness of Homer in ancient busts of the poet and the agony of the ancient *Laocoön* group, on whose restoration Michelangelo had worked. Unexpectedly old (St. Paul was a young man at the time of his conversion), the face with its snowy, two-tailed beard was probably intended to suggest that of Pope Paul III (see Titian's portrait, fig. 632).

The difficult subject of the *Crucifixion of St. Peter* is handled by Michelangelo as an elevation of Peter's cross. The configuration becomes a hollow square, tilted up with the rising movement of the landscape and traversed by the powerful diagonal of the cross. Yet for all the massiveness of the figures, they are strangely weightless and floating. The foreground figures now stand on the ground, or rise from nowhere, or are cut off at the waist or knee by the frame. Renaissance perspective, which is always less interesting to an artist who is more responsive to tangible than to optical effects, is abandoned, and, with an archaistic disregard of illusionistic space, what is behind is here represented as above. The strange composition, with its ranks of figures floating upward, generally facing the observer, culminates in an awestruck group silhouetted against distant promontories. They look down, or at each other, with expressions of trance-like wonder that are even shared by the soldiers and exe-

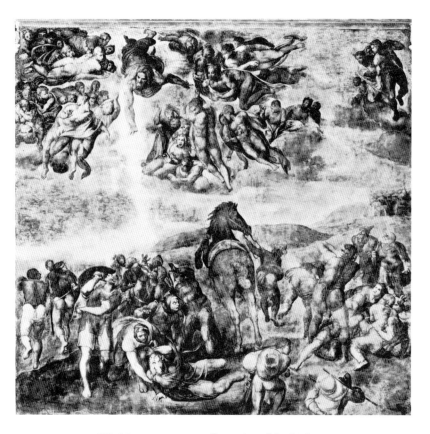

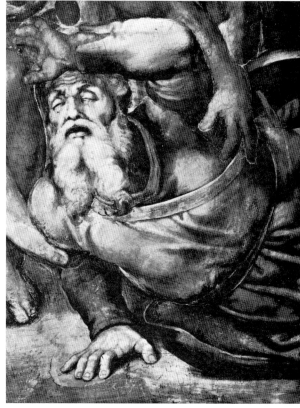

678. MICHELANGELO. *Conversion of St. Paul.*
1542–45. Fresco, 20' 4" x 22'. Pauline Chapel, Vatican,
Rome. Commissioned by Pope Paul III

679. Detail of fig. 678

cutioners. Few figures are shown in action, and *contrapposto* has disappeared almost entirely. So have hatred, anger, and all emotions save awe and fear. As in a Passion play in which the actors are all townsfolk, there is little distinction between executioner and martyr, pagan and Christian. The scene becomes strangely intimate and personal, the drama a ritual.

When he finished the Pauline frescoes in 1550, Michelangelo was seventy-five. His failing eyesight and general ill health prevented him from undertaking monumental pictorial commissions, but he could still carve stone and design buildings. As his control of the immediate circumstances of practical existence and visual reality faded, his architectural forms became grander and more richly articulated, as if the sense of mass, which in his earlier art had arisen from the human figure, had outgrown it and could function on its own in the abstract shapes of architecture. Aside from his continued long-distance supervision of the details of the Laurentian Library (see figs. 562, 563), two of Michelangelo's three most important late architectural projects had been commenced by Antonio da Sangallo the Younger (see pp. 577–78).

We have seen the effect Michelangelo's central window and colossal cornice had on Antonio's façade of the Palazzo Farnese (see fig. 604). But it was in Antonio's courtyard that Michelangelo intervened with revolutionary results (fig. 680). He carried out Antonio's sec-

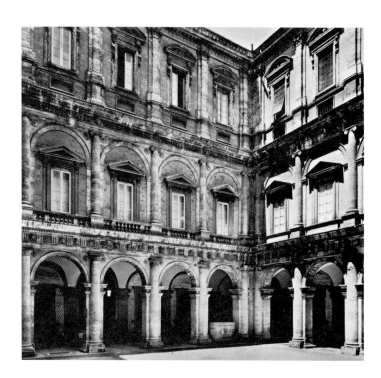

680. ANTONIO DA SANGALLO THE YOUNGER and MICHELANGELO. Courtyard, Palazzo Farnese, Rome. 1517–46 and 1547–50. Commissioned by Alessandro Farnese, who later became Pope Paul III

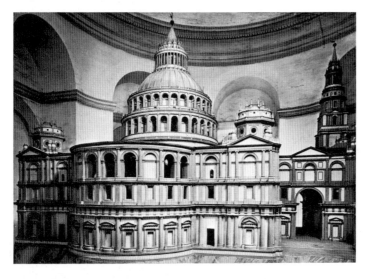

681. ANTONIO DA SANGALLO THE YOUNGER. Model for St. Peter's,
Vatican, Rome. 1539–46. Wood. Museo Petriano, Vatican, Rome.
Commissioned by Pope Paul III

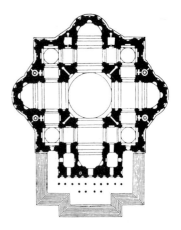

682. MICHELANGELO. Plan of
St. Peter's, Vatican, Rome. 1546–64.
Michelangelo's work on St. Peter's was
commissioned by Pope Paul III

ond, Ionic story with only minor changes. But in the third story he demonstrated his originality by abandoning engaged columns and substituting pilasters on lofty bases whose height was governed by the mezzanine story for servants' quarters. Each pilaster is flanked by half-pilasters. These clustered pilasters, the architectural counterpart of the clustered, vibrating figures of Michelangelo's pictorial and sculptural compositions, introduce a new organic richness and near-human vibrancy to the static, almost inert quality of the architectural elements designed by Antonio. This new vitality was especially admired by the architects of the seventeenth century, and in a sense Michelangelo was here helping to sow the seeds of Baroque architecture. He communicated the same quality of tension and inner life to the windows he designed for the third story, with their broken sills with pendant moldings at the corners, fantastic consoles, lions' heads, and broken moldings inside arched pediments. These are all related to the bold, dramatic effects Michelangelo obtained in his articulation of the exterior of St. Peter's.

Here Michelangelo took over totally. Antonio the Younger had continued the construction of Bramante's basic project, whose four piers and arches to uphold the dome had been built and could not be changed in any essential respect (see fig. 503). Vasari's fresco (see fig. 704) shows the state of affairs at that time, with Paul III directing it all. The Albertian coupled pilasters are already built according to Bramante's designs; the barrel vaults of the transept still have their wooden centering; Bramante's colossal temporary Doric construction around the apse appears at the left of the building, and at the right a portion of the nave of the old Constantinian Basilica of St. Peter's still stands. But in the center, masons are laying the stones of a feature Michelangelo particularly disliked, a huge ambulatory added by Antonio.

It can also be seen on the plan being presented to the pope. This system of galleries and loggie would have inflated the church to almost double its already gigantic size; the model (fig. 681) shows that the Doric ambulatory would have supported a high mezzanine and a higher Ionic second story, whose largely open arches had no other purpose than show. An open gallery would have connected the main building to an almost independent façade that culminates in two campanili as lofty as the dome.

Admittedly, Antonio's design is fantastic. At no point can the eye select a single dominant feature; always it has to choose between two of apparently equal importance. Even the dome has two superimposed peristyles, and the ribbed shell (instead of Bramante's hemisphere; see fig. 501) is crushed between the peristyles and the outsize lantern. Bramante's corner towers are converted into strange octagonal structures lighted by oculi, and these excrescences—including the peristyles, the lantern, and the campanili—bristle with obelisks.

Michelangelo wrote a devastating letter criticizing the design as Germanic, pointing out that it would take an army of guards to clear the open loggie at nightfall, that they would provide shelter for all kinds of crime, and that in order to construct the ambulatories, whole sections of the Vatican, including the Sistine and Pauline chapels, would have to be demolished. Whoever departed from Bramante, Michelangelo said, "departed from the truth." He accepted the commission to complete St. Peter's without pay, for the salvation of his soul, and he developed a new, unified plan. First went the ambulatories, then the façade with its towers. The Greek-cross plan of Bramante was reinstated (fig. 682; see also fig. 502), along with the colossal order on the exterior. In the interests of the stability of the dome, however, Michelangelo also suppressed Bramante's smaller Greek crosses,

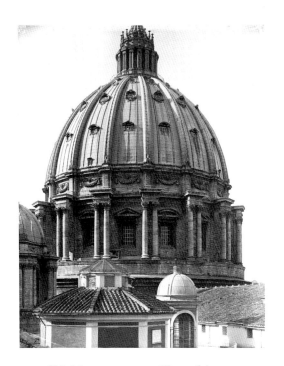

683. MICHELANGELO. View of dome,
St. Peter's, Vatican, Rome
(see colorplate 13, p. 21). 1546–64

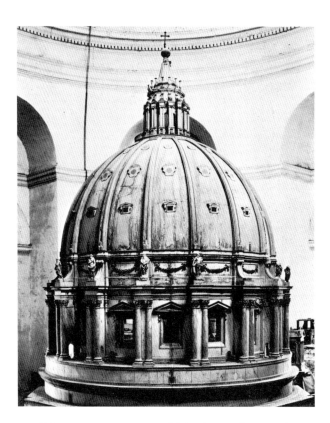

684. MICHELANGELO. Model for dome of St. Peter's,
Vatican, Rome. 1558–61. Wood. Museo Petriano, Vatican,
Rome. Commissioned by Pope Paul III

substituting simpler domed spaces (two exterior domes, built later, probably reflect Michelangelo's designs) and increasing the bulk of the piers. The façade was to have been a temple shape of freestanding columns, subordinate to the crowning effect of the dome.

In order to unify the exterior (colorplate 13, p. 21), Michelangelo adopted a single embracing theme, the idea of a coupled Corinthian order, using pilasters in the main mass of the church and columns in the peristyle and lantern of the dome (fig. 683). He designed a Florentine ribbed dome instead of Bramante's hemisphere, dividing it by twice the number of ribs in the Florentine dome, and even these and the ribs of the culminating lantern are paired (fig. 684). Thus the entire church, from the ground to the sphere on the lantern, gives the impression of a colossal monolith. To increase its unity and density, Michelangelo cut across the reentrant angles of the transept with diagonal masses and even intended to fill the angles of the entablatures projecting from the peristyle of the dome with consoles that would curl upward from the pedestals of statues. Unfortunately, these were never carried out. At his death, in fact, the drum and the peristyle of the dome were still under construction. The shell as finally built was heightened somewhat from Michelangelo's original design, which was closer to a hemisphere, but by and large the effect of the building, seen from the sides or back, follows his intentions. Unfortunately, the unified dome, which was all important as the centralizing ele-

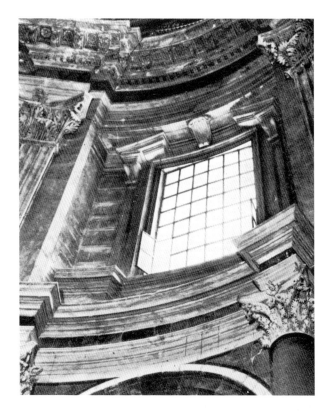

685. MICHELANGELO. Window in north transept,
St. Peter's, Vatican, Rome. 1546–64

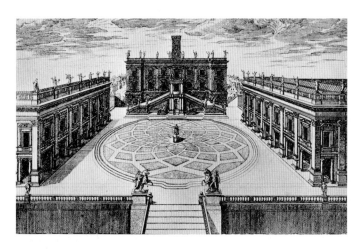

686. MICHELANGELO. Campidoglio, Rome. 1538–64.
Engraving by ÉTIENNE DUPÉRAC, 1569

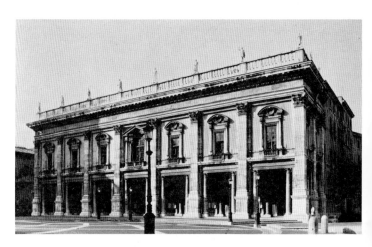

687. MICHELANGELO. Palazzo dei Conservatori,
Campidoglio, Rome. Begun 1563

ment in Bramante's and Michelangelo's conception, can now hardly be seen from the façade because the nave was prolonged in the seventeenth century.

The grand unity of the structure embraces immense complexities, but in the warfare between wall and column that had reached a deadlock in the Medici Chapel and Laurentian Library, the column has at last won. Nonetheless, the struggle continues in many details of the interior. The apse windows, for example, are capped by broken pediments that seem crushed by the concave entablatures above them (fig. 685). While the basic forms and spaces of the interior were decided by Bramante (save for the floor level, which was raised by Antonio, thereby shortening Bramante's giant pilasters), Michelangelo was able to alter the apse vaults, which he turned into neo-Gothic ribbed vaults instead of the semidomes Bramante planned. Since Michelangelo was unable to ride a horse across Rome to supervise the construction in person, one of these vaults was built incorrectly and had to be torn down and redone. The plastic effect of the interior, which he would surely have left quite severe, is diminished by the seventeenth-century addition of inlaid designs in colored marble and gold mosaic (see fig. 505).

Michelangelo's single but influential contribution to civic design was his coordinated scheme for the Capitoline Hill—the center of ancient Rome (fig. 686). Much against his will, he was constrained in 1538 to move the Roman bronze equestrian statue of Marcus Aurelius, then considered a portrait of Constantine, from its original position near St. John Lateran to the Campidoglio; at that time he provided the statue with its ovoid base and designed a double flight of steps to the Palazzo Senatorio at the back of the piazza. Michelangelo probably made no further designs before 1561, when real work on the Capitoline project began. Certainly he was responsible for the general idea of the project, whose two facing palaces, the Palazzo dei Conservatori and Palazzo Nuovo, are at an angle to each other because of the configuration of the terrain and preexisting structures that had to be incorporated. The design of the pavement, with its pattern of radiating, interlocking petals that symbolize Roman rule at the center or umbilicus of the world, is Michelangelo's.

The Palazzo dei Conservatori (fig. 687) was built from his drawings under the supervision of Tommaso Cavalieri. The central window is a misunderstood version by his follower Giacomo della Porta of Michelangelo's own window in the second story of the Palazzo Farnese (see fig. 604). Nonetheless, the revolutionary design of the

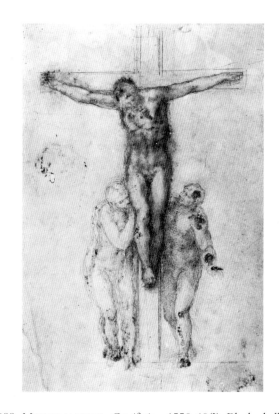

688. MICHELANGELO. *Crucifixion*. 1550–60(?). Black chalk,
16³/₈ x 11". British Museum, London

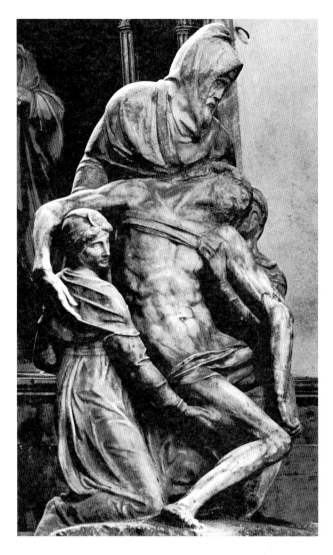

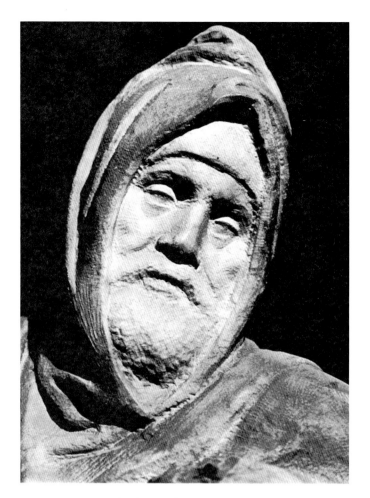

690. Joseph of Arimathea, detail of fig. 689

689. MICHELANGELO. *Pietà*. Before 1555. Marble, height 92". Museo dell'Opera del Duomo, Florence. Begun by Michelangelo for his own tomb

building is Michelangelo's. Like St. Peter's, the structure is embraced by a colossal Corinthian order, within which a small Ionic order seems imprisoned. The straight entablature of the portico, in preference to an arcade, is a typical Michelangelism.

In the aged artist's last letters and poems, death is always near. But he no longer dreams of the mighty Creator, nor even of the awesome Judge, but rather of the merciful Redeemer. His drawings of the crucified Christ are dedicated to

That Love divine
Which opened to embrace us
His arms upon the Cross.

Sometimes the figures are unable to bridge the gap that separates them from God, and cry soundlessly in the void below the cross; sometimes (fig. 688) the same last shudder that pierces the crucified unites them with him, as they embrace him, pressing themselves against him, trying to merge their being in his. Michelangelo's eye-

sight is no longer clear, his hand shakes, and the contours tremble, but vague though the shapes are, their masses are almost architectural, and the mighty forms and tensions group the misty figures into shapes of a grand simplicity.

Two unfinished and broken *Pietàs* remain as sculptural witnesses of Michelangelo's inner life in his last years. One, carved before 1555 (fig. 689), was meant for his own tomb. He had already carefully removed the left leg, apparently to replace it, when, in a fit of desperation—he claimed the stone was too hard and would not obey him, but doubtless there were psychological reasons as well—he started to destroy the work. He smashed the group in several places before his pupils stopped him. They pieced together the breaks, but the leg has completely disappeared. In spite of this mutilation, and an attempt by one of the pupils to finish the Magdalen so that she is now out of proportion with the other figures, the effect of the group is immensely moving. The theme is the relentless power of death, which seems to be drawing Christ downward into the tomb with a force that the human figures are powerless to prevent; the Magdalen, the Virgin, and Joseph of Arimathea, the rich man who allowed Christ to be buried in his tomb, sink with him. The features are Michelangelo's own (fig. 690); he presses Christ's head to his

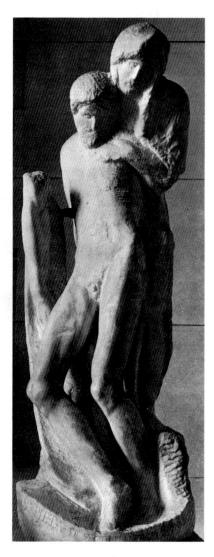

691. MICHELANGELO. *Pietà*. 1554–64. Marble, height 63³/8". Castello Sforzesco, Milan. Intended by Michelangelo for his own tomb

chest, merging his identity with that of divinity. The difference between this gentle, controlled self-image and the agonized one on the empty skin in the *Last Judgment* (see fig. 675) gives us new insight into the final period of Michelangelo's life and art. Rough though the unfinished surfaces may be, the emotional and spiritual relationships and the power and beauty of the forms and composition need no analysis.

Only a few days before his death in February 1564, Michelangelo began to work again on a *Pietà* that he had started ten years or so earlier (fig. 691). It went through at least two main stages. The original version, which was probably very nearly finished, consisted of the Virgin holding the slender dead Christ in her arms, as if lifting him up before us in the spirit of the *Sistine Madonna* with her infant Son (see fig. 527) or of Michelangelo's own designs for the Virgin on the tomb of Julius II. But in a last feverish burst of activity, he cut away the head and shoulders of the Christ, leaving the

right arm still hanging, and began to fashion a new head for Christ out of the Virgin's shoulder and chest. In the beginnings of a third stage he cut into the new heads, drawing them even closer together in an intensification of the process of merging we have seen in all his late work. One gets the feeling not that they are sinking into the grave, but that the Virgin is standing at its brink and that Christ floats weightlessly in her arms.

Through the successive ghostly stages of shattered marble, the chisel—the love for which Michelangelo drank in with his foster-mother's milk—seeks the riddle of identity between Son and Mother and gives Michelangelo's own features to the sacrificed Christ. Six days before his death, at nearly eighty-nine, he was still working on the group. He fell ill after exposure to the rain, and at first refused his pupils' counsel to go to bed; he eventually succumbed, probably to pneumonia. In his will he consigned his soul to God, his body to the earth, his belongings to his nearest relatives, and asked the friends around him, including Tommaso Cavalieri, to remember in his death the death of Christ.

THE *MANIERA*

After such disclosures, one turns with some difficulty to the artists of the *maniera*, who believed that they stood, with Michelangelo, at the summit achieved by art since antiquity. Vasari writes that he and his contemporaries had discovered the perfect formula for grace of body and feature and for beauty of composition. Their contemporaries in Venice, where the Renaissance still flourished, were by no means convinced. The Venetian Ludovico Dolce uses the word *maniera* derogatorily to refer to artists in whose paintings the faces and figures looked too much alike; to Vasari, this was an advantage because it speeded up production time. In the last analysis one's estimate of the *maniera* is a matter of personal taste and judgment, but it is hardly open to question that by the middle of the Cinquecento in central Italy the Renaissance, in its etymological sense of "rebirth," was over. Snatches of Michelangelesque and Raphaelesque, even Leonardesque, melodies linger on, whole motives are sometimes borrowed, but the world has changed: the artist no longer experiences the excitement of discovery, and Nature, the ultimate reference point for Masaccio, Alberti, Antonio del Pollaiuolo, and Leonardo, takes second place to the refined inventions of the cultivated artist. What follows, therefore, is in a sense an epilogue.

THE MICHELANGELESQUE RELIEF

Michelangelo is known to have planned a number of sculptural reliefs for inclusion in the tomb of Julius II and other undertakings, but scholars are still uncertain about what their style might have been, since the only reliefs by his hand are the *Battle of Lapiths and Centaurs* and the three Florentine *Madonnas* (see figs. 468, 467, 476, 511). Would the marble panels for Julius's tomb

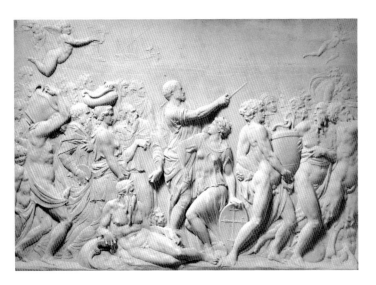

692. PIERINO DA VINCI. *Cosimo I as Patron of Pisa.*
1549. Marble, 28⅞ x 63". Museo Vaticano, Rome. Probably
commissioned by Duke Cosimo de' Medici

have been in low or high relief? And what would have
been the appearance of those in bronze? Some insight
may be provided by a large marble low-relief panel representing *Cosimo I as Patron of Pisa* (fig. 692) by Pierino
da Vinci (probably 1521–54), a young Florentine *maniera*
sculptor deeply influenced by Michelangelo, whom he
had met in Rome.

The relief shows the duke lifting a figure representing
Pisa. With a general's baton, Cosimo drives away Pisa's
enemies, who are laden with plunder. Behind him reclines the bearded River Arno, water gushing from his
enormous jar and doubtless derived from one of Michelangelo's river-gods planned for the Medici Chapel.
This figure is a reference to Cosimo's plans to deepen
the Arno, rebuild the port of Pisa, and connect it with a
canal to the new port at Livorno. Among the other allegorical figures, the University of Pisa, which Cosimo reorganized and reestablished, is shown holding a great

book. The relief is carved in emulation of Michelangelo's *Madonna of the Stairs* (see fig. 467), and the polished Michelangelesque figures in low and still lower
relief are defined with linear perfection. In the left background a galley can be seen, and the sculpture would, if
finished, doubtless have shown other vessels. The fact
that Pierino's groups in the round are almost slavishly
dependent on the *Victory* for Julius's tomb (see fig. 566)
supports the suggestion that Michelangelo's marble reliefs might have looked like this.

A possibility for those in bronze is suggested by the
work of another Michelangelo imitator, Vincenzo Danti
from Perugia (1530–76), who also produced groups
based on the *Victory*. His *Moses and the Brazen Serpent*
(fig. 693) suggests the hazy, sketchy style of Michelangelo's composition drawings translated into bronze.
The relief offers a wide variety of projections and a free
handling of detail that produce, as light moves over the
glossy bronze, an equivalent of the *chiaroscuro* effects and
floating contours of rapid drawing in charcoal or chalk
(see fig. 558). The composition is based on Michelangelo's spandrel for the Sistine Ceiling (see colorplate
101, p. 496) but there Moses is relegated to the background. Danti, instead, has placed the tall, bony figure
of the lawgiver so that his right hand, and the staff
around which the Brazen Serpent is entwined, are centered. Around and behind him are heaped the writhing
figures of the children of Israel, the men mostly nude,
their poses often borrowed from the *Last Judgment* to
display Danti's prowess as an anatomist and to reveal his
intimate knowledge of the works of the master. The
effect of distance, into which the figures recede, is
achieved by the spontaneity of hand and tool in modeling the original clay or wax—probably the latter—from
which a mold was taken for the cast in bronze, and the
suggestiveness and accidental effects of the model are
preserved even in the figures and drapery. As a result,
Danti suggests less an historical event than a vision of
healing and salvation that is revealed in a thunderclap.

693. VINCENZO
DANTI. *Moses
and the Brazen Serpent.*
1559. Bronze,
32⅜ x 67¾".
Bargello, Florence.
Commissioned
by Duke Cosimo de'
Medici

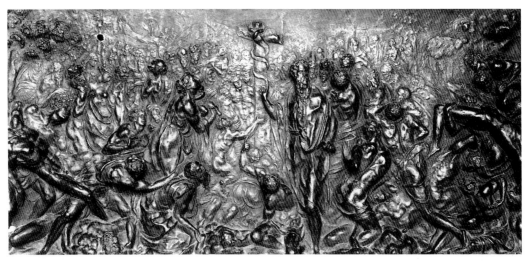

BENVENUTO CELLINI

Among the sculptors who found work in Florence under the Medici rulers of the middle and later Cinquecento, the most familiar figure is Benvenuto Cellini (1500–1571), partly because his vivid *Autobiography* is still widely read. After many years of activity as a goldsmith in Rome, including hair-raising adventures during the Sack of 1527, and a prolonged stay in France, Cellini settled in Florence, where he attracted the attention of Duke Cosimo I. In 1545 Cosimo commissioned him to do the *Perseus and Medusa* (fig. 694); owing to the difficulty of casting a figure of this size in bronze by means of a novel experimental technique, it occupied him until 1554. Although the proportions of this work are heavier than those of Cellini's earlier models, the statue is one of the most successful sculptural creations of the *maniera*.

The destination of the work for the Loggia dei Lanzi (see colorplate 16, p. 24), where Donatello's *Judith and Holofernes* (see fig. 292) was then installed, probably caused Cellini to devise a rough parallelism between the triumphant figures, the defeated enemies, and even the cushions of the bases—iconographically justifiable for *Judith* but hard to understand for *Perseus*. The modeling of the nude figure shows Cellini's study of anatomy, while the play of light on the surfaces and the infinity of possible viewpoints are in the tradition of Michelangelo's marble nudes. But, unlike Donatello, there is no attempt to evoke horror at the decapitation; the perfection of workmanship, born of Cellini's training as a goldsmith, seems to congeal the possibility of drama. The rich locks of Perseus's hair, the writhing serpents, even the torrents of blood gushing from the truncated neck are transformed into ornamental shapes similar to those that animate the extravagant decoration of the pedestal. Like Michelangelo in the *Pietà* in St. Peter's, Cellini placed his signature on a strap crossing Perseus's breast.

BARTOLOMMEO AMMANATI

A sculptor closer to Michelangelo, in fact protected and often supervised by him, was Bartolommeo Ammanati (1511–92). The marble and bronze *Fountain of Neptune* occupied Ammanati and his shop from 1560 to 1575, and a Sea Nymph (fig. 695) on the fountain, probably executed by an assistant using Ammanati's model, is instructive with regard to the relation of *maniera* artists to Michelangelo. Obviously derived from the Medici Chapel *Dawn* (see fig. 560), it is also very different. Where Michelangelo is tense, Ammanati is relaxed; where Michelangelo is tragic, Ammanati is serene. Michelangelo's devices, including even the famous pose "slipping off" the support, have been ornamentalized. The motive is Michelangelesque, but the drama is gone. This is true of much of Ammanati's sculpture, and, as will be seen, of many paintings by Vasari and Alessandro Allori as well.

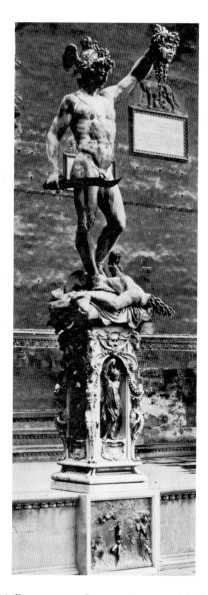

694. BENVENUTO CELLINI. *Perseus and Medusa* (see colorplate 16, p. 24). 1545–54. Bronze with marble pedestal, height 18'. ⬛ Loggia dei Lanzi, Florence. Commissioned by Duke Cosimo de' Medici

Characteristic of the grandiosity of late Cinquecento architecture is the courtyard of the Palazzo Pitti (fig. 696), which Ammanati added in 1558–70 to the original Quattrocento structure, which had been purchased by Cosimo in 1549 for his duchess, Eleonora da Toledo. It was when the Medici moved to the Palazzo Pitti, leaving behind their former living quarters in the Florentine republican city hall, that the Palazzo dei Priori became known as the "old palace"—Palazzo Vecchio— a name that has stuck to the present day. Ammanati had worked in Venice under Jacopo Sansovino, and doubtless he had the Zecca (see fig. 663) in mind when designing the Pitti courtyard, but he carried the rustication further, embracing three stories of columns and also walls, arches, and lintels. Only capitals, bases, entablatures, and ornamental window frames escape. Although the rusticated blocks are rough in contrast to Sansovino's smooth ones, they have none of the rude, formless qual-

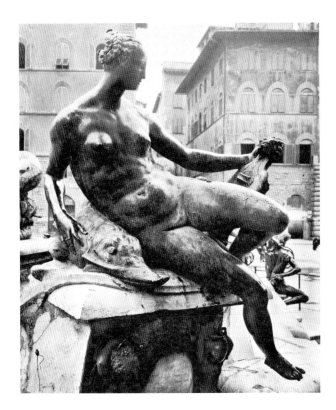

695. BARTOLOMMEO AMMANATI. Sea Nymph, on
the *Fountain of Neptune*. 1560–75. Bronze, over-life-sized.
🏛 Piazza della Signoria, Florence. Commissioned by
Duke Cosimo de' Medici

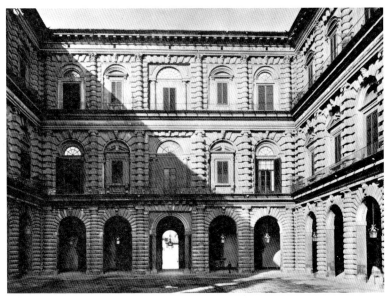

696. BARTOLOMMEO AMMANATI. Courtyard,
Palazzo Pitti, Florence. 1558–70. Commissioned by
Duke Cosimo de' Medici

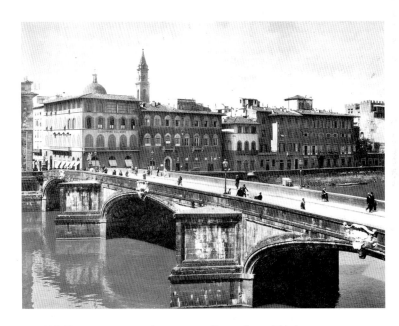

697. BARTOLOMMEO AMMANATI. Ponte Santa Trinita,
Florence. Begun 1566 (rebuilt after 1945). Commissioned
by Duke Cosimo de' Medici

ity so disturbing in the architecture of Giulio Romano
(see fig. 610). On the ground story (Tuscan) the blocks
are rounded and contiguous, on the second (Ionic)
square and separated, on the third (Corinthian) rounded
and separated. For all its colossal scale, the courtyard is
ultimately ornamental. The window tabernacles of the
second story bear the same relationship to Michelangelo's originals in the vestibule of the Laurentian Library (see fig. 562) as does Ammanati's Sea Nymph to
Michelangelo's *Dawn*.

Ammanati took his original designs for the Ponte
Santa Trinita (fig. 697) to Michelangelo shortly before
the latter's death, and the master criticized and corrected
them. The soaring flight of the roadway above the river,
the tension and power of the flattened arches, and the
potent simplicity of the wedge-shaped pylons should be
credited to Michelangelo, even if the details were perhaps softened by Ammanati. Ammanati's Ponte Santa
Trinita was blown up by the retreating Germans in 1944
and rebuilt after the war.

GIOVANNI BOLOGNA

The swan song of Late Renaissance sculpture in Florence was performed by a foreigner, in fact a non-Italian
who for more than half a century was active in Italy.
Jean Boulogne (1529–1608) was born in Douai in Flanders but is generally known by the Italianized version of

his name, Giovanni Bologna or even Giambologna. He
rapidly absorbed a variety of Italian sources, including
Donatello, Ghiberti, Verrocchio, Michelangelo, and the
sculptors of the *maniera*, but in freedom of invention and
skill of execution he surpassed his contemporaries. Is
Giambologna an Italian or a Fleming? Is he a Renaissance artist at all? It can be argued that his relief compositions lead us in the direction of the paintings of the
Northerners Rubens and Poussin, his new pictorial
treatment of pulsating human flesh, flashing eyes, and
silky hair directly to Gianlorenzo Bernini.

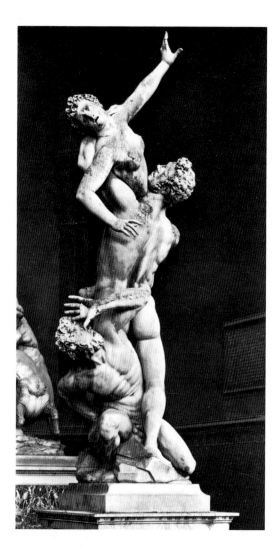

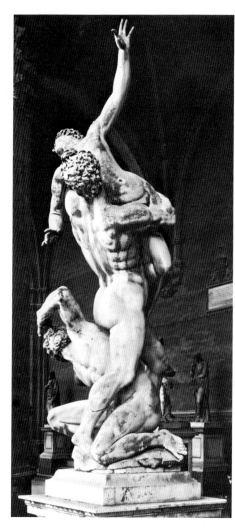

If there is a transition from the Italian Late Renaissance to the European Baroque, it is in the sculpture of Giovanni Bologna that we can find it, and it could even be argued that he does not belong in this book. Although he was as much an anachronism as Leonardo in Lombardy forty years before, he was physically present in late Cinquecento Tuscany, and in the stiff intellectual climate of the *maniera* and the Academy, his vitality appears as a refreshing antidote.

Giovanni Bologna added his own contributions to the statuary of the Piazza della Signoria, including the *Rape of the Sabine Woman* (figs. 698, 699), placed in 1583 by Grand Duke Francesco I under the Loggia dei Lanzi (see colorplate 16, p. 24) in the spot once occupied by Donatello's *Judith and Holofernes*. The identification of the subject mattered so little to Giambologna that he called earlier versions of the same group Paris and Helen, Pluto and Proserpina, and Phineus and Andromeda. His chief interest lay in the energy of the spiral movement and the vitality of the male and female figures, and he succeeded so well in their rendition that Baroque sculptors, particularly Bernini, never forgot this group.

BRONZINO

After Pontormo, the leading painter in Tuscany was his pupil Agnolo Tori, called Bronzino (1503–72), who is the boy in a cloak seated on the steps in Pontormo's *Joseph in Egypt* (see fig. 578). Although Bronzino absorbed much from his master, he does not seem to have responded to Pontormo's poetry and imagination. "Cold" and "hard" are the adjectives that come to mind as we attempt to characterize Bronzino's style; metal, marble, and porcelain are the substances his pictures suggest. His early style, during or soon after the period when he was Pontormo's assistant at the Capponi Chapel, is represented by the *Pietà* (fig. 700), once attributed to Pontormo but now given to Bronzino.

Instead of the soaring fountain of figures in Pontormo's Capponi *Entombment* (see colorplate 108, p. 518), Bronzino reverts to a closed composition of sculptural masses recalling rather the Luco *Lamentation* (see fig. 576) by Andrea del Sarto. Yet Pontormo's polished surfaces persist—if anything they seem congealed by his pupil's emotional reserve. Linear contours, sometimes

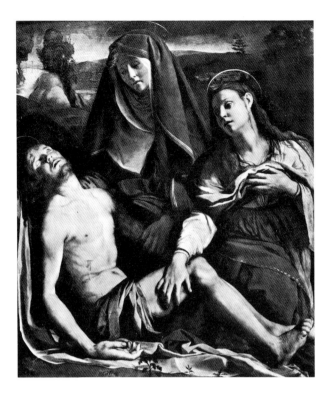

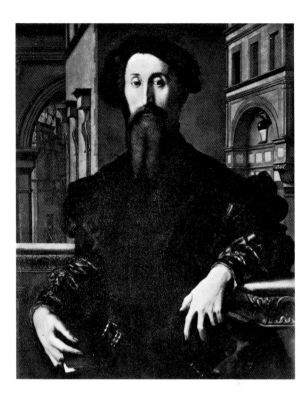

700. BRONZINO. *Pietà*. c. 1530. Panel, 41¼ x 39½".
Uffizi Gallery, Florence. Perhaps commissioned
for Sta. Trinita, Florence

701. BRONZINO. *Bartolommeo Panciatichi*. c. 1540.
Panel, 41⅜ x 33½". Uffizi Gallery, Florence. Probably
commissioned by the sitter

precisely drawn in Quattrocento style, isolate features, anatomical details, and drapery folds. Even the distant landscape—a rare feature in Bronzino's art—looks Quattrocentesque in the stylization of trees and hills. Calvary at the left and a small woods at the right anchor the arc of the horizon, locking it to the upper corners of the frame; in the lower corners Christ, his limbs stiffened in rigor mortis, fits into the left, and the Magdalen into the right. Yet for all Bronzino's chill, it would be a mistake to suppose that he is an unemotional artist. Within the rigidity of compositional arrangements and metallic surfaces lives the possibility of intense feeling. The cross-light reveals this as it plays on the distraught eyes and open mouth of the Magdalen and illuminates the dead features of Christ from below.

Bronzino was the perfect artist for the newly established regime of Cosimo I, who was installed as second duke of Florence after the murder of Alessandro de' Medici in 1537 and who eventually, in 1569, became grand duke of Tuscany. Again and again, Bronzino and his pupils portrayed the new monarch, his family, and his court in elegant images that nonetheless seem to betray the terror of Cosimo's absolutism. The melancholy stare of Bronzino's portrait of *Bartolommeo Panciatichi* (fig. 701) issues from a frozen mask, and every surface and detail are drawn with pitiless accuracy. The haughty young man stands, his elbow propped on a pedestal, against a background of utter unreality. Fragments of buildings, incommensurable in character, style, and scale, deprived of bases, entrances, or connecting streets, and

arranged at baffling angles in depth, are drawn with inhuman hardness—a world of carved stone without a living being or a plant and almost without sky.

An astounding picture, probably painted in the mid-1540s, is Bronzino's *Allegory with Venus and Cupid* (colorplate 132, p. 653). Ordered by Cosimo de' Medici and given by him as a present to King Francis I of France, the painting can be seen as a summary of the stylistic tendencies and moral dilemmas of the age. Its intricate symbolism continues to provoke scholarly interest and controversy; two recent theories have identified the main theme as the *Exposure of Luxury* and *Venus Disarming Cupid*. The bald, winged figure at the upper right is almost certainly Father Time; assisted by a figure who may represent Truth or Fraud at the opposite corner, Time draws back a curtain to unveil a scene that seems to represent incipient incest. An older-than-childish Cupid rubs against his mother, Venus, kissing her and squeezing her nipple while a putto (Jest or Folly?) pelts the shameless pair with roses. At the lower left, Venus's doves bill and coo. The screaming figure at the left edge has been identified as the female allegory of Jealousy, but a new interpretation suggests that this is a male allegory of Syphilis. To the right, with the face of a beautiful girl, is a monster with a serpent's tail and the hind legs and claws of a lion. She wears a green dress and carries a honeycomb in one hand and a scorpionlike stinger in the other.

The cold and fanatical perfection of the artist's draftsmanship projects and models the figure of Venus in crys-

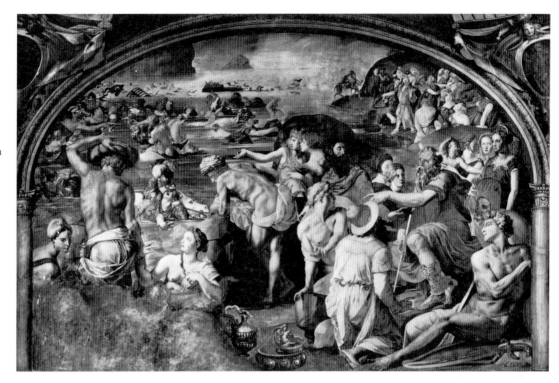

702. BRONZINO. *Crossing of the Red Sea.* c. 1540. Fresco, size of chapel 16' 1" deep x 12' 7" wide. Chapel of Eleonora da Toledo, Palazzo Vecchio, Florence. Commissioned by Duke Cosimo de' Medici

talline light. The variety of anatomies—male, female, young, old—the pearls and the shining locks of hair, and the glittering masks belonging to the figure identified as Fraud or Truth are set against silks of piercing green, blue, and violet. What seems here to be deliberate lasciviousness should be compared with the purity of Michelangelo's nudes, who come to us unclothed as from the mind of God. It is characteristic of the period that the same society that accepted such dubious pictures as this also enforced bits of drapery on Michelangelo's *Last Judgment*; Michelangelo was even condemned as salacious by Pietro Aretino, who was one of the most scandalous figures of the age. In one variation or another, the Venus and Cupid theme was repeated again and again in the mid-Cinquecento, including several times by Bronzino.

Bronzino decorated the walls and ceiling of a chapel erected for Cosimo's duchess Eleonora da Toledo in the Palazzo dei Priori, which the Medici had taken over as living quarters, using a technique far more time-consuming than the traditional one. Damaged portions seem to indicate that the underpainting was in true fresco and the detailed finished layer was added in tempera. The *Crossing of the Red Sea* (fig. 702) was intended to recall Michelangelo's *Deluge* (see colorplate 88, p. 489). This kind of quotation lent authority to the learned *maniera* style, but none of Michelangelo's poses are exactly, or even approximately, repeated, and Bronzino shows that he can vary the vocabulary and improvise on a Michelangelesque theme. He tosses figures about with abandon in the rising sea, along with the floating baggage of pharaoh's army. The well-preserved portions show muscular anatomies that, although devoid of Michelangelo's energy, are rendered with all the uncan-

ny delicacy of Bronzino's panel paintings and glow with the same cold, pearly light.

FRANCESCO SALVIATI

Approximately contemporary with Bronzino's frescoes in the chapel of Eleonora da Toledo are those by Francesco Salviati (1510–63) in the Sala dell'Udienza, in another part of the Palazzo dei Priori. Salviati, a boyhood companion and lifelong friend of Giorgio Vasari, retained his own striking and often delightful individuality in decorative frescoes in Rome and Florence. The *Triumph of Camillus* (fig. 703) in the Sala dell'Udienza displays his erudition and virtuosity. The general on his triumphal car, the barbarian captives, the trophies and standards, and even the altar to Juno with its smoking lamps are based on Salviati's study of ancient Roman historical reliefs rather than on direct observation of nature. The ornamentalized and archaistic horses, for example, are imitated from Imperial Roman reliefs. The procession is compressed into the foreground plane in the manner of Salviati's ancient prototypes, yet he allowed himself imaginative freedom in the mountain landscape and the low, luminous clouds. Out of the profusion of archaeological elements, an occasional contemporary portrait stands out with clarity.

The point of no return in *maniera* complexity is exemplified by the frescoes with which Salviati decorated the salone of the Palazzo Sacchetti in Rome (colorplate 133, p. 654). Probably representing the havoc wrought by the Ark of the Lord when carried off by the Philistines (I Samuel: 5–6), the frescoes simulate wall paintings of different proportions and deliberately do not harmonize with the shapes of the upper windows.

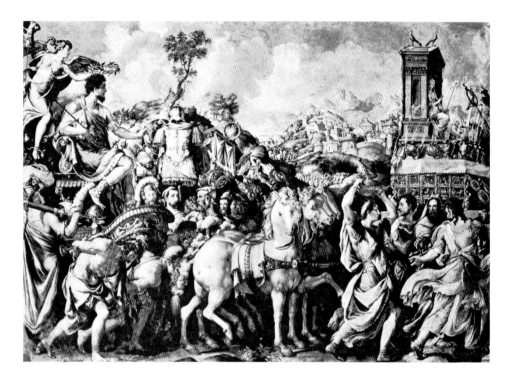

703. FRANCESCO SALVIATI. *Triumph of Camillus*. Mid-1540s. Fresco, 13' 10" x 19' 4". Sala dell'Udienza, Palazzo Vecchio, Florence. Commissioned by Duke Cosimo de' Medici

These "paintings" are scattered about the wall like the paintings-within-paintings in Pompeiian murals, which Salviati could not have seen, although he may have known similar examples in Rome or elsewhere that are now lost. All are enclosed in fantastic painted frames, all different, intertwined with a jumble of garlands and sculptured figures. Out of the darkness under the helmet, jar, and vegetables that dangle from one of the frames emerges Father Time, and his hands overlap the simulated marble frame of the lower windows as he steps from his pedestal as if into the very space of the room. Above the lower window frames, nudes—like Michelangelo nudes in a drugged torpor—languish in poses of abandoned sensuality, one seen from the back, the other from the front, on draped cloths that almost cover the tops of the window frames. Nothing more contrary to principles of Renaissance harmony could be imagined, yet all is done with exquisitely refined colors and draftsmanly skill.

GIORGIO VASARI

The prince of the Florentine *maniera* was Giorgio Vasari (1511–74), into whose *Lives of the Most Eminent Painters, Sculptors, and Architects*, an immense reservoir of knowledge, tradition, opinion, theory, and legend, we have dipped from time to time. So successful was Vasari's formula for inventing figures and compositions, so slight his necessity for further study from nature, so well disciplined his army of assistants, that with their aid Vasari was able to cover many Florentine and Roman walls and ceilings with frescoes and oil paintings. While these are often unreal and pompous, they seldom lack decorative effect or historical interest. Enormous altarpieces from

his studio line the side aisles of Santa Croce, Santa Maria Novella, and other Florentine churches; vast battle scenes and smaller decorative works fill the halls and smaller chambers of the Palazzo dei Priori. The fresco of *Paul III Directing the Continuance of St. Peter's* (fig. 704), painted before Michelangelo was appointed architect by Pope Paul III, is typical of his style. It forms a part of the decorations of the Cancelleria in Rome (see fig. 231), a building begun as a cardinal's palace and converted in the Cinquecento into offices for the pontifical government. Vasari and his pupils painted the frescoes lining the great hall in just one hundred working days, and when he boasted of this fact to Michelangelo, the latter replied, "*Si vede bene*" ("So one sees").

A Roman Doric portico at either side encloses a flight of concave, semicircular steps, based on Bramante's design for the fountain of the Vatican Belvedere. On one side can be distinguished a statue labeled Magnificentia, on the other Sinceritas opens a door in her body to display her heart. The pope is followed by Renaissance architects, one of whom is a portrait of Bramante, but the pontiff's attendants are allegorical figures in classical costume. Paul III lifts one Michelangelesque hand to point to the unfinished St. Peter's (see p. 636), while with the other he approves the plan of Antonio da Sangallo the Younger, held up by figures characterized as the Arts of Design and Construction by the drawing and stonecutting tools that they hold or that lie on the steps below. At the right Father Tiber, his elbow and foot propped on books, reclines on the steps, embracing the papal tiara and holding an umbrella sheltering the crossed keys. The style is standard—linear, elaborate, and learned. Many of the figures are borrowed from Michelangelo and Raphael, and the composition skill-

right: 704. GIORGIO VASARI. *Paul III Directing the Continuance of St. Peter's,* from a cycle of the Life of Pope Paul III. 1544. Fresco. Great Hall, Palazzo della Cancelleria, Rome. Commissioned by Cardinal Alessandro Farnese

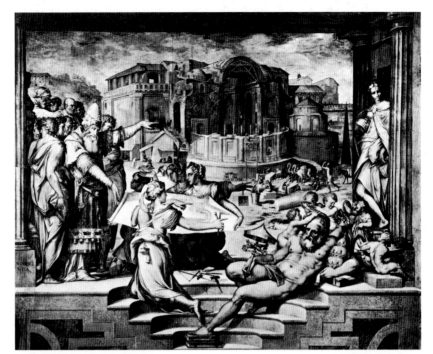

below: 705. GIORGIO VASARI. Uffizi, Florence. 1560–80. Finished by BERNARDO BUONTALENTI and ALFONSO PARIGI. Commissioned by Cosimo I de' Medici

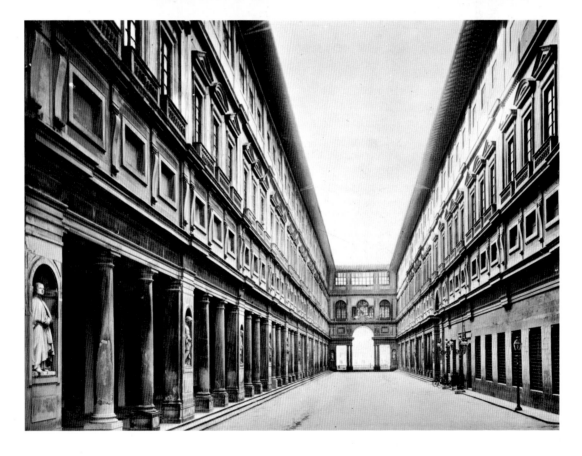

fully interweaves numerous linear elements. One's judgment of such rhetorical paintings depends on personal preferences, but what seems odd is that Vasari's taste is not that of the Renaissance, about which he knew more than any of his contemporaries.

The supreme example of Vasari's architecture is the Uffizi (Offices), commissioned by Cosimo to house the governmental functions and records of the duchy of Florence, later the grand duchy of Tuscany (fig. 705).

The building's four lofty stories line three sides of a space that is more like a street than a piazza. Centrality is avoided and the Uffizi derives its cumulative effect from the repetition of elements: two Tuscan columns and a pier on the ground story, while on the second story a triplet of mezzanine windows alternates with Michelangelesque consoles. The third story features another triad of windows, and the open loggia of the fourth (now unfortunately glazed) reflects the Tuscan columns

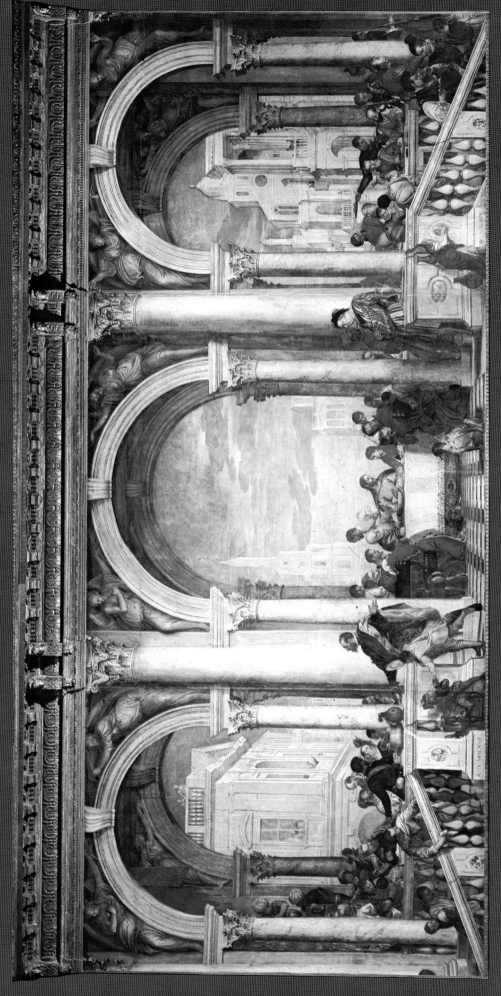

Colorplate 128. VERONESE. *Feast in the House of Levi*. 1573. Canvas, 18' 3" x 42'. Accademia, Venice. Commissioned for the refectory of the Dominican Monastery of SS. Giovanni e Paolo, Venice; the patron was probably Andrea Buono, a friar in the monastery

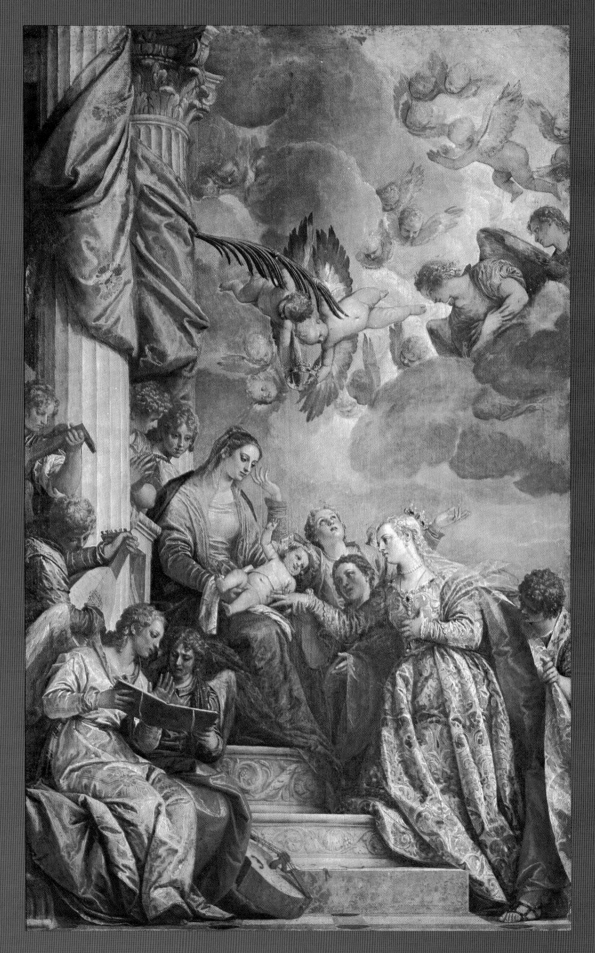

Colorplate 129. VERONESE. *Mystical Marriage of St. Catherine*. Probably 1570s. Canvas, 12' 5" x 7' 11".
Accademia, Venice. Commissioned for the high altar of S. Caterina, Venice

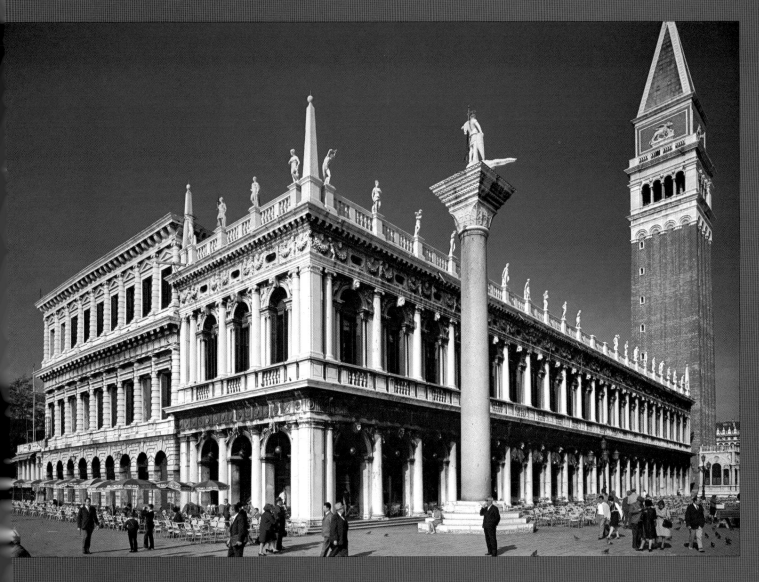

Colorplate 130. JACOPO SANSOVINO. Library of S. Marco, Venice. Begun 1537.
Finished by VINCENZO SCAMOZZI. Commissioned by the Procurators of St. Mark's; to the left is
Sansovino's Zecca (Mint); see fig. 663

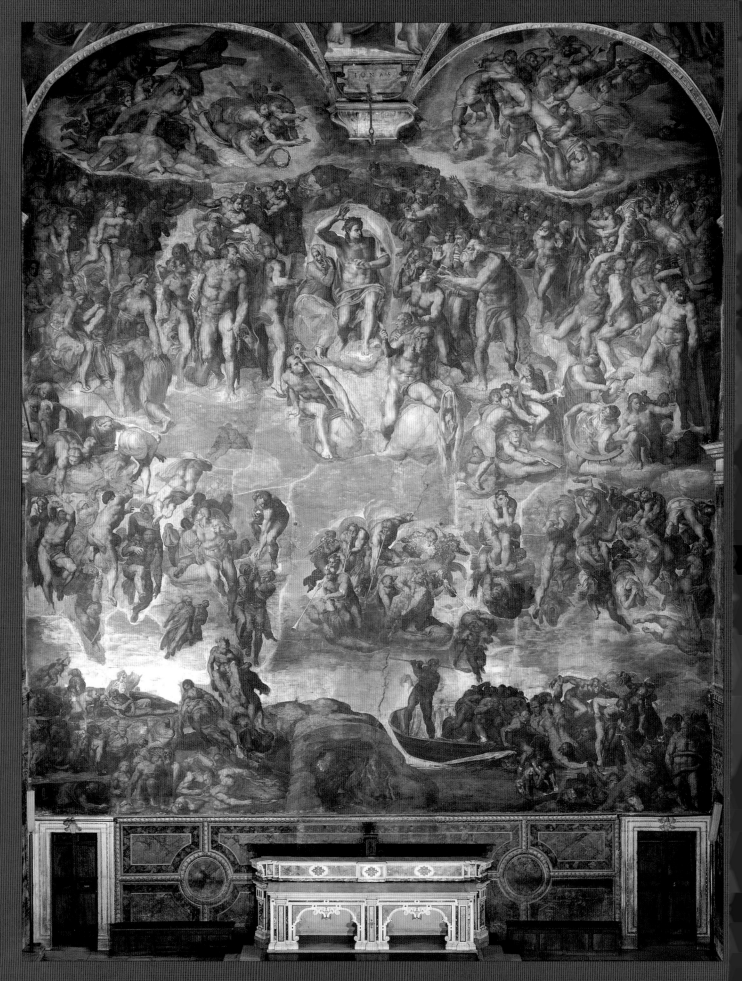

Colorplate 131. MICHELANGELO. *Last Judgment*. 1536–41. Fresco, 48 x 44'. Sistine Chapel,
Vatican, Rome. Commissioned by Pope Paul III

Colorplates 128–35
652

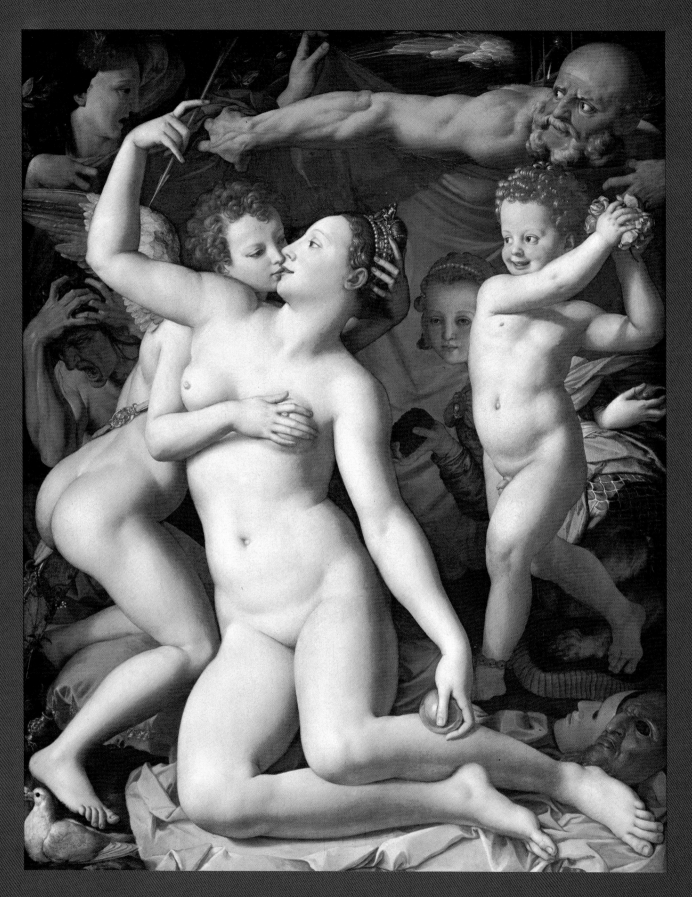

Colorplate 132. BRONZINO. *Allegory with Venus and Cupid*. Mid–1540s. Panel, 61 x 56¾". National Gallery, London. Commissioned by Cosimo de' Medici; given by him to King Francis I of France

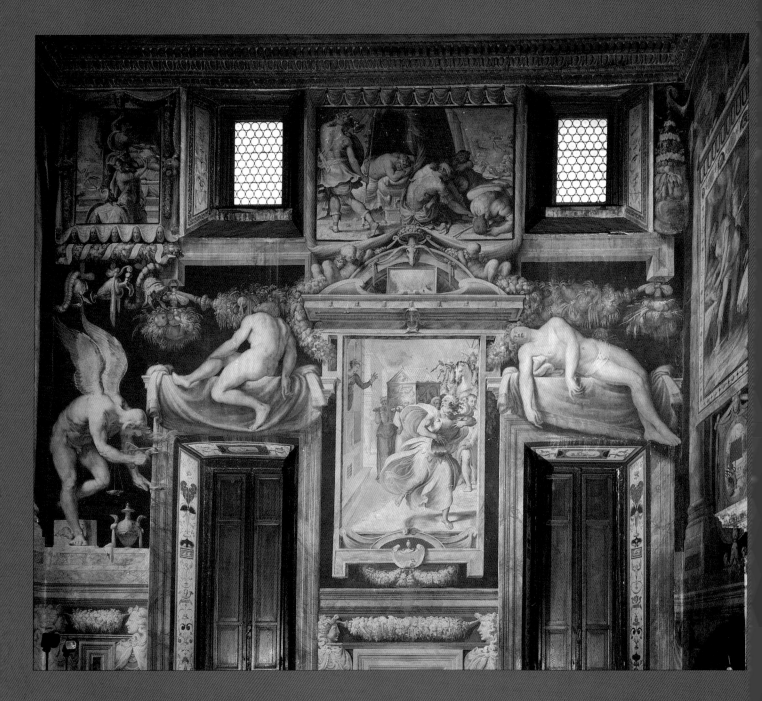

Colorplate 133. FRANCESCO SALVIATI. Fresco decoration. c. 1553. Salone, Palazzo Sacchetti, Rome. Probably commissioned by Cardinal Ricci da Montepulciano

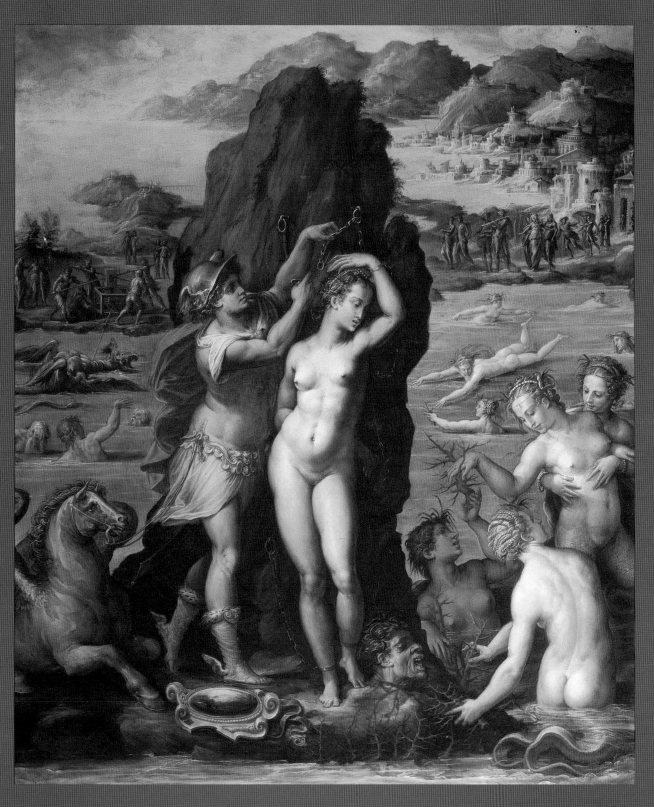

Colorplate 134. GIORGIO VASARI. *Perseus and Andromeda*. 1570–72. Oil on slate, 45¹/₂ x 34".
🏛 Studiolo, Palazzo Vecchio, Florence. Commissioned by Francesco I de' Medici

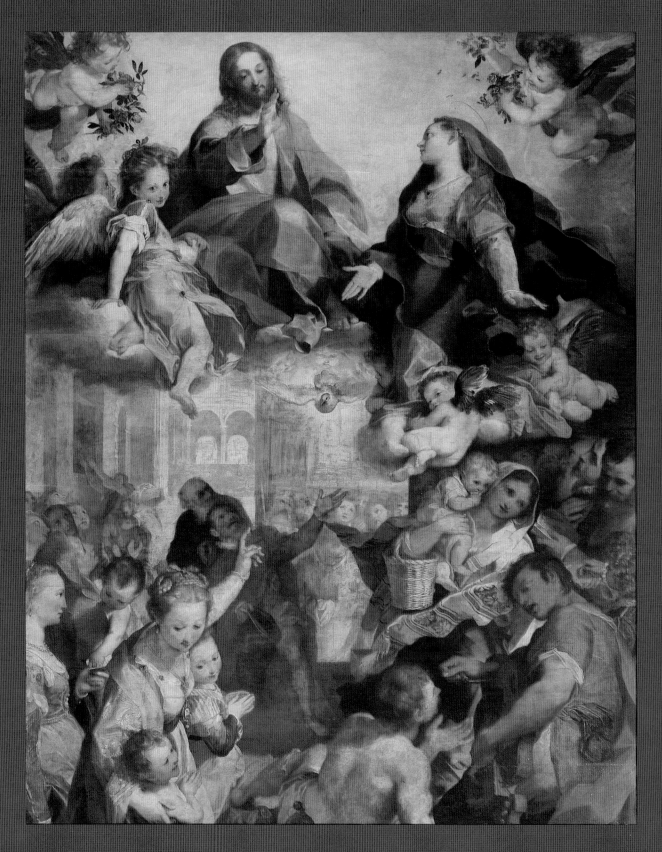

Colorplate 135. FEDERICO BAROCCI. *Madonna del Popolo*. 1575–79. Panel, 11' 9³⁄₈" x 8' 3¹⁄₄". Uffizi Gallery, Florence. Commissioned by the Confraternity of the Misericordia, Arezzo

of the ground story. The only break in the uniformity comes at the end, where a central arch with a Palladian motive above it opens the vista in the direction of the Arno River. Vasari's governmental structure incorporated existing buildings, including private houses and almost the entire Church of San Piero Scheraggio, where Dante had spoken and so many important events of Republican Florence had taken place. The imposing façades of the Uffizi, whose *pietra serena* trim outweighs the few remaining *intonaco* wall surfaces, mask the disparity of old and new buildings that is visible when one looks at the structure from the back. The huge complex, so rapidly remodeled, strung together, and refaced, contained such extensive openings and reached such a height that Vasari was constrained to use steel girders to reinforce it, one of the earliest known instances of metal architecture.

THE STUDIOLO

It is fitting that our consideration of Florentine art should draw toward a close with a characteristic invention of the *maniera*, the Studiolo of Francesco I de' Medici, son and successor of Cosimo I. This tiny chamber within the Palazzo dei Priori (see fig. 54) was dedicated to the geological, mineralogical, and alchemical interests of this self-centered and ineffective ruler. Its walls are lined with two tiers of paintings that act as doors for cupboards containing Francesco's scientific books, specimens, and instruments. Two doors, not distinguished in any way from the cupboard doors, cover the only windows: Francesco preferred to work by candlelight. The intimate scale of the project allowed Vasari and his pupils to develop their imaginative abilities, technical skill, and jewel-like delicacy of color. Eight sculptors contributed bronze statues, and the paintings were done by no fewer than twenty-four masters.

Vasari's own contributions are charming, especially the *Perseus and Andromeda* (colorplate 134, p. 655); legend states that when Perseus held up the head of Medusa and plunged his sword into the dragon that was about to attack Andromeda, the dragon turned to stone and its blood, streaming through the water, turned to coral. In the foreground Andromeda is chained to the rock while mermaids sport about in—and even on—the green sea and retrieve branches of coral. In the background, stylized promontories that recall the mountainous seacoast north of Pisa sparkle with classical buildings, and on the beach workmen draw the dragon onto land with a huge winch.

Just as toylike in its unreality is the *Pearl Fishers* (fig. 706) by Bronzino's follower Alessandro Allori (1535–1607), whose style is imitated from the cool, smooth manner of his master. Exquisite male and female nudes, human and mythological, play about on rocks, dive off boats, and bring up shells overflowing with sea water and pearls. Over and over the figures quote Michelangelo (the central nude seen from the back comes

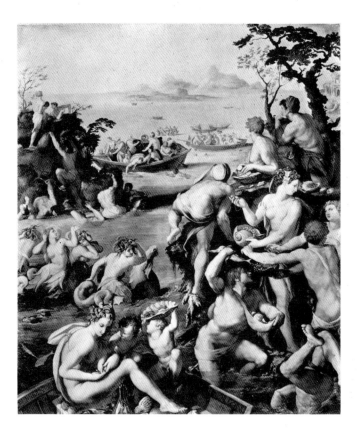

706. ALESSANDRO ALLORI. *Pearl Fishers*. 1570–72. Oil on slate, 45½ x 34". ▪ Studiolo, Palazzo Vecchio, Florence. Commissioned by Francesco I de' Medici

straight out of the *Battle of Cascina*; see fig. 479), but in the most playful way, and the echoes of the *Deluge* on the Sistine Ceiling are transformed by Allori's predominantly pink and blue coloring.

The artists who contributed to the Studiolo, including even a Netherlander, created a surprising variety of changes on the *maniera* formula. Three among them, nonetheless, seem to have harbored the ideal of a reform—Santi di Tito and two painters hardly known outside the Studiolo, Mirabello Cavalori (before 1520–72) and Girolamo Macchietti (1535/41–92). Their styles and their outlook on the nature and purpose of painting are similar, but due to the age gap between them Cavalori should probably be credited as the innovator. But any argument about him is difficult to sustain, because his production is an enigma: only four pictures by him are known, two of them in the Studiolo, and all four were painted in the last four years of his life. After the artificiality of the *maniera* paintings in the Studiolo, his pictures and those of Macchietti are like windows into the Cinquecento. Neither artist was able to transfer his naturalism to hieratic themes, as Caravaggio was to do only twenty years later, but here they were assigned or they selected subjects from daily life, to which their only possible addition appears to be the architectural setting, a severe Tuscan order remarkably similar in both.

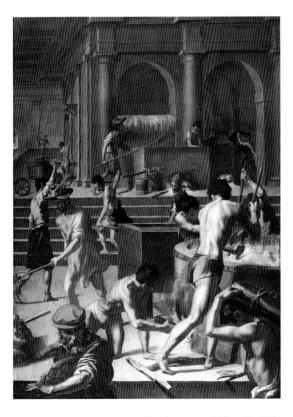

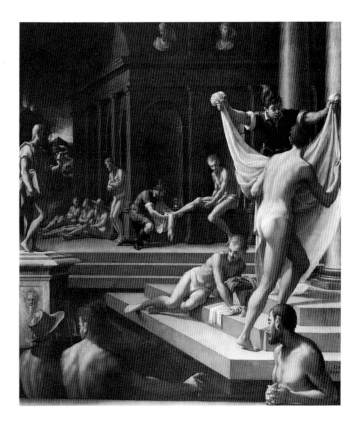

707. MIRABELLO CAVALORI. *Wool Factory*. 1570–72. Oil on slate. 🏛 Studiolo, Palazzo Vecchio, Florence. Commissioned by Francesco I de' Medici

708. GIROLAMO MACCHIETTI. *Baths at Pozzuoli*. 1570–72. Oil on slate. 🏛 Studiolo, Palazzo Vecchio, Florence. Commissioned by Francesco I de' Medici

The devotion to naturalism in Cavalori's *Wool Factory* (fig. 707) cannot be paralleled, even in Lombardy. It is hard to imagine that the figures were unposed, but the artist has done his utmost to make them look as if they were. Probably he made sketches in a wool factory, of which there were many in Florence, and models—perhaps even the workmen themselves—could have been posed later in Cavalori's studio. Here people do what they are doing because they have to, not because they are forced into artistic poses, and the men are not nude to display the beauty of their anatomy; they have stripped because they are hot, displaying far-from-ideal bodies wearing typical Cinquecento undershorts. In fact, the only "nudes" are those who are carrying firewood, stuffing it into the flames, or churning the masses of wool in the boiling caldron. Next behind them a wringer is being twisted, and at the top of the steps the wool, wound on a huge spindle, is being carded. Cavalori seems to have taken special pleasure in the felt hats and peaked caps of the workmen.

No abstract scheme, either imposed upon the figures or derived from them, unites their activities, but a strong side light gives deep shadows, a uniformly smooth brushwork suggests textures, and a hectic sense of hard labor under pressure is expressed. One can see, feel, hear, and even, it seems, smell the factory; endowed with hindsight, we may think of Edgar Degas or George Bellows. Yet there is a grand architectural setting and, in spite of everything, an indefinable Renaissance nobility. Grand Duke Francesco may have liked such proletarian pictures as oddities, especially since the wealth of his dominion still depended largely on wool, but the *Wool Factory* was not the kind of picture calculated to gain Cavalori lucrative public commissions.

Girolamo Macchietti's *Baths at Pozzuoli* (fig. 708) is similar to the *Wool Factory* in its naturalistic concept and smooth pictorial style. One can hardly expect that these hot-spring baths, not far from Naples, were set in architecture of such grandeur, and most likely Macchietti had never seen them. He could, however, have studied and sketched in the Florentine public baths, as did Leonardo and Michelangelo. The resemblance between the youth reclining on the steps and the seated figure having his leg toweled in Macchietti's picture and their counterparts in Michelangelo's *Battle of Cascina* (see fig. 479) are due not to imitation on Macchietti's part, for the figures are in no sense imitations, but, most probably, to the fact that such poses could be seen daily in the Stufa. A statue of Aesculapius, god of health, presides over the scene from the left, but so unobtrusively that he almost seems one of the bathers. Here, too, one feels the temperature; the half-figures in the foreground, cut off by the edge of the marble baths, stand happily in the warm, medicinal water. Mavericks such as Cavalori and Macchietti were ahead of their time indeed, but in 1564 Vasari included them among the painters selected to provide pictures for the catafalque to solemnize Michelangelo's funeral in San Lorenzo. Their Studiolo pictures point the way out of the *maniera*, and one wonders if Caravaggio gained admittance to this arcane chamber on his way to Rome.

We have come full circle. From the moment of its construction the Palazzo dei Priori had been the home of the Florentine Republic, and its simplicity and power had symbolized the qualities of individual character that the Republic exalted. Through two and a half centuries these qualities, in crisis and in triumph, in failure and in success, had inspired one of the great periods in the history of human artistic imagination. Now that the Republic was over, it is symbolic that the massive building, deprived of its meaning, should provide the setting for an absolutist ruler to divine secret mysteries by artificial light. The fortress from which the Florentines of the Renaissance had issued to conquer reality has become both the refuge for a Mannerist flight from reality and a womb for the germination of a new vision of reality.

POSTLUDE

For the absolutist elegance of grand-ducal Florence, the *maniera* was an appropriate vehicle. But even Counter-Reformation Rome was populated by *maniera* artists of intense productivity, great authority, high position, and, it might be argued, limited talent and taste. In this context, the last paintings, sculpture, and architecture of Michelangelo are exceptional. In retrospect, the dramatic architectural style created by Michelangelo in his last Roman works seems to point the way toward the architectural triumphs of the Roman Baroque, and in a sense it did, because some of his pupils were instrumental in laying the groundwork of Early Baroque architecture.

Strong countercurrents to the maniera in central Italy were led by two outsiders to Rome, the architect Vignola and the painter Barocci, neither of whom owes much to Michelangelo. Whether either of them belongs in a book on Renaissance art is as debatable as whether they should appear in the Baroque, but even if they elude classification, these masters are too important to omit from a period in which, chronologically at least, they lived and worked.

GIACOMO DA VIGNOLA

Jacopo Barozzi (1507–73), known as Giacomo da Vignola, was born in Vignola, near Bologna. He started out as a painter under the tutelage of Sebastiano Serlio, the architect and perspective painter who is best known for his treatise *Regole generali di architettura* and for his role in transporting the Renaissance to France. Serlio had studied under Peruzzi in Rome, and thus Vignola was brought into contact with High Renaissance tradition before he arrived in Rome in 1530. He worked with Peruzzi and Antonio da Sangallo the Younger in the Vatican and was employed in finishing the Palazzo Farnese and, after 1564, St. Peter's itself.

His work reveals his desire to revive and codify the Bramantesque tradition, an ambition not unusual for this era of treatises and standardization. Instead of inventing their own capitals, as had so many Quattrocento architects and indeed Michelangelo himself, *maniera* architects generally were content with copies of Bramante's capitals for St. Peter's. But Vignola settled the course of classical architecture for the next three and a half centuries with his *Regola delli cinque ordini di architettura*, first published in 1562 and reprinted in innumerable editions that came to an end only when the tradition of classical architectural training died out in the second quarter of the twentieth century. In this work, thirty-two plates, with instructions, laid down principles for the design, proportions, and employment of the orders then recognized—Tuscan, Doric, Ionic, Corinthian, and Composite—including shafts, capitals, bases, and entablatures. All were based on the ancient Roman models that were considered most beautiful, thus imposing Bramantesque taste on posterity and eliminating from consideration those fantasies of Roman architecture that so delight twentieth-century students.

Neither experience in completing Michelangelo's buildings nor collaboration with the Florentine *maniera* architects Vasari and Ammanati seems to have had any effect on Vignola other than to reinforce his classicism. He is best known today for the interior of the Gesù, the mother church of the Jesuit Order, in Rome. Often considered the earliest Baroque church, the Gesù was derived from Alberti's Sant'Andrea in Mantua.

Vignola's Villa Farnese at Caprarola is perhaps the most overwhelming secular building of the Renaissance in absolute dimensions (about 150 feet on each side), in its hilltop site, and in the grandeur of its proportions (fig. 709). Vignola was faced with an unusual problem: in 1559 Pope Paul III commissioned him to erect a palace for his son, Pierluigi Farnese, whom he had made duke of Castro and Nepi, on top of a pentagonal fortress the pope himself had built while a cardinal. In 1581 Michel de Montaigne stated that the villa was "pentagonal in form, but looks like a pure rectangle. Inside it is perfectly round." The tension maintained between the five sides of the fortress pedestal and our expectation of four for the villa is the source of much of our pleasure in the design. This sublimated conflict is analogous to those we have seen in the work of Palladio. Vignola reinforced the angles of the fortress with quoins, crowned it with a cornice and parapet, and provided it with two superimposed, rusticated, and arched entrances connected by balustraded ramps and flanked by pedimented windows. The motive of the corner bastions is continued, still with quoins, in the upper stories. Between these towering corners a seven-bay order stretches across each façade, with Ionic on the second story and Corinthian on the third. The pilaster sequence of the second story embraces a loggia (now glazed) of arches that affords a view over the hills and valleys of northern Latium. Windows fill these bays on the other sides. The

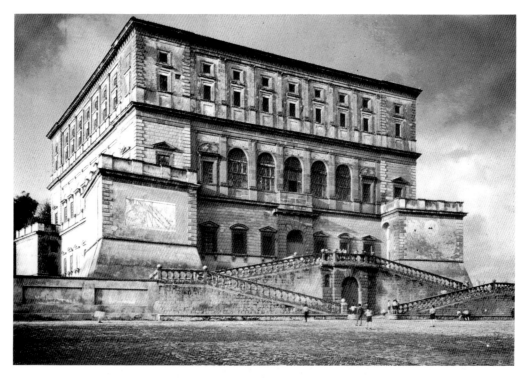

709. GIACOMO DA VIGNOLA. Façade, Villa Farnese, Caprarola. Begun 1559.
Commissioned by Pope Paul III for his son, Pierluigi Farnese

final story is subdivided into a row of oblong windows below a mezzanine of square ones, embraced by the same giant order.

The circular courtyard (fig. 710) consists of rusticated arches upholding a majestic *piano nobile* of paired Ionic engaged columns flanking arches that culminate in a balustrade with urns that conceals the setback third story. The courtyard thus appears as a revival in circular form of the two-story scheme of Bramante's Palazzo Caprini (see fig. 509). The villa's spiral staircase (fig. 711), composed of paired Tuscan columns, recalls Bramante's spiral ramp for the Vatican Belvedere.

FEDERICO BAROCCI

Ironically enough, the Emilian architect Vignola based his style on that of Bramante of Urbino, while the Urbinate painter Federico Barocci (1526–1612) dedicated much of his life to a revival of the inventions of the Emilian Correggio. And as Vignola was the most powerful architect in central Italy during the 1550s and 1560s except for Michelangelo, so Barocci was the most significant painter in that region between the death of Michelangelo and the arrival in Rome of the Carracci and Caravaggio in the 1590s. His long career overlapped the beginnings of the Baroque style, and he appears to have had considerable effect on Baroque painting, especially Rubens.

Although Barocci was profoundly influenced by the work of Correggio, he experienced it elsewhere than in

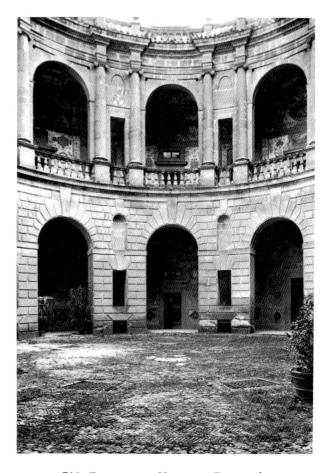

710. GIACOMO DA VIGNOLA. Courtyard,
Villa Farnese, Caprarola

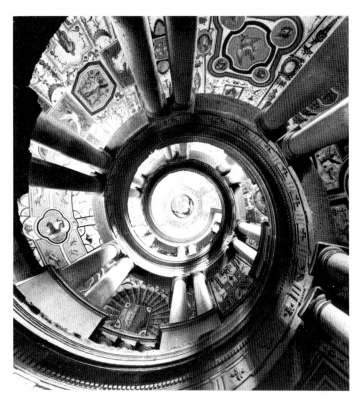

711. GIACOMO DA VIGNOLA. Spiral staircase, Villa Farnese, Caprarola

Parma, where there is no record of his presence. Nor, for that matter, does he seem to have been anywhere else in northern Italy, in spite of the considerable Venetian influence in his work. He did make two trips to Rome, where he studied particularly the work of Raphael and was protected by Federico Zuccari, the accomplished but monotonous leader of the Roman *maniera*. He worked in the little *casino* (garden house) built for Pope Pius IV in the Vatican Gardens. He left Rome in 1563, in poor health and with the suspicion that he had been poisoned, presumably by a jealous rival. Thereafter, he seldom left his mountain home at Urbino, where the classicism of his illustrious forebears, Piero della Francesca, Bramante, and Raphael, seems to have held little meaning for him.

In an era that sought rules and standards, Barocci acknowledged none save his own sensibility. In a period of stasis he was as enthralled by the mysteries of motion as was his Venetian contemporary Tintoretto (whom there is no possibility of his ever having met). But Correggio is uppermost in his mature work, especially his celebrated *Madonna del Popolo* (colorplate 135, p. 656). In Piero's altarpiece for a similar confraternity in Sansepolcro more than a century before (see figs. 277–79), the decisive principle had been the Virgin's protection of a group of mortals. For Barocci the essential was the dramatic instant of the Virgin's intercession for her people before a loving Christ.

The whole scene is caught up in a bewitching fusion of everyday experience with otherworldly rapture. Below surges a crowd worthy of Tintoretto, yet free of his urgency and violence. At the left an elegantly dressed young mother tries to interest her children in the heavenly apparition, but they are attracted by the beggar in the foreground and the player of the *vielle*—a four-stringed popular instrument operated by a crank—who in turn resists the beggar's request for charity. At the extreme lower right a brown-and-white puppy appeals to the spectator. With no gap between earthly byplay and heavenly apparition, one ascends over the heads of mothers with baskets and babies to child-angels, who support a beautiful Virgin, her hands spread gracefully in appeal. From a nearby Heaven of golden light, a youthful Christ blesses the crowd, over whose heads soars the dove of the Holy Spirit. Despite the powerfully modeled anatomy of the male figures, nothing has much weight or substance. Light plays over figures, faces, and bright garments as if through colored mists, as lightly as the Correggiesque smiles that move across the faces. Barocci's studies for this and other paintings include unprecedented color drawings made with pastels (sticks of dry color) or with colored chalks that glow in opalescent tones on paper generally tinted a rich robin's-egg blue. In the dissolving colors and smiling charm of the subjects, we seem to have left the solemnity and tensions of the late Cinquecento far behind.

Glossary

This glossary is limited to the most important terms. For definitions of architectural terminology not included here or for more detailed information, see Nikolaus Pevsner, John Fleming, and Hugh Honour, *The Penguin Dictionary of Architecture*, 4th ed., London, 1991. For symbols and iconographic themes, see James Hall, *Dictionary of Subjects and Symbols in Art*, New York, 1979. Cross-references are indicated by the use of SMALL CAPITALS.

ALTARPIECE. A painted or sculpted work of art that stands as a religious image upon and at the back of an altar; for a typical example, see Orcagna's altarpiece (colorplate 33, p. 119). It may depict the CRUCIFIXION, the Virgin and Child, and/or various saints, including the saint to whom the particular church or altar is dedicated. In certain periods it includes decorated gables and PINNACLES, as well as a PREDELLA. See also MAESTÀ.

ANNUNCIATION. The announcement by the angel Gabriel to the Virgin Mary of the Incarnation of Jesus Christ (Luke 1:26–38). In many representations of this scene a dove appears, to indicate that the Virgin has conceived by the Holy Spirit and will bear the Son of God; see the examples by Ghiberti, Fra Angelico, and Lorenzo Lotto (figs. 154, 206, and 640). The Annunciation to the Shepherds is the scene in which angels announce to shepherds the birth of Christ (Luke 2:8–14); see the example by Taddeo Gaddi (fig. 82).

ANTIPOPE. A rival pope, elected in opposition to another, who is later judged not to be a part of the accepted succession of popes. In general, it refers to the popes elected at Avignon in opposition to those at Rome during the Great Schism (1378–1417), and to a series of popes elected at Pisa and Basel.

APOCALYPSE. The Book of Revelation, the last book of the New Testament, in which St. John narrates the visions he experienced on the island of Patmos.

APOCRYPHA. A group of writings once included in versions of the Bible, but now generally excluded.

APSE. A large semicircular or polygonal niche, as seen in Leonardo's drawing of churches (fig. 449), at Sta. Maria della Consolazione in Todi (fig. 506), and behind the Virgin in Domenico Veneziano's St. Lucy altarpiece (colorplate 48, p. 258).

ARCADE. A series of ARCHES with their supporting COLUMNS or PIERS, as in the courtyard of the Palazzo Ducale at Urbino (colorplate 70, p. 359).

ARCH. A means of construction in which an opening, usually semicircular, is spanned by a series of wedge-shaped elements. It is supported from below by walls, PIERS, or COLUMNS, and by BUTTRESSING at the sides. See the courtyard of the Palazzo Ducale at Urbino (colorplate 70, p. 359).

ARCHITRAVE. The LINTEL and the lowest part of an ENTABLATURE; see Bramante's Tempietto (fig. 498).

ARRICCIO. The layer of relatively coarse plaster that is the first layer applied to a wall in the making of a FRESCO; see fig. 13.

ARTE (pl. *ARTI*). See GUILDS.

ARTS, LIBERAL. The seven liberal arts, which are derived from the curriculum for secular learning during the Middle Ages, are grammar, rhetoric, logic, arithmetic, music, geometry, and astronomy. They were frequently represented allegorically during the Middle Ages and the Renaissance; see Pollaiuolo's tomb of Pope Sixtus IV (figs. 329, 330).

ARTS, MECHANICAL. Practical occupations that involved working with the hands. During the Middle Ages, the mechanical arts included painting, sculpture, and architecture. Contrasted to the LIBERAL ARTS.

A SECCO. See FRESCO.

ASCENSION. The ascent of Christ into Heaven, as witnessed by his disciples forty days after the RESURRECTION (Luke 24:51 and Acts of the Apostles 1:9–12); see the example by Mantegna (fig. 408).

ASSUMPTION. The ascent of the Virgin Mary to Heaven after her death and burial when, according to Roman Catholic belief, her soul was reunited with her body; see the example by Titian (colorplate 118, p. 575).

AVELLO (pl. *AVELLI*). Italian word for tomb, generally used by art historians to refer to a tomb surmounted by a Gothic arch and often built into an opening between two chapels or as a series in a wall, as across the façade of Sta. Maria Novella (fig. 226).

BARREL VAULT. A semicylindrical VAULT; see the barrel vaults surmounting the nave and side chapels of Sant'Andrea in Mantua (fig. 229).

BASE. The lowest element of a COLUMN, wall, or DOME, occasionally of a statue; see the base of the column in Piero della Francesca's *Annunciation* (fig. 285) or the elaborately worked base of Cellini's statue of Perseus (fig. 694).

BASILICA. A general term applied to any church that, like Early Christian basilicas, has a longitudinal NAVE that terminates in an APSE and is flanked by SIDE AISLES; see figs. 137, 140–42.

BAY. An individual unit of space defined by PIERS and VAULTS in a vaulted structural system; the term also refers to the vertical definitions of these same units on the exterior or interior surfaces of a building, as indicated by such elements as BUTTRESSES and COLUMNS. The individual bays are evident in the plan of Brunelleschi's Sto. Spirito (fig. 142).

BEATO (fem. *BEATA*). Italian word for blessed. Specifically, beatification is a papal decree that declares a deceased person to be in the enjoyment of heavenly bliss (*beatus*) and grants a form of veneration to him or her. It is usually a step toward canonization.

BENEDICTINE ORDER. Founded by St. Benedict of Nursia (c. 480–c. 543) at Subiaco near Rome, the Benedictine rule spread to England and much of Western Europe in the next two centuries. Less austere than other early ORDERS, the Benedictines divided their hours among religious worship, reading, and work, generally either educational or agricultural.

BIRETTA. The square cap worn by ecclesiastics, that of priests being black, of bishops purple, and of cardinals red; see Raphael's *Pope Leo X with Cardinals* (fig. 530).

BLIND ARCADE. A closed ARCADE, as above the entrance door of Codussi's S. Zaccaria (fig. 433).

BOTTEGA. Italian word for shop, used to describe both the group of assistants who worked with an artist and the place where they worked.

BRACCIO (pl. *BRACCIA*). Italian word for arm. A unit of linear measurement used in many Italian centers, but varying from place to place; in Florence a *braccio* is approximately 1.913 feet.

BUTTRESS. A masonry support that counteracts the outward thrust of an ARCH or VAULT; diagonal buttresses are visible in the exterior view of the Cathedral of Florence (fig. 132).

CALVARY. See GOLGOTHA.

CAMALDOLITE ORDER. An independent branch of the BENEDICTINE ORDER founded by St. Romuald to establish the Eastern eremitic form of monasticism in the West. St. Romuald was born in Ravenna about 950 and died in 1027.

CAMPANILE. From the Italian word *campana* (bell). A bell tower either attached to a church or freestanding nearby; see figs. 132, 550.

CAMPO. Italian word for field; used in Siena, Venice, and other cities to denote certain public squares; for the irregularly shaped Campo in Siena, see fig. 4. See also PIAZZA.

CAPITAL. The decorated, crowning member of a COLUMN or PILASTER, on which rests the LINTEL or the arches of an ARCADE; see the courtyard of the Palazzo Ducale in Urbino (colorplate 70, p. 359). See also ORDER.

CAPOMAESTRO. Italian word for headmaster, used for the person in charge of design and construction for a cathedral or major governmental structure.

CARMELITE ORDER. Begun in the mid-twelfth century by a crusader named Berthold and his followers, who settled in caves on Mt. Carmel and led lives of silence, seclusion, and abstinence. About 1240 they migrated to Western Europe, where the rule was altered, the austerities mitigated, and the ORDER changed to a mendicant one, analogous to the DOMINICAN and FRANCISCAN ORDERS.

CARTHUSIAN ORDER. Founded by St. Bruno (c. 1030–1101) at Chartreuse near Grenoble in 1084. Carthusians follow a life of prayer, silence, and extreme austerity.

CARTOON. Full-scale preparatory drawing on one or more sheets of heavy paper.

CARYATID. A female figure that structurally or decoratively takes on the function of a COLUMN or PILASTER.

CASINO. A garden house.

CATHEDRAL. The church in which the bishop of a diocese has his permanent *cathedra*, or episcopal throne; not all large churches are cathedrals, and a town or city, no matter its size, can have only one cathedral.

CENACOLO. Italian word for supper room or REFECTORY, as in the Cenacolo of Sant'Apollonia, location for Castagno's *Last Supper* (colorplate 50, p. 260). The term is also used to refer to a representation of the Last Supper.

CERTOSA. Italian title for a Carthusian monastery (see figs. 437–39). Derived from Chartreuse, where St. Bruno founded a monastery in 1084.

CHALICE. Generally, a drinking cup, but specifically the cup used to hold the wine consecrated during the EUCHARIST; see the chalice in the foreground of Andrea del Sarto's *Lamentation* (fig. 576).

CHANCEL. The space in a church that is reserved for the clergy and choir; it is set off from the NAVE by steps and occasionally by a screen; see Palladio's S. Giorgio Maggiore (figs. 668, 669).

CHASING. The ornamenting of metal by engraving; see Ghiberti's bronze *Gates of Paradise* (colorplate 46, p. 257).

CHERUB (pl. CHERUBIM). One of an order of angelic beings ranking second to the SERAPHIM in the celestial hierarchy, usually represented as a baby angel; see Donatello's *Cantoria* (figs. 243, 244).

CHIAROSCURO. In painting, the contrast of light and shade—from the Italian *chiaro* (light) and *oscuro* (dark)—to enhance modeling, as in Masaccio's *Expulsion of Adam and Eve* (colorplate 5, p. 13, and figs. 196, 197).

CHRISTUS MORTUUS. Latin phrase for dead Christ, as in Giotto's *Crucifixion* in the Arena Chapel (fig. 66).

CHRISTUS PATIENS. Latin phrase for suffering Christ. A cross with a representation of the dead Christ, as seen in Coppo's *Crucifix* (figs. 27, 28). This type in general superseded representations of the CHRISTUS TRIUMPHANS type.

CHRISTUS TRIUMPHANS. Latin phrase for triumphant Christ. A cross with a representation of a living Christ, eyes open and triumphant over death, as seen in the *Crosses* in figs. 20 and 25. Scenes of the PASSION are usually depicted at the sides.

CINQUECENTO. Italian word for five hundred, used to refer to the 1500s—the sixteenth century.

CISTERCIAN ORDER. A reform movement in the BENEDICTINE ORDER, it was started in France in 1098 by St. Robert of Molesme for the purpose of reasserting the original BENEDICTINE ideals of field work and a life of severe simplicity.

CLAUSURA. Latin word for closure, used to signify the restriction of certain orders of monks and nuns to sections of their convents and to their prohibition against speaking to lay persons.

CLERESTORY. An area that is elevated above adjacent rooftops, usually along a central axis; it has windows on the sides, and its purpose is to allow light into the interior. In many churches the clerestory is in the NAVE, which is higher than the SIDE AISLES; for example, see Sta. Maria Novella (fig. 50).

CLOSED DOOR. See *PORTA CLAUSA.*

CLOSED GARDEN. See *HORTUS CONCLUSUS.*

COFFER. In architecture, a recessed panel in a ceiling or vault, as seen in Sant'Andrea in Mantua (fig. 229), Piero della Francesca's *Madonna and Child with Saints* (fig. 287), and Melozzo da Forlì's *Sixtus IV, His Nephews, and Platina, His Librarian* (fig. 382).

COLONNADE. A continuous row of COLUMNS supporting an ENTABLATURE, as in Domenico Veneziano's *Annunciation* (fig. 266) and Bramante's Tempietto (fig. 498).

COLONNETTE. A slender, columnar decorative motif, as seen in Donatello's *Cantoria* (fig. 243).

COLUMN. A freestanding cylindrical support, usually consisting of a BASE, a rounded SHAFT, sometimes fluted, and a CAPITAL; for examples see figs. 140, 665, 666. See also ORDER.

COMPANY (Italian: *compagnia*). In Renaissance terms, a fraternal organization under ecclesiastical auspices and dedicated to good works. In Venice it was usually called a *scuola* (school), though it had no educational function, and in Tuscany it was sometimes called a confraternity.

CONDOTTIERE. Italian term meaning mercenary military leader; see the monuments to Gattamelata (fig. 249), Hawkwood (fig. 259), Tolentino (fig. 276), and Colleoni (fig. 337).

CONFRATERNITY. See COMPANY.

CONSOLE. A bracket, usually formed of VOLUTES that project from a wall to support a LINTEL, CORNICE, or other member, as on the Palazzo Medici cornice (fig. 147), or in Michelangelo's Laurentian Library entrance hall (fig. 562).

CONTADO. Countryside or rural area around a city.

CONTRAPPOSTO. Italian word for set against. A term describing the position assumed by the human body when the weight is borne on one leg while the other is relaxed. *Contrapposto* can suggest that a figure has the potential for movement; see Donatello's *St. Mark* (fig. 162).

COPE. A semicircular cloak or cape worn by ecclesiastics in processions and on other solemn ceremonial occasions; see St. Martin of Tours in Masolino's Sta. Maria Maggiore altarpiece (fig. 191).

CORBEL. An arrangement of stones that projects from the surface of a wall to provide support; see the corbels on the Palazzo dei Priori (fig. 54).

CORNICE. The crowning, projecting architectural feature, especially the uppermost part of an ENTABLATURE. See the Palazzo Medici cornice (fig. 147).

CORPUS CHRISTI. Latin phrase for body of Christ. At the Feast of Corpus Christi, the presence of Christ in the EUCHARIST is honored, and there is a procession of the HOST.

CORPUS DOMINI. Latin phrase for body of God. See also *CORPUS CHRISTI.*

CROSS VAULT. See GROIN VAULT.

CRUCIFIX. From the Latin word *crucifixus* (an object made in the shape of a cross). A painted or sculpted representation of a cross with the figure of Christ crucified on it; see figs. 27, 251.

CRUCIFIXION. The death of Christ on the cross, described in all four of the gospels (e.g., Matthew 27:33–56). In Christian theology, the Crucifixion represents Christ's sacrifice for the sins of the world, an act that made it possible for humanity to gain access to Paradise. Because it is the central mystery in Christianity, it is frequently represented; see examples by Masaccio, Mantegna, and Tintoretto (colorplate 40, p. 205; fig. 404; colorplate 127, p. 616).

CUPOLA. Another word for DOME: a rounded, convex roof or vaulted ceiling, usually hemispherical on a circular BASE and requiring BUTTRESSING; see Brunelleschi's cupola for Florence Cathedral (fig. 132) and Michelangelo's for St. Peter's (fig. 684).

DALMATIC. An ecclesiastical vestment with wide sleeves and a skirt slit at the sides, worn in the Western church by deacons at High Mass; see Fra Angelico's fresco in the Chapel of Nicolas V (fig. 214). A similar garment was also worn by kings at coronation.

DENTILS. A decorative molding derived from antiquity that consists of a row of small, projecting blocks used as a motif on Ionic and Corinthian cornices, as on the Palazzo Medici (fig. 147).

DEPOSITION. The removal of Christ's body from the cross after the CRUCIFIXION; also known as the Descent from the Cross. See the examples by Pietro Lorenzetti and Rosso Fiorentino (colorplate 2, p. 11; colorplate 109, p. 519).

DESCENT FROM THE CROSS. See DEPOSITION.

DIPTYCH. ALTARPIECE or devotional picture consisting of two wooden panels joined together.

DI SOTTO IN SÙ. Italian phrase that refers to the idea of looking up from below. A type of illusionism in painting, achieved by means of sharp foreshortening, in which the figures and architecture seem to be high above and receding from the spectator; see Mantegna's frescoes in the Camera Picta (fig. 411) and Correggio's *Vision of St. John the Evangelist* (fig. 591).

DOGE. Italian dialect word for the elected head of state in Venice and Genoa.

DOME. A large CUPOLA supported by a circular wall or DRUM, or, over a noncircular space, by corner structures; see figs. 132, 683. See also PENDENTIVE, SQUINCH.

DOMINICAN ORDER. Founded as a preaching ORDER at Toulouse in 1216 by St. Dominic. The Dominicans lived austerely and believed in having no possessions, surviving by charity and begging. After the FRANCISCANS, they became the second great mendicant (begging) order.

DONOR. The person or group who commissions and pays for a work of art or architecture for public display, usually as a religious donation to a church or monastery. The donor is occasionally represented in the work, as in Giotto's Arena Chapel (fig. 68), Masaccio's *Trinity* (colorplate 41, p. 205), and Mantegna's *Madonna of the Victory* (fig. 412). See also PATRON.

DRUM. One of several sections composing the SHAFT of a COL-

UMN. Also, a cylindrical wall supporting a DOME; see Bramante's Tempietto (fig. 500) and St. Peter's (fig. 504).

DUECENTO. Italian word for two hundred, used to refer to the 1200s—the thirteenth century; also called *DUGENTO.*

DUOMO. Italian word for CATHEDRAL.

EGG-AND-DART. A decorative molding derived from antiquity that consists of alternating oval and pointed, arrowlike forms, as in the FRIEZE of Donatello's *Annunciation* (fig. 245).

ENTABLATURE. The upper part of an architectural ORDER; see the portico of the Villa Medici at Poggio a Caiano (fig. 312).

EUCHARIST. From the Greek word for thanksgiving. The sacrament of the Lord's Supper, celebrated in the MASS. Eucharist can refer to the consecrated bread and wine used in the rite of Communion, or to the rite itself.

EX-VOTO. Latin phrase meaning from a vow. An ex-voto is an offering made to fulfill a vow. It is frequently a painting presented to a church in hope of or gratitude for divine help.

EXEDRA. A semicylindrical architectural space or shape surmounted by a half-dome; see the exedrae on Brunelleschi's dome for Florence Cathedral (fig. 133).

FATHERS OF THE CHURCH. The four Latin Fathers of the Church are Sts. Jerome, Ambrose, Augustine, and Gregory. They were early teachers and defenders of Christianity; they are represented, with the four evangelists, in the bottom panels of Ghiberti's North Doors (see fig. 153).

FRANCISCAN ORDER. Founded by St. Francis of Assisi (Giovanni di Bernardone, 1181/82–1226) for the purpose of ministering to the spiritual needs of the poor and imitating as closely as possible the life of Christ, especially in its poverty. The first great mendicant (begging) ORDER.

FRESCO. Italian word for fresh. A painting made on wet plaster with pigments suspended in water so that the plaster absorbs the colors and the painting becomes part of the wall; see fig. 13. *FRESCO A SECCO*, or painting on dry plaster (*secco* is Italian for dry), was also used, but it is a much less durable technique, and the paint tends to flake off with time.

FRIEZE. The middle part of the ENTABLATURE; also, any horizontal band decorated with moldings, RELIEF sculpture, or painting. The frieze of Donatello's *Annunciation* (fig. 245) is decorated with several motifs drawn from classical antiquity.

GENIUS (pl. GENII). In Roman and Renaissance art, usually the guardian spirit of a person, place, or thing, though it may be purely decorative. Genii are represented in human form, frequently seminude and winged; see the genii on the base of the tomb of the Cardinal of Portugal (fig. 300).

GESSO. A mixture of finely ground plaster and glue used to prepare the surface of a wooden panel for TEMPERA painting (see fig. 8), or to prepare a wooden sculpture for polychromy, as in Donatello's *Penitent Magdalen* (colorplate 56, p. 297).

GILDING. Coating with gold, gold leaf, or some gold-colored substance; see Orcagna's altarpiece (colorplate 33, p. 119); for a diagram, see fig. 8. Techniques were devised in Italy for gilding on painting, sculpture, and architectural ornament.

GLAZES. In oil painting, thin layers of superimposed translucent varnish, often with a small amount of pigment added, to modify color and build up a rich, sonorous effect. Titian used glazes extensively in such later pictures as the *Rape of Europa* (colorplate 120, p. 609).

GOLDEN LEGEND. A collection of saints' lives written in the thirteenth century by Jacopo da Voragine, archbishop of Genoa.

GOLGOTHA. Aramaic word for skull; thus, the Place of the Skull. Golgotha is the site outside Jerusalem where Christ was crucified (Matthew 27:33). CALVARY, another name for the same place, is from the Latin word for skull, *calvaria*.

GONFALONIERE. Italian for standard-bearer; the title given an important Florentine political official; the male DONOR in

Masaccio's *Trinity* is dressed in the robes of a *gonfaloniere* (see colorplate 41, p. 205).

GOSPEL. In Christian usage, the name given to the first four books of the New Testament, which relate the story of Christ's life and teachings. These books are traditionally ascribed to the evangelists Matthew, Mark, Luke, and John.

GRISAILLE. Monochromatic painting in shades of gray; see Giotto's Virtues and Vices in the Arena Chapel (figs. 69–71).

GROIN VAULT. A VAULT formed by the intersection at right angles of two BARREL VAULTS of equal height and diameter; where they meet the groins form a diagonal cross. See Sta. Maria Novella (fig. 50). Also known as a cross vault.

GROTTESCHI. A Renaissance decorative scheme in paint or stucco that uses motifs discovered during the Renaissance in an ancient Roman setting that seemed to be a grotto, hence the name. These motifs were interwoven into a variety of patterns to cover walls or PILASTERS; see Pintoricchio's Piccolomini Library frescoes (colorplate 68, p. 357) and Raphael's Villa Madama (fig. 533).

GUILDS. *Arti* (sing. *Arte*) in Italian. Independent associations of bankers and of artisan-manufacturers. The seven major guilds in Florence were: Arte di Calimala—refiners of imported wool; Arte del Cambio—bankers and money changers; Arte dei Giudici e Notai—judges and notaries; Arte della Lana—wool merchants who manufactured their own cloth; Arte dei Medici e Speziali—doctors, pharmacists, and painters; Arte della Seta— silk weavers and sculptors in metal; Arte dei Vaiai e Pellicciai— furriers. Other guilds include the Arte dei Corazzai e Spadai—armorers and swordmakers; the Arte dei Linaioli e Rigattieri—linen drapers and peddlers; and the Arte di Pietra e Legname—workers in stone and wood, including stone sculptors. See also MERCANZIA.

GUILLOCHE. An ancient decorative motif composed of a curvilinear motif of interlaced lines; it is used for the frieze in Castagno's *Last Supper* (fig. 269).

HARPY (pl. HARPIES). From the Greek word meaning snatcher. A female monster who carries souls to Hell; a combination of a woman's head and body with a bird's wings, legs, claws, and tail; see the harpies on the base of the Madonna's pedestal in Andrea del Sarto's *Madonna of the Harpies* (fig. 575). Harpies occasionally appear as more benign spirits who carry souls to another world.

HERM. The torso of a male figure emerging from a pedestal; sometimes used as a PILASTER; see the final version of Michelangelo's tomb of Julius II (fig. 676).

HORTUS CONCLUSUS. Latin phrase for closed garden; refers to the phrase "A garden inclosed is my sister, my spouse; a spring shut up, a fountain sealed" (Song of Solomon 4:12). Often used as a symbol of Mary's virginity in scenes of the ANNUNCIATION; see the example by Fra Angelico (fig. 206).

HOST. From Latin *hostia* (sacrificial victim). In some Christian denominations the term Host is used to designate the bread or wafer consecrated in the EUCHARIST or MASS and regarded as the body of Christ. The priest is holding up the Host in Raphael's *Mass of Bolsena* (fig. 524).

ICON. From the Greek term for image or likeness, but commonly used in the Orthodox denominations to designate a panel painting representing Christ, the Virgin Mary, a saint, or a religious narrative.

IMPASTO. Raised brushstrokes of thick paint, as in Titian's *Rape of Europa* (colorplate 120, p. 609, and fig. 635).

INTARSIA. Inlaid cabinetwork composed of various woods; see the Duke of Urbino's Studiolo (colorplate 9, p. 17, and fig. 387).

INTONACO. The layer of smooth plaster on which a FRESCO is painted; see fig. 13.

ISTORIA. Italian term for history or historical narrative. See also *STORIA.*

LAMENTATION. The mourning of Christ's mother and his followers over the body of Christ after the DEPOSITION. Not mentioned in biblical accounts of the CRUCIFIXION; see the example by Botticelli (fig. 354).

LAST JUDGMENT. The second coming of Christ, when he will judge souls to determine whether individuals will be sent to Heaven or to Hell. Representations of this subject are usually accompanied by a multitude of saints and angels, and there are scenes from Heaven and Hell. See the examples by Giotto and Michelangelo (colorplate 1, p. 10, and colorplate 131, p. 652).

LINTEL. The horizontal beam spanning an opening, as on the façade of Peruzzi's Palazzo Massimo alle Colonne (fig. 607).

LITANY. A form of group prayer consisting of a series of supplications by the clergy with responses from the congregation.

LITURGY. The ceremonies of public worship, including the prescribed prayers and other readings.

LOGGIA (pl. *LOGGIE*). A gallery or ARCADE open to the air on at least one side; see Brunelleschi's Ospedale degli Innocenti (fig. 136).

MACHICOLATIONS. Openings in a projecting wall or parapet through which pitch or molten lead might be cast upon the enemy beneath; see the machicolations across the top of the Palazzo dei Priori in Florence (fig. 54).

MADONNA OF MERCY. A representation of the standing Virgin Mary protecting worshipers, usually kneeling, under her mantle. In Italian, *Madonna della Misericordia.* See the example by Piero della Francesca (fig. 278).

MAESTÀ. Italian term meaning Virgin in Majesty. A large altarpiece of the Virgin enthroned, adored by saints and angels; see Duccio's *Maestà* for Siena Cathedral (colorplate 28, p. 115).

MANDORLA. From the Italian word for almond. An oval or almond-shaped halo that surrounds the body of a figure to indicate divinity or holiness; see the Florentine Baptistery mosaic (colorplate 19, p. 59), Giotto's *Last Judgment* (colorplate 1, p. 10), Orcagna's Strozzi altarpiece (colorplate 33, p. 119), and Nanni di Banco's *Assumption* (fig. 169). In Torriti's *Coronation of the Virgin,* the Virgin and Christ share a mandorla (fig. 33), but in Traini's *Last Judgment* (fig. 123) they have individual mandorlas.

MASS. The celebration of the EUCHARIST to perpetuate the sacrifice of Christ upon the cross, including readings from one of the GOSPELS and an epistle; also the form of LITURGY used in this celebration.

MAZZOCCHIO. A wire or wicker frame around which a hood or *cappuccio* was wrapped to form a headdress commonly worn by fifteenth-century Florentine men; see Uccello's *Deluge* (fig. 260).

MERCANZIA, MERCATANZIA. The merchants' GUILD.

MINORITES. A name once used for the Franciscan Friars Minor, the largest of the three branches of the FRANCISCAN ORDER.

MITRE. A hat terminating in tall peaks at the front and back—the distinctive headdress of the pope, bishops, and abbots; see Simone Martini's *Funeral of St. Martin* (fig. 97) and the tomb of the Cardinal of Portugal (fig. 302).

MONSTRANCE. An open or transparent receptacle of gold or silver in which the consecrated HOST is exposed for adoration; one is shown on the altar in Raphael's *Disputà* (fig. 519).

MOZZETTA. A cape with a hood worn by the pope and other dignitaries of the Church; see Titian's *Pope Paul III* (fig. 632).

MULLION. A vertical COLONNETTE or support dividing a window into two or more openings; see the Palazzo Medici (fig. 146).

NAVE. The large central hall, usually AXIAL and often with a CLERESTORY, that characterizes the BASILICA plan; see Brunelleschi's Sto. Spirito (fig. 141).

NEOPLATONISM. A school of Greek philosophy established in

Alexandria in the third century A.D. that was revived by Italian humanists in the fifteenth century. These scholars translated the works of Plato and Plotinus and tried to evolve a system that would reconcile Christian beliefs with Neoplatonic mystical thought. How much impact this movement had on art is still debated. See also PLATONIC ACADEMY.

OCULUS (pl. OCULI). A circular opening in a wall, as in the CLERESTORY and DRUM of the Cathedral of Florence (fig. 132) or at the apex of a DOME, as at Sta. Maria delle Carceri in Prato (fig. 315).

OIL PAINT. Pigments mixed with the slow-drying and flexible medium of oil and applied to a panel covered with GESSO, as in TEMPERA painting, or to a stretched canvas strengthened with a mixture of glue and white pigment.

OPERA DEL DUOMO. Board of Works of a CATHEDRAL, the body that often functions as the patron for works of art created for the Cathedral. A cathedral museum is sometimes known as the Museo dell'Opera del Duomo.

ORATORY OF DIVINE LOVE. A confraternity, founded in Rome, which had the grudging approval of Pope Leo X by 1517. Its goal was the reform of the Church from within, and it was pledged to the cultivation of the spiritual life of its members by prayer and frequent Communion and to the performance of charitable works. Dissolved in 1524. Its members expanded their original work into the newly founded THEATINE ORDER.

ORDER (architectural). A series of Greek and Roman architectural systems that give aesthetic definition and decoration to the post-and-lintel system; an order is characterized by a COLUMN (usually including BASE, SHAFT, and CAPITAL) and its ENTABLATURE (including ARCHITRAVE, FRIEZE, and CORNICE). The five classical orders are the Doric (fig. 498), Ionic (figs. 666, 710), Corinthian (fig. 505; colorplate 15, p. 23), Tuscan (fig. 607), and Composite (fig. 210).

ORDER (monastic). A religious society or fraternity living under a particular rule. See BENEDICTINE, CAMALDOLITE, CARMELITE, CARTHUSIAN, CISTERCIAN, DOMINICAN, FRANCISCAN, SYLVESTRINE, and THEATINE.

ORTHOGONALS. Lines running at right angles to the plane of the picture surface but, in a representation using one-point perspective, converging toward a common vanishing point in the distance; the orthogonals are clearly visible in the piazza of Perugino's *Christ Giving the Keys to St. Peter* (colorplate 67, p. 356). For a diagram see fig. 235.

PALAZZO (pl. *PALAZZI*). Italian word for palace, but during the Renaissance and later the word was also used for large civic or even religious buildings, as well as for relatively modest town houses.

PALLADIAN MOTIF. An arched opening supported by columns and flanked by narrow, flat-topped openings. This motif was popularized by Palladio (see his Basilica, fig. 664).

PASSION OF CHRIST. The sufferings of Christ during the last week of his earthly life or the representation of his sufferings in narrative or pictorial form, as at Giotto's Arena Chapel (fig. 66), or in the cycle assigned to Barna da Siena in the Collegiata at San Gimignano (figs. 119, 120).

PATEN. The shallow dish, usually circular, on which the HOST is laid during the EUCHARIST or MASS; see the paten resting atop the chalice in Andrea del Sarto's *Lamentation* (fig. 576).

PATRON. The person or group who commissions and pays for a work of art or architecture. The patron is sometimes represented in the work, as in Giotto's Arena Chapel (fig. 68), Masaccio's *Trinity* (colorplate 41, p. 205), and Mantegna's *Madonna of the Victory* (fig. 412).

PENDENTIVE. In a domed structure, the four curved triangular segments that provide a transition from the four supporting piers to the DRUM or to the circular base of the DOME; see Brunel-

leschi's Pazzi Chapel (colorplate 37, p. 202) and Bramante's Santa Maria presso S. Satiro (fig. 493).

PERISTYLE. A COLONNADE or ARCADE around a building or open court; see the courtyard of the Palazzo Ducale at Urbino (colorplate 70, p. 359).

PIANO NOBILE. Italian phrase meaning noble floor or floor for the nobles. It refers to the second story of a building (American style; in European style this is called the first story), intended for the owner and family; see Bramante's Palazzo Caprini (fig. 509).

PIAZZA (pl. *PIAZZE*). Italian word for public square; see the huge *piazza* in Perugino's *Christ Giving the Keys to St. Peter* (colorplate 67, p. 356). See also *CAMPO*.

PIER. A vertical architectural support used in an arched or vaulted structural system. Piers are usually rectangular in section, but if used with an ORDER, they may be decorated with half-columns or PILASTERS with BASES and CAPITALS of the same design.

PIER BUTTRESS. An exterior PIER in Romanesque and Gothic architecture, buttressing the thrust of the VAULTS within.

PIETÀ. Italian word meaning both pity and piety. It designates a representation of the dead Christ generally, but not always, mourned by the Virgin, and with or without saints and/or angels; see Michelangelo's Florence *Pietà* (fig. 689). When the representation shows a larger group of figures, it is usually termed a LAMENTATION; see the example by Andrea del Sarto (fig. 576).

PIETRA FORTE. The tan stone traditionally employed by Florentine builders. The Palazzo dei Priori in Florence is built of *pietra forte*; see fig. 54.

PIETRA SERENA. The gray Tuscan limestone used in Florence. Brunelleschi used *pietra serena* in the Ospedale degli Innocenti, the Pazzi Chapel, and many other structures (see figs. 136–42; colorplate 37, p. 202).

PILASTER. A shallow, virtually flat vertical element having a CAPITAL and BASE. A pilaster is engaged in a wall, from which it projects, and is decorative rather than structural. See the exterior and interior of Sant'Andrea in Mantua (figs. 227, 229) and of St. Peter's in Rome (fig. 505; colorplate 13, p. 21).

PINACOTECA. Italian word for picture gallery.

PINNACLE. A pointed ornamental motif used along the crest of paintings, sculptural niches, and buildings. It is mainly decorative and is especially common in the Gothic period; see the Siena Cathedral façade (colorplate 23, p. 62), Giotto's design for the Campanile in Florence (fig. 76), and the niche for Nanni di Banco's *Four Crowned Martyrs* (fig. 168).

PINXIT. Latin word for "he/she painted"; often used in artists' signatures.

PLATONIC ACADEMY. An informal group of Florentine humanists and scholars, founded by Marsilio Ficino, who translated Plato and Plotinus into Latin. The academy's history is uncertain, but it was apparently encouraged by Cosimo de' Medici. See also NEOPLATONISM.

POLYPTYCH. An ALTARPIECE or devotional object consisting of more than three sections joined together; see Pietro Lorenzetti's Pieve altarpiece (fig. 101) and Orcagna's Strozzi Chapel altarpiece (colorplate 33, p. 119).

PORPHYRY. A rare, hard, purplish-red stone; the wall behind the tomb of the Cardinal of Portugal is porphyry (fig. 300). Sometimes Renaissance sculptors and architects used red marble or even red sandstone as a substitute.

PORTA CLAUSA. Latin phrase for closed door; refers to Ezekiel's vision of the door of the sanctuary in the Temple that was closed because only the Lord could enter it (Ezekiel 44:1–4). Interpreted as a prophecy and used as a symbol of Mary's virginity, often in scenes of the ANNUNCIATION; see the example by Piero della Francesca (fig. 285).

POUNCING. A method of transferring a CARTOON to a surface preparatory to painting. Small holes pricked along the outlines of the drawing are dusted with powdered charcoal so that the lines of the composition are transferred to the surface beneath. The cartoon used in this method is called a *SPOLVERO*.

PREDELLA. Pedestal of an ALTARPIECE, usually decorated with small narrative scenes; see Orcagna's Strozzi Chapel altarpiece (colorplate 33, p. 119), Lorenzo Monaco's *Coronation of the Virgin* (colorplate 35, p. 201), and Gentile da Fabriano's *Adoration of the Magi* (colorplate 38, p. 203).

PRIE-DIEU. French phrase literally meaning pray God. A small prayer desk with a footpiece on which to kneel and a support to hold a book; a *prie-dieu* is visible behind the Virgin Mary in Lotto's *Annunciation* (fig. 640).

PRIORI. Italian word for priors, the council or principal governing body of a town.

PUTTO (pl. *PUTTI*). A figure of a male baby, often winged, that is used in Renaissance painting, sculpture, and architectural decoration. Sometimes these figures personify love and are called cupids or *amoretti*; sometimes they are intended to represent angels and are called *angeletti*. Often they are purely decorative. The term *putto* is of modern application; documents sometimes refer to these figures as *spiritelli*. They are especially common in the art of Donatello; see his *Annunciation* (fig. 245) and also the putti on Desiderio's Marsuppini tomb (figs. 296, 297).

QUATTROCENTO. Italian word for four hundred, used to refer to the 1400s—the fifteenth century.

REFECTORY. The dining hall of a monastery. See also CENACOLO.

RELIEF. Sculpture in which the figures or forms are united with a background and project from it. It is called high relief (fig. 47) or low relief (figs. 253, 254) depending on the amount of projection. Ghiberti and Donatello evolved a kind of relief that combined high and low relief to develop pictorial relief (see fig. 173 and colorplate 46, p. 257). See also *RILIEVO SCHIACCIATO*.

RESURRECTION. The rising again of Christ on the third day after his death and burial, a scene mentioned in the GOSPELS but not directly described; see the examples by Piero della Francesca and Michelangelo (figs. 281 and 558).

RIBBED VAULT. A GROIN VAULT whose groins are accentuated by projecting stone ribs; see Sta. Maria Novella (fig. 50).

RILIEVO SCHIACCIATO. Italian term for flattened RELIEF; refers to a kind of sculpture initiated by Donatello in which distance and perspective are achieved by optical suggestion rather than sculptural projection; see Donatello's *St. George and the Dragon* (fig. 166).

ROSARY. A string of beads ending in a crucifix. The form in present use was developed by the DOMINICAN ORDER as an aid to memory in the recitation of prayers. In the fifteenth and sixteenth centuries there were many forms of rosaries; see fig. 441.

RUSTICATION. Protruding masonry, frequently with a roughened surface; see the Palazzo dei Priori (fig. 54), the Palazzo Pitti (fig. 234), Giulio Romano's Palazzo del Te (fig. 610), and Ammanati's courtyard of the Palazzo Pitti (fig. 696).

SACRA CONVERSAZIONE. Italian term for sacred conversation. A Madonna and Child accompanied by four or more saints either conversing or silently communing; see Mantegna's S. Zeno altarpiece (colorplate 73, p. 410) and Bellini's S. Zaccaria altarpiece (colorplate 79, p. 416).

SALA. Italian word for room or hall.

SCUOLA (pl. *SCUOLE*). See COMPANY.

SERAPH (pl. SERAPHIM). A celestial being or angel of the highest order, usually represented with three sets of wings and sometimes shown as a head with wings; see the seraphim that compose the MANDORLA of Christ in Orcagna's Strozzi altarpiece (colorplate 33, p. 119) and of Sassetta's *St. Francis* (colorplate 66, p. 355). See also CHERUB.

SFUMATO. Italian term for smoky, used for the method developed by Leonardo da Vinci of modeling figures by virtually imperceptible gradations from light to dark; see the *Madonna of the Rocks* (colorplate 82, p. 451).

SGRAFFITO (pl. *SGRAFFITI*). A technique of scratched and tinted designs in plaster used for Florentine house façades; seen in the frieze of the Palazzo Medici courtyard (fig. 148). Also any drawings or writings scratched on a wall.

SHAFT. A cylindrical form; in architecture, the part of a COLUMN or PIER between BASE and CAPITAL; see the courtyard of the Palazzo Ducale at Urbino (colorplate 70, p. 359).

SIBYLS. Greek and Roman prophetesses who were thought to have foretold the coming of Christ; see Michelangelo's Sistine Ceiling (fig. 513).

SIDE AISLE. One of the corridors parallel to the NAVE of a church, separated from it by an ARCADE or COLONNADE; see the side aisles flanking the nave in Brunelleschi's Sto. Spirito (fig. 141).

SIGNORIA. Italian word for lordship, used to refer to the governing bodies of Florence.

SILVERPOINT. A drawing made with a slender silver rod or wire on paper coated with a colored, slightly grainy preparation; see Leonardo's *Study of Drapery* (fig. 454).

SINOPIA. Preliminary brush drawing, in red earth mixed with water, for a painting in FRESCO; usually done on the ARRICCIO of the wall; see figs. 13, 14. This Italian term derives from the city of Sinope in Asia Minor that was famous for its red earth.

SPANDREL. The roughly triangular area between two adjoining arches; see the sequence of spandrels in the courtyard of the Palazzo Ducale at Urbino (colorplate 70, p. 359) and the spandrels on either side of the arch in Foppa's *Crucifixion* (fig. 435).

SPOLVERO. Italian term for dust off, used for a preparatory drawing employed to transfer a CARTOON to a surface for painting in the method known as POUNCING. Small holes pricked along the outlines of the drawing are dusted with powdered charcoal so that the lines of the composition are transferred to the surface beneath.

SQUINCH. A construction using ARCHS, LINTELS, or CORBELS that jut across the corners of a square space to support a DOME.

STANZA (pl. *STANZE*). Italian word for room, as in the *stanze* that Raphael painted for Pope Julius II (see figs. 519–27).

STIGMATA. Marks corresponding to the wounds of the crucified Christ that appear on the hands, feet, and side of religious persons after prolonged meditation. They are believed to be a token of divine favor. St. Francis, the example most frequently represented, is said to have received the stigmata in 1224; see Giotto's and Giovanni Bellini's representations of this scene (figs. 75, 426).

STORIA. Italian term for story or history, used by Alberti to refer to a representation of an historical narrative or episode.

STUDIOLO. Italian for small study; used to describe the small, specially decorated chambers in Renaissance PALAZZI where books, works of art, and objects of historical and scientific interest were kept; see the Studiolo of Federico da Montefeltro in the Palazzo Ducale, Urbino (colorplate 9, p. 17).

STYLOBATE. The platform on which COLUMNS rest.

SYLVESTRINE ORDER. A monastic ORDER founded in 1231 at Montefano by St. Sylvester Gozzolini. Although the order was under the BENEDICTINE rule, its practice was much stricter in regard to poverty and abstinence.

TEMPERA. Ground colors mixed with yolk of egg; see fig. 8 for a diagram of a typical tempera painting. Tempera was widely used for Italian panel painting before the sixteenth century.

TERRA-COTTA. Italian word for baked earth. A hard glazed or unglazed earthenware used for sculpture and pottery or as a building material. The word can also mean something made of this material or the color of it, a dull brownish-red. Terra-cotta PUTTI decorate the top of Donatello's *Annunciation* (fig. 245).

TERRA VERDE. Italian for green earth, the color used for the underpaint of flesh tones in TEMPERA painting and sometimes as the main color for FRESCOES, as in Uccello's Chiostro Verde frescoes (figs. 260–62).

THEATINE ORDER. Founded jointly in 1524 by St. Cajetan and Giovanni Carafa (later Pope Paul IV). Also called the Society of Clerks Regular. It presented a new model of deportment marked by extreme austerity, a devotion to pastoral work, and a strong emphasis on prayer and EUCHARISTIC devotion.

TIARA (papal). The pope's pointed crown, which is surmounted by the orb and cross; earlier it was quite simple, as is shown in Maso di Banco's fresco of St. Sylvester (fig. 79), but later examples have three crowned tiers, as in Raphael's *Sistine Madonna* (fig. 527). An emblem of the pope's sovereign power, it has little sacred character and is not worn during celebrations of the MASS, at which time the pope wears a MITRE.

TIE-ROD. An iron rod used structurally to keep the base of an ARCH or VAULT from spreading; tie-rods are visible at the Arena Chapel (fig. 55) and in the nave and side aisle of Florence Cathedral (see fig. 126), and there is even one in Giovanni Bellini's S. Zaccaria altarpiece (colorplate 79, p. 416).

TITULUS. Latin term for inscription; also the name given to the label that Pilate ordered to be placed on the cross of Christ (John 19:19–20). In paintings and sculptures it often bears the initials INRI, the abbreviation for Jesus Nazarenus Rex Judaeorum—Jesus of Nazareth, King of the Jews. For examples see paintings by Coppo di Marcovaldo (fig. 27), Perugino (fig. 379), Mantegna (fig. 404), and Antonello da Messina (fig. 419).

TONDO. Italian term for circular painting; see Domenico Veneziano's *Adoration of the Magi* (fig. 265) and Michelangelo's *Doni Madonna* (colorplate 85, p. 454).

TRANSEPT. In a cross-shaped Christian church, the crossarms placed perpendicular to the NAVE. The transepts usually separate the NAVE from the CHANCEL or APSE; see the plans in figs. 142, 228.

TRANSVERSALS. In a scientific perspective composition, the horizontal lines that run parallel to the picture plane and intersect the ORTHOGONALS; the transversals are clearly visible in the piazza in Perugino's *Christ Giving the Keys to St. Peter* (colorplate 67, p. 356). For a diagram see fig. 235.

TRAVERTINE. A light-colored porous limestone used in Italy, es-

pecially Rome, for building. The exteriors of St. Peter's and of the Palazzo dei Conservatori on the Capitoline are largely of travertine; see fig. 687 and colorplate 13, p. 21.

TRECENTO. Italian word for three hundred, used to refer to the 1300s—the fourteenth century.

TRIPTYCH. An ALTARPIECE or devotional object consisting of three sections; see Nardo's *Madonna and Child with Saints* (colorplate 17, p. 57) and also figs. 11, 105, 106, 187.

ULTRAMARINE. An intense blue pigment made from pulverized lapis lazuli, a semiprecious stone found in the Near East. Documents of commission often specified that painters use ultramarine for such important areas as the Virgin Mary's mantle.

VAULT. A structural system based on the ARCH and including the BARREL VAULT, GROIN VAULT, RIBBED VAULT, and DOME.

VICES. Coming from the same tradition as the VIRTUES, and frequently paired with them, they are more variable but usually include Pride, Avarice, Wrath, Gluttony, and Lust. Others such as Folly, Inconstancy, and Injustice are selected to make a total of seven. Seven virtues and seven vices are paired in the bottom register of Giotto's Arena Chapel (see figs. 69–71 and colorplate 1, p. 10).

VIRTUES. Divided into the three Theological Virtues of Faith, Hope, and Charity, and the four Cardinal Virtues of Prudence, Justice, Fortitude, and Temperance. As with the VICES, the allegorical representation of the Virtues as human figures in the Renaissance derives from a long medieval tradition in manuscripts and sculpture and from such literary sources as the *Psychomachia* of Prudentius and writings of St. Augustine, with their commentaries. Seven virtues and seven vices are paired in the bottom register of Giotto's Arena Chapel (see figs. 69–71 and colorplate 1, p. 10).

VOLGARE. Italian word for vulgar or "of the people"; used to denote the developing Italian language as distinct from Latin.

VOLUTE. Ornament resembling a rolled scroll. Especially prominent on CAPITALS of the Ionic and Composite ORDERS; see figs. 138, 210, 666, 710.

VULGATE. The Latin version of the Bible that St. Jerome prepared at the end of the fourth century A.D.

WASH. A broad thin layer of diluted pigment or ink used in some drawings to enchance the effect of shadow. Also refers to a drawing made in this technique. Wash is used in Leonardo da Vinci's preparatory drawing of the *Adoration of the Magi* (fig. 455).

Bibliography

Because of the extensive recent publications in the field of Renaissance art, the bibliography has been radically updated for this edition; many of the newest books here have not been used in the preparation of this revision. Preference has been given to the most important recent books and to books in English, and although a book may qualify for inclusion in several sections, no book—with three exceptions—is listed more than once. Additional bibliographies in greater depth can be found in virtually all the volumes listed here. Sources for periodical articles, which often offer the most important updated ideas about the period and its artists, include the *Bibliography of the History of Art* and the *Art Index* (available on CD-ROM). Two important earlier sources, *RILA* and *Répertoire d'art et d'archéologie*, ceased publication in 1989. *Dissertation Abstracts*, another useful tool in the search for new research, is also available on line.

I. BIBLIOGRAPHIES

DUNKELMAN, MARTHA LEVINE. *Central Italian Painting, 1400–1465: An Annotated Bibliography*. Boston: G. K. Hall, 1986.

KARPINSKI, CAROLINE. *Italian Printmaking, Fifteenth and Sixteenth Centuries: An Annotated Bibliography*. Boston: G. K. Hall, 1987.

ROSENBERG, CHARLES M. *Fifteenth-Century North Italian Painting and Drawing: An Annotated Bibliography*. Boston: G. K. Hall, 1986.

STUBBLEBINE, JAMES H. *Dugento Painting: An Annotated Bibliography*. Boston: G. K. Hall, 1983.

WILK, SARAH BLAKE. *Fifteenth-Century Central Italian Sculpture: An Annotated Bibliography*. Boston: G. K. Hall, 1986.

II. THE SOCIAL, HISTORICAL, AND CULTURAL BACKGROUND OF ITALIAN ART

ANTAL, FREDERICK. *Florentine Painting and Its Social Background*. London: Kegan Paul, 1948.

Art and Politics in Late Medieval and Early Renaissance Italy. Ed. Charles M. Rosenberg. Notre Dame, Ind.: University of Notre Dame Press, 1990.

BAROLSKY, PAUL. *Giotto's Father and the Family of Vasari's Lives*. University Park, Pa.: Pennsylvania State University Press, 1991.

———. *Why Mona Lisa Smiles and Other Tales by Vasari*. University Park, Pa.: Pennsylvania State University Press, 1991.

BARON, HANS. *The Crisis of the Early Italian Renaissance*. Rev. ed. 2 vols. Princeton, N.J.: Princeton University Press, 1966.

BAXANDALL, MICHAEL. *Giotto and the Orators*. Oxford: Clarendon Press, 1971.

———. *Painting and Experience in Fifteenth-Century Italy: A Primer in the Social History of Pictorial Style*. 2d ed. New York: Oxford University Press, 1988.

BRUCKER, GENE A. *Renaissance Florence*. Berkeley: University of California Press, 1983.

BURCKHARDT, JAKOB C. *The Civilization of the Renaissance in Italy*. Trans. S. G. Middlemore. Oxford: Phaidon, 1965.

BURKE, PETER. *The Italian Renaissance: Culture and Society in Italy*. Cambridge, Eng.: Polity Press, 1987.

CHASTEL, ANDRÉ. *The Age of Humanism: Europe 1480–1530*. Trans. K. M. Delavenay and E. M. Gwyer. New York: McGraw-Hill, 1964.

———. *The Crisis of the Renaissance, 1520–1600*. Trans. P. Price. Geneva: Skira, 1968.

———. *The Sack of Rome, 1527*. Princeton, N.J.: Princeton University Press, 1983.

Circa 1492: Art in the Age of Exploration. Ed. Jay A. Levenson. New Haven: Yale University Press, 1991.

CLARKE, PAULA C. *The Soderini and the Medici: Power and Patronage in Fifteenth-Century Florence*. Oxford: Clarendon Press, 1991.

EDGERTON, SAMUEL Y. *Pictures and Punishment: Art and Criminal Prosecution During the Florentine Renaissance*. Ithaca, N.Y.: Cornell University Press, 1985.

FREMANTLE, RICHARD. *God and Money: Florence and the Medici in the Renaissance, Including Cosimo I's Uffizi and Its Collections*. Florence: Olschki, 1992.

GOLDTHWAITE, RICHARD A. *The Building of Renaissance Florence: An Economic and Social History*. Baltimore: Johns Hopkins University Press, 1980.

HALE, J. R. *Artists and Warfare in the Renaissance*. New Haven: Yale University Press, 1990.

HARTT, FREDERICK. "Art and Freedom in Quattrocento Florence." *Marsyas: Studies in the History of Art*. Suppl. 1: *Essays in Memory of Karl Lehmann*, Institute of Fine Arts, New York University (1964): 114–31.

———. "Power and the Individual in Mannerist Art." In *Studies in Western Art: Acts of the 20th International Congress of the History of Art*. Vol. 2, *The Renaissance and Mannerism*, 222–38. Princeton, N.J.: Princeton University Press, 1963.

HAUSER, ARNOLD. *The Social History of Art*. Trans. S. Goodman, in collaboration with the author. New York: Knopf, 1951.

HERLIHY, DAVID, and CHRISTIANE KLAPISCH-ZUBER. *The Tuscans and Their Families*. New Haven: Yale University Press, 1985.

HOLMES, GEORGE. *Florence, Rome, and the Origins of the Renaissance*. Oxford: Clarendon Press and Oxford University Press, 1986.

KEMP, MARTIN. *The Science of Art: Optical Themes in Western Art from Brunelleschi to Seurat*. New Haven: Yale University Press, 1989.

KING, MARGARET L. *Women of the Renaissance*. Chicago: University of Chicago Press, 1991.

KLAPISCH-ZUBER, CHRISTIANE. *Women, Family, and Ritual in Renaissance Italy*. Chicago: University of Chicago Press, 1985.

KRISTELLER, PAUL O. *Renaissance Thought and Its Sources*. New York: Columbia University Press, 1979.

LARNER, JOHN. *Culture and Society in Italy, 1290–1420*. New York: Scribner's, 1971.

LESNICK, DANIEL R. *Preaching in Medieval Florence: The Social World of Franciscan and Dominican Spirituality*. Athens: University of Georgia Press, 1989.

MIGIEL, MARILYN, and JULIANA SCHIESARI, eds. *Refiguring Woman: Perspectives on Gender and the Italian Renaissance.* Ithaca, N.Y.: Cornell University Press,1991.

Rome Reborn: The Vatican Library and Renaissance Culture. Ed. Anthony Grafton. New Haven: Yale University Press, 1993.

RUSSELL, H. DIANE, with BERNADINE BARNES. *Eva/Ave: Woman in Renaissance and Baroque Prints.* Washington, D.C.: National Gallery of Art, 1990.

SASLOW, JAMES M. *Ganymede in the Renaissance.* New Haven: Yale University Press, 1986.

SEZNEC, JEAN. *The Survival of the Pagan Gods: The Mythological Tradition and Its Place in Renaissance Humanism and Art.* Trans. B. Sessions. Princeton, N.J.: Princeton University Press, 1953.

STARN, RUDOLPH, and LOREN PARTRIDGE. *The Arts of Power: Three Halls of State in Italy, 1300–1600.* Berkeley: University of California Press, 1992.

STEPHENS, JOHN. *The Italian Renaissance: The Origins of Intellectual and Artistic Change Before the Reformation.* London: Longman, 1990.

TREXLER, RICHARD C. *Public Life in Renaissance Florence.* New York: Academic Press, 1980.

WIND, EDGAR. *Pagan Mysteries in the Renaissance.* New Haven: Yale University Press, 1958.

III. SOURCES: ANTHOLOGIES

CHAMBERS, DAVID. *Patrons and Artists in the Italian Renaissance.* Columbia: University of South Carolina Press, 1971.

GILBERT, CREIGHTON E. *Italian Art, 1400–1500: Sources and Documents in the History of Art.* Evanston, Ill.: Northwestern University Press, 1992.

GLASSER, HANNELORE. *Artists' Contracts of the Early Renaissance.* New York: Garland, 1977.

HOLT, ELIZABETH, ed. *Literary Sources of Art History.* Princeton, N.J.: Princeton University Press, 1947 (paperback edition entitled *A Documentary History of Art*).

KLEIN, ROBERT, and HENRI ZERNER. *Italian Art, 1500–1600: Sources and Documents in the History of Art.* Englewood Cliffs, N.J.: Prentice Hall, 1966.

Splendors of the Gonzaga. Ed. David Chambers and Jane Martineau. London: Victoria and Albert Museum, 1982.

IV. SOURCES: WRITINGS BY RENAISSANCE INDIVIDUALS

ALBERTI, LEONBATTISTA. *On Painting and on Sculpture, the Latin Texts of De Pictura and De Statua.* Ed. with trans., intro., and notes by Cecil Grayson. London: Phaidon, 1972.

———. *Ten Books on Architecture.* Ed. J. Rykwert; trans. J. Leoni. London: Tiranti, 1955.

ANTONINE OF FLORENCE, SAINT. *Lettere.* Florence, 1736. Reprint. Florence: Tipografica Barbèra, Bianchi e c, 1859.

———. *Opera a benvivere.* Venice, 1578. Reprint. Florence: Libreria editrice fiorentina, 1923.

———. *Opus chronicorum.* Venice, [1480?]; Lyons, 1587.

———. *Summa theologica.* Venice, 1480. Reprint. Verona, 1740. Reprint. Graz: Akademische Druck und Verlagsanstalt, 1959.

BAROCCHI, PAOLA. *Trattati d'arte del Cinquecento fra Manierismo e Controriforma.* 3 vols. Bari: Laterza, 1960–62.

CASTIGLIONE, BALDASSARE. *The Book of the Courtier.* Trans. L. E. Opdycke. New York: Scribner's, 1903.

CELLINI, BENVENUTO. *Autobiography.* Ed. J. Pope-Hennessy. London: Phaidon, 1960.

CENNINI, CENNINO. *The Craftsman's Handbook (Il libro dell'arte).* Trans. D. V. Thompson, Jr. New York: Dover, 1954.

CONDIVI, ASCANIO. *The Life of Michelangelo.* Ed. Hellmut Wohl; trans. Alice Sedgwick Wohl. Baton Rouge: Louisiana State

University Press, 1976.

FILARETE (ANTONIO AVERLINO). *Treatise on Architecture.* Trans. with intro. and notes by J. R. Spencer. 2 vols. New Haven: Yale University Press, 1965.

LEONARDO DA VINCI. *Leonardo da Vinci on Painting: A Lost Book (Libro A).* Ed. C. Pedretti. Berkeley: University of California Press, 1964.

———. *Leonardo on Painting: An Anthology of Writings by Leonardo da Vinci with a Selection of Documents Relating to his Career as an Artist.* Ed. Martin Kemp and Margaret Walker. New Haven: Yale University Press, 1989.

———. *The Literary Works of Leonardo da Vinci.* Ed. J. P. Richter and Carlo Pedretti. 2 vols. Berkeley: University of California Press, 1977.

———. *The Notebooks of Leonardo da Vinci.* Ed. E. MacCurdy. New York: Braziller, 1955.

———. *Treatise on Painting.* Trans. and annotated by A. P. McMahon. 2 vols. Princeton, N.J.: Princeton University Press, 1956.

MANETTI, ANTONIO DI TUCCIO. *The Life of Brunelleschi by Antonio di Tuccio Manetti.* Ed. Howard Saalman.University Park: Pennsylvania State University Press, 1970.

MARTINI, FRANCESCO DI GIORGIO. *Trattati di architettura, ingegneria e arte militare.* Ed. C. Maltese. 2 vols. Milan: Il Polifilo, 1967.

MICHELANGELO. *Complete Poems and Selected Letters of Michelangelo.* Ed. R. N. Linscott; trans. C. Gilbert. 2d ed. New York: Random House, 1965.

———. *The Letters of Michelangelo.* Ed. and trans. E. H. Ramsden. Palo Alto, Cal.: Stanford University Press, 1963.

———. *The Poetry of Michelangelo.* Ed. James Saslow. New Haven: Yale University Press, 1991.

PALLADIO, ANDREA. *I quattro libri dell'architettura.* Venice, 1570. Facsimile reprint. Milan: Hoepli, 1951.

SERLIO, SEBASTIANO. *Regole generali di architettura sopra le cinque maniere degli edifici.* Venice, 1537 and 1551. Books 1–5 and *Libro straordinario*, Venice, 1566 and 1584. Book 6, ed. M. Rosci. Milan, 1967.

VASARI, GIORGIO. *Lives of the Most Eminent Painters, Sculptors and Architects.* Trans. G. du C. De Vere. 10 vols. London: Medici Society, 1912–15.

———. *Vasari on Technique.* Ed. G. B. Brown; trans. L. S. Maclehose. New York: Dover, 1960.

VIGNOLA, GIACOMO BAROZZI DA. *Regola delli cinque ordini di architettura.* Rome, 1562.

V. THEORY

BLUNT, ANTHONY. *Artistic Theory in Italy, 1450–1600.* Oxford: Clarendon Press, 1966.

EDGERTON, SAMUEL Y. *The Heritage of Giotto's Geometry: Art and Science on the Eve of the Scientific Revolution.* Ithaca. N.Y.: Cornell University Press, 1991.

———. *The Renaissance Rediscovery of Linear Perspective.* New York: Basic Books, 1975.

PANOFSKY, ERWIN. *Meaning in the Visual Arts.* Garden City, N.Y.: Doubleday, 1957.

———. *Studies in Iconology: Humanistic Themes in the Art of the Renaissance.* Oxford: Oxford University Press, 1939.

SUMMERS, DAVID. *The Judgment of Sense.* Princeton, N.J.: Princeton University Press, 1987.

———. *Michelangelo and the Language of Art.* Princeton, N.J.: Princeton University Press, 1981.

VI. PATRONAGE

GOFFEN, RONA. *Piety and Patronage in Renaissance Venice: Bellini, Titian, and the Franciscans.* New Haven: Yale University Press, 1986.

KEMPERS, BRAM. *Painting, Power, and Patronage: The Rise of the Professional Artist in the Italian Renaissance.* London: Penguin, 1992.

NOVA, ALESSANDRO. *The Artistic Patronage of Pope Julius III (1550–1555): Profane Imagery and Buildings for the De Monte Family in Rome.* New York: Garland, 1988.

Patronage, Art, and Society in Renaissance Italy. Canberra: Humanities Research Centre Australia and Oxford University Press, 1987.

ROBERTSON, CLAIRE. *Il Gran Cardinale: Alessandro Farnese, Patron of the Arts.* New Haven: Yale University Press, 1992.

ZERVAS, DIANE FINIELLO. *The Parte Guelfa, Brunelleschi and Donatello.* Locust Valley, N.Y.: J. J. Augustin, 1988.

VII. GENERAL

AMES-LEWIS, FRANCIS, and ANKA BEDNAREK, eds. *Decorum in Renaissance Narrative Art.* London: Birbeck College, 1992.

ANDRES, GLENN M. *The Art of Florence.* New York: Abbeville Press, 1988.

BOBER, PHYLLIS PRAY, and R. O. RUBINSTEIN. *Renaissance Artists and Antique Sculpture: A Handbook of Sources.* New York: Oxford University Press, 1986.

BURCKHARDT, JACOB. *The Altarpiece in Renaissance Italy.* Oxford: Phaidon, 1988.

CAFRITZ, ROBERT. *Places of Delight: The Pastoral Landscape.* Washington, D.C.: Phillips Collection in association with the National Gallery of Art, 1988.

CAMPBELL, LORNE. *Renaissance Portraits.* New Haven: Yale University Press, 1990.

CHAMBERS, DAVID S. *The Imperial Age of Venice, 1380–1580.* New York: Harcourt Brace Jovanovich, 1971.

CHASTEL, ANDRÉ. *Studios and Styles of the Italian Renaissance.* Trans. J. Griffin. New York: Odyssey Press, 1966.

COLE, BRUCE. *Italian Art, 1250–1550: The Relation of Renaissance Art to Life and Society.* New York: Harper and Row, 1987.

———. *The Renaissance Artist at Work, from Pisano to Titian.* New York: Harper and Row, 1983.

COSGROVE, DENIS. *The Palladian Landscape: Geographical Change and Its Cultural Representations in Sixteenth-Century Italy.* University Park: Pennsylvania State University Press, 1993.

FRANZOI, UMBERTO. *Palaces and Churches on the Grand Canal in Venice.* Venice: Storti, 1991.

GOMBRICH, ERNST H. *New Light on Old Masters.* Oxford: Phaidon, 1986.

———. *Norm and Form: Studies in the Art of the Renaissance.* London: Phaidon, 1966.

HAGER, SERAFINA, ed. *Leonardo, Michelangelo, and Raphael in Renaissance Florence from 1500 to 1508.* Washington, D.C.: Georgetown University Press, 1992.

HARTT, FREDERICK. *Florentine Art Under Fire.* Princeton, N.J.: Princeton University Press, 1949.

HAYWARD, J. L. *Virtuoso Goldsmiths and the Triumph of Mannerism.* New York: Sotheby Parke-Bernet, 1976.

HERSEY, GEORGE L. *High Renaissance Art in St. Peter's and the Vatican: An Interpretive Guide.* Chicago: University of Chicago Press, 1993.

HOLMES, GEORGE. *Florence, Rome, and the Origins of the Renaissance.* Oxford: Clarendon Press, 1986.

HUSE, NORBERT, and WOLFGANG WOLTERS. *The Art of Renaissance Venice: Architecture, Sculpture, and Painting.* Chicago: University of Chicago Press, 1990.

Italian Church Decoration of the Middle Ages and Early Renaissance: Functions, Forms and Regional Traditions: Ten Contributions to a Colloquium Held at the Villa Spelman, Florence. Ed. William Tronzo. Bologna: Nuova Alfa Editoriale, 1989.

LEVEY, MICHAEL. *High Renaissance.* Harmondsworth: Penguin, 1975.

MASSINELLI, ANNA MARIA, and FILIPPO TUENA. *Treasures of the Medici.* New York: Rizzoli, 1992.

PANOFSKY, ERWIN. *Renaissance and Renascences in Western Art.* 2 vols. Stockholm: Almqvist and Wiksell, 1960.

POPE-HENNESSY, JOHN. *The Portrait in the Renaissance.* New York: Bollingen Foundation, 1966.

SCHULTZ, BERNARD. *Art and Anatomy in Renaissance Italy.* Ann Arbor, Mich.: UMI Research Press, 1985.

SHEARMAN, JOHN. *Mannerism.* Harmondsworth and Baltimore: Penguin Books, 1967.

———. *Only Connect—Art and the Spectator in the Italian Renaissance.* Princeton, N.J.: Princeton University Press, 1992.

SMYTH, CRAIG H. *Mannerism and Maniera.* Locust Valley, N.Y.: J. J. Augustin, 1961.

THORNTON, PETER. *The Italian Renaissance Interior 1400–1600.* New York: Harry N. Abrams, 1991.

VENTURI, ADOLFO. *Storia dell'arte italiana.* 11 vols. in 25 parts. Milan: Hoepli, 1901–40.

WACKERNAGEL, MARTIN. *The World of the Florentine Renaissance Artist: Projects and Patrons, Workshop and Art Market.* Trans. Alison Luchs. Princeton, N.J.: Princeton University Press, 1981.

WHITE, JOHN. *Art and Architecture in Italy, 1250–1400.* 3d ed. New Haven: Yale University Press, 1993.

———. *Studies in Late Medieval Italian Art.* London: Pindar Press, 1984.

WÖLFFLIN, HEINRICH. *Classic Art.* 2d ed. London: Phaidon, 1953.

VIII. ARCHITECTURE

ACKERMAN, JAMES S. *The Villa: Form and Ideology of Country Houses.* Princeton, N.J.: Princeton University Press, 1990.

BURCKHARDT, JACOB. *The Architecture of the Italian Renaissance.* Ed. Peter Murray. Chicago: University of Chicago Press, 1985.

COFFIN, DAVID R. *Gardens and Gardening in Papal Rome.* Princeton, N.J.: Princeton University Press, 1991.

———. *The Villa in the Life of Renaissance Rome.* Princeton, N.J.: Princeton University Press, 1979.

GOY, RICHARD J. *Venetian Vernacular Architecture: Traditional Housing in the Venetian Lagoon.* New York: Cambridge University Press, 1989.

HEYDENREICH, LUDWIG H., and WOLFGANG LOTZ. *Architecture in Italy, 1400 to 1600.* Baltimore: Penguin Books, 1974.

LAZZARO, CLAUDIA. *The Italian Renaissance Garden.* New Haven: Yale University Press, 1990.

LIEBERMAN, RALPH. *Renaissance Architecture in Venice, 1450–1540.* New York: Abbeville Press, 1982.

MURRAY, PETER. *Renaissance Architecture.* New York: Harry N. Abrams, 1971.

VAN DER REE, PAUL; GERRIT SMIENK; and CLEMENS STEENBERGER. *Italian Villas and Gardens.* Munich: Prestel, 1992.

WITTKOWER, RUDOLF. *Architectural Principles in the Age of Humanism.* 3d ed., rev. London: Tiranti, 1962.

IX. PAINTING

BERENSON, BERNARD. *Italian Painters of the Renaissance.* Rev. ed. London: Phaidon, 1967.

———. *Italian Pictures of the Renaissance.* 7 vols. London: Phaidon, 1957–68.

BOLOGNA, FERDINANDO. *Early Italian Painting: Romanesque and Early Medieval.* Princeton, N.J.: Van Nostrand, 1964.

BOMFORD, DAVID, ed. *Italian Painting Before 1400.* London: National Gallery Publications, 1989.

BORSOOK, EVE. *The Mural Painters of Tuscany from Cimabue to Andrea del Sarto.* 2d ed. Oxford: Oxford University Press, 1979.

BURCKHARDT, JACOB. *The Altarpiece in Renaissance Italy.* Ed. Peter Humfrey. Cambridge, Eng.: Cambridge University Press, 1988.

CAST, DAVID. *The Calumny of Apelles: A Study in the Humanist Tradition*. New Haven: Yale University Press, 1981.

CHRISTIANSEN, KEITH. *Painting in Renaissance Siena, 1420–1500*. New York: The Metropolitan Museum of Art, 1988.

COLE, BRUCE. *Sienese Painting, from Its Origin to the Fifteenth Century*. New York: Harper and Row, 1980.

———. *Sienese Painting in the Age of the Renaissance*. Bloomington: Indiana University Press, 1985.

CROWE, JOSEPH A., and GIOVANNI B. CAVALCASELLE. *A History of Painting in Italy*. Ed. L. Douglas. 2d ed. 6 vols. London: John Murray, 1903–14.

———. *A History of Painting in North Italy*. Ed. T. Borenius. 3 vols. New York: Scribner's, 1912.

DEWALD, ERNEST T. *Italian Painting, 1200–1600*. New York: Holt, Rinehart and Winston, 1961.

DUNKERTON, JILL, ed. *Giotto to Durer: Early Renaissance Painting in the National Gallery*. New Haven: Yale University Press in association with National Gallery Publications, London, 1991.

FREEDBERG, S. J. *Painting in Italy, 1500–1600*. Harmondsworth: Penguin Books, 1990.

———. *Painting of the High Renaissance in Rome and Florence*. New York: Harper and Row, 1972.

FREMANTLE, RICHARD. *Florentine Gothic Painters from Giotto to Masaccio*. London: Martin Secker and Warburg, 1975.

FRIEDLAENDER, WALTER F. *Mannerism and Anti-Mannerism in Italian Painting*. New York: Columbia University Press, 1957.

GARRISON, EDWARD, B. *Italian Romanesque Panel Painting: An Illustrated Index*. Florence: Olschki, 1949. Reprint. New York: Hacker Art Books, 1976.

HALL, MARCIA B. *Color and Meaning: Practice and Theory in Renaissance Painting*. New York: Cambridge University Press, 1992.

———. *Color and Technique in Renaissance Painting*. Locust Valley, N. Y.: J. J. Augustin, 1987.

HUMFREY, PETER, and MARTIN KEMP, eds. *The Altarpiece in the Renaissance*. Cambridge, Eng.: Cambridge University Press, 1990.

LAVIN, MARILYN ARONBERG. *The Place of Narrative: Mural Decoration in Italian Churches, 431–1600*. Chicago: University of Chicago Press, 1990.

LEWINE, CAROL F. *The Sistine Chapel Walls and the Roman Liturgy*. University Park: Pennsylvania State University Press, 1993.

MARLE, RAIMOND VAN. *The Development of the Italian Schools of Painting*. 19 vols. The Hague: Nijhoff, 1923–38.

MARTINEAU, JEAN, and CHARLES HOPE, eds. *The Genius of Venice 1500–1600*. London: Royal Academy of Arts, 1983.

MEISS, MILLARD. *The Great Age of Fresco: Discoveries, Recoveries and Revivals*. New York: Braziller, 1970.

———. *Painting in Florence and Siena After the Black Death*. Princeton, N.J.: Princeton University Press, 1951.

NEWBERRY, TIMOTHY J.; GEORGE BISACCA; and LAURENCE B. KANTER. *Italian Renaissance Frames*. New York: The Metropolitan Museum of Art, 1990.

NICOLSON, BENEDICT. *The Painters of Ferrara: Cosmè Tura, Francesco del Cossa, Ercole de' Roberti and Others*. London: Elek, 1950.

OFFNER, RICHARD A. *A Critical and Historical Corpus of Florentine Painting*. New York: New York University Press, and Florence: Barbera, 1930–.

———. *Studies in Florentine Painting: The 14th Century*. New York: Sherman, 1927; Reprint. New York: Junius Press, 1972.

OS, H. W. VAN. *Sienese Altarpieces, 1215–1460*. Groningen: Bouma's Boekhuis, 1984.

POPE-HENNESSY, JOHN. *Sienese Quattrocento Painting*. Oxford: Phaidon, 1947.

SOUTHARD, EDNA CARTER. *The Frescoes in Siena's Palazzo Pubblico, 1289–1539: Studies in Imagery and Relations to Other Communal Palaces in Tuscany*. New York: Garland, 1979.

STEER, JOHN. *Venetian Painting: A Concise History*. London: Thames and Hudson, 1970.

TOESCA, JOHN. *Florentine Painting of the Trecento*. New York: Harcourt, Brace, 1929.

VAVALÀ, EVELYN SANDBERG. *Studies in the Florentine Churches*. Florence: Olschki, 1959.

———. *Uffizi Studies: The Development of the Florentine School of Painting*. Florence: Olschki, 1948.

WHITE, JOHN. *The Birth and Rebirth of Pictorial Space*. London: Faber and Faber, 1987.

WILDE, JOHANNES. *Venetian Art from Bellini to Titian*. New York: Oxford University Press, 1974.

WOLLESON-WISCH, BARBARA. *Italian Renaissance Art: Selections from the Piero Corsini Gallery*. University Park: Museum of Art, Pennsylvania State University, 1986.

ZAMPETTI, PIETRO. *Paintings from the Marches: Gentile to Raphael*. London: Phaidon, 1971.

X. SCULPTURE

OLSON, ROBERTA J. M. *Italian Renaissance Sculpture*. New York: Thames and Hudson, 1992.

POPE-HENNESSY, JOHN. *Italian Gothic Sculpture*. 3d ed. Oxford: Phaidon, 1986.

———. *Italian High Renaissance and Baroque Sculpture*. 3d ed. Oxford: Phaidon, 1986.

———. *Italian Renaissance Sculpture*. 3d ed. Oxford: Phaidon, 1986.

SEYMOUR, CHARLES. *Sculpture in Italy, 1400–1500*. Pelican History of Art. Harmondsworth and Baltimore: Penguin Books, 1966.

XI. DRAWINGS

AMES-LEWIS, FRANCIS. *Drawing in the Italian Renaissance Workshop*. London: Victoria and Albert Press, 1983.

BERENSON, BERNARD. *The Drawing of the Florentine Painters*. 3 vols. Chicago: University of Chicago Press, 1938.

DEGENHART, BERNHARD, and ANNEGRIT SCHMITT. *Corpus der italienischen Zeichnungen, 1300–1450*. Berlin: Gebrüder Mann Verlag, 1968–.

FEINBERG, LARRY J. *From Studio to Studiolo: Florentine Draughtsmanship Under the First Medici Grand Dukes*. Oberlin, Ohio: Allen Memorial Art Museum, 1991.

Italian Drawings in the Department of Prints and Drawings in the British Museum. 4 vols. London: British Museum. Vol. I: POPHAM, ARTHUR E., and PHILIP POUNCEY. *The 14th and 15th Centuries*. 2 vols. 1950; VoI. II: WILDE, JOHANNES. *Michelangelo and His Studio*.1953; Vol. III: POUNCEY, PHILIP, and JOHN A. GERE. *Raphael and His Circle*. 2 vols. 1962; Vol. IV: POPHAM, ARTHUR E. *Artists Working in Parma in the 16th Century*. 2 vols. 1967.

POPHAM, ARTHUR E. *The Italian Drawings of the XV and XVI Centuries in the Collection of His Majesty the King at Windsor Castle*. London: Phaidon, 1949.

TIETZE, HANS, and ERICA TIETZE-CONRAT. *The Drawings of the Venetian Painters in the 15th and 16th Centuries*. Locust Valley, N.Y.: J. J. Augustin, 1944.

XII. OTHER ARTS

Early Italian Engravings from the National Gallery of Art. Washington, D.C.: National Gallery of Art, 1973.

LADIS, ANDREW. *Italian Renaissance Maiolica from Southern Collections*. Athens: Georgia Museum of Art, University of Georgia, 1989.

MARCHINI, GIUSEPPE. *Italian Stained Glass Windows*. New York: Harry N. Abrams, 1956.

REED, SUE WALSH. *Italian Etchers of the Renaissance and Baroque*. Boston: Northeastern University Press, 1989.

XIII. STUDIES OF MAJOR PROJECTS AND INDIVIDUAL WORKS OF ART

ACKERMAN, JAMES S. *The Cortile del Belvedere*. Vatican City: Biblioteca apostolica vaticana, 1954.

CHELES, LUCIANO. *The Studiolo of Urbino: An Iconographic Investigation*. University Park: Pennsylvania State University Press, 1986.

ETTLINGER, L. D. *The Sistine Chapel Before Michelangelo*. Oxford: Clarendon Press, 1965.

HARTT, FREDERICK; GINO CORTI; and CLARENCE KENNEDY. *The Chapel of the Cardinal of Portugal, 1434–1459, at San Miniato in Florence*. Philadelphia: University of Pennsylvania Press, 1964.

MUCCINI, UGO. *The Salone del Cinquecento of Palazzo Vecchio*. Florence: Le Lettere, 1990.

———, and ALESSANDRO CECCHI. *The Apartments of Cosimo in Palazzo Vecchio*. Florence: Le Lettere, 1991.

ROTONDI, PASQUALE. *The Ducal Palace of Urbino*. London: Tiranti, 1969.

SMITH, GRAHAM. *The Casino of Pius IV*. Princeton, N.J.: Princeton University Press, 1977.

VERHEYEN, EGON. *The Paintings in the Studiolo of Isabella d'Este at Mantua*. New York: New York University Press, 1971.

———. *The Palazzo del Te*. Baltimore: Johns Hopkins University Press, 1977.

WESTFALL, CARROLL WILLIAM. *In This Most Perfect Paradise: Alberti, Nicholas V, and the Invention of Conscious Urban Planning in Rome, 1447–55*. University Park: Pennsylvania State University Press, 1974.

XIV. ARTISTS

Alberti

BORSI, FRANCO. *Leon Battista Alberti: The Complete Works*. New York: Electa/Rizzoli, 1989.

GADOL, JOAN. *Leon Battista Alberti, Universal Man of the Renaissance*. Chicago: University of Chicago Press, 1969.

JARZOMBEK, MARK. *On Leon Battista Alberti: His Literary and Aesthetic Theories*. Cambridge, Mass.: MIT Press, 1989.

JOHNSON, EUGENE J. *S. Andrea in Mantua: The Building History*. University Park: Pennsylvania State University Press, 1975.

Fra Angelico

HOOD, WILLIAM. *Fra Angelico at San Marco*. New Haven: Yale University Press, 1993.

POPE-HENNESSY, JOHN. *Fra Angelico*. 2d ed. Ithaca, N.Y.: Cornell University Press, 1974.

———. *Fra Angelico*. Florence: Scala, 1981.

Anguissola

PERLINGIER, ILYA SANDRA. *Sofonisba Anguissola: First Great Woman of the Renaissance*. New York: Rizzoli, 1992.

Antonello da Messina

BOTTARI, STEFANO. *Antonello da Messina*. Trans. G. Scaglia. Greenwich, Conn.: New York Graphic, 1955.

VIGNI, GIORGIO. *All the Paintings of Antonello da Messina*. Trans. A. F. O'Sullivan. New York: Hawthorn, 1963.

Baldovinetti

KENNEDY, RUTH W. *Alesso Baldovinetti: A Critical and Historical Study*. New Haven: Yale University Press, 1938.

Barocci

OLSEN, HARALD. *Federico Barocci*. Copenhagen: Munksgaard, 1962.

Fra Bartolommeo

FISCHER, CHRIS. *Fra Bartolommeo, Master Draughtsman of the Renaissance*. Rotterdam: Museum Boymans-van Beuningen, 1990.

Beccafumi

Domenico Beccafumi e il suo tempo. Milan: Electa, 1990.

Giovanni Bellini

GOFFEN, RONA. *Giovanni Bellini*. New Haven: Yale University Press, 1989.

ROBERTSON, GILES. *Giovanni Bellini*. Oxford: Clarendon, 1968.

WIND, EDGAR. *Bellini's Feast of the Gods: A Study in Venetian Humanism*. Cambridge, Mass.: Harvard University Press, 1948.

Jacopo Bellini

EISLER, COLIN T. *The Genius of Jacopo Bellini: The Complete Paintings and Drawings*. New York: Harry N. Abrams, 1989.

Benedetto da Maiano

LEIN, EDGAR. *Benedetto da Maiano*. New York: Lang, 1988.

Bertoldo di Giovanni

DRAPER, JAMES DAVID. *Bertoldo di Giovanni, Sculptor of the Medici Household: Critical Reappraisal and Catalogue Raisonné*. Columbia: University of Missouri Press, 1992.

Botticelli

BALDINI, UMBERTO, et al. *Primavera: The Restoration of Botticelli's Masterpiece*. New York: Harry N. Abrams, 1986.

CLARK, KENNETH. *The Drawings of Sandro Botticelli for Dante's Divina Commedia*. New York: Harper and Row, 1976.

DEMPSEY, CHARLES. *The Portrayal of Love: Botticelli's Primavera and Humanist Culture at the Time of Lorenzo the Magnificent*. Princeton, N.J.: Princeton University Press, 1992.

ETTLINGER, LEOPOLD DAVID, and HELEN S. ETTLINGER. *Botticelli*. London: Thames and Hudson, 1976.

LIGHTBOWN, RONALD. *Botticelli*. 2 vols. Berkeley: University of California Press, 1978.

———. *Sandro Botticelli: Life and Work*. New York: Abbeville Press, 1989.

Bramante

BRUSCHI, ARNALDO. *Bramante*. London: Thames and Hudson, 1977.

Bronzino

COX-REARICK, JANET. *Bronzino's Chapel of Eleanora in the Palazzo Vecchio*. Berkeley: University of California Press, 1993.

McCOMB, ARTHUR K. *Agnolo Bronzino, His Life and Works*. Cambridge, Mass.: Harvard University Press, 1928.

McCORQUODALE, CHARLES. *Bronzino*. New York: Harper and Row, 1981.

SMYTH, CRAIG HUGH. *Bronzino as a Draughtsman: An Introduction*. Locust Valley, N.Y.: J. J. Augustin, 1931.

Brunelleschi

KEMP, MARTIN. *Geometrical Perspective from Brunelleschi to Desargues: A Pictorial Means or an Intellectual End?* Oxford: Oxford University Press, 1985.

KLOTZ, HEINRICH. *Filippo Brunelleschi: The Early Works and the Medieval Tradition*. London: Academy Editions, 1990.

PRAGER, FRANK D., and GIUSTINA SCAGLIA. *Brunelleschi: Studies of His Technology and Inventions*. Cambridge, Mass.: MIT Press, 1970.

SAALMAN, HOWARD. *Filippo Brunelleschi: The Cupola of Santa Maria del Fiore*. London: Zwemmer, 1980.

Carpaccio

BROWN, PATRICIA FORTINI. *Venetian Narrative Painting in the Age of Carpaccio*. New Haven: Yale University Press, 1988.

LAUTS, JAN. *Carpaccio: Paintings and Drawings*. London: Phaidon, 1962.

Andrea del Castagno

HORSTER, MARITA. *Andrea del Castagno: Complete Edition with a Critical Catalogue*. Oxford: Phaidon, 1980.

SPENCER, JOHN R. *Andrea del Castagno and His Patrons*. Durham, N.C.: Duke University Press, 1991.

Cavallini

HETHERINGTON, PAUL. *Pietro Cavallini: A Study in the Art of Late Medieval Rome*. London: Sagittarius Press, 1979.

Cellini

POPE-HENNESSY, JOHN. *Cellini.* New York: Abbeville Press, 1985.

Cimabue

BATTISTI, EUGENIO. *Cimabue.* Trans. R. Enggass and C. Enggass. University Park: Pennsylvania State University Press, 1966.

CHIELLINI, MONICA. *Cimabue.* Scala Books. Florence: Harper and Row, 1988.

Correggio

The Age of Correggio and the Carracci: Emilian Painting in the Sixteenth and Seventeenth Centuries. Washington, D.C.: National Gallery of Art, 1986.

BROWN, DAVID ALAN. *The Young Correggio and His Leonardesque Sources.* New York: Garland, 1981.

GHIDIGLIA QUINTAVALLE, AUGUSTA. *Correggio: The Frescoes in San Giovanni Evangelista in Parma.* Trans. Olga Ragusa. New York: Harry N. Abrams, 1964.

GOULD, CECIL. *The Paintings of Correggio.* London: Faber, 1977.

POPHAM, ARTHUR E. *Correggio's Drawings.* London: Oxford University Press, 1957.

Daddi

OFFNER, RICHARD. *A Critical and Historical Corpus of Florentine Painting.* Section 3. Vols. 3 and 4. New York: New York University Press, 1930 and 1934.

Vincenzo Danti

SUMMERS, DAVID. *The Sculpture of Vincenzo Danti: A Study in the Influence of Michelangelo and the Ideals of the Maniera.* New York: Garland, 1979.

Domenico Veneziano

WOHL, HELLMUT. *The Paintings of Domenico Veneziano: A Study in Florentine Art of the Early Renaissance.* New York: New York University Press, 1980.

Donatello

BENNETT, BONNIE A., and DAVID G. WILKINS. *Donatello.* Oxford: Phaidon, 1984.

HARTT, FREDERICK. *Donatello, Prophet of Modern Vision.* New York: Harry N. Abrams, 1973.

HERZNER, VOLKER. "Regesti Donatelliani." *Rivista dell'Istituto Nazionale d'Archeologia e Storia dell'Arte,* 3, vol. 2 (1979): 169–228.

Italian Renaissance Sculpture in the Time of Donatello: An Exhibition to Commemorate the 600th Anniversary of Donatello's Birth and the 100th Anniversary of the Detroit Institute of Arts. Detroit, Mich.: Founders Society, Detroit Institute of Arts, 1985.

JANSON, H. W. *The Sculpture of Donatello.* 2 vols. Princeton, N.J.: Princeton University Press, 1957.

MUNMAN, ROBERT. *Optical Corrections in the Sculpture of Donatello.* Philadelphia: American Philosophical Society, 1985.

Dosso Dossi

GIBBONS, FELTON. *Dosso and Battista Dossi, Court Painters at Ferrara.* Princeton, N.J.: Princeton University Press, 1968.

Duccio

STUBBLEBINE, JAMES H. *Duccio di Buoninsegna and His School.* 2 vols. Princeton, N.J.: Princeton University Press, 1979.

WHITE, JOHN. *Duccio: Tuscan Art and the Medieval Workshop.* New York: Thames and Hudson, 1979.

Ercole de' Roberti

MANCA, JOSEPH. *The Art of Ercole de' Roberti.* New York: Cambridge University Press, 1992.

Francesco di Giorgio

WELLER, ANDREW STUART. *Francesco di Giorgio, 1439–1501.* Chicago: University of Chicago Press, 1943.

Agnolo Gaddi

COLE, BRUCE. *Agnolo Gaddi.* Oxford: Clarendon Press, 1977.

Taddeo Gaddi

LADIS, ANDREW. *Taddeo Gaddi: Critical Reappraisal and Catalogue Raisonné.* Columbia: University of Missouri Press, 1982.

Gentile da Fabriano

CHRISTIANSEN, KEITH. *Gentile da Fabriano.* Ithaca, N.Y.: Cornell University Press, 1982.

Ghiberti

KRAUTHEIMER, RICHARD, and TRUDE KRAUTHEIMER HESS. *Lorenzo Ghiberti.* 2d ed. Princeton, N.J.: Princeton University Press, 1970.

Ghirlandaio

BORSOOK, EVE. *Francesco Sassetti and Ghirlandaio at Santa Trinità, Florence: History and Legend in a Renaissance Chapel.* Doornspijk: Davaco, 1981.

DAVIES, GERALD S. *Ghirlandaio.* New York: Scribner's, 1909.

Giambologna

AVERY, CHARLES. *Giambologna: The Complete Sculpture.* Oxford: Phaidon Christie's, 1987.

Giambologna, 1529–1608, Sculptor to the Medici. London: Victoria and Albert Museum, 1978.

Giorgione

BALDASS, LUDWIG VON. *Giorgione.* Trans. J. M. Brownjohn. New York: Harry N. Abrams, 1965.

PIGNATTI, TERISIO. *Giorgione.* Trans. Clovis Whitfield. London: Phaidon, 1971.

RICHTER, GEORGE M. *Giorgio da Castelfranco, called Giorgione.* Chicago: University of Chicago Press, 1937.

SETTIS, SALVATORE. *Giorgione's Tempest: Interpreting the Hidden Subject.* Chicago: University of Chicago Press, 1990.

Giotto

BACCHESCHI, EDI, and ANDREW MARTINDALE. *The Complete Paintings of Giotto.* New York: Harry N. Abrams, 1966.

BARASCH, MOSHE. *Giotto and the Language of Gesture.* Cambridge, Eng.: Cambridge University Press, 1987.

COLE, BRUCE. *Giotto and Florentine Painting, 1280–1375.* New York: Harper and Row, 1976.

GNUDI, CESARE. *Giotto.* Milan: Martello, 1959.

GOFFEN, RONA. *Spirituality in Conflict: Saint Francis and Giotto's Bardi Chapel.* University Park: Pennsylvania State University Press. 1988.

SMART, ALISTAIR. *The Assisi Problem and the Art of Giotto.* London: Oxford University Press, 1971.

STUBBLEBINE, JAMES H. *Assisi and the Rise of Vernacular Art.* New York: Harper and Row, 1985.

———, ed. *Giotto: The Arena Chapel Frescoes.* New York: Norton, 1969.

TINTORI, LEONETTO, and EVE BORSOOK. *Giotto: The Peruzzi Chapel.* New York: Harry N. Abrams, 1965.

TRACHTENBERG, MARVIN L. *The Campanile of Florence Cathedral: "Giotto's Tower."* New York: New York University Press, 1971.

Giovanni di Paolo

POPE-HENNESSY, JOHN. *Giovanni di Paolo, 1403–1483.* New York: Oxford University Press, 1937.

Giovannino de' Grassi

The Visconti Hours, National Library, Florence. New York: G. Braziller, 1972.

Giulio Romano

HARTT, FREDERICK. *Giulio Romano.* 2 vols. New Haven: Yale University Press, 1958.

Guido da Siena

STUBBLEBINE, JAMES H. *Guido da Siena.* Princeton, N.J.: Princeton University Press, 1964.

Leonardo da Vinci

CLARK, KENNETH. *The Drawings of Leonardo da Vinci in the Collection of Her Majesty the Queen at Windsor Castle.* 2d ed. 3 vols. Rev. with the assistance of Carlo Pedretti. London:

Phaidon, 1968.

———. *Leonardo da Vinci*. Rev. ed. London: Penguin Books, 1988.

KEMP, MARTIN. *Leonardo da Vinci: The Marvelous Works of Nature and Man*. Cambridge, Mass.: Harvard University Press, 1981.

———, and JANE ROBERTS, with PHILIP STEADMAN. *Leonardo da Vinci*. New Haven: Yale University Press, 1981.

Leonardo da Vinci. New Haven: Yale University Press, 1989.

MAIORINO, GIANCARLO. *Leonardo da Vinci, The Daedalian Mythmaker*. University Park: Pennsylvania State University Press, 1992.

POPHAM, ARTHUR E. *The Drawings of Leonardo da Vinci*. New York: Reynal and Hitchcock, 1945.

WASSERMAN, JACK. *Leonardo da Vinci*. New York: Harry N. Abrams, 1975.

Filippino Lippi

NEILSON, KATHERINE B. *Filippino Lippi*. Cambridge, Mass.: Harvard University Press, 1938.

Fra Filippo Lippi

FOSSI, GLORIA. *Filippo Lippi*. New York: Scala, 1989.

RUDA, JEFFREY. *Fra Filippo Lippi: Life and Work with a Complete Catalogue*. New York: Harry N. Abrams, 1993.

Ambrogio Lorenzetti

ROWLEY, GEORGE. *Ambrogio Lorenzetti*. 2 vols. Princeton, N.J.: Princeton University Press, 1958.

Pietro Lorenzetti

DEWALD, ERNEST T. *Pietro Lorenzetti*. Cambridge, Mass.: Harvard University Press, 1930.

Lotto

BERENSON, BERNARD. *Lorenzo Lotto*. London: Phaidon, 1956.

BIANCONI, PIERO. *All the Paintings of Lorenzo Lotto*. Trans. P. Colacicchi. 2 vols. New York: Hawthorn, 1963.

Mantegna

BOORSCH, SUZANNE, et al. *Andrea Mantegna*. New York: Harry N. Abrams, 1992.

FIOCCO, GIUSEPPE. *The Frescoes of Mantegna in the Eremitani Church, Padua*. 2d ed. Oxford: Phaidon, 1978.

GREENSTEIN, JACK M. *Mantegna and Painting as Historical Narrative*. Chicago: University of Chicago Press, 1992.

LIGHTBOWN, R. W. *Mantegna: With a Complete Catalogue of the Paintings, Drawings and Prints*. Oxford: Phaidon Christie's, 1986.

Simone Martini

MARTINDALE, ANDREW. *Simone Martini: Complete Edition*. New York: New York University Press, 1988.

Masaccio

BALDINI, UMBERTO, and ORNELLA CASAZZA. *The Brancacci Chapel*. New York: Harry N. Abrams, 1992.

BERTI, LUCIANO. *Masaccio*. University Park: Pennsylvania State University Press. 1967.

COLE, BRUCE. *Masaccio and the Art of Early Renaissance Florence*. Bloomington: Indiana University Press, 1980.

JOANNIDES, PAUL. *Masaccio and Masolino: A Complete Catalogue*. New York: Harry N. Abrams, 1993.

SHULMAN, KEN. *Anatomy of a Restoration: The Brancacci Chapel*. New York: Walker, 1991.

Maso di Banco

WILKINS, DAVID G. *Maso di Banco: A Florentine Artist of the Early Trecento*. New York: Garland, 1985.

Masolino

BALDINI, UMBERTO, and ORNELLA CASAZZA. *The Brancacci Chapel*. New York: Harry N. Abrams, 1992.

JOANNIDES, PAUL. *Masaccio and Masolino: A Complete Catalogue*. New York, Harry N. Abrams, 1993.

ROBERTS, PERRI LEE. *Masolino da Panicale*. Oxford: Clarendon Press, 1993.

Melozzo da Forlì

CLARK, NICHOLAS. *Melozzo da Forlì, Pictor Papalis*. London: Sotheby's, 1990.

Michelangelo

ACKERMAN, JAMES S. *The Architecture of Michelangelo*. Chicago: University of Chicago Press, 1986.

BAROLSKY, PAUL. *Michelangelo's Nose: A Myth and Its Maker*. University Park: Pennsylvania State University Press, 1990.

CAMESASCA, ETTORE. *The Complete Paintings of Michelangelo*. Intro. L. D. Ettlinger. New York: Harry N. Abrams, 1969.

CLEMENTS, ROBERT J. *Michelangelo's Theory of Art*. New York: New York University Press, 1961.

DE TOLNAY, CHARLES, ed. *The Art and Thought of Michelangelo*. Trans. N. Buranelli. New York: Pantheon, 1964.

———. *The Complete Works of Michelangelo*. New York: Reynal, 1965.

———. *Michelangelo*. 5 vols. Princeton, N.J.: Princeton University Press, 1943–60.

GOLDSCHEIDER, LUDWIG. *Michelangelo: Paintings, Sculpture, and Architecture*. 5th ed. New York: Phaidon, 1962.

HARTT, FREDERICK, *David by the Hand of Michelangelo: The Original Model Discovered*. New York: Abbeville, 1987.

———. *Michelangelo*. New York: Harry N. Abrams, 1984.

———. *Michelangelo Drawings*. New York: Harry N. Abrams, 1971.

———. *Michelangelo: The Complete Sculpture*. New York: Harry N. Abrams, 1969.

———. *The Sistine Chapel*. 2 vols. London: Barrie and Jenkins in association with Nippon Television Network Corp., 1991.

———, and DAVID FINN. *Michelangelo's Three Pietàs*. New York: Harry N. Abrams, 1976.

HIBBARD, HOWARD. *Michelangelo*. 2d ed. New York: Harper and Row, 1985.

HIRST, MICHAEL. *Michelangelo and His Drawings*. New Haven: Yale University Press, 1988.

MILLON, HENRY A. *Michelangelo Architect: The Facade of San Lorenzo and the Drum and Dome of St. Peter's*. Milan: Olivetti, 1988.

PIETRANGELI, CARLO, et al. *The Sistine Chapel, A New Light on Michelangelo: The Art, the History, and the Restoration*. New York: Harmony Books, 1986.

RICHMOND, ROBIN. *Michelangelo and the Creation of the Sistine Ceiling*. London: Barrie and Jenkins, 1992.

SEYMOUR, CHARLES, JR., ed. *Michelangelo: The Sistine Chapel Ceiling*. New York: Norton, 1972.

STEINBERG, LEO. *Michelangelo's Last Paintings: The Conversion of St. Paul and the Crucifixion of St. Peter*. New York: Oxford University Press, 1975.

WEINBERGER, MARTIN. *Michelangelo the Sculptor*. 2 vols. New York: Columbia University Press, 1967.

Michelozzo di Bartolommeo

CARLOW, HARRIET McNEAL. *Michelozzo*. 2 vols. New York: Garland, 1977.

Lorenzo Monaco

EISENBERG, MARVIN. *Lorenzo Monaco*. Princeton, N.J.: Princeton University Press, 1989.

Nardo di Cione

OFFNER, RICHARD. *A Critical and Historical Corpus of Florentine Painting*. Section 4. Vol. 2. New York: New York University Press, 1960.

Orcagna

OFFNER, RICHARD. *A Critical and Historical Corpus of Florentine Painting*. Section 4. Vol. 11. New York: New York University Press, 1962.

Palladio

ACKERMAN, JAMES S. *Palladio*. Rev. ed. New York: Penguin, 1978.

HOLBERTON, PAUL. *Palladio's Villas: Life in the Renaissance Countryside*. London: Murray, 1990.

TRAGER, PHILIP. *The Villas of Palladio*. Boston: Little Brown, 1986.

TRAVENOR, ROBERT. *Palladio and Palladianism*. New York: Thames and Hudson, 1991.

SCULLY, VINCENT. *The Villas of Palladio*. Boston: Little Brown, 1986.

Palma Vecchio

RYLANDS, PHILIP. *Palma Vecchio*. New York: Cambridge University Press, 1990.

Paolo Veneziano

MURARO, MICHELANGELO. *Paolo da Venezia*. University Park: Pennsylvania State University Press, 1970.

Parmigianino

FREEDBERG, SYDNEY J. *Parmigianino, His Works in Painting*. Cambridge, Mass.: Harvard University Press, 1950.

POPHAM, ARTHUR E. *The Drawings of Parmigianino*. New York: Beechhurst Press, 1953.

Piero della Francesca

BERTELLI, CARLO. *Piero della Francesca*. New Haven: Yale University Press, 1992.

CLARK, KENNETH. *Piero della Francesca*. New York: Phaidon, 1951.

COLE, BRUCE. *Piero della Francesca: Tradition and Innovation in Renaissance Art*. New York: Icon Editions, 1991.

GILBERT, CREIGHTON. *Change in Piero della Francesca*. Locust Valley, N.Y.: J. J. Augustin, 1968.

LAVIN, MARILYN ARONBERG. *Piero della Francesca*. New York: Harry N. Abrams, 1992.

———. *Piero della Francesca's Baptism of Christ*. New Haven: Yale University Press, 1981.

———. *Piero della Francesca: The Flagellation*. London: Penguin, 1972.

LIGHTBOWN, R.W. *Piero della Francesca*. New York: Abbeville Press, 1992.

POPE-HENNESSY, JOHN. *The Piero della Francesca Trial*. London: Thames and Hudson, 1992.

Piero di Cosimo

FERMOR, SHARON. *Piero di Cosimo: Fiction, Invention and Fantasia*. London: Reaktion, 1993.

Pisanello

PACCAGNINI, GIOVANNI. *Pisanello*. Trans. Jane Carroll. London: Phaidon, 1973.

SINDONA, ENIO. *Pisanello*. Trans. J. Ross. New York: Harry N. Abrams, 1961.

WOODS-MARSDEN, JOANNA. *The Gonzaga of Mantua and Pisanello's Arthurian Frescoes*. Princeton, N.J.: Princeton University Press, 1988.

Andrea and Nino Pisano.

MOSKOWITZ, ANITA FIDERER. *The Sculpture of Andrea and Nino Pisano*. Cambridge, Eng.: Cambridge University Press, 1986.

Giovanni Pisano

AYRTON, MICHAEL. *Giovanni Pisano*. London: Thames and Hudson, 1969.

Nicola Pisano

ANGIOLA, ELOISE. *Nicola Pisano: The Pisa Baptistery Pulpit*. Ann Arbor: University Microfilms, 1975.

CRICHTON, GEORGE H., and ELSIE R. CRICHTON. *Nicola Pisano and the Revival of Sculpture in Italy*. Cambridge, Eng.: Cambridge University Press, 1938.

Antonio and Piero del Pollaiuolo

ETTLINGER, LEOPOLD D. *Antonio and Piero Pollaiuolo: Complete Edition with Critical Catalogue*. New York: Phaidon, 1978.

Pontormo

CLAPP, FREDERICK M. *Jacopo Carucci da Pontormo, His Life and Work*. New Haven: Yale University Press, 1916.

COX-REARICK, JANET. *The Drawings of Pontormo*. 2 vols. Cambridge, Mass.: Harvard University Press, 1964.

———. *Dynasty and Destiny in Medici Art: Pontormo, Leo X, and the Two Cosimos*. Princeton, N.J.: Princeton University Press, 1984.

NIGRO, SALVATORE S., ed. *Pontormo Drawings*. New York: Harry N. Abrams, 1992.

Jacopo della Quercia

BECK, JAMES H. *Jacopo della Quercia*. New York: Columbia University Press, 1991.

HANSON, ANNE C. *Jacopo della Quercia's Fonte Gaia*. Oxford: Clarendon Press, 1965.

SEYMOUR, CHARLES. *Jacopo della Quercia*. New Haven: Yale University Press, 1973.

Raphael

AMES-LEWIS, FRANCIS. *The Draftsman Raphael*. New Haven: Yale University Press, 1986.

BECK, JAMES. *Raphael*. New York: Harry N. Abrams, 1976.

ETTLINGER. LEOPOLD D. *Raphael*. Oxford: Phaidon, 1987.

FISCHEL, OSKAR. *Raphael*. Trans. B. Rackham. 2 vols. London: Kegan Paul, 1948.

JOHANNIDES, PAUL. *The Drawings of Raphael with a Complete Catalog*. Berkeley: University of California Press, 1983.

JONES, ROGER, and NICHOLAS PENNY. *Raphael*. New Haven: Yale University Press, 1983.

PEDRETTI, CARLO. *Raphael: His Life and Work in the Splendors of the Italian Renaissance*. Florence: Giunti, 1989.

POPE-HENNESSY, JOHN. *Raphael*. New York: New York University Press, 1970.

SALMI, MARIO, et al. *The Complete Works of Raphael*. New York: Reynal, 1969.

SHEARMAN, JOHN, *Raphael's Cartoons in the Collection of Her Majesty the Queen and the Tapestries for the Sistine Chapel*. London: Phaidon, 1972.

———, and MARCIA B. HALL, eds. *The Princeton Raphael Symposium: Science in the Service of Art History*. Princeton, N.J.: Princeton University Press, 1990.

Luca della Robbia

POPE-HENNESSY, JOHN. *Luca della Robbia*. Ithaca, N.Y.: Cornell University Press, 1980.

Antonio and Bernardo Rossellino

SCHULZ, ANNE MARKHAM. *The Sculpture of Bernardo Rossellino and His Workshop*. Princeton, N.J.: Princeton University Press, 1977.

Rosso Fiorentino

CARROLL, EUGENE A. *Rosso Fiorentino: Drawings, Prints and Decorative Arts*. Washington, D.C.: National Gallery of Art, 1987.

Jacopo Sansovino

BOUCHER, BRUCE. *The Sculpture of Jacopo Sansovino*. New Haven: Yale University Press, 1991.

HOWARD, DEBORAH. *Jacopo Sansovino: Architecture and Patronage in Renaissance Venice*. New Haven: Yale University Press, 1987.

Andrea del Sarto

FREEDBERG, SYDNEY J. *Andrea del Sarto*. 2 vols. Cambridge, Mass.: Harvard University Press, 1963.

SHEARMAN, JOHN. *Andrea del Sarto*. 2 vols. Oxford: Clarendon Press, 1965.

Sassetta

POPE-HENNESSY, JOHN. *Sassetta*. London: Chatto & Windus, 1939.

Savoldo

BOSCHETTO, ANTONIO. *Gian Girolamo Savoldo*. Milan: Bramante, 1963.

GILBERT, CREIGHTON. *The Works of Girolamo Savoldo: The*

1955 Dissertation, with Review of Research. New York: Garland, 1986.

Sebastiano del Piombo

HIRST, MICHAEL. *Sebastiano del Piombo.* New York: Oxford University Press, 1981.

Signorelli

KURY, GLORIA. *The Early Work of Luca Signorelli, 1465–1490.* New York: Garland, 1978.

PAOLUCCI, ANTONIO. *Luca Signorelli.* Florence: Scala, 1990.

Sodoma

HAYUM, ANDRÉE. *Giovanni Antonio Bazzi—"Il Sodoma."* New York: Garland, 1976.

Tintoretto

RIDOLFI, CARLO. *The Life of Tintoretto and of His Children Domenico and Marietta.* Trans. and intro. Catherine Enggass and Robert Enggass. University Park: Pennsylvania State University Press, 1984.

ROSAND, DAVID. *Painting in Cinquecento Venice: Titian, Veronese, Tintoretto.* New Haven: Yale University Press, 1982.

TIETZE, HANS. *Tintoretto: The Paintings and Drawings.* New York: Phaidon, 1948.

VALCANOVER, FRANCESCO. *Tintoretto.* New York: Harry N. Abrams, 1985.

Titian

NASH, JANE C. *Veiled Images: Titian's Mythological Paintings for Philip II.* Philadelphia: Art Alliance Press and Associated University Presses, 1985.

PANOFSKY, ERWIN. *Problems in Titian, Mostly Iconographic.* New York: New York University Press, 1969.

ROSAND, DAVID. *Painting in Cinquecento Venice: Titian, Veronese, Tintoretto.* New Haven: Yale University Press, 1982.

———. *Titian.* New York: Harry N. Abrams, 1978.

———. *Titian and the Venetian Woodcut.* Washington, D.C.: National Gallery of Art, 1976.

Titian, Prince of Painters. Venice: Marsilio, 1990.

WETHEY, HAROLD E. *The Paintings of Titian.* 3 vols. London: Phaidon, 1969–75.

———. *Titian and His Drawings: With Reference to Giorgione and Some Close Contemporaries.* Princeton, N.J.: Princeton University Press, 1987.

Tura

RUHMER, EBERHARD. *Tura: Paintings and Drawings.* London: Phaidon, 1958.

Uccello

POPE-HENNESSY, JOHN. *The Complete Work of Paolo Uccello.* London: Phaidon, 1950; 2d ed., 1959.

Vasari

BAROLSKY, PAUL. *Giotto's Father and the Family of Vasari's Lives.* University Park: Pennsylvania State University Press. 1991.

———. *Why Mona Lisa Smiles and Other Tales by Vasari.* University Park: Pennsylvania State University Press. 1991.

BOASE, T. S. R. *Giorgio Vasari, The Man and the Book.* Princeton, N.J.: Princeton University Press, 1979.

CABLE, CAROLE. *Giorgio Vasari, Architect: A Selected Bibliography of Books and Articles.* Monticello, Ill.: Vance Bibliographers, 1985.

Veronese

COCKE, RICHARD. *Veronese's Drawings.* Ithaca, N.Y.: Cornell University Press, 1984.

DELOGU, GIUSEPPE. *Veronese: The Supper in the House of Levi.* Milan: Pizzi, 1948.

REARICK, WILLIAM R. *The Art of Paolo Veronese.* Cambridge, Eng.: Cambridge University Press, 1988.

ROSAND, DAVID. *Painting in Cinquecento Venice: Titian, Veronese, Tintoretto.* New Haven: Yale University Press, 1982.

Verrocchio

BULE, STEVEN, ed. *Verrocchio and Late Quattrocento Sculpture.* Florence: Le Lettere, 1992.

PASSAVANT, GUNTER. *Verrocchio: Sculptures, Paintings, and Drawings.* Trans. Katherine Watson. London: Phaidon, 1969.

SEYMOUR, CHARLES. *The Sculpture of Verrocchio.* London: Studio Vista, 1971.

Vignola

ACKERMAN. JAMES S., and WOLFGANG LOTZ. *Vignoliana.* Locust Valley, N.Y.: J. J. Augustin, 1965.

WALCHER CASOTTI, MARIA. *Il Vignola.* 2 vols. Trieste: Università, Instituto di storia dell'arte antica e moderna, 1960.

Index

G

Michelangelo, 463, 465, 468, 488, 501, 506; on Parmigianino, 563, 564; on Perugino, 367; on Piero della Francesca, 275–76, 280, 289; on Pollaiuolo, 320; on Pontormo, 550, 552, 554; on Quercia, 183; on Raphael, 468; on Rosso Fiorentino, 555; on Sangallo, A., the Younger, 578; on Sarto, 549; on sculptural technique, 175; on Signorelli, 474; on sketching process, 34–35; on Titian, 586; on Uccello, 252; *Paul III Directing the Continuance of St. Peter's,* Palazzo della Cancelleria, Rome, 636, 647; *704; Perseus and Andromeda,* Studiolo, Palazzo Vecchio, Florence, 657; colorplate 134, p. 655; Uffizi, Florence (finished by Buontalenti and Parigi), 578, 648, 657; *705*

Vatican
 Belvedere (Bramante), 485–87, 660; *507, 508*
 Chapel of Innocent VIII, frescoes (Mantegna), 394
 Chapel of Nicholas V, frescoes: (Angelico, Fra), 220–21, 285, 311; *214;* (Gozzoli), 311
 Library, frescoes: (Ghirlandaio, D. and D.), 372; (Melozzo da Forlì), 236, 372–73, 393; *382*
 Old St. Peter's (Basilica of St. Peter's), 479, 482; bronze and silver doors (Filarete), 422; frescoes (Cavallini), 56
 Pauline Chapel, frescoes (Michelangelo), 634–35; *677–79*
 St. Peter's, 163; (Bramante), 41, 235, 480, 482–85, 487, 488, 509, 526, 568, 577, 578, 636, 659; *501–5;* (Michelangelo), 235, 462–63, 482, 485, 636–38; colorplate 13, p. 21; (Raphael), 523, 526; (Rossellino, B.), 236, 482; (Sangallo, A., the Younger), 636; *681;* (Vignola), 659; frescoes (Angelico, Fra), 220; sculpture (Michelangelo), *472, 473, 682–85*
 Sistine Chapel: frescoes, 328; colorplate 11, p. 19; (Botticelli), 327, 328–31, 345, 393, 501, 504; *342–45;* (Ghirlandaio), 328, 345, 393, 504; *360;* (Michelangelo; ceiling), 71, 277, 320, 328, 448, 458, 459, 461, 463–65, 488, 497–503, 504, 508, 540, 542; *512;* colorplates 88–102, pp. 489–96; (Michelangelo; wall), 497, 631–38; *673–75;* colorplate 131, p. 652; (Perugino), 41, 328, 367–68, 371, 393, 504, 631; *378;* colorplate 67, p. 356; (Signorelli), 474, 504; tapestries (Raphael), 523–25, 620; *531, 532;* colorplate 105, p. 515
 Stanza d'Eliodoro, frescoes (Raphael), 510–12; *524–26;* colorplates 103, 104, pp. 513, 514
 Stanza della Segnatura, frescoes: (Raphael), 506–10, 530; colorplate 12, p. 20; (Sodoma), 506
 Stanza dell'Incendio, frescoes (Raphael), 523
VECCHIETTA (LORENZO DI PIETRO) 364; *Risen Christ,* Sta. Maria della Scala, Siena, 364; *372*
Vecellio, Francesco, 586
Vecellio, Orazio, 598
Velázquez, Diego, 406
Vendramin, Gabriel, 584
VENEZIANO, DOMENICO, *see* DOMENICO VENEZIANO
VENEZIANO, PAOLO, *see* PAOLO VENEZIANO
Venice, 29, 44, 54, 76, 290, 582, 601, 603, 623, 624
 aerial view of, *5*

Doges' Palace, 404, 617; altarpiece (Jacobello del Fiore), 381; *391;* frescoes: (Gentile da Fabriano), 187, 378; (Pisanello), 378; Sala del Gran Consiglio, 622; *659;* colorplate 14, p. 22; frescoes (Gentile da Fabriano), 187; paintings: (Pordenone), 565; (Tintoretto), colorplate 14, p. 22; (Veronese), 622; *659;* colorplate 14, p. 22
Fondaco dei Tedeschi, frescoes (Giorgione and Titian), 586
history and founding of, 146
Library of S. Marco (Sansovino and Scamozzi), 601, 622, 624, 626, 628; colorplate 130, p. 651
palaces of, 624
Palazzo Vendramin-Calergi, façade (Codussi), 420–21; *434*
political and economic development of, 28, 146–48, 152, 378
S. Giobbe, Hospital of, altarpiece (Bellini, Giovanni), 404, 406; *425*
S. Giorgio Maggiore (Palladio and Scamozzi), 628–29; *668, 669;* façade, colorplate 15, p. 23; paintings: (Tintoretto), 617; *651;* (Veronese), 620; *656–58*
SS. Giovanni e Paolo, painting (Veronese), 620–22; colorplate 128, p. 649
S. Marco, 419; mosaics, 147; (Castagno and Giambono), 267–68, 422; *267;* (Uccello?), 252
Sta. Maria della Salute, Sacristy, ceiling paintings (Titian), 594–95, 598; *629–31*
Sta. Maria Gloriosa dei Frari: altarpieces (Titian), 587–88, 591, 598; *618, 623;* colorplate 118, p. 575; Cappella del Crocifisso, tomb of Titian, 598–99; Frari altarpiece (Bellini, Giovanni), *424;* Sacristy, altarpiece (Bellini, Giovanni), 402–3
S. Pantaleone, altarpiece (Vivarini and Giovanni d'Alemagna), 381; *392*
S. Sebastiano, ceiling painting (Veronese), 619–20, 622; *654*
Sto. Spirito in Isola, 594
S. Zaccaria: altarpiece (Bellini, Giovanni), 286, 399, 406; colorplate 79, p. 416; façade (Codussi), 419–20; *433*
Scuola della Carità, mural (Titian), 592–93; *626, 627*
Scuola di S. Fantin, sculpture (Vittoria), 630; *672*
Scuola di S. Giovanni Evangelista, painting (Bellini, Gentile), 395–96; *414*
Scuola di Sant'Orsola, paintings (Carpaccio), 406–8, 417; *428;* colorplate 80, p. 449
Scuola di S. Rocco, paintings (Tintoretto), 604, 606–8; Sala dell'Albergo, 606; *646;* colorplate 127, p. 616; Sala Grande, 607–8; *647–50*
Scuola Grande di S. Marco, paintings (Tintoretto), 604; *644, 645;* colorplate 126, p. 615
Zecca, La (Sansovino), 601, 625, 642; *663*
Venus Anadyomene (Sansovino), 625; *662*
Venus and Mars (Botticelli), 333–34; *348*
Venus and the Lute Player (Titian), 596–97; *634*
Venus of Urbino (Titian), 593, 596; *628*
Vergerio, Pier Paolo, 32
Vermeer, Jan, 406
Verona, 378, 601, 623; cathedral, frescoes (Romano), 622; Palazzo Bevilacqua (Sanmicheli), 623–24; *661;* Sant'Anastasia, fresco (Pisanello), 378, 379; Sant'Anastasia, Pellegrini Chapel, fresco (Pisanello), *388;* S. Zeno, altarpiece (Mantegna), 286, 387–89, 393, 401, 422; *403, 404;*

colorplates 73, 74, pp. 410, 411
VERONESE, PAOLO (PAOLO CALIARI), 327, 384, 582, 601, 622, 630; *Abundance, Fortitude, and Envy,* Villa Barbaro, Maser, 620; *655; Feast in the House of Levi,* 620–22, 625; colorplate 128, p. 649; *Marriage at Cana,* 620; *656–58; Mystical Marriage of St. Catherine,* 622; colorplate 129, p. 650; *Triumph of Mordecai,* S. Sebastiano, Venice, 619–20, 622; *654; Triumph of Venice* (with pupils), Doges' Palace, Venice, 622; *659;* colorplate 14, p. 22
VERROCCHIO, ANDREA DEL, 209, 317, 319, 323–26, 344, 349, 367, 476, 643; *Baptism of Christ* (with Leonardo da Vinci), 323–24, 436, 447; *332; Bust of a Young Woman,* 324–25; *335; David,* 325–26, 335, 467; *336; Doubting of Thomas,* Orsanmichele, Florence, 324, 342; *333, 334; Equestrian Monument of Bartolommeo Colleoni* (with Leopardi), 149, 326, 441; *337–39;* influence of, 323, 327, 332, 344, 368, 370; relationship with Leonardo da Vinci, 370
Vertumnus and Pomona (Pontormo), 309, 553, 555; *579*
Vespucci, Simonetta, 334; portrait of (Piero di Cosimo), *491*
Vespucci family, 334
Vicenza, 378, 601, 623; Basilica/Palazzo della Ragione (Palladio), 625–27; *664;* Olympian Theater (Palladio and Scamozzi), 629–30; *670, 671;* Palazzo Chiericati (Palladio), 627; *665;* Villa Rotonda/Villa Capra (Palladio and Scamozzi), 627–28; *666, 667*
Victory (Michelangelo), 545–46, 641; *566, 567*
View of an Ideal City (Laurana, L., and Piero della Francesca), 41, 231, 236, 238, 310, 376–77, 487; *386*
Vigerio della Rovere, Marco, 497, 500, 501
Vigevano, piazza (Bramante), 423
VIGNOLA, GIACOMO DA (JACOPO BAROZZI), 659–60; Villa Farnese, Caprarola, 659–60; *709–11*
Villa: Barbaro, *see* Maser; Capra, *see* Vicenza, Villa Rotonda; Carducci, *see* Legnaia; Farnese, *see* Caprarola; Farnesina, *see* Rome; La Gallina, *see* Florence; Madama, *see* Rome; Medici, *see* Poggio a Caiano; Rotonda, *see* Vicenza
Villani, Filippo, 32
Villani, Giovanni, 76
Virgil, 333, 553
Virgin Adoring the Child (Perugino), 369–70; *381*
Virgin and Child Between St. John the Baptist and a Female Saint (Bellini, Giovanni), 405–6; *427*
Virgin and Child with Angels (Lippi, Filippino), 340–41, 437; *356*
Virgin Annunciate (Antonello da Messina), 398; *417*
Visconti, Bernabò, 149; tomb monument of (Bonino da Campione), 149, 246; *131*
Visconti, Federigo, 65–69
Visconti, Filippo Maria, 153, 195, 421, 447
Visconti, Giangaleazzo (duke of Milan), 146, 149–50, 152, 167, 209, 350, 423; portrait of (Giovannino de' Grassi), 150; colorplate 36, p. 202
Visconti family, 149, 152, 378, 423, 441
Visconti Hours (Giovannino de' Grassi), 150; colorplate 36, p. 202
Vision of Anna (Giotto), 80, 106; *57*
Vision of Constantine (Piero della Francesca), 285; *286*
Vision of St. Bernard: (Bartolommeo, Fra), 472–73, 521; *486;* (Lippi, Filippino), 341–42, 472,

Credits

The author and publisher wish to thank the libraries, museums, galleries, and private collectors named in the picture captions for permitting the reproduction of works of art in their collections and for supplying the necessary photographs. Photographs from other sources are gratefully acknowledged below. Colorplates are followed by figures.

Alinari, including Anderson and Brogi, Florence: color-plates 24, 35, 74; title page and pages 9, 25, 151, 429; figures 4–7, 9, 16–18, 21, 23, 24, 30, 31, 38–42, 44–49, 52, 54–63, 65, 66, 68–72, 74, 76–78, 80, 81, 84–86, 88–90, 93, 94, 96–99, 101, 103, 106–11, 113–15, 118–27, 129, 130, 132–34, 138–41, 144, 146–48, 150–55, 157, 159, 160, 162, 165, 167, 169–86, 204, 205, 209, 210, 212–15, 217–20, 222, 223, 225, 226, 230, 234, 236, 237–57, 263, 264, 267, 268, 270–72, 282, 287–89, 291–97, 300, 304–7, 309, 312, 313, 315–18, 324, 326, 328, 329, 331, 332, 334, 336–41, 343, 345, 347, 349–53, 356–59, 361, 362, 364, 369–71, 373–75, 378, 380–86, 388, 391–93, 395–404, 406–12, 414, 417, 423, 425, 427–29, 432, 434, 435, 437, 438, 440–42, 453–58, 460–62, 465, 467, 469, 471, 474, 477, 478, 484–86, 488, 489, 491, 498, 505, 507, 511, 516, 519, 520, 523–28, 530, 534, 536, 539–43, 548, 549, 551, 553–56, 559, 561, 562, 566–68, 570, 571, 574–77, 579, 582, 584, 586–88, 590, 593, 594, 599, 600, 602, 603, 607, 610, 614–16, 618, 620, 625–33, 639, 640, 644–51, 654, 655, 657–59, 661, 663–65, 670, 671, 673–81, 684, 689, 690, 694–705. De Antonis: 35. Aragozzini, Milan: 493–96. Archives Photographiques, Paris: 508. Archivio Fotografico dei Musei e Gallerie Ponti-ficie, Vatican City, Rome: colorplates 14, 103; figures 330, 521. Raffaeli Armoni & Moretti: colorplate 36; figure 112. Art Resource, New York: colorplates 33, 107. Art Resource/Bildarchiv Foto Marburg: 552. Art Resource/Scala: colorplates 1, 9, 16, 61. Vincenzo Bertotti-Scamozzi, *L'Idea dell' architettura universale:* 667. Biblioteca Nazionale, Florence: 436. Calzolari, Mantua: 611, 612. Cameraphoto, Venice: jacket; colorplates 15, 79, 118; figures 424, 479, 623, 638, 641. Canali Photobank, Capriolo: colorplates 8, 10–12, 18, 22, 23, 27, 28, 30, 38, 41, 43, 50, 60, 64, 108, 123, 124, 127, 131, 133; figures 67, 166, 207, 211, 231, 233, 269, 549, 672. Pedicini/Canali, Capriolo: 95. Pelazza/Canali Photobank, Capri-olo: colorplate 42. Tomba/Canali Photobank, Capriolo: colorplate 73. Eugenio Cassin, Florence: 506, 604. Fondazione Giorgio Cini, Venice: 668. Giancarlo Costa, Milan: 131. Edizione Giusti di S. Becocci, Florence: 75. *Encyclopedia of World Art* (New York: McGraw Hill, 1967): 2, 308, 314, 376, 537, 601. David Finn, New York: 161. Fotostudio Grassi, Siena: 43, 372. Fototeca Unione, Rome: 310, 538, 544, 685, 687. Gabinetto Fotografico Nazionale, Florence: 11, 12, 14, 20, 25–29, 73, 79, 82, 83, 87, 116, 117, 149, 163, 187, 206, 208, 258–62, 274–79, 283–86, 319, 320, 333, 335, 363, 377, 468, 470, 503, 557, 564, 569, 573, 580, 581, 583, 693, 706. Gabinetto Fotografico Nazionale, Rome: 34, 475, 686. Lydia Gershey, Communigraph, New York: 8, 13. Giraudon, Paris: 100, 365, 413. Frederick Hartt: 517, 518. Hirmer Verlag, Munich: 64, 158, 164, 168. Institut de France, Paris: 449. Instituto Centrale del Restauro, Rome: 105. Paul Letarouilly, *Les Edifices de Rome moderne* (London: J. Tiranti, 1928–31?), vol. 2, pl. 116: 605. Massimo Listri, Florence: colorplate 7; 387. Bates Lowry, *Renaissance Architecture* (New York: George Braziller, 1962): 609. Magellan Geographix SM/Santa Barbara, California: endpaper maps. Mansell Collection, London: 281. MAS, Barcelona: 621. Leonard von Matt, Buochs: 606. Rollie McKenna, New York: 227. Pepe Merisio, Bergamo: 710, 711. Takashi Okamura/Nippon Television, Tokyo: colorplates 13, 88–102; figure 513. Takashi Okamura, Rome: colorplates 2, 19, 104; figure 490. Palazzo del Te, Mantua: colorplate 114. E. Peets and W. Hegemann, *Civic Art*, p. 25: 232. N. Pevsner, *Outline of European Architecture* (Baltimore: Penguin): 228. Piccolomini Library, Siena: 68. Pinacoteca, Vatican, Rome: colorplates 106, 109, 110. Eric Pollitzer, New York: 509. Josephine Powell, Rome: 19, 22. Antonio Quattrone (Olivetti), Florence: 192–201. Mario Quattrone, Florence: colorplates 3–6, 20, 31, 34, 39, 54–56, 85, 135; figures 707, 708. Gerhard Reinhold, Berlin: colorplate 75. Sta. Maria delle Grazie, Milan: colorplate 83. Umberto Sciamanna, Rome: 545–47. Mario Semprucci & C., Pesaro: 422. Service Photographique de la Réunion des Musées Nationaux, Paris: colorplates 58, 65, 72, 82, 84, 116; figures 15, 216, 389, 394, 464, 529, 624, 656. Walter Steinkopf, Berlin: 203, 221, 265, 443. Studio Rapuzzi, Brescia: 642. Dusan Tasic, Belgrade: 36. Marvin Trachtenberg, New York: 50, 136, 229, 311, 433, 666. Nadir Tronci, Florence: 32, 102. Vaghi, Parma: 591, 592. Villa I Tatti, Florence: colorplate 66. Roger Viollet, Paris: 463. John White, *Art and Architecture in Italy: 1250–1400* (Middlesex: Penguin, 1987), fig. 3: 51